THE DRAVIDIAN LANGUAGES

The Dravidian languages are spoken by over 200 million people in South Asia and in diaspora communities around the world, and constitute the world's fifth largest language family. It consists of about twenty-six languages in total including Tamil, Malayāḷam, Kannaḍa and Telugu, as well as over twenty non-literary languages. In this book, Bhadriraju Krishnamurti, one of the most eminent Dravidianists of our time and an Honorary Member of the Linguistic Society of America, provides a comprehensive study of the phonological and grammatical structure of the whole Dravidian family from different aspects. He describes its history and writing system, discusses its structure and typology, and considers its lexicon. Distant and more recent contacts between Dravidian and other language groups are also discussed.

With its comprehensive coverage this book will be welcomed by all students of Dravidian languages and will be of interest to linguists in various branches of the discipline as well as Indologists.

BHADRIRAJU KRISHNAMURTI is a leading linguist in India and one of the world's renowned historical and comparative linguists, specializing in the Dravidian family of languages. He has published over twenty books in English and Telugu and over a hundred research papers. His books include *Telugu Verbal Bases: a Comparative and Descriptive Study* (1961), *Koṇḍa or Kūbi, a Dravidian Language* (1969), *A Grammar of Modern Telugu* (with J. P. L. Gwynn, 1985), *Language, Education and Society* (1998) and *Comparative Dravidian Linguistics: Current Perspectives* (2001).

CAMBRIDGE LANGUAGE SURVEYS

General editors
P. Austin (*University of Melbourne*)
J. Bresnan (*Stanford University*)
B. Comrie (*Max Planck Institute for Evolutionary Anthropology, Leipzig*)
W. Dressler (*University of Vienna*)
C. Ewen (*University of Leiden*)
R. Lass (*University of Cape Town*)
D. Lightfoot (*University of Maryland*)
I. Roberts (*University of Cambridge*)
S. Romaine (*University of Oxford*)
N. V. Smith (*University College, London*)

This series offers general accounts of the major language families of the world, with volumes organised either on a purely genetic basis or on a geographical basis, whichever yields the most convenient and intelligible grouping in each case. Each volume compares and contrasts the typological features of the languages it deals with. It also treats the relevant genetic relationships, historical development and sociolinguistic issues arising from their role and use in the world today. The books are intended for linguists from undergraduate level upwards, but no special knowledge of the languages under consideration is assumed. Volumes such as those on Australia and the Amazon Basin are also of wider relevance, as the future of the languages and their speakers raises important social and political issues.

Volumes already published include
Chinese *Jerry Norman*
The languages of Japan *Masayoshi Shibatani*
Pidgins and Creoles (volume I: Theory and structure; volume II: Reference survey) *John A. Holm*
The Indo-Aryan languages *Colin Masica*
The Celtic languages *edited by Donald MacAulay*
The Romance languages *Rebecca Posner*
The Amazonian languages *edited by R.M.W. Dixon and Alexandra Y. Aikhenvald*
The languages of Native North America *Marianne Mithun*
The Korean language *Ho-Min Sohn*
Australian languages *R.M.W. Dixon*

THE DRAVIDIAN LANGUAGES

BHADRIRAJU KRISHNAMURTI

CAMBRIDGE
UNIVERSITY PRESS

PUBLISHED BY THE PRESS SYNDICATE OF THE UNIVERSITY OF CAMBRIDGE
The Pitt Building, Trumpington Street, Cambridge, United Kingdom

CAMBRIDGE UNIVERSITY PRESS
The Edinburgh Building, Cambridge CB2 2RU, UK
40 West 20th Street, New York, NY 10011–4211, USA
477 Williamstown Road, Port Melbourne, VIC 3207, Australia
Ruiz de Alarcón 13, 28014 Madrid, Spain
Dock House, The Waterfront, Cape Town 8001, South Africa

http://www.cambridge.org

First published 2003

Printed in the United Kingdom at the University Press, Cambridge

Typeface Times New Roman 9/13 pt *System* $\LaTeX 2_\varepsilon$ [TB]

A catalogue record for this book is available from the British Library

ISBN 0 521 77111 0 hardback

To M. B. Emeneau, my guru

and to

Henry M. Hoenigswald, my teacher in historical linguistics

CONTENTS

ILLUSTRATIONS

Map

Figures

TABLES

PREFACE

This volume is the result of two years of concentrated reading, reflection and writing, from September 1999 to October 2001, with many years of research and study prior to it. This work differs somewhat in focus and scope from the other volumes in the Cambridge Language Surveys series. My focus is on historical and comparative aspects of the Dravidian languages, although I have not altogether neglected descriptive and typological ones. There have been several descriptive studies of the Dravidian languages, though they are not comprehensive, for instance, Andronov's *Dravidian Languages* (1970) and, more recently, *The Dravidian Languages* (1998) edited by Sanford B. Steever. The second book is more substantial, although it covers only ten out of twenty-six or so known Dravidian languages; it has two chapters each devoted to Tamil and Telugu, representing old and modern varieties. Caldwell's pioneering work of 1856 (revised in 1875 and 1919, reprinted 1956, 1961) has remained the solitary model in the field for nearly a century. Jules Bloch's *Structure grammaticale des langues dravidiennes* (1946; English translation by R. G. Harshe 1954) has a descriptive title, but a comparative focus; it deals with specific problems of morphology based on data of newly studied languages like Gondi, Kui, Kuṛux, Malto, Brahui etc. Zvelebil's survey monograph of 1990 is a broad sketch (156 pages) of major issues in phonology and morphology up to that period. It has a useful summary for the kind of interest that scholars outside hardcore linguistics have in comparative Dravidian studies, under the titles 'Dravidian and Harappan', 'Dravidian and Ural Altaic', 'Dravidian and Elamite' and 'Dravidian and Japanese', although these topics take up half of the volume.

Research and publication in Dravidian studies during the twentieth century was concerned mostly with problems of comparative phonology and we are now fairly certain about the phonological system of Proto-Dravidian and how it has developed in individual languages. The publication of the monumental *Dravidian Etymological Dictionary* (1961, 2nd revised edition 1984) by T. Burrow and M. B. Emeneau as well as R. L. Turner's *Comparative Dictionary of the Indo-Aryan Languages* (1966) has both promoted and facilitated studies in comparative phonology (see my survey articles 1969b, 1980, 2001b). There were, however, several articles on different aspects of morphology by a wide range of scholars: L. V. Ramswami Aiyar, M. B. Emeneau, Bh. Krishnamurti, K. V. Zvelebil, P. S. Subrahmanyam, S. B. Steever, etc. but much remains to be done. There were only two publications covering comparative morphology: *Dravidian Verb Morphology: a Comparative Study* by P. S. Subrahmanyam (1971) and *Dravidian Nouns: a Comparative Study* by S. V. Shanmugam (1971a). These works are quite comprehensive but they are the first of their kind in the field. There has not been much study and discussion of these monographs during the past three decades. These books have been my primary sources for comparative data on noun and verb morphology, although I have not always accepted their reconstructions or conclusions. Then came Steever's groundbreaking work on serial verbs (1988, 1993), which has widened our understanding of composite verbs, mainly in South Dravidian II, but I have reservations on some of his proposals and reconstructions. The Chomskyan revolution has attracted many young linguists into looking at their own language data from a generative-transformational point of view. In the second half of the twentieth century, the Linguistics Departments in India could not get many young scholars interested either in fieldwork and study of new, unexplored languages, or in historical and comparative linguistics.

Emeneau's *Kota Texts* (1944–6) was the major work after the publication of volume IV: *Muṇḍā and Dravidian Languages* in 1906 by George Grierson as part of the Linguistic Survey of India. A number of new languages of central India were studied and described by T. Burrow and S. Bhattacharya (1953: Parji, 1970: Pengo; notes on Kui–Kuvi 1961, 1963). Bhattacharya published sketches of Ollari (1957) and Naiki (1961). Emeneau's Kolami (1955b), Krishnamurti's Koṇḍa (1969a), Israel's Kuvi (1979) and Bhaskararao's Koṇekor Gadaba (1980) have added to the enrichment of our knowledge of the Dravidian languages of central India. They also provided us with an opportunity to look at the problem of subgrouping of the Dravidian languages afresh.

During 1960–85, the Department of Linguistics of Annamalai University brought out many studies on comparative aspects of Dravidian as well as descriptions of individual languages of southern India, namely Irula, Toda, Kota, Koḍagu etc. Dieter B. Kapp has a voluminous study of the grammar and vocabulary of Ālu Kuṟumba Nāya^{n} (1984a). Emeneau's comprehensive grammar and texts of Toda came out in 1984. B. P. Mahapatra presented a modern description of Malto (1979). The founding of the *International Journal of Dravidian Linguistics* in 1972 by V. I. Subramoniam of Kerala University has provided an organ for publication of research on Dravidian linguistics. It is a bi-annual and is issued regularly, although on an austere budget. It does require improvement in quality of production. There have been several unpublished dissertations on different tribal languages at universities and institutes, Indian and foreign, some of which are not easily accessible, for instance, Diffloth's Irula, Garman's Koḍagu, Andrea's Muria Gondi, Ekka's Kuṟux, and Pilot-Raichoor's Baḍaga. Some significant dissertations on a comparative study of South Dravidian II and Central Dravidian were produced at

Osmania University in the 1980s, especially Sumati (1982), Suvarchala (1984) and G. U. Rao (1987b).

We see that, in the latter half of the twentieth century, many new Dravidian languages have come to light and there has also been considerable research on the major literary languages. Therefore, the time is ripe to take a look at the structural, typological and historical linkages relating different Dravidian languages. T. Burrow, while writing a foreword to my *Koṇḍa or Kūbi, a Dravidian Language* (1969a), says: 'The book provides a solid basis for comparative Dravidian studies. The time is approaching when a serious attempt at a comparative grammar of Dravidian can be made, and pioneering works of this kind will make this achievement possible' (p. xvii). I do not claim this book to be a comparative grammar of the Dravidian languages, but it does, I hope, lay the foundation for such a comprehensive work in the future.

I dedicate this book, a lifetime labour of love, to my teacher, mentor and Guru (since 1955), M. B. Emeneau, the leading living Indologist and a renowned authority on comparative Dravidian, and to my teacher in historical linguistics at the University of Pennsylvania and my well-wisher, ever since, Henry M. Hoenigswald, whose scholarly contribution, I consider, has brought scientific rigour to the field of historical and comparative linguistics.

ACKNOWLEDGEMENTS

It is my pleasure and privilege to acknowledge the help and support that I have received from many institutions and individuals during the past two years. First of all, I must thank Katherina Brett, Commissioning Editor, Language and Linguistics, Cambridge University Press, for inviting me to write this book. She has graciously put up with the delays in submitting the final typescript.

I am grateful to the Director of the Institute for Advanced Study, Princeton, and its Faculty of the School of Historical Studies, for awarding me a Membership of the Institute for the year 1999–2000. During that period I was able to complete chapters 1 to 5 of the book. The intellectual ambience of the Institute, access to the libraries of Princeton University and of the University of Pennsylvania and the availability of my former teacher Henry M. Hoenigswald and my friend George Cardona for frequent consultation – all these strengthened my self-confidence and facilitated my work at Princeton.

I was awarded a Fellowship for the fall semester of 2000 at the Center for Advanced Study in the Behavioral Sciences (CASBS), Stanford, where I spent four months, September to December 2000, and could complete chapter 6 and write most of chapter 7, the longest in the book. Neil Smelser, the Director of the Center, and Robert Scott, the Associate Director, were very considerate and gracious in awarding me a Fellowship there, when I approached them for support to continue my project. I thank the Ford Foundation (Grant #1000-0287) for providing financial support, which made my stay at the Center possible.

While I was at Princeton, I was delighted to receive an invitation from R. M. W. (Bob) Dixon, Director of the Research Centre for Linguistic Typology (RCLT), La Trobe University, Australia, to spend six months at the Centre as a Visiting Fellow in 2001 and finish my book-writing there. I considered it a privilege and readily accepted the invitation. Bob Dixon, whom I have known for over twenty-seven years, has been my friend, philosopher and guide throughout this project, from reading the book-proposal submitted to Cambridge University Press in 1998 to reading, thoroughly and critically, the complete typescript of this volume. I do not have adequate words to thank him, not only for his keen interest in the successful completion of this book by inviting me here but also for his many insightful and valuable comments to improve the organization and quality of this volume. After writing the unfinished part of chapter 7, I added four more chapters, 8, 9, 10 and 11, revised all other chapters, and put them all into book form during my fellowship period at La Trobe University. I express my sincere thanks to Alexandra Y. (Sasha) Aikhenvald, Associate Director of the RCLT, who has thoroughly read the whole typescript and made many perceptive comments, which I gratefully acknowledge. The Centre is a meeting place of several young researchers in linguistics and some senior Fellows, with whom I could usefully interact. It has been an ideal place for me to continue my project and complete it successfully. I thank the Vice-Chancellor for making my stay at La Trobe University possible. I also thank Gilah Leder, Director of the Institute for Advanced Study, of which RCLT is a constituent, for making me a Fellow of the IAS and providing us with housing on the campus.

I owe a special debt of gratitude to Bernard Comrie (one of the General Editors, Cambridge Language Surveys), who has kindly read through the whole book and sent me his valuable comments promptly. I have no doubt that the structure and quality of this monograph owe a lot to his insightful remarks and encouragement. I gratefully acknowledge William Bright for his suggestions on the draft book-plan of this volume.

During the past two years, I have requested a number of scholars to read different chapters of the book for comments and I thank them by name for their gracious acceptance of my request and for many useful suggestions and comments: Henry M. Hoenigswald (chapters 1, 2, 4), George Cardona (chapters 1, 2, 4), Jane Grimshaw (chapters 6, 9), Merritt Ruhlen (chapter 1), Paul Kiparsky (chapter 4), G. U. Rao (chapter 6), Andrew Ingram (chapter 7), Brian Joseph (chapters 2, 4), Sanford B. Steever (chapters 7, 8, 9), Hilary Chappel (chapters 5, 6), K. A. Jayaseelan (chapter 9). Thanks are due to Ms Priti Samyukta for the artwork in tables 3.1a and 3.1b. M. B. Emeneau read chapter 4 on historical phonology and suggested improvements, which I gratefully acknowledge. For any flaws and deficiencies still remaining I take the responsibility.

Last, but not least, I must thank my wife, Syamala, for her positive and supportive role during the two long years of my *tapas* 'penance'.

NOTE ON TRANSLITERATION AND SYMBOLS

Transliteration

The citation forms from different languages are phonemic for all the literary languages, and for Toda, Kota, Koḍagu of South Dravidian, Koṇḍa and Pengo of South-Central Dravidian, Kolami, Parji, Ollari and Konḍekor Gadaba of Central Dravidian, and Malto (Mahapatra) of North Dravidian. For the rest of the languages, the forms are apparently written in a 'broad transcription' bordering on truly phonemic representation, in some cases, e.g. Israel's Kuvi and Bray's Brahui. Some are not reliable, like the transliteration of different Gondi dialects described by various administrators and missionaries, e.g. Kuvi (F), (S) and Droese's Malto. In general, the plan of Burrow and Emeneau in copying the spellings as they occurred in different sources in citing cognates in *DEDR* is followed, except for two important changes, i.e. (1) and (2) below; (3) to (9) explain the symbols which do not differ from the ones also used in *DEDR*.

(1) Long vowels are marked with different diacritics in *DEDR* (copied as they were in source materials). Here they are normalized by the use of a macron over the vowel, e.g. ā, ī, ū, ē, ō; with umlauted vowels ï, ë, ü, ö, ï̄, ë̄, ǟ, ǖ. Phonetic vowel-length is sometimes indicated by [:].

(2) Retroflex consonants are indicated by a subdot: stops ṭ, ḍ, nasal ṇ, lateral ḷ, flap ṛ, sibilant ṣ, and frictionless continuant or approximant ẓ. This last one replaces a number of symbols used in the literature since Caldwell's time (1856), namely ṛ, l̤, ḻ, ẓ, r̤; the last symbol is used by *DEDR*. Old Tamil āytam [∴] is marked by [ḥ]. For the reconstructed stages of Proto-Dravidian or other proto-stages, I have used [w] to represent the bilabial semivowel consistently, and not [v]. I consider the Proto-Dravidian semivowel to be a bilabial. Similarly I preferred for Telugu /w/ instead of /v/. It must be noted that in no Dravidian language do [w] and [v] contrast.

(3) Alveolars are marked by a subscript bar where they are distinguished from dentals which do not carry any diacritic: dentals t, d, n, alveolars ṯ, ḏ, ṉ; in the literary languages of south India, alveolar [ḏ] became a voiced alveolar trill, marked [ṟ]. Normally only [n] without a diacritic is used if dental–alveolar contrast is not present, as in Proto-Dravidian. Both Old and Modern Tamil distinguish the two nasals in orthography because of a few contrasts in Old Tamil; these are indicated as [n] dental and [ṉ] alveolar.

(4) The velar nasal is represented by two symbols [ṅ] for the literary languages Koḍagu and Tuḷu, where it is conventionally used, and [ŋ] in the case of the other non-literary languages of South Dravidian II and Central Dravidian; [ñ] is a palatal nasal.

(5) In the Nilgiri languages: [ï] = high back unrounded vowel (it is also used to represent the word-final enunciative vowel in Tamil, Koḍagu and Tuḷu), [ü] = high front rounded vowel, [ë] = mid central unrounded vowel, [ö] = mid central rounded vowel; Tuḷu [è] = [æ] higher low front unrounded vowel. In Toda c = [ts], z, = [dz] , č = [tš], ǰ = [tž]; θ = voiceless dental fricative, x = voiceless velar fricative; ł and ɬ̣ are voiceless laterals of alveolar and retroflex series, respectively; among the sibilants s̲, z̲ are alveolar, š, ž are alveolo-palatal and ṣ, ẓ are retroflex.

(6) [ʔ] marks a glottal stop in South Dravidian II; Gondi -rr is of uncertain phonetic value; it could be either a geminated flap or an alveolar trill -r̲- contrasting with flap -r-. Kuvi (S) ẓ = [ts], ch = [č]. We do not know how to interpret Fitzgerald's word-initial vw-. In the Hill-Maṛia dialect of Gondi [r̥] represents a uvular *r* corresponding to South Dravidian [-r̲-] or Proto-Dravidian *t̲. In Koṇḍa the voiceless alveolar trill is transcribed [R].

(7) Kuṛux and Brahui k̲h̲ = [x] voiceless uvular fricative; Malto q = [q] voiceless uvular stop; the corresponding voiced ones are written g̲h̲ = [ɤ] and [g̣], respectively. What is written as [n̲] in Malto by Droese appears to be a palatal nasal [ñ].

(8) The name of the language which used to be spelt Kuruk̲h̲ has been changed here to the way it is pronounced [Kuṛux].

(9) Whenever a phonetic representation of a cited form is given within [ ], I have followed a combination of IPA symbols with established Roman types used in Indological publications. For instance, IPA uses a diacritic for dental stops and leaves alveolars unmarked, whereas in Dravidian a subscript bar is used for alveolars and the dentals are left unmarked because phonemically /n/ goes with dental stops in South Asian languages, in most of which dental and alveolar stops do not contrast.

(10) Sometimes the verbs are given in the entries with their infinitive morphs, Ma. *-ka/-kka*, Tu. *-uni/-pini*, *-vuni/-puni*, Go. *-ānā*, Kui *-pa/-ba/-va*, Kuvi (F) *-ali*, (S) *-nai/-inai*, Kuṛ. *-ānā*, Malt. *-e*. While studying the comparative etyma these elements have to be eliminated. The form in parentheses cited after a verb root in any language is the past stem of the root, unless stated otherwise, e.g. Ta. *cel-* (*cen̲-r̲-*) 'to go'.

Symbols

-	Marks etymological or morphological break
#	Marks the beginning or end of a word or any free form
*	Precedes a hypothetical form reconstructed for a proto-stage. In synchronic description it stands for an ungrammatical expression
**	A form reconstructed on the basis of reconstructed forms (represents greater time-depth)

/ /	Enclose phonemic transcription
[ ]	Enclose phonetic transcription; morpheme-by-morpheme glossing of text; the entry no. of *DEDR*; other uses as indicated in the text
< >	Enclose orthographic representation
[X	Following environment X
X]	Preceding environment X
+	Morpheme boundary
A > B/__C	A is historically replaced by B in the environment of a following C
A≫B	A is morphologically replaced by B
B, D	Symbolize a voiced stop
L	A sonorant including nasals
N	A nasal homorganic with a following stop
P, T	Symbolize a voiceless stop
R	A liquid (trill, lateral, approximant)
V^n	Nasalized vowel = $\tilde{V}$
X ~ Y	X alternates with Y, or X varies with Y
X < Y	X is historically derived from Y
X > Y	Y is historically derived from X
X → Y	X becomes, or is replaced by, Y (descriptively)
X/Y	X or Y

ABBREVIATIONS

Books (details in bibliography)

CDIAL	*A Comparative Dictionary of the Indo-Aryan Languages,* R. L. Turner (1966)
CDL	*Comparative Dravidian Linguistics,* Bh. Krishnamurti (2001a)
DBIA	*Dravidian Borrowings from Indo-Aryan,* M. B. Emeneau and T. Burrow (1962)
DCP	*Dravidian Comparative Phonology,* P. S. Subrahmanyam (1983)
DED	*A Dravidian Etymological Dictionary,* T. Burrow and M. B. Emeneau (1961)
DEDR	*A Dravidian Etymological Dictionary,* T. Burrow and M. B. Emeneau (revised edition 1984)
DNM	*Deśīnāmamālā* (Prakrit dictionary), M. Banerjee (1931)
DVM	*Dravidian Verb Morphology,* P. S. Subrahmanyam (1971)
LSI	*Linguistic Survey of India, vol. IV,* George Grierson (1906)
TVB	*Telugu Verbal Bases,* Bh. Krishnamurti (1961)

Journals

AO	*Archiv Orientální*
BDCRI	*Bulletin of the Deccan College Research Institute*
BSO(A)S	*Bulletin of the School of Oriental (and African) Studies*
IA	*Indian Antiquary*
IIJ	*Indo-Iranian Journal*
IJDL	*International Journal of Dravidian Linguistics*
IL	*Indian Linguistics*
JAOS	*Journal of the American Oriental Society*
JOR	*Journal of Oriental Research*
JTS	*Journal of Tamil Studies*
PAPS	*Proceedings of the American Philosophical Society*
QJMS	*Quarterly Journal of Mythic Society*

SII	*South Indian Inscriptions*
TC	*Tamil Culture*
TPS	*Transactions of the Philological Society*
	Series
UCPL	University of California Publications in Linguistics
	Literary texts (Tamil)
Aiṅk.	Aiṅkuṟunūṟu
Cil.	Cilappatikāram
KT	Kuṟuntokai
Naṟṟ.	Naṟṟiṇai
Pat.	Patiṟṟuppattu
PN	Puṟanāṉūṟu
Tolk.	Tolkāppiyam
	Languages
ĀKu.	Ālu Kuṟumba
Bal.	Balochi
Br.	Brahui
CD	Central Dravidian
Eng.	English
Gad.	(Koṇḍekor) Gadaba
Go.	Gondi
IA	Indo-Aryan
IE	Indo-European
Ir.	Iruḷa
Ka.	Kannaḍa
Koṇḍa	–
Koḍ.	Koḍagu
Ko.	Kota
Kol.	Kolami
Kui	–
Kuṟ.	Kuṟumba
Kuṛ.	Kuṛux
Kuvi	–
Ma.	Malayāḷam
Malt.	Malto
Manḍa	–

ND	North Dravidian
Nk. (Ch.)	Naiki (Chanda)
Nk.	Naiki/Naikṛi
Oll.	Ollari
Pa.	Parji
Pali	–
PD	Proto-Dravidian
Pe.	Pengo
Pers.	Persian
Pkt.	Prakrit(s)
PKu.	Pāl Kuṟumba
SCD	South-Central Dravidian (same as SD II)
SD I	South Dravidian I
SD II	South Dravidian II
Skt.	Sanskrit
Ta.	Tamil
Te.	Telugu
To.	Toda
Tu.	Tuḷu
Ur.	Urdu

General

1	1st person
2	2nd person
3	3rd person
A	Subject of a transitive sentence
abl	ablative
adj	adjective
adjl	adjectival
AdjP	Adjectival Phrase
adv	adverb
advl	adverbial
AdvP	Adverbial Phrase
aux	auxiliary
caus	causative
cent	century
cl	clitic
class	classifier
com	comitative

comp	complement
conc	concessive
cond	conditional
conj	conjunction
coor	coordinator
dat	dative
dial	dialectal
dis	distal
dur	durative
emph	emphatic (particle)
ety.	etymological group serially numbered in the text of a chapter
excl	exclusive
f	feminine
fut	future
gen	genitive
h/hum	human
hon	honorific
imper	imperative
incl	inclusive
inf	infinitive
instr	instrumental
intr	intransitive
irreg	irregular
loc	locative
lw	loanword
m	masculine
M	Middle
Mdn	Modern
n	noun
neg	negative
neu.	neuter
n-h	non-human
n-m	non-masculine
noml	nominal
NP	Noun Phrase
n-past	non-past
num	numeral
O	Old (before language names); Object
obl	oblique

PE	personal ending
perf	perfective (tense/aspect)
pers	person
pl	plural
pol	polite
poss	possessive
pp	postposition
PP	Postpositional Phrase
ppl	perfective participle
pres	present
proh	prohibitive
prox	proximal
Pst	Past
S	Sentence; Subject of an intransitive sentence
sg	singular
soc	sociative
subj	subject
tr	transitive
v.i.	verb intransitive
Vst	Verb stem
v.t.	verb transitive

1

Introduction

1.1 The name Dravidian

Robert Caldwell (1856, 3rd edn, repr. 1956: 3–6) was the first to use 'Dravidian' as a generic name of the major language family, next to Indo-Aryan (a branch of Indo-European), spoken in the Indian subcontinent. The new name was an adaptation of a Sanskrit term *draviḍa-* (adj *drāviḍa-*) which was traditionally used to designate the Tamil language and people, in some contexts, and in others, vaguely the south Indian peoples. Caldwell says:

> The word I have chosen is 'Dravidian', from Drāviḍa, the adjectival form of Draviḍa. This term, it is true, has sometimes been used, and is still sometimes used, in almost as restricted a sense as that of Tamil itself, so that though on the whole it is the best term I can find, I admit it is not perfectly free from ambiguity. It is a term which has already been used more or less distinctively by Sanskrit philologists, as a generic appellation for the South Indian people and their languages, and it is the only single term they ever seem to have used in this manner. I have, therefore, no doubt of the propriety of adopting it. (1956: 4)

Caldwell refers to the use of Drāviḍa- as a language name by Kumārilabhaṭṭa's Tantravārttika (seventh century AD) (1956: 4). Actually Kumārila was citing some words from Tamil which were wrongly given Sanskritic resemblance and meanings by some contemporary scholars, e.g. Ta. *cōṟu* 'rice' (matched with Skt. *cora-* 'thief'), *pāmpu* 'snake', adj *pāppu* (Skt. *pāpa-* 'sin'), Ta. *atar* 'way' (Skt. *atara-* 'uncrossable'), Ta. *māḷ* 'woman' (Skt. *mālā* 'garland'), *vayiṟu* 'stomach' (Skt. *vaira-* 'enemy')[1] (Zvelebil 1990a: xxi–xxii). Caldwell further cites several sources from the scriptures such as the

[1] The actual passage cited by Zvelebil (1990a: xxii, fn. 21), based on Ganganatha Jha's translation of the text:

> tad yathā drāviḍa-bhāṣāyām eva tāvad vyanjanānta-bhāṣāpadeṣu svarānta-vibhakti-strīpratyayādi-kalpanābhiḥ svabhāṣānurūpān arthān pratipadyamānāḥ dṛśyante; tad yathā ōdanam cōr ityukte cōrapadavācyam kalpayanti; panthānam atara iti

Manusmr̥ti, Bharata's *Nāṭyaśāstra* and the *Mahābhārata* where Drāviḍa- is used as a people and Drāviḍī as a minor Prakrit belonging to the Paiśācī 'demonic' group. Since Tamiẓ was the established word for the Tamil language by the time Caldwell coined the term Dravidian to represent the whole family, it met with universal approval. He was aware of it when he said, 'By the adoption of this term "Dravidian", the word "Tamilian" has been left free to signify that which is distinctively Tamil' (1956: 6). Dravidian has come to stay as the name of the whole family for nearly a century and a half.[2]

1.2 Dravidians: prehistory and culture

1.2.1 *Prehistory*

It is clear that 'Aryan' and 'Dravidian' are not racial terms. A distinguished authority on the statistical correlation between human genes and languages, Cavalli-Sforza (2000), refuting the existence of racial homogeneity, says:

> In more recent times, the careful genetic study of hidden variation, unrelated to climate, has confirmed that homogenous races do not exist. It is not only true that racial purity does not exist in nature: it is entirely unachievable, and would not be desirable . . . To achieve even partial 'purity' (that

> kalpayitvā āhuḥ, satyam dustaratvāt atara eva panthā iti; tathā pāpaśabdam pakārāntam sarpavacanam; a kārāntam kalpayitvā satyam pāpa eva asau iti vadanti. evam māl śabdam strīvacanam mālā iti kalpayitvā satyam iti āhuḥ; vairśabdam ca rēphāntam udaravacanam, vairiśabdena pratyāmnāyam vadanti; satyam sarvasya kṣudhitasya akārye pravartanāt udaram vairikārye pravartate it . . .
>
> (Thus, in the Drāviḍa language, certain words ending in consonants are found to be treated as vowel-ending with gender and case suffixes, and given meanings, as though they are of their own language (Sanskrit); when food is called *cor*, they turn it into *cora*..('thief'). When a 'path' is called *atar*, they turn it into *atara* and say, true, the 'path' is *atara* because it is *dustara* 'difficult to cross'. Thus, they add *a* to the word *pāp* ending in *p* and meaning 'a snake' and say, true, it is *pāpa* 'a sinful being'. They turn the word *māl* meaning 'a woman' into *mālā* 'garland' and say, it is so. They substitute the word *vairi* ('enemy') for the word *vair*, ending in *r* and meaning 'stomach', and say, yes, as a hungry man does wrong deeds, the stomach undertakes wrong/inimical (*vairi*) actions . . .)

The items cited were actually of Tamil, namely *cōṟu* 'rice', *atar* 'way', *pāppu* adj of *pāmpu* 'snake', *māḷ* 'woman' < *makaḷ*; *vayiṟu* 'belly'. Since these did not occur as such in Kannaḍa or Telugu, Kumārilabhaṭṭa was referring to Tamil only in this passage by the name *drāviḍa-*.

[2] Joseph (1989) gives extensive references to the use of the term *draviḍa-*, *dramila-* first as the name of a people, then of a country. Sinhala inscriptions of BCE cite *dameḍa-*, *damela-* denoting Tamil merchants. Early Buddhist and Jaina sources used *damiḷa-* to refer to a people in south India (presumably Tamil); *damilaraṭṭha-* was a southern non-Aryan country; *dramiḷa-*, *dramiḍa-* and *draviḍa-* were used as variants to designate a country in the south (*Br̥hatsamhita-*, *Kādambarī*, *Daśakumāracarita-*, fourth to seventh centuries CE) (1989: 134–8). It appears that *damiḷa-* was older than *draviḍa-*, which could be its Sanskritization. It is not certain if *tamiẓ* is derived from *damiḷa-* or the other way round.

> is a genetic homogeneity that is never achieved in populations of higher animals) would require at least twenty generations of 'inbreeding' (e.g. by brother–sister or parent–children matings repeated many times) . . . we can be sure that such an entire inbreeding process has never been attempted in our history with a few minor and partial exceptions. (13)
>
> There is some indirect evidence that modern human language reached its current state of development between 50,000 and 150,000 years ago . . . . Beginning perhaps 60,000 or 70,000 years ago, modern humans began to migrate from Africa, eventually reaching the farthest habitable corners of the globe such as Tierra del Fuego, Tasmania, the Coast of the Arctic Ocean, and finally Greenland. (60)
>
> Calculations based on the amount of genetic variation observed today suggests that the population would have been about 50,000 in the Paleolithic period, just before expansion out of Africa. (92)

He finds that the genetic tree and the linguistic tree have many 'impressive similarities' (see Cavalli-Sforza 2000: figure 12, p. 144). The figure, in effect, supports the Nostratic Macro-family, which is not established on firm comparative evidence (Campbell 1998, 1999). Talking about the expansion of the speakers of the Dravidian languages, Cavalli-Sforza says:

> The center of origin of Dravidian languages is likely to be somewhere in the western half of India. It could be also in the South Caspian (the first PC center), or in the northern Indian center indicated by the Fourth PC. This language family is found in northern India only in scattered pockets, and in one population (Brahui) in western Pakistan. (157)

He goes on to suggest a relationship between Dravidian and Elamite to the west and also the language of the Indus civilization (137), following the speculative discussions in the field. Still there is no archeological or linguistic evidence to show actually when the people who spoke the Dravidian languages entered India. But we know that they were already in northwest India by the time the R̥gvedic Aryans entered India by the fifteenth century BCE.

In an earlier publication Cavalli-Sforza et al. (1994: 239) have given a genetic tree of twenty-eight South Asian populations including the Dravidian-speaking ones, which is reproduced below as figure 1.1 (their fig. 4.14.1). They say:

> A subcluster is formed by three Dravidian-speaking groups (one northern and two central Dravidian groups, C1 and C2) and the Austro-Asiatic speakers, the Munda. The C1 Dravidian group includes the Chenchu–Reddi (25,000), the Konda (16,000), the Koya (210,000), the Gondi (1.5million),

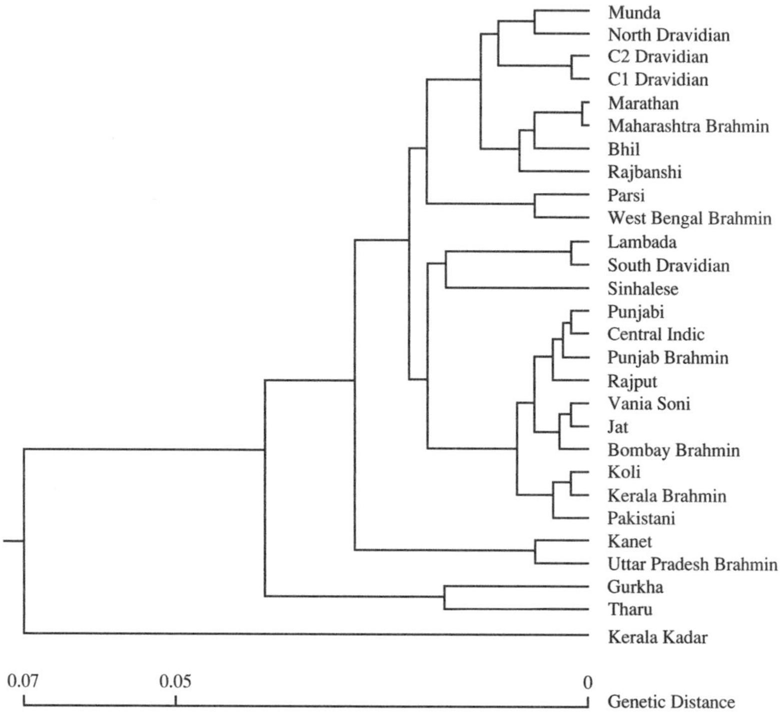

Figure 1.1 Genetic tree of South Asian populations including the Dravidian-speaking ones

and others, all found in many central and central-eastern states, though most data come from one or a few locations. The C2 Dravidian group includes the Kolami–Naiki (67,000), the Parji (44,000) and others; they are located centrally, a little more to the west. North Dravidian speakers are the Oraon (23 million), who overlap geographically with some of the above groups and are located in a more easterly and northerly direction. (239)

The second major cluster, B, contains a minor subcluster B1 formed by Sinhalese, Lambada, and South Dravidian speakers . . . The South Dravidian group includes a number of small tribes like Irula (5,300) in several southern states but especially Madras, the Izhava in Kerala, the Kurumba (8,000) in Madras, the Nayar in Kerala, the Toda (765), and the Kota (860 in 1971) in the Nilgiri Hills in Madras (Saha et al. 1976). (240)[3]

[3] Based on earlier writings, Sjoberg (1990: 48) says, 'the Dravidian-speaking peoples today are a mixture of several racial sub-types, though the Mediterranean Caucasoid component predominates. No doubt many of the subgroups who contributed to what we call Dravidian culture will

Several scholars have maintained, without definite proof, that Dravidians entered India from the northwest over two millennia before the Aryans arrived there around 1500 BCE. Rasmus Rask 'was the first to suggest that the Dravidian languages were probably "Scythian", broadly representing "barbarous tribes that inhabited the northern parts of Asia and Europe"' (Caldwell 1956: 61–2). There have been many studies genetically relating the Dravidian family with several languages outside India (see for a review of earlier literature, Krishnamurti 1969b: 326–9, 1985: 25), but none of these hypotheses has been proved beyond reasonable doubt (see section 1.8 below).

Revising his earlier claim (1972b) that Dravidians entered India from the northwest around 3500 BC, Zvelebil (1990a: 123) concludes: 'All this is still in the nature of speculation. A truly convincing hypothesis has not even been formulated yet.' Most of the proposals that the Proto-Dravidians entered the subcontinent from outside are based on the notion that Brahui was the result of the first split of Proto-Dravidian and that the Indus civilization was most likely to be Dravidian. There is not a shred of concrete evidence to credit Brahui with any archaic features of Proto-Dravidian. The most archaic features of Dravidian in phonology and morphology are still found in the southern languages, namely Early Tamil *āytam*, the phoneme *ẓ*, the dental-alveolar-retroflex contrast in the stop series, lack of voice contrast among the stops, a verbal paradigm incorporating tense and transitivity etc. The Indus seals have not been deciphered as yet. For the time being, it is best to consider Dravidians to be the natives of the Indian subcontinent who were scattered throughout the country by the time the Aryans entered India around 1500 BCE.

1.2.1.1 *Early traces of Dravidian words*

Caldwell and other scholars have mentioned several words from Greek, Latin and Hebrew as being Dravidian in origin. The authenticity of many of these has been disputed. At least two items seem plausible: (1) Greek *oruza/oryza/orynda* 'rice' which must be compared with Proto-Dravidian **war-inci* > Ta. Ma. Te. *wari*, Pa. *verci(l)*, Gad. *varci(l)*, Gondi *wanji* 'rice, paddy' [*DEDR* 5265] and not with Ta. *arisi* (South Dravidian **ariki*) as proposed by Caldwell. Old Persian *virinza* and Skt. *vrīhi-* 'rice' which have no Indo-European etymology pose a problem in dating the borrowing from Dravidian; (2) Greek *ziggiberis/zingiberis* 'ginger' from South Dravidian nominal compound **cinki-wēr* (PD **wēr* 'root') > Pali *singi*, *singivera*, Skt. *śṛṅgavera-*; Ta. Ma. *iñci* was derived from **cinki* by **c* [>*s* >*h* >] > Ø, and by changing *-k* to *-c* before a front vowel.[4] A number of place names of south India cited by the Greek geographers

be forever unknown to us.' Basham (1979: 2) considers that 'the Dravidian languages were introduced by Palaeo-Mediterranean migrants who came to India in the Neolithic period, bringing with them the craft of agriculture'.

[4] I am indebted to Professor Heinrich von Staden of the Institute for Advanced Study, Princeton, for providing me with dates for these words in early Greek texts: *oryza* 'rice' (earliest occurrence in

Pliny (first century AD) and Ptolemy (third century AD) end in *-our* or *-oura* which is a place name suffix *ūr* 'town' from PD *_ūr_.

It is certain that Dravidians were located in northwestern India by the time the Aryans entered the country around the middle of the second millennium BC. R̥gvedic Sanskrit, the earliest form of Sanskrit known (c.1500 BC), already had over a dozen lexical items borrowed from Dravidian, e.g. *ulūkhala-* 'mortar', *kuṇḍa* 'pit', *khála-* 'threshing floor', *kāṇa-* 'one-eyed', *mayūra* 'peacock' etc. (Emeneau 1954; repr. 1980: 92–100). The introduction of retroflex consonants (those produced by the tongue-tip raised against the middle of the hard palate) from the R̥gvedic times was also credited to the contact of Sanskrit speakers with those of the Dravidian languages. (For more on this theme, see section 1.7 below.)

A Russian Indologist, Nikita Gurov, claims that there were as many as eighty words of Dravidian origin in the *R̥gveda*, 'occurring in 146 hymns of the first, tenth and the other maṇḍalas', e.g. *R̥V* 1.33.3 *vaila* (*sthāna-*) 'open space': PD *_wayal_ 'open space, field' [5258], *R̥V* 10.15 *kiyāmbu* 'a water plant': PD *_keyampu_ (<*_kecampu_) 'Arum colacasia, yam' [2004], *R̥V* 1.144 *vríś* 'finger': PD *_wirinc-_ [5409], *R̥V* 1.71, 8.40 *vīḷú* 'stronghold': PD *_wīṭu_ 'house, abode, camp' [5393], *sīrá* 'plough': PD *_cēr_, *R̥V* 8.77 *kāṇukā*: PD *_kāṇikkay_ 'gift' [1443]; 'T.Ya. Elizarenkova: *kāṇuka* is a word of indistinct meaning, most probably of non-Indo-European origin.' Gurov also cites some proper names, *namuci*, *kīkaṭa*, *paramaganda*, as probably of Dravidian origin.[5]

1.2.2 *Proto-Dravidian culture*

The culture of the speakers of Proto-Dravidian is reconstructed on the basis of the comparative vocabulary drawn from *DEDR* (1984). Something similar to this has been done for the other language families (Mallory 1989: ch. 5). However, in the case of Dravidian, there are certain limitations to be taken into account:

1. Only four of the Dravidian languages have recorded history and literature starting from pre-CE to the eleventh century. The available dictionaries of the literary languages are extensive, running to over 100,000 lexical items in each case. The vocabulary of the non-literary languages is not commensurate. Now Tuḷu has a six-volume lexicon, but there is no comparable dictionary for Koḍagu, which is also semi-literary in the sense that Tuḷu is. *The Baḍaga–English Dictionary* of 1992 by Hockings and Pilot-Raichoor is fairly large. The remaining twenty or so non-literary languages spoken by 'scheduled tribes' do not have recorded lexicons/word lists of even one-twentieth of the above size. Therefore, most of the cognates turn up in the four literary languages, of which Tamil,

the fourth century BC), *orindes* 'bread made of rice flour' (earliest fifth century BC), *zingiberis*(*s*) 'ginger' (first century BC in *Dioscurides*). There is evidence of sea-trade between south Indian ports on the west coast and Rome and Greece in the pre-Christian era.

5 Based on a manuscript handout of a paper, 'Non-Aryan elements in the early Sanskrit texts (Vedas and epics)', submitted to the Orientalists' Congress in Budapest, July 1997 (see Gurov 2000).

Malayāḷam and Kannaḍa belong to South Dravidian I and Telugu to South Dravidian II. The absence of cognates in the other subgroups cannot be taken to represent the absence of a concept or a term in Proto-Dravidian. The presence of a name (a cognate) in the minor languages and its exclusion in the major languages should lead to a significant observation that the cognate could be lost in the literary languages, but not vice versa.

2. Semantic changes within the recorded languages do not give us, in certain cases, a clue to identify the original meaning and the path of change. We need to apply certain historical and logical premises in arriving at the original meaning and there is a danger of some of these being speculative. For instance, certain items have pejorative meaning in South Dravidian I (sometimes includes Telugu), while the languages of South Dravidian II have a normal (non-pejorative) meaning: e.g. **maṯ-i(nṯu)* 'the young of an animal' in South Dravidian I, but 'a son, male child' in South Dravidian II [4764]. Similarly, **pē(y)/*pēṇ* 'devil' in South Dravidian I, but 'god' in South Dravidian II [4438]. We do not know which of these is the Proto-Dravidian meaning. We can speculate that the pejorative meaning could be an innovation in the literary languages after the Sanskritization or Aryanization of south India. There are, however, cases of reversal of this order, e.g. Ta. *payal* 'boy', so also all others of South Dravidian I; in Central Dravidian and South Dravidian II languages, *pay-*~*peyy-*V- 'a calf' [**pac*-V- 3939].

3. While the presence of a cognate set is positive evidence for the existence of a concept, the absence of such a set does not necessarily indicate that a given concept had never existed among the proto-speakers. It could be due to loss or inadequacies of recording. In addition to one of the literary languages (South Dravidian I and South Dravidian II), if a cognate occurs in one of the other subgroups, i.e. Central Dravidian or North Dravidian, the set is taken to represent Proto-Dravidian. In some cases a proto-word is assumed on the basis of cognates in only two languages belonging to distant subgroups.

4. Where there are several groups of etyma involving a given meaning, I have taken that set in which the meaning in question is widely distributed among the languages of different subgroups. For some items two or more reconstructions are given which represent different subgroups. It is also possible that in some cases there were subtle differences in meaning not brought out in the English glosses available to us, e.g. curds, butttermilk; paddy, rice etc. in section 1.2.2.2.

Keeping these principles in view we reconstruct what the Proto-Dravidian speakers were like.[6]

1.2.2.1 *Political organization*

There were kings and chiefs (lit. the high one) [**eṯ-ay-anṯu* 'lord, master, king, husband' 527, **kō/*kōn-ṯu* 'king (also mountain)' 2177, **wēnt-anṯu* 'king, god' 5529, 5530],[7] who

[6] If readers want to read the running text, they may skip the material in square brackets.

[7] Some of the words have plausible sources, e.g. **ēṯ-* 'to rise, be high' [916], **kō* 'mountain' [2178, given as a homophonous form of the word meaning 'king, emperor' 2177, but it could as well be

ruled [*$y\bar{a}\d{l}$, 5157]. They lived in palaces [*kōy-il 2177] and had forts and fortresses [*kōṭṭ-ay 2207a], surrounded by deep moats [*akaẓ-tt-ay 11] filled with water. They received different kinds of taxes and tributes [*ar-i 216, *kapp-am 1218]. There were fights, wars or battles [*pōr, 4540] with armies arrayed [*aṇi 117] in battlefields [*mun-ay 5021, *kaḷ-an 1376]. They knew about victory or winning [? *gel-/*kel- 1972] and defeat or fleeing [*ōṭu v.i., ōṭ-ṭam n. 1041, 2861]. Proto-Dravidians spoke of large territorial units called *nāṭu (>*nāṯu in South Dravidian II, 3638) for a province, district, kingdom, state [3638], while *ūr [752] was the common word for any habitation, village or town. A hamlet was known as *paḷḷ-i [4018]. [The highest official after the king was the minister *per-kaṭa [4411] 'the one in a high place' (a later innovation in Kannaḍa and Telugu).]

1.2.2.2 *Material culture and economy*

People built houses to stay in [*wīṭu 5393,[8] *il 494, man-ay 4776, ir-uwu 480]; most of these derive from the root meaning 'to settle, stay, live'. Houses had different kinds of roofing, thatched grass [*pīr-i 4225, *pul 4300, *wēy 'to thatch' 5532], tiles [*peṇ-kk- 4385] or terrace [*mēṭ-ay, *māṭ-V- 4796 a,b].

There were umbrellas [*koṭ-ay 1663] and sandals [*keruppu 1963] made of animal skin/hide [*tōl 3559] that people used. Among the domestic tools, the mortar [*ur-al/-aḷ 651], pestle [*ul-akk-V- 672, *uram-kkal 651, from *ur- 'to grind' 665 and *kal 'stone' 1298], grinding stone, winnowing basket [*kēṯṯ- 2019] and sweeping broom [*cī-pp-/ *cay-pp- 2599] existed. Different kinds of pots made of clay [*kā-nk- 1458, *kur-Vwi 1797, *caṭṭi 'small 'pot' 2306] or of metal [*kiṇṭ-V 1540, 1543, *kem-pu 'copper vessel' 2775] were used for cooking and storing. Cattle [*toṯ-V-] consisting of cows and buffaloes were kept in stalls [*to ẓ-V-]. Milk [*pāl 4096] and its curdled [*pēṯ-/*peṯ-V- 4421] form curds, buttermilk [*caḷ-V- 2411, *moc-Vr 4902, *peṟ-uku 4421] were churned [*tar-V-] to make butter/white oil [*weṇ-ṇey < *weḷ-ney 5496b].

Cloth woven [*nec-/*ney- 'to weave' 3745] from spun [*oẓ-ukk- 1012] thread [*ēẓ-/ *eẓ-V- 506, *nūl 3728], drawn from dressed [*eHk- 765] cotton [*par-utti 3976] was used, but different types of garments by gender were not known.

Among the native occupations, agriculture [*uẓ-V- 'to plough' 688] was known from the beginning. There were different kinds of lands meant for dry and wet cultivation [*paṇ-V- 'agriculture land' 3891, *pun 'dry land' 4337 (literally 'bad', as opposed to *nan- 'good'), *pol-am 'field' 4303, *kaẓ-Vt- 1355, *key-m 'wet field' 1958, *wāy/

the original meaning]; the last one seems to be related to *wēy 'extensiveness, height, greatness' [5404]. The meanings 'emperor, king' are based apparently on their later usage in the literary languages. The basic meaning seems to be the person who is the 'highest, tallest and the most important'.

[8] *DEDR* should have separated the set of forms *wiṭ-V- 'to lodge' and its derivative 'house' from the homophonous root wiṭu 'to leave' and its derivatives.

way-V- 5258]. Cattle dung [**pēṇṭ*-V (<**pēḷ-nt-*) 4441a, b] was used as manure. The word for a plough [**ñāñ-k*V*l*][9] was quite ancient. A yoked plough [**cēr* 2815] and a ploughed furrow [**cāl* 2471] had basic words. Some parts of the plough had basic terms like the shaft [**kōl* 2237], plough-share [**kāṯ-* 1505], and plough handle [**mēẓ-i* 5097]. Seedlings [**ñāṯ-u* 2919] were used for transplantation. Harvesting was by cutting [**koy* 2119] the crop. Threshing in an open space [**kaḷ-am* /**kaḷ-an* 1376] separated the grain from the grass. Grain was measured in terms of a unit called **puṭṭ-i* [4262], about 500 lbs, and stored in large earthen pots [*wān-ay* 4124, 5327].

Paddy [**kūl-i* 1906, **nel* 3743, **war-iñc-* 5265] and millets [**ār*/**ar-ak* 812, **koṯ-V-* 2165] of different kinds were grown. The cultivation of areca nut [**aṭ-ay-kkāy* 88, **pānkk-* 4048], black pepper [**miḷ*-V*ku* 4867], and cardamom [**ēl*-V 907] seem native to the Dravidians, at least in south India.

Milk [**pāl* 4096], curds [**per*-V-*ku*/-*ppu* 1376], butter [**weḷ-ney* 5496b], ghee, oil [**ney* 3746], rice [*war-inc* 5265] and meat [**iṯ-aycci* 529] were eaten. Boiling, roasting [**kāy* 1438, **wec-*/*wey-* 5517] and frying [**waṯ*-V- 5325] were the modes of cooking [**aṭ-u* 76, **wanṯ-* 5329] food on a fire-place [**col* 2857] with stones arranged on three sides. Toddy (country liquor from the toddy palm tree)[**īzam* 549, **kaḷ* 1374] and Mahua liquor (brewed from sweet mahua flowers) [**ir-upp-a- Bassia longifolia* 485] were the intoxicating beverages.

People carried loads [**mūṭṭ-ay* 'bundle' 5037] on the head with a head-pad [**cum*-V-2677] or on the shoulder by a pole with ropes fastened to both ends with containers on each [*kā-waṭi* 1417].

Different tools were used for digging [**kun-tāl* 'pick-axe', **pār-ay* 'crowbar' 4093], cutting and chopping [**katti* 'knife' 1204]. People used bows [**wil* 5422] and arrows [**ampu* 17a] in fighting [**pōr*/**por-u-* 4540] or hunting [**wēṇ-ṭṭ-a-* 5527]. They had the sword [**wāḷ* 5376, **wāy-cc-i* 5399], axe [**maẓ*-V-/**maṯ*-V*cc* 4749] and the club [**kut*-V 1850b]. There was no word for a cart and a wheel until much later.[10] In the literary languages there is an ancient word **tēr* 'chariot' [3459] used on the battle-field or as a temple car.[11] Buying [**koḷ-*/**koṇ-* 215], selling [**wil-* 5421] and barter [**māṯṯ-* 4834] were known. 'Price' is derived from 'sell' [**wilay* 5241].

[9] Obviously a compound derived from *ñam* + *kōl* 'our shaft'; *kōl* is used in the sense of a plough shaft in some of the languages. Its general meaning, however, is 'stick, pole, staff'. In unaccented position the vowel has undergone variation as *-kāl*, *-kēl*, *-kil* (*-cil* with palatalization in Tamil), *-kal*, etc.

[10] The widely used set in the literary languages is Ta. Ma. *vaṇṭi*, Ka. Te. *baṇḍi* 'cart', which is traced to Skt. *bhāṇḍa-* 'goods, wares', Pkt. *bhaṇḍī* (see *DEDR* Appendix, Supplement to *DBIA*, 50). A native-like word for wheel is Ta. *kāl*, Ka. Tu. *gāli*, Te. *gānu*, *gālu* [1483] is probably related to **kāl* 'leg' [1479].

[11] This word occurs in South Dravidian I and Telugu. In Kota *dēr* 'god, possession of a diviner by god', *tēr kārn* 'diviner', To. *tör ōḍ-* '(shaman) is dancing and divining', Tu. *tēri* 'idol car, the car festival'. The origin of this word is not clear.

People used medicines [**mar-untu* 4719], presumably taken from tree [**mar-an* 4711a] products. The expression 'mother', denoting mother goddess, was used for the virus smallpox. The rash on skin through measles etc. [**taṭṭ-*/**taṭ-V-* 3028] had a name. Not many words are available for different diseases. Some disorders had expressions such as blindness [**kur-uṭu* 1787], deafness [**kew-iṭu*, **kep-* 1977c], being lame [**coṭṭ-* 2838], cataract [**por-ay* 'film' 4295] and insanity [**picc-*/**pic-*V- 4142].

Certain items of food can be reconstructed for the literary languages of the south, the pancake made of flour [**aṭṭu* 76, **app-am* 155, **tōc-ay* 3542]. The staple food was cooked rice, thick porridge [*kūẓ* 1911,?**amp-ali* 174], or gruel [**kañc-i* 1104] and meat [**iṯ-aycci* 528, **ū/ ūy* 728]. Proto-Dravidians sang [**pāṭ-u* 4065] and danced [**āṭ-u* 347].

They knew of iron [**cir-umpu* 2552], gold [**pon* 4570, **pac-*V*ṇṭ-* 3821] and silver [**weḷ-nt-* 5496] derived from the colour terms for 'black' [**cir-*V- 2552], 'yellow' [**pac-* 3821] (not **pon*), and 'white' [**weḷ* 5496].

1.2.2.3 *Social organization*

The Dravidian languages are rich in kinship organization. Separate labels exist for the elder and younger in ego's generation; but for the ones (one or two generations) above and below, descriptive terms 'small' (younger) and 'big' (older) are used, e.g. **akka-* 'elder sister' [23], **tam-kay* [3015], **cēl-āḷ* 'younger sister' [2783], **aṇṇa-* 'elder brother' [131], **tamp-V-* 'younger brother' [3485]; **app-a-* [156a] **ayy-a-* [196]/*tan-tay* ~ **tan-ṯi* 'father' [3067; *tam* + *tay* vs. *tan* + *ṯi* (< ? *-tay*)], **amm-a-* [183]/**āy* [364]/ **aww-a*[273]/ **taḷḷ-ay*/*-i* 'mother' [3136], **mak-anṯu* [4616]/ **koẓ-V-* [2149]/ *maṯ-in-ṯu* 'son' [4764];[12] **mak-aḷ* [4614] /**kūn-ttu, -ccu, -kku* [1873] 'daughter'. The same words are used for father's sister/mother's brother's wife/mother-in-law **atta-* [142], so also for their respective husbands **māma-* [4813] 'father's sister's husband/mother's brother/father-in-law'. This is because of the custom of their daughter/son being eligible for marriage by ego. If we go to another generation higher or lower we find both neutralization of categories and a wide variation of particular terms in usage; examples: mother's father/father's father are indicated by the same term **tātt-a-* [3160] or *pāṭṭ-āṉ* [4066], but their spouses were distinguished descriptively in different languages, Ta. Ma. *pāṭṭ-i* [4066] 'grandmother', Te. *amm-amma* 'mother's mother', *nāyan* (*a*)*-amma* 'father's mother'. Corresponding to Ta. *mūtt-app-aṉ* 'father's father', *muṟṟ-avai* 'grandmother', Ma. *mutt-app-an* 'grandfather', *mūtt-app-an* 'father's father' (also 'father's elder brother'), *mūtt-amma* 'mother's mother' (also 'elder sister of father or mother')

[12] The root **maṯ-* underlies another set of kinship terms only found in South Dravidian II and borrowed from Telugu into Central Dravidian, e.g. Te. *maṟ-a*^{n}*di* [Mdn. Te. *maridi*] 'spouse's younger brother, younger sister's husband, younger male cross-cousin'; the corresponding female kin is *maṟa*^{n}*d-alu* 'spouse's younger sister, younger brother's wife, younger female cross-cousin'. Cognates occur in Gondi, Kui and Kuvi [see 4762].

[4954], Telugu, Tuḷu and Koḍagu have independently developed expressions with **mut-* 'old' added to words meaning 'grandfather/grandmother' to refer to kinship two generations higher ('great-'): Te. *mut-tāta* 'great grandfather', *mutt-awwa* 'great grandmother', Tu. *mutt-ajje*, *mutt-ajji*, Koḍ. *mutt-ajjë*, *mut-tāy* id. [4954]. Even in the terms referring to one generation above, there is local specialization as well as variation in generation overlap. Thus it is not unusual to find a term meaning mother/father in one language means grandmother/grandfather in another language. Thus *tāta*, *appa*, *ayya* have overlapping meanings regionally. The words for husband and wife are synonymous with man/woman **āḷ* [399], **kaṇṭ-a-*, **maẓc-a-* [4756], **māy-tt-/*mā-cc-* [4791] 'man';**āḷ* [400], **peṇ-(ṭṭ-)* [4395] 'woman'. The word for son-in-law and nephew were the same [**cāḷ-iy-anṯu* 2410].[13]

Marriage [**mat-al/-uw-ay*, 4694 SD I, *peṇḍ-ili*, 4395a SD II, **wet-V-* 'to search, marry', ND 5483] was an established institution. We do not know at what stage the tying of *tāli* 'marriage necklace' [3175] was introduced into the marriage ritual.

There are no reconstructible words for caste or caste names. Native terms can be identified for farming [**uẓ-a-tti* 688], pot making [**koc*-V- 1762], smithy [**kol* 2133] and toddy tapping [**īẓ-a-wanṯ-* 'toddy-tapper' 549, from **īẓ-am* 'toddy']. There is an item meaning a weaver [**cāl*-V*y-anṯu* 2475]. Several occupational terms came later as borrowings from Indo-Aryan, e.g. Te. *kamm-ari* 'blacksmith', *kumm-ari* 'potter'.

Lying [**poc-V-*, **poy-nkk-* 4531] and theft [**kaḷ* 1372] were known. There were expressions for service or work [**paṇ* 3884] and slavery [**toẓ-V-* 3523], but no clear words for the rich and the poor.

1.2.2.4 *Religion*

There were words for god [**pē(y)*, **pēṇ* 4438, in SD II, but in SD I 'devil'] and **kō/*kōnṯ-* [2177] 'king, god'. There were animal sacrifices to attain wishes [**wēḷ* 5544]; this word has changed its meaning to 'offerings made in fire' after perhaps the Aryanization of South India. In Telugu *wēl-cu* is 'to sacrifice in fire' and *wēlpu* 'god'. The basic meaning of **wēḷ* [ultimately from **weH-ḷ*, see Krishnamurti 1997b: 150] was 'to wish, desire'. There is a special verb to denote animal sacrifices, *aḷ-V-kk-* found in South Dravidian II and Brahui [297]. Pollution [**pul*-V- 4547] was observed on different occasions, menstruation [**muṭṭu* 4934], birth [**pur-uṭu*], death etc. Not much is known about the religious rituals of Proto-Dravidians. Scholars have speculated about them in terms of the current ritual practices.

[13] Trautmann (1981: 229–37) has reconstructed a paradigm of Proto-Dravidian kinship organization, using four semantic contrasts, 'sex, generation, relative age and crossness'. He has not illustrated the contrasts in terms of linguistic categories used in different subgroups; he claims to have used the method of reconstruction of historical linguistics.

1.2.2.5 *Flora and fauna*

Words for tropical trees can be traced to Proto-Dravidian. Big trees like the banyan [**āl,* 382], neem [**wē-mpu* 5531], palmyra [**tāẓ* 380, **pan*-V- 4037], tamarind [**cin-tta* 2529], pipal [**ar-ac-/-aḷ* 202, **cuw-* 2697], mango [**mām-* 4782, **maṯ-kāy* 4772], jack fruit [**pal-ac-* ~ **pan-ac* 3987] and myrobalan [**nel*-V- 3755] were part of the immediate environment of people. The small trees included the coconut [**ten-kāy* 3408], the date palm [**cīnt*(*t*)- 2617] and the soap-nut [**cīk-kāy* 2607a].

Wild trees growing in forests included teak [**tēnkk-* 3452], *Belleric myrobalan* [**tānṯ-i* 3198], *Schleichera trijuga* [**puc-/*puy-* 4348], mastwood [**punn-ay* 4343], *Eugenia jambolana* [**ñānṯ*-Vl 2917] and *Terminalia tomentosa* [**mar*-V*t*- 4718], etc.

A number of vegetables, cereals and fruit were used: greens [*kucc-/*kuc*-V- 1760], tubers, roots [**kiẓ*-V*nk* 1347], fruit/pod [**kāy* 1459], mushroom [**kūnt* (*t*)- 1893], onion [**uḷḷi* 705], ginger [**cink-i* 429], yam, *Colacasia antiquorum* [**kic-ampu* 2004], brinjal [**waẓ*-V*t*- 5301], fenugreek [**mentt-i* 5072], radish [**mūḷ-/*muḷḷ*-V- 5004], black gram [**uẓ-untu* 690], green gram [**pac*-V*ṯ/*-V*l* 3941], red gram or tuwar [**kar*-V*nti* 1213], sesame [**nū*(*w*) 3720], plantain, banana [**wāẓ-a-* 5373, *ar-Vṇṭi* 205], wood-apple [**weḷ*-V- 5509] and sugar-cane [**kar-umpu* 1288, **ceṯ-Vkk-* 2795].

The following domestic animals were known: cat [**wer-uku* 5490, **pill*-V 4180], rat [**el-i* 833], dog [**naH-ay/-att/-kuẓi* 3650], pig [**pan-ṯi* 4039], donkey [**kaẓ-ut-ay* 1364], cow [**ā*(*m*)- 334], ox [**er-utu* 815, **ēṯu* 917], buffalo [**er-um*V- 816], sheep [**koṯ-i* 2165]/ram, goat [**yāṭu* 5152, **tak-ar* 3000, *mēnkk*-V- 5087] and also the young of these [**kaṭ-ac-* 1123]. There have been native words for horse [**kut-ir-ay* SD I, 1711a from **kut-i* 'to jump', Te. *guṟṟ-am* 1711b, *māwu* 4780] but their etymologies are doubtful.

Proto-Dravidians knew of reptiles such as the snake [*pāmpu* 4085], cobra [**car-ac-* 2359], scorpion [**tēḷ* 3470], chameleon [**oṭ*-V*kk*- 2977, *toṇṭ*-V- 3501] and different types of lizards [**pall-i* 3994, **kaw-uḷi* 'house lizard' 1339; **ōn-tti* 'bloodsucker lizard' 1053]. There were mosquitoes [**nuẓ*-V*-ḷ/-nk* 3715] and insects [**puẓ-u-* 4312] of different kinds.

The wild animals which lived in the hills [**kunṯ-am* 1864] and forests [**kā*(*n*)- 1418; *kāṭu* 1438] included the iguana [**uṭ-ump-* 592], mongoose [**mūnk-ūc-* 4900], cheetah, panther [**kiṯ-u-tt-/-mp-* 1599, 2589], tiger [**pul-i* 4307, **uẓ-uw-* 692], elephant [**yĀnay* 516], black bear [**eḷ*-V*-ñc-* 857], porcupine [**cey-t-/*coy-t-* 2776, 2852], wild buffalo [**kaṭ*-V- 1114], wolf [**tōẓ*-V, **tōẓ-nt-* 3548], jackal [**nari* (*-kkV*) 306], stag [**kaṭ*-V*-ncc/-ntt* 1114, **uẓ-u-pp-* 694], deer [**kur*-V*-c-* 1785, *mā-y* 4780], hare [**muc*-V*l* 4968], langur, black-faced monkey, baboon [**muy-cc-* 4910] and monkey [**kor*-V*-nk-/-ntt-* 1769]. I could not find any word for lion[14] or rhinoceros.

[14] *DEDR* 5158: *yāḷi, āḷi* 'a lion; a mythological lion-faced animal with elephantine proboscis and tusks'; Ma. *yāẓi* 'lion, panther'; *āḷi* 'a fabulous animal'. This is a doubtful etymology, as there are no cognates in any other language and the figure of this is found only in temple sculpture.

The known birds included the chicken [**kōẓ-i* 2248, **koṯ-u* 2160 in SD II], peacock [**ñam*-V-*l* 2902], pigeon, dove [**puṯ*-V*c*- 4334, **kūm*-/**kum*-V- 1930], 'imperial pigeon' [**pok*-V*ḷ* 4454], parrot [**kiḷ*-V- 1584], crane [**kor*V-*nk*-/-*nkk* 2125], eagle [**kaẓ*-V-*ku*/-*tu* 1362], vulture [**par*-V*ntu* 3977], crow [**kā-kk*-/-*w*- 1425], sparrow [**piẓ*-V*cc*- 4190, **kur*-V-*wi* 1793] and owl [**ānt-ay* SD I, 359]. A male of an animal or a bird was called **pō-ntt*-V [4586] and a female **peṇ-ṭṭ*-V- [4395a, b].

Aquatic animals (amphibians) included the frog [**kapp-a* 1224, **par*-V*ṇṭu* 'bull-frog' 3955], crab [**ñaṇṭ*- 2901], different kinds of fish [**kay*-V- (*l*/-*kk*-/*mpp*-)1252, **mīn* 4885], prawn [**eṯ*-V-*y* 533], shark [**coṯ-ac*- 710], tortoise [**yām-ay*, **cām-p*- 5155] and crocodile, alligator [**mōc*-/**moc*-V*ḷ* 4952, **nek*-V*ḷ* 3732]. There is no native word for goose or swan. A male of an animal or bird was **pōntt*- [4586] and a female **peṇ-ṭṭ*- [4395 a].

1.2.2.6 *Climate and water sources*

Words for sun [**pōẓ*/ **poẓ*-V*tu* 4559, **ñāc*-V*ṯu* 2910], moon [**nel-a-nc*/-*ncc* 3754, **tin-kaḷ* 3213 in SD I], stars [**cukk*-V 2646, **miHn* 4876], sky [**wān-am* 5381], clouds [**muy-il* 4892], wind [**wal*-V- 5312], rain [**maẓ-ay* 4753 SD I, **piṯ-u* 4199 SD II, ND, **tuw-Vṯ* 'to drizzle' 3398], night [**cir-a*-, **cir*-V-*ḷ*/-*nk*- 'darkness' 2552, **cīnkk*- 2604, **nāḷ*/**naḷ*-V-'night' 3621] and day [**pak-al* 'daylight' 3805, **ñān-ṯu* 'day' 2920, **cir* 'day' 2553, only in CD] existed. There were words apparently denoting dew, fog, frost [**pan-i*- (*kil*) 4035, **may-nt* (*t*)- 4641] which were used with extended meanings. Clear distinction was not made among 'snow', 'ice' and 'dew'. Only Kuṛux and Malto have words for snow, ice [**kīw*-/**kiw*-V- 1618], but their etymology is not known. Being hot [**wec*-/**wey*- 5517] and cold [**caḷ*-/**caṇ*- 3045] had expressions. There are no basic expressions for seasons, except perhaps for monsoon, or the rainy season [**kār* 'dark clouds' 1278, **kōṭ-ay* 'west wind, monsoon' 2203 in SD I].

Water sources such as the sea [**kaṭ-al* 1118], river, stream [**yĀṯu* 5159], canal [**kāl* 1480], tank [**keṯ-ay*/-*uwu* 1980], lake [**kuḷ-am*/-V*ñc* 1828] and well [**nūy* 3706] were known. There were ships [**kal-am* 1305] and boats [**amp-i* 177, **kapp-al* 119, **paṭ*-V*ku* 3838] for navigation. There were floats [**tepp*-V- 3414] presumably used for sport or for short distances. Tubular tunnels for drainage [**tūmpu* 3389] and covered sluices [**mat-Vku* 4688, **kal-Vnk*- 1309] to drain surplus water from tanks were built. Only the southern languages have a word for navigator or boatsman [**taṇṭ-al* 3049], but it is difficult to know its source.

1.2.2.7 *Abstract concepts*

The word for 'mind' was 'the one inside, the pith' [**uḷḷ-am*, **neñ-cu*, see above] and 'to think' was a semantic extension of 'to see, consider' [several verbs: **kaHṇ*- 'to see' 1443, **cū-ẓ* 'to see, deliberate' 2735, **pār* 'to perceive, see, know' 4091, **tōn-ṯu* 'to appear, strike to mind' 3566] and 'to count' [**eṇ*- 793]. In Telugu, moreover, 'to say to oneself' [*anukon-*] is 'to think'. There are some basic forms like Ta. *ninai* 'to think' [<**nen-ay*, see *neñ-cu* above; 3683 SD I], **wak-ay* 'to consider, deliberate' [SD I, Te.] which are not semantically related to 'see' words. Kui and Brahui share a word which reconstructs to **ēl* 'mind, reason, knowledge' [912]. Another pair of forms, restricted to South Dravidian I and Telugu, is **kar*-V-*nt*- 'to intend, consider', *kar*-V-*ntt*- n. 'will, mind' [1283]. There are basic verbs meaning 'to know' [**aṯ*-V- 314, SD I, II, ND] and 'to learn' [**kal-*/**kaṯ*- 1297, SD I, II, CD]. Understanding and knowledge are semantically related to 'becoming clear or white' [**tēr*/*ter*-V- 3419, **teḷ*-*V*- 3433, **weḷ* 5496]. Writing was 'scratching, drawing lines, painting' [**war*-V- 5263, **kī-ṯ*- 1623] perhaps on palm leaves with a stylus; there were words for 'reading, reciting' [**ōtu* 1052, **cat-u*- 2327] and 'singing' [**pāṭ*- 4065]. Forgetting was 'being hidden, obscure' [**maṯ*-V- 4760]. There were basic expressions for fear, shame, beauty, strength etc.

There were basic numerals up to ten and one hundred; only Telugu has a native number word for 'thousand' *wēyi*, which *DEDR* relates to **wey-am* 'extensiveness, height' (cognates only in Ta. Ma. and Go. 5404). The number nine [**toṇ-*/*toḷ*- 3532] is also expressed as ten minus one. The numeral 'eight' and the verb 'to count' [**eṇ* 793] are homophonous. This has led some to say that Dravidians counted in terms of 'eight'. But the system is clearly decimal, $11 = 10 + 1$, $12 = 10 + 2$ etc., 21 = 2-10-1, 22 = 2-10-2. The preceding digit of a higher number signalled multiplication and the following one addition.

Time [**nēr-am* 'sun' 3774, **pōẓ-*/**poẓ-utu* 'time, sun' 4559] was referred to in terms of units of the day [**nāḷ* 'day' 3656, **nāṇ-ṭ*- < ***nāḷ-nt*- SD II], month [**nel*-V- 3754] and year [**yĀṇṭu* 5153]; there were descriptive expressions for yesterday and the day-before-yesterday; similarly for tomorrow and the day-after-tomorrow. East and west have several reconstructible names, while north and south have one reconstruction each: east [**cir*-V-*tt*- 'the low area' 2584, **kīẓ*/**kiẓ*-V*kku* 'the area below' in SD I], west [**mē-l* 'high place', *mēṯ-kku*, **mel*-V*kku* 5086, **koṭ*-V*kku* 1649; the last one looks more basic], south [**ten*, *teṯ-kku* 3449] and north [**waṭ-akku* 5218].

1.2.2.8 *Miscellaneous*

There were basic words for all visible parts of the (human) body such as head, hair, face, eye, eyelid, eyeball, mouth, tongue, tooth, nose, ear, neck, trunk, chest, breast, stomach, hand, hip, leg, finger, nail, thigh, foot etc. Some invisible parts were also named, like the lungs [**poṯ*-V*ḷ* 4569, *tor*-V*mp*- 3515], bone [**el*-V-*mp*- 839], liver [**taẓ*-V*nk*- 3120], heart [**kuṇṭ*-V 1693, **uḷḷ-am* 'heart, mind' 698], brain [**mit*-V*ẓ* 5062, **neñc*-V 'brain, mind, heart, pith' 3736], bone-marrow [**mūḷ*-V- 5051], intestines [**wac*-V*ṯu* 'belly, intestines, foetus', **kar*-V*ḷ* 'intestines, bowels' 1274] and nerves [**ñar*-V*mpu* 2903], possibly known and seen from killing animals for food and in sacrifices to gods.

The colour spectrum was divided into four: white [**weḷ* 5496], black [**kār*/**kar*-V- 1278a], green–yellow [**pac*-V- 3821] and red [**kem*- 1931, **eṯ*-V- 865].

There were several words for speech acts, namely **aHn-* 'to say' [869], **pēc-/pēẓ-* 'to talk, prattle' [4430], **kēḷ-* 'to ask, to hear' [2017a], **kep-* 'to tell, scold' [1955], **col-* 'to speak, relate' [2855], **pāṇ/paṇ*-V- 'to question, commission, inquire', **pok*-Vẓ 'to praise' [4235], **noṭ*-V- 'to say' [3784], **moẓ*-V- 'to say, speak (loudly)' [4989]. It is difficult to sort out the minute differences in meaning or the precise contexts requiring the use of different terms.

Words for excrement or faeces [**pīy* 4210] and 'breaking wind' [**pī-t-/*pi-tt-* 4167] can be reconstructed for all subgroups.[15]

Names for precious stones include coral [**tuw*-V*r* 3284, **paw-aẓ* 3998] and pearl [**mutt-* 4959].

1.2.2.9 *Observations*

The foregoing outline of Proto-Dravidian culture gives a glimpse of a highly civilized people, who lived in towns in tiled or terraced houses, with agriculture as the main occupation. They drew water from wells, tanks and lakes, and knew drainage. They also carried trade by boat in the sea. However, there is no indication of the original home of these people. At least, it is certain that they do not have terms for flora and fauna not found in the Indian subcontinent. It is significant that Proto-Dravidians have not 'retained' any expressions for snow and ice and they do not have a name for the lion, rhino and camel. In view of this situation it would be safe to consider the speakers of the Dravidian languages as native people of India. This does not rule out the possibility of Proto-Dravidians being the originators of the Harappa civilization. In the third millennium BCE they must have been scattered all over the subcontinent, even as far as Afghanistan in the northwest where they came in contact with the early R̥gvedic Aryans. After some groups had moved to the periphery of the Indo-Gangetic plains with the expansion of Aryans, several other groups must have been assimilated into the Aryan society. The major structural changes in Middle or Modern Indic strongly suggest a Dravidian substratum for over three millennia.[16]

There have been Dravidian lexical items borrowed into Sanskrit and Prakrits during the Middle Indic period but most of these refer to concepts native to Dravidian: see table 1.1. The list shows that, during the long period of absorption and shift to Indo-Aryan

[15] 'Proto-Indo-Europeans .... were far more obliging in passing on to us no less than two words for 'breaking wind'. English dictionaries may occasionally shrink from including such vulgar terms as "fart" but the word gains status when set within the series: Sanskrit *pardate*, Greek *perdo*, Lithuanian *perdzu*, Russian *perdet'*, Albanian *pjerdh* "to fart loudly" (distinguished from Proto-Indo-European **pezd-* "to break wind softly")' (Mallory 1989:126).

[16] After completing this section I have read Southworth (1995) in which he has given a brief outline of Proto-Dravidian culture in three chronological layers. It was interesting reading, although I could not find evidence for his setting up three chronological stages in the evolution of Dravidian culture. I also do not find any reason to revise any part of this section in the light of the contents of that article.

Table 1.1. *A sample list of Dravidian borrowings into Middle Indo-Aryan*

Proto-Dravidian [*DEDR*]	Classical Skt./Middle-Indic	*CDIAL*
**aḷ-amp-* 'mushroom' [300]	Pkt. *ālamba- DNM*	1365
**kaẓ-*V*t-* 'paddy field' [1355]	Skt. *karda-*, *kardama-* 'mud'	2867–70
**kap-*Vḷ 'cheek' [1337]	Skt. *kapola-* 'cheek'	2755
kuṭ-*V/kuṇṭ-*V 'eyeball' [1680]	Skt. *guḍa-* 'globe'	4181
**kaṭ-ac-* ' young male animal' [1123]	MIA **kaḍḍa-* id.	2645
**kay* 'fish' [1252]	Skt. *kaivarta-*/**kevarta-*[17] 'fisherman'	3469
**kaw-*V*ḷi* 'gecko' [1338]	Skt. *gaulī-* 'a house lizard'	4324
**kunṯ-i* 'crab's eye, a plant' [1865]	Skt. *gunjā-* id.	4176
**kor-*Vnk-/*-nkk-* 'a stark, crane' [2125]	Skt. *kaṅka-* id.	2595
SD II: **paḍḍ-*V 'female buffalo' [3881]	Skt. *paḍḍika-* 'female cow' DNM *peḍḍa-* 'buffalo'	8042
**cink-i* 'ginger' [429]	Pkt. *singi/ī* 'ginger root' Skt. *śr̥ṅga-vera-*	12588
**uẓ-*V*ntu* 'black gram' [690]	Pkt. *uḍida-* id.	1693
**kaṭ-ampu Anthocephalus cadamba* [1116]	Skt. *kādamba-* id.	2710
**kā*, **kā-n* 'forest' [1418]	Skt. *kānana-* id.	3028
**kar-*V*nk- Pongamia glabra* [1507]	Skt. *kárañja-* id.	2785
**koṯ-aṇṭ-/-añc-* 'henna', *Barleria* sp. [1849]	Skt. *kuraṇṭa(ka)-* id.	3322, 3326
**kay-tay* 'fragrant screw-pine' [2026]	Skt. *ketaka-* id	3462
**koẓ-*V- 'young' [2149]	Skt. *kuṇaka-*, *kuḍa-* 'boy'	3527, 3245
**aṭ-a-ppay* 'betel pouch' [64]	Pkt. *haḍapp(h)a-*	1948
**kañc-i* 'rice water, gruel' [1104]	Skt. *kāñjī-* 'gruel'	3016
**kaḷ* 'toddy, liquor' [1372]	Skt. *kalyā-* 'spirituous liquor' Pkt. *kallā*	2950–1

by the Dravidian speaking tribes, only specialized lexical items from Dravidian were borrowed into Indo-Aryan, mainly items of need-based borrowing. However, the grammatical changes which had swept through Indo-Aryan were far-reaching, mainly because of transplanting the Dravidian structure onto Indo-Aryan (see section 1.7 below).

1.3 The Dravidian languages as a family

As early as 1816, Francis Whyte Ellis, an English civil servant, in his *Dissertation on the Telugu Language*,[18] asserted that 'the high and low Tamil; the Telugu, grammatical and vulgar; Carnataca or Cannadi, ancient and modern; Malayalma or Malayaḷam . . . and Tuluva' are the members 'constituting the family of languages which may be appropriately called the dialects of South India'; 'Codagu', he considered 'a local dialect of the same derivation'. Speaking about Malto, he says, 'the language of the Mountaineers of Rajmahal abounds in terms common to the Tamil and Telugu'. His purpose

[17] The alternation *kai-/kē-* indicates Dravidian origin; *varta-/vaṭṭa-* is an Indo-Aryan stem.

[18] Published as a 'Note to the Introduction' of A. D. Campbell's *A Grammar of Teloogoo Language Commonly Called the Gentoo*, printed in Madras in 1816. This note was reprinted with an editorial note by N. Venkata Rao (1954–5).

was to show that Tamil, Telugu and Kannaḍa 'form a distinct family of languages', with which 'the Sanscrit has, in later times, especially, intermixed, but with which it has no radical connection'. He presented considerable illustrative material, mainly lexical and some grammatical, from Telugu, Kannaḍa and Tamil in support of his hypothesis (Krishnamurti 1969b: 311–12). Ellis recognized the Dravidian languages as a family, thirty years after Sir William Jones had floated the concept of the language family in his famous lecture to the Asiatic Society of Bengal in Calcutta, on 2 February, 1786.

Zvelebil (1990a: xiv–vii) gives a detailed account of the first contact of Western missionaries with the Dravidian languages. In 1554 Fr. Anrique Anriquez (1520–1600), a Jewish Portuguese missionary of the Jesuit order, published the first book on Tamil in Roman script. First published in 1554, *Cartilha em Tamul e Português* was reprinted in 1970 by the Museu Nacional de Arquelogia e Ethnologia, Lisbon. Herbert Herring (1994) discusses, at length, the contribution of several German missionaries/scholars to Dravidian studies. Ziegenbalg (1682–1719), a Protestant German missionary, published the first Tamil grammar by a westerner, *Grammatica Damulica*, in Latin (1716) in Halle, Germany. Tamil was also called the Malabarian language. Karl Graul (1814–64) published an *Outline of Tamil Grammar* (1856) and brought out four philosophical treatises on Tamil. Graul translated Kuṟaḷ into German and Latin (1856).[19]

Robert Caldwell (1814–91) brought out the first edition of his *Comparative Grammar* in 1856, which marked the first, pioneering breakthrough in comparative Dravidian studies. Caldwell enumerated only twelve Dravidian languages[20] and, as the title of his work suggests, he mainly drew upon the literary languages of the south with greater attention paid to Tamil, which he had studied for over thirty-seven years by the time he brought out the second edition of the book in 1875. With inadequate sources and with the comparative method and reconstruction of the proto-language still in their infancy,[21] Caldwell could not have done better. He succeeded in showing family likeness among the Dravidian languages in phonology and morphology and in disproving the Sanskrit origin of the Dravidian languages, a view strongly advocated by many Oriental as well as Western scholars both before and after him. He also attempted to show a possible affinity between Dravidian and the so-called 'Scythian' languages.[22]

[19] Bibliographical details of these early works can be found in the *Linguistic Survey of India*, vol. IV (1906; repr. 1967, 1973 Delhi: Motolal Banarsidass).

[20] Tamil, Malayāḷam, Telugu, Canarese (Kannaḍa), Tuḷu, Kudagu or Coorg (Koḍagu), Tuda (Toda), Kota, Goṇḍ (Gondi), Khond or Ku (Kui), Orāon (Kuṛux or Oraō^{n}), Rajmahāl (Malto). The modern spellings are given in parentheses. Caldwell adds a note on Brahui in the Appendix to the 2nd edition in 1875 (in the 3rd edition reprinted in 1956: 633–5).

[21] He was a contemporary of August Schleicher (1821–68) of Germany who initiated the method of reconstructing the parent of the Indo-European languages.

[22] '. . . a common designation of all those languages of Asia and Europe which do not belong to the Indo-European or Semitic families' *LSI* 4. 282 (1906).

C. P. Brown (1798–1884), a British administrative officer in the Telugu-speaking area, spent the bulk of his income on preparing edited texts of classics and published a grammar of Telugu and *A Dictionary, Telugu and English* (the last in 1852). Rev. Winslow's *Comprehensive Tamil and English Dictionary* was published in 1862. Rev. Hermann Gundert (1814–93) published a monumental *Malayāḷam–English Dictionary* (1872) and,

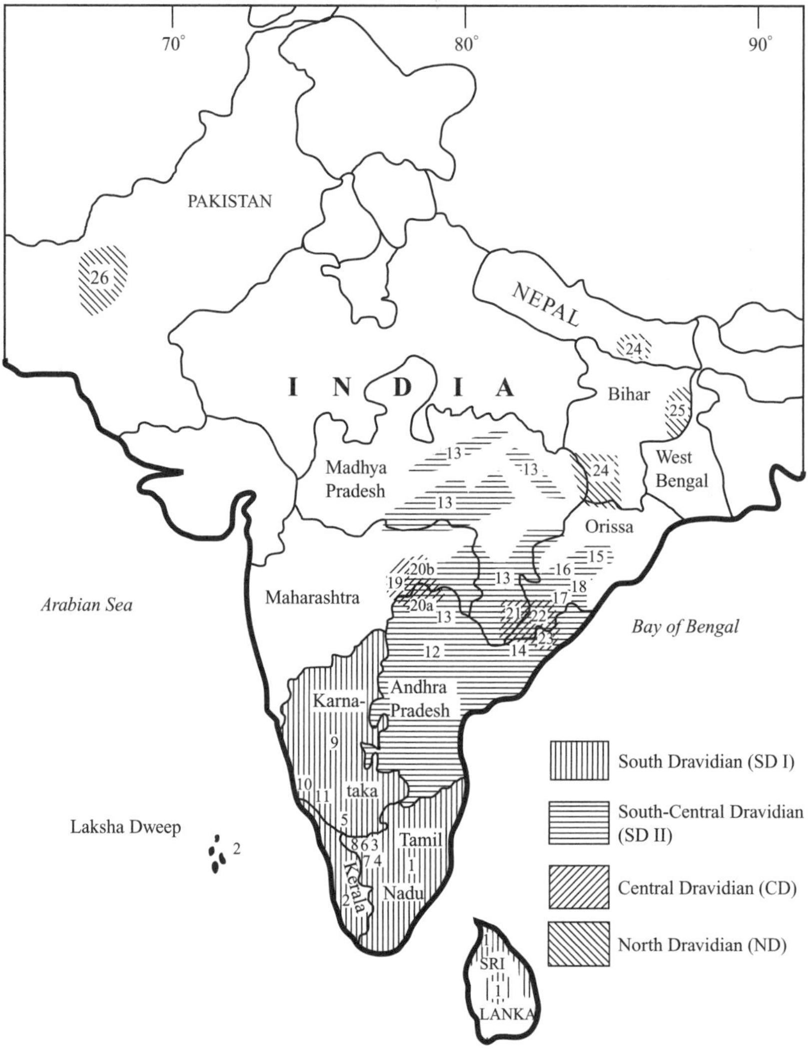

Map 1.1 Geographical distribution of the Dravidian languages in South Asia

Southern group (SD I)	South-Central group (SD II)
1. Tamil	**12. Telugu**
2. Malayāḷam	13. Gondi
3. Iruḷa	14. Koṇḍa
4. Kuṟumba	15. Kui
5. Koḍagu	16. Kuvi
6. Toda	17. Pengo
7. Kota	18. Manḍa
8. Baḍaga	
9. Kannaḍa	
10. Koraga	
11. Tuḷu	
Central group (CD)	
19. Kolami	
20a. Naikṛi	
20b. Naiki (Chanda)	
21. Parji	
22. Ollari	
23. (Koṇḍēkōr) Gadaba	
Northern group (ND)	
24. Kuṛux	
25. Malto	
26. Brahui	

Note: The major literary languages are indicated in bold face.

earlier, a grammar of the Malayāḷam language (1859). Ferdinand Kittel's (1832–1903) *Kannaḍa–English Dictionary* (1894) and Männer's *Tuḷu-English Dictionary* (1886) are still considered standard tools of reference for linguistic and literary studies in these languages. Grammatical sketches and vocabularies appeared on several minor Dravidian languages during the later half of the nineteenth century: Gondi (Driberg 1849), Kui (Letchmajee 1853), Kolami (Hislop 1866), Koḍagu (Cole 1867), Tuḷu (Brigel 1872) and Malto (Droese 1884). Toda was identified in 1837 (Bernhard Schmidt) and Brahui in 1838 (Leech). Some of these materials are not easily accessible to scholars and are also inadequate for a comparative study.

1.4 Names of languages, geographical distribution and demographic details

There are over twenty-six Dravidian languages known at present. They are classified into four genetic subgroups as follows (see map 1.1):

1. South Dravidian (SD I): Tamil, Malayāḷam, Iruḷa, Kuṟumba, Koḍagu, Toda, Kota, Baḍaga, Kannaḍa, Koraga, Tuḷu;
2. South-Central Dravidian (SD II): Telugu, Gondi (several dialects), Koṇḍa, Kui, Kuvi, Pengo, Manḍa;

3. Central Dravidian (CD): Kolami, Naikṛi, Naiki, Parji, Ollari, (Koṇḍekor) Gadaba;
4. North Dravidian (ND): Kuṛux, Malto, Brahui.

South Dravidian I and South Dravidian II must have arisen from a common source, which is called Proto-South Dravidian. The shared innovations include two sound changes: (a) PD **i* **u* became **e* **o* before a low vowel **a* (section 4.4.2), (b) PD **c* became (**s* and **h* as intermediate stages) zero in SD I; this change is now in progress in SD II (section 4.5.1.3). Morphological innovations include (c) the back-formation of **ñān* from Proto-Dravidian inclusive plural **ñām*/*ñam-* as the first person singular, beside PD **yān* 'I', (d) the development of paired intransitive and transitive stems with NP/NPP alternation in verbs (section 7.3.6), and (e) the use of the reflexes of **-ppi* as a causative marker (section 7.3.3). There are several innovations within each subgroup. The typical ones for South Dravidian I are: (a) loss of the final -CV of 3msg pronouns **awan* 'that man', **iwan* 'this man' (<**awan-ṯu*, **iwan-ṯu*), (b) the creation of 2fsg in *-aḷ* (section 6.2.3–4) and (c) the use of reflexive pronoun **tān* as emphatic marker beside **-ē* (section 8.4.2). The typical innovations of South Dravidian II are: (a) the generalization of **-tt* as past-tense marker, and (b) the creation of new oblique stems **nā-*/**mā-* and **nī-*/**mī-* for the first and second personal pronouns. The other subgroups are already the established ones in Dravidian. The details of subgrouping will be consolidated and reviewed in the last chapter.

See map 1.1 for the geographical distribution of these languages. A family tree diagram of the Dravidian languages is given as figure 1.2. Justification for setting up the subgroups will be seen in the succeeding chapters of this book.

General information about each of the Dravidian languages is provided in the following order: modern name (other names in extant literature); population figures (1991 Census where available); area where the language is spoken; in the case of literary languages, the earliest inscription discovered and the earliest literary work; miscellaneous information; main bibliographical sources for comparative study in the case of non-literary languages.

1.4.1 *Major literary languages*[23]

There are four languages with long traditions of written literature, namely Tamil, Malayāḷam, Kannaḍa and Telugu. Tuḷu is said to have some literary texts of recent origin. Both Tuḷu and Koḍagu are spoken by civilized, literate communities, unlike

[23] There have been speculative etymologies for the names Tamiẓ, Malayāḷam and Telugu. I have not given much thought or space to these. Zvelebil says (1990a: xxi) that *tam-iẓ* was derived from *taku-* 'to be fit, proper' with *-k-* > *-w-* > *-m-*, but the *-k-* and *-w-* variants are nowhere attested. Koskinen (1996) relates *tamiẓ* to the lotus word *tāmarai*. Southworth (1998) suggests **tam-miẓ* > *tam-iẓ* 'self-speak', or 'one's own speech' by deriving **miẓ-*/*muẓ-* as the underlying

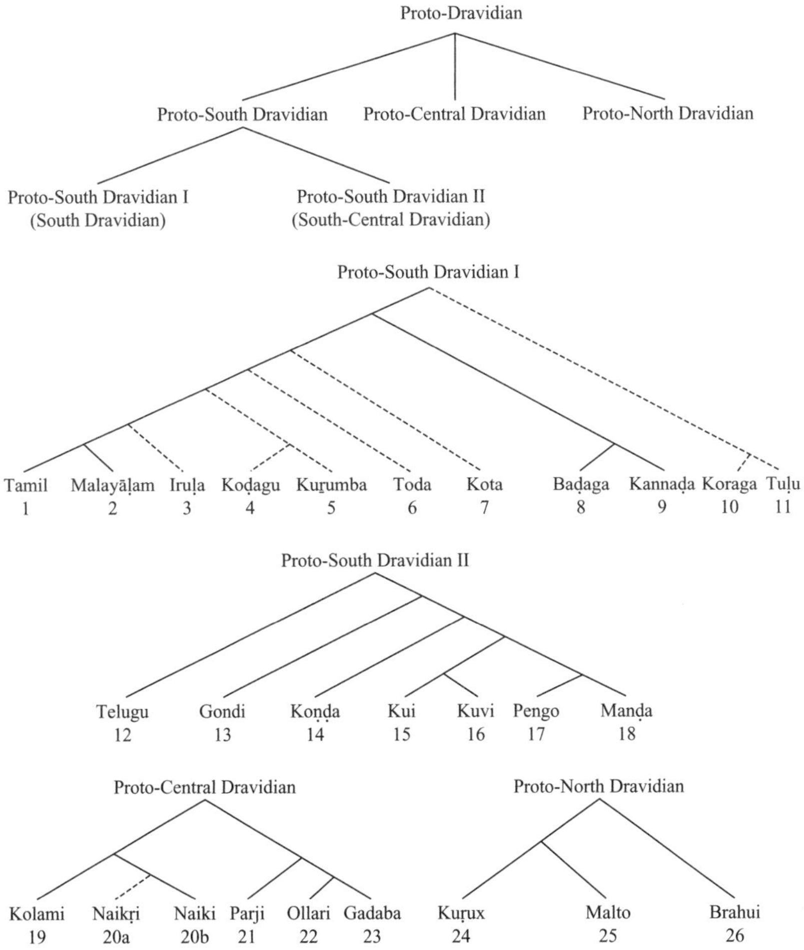

Broken lines reflect uncertainty as to a language's position within the group.

Figure 1.2 Family tree of the Dravidian languages

the remaining non-literary languages, some of which are spoken by pre-literate, tribal populations.

root of *moẓi* 'word'. The root must be **moẓ-* and not **muẓ-*. In Malayāḷam, one can be sure of *malai* 'mountain' and *āḷ* 'man', i.e. 'mountain dweller'; alternatively, *āẓ-am* 'depth, ocean', 'the land between the mountains and the ocean'. *Tenungu/telungu* with *l/n*-alternation have several suggested sources derived from Skt. *triṇaga* 'three hills', *triliṅga* 'three lingas of Siva', besides deriving them from **ten-* 'south'. **teḷ-/teṇ-* 'sesame' < **ceḷ-* meaning the place where oilseeds grow. Kannaḍa is plausibly derivable from *kar(u)-* 'black', *nāḍu* 'country', i.e. 'the land of black soil'.

1. Tamil (true native name Tamiẓ; other names: Malabāri, Drāviḍī, Tamul, Aravam). Pop. 53,006,368; 3.35 million in Sri Lanka and over 2 million in South Africa, Malaysia, Singapore, Mauritius, Fiji and Burma. Cave inscriptions (some seventy-six) in Tamil Brāhmī script were found in Madurai and Tirunalvēli districts c. second century BC (Mahadevan 1971: 83–4). The first known work, *Tolkāppiyam*, is a treatise on grammar and poetics ascribed to the early pre-Christian era, presupposing a large body of literature before it, available in the form of anthologies. Although the influence of early Sanskrit grammars (fifth century BC) is obvious in certain grammatical concepts like Tamil *kālam* 'tense, time' (Sanskrit *kāla-* 'time, tense'), Tamil *peyar* 'name' for the noun (Sanskrit *nāman-* 'name, noun'), Tamil *vēṟṟumai* 'separation, division' for 'case' (Sanskrit *vibhakti-* 'case marker', literally 'division'), there is much that is original in *Tolkāppiyam*.

As in the case of Pre-Modern Greek and Arabic, Tamil has 'diglossia' (Ferguson 1964), which means that the standard written and spoken variety of Tamil, called *centamiẓ* 'beautiful Tamil', is based on the classical language of an earlier era and not on any of the contemporary regional dialects. The spoken variety is called *koṭuntamiẓ* 'crooked/vulgar Tamil' and is not used for formal roles in speech and writing. The newspaper language and the language of political speeches are 'high'. The 'low' variety is used in conversations and lately for movie dialogues. There are both geographical and social dialects of the 'low' variety. Some of the social dialects are distinguished on the basis of caste (Asher 1982: ix–x). The writing system of the 'high' variety is used even for the spoken 'low' varieties in plays, etc.; this practice naturally leads to many problems of spelling. The rate of literacy in Tamil Nadu for all ages in 7+ was 63.7 per cent (1991). There were 1,863 newspapers published in Tamil in 1999, of which 353 were dailies (*India 2001*).

2. Malayāḷam (Malayāẓma). Pop. 30,377,166; west-coast dialect of Tamil till about the ninth century AD; official language of Kerala state. The Vāẓappaḷḷi inscription of Rajaśēkhara of the ninth century AD is considered the earliest document (Gopalakrishnan 1985: 31). The first literary work is *Rāmacaritam* (c. twelfth century) and the first grammar, *Līlātilakam* (fourteenth century), written in Sanskrit. More than Kannaḍa and Telugu, and unlike Tamil, Malayāḷam has borrowed liberally from Sanskrit not only words but even inflected words and phrases. A new style called Maṇipravāḷa (diamond and coral) was a literary innovation in Malayāḷam, representing a harmonious blend of *bhāṣa* 'native language' and *samskṛta* 'Sanskrit'. Kerala has the highest rate of literacy in India, 90.6 per cent (1991). Because of a high rate of literacy, the publishing and newspaper industry has been flourishing in Malayāḷam. The religious minorities, though comparatively very high, Muslims (21.3 per cent) and Christians (20.6 per cent), mostly speak Malayāḷam; the linguistic minorities constitute only 5.2 per

cent. Malayāḷam had 1,373 newspapers (dailies 213) in 1999 (*India 2001*). Malayāḷam does not have diglossia of the Tamil kind.

There has been no good description of Malayāḷam dialects. 'Malayāḷam has many different regional and social dialects . . . since the 1930s or earlier, distinguished creative writers have in narrative passages deliberately used a language that is close to what they use in normal conversation . . . examples provided aim to be as dialectally neutral as possible, though there may be a slight bias toward the variety used by educated speakers in central Kerala' (Asher and Kumari 1997: xxv). This is what we tentatively take as Modern Standard Malayāḷam.

3. Kannaḍa (Kanarese, Canarese, Karṇāṭaka). Pop. 32,753,676; the official language of Karnataka state; the first inscription is dated 450 AD by Kadamba Kākutstha Varma from Halmiḍi, Belur Taluq, Mysore district; the first literary work *Kavirājamārga*, a treatise on poetics, belongs to the ninth century: *S'abdamaṇidarpaṇa* is the first comprehensive grammar written in Kannaḍa (thirteenth century). Modern Standard Kannaḍa is based on the educated speech of southern Karnataka (Mysore–Bangalore) and differs considerably from the northern (Dharwar) and coastal varieties. There are also caste dialects reported within each of the regions. The literacy rate of Karnataka was 56 per cent (1991). There were 1,561 newspapers published in the Kannaḍa language in 1999, including 314 dailies (*India 2001*).

4. Telugu (Telũgu, Tenũgu, Āndhram, Gentoo, Waḍugu, Warugī). Pop. 66,017,615; official language of Andhra Pradesh. Telugu place names occur in Prakrit inscriptions from the second century AD onwards. The first Telugu inscription is dated 575 AD from Erraguḍipāḍu of the Kaḍapa district by a prince of the Cōḍa dynasty; the first literary work, a poetic translation of a part of the *Mahābhārata*, belongs to the eleventh century AD. The first Telugu grammar written in Sanskrit, *Āndhraśabdacintāmaṇi*, is said to have been composed by the author of the first literary work. There are four regional dialects in Telugu, namely (i) northern, nine Telugu-speaking districts of the old Nizam's Dominions, called Telangāṇā, merged with Andhra Pradesh in 1956, (ii) southern, four southern districts called Rāyalasīma plus two coastal districts of Nellore and Prakasham, (iii) eastern, three northeast districts, Visakhpatnam, Vijayanagaram and Srikakulam, adjoining Orissa, called the Kalinga country, and (iv) four central coastal districts, Guntur, Krishna, East Godavari and West Godavari. Modern Standard Telugu (Krishnamurti and Gwynn 1985) is based on the speech and writings of the elite of the central coastal dialect (Krishnamurti 1998c: 51–108). In the case of social dialects the main criterion is the level of education. There are differences between educated and uneducated speech in phonology, morphology and lexicon (Krishnamurti 1998c: 110–20).

Although it is genetically closer to its northern neighbours, as a literary language Telugu has a great measure of give and take with Kannnaḍa; Telugu and Kannaḍa have a common stage of evolution in their script called the Telugu–Kannaḍa script (seventh to thirteenth century). There were several Saivite poets who wrote both in Telugu and Kannaḍa. The Vijayanagara King Krishnadevaraya patronized both Kannaḍa and Telugu poetry. Consequently, there are extensive lexical borrowings between Telugu and Kannaḍa both ways. Literacy in Andhra Pradesh was 45.1 per cent (1991). There were 1,106 newspapers published in Telugu in 1999, of which 151 were dailies (*India 2001*).

1.4.2 *Minor literary and non-literary languages*

I. *South Dravidian (SD I)* 5. Tuḷu (Tuluva). Pop. 1.6 million; Dakshiṇa Kannaḍa district of Karnataka and the Kasaragode Taluk of Kerala on the west coast. Kannaḍa script is adopted; the Brahmin dialect is heavily influenced by Kannaḍa. All educated people are bilingual in Kannaḍa which is used for formal communication. The widely used common Tuḷu is the variety of the non-Brahmin castes. There are two major regional dialects (north and south) and two major social dialects (Brahmin and Common), which together give rise to a four-way dialect division, North Brahmin (NB), North Common (NC), South Brahmin (SB), and South Common (SC). The first Tuḷu inscription was dated to the fifteenth century. Two epic poems are said to have been composed in the seventeenth century, but there has been no continuous literary tradition (Bhat 1998: 158–60). There is now a growing modern literature in Tuḷu.

Tuḷu seems to share several phonological, grammatical and lexical features with the members of the Central Dravidian subgroup, namely Kolami-Parji, etc. An elementary grammar was published by Brigel (1872) and a Tuḷu–English Dictionary by Männer (1866). Bhat (1967) analyses the current language. *Tuḷu Lexicon* (1987–97), a new dictionary in six volumes, edited by Haridas Bhat and Upadhyaya, has been published recently by Rashtrakavi Govinda Pai Samshodhan Kendra, Udupi.

6. Koḍagu (Coorgi, Koḍagï, Koḍava). Pop. 93,000 in the Koḍagu (Coorg) district of Karnataka bordering on Kerala. Koḍagus use Kannaḍa as their official language and as the language of education. A grammar by Cole (1867) and fieldnotes by Emeneau (1935–8) were the earlier sources. Balakrishnan's two volumes (1976, 1977) deal with the phonology, grammar and vocabulary of Koḍagu. Recently a short descriptive sketch of 'Koḍava' by Karen Ebert (1996) was published in the series entitled *Languages of the World* (Materials 104).

7. Iruḷa (Irula, Ërla). Pop. 5,200. Nilgiri hills. Diffloth (1968), Zvelebil (1973, 1979, 1982b), Perialwar (1978a,b).

8. Kuṟumba (several dialects). Pop. about 5,000. Nilgiri hills. Kapp (1984, 1987), Zvelebil (1982a, 1988).

9. Toda (Tuda). Pop. 1,600. Western regions of Nilgiri Hills. Emeneau (1957, 1984). Earlier accounts are not reliable.

10. Kota. Pop. 1,400. Mainly craftsmen among the Nilgiri tribes. Emeneau (1944–6).

11. Baḍaga (Badagu, Vadagu). Pop. 125,000. Nilgiri hills. It was considered a dialect of Kannaḍa after the sixteenth century, but Pilot-Raichoor claims an idependent status for it as a language. Hockings and Pilot-Raichoor (1992).

12. Koraga. Pop. about 1,000. Basket makers in the South Kanara district. A number of them are bilingual in Tuḷu. It looks more like an off-shoot of Tuḷu at a recent past, although Bhat suggests genetic closeness with North Dravidian (Bhat 1971: 3).

Kota, Toda, Iruḷa and Kuṟumba have preserved the three-way distinction of the coronal stop consonants, namely *t* (dental), *ṯ* (alveolar) and *ṭ* (retroflex), which was a feature of Proto-Dravidian. Toda has the largest number of vowels (14) and consonants (37) which have developed through numerous sound changes and not through borrowing. Baḍagas, supposed to speak a dialect of Kannaḍa, moved to the Nilgiri hills in the sixteenth century. They are the dominant community both in numbers and in the economy of the area. A great deal has been published on the languages, geography and ethnography of the Nilgiris during the past two decades (see Hockings 1989, 1997).

II. *South Central Dravidian (SD II)* 13. Gondi (native name Kōytor). Pop. 2,395,507 (includes the Koya dialect spoken in Andhra Pradesh); it has many dialects scattered over four neighbouring states, Madhya Pradesh, Maharashtra, Orissa and Andhra Pradesh. The main dialect division is between west, north and northwest, on the one hand, and south and southeast, on the other. Some of these dialects are probably mutually unintelligible, particularly Maria Gondi and Koya in the south and southeast to the speakers of the other dialects. The earliest writings include Driberg and Harrison (1849), Hislop (1866) and Williamson (1890). In the twentieth century Lind (1913), Trench (1919, 1921), Mitchell (1942), Moss (1950), Subrahmanyam (1968b), Tyler (1969) and Natarajan (1985). The last three descriptive grammars cover different dialects. Several PhD dissertations from Indian universities treat various aspects of Gondi grammar. Burrow and Bhattacharya (1960) is the main source of comparative vocabulary drawing on the sources available up to that period.

14. Kūi (Kūinga, Kandh, Khond, Kōdu). Pop. 641,662; spoken in Ganjam and Phulbani districts of Orissa. Census reports confuse Kui and Kuvi, both of which are called Khond or Kandh. Lingum Letchmajee (1853) wrote the first grammar. Winfield's grammar and vocabulary (1928, 1929) are still the main source of information on grammar and vocabulary. Winfield (1928: 226–9) discusses the history and etymology of the names of the tribes and languages 14 and 15.

15. Kūvi (Kūvinga, Khond, Kondh, Kōdu, Kōju, Sāmantu, Jātāpu). Pop. 246,513. Spoken in the districts of Ganjam, Kalahandi and Koraput of Orissa, Visakhapatnam and Srikakulam of Andhra Pradesh. Most published sources are neither comprehensive nor reliable. Schultze (1911, 1913), Fitzgerald (1913). The most recent is Israel (1979).

16. Koṇḍa (Koṇḍa Dora, Kūbi, Kūbiŋ). Pop. 17,864; mainly spoken in the hills of the northeastern districts of Andhra Pradesh, and is linguistically closer to Telugu than Kui or Kuvi. Krishnamurti (1969a) is the main source.

17. Pengo. Pop. 1,300. It is spoken in the Navrangpur district of Orissa. Burrow and Bhattacharya (1970) is the only source for Pengo.

18. Manḍa. Pop. not known; spoken near Thuamul Rampur of the Navrangapur district of Orissa; closely related to Pengo. A grammatical sketch by Burrow (1976) and the vocabulary available from *DEDR* (1984) based on the fieldnotes of Burrow and Bhattacharya.

III. *Central Dravidian* 19. Kolami (Kōlāmī). Pop. 99,281. Adilabad district of Andhra Pradesh, Yeotmal and Wardha districts of Maharashtra. Main sources Sethumadhava Rao (1950), Emeneau (1955b). It has borrowings from Telugu from a very early period.

20a. Naikṛi. Pop. 1,500 (1961). Spoken in Andhra Pradesh and Maharashtra in the vicinity of Kolami. Burrow and Bhattacharya considered this a dialect of Kolami without any supporting arguments. I am considering Naikṛi and Naiki of Chanda as related languages. Thomasiah's (1986) unpublished PhD thesis is the main source, besides the cognate list in *DEDR*.

20b. Naiki (Chanda). Pop. (?) 54,000. Chanda district of Madhya Pradesh. Bhattacharya's article (1961) is the main source.

21. Parji (Poroja, Dhurwa). Pop. 44,001 in the Bastar district of Madhya Pradesh and the adjacent hills of the Koraput district of Orissa. Burrow and Bhattacharya (1953).

22. Ollari (Hallari). Pop. 9,100. Burrow and Emeneau treat Ollari; and Gadaba as dialects of the same language, but I have kept them apart as languages. Bhattacharya's monograph (1957) is the only source.

23. Gadaba (Konḍekor Gadaba). Pop. 9,197 in Census 1981; in 1991 ?54,000. Srikakulam District of Andhra Pradesh and Koraput district of Orissa. There is a Mundarian Gadaba called Gutob Gadaba. The Census reports do not distinguish the two although they belong to different families. If we take only the population figures of Andhra Pradesh they number less than 10,000. Fieldnotes of Krishnamurti of the 1950s included in *DED* (1961) and P. Bhaskararao (1980).

IV. *North Dravidian* 24. Kuṛux (Kurukh, Oṛāō^{n}). Pop. 1,426,618. Bhagalpur and Chota Nagpur districts of Bihar, Raygarh, Sarguja districts of Madhya Pradesh, Sundargarh, Sambalpur districts of Orissa. Kuṛux is in contact with both Indo-Aryan and Munda languages. There is a dialect of Kuṛux, called Dhangar, spoken by 10,000 persons in Nepal. The earliest grammar is by Hahn (1911). The main sources are Grignard's grammar (1924a) and dictionary (1924b).

25. Malto (Rājmahālī, Mālerī). Pop. 108,148. Spoken in the Rajmahal hills in the Santal Paraganas (northeast) of Bihar. Not geographically adjacent to Kuṛux now. Droese (1884), Mahapatra (1979).

26. Brahui (Brāʔūī, Brāhūī). Pop. 1.7 million (*International Encyclopedia of Linguistics* 1991); 1.4 million (estimate by Breton 1994: 204). Spoken in Baluchistan of Pakistan. Bray (1909, 1934), Emeneau (1962d), Elfenbein (1997, 1998). This is the farthest removed of the Dravidian languages. Some writers considered Brahui as the first column (?) of speakers to branch off in the third millennium BC. Since it does not retain any archaic features of Proto-Dravidian, it is likely that the speakers of Brahui had migrated westward from the mainland where they were together with the speakers of Kuṛux and Malto. Some sound changes shared by these three languages suggest a common undivided stage deeper in history. Surrounded by Indic and Iranian languages for many centuries, Brahui is said to have only 10 per cent of Dravidian words, 20 per cent Indo-Aryan, 20 per cent from Balochi, 30 per cent from Perso-Arabic and 20 per cent of unknown origin (Elfenbein 1997: 810).

For a better idea of the geographical location of the Dravidian languages, see map 1.1. A number of other Dravidian languages are listed in the *Encyclopedia of Linguistics* (1991) and most recently by Zvelebil in an article (1997). Most of the names represent dialects of the main languages listed above. Koraga (Bhat 1971) is almost like Tuḷu in most respects and is tentatively shown as an off-shoot of Pre-Tuḷu.

1.5 Typological features of the Dravidian languages

1.5.1 *Phonology*

There are five short and five long vowels in Dravidian /i e a o u ī ē ā ō ū/; the long vowels are indicated with a suprasegmental phoneme of length [ː], marked by a macron here. Only some of the languages of the Nilgiris and Koḍagu have phonemic centralized vowels /ï ë/, which have developed from retracted allophones of the front vowels before retroflex consonants. Only Toda and Iruḷa have also developed front rounded vowels /ü ö/ (see chapters 3 and 4 for descriptive and historical details). The favoured syllable pattern of the word (free form) in Dravidian is (C)V̄CV/(C)VCCV/(C)VCVCV (three morae each). The other types are infrequent. There is no phonemic stress in any of the Dravidian languages. Normally stress (loudness) falls on the initial syllable of a word, short or long. A non-initial long vowel is louder than short vowels. Words can begin with vowels or consonants.

There are seventeen consonantal segments in Proto-Dravidian, six stops, four nasals, two laterals, one trill, one approximant (frictionless continuant) and three semivowels including a laryngeal, which patterns with semivowels. Voicing and aspiration are not phonemic. The three-way distinction, dental-alveolar-retroflex /t ṯ ṭ/ in the stop series, a separate series of phonemic retroflexes with different articulatory effort /ṭ ṇ ḷ ẓ/ (stop, nasal, lateral, approximant), absence of voice contrast in the stop series are the typologically important features of the Proto-Dravidian consonantal system. Alveolars and retroflexes occurred only in the medial position in Proto-Dravidian. Voicing was subphonemic to start with, but it became phonemic in most of the languages, due to internal changes and borrowing from Indo-Aryan. Consonant clusters occur non-initially, mainly geminates or nasal + stop series. Qualitative changes of segments in radical syllables are not common. Short vowels in non-root syllables (in unaccented position) tend to be lost. Among apical consonants alveolar **ṯ*, and the retroflex approximant **ẓ* are the most marked segments.

1.5.2 *Morphology*

The Dravidian languages are agglutinating in structure. There are no prefixes or infixes. Grammatical relations are expressed only by suffixation and compounding. A Dravidian root is (C)V, or (C)VC in which the V can be short or long in the case of verbs. These are followed by suffixes, which originally denoted tense–voice contrasts; a number of languages have lost their original meaning and they have become only voice markers in some, or mere formatives (without any discernible meaning) in others (see chapter 5). These are NP (nasal + stop) in intransitive or NPP (nasal + stop + stop in transitive) following (C)V-roots; a V_2 (*i a u*) is inserted when these follow (C)VC-roots. Many other suffixes are added to the roots and stems described above in different languages to form words.

1.5.2.1 *Nouns, adjectives*

Nominals (including nouns, pronouns, numerals and adverbs of time and place) are all inflected for case. In several classes of nominals the nominative stem is the basic form. An oblique stem, which occurs before case suffixes, is different from the nominative; a series of oblique suffixes is added to form it. In most languages, the genitive and the oblique stems are identical. Case relations are expressed by bound morphs (accusative, dative, genitive, instrumental/locative) or by inflected words, which have become grammaticalized, e.g. instrumental, sociative, ablative, some genitive and locative. This latter set are known as postpositions. Different Dravidian languages have developed independent postpositions meaning 'by means of, from (being in a place/time), before, after, above, below, up to, until, through' etc. Case markers and postpositions are added to the oblique stems of nouns, in the singular and in the plural.

Gender and number are interrelated categories. Singular (unmarked) and plural (marked) are the numbers denoting 'one' and 'more than one'. The plural is differentiated originally between human and non-human categories. The categories ±Animate, ±Human, ±Male human underlie gender classification, which is mainly based on meaning and not on form. There are two plurals of the first-person pronoun, one including the person addressed (inclusive) and the other excluding the person addressed (exclusive). Adverbial nouns have no gender or number; personal pronouns (first and second) are distinguished for number and not gender. Gender and number are relevant only in the third person. Gender-number-person agreement is expressed by finite verbs. An inflected noun has the structure Stem + number + oblique + case. By adding personal suffixes to nouns and adjectives, pronominalized nouns (Caldwell's 'appelative verbs or conjugated nouns') are formed.

Adjectives precede the noun head that they qualify. Adjectives do not agree with the noun head in gender and number. Adjectives are mainly a syntactic class. Numerals and adverbs of time and place can become adjectives by suffixation. There is no morphological device for comparative and superlative degrees.

1.5.2.2 *Verbs, adverbs*

The verb in Dravidian is finite or non-finite. The finite verb has the structure Stem (Root + (transitive) + (causative)) + Tense + Gender–Number–Person (gnp). A stem can be complex (as above) or compound. A compound stem has one or more coverbs attached to an uninflected noun, or an inflected (infinitive or perfective) main verb; in the latter case, the coverb is either an explicator/operator/vector type (lexical) or a modal auxiliary (grammatical) (section 7.15). Basically there are two tenses in Dravidian, past and non-past. A finite verb may carry negation as part of its tense category (mainly non-past). A non-finite verb heads subordinate clauses, like the durative, perfective, conditional, concessive, etc. Certain finite verbs may not carry agreement in gnp.

Adverbs of time and place function as nominals morphologically. Only manner adverbs derived by adding an inflected form of the verb 'to be' or iteratives (*gaṇagaṇa* 'ring of bells') are true adverbs. Adverbs precede verbs syntactically.

There are clitics (grammaticalized words) which are added to autonomous syntactic units – words, phrases, clauses – to signal a variety of meanings, tag questions, emphasis, interrogation, surprise, doubt, etc.

1.5.3 ***Syntax***

The Dravidian languages are of the OV type, head-final and left-branching. A simple sentence consists of a subject and a predicate. The subject argument is generally expressed by a noun phrase (NP), but a postpositional or casal phrase with the head nominal in the dative case can also function as the subject. The latter is called a dative subject sentence. The predicate has either a verb or a nominal as head. Sentences with nominal predicates are equative sentences, which lack the copula or the verb 'to be' in most of the languages. A noun phrase (NP) has a nominal head, optionally preceded by one or more adjectives and/or a relative clause, in a fixed order. A verb phrase (VP) has a verb as head, optionally preceded by one or more complements, carrying different case markers or postpositions, encoding different grammatical relations with the verb. I call these postpositional phrases (PP = NP + case/postposition). A subordinate clause can be either verbal (with a non-finite verb as head) or nominal, i.e. a pronominalized verb or a relative clause with a noun head.

Interrogative sentences are formed either by the addition of an interrogative particle (yes–no type) or by using an interrogative word substituted for the questioned noun. Any head nominal can be questioned whether it is a constituent of the main clause or subordinate clause.

Nominal and verbal predicates have different negative words to express sentence negation. A negative word is an inflected verb meaning 'to be' or 'to be not'. Non-finite verbs, which head subordinate clauses, have affirmative and negative counterparts.

The argument NPs which occur as complements to a verb derive from the semantic structure of the verb; for instance, an intransitive verb requires only one argument, Agent/Object/Experiencer/Source. A transitive verb requires an Agent + Object (Patient); a causative verb, Agent (causer) + Agent (causee) + Instrument + Object. Reflexivity and reciprocity are expressed in the verb by an auxiliary or by reflexive pronouns. The passive voice is rarely used in modern Dravidian languages.

A quotative clause is embedded in the main clause as NP by an inflected complementizer of the verb 'to say'. The difference between direct and indirect (reported) speech is sometimes noticed in the change of the subject/object pronoun of the quoted clause. The quotative particle is used to signal a variety of meanings including 'like, because', etc.

1.6 Dravidian studies, past and present[24]

1.6.1 *1856–1950*

During the nineteenth century, after Caldwell's work (1856), there were grammars and bilingual dictionaries of the major Dravidian languages prepared by missionaries and administrative officials. Some of these became standard reference works (see section 1.3 above). Among the minor languages, Männer's dictionary (1886) and Droese's grammar and vocabulary lasted as standard writings into the twentieth century. The *Linguistic Survey of India* edited by Sir George A. Grierson has brought out short accounts of the Dravidian languages (1906: *LSI* IV) outside southern India, which was not covered by the Survey.[25] Traditional scholars of the major languages took for granted the Sanskrit origin of the Dravidian languages and this fact was presumably responsible for the long spell of disinterest in pursuing Caldwell's ground-breaking study for nearly five decades.

[24] What follows is a summary of three survey articles that I have published (see Krishnamurti 1969b, 1985, 2001b: ch. 21).

[25] The Madras Presidency, the princely states of Mysore, Travancore and Cochin, Coorg and the Nizam's Dominions (*LSI* 1: 1. 25 [1927]).

Between 1900 and 1950, scholars from different parts of the world pursued a comparative study of the Dravidian languages, besides preparation of grammars and vocabularies of individual languages. Subbaiya (1909–11) dealt with a number of phonological problems (involving alternations *i*/*e*, *u*/*o*, *p*-/*h*-, *k*-/*c*-, *ā*-/*ē*-, metathesis in South Central Dravidian etc.) and attempted the reconstruction of 'Primitive Dravidian'. The conditions of change in many cases were not formulated correctly. During the period 1925–50, L. V. Ramaswami Aiyar was the major contributor to comparative Dravidian studies, publishing over a hundred articles and some monographs on Malayāḷam and Tuḷu. In my opinion the most significant of his papers were 'Dravidic sandhi' (1934–8: *QJMS* 26–28), 'Aphaeresis and sound displacement in Dravidian' (1931–2: *QJMS* 22), and 'The history of Tami-Malayāḷam alveolar plosive' (?1937: *JOR* 8.3: 1–32; 4). Jules Bloch's postwar book on Dravidian (1946) advanced our knowledge of comparative morphology, since he brought data from non-literary languages (Tuḷu, Gondi, Kui, Kuṛux and Brahui) into his analysis and argumentation. S. K. Chatterji (1926: 170–8) and Bloch (1934: 321–31) clearly spoke of a Dravidian substratum in the evolution of Middle and New Indo-Aryan. E. H. Tuttle's *Dravidian Developments* (1930) created interest in the Dravidian phenomena in North America. His reconstructions of Proto-Dravidian forms were methodologically flawed, but he made some insightful remarks on subgrouping. Burrow's 'Dravidian studies I to VII' (*BSOAS* 9–12) marked the true beginning of comparative phonology of Dravidian. He traced the developments of PD **k*, **c*, **y*, **ñ* (word-initially), alternations *i*/*e* and *u*/*o* in South Dravidian and defended the reconstruction of a voiceless stop series for Dravidian. He systematically demonstrated Dravidian loanwords in Sanskrit from Ṛgvedic times (1945, 1946b, 1948).

Emeneau spent three years in India doing linguistic and anthropological fieldwork on the Nilgiri languages Toda and Kota; he also worked on Koḍagu and later on Kolami for a short period. His *Kota Texts* was published in four volumes during 1944–6. Madras University published the comprehensive *Tamil Lexicon* (1924–39). In Telugu, *Sūryarāy*(*a*)-*āndhra-nighaṇṭuwu*, a six-volume monolingual dictionary, was started by an assembly of scholars in 1936 and published four volumes by 1944. The work was continued to completion under the aegis of the Andhra Pradesh Sahitya Akademi in the 1960s. Several descriptive grammars were prepared by missionaries and administrative officials for Gondi, Kui, Kuvi, Kuṛux and Brahui (see section 1.4). Those of Kui, Kuṛux and Brahui are still considered the best accounts.

1.6.2 ***1950–2000***

Since India became independent in 1947, and a Democratic Republic in 1950, there has been greater interest in the study of major languages and linguistics at the university level. This was facilitated by the creation of linguistic states in 1956. The Deccan College Project (1955–9), supported by the Rockefeller Foundation, created facilities for the training and exchange of scholars in linguistics between India and the United States. Consequently a cadre of trained linguists in modern descriptive and historical linguistics emerged in the early 1950s from the universities of India and the USA.

Burrow and Bhattacharya concentrated on fieldwork in central India and brought out grammars and vocabularies of Parji (1953) and Pengo (1970), besides articles on Kui and Kuvi (1961, 1963). They have also compiled a comparative vocabulary of the Gondi dialects from many published sources (1960). Burrow continued his interest in Dravidian loanwords in Sanskrit (1955, 1960, 1983). He wrote a short sketch of the Manḍa grammar (1976). The Manḍa vocabulary collected by Burrow and Bhattacharya was incorporated in *DEDR* (1984). Bhattacharya's book on Ollari (1957) and his article on Naiki of Chanda (1961) have resulted from his independent fieldwork.

Emeneau's contribution during this period has been in various directions. (i) He has discussed problems of comparative phonology of several non-literary languages – Brahui: velar stops (1961b), developments of PD **ẓ* (1971b, 1980c); Koḍagu: centralization of vowels before apicals (1970b); Toda: development of PD **c*- (1953a), non-initial vowels (1979); and Kota: the developments arising from PD -*ay* (1969b); a comprehensive treatment of **c*- in different subgroups (1988) and a revision of the palatalizing rule in South Dravidian (1995). His monograph on Brahui (1962d) deals with phonological and morphological problems comparatively. (ii) As to Emeneau's contribution to comparative morphology, mention must be made of Dravidian kinship terms (1953b), Dravidian numerals (1957), Brahui demonstratives (1961a), verb inflection in Brahui (1962d), Dravidian verb stem formation (1975), Indian demonstrative bases: a revision (1980a), and expressives (intensives) in Dravidian (1987). (iii) He defined India as a 'linguistic area' (1956), which implies mainly inter-influences between Dravidian and Indo-Aryan creating in each the structural influences of the other over a long period of bilingualism (particularly see 1962a, 1964, 1965, 1969a, 1971a, 1974b, culminating in a collection of his articles in book form in 1980). These essays include studies of features, which are phonological, morphosyntactic and ethno-semantic (like the use of quotatives, onomatopoetic expressions, 'right hand as the eating hand', etc.). This theme has developed into a rich area of research in South Asia (for more on this see section 1.7 below). (iv) Emeneau published books on the grammar, texts and vocabulary of Kolami (1955b), a grammar and texts of Toda (1984) and a sketch of comparative phonology (1970a).

The most monumental work of the century in Dravidian linguistics is the collaborative comparative/etymological dictionary of the Dravidian languages by Burrow and Emeneau, first published in 1961 (with supplements in1968 and 1972); the second edition came out in 1984 incorporating the supplements and much new material. The field of South Asian linguistics is enriched by another monumental work by Sir Ralph Turner, *A Comparative Dictionary of the Indo-Aryan Languages*, which also came out about the same time (1966). For a review of *DED*(*R*) see Krishnamurti 1963 and 2001b (ch. 21).

Bh. Krishnamurti's major work (revised PhD dissertation with two additional chapters), *Telugu Verbal Bases: a Comparative and Descriptive Study*, was published in 1961 by the University of California Press as UCPL 24. It deals with many topics in comparative Dravidian for the first time: a systematic analysis of Proto-Dravidian roots and formatives, a comparative phonology of Dravidian with Telugu as the main focus, an original discussion and resolution of many phonological problems, such as (C)V̄C-/ (C)VCC- becoming (C)VC- in the environment of [V in the formative syllable, alternations *i*/*u* and *e*/*o* in South Dravidian in the environment [C-*a*, rules for the formation of initial apicals as well as consonant clusters initially and non-initially, the incorporation of tense suffixes in stem morphemes, etc. Krishnamurti made pioneering observations on the formation of subgroups within Dravidian. An etymological index of 1,236 primary verbal bases is given in the Appendix with reconstructions. He published several papers on phonological problems: alternations *i*/*e* and *u*/*o* in South Dravidian (1958a), the developments of Proto-Dravidian **ẓ* (1958b), the split of PD **n*- and **m*- to *d*-/*n*- and *b*-/*m*- in Brahui before front vowels (1969c), raising of *ā̆* to *ē̆* before Pre-Parji alveolars (1978b), a quantitative study of 'apical displacement' in South Central Dravidian (1978a), and a peculiar vowel-lowering rule in Kui–Kuvi (1980), the elimination of a super-heavy syllable in Dravidian through a change of (C)V̄CCV to (C)V̄CV (1991a) with structural parallels in Indo-Aryan, using the evidence of Early Tamil *āytam* to reconstruct a Proto-Dravidian laryngeal **H*(1997b), and finally a two-step sound change *s* > *h* > *Ø* in Gondi dialects (1998b). In another paper (1998a) he has summarized the major sound changes in Dravidian and has proposed that typologically motivated sound changes tend to be more regular than simple historical changes. In four papers (1978a, 1978b, 1983, 1998b) he has established, with Dravidian case material, that lexical diffusion can lead to a regular sound change, and that one innovation was enough to set up subgroups within a language family, in terms of the model of lexical diffusion.

In comparative morphology, Krishnamurti published papers on the personal pronouns (1968b), on the reconstruction of gender–number categories in Proto-Dravidian (1975a), and on the origin and evolution of formative suffixes in Dravidian (1997a). In the last one, Krishnamurti sought to establish that the so-called formative suffixes, which currently signal intransitive vs. transitive (derivatively noun vs. adjective) in some of the languages of South and South-Central Dravidian, were originally tense and voice morphemes. Some languages lost tense but not voice; others have lost both the grammatical functions, thereby converting them into mere stem-formatives. In another paper (1989, with G. U. Rao) he reconstructed the third-personal pronouns in different Gondi dialects with focus on the interaction between phonological and morphological rules in language change.

During this period Krishnamurti suggested a revision of the subgrouping that he had proposed earlier in *TVB*. The subgroup Telugu–Gondi–Kui–Kuvi–Pengo–Manḍa is now attached to Proto-South Dravidian as South Dravidian II, while Tamil–Malayāḷam–Kannaḍa–Tuḷu–Koḍagu–Toda–Kota–Iruḷa are taken as South Dravidian I. South Dravidian II is also called South-Central Dravidian. He has given supporting evidence for this regrouping in his papers since 1970 (1975a,b, 1976, 1980). A number of scholars have accepted this regrouping since then (see figure 1.2).

He has published a grammar, texts and a lexicon of a South-Central Dravidian language, Koṇḍa (also known as Kūbi), in 1969 (1969a) and a grammar of Modern Telugu (with J. P. L. Gwynn) in 1985. He has further published three papers in encyclopedias, one on the 'Dravidian languages' (1992a), one on 'Dravidian lexicography' (1991b) and the other on 'Indian names: Dravidian' (1994a).

P. S. Subrahmanyam (1971) has published his PhD dissertation on Dravidian verb morphology, and S. V. Shanmugam, a comparative study of Dravidian nouns (1971a). These two works provide comparative data and attempt reconstruction of the inflectional categories of verbs and nouns. Subrahmanyam (1976b, 1977a,b) has a series of articles dealing with the developments of PD **a*, **ā*, **l*, **ḷ* and **r* in Toda. These changes go to the Pre-Toda stage and the conditioning environments have also to be reconstructed to the same stage. Subrahmanyam (1983) has brought out a monograph on comparative Dravidian phonology, which takes into account all publications until 1980. It is an advancement on Zvelebil (1970b), but it has too many misprints. The etymologies are based on *DED* (1961) and not on *DEDR* (1984). It also lacks rigour in formulating the sound changes for Proto-Dravidian.

Zvelebil (1970b) published a book on comparative Dravidian phonology about the same time as Emeneau (1970a). Both these were reviewed by Krishnamurti (1976, 1975b). Zvelebil's short monograph on comparative morphology (1977) does not add anything new to what has already been covered in Subrahmanyam (1971) and Shanmugam (1971a). Zvelebil has published his description of Iruḷa in three parts (1973, 1979, 1982b) and several short articles on Kuṟumba dialects (1982a, 1988) and one on Shōlega (1990b). He has an introduction to Dravidian linguistics in a monograph (1990a), in which he has devoted considerable space to the question of long-range comparison between Dravidian and other language families, as well as to the question of the language of the Indus seals being a form of Early Dravidian.

Kumaraswami Raja (1969b) has proposed *NPP for Proto-Dravidian to account for the correspondence NP (Kannaḍa–Telugu): PP (Tamil–Malayāḷam), as opposed to *NP, which accounts for NB (Kannaḍa–Telugu): NP [NB] (Tamil–Malayāḷam). He has written a monograph covering the whole family and showing how this solution helps in explaining the correspondences even outside the southern group better than the earlier writings. Sanford Steever's *Analysis to Synthesis* (1993) is a collection of his earlier papers in which he shows how two serial verbs of which the second is an auxiliary ('to be', 'to give', etc.) got fused into a single finite verb in South-Central and Central Dravidian languages (presumably a Proto-Dravidian phenomenon). Steever's research breaks new ground in Dravidian in the reconstruction of morphology and syntax. He edited a volume (1998) in which descriptive accounts of three literary and seven non-literary languages occur. Suvarchala's comparative study of the morphology of Central Dravidian (1992) and G. U. Rao's unpublished PhD thesis (1987b) on a comparative study of the phonology and morphology of Gondi dialects are useful additions to comparative Dravidian studies.

During the last two decades grammars of the literary languages have been published: Spoken Tamil by Asher (1982/1985), Modern Telugu by Krishnamurti and Gwynn (1985), Kannaḍa by Sridhar (1990), Old Tamil (1991b) and Modern Tamil (1989) by T. Lehmann, Malayāḷam by Asher and Kumari (1997), and spoken Tamil by Schiffman (1999); also dictionaries of contemporary Telugu by Gwynn (1991) and of Tamil by P. R. Subramanian (1992) need to be mentioned. All these are useful for linguistic and philological studies.

1.6.3 *What remains?*

A description of Manḍa is yet to be written and published by a former faculty member of Osmania University. A more thorough study of the dialects of Kui, Kuvi and Gondi is a desideratum. We need to decide the position of the Nilgiri languages (mainly Toda, Kota, Iruḷa, Baḍaga and Kuṟumba) in relation to Tamil and Kannaḍa. The absence of centralized vowels in Kota casts a suspicion on its closeness to Toda. The location of Tuḷu in the family tree is doubtful and Koraga needs to be appropriately located in the subgrouping scheme. Comparative morphology and syntax are still unexplored areas. It is hoped that this volume triggers future research in these areas.

1.7 Dravidian and Indo-Aryan

1.7.1 *Early contacts, scriptural evidence, language shift*

There has been a great deal of speculation on the time, the place and the nature of the earliest contact between the speakers of the Dravidian languages and those of Indo-Aryan. All this is part of prehistory and no archeological evidence is available to clinch the issue.

On the basis of lexical and syntactic evidence found in the language of the Ṛgveda, historians and linguists believe that 'the Ṛgvedic society consisted of several different ethnic components, who (sic!) all participated in the same cultural life' (Kuiper 1991: 8). Therefore, the term 'Aryan' was not used as a racial term; it referred to a people who were basically a pastoral community keeping herds of cattle as its economic mainstay, speaking a form of Old Indo-Aryan and practising certain rituals.[26] The non-Aryans

[26] I am indebted to Romila Thapar for lending me the manuscript of her paper, 'The Ṛgveda: encapsulating social change'. It is now published as a chapter in a book (see Bibliography under Thapar 2000).

with whom they came in contact and who did not rise to their level were called *dāsa-* or *dasyu-*; they were dark-skinned (*tvacaṃ kr̥ṣṇām*) and spoke indistinctly (*mr̥dhrawācaḥ*). Very likely these could be the speakers of the Dravidian languages; some tribes probably also spoke the Munda languages. Several clans of Aryans migrated from Iran under the leadership of Indra who helped the Bharatas, Yadu, Turvaśa, Pūru, Marut and Ayu to move eastward and cross the rivers Paruṣṇī (Ravi), Vipāś (Beas) and Śutudrī (Sutlej). 'Indra leads the clans of the *āryas* across regions difficult to traverse' (*R̥V* 6.22.7). Some of these clans seemed to have a mixed origin, possibly through intermarriage with non-Aryans, e.g. the Pūrus, Yadu and Turvaśa, who were accepted into the Aryan society. The Pūrus were also described as *mr̥dhravāc* and this meant that they could not speak the language as well as the Bharatas, but they were friendly with Indra who helped them.

Reference to *ārya-varṇa* and *dāsa-varṇa* in the *R̥gveda* gave rise to theories giving a racial connotation to Ārya and Dāsa based on skin-complexion (*varṇa-* 'colour'). Whatever the original meanings, the labels came to represent different cultural groups with different languages and religious practices. Kuiper (1991: 6) and Thapar (2000: 16–17) assert that 'black' was used as a metaphor for a people devoid of good pronunciation, and good religious practices (*avratān*), because they were phallic worshippers (*śiśna-devāḥ*). Kuiper (1991: 6) cites *'ambarīṣa'* as a non-Aryan name given 'to a son born in a family in which Indo-Aryan names were the rule'. A Vedic 'priest is said to have received a hundred camels from the *dāsá-*, Balbūthá-, Tárukṣa-'. Kuiper further gives a sample list of thirty-five 'names of some individuals, families and peoples' of non-Aryan origin, who had 'won access to the higher strata of Rigvedic society' (1991: 8).

The Dāsas were said to be numerous, running into hundreds of thousands, while the Aryans were fewer in number. The Pūrus among the Aryans and Balbūthá- among the Dāsas were treated differently from the parent groups. The Pūrus were also *mr̥dhra-vācaḥ*, but still Indra helped them (1.30.7). 'In the later Brāhmaṇas the Pūrus were said to have an *asura/rākṣasa* ancestry', and this means that they were assimilated into the Aryan fold from non-Aryan groups because of their changed life style, language or intermarriage with Aryans.

Deshpande (1979b: 2) says that Aryans considered non-Aryans as 'substandard human beings'. They called their enemies 'godless (*adeva*)', 'non-sacrificers (*ayajyavaḥ*)', 'non-believers in Indra (*anindra*)', 'worshippers of dummy gods (*mūradeva*)' and 'phallic gods (*śiśna-deva*)' and 'those whose language was obscure and unintelligible (*mr̥dhra-vācaḥ*)'. This runs counter to Kuiper's (see above) thinking, since the R̥gvedic language has a large number of loanwords from non-Aryan sources, over 380, of which 88 had retroflex phonemes! Besides, the *R̥gveda* has used the gerund, not found in Avestan, with the same grammatical function as in Dravidian, as a non-finite verb for 'incomplete' action. Ṛgvedic language also attests the use of *iti* as a quotative clause complementizer. All these features are not a consequence of simple borrowing, but they indicate substratum influence (Kuiper 1991: ch. 2).

Deshpande (1979b: 3) says that by the time of 'the late Saṃhitas and the Brāhmaṇa literature', Vedic Sanskrit was 'becoming archaic, and new forms of Sanskrit had begun to develop'. Pāṇini (fifth century BC) marked the end of this phase. Spoken varieties such as Pali and Prakrits were becoming popular. With the ascendancy of Buddhism and Jainism under royal patronage, Prakrits became standard and Sanskrit gradually ceased to be the first language. By the time of Katyāyana (300 BC) and Patañjali (100 BC), the first language of the Brahmins was Prakrit, while Sanskrit was confined to ritual purposes (Deshpande 1979b: chs. 2 and 3). Such a rapid transformation within a span of one millennium could not have happened unless most of the speakers of the non-Aryan languages (mainly the speakers of the Dravidian languages) had merged with the 'Aryan' speech community and accepted their language as the lingua franca, but 'learnt it imperfectly', giving rise to regional Prakrits. This explains the background of convergence and cultural fusion between Indo-Aryan and Dravidian, through language shift and adoption of a new medium by the erstwhile Dravidian speakers, and not through simple bilingualism and borrowing. By that time it was perhaps impossible to distinguish an 'Aryan' from a 'non-Aryan' person by skin colour or by speech.

Loanwords from Dravidian into Old Indo-Aryan have been identified from the nineteenth century onwards by scholars such as Gundert, Kittel and Caldwell without laying down the principles underlying such borrowings. Most of their suggestions were ignored by Indo-European scholars. Then followed the more sophisticated writings of Jules Bloch (1930) and T. Burrow (1945, 1946b, 1948) during the first half of the twentieth century. Having examined all these, Emeneau (1954/1980b) says that 'it is clear that not all of Burrow's suggested borrowings will stand the test of his own principles' (1980b: 91). Emeneau filters the alleged borrowings from Dravidian into Sanskrit and comes up with a list of twelve which he considers very definite, e.g. Skt. *ketaka-*, *ketakī-*: PD **kay-t-*V*kk-* 'screw-pine', Skt. *ēlā-*: PD **ēl-*V- 'cardamom', Skt. *pallī-*, *pallikā-*: PD **palli* 'house lizard', Skt. *mayūra-*: PD **may-*V*r* 'peacock', Skt. *puṭa-*, *puttikā-*: PD **puntt̲-* 'white anthill', etc. With the exception of three items, i.e. Skt. *mayūra-*, *khála-* 'threshing floor' and *phála-* which occur in the *Ṛgveda*, the rest are late borrowings found either in later literature or attested only as lexical entries (1980b: 93–9). Elsewhere in the article he thinks that Skt. *bála-* 'strength' (*ṚV*) must be traced to PD **wal-* 'to be strong' (93). Southworth (1979: 210–12) takes twenty words from Burrow's list with clear Dravidian etymologies as evidence of the earliest borrowings from Dravidian into Ṛgvedic Sanskrit.

In a monograph entitled 'Substrate languages in Old Indo-Aryan (Ṛgvedic, Middle and Late Vedic)' circulated as volume 5 of the electronic *Journal of Vedic Studies*,

Michael Witzel proposed three chronological phases (pp. 4–5) in the composition of the *R̥gveda*: I. the earliest books (4, 5, 6, 2) of the *R̥gveda* go back to 1700 to 1500 BCE; II. the Middle R̥gvedic period is c. 1500–1350 BCE (books 3, 7, 8); and III. the late R̥gvedic period 1350–1200 BCE (books 1.1–50, 8.67–103, 10.1–854, 10.85–191). He asserts that Dravidian loanwords appear only in the late R̥gvedic phases II and III. There are 300 non-Indo-European words in the first two phases, which Witzel traces to a substrate language, that he calls Para-Munda. He identifies certain non-Sanskritic prefixes during this period which could not be Dravidian since prefixes cannot be reconstructed for Proto-Dravidian. He illustrates several lexical items which had such prefixes as *ka-*, *ki-*, *ku-* etc. which he compares with Khasi articles masculine *u-*, feminine *ka-*, plural *ki-* followed by examples such as *ka-kardu* 'wooden stick', *kī-kaṭa-* 'a tribe', *kī-lāla-* 'biestings, a sweet drink', *ka-rambha-* 'gruel' etc. (pp. 8–12). He even considers the language of the Indus Valley civilization as Para-Munda.

The main flaw in Witzel's argument is his inability to show a large number of complete, unanalysed words from Munda borrowed into the first phase of the *R̥gveda*. Such an extensive lexical borrowing must precede any effort on the part of the borrowers proceeding to the next stage of isolating the prefixes and using them creatively with native stems. It would have been better if he said that we did not know the true source of 300 or so early borrowings into the *R̥gveda*. Nikita Gurov, a Russian linguist, has shown several of these to have Dravidian etymologies based on compounding and not prefixing, e.g. *kīkaṭa-* 'n. pr. of a tribe' from PD **kīẓ* 'low, bottom, mean', **kaṭa* 'place', with loss of **ẓ* from the compound **kīẓ-kkaṭṭ-ar* 'mean persons', *pra-maganda-* 'the name of a tribal chief, who was friendly with Indra' from PD **per*-V- 'big', + PD **makanṯu* [*magaṉḏu*] 'man, warrior' (see section 1.5 last paragraph). Witzel generalizes that 'the Pre-R̥gvedic Indus civilization, at least in the Panjab, was of (Para-)Austro-Asiatic nature' (p. 18).

1.7.2 *India as a linguistic area*

In 1956 Emeneau published an epoch-making paper, 'India as linguistic area'. He defines a linguistic area as 'an area which includes languages belonging to more than one family but showing traits in common which are not found to belong to the other members of (at least) one of the families'. He explains this phenomenon as a consequence of structural borrowing through extensive bilingualism, in the present context, 'Indianization of the immigrant Indo-Aryan' (Emeneau 1971a; repr. 1980b: 168). Earlier Chatterji (1926) and Jules Bloch (1930) had discussed the impact of non-Aryan on Indo-Aryan in phonology and morphology.

Emeneau has mentioned many features shared between Dravidian and Indo-Aryan, namely the use of retroflex consonants, distinction between dental and palatal affricates [ts dz č ǰ] in Telugu, Southern Oriya, Northern Kannaḍa and Marathi, the addition of the same set of case morphemes to the singular and plural oblique stems, the use of verbal participles as heads of subordinate clauses, changing finite verbs into verbal adjectives (relative participles) before noun heads, extensive use of echo words, and the use of classifiers and quantifiers (the last one Emeneau's exclusive discovery), a feature of Tibeto-Burman languages shared by Northeastern Indo-Aryan and transmitted to Dravidian. Emeneau (1965) examines the occurrence of retroflexes *ṭ*, *ḍ*, *ṛ*, *ṇ*, *ḷ* in several languages of the Iranian group – Balochi, Pashto, Ormuri, Parachi, Yidhga, Sanglechi–Ishkashmi, Wakhi – and the unique Burushaski. He says 'the isogloss then runs roughly north to south through Afghanistan and Baluchistan . . . Bilingualism, involving Indo-Aryan languages must be the answer' (Emeneau 1965; repr.1980b: 128–30). In further studies, Emeneau (1969a, 1971a, 1974b) discusses syntactic parallels between PD **-um* 'also, and, even, (with numerals) indefiniteness' and Skt. *api* with the same meaning range (see section 8.4.1 below), the Dravidian use of the past participle derived from the verb 'to say' **an-/*en-/*in-* (now in my reconstruction **aHn-*) and the use of Skt. *iti* as a quotative particle, and using phonological strategies in distinguishing male and female members of various castes and subcastes etc. (Sjoberg 1992: 510).

Andronov (1964b) thinks that the replacement of negative verbs by 'special negative words' is a feature of Indo-Aryan found in Dravidian. William Bright (1966) notices a phenomenon, similar to the Proto-South Dravidian rule *i u* > *e o* in the environment [*a* (umlaut, vowel harmony), which he calls 'Dravidian metaphony', also in some Modern Indo-Aryan and Munda languages extending from Assam to Ceylon which he calls a 'linguistic area' (see Krishnamurti 1969b: 324). Kuiper (1967) particularly discusses the use of *iti* 'thus' as a complementizer of onomatopoetic expressions from the Vedic times as strikingly Dravidian in origin. Most writers (Bloch, Emeneau, Kuiper) are agreed on the use of the absolutive form of the verb, the gerund, as head of non-finite clauses as a typical Dravidian feature of Indo-Aryan syntax. Masica's typological study of shared features (1976) has led him to isolate at least four, typically marking the South Asian area from the rest, namely retroflex consonants, Skt. *api*/Dravidian *-um* meaning 'even, also, and, indefinite', dative-subject constructions, and finally echo-words. He has a qualified 'yes' for nine features, because typologically they extend to much larger areas outside South Asia. These include the conjunctive particle, morphological causatives etc. (187–90) (see Krishnamurti 1985: 224).

Emeneau has continued to add to the 'areal features' in his papers on onomatopoetics (1969a; this is not specifically South Asian), onomastics (1978), and intensives (which he prefers to call 'expressives' now; 1987a). He has further looked at different kinds of phenomena in ethno-semantics, which have an areal bias, in his papers ' "Arm" and "leg" in the Indian linguistic area' (1980b: 294–314), and 'The right hand is the "eating hand": an Indian areal linguistic inquiry' (1987b).

In a comprehensive and well-documented paper, Andrée Sjoberg (1992) discusses the impact of Dravidian on Indo-Aryan. She has added to the observations of Emeneau and

Masica, the recent work of Fairservis and Southworth on linguistic archeology (unpublished paper of 1986) and that of a number of other linguists who have traced Dravidian influences in the syntax of New Indo-Aryan, particularly Marathi, Gujarati, Oriya and Bengali (Sjoberg 1992: 520–5). She points to the 'analytical grammatical'[27] type of NIA which she considers 'mainly to have resulted from Dravidian influences' (1992: 520), namely OV as opposed to English VO, postpositions as opposed to prepositions, the order Standard-Marker-Adjective as opposed to Adjective-Marker-Standard, adjective and adverb preceding noun and verb, respectively, as opposed to their inverse order in European languages. All these are typical of Dravidian, although the Dravidian languages are 'agglutinating-synthetic'. Jhungare (1985) considers 'topic prominence' in sentence structure is a shared feature of Indo-Aryan and Dravidian (Sjoberg 1992: 521). Klaiman (1987) has cited several syntactic parallels between Dravidian and Bengali, e.g. the use of an inflected verb 'say' as a clitic, the use of an invariant negative marker *nei* like Ta. *illai*, besides negative verbs, restructuring gender on the model of Dravidian; all such features indicate a Dravidian substratum in Bengali (Sjoberg 1992: 520–1). Krishnamurti (1991a) has demonstrated that there has been convergence in creating two favoured syllable types, V̄C or VCC in Dravidian and Indo-Aryan around the beginning of the CE; super-heavy syllable types had merged with one or the other in both. Thus PD **pāṭu* 'to sing': **pāṭ-ṭam* 'song', preserved in Early Tamil, became *pāḍu*: *pāṭ*-V- in almost all languages including Middle and Modern Tamil. Thus single vs. double contrast was reorganized as voiced and voiceless; in Skt. *dīrgha-* 'long' > Pali *dīgha*, Pkt. *diggha* (but not **dīggha* which must have been the intermediate form). Also the alternation between these two types (NIA *kamma*/*kām* 'action' < *Skt. *karman-*) has become internal to each of these families.

In conclusion, Sjoberg raises an important question:

> Thus the Dravidian grammatical impact on Indo-Aryan has been far greater than the Indo-Aryan grammatical impact on Dravidian – a point that specialists on Indian linguistic history seem not to have appreciated. How can we account for this pattern?
>
> Even after three millennia or more of Indo-Aryan-Dravidian contact the Dravidian languages have changed relatively little in their grammatical structure, whereas Indo-Aryan has undergone major grammatical restructure. (1992: 524)

Her hypothetical answer to this question is that 'agglutinative languages also seem highly resistant to syntactic change'. Sjoberg did not notice that I raised a similar question

[27] 'Agglutinative' would have been a better choice than calling it 'analytical'.

and provided a more acceptable answer in my first survey article (Krishnamurti 1969b: 324–5):

> It is the Dravidian languages (particularly South Dravidian) which show evidence of extensive lexical borrowing but only a few traits of structural borrowing from Indo-Aryan. On the contrary, Indo-Aryan (particularly Middle and Modern) shows large scale structural borrowing from Dravidian, but very little lexical borrowing. How can we reconcile these conflicting facts in order to work them into a framework of a bilingual situation?

I proposed an answer in a long footnote, as follows, which many subsequent researchers seem to have missed:

> That Middle Indo-Aryan and New Indo-Aryan have been built on a Dravidian substratum seems to be the only answer. The fact that the invading Aryans could never have outnumbered the natives, even though they politically controlled the latter, is a valid inference. We may formulate the situation as follows: If the speakers of L_1 (mother tongue) are constrained to accept L_2 (2nd language) as their 'lingua franca', then an L_3 will develop with the lexicon of L_2 and with the dominant structural features of L_1 and L_2; L_1 = Dravidian languages, L_2 = Varieties of Sanskrit, L_3 = Middle Indic. This is also true of modern Indian varieties of English, which have an English (L_2) lexicon but a large number of structural features of Indian languages (L_1). Here, of course, the situation is different since the native languages have not been abandoned. But what is interesting is that Indian languages have freely 'borrowed' words from English but no structural features; transfer of only structural features excluding the lexicon is evident when Indians speak English as a second language.
>
> The hypothesis that most of the present New Indo-Aryan speakers should have been originally Dravidians and also presumably Kolarians (Munda speakers) was suggested long ago (see Caldwell 1956: 52–61). Quoting Hodgson, Caldwell says, '. . . the North Indian vernaculars had been derived from Sanskrit, not so much by the natural process of corruption and disintegration as through the overmastering, remoulding power of the non-Sanskritic elements contained in them' (p. 53). Emeneau says, 'In the case of Sanskrit, however, the Dravidian substratum is easily accessible in its dozen or more living languages, and in that a Proto-Dravidian can be worked out, given enough scholars interested in the matter' (1954: 285); also see S. K. Chatterji (1957), see particularly, pp. 212–13 in which he speaks of non-Aryan substratum of Aryan.

Recently, Thomason and Kaufman (1988: chs. 2, 3) have made a distinction between 'borrowing' and 'interference through shift'. They consider the Dravidian and Indo-Aryan situation comes under the latter type. Commenting on Emeneau's (1956) remark that 'absorption, not displacement, is the chief mechanism in radical language changes of the kind we are considering', they say:

> . . . the two basic assumptions are that Dravidian speakers, shifting in considerable numbers to the language of the Indo-Aryan invaders, imposed their own habits of (among other things) retroflex vs. dental articulation on Indic as they learned it; and they were numerous enough to influence Indic as a whole, through the eventual imitation of their flawed Indic by original Indic speakers. The interference in Indic from Dravidian is striking in view of the fact that, as has frequently been observed, there are few old Dravidian loanwords in Indic. In sharp contrast, Sanskrit influence on some literary Dravidian languages has come about through borrowing – native speakers of Dravidian languages are initiators of the structural changes – and accordingly we expect, and indeed find, large numbers of Sanskrit loanwords in Dravidian. (1988: 39–40)

Apparently they also did not notice that I made a similar observation two decades earlier, though I used different labels, lexical borrowing vs. structural borrowing.

Hock (1975, 1982, 1996) has persistently questioned the theory of a Dravidian substratum in Indo-Aryan from pre-historic times. This is questioning over one-and-a-half centuries of scholarship in comparative studies. While Kuiper has provided evidence for the integration of some accomplished Dravidians into the Aryan fold (see section 1.7.1), Hock (1996: 57–8) uses this evidence to suggest that R̥gvedic Aryans and non-Aryans met as 'near-equals'. There is no such implication from the way that non-Aryans were described as 'dark-skinned', 'indistinct speakers' and 'godless'. In conformity with his line of thinking, Hock calls the substratum theory a 'subversion' and supporters of it 'subversionists'. His approach ignores both the history and geography of Aryan and Dravidian contact, and the fact that the evolution of Middle and Modern Indo-Aryan has been a slow and unconscious process and is not the consequence of the Dravidian natives deliberately 'subverting' the structure and system of Indo-Aryan. The scenario with three Dravidian languages scattered at distant points on the northern periphery, with several islands in central India, and with thick concentration in the south indicates that most of the early native Dravidian speakers in the north and centre had merged with local speech communities within Indo-Aryan. Constraints of space prevent me from countering his arguments, which sound clearly strained and biased.

1.8 Affinity between Dravidian and languages outside India

In a short but well-informed paper Austerlitz (1971) has characterized most of the comparisons made between Dravidian and the other families/languages such as Uralic, Altaic, African, Basque, Sumerian, etc. as 'unprofessional', 'typological', 'wrong', 'experiments without intent to convince', 'unsystematic' etc. (1971: 254–6). He suggests first the reconstruction of proto-languages of established families, and then proceeding to compare the proto-languages as a method of making long-range comparisons to reconstruct macro-families. He says, 'In so doing we can collate our results with information about migrations, paleontology, archaeology, and other fields and thus attempt to capture a more realistic picture of the linguistic past of the continents' (1971: 257–8).

1.8.1 *Dravidian and Ural-Altaic*

Caldwell hypothesized about the genetic connection between Dravidian and the so-called 'Scythian' or 'Turanian' (see fn. 5). He said that the Dravidian languages 'bear a special relationship to a particular family included in the group, the Finno-Ugrish' (1956: 65). During the twentieth century several scholars pursued the idea of a genetic relationship between Dravidian and Ural-Altaic. Burrow, in one of his earlier papers (1944), gave a brief history of the theory with 72 etymologies referring to body parts in Dravidian and Uralian. Zvelebil (1990a: 99–103) has surveyed the history of this theme with bibliographical references, but he has not cited the line of argumentation of each contributor. Krishnamurti (1969b: 326, 328–9) has reviewed the arguments of Karl Bouda (1953, 1956) and Menges (1964). Earlier F. O. Schrader pursued the theory (1937). Subsequent contributions, according to Zvelebil, include Pentti Aalto (1971), Karl Menges (1977), S. A. Tyler (1968), and several recent publications of J. Vachek including two in *Archív Orientální* (1978, 1987).

Zvelebil says that 'the most important agreements are in morphology'. This matter has to be established in terms of identified morphs with similar function, or else the similarities could be just typological. Zvelebil does mention such identities without any example (1990a: 101). Pentti Alto (1971: 63–5) points out that some case suffixes like Fenno-Ugric lative *-*k*(*a*), Proto-Uralian *-*m* for accusative sg. compare favourably with Dravidian dative *-*kk*(V) and accusative *-V*n*. Vacek suggests the possibility of 'prolonged ancient contact' leading to borrowing and diffusion (Zvelebil 1990a: 103). Zvelebil concludes that the 'Uralaltaic-Dravidian hypothesis remains the most promising' (103). In reviewing Lahovary's various studies relating Dravidian with 'peri-Mediterranean', I called it a 'colossal adventure in time and space' (Krishnamurti 1969b: 329). The method that most scholars have followed is not comparing one proto-system with the other, but showing parallels in selected features between some languages of one family and some of the other family.

1.8.2 *Dravidian and Elamite*

Zvelebil (1990a) devotes considerable space to survey the claims made by scholars relating Dravidian to Elamite (104–15) and Japanese (116–22). I also reviewed McAlpin's papers (1974, 1975, 1979) in my 1985 survey of comparative Dravidian studies. His book was published in 1981 and not included in my survey article written in 1980. I quote the following (1985: 225–6):

> (1) Many of the rules formulated by McAlpin lack intrinsic phonetic/phonological motivation and appear *ad hoc*, invented to fit the proposed correspondences: e.g. Proto-Elamo-Dravidian **i*, **e* > Ø Elamite, when followed by *t*, *n*, which are again followed by *a*; but these remain undisturbed in Dravidian (1974: 93). How does a language develop that kind of sound change? This rule was dropped a few years later, because the etymologies were abandoned (see 1979: 184).
>
> (2) He set up retroflexes as an innovation in Dravidian resulting from PED **rt* (1974: 94). Later he abandoned this rule and set up retroflexes and dentals for PED and said that Elamite merged the retroflexes with dentals (1979: see chart on 184–5). But the following statement in the body of the article, referring to his updated version of correspondences, is puzzling: 'The major additions have been . . . the splitting of the Proto-Elamo-Dravidian dental series into dental and post-dental series reflecting the dental-retroflex contrast in Dravidian.' But the chart shows merger in Elamite and not split of PED dental into dental and retroflex in Dravidian! The correspondences between 1974 and 1979 have undergone total change, which meant that earlier 'etymologies' were abandoned and new ones commissioned. The 1979 correspondences sound more plausible, but the etymologies are weak; e.g. PDr. *īn* 'to bear young (of animal), to yean' is said to be cognate with Elamite *šinni* 'to arrive' by positing loss of PED **š* in PDr. This semantic connection is perhaps dictated by the author's English language background in which people refer to 'the arrival of a baby'. But it is extremely odd to attribute this adhoc semantic connection to PDr. For those who know Dravidian, this meaning shift is extremely spurious and adhoc.

Zvelebil (1990a) reviews McAlpin's study in greater detail, but ends saying 'I am also convinced that much additional work is to be done and many alterations will have to be made to remove the genetic cognation in question from the realm of sheer hypothesis and establish it as a fact acceptable to all' (115). In his book (1981) McAlpin shows only 81 items, out of a corpus of 5,000 lexical items of Elamite, as possible cognates with Dravidian. The basic problem is the small size of the database, and the fact that it belongs to the sixth century BC, by which time the major Dravidian languages had already split (mainly Telugu and Tamil). In my recent research in reconstructing a Proto-Dravidian laryngeal, I noticed two important cognates that have *h-* in Elamite,[28] the deictic roots **ah* 'that, not far', *(*h*) *ih* 'this' and **huh* 'that (remote)' (McAlpin 1981: 81–2, A3-6; also 26, § 221.31 (5); Krishnamurti 1997b: 149, fn. 2; also see Zvelebil 1990a: 111); secondly, the Proto-Dravidian verb **caH-* 'to die' has a close cognate in Middle Elamite *sa-* 'life to be cut off', *sahri* 'death' (McAlpin reconstructs **cah-* for PED, see 1981: 99). We need more cognates of an atypical kind to rule out the possibility of chance.

1.8.3 *Dravidian and Japanese*

Susumu Ohno has been a persistent writer on the relationship between Japanese and Tamil. It was pointed out to him that any relationship with Japanese should go back to an earlier stage than Tamil (i.e. Proto-Dravidian). He published a book (1980) dealing with the so-called correspondences between Tamil and Japanese without any reference to the external history or archeology of the two speech communities to support his hypothesis. Zvelebil says that there is 'evidence' of relationship but no 'proof' (1990a: 117). Some are 'false cognates', he says, Ta. *cēttu* 'red' [*DEDR* 1931 *cē-* (<**kē-*)] with Japanese *sita* 'red'. This change is dateable to the third century BC in Tamil. Zvelebil concludes saying, 'there is strikingly close typological affinity between Dravidian (particularly Modern Tamil) and Japanese in their morpho-syntactic structure' (1990a: 121–2). The typological similarities arise from the hypothesis that Japanese was also considered an offshoot of the Altaic stock.

1.8.4 *Dravidian and Nostratic*

Holger Pedersen, the Danish linguist, as early as 1903, proposed that the Indo-European languages could be genetically related to Semito-Hamitic/Afro-Asiatic, Uralic, Altaic, Yukagir and Eskimo and called this macro-family 'Nostratic', from Latin *noster* 'our', meaning 'our primordial tongue'. Former Soviet linguists, Illič-Svityč, Dolgopolsky, Shevoroshkin, etc., working independently, expanded the hypothesis to include some other families including Dravidian under Nostratic. There is no agreement even among the supporters of the hypothesis on what language families make up Nostratic. There has been a great deal of writing on this hypothesis during the past three decades. Illič-Svityč (b.1934–d.1966) compiled an etymological dictionary of 607 items from these families with a statement of phonological correspondence before his premature tragic death. The Nostratic hypothesis has its adherents as well as detractors. Greenberg (2000) proposed the reconstruction of a Eurasiatic family and provided reconstructions of grammatical

[28] McAlpin has apparently based his reconstructions on my proposal for a Proto-Dravidian laryngeal in my 1963 review of Burrow and Emeneau (1961). I made that observation purely on the basis of internal evidence based on Old Tamil *āytam*.

morphemes. He excluded Afro-Asiatic and Dravidian from Eurasiatic, but included Uralic–Yukaghir, Altaic, Eskimo-Aleut, and Korean–Japanese–Ainu. In a personal communication in October 2000 at Stanford, he said that Dravidian could be a sister of Eurasiatic and not a daughter.

I will confine myself to examining Dravidian data in relation to Nostratic. Dolgopolsky (1986) has proposed 'morphemic stability' as a criterion for selecting the lexical items for comparison. He arrived at fifteen items with very high 'morphemic stability' cross-linguistically. He then goes on to cite 'phonetic similarities' among the lexical items representing these fifteen from different families. Unfortunately Dravidian is not given in this listing, because he does not believe Dravidian to be a member of Nostratic (Campbell 1998: 110), but Bomhard and Kerns (1994) include it. I give the Proto-Dravidian reconstructions of these and cite some of the reconstructions of Illič-Svityč from Proto-Nostratic (PN) cited by Campbell (1998: 124–8). The Eastern branch is said to include Uralic, Altaic and Dravidian.

Dolgopolsky's items	Proto-Dravidian reconstructions [*DEDR*]
(1) first-person marker	**yā-n*/**ya-n-* (mine: **yAH-n-*) [5160, 5154]
(2) '2'	**īr*/**ir-* [474]
(3) second-person marker	**nī-n* [3684, 3688]
(4) 'who' 'what'	**yā-w-anṯ*/*-at* (mine **yĀ̌H-a-*) [5151]
(5) 'tongue'	**nā-l* [3633]
(6) 'name'	**pin-cc*-V-*r* [4410]
(7) 'eye'	**kaṇ-* [1159a]
(8) 'heart'	**kuṇṭ*-V- [1693]
(9) 'tooth'	**pal* [3986]
(10) verbal neg (both negative proper and prohibitive)	***-aH-*/***aH-aH*
(11) 'finger/toe nail'	**ok*-V*r*, **kōr-* [561]
(12) 'louse'	**pēn* [4449]
(13) 'tear' (noun)	**kaṇ-nīr* 'eye-water' [1159b]
(14) 'water'	**nīr* [3690]
(15) 'dead'	**caH-* 'to die' [2426]

The reconstructions from other families do not match most of these. There is no adjective 'dead' in Dravidian. Instead the past particiciple 'the dead . . . ' from the verb 'to die' is used. It is not clear what (13) means. There is a comment 'no correspondences' (Dolgopolsky 1986: 43). I have taken it to mean 'a tear drop' not 'a cut'. Illič-Svityč's reconstructions: Uralic **mi* (1); in Dravidian *-n*/*-m* are sg/pl suffixes in items (1) and (3), PN ***to* 'two' (2), Proto-Uralic **ti* 'thou/you' (3), PN ***K'e* 'who' (4), ***K'ä*/*lH*/*ä* 'tongue'(5), ***nimi* 'name'(6), ***HuK'a* 'eye'(7), ***k'Erd*V- (8) 'heart', ***p'*/*al*V 'tooth'(9), VERBAL NEG ***ʔäla* (10), ***p/a/r/ä* 'nail'(11), ***t' äj*V 'louse'(12), ***wete* (14) 'water', ***m/ä/r*V 'die'(15). <K> is a cover symbol for any velar consonant; <'> a glottallized stop. Among these only item (9) 'tooth' matches, but the reconstruction does not explain Indo-European: Lat. *dent-*, OIA *dant-*. South Dravidian I has **al* as a negative verb, which looks like the reconstruction in (10). Even then two out of fifteen (6.5 per cent) can be simply chance resemblances.

Zvelebil (1999) says, 'There are, from Dravidian perspective, reconstructions which I would not certainly hesitate to accept' and gives some specific reconstructions. The foregoing is enough to show that the question is still very speculative.

1.8.5 *Dravidian and Harappan*

There is no decisive support to the recent proposals that Aryans were native to the Indian subcontinent. The hypothesis that the Indus civilization was Indo-Aryan is also rejected by knowledgeable historians, because of several factors: the Indus civilization around Harappa ended before the Aryans entered India; the seals bear evidence of a non-prefixing language; it 'had an extensive agrarian base and an urban population dependent on food production in rural areas' (Thapar 2000:13); there is no evidence that the Indus valley people (like the Dravidians) knew of the lion and the horse; for the Aryans, the knowledge of the tiger and the elephant came much later.

Zvelebil gives the history of the hypothesis tracing the Harappa culture to proto-Dravidian as well as a summary of the present state of the art (1990a: 84–98). The period of the Indus civilization is broadly placed between 2500 and 1700 BC. There were over 3,000 seals written in a script with 419 signs. It was likely to be logosyllabic with some signs (pictograms) representing full words. Russian and Finnish scholars computerized the data and made an effort to relate meaning to the signs in the 1960s. In India Mahadevan (1977) published a concordance of the signs, with a listing of the sequences and frequencies of all those that co-occur with a given sign. The Finnish scholars also prepared another concordance. The writing was right to left, sometimes both right to left and left to right. Numerous attempts have been made at decipherment but none of these has borne fruit. The latest book-length treatment of decipherment of the Indus script is by Asko Parpola (1994) but it only explains certain hunches with no decipherment.

Possehl (1996) has critically reviewed different attempts at decipherment by thirty-five scholars between 1924 and 1992 and concludes: 'Since there is little basic research on the script and so little sharing of programmatic visions, it is scarcely a wonder that the writing system has not yet been understood' (168).

The subtitles of the above four subsections as well as much of the contents are taken from Zvelebil's recent, painstaking study of these problems. Since even by Zvelebil's own confession they are all speculative studies, I have not made an original study of these except where I have given references to works that I have consulted.

2

Phonology: descriptive

2.1 **Introduction**

The Dravidian languages retain most of the contrasts of Proto-Dravidian vowels and consonants. Proto-Dravidian had five vowels /i e a o u/ with length contrast /7. Alternatively, one can set up ten vowels for Proto-Dravidian, five short and five long. Diphthongs [ai au] can be treated as sequences of a vowel + a semiconsonant, i.e. /ay aw/ patterning with VC. There were seventeen consonants in Proto-Dravidian: six stops /p t t̲ ṭ c k/, four nasals /m n ṇ ñ/, two laterals /l ḷ/, one flap /r/, one retroflex frictionless continuant /ẓ/, three semivowels /w y H/. The last one is a laryngeal, which patterns phonologically with semivowels. All departures from this system can be traced to two sources: (a) certain sound changes within the historical period of individual languages or subgroups; (b) borrowing from contact languages, either of the same family or of a different family.

The five-vowel system is fairly stable in all subgroups; new centralized vowels have been added, through splits, to the list of phonemes of several of the Nilgiri languages, namely Toda, Iruḷa, Kur̲umba of South Dravidian I. Long vowels are less subject to change than the short vowels. Four of the stops have remained stable in the whole family: /p t ṭ k/. The affricate /c/ gets variable treatment in different subgroups, represented as [ts c s]. The alveolar /t̲/ also has undergone change and has been eliminated as a distinctive unit outside South Dravidian. Voiced or lenis allophones of stop phonemes have developed within the native element in all languages and subsequently they became phonemic, except in Old Tamil and Malayāḷam. For all other subgroups, both voiceless and voiced stops need to be reconstructed. Among nasals /m n/, and among liquids /r l/ have been the most stable. Retroflex /ḷ ṇ/ have been gradually replaced by /l n/ in all but the languages of South Dravidian I, while the frictionless continuant /ẓ/, a highly marked segment, has vanished in most languages, having merged with different phonemes in different languages; it has lost its phonemic identity, except in Tamil (dialectally) and Malayāḷam. Aspirated stops and affricates, voiceless and voiced, have been added to the inventories of Kannaḍa, Telugu and Malayāḷam from the beginning of literature in these languages, owing to extensive borrowing from Sanskrit and the Prakrits (see sections 10.2–3). Even some non-literary languages (particularly Kolami, Naiki,

Kuṟux) have added aspirated stops through bilingualism in surrounding Modern Indo-Aryan languages. The Indo-Aryan-like completeness in the stop series in five points of articulation – labial, dental, retroflex, palatal and velar – could have been a typologically based reason why alveolar **ṯ* was eliminated from the system, since there could not have been aspirated series involving it. Also note that the alveolar **ṯ* is the most highly marked segment in the series dental–alveolar–retroflex among the Dravidian languages and the languages of the South Asian area.

Alveolar and retroflex consonants did not begin a word in Proto-Dravidian and this feature is preserved in all except in one subgroup (South Dravidian II). In South Dravidian I, during recent times, words beginning with *r* and *l* appear through loss of the first syllable, e.g. Ta. Ma. *raṇḍu* (<**iraṇṭu*) 'two'; in Iruḷa and Tuḷu this change has spread to several lexical items, creating words with initial *r*, *ḍ* and *l*. Consonant clusters did not occur word-initially in Proto-Dravidian. Even here only one subgroup (South Dravidian II) makes a departure. The Proto-Dravidian laryngeal /H/ was preserved in a few cases in early Tamil as a distinct sound, called *āytam* [aːydam] (section 4.5.7.2 (c)). Its presence is inferred from the lengthening of a preceding short vowel in most cases (Krishnamurti 1997b; see section 4.5.7.2c). The descriptive and typological changes in vowels and consonants in different subgroups and languages are dealt with in greater detail below.

2.2 Vowels

2.2.1 *South Dravidian (SD I)*

The inherited system of ten vowels /i e a o u ī ē ā ō ū/ is retained intact in Tamil and Malayāḷam, both old and modern. Koḍagu and most of the Nilgiri languages (Toda, Iruḷa, Kuṟumba, etc.) have developed the centralized vowels *ï ī̈ ë ē̈* when followed by retroflex (sometimes alveolar) consonants. These apparently were allophonic to start with but became phonemic with the obliteration or modification of the conditioning environments.

Modern Tamil and Malayāḷam have added /ǣ/ (lower mid front vowel) through borrowing from English words such as 'bank'. Modern Tamil also has nasalized vowels developing from word-final V*m*/*n* sequences, but final *m*/*n* are retained when a vowel follows, e.g. *avā̃*/*avan-* 'he' (the nasalized vowel is fronted dialectally [ε^{n}]), *marā̃*/*maram-* 'wood' (following vowel rounding [o^{n}/$ɔ^{n}$], dialectally). Most words in Modern Tamil end in vowels. Words beginning with a front vowel have a [y] onglide in speech; similarly, a rounded vowel has a [w] onglide (Annamalai and Steever 1998: 102, Asher and Kumari 1997: 406, Schiffman and Eastman 1975: xix). A short /u/ following a word-final stop (in Modern Tamil any consonant) is phonetically a back unrounded vowel [ï] which was called the 'enunciative vowel' (Bright 1975: §§ 3ff.). This is regularly lost when followed by a vowel across a morph or word boundary, *nāṭu* 'country' + *iṉ* → *nāṭ-iṉ-*, obl of *nāṭu*.

The only exception is stems of the CVP-*u* type (P = voiceless stop; Kumaraswami Raja 1975).

Toda has the following vowels in addition to the ten-vowel system: *ü ǖ ï ï̄* (front rounded and back unrounded vowels) and *ö ö:*, mid central rounded vowels (Emeneau 1957: 21, 1984:7). Shalev et al. (1994) confirm the phonemic analysis of Emeneau and set up sixteen vowels for Toda, despite the gap of sixty years in the collection of field data. They consider, on acoustic grounds, that *ï ï̄* are 'high-mid central unrounded vowels' and *öȫ*, 'central, mid rounded vowels'. They add [æː], which Emeneau treated as an allophone of /eː/. They have further discussed the variation in allophonic quality and duration of vowels before voiceless and voiced consonants: 'the V/Vː ratio of 50% is maintained even when other factors (the voicing value of the following consonant) affect vowel duration, which indicates that this ratio is the cue for quantity' (Shalev et al. 1994: 28). They say that no other Dravidian language has *ï ü ö* (central high unrounded, front high and mid rounded vowels) as described here, which are unique to Toda with restricted distribution (1994: 29–30). This is not true since Iruḷa also has similar vowels (Zvelebil 1973: 11–12).

Unlike the other Nilgiri languages (Emeneau 1944, vol.1: 15ff.), Kota has no centralized vowels and it is puzzling since its closest sister Toda has them.

Iruḷa has *ï ë ü ö*, short and long. According to Zvelebil (1971a: 116–17), these are 'central (unrounded and rounded) vowels, respectively high and mid'. He says, 'the feature "rounded: unrounded" is not entirely clear so far. What is clear is the position of *ü* and *ö* which are further back than *ï* and *ë*, respectively'. He added *ä ǟ* to his earlier (1971a, 1973) inventory of Iruḷa phonemes in *The Irula (Ërla) Language*, Part II (1979: 23), e.g. *päṉḏi* 'pig', *ǟne* 'elephant'. Perialwar (1978b: ch. 2) sets up five centralized vowels corresponding to the inherited five non-centralized vowels. He adds *ä* to the list of Zvelebil. He says that the feature of rounding is present in *ü* and *ǖ*. It is not certain if the centralized *ä* and *ǟ* are phonetically [ə] shwa-like. Clarity of phonetic definition is lacking in the descriptions of Zvelebil, Kapp and Perialwar. Diffloth (1968 [1976]: 129) describes *ü* as 'a centralized rounded back vowel' and he calls it the enunciative vowel. In Tamil the enunciative vowel is the unrounded back vowel [ï].

Zvelebil gives the following examples, to which I have added the Tamil cognates and references to *DEDR*:

> *piyë* 'crime': Ta. *piḻai* 'fault' [4187]
> *kï̄ye/kï̄ë-* 'down, below': Ta. *kīḻ* 'below' [1619]
> *vüyu* 'to fall': Ta. *viḻu* 'to fall' [5430]
> *mǖy* 'to surround': Ta. *mūḻ* [5030]
> *ëṭu* 'eight': Ta. *eṭṭu* 'eight' [784]
> *kë̄kka* 'to hear': Ta. *kēḷ* 'to hear, to ask' [2017]
> *köttu* 'neck': Ta. *kaḻuttu* 'neck' [1366]
> *ȫḷu* 'seven': Ta. *ēḻ* 'seven' [910]

Centralization of front vowels before retroflexes is accompanied by rounding in some cases and not in others, e.g.**ēẓ* >**ōẓ* > *ȫḷu* as opposed to *ë̄* in *kë̄-* (< **kēḷ-*) 'to hear'.

The Kuṟumba (Kapp 1978, 1987) dialects have two centralized vowels *ï* and *ë* (short and long) which in effect are *i* and *e* retracted to central position when followed by retroflex and alveolar consonants originally, e.g. *kïḷi* 'parrot': Ta. *kiḷi* 'parrot'[584], *ëṭṭu* 'eight': Ta. *eṭṭu* 'eight'[784]; recent loanwords from English, in which /t d/ are pronounced as retroflexes, do not show this change. Retroflex /ḷ ẓ/ are lost word-finally after centralizing the preceding vowels, e.g. *kë̄* (*-p*, *-t*) 'hear': Ta. *kēḷ* (*kēṭp-*, *kēṭṭ-*), *kï̄e* 'place below': Ta. *kīẓ* [1619]. In Pālu Kuṟumba, retroflex *ẓ* and *ḷ* merge with *y* (< * *y*) or are assimilated to the following obstruents, promoting the allophones to a phonemic status. In Ālu Kuṟumba also the cause of centralization is practically the same, e.g. *ïḍe* 'place': Ta. *iṭai* 'place, space'[434]. Jēnu Kuṟumba has *ï ë ü* and *ä*, of which the conditioning factors for *ü* and *ä* are not clear (Zvelebil 1988).[1]

Koḍagu also has four front centralized vowels *ï* and *ë* (short and long) in root syllables (when not preceded by palatal or labial consonants), conditioned by following retroflexes and alveolar **ṟ* (Emeneau 1970b, Balakrishnan 1976). Emeneau calls these 'back unrounded vowels', high and mid (1970b: 145). Word-finally it has *ï* corresponding to the Tamil enunciative vowel (1970b: 147ff.).

Baḍaga, another Nilgiri language with 125,000 speakers, is the largest of the Nilgiri tribes, but it has only the inherited ten vowels (Hockings and Pilot-Raichoor 1992: xvi). Badagas are said to have moved to their new habitat from Mysore around the sixteenth century. Hockings and Pilot-Raichoor further maintain that it is not a dialect of Kannaḍa as presumed by several scholars earlier. None of the dialects studied by these authors shows any evidence of retracted (retroflexed) vowels that Emeneau had alluded to in his 1939 paper. For instance, they have given several variants for the word meaning 'seven' (PD **ēẓ*), namely *iu*, *īu*, *īyu*, *iyyu*, *iḷu* (in Merkunāḍ dialect) besides *ēḷu* (Todanāḍ dialect). It was in the Merkunāḍ dialect that Emeneau recorded, sixty years ago, [ī̈ ü], [ē̈ ü] for this word. In his foreword to the book cited above, Emeneau suggests that further fieldwork is needed to sort out this problem. The huge *Baḍaga–English Dictionary* by Hockings and Pilot-Raichoor has no evidence of retracted vowels.

Emeneau (1989: 135) thinks that the Nilgiri languages must have split from Pre-Tamil before palatalization of velars (in the environment [+V, +Front]) started in Tamil–Malayāḷam, i.e. 'round about the beginning of the Tamil recorded texts' (first to third century BCE). The absence of palatalization in Old Tamil (and Malayāḷam) when front vowels were followed by retroflex (some alveolar) consonants suggests that the centralization of the front vowels was an inherited feature of all these languages, originally at the subphonemic level. The only puzzle is that Kota does not show this feature.

[1] Zvelebil calls it an independent language, 'rather Kannaḍa like', but without supporting arguments.

Old Kannaḍa has the inherited ten vowels /i e a o u ī ē ā ō ū/. Modern Kannaḍa, like Tamil–Malayāḷam, has added /ǣ/ through borrowings from English. Tuḷu has the same core system but it has added *ɛ* (front low unrounded vowel, historically from *-ay* word-finally) and *ï* (high central unrounded) (Bhat 1998), which mainly occur finally. *ï* and *u* result from a split of older /u/ and *ï* corresponds to the enunciative vowel of the other Southern languages (also see K. P. Kekunnaya 1994: 21–2). The long counterparts of *ï* and *ɛ* are extremely restricted.

2.2.2 *Other subgroups*

South-Central Dravidian (SD II), namely Telugu, Gondi, Koṇḍa, Kui, Kuvi, Pengo and Manḍa, all have five short vowels and five long vowels, the core inherited system. Modern Telugu, however, has added /ǣ/ derived from internal changes as well as from loanwords from English, e.g. *cǣru* 'tamarind soup', *tāṭǣku* (*tāṭi* + *āku*) 'palm leaf', *bǣnku* 'bank' (Krishnamurti and Gwynn 1985: 29–30). In some of the non-literary languages (Gondi, Koṇḍa, Kui), short and long vowels contrast only in word-initial (root syllable) position. In speech, Telugu, like the other literary languages, has subphonemic glides [y w] added to word-initial front and back (rounded) vowels respectively. Winfield (1928: 1–2) talks of a hiatus in Kui when 'vowels come together, *laa* young woman'; this hiatus is 'prevented by the insertion of *v* or *j* or *n*, between the contiguous vowels, e.g. *lāvenju* (*lā-v-enju*), young man'. Winfield perhaps meant a glottal stop while referring to hiatus. He also suggests that vowel sequences *au* and *ai* are rendered *av* and *ay*, e.g. *kāu* → *kāv* 'a fruit', *māi* → *māy* 'our' (Winfield 1928: 2). Kuvi and Koṇḍa have a phonemic glottal stop.

The five-vowel system with an additional phoneme of length also occurs in Central and North Dravidian languages. The only exception is Brahui which does not have short *e* and *o* owing to the influence of surrounding Indo-Aryan and Iranian languages, which lack contrast between *e*/*ē* and *o*/*ō* (Emeneau 1962d: 7–20; Elfenbein 1998: 391–2). Emeneau says that in non-initial (unaccented) syllables only, short *e* and *o* occur as allophones of /e o/ which are always long in initial (accented) syllables. Emeneau draws attention to limited contrasts between *e* and *ē* in inflected forms, non-initially (1962d: 7, fn.2).

2.3 **Consonants**

There is greater variation among the consonants of different subgroups. In Proto-Dravidian voicing and aspiration were not distinctive features among the consonants. Word-initially apical (alveolar and retroflex) consonants did not occur. There were no initial consonant clusters. Medial clusters were usually geminate obstruents or sequences of nasal + a homorganic stop (+ a homorganic stop); a semivowel or liquid followed by an obstruent also occurred less frequently.

2.3.1 ***South Dravidian (SD I)***

The inventory of consonants of Old Tamil is very similar to that of Proto-Dravidian. It has seventeen consonants, viz. /p t ṯ c ṭ k, m n ñ ṇ, r ẓ, l ḷ, y w ḥ/. The last segment is my transliteration of Tamil *āytam* ([k̲] in *Tamil Lexicon*), which is derived from a Proto-Dravidian laryngeal **H* (see section 4.5.7.2.3 below; also Krishnamurti 1997b). The rest are represented by the same symbols. Old and Modern Tamil write both dental [n] and alveolar [ṉ] nasals but evidence for their contrast is insignificant. Lehmann (1998: 77) and Steever (1998: 14, 16) considered *āytam* an allophone of Tamil /y/ before obstruents, but there is no real evidence for this assumption. Old Tamil has *eytu* 'to approach' [*DEDR* 809], and *cey-tu* 'having done' where /y/ is not phonetically [ḥ]. It is important to notice that Old Tamil had three distinct coronal obstruents – *t ṯ ṭ* (dental, alveolar and retroflex); the system is also preserved by Malayāḷam, old and modern. Modern Tamil has only dental and retroflex stops. Also Modern Tamil shows voice contrast in the stop series, mainly in borrowed words. The stops were lenis medially in old Tamil allophonically [w ð ṟ s ṛ ɤ] and voiced in postnasal position. Old Tamil had nine consonants in word-initial position /p t c k m n ñ y v/, and nine in word-final position /m n ṇ r l ḷ ẓ v y/. Words end in vowels in Modern Tamil. Malayāḷam has developed voiced and aspirated stops (voiced and voiceless) through extensive borrowing from Sanskrit. It also has six phonemic nasals corresponding to six stops /p t ṯ ṭ c k/, because they contrast in postvocalic gemination /mm nn ṉṉ ṇṇ ññ ṅṅ/. Only /m n/ occur word-finally; an optional [ə] is added to words ending in /ṇ r ṟ l ḷ y/, e.g. *kāl* → *kālə* 'leg'. Proto-Dravidian retroflex frictionless continuant /ẓ/, which occurred in all the literary languages until the medieval period, remains only dialectally in Modern Tamil but is preserved intact in Malayāḷam. In most Tamil dialects it has merged with /ḷ/ or /y/ (Lehmann 1998: 75–99, Annamalai and Steever 1998: 100–28, Asher and Kumari 1997: 405–50).

Kota (Emeneau 1944: 15ff.) has six pairs of voiceless and voiced stops /p b t d ṯ ḏ ṭ ḍ č j k g/, four nasals /m n ṇ ñ/, two laterals /l ḷ/, one flap /r/ and two semivowels /v y/. /č/ can be replaced freely by [s] and /j/ by [z]; before a retroflex, [s] is pronounced as [ṣ].

The Toda consonantal system is atypical and unique (Emeneau 1957, 1984). It has seven pairs of stops, voiceless and voiced /p b t d c j ṯ ḏ č ǰ ṭ ḍ k g/, [c = ts, j = dz], four nasals /m n ṇ (ŋ)/, seven fricatives, i.e. three voiceless /f θ x/ and four pairs of voiceless and voiced sibilants /s z s̱ ẕ š ž ṣ ẓ/, three trills /r ṟ ṛ/, two pairs of voiceless and voiced laterals /ɫ l ḷ ɫ̣/, and two 'continuants', palatal and velar /y w/. Emeneau classifies these into variable and invariable series with the feature +/– voice. The variable voiceless consonants are /f θ x ṟ ṛ ɫ ɫ̣ s s̱ š ṣ/ and the variable voiced consonants, /m n ṇ y/. The variable consonants have variable voice feature allophonically (Emeneau 1984: 14, Shalev et al. 1994: 32). In Toda voiced obstruents (stops and fricatives) do not occur word-initially. Shalev et al. have discussed at length the acoustic and articulatory analysis of the sibilants to answer the question how so many sibilants could be distinguished in Toda and what cues are used for such distinction.

Many of the Nilgiri languages preserve the three coronal stops, *t ṯ* and *ṭ*. Kota (Emeneau 1944–6), Iruḷa (Zvelebil 1973) and Pālu Kuṟumba (Kapp 1978), Ālu Kuṟumba (Kapp 1987), Shōlega (Zvelebil 1990b), Jēnu Kuṟumba (Zvelebil 1988) retain the distinction between *r* and *ṟ*, of which the latter is derived historically from PD **ṯ* in intervocalic position. None of the Nilgiri languages preserves PD **ẓ*. They all retain the other retroflex consonants *ṭ ṇ ḷ*. The stops in five positions have phonemic voiced counterparts /p b t d (ṯ ḏ) c j ṭ ḍ k g/ in all Nilgiri languages and Koḍagu. In Pālu Kuṟumba there is no reason to represent *ṯ*, *ḏ* and *ṟ* as separate phonemes (see Kapp 1978). It is also not necessary to have two *n*'s [n] and [ṉ] as is done in Tamil.[2] Kapp gives a pair of forms to indicate a *ṯ ṟ* contrast, *niṟa(mu)* 'colour': *nāṯa(mu)* 'stench'(1978: 520), but it is highly suspicious since, historically, [ṟ] is an allophone of /ṯ/ in intervocalic position.

Koḍagu has three sibilants /s ṣ š/ because of borrowings from Sanskrit, and five nasals /m n ṇ ñ ṅ/, corresponding to the five stops (Balakrishnan 1976: 1–12). All the nasals contrast intervocalically in gemination, e.g. *caṅṅāti* 'friend', *aññāna* 'ígnorance'. Word-initially /ñ/ occurs in Koḍagu as in Malayāḷam in native vocabulary (Balakrishnan 1976: 11, 26).

Old Kannaḍa had five stops with a four-way distinction – voiceless unaspirated, voiceless aspirated, voiced unaspirated and voiced aspirated – four fricatives /s ś ṣ h/, three nasals /m n ṇ/, two laterals /l ḷ/, two trills /r ṟ/ and one retroflex approximant /ẓ/ which was becoming archaic (Ramachandra Rao 1972: 1–29). Kēśirāja also listed [ṅ] and [ñ] following the Sanskrit model, but they were not phonemic. Modern Kannaḍa has added /ǣ/ among the vowels and /z f/ among the consonants. Older /ṟ/ and /r/ were replaced by /r/ (Steever 1998: 130). Ramachandra Rao (1972: 4) treats [ṅ] as an allophone of /m/, and [ñ] as an allophone of /n/. Word-initially /ṇ y r/ did not occur in Old Kannaḍa. Initial /ṭ ḍ/ occurred only in loanwords; only one case of word-initial *ṟ* and a few of *ḷ* are found in Pampa Bhārata (tenth century CE). All consonants except /r ṟ ẓ s/ could occur double in Old Kannaḍa (1972: 10–11).

Tuḷu (D. N. S. Bhat 1998: 160–1, Kekunnaya 1994: 11) has five pairs of stops, voiceless and voiced /p b t d ṭ ḍ c j k g/, five nasals /m n ṇ ñ ṅ/, one sibilant /s/ and two semivowels and two liquids /v y l r/. The Brahmin dialects add three more fricatives /ś ṣ h/ and /ḷ/ besides the aspirated stops in both the voiceless and voiced series. Word-initial front vowels have a *y*-onglide and the rounded vowels a *w*-onglide in speech. Bhat says the aspirated stops are in free variation with the corresponding unaspirated ones even in the Brahmin dialect (1998: 161). The South Common (non-Brahmin) dialect is said to preserve the contrast of *l* and *ḷ*; /ṅ ṇ ḷ/ do not begin a word. All unaspirated stops and sonorants have

[2] The author said, in a private communication to me in August 1998, that it was a mistake.

a contrast between single and double, including the four nasals (Kekunnaya 1994: 29). No consonant occurs in final position.

2.3.1.1 *Phonotactics*

The first syllable of a word can be either V_1 or C_1V_1; any short or long vowel can occur as V_1; C_1 is not usually an apical [−Distributed] consonant /*ṯ* ṭ l ḷ r ẓ/; in Modern Tamil, Malayāḷam, Kannaḍa, Tuḷu, Iruḷa and Koḍagu, in recent times, a limited number of words with word-initial apicals have started emerging through aphaeresis or loss of a short word-initial vowel, e.g. Ta. *reṇḍu* (OTa. *iraṇṭu*), Ma. *raṇḍu* 'two', Iruḷa *raṇḍu*, *reṇḍu*, Koḍagu *daṇḍï*, Tuḷu *raḍḍï*. This tendency is much more widespread in Iruḷa and Tuḷu. The diphthongs are treated as long vowels metrically in the literary languages because of their equivalence to long vowels in the duration of articulation (two morae). Phonologically they can be considered sequences of a vowel + consonant, where the C = semivowel. There are no word-initial consonant clusters in the native element.

2.3.2 ***South Dravidian II (SD II)***

These languages have word-initial apicals /ṟ r ẓ l ḷ ḍ/ and consonant clusters unlike South Dravidian I. All languages of this subgroup developed word-initial consonant clusters with obstruents as first members and sonorants as second members. Gondi and Koṇḍa do not show such initial clusters now, but there is evidence that they once existed and were simplified. Old Telugu had such clusters with *Cr-* (C = an obstruent other than an affricate, *s* and *w*), but they are simplified by loss of *-r-* (< **ṯ r ẓ*) in Modern Telugu. The remaining languages, Kui, Kuvi, Pengo and Manḍa, still have initial consonant clusters and the sound change is still in progress (Krishnamurti 1978a).

In Old Telugu, the inherited consonantal system was fairly well preserved except for incorporating the feature of voicing from the earliest known period: /p b t d ṭ ḍ c j k g s m n ṇ r ṟ l ḷ ẓ y w/; Sanskrit borrowings from a very early period added two more sibilants /ś ṣ/ and the voiced and voiceless aspirated series /ph bh th dh ch jh ṭh ḍh kh gh/. In Modern Telugu there is only an alveolar flap /r/; even by the thirteenth century /ẓ/ was totally eliminated as a distinctive sound after it had merged with /ḍ r/ in different environments. A new phoneme /f/ is added to Modern Telugu in such loanwords as /āfīsu/ 'office', and /kāfī/ 'coffee'. /ṇ ḷ/ do not begin a word. All words ended in vowels in Old Telugu. In Modern Telugu only /m n w y/ can occur word-finally.

Gondi has several dialects, but there are only a few systematic descriptions. Natarajan (1985: 32–3) set up the following consonants for Abhuj Maria, a Southern dialect of Bastar: /p b t d ṭ ḍ c j k g m n ṅ s l r ṛ w y/. According to G. U. Rao (1987b: §2), the South Bastar Gondi has an overall pattern of twenty-one consonants; he adds /ṇ h/ to Natarajan's list. Hill Maria has, in addition to the above, three new segments: uvular /R/, a glottal stop /ʔ/ and a retroflex /ṇ/. Western Gondi has twenty consonantal segments including a phonemic /h/ and no retroflex /ṇ/. Adilabad Gondi has twenty consonants including a phonemic /h/. Adilabad Gondi described by Subrahmanyam (1968a) has also aspirated consonants. Even some native words have the feature of aspiration, e.g. *phō̃ṛd* 'sun' (cf. Ta. *poẓutu*). The Southeastern Gondi has twenty phonemes including /ṇ/, but with a marginal status for /h ŋ/. G. U. Rao (1987b: §3) set up twenty-three consonants for Proto-Gondi: /p b t d ṭ ḍ c j k g m n ṇ ŋ s h r ṛ ṟ l ḷ w y/.

Koṇḍa has twenty-three consonantal segments /p b t d ṭ ḍ k g ʔ s z h R ṟ m n ṇ ŋ r ṛ l v y/. /ʔ R ṇ ŋ/ do not occur word-initially. Voiceless and voiced sibilants and trills /s z R ṟ/ pattern with stops. In consonant clusters /ʔ/ is never the first member and /R/ is never the second member of a consonant cluster (Krishnamurti and Benham 1998).

Kui has eighteen consonants /p b t d s j ṭ ḍ k g (s) h m n ṇ r ṛ l v/. Winfield lists [s] twice, as a palatal [s] with a corresponding voiced [j], the second a sibilant [s], but there is no phonological difference between the two. There is no semivowel /y/ in Winfield's Kui. Where it is expected on the basis of PD **y*, it is replaced by *i* or *j* in Kui; *v* ~ *b* occurs in dialects mostly influenced by Oriya. Winfield calls the stops 'strong consonants', and the sonorants, 'weak consonants', because the sonorants 'may be lost in declension or conjugation'. In the case of obstruents, only voice feature changes (Winfield 1928: §1).

The Kuvi consonantal system is essentially similar to that of Kui: /p b t d ṭ ḍ k g ʔ c j, s h, m n ṇ ŋ, l, r ṛ, v y/; /c j/ are phonetically /ts ds/ freely varying with /s z/ (Israel 1979: §1); /ʔ ŋ/ do not begin a word; only /ŋ y m/ occur finally.

Pengo has twenty-two consonants: /p b t d ṭ ḍ c j k g s z h m n ṇ ŋ r ṛ l v y/. Nasalized vowels occur in Indo-Aryan loanwords like *gō̃* 'wheat'. Aspiration occurs in Oriya loanwords, e.g. *dhan* 'wealth'. Native *h* can combine with stops, e.g. *kūk-hi-* 'having heard', where *-hi* is perfective participial sign. We do not know if the sequence is pronounced as a single aspirated stop or as a sequence of *k* + *h* (Burrow and Bhattacharya 1970: §1).

Manḍa is closer to Pengo than to any other member (Burrow 1976), but we do not know much about the phonological system. It has /r ṛ l/ besides five pairs of voiceless and voiced stops.[3]

2.3.3 *Central Dravidian (CD)*

None of the Central Dravidian languages shows either apical consonants or consonant clusters word-initially in native vocabulary. This feature distinguishes them from the South Dravidian II subgroup. Except for the Kolami–Naiki subgroup, aspirate consonants are not phonemic. Particularly Naiki shows voiceless and voiced aspirated stops initially in native words (see section 2.3.3.1).

[3] B. Ramakrishna Reddy collected data on Manḍa over a decade ago but he has not published his analysis of the language yet. He also reported that there were two other dialects or languages closely allied to Pengo and Manḍa, which he called Indi and Āwe.

Kolami has four pairs of stops, voiceless and voiced /p b t d ṭ ḍ k g/, two affricates /c j/, two sibilants /s z/, three nasals /m n ŋ/, two liquids /r l/ and two fricatives /v y/. In loanwords from Marathi [ts ḷ] are used (Emeneau 1954: §1). Subrahmanyam (1998) represents Emeneau's /z/ by /j /. Naikṛi has a four-way distinction of stops or affricates with features of voicing and aspiration like /p ph b bh/ in all five positions . It also has an alveolar /c/, three fricatives /v s h/, three nasals /m n ŋ/ two laterals /l ḷ/, a trill /r/ and a semivowel /y/. /c/ is said to be an alveolar affricate /ts/. Palatal affricates /č j/ occur mainly in Marathi loans. Contrast between long and short vowels seems to be confined to root syllables (Thomasiah 1986: §1). In this work I have treated Naikṛi and Naiki (Chanda) as dialects of the same language, distinct from Kolami (see section 2.3.3.1).

Parji has nineteen consonantal segments of normal status /p b t d ṭ ḍ c j k g m n ñ ŋ r ṛ l v y/; /s h/ are marginal phonemes heard in rendering Halbi words (Burrow and Bhattacharya 1953: 1–8). It appears that /ñ ŋ/ could be phonemically represented as /nj ng/, although Burrow and Bhattacharya say that the stop element is lost word-finally but is restored (in the case of *g* of *ŋg* when followed by a vowel) (1953: 7).

Ollari has four pairs of stops /p b t d ṭ ḍ k g/, two pairs of affricates /ts dz c j/, five nasals /m n ṇ ñ ŋ /, three liquids /r ṛ l/, two sibilants /s z/ and two fricatives /v y/. The segments /ts dz c j/ are said to have a marginal status, occurring mainly in loanwords (Bhattacharya 1957: 10). As in Parji, it seems possible to represent /ŋ ñ/ as sequences of /ng nj/ with phonetic realization as simple nasals in word-final position (Bhattacharya 1957: 1–14).

Konḍekor Gadaba has nineteen consonantal segments: /p b t d ṭ ḍ c j k g s m n ṇ ŋ r l w y/; /ṇ ŋ/ do not begin a word. There are no word-initial consonant clusters (Bhaskararao 1980).

2.3.3.1 *Voiced aspirate stops*

A puzzling feature of Central Dravidian is the presence of many words with voiced (some voiceless) aspirated stops in Naikṛi (which Burrow and Emeneau have listed as a dialect of Kolami in *DEDR*, see index, pp. 688–91), corresponding to unaspirated voiced stops of several other languages in native words. There are eighteen items of this kind, most of which have etymologies, e.g. *ghurrum* 'horse': OTe. *gurṟamu*, Mdn Te. *gurram* [1711], *ghāḷi* 'wind': Te. *gāli* id.[1499], *dhāv* 'distance': Te. *davvu*, Kol. [SR] *davva* [446] (from **iṭ-a-* does not seem to be an appropriate etymology.) Even the items with voiceless aspirated stops in Naikṛi have cognates in voiced unaspirated stops in many other languages, e.g. *khīr* 'line' [1623] has cognates with *g-* in Ka., Koḍ., Tu., Te., Kol. [SR], Koṇḍa, Kui and Kuvi. This situation leads one to suspect that we have evidence of a voicing laryngeal of Proto-Dravidian retained here. Naikṛi is definitely not a dialect of Kolami and it preserves some archaic features which Kolami has lost, e.g. *nēm* 'we (inclusive)' from PD **ñām* [3647]. Note that there are three lexical items in Naikṛi which begin with *h-* before word-initial vowels corresponding to its absence in the other languages, namely *heḍḍ* 'bull, ox': Ka. *eẓtu*, Ta. *erutu*, Te. *eddu*, pl *eḍlu* (aberrant phonology [815]), *hegar* 'watchman's raised platform': Kol. *ēgar* id. (no other language has cognates; [877]) and *huṛug* 'iguana' (Te. *uḍumu* id. [592]). There are forms beginning with vowels, which contrast with these. No explanation has been given for this phenomenon.

2.3.4 *North Dravidian (ND)*

Kuṛux has the following consonants: *k kh x g gh c ch j jh ṭ ṭh ḍ ḍh ṛ ṛh t th d dh p ph b bh s h m n r l y w*. Grignard (1924a: §1) considers [ñ ṇ ŋ] as positional variants (i.e. allophones) of /n/ before palatal, retroflex and velar consonants. He calls them 'purely accidental modifications of the "n" sound' (1924a: 3).

Malto has five pairs of voiceless and voiced stops /p b t d ṭ ḍ c j k g/, a voiceless uvular stop /q/, four fricatives /ð s ɤ h/, four nasals /m n ñ ŋ/, three liquids (trill, lateral, flap) /r l ṛ/ and two semivowels /w y/ (Mahapatra 1979: §2). In consecutive syllables (except when they are separated by a 'formative boundary') an initial consonant as onset of a syllable is followed by an identical segment as the onset of the next syllable, *qeqeldu* 'earth', *kake* 'comb', *ṭuṭuwa* 'leper', etc. (1979: 38–40). /ð ɣ/ do not occur word-initially. There are no word-initial clusters in Malto.

Brahui has four pairs of stops + a glottal stop and two affricates: /p b t d c j ṭ ḍ k g ʔ/, eight fricatives /f s z š ž x ɤ h/, four nasals /m n ṇ ŋ/, two laterals /ɬ l/, two flaps /r ṛ/, and two semivowels /w y/ (Elfenbein 1997, 1998). The large number of fricatives is owing to the influence of Balochi. It is reported that two-thirds of Brahuis are bilingual in Balochi. Words with /f x ɬ/ have good Dravidian cognates. Word-initially /f/ does not occur. Voiceless lateral /ɬ/, transcribed by Bray and Elfenbein as [l̲h̲], is internal to Brahui as are the retroflexes, which are not found in Balochi; /ŋ / occurs only before velar stops and can be replaced by /nk, ng/. Voiceless stops can optionally be aspirated in speech. Voiced aspirates occur only in loanwords from Indo-Aryan. Northern Brahui has /h/ which is replaced in the Southern dialects by a glottal stop [ʔ] initially and between vowels; it is lost finally and before consonants. 'It is often prefixed to word-initial words in the south' (Elfenbein 1997: 800–4, 1998: 392–4).

2.4 **Suprasegmental features**

Vowel length is the only stable suprasegmental feature in all Dravidian languages. In single morphemes (roots), which are monosyllabic, short and long vowels contrasted in the proto-language. This feature is inherited by all Dravidian languages with the exception of Brahui, which has lost the contrast in mid vowels *e*/*ē* and *o*/*ō* under the influence of the neighbouring Indo-Aryan and Iranian languages. In non-radical syllables also, in the literary languages, long and short vowels contrast in inflection and derivation. In many non-literary languages, short and long vowels contrast only in the root syllable.

2.4.1 *Stress and intonation*

Very little has been written about stress and intonation. The following statement is typical: 'Stress in Tamil is non-contrastive, and falls on the first syllable of a word. Intonation patterns have yet to be studied satisfactorily' (Annamalai and Steever 1998: 104). Andronov (1969: 33) says that 'the place of a stressed syllable in a word is not fixed' in Tamil and marks words differently, *péyar* 'name' vs. *virál* 'finger', *ávaṉ* vs. *tamíẓ*. In that case, stress becomes phonemic, but there is little supporting evidence for such an analysis. Asher (1982: 230–4) says the role of stress is 'to express emphasis'. It does not distinguish words. 'The main correlate of stress is greater intensity.' Syllables with longer vowels when stressed have extra duration. Statements, commands and question-word questions have a falling intonation [↘]; if the question is repeated with surprise, it has a rising intonation [↗]. Yes–no question sentences ending in an interrogative particle have a rise–fall on the particle [↗↘]. Exclamatory sentences have a mid-level intonation [→].

In Malayāḷam stress does not distinguish one lexical item from another. Citing K. P. Mohanan, Asher and Kumari (1997: 436–7) say that position and vowel-length play a role in determining the placement of primary stress. The stress falls on the first syllable if it is short; it falls on the second syllable which follows a short syllable and if it has a long vowel. 'All syllables after the second which have a long vowel carry secondary stress', *ku̳dira* 'horse', *paṭṭā̳ḷakkā̲ran* 'soldier'. Declarative sentences end with a rising pitch. Questions which end in interrogative particles *-ē* or *-ō* end with a falling pitch. Question-word questions carry a rising tone. Non-final clauses end on 'level or rising tone'. Commands end with falling pitch. Asher and Kumari say that intonation 'ís very much a primary area where research is needed' (436). According to Mohanan 'stress is associated with word melody'.

Emeneau (1984: 18) makes some significant remarks on intonation in Toda: 1. A declarative sentence has 'a slight drop of pitch on the syllable or syllables after the last strong stress of the sentence'. 2. 'Imperative or prohibitive sentences have level pitch continued to the end.' 3. 'Questions ending in an interrogative particle, imperatives in *-ō* or *-mō*, vocatives in *-ā* or *-ō*, . . . some interjections . . . have on the final syllables a pitch that is somewhat higher (level or slightly rising) than the pitch of the preceding syllables.'

Lisker and Krishnamurti (1991) make the following observations about Telugu stress based on an experimental study in which two groups of speakers participated, ten native Telugu speakers who also knew English and fifteen native English speakers who had no knowledge of Telugu. The judgements on placement of stress are broadly similar in both the groups. The first syllable carries a phonetic stress in words of two short syllables (SS), e.g. *gádi* 'room' (SS – [mean value of responses of Telugu speakers by the syllable 1st: 2nd: non-definite] 57% : 35 % : 8%]), or when the first syllable is long and the second short, e.g. *tā́ta* 'grandfather' (LS – 77% : 20% : 3%). If the second syllable is long or if both syllables are long, stress falls on the second syllable, e.g. *dagā́* 'deceipt' (SL – 40% :

59% : 1%), *bākī́* 'debt', *rūpā́y* 'rupee'(LL – 21% : 76% : 4%). In the case of trisyllabic words, the first syllable is stressed if it is long; otherwise, it is the penultimate syllable that carries stress, e.g. *kū́turu* 'daughter' (LSS – 59% : 26% : 9% : 5%; the last value for undecided or non-definite): *paláka* 'slate' (SSS – 25% : 59% : 10% : 5%), *tapássu* 'penance' (SLS – 26% : 63% : 0% : 11%), *tupā́kī* 'gun' (SLL – 15% : 57% : 21% : 7%), *sātā́ni* 'a weaver caste' (LLS: 25% : 64% : 0% : 11%). The difference in scores among the English speakers is sharper for the same classes of items. There is a greater degree of variation in repeated tests among Telugu speakers than among the English speakers. 'If Telugu were a stress language like English, we might expect distributions showing either constant values of 0 or 100% or having the shape of step functions with values shifting from 0 to 100%. Instead we find distributions that, particularly for Telugu speakers, are closer to being continuously variable between those extremes'(4). '. . . the Telugu group's behaviour is a consequence of the nondistinctive function of word-stress in the language'(5).

In Koṇḍa, short and long vowels contrast only in the initial syllable (Krishnamurti 1969a: 188–92) of a 'phonological word'. A phonological word occurs between two marked junctures /# + ,/ (# marks silence before or after an utterance; + boundary of phonological word; /, / = marks a phonological phrase which is part of a higher structure). A vowel in the first syllable is stressed if it is long; if it is short the second syllable is phonetically longer and louder and carries primary stress. All alternate syllables from the stressed one carry 'a second degree loudness' or prominence, [ū́s.pa.zì.nad] 'she is applying oil', [aṛ.bá.zi.nàd] 'she is crying'. A stop preceding a stressed vowel is markedly fortis. 'Once the word boundaries are indicated and the contrast of short and long vowels in initial syllables marked, features of stress and length in the remaining syllables within a phonological word become automatic and predictable' (190). A morphological word can be two phonological words, e.g. *#nā + rāyna#* 'Oh God!' (name of a Hindu God *nārāyaṇa*) is one morphological word, but two phonological words, because there are two long vowels. A phonological word has only one phonemic long vowel. In Koṇḍa phonological and morphological words have been defined differently (for details, see Krishnamurti 1969a: 186–92).

It is clear from the existing descriptions that the first syllable is stressed irrespective of vowel length. If it is short and followed by a heavy syllable it is the latter that receives primary stress. Sentences ending in an interrogative particle /ā ō ē/ have a rising intonation (section 8.4). Imperatives have a falling pitch when they end or constitute whole utterances.

2.5 Sandhi or morphophonemics

Both internal (intra-word) and external (inter-word) sandhi is widely prevalent in Dravidian. Since some of the processes are idiosyncratic to individual languages, only generalized and widely used processes are covered here. (1) Loss of a word-final short vowel, especially the 'non-morphemic' /u/ before another vowel either within the same word or between words, is a rule which has validity in most languages of the family. (2) Where there is no sandhi (or hiatus between V + V across a morph or word boundary), a glide *y* or *w* is inserted, predictable in terms of the qualities of the preceding and following vowels, e.g. Ta. *pala* + *-v-iṉ* → *pala-v-iṉ-*, *moẓi-iṉ-* → *moẓi-y-iṉ-*; Mdn Ta. *katti-y-āl* 'by knife'. (3) A number of assimilative changes take place among the consonants, e.g. Ta. *kēḷ* + *ttu* → *kēṭṭu* 'having heard', *kal* + *ttu* → *kaṯṯu* 'having learnt', *āḷ* + *ntu* → *āṇṭu* 'having ruled'. These changes had their origin in Proto-Dravidian. (4) The other type is gemination of CVC to CVCC when followed by a vowel, e.g. Ta. *kal* 'stone': *kall-āl* 'by stone' (Lehmann 1998, Steever and Annamalai 1998).

Kannaḍa, old and modern, has both vowel-loss and glide-insertion rules operating, e.g. *hōguvudu* + *illa* → *hōgvudilla* 'does not go', *huli-y-inda* 'from tiger', *hū-v-inda* 'from flower'. (For Old Kannaḍa, see Ramchandra Rao 1972: 31–3.) (5) In compound sandhi the literary language changes initial voiceless stops of the second member to voiced stops, Ka. *hosa* + *kannaḍa* → *hosa-gannaḍa* 'new Kannaḍa' (Ramachandra Rao 1972: 34–6, Sridhar 1990: 284); Te. *anna-dammulu* 'elder and younger brothers' (*-tammuḍu* 'younger brother', *-lu* pl suff.).

In Tuḷu word-final *ï* is lost when a vowel follows; glide insertion is also common, e.g. *mugi-y-ontu* 'finishing', *pō-v-arɛ* 'in order to go' (D. N. S. Bhat 1998: 162–3).

In Old Telugu, word-final *u*-loss is regular before another vowel; in modern Telugu any word-final short vowel is lost before another vowel, obligatorily across a morph boundary, but optionally across a word boundary: *amma* + *ekkaḍa* → *amm*(*a*) *ekkaḍa* 'where is mother?'(external sandhi), *rāma* + *anna* → *rāmanna* 'Ramanna' (male name) (internal sandhi). Where the vowel is not lost, only traditional Telugu grammarians mentioned the insertion of a *-y* glide, *mā* + *amma* → *mā-y-amma* 'our mother'. No such insertion takes place in modern standard Telugu even after a long vowel. A short vowel is lost between consonants having the same point of articulation or between two coronal consonants with different points of articulation, *nāku* + *kāwāli* → *nāk* + *kāwāli* 'I want it', *pāla* + *rāyi* → *pāl-rāyi* 'marble (lit. milky stone)' (Krishnamurti 1998d: §8.2).

Appendix. Phonemic inventories of individual languages

Inventories of vowels and consonants are given by the subgroup and language, as they are represented by the cited authors and sources. Long vowels are represented by a macron, or occasionally by /ː/ where it is cited as a separate suprasegmental phoneme. Some of the authors have not tabulated the segments or given articulatory labels. They are arranged in tabular form. Where the authors have not given the labels, the relative positioning of the segments has to be taken as indicative of articulatory labels.

South Dravidian (SD I)

1a Old Tamil (Lehmann 1998: 75–99)

Consonants[4]

	Labial	Dental	Alveolar	Retroflex	Palatal	Velar
Stops	p	t	ṟ	ṭ	c	k
Nasals	m	n	ṉ	ṇ	ñ	(ṅ)
Laterals		l		ḷ		
Glides	v				y	
Taps			r			
Approximant				ẓ		

Vowels

i	ī			u	ū
e	ē			o	ō
		a	ā		

1b Modern Tamil (Annamalai and Steever 1998: 100–28)

Consonants

	Labial	Dental	Alveolar	Retroflex	Palatal	Velar	Glottal
Stops:							
Voiceless	p	t		ṭ	c	k	
Voiced	(b)	(d)		(ḍ)	(j)	(g)	
Tap		r	[ṟ]				
Nasal	m	n	[ṉ]	ṇ	ñ	ṅ[5]	
Lateral		l		ḷ			
Glide	v				y		

[4] Lehmann treats [ṅ] as an allophone of /n/; /l/ should have been given under alveolars. Old Tamil sandhi *l* + *t* → *ṯ* (*kal* 'learn' + *tt*- past → *kaṯṯ*-) suggests that /l/ was an alveolar. Alveolars and retroflexes do not begin a word, but dentals do. Even by this criterion /l/ should have been listed in the alveolar column; *āytam* /ḵ/ should have been included in the table.

[5] Only one or two words have double velar nasal /aṅṅāṉam/ 'that manner' (Annamalai and Steever 1998: 103). In the spoken language virtually all words end in vowels (as against OTa.). Voiced/ voiceless stops contrast in spoken Tamil.

Vowels and diphthongs

	Front		Mid		Back	
	Short	Long	Short	Long	Short	Long
High	i	ī			u	ū
Mid	e	ē	ʌ		o	ō
Low		(ǣ)	a	ā		

2 *Malayāḷam (Asher and Kumari 1997: 405–50)*

Consonants

	Labial	Dental	Alveolar	Retroflex	Palatal	Velar	Glottal
Stops Voiceless	p	t	t̠	ṭ	c	k	
Voiceless asp	ph	th		ṭh	ch	kh	
Stops Voiced	b	d		ḍ	j	g	
Voiced asp	bh	dh		ḍh	jh	gh	
Fricative	(f)		s	ṣ	ś		h
Nasal	m	n	n̠	ṇ	ñ	ṅ	
Liquid							
Tap/trill			r, r̠				
Lateral			l	ḷ			
Approx.				ẓ			
Glide	v				y		

Vowels

i	ī				u	ū
e	ē				o	ō
		(æ)				
			a	ā		

Consonants in the native system

	Labial	Dental	Alveolar	Retroflex	Palatal	Velar
Stop	p	t	r̠	ṭ	c	k
Nasal	m	n	n̠	ṇ	ñ	ṅ
Liquid:						
Tap/trill			r, r̠			
Approx.				ẓ		
Lateral			l	ḷ		
Glides	v				y	

3 Koḍagu (Balakrishnan 1976: 1–4 ff.)

Vowels

i	ï	u
e	ë	o
	a	

Consonants

p b	t d	ṭ ḍ	c j	k g	
m	n	ṇ	ñ	ṅ	
	s	ṣ	š		h
	l	ḷ			
	r				
v			y		

4 Ālu Kuṟumba (Kapp 1987: 409)

Vowels

i		ï	u
e		ë	o
	a		

Length of vowels /ː/

Consonants

p	t		c	ṭ	k
b	d		j	ḍ	g
m	n	.		ṇ	ŋ
		r ṟ			
		l		ḷ	
v		s	y		

Nasalization / ˜ /

5 Iruḷa (Zvelebil 1973: §1)

Vowels[6]

i		ï				ü		u
	e		ë		ö		o	
				a				

Consonants[7]

p	t	ṯ	ṭ	c	k
b	d	ḏ	ḍ	j	g
m		n	ṇ		
			ḷ		
		l			
		r			
		ṟ	ṛ		
v				y	

6 Kota (Emeneau 1944, Kota Texts, UCPL 2: 1.5–18)

Vowels

i	ī			u	ū
e	ē			o	ō
		a	ā		

Consonants

p	t	ṯ	ṭ	č	k
b	d	ḏ	ḍ	j	g
m	n		ṇ		ṅ
		l	ḷ		
		r			
v				y	

6 The four centralized vowels occur both short and long; *ï* and *ë* are unrounded high and mid; *ü* and *ö* are rounded, high and mid (Zvelebil 1973: 11).

7 Zvelebil writes alveolars next to labials followed by dentals! He says that *ḏ* and *ṟ* are historically from **ṯ* [-ṟ-] intervocalically and -*ḏ* after a nasal, e.g. *panḏi* 'pig'. It is not clear why they are given as two phonemes. His lexicon of 484 items shows *r*/*ṟ* merger in some cases, contrast in others.

7 Toda (Emeneau 1958: 15–66, 1984:7,11; Shalev et al. 1994: 19–56)[8]

Vowels

	Front				Central		Back			
	Unrounded		Rounded		Rounded		Unrounded		Rounded	
High	i	i:	ü	ü:			ï	ï:	u	u:
Mid	e	e:			ö	ö:			o	o:
Low						a	a:			

Consonants

	Labial		Dental		Post-dental		Alveolar		Alveolo-palatal		Retroflex		Velar	
Stop and Affricate	p	b	t	d	c [ts	z, dz]	t̲	d̲	č [tš	ǰ dž]	ṭ	ḍ	k	g
Nasal		m						ṅ				ṇ		(ŋ)
Fricative	f		θ										χ	
Trill						r	r̲				ṛ			
Lateral							ł	l			ɫ̣	ḷ		
Sibilant					s	(z)	s̲	(z̲)	š	ž	ṣ	ẓ		
Continuant									y				w	

8 Modern Kannaḍa (Sridhar 1990: 291–313)

Vowels

	Front		Central		Back	
High	i	ī			u	ū
Mid	e	ē			o	ō
Lower-mid	æ					
Low			a	ā		

[8] In his 1984 book Emeneau puts fricatives and alveolar and retroflex trills in one row; there is one whole row for the postdental trill /r/. I have put all the trills in one row and fricatives in another. Shalev et al. have combined the sibilants and fricatives and put them in one row. [z z̲], according to Emeneau, are used in 'fast speech' and he puts them on the last row in his table, implying that they are a phonetic phenomenon; Shalev et al. have no voiced sibilants at all in their table. /y/ is put under alveolo-palatal and /w/ under velar by both. These are called approximants by Shalev et al. and continuants by Emeneau.

Consonants

	Labial	Dental–alveolar	Retroflex	Palatal	Velar–glottal
Stop-vl	p	t	ṭ	c	k
Stop-vd	b	d	ḍ	j	g
Fricative	f	s z	ṣ	ś	h
Nasal	m	n	ṇ		
Lateral		l	ḷ		
Semivowel	v			y	

/æ f z/ occur only in loanwords. Old Kannaḍa had an archaic phoneme / ẓ / under retroflexes in early inscriptions and it maintained the contrast between two trills /ṟ/ (< PD */ṯ/) and /r/ from (< PD */r/). The trill *ṟ* merged with *r* in Medieval and Modern Kannaḍa.

9 Baḍaga[9] (Hockings and Pilot-Raichoor 1992: xvi)

Vowels

ī	i			u	ū
ē	e			o	ō
		a	ā		

Consonants

p	t	ṭ	c	k
b	d	ḍ	j	g
			s	(h)
m	n	ṇ		
	r			
	l	ḷ		
v			y	

10 Tuḷu (D. N. S. Bhat 1998)

Vowels

i	ī	ï		u	ū
e	ē			o	ō
ɛ	ɛ̄	a	ā		

9 The authors have put /v l ḷ y/ in one row and /r/ only in the last row without any discussion of criteria.

Consonants

	Labial	Dental	Retroflex	Palatal	Velar
Stops :					
Voiceless	p	t	ṭ	c	k
Voiced	b	d	ḍ	j	g
Sonorants:					
Nasal	m	n	ṇ	ñ	ṅ
Oral	v			y	
Lateral		l	ḷ		
Trill		r			
Fricative		s			h

11 Koraga (D. N. S. Bhat 1971: 4)

Vowels

i	ī	ï		u	ū
e	ē			o	ō
		a	ā		

Consonants

p	t	ṭ	c	k
b	d	ḍ	j	g
m	n			ŋ
v	r		y	
	l			
	s			

Bhat writes the high back unrounded short vowel as /ɨ/ (barred i), represented here as /ï/.

South Dravidian II (South-Central Dravidian)
12 Telugu (Krishnamurti 1998d: 260)

Vowels

i	ī			u	ū
e	ē			o	ō
	(ǣ)[10]				
		a	ā		

[10] Only modern Telugu has /ǣ/. The rest is shared by old as well as modern Telugu.

Consonants[11]

	Labial		Denti-alveolar		Retroflex		Palatal		Velar	
Stops:										
Voiceless	p	ph	t	(th)	ṭ	ṭh	c	ch	k	kh
Voiced	b	bh	d	dh	ḍ	ḍh	j	jh	g	gh
Fricative	f		s		ṣ		ś		h	
Nasal	m		n		ṇ					
Lateral			l		ḷ					
Flap			r							
Semivowel	w								y	

13 Gondi (overall pattern of different dialects) (Rao 1987b: 101)

Vowels

i	ī			u	ū
e	ē			o	ō
		a	ā		

Consonants

p	b	t	d		ṭ	ḍ	c	j	k	g	
				s							h
				r	ṛ						
				ṟ							
				l	ḷ						
	m			n	ṇ				ŋ		
	w						y				

14 Koṇḍa/Kūbi (Krishnamurti 1969a: 185–6)

Vowels

i	ī			u	ū
e	ē			o	ō
		a	ā		

[11] The aspirated stops and *f ṣ, ś* and *h* mainly occur in loanwords from Indo-Aryan, Perso-Arabic and English.

Consonants

Obstruents													
Stop	p	b	t	d					ṭ	ḍ	k	g	
Fricative					s		z						(h)
Trill					R		ṟ						
Sonorants													
Flap						r			ṛ				
Nasal	m					n			ṇ			ŋ	
Lateral			l			ḷ							
Semiconsonant	w							y					

15 Kui (Winfield 1928: 1–5)

Vowels

i	ī			u	ū
e	ē			o	ō
		a	ā		

Consonants[12]

p	b	t	d	ṭ	ḍ	s	j	k	g	
		s								h
m		n				ṇ				
		l								
		r				ṛ				
v										

[12] In Winfield's listing there is no /y/. *DEDR* (in correspondences list) says **y* = Kui *j*. The Kui vocabulary also does not show any case of /y/; where it is expected Kui shows a long vowel with compensatory lengthening for PD *cV*y*-, e.g. Kui *kō-va* (*kō-t-*) 'to reap'; *kō-eri* 'harvest' (? missing); *ēs-pa* (*ēs-t-*) 'to weave'; *nō-va* (*nō-t-*) 'be painful'; *pū-pa* (*pū-t-*) 'to flower', *vī-ka*, *vī-nja* 'to blow'; *vē-pa* (*vē-t-*) 'to strike', or the source of *-y* , i.e. source *-s* in some cases, *mus-pa* (*mus-t-*); or a [g] replacing [y], e.g. *rāg-a* 'rub' (<**ar-ay*), *pāg-a* 'to pounce upon' (Ta. *pāy* 'to spring'); **kay* 'hand': Kui *kaju* (pl *kaka*) 'hand' is the only case of a direct correspondence of **y* = [j]. Palatal *s* and 'sibilant *s*' have the symbol !.

16 Kuvi (Israel 1979: §1)

Vowels

i		u
e		o
	a	

Length /ː/, Nasalization[13] /~/

Consonants

Stop	p	t		ṭ		k	ʔ
	b	d		ḍ		g	
Affricate					c		
					j		
Sibilant				s			
Nasal	m	n		ṇ		ṅ	
Lateral		l					
Flap		r	ṛ				
Fricative	v			y		h	

17 Pengo (Burrow and Bhattacharya 1970:1)

Vowels

i	ī			u	ū
e	ē			o	ō
		a	ā		

Consonants

p	b	t	d	ṭ	ḍ	c	j	k	g	
		s	z							h
	m		n		ṇ				ŋ	
					ṛ					
					r					
					l					
	v					y				

[13] In the dialect reported by Burrow and Bhattacharya (1963), retroflex and velar nasals do not occur. Spontaneous nasalization of vowels before *y* is reported, $kriy^ny^na$ 'bee', $kriy^n y^n u$ 'ear' (Burrow and Bhattacharya 1963: 244).

Central Dravidian

18 Kolami (Emeneau 1961: §1)

Vowels

i	ī			u	ū
e	ē			o	ō
		a	ā		

Consonants

	Labial	Labio-dental	Dental	Post-dental	Retroflex	Palatal	Velar
Stop	p b		t d		ṭ ḍ		k g
Affricate						c j	
Sibilant				s z			
Trill				r			
Lateral				l			
Nasal	m		n				ŋ
Fricative		v				y	

19 Naikṛi (Thomasiah 1986: §1)

Vowels

i	ī			u	ū
e	ē			o	ō
		a	ā		

Consonants

	Labial	Dental	Alveolar	Retroflex	Palatal	Velar	Glottal
Stop	p b	t d		ṭ ḍ		k g	
	ph bh	th dh		ṭh ḍh		kh gh	
Affricate			c		č j		
					jh		
Nasal	m		n			ŋ	
Fricative	v		s				h
Lateral			l	ḷ			
Trill			r				
Semivowel					y		

20 Parji (Burrow and Bhattacharya 1953: §1)

Vowels

i	ī			u	ū
e	ē			o	ō
		a	ā		

Consonants

p	b	t	d	ṭ	ḍ	c	j	k	g		
	m		n				ñ		ŋ		
		[s									h]
			r		ṛ						
			l								
	v						y				

21 Ollari (Bhattacharya 1957: part I)

Vowels[14]

i	ī			u	ū
e	ē			o	ō
		a	ā		

Consonants

	Labial	Labio-dental	Dental	Post-dental	Retroflex	Palatal	Velar
Stop	p b		t d		ṭ ḍ		k g
Affricate				ts dz		c j	
Nasal	m		n			(ñ)	ŋ
Rolled				r			
Flapped				ṛ			
Lateral				l			
Fricative		v				y	
Sibilant				s z			

[14] There are some nasalized vowels of rare occurrence.

22 Gadaba (Bhaskararao 1998: 329ff.)

Vowels

i	ī			u	ū
e	ē			o	ō
		a	ā		

Consonants

	Labial	Dental	Retroflex	Palatal	Velar
Stops:					
Voiceless	p	t	ṭ	c	k
Voiced	b	d	ḍ	j	g
Nasal	m	n	ṇ		ŋ
Fricative		s			
Trill		r			
Lateral		l			
Glide	v			y	

North Dravidian

23 Kuṛux (Grignard 1924a: 1–15. Grignard's classification of consonants is given as it is.)

Vowels

i	ī			u	ū
e	ē			o	ō
		a	ā		

Nasalized vowels[15]

ĩ	ī̃			ũ	ū̃
ẽ	ē̃			(õ)	ō̃
		(ã)	ā̃		

[15] There are some nasalized vowels of rare occurrence. Grignard reports that oral and nasal vowels vary dialectally, e.g. *eō̃dā* 'how many?', *muī̃* 'face'. Grignard does not give any examples of nasalized short vowels. So it appears that nasalization goes with length; diphthongs are treated as a V + *y*, both oral and nasal.

Consonants[16]

Gutturals	k	kh, <u>kh</u>	g	gh
Palatals	c	ch	j,y	jh
Cerebrals	ṭ	ṭh	ḍ, ṛ	ḍh, ṛh
Dentals	t	th	d	dh
Labials	p	ph	b	bh
Liquids	l	m	n	r
Sibilants, etc.	s	h	w	

Pfeiffer (1972: 8–11), following Pinnow (1964; *IIJ* 8: 32–59), sets up the Kuṛux phonemes as follows:

Vowels

/i	ə	u
e	a	o/

Nasalization /~/ occurs with all vowels except /ə/. Grignard's auxiliary vowels are not phonemic.

Consonants

Stops:						
Voiceless	p	t	ṭ	c	k	ʔ
Voiced	b	d	ḍ	j	g	
Nasals	m	n	(ṇ)		ŋ	
Fricatives	s			x	h	
Lateral	l					
Trills	r	(ṛ)				
Semivowels	w			y		

16 The transcription is not phonemic nor is it purely phonetic. Notice the following statements of Grignard: ' "<u>kh</u>" , though totally different in pronunciation from "kh", is really the same letter, as is proved by the facility with which they interchange'. [footnote: mō<u>kh</u>nā 'to eat' mokhan 'I ate', nēkhai or nē<u>kh</u>ai 'of whom?'.] Apparently there is free variation between *<u>kh</u>* = [x] and *kh* confined to some lexical items. He says further, 'The surest method for correctly sounding n, ṅ, ñ, ṇ is to give them no thought whatever . . . these three extra sounds are automatic and purely accidental modifications of the "n" sound which alone, all the time, is intended' (1924a: 3). Therefore, the nasals listed in the chart above are not phonemic. Grignard speaks of a vowel hiatus, which is a name he gave to a 'glottal stop'. It does vary with certain consonants /p k g/. It occurs between vowels, e.g. *ci'on* [ciʔon] 'I shall give', *ban'nā* 'to succeed', *ba'nā* 'to say'. The 'hiatus' is filled by 'a very short vowel sound for the sake of euphony' (1924a: 6). 'This fleeting sound is always, in nature, the reproduction (or anticipation) of the vowel; . . . e.g. *ba'anā*, *nē'enā*, *ci'inā*, etc.' He suggests that the 'euphonic' vowel need not be written (1924a: 7).

24 Malto (Mahapatra 1979: 19–20)

Vowels

i	ī			u	ū
e	ē			o	ō
		a	ā		

Consonants[17]

	Labial	Dental	Alveolar	Retroflex	Palatal	Velar	Uvular	Glottal
Stop								
Voiceless	p	t		ṭ	c	k	q	
Voiced	b	d		ḍ	j	g		
Nasal	m	n			ñ	ṅ		
Fricative		ð	s				ɣ	h
Trill			r					
Lateral			l					
Flap				ṛ				
Semivowel	w				y			

25 Brahui[18] *(Emeneau 1962d; Elfenbein 1997: 798–800, 1998: 392)*

Vowels

i	ī			u	ū
	ē				ō
		a	ā		

17 Consonant-ending words in isolation take an enunciative *u* (Mahapatra 1979: 360). No aspirated stops or nasal vowels are reported.

18 Short *e o* are allophones of *ē ō* before conjunct consonants (Elfenbein 1998: 391–2).

Consonants[19]

Stops	p	b	t	d			ṭ	ḍ	k	g	?
Affricate					č	j					
Fricative	f								x	ɣ	h
Spirant			s	z	š	ž					
Nasal	m			n			ṇ			(ŋ)	
Lateral			ɬ	l							
Flap			r				ṛ				
Semivowel	w		y								

19 Elfenbein 1998 shows /y/ under velars, but in 1997 under dentals; the former must be a misprint; [h] of north corresponds to glottal stop of south initially and intervocalically; before a C in word-final position it is lost (1998: 393). Non-phonemic glottal stop before word-initial vowels, e.g. *hust* (N), *ʔust* (S) 'heart'; [ɬ] and [l] freely vary in many cases; contrast is limited to two or three items. Conditions for the emergence of [ɬ] are not clear. Bray transcribes the voiceless [ɬ] as *l̲h̲*. [ŋ] is not phonemic. [ṛ] does not occur word-initially. The consonants [p t k] freely alternate with aspirated counterparts in the northeast. r → ṛ before t d s z in northern Brahui (Elfenbein 1998: 394), e.g. *xūrt* → *xūṛt* 'tiny'. Aspirated stops word-initially occur in loanwords in the south, where they freely vary with unaspirated stops.

3

The writing systems of the major literary languages

3.1 **Origins**

The Aśokan Brāhmī of the third century BCE is the mother of all major Indian scripts, both Indo-Aryan and Dravidian. It was an alpha-syllabic script with diacritics used for vowels occurring in postconsonantal position. It has separate symbols for the five primary vowels a i u e o, twenty-five occlusives and eight sonorants and fricatives. The Brāhmī script was used in the rock edicts set up by the Mauryan Emperor Aśoka to spread the Buddhist faith in different parts of the country. The languages represented were Pali and certain early regional varieties of Middle Indic. The origin of the Brāhmī script is controversial; nearly half of the characters are said to bear similarity to the consonant symbols employed in the South Semitic script, eventually traceable to Aramaic script of 2000 BCE (Daniels and Bright 1996: §30, 373–83).

The writing was based on the concept of *akṣara* or the 'graphic syllable', which has a vowel as the final constituent, i.e. V, CV, CCV, CCCV etc. Word-initial V is written in its primary form; in the postconsonantal position, the vowel is represented by a diacritic. Similarly the first consonant of a syllable has the primary consonant and all other consonants following the first one are represented by their secondary (diacritic) forms, e.g <i> = 𑀇, <k> = 𑀓; but <ki> = 𑀓𑀺; <kt> = 𑀓𑁆𑀢 as opposed to <kata> 𑀓𑀢. The Aśokan script got diversified into regional scripts over the next two thousand years. 'Most of the modern Indic scripts achieved their distinct forms between the tenth and fifteenth centuries.' It originally developed into three major branches, western, northern and southern. The southern branch led to two parent scripts, the Telugu–Kannaḍa script on the one hand, and the Tamil–Malayāḷam script, on the other (Daniels and Bright 1996: 373–9).

3.2 **Telugu–Kannaḍa script**

A variety of Southern Brāhmī script was earlier employed in Prakrit inscriptions and later developed into Proto-Telugu–Kannaḍa script by the sixth century AD, when the Telugu and Kannaḍa inscriptions begin to appear. This variety continued up to the fifteenth

Table 3.1a. *Evolution of the Telugu–Kannaḍa script from the third century BC to the sixteenth century AD [a–ḍ]*

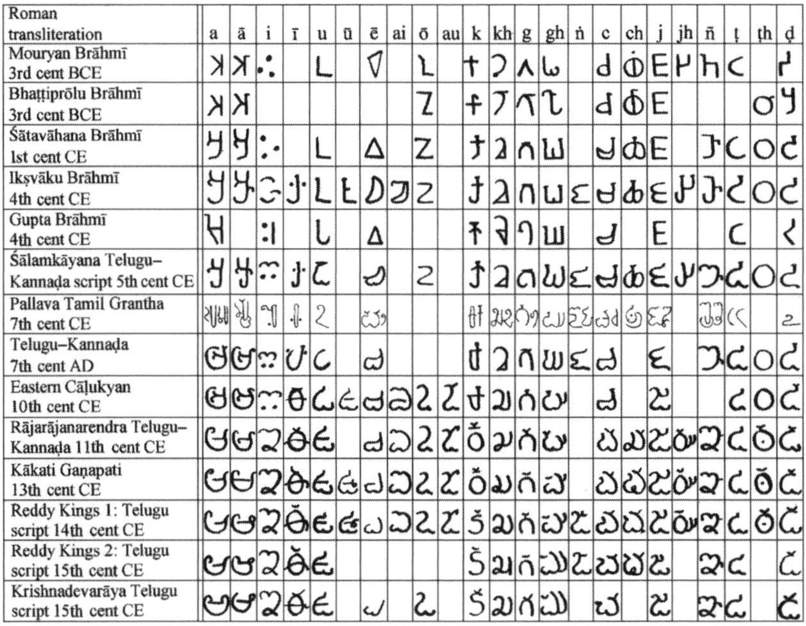
Roman transliteration
a ā i ī u ū ē ai ō au k kh g gh ṅ c ch j jh ñ ṭ ṭh ḍ
Mouryan Brāhmī 3rd cent BCE
Bhaṭṭiprōlu Brāhmī 3rd cent BCE
Śātavāhana Brāhmī 1st cent CE
Ikṣvāku Brāhmī 4th cent CE
Gupta Brāhmī 4th cent CE
Śālamkāyana Telugu–Kannaḍa script 5th cent CE
Pallava Tamil Grantha 7th cent CE
Telugu–Kannaḍa 7th cent AD
Eastern Cāḷukyan 10th cent CE
Rājarājanarendra Telugu–Kannaḍa 11th cent CE
Kākati Gaṇapati 13th cent CE
Reddy Kings 1: Telugu script 14th cent CE
Reddy Kings 2: Telugu script 15th cent CE
Krishnadevarāya Telugu script 15th cent CE

century AD with shared changes, after which Telugu and Kannaḍa scripts diverged and developed independently. The Chalukyan script of the last quarter of the eleventh century represented the transitional phase which was used both for Kannaḍa and Telugu records. By the fourteenth century the Old Telugu and the Haḷagannaḍa scripts had distinct differences. Aspirated stops had a vertical stroke underneath the letter in Telugu which was absent in Kannaḍa. The serif developed into a talakaṭṭu (check mark) in Telugu and the bottom portions of all letters have developed circularity. New symbols were attested in the inscriptions for <ṟ> = ఱ, and <ẓ> = ఴ peculiar to the Dravidian languages, from the fifth century CE (T. Ramchandra 1993: chart opp. p.144). The phoneme /ẓ/ was gradually replaced in speech by /ḍ r/ in Telugu and by /ḷ r/ in Kannaḍa in complementary environments even by the eleventh century, but the old symbol <ẓ> continued in the writing system for a long time even after the merger with the other phonemes was completed. It was gradually discontinued after the thirteenth century. Burnell says ‘these additional signs were the inventions of the people from the North’ (1968: 28). Distinct symbols for /r ṟ/ have continued into the modern period in Telugu

Table 3.1b. *Evolution of the Telugu–Kannaḍa script from the third century BC to the sixteenth century AD [ḍh–ẓ]*

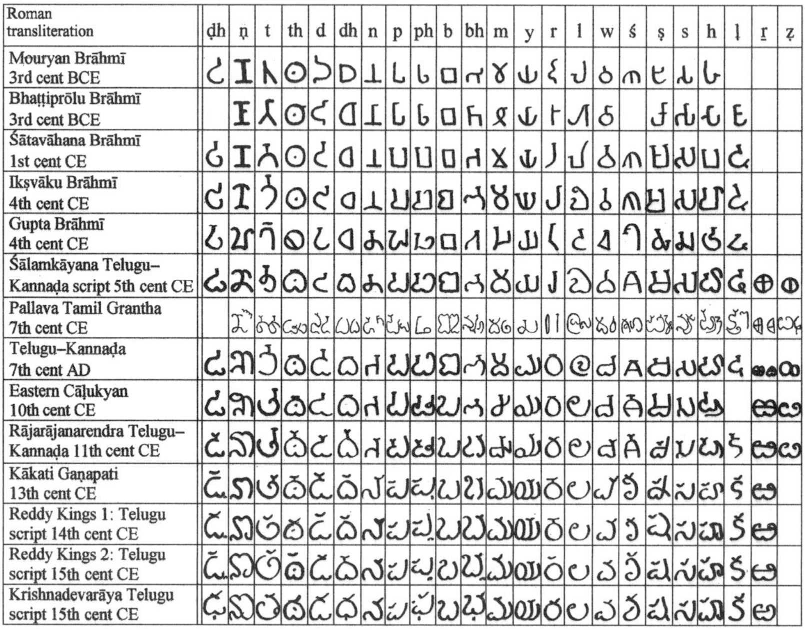
Roman transliteration
ḍh ṇ t th d dh n p ph b bh m y r l w ś ṣ s h ḷ ṟ ẓ
Mouryan Brāhmī 3rd cent BCE
Bhaṭṭiprōlu Brāhmī 3rd cent BCE
Śātavāhana Brāhmī 1st cent CE
Ikṣvāku Brāhmī 4th cent CE
Gupta Brāhmī 4th cent CE
Śālamkāyana Telugu–Kannaḍa script 5th cent CE
Pallava Tamil Grantha 7th cent CE
Telugu–Kannaḍa 7th cent AD
Eastern Cāḷukyan 10th cent CE
Rājarājanarendra Telugu–Kannaḍa 11th cent CE
Kākati Gaṇapati 13th cent CE
Reddy Kings 1: Telugu script 14th cent CE
Reddy Kings 2: Telugu script 15th cent CE
Krishnadevarāya Telugu script 15th cent CE

although the phonological difference between the two was lost nearly ten centuries ago. The introduction of the printing mode has standardized the differences between the Telugu and Kannaḍa writing systems.

The following observations relate to modern scripts of Telugu and Kannaḍa:

1. The vowels are written in their primary form when they occur at the beginning of a word. In all postconsonantal positions only the secondary forms or diacritics are used, e.g. <a ā> Te./Ka. అ ఆ/ಅ ಆ, but <ka kā> క కా /ಕ ಕಾ.
2. The first member of a consonant cluster occurs in its primary form, all other consonants that follow it occur in their secondary (diacritic) form. The vowel which ends the orthographic syllable is added to the first member of the cluster, e.g. Te./Ka. <ty> త్య /ತ್ಯ.

   Exception: in Kannaḍa consonant clusters beginning with r- show this as a diacritic at the end of the cluster, e.g. <karta> Te. కర్త, Ka. ಕರ್ತ.
3. Kannaḍa and Telugu differ in their diacritics for long vowels, mainly in the case of high and mid vowels, e.g. <kī, kū, kē, kō> = Te. కీ కూ కే కో; Ka. ಕೀ ಕೂ ಕೇ ಕೋ.
4. When the consonant is intended to be represented in its pure form, the check is replaced by ్ in Te. as in క్ and Ka. ಕ್.

Table 3.2a. *Primary vowels and consonants of Telugu*

అ	ఆ	ఇ	ఈ	ఉ	ఊ	ఋ	ఎ	ఏ	ఐ	
a	ā	i	ī	u	ū	ṛ	e	ē	ai	
		ఒ	ఓ	ఔ	అం		అః			
		o	ō	au	aṃ		aḥ			
క	ఖ	గ	ఘ	ఙ						
k	kh	g	gh	ṅ						
చ	ఛ	జ	ఝ	ఞ						
c	ch	j	jh	ñ						
ట	ఠ	డ	ఢ	ణ						
ṭ	ṭh	ḍ	ḍh	ṇ						
త	థ	ద	ధ	న						
t	th	d	dh	n						
ప	ఫ	బ	భ	మ						
n	ph	b	bh	m						
య	ర	ల	వ	శ	ష		స	హ	ఱ	ళ
y	r	l	w	ś	ṣ		s	h	ṟ	ḷ

Table 3.2b. *Primary vowels and consonants of Kannaḍa*

ಅ	ಆ	ಇ	ಈ	ಉ	ಊ	ಋ	ಎ	ಏ	ಐ	ಒ	ಓ	ಔ	ಅಂ	ಅಃ
a	ā	i	ī	u	ū	ṛ	e	ē	ai	o	ō	au	aṃ	aḥ
ಕ	ಖ	ಗ	ಘ	ಙ										
k	kh	g	gh	ṅ										
ಚ	ಛ	ಜ	ಝ	ಞ										
c	ch	j	jh	ñ										
ಟ	ಠ	ಡ	ಢ	ಣ										
ṭ	ṭh	ḍ	ḍh	ṇ										
ತ	ಥ	ದ	ಧ	ನ										
t	th	d	dh	n										
ಪ	ಫ	ಬ	ಭ	ಮ										
p	ph	b	bh	m										
ಯ	ರ	ಲ	ವ											
y	r	l	v											
ಶ	ಷ	ಸ	ಹ	ಳ										
ś	ṣ	s	h	ḷ										

5. The vowel diacritics are added to the consonant symbol to the top or right, but the secondary consonants are not allowed to touch the body of the consonantal symbol. One clear exception to this rule is vocalic <ṛ> which is treated as a consonant phonologically in Telugu and Kannaḍa. In Kannaḍa the diacritic for vowel length is a separable symbol.

Table 3.3a. *Combination of primary consonants with secondary vowels in Telugu*

	a	ā	i	ī	u	ū	ṛ	e	ē	ai	o	ō	au
k	క	కా	కి	కీ	కు	కూ	కృ	కె	కే	కై	కొ	కో	కౌ
kh	ఖ	ఖా	ఖి	ఖీ	ఖు	ఖూ	ఖృ	ఖె	ఖే	ఖై	ఖొ	ఖో	ఖౌ
g	గ	గా	గి	గీ	గు	గూ	గృ	గె	గే	గై	గొ	గో	గౌ
gh	ఘ	ఘా	ఘి	ఘీ	ఘు	ఘూ	ఘృ	ఘె	ఘే	ఘై	ఘొ	ఘో	ఘౌ
c	చ	చా	చి	చీ	చు	చూ	చృ	చె	చే	చై	చొ	చో	చౌ
ch	ఛ	ఛా	ఛి	ఛీ	ఛు	ఛూ	ఛృ	ఛె	ఛే	ఛై	ఛొ	ఛో	ఛౌ
j	జ	జా	జి	జీ	జు	జూ	జృ	జె	జే	జై	జొ	జో	జౌ
jh	ఝ	ఝా	ఝ2	ఝ3	ఝు	ఝూ	ఝృ	ఝె	ఝే	ఝై	ఝొ	ఝో	ఝౌ
ṭ	ట	టా	టి	టీ	టు	టూ	టృ	టె	టే	టై	టొ	టో	టౌ
ṭh	ఠ	ఠా	ఠి	ఠీ	ఠు	ఠూ	ఠృ	ఠె	ఠే	ఠై	ఠొ	ఠో	ఠౌ
ḍ	డ	డా	డి	డీ	డు	డూ	డృ	డె	డే	డై	డొ	డో	డౌ
ḍh	ఢ	ఢా	ఢి	ఢీ	ఢు	ఢూ	ఢృ	ఢె	ఢే	ఢై	ఢొ	ఢో	ఢౌ
ṇ	ణ	ణా	ణి	ణీ	ణు	ణూ	ణృ	ణె	ణే	ణై	ణొ	ణో	ణౌ
t	త	తా	తి	తీ	తు	తూ	తృ	తె	తే	తై	తొ	తో	తౌ
th	థ	థా	థి	థీ	థు	థూ	థృ	థె	థే	థై	థొ	థో	థౌ
d	ద	దా	ది	దీ	దు	దూ	దృ	దె	దే	దై	దొ	దో	దౌ
dh	ధ	ధా	ధి	ధీ	ధు	ధూ	ధృ	ధె	ధే	ధై	ధొ	ధో	ధౌ
n	న	నా	ని	నీ	ను	నూ	నృ	నె	నే	నై	నొ	నో	నౌ
p	ప	పా	పి	పీ	పు	పూ	పృ	పె	పే	పై	పొ	పో	పౌ
ph	ఫ	ఫా	ఫి	ఫీ	ఫు	ఫూ	ఫృ	ఫె	ఫే	ఫై	ఫొ	ఫో	ఫౌ
b	బ	బా	బి	బీ	బు	బూ	బృ	బె	బే	బై	బొ	బో	బౌ
bh	భ	భా	భి	భీ	భు	భూ	భృ	భె	భే	భై	భొ	భో	భౌ
m	మ	మా	మి	మీ	ము	మూ	మృ	మె	మే	మై	మొ	మో	మౌ
y	య	యా	యి	యీ	యు	యూ	యృ	యె	యే	యై	యొ	యో	యౌ
r	ర	రా	రి	రీ	రు	రూ	రృ	రె	రే	రై	రొ	రో	రౌ
l	ల	లా	లి	లీ	లు	లూ	లృ	లె	లే	లై	లొ	లో	లౌ
v	వ	వా	వి	వీ	వు	వూ	వృ	వె	వే	వై	వొ	వో	వౌ
ś	శ	శా	శి	శీ	శు	శూ	శృ	శె	శే	శై	శొ	శో	శౌ
ṣ	ష	షా	షి	షీ	షు	షూ	షృ	షె	షే	షై	షొ	షో	షౌ
s	స	సా	సి	సీ	సు	సూ	సృ	సె	సే	సై	సొ	సో	సౌ
h	హ	హా	హి	హీ	హు	హూ	హృ	హె	హే	హై	హొ	హో	హౌ
ḷ	ళ	ళా	ళి	ళీ	ళు	ళూ	ళృ	ళె	ళే	ళై	ళొ	ళో	ళౌ

Table 3.3b. *Combination of primary consonants with secondary vowels in Kannaḍa*

	a	ā	i	ī	u	ū	ṛ	e	ē	ai	o	ō	au
k	ಕ	ಕಾ	ಕಿ	ಕೀ	ಕು	ಕೂ	ಕೃ	ಕೆ	ಕೇ	ಕೈ	ಕೊ	ಕೋ	ಕೌ
kh	ಖ	ಖಾ	ಖಿ	ಖೀ	ಖು	ಖೂ	ಖೃ	ಖೆ	ಖೇ	ಖೈ	ಖೊ	ಖೋ	ಖೌ
g	ಗ	ಗಾ	ಗಿ	ಗೀ	ಗು	ಗೂ	ಗೃ	ಗೆ	ಗೇ	ಗೈ	ಗೊ	ಗೋ	ಗೌ
gh	ಘ	ಘಾ	ಘಿ	ಘೀ	ಘು	ಘೂ	ಘೃ	ಘೆ	ಘೇ	ಘೈ	ಘೊ	ಘೋ	ಘೌ
c	ಚ	ಚಾ	ಚಿ	ಚೀ	ಚು	ಚೂ	ಚೃ	ಚೆ	ಚೇ	ಚೈ	ಚೊ	ಚೋ	ಚೌ
ch	ಛ	ಛಾ	ಛಿ	ಛೀ	ಛು	ಛೂ	ಛೃ	ಛೆ	ಛೇ	ಛೈ	ಛೊ	ಛೋ	ಛೌ
j	ಜ	ಜಾ	ಜಿ	ಜೀ	ಜು	ಜೂ	ಜೃ	ಜೆ	ಜೇ	ಜೈ	ಜೊ	ಜೋ	ಜೌ
jh	ಝ	ಝಾ	ಝಿ	ಝೀ	ಝು	ಝೂ	ಝೃ	ಝೆ	ಝೇ	ಝೈ	ಝೊ	ಝೋ	ಝೌ
ṭ	ಟ	ಟಾ	ಟಿ	ಟೀ	ಟು	ಟೂ	ಟೃ	ಟೆ	ಟೇ	ಟೈ	ಟೊ	ಟೋ	ಟೌ
ṭh	ಠ	ಠಾ	ಠಿ	ಠೀ	ಠು	ಠೂ	ಠೃ	ಠೆ	ಠೇ	ಠೈ	ಠೊ	ಠೋ	ಠೌ
ḍ	ಡ	ಡಾ	ಡಿ	ಡೀ	ಡು	ಡೂ	ಡೃ	ಡೆ	ಡೇ	ಡೈ	ಡೊ	ಡೋ	ಡೌ
ḍh	ಢ	ಢಾ	ಢಿ	ಢೀ	ಢು	ಢೂ	ಢೃ	ಢೆ	ಢೇ	ಢೈ	ಢೊ	ಢೋ	ಢೌ
ṇ	ಣ	ಣಾ	ಣಿ	ಣೀ	ಣು	ಣೂ	ಣೃ	ಣೆ	ಣೇ	ಣೈ	ಣೊ	ಣೋ	ಣೌ
t	ತ	ತಾ	ತಿ	ತೀ	ತು	ತೂ	ತೃ	ತೆ	ತೇ	ತೈ	ತೊ	ತೋ	ತೌ
th	ಥ	ಥಾ	ಥಿ	ಥೀ	ಥು	ಥೂ	ಥೃ	ಥೆ	ಥೇ	ಥೈ	ಥೊ	ಥೋ	ಥೌ
d	ದ	ದಾ	ದಿ	ದೀ	ದು	ದೂ	ದೃ	ದೆ	ದೇ	ದೈ	ದೊ	ದೋ	ದೌ
dh	ಧ	ಧಾ	ಧಿ	ಧೀ	ಧು	ಧೂ	ಧೃ	ಧೆ	ಧೇ	ಧೈ	ಧೊ	ಧೋ	ಧೌ
n	ನ	ನಾ	ನಿ	ನೀ	ನು	ನ	ನೃ	ನೆ	ನೇ	ನೈ	ನೊ	ನೋ	ನೌ
p	ಪ	ಪಾ	ಪಿ	ಪೀ	ಪು	ಪೂ	ಪೃ	ಪೆ	ಪೇ	ಪೈ	ಪೊ	ಪೋ	ಪೌ
ph	ಫ	ಫಾ	ಫಿ	ಫೀ	ಫು	ಫೂ	ಫೃ	ಫೆ	ಫೇ	ಫೈ	ಫೊ	ಫೋ	ಫೌ
b	ಬ	ಬಾ	ಬಿ	ಬೀ	ಬು	ಬೂ	ಬೃ	ಬೆ	ಬೇ	ಬೈ	ಬೊ	ಬೋ	ಬೌ
bh	ಭ	ಭಾ	ಭಿ	ಭೀ	ಭು	ಭೂ	ಭೃ	ಭೆ	ಭೇ	ಭೈ	ಭೊ	ಭೋ	ಭೌ
m	ಮ	ಮಾ	ಮಿ	ಮೀ	ಮು	ಮೂ	ಮೃ	ಮೆ	ಮೇ	ಮೈ	ಮೊ	ಮೋ	ಮೌ
y	ಯ	ಯಾ	ಯಿ	ಯೀ	ಯು	ಯೂ	ಯೃ	ಯೆ	ಯೇ	ಯೈ	ಯೊ	ಯೋ	ಯೌ
r	ರ	ರಾ	ರಿ	ರೀ	ರು	ರೂ	ರೃ	ರೆ	ರೇ	ರೈ	ರೊ	ರೋ	ರೌ
l	ಲ	ಲಾ	ಲಿ	ಲೀ	ಲು	ಲೂ	ಲೃ	ಲೆ	ಲೇ	ಲೈ	ಲೊ	ಲೋ	ಲೌ
v	ವ	ವಾ	ವಿ	ವೀ	ವು	ವೂ	ವೃ	ವೆ	ವೇ	ವೈ	ವೊ	ವೋ	ವೌ
ś	ಶ	ಶಾ	ಶಿ	ಶೀ	ಶು	ಶೂ	ಶೃ	ಶೆ	ಶೇ	ಶೈ	ಶೊ	ಶೋ	ಶೌ
ṣ	ಷ	ಷಾ	ಷಿ	ಷೀ	ಷು	ಷೂ	ಷೃ	ಷೆ	ಷೇ	ಷೈ	ಷೊ	ಷೋ	ಷೌ
s	ಸ	ಸಾ	ಸಿ	ಸೀ	ಸು	ಸೂ	ಸೃ	ಸೆ	ಸೇ	ಸೈ	ಸೊ	ಸೋ	ಸೌ
h	ಹ	ಹಾ	ಹಿ	ಹೀ	ಹು	ಹೂ	ಹೃ	ಹೆ	ಹೇ	ಹೈ	ಹೊ	ಹೋ	ಹೌ
ḷ	ಳ	ಳಾ	ಳಿ	ಳೀ	ಳು	ಳೂ	ಳೃ	ಳೆ	ಳೇ	ಳೈ	ಳೊ	ಳೋ	ಳೌ

3.2.1 *Writing vs. pronunciation*

1. The vocalic <r̥> is written but is not pronounced as a syllabic; it is pronounced as [ru/ri] in Te. ఋ తు వు *r̥tuwu* [rutuwu], Ka. ಋತು *r̥tu* [ritu] 'season'.
2. The *anusvāra* <o> transliterated as [ṃ] is used as a cover symbol of all nasals before homorganic stops where it is pronounced like the homorganic nasal, e.g. Te. <gaṃga> గ ం గ, Ka. <gaṃge> ಗ ಂ ಗೆ, Te. <paṃpa> ప ం ప, Ka. <paṃpa> ಪ ಂ ಪ. In Telugu it also occurs in the word-final position and before /w s ś h/ of loans from Sanskrit, with the phonetic value of [m].
3. The Sanskrit *visarga* <ః>, transliterated <ḥ>, is pronounced as a voiceless [ḥ] after a long vowel, and as [ḥV] after a short vowel; the final vowel has the same quality as the preceding vowel, e.g. <muniḥ> = Te. ము ని ః [munihi] 'an ascetic', Ka. ಪುನ ಃ [punəha] 'again'.
4. In loanwords beginning with <jñ> the palatal is pronounced like a stop and <ñ> as [ny]; Te. జ్ఞాన ం [ɟɲaːnaṃ], Ka. ಜ್ಞಾ ನ *jñāna* [ɟɲaːna], 'knowledge'.
5. In standard Telugu, the contrast between /ā/ and /ǣ/ is not indicated in writing. It is represented by long <ā> in verbs చెప్పా ం [ceppæːm] 'we said'.
6. In Telugu /c j/ are pronounced as palatal affricates [tʃ dʒ] before front vowels /i e æ/ and as alveolar affricates [ts dz] before non-front vowels /a u o/: చిలక *cilaka* [tʃilʌkʌ] 'parrot', చా లా *cālā* [tsaːlaː] 'much'. In Sanskrit loanwords <c j> are pronounced as palatal affricates even when followed by a low vowel, చ క్ర ం <cakram> [tʃakrʌm] 'wheel'. The vowel following the palatal is however fronted and becomes indistinguishable from [e].

Tables 3.2a, b show the primary forms of vowels and consonants of Telugu and Kannaḍa, respectively. Tables 3.3a, b show combination of primary consonants with secondary vowels in Telugu and Kannaḍa. Note that the combinations given in the tables are the possible ones and only some of those (over 50 per cent) are the actual ones.

3.3 Tamil and Malayāḷam scripts

Certain new symbols were innovated and added to the Aśokan Brāhmī to represent the sounds peculiar to Tamil like [ḷ, ṟ ẓ ṉ]. The innovation consisted in the use of diacritics added to the symbols representing *l*, *t*, *ṭ*, and *n*. One can see in this the phonetic similarity between the old and new symbols – alveolar *l* and retroflex *ḷ* (both laterals with place difference), dental *t* and alveolar *ṯ* (both stops with place difference), retroflex stop *ṭ* and continuant *ẓ* (same place with manner difference), dental *n* and alveolar *ṉ* (place difference, but actually allophones of the same phoneme). The adapted script is now called the Tamil Brāhmī. This script was used in seventy-six cave inscriptions in the Madurai–Tirunalveli districts. These inscriptions were dated to the second century BC. The language of these inscriptions was clearly Tamil with a mixture of Prakrit words. They described grants made to Jaina and Buddhist monks by the kings and chieftains of the Pandyan era. Later this script spread to the entire Tamil-speaking area. By the seventh to eighth centuries, a transitional variety called Vaṭṭeẓuttu had evolved which became the parent of Tamil and Malayāḷam scripts. Mahadevan (1971) has thoroughly described the language of the Tamil-Brāhmī inscriptions and shown how the new symbols had been innovated.

Vaṭṭeẓuttu was replaced by another Tamil script from the seventh century AD in the Pallava court, by simplifying the Grantha script (which itself was derived from the Southern Brāhmī) and adding to it necessary symbols from Vaṭṭeẓuttu. This continued in the Tamil country as the Tamil script from the eleventh century onwards. On the west coast, in Malayāḷam, Vaṭṭeẓuttu continued for a much longer period by adding symbols from the Grantha script to represent Indo-Aryan loanwords. This eventually developed into the present-day Malayāḷam script.[1]

Tamil and Malayāḷam are genetically closer than Telugu and Kannaḍa, but the writing systems of Telugu and Kannaḍa are much closer than those of Tamil and Malayāḷam. This is a good case to show that orthographic proximity does not imply genetic proximity.[2] Other differences are:

1. Unlike in Kannaḍa and Telugu, in Tamil and Malayāḷam vowel diacritics are generally added to consonantal symbols in a linear order and not above or below the consonantal letter:

Tamil		*Malayāḷam*	
pa	ப	pa	പ
pā	பா	pā	പാ
pi	பி	pi	പി
pī	பீ	pī	പീ
pu	பு	pu	പു
pū	பூ	pū	പൂ
pe	பெ	pe	പെ
pē	பே	pē	പേ
pai	பை	pai	പൈ
po	பொ	po	പൊ
pō	போ	pō	പോ
pau	பௌ	pau	പൗ

[1] I am grateful to Iravatham Mahadevan for suggesting some changes regarding the history of Tamil and Malayāḷam scripts.

[2] In the 1950s and 1960s, the Government of Andhra Pradesh made efforts through committees to recommend changes in the writing systems of Telugu and Kannaḍa so that they could be printed in the same script. There were many at that time who thought that, by bringing the scripts together, the differences between the two languages would get submerged. Fortunately, these efforts have not succeeded. The talk of reform of a script is an anachronism now with the emergence of the computer as a printing tool.

Table 3.4a. *Combination of primary consonants with secondary vowels in Tamil*

	a	ā	i	ī	u	ū	e	ē	ai	o	ō	au
k	க	கா	கி	கீ	கு	கூ	கெ	கே	கை	கொ	கோ	கௌ
c	ச	சா	சி	சீ	சு	சூ	செ	சே	சை	சொ	சோ	சௌ
ṭ	ட	டா	டி	டீ	டு	டூ	டெ	டே	டை	டொ	டோ	டௌ
ṇ	ண	ணா	ணி	ணீ	ணு	ணூ	ணெ	ணே	ணை	ணொ	ணோ	ணௌ
t	த	தா	தி	தீ	து	தூ	தெ	தே	தை	தொ	தோ	தௌ
n	ந	நா	நி	நீ	நு	நூ	நெ	நே	நை	நொ	நோ	நௌ
p	ப	பா	பி	பீ	பு	பூ	பெ	பே	பை	பொ	போ	பௌ
m	ம	மா	மி	மீ	மு	மூ	மெ	மே	மை	மொ	மோ	மௌ
y	ய	யா	யி	யீ	யு	யூ	யெ	யே	யை	யொ	யோ	யௌ
r	ர	ரா	ரி	ரீ	ரு	ரூ	ரெ	ரே	ரை	ரொ	ரோ	ரௌ
l	ல	லா	லி	லீ	லு	லூ	லெ	லே	லை	லொ	லோ	லௌ
v	வ	வா	வி	வீ	வு	வூ	வெ	வே	வை	வொ	வோ	வௌ
ẓ	ழ	ழா	ழி	ழீ	ழு	ழூ	ழெ	ழே	ழை	ழொ	ழோ	ழௌ
ḷ	ள	ளா	ளி	ளீ	ளு	ளூ	ளெ	ளே	ளை	ளொ	ளோ	ளௌ
ṟ	ற	றா	றி	றீ	று	றூ	றெ	றே	றை	றொ	றோ	றௌ
ṉ	ன	னா	னி	னீ	னு	னூ	னெ	னே	னை	னொ	னோ	னௌ
ṣ	ஷ	ஷா	ஷி	ஷீ	ஷு	ஷூ	ஷெ	ஷே	ஷை	ஷொ	ஷோ	ஷௌ
s	ஸ	ஸா	ஸி	ஸீ	ஸு	ஸூ	ஸெ	ஸே	ஸை	ஸொ	ஸோ	ஸௌ
j	ஜ	ஜா	ஜி	ஜீ	ஜு	ஜூ	ஜெ	ஜே	ஜை	ஜொ	ஜோ	ஜௌ
kṣ	க்ஷ	க்ஷா	க்ஷி	க்ஷீ	க்ஷு	க்ஷூ	க்ஷெ	க்ஷே	க்ஷை	க்ஷொ	க்ஷோ	க்ஷௌ
h	ஹ	ஹா	ஹி	ஹீ	ஹு	ஹூ	ஹெ	ஹே	ஹை	ஹொ	ஹோ	ஹௌ

2. Tamil is much more conservative than Malayāḷam. It has only one set of symbols for each stop, the voiceless one, without marking voice and aspiration. But Malayāḷam has separate symbols for voiced stops and also for aspirated consonants in voiced and voiceless series. The combination of primary consonants with secondary vowels in Tamil is illustrated in table 3.4a.
3. The underlined letters in table 3.4a have been reformed, at the initiative of the Government of Tamil Nadu, to fall in line with the other letters in their shapes and modern Tamil writings have switched to new spellings, namely:

	old form(s)	**new form(s)**
ṇā, ṇai, ṇo, ṇō	ணா ணை ணொ ணோ	ணா, ணை, ணொ, ணோ
lai	லை	லை
ḷai	ளை	ளை
ṟā, ṟo, ṟō	றா றொ றோ	றா, றொ, றோ
ṉā, ṉai, ṉo, ṉō	னா னை னொ னோ	னா, னை, னொ, னோ

4. In the case of consonant clusters also linearity is more widely the pattern than combining the diacritics with the body of the first member of the cluster. Tamil exploits the linearity principle more than Malayāḷam, e.g.:

Tamil		
ciṟṟil	சிற்றில்	'small house'
yāṇṭu	யாண்டு	'year'
cērntu	சேர்ந்து	'having joined'
tōnṟuvan	தோன்றுவன்	'the one who appears'
Malayāḷam		
niyantriccitṭum	നിയന്ത്രിച്ചിട്ടും	'despite controlling'
vyāyāmam	വ്യായാമം	'exercise'
hr̥drōgaṃ	ഹൃദ്രോഗം	'heart disease'

5. Earlier Tamil used five Grantha letters to represent some spellings of Sanskrit:

j	ஜ
ṣ	ஸ
s	ஷ
h	ஹ
kṣ	க்ஷ

6. In Modern Tamil they use the ancient symbol for *āytam* by combining it with other symbols to indicate fricative sounds; thus *āytam* + <p> = [f], e.g. ஃபீசு [fīcu] 'fees'.

Table 3.4b gives the Malayāḷam primary consonants with secondary vowels. Table 3.5 shows the combination of primary consonants with secondary consonants, for three languages. More details on south Indian scripts can be found in Bright (1998).

3.4 Writing in non-literary languages

We do not have clear data on the non-literary languages. But we know that no special scripts have evolved in these. Tuḷu and Koḍagu use Kannaḍa script. Some Tuḷu speakers in Kerala may be using the Malayāḷam writing system. In the Nilgiris Tamil is used as a language of literacy. In Andhra Pradesh Telugu script is used to teach the Gonds, Kolam and Konda Doras. Gondi is spread in Maharashtra and Madhya Pradesh where they use the scripts of the dominant languages. It appears that Oriya script is used for Kui–Kuvi and Devanagari for Kuṛux and Malto. Brahuis use different scripts in different countries, but, certainly, the Urdu writing system in Pakistan. It would be interesting to know how the sounds for which symbols are not available in the dominant regional languages are represented in writing in teaching literacy to the tribal children. At least for Koṇḍa I have proposed new symbols for the voiceless and voiced alveolar trill and the glottal stop based on Telugu /R ṟ ʔ/ = ఱ్వ°ఱ ʔ.

Table 3.4b. *Combination of primary consonants with secondary vowels in Malayāḷam*

	a	ā	i	ī	u	ū	r̥	e	ē	ai	o	ō	au
k	ക	കാ	കി	കീ	കു	കൂ	കൃ	കെ	കേ	കൈ	കൊ	കോ	കൌ
kh	ഖ	ഖാ	ഖി	ഖീ	ഖു	ഖൂ	ഖൃ	ഖെ	ഖേ	ഖൈ	ഖൊ	ഖോ	ഖൌ
g	ഗ	ഗാ	ഗി	ഗീ	ഗു	ഗൂ	ഗൃ	ഗെ	ഗേ	ഗൈ	ഗൊ	ഗോ	ഗൌ
gh	ഘ	ഘാ	ഘി	ഘീ	ഘു	ഘൂ	ഘൃ	ഘെ	ഘേ	ഘൈ	ഘൊ	ഘോ	ഘൌ
c	ച	ചാ	ചി	ചീ	ചു	ചൂ	ചൃ	ചെ	ചേ	ചൈ	ചൊ	ചോ	ചൌ
ch	ഛ	ഛാ	ഛി	ഛീ	ഛു	ഛൂ	ഛൃ	ഛെ	ഛേ	ഛൈ	ഛൊ	ഛോ	ഛൌ
j	ജ	ജാ	ജി	ജീ	ജു	ജൂ	ജൃ	ജെ	ജേ	ജൈ	ജൊ	ജോ	ജൌ
jh	ഝ	ഝാ	ഝി	ഝീ	ഝു	ഝൂ	ഝൃ	ഝെ	ഝേ	ഝൈ	ഝൊ	ഝോ	ഝൌ
ṭ	ട	ടാ	ടി	ടീ	ടു	ടൂ	ടൃ	ടെ	ടേ	ടൈ	ടൊ	ടോ	ടൌ
ṭh	ഠ	ഠാ	ഠി	ഠീ	ഠു	ഠൂ	ഠൃ	ഠെ	ഠേ	ഠൈ	ഠൊ	ഠോ	ഠൌ
ḍ	ഡ	ഡാ	ഡി	ഡീ	ഡു	ഡൂ	ഡൃ	ഡെ	ഡേ	ഡൈ	ഡൊ	ഡോ	ഡൌ
ḍh	ഢ	ഢാ	ഢി	ഢീ	ഢു	ഢൂ	ഢൃ	ഢെ	ഢേ	ഢൈ	ഢൊ	ഢോ	ഢൌ
ṇ	ണ	ണാ	ണി	ണീ	ണു	ണൂ	ണൃ	ണെ	ണേ	ണൈ	ണൊ	ണോ	ണൌ
t	ത	താ	തി	തീ	തു	തൂ	തൃ	തെ	തേ	തൈ	തൊ	തോ	തൌ
th	ഥ	ഥാ	ഥി	ഥീ	ഥു	ഥൂ	ഥൃ	ഥെ	ഥേ	ഥൈ	ഥൊ	ഥോ	ഥൌ
d	ദ	ദാ	ദി	ദീ	ദു	ദൂ	ദൃ	ദെ	ദേ	ദൈ	ദൊ	ദോ	ദൌ
dh	ധ	ധാ	ധി	ധീ	ധു	ധൂ	ധൃ	ധെ	ധേ	ധൈ	ധൊ	ധോ	ധൌ
n	ന	നാ	നി	നീ	നു	നൂ	നൃ	നെ	നേ	നൈ	നൊ	നോ	നൌ
p	പ	പാ	പി	പീ	പു	പൂ	പൃ	പെ	പേ	പൈ	പൊ	പോ	പൌ
ph	ഫ	ഫാ	ഫി	ഫീ	ഫു	ഫൂ	ഫൃ	ഫെ	ഫേ	ഫൈ	ഫൊ	ഫോ	ഫൌ
b	ബ	ബാ	ബി	ബീ	ബു	ബൂ	ബൃ	ബെ	ബേ	ബൈ	ബൊ	ബോ	ബൌ
bh	ഭ	ഭാ	ഭി	ഭീ	ഭു	ഭൂ	ഭൃ	ഭെ	ഭേ	ഭൈ	ഭൊ	ഭോ	ഭൌ
m	മ	മാ	മി	മീ	മു	മൂ	മൃ	മെ	മേ	മൈ	മൊ	മോ	മൌ
y	യ	യാ	യി	യീ	യു	യൂ	യൃ	യെ	യേ	യൈ	യൊ	യോ	യൌ
r	ര	രാ	രി	രീ	രു	രൂ		രെ	രേ	രൈ	രൊ	രോ	രൌ
l	ല	ലാ	ലി	ലീ	ലു	ലൂ	ലൃ	ലെ	ലേ	ലൈ	ലൊ	ലോ	ലൌ
v	വ	വാ	വി	വീ	വു	വൂ	വൃ	വെ	വേ	വൈ	വൊ	വോ	വൌ
ś	ശ	ശാ	ശി	ശീ	ശു	ശൂ	ശൃ	ശെ	ശേ	ശൈ	ശൊ	ശോ	ശൌ
ṣ	ഷ	ഷാ	ഷി	ഷീ	ഷു	ഷൂ	ഷൃ	ഷെ	ഷേ	ഷൈ	ഷൊ	ഷോ	ഷൌ
s	സ	സാ	സി	സീ	സു	സൂ	സൃ	സെ	സേ	സൈ	സൊ	സോ	സൌ
h	ഹ	ഹാ	ഹി	ഹീ	ഹു	ഹൂ	ഹൃ	ഹെ	ഹേ	ഹൈ	ഹൊ	ഹോ	ഹൌ
ḷ	ള	ളാ	ളി	ളീ	ളു	ളൂ		ളെ	ളേ	ളൈ	ളൊ	ളോ	ളൌ
ẓ	ഴ	ഴാ	ഴി	ഴീ	ഴു	ഴൂ		ഴെ	ഴേ	ഴൈ	ഴൊ	ഴോ	ഴൌ
ṟ	റ	റാ	റി	റീ	റു	റൂ		റെ	റേ	റൈ	റൊ	റോ	റൌ

Table 3.5. *Combination of primary consonants with secondary consonants for Telugu, Kannaḍa and Malayāḷam*

Telugu		Kannaḍa		Malayāḷam	
క k	క్క kk, ట్క ṭk, స్క sk	ಕ k	ಕ್ಕ kk, ತ್ಕ tk, ಸ್ಕ sk	ക k	ക്ക kk, ങ്ക ṅk, ല്ക lk, സ്ക sk
ఖ kh	క్ఖ kkh, స్ఖ skh	ಖ kh	ಕ್ಖ kkh, ಸ್ಖ skh	ഗ g	ഗ്ഗ gg
గ g	గ్గ gg, డ్గ ḍg	ಗ g	ಗ್ಗ gg, ಡ್ಗ ḍg	ങ ṅ	ങ്ങ ṅṅ
ఘ gh	ద్ఘ dgh	ಘ gh	ದ್ಘ dgh	ച c	ച്ച cc, ഞ്ച ñc, ശ്ച śc
చ c	క్చ kc, చ్చ cc, శ్చ śc	ಚ c	ಕ್ಚ kc, ಚ್ಚ cc, ಶ್ಚ śc	ഛ ch	ച്ഛ cch
ఛ ch	క్ఛ kch, చ్ఛ cch	ಛ ch	ಕ್ಛ kch, ಚ್ಛ cch	ജ j	ജ്ജ jj
జ j	జ్జ jj	ಜ j	ಜ್ಜ jj	ഝ jh	ജ്ഝ jjh
ఞ ñ	జ్ఞ jñ	ಞ ñ	ಜ್ಞ jñ	ഞ ñ	ഞ്ഞ ññ
ట ṭ	ట్ట ṭṭ, ష్ట ṣṭ	ಟ ṭ	ಟ್ಟ ṭṭ, ಷ್ಟ ṣṭ	ട ṭ	ട്ട ṭṭ, ണ്ട ṇṭ, ഷ്ട ṣṭ
ఠ ṭh	ష్ఠ ṣṭh	ಠ ṭh	ಷ್ಠ ṣṭh	ഡ ḍ	ഡ്ഡ ḍḍ
డ ḍ	డ్డ ḍḍ	ಡ ḍ	ಡ್ಡ ḍḍ	ണ ṇ	ട്ണ ṭṇ, ണ്ണ ṇṇ
ఢ ḍh	డ్ఢ ḍḍh	ಢ ḍh	ಡ್ಢ ḍḍh	ത t	ക്ത kt, ത്ത tt, ന്ത nt, സ്ത st
ణ ṇ	ట్ణ ṭṇ, ణ్ణ ṇṇ	ಣ ṇ	ಟ್ಣ ṭṇ, ಣ್ಣ ṇṇ	ഥ th	ത്ഥ tth, സ്ഥ sth
త t	క్త kt, త్త tt, స్త st	ತ t	ಕ್ತ kt, ತ್ತ tt, ಸ್ತ st	ദ d	ദ്ദ dd
థ th	త్థ tth, స్థ sth	ಥ th	ತ್ಥ tth, ಸ್ಥ sth	ധ dh	ദ്ധ ddh
ద d	ద్ద dd	ದ d	ದ್ದ dd	ന n	ഘ്ന ghn, ന്ന nn
ధ dh	బ్ధ bdh	ಧ dh	ಬ್ಧ bdh	പ p	പ്പ pp, മ്പ mp, ഷ്പ ṣp, സ്പ sp
న n	క్న kn, ఘ్న ghn, త్న tn, న్న nn, స్న sn	ನ n	ಕ್ನ kn, ಘ್ನ ghn, ತ್ನ tn, ನ್ನ nn, ಸ್ನ sn	ബ b	ബ്ബ bb
ప p	ప్ప pp, ల్ప lp, ష్ప ṣp	ಪ p	ಪ್ಪ pp, ಲ್ಪ lp, ಷ್ಪ ṣp	മ m	മ്മ mm, ശ്മ śm, ഷ്മ ṣm, സ്മ sm
ఫ ph	ష్ఫ ṣph	ಫ ph	ಸ್ಫ sph	യ y	ക്യ ky, ഖ്യ khy, ഭ്യ bhy, യ്യ yy
బ b	బ్బ bb	ಬ b	ಬ್ಬ bb	ര r	ക്ര kr, ഗ്ര gr, മ്ര mr
భ bh	ద్భ dbh	ಭ bh	ದ್ಭ dbh	ല l	ക്ല kl, പ്ല pl, ല്ല ll
మ m	క్మ km, గ్మ gm, మ్మ mm, స్మ sm	ಮ m	ಕ್ಮ km, ಗ್ಮ gm, ಮ್ಮ mm, ಸ್ಮ sm	വ v	ക്വ kv, ല്വ lv, വ്വ vv
య y	క్య ky, ఖ్య khy, భ్య bhy, య్య yy	ಯ y	ಕ್ಯ ky, ಖ್ಯ khy, ಭ್ಯ bhy, ಯ್ಯ yy, ಳ್ಯ ḷy	ശ ś	ശ്ശ śś
ర r	క్ర kr, గ్ర gr, ప్ర pr, మ్ర mr	ರ r	ಕ್ರ kr, ಗ್ರ gr, ಪ್ರ pr, ಮ್ರ mr	ഷ ṣ	ക്ഷ kṣ
ల l	క్ల kl, ప్ల pl, మ్ల ml, ల్ల ll	ಲ l	ಕ್ಲ kl, ಪ್ಲ pl, ಮ್ಲ ml, ಲ್ಲ ll	സ s	പ്സ ps, സ്സ ss
వ v	క్వ kv, ల్వ lv, వ్వ vv	ವ v	ಕ್ವ kv, ಲ್ವ lv, ವ್ವ vv	ള ḷ	ള്ള ḷḷ
శ ś	శ్శ śś	ಶ ś	ಶ್ಶ śś	റ ṟ	റ്റ ṟṟ
ష ṣ	క్ష kṣ, ష్ష ṣṣ	ಷ ṣ	ಕ್ಷ kṣ, ಷ್ಷ ṣṣ		
స s	త్స ts, స్స ss	ಸ s	ತ್ಸ ts, ಸ್ಸ ss		
		ಳ ḷ	ಳ್ಳ ḷḷ		

4

Phonology: historical and comparative

4.1 The phonemes of Proto-Dravidian

Proto-Dravidian (PD) had ten vowels (five short with a co-vowel of length, or five short and five long) and seventeen consonants (Krishnamurti 1961: §4.3) (see tables 4.1 and 4.2).

The low vowels pattern with the ones marked [+Back]; they can be called either central or back in phonetic terms. They carry the features [+Back, −Rounded, +Low]. /a ā/ do not cause palatalization of a velar or a dental found in several of the Dravidian languages. Only unrounded vowels occur after word-initial /w/ and this provides a grouping of low and front vowels together. There are no diphthongs in Dravidian. Traditional grammars treat *ai au* as diphthongs but they can be treated as sequences of *a* + glide *y/w*. There are sequences of *iy uy ey oy* and *iw uw ew ow* which are not treated as diphthongs in traditional records, but are treated as (C)VC. By also writing *ai au* as *ay aw*, we would be normalizing the writing system and bringing about phonological symmetry for Proto-Dravidian. Roots of (C)V*y* type, e.g. **kay* 'hand', **koy* 'to cut', pattern with (C)VC-type where the final segment is a sonorant, e.g. **man* 'live', **cal* 'go'. Not much is known about the phonetics of the Proto-Dravidian vowels beyond what is already indicated in the table.

4.2 Phonotactics

A Proto-Dravidian root is monosyllabic and is either open or closed; open: V_1, CV_1, $\bar{V}_1$, $C_1\bar{V}_1$; closed: V_1C_2, $C_1V_1C_2$, $\bar{V}_1C_2$, $C_1\bar{V}_1C_2$. All these eight canonical forms can be captured in the formula $(C_1)\,\breve{\bar{V}}_1(C_2)$ in which the elements in brackets have optional occurrence; the vowel may be long or short. Extended stems are formed by the addition of formative suffixes of the type -C (V), -CC (V) or -CCC (V) to open syllable roots without any change. Closed syllable roots take a vowel (V_2), i.e. /i u a/, as the first layer of formative suffixes; V_2 may be followed by -C -CC, or -CCC. C = an obstruent P (one of the stops) or a sonorant L (nasal, lateral, flap/approximant, a glide). CC = PP, NP (N = nasal), CCC = NPP. If the stem ends in a stop, it is followed by a non-morphemic or enunciative vowel /u/. Roots of (C)VC- and (C)VCC- contrast when followed by

Table 4.1. *Proto-Dravidian vowels*

	−Back		+Back
High	i ī		u ū
Mid	e ē		o ō
Low		a ā	

Table 4.2. *Proto-Dravidian consonants*[1]

	Labial	Dental	Alveolar	Retroflex	Palatal	Velar	Glottal
Stops	p	t	ṯ	ṭ	c	k	
Nasals	m	n		ṇ	ñ		
Laterals			l	ḷ			
Flap/Approximant			r	ẓ			
Glides	w				y		H

formatives or derivative suffixes beginning with vowels. It is not clear if the difference between root-final C and CC is determined by the nature of the derivative suffix that follows. When roots in final obstruents are free forms, the final consonant is geminated followed by a non-morphemic (enunciative) *u*. When roots of the type (C)V̄C- or (C) VCC- are followed by a formative vowel, V_2 = /i u a/, they merge with (C)VC-.[2]

1 I proposed earlier the following feature matrix to define the consonantal phonemes of Proto-Dravidian (Krishnamurti 1978a:2, fn.2). I have now added to the list the features of the laryngeal *H*. In terms of these, most sound changes in Dravidian can be shown to require changes in one or two features only.

	p	t	ṯ	ṭ	c	k	m	n	ṇ	ñ	l	ḷ	r	ẓ	w	y	H
syllabic	−	−	−	−	−	−	−	−	−	−	−	−	−	−	−	−	−
consonantal	+	+	+	+	+	+	+	+	+	+	+	+	+	+	−	−	−
sonorant	−	−	−	−	−	−	+	+	+	+	+	+	+	+	+	+	−
continuant	−	−	−	−	−	−	−	−	−	−	+	+	+	+	+	+	+
anterior	+	+	+	−	−	−	+	+	−	−	+	−	+	−	+	−	−
coronal	−	+	+	+	+	−	−	+	+	+	+	+	+	+			
apical		−	+	+	−			−	+	−	+	+	+	+			
nasal							+	+	+	+	−	−	−	−			
lateral											+	+	−	−			

2 Subrahmanyam (1983: 22) proposes superheavy syllables such as **kākk-ay* 'crow' [1425], **tāṇṭu* 'to dance, jump over' [3158], and **pāmpu* 'snake' [4085] also as roots of Proto-Dravidian. This is not justified in terms of the overall pattern of root structure in Dravidian; *kā-kk-ay* has a root **kā-* (onomatopoetic) with *-kk-ay* as formative suffixes, cf. Go. *kā-w-āl*, Kui, Kuvi *kāwa*, Pe. *kāv*; similarly,**tāṇ-ṭu*/**tā-ḷ-nt-* cf. Ta. Ma. *tā-vu* 'to jump, leap', Ka. *tā-gu* [3177], *pā-mpu* presumably from *pāy* 'to spring, attack' [4087]. Our inability to find immediate sources within Dravidian does not necessarily make the above roots.

Root	Formative		
# $(C_1)\breve{\bar{V}}_1$		Ø	(u)#
# $(C_1)V_1C_2$	V_2	L P PP NP NPP	u#
# $(C_1)\breve{\bar{V}}_1N$		P PP	

C_1 = any consonant other than a member of the alveolar and retroflex series /ṯ l r ṭ ṇ ḷ ẓ/;
V_1 = any vowel, short or long;
C_2 = any consonant (except *ñ);
V_2 = *a i u* (rarely long);
L = a sonorant, i.e. any consonant other than a stop (L includes N);
P = any obstruent (includes **c* which was probably an alveolo-palatal affricate in Proto-Dravidian);
N = nasal homorganic with the following stop.

Figure 4.1 Structure of Proto-Dravidian roots and stems

A root can be a free form (word) without a formative, i.e. with a zero formative, e.g. PD **kal* 'stone' [1298], **ān* 'cow' [334], **pū* 'flower' [4345]; or it may take the first layer of formative suffixes V_2, *i a u*, e.g. **keṭ-u* 'to perish' (also imperative sg) [1942] and still be a free form; extended stems are such as **tir-a-ḷ*, **tir-u-ku*, **tir-u-ntu*, **tir-u-mpu*, **tir-u-mppu* etc. all with an underlying root *tir-* 'to turn, revolve' [3246, 3244, 3245, 3251]. The *NPP sequence is not preserved in any descendant language as such. Some languages developed it to NP contrasting with NB (< *NP), and others to PP, e.g. **eṇ-ṭṭu* 'eight' > Ta. *eṭṭu*, Ka. *eṇṭu* [784]. The other three-consonant clusters may include a liquid/approximant/glide + NP or PP. The syllable structure of Proto-Dravidian is preserved intact in Old Tamil and Malayāḷam. Figure 4.1 captures the structure of Proto-Dravidian roots and stems with formative suffixes. No meaning can be assigned to the formative suffixes. It will be shown later that these represented tense and voice markers at an early stage of Proto-Dravidian and were already losing that significance within Proto-Dravidian in different subgroups (Krishnamurti 1997a). The last row in figure 4.1 represents stems ending in a nasal followed by P or PP.

Alveolar and retroflex consonants do not begin a word in Proto-Dravidian. Any consonant may occur root-finally. Word-initial **y-* and **ñ-* are followed generally by *a*/*e* and *ā*/*ē* representing neutralization of the two qualities (an archi-phoneme **ă*/**ĕ* in Prague School parlance), and rarely by *i* and *o*. Initial **w* is not followed by rounded vowels. There are no consonant clusters word-initially. Single and double consonants contrast in non-initial position with the exception of *r and *ẓ which occur only singly. Proto-Dravidian *n had two allophones: a dental [n] word-initially and before dental stops, [ṉ] alveolar elsewhere. This distribution is preserved in Classical Tamil and Old and Modern Malayāḷam. Proto-Dravidian *n is put in the dental column and not in the alveolar one, because words may begin with *n*- and not with any member of the alveolar series. The stops had lenis allophones between vowels, i.e. [w d ḏ/ṟ ḍ s g]; after a homorganic nasal, all stops were voiced [b d ḏ ḍ j g]. Initially and in gemination all stops were voiceless. All sonorants occur as root/stem-final segments. When an obstruent occurs in the final position of a root or an extended stem, a non-morphemic -*u* occurs at the end; the final obstruent following a radical short vowel is geminated, when the root occurs as a free form, e.g. **kaṭ* = *kaṭṭu* 'to tie', n. 'a tie', Laryngeal /H/ had a restricted distribution within Proto-Dravidian in which it occurred non-initially (i.e. within a root and/or in its final position). It also occurred in certain formative and inflectional morphs. It survives as [ḥ] only in a few lexical items in Ancient Tamil (see section 4.5.7.2.3; Krishnamurti 1997b).

Voicing was not phonemic in Proto-Dravidian. This system is still preserved by Old Tamil and Malayāḷam in so far as the native element is concerned. Toda also has no initial voiced stops. Voicing became distinctive in almost all other languages through internal changes and borrowing from Indo-Aryan. Middle and Modern Tamil have also developed distinctive voicing in loanwords. Some languages also developed aspiration in both voiceless and voiced series.

In the following sections, major sound changes have been given in the form of serially numbered rules followed by serially numbered etymologies with *DEDR* entry number indicated at the end of each group in square brackets. Within each etymology the languages are listed in the genetic order adopted in this book within each subgroup from south to north, namely South Dravidian I, South Dravidian II, Central Dravidian and North Dravidian. One can therefore notice justification of the subgrouping wherever shared innovations are involved.

4.3 Proto-Dravidian morphophonemics

In external sandhi the word-final enunciative vowel is lost before a word beginning with a vowel. This is certainly true of the literary languages and some non-literary languages in South and South Central Dravidian. But internal sandhi is partly reconstructible to a stage preceding Proto-Dravidian, maybe to a stage when Proto-Dravidian already had dialect variation before it split into subgroups. A study of etymologies from languages cutting across genetic subgroups shows stem alternations that recur in derivation and inflection requiring their reconstruction in Proto-Dravidian. Such reconstructions are reflected in the verb-inflection of Old Tamil with reflexes in other subgroups (for sandhi in Old Tamil, see Rajam 1992: 103–9).

4.3.1 ***Apical obstruent formation (+ stands for a morph boundary)***

(a) l + t → ṯ
l + tt → ṯṯ
l + nt → nṯ
l + ntt → nṯṯ
(b) n + t → nṯ
n + tt → nṯṯ
(c) ḷ + t → ṭ
ḷ + tt → ṭṭ
ḷ + nt → ṇṭ
ḷ + ntt → ṇṭṭ
(d) ṇ + t → ṇṭ
ṇ + tt → ṇṭṭ

(b) and (d) are cases of progressive assimilation and (a) and (c) are cases of reciprocal feature assimilation, producing alveolar and retroflex consonants secondarily. There are, however, many more lexical items in which alveolar and retroflex obstruents are primary. The following alternations are attested and distributed widely in different subgroups:

Rule 1a. *Alternations in root-final consonants* {l, n}: ṯ: ṯṯ: nṯ

(1) PD **nil-* (past *ninṯ-*, *niṯṯ-*, *nil-tt-*) 'to stand'. SD I: Ta. *nil-* (*ninṟ-*), Ma. *nil* (*ninn-*), Ko. *nil-/nin-* (*ninḏ-*), To. *nil-* (*niḏ-*), Kod. *nil-* (*nind-*), Ka. *nil-* (*nind-*); SD II: **nil* (past *niṯṯ-*), Go. *nil-* (*nitt-*), Koṇḍa *nil-* (*niR-*);
PD **nil-* (past *nil-tt-*); SD I: Ka. *nil* (*nilt-*); CD: Pa. Oll. Gad. *nil-* (*nilt-*), Kol. Nk. *nil-* (*nilt-*); (SD II): Pe. *nil* (*nilt-*), Manḍa *li-* (*lit-*); ND *il-* (*il-c-*).
PD **niṯ-*(<**nil-t-*). SD I: Ta. Ma. *niṟu* 'to put, place';
PD **niṯṯ-*. SD II: Go. *nitt-/nit-* 'to stand', Kui *nisa* (*nisi*); CD: Pa. *nit-* (*nit-it-*) [3675].

Another such case is **kal* (*kaṯṯ-*) beside **kaṯ-*'to learn', the former in South Dravidian I and the latter in South Dravidian II and Central Dravidian [1297]. Note that in the above cases, **niṯ*, **niṯṯ-* and **kaṯ-* are represented as bases within Proto-Dravidian, perhaps restructured with the past suffix incorporated as a derivative at a later stage, still within Proto-Dravidian. Such alternations are also noticed in non-verbs, e.g. PD **kil*/ **kiṯ*-V 'small' with cognates in South Dravidian I and South Dravidian II [1577, 1594].

(2) PSD **kil-* (*kinṯ-*) 'to be able'. SD I: Ta. *kil-* (*kiṟp-*, *kiṟṟ-*) 'to be able', *kiṟ-pu* 'strength', *kiṟṟal* (< **kil-tt-al*) 'being able to do', Ma. *kelpu* 'strength', To. *kïs̱-*(*kïḏ-*) 'to be able'; Toda past presupposes **kin-ṯ-* [1570].

Tamil present-tense suffix *-kiṟ-/-kinṟ-* is traced to this root (Steever 1994: 172–8).

(3) PD **el, *en-ṯu* 'sunshine, sun'. SD I: Ta. *el* 'lustre, splendour, sun, day time', *eṟ-i* (< **el + t + i*) 'to shine, glitter', Ma. *el* 'lustre', Ma. *eṟikka* 'to shine' [829, 861], Ta. *eṉṟu* 'sun', To. *eṟ* 'sun'; SD II: Te. *eṇḍa* 'sunshine', *eṇḍu* 'to dry in sun', Go. *eddi, addi* 'sunshine'; CD: Nk. *edde*, Pa. *nendi, nenḍi* [869].

(4) a. PD **niṯ-V-* 'to be full'. SD I: Ta. *niṟ-ai* (*-v-, -nt-*) 'to become full', Ma. *niṟay-uka*, Ko. *nerv-* (*nerd-*), To. *neṟ-* (*neṟ-θ-*), *nere-* (*nerv-, nerend-*), Ka. *neṟ-e* (*neṟe-d-*), Tu. *nerevuni* 'be full'; SD II: Te. *neṟayu* v.i.

b. PD **nin-ṯ-* v.i., *nin- ṯṯ-* v.t. 'to be full'. SD I: Tu. *diñj-uni* 'to be full', Koraga *jiñji*; SD II: Te. *niṇḍu* 'be full', *nincu, nimpu* v.t., Go. *nind-* v.i., *niht-, nih-* (< **ni-ṯṯ-* with loss of nasal) v.t., Koṇḍa *ninṟi-* v.i., *niR-* v.t., Kui-Kuvi *nenj-* v.i., *nes-/neh-* v.t., Pengo *nenj-* v.i., *nec-* v.t., Maṇḍa *neh-* v.t.; ND: Kuṛ. *nind-* v.i. 'to be spread over', Malt. *nind-* [3682].

(5) PD **aHn-* (>**ayn-*>**eyn-* >**iyn-*) 'to say'. SD I: **en/*in/*an* (with *y*-loss and *e > i*): Ta. *eṉ-* (*eṉṟ-*), Ma. *ennuka*, Ko. *in-* (*iḏ-*), To. *ïn-* (*ïḏ-*), Koḍ. *enn-* (*end-*), Ka. *en-, an-*, Tu. *anpini, inpini*; SD II: **an/ *in* (*an-ṯṯ-/in-ṯṯ-*): Te. *an-* (*aṇ-ṭ-*), Go. *ind-, in-* (*itt-, it-*), Koṇḍa *in-* (*iR-*), Kui *in-* (*is-*), Kuvi *in-* (*icc-*), Pe., Maṇḍa *in-* (*ic-*); the past stem for South-Central Dravidian (South Dravidian II) was *an-ṯṯ-, in-ṯṯ-* with nasal loss in Go. Koṇḍa, Kui, Kuvi, and Pe.–Maṇḍa; ND: *ān* (<**aHn-*): Kuṛ.–Malt. *ān-* [868].

For the reconstruction of a laryngeal **H* see Krishnamurti (1997b).

Rule 1b. *Alternations in root-final consonants* {ḷ, ṇ}: ṭ: ṭṭ: ṇṭ

(6) PD **koḷ* (*koṇṭ- < koḷ-nt-*) 'to receive, seize, buy'. SD I: Ta. Ma. *koḷ* (*koṇṭ-*), Ko. *koḷ-/koṇ-* (*koḍ-*), To. *kwïḷ-* (*kwïḍ-*), Kod. *koḷḷ-* (*koṇḍ-*), Ka. *koḷḷ-* (*koṇḍ-*), Tu. *koṇ-* (*koṇḍ-*); SD II (past **koḷ-ntt-*):Te. *koṇ-* (*koṇṭ-*), tr. *kolupu*, Koṇḍa *koṛ-/koḷ-* (*koṇ-, koṭ-*), Kui *koḍa* (*koḍi*), Kuvi *koḍ-* (*koḍ- it-*), Pe. *koṛ-* (*koṛ-t-*), Maṇḍa *kṛag-* (*kṛakt-*); CD: Kol. Nk. *kor-/ko-(kott-)* [2151].

Similarly, PD **kaḷ-* (*kaṭṭ-*) 'to steal', cf. Tu. *kaṇḍ-uni* [1372]; **kēḷ-* (*kēṭṭ-, kēṇṭṭ-*) 'to hear, ask', Tu. *kēṇuni*, Go. *kēnj-* [2017a];**wēḷ* (*wēṇṭ-, wēṇṭṭ-*; from ***weH-ḷ-*) 'to desire, want' [5528]; **kāṇ-* (*kaṇṭ-*) 'to see', **kāṇ-ṭṭu* (*-ṭṭu* caus. marker) 'to show', ultimately from ***kaHṇ-* [1443] widely represented in different subgroups with long and short vowels.

4.3.2 *Alternations in syllable length or weight*

Proto-Dravidian syllables are heavy (H) or light (L). Heavy syllables have a long vowel (C)$\bar{V}$ or a short vowel followed by a consonant (C)VC-. A light syllable has a short V as in (C)V. A heavy syllable is equivalent to two light syllables, i.e. (C)$\bar{V}$ = (C)VCV. Both these types can be followed by a sonorant consonant in which case they maintain the same weight, e.g. Ta. *pē-r* (H+ Margin *r*) 'name' from older *pe-ya-r* (LL+ Margin *r*) 'name'. When these change to vowel-final stems a new light syllable is created with *r* as onset, Ta. *pē- rï*. When an obstruent or a cluster ending in an obstruent follows, an enunciative vowel is added constituting a new syllable, e.g. **pe.ru.ku* (LLL) 'to grow', **i.raṇ.ṭu* (LHL) 'two'.

4.3.2.1 *Syllable contraction*

Contraction of two syllables into one, i.e. $(C_1)V_1C_2V_2$ to $(C_1)\bar{V}_1$ (where C_2 is **y*, **w* or **k*) is reconstructible within Proto-Dravidian, although it continues as a change in subgroups and languages in later periods also (Krishnamurti 1955), e.g.

Rule 2. *Syllable contraction*

$(C_1)V_1$ {*y, w, k*}-V_2- > (C_1) V_1 [+long]

(7) PD **tiy-am* > **tī-m* 'honey'; PSD **tey-am* > *tē-m*. SD I: Ta. Ma. *tēn*, Ko. *tēn*, To. *tēn*, Kod. *tēni*, Ka. *tēnu*, *jēn*. Tu. *tīya*; SD II: Te. *tēne*, Go. Koṇḍa *tēne*; CD **tiy-am* > *tī-m*, Pa., Oll., Gad. *tīn* (Kol. Nk. borrowed *tēne* from Telugu); ND **tiyam* > *tīn*, Kuṛ. *tīn-ī* 'bee', Malt. *tēni* 'honey, bee' [3268b].

(8) PD **kic-ampu* > **kiy-ampu* > PSD **key-ampu* < **kec-ampu*; SD I: Ta. *cēmpu*, *cēmpai Colocasia indica*, 'yam', Ma. *cēmpu*, *cēmpa*, Ka. *kesavu*; SD II: Te. *cēma*; PD > CD: Pa. *kībi*, Gad. *kiyub*; ND: Kuṛ. *kisgō*. Note that Central Dravidian and North Dravidian have *i*/*ī* and not *ē* as expected [2004].

Other such cases are **tok-al* > **tōl* 'skin, peel' in South Dravidian I and South Dravidian II [3559], **mic-al*/**miy-al* >**mē-l* 'above, high', which occurs in all subgroups [4841, 5086]. The contraction rule originated in Proto-Dravidian and continues into subgroups and individual languages to date. Only comparative evidence will help in identifying the relative chronology of the change.

4.3.2.2 *Alternations between long and short vowels*

All Dravidian languages carry evidence of alternation between heavy and light root syllables, when a 'formative' vowel follows as V_2, or when a monosyllabic root becomes disyllabic:

$(C)\bar{V}_1C$: $(C)V_1C$-V_2-

$(C)V_1CC$-: (C) V_1C-V_2-

Contrasting with the above, there are non-alternating pairs like

$(C)V_1C$-: (C) V_1C-V_2-

Therefore, in the neutralizing environment, i.e. -V_2, a heavy syllable is said to have merged with a light syllable, by internal reconstruction within Proto-Dravidian.

Rule 3. *Quantitative variation*

$$\text{(C)}\bar{V}_1\text{C-/(C) }V_1\text{CC-} \rightarrow \text{(C) }V_1\text{C-/\#\_\_+}V_2\text{-}$$

(9) PD **pāṯ-*: **paṯ-V-* ‘to run, flee’. SD I: Ta. Ma. *pāṟu, paṟ-a*, Ko. *parn-*, To. *pōṟ-*, Koḍ. *pār*, Ka. *pāṟu, paṟi*, Tu. *pāruni*; SD II: Te. *pāṟu, paṟacu*, Go. *parī-*, Kui *pāsk-*, Kuvi *prāḍ-* [4020].

(10) PD **cup*: **cuw-ar* (<**cup-ar*) ‘salt’. SD I: **up*:**owar* > Ta. Ma. Ka. Tu. (Te. *uppu*) Ko. To. *up*, Kod. *uppï*; also Ta. *uvar* ‘to taste salty, brackish’; n. ‘brackishness, saltiness’, Ma. *uvar*, n., Ka. *ogar*, Tu. *ubarï, ogarï* ‘brackishness’; SD II: Te. *ogaru* ‘astringent taste’, perhaps a loanword from Ka.; **cow-ar* > Go. *sovar, sawwor* (with vowel metathesis), *hovar, ovar* (dial), Koṇḍa *sōru*, Kui *sāru*, Kuvi *hāru*, Pe. *hōr*, Manḍa *jār*; CD: Kol. Nk. *sup*, Pa. *cup*, Oll. *sup*, Gad. *cuppu* [2674a,b].

Although these rules work extensively in verbs (Krishnamurti 1955), they apply to the other form classes also, being phonological in origin and not grammatical, e.g. **īr*: **ir-u* ‘two’, **pēr-*: **per-u* adj. ‘big’.

G. Sambasiva Rao (1973, 1977) suggested that Rule 3 operated systematically if the underlying and derived forms belonged to the same grammatical class, e.g. both verbs, or both nouns, etc. Where a verb is derived from a noun or vice versa, the rule did not operate (for further details, see Subrahmanyam 1983: 182–6). V_2 added to consonant-ending roots is called here a formative and not a derivative suffix. It apparently had an epenthetic role of splitting clusters without affecting the syllable weight as in the case of **muẓ-u-nk* v.i., **muẓ-u-nkk* v.t. ‘to sink, drown’ [4993] as opposed to **mūẓ-nk/-nkk*. I would call the three vowels *i u a* (V_2) phonological facilitators. Therefore, the input and output forms belong to the same form class. They do not naturally behave like noun-forming suffixes such as *-am* in Ta. *kār* ‘to be pungent’: *kār-am* ‘pungency’ (the verb occurs only in Tamil and could be even a back-formation from an original noun). A counter-example to Sambasiva Rao’s claim is Ta. *kāṉ* ‘jungle’: *kāṉ-al, kāṉ-am* ‘forest, grove’ [1418] in which there is no length reduction, although the underlying and derived forms belong to the same grammatical category. The reason is that *-al* and *-am* here are denominal suffixes, which are added to nouns to derive other nouns and are historical within each of the literary languages. Similarly, Ta. *kaṭṭ- ai* ‘dam’, *kaṭṭ-aṇ-am* ‘building’, *kaṭṭ-aḷ-ai* ‘code, rule’ are derivable from *kaṭṭu* v. ‘to tie, build’, n. ‘tie, band’ [1147]. Here I would reconstruct the root as **kaṭ-*, and the final obstruent automatically gets geminated, with the non-morphemic *-u* added to it, if it occurs as a free form, or if it is followed by a word-forming suffix in derivation or compounding. Thus we obtain [kaṭṭu] ~ [kaṭṭ-]. Consequently most of the languages in this etymological group point to a reconstruction with **ṭṭ*. The geminate is not simplified in the above case, because (a) the root itself is a free form, or (b) a derivative suffix or suffixes are added which are clearly noun-forming morphs. Contrast this with:

(11) PD **kaṭ*-V 'be bitter, pungent': Ta. Ma. *kaṭu*, Koḍ. *kaḍïpa*, Ka. *kaḍu*, *kaṭṭa* 'intensity', *kaḍupu*, *kaḍime* 'intensity', Tu. *kaḍu* 'pungency', *kaḍuve* 'hero', Te. *kaḍu* 'much', *kaṭṭ-* bound adj in *kaṭṭ-aluka* 'peak of anger', Nk. *kaṛu* 'bitter', Kuṛ. *xaṛxā* 'bitter', Malt. *qaṛq-*, Br. *xarēn* 'bitter' [1135].

In this case, the reconstruction presupposes an intervocalic *ṭ*, as in **kaṭ*-V- because the stop is not geminated and the final *-u* is not an enunciative vowel. Only where it loses the formative V before a derivational suffix or a word beginning with a vowel does it get geminated; see the Telugu example. *DEDR* 2674 has both formative and derivative suffixes occurring after the reconstructed root PD **cup* 'salt': PSD **cup*: **cow-ar*/ **ow-ar*, SD I *up-*: *owar*, SD II **cowar*; CD **cup* (see (10) above). But notice the occurrence of geminate *pp* when true derivational suffixes follow, e.g. Ta. Ma. *uppu* 'salt', *upp-aḷ-am* 'salty soil', Ka. *uppu* 'salt', *upp-al-iga* 'a man of salt-maker caste', Koḍ. *uppï*, Tu. *uppu* 'salt', *upp-aḍa* 'salted fish', Te. *uppu* 'salt', *upp-ana* 'saltish', Pa. *cup*, Kol. Nk. Oll. Gad. *sup* [2674 a, b]. We reconstruct Proto-Dravidian **cup* and say that it assumes the form **cupp-* when it occurs as a free form or when it is followed by meaningful derivative suffixes. We can see in this case clearly that it is the nature of the suffixes added that would determine the length of the root-final obstruent. Another such case is PD **keṭ-u* 'to perish' in South Dravidian I and II and CD [1942]. The formatives, as opposed to derivative suffixes, belong to a deeper chronological layer within Proto-Dravidian. The criteria determining the alternations in syllable weight are prosodic and not morphological (for further discussion, see Krishnamurti 2001a: postscript to ch. 1).

Following the foregoing criteria, alternation between single or double obstruents in the root-final position could be widespread in the family, e.g. PD **kap-* ~ **kapp-* (all subgroups): **kaw*-V- 'to cover, overspread' (SD I, SD II) [1221], **waṯ* - ~ **waṯṯ*-: **waṯ*-V- 'to dry up': Ta. *vaṟṟ-am* 'dryness', *vaṟ-al* 'drying up', *vaṟṟu* 'to go dry', *vaṟ-a* 'to dry up'. South Dravidian has forms requiring single and double consonants in the root; South-Central Dravidian (South Dravidian II), Central Dravidian and North Dravidian show reflexes of **ṯṯ* in the root [5320]. Because of such cases, there is reason to posit contrast between single and double consonants in the medial position of words in Proto-Dravidian.

4.4 Historical phonology: vowels

In the following sections the history of the vowels and consonants of Proto-Dravidian is given in terms of the sound changes that they have undergone. The developments are given with only one or two examples for each, drawing cognates from the principal members of each subgroup. Cross-reference to the entry numbers in _DEDR_ is given in square brackets for those who want to look up full details. Shared innovations of whole subgroups are treated first, followed by changes confined to smaller subgroups or individual members of a given subgroup.

Generally long vowels are more stable than short vowels. Only the vowels in the root syllables are discussed in these sections, since the vowels in non-initial syllables are lost in most of the languages. The general rule is that vowels in the root syllables remain unchanged in most of the languages. There is no difference between word-initial and postconsonantal vowels in the radical syllables. PD *_y_-, *_ñ_-, *_c_- cause variation in the height of the following low and mid vowels *_a_/*_e_, *_ā_/*_ē_; labials *_p_, *_m_, *_w_ cause rounding of unrounded vowels sporadically in some of the languages. PD *_H_ lengthens the preceding vowel in free forms. PD *_y_- was preserved in ancient Tamil and sporadically in a few other languages like Tuḷu. Corresponding to Early Tamil _yā_- the other South Dravidian I languages have _ā_- (with loss of _y_-), South Dravidian II have _ē_/_ā_, Central Dravidian _ā_ and North Dravidian _ē_. There is reason to believe that Proto-Dravidian has neutralization of *_ā̆_ and *_ē̆_ after *_y_, resulting in a variation between these two qualities (Burrow 1946a, Krishnamurti 1961: § 1.216), e.g. PD *_yĀn_/ *_yᴀn_- 'I': SD I *_yān_/*_yan_-, SD II _ēn_/_ān_, CD *_ān_/*_an_-, ND *_ēn_/*_en_- [5160]. Word-initial PD *_c_ also occasionally causes *_ā_/*_ē_ alternation, *_cār_/*_cēr_ 'to go, reach' [2484] (Krishnamurti 1961:§ 1.240). PD *_ñ_- merges with _n_- in almost all the languages, except Old Tamil, Malayāḷam and, to some extent Koḍagu; the vowels following *_ñ_ alternate between *_ā̆_ and *_ē̆_ (Burrow 1946a). These developments will be treated under respective consonants.

Two major sound changes are treated below, following the illustrations of retention, namely (i) the merger of high vowels with mid vowels before formative -_a_ (V_2) in Proto-South Dravidian (SD I and II), (ii) contraction of root and formative vowels into long vowels following metathesis in the South-Central Dravidian (SD II) subgroup. Among individual languages that have change, Toda has the most complex set of changes, mainly caused by root vowels being harmonized to the following open or closed vowels (V_2) at the Pre-Toda stage with subsequent loss of the conditioning vowels. The consonants, which intervene between V_1 and V_2, are also significant. Root-initial bilabials cause rounding of unrounded vowels in Tuḷu and Koḍagu. The other Nilgiri languages (Toda, Iruḷa, Kuṟumba) have centralization of front vowels when followed by retroflex (and some alveolar) consonants which require a raised apex and retracted body of the tongue. The quality of the vowel, which follows in the formative syllable (V_2) also, plays a role. These allophonic changes became phonemic with the loss of conditioning environments. It is shown that these changes originated over two thousand years ago in Pre-Tamil itself and got concretized in the Nilgiri area. Kui–Kuvi of South-Central Dravidian, Parji of Central Dravidian and Brahui of North Dravidian have idiosyncratic changes, treated in appropriate sections.

4.4.1 *Examples for the retention of Proto-Dravidian vowels in radical syllables*

(12) PD **kaṇ* 'eye'. SD I: Ta. Ma. Ka. *kaṇ*, Ko. *kaṇ*, Koḍ. Tu. *kaṇṇï*; SD II: Te. *kan(n)u*, Go. *kan*, *kaṛ*, Koṇḍa *kaṇ*, Kui *kanu*, Kuvi *kannu*, Pe. *kaṇga*, Manḍa *kan*; CD: Kol. Nk. Pa. *kan*, Gad. *kanu*, Oll. *kaṇ*; ND: Kuṛ. *xan*, Malt. *qanu*, Br. *xan* [1159a].

(13) PD **pāl* 'milk'. SD I: Ta. Ma. Ka. Kota *pāl*, Koḍ. *pālï*, Tu. *pērï*; SD II: Te. *pālu*, Go. *pāl*, Koṇḍa *pāl(u)* 'milk, breast', Kui, Kuvi *pālu*, Pe. *pāl*; CD: Kol. Nk. Gad. *pāl*, Pa. *pēl* 'milk'; ND: Br. *pāl̲h̲*. Tuḷu **ā* > *ē* and **l* > *r* are irregular changes (Kekunnaya 1994: 58) [4096].

(14) PD **wil* 'bow'. SD I: Ta. Ma. *vil*, Koḍ. *billï*, Ka. *bil*, *billu*, Tu. *billï*, *biru*; SD II: Te. *willu* (pl *wiṇḍ-lu*), Go. Koṇḍa, Pe. Manḍa *vil*, Kui *vilu*, Kuvi *velu*; CD: Kol. Pa. *vil*, Gad. *vinḍu*, Oll. *vinḍ*; ND: Br. *bil* [5422].

(15) PD **piy* /**pī* 'excrement, faeces'. SD I: Ta. Ma. Ka. Ko. Tu. *pī*; SD II: Te. *pīyi/piyyi*, Go. *pīŋgu*, Koṇḍa *pīŋu*, Kui *piu* (pl *pīnga*), Kuvi *piŋa*, *piŋga*, Pe. Manḍa *pīŋ*; CD: Kol. *pīya* (lw < Te.), Pa. Oll. *pī*, Gad. *piyu*; ND: Kuṛ. *pīk*, Malt. *pīku*, Br. *pī* (note in some of the languages only the plural form occurs) [4210].

(16) PD **puṯ(ṯu)* 'anthill'. SD I: Ta. *puṟṟu*, Ka. *puttu*, *putta*, *huttu*, *hutta*, Koḍ. *puttï*; ?Tu. *puñca*, Koraga (dial) *huñca*, *huntu*; SD II: Te. *puṭṭa*, Go. *puttu*, *puttī*, Koṇḍa *puRi*, Kui *pusi*, *pucci*, Kuvi *puci*, *pucci*, Pe. *puci*; CD: Kol. Nk. *puṭṭa*, Pa. *putta*, *puṭṭa*, Oll. *puṭkal*. The Tuḷu and Koraga forms presuppose a reconstruction with a pre-consonantal nasal **pun-ṯṯ-*, but it is puzzling that no other language preserves the nasal [4335].

(17) PD **puy*/**pū* (< ***puH*) 'flower'; v. 'to blossom'. SD I: Ta. *pū* n. and v., Ma. *pū*, *pūvu* n., *pūkka* v., Ko. *pū* n., To. *pūf* n., Koḍ. *pū*, *pūvï*, Ka. *pū* n. and v., *pūvu*/*puvvu* n.,Tu. *pū*; SD II: Te. *pū*, *pūwu*/*puwwu* n., *pūc-* v., Go. *puŋgar* n., *pūy-*/*puy-* v., Koṇḍa *puyu*, n. *pū* v., Kui *pūju* n., *pū-* v., Kuvi *pūyu* n., Pe. Manḍa *puy* n.; CD: Kol. Nk. *pūta* n. Pa. Oll. *pū* n., *pūp-*/ *pūt-* v., Gad. *puvvu* n., *pūk-* (*pūt-*) v.; ND: *pūmp* n., *puyd-* v., Malt. *pūpu* n., *puth-* v. (Metaphorical extension of meaning to 'cataract' occurs in all subgroups and perhaps goes to the Proto-Dravidian stage. Variable length of the root vowel and the occurrence of glides *y* and *w* suggest an original laryngeal in the reconstruction as **puH-*) [4348].

(18) PD **kew-i* 'ear'. SD I: Ta. Ma. *cevi*, Ma. also *ceppi*, Ko. *kev*, Koḍ. *kevī*, Ka. *kivi* (< **kew-i*), Tu. *kebi*; SD II: Te. *cevi*, Go. *kevi*, *kavi*, Koṇḍa *gibi*, *kibi*, Pe. *kitul*, Manḍa *giy*; CD: Kol. Nk. *kev*, Pa. Oll. *kekol*, Gad. *kekkōl*; ND: Kuṛ. *xebdā*, Malt. *qethw-* [1977a].

(19) PD **tēḷ* 'scorpion'. SD I: Ta. Ma. *tēḷ*, Koḍ. *tēḷï*, Ka. *cēẓ(u)*, *tēẓ* (*ẓ* instead of *ḷ* could be a hyper-standard form after *ẓ* became *ḷ*), Tu. *tēḷï*, *cēḷï*, *tēlï*; SCD (SD II): Te. *tēlu*. ND: Malt. *tēle*, Br. *tēl̠h*. (No cognates from most of SD II and CD) [3470].

(20) PD *on-t̠u* (*-tu* neuter sg suffix) 'one'. SD I: Ta. *on̠r̠u* (> Mdn Ta. *oṇṇu*), Ma. *onnu*, Ko. *oḏ*, Koḍ. *ondï*, Ka. *ondu*, Tu. *oñji*; SD II: OTe. *oṇḍu*, Mdn Te. *oṇṭi* 'single, alone', Go. *undī*, *unḍī*, Koṇḍa *unr̠i*; ND: Kuṛ. *ōn*, *ōnd*, Malt. *-ond*, Br. *asi* [990 d].

(21) PD **kōl* 'stick'. SD I: Ta. Ma. Ko. *kōl*, Koḍ. *kōlï*, Ka. *kōl*, *kōlu*, Tu. *kōlï*, *kōlu*; SD II: Te. *kōla*, Go. *kōla*, Koṇḍa *kōl*, Kui *kōḏu*, Kuvi *kōlu*, Pe. *kōl* 'pestle', Manḍa *kūl*; CD: Kol. *kōla*, Nk. Pa. *kōl* 'pestle' [2237].

4.4.2 *Alternations i/e and u/o in Proto-South Dravidian (SD I and SD II)*

It has already been stated that -V_2 is a part of the formative syllable and only three vowels can occur in this position, namely *i a u*, and not all the five vowels of Proto-Dravidian which occur in V_1 position. The following sound changes are significant in that Rule 4a represents the Proto-South Dravidian stage which includes South Dravidian I and South Dravidian II, while 4b occurred only in a subgroup of South Dravidian I, i.e. Proto-Tamil, and 4c in Early Kannaḍa. The sound changes in question have been discussed thoroughly by Burrow (1940) and Krishnamurti (1958a, 1961, 1980, 2001a: ch. 2 Postscript) and we now know their profile from the Proto-South Dravidian stage through Early Tamil (which included Malayāḷam also). For subsequent adoption of the principles of reconstruction of this change, see Emeneau (1970a), Zvelebil (1970b) and Subrahmanyam (1983).

Rule 4. *South Dravidian umlaut*

(a) PD **i *u* > **e *o* / # (C_1)__C_2-*a* (Proto-South Dravidian)
(b) PSD **e *o* > *i u* / # (C_1)__C_2-*a* (Proto-Tamil).

Rule 4a merges high vowels with mid vowels when followed by *-a* in the next syllable. This means that PSD **e* represents PD **i* and **e* and PSD **o* represents PD **u* and **o*, when followed by *-a* in the next syllable. At a much later stage, by Rule 4b these instances of **e*, **o* became *i*, *u*, respectively, in Early Tamil. As a consequence of these two changes, Tamil and Malayāḷam have *i*, *u* corresponding to Telugu and Kannaḍa *e*, *o* in the environment [C-*a*. By looking only at etymologies in which Tamil and Malayāḷam have *i*, *u*C-*a* and Telugu and Kannaḍa *e*, *o*C-*a*, there is no way one can reconstruct the Proto-Dravidian vowel qualities. When high vowels or a Ø formative occur as V_2, all Proto-Dravidian vowels remain in all the languages concerned. Similarly, if any of the languages preserves a long vowel in cognates, its quality can be taken to represent the quality of the Proto-Dravidian vowel (see ety. (13), (15), (17), (19), (21)). Since this is a change that covered mainly South Dravidian I and South Dravidian II languages, evidence from the other subgroups like Central Dravidian and North Dravidian would also help in reconstructing the Proto-Dravidian vowel qualities in doubtful cases, i.e. if none of the South Dravidian languages has cognates with high vowels or zero beginning the formative syllable or with a long radical vowel. The following examples attest the application of Rules 4a and b and also identify the diagnostic environments for the reconstruction of the Proto-Dravidian vowel qualities:

(22) PD **iṯ*-V- 'meat'. PSD **eṯ-a*-V-; SD I: Ta. *iṟacci* 'meat', Ma. *iṟacci*, Koḍ. *eraci*; SD II: OTe. *eṟaci*, Pe. *jey* 'meat' (< **ṟey*- < **iṟ- ay*) [529].

The Proto-Dravidian quality is preserved in Ta. *iṟṟi* 'flesh' where **i* occurs in a closed syllable.

(23) PD **kēḷ* / **keḷ*-V- n. 'family', v. 'to ramify'. PSD **kēḷ* /**keḷ-a-*; SD I: Ta. *kēḷ* 'kindred', *kēḷ-mai* 'friendship', *kiḷ-ai* v.i. 'to multiply', n. 'kindred, relations', Ko. *kēḷ*, To. *keɬ̣* 'partnership', Ka. *keḷ-e*, *geṇ-e* 'companionship', *kēḷ-a* 'companion', Tu. *geṇ-e* 'coupling'; SD II: Kui *klāmba* 'family, lineage, kin' (Kui *ā* < **ē*) [2018].

The Proto-Dravidian vowel quality is based on the long vowel stems in Tamil and Kannaḍa.

(24) PD **col* 'fireplace'. PSD *col*-V-; SD I **ol*-V- > Ta. *ul-ai*, Ma. *ul-a*, Ko. *elkāl* 'fireplace between two stones', To. *was̲* (<**ol-*), Koḍ. *ol-e*, Ka. *ol-e*, Tu. *ul-e* (loss ọf **c*- in SD I); SD II **col* > Koṇḍa *solu*, Kui *soḍu*, Pe. *hol*, Manḍa *huli*; CD: Pa. *colŋgel* (*-kel* 'stone'), Gad. *soygel* [2857].

The Proto-Dravidian vowel quality can be established on the basis of cognates from South Dravidian II and Central Dravidian.

(25) PD **nūẓ* /**nuẓ*-V- 'to squeeze through'. PSD **nūẓ*/ ** noẓ-a* > Ta. *nuẓ-ai* v.i. 'to creep in', v.t. 'to insert', n. 'a narrow passage', Ma. *nuẓ-ayuka* 'to creep in, squeeze through', Ka. *noẓ-e*, *nurgu*, *nuggu* (<**nuẓ-ung-*) 'to squeeze through', Tu. *nurguni* 'pass through'; ND: **nuẓ*- > Kuṛ. *nuṛ*- (*nuḍḍ*-) 'to hide', Malt. *nuḍ*-. Also cf. Ta. *nuẓ-u-ntu*, *nuẓ-u-tu* 'to insert', *nūẓ-ai* 'hole' [3714].

Long root-vowel, high vowel as V_2 and evidence from ND attest to Proto-Dravidian vowel quality and quantity.

There are a few residual forms for which it may not be possible to reconstruct the Proto-Dravidian vowel quality for want of diagnostic environments as defined above, e.g.

(26) PSD **el-a-* > Ta. *il- ai* 'leaf, petal', Ma. *il-a*, Ko. *el*, To. *e<u>s</u>*, Koḍ. *elakaṇḍa*, Ka. *el-e, el-a*; ?Go. (Mu.) *koṛk-ila* 'new leaf' [497].

It is not certain what the original quality of vowel was before the merger in Proto-South Dravidian. For other such cases, see Subrahmanyam (1983: 209–10).

4.4.2.1 *Reconstruction of Proto-Dravidian vowel qualities after merger*

It was established beyond doubt that PD **i *u* merged with **e *o* in Proto-South Dravidian and not vice versa (Krishnamurti 1958a: 464–65). It was shown as part of Proto-Dravidian morphophonemics that $(C_1)V_1C_2$-V_2- (where C_2 = **y*, **w*, **k*) produce $(C_1)\bar{V}_1$- by syllable-contraction rule (Rule 2). When V_2 is a high vowel /i u/, the resultant long vowel has the same quality as V_1; but when V_2 is /a/, the resultant long vowel is **ē* for both **i* and **e* as V_1 and **ō* for both **u* and **o* as V_1. From this it is clear that when the formative vowel was *-a*, PSD **e* replaced PD **i*, **e* and **o* replaced **u*, **o* respectively, before the contraction rule operated (see Krishnamurti 1958a: 464–5), e.g. PSD **tē-* < *tiy-a-* 'sweet' (see ety. 7), PSD **kē-mp-* < **kiy-a-mp* (ety. 8).

(27) PD **tē-* < **tew-i* 'to be full, satiated; to belch'. PSD **tew-*V- > Ta. *tev-iḷ* 'to be full', *tev-iṭṭu, tek-uṭṭu* 'to be cloyed, sated', *tev-iṭṭu* 'loathing of food from satiation', *tevvu* 'to fill', *tik-ai* v.i. 'to be complete'; Ma. *tikaṭṭ-uka* 'to become full to the throat, to belch', *tēṭṭ-uka* 'to belch, ruminate' [3405, 3453]. Cf. Ta. *tē-nku* (or ?*tēṇ-ku*) 'to become full', *tē-kku* 'to be sated, to belch', Ma. *tēṅṅ-uka* 'to feel nausea', *tēkk-uka* 'to belch', Ko. *tēkl* 'a belch', To. *tȫ̄k-* 'to belch', Koḍ. *tē̈kïlï* 'a belch', Ka. *tēgu, tē̆ku* 'a belch' Tu. *tēkɛ* 'brimful'; SD II: Te. *tēncu* 'to belch', Koṇḍa *dēk-* 'to belch', Kui *tēk-*; ND: Kuṛ. *tē^n kh tē^n khrnā* 'to feel heavy after a dinner' [3451, 3453].

DEDR puts the relevant cognates in three entries, but items under 3453 illustrate the contraction rule given at the head of the entry.

(28) PD **tō-l* < **tok-al* 'skin, hide'. SD I: Ta. Ma. Ko. *tōl*, To. *twī̈<u>s</u>*, Koḍ. *tōlï*, Ka. *tō-l*; SD II : Te. *tōlu*, Go. *tōl*, Koṇḍa *tōlu*, Kui *tōḍu*, Kuvi *tōlu*, Pe. *tōl*; CD: Kol. Nk. Pa. Oll. Gad. *tōl*. Compare these with Ta. *tuk-al, tokku* 'skin of fruit', Ka. *togal, toval* 'leather, skin of fruit', Te. *tokka* 'skin of fruit', Oll. *tokka*, Gad. *tokkā* [3559].

(29) PD **pō*< **puk-a-* 'to go'. SD I: Ta. *puk-u* (*pukk-*) 'to enter, go', Ma. *puku-ka*, To. *pux-* (*puk-*), Ka. *puku, pogu* (*pokk-*), Tu. *pogg- uni* 'to enter' [4238]. This item is related to 4572 PD **pō* 'to go': SD I >Ta. Ma. *pō* 'to go', *pōkku* 'to cause to go', To. *pī̈x-* v.i., Ka. *pō, pōgu, hōgu*, Tu. *pō-pini*; SD II > Te. *pō*(*wu*), Koṇḍa, Pe. *pōk-* 'to send', Manḍa *pūk-* [4572].

DEDR separates these two sets on the basis of the differences in their surface phonology.

Contrasting with the above are cases of lengthening of the root vowel without change after contraction, if the underlying formative vowel (V_2) is **i* or **u*, e.g. OTe. *nī-ṟu*, *niw-uṟu* 'ashes': Ta. Ma. Ka. *nī-ṟu*, Go. *nī-r*, Koṇḍa *nī-ṟu*, Pe. *nīz*/*nīs* [3693].

(30) PD **niw-i*/*u-* > *nī-* 'to be elongated, to stretch out'. PSD **niw-i*/*u-*, **nī-*; SD I > Ta. *nim-ir* 'to be straight', Ma. *nivir-uka*, Ka. *nimir*, *nigur* 'to be stretched out', *nig-uḷ* 'to stand erect', *nig-ur* 'to lengthen out', Tu. *nigacuni*; SD II: Te. *nig-uḍu* 'to stretch out', Koṇḍa *nig-ṛi-* 'become erect'; CD: Pa. *nikip-* (*nikit-*) 'to stretch out' [2922]: SD I> Ta. Ma. *nī-ḷ* 'to grow long', *nī-ṭu* id., Ko. To. *nīṛ* v.i., *nīṭ* v.t., Koḍ. *nīḏ-*, v.i., *nīṭ-* v.t., Tu. *nīṭ-uni*, *nīḍ-uni*, Ka. *nī-ḷ* ; SD II > Te. *nī-lugu*, Kui *nīl-* (*nīṭ-*) 'to stand up', *ḍrīnj-*(< **nḍīnj-* <**niḍ-inj-*) [3692].

PD *-*w*- changes to -*m*- or -*g*- in different languages (see section 4.5.7.2.1).

4.4.2.2 *Exceptions and extensions to the umlaut rule*

1. Tamil: in Old Tamil there are some thirteen residual forms which appear not to have undergone the dissimilatory rule (Rule 4b). Almost all these forms are attested in early literary texts (see Krishnamurti 1958a: 465–8), e.g. Ta. *cey-al* 'action': *cey* 'to do', *cel-avu* 'going': *cel* 'to go', *ceṟ-al* 'anger': *ceṟ-u* 'to be angry', *koḷ-ai* 'hold, determination': *koḷ* 'to hold', *kol-ai* 'killing, murder': *kol* 'to kill', *toṭ-aṅku* 'to begin': *toṭ-u* 'to begin'. Do these represent retention of the Proto-Dravidian stage or the Proto-South Dravidian stage? At least one etymology is diagnostic in pointing to these as retentions of the Proto-South Dravidian stage:

(31) PD **pic-ar* 'name'. PSD **pec-ar* [*pes-ar*] > **pey-ar*; SD I: Ta. *pey-ar*, *piy-ar*, *pē-r* 'name', Ma. *pey-ar*, *piy-ar*, *pē-r*, Ko. *pēr*, To. *pȫr* n., *pȫšf* v.t. 'to name', Koḍ. *peda* (*r*-loss), Ka. *pesar* (*u*), *hesaru*, Tu. *pudarï*, Koraga *podari*, *hudari*; SD II: Te. *pēru*, Go. *parōl*, *padur* (< *pedur*), Koṇḍa *pēr*(*u*), Kui *pāru*; CD: Kol. Nk. *pēr* (lw < Te.), Pa. Oll. Gad. *pidir*; ND: Kuṛ. Malt. *pinj-* 'to name', Br. *pin* 'name' [4410].

The Central Dravidian and North Dravidian forms are diagnostic in that they show **i* as the Proto-Dravidian vowel. The ultimate connection could be **pin-cc-* > * *picc-ar* > **pic-ar* whence Ka. *pes-ar*. The Tuḷu, Koḍagu and Central Dravidian forms point to -*d*- (< -*t*- < -*c*-). In that case Tamil–Malayāḷam *pey-ar* represents the Proto-South Dravidian stage and not the Proto-Dravidian stage (see Krishnamurti 1958a: 466). The few residual forms have to be taken as exceptions to the dissimilatory rule. That these are nouns formed synchronically from verb roots within Tamil does not qualify them as exceptions (as proposed by Subrahmanyam 1983: 214–16), because forms like Ta. *veḷ* 'white':

viḷanku 'to shine', *viḷ-ar* 'to become pale' [5496a], Ta. *peṟ-u* 'to beget, bear': *piṟ-a* 'to be born', *piṟ-avi* 'birth' [4422] are similarly related, except that Rule 4a applies to them.

Kota, Toda, Iruḷa and Kuṟumba dialects (except Pālu Kuṟumba) and Baḍaga conform to the rule by showing only *e* and *o* before C-*a*. Kapp (1978) says that Pālu Kuṟumba does not show the implementation of *i*, *u* [C-*a* > *e*, *o* [C-*a*, e.g. *nila*, *nilamu* 'ground, soil', *muḷamu* 'cubit', *ile* 'leaf'. The fact seems to be that this dialect shares with Early Tamil the dissimilation rule (Rule 4b), i.e. *e*, *o* [C-*a* > *i*, *u* [C-*a*, because of the presence of such forms as *ule* 'fireplace': Ta. *ulai* (< **ol-ay* < PD**col-ay*; see ety. (24)), and *puge* 'smoke': Ta. *pukai* (< PD **pokai*).

2. Tuḷu: Rules 4a and b require that all other languages of South Dravidian I and II have only *e*, *o*C-*a* while Tamil and Malayāḷam have *i*, *u*C-*a* after the operation of the rule. All Nilgiri dialects which branched from Pre-Tamil at different points in time show the inherited qualities as expected. So do Koḍagu and Kannaḍa. Tuḷu has two regional dialects, North (N) and South (S), and two caste dialects, Brahmin (B) and Common (C). A recent study of Tuḷu dialects demonstrates that the NB, SB and SC attest the inherited qualities (*e*, *o*C-*a*), while the NC has changed these to high vowels (*i*, *u*C-*a*). This must be a recent dialectal change, which is not related to what happened in Early Tamil (Rule 4b); e.g. Tu. *es-aḷu* 'petal', *moḷampu* 'knee' (SB, SC, NB): *is-aḷu*, *mur-ampu* (NC) (Kekunnaya 1994: 42).

3. Kui–Kuvi: it has already been demonstrated (Krishnamurti 1958a: 465) that the umlaut rule (Rule 4a) preceded the syllable contraction rule (Rule 2) in all South Dravidian languages; therefore, it is a shared innovation of South Dravidian I and South Dravidian II. It also preceded the metathesis and vowel-contraction rules of South-Central Dravidian (South Dravidian II), perhaps going back to over a millennium BCE. These require us to reconstruct **ē* and **ō* in South Dravidian II also for older ****i*** / **e*C-*a*, **u*/ **o*C-*a*. The metathesis and vowel-contraction rule (see section 4.4.3, Rule 6 below) is still an ongoing sound change in Kui–Kuvi–Pengo and Manḍa (Krishnamurti 1978a). The long mid vowels which resulted from Rule 2 or Rule 6 (metathesis and vowel contraction) are retained in the other South-Central Dravidian (South Dravidian II) languages but lowered to -*ā*- in Kui–Kuvi (Krishnamurti 1980), e.g.

Rule 4c. *Lowering of long mid vowels in Kui–Kuvi*

ē, *ō* > *ā* / # $(C_1)(C_2)$__(Pre-Kui–Kuvi)

PSD **cow-ar* (<**cup* + *ar*) 'salt'. SD I **ow-ar*: Ta. Ma. *uvar*, Ka. *ogar*, Tu. *ubarï*, *ogarï*; SD II: **cow-ar* > (Te. *ogaru* 'astringent', lw from Ka.), Go. *sovar*, *hovar*, *ovar*, Koṇḍa *sōru*, Pe. *hōr*, Kui *sāru*, Kuvi *hāru*, Manḍa *jār* [2674a,b; see ety. (10)].

(32) PD **kuẓ*-V n. 'pit, hollow', v.i. 'to form pit'. PSD *kuẓ-i*/*-u*, *koẓ-a*-; SD I: Ta. Ma. *kuẓ-al* 'flute', Ko. *korl* 'tube', *kuy* 'pit', To. *kwēṭ* 'clarinet', Koḍ.

koḷ-a, Ka. *koẓ-al*, *koẓ-avi* ‘flute, tube’, Tu. *koḷ-avɛ*; SD II: OTe. *krō-lu*, *krō-wi*, Pe. *kṛoy* ‘pit’, Kui *kṛāu* (*kṛānga*, pl) ‘pit, hole’, Kuvi (F) *graiyū* (*grānga*, pl), *gṛāyu* ‘hole’ [1818].

Since this sound change occurs only in the case of long vowels resulting from contraction *e*C-*a*, *o*C-*a*, and not in original **ē*, **ō*, it was possible that the qualities of these vowels could have been phonetically opener and lower than mid vowels, somewhat like ɛ̄ and ɔ̄ before they merged with *ā* (Krishnamurti 1980: 502–3). There are seven cases shared by Kui and Kuvi, eight in Kui alone and three in Kuvi alone.

4. Modern literary languages: Rules 4a and 4b are not operative in Modern Tamil, Kannaḍa and Telugu. Tamil and Malayāḷam have changed older *i*, *u*C-*a* to modern *e*, *o*C-*a*, e.g. OTa. *il-ai* > Mdn Ta. *elɛ* ‘leaf’, *iṭ-am* > *eḍ-am* ‘space’, *puk-ai* ‘smoke’ > *poh-ɛ*. These forms violate 4b, which ceased to operate by the Middle Tamil period. Therefore they appear to go back to the old pre-assimilatory stage. Mdn Kannaḍa has *tig-aṭu* ‘rind’, *huḷ-a* ‘worm’, *nil-avu* ‘standing’; so also Te. *cil-aka* < *cil-uka* ‘parrot’, *uḍ-ata* < *uḍ-uta* ‘squirrel’. These violate Rule 4a, which is no longer operational in these languages. Notice in all such cases in Telugu and Kannaḍa it is the formative vowel which has changed from high to low (Krishnamurti 1958a: 468).

4.4.2.3 *Kannaḍa umlaut*

Around the eighth century CE, Kannaḍa independently introduced a sound change: radical mid vowels became high when followed by a high vowel, before written literature emerged in the language (Krishnamurti 1958a: 467; earlier Sreekanthaiya 1935, Burrow 1940: 296–7 and Gai 1946: 5–6 mentioned this change).

Rule 5. *Mid-to-high vowel harmony*

$$e, o > i, u \,/\, \#\,(C_1)\_\_C_2\text{-}V_2\ (V_2 = [+\text{high}])$$

id-ir ‘opposite’ (<**ed-ir*): Ta. *et-ir*, Te. *ediri* ‘opponent’, *ed-uru* ‘opposite’, *sur-i* ‘to pour down’ (< **cor-i*): Ta. *cor-i* id., Te. *tor-ãgu* ‘to spill’, *pur-i* ‘to fry’ (< *por-i*): Ta. *por-i*, Te. *por-ãṭu* id. Here, the umlauted *e*, *o* are not involved in the change.

4.4.3 *Long vowels through metathesis and vowel-contraction in South-Central Dravidian (SD II)*

After high vowels had merged with mid vowels in South Dravidian II (Telugu, Gondi, Koṇḍa, Kui, Kuvi, Pengo and Manḍa), a sound change came about as an innovation in this subgroup. One of the consequences of this sound change was to shift non-nasal apical consonants /*ṯ *ṭ *l *ḷ *r *ẓ/ which occurred as $^*C_2$ in Proto-Dravidian stems $(C_1)V_1C_2$-V_1- to the position before V_1, allowing V_1 and V_2 to contract into long $\bar{V}_1$ (Krishnamurti 1955, 1961: 51–68, 1978a: 18–19).

Rule 6. *Metathesis and vowel contraction*

PD		PSD
$(C_1)V_1C_2$-V_2-	>	$(C_1)C_2\bar{V}_1$
i i	>	ī
u u	>	ū
a a	>	ā
i/e a	>	ē
u/o a	>	ō

If the proto-form had no initial consonant, then C_2 would become C_1, creating words with alveolar and retroflex consonants in this subgroup. Where the proto-form had an initial consonant, the resulting form would have a consonant cluster with an apical resonant as the second member. Since this change took place in Proto-South Dravidian after the umlaut rule (Rule 4), PSD **e* and **o* represent PD *i/e* and *u/o* respectively; after contraction we have *ē* and *ō* from **e-a* and **o-a*, respectively. This is a major historical and typological change leading to innovative phonotactics in South Dravidian II. Examples:

(33) PD **aṭ-ank-* 'to be compressed, to hide'. PSCD **aḍ-ang-/*ḍā-ng*: OTe. *ḍā̃-gu* 'to lie hidden', *ḍā̃-cu* v.t. 'to hide' (beside *aḍ-ãgu, aḍ-ãcu*), Mdn Te. *ḍā-gu, ḍā-cu* (beside *aṇugu, aṇuc-*), Koṇḍa *ḍāŋ-* v.i., *ḍāp-*, v.t., Kui *ḍāpa* (*ḍāt-*) 'to lie in wait for' (Kol. *ḍāŋg-*, *ḍāp-* and Nk. *ḍhāŋg-*, *ḍhāp-* were apparently borrowed with *ḍ-* from Early Telugu); SD I: Ta. *aṭanku, aṭakku*, Ma. *aṭaṅṅu, aṭakku*, Koḍ. *aḍak-* v.t. Ka. *aḍangu, aḍaku*; ND: Malt. *aṛg-* 'to press down', Kuṛ. Malt. *aṛk-* 'to press down' [63].

(34) PD **eḷ-V-* 'young, tender'. PSD **eḷ-a-/ *ḷē-* : Te. *lē-* 'tender', also *el-a*, Go. *leyor, leyonḍ* , *ḍiyyōr* 'young man', *leya, ḍiyyā* 'young woman', Kui *lāvenju* 'young man', *lāa, rāʔa* 'young woman' (*lā- < lē-*), Kuvi *rāʔa, ṛaʔa* 'young woman, virgin'; SD I: Ta. *iḷ-a, iḷ-ai* 'young', Ma. *iḷ-a*, Ko. To. *eḷ* 'young', Koḍ. *ëḷeë* 'youth', Ka. *eḷ-a, eḷ-e* 'tenderness, youth', Tu. *eḷ-e* [513].

(35) PD **mar-am/n* 'tree'. PSD **mar-an/*mrā-n*: OTe. *mrānu* 'tree', Mdn Te. *mānu*, Koṇḍa *maran, mrānu*, Kui *mrānu*, Kuvi *mrānu, mṛānu*; SD I: Ta. Ma. *maram*, Koḍ. Ka. *mara*; CD: Pa. *meri*, Oll. *marin*, Gad. *māren*; ND: Kuṛ. *mann*, Malt. *man* [4711a].

(36) PSCD **por-a-/*prō-* 'to sell': Koṇḍa *por-* (*port-*), Kui, Kuvi *prā-* (*prāt-*), Pe. *pro-* (*prot-*), Manḍa (BB) *pre-* (*pret-*)[4536].

Further examples can be seen in *DEDR* 1278, 4973, 3949, 3174, 3340, 4283, etc. Krishnamurti (1978a, 1983) discusses this sound change and shows that it has spread through the mechanism of 'lexical diffusion' and has not completed its course in some of the languages, particularly, Kui–Kuvi–Pengo–Manda. It has ceased to be an ongoing change in Telugu, Gondi and Koṇḍa (1978a: 9). Even South Dravidian I languages show loss of word-initial vowels before alveolar and retroflex consonants, thereby promoting the apical consonants to word-initial position; Iruḷa and Tuḷu have over two dozen items beginning with non-nasal apicals (Krishnamurti 1978a: 18, fn.14). This phenomenon is discussed in greater detail under consonants.

4.4.4 *Vowel changes in individual languages: South Dravidian I*

4.4.4.1 *Toda*

Emeneau (1957b, 1970a) and Subrahmanyam (1976b, 1983) have attempted to identify the conditions of the most complex changes in Toda vowels. There are still a number of exceptions to the rules proposed. Subrahmanyam (1983: 53–60) describes the conditions for retention and says that 'change' occurs elsewhere. Normally we notice conditions (in the environment of a given segment) for change and not necessarily for retention. In the following sections I have tried to recast the rules of Subrahmanyam into those specifying the conditions of change and not of retention.

Rule 7a. *Low vowel rounding in Pre-Toda*

$$\text{PD } {}^*a\ {}^*\bar{a} > o, \bar{o}\ /\#\ (C_1)\_\_(C_2)\text{-}V_2$$

(V_2 is [−low]; in the case of *a, $C_2 \neq$ an alveolar *ṯ, *l, *r [+ apical, + anterior]; or C_2 is not a single retroflex *ṭ, *ḷ, *ẓ [+apical, −anterior] of Pre-Toda followed by a vowel which is [+low] as (V_2); elsewhere, *a and *$\bar{a}$ will remain unchanged.)

Examples: PD **kaṇ* 'eye' > To. *koṇ* (C_2 is a retroflex but not followed by *-a*/*-ay*) [1159], but **pal* 'tooth' > To. *pas̱* (alveolar *l* is an anterior, i.e. a non-back consonant retains *a*) [3986], PSD **nakk-* 'to lick' > To. *nok* [4353]; here, the consonant following the root vowel is back and high, hence the change; **pāṯ-u* 'to fly' > To. *pōṟ-* (not followed by *-a*/*-ay*) [4020]. There are a number of exceptions to the rules stated above: (1) To. *koṛṇ* 'loan': Ta. *kaṭ-aṉ* [1113], To. *koḷṇ* 'threshing floor': Ta. *kaḷ-aṉ* [1376], To. *oḍg-* 'be quiet', *oṛk-* 'to subdue': Ta. *aṭanku* v.i., *aṭakku* v.t. [63] all have a single retroflex followed by *-*a* but still they do not retain the original **a* root vowel; (2) deictic *aθ-* 'he, she, it', pl *aθ-ām*, *at* 'that much', *atfok* 'then', etc. do not change *a* to *o* [1], and *tan-*, *tam-* reflexive pronoun obliques have retained the original vowel – perhaps a grammatical constraint on the operation of the sound change; (3) through contraction with the suffix vowel, the root vowel is lengthened in a few cases, To. *kāl* (*kāḏ-*) 'fall from height': Ta. *kaẓal* 'slip' [3582], To. *pāw*, *pā*, *pāfn* 'old' : Ta. *paẓa* [3999], To. *pāg* 'to use': Ta. *paẓ-aku* 'be used' [4000] (Subrahmanyam 1983: 51–60, 63–70).

PD **i* split into *ï* and *i*; *ï* before and after consonants other than *c*, *č* and *s*, and *i* elsewhere.

Rule 7b. *Splits of front and back vowels* (Emeneau 1970a: 36–46; Subrahmanyam 1983: chs. 4–13, pp. 51–157)

(i) **i* > *ï*/ # (C_1)__C_2 (C_1 and C_2 are not palatal or sibilant in pre-Toda)

PSD **ir-u* 'to be' > Ta. *iru-* (*iru-nt-*): To. *ïr-* (*ïθ-*) 'to sit, live' [480], PD **tin* (*tin-ṯ*) 'to eat' > Ta. *tiṉ-* (*tiṉ-ṟ-*): To. *tïn* (*tïḏ-*) [3263]; PD **kil-* 'to sound' > Ta. *cilai* 'to sound': To. *kis̱-* (*kis̱-θ-*) 'to crow' [1574]. The conditions of split are not clear although *ï* appears mostly before pre-Toda alveolar consonants. In contrast *i* remains in PD **cil-* 'to be not' > Ta. *il* 'non-existence', *illai* 'no, not': To. *il-* 'not to exist' [2559], Ta. *kiḷḷu* 'to pinch': To. *kiṭ* [1589], To. *kic*, *kič* 'fire' (< **kic-*) [1514], To. *siry* 'joy' (< *ciri* 'laughter') [1562], etc.

(ii) **e* > *ö*/ #(C_1)__C_2 (C_2 = [–alveolar]; Pre-Toda) [784]

Ta. *eṭṭu* 'eight' : To. *öṭ*, but *kerf* 'shoe' (<* *kerpu* [*DED* 1963]). There are 41 examples given: 29 follow the rule and 12 violate it. Subrahmanyam invariably calls all exceptions loanwords without any evidence from external history, like *peṇ* 'butter' (cf. Ta. *veṇṇey*).

(iii) **e* > *i*/#(C_1)__C_2-V_2 (V_2 = [+high] or C_2 is [+palatal])

E.g. To. *nis̱* 'emblic myrobalan' : Ta. *nelli* [3755],To. *iṟ-* (*iṟθ-*): Ta. *eṟi* 'to throw a weapon' [859] Subrahmanyam gives 16 examples that conform to the rule and 6 that violate it.

(iv) **e* > *ï* is said to occur in the remaining environments. But the specific conditions are not clear (Subrahmanyam 1983:125). In most cases C_2 is an alveolar, retroflex, velar or the glide /y/, i.e. [+apical] or [+high], e.g. To. *ïr* 'female buffalo': Ta. *erumai* [816], *kïy* (*kis̈-*) 'to do': Ta. *cey* [1957]. In a few cases **e* > *ü*, e.g. To. *tüḷc-* (*tüḷ č-*) 'to become clear': Ta. *teḷ-i*, Ka. *tiḷ-i* [3433].

(v) a. *ē* > ȫ / #(C_1)__C_2-V_2 (C_2 ≠ *y*); elsewhere, *ē* remains.

In the 26 etymologies provided, roots end in *-y* only in three cases, derivative *-y* (< *-i*) occurs in 6; the rest are shown to retain *ē* either because they are loanwords from Tamil, Kannaḍa and Baḍaga, or cannot be explained at present (Subrahmanyam 1983: 131–6). Out of the 13 examples given for the sound change, 11 have an apical consonant. It appears that the rule can be reformulated as

(v) b. *ē* > ȫ / # (C_1)__C_2-V_2 (C_2 =[+apical])

To. *pēy* 'to thatch': Ta. *vēy* [5532], To. *ȫṟ* 'to rise': Ta. *ēṟu* [916], To. *sȫr* (*sȫd-*) 'to arrive': Ta. *cēr* (*cēr-nt-*) [2814].

(vi) **u* > *ü* / # (C_1)__C_2-V_2 (C_2 = **y*, **cc*; or, V_2 = **i*)

PSD **pul-i* 'tiger' > Ta. *pul-i*, To. *pus̱-y* [4307], PD **muc-* 'to cover' > Ta. *muccu*, To. *müc* [4915]. Eleven cases have been shown of which three have long vowels through compensatory lengthening, e.g. Ta. Ma. *ukir*, To. *ǖr* 'finger nail' [561].

(vii) **u* > *ï* / # (C_1)__(C_2)C_3-V_2 (C_1 or (C_2)C_3 = [+labial], V_2 = [+low])

The segment(s) preceding V_2 may be a single consonant or a consonant cluster (PP or NP), e.g. To. *pi̥ḷ* 'hole in a wall': Ta. *puẓai* [4317], To. *kïp* 'rubbish': Ta. *kuppai* 'heap' [1731a]. All the 12 examples fit the description including one with compensatory lengthening, To. *pī̈ḷ* 'to tumble over': Ta. *puraḷ*, *piraḷ* [4285]. There are two exceptions to the above rule (see Subrahmanyam 1983: 6, fn2).

(viii) (**u* >) **o* > *wa*/ #(C_1)__C_2-V_2

(C_2 = alveolar [+apical, −back], V_2 = [+low]: one of the environments is enough for the change)

(ix) **o*> *wï*/ # (C_1)__C_2-V_2 (V_2 = [−low])

Here, we can ignore the first stage. Toda has inherited the Proto-South Dravidian change of *i*, *u* > *e*, *o* [C-*a* (see below). Rules (viii) and (ix) are complementary. They reflect the developments of PD **o* with which **u* had merged in Proto-South Dravidian before [C-*a*. PSD **koṯ-a* 'to become short' > Ta. *kuṟai* (*-nt-*), To. *kwaṟ-* (*kwaṟθ-*) [1851], PSD **koṭ-ay* 'umbrella' > Ta. *kuṭai*, To. *kwaṛ* [1663]; PSD **kuṭ-i* 'house' > Ta. *kuṭi*, To. *kwïs̠* 'shed for calves' [1655].

(x) **u* > *u* / # (C_1)__C_2-*u*/ C_2C_2*u*/C_2-Ø

**u* remains unchanged when no vowel occurs, or *-u* occurs in V_2 position. PD **uṇ* 'to drink' > Ta. *uṇ*, To. *uṇ* (*uḍ-*) [600], PD *puẓ-u* 'worm' > Ta. *puẓu*, To. *puf* [4312].

(xi) a. **o*, **ō* > *wa*, *wā*/# (C_1)__C_2-V_2 (C_2 = alveolar or retroflex, i.e. [+apical], V_2 = [+low])

Examples: PSD **oṭ-ay* v.i. 'to break' > Ta. *uṭ-ai* (*-nt-*), To. *waṛ-* (*waṛ-θ-*) [946], PSD **koṯ-ay* 'to pierce' > Ka. *koṟ-e* 'to pierce as cold', To. *kwaṟ-* (*kwaṟ-θ-*) 'to feel cold' [2168, 1859], SD **kōṭ-ay* 'west wind' > Ta. *kōṭay*, To. *kwāṛ* [2203].

(xi) b. **o*, **ō* > *wï*, *wī̈*/ # (C_1)__Co_2-V_2 (Co = one or more than one consonant; V_2 = [+high] or zero)

PSD **oṭ-unku* 'to be restrained' > Ta. *oṭ-unku* v.i, *oṭ-ukku* v.t., To. *wïṛg-* (*wïṛgy-*) 'be crushed', *wïṛk-* 'to crush' [954], PD **onṯu* 'one' > Ta. *onṟu*, To. *wïḏ* [990d], PD **kōṭu* 'horn' > Ta. *kōṭu*, To. *kwī̈r* [2200].

(xi) c. **w* > Ø / # *p*__

The sequence *pw-* created by the Rules (xi) and (xii) is simplified to *p*, e.g. Ta. *poṟai* 'load': To. *paṟ* [4042], Ta. *pukai* 'smoke': To. *pax* 'smoke, tobacco' [4240]; PSD *pon* 'gold' > Ta. *pon*, To. *pïn* [4570], Ta. *ponku* 'to boil': To. *pïg* 'to bubble up', PD **pōr* n. 'fight' > Ta. *pōr*, To. *pī̈r* 'quarrel' [4540], PSD **pō* 'to go' > Ta. *pō* (*pōy-i*), To. *pī̈x pī̈* [4572].

(xii) **o* > *ü* / # (C_1)__C_2 (C_2 = y)

PSD **moyal* > Ta. *muyal* 'hare': To. *müːs̠* [4968], Ta. *toy* 'to breathe hard as in asthma', Ka. *suy* 'to breathe': To. *tüs̠* 'to breathe heavily' [2680, 3512]; there are exceptions and the conditions of change are not clear.

There are a few items of Pre-Toda **o* > *u* which are considered borrowings from the neighbouring languages. Pre-Toda **o* remains in six items only including the name of the tribe, To. *toz*, *mox* 'a Toda woman' (Subrahmanyam 1983: 145–6). All the rules formulated to explain the developments in Toda belong to the Pre-Toda stage when the formative vowel was still identifiable, since it is the quality of this vowel that seems to determine a number of changes. We need to recognize a further rule dropping V_2 between Pre-Toda and Toda:

(xiii) $V_2 > \emptyset \, / \, (C_1)V_1C_2\text{-}\_\_$

There are also other changes like contraction of root and formative syllables, loss of preconsonantal nasal, etc., which are obvious from the examples given. In almost all cases where he encountered exceptions, Subrahmanyam has invoked a loanword explanation without further discussion. In many of such exceptions it can be that the sound change is still in progress and has not covered the whole lexicon. For instance **o* remains in the name of the Todas as *toz* [todz], which does not seem to be a borrowing from any other language.

4.4.4.2 *Centralized vowels in Nilgiri languages (NL)*

With the exception of Kota, all the other Nilgiri languages have centralized vowels (see section 2.1.1). Toda has high and mid central vowels (short and long), *ï ï̄ ö ȫ*; it also has front rounded *ü* and *ǖ*. Zvelebil 1973 (11–12) set up four centralized vowels *ï ï̄, ë ë̄, ü ǖ, ö ȫ* (central unrounded and rounded) for Iruḷa, but in 1979 (ch. 4) he adds *ä* and *ǟ*; Perialwar (1979: ch. 2) has five centralized vowels, short and long, for Iruḷa, corresponding to the five non-centralized ones, short and long. Kuṟumba dialects (Kapp 1978, 1987; Zvelebil 1982a, 1988) also have *ï* and *ë*, short and long. With the exception of Kota, most of the Nilgiri languages have centralized vowels caused by splits of *i* and *e* when followed by retroflexes (or alveolars in some cases); this statement does not completely define the environments that centralize vowels in Toda. In all cases, original allophonic differences became phonemic when the conditioning factors became obscure or lost. This phenomenon has not influenced one Nilgiri language, namely Kota. Koḍagu, which is not a Nilgiri language, also has centralized vowels. First, examine the following examples:

(37) PD **kiḷi* 'parrot'. Ta. Ma. *kiḷi*, Ka. Tu. *giḷi*, *giṇi*, Koḍ. *gïṇi*; NL: Ko. *kiḷi vaky*, To. *kiḷy* [1584], Ir. *kï̄ḷi*, ĀKu., PKu *kï̄ḷi*.

(38) PD **kīẓ/kiẓ*-V- 'below'. Ta. Ma. *kīẓ/kiẓ*-V, OKa. *kīẓ/kiẓ*-(V)-, *keḷagu* 'bottom', Koḍ. *kï̄ḷï*, *kï*-, Tu. *kīḷï* ; NL: Ko. *kī*-, *kīṛm* 'monsoon clouds' (from the western side), To. *kī*- 'lower, below', *kï̄e*, *kï̄ye* 'down, below' [1619], ĀKu. *kï̄e (kï̄*-, *kï̄a*- in cpds.).

(39) PSD I **eṇ-ṭṭu* 'eight'. Ta. Ma. *eṭṭu*, Ka. *eṇṭu*, Koḍ. *ëṭṭï*, Tu. *eṇma*; NL: Ko. *eṭ*, To. *öṭ* [784], ĀKu. *ëṭṭu*.

(40) PSD ***ēẓ-*: **eẓ*-V- ‘seven’. Ta. Ma. *ēẓ(u)*/ *eẓ-u*, OKa. *ēẓu*/ *eẓ-u*, *ēḷ-*/*eḷ-u*, Koḍ. *ё̄ḷï*, Tu. *ēḷï*; NL: Ko. *ēy*, *eḷ-*, *e-*, To. *öw*, *ȫ*, Ir. *ȫḷu* , ĀKu. *ё̄ḷu* [910].

The above data are important to establish two facts. First, centralization is not a phenomenon of all Nilgiri languages, because Kota has no centralized vowels and a non-Nilgiri language like Koḍagu also has centralized vowels. Second, the conditioning factors of centralization are not the same among different Nilgiri languages. Therefore, centralization of vowels cannot be cited as an areal feature of all the Nilgiri languages (Zvelebil 1980).

The Nilgiri languages are all non-palatalizing, unlike Tamil and Malayāḷam (see section 4.5.1.4, Rule 14b). They must have separated from Pre-Tamil before the rule of palatalization set in, i.e. before recorded literature evolved in Early Tamil, about the third century BCE (Emeneau 1989: 135). We notice that palatalization did not occur in early Tamil before retroflexes and also some alveolars, especially *-*ṟ* (Emeneau 1995: §14, 18). This means that the front vowels /i ī e ē/ were retracted and centralized before retroflexes and possibly some alveolar consonants at that point in time, as shown by applying the principle of phonetic reconstruction inferred from the results of sound change. Firth (1934) says that even in modern Tamil the front vowels are retracted before retroflex consonants ‘giving the vowels a centralized obscure quality’ (cited by Emeneau 1994: 194). This phenomenon must have been shared by all those languages that have developed centralized vowels by the loss of retroflex and alveolar consonants that caused the allophones. Toda, Iruḷa and Kuṟumba must have split from Pre-Tamil after it developed the centralized allophones of front vowels, but before palatalization took place. The environments causing centralization of front vowels (following retroflexes and **ṯ*) are mostly similar between Koḍagu and Kuṟumba. Toda and Iruḷa also have centralized front and back rounded vowels, not shared by Koḍagu and Kuṟumba. Iruḷa also has lost initial short vowels before alveolar **r*, **ṟ* and **l*, not found in Toda. They do not seem to have a common stage of development. Kota must have separated at a still earlier point in time, i.e. before Pre-Tamil developed centralized allophones of the front vowels when followed by retroflex consonants. We will review this hypothesis in the concluding chapter. The successive splits of Pre-Tamil are represented in figure 4.2.

4.4.4.3 *Koḍagu developments*

Koḍagu registers the split of Pre-Koḍagu *i* to *i*/*ï* and *e* to *e*/*ë*; the centralized vowels occur before retroflex consonants and *r* (<*-*ṯ*- [-ṟ-]). At a later period, the consonants that conditioned the original allophones were lost through assimilation to the following obstruents. After bilabial consonants front vowels become the corresponding back vowels which bleed all such instances from centralization. Root vowel **e* becomes *a* when

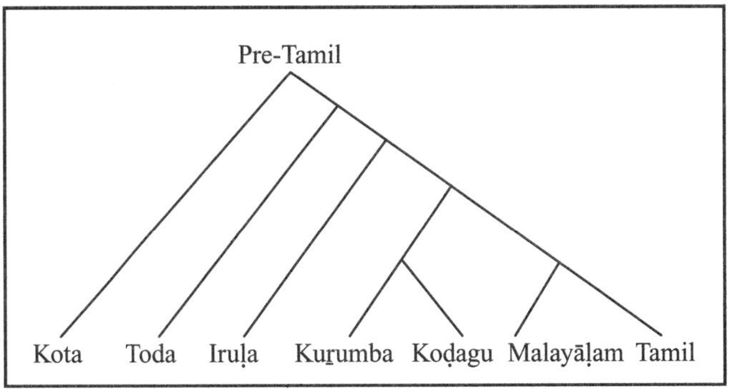

Figure 4.2 The Pre-Tamil sub-branch of South Dravidian I

followed by retroflexes followed by V_2, that is [+low] (Emeneau 1970a: 46–9, 1970b: 145–58, repr. 1994: 183–201).

Rule 8a. *Lowering of front mid vowel*

**e > a*/# (C_1)__C_2-V_2(C_1 = **p, *m, *c, *k*; V_2 = [+low]) Pre-Koḍagu to Koḍagu change

PSD **keḷ-ay* >Ta. *kiḷai* 'to dig up', Koḍ. *kaḷ-a* [1588]; PSD **peṭ-a-* >Ta. *piṭ-ar* 'nape of neck', Ka. *peḍa*: Koḍ. *paḍa maṇḍe* 'back of head', Pa. *piḍtel* 'behind' [4146].

Rule 8b. *Retraction and rounding of front vowels after labials*

i ī e ē >*u ū o ō* / # C_1__C_2-V_2(C_1 = *p, m, b*[<**w*])

PSD **wiṭ-u* 'to leave, release' > Ta. *viṭu* (*viṭṭ-*): Koḍ. *buḍ-* (*buṭ-*), PSD **wīẓ-*/**wiẓ*-V- >Ta. *vīẓ* (*-v-*, *-nt-*)/*viẓ-u*(*-v-*, *-nt-*) 'to fall': Koḍ. *būḷ-* (*būv-*, *budd-*) [5430], **peṭṭi* 'box' >Ta. Ma. *peṭṭi*: Koḍ. *poṭi* 'box', PSD **vēḷ-nt-* 'to want' >Ta. *vēṇṭu* 'to want': Koḍ. *bōḍ-* 'to beg' [5528].

Rule 8c. *Centralization of front vowels*

i, ī, e, ē > *ï, ī̈, ë, ē̈* / # (C_1)__C_2-V_2 (C_1 ≠ labial or palatal; C_2 = Retroflex or **ṯ*) Pre-Koḍagu to Koḍagu.

PD **iṭ-u* 'to put, place': PSD **iṭ-u* > Ta. *iṭu* (*iṭṭ-*): Koḍ. *ïḍ-* (*ïṭṭ-*) [442], PD **kīẓ* 'below' > Ta. *kīẓ* > Koḍ. *kī̈ḷï* [1619], PSD **eṇ-ṭṭu* 'eight' > Ta. *eṭṭu*, Koḍ. *ëṭṭï* [784], PD **tēṯ-* 'to be thorough, to recover' > Ta. *tēṟu*, Koḍ. *tē̈r-* (*tē̈ruv-*, *tē̈nd-*) '(man) becomes fully grown' [3471]. The centralization here took place before **ṯ* [-ṟ] merged with *r* (<**r*), because it does not take place before *r* < **r* or before the reflex of geminated **ṯṯ*. Rule 8c applies to items that have been left out after Rules 8a and 8b have applied. It is in a bleeding relation to those rules. They also indicate the chronological profile of the changes.

4.4.4.4 *Kota vowel shift*

Kota has no centralized vowels like the other Nilgiri languages. This has been explained as due to its earlier separation from Pre-Tamil. It has, however, another idiosyncratic change of the root vowel being harmonized to the formative vowel **-e* (< **-ay*) which was later lost (Emeneau 1970a: 49–50, 1969b: 21–34, repr. 1994: 175–82).

Rule 9a. *Fronting and raising of formative* -ay

ay > *e*/ # (C_1) *o*, *u* (C_2)C_2-__# (C_2 = any consonant admissible in the intervocalic position: (C_2)C_2 = a geminate stop or a nasal + stop; stem-final **-ay* becomes *-e* in Pre-Kota)

Rule 9b. *Root-vowel assimilation*

**o*, **u* > *e*, *i* / # (C_1)__(C_2)C_2-V_2 (V_2 = *e* from Rule 9a)

Root vowels *o*, *u* become *e*, *i* respectively, before formative *e* in Pre-Kota.

Rule 9c. *Loss of the formative vowel*

**e* > Ø / #(C_1)*e*, *i* (C_2)C_2-__#

Stem-final, formative *-e* derived from Rule 9a is lost; Pre-Kota to Kota.

Rule 9d. *Simplification of final consonant cluster*

(C_2)C_2 > C_2/# (C_1)*e*, *o*__#

The final cluster resulting from Rule 9c is simplified, or (C_2) is lost between Pre-Kota and Kota.

This is a three-step sound change: (1) stem-final formative *-ay* becomes *-e* in Pre-Kota; (2) radical vowels *o*, *u* are fronted to corresponding height, being assimilated to the following formative vowel *-e*; (3) the loss of the formative vowel *-e* and the simplification of the preceding consonant cluster. The root vowel can be short or long and the intervening consonant can be single or a cluster. The consonant clusters in the intervening position are PP (geminate stops) or NP nasal + stop.

Examples: PSD **koṭ-ay* 'umbrella' > Ta. *kuṭ-ay*: Ko. *keṛ* (<**keṛ-e* <**koḍ-e* <**koḍ-ay*) [1663]; the relative chronology of what happened to the medial consonant(s) is not relevant to the sound changes in question; PSD **koṭṭ-ay* 'stone of fruit' >Ta. *koṭṭay*: Ko. *keṭ* 'testes' [2069]; Ta. *kōṭay* 'west wind': Ko. *kēṛ* 'SW monsoon' [2203]; PSD **ol-a-kk-ay* 'pestle' > Ta. *ulakkai*: Ko. *elk* (also loss of *-a-* between *-l-* and *-kk-*) [672]; PD **kupp-ay* 'heap' > Ta. *kuppai*: Ko. *kip* [1731a]; Ta. *puṇṭai* 'male organ': Ko. *piḍ* 'vulva' [4273]; PSD **mūḷay* 'brain, marrow' > Ta. *mūḷai*, Ko. *mīḷ*. [5051].

Emeneau (1994: 178–82) has noted that there are many exceptions to the above sound changes. Seven out of 26 items which register the changes as proposed have doublets like *peg, pog* 'smoke' (< **pokay*), *mel, mol* 'breast' (< **molay*). Besides, there are 22 nouns and 9 verbs with unchanged vowels under the conditions of expected change, e.g Ko. *ōl* 'palm leaf': Ta. *ōlai* [1070], Ko. *koḷv-* (*koḷd-*) 'to rot': Ta. *kuẓai* (*-v-*, *-nt-*) [1822]. For some of these Emeneau invoked borrowing from neighbouring languages like Baḍaga, Kannaḍa and Tamil (179). It is possible that the order in which the above sound changes applied could be different, producing different results. If Rules 9b and 9c started from different ends of the Kota territory, it is possible that loss applied first and blocked assimilation of the root vowel in the overlapping area, leading to what is called rule reordering. The large number of doublets support this alternative. In the case of verbs *-e-* < **-ay* occurs medially and its loss must have preceded the assimilation rule (Krishnamurti 1994a: xvi–xvii). It is also possible that the sound change had ceased midway.

4.4.4.5 *Tuḷu development*

A rule similar to Rule 8b in Koḍagu also occurred in Tuḷu independently whereby front unrounded vowels of the root syllable became rounded after bilabial consonants /p b m/ (Emeneau 1994: 199–200; earlier Ramaswami Aiyar 1936: *IL* 6.385–439):

Rule 10a. *Rounding of front vowels after labials*

$[+\text{V}, -\text{back}, -\text{rounded}] > [+\text{back}, +\text{rounded}] / \# C_1 \_\_ C_2$ ($C_1 = [+\text{labial}]$, $C_2 =$ retroflex $[+\text{apical}, -\text{anterior}]$)

This rule must have been quite native and old to Tuḷu, since it occurs in all regional and social dialects (Kekunnaya 1994: 50–1). Emeneau thinks that this change could be basic to Tuḷu and that it spread to Koḍagu later through areal diffusion, creating a state of sharing an isogloss (1994: 199–200).

PSD **piṭi* 'handle' > Ta. *piṭi*, Ka. *piḍi*: Tu. *puḍi*; PSD **wiṭu* 'to leave' > Ta. *viṭu*, Ka. *biḍu*: Tu. *buḍu*, PSD **wīẓ* 'to fall' > Ta. *vīẓ*, Ka. *bīḷu*: Tu. *būḷu*; PSD **peṇ* 'woman' >Ta. *peṇ*, Ka. *peṇ*, *heṇṇu*: Tu. *poṇṇu*; PSD **wēṇṭu* 'to wish' > Ta. *vēṇṭu*, Ka. *bēḍu* 'to beg': Tu. *bōḍu* 'to wish, want'. The sound change is different from that in Koḍagu in that a following **ṯ* does not behave like a retroflex. It appears that the sound change is now spreading to environments where no retroflex is involved as C_2, e.g. PSD **wittu* 'seed' > Ta. *wittu*: Tu. *buttu*. In one case a reverse change **u* > *i*/#*p–* is noticed, which is dissimilatory, e.g. PSD **puli* 'tiger' > Ta. *puli*: Tu. *pili*, PSD **molay* 'breast' > Ta. *mulai*: Tu. *mirɛ* (Kekunnaya 1994: 51).

4.4.4.6 *Aphaeresis in Iruḷa and Tuḷu*

Aphaeresis is the loss of a word-initial vowel before an accented or heavy syllable. Iruḷa shows evidence of such a loss after it had branched off from Pre-Tamil. This sound change mainly occurred before Proto-South Dravidian intervocalic **r*, **ṟ* and

**l*. Zvelebil (1979: 68) gives 5 words with *r*-, 1 with *ṟ*- and 2 items with *l*-. Perialwar (1979: 228–9) has listed 9 different lexemes with *r*- and 7 with *l*-, all native. *DEDR* index has incorporated 8 items with *r*-, 1 with *ṟ*- and 2 with *l*-. I have not taken into account the loanwords from Indo-Aryan, e.g. Ir. *raṇḍu*, *reṇḍu* (the latter lw from Mdn Ta.?) 'two': Ta. *iraṇṭu* (>spoken *reṇḍu*) [474], Ir. *rāvu*, *rāpodu* 'night': Ta. *ir-ā*, *ir-avu*, *rā* 'night' [2552], Ir. *ṟangu* 'to descend': Ta. *iṟ-anku* [516], Ir. *rongu* 'to sleep': Ta. *uṟanku* id. (< PSD **oṯ-a-nku*) [707], Ir. *lē*- (*lēnd*-) 'to wander': Ta. *alai* (*-nt-*) 'to wander' [240]. Besides the vowel loss, we notice change in vowel quality in *reṇḍu*, *rongu*. The form *reṇḍu*, being a doublet beside the normal *raṇḍu*, and the representation of *r* for *ṟ* in *orangu* make the history of these two items suspicious.

The tendency to lose an initial short vowel is also found, on a limited scale, in all South Dravidian languages, but the change apparently is intensified in Iruḷa and Tuḷu, independently. Kota has one form *rek* 'wing' [2591] and Toda has none beginning with *r*- or *l*-. Tuḷu not only has entries with *l*- (14) and *r*- (15), but also with *ḍ* (11) – indicating a wider application of the rule of initial short vowel loss. Koḍagu has three items with *r*- [489, 2591, 5169] all of which look like loanwords from Kannaḍa and one with *l*-, onomatopoetic [5195]. Kannaḍa has 18 entries with *r*-, 6 with *ṟ*- and 18 with l-, several of which seem to be native and not loanwords. Under Tamil there are 7 with *r*- and one with *l*- indicating initial short vowel loss, some time between Middle and Modern Tamil (three more items with *l*- are onomatopoetic, like *loṭa loṭa*).

In Tuḷu aphaeresis takes place dialectally. In the Northern Common dialect the following rule operates (Kekunnaya 1994: 42–4):

Rule 10b. *Word-initial short vowel loss before apicals*

$V_1 \rightarrow Ø/\#\_[C_1\text{-}V_2C_2C_2\text{-}$ (V_1 = *a*, *e*, *o*; less frequently *i*, *u*; C_1 = a retroflex consonant *ḍ*, *ṇ*, *ḷ* [+apical, −anterior] ; C_2C_2= geminate or nasal +stop sequence), e.g.

Gloss	SB	SC	NB	NC
'to throw'	*aḍkkï*	*aḍakkï*	*aḍakï*	*dakkï*
'to measure'	*aḷappu*	*aḷappu*	*aḷapu*	*lappu*
'to dry'	*uṇuṅgu*	*uṇuṅgu*	*uṇuṅgu*	*nuṅgu*

In some cases the SC also drops the short vowel:

Gloss	SB	SC	NB	NC
'to stumble'	*eḍeṅku*	*ḍaṅku/daṅku*	*eḍaṅku*	*daṅku*
'to call'	*oḷeppu*	*leppu*	*oḷepu*	*leppu*

The rule of vowel loss now extends to environments in which non-retroflex consonants occur as C_2 (Kekunnaya 1994: 44):

Gloss	SB	SC	NB	NC
'without'	*idyantɛ*	*idyantɛ, idyāntɛ*	*dantɛ*	*dāntɛ*
'fasting'	*upasso*	*pāso*	*upāsa*	*pāsa*

The last item, obviously a borrowing from Indo-Aryan (Skt. *upavāsa-*), has suffered vowel loss in the common dialects of south and north. Kekunnaya gives seventeen examples of vowel loss in all. I discussed this 'trend' in South Dravidian I, which could be interpreted as an example of what Sapir (1921: 172) called 'drift'. The typological design underlying the drift could be to maintain the CVC structure of the root syllable while at the same time giving apical consonants an even distribution with the other consonants by promoting them to the word-initial position (Krishnamurti 1978a: 17, 18 fn. 14). It is probably not possible to say that the South Dravidian II rules of metathesis and vowel contraction are related to the above rule historically as a shared innovation.

4.4.5 *Vowel changes in Central Dravidian: Parji*

In Pre-Parji PCD **a*, **ā* became *e*, *ē* in radical syllables (V_1) when followed by an alveolar consonant, PCD **ḏ*, **nḏ*, **ṯṯ*, **n*, **r*, **l* deriving from PD **ṯ*, **n*, **r*, **l* (Krishnamurti 1978b):

Rule 11. *Low vowel fronting and raising before apicals in Pre-Parji*

[+V, +low] > [−back, −low, −high]/# (C_1)__C_2 (C_2 = alveolars [+anterior, +apical])

PD **āṯ-* 'to cool'. PCD **āḏ-*/**āṟ*: Pa. *ēd*, NE *ēḍ* 'to cool, cool off', Kol. Nk. *ār-* 'to dry up'; PSD **āṯ- u* [āṟ-u] id. [404], PD **panṯi* [panḏi] 'pig' > PCD **panḏi*: Pa. *pend*, (NE) *penḍ*, Oll. *panḍ*, Gad. *panḍu*; PSD **panṯi* [panḏi/panṟi] [4039], PD **man-* (*man-ṯ-*) 'to be', PCD **man-* (*man-ḏ-*, *man-ṯṯ-*): Pa. *men-* (*mend-*, *mett-*) 'to stay', Oll. *man-*, Gad. *man-*, Nk. *man-*; PSD *man-* (*man-ṯ-*/*man-ṯṯ-*); PND **man* (*n*)- [4778]. There are forty-seven etymologies in which the rule operates. This shows that, until the separation of the Parji–Ollari–Gadaba subgroup, Proto-Dravidian alveolar stop sequences remained intact. Only after Rule 11 did the rule of dialect split take place in Parji, which merged the Pre-Parji alveolar stop with dental and retroflex stops respectively in different regional dialects. Exceptions to the rule are motivated by grammatical criteria, namely pronouns ending in *-n*, *-r* or are clearly identifiable loanwords from Indo-Aryan. True exceptions, which are less than a dozen, have been discussed in detail in Krishnamurti (1978b: 258–9). The vowel raising rule does not apply to *a* and *ā*, preceding *l*, *n* which derived from **ḷ*, **ṇ* later (for detailed discussion, see Krishnamurti 1978b).

In five lexical items we notice a change of **e* **ē* to *a ā* in Parji before **r* **ṟ* and **l*; none of the items which are the output of Rule 7 is involved in this, e.g. Pa. *vār* 'root' < **wēr*

[*DEDR* 5535], Oll. Gad. Kol. Nk. *vēr* id. For some of these items only the southern dialect shows the low vowel form (Krishnamurti 1978b: 259).

4.4.6 *Vowel changes in North Dravidian: Brahui*

Brahui has inherited Proto-Dravidian high and low vowels, short and long /a ā i ī u ū/. Among the mid vowels, Bray gives short and long *e ē*, but only *ō*. Emeneau (1962d: §2.1) has established that short *o* occurs only in unaccented non-root syllables and that there is no contrast between *e* and *ē*. Therefore, he sets up only long mid vowels phonemically /ē ō/, accounting for this situation because of the influence of neighbouring Indo-Aryan and Iranian languages. Emeneau shows that PD **e* is replaced by *a* and *i*, and **o* by *ō*, *u* and *a* in root syllables. The conditions of the split are not clear. In a recent article (1997: 441–3), he has provided evidence for PD **e* being represented by *ē* in root syllables, which fills in a phonological gap. Examples: PND **e* > Br. *a*, e.g. *hal* 'rat' < **el-i* [833], *kah-* 'to die' (< PND **keh-* < PD **caH-*~**ceH-*'to die'); in this case only Brahui preserves the Proto-Dravidian laryngeal as /h/: PND **e* > Br. *i*, e.g. *pir* 'to swell' <**per*-V- [4411], *mir-* 'to plaster' <**meẓ*-V- [5082]. Emeneau gives 15 instances of **e* > *a* and 7 of **e* > *i*; from new material PND **e* > *ē* in Br. *bē<u>gh</u>* 'knead': PD **mel-k-*, cf. Ta. *melku* 'to become soft (by soaking, etc.)' [5078], with loss of *l* before *k* and lengthening of the preceding vowel (1997: 442). There are 13 certain cases of retention of PD **ē* as Br. *ē* (Emeneau 1962d: §§ 2.13–21). PND **o* > Br. *ō* (4 cases), e.g. *tōr-* (*tōn-*, *tō-*) 'to hold, keep' < **toṭ*-V- [3480], PND **o* > Br. *u* (5 cases), e.g. *cuṭ* 'a drop', *cuṭṭing-* 'to drip' <**coṭ-*: Ta. *coṭṭu* 'to fall in drops', n. 'a drop' [2835], **o* > *a* (2 cases), Br. *xall-* 'to strike, kill' <**kol-* 'to kill' [2132]. There are 8 clear cases of **ō* > Br. *ō*, e.g. Br. *tōla* 'jackal', Ka. *tōḷa*, Tu. *tōḷï* [3548] (see Emeneau 1962d: §§ 2.22–7).

4.4.7 *Diphthongs* ai *and* au

Literary languages have treated *ai* and *au* as diphthongs rhyming with long vowels metrically. But in terms of reconstruction, roots and extended stems ending in *ai* and *au* are structurally parallel to $(C_1)V_1C_2$-(V_2C_3) where C_2/C_3 is L = nasal or liquid, e.g. **kay* 'hand' parallels **man* 'to live', **cal* 'to go', **kal* 'stone' and **ur-ay* 'to rub' parallels **tir-uḷ* 'to turn', **mar-am* 'tree', etc. In many cases, root-final -*y* comes from an older *-*c*, **wey-* 'to be hot' <**wec-*. The traditional grammarians of the literary languages rightly treat the non-syllabic vowels *i* and *u* as equivalent to *y* and *w*, respectively (Krishnamurti 1961: §§1.121–2, 119–21). Proto-Dravidian roots ending in *aw* are rare.

PD **ay* has different developments in root and formative syllables. The languages of South Dravidian I preserve **ay-*; in South Dravidian II Te. has *ay-/ey-*>*ē-* and Gondi has *ay-*; most of the languages of South Dravidian II, Central Dravidian and North Dravidian develop it to *ey/ē* and *iy/ī* with loss of -*y* before consonants, e.g.

(41) PD **kay* 'hand'. SD I: Ta. *kai*, Ma. *kai*, *kayyi*, Ko. *kay*, To. *koy*, Koḍ. *kay*, Ka. *kayi*, *kayyi*, *kayyi*, *key*, Tu. *kai*; SD II: Te. *cēyi*; in classical texts, also *kai-* in compounds and *kēlu* 'hand', Go. *kay*, Koṇḍa *kiyu* (pl *kiku*), Kui *kaju*, *kagu* (pl *kaska*, *kaka*), Kuvi *keyu* (pl *keska*), Pe. *key*, Manḍa *kiy*; CD: Kol. *key*, *kiy*, *kī* (dial), Nk. *kī*, Pa. *key*, Oll. *ki* (pl *kil*), Gad. *kiy*, *kiyyū* (pl *kiyyl*, *kiykīl*); ND: Kuṛ. *xekkhā*, Malt. *qeqe* [2023].

(42) PD **kac->*kay-* 'to be bitter', 'bitterness'. SD I: Ta. *kai*, *kay-a*, *kac-a* 'to be bitter', *kac-appu*, *kay-appu*, *kacc-al*, *kai-ppu* 'bitterness', Ma. *kai-kka*, *kas-akka* v.i., *kaippu* 'bitterness', Ko. *kac-* v., To. *koy-*, v., Koḍ. *kay-* v., Ka. *kay*, *kayi*, *kayyi*, *kaypu* n., Tu. *kaipɛ*, *kaipe* n.; SD II: *cẽ̄du* 'bitterness', *kasu-* 'unripe', Go. *kay-*, *kaitt-* v., *kaitā*, *kehtā* adj, Kuvi *kam-beli* adj, Pe. *ke-* v., Manḍa *kem-bel* adj; CD: Nk. *kayek* 'unripe', Pa. *kēp-* (*kēt-*) v., Gad. *keym-bur*, *kēm-bur* adj [1249].

This example shows that **-c* ~**-y* was part of Proto-Dravidian variation since it is reflected in all the subgroups. These contrast with radical **ey* in South Dravidian I and the languages that maintain **ay*/**ey* contrast, Telugu, Gondi etc.:

(43) PD **ney* 'oil, ghee'. SD I: Ta. Ma. *ney*, Ko. *nay*, To. *nïy*, Koḍ. *ney*, Ka. *ney*, *nēy*, Tu. *neyi*, *nēyi*; SD II: Te. *neyyi*, *nēyi*, Go. *ney*, *nīy*, *nī*, Koṇḍa *niyu*, Kui *nīju*, Kuvi *nīyu*, Manḍa *ney*; CD: Kol. Nk. Pa. Oll. *ney*, Gad. *ney*(*yu*); ND: Kuṛ. *nẽ̄tā* 'grease, fat', Malt. *neṉya* 'fat of animal' [3746].

The formative *-ay* becomes *-a* in Malayāḷam and Telugu. Kannaḍa, Pre-Kota, Koḍagu and Tuḷu change it to *-e*. The rest of the languages lose formative vowels (see Krishnamurti 1961: §1.285, p. 121; ety. (23), (24), (26) and section 4.4.4.4).

4.5 Historical phonology: consonants

The Proto-Dravidian consonants are presented in a chart in table 4.2. Only nine consonants occur word-initially (C_1), namely four stops /p t c k/, three nasals /m n ñ/ and two semivowels /w y/. A phonologically significant statement is that apical consonants (alveolars and retroflexes) are excluded from word-initial position in Proto-Dravidian. All consonants except **ñ* occur in intervocalic position, i.e. as C_2 in bound Proto-Dravidian root syllables. Consonant-clusters which follow V_1 are PP or NP [NB]; in the latter case, the first segment (N) can also be a part of the root, established on comparative grounds. There is also evidence for the occurrence of NP-P/N-PP with a morphological boundary between NP and P, or N and PP. In the case of words ending in stops a non-morphemic /u/ is added at the end. Single and double obstruents contrast in Proto-Dravidian. In the case of sonorants, there is marginal evidence to propose contrast between single and double laterals **l* and **ḷ* (Emeneau 1970a:7,121;

Table 4.3. *Distribution of Proto-Dravidian phonemes*

Stop	#__	V_1__+V_2	V_1__(V)#	V_1__(V)#	V_1__(V)#	$\bar{V}_1$__(V)#
	p-	-w-	-pp	-mb	-mp-p	-p
	t-	-d-	-tt	-nd	-nt-t	-t
	–	-ḏ- /-ṟ-	-ṯṯ	-nḏ	-nṯ-t	-ṯ
	–	-ḍ-	-ṭṭ	-ṇḍ	-ṇṭ-ṭ	-ṭ
	c-	-s-	-cc	-ñj	-ñc-c	-c
	k-	-g-	-kk-	-ng	-nk-k	-k
Nasal						
	m-	-m-	–			-m
	n-	-n-	–			-n
	–	-ṇ-	–			-ṇ
	ñ-	–	–			?-ñ
Lateral						
	–	-l-	?-ll-			-l
	–	-ḷ-	?-ḷḷ-			-ḷ
Approximant						
	–	-r-	–			-r
	–	-ẓ-	–			-ẓ
Semivowel						
	y-	-y-	–			-y
	w-	-w-	–			-w
	–	-H-	[P			-H

Subrahmanyam 1983:49);[3] **r*, **ẓ* occur only singly both in Proto-Dravidian and in the descendant subgroups. Single and double sonorants contrast synchronically in many Dravidian languages, but the contrast is not traceable to Proto-Dravidian. Table 4.3 shows the segments and sequences that can be reconstructed for Proto-Dravidian. Phonetic representations at the Proto-Dravidian stage are given below. The symbols in the first column can be taken to represent both phonemic and phonetic values.

4.5.1 ***Initial consonants: voiceless stops***

4.5.1.1 *p-

Rule 12. *Laryngealization of bilabial stop*

**p > h/#*__ . . . (Middle Kannaḍa)

Within the historic period of Kannaḍa, PSD **p-* became *h-* around the tenth century AD. The change was completed by the fourteenth century, but both *p-* forms and *h*-forms coexisted, with the unchanged forms slowly declining. In 931 CE only two words occur with *h-* in Kannaḍa inscriptions and by the end of the tenth century the

[3] Zvelebil (1970b: 77) lists single and double *l*, *y*, *v* but he does not give any examples for the double consonants in Proto-Dravidian.

sound change had spread to the entire Kannaḍa-speaking area (Gai 1946: 13–14). In *Pampabhārata*, the first literary work of mid tenth century, the sound change was not attested. In uneducated Kannaḍa *h-* started getting lost as early as the beginning of the thirteenth century and this distinguishes standard from non-standard in Modern Kannaḍa: words involving this change occur in neighbouring languages Tuḷu, Baḍaga, different Kuṟumba dialects, Ālu Kuṟumba, Bëṭṭï Kuṟumba, Jēnu Kuṟumba and Shōlega. Examples: OKa. *pālu* > Middle and Mdn. Ka. *hālu* 'milk', OKa. *pū(vu)* 'flower' > *hūvu*, OKa. *putta* 'anthill' > *hutta* (see etymologies (13), (16), (17)). Ālu Kuṟumba has many forms with Ø corresponding to *h-* of Mdn Kannaḍa, e.g ĀKu. *ōg* 'to go' (< Ka. *hōgu* < *pōgu*), Jēnu Kuṟumba has both zero and *h-* forms, e.g. *ëṇṇu* 'female, woman' (< Mdn Ka. *eṇ* < *heṇṇu*), *hëṇḍi* 'pig'[4] (< OKa. *pandi*, *handi*). Some Kuṟumba dialects also show the *h-* forms and *p-* forms beside Ø- forms. It is not possible to conclude anything since clear data are lacking on word history. Kota and Toda have hardly any direct borrowings from Kannaḍa involving this change; Kota has *hāḷ* 'ruin' (< Baḍaga) from Ka. *pāẓ*, *hāḷ*, *āḷ* 'ruin' [4110]. Baḍaga has variants with *h-*/*Ø-*, e.g. *heṇṇu*/*eṇṇu* (Pilot-Raichoor 1997: 137). Baḍaga also has many more native items with *p-* (*pōgu* 'to go', *pui*/*poi* 'false', etc.) which make us doubt if they really migrated to the Nilgiris in the sixteenth century as proposed (Hockings and Pilot-Raichoor 1992, Foreword by Emeneau: viii–ix), and not much earlier, i.e. after the sound change **p* > *h-* began (tenth century CE) but had not run its full course (fourteenth century CE). Emeneau also mentions the 'disquieting statement of Francis' that Baḍaga has two forms of *r* (*r* and *ṟ*), of course not in the dialects covered by the authors (ix).

4.5.1.2 *t-

PD **t-* remains *t-* (or *d-*) in all the languages (see ety. (19), (27), (28)); one more basic item:

(44) PD **talay* 'head, top, hair'. SD I: Ta. *talai*, Ma. *tala*, Ko. *tal*, To. *tal* 'head', *taṣm* 'top', Koḍ. *tale* 'end', Ka. *tale*, *tala*, Tu. *tarɛ*; SD II: Te. *tala*, Go. *tal*, *tala*, *talā*, *talla*, Koṇḍa *tala*, Kui *tlau* (pl *tlāka*), Kuvi *trāyu* (pl *trāka*); CD: Kol. Nk. *tal*, Pa. *tel*, Oll. *tal*, Gad. *tallu*; ND: Malt. *tali* 'hair of head' [3103].

Also compare **tiyam* 'sweet' (7), **tew-i-* 'to be sated' (27), **tokal* 'skin' (28).

4.5.1.3 *c-

PD **c-* remains in a large number of etymologies in all the languages. It has, however, undergone certain irregular (incomplete) sound changes, **c-* >*Ø-*/*t-*/*k-*. In all South

[4] This form makes me doubt if it is inherited. Ka. *nd* and not *ṇḍ* corresponds to PD **ṉḏ*. Does this indicate that JKu. borrowed this form after *h-* < *p-* and before *nd-* < **ṉḏ*, or is it only a problem of recording (Zvelebil 1988)?

Dravidian I languages it is lost in a number of items, perhaps through two intermediate stages such as **c- > *s- > h- > Ø-*. Since *h-* was not phonemic in South Dravidian I it was not recorded. This sound change was shared by South Dravidian I and South Dravidian II and it is still an ongoing change in south and southeastern Gondi dialects. The change apparently spread from Telugu to Gondi through Koya and Maṛia dialects in which it is a completed regular sound change with Ø corresponding to *s* and *h* of the other dialects. It ceased to operate in the northern and western dialects after a few items had passed through the first phase of change (see Krishnamurti 1998b for a comprehensive treatment of this sound change in Gondi dialects). This change, insofar as South Dravidian I is concerned, was first treated in great detail by Meile (1943–5) and Burrow (1947), independently. The changes affecting PD **c-* were examined later by Krishnamurti (1961:§§1.15–21), Zvelebil (1970b: 109–15) and Subrahmanyam (1983: 317–34). The most recent comprehensive treatment of the developments of **c* occur in Emeneau 1988 (repr. 1994: 307–85). The irregular changes may be formulated as follows:

Rule 13. *Affricate weakening, loss, irregular merger with dentals and velars*

a. **c* > (**s* > **h*) > Ø/ #___... (South Dravidian I; Telugu)

The number of items subject to Rule 13a is 14 per cent of the total number of items (500) that require PD **c-*. The rule implies that *c* > Ø passed through successive stages of weakening in South Dravidian I also although there is no direct attestation of these stages since /h/ was not phonemic (Krishnamurti 1961: §1.53, p. 23, 1998b: 69). The representation of **c* as [s-] in some of the southern languages is well attested, e.g. spoken Tamil, Kota, Kannaḍa, Tuḷu, non-standard Telugu and all languages of South-Central Dravidian (SD II), Kolami, Naiki and Gadaba of Central Dravidian. Emeneau is inclined to delink the South Dravidian I change from the scope of **s- > h->Ø-* in Gondi dialects and says that it was a one-step change in South Dravidian I, i.e. **c>Ø* (Emeneau 1994: §16, p. 355). It is difficult to visualize phonetically a jump from **c-* to *Ø-*, that too in the initial position of a root syllable. The sharing of this sound change is one of the crucial arguments in favour of South Dravidian I and South Dravidian II being sub-branches of Proto-South Dravidian. At about the same time (second century BCE) Sinhala changed *s* to *h* in non-final positions, perhaps prompted by a similar change in the Tamil area (Masica 1991: 205–7).[5] In 13 groups all SD I languages and Telugu have lost **c-*; the

[5] Early Tamil attests the loss of Sanskrit and Prakrit sibilants *ś, ṣ, s* in loanwords (Burrow 1943: 132–5) more than any other southern language. It is reasonable to assume that, even in loanwords, *s* first became *h* as it happened in Sinhala before it became Ø. There is crucial evidence in Tamil lexical phonology which supports this assumption. Only Tamil has *-ā* as V_2 and no other member of SD I. In several lexical items where Ta. has *-ā*, the other languages point to an older *-ac*V- [-asu] which, we can suppose, became *-ah*(V) that resulted in *-ā* through contraction. Examine:

(1) PD **car-ac-* [sar-asu] > SD I: Ta. *ar-ā* 'snake' (also *ara*, *aravu*), Ma. *aravu*; SD II: Te. *trā̆cu* (<**tar-a-ncc-*) 'cobra', Go. *taras*, *taranj*, Koṇḍa *saras*, *srāsu*, Kui

remaining 57 cases have irregular loss beside *c*- in one or more languages. It is possible that items which had developed *s*- variants in social dialects were the ones which suffered change but it is impossible to retrieve the sociolinguistic aspects involved in the change.

(45) **ciy-/*cī-* 'to give'. South Dravidian I: Ta. *ī* (*-v-*, *-nt-*) 'to give to inferiors', *īvi* 'gift', Ka. *ī-* (*itt*),Te. *icc-* (*ī-*, *īy-/iyy-*, *iww-*), *īvi* 'gift': South Dravidian II: Go. *sī-*, *hī-*, *ī-*, Koṇḍa *sī-* (*sit-*), Kui *sīva* (*sīt-*), (K.) *hī-*, Kuvi *hī-*(*hīt-*), Pe. *hī-* (*hīt-*), *sī-* (in songs), Manḍa *hī*; CD: Kol. Nk. *sī-*, Pa. *cī-* (past *ciñ-* < **ciy-nd-*), Oll. Gad. *sī-* (*sīd-*); ND: Kuṛ. *ci'* (*cicc-*), Malt. *ciy-* (*cic-*) [2598].

Also see **cup*: **cuw-ar* 'salt' (10), **col-ay* 'fireplace' (24).

Emeneau considers this sound change as a possible case of lexical diffusion, which failed to cover all eligible lexical items before it ceased to operate (1994: §§12–14) (see table 4.4).

srāsu, *srācu*, Kuvi *rācu*, Pe. *rāc*, Manḍa *trehe*. Pkt. DNM *sarāhaya-* [2359]. The Proto-Dravidian reconstruction would be **car-a-ncc-* > **car-a-cc-* > **car-a-c-* [car-as-V]. *-as* > *-ah* > *-ā* to account for the long *-ā* in Ta. The *-h* element is reflected in Deśīnāmamālā's borrowing and also in Manḍa *trehe*. Note that Tamil adds a further formative suffix *-vu* whenever it ends in a long vowel in V_2 position and the long vowel in the unaccented position gets shortened.

(2) PD **kal-ac-* 'to quarrel' > SD I: Ta. *kal-ā-vu* 'to be angry', *kal-ā-y* 'to quarrel', *kal-ā-m* 'war, battle' (< **kal-ah-* < **kal-ac-*), Ma. *kalacuka* 'be disturbed', *kalacal* 'quarrel'; SD II: Kui *glahpa* (*glah-t-*) 'to confuse' ||>Skt. *kal-aha-* 'quarrel, fight' [1303; also see Burrow 1948: 371]. Cognates occur in all subgroups, but only the diagnostic ones are given; the occurrence of *-s* form in Ma., *h-* form in Kui, and *-h* in Skt. borrowing point to *-as* > *-ah* > *-ā*.

(3) PD **kan-ac*V 'dream, to dream' > SD I: Ta. *kaṉ-ā* (< **kan-ah-* < **kan-ac-*), *kaṉ-avu* 'dream', v.i. 'to dream', Ma. *kan-āvu*, *kin-āvu*, *kan-avu* n., *kan-avu* v.i., Ko. *kancn* 'dream', Koḍ. *kenaci*, Ka. *kanasu*, *kanasa* n.; SD II: Go. *kansk*, *kansk-*, *kanjk-* v.i. [1407].

(4) PD **tuḷ-ac*V 'sacred basil' > SD I: Ta. *tuẓ-āy*, *tuḷ-aci*, *tuḷ-avu*, Ma. *tuḷ-asi*, Koḍ. *toḷ-asi*, Ka. *toḷ-aci*, *toḷ-asi*, Tu. *tuḷ-asi*, *tul-asi*; SD II: Te. *tul-asi*; CD: Pa. *tul-ca* ||>Skt. *tulasī*; some of the Modern Dravidian forms could have been reborrowed from Skt. [3357].

(5) PD **nel-a-nc*/ **nel-a-ncc-*'moon, moon-light' > SD I: Ta. *nil-ā* (<**nel-ah-* <**nel-ac-*<**nel-acc-*), *nil-avu*, Ma. *nil-ā*, Koḍ. *nel-aci*; SD II: Go. *nelanj*, Kui, Kuvi, Pe. Manḍa *lēnj-* (<**nlēnj* < *nelanj-*), Kui *ḍānju* (<**lānj-* <**lēnj-*); CD: Pa. *neliñ* [nelinj-], Gad. *neliŋ*. This compares well with **car-a-ncc-* in (1) above [3754].

(6) **pal-ac*V/**pan-ac*V 'jack fruit tree' > SD I: Ta. *pal-ā*, *pil-ā*, *pal-avu*, Ma. *pal-āvu*, *plāvu*, Koḍ. *palaci*, Ka. *panasa*, *palasa*, *palasu*; SD II: Te. *panasa*, Kuvi *panha*, *paṇha*; CD: Pa. *penac*, Gad. *panis* ||>lw. Skt. *panasa-*, *palasa-*, *phanasa-*, *phalasa-* [3988].

(7) **kaṭ-aca-* [kaṭ-asV-] 'male of cattle, heifer' > SD I: Ta. *kaṭ-ā*, *kaṭ-āy*, *kaṭ-avu*, *kiṭ-ā*, *kiṭ-āy*, Ma. *kaṭ-ā*, *kiṭ-ā*(*vu*), *kaṭ-acci* 'young cow', Ko. *karc nāg*/*kurl* 'calf of buffalo/cow', Koḍ. *kaḍ-ïci*, Tu. *gaḍ-asu*, Ka. *kaḍ-asu*; SD II: Go. *kāṛ-ā*, Koṇḍa *gṛālu*, Kui *grāḍu*, *kṛai*, Kuvi *ḍālu*; ND: Kuṛ. *kaṛ-ā* 'young male buffalo', *kaṛ-ī*

Table 4.4. *Number of lexical items showing* c-/ Ø- *alternation*

DEDR entry nos.	*c-*	*Ø-*
2341, 2391, 2410, 2485, 2552, 2559, 2598, 2617, 2674, 2776, 2798, 2826, 2857 (13)		SD I, SD II: Te.
2335 + 157, 2342 + 162 + 271 2698 (3)	SD II: other than Te., CD	SD I, SD II: Te.
2684 + 664 (1)	SD I	SD I, SD II: Te.
(28)	one or more of the languages with doublets in *c-*	and Ø, or *c* or Ø
(25)	Sporadic loss or retention of *c-*	

Rule 13b.

$^{*}c$- > *t*- (Toda – regular)
(Other languages – irregular)

This is a fairly regular sound change treated in detail by Emeneau (1957b; 1988 repr. 1994: §§18–23). In the latter article, Emeneau has added more examples of the operation of Rule 13b and explained the exceptions. The irregular development of *t*- from $^{*}c$- was

'young female buffalo' (final vowels are gender markers borrowed from IA), Br. *xarās* 'bull' || > Skt. *kaṭāha*- 'young female buffalo' [1123; also Burrow 1948: 368]. Note the occurrence of -*c*V/-*s*V in SD and Brahui and Sanskrit loanword with -*ha*.

In all these cases and similar ones, Old Tamil formative -*ā* which is unique can be interpreted to have developed from the contraction of an older *-*ah* <*-*as*. These examples provide the missing phonetic links otherwise shrouded in history, because -*h* was subphonemic. The laryngeal **H* had already gone out of the Tamil speech except in some relic forms with restricted distribution. All this evidence supports the view that the change *s* > *h* > *Ø* occurring in South Dravidian I had spread to Gondi dialects in South Dravidian II from Telugu. The sound change is still running its course dialectally in South Dravidian II. Also notice that *s* > *h* occurs dialectally in the other members of South Dravidian II also, namely Kui, Kuvi, Pengo and Manḍa. Burrow (1947: 133) cited items (4) and (6) as instances of Sanskrit words losing -*s* > -*Ø* in early Tamil. In *DEDR* these are included as native groups indicating Sanskrit as the borrower with cross references to *CDIAL* entries. Further Burrow mentioned categorically the loss of Sanskrit sibilants, but only a few items with Sanskrit affricate *c*- (p. 134). The examples given by Burrow showed the loss of sibilants irrespective of their position in a word. Another point which receives indirect support from these examples is the possible merger of the Proto-Dravidian laryngeal **H* with **h* < **s* leading to parallel phonetic developments (see Krishnamurti 1997b).

Table 4.5. *Languages showing* c-/t- *alternation*

c-	*t-*
SD I: Ta. Ma. Ko. Ka. Tu.	Ta. To. Ko. Koḍ. Ka.Tu.
SD II: Te.Go, Koṇḍa, Kui, Kuvi, Manḍa	Te. Kui
CD: Kol. Nk. Pa. Gad	Kol. Nk. Pa. Gad.
ND: Kuṛ. Br.	

Table 4.6. *Languages showing* c-/t-/Ø- *alternation*

c-	*t-*	*Ø-*
SD I: Ta. Ma. Ko. Ka. Koḍ.	Ta. Ma. Ko. To. Koḍ. Ka.	Ta. Ma. Ko. Ir. ĀKu., Koḍ. Ka.Tu.
SD II: Te. Go. Koṇḍa, Kui, Kuvi, Manḍa	Te. Go.Koṇḍa, Kui, Manḍa	Te. Go.
CD: Kol. Gad.	Gad. Pa.	
ND: Kuṛ. Malt.	–	–

mentioned earlier by Burrow (1947: 142) and Krishnamurti (1961: 12–13, 89–90). Emeneau has surveyed all the relevant lexical items and illustrated many examples for the irregular change of **c- > t-* in many Dravidian languages which defy generalization (§§21–3). The oppositions shown in table 4.5 are noticed, based on Emeneau's data and discussion. Tables 4.5 and 4.6 summarize Emeneau's analysis of irregular reflexes involving zero and *t-*, beside retention of PD **c-* in different subgroups. The gaps in the tables like the absence of *t-* forms in North Dravidian seem to be significant since a whole subgroup does not show a dental reflex for PD **c-*. It is clear that Ø is confined to South Dravidian I spreading into Telugu and more recently Gondi of South Dravidian II. Krishnamurti (1961: §1.90, p. 40) proposed that **c- > t-* would have preceded in point of time **c- (s- > h-) >Ø-*, since an occlusive *t-* was more likely to arise from the affricate in Proto-Dravidian than when it became a sibilant at least in a part of the lexicon that was affected by other changes leading to its loss.

Rule 13c.

**c > k/#__* [+syllabic, −low] (North Dravidian)

Emeneau (1961b: 371–88; repr. 1994:1–15) proposed a rule that PD **c-* becomes a velar voiceless stop *k-* in North Dravidian before *u, ū* and *e, ē*; he gave four cases of *k* [*u, ū* and four for *k* [*e, ē*. Actually the instances involving the mid vowels were not as clear as the ones with high back vowels. In 1988 (repr. 1994) he noticed that besides North

Dravidian several other Dravidian languages also showed *k*- sporadically. He called this sound change 'sporadic' and irregular and not specific to North Dravidian only. I have restated Rule 13c by including all high and mid vowels in the environment in view of ety. (46) below. Some of the etymologies involved follow (see Emeneau 1994: §§28, 29):

(46) PD **cīnt*- 'date-palm'. SD I: Ta. *īntu*, *īñcal*, Ma. *īntal*, Ka. *īcal* (<**īn-ccal* <**īntt-al*); SCD (SD II): Te. *ī̃ta* (< **īn-tt-*), Go. *sīndi*, *hīndi*, *īndi*, Koṇḍa *sīntel*, Kui *sīta*, Kuvi *sīndi*; CD: Pa. Gad. *sīndi*: ND Kuṛ. *kī̃ndā* [2617].

PD **cuṭ-u* 'to burn': SD I and II, CD have cognates: Kuṛ. Malt. *kuṛ*- [2654]; PD **cur*-V 'to shrink, shrivel'. South Dravidian I, Te. and Central Dravidian have cognates: ND: *kurr*- [2687]; PD **cum*-V- 'to carry on head'. South Dravidian I, South Dravidian II, Central Dravidian have cognates: ND: Kuṛ. Malt. *kum*-, Br. *kubēn* 'heavy' [2677]; PD **cūr*/**cur*-V- 'to curl, roll up'. South Dravidian I, South Dravidian II, Central Dravidian have cognates: ND: Kuṛ. *kūr*, Malt. *kuṛg*-, Br. *kūr*-[2684]; South Dravidian I and Te. also have forms traceable to **kur-uḷ* with the same meaning in [1794]. The North Dravidian forms can match both the etymologies. For the forms with **c* [*ĕ̄* Emeneau gives 9 examples, not all of which are clearly reconstructable to **ĕ̄*, e.g. **cer*- 'to insert'. South Dravidian I and South Dravidian II have cognates; ND: Kuṛ. *xerr*-, Malt. *qer*-. The North Dravidian consonant points to PD **k*- rather than **c*-, but Ka. has no *k*-. Emeneau has given *k*- forms for **c*- sporadically in Toda [2599], Parji [2484], suggesting *c*-> Ø-, *t*-, *k*- [2591] etc. Since there is no pattern in these changes, one cannot be certain of the cognates grouped under the same entry. For instance, I would separate the words meaning 'wing' in the following etymology into two groups:

(47) a. PD **ceṯ-ank-*/*-ankk-* 'wing'. SD I: Ta. *ciṟai*, *ciṟaku*, *iṟai*, *iṟaku*, *iṟakkai*, Ma. *ciṟaku*, To. *tergy*, Ka. *eṟanke*, *eṟake*, *ṟakke*, *ṟekke*, Koḍ. *teṟake*, Tu. *ediṅke*, *reṅke*; SD II: Te. *eṟaka*, *ṟekka* (some South Dravidian II and Central Dravidian languages have borrowed from Telugu).
b. PD **keṯ*-V- 'wing, feather': Ko. *kera* (*ŋ*)*l*, Tu. *keduṅke* 'tip of wing', *kedi* 'feather', Go. *gerŋ*(*g*) [2591].

In any case there are clear etymologies suggesting PD **c* > ND *k*- before non-low vowels. A very valuable etymology pointing to **c* > *k* [*ay* ~ *ey* is the group meaning 'die' which seems to involve a Proto-Dravidian laryngeal **H* because it is preserved as a laryngeal fricative in Brahui and also because of the aberrant vocalism in different languages (Krishnamurti 1997b: 152):

(48) PD **caH*- 'to die', PSD **caH-*/**cā*-. SD I: Ta. *cā* (non-past *cā-v-*, past *ce-tt-*<**ca-tt*), Ma. *cā*- (*catt*-); with **H* > *y*, To. *soy*- (*sot*-) (borrowing

from Badaga), Ka. sāy- (satt-), Tu. sai- 'to die'; all the South Dravidian languages also have a noun in *cāw (<*caH-w-) 'death'; SD II: Te. cacc- (past cacc- < *caH-cci, non-past [imper/inf] cā-/cāw-, by contraction of *aH to ā) 'to die', ca-mpu (<*caH-mpp-) v.t. 'to kill', cāwu n. 'death', Go. sai-, sāy-, sā-, hā-, Koṇḍa sā- (sā-t-), Kui sā- (sā-t-), Kuvi hai-, hā- (hā-t-), Pengo–Manḍa hā- (hā-t-). PCD *cay-/*cāy-: Pa. cay- (ca-ñ- < cay-nj- <*cay-nd-), Oll. say-, Gad. cay- 'to die'. ND *keH-, *key-: Kuṛ. khē-~*kē (ke-cc-), Malt. key- (kec-) 'to die', keype n. 'death', Br. kah- (kask-, neg, kas-) 'to die', kas-if- 'to kill' [2425].

4.5.1.3.1 *c- and *t- merger in Tuḷu PD *c- and *t- merged into *c- in 'Proto-Non-Brahmin Tuḷu' which later changed into c-, s-, h- and Ø- in different Tuḷu dialects, the exact demarcation of which is not known (Subrahmanyam 1983: 321–2, based on Shankar Bhat's observations). Kekunnaya (1994: 52–3) says that PD *c-, *t- = Tu. s-, t- in North Brahmin and South Brahmin dialects. PD *c-, *t- > *c- in the Common (non-Brahmin) dialects leading to the representation of this *c- as s- in SC and as t- in NC:

	SB	NB	Proto-C	SC	NC
*c- Ta. cappu 'leaves'	sappu	sappu	*c	sappu	tappu
*t- Ta. talai 'head'	tarɛ	tarɛ		sarɛ	tarɛ

The result of *t-, *c- >*c- is further represented as c- in the Harijan dialect (south-west and south-central) and as h- in the Jain dialect; s-/h- vary in south-central B and C dialects and it is represented as Ø- in southeast Common and Harijan dialects. Interdialectal borrowing makes this picture further confusing, replacing s- of southern dialects by t- of northern dialects (see Emeneau 1994: 370–2).

4.5.1.3.2 *c- > s- > h- > Ø in Gondi dialects PD *c- is represented in different Gondi dialects as s-, h-, Ø-. There are three items that have c- instead of s- in Adilabad and Yeotmal districts [2391, 2677, 2865] and it could be due to the influence of Marathi. In most of the items even these western dialects have only s-. The western and northern dialects represent Proto-Gondi *s- by s-, the farther eastern and southern dialects show Ø, and the middle dialects have h-. Though this sound change is still in progress, it is a completed sound change in the southern dialects of Hill-Maṛia, other Gondi dialects of Bastar, and Koya of Andhra Pradesh. This change has been treated by Krishnamurti (1998b) to establish that lexical diffusion can result in a regular sound change. The second aspect is that the Gondi change is a continuation of the change of *c > Ø in SD I and Telugu and it provides the missing phonetic links in the final output, i.e. *c- > [s- > h->] Ø.

4.5.1.4 *k-

Burrow (1943) has dealt with this problem systematically followed by Krishnamurti (1961: §§1.17–21, pp. 10–11). Burrow's statements can be formulated as a set of rules:

Rule 14. *Palatalization of velars*

a. **k* > *c*/ #__[+V, −back] (Telugu)

b. **k* > *c*/ #__[V_1C_2] (V_1 = [−back], $C_2 \neq$ retroflex consonant) (Pre-Tamil)

The sound change occurred in Telugu and Tamil–Malayāḷam, independently, because the environments are different. Tamil and Malayāḷam palatalize, if the **k*- is not followed by a retroflex consonant in the next syllable. Telugu has no such constraint. Before Proto-Dravidian front vowels as well as derived front vowels, Telugu palatalizes the velar **k*-. For instance, **ay* > *ē* causes palatalization in Telugu and not in Tamil and Malayāḷam (Burrow 1943: 128), e.g. Te. *cĕ̄yi* 'hand' < **key* < **kay* (ety. (41)), *cēnu* 'field' (< *key-m-* < *kay-m-*) [1958], *cĕ̄du* 'bitter' (< **key-nd-* < **kay-nd-*), see (42). Krishnamurti (1961: §1.18, p. 10) showed that palatalization occurred after another sound change, namely metathesis and vowel contraction, which blocked palatalization by removing the front vowel from the immediate environment of **k*-. Forms such as *krinda* (<**kiẓ-nd-*) 'below' do not show palatalization; similarly, a number of words beginning with *gi-*, *gī-*, *ge-*, *gē-* are also not palatalized, *giccu* 'to pinch', *gĩku* 'to scribble', *gīṟu* 'to scratch', *geṇṭu* 'to push out by neck' etc. (Krishnamurti 1961: §1.59, p. 25). Obstruent voicing could have preceded palatalization and, therefore, inhibited its occurrence. E. Annamalai (1968) has provided solid evidence for the non-operation of the palatalization rule in echo-words. In a recent article Emeneau (1995) has illustrated the non-operation of palatalization in several forms which had an alveolar as C_2 in Pre-Tamil. Therefore, the environment in Rule 14b can be expanded to include alveolars, i.e. $C_2 \neq$ [+apical]. Examples:

(49) PD **key* 'to do, make, create'. SD I: Ta. Ma. *cey*, To. *kïy*, Ko. *key*, *gey*, Koḍ. *key*, Tu. *geyi-*, *gai-*; SD II: Te. *cēy-*, Go. *kiy-*, *kī-*, Koṇḍa *ki-*, Kui *ki-*, *gi-*, Kuvi *kī-*, Pe. *ki-*, Manḍa *ki-*; CD: Pa. Oll. Gad. *key-*; ND: Br. *kē-* [1957].

(50) PD **keṭ-u* 'to perish, decay, be spoiled'. SD: Ta. Ma. *keṭ-u*, Ko. *keṛ-*, To. *köṛ-*, Koḍ. *këḍ-* 'to be spoiled', Ka. *keḍu*, *kiḍu* (*keṭṭ-*); SD II: Te. *ceḍu* [1942].

PD **kiḷ-i* 'parrot'. SD I: Ta. Ma. *kiḷi*, To. Ko. *kiḷy*, Koḍ. *giṇi*, Ka. Tu. *giḷi*, *giṇi*; SD II: Te. *ciluka*; (Go. *siṛī*, Koṇḍa *siṛa*, Pe. *hiṛa* are plausibly loanwords from Pre-Telugu in the form **ciḷi* >**siḷi*); CD: Pa. *kil*, Gad. *killiŋ* [1584, see (37)].

(51) ?PD **kic*-V *kic*-V 'chirping, squeaking' (onomatopoetic expression). SD I: Ta. Ma. *kiccu kiccu*, *kīccu*, Ka. *kica kica*, Tu. *kicikici* n. 'screaming', *kīc-* 'to squeak'; SD II: Te. *kicakica* adv., *kīcurāyi* 'an insect making noise'.

Etymologies (49) [earlier see (8) and (18)] illustrate Rule 14a, (37) and (50), Rule 14b. Ety. (51) exemplifies the non-occurrence of palatalization in expressives.

Emeneau (1995: §§5–17) has noticed that in Tamil and Malayāḷam even alveolars /ṯ ṯṯ nṯ l n r/ have blocked palatalization in a considerable number of cases, if not all. He gives five examples with *ṟ*, one with *n* and two with *l* as C_2, Ta. *kiṟāvu* 'to cry' [1590], *kiṟukku*, *kēṉam* 'craziness' [1596, 2021], *kil* 'to be able'[1570], etc. There are cases for non-palatalization in Telugu, but these look like early borrowings from Kannaḍa in the literary texts: *kelasamu* 'work' [1970], *kelanu* 'side' [1969] (cf. Ka. *kelasa*, *kela*); several expressives are anyway exceptions to palatalization: Ta. *kila kila* [1575], Ta. *kiṟa kiṟa* [1593]; for another expressive Emeneau reconstructs a voiced stop for PSD **giṟu giṟu* [1595] 'go round and round' with cognates from Kannaḍa, Tuḷu and Telugu. Further, Emeneau cites six forms where the palatalization rule is not blocked even when C_2 is an alveolar, *ceṟi* 'be tight, crowded', *ceṟu* 'to control' [1980], *ciṟukku* 'be angry with' [1597] with cognates from Kannaḍa, Telugu, Kui and Brahui which, according to Emeneau, are related to **kiṉ*- 'to be angry': Ta. *ciṉa* v.i. 'be angry', Ma. *ciṉam* 'anger', Ka. *kinisu*, Te. *kiniyu* 'be angry' [1600], Ta. *ceṟu* (*ceṟṟ*-) 'to kill' [1981], Ta. *cil-/ciṟ*- 'small'(<**kil-*/**kiṯ*-) [1571, 1594] with cognates mainly from SD I, Ta. *cil* 'sound, noise' (<**kil*-) [1574], Ta. *cil* 'small piece' [1577], Ta. *cēṟu* 'mud' (< **kec-aṯ*-) [2020], Ta. *cēṉai* 'yam' (<**kēn*-) [2022]. In two entries Ma. *kiṟ*- lacks palatalization [1591,1562]. Two more cases where *-*r* seems to block palatalization are Ta. *kīri* 'mongoose' [1614], *kīrai* 'greens' [1617].

It is important to note that most of the instances where palatalization is blocked seem to be confined to South Dravidian I. Emeneau's paper gives one more reason for alveolars and retroflexes to be grouped as a natural class at the proto-level (see sections 4.2, 4.5 above). In the case of Koḍagu and the Nilgiri languages we have noticed that vowel-centralization is caused by the following retroflexes and alveolars, mainly **ṯ* (Krishnamurti 1975b; Emeneau 1995: 407–8).

Rule 15. *Spirantization/retraction of the velar* (*North Dravidian*)

PD *$k > x, q$/#__ V_2(V_2 = All but the high front vowels *i ī* [+V, −[+high, −back]]).

When Burrow (1943: 132–9) formulated this change he said that only before high front vowels *i*, *ī*, **k*- remained *k*-; before all other vowels it became /x/ (spelt as *kh̲*-) in Kuṛux and Brahui, and as *q*- in Malto[6] in North Dravidian. He discussed this change in great detail and also tried to explain the few exceptions to the rule framed by him. He gave 24 items where the rule operated and 8 where **k*- remained unchanged before high

[6] Originally it was thought that Malto *q* was also a postvelar spirant, but Burrow and Bhattacharya in a field trip in 1957–8 discovered that *q* is a uvular stop and not a spirant (see Emeneau 1994: 14). Mahapatra (1979: 25) confirms this fact.

front vowels. Pfeiffer (1972: 63–7) demonstrated that the rule was generalized in Kuṛux and Malto extending the environments to all high vowels, i.e. **k* remains *k-* before all high vowels, but Brahui still retains the original environment (Emeneau 1994: 14, fn.1). Examples for this rule can be seen in ety. (8), (11), (12), (18), (38) and (41), to which the following may be added:

(52) PD **kāy* 'to grow hot'. SD I: Ta. *kāy*, Ma. *kāyuka*, Ko. *kāy*, To. *kōy*, Koḍ. *kāy*, Tu. *kāy*, Ka. *kāy*; SD II: Te. *kā̃gu* v.i., *kā̃cu* v.t., Go. *kās-* v.i., *kāp* v.t., Koṇḍa *kāy-*, v.i., *kāp-* v.t., Kui *kāg-*, *kānd-* v.i., *kās-* v.t., Kuvi *kāy-*, *kād-* v.i., *kāp-* v.t. Pe. Manḍa *kāy* v.i.; CD: Kol. Nk. *kāng-* v.i., *kāp-* v.t., Pa. *kāp-* v.t., Oll. *kāyp-* v.t.; ND: Kuṛ. *xāy-*, Malt. *qāy-* v.i., Br. *xāxar* 'fire' [1458].

(53) PD **kū-r-* 'to sleep'. SD I: Tu. *kūr-uni*; SD II: Te. *kūru* v.i., *kūrku* 'a nap', Go. *kūrk-* 'to doze'; CD: Pa. Gad. *kūrk-* 'to nod in sleep'; ND: Kuṛ. Malt. *kūg-* 'to doze' [1902].

4.5.2 *Initial consonants: voiced stops*

Burrow (1938) discussed the question of initial voiced stops, comparing etymologies involving this feature in the literary languages of South India, mainly Telugu and Kannaḍa. He concluded that voicing was secondary in Dravidian and the Proto-Dravidian condition is preserved in Old Tamil and Malayāḷam. He was supported with further arguments by Krishnamurti (1961: §§1.55–9, 1.70–3, pp. 24–5, 28–9). Zvelebil (1970b), Emeneau (1970a) and Subrahmanyam (1983) have endorsed this position but have not added anything new. Krishnamurti gives the environments which seem to promote secondary/sporadic voicing in word-initial obstruents, in so far as Telugu is concerned, but the observations apply to a number of other languages also in different etymological groups: (1) when the root syllable ends in a phonetic sonorant as opposed to a voiceless obstruent, Te. *gillu* 'to pluck', *jarugu* 'to slide', etc.; (2) where a sonorant occurs as the second member of a word-initial cluster which converts an initial obstruent to a voiced one, e.g. Te. *kruccu*/ *gruccu* 'to pierce', etc.; (3) when a radical liquid is assimilated to a voiced obstruent, e.g. Te. *diddu* 'to rectify' (< **tirdu*); (4) where a root-final semivowel or liquid is lost before a nasal–stop combination, Te. *bonku* 'to lie' (< *poy-nkk-*), also where a root-final nasal is joined to an obstruent, e.g. *janku* 'to fear' (< *caṇ-kk-*).

> While the general principle seems to be the extension to initial voiceless stop of voicing occurring in the succeeding syllables, there are also innumerable cases where initial voicing is not produced under the same circumstances. However, voicing is more wide-spread in constructions, which are capable of being analysed (in PDr.) into a base plus a derivative suffix than in unsuffixed stems as *kappu*, *tappu*, *tannu*, etc. Again the relative susceptibility of the various voiceless stops to the assimilative influence of

> the succeeding sonorants is also to be taken into account. Thus *k*- is more easily influenced to alternate with *g*-, than *c*- with *j*- and *t*- with *d*-; *p*-> *b*- is extremely rare, while *ṭ*- > *ḍ*- never occurs on account of lack of forms with *ṭ*- in Dravidian (Krishnamurti 1961: 28–9).

Zvelebil's (1972a) study of initial voiced stops based on *DED* showed that the ratio between voiced and voiceless stops in Dravidian was 1:10. The highest rate of voicing was found in South Dravidian II and Central Dravidian, while in North Dravidian the ratio was 1:14. The study was useful, but we need to remember that languages studied have different sized lexicons. It may be rewarding to take a list of two hundred or so words with initial stops for which cognates are available in most of the languages in all the subgroups and study the pattern of voicing in these. Emeneau's study of expressives (1969a, 1993) shows that in this category of words one can expect voiced stops to be reconstructed for Proto-Dravidian, at least for some of the small subgroups:

**g*-:	*gala gala*	Ka. Tu.; Te. [1302]
	guḍu guḍu	Ko. Ka. Tu.; Go.; Kol. Pa. [1659]
	gaṇa gaṇa	Ka. Tu.; Te. [1162]
	gama gama	Ko. Ka. Tu.; Te.; Kuṛ. [1247]
**d*-:	*daga daga*	Ko. Ka. Tu.; Te.; Kuṛ. Malt. (<? IA) [2998]

It is also a question of how old these expressions are in the literary languages to make sure that they have not culturally diffused during recent times.

Another area to look for is a possible 'voicing laryngeal' in early Dravidian. Several etymologies with widely distributed voiced stops in many languages have unexplained aspiration associated with stops, both voiced and voiceless, in Naikṛi, a Central Dravidian language, and in Naiki (Chanda). These are not borrowed items from Indo-Aryan, e.g. Naikṛi:

(54) *ghaḍḍi* 'grass, straw', Kol. *gaḍḍi*; Te. *gaḍḍi*, Go. *gaḍḍi*, *gaḍḍu*, Koṇḍa *gaḍi*, Kuvi *gaṇḍrī* || IA *khaṭa*-, *khaḍa*- *CDIAL* 3769 [1158].

(55) *ghāḷi* 'wind, air', Nk. (Ch.) *ghāy* id., Kol. *gāli*; Ka. Koḍ. Tu. *gāḷi*; Te. *gāli*, Go. *gāl*, Koṇḍa *gāli*, Kuvi *gāli* [1499].

(56) *ghel* 'to win', Kol. *gell*-; Ta. *keli* 'to conquer', Ko. *gel*- (*geḏ*-), To. *kelc*-, Koḍ. *gel*- (*gedd*-), Tu. *gelpuni*, *genduni*, Ka. *gel*- (*gedd*-); Te. *gelucu*, Koṇḍa *gels*-, Kuvi *gelh*- [1972].

(57) *ghummi* 'storage basket for grain'; Te. *gummi* id. Ta. Ka. Koḍ. forms with *k*- mean something else [2117].

(58) *ghunḍ* 'stone', Kol. *gunḍ*; Ta. *kuṇṭu* 'ball, anything globular, bullet', Ko. *guṇḍ gal* 'a huge round stone', Ka. Tu. *guṇḍu*; Te. *guṇḍu* 'rock, bullet, anything spherical', *guṇḍr-ani* adj. 'round', Go. *gonḍra* 'round' [1695].

(59) *ghurram* 'horse', Nk. (Ch.) *kurmam*, Kol. *gurram*, Pa. *gurrol*; Te. *guṟ(ṟ)am*, Go. *gurram*, Koṇḍa *guṟam*, Kuvi *gurromi* [1711b].

SD I: **kut-ir-ay* forms do not seem to be phonologically related to the above set.

(60) *dhāv* 'distance', Kol. *davva, dautān* 'distant'; Te. *dawwu* 'distance', Nahali *dhava* 'distance' [?446].

The other cognates given by *DEDR* looking to **eṭ-ay* do not fit phonologically. A related form in Nahali suggests another substrate language as the ultimate source. Naiki (Chanda):

(61) *khaj* 'itch', Pa. *kajra*; Koḍ. *kajji*, Tu. *gajji*, Ka. *kajji*, *gajji* 'scab, itch'; Te. *gajji* 'itch', also *kasi*, Go. *gajji*, *gajju*, Koṇḍa *gazi*, Kui *kas*; Kuṛ. *khasrā* id., *xā*^{n}*snā* 'to scratch for relief' ||>Pkt. *khajjū CDIAL* 3827 [1104].

(62) *khīr* 'line', Kol. *kīra*, Pa. *gīr*, Gad. *gīri*; Koḍ. *gīc*- 'to make a mark by scratching', Ka. *gīṟu* 'to scratch', n. 'a line', *gīku*, *gīcu* v.t., *gīṭu* n., Tu. *gīruni* v.t., *gīṭï* 'line, scratch'; Te. *gīṟu* v.t., *gī̃ku*, *gīcu*, *gīyu* 'to scratch', *gī̃ta*, *gīṭu* 'stroke, line', Go. 'line', Koṇḍa *gīr* n., Kui–Kuvi *gīra* 'line'; A number of languages have *k*- forms: Ta. Ma. Ko. Tu. ||>? Skt. *kīraka*- 'a scribe' [1623].

(63) *phar* 'big, elder', Pa. *berto* 'big', Oll. *berit*; Te. *bebbuli* (< *per-puli*) 'tiger', Go. *ber*- 'big', Kui *beri beri inba* 'to swell, increase in size'. Most other languages have *p*- [4411].

Why does Naikṛi have aspirated voiced stops in native words, and that, moreover, where the aspirates correspond to voiced stops in many subgroups, mainly in South Dravidian and Central Dravidian? It has unaspirated *g*- (16 items) contrasting with *gh*- (10 items); similarly, *dh*- (3 items): *d*- (2 items), *ḍh*- (3 items): *ḍ*- (8) all of which appear to be loanwords from Early Telugu, *kh*- (8 items): *k*- (c. 80 items), *ph*- (2 items) *p*- (70 items). The cognates in the case of *kh*- and *ph*- have no voiced counterparts. The related words in IA and Nahali (perhaps borrowings from Dravidian) for ety. (54), (60) and (61) also show aspirated stops. The evidence is preponderantly with *gh*- corresponding to voiced *g*- in most other languages. It is better to leave the matter here without any conclusion, until more fieldwork is done on Naikṛi and Naiki.

4.5.2.1 *A quantitative study: voiced or voiceless stops in Proto-Dravidian?*

Methodology I have adopted a quantitative approach to determine if Proto-Dravidian had a contrast between voiced and voiceless stops in word-initial position.[7] The first step:

[7] I am indebted to Lincoln Moses, my former research collaborator (see Krishnamurti 1983) and Statistical Consultant at the Center for Advanced Study at Stanford, who suggested this approach to me in October 2000. It is a fairly standardized technique.

using *DEDR* (1984) as the source, I listed separately the entries with initial stops *k/g, c/j, t/d, p/b* that have cognates in all *four* subgroups. Even if one language in a subgroup has a clear cognate, I have taken the subgroup as represented. This criterion has naturally limited the list to a manageable few. *DEDR* has a total of 5,558 numbered entries. The number of entries with initial stops and the ones represented in all four subgroups are as follows:

Initial segment	DEDR entries	Difference	Entries in all subgroups
k/g	1075–2263	1189	37
c/j	2264–2900	637	18
t/d	2995–3567	573	20
p/b	3801–4614	814	44
Total		3213	119

These figures show that entries beginning with stops constitute 57.81 per cent of the total of 5,558 entries in *DEDR* and the ones represented in all subgroups make up 3.7 per cent of this total. I have not considered initial *ṭ/ḍ* (*DEDR* 2938–94) 57 entries since none of them is represented in all four subgroups. Note that Proto-Dravidian had no words beginning with apical (alveolar and retroflex) stops.

The second step was to set up three possible representations of stops initially and give them numerical values, e.g. *k-* = 3, *k-/g-* = 2, *g-* = 1. I prepared a table with all languages listed at the top according to subgroups from Tamil to Brahui, as follows: Tamil, Malayāḷam, Koḍagu, Toda, Koṭa, Kannaḍa and Tuḷu (seven languages: SD I); Telugu, Gondi, Koṇḍa, Kui, Kuvi, Pengo, Manḍa (seven languages: SD II); Kolami, Naikṛi/Naiki, Parji, Ollari, Gadaba (five languages: Central Dravidian); Kuṛux, Malto, Brahui (three languages: North Dravidian) = twenty-two languages. For each entry in a row I marked under each language if the cognate has one of the possible reflexes of a given segment, e.g. *k-*, or *k-/g-* or *g-*. In the vertical column at the end of each language, it would then be possible to list the total number of entries that have different reflexes: *k-* or *k-/g-* or *g-*.

The third step was to multiply each variant with a numerical value already assigned, say, k 5 × 3 = 15, k/g 5 × 2 = 10, g 5 × 1 = 5; the aggregate value for fifteen entries is 15 + 10 + 5 = 30. Therefore, the average voicing index is this total value divided by the number of entries available, i.e. 30/15 = 2. This procedure was repeated for each language and subgroup; then, for the whole family, the score for a given segment could be computed. After doing this for the four stops, an average index of the four indexes could be arrived at by dividing the total index value by four, standing for the four stop segments. That is the index for the whole family and is taken to represent the status of the proto-stage.

The fourth step was interpreting the results. The final score for all the entries for the whole family should range between 3 and 1. Any final score above 2.5 would suggest that Proto-Dravidian had only voiceless stops to start with, and voicing has infiltrated into some languages, owing to internal changes and/or borrowing from other families, like Indo-Aryan or Munda. If the final score was 1.5 or below, it would suggest that Proto-Dravidian had primarily voiced stops, and voiceless stops must have infiltrated into the system through the same factors. If the score was between 1.51 and 2.49 the result would be indecisive: it would show that Proto-Dravidian had both voiceless and voiced stops, with a higher score suggesting more words with initial voiceless stops and a lower score suggesting more words with voiced stops. Circumstances leading to developing voicing secondarily are greater and more natural in linguistic change than the reverse. It is also possible to work out scores for individual entries by language, subgroup or family and discover the ones that have tilted the scores one way or the other. Similarly, the average index by language would show which language and which subgroup registers a lower or higher score in voicing phenomena. It would also be possible to find out historical explanations for such variation. For instance, Telugu has cognates for 35 out of 37 entries with *k-/g-*; out of these there are 26 items with *k-* ($26 \times 3 = 78$), 7 items with *k-/g-* ($7 \times 2 = 14$) and 2 items with *g-* ($2 \times 1 = 2$); the total value for 35 cognates is $78 + 14 + 2 = 94$; the average score is $94/35 = 2.685$. The average scores for all four segments give the total voicing score for the whole language.

Before we look at the results, certain clarifications would be in order. I have reconstructed the proto-phonemes for each entry under velar, palatal, dental and labial, only to make sure that items belonging to one phoneme are not listed under another. There are sound changes, which affected the word-initial phonemes in different languages, e.g. palatalization of **k* (section 4.5.1.4) gives either *c/s* or *j* in one or more languages which had this sound change, namely Tamil, Malayāḷam and Telugu. If the changed phoneme is voiced, the proto-phoneme is also counted as voiced, although it is possible for voicing to have developed after palatalization. Such cases are numerically so rare that the score will not be affected by them. In South Dravidian I, PD **c-* became Ø in some items, presumably through intermediate **s* and **h*; therefore, *c-/Ø-* alternation comparatively would suggest the segment as a voiceless one in a given language. Similarly, if there is *s/h/Ø* (dialectally in Gondi), it is taken to represent a voiceless phoneme for the relevant item (section 4.5.1.3.2). Palatalized velars are not involved in loss. Another such change is **p- >h-* in Early Medieval Kannaḍa. *DEDR* mostly takes only the older forms with *p-*, but where only *h-* occurs corresponding to *p-* in other languages, it is also taken as a voiceless stop (section 4.5.1.1). Alternations *k-/g-*, *t-/d-*, etc. are set up even if there is one item derived from the same root which shows a voiced stop, while several others show a voiceless stop; the relative frequency of the alternation for a given etymology is not taken into account. Sometimes the alternation could be between social dialects. Not all circumstances of such alternations are retrievable from mere listings in *DEDR*.

Table 4.7a *Voicing index (VI) of word-initial stops in South Dravidian I and II for 119 entries*

Seg	Ta	Ma.	To.	Ko.	Koḍ	Ka.	Tu.	Te.	Go	Kon.	Kui	Kuvi	Pe.	Manḍa
k/g	3.00	2.97	2.97	2.67	2.93	2.72	2.72	2.69	2.74	2.41	2.57	2.50	2.83	2.77
c/j	3.00	3.00	3.00	2.77	3.00	2.88	2.78	2.84	3.0	3.00	2.70	2.69	3.00	2.66
t/d	3.00	3.00	3.00	2.70	2.70	2.63	2.68	2.68	2.58	2.67	2.50	2.60	2.70	3.00
p/b	3.00	3.00	3.00	3.00	2.90	3.00	2.89	2.90	2.85	2.93	2.92	2.81	3.00	3.00
VI	3.00	2.99	2.99	2.78	2.88	2.81	2.77	2.77	2.83	2.75	2.67	2.65	2.88	2.86

Table 4.7b *Voicing index of word-initial stops in Central Dravidian for 119 entries*

Segment	Kol.	Nk.	Pa.	Oll.	Gad.	Subgroup
k/g	2.80	2.90	2.80	2.80	2.90	2.84
c/j	2.83	3.00	3.00	3.00	3.00	2.97
t/d	2.90	2.82	2.84	3.00	2.77	2.87
p/b	2.86	2.90	2.74	3.00	2.92	2.89
VI by lang.	2.85	2.90	2.85	2.95	2.89	2.89

Results Tables 4.7a-d give the voicing index for each segment, language, subgroup and the whole family. VI = voicing index by language (average of the four rows under each column).

From table 4.7a, the voicing index for South Dravidian I is 2.89 and for South Dravidian II is 2.77. For the whole branch, the voicing index is 2.86. Tamil has the maximum score, i.e. no voiced stops in word-initial position. The lowest score in South Dravidian I is that of Tuḷu. In South Dravidian II, Pengo–Manḍa show the highest score (fewer words with initial voicing) and Kui–Kuvi the lowest (more words with initial voicing). On the whole South Dravidian II has more words with word-initial voicing than South Dravidian I.

In table 4.7b the voicing index is like that of South Dravidian I. Naiki and the Ollari–Gadaba subgroup have fewer words with initial voiced stops.

In table 4.7c all members show a high score, suggesting more voiceless stops word-initially, despite their exposure to Indo-Aryan for over two millennia.

Scores for each of the segments, by subgroup and family, are given in table 4.7d.

The score for the whole family is 2.855 or 2.86, which clearly proves that Proto-Dravidian had primarily only voiceless stops and it is still the dominant feature in native lexical items. We also notice that velar and dental series are more prone to voicing than palatal and labial series. South Dravidian II has a lower score than all other sub-groups suggesting a higher degree of voicing than other languages. This coincides with

Table 4.7c *Voicing index of word-initial stops in North Dravidian for 119 entries*

Segment	Kuṛux	Malto	Brahui	Subgroup
k/g	2.90	2.90	2.70	2.83
c/j	3.00	2.85	3.00	2.95
t/d	2.75	2.82	2.78	2.78
p/b	2.87	2.82	3.00	2.90
VI	2.88	2.85	2.87	2.865

Table 4.7d *Voicing index of word-initial stops in the whole family*

Segment	SD I	SD II	CD	ND	Family
k/g	2.85	2.64	2.84	2.83	2.79
c/j	2.92	2.84	2.97	2.95	2.92
t/d	2.82	2.68	2.87	2.78	2.78
p/b	2.97	2.92	2.89	2.90	2.92
Final VI	2.89	2.77	2.89	2.87	2.855

Zvelebil's study reported earlier. South Dravidian I still leads in voiceless stops, because Tamil–Toda have only voiceless stops in word-initial position; Malayāḷam has internal voicing sparingly.

Voicing can be accounted for through borrowing from Indo-Aryan or Munda, and also through voicing assimilation within native words, which I explained earlier as extension of the feature of voicing from non-initial segments to the initial segment, e.g. Ta. Ma. *tiruttu*, Ka. *tirdu, tiddu* (<**tir-t-* <**tir-utt-*) 'correct', Koḍ. *tidd-*, Tu. *tird-/tidd-*, but Te. *diddu* [3251]. I give below the lexical items that have only voiced stops in more than one subgroup; these naturally exclude Tamil, which represents even initial voiced stops as voiceless because of the limitation of its orthography. In the whole data there are three onomatopoetic items and two have decidedly voiced initials across subgroups, namely **guḍ*V *guḍ*V 'rumbling noise, thunder' [1659], **gur*V *gur*V 'snore, growl' [1852], **caṭ*V *caṭ*V 'cracking sound' [2796]. The last one has no voiced stop representation in any language. All the three occur in Indo-Aryan also and *CDIAL* has Middle Indic reconstructions:

(64) a. **guḍ*V *guḍ*V onom. 'gurgling or rattling sound'. SD I: Ta. Ma. *kuṭukuṭu*, To. *kuḍx-* v.i. 'stomach rumbles', Ko *guṛg, guṛ guṛ in-* (*in-* 'say'), Ka. *guḍuguḍu* onom., *guḍugu* n. 'thunder, roar', Tu. *guḍuguḍu*; SD II: Te. *guḍaguḍa* onom. of drinking fast, Go. *guṛnj-* 'to thunder', Koṇḍa *guṛuguṛu* 'running fast', Kui *ḍṛū* 'thunder', Kuvi *gṇu-* 'to thunder';

CD: Kol. *guḍm-* 'make noise', Pa. *guṛi, guḍr-* 'to thunder'; ND: Kuṛ. *guṛguṛur-* v.i. 'make noise like thunder' || *CDIAL* 4180 cites IA etymologies and reconstructs for IA **guḍuguḍu-* [1659].

b. **gur*V *gur*V onom. 'sound of snoring, growling'. SD I: Ta. *kuṟukuṟuppu, koṟukk-ai* 'snoring', Ma. *kuṟukuṟukka* 'breathe hard', *kurkku* 'a snore', Ka. *guṟuguṟu* 'sound of snoring', *gu/oṟuku, gorke* 'snoring', Tu. *guranè* 'snarling of dog', *gurru kore-* 'to snore'; SD II: Te. *guṟaka, guṟṟu* 'snoring', Go. *gurr-*'to snore', Koṇḍa *gōr-* v.i 'snore', *gōr-uṇ* 'snoring', Kui *ḍrōka* (<**grō-* <**gor*-V-) 'snoring', Kuvi *ḍruk-, gurr-* v.i. 'snore'; CD: Kol. *gurgaḍil-* 'dog growls', Pa. *gurr-* 'to hiss', *gurj-* 'to squeak'; ND: Kuṛ. *gurr-* 'roar as tiger, shout', Br. *g̲hurr-* 'to growl' || **guragura CDIAL* 4486, Skt. *ghuraghurā-yate* 'it growls' 4489 [1852].

At this point we do not know the historic source of such onomatopoetic expressions, in the absence of comparative and etymological data from Munda languages. Since onomatopoetic expressions tend to fall outside the normal phonological system of a language (see Emeneau 1993: 83), we cannot generalize that voiced and voiceless stops contrasted in Proto-Dravidian and the contrast is confined only to onomatopoeia. We can safely conclude from the quantitative study that Proto-Dravidian had only voiceless stops and voicing originated in the descendant languages through internal changes and borrowing. We have shown that infiltration of voicing in the whole family stands at .16 out of 3.00, i.e. .005 per cent. It is remarkable that the proto-feature is so persistent even after about 3,000 years of breakup of Proto-Dravidian.

4.5.3 *Initial consonants: nasals*

4.5.3.1 *m-

PD * *m-* remains in all languages, except Brahui in which it splits into *m-* and *b-*; *b-* when followed by front vowels, and *m-* elsewhere. This split is parallel to the split of **n-* into *d-* and *n-* (Krishnamurti 1969c).

Rule 16a. *Nasal split in Brahui*

m > *b*/ #__[+V, −back] (Brahui)

(65) PD **mē, mē-l* 'above, high, excellence'. SD I: Ta. *mē, mēl* n. 'height, high place, above, sky', Ma. *mē, mēn*, Ko. *mē*, To. *mēl* 'up', Koḍ. *mē, mēm-* adj, Ka. *mē, mēgu* n., *mēm-* adj., Tu. *mēlï* 'upper part'; SD II: Te. *mēlu* 'high, excellent, good', Go. *mēlta* 'good'; ND: Br. *bē* 'up, over, on (verbal prefix)', *bē-haṛsing* 'to turn over' [5086].

(66) PD **mēy* 'to graze'. SD I: Ta. *mēy* 'to graze', Ma. *mēy*, Ko. *mēy*, To. *mīy*, Koḍ. *mēy*, Ka. *mē-, mēyu* (past *mēdu*), Tu. *mēyuni* v.i., *mēpuni* v.t.; SD II:

Te. *mēyu* v.i, *mēpu* v.t., Go. *mēy-*, Koṇḍa *mēy-*, Kuvi *mēy*, *mē-*; CD: Kol. Nk. *mī-* v.i., *mīp-* v.t. Pa. *mēy-* v.i., *mēp-* v.t.; ND: Kuṛ. *men-* v.i, *menta-* v.t., Malt. *min-* v.i., Br. *bei* 'grass fit for grazing' [5093].

Krishnamurti (1969c) examined fourteen etymologies to establish a split of *n-* into *d-/n-* with one exception and *m-* > *b-/m-* also with one exception. The authors of *DEDR* have accepted the above rules. For retention of **m-* in different subgroups, see **maram* 'tree' (35).

4.5.3.2 *n-

PD **n-* remains unchanged in all languages except Brahui before all vowels (Krishnamurti 1961: § 1.24; 1969c). Old Tamil distinguished between dental and alveolar nasals; word-initially and before a dental stop, dental [n] occurred, in all other non-initial positions (intervocalically, in gemination, before **ṯ*, and finally) the alveolar nasal [ṉ] occurred. However, according to Tolkāppiyam there were few contrasts between the two in non-initial positions, e.g. *verin* 'back': *var-iṉ* 'if one comes', both from Cankam texts; there are text variants to the contrary in some cases (Shanmugam 1971b: 32–3, also fn. 11). Malayāḷam developed contrast secondarily in geminates, **nt*, **nṯ* [nd/nḏ] >*nn* (dental), **nn* [ṉṉ] > *ṉṉ*, e.g. *puṉṉa* 'mast-wood' vs. *kunnu* 'hill' (<**kunṯu*) (see Subrahmanyam 1983: 380). It appears that the nasal+ alveolar sequence merged with nasal +dental and both these developed into a geminate dental stop in Malayāḷam. In any case there is no comparative evidence to set up two n-phonemes for Proto-Dravidian. As in Tamil there could have been a phonetic difference between initial dental [n] and non-initial alveolar [ṉ] in Proto-Dravidian also, because /n/ occurs word-initially in Proto-Dravidian reconstructions unlike the alveolar phonemes /ṯ l r/. For this reason /n/ is put in the dental column in the chart (see table 4.2).

Rule 16b.

**n* > *d*/#__[+V, −back] (Brahui)

(67) PD **nīr* 'water'. SD I: Ta. Ma. Ko To. *nīr*, Ta. *īr* 'moisture', Ma. *īrppam* 'dampness', Koḍ. Tu. *nīri*, Ka. *nīr*, *nīru*; SD II: Te. *nīru*, Go. *nīr*, Koṇḍa *nīr masu* 'dew', Kui *nīru* 'juice, sap, essence', CD: Kol. Nk. *īr*, Pa. Oll. Gad. *nīr*; ND: Br. *dīr* 'water, flood-water' || >Skt. *nīr* 'water, juice, liquor' [3690].

There are six certain etymologies, Br. *ditar* 'blood' < **ney-tt-*V*r* [*DED* 3798], Br. *darō* 'yesterday' <**ner*-V- (Br. *a-* <**e-*) [3758], Br. *dē* 'sun' <**nēr-* [3744], etc. There is a much larger number preserving **n-* before non-front vowels. The only exception to the split rule is second sg pron. *nī* in Brahui which could have been analogically restructured on *n*- allomorphs of the paradigm, *n-ā* gen sg, *num*- pl nom. and obl. (Krishnamurti 1969c). For other cases of retention of **n*- see ety. (4b), (25) and (43).

There is a sporadic loss of **n*- in various languages (Krishnamurti 1961: §§1.32, 1.218–20, pp. 17, 91–2), but its loss is more common in the Kolami–Naiki subgroup (see (67)). It is almost a regular sound change in Naiki (Suvarchala 1992: 20).

4.5.3.3 *ñ-

Proto-Dravidian **ñ* occurred only word-initially mainly before *ă* and *ĕ* (short or long). It is phonemically preserved in Old Tamil, Old and Modern Malayāḷam, Koḍagu and Tuḷu. Not all items that require the reconstruction of **ñ* are preserved in all these languages. Tamil and Malayāḷam give evidence of contrast between this and the other nasals. This phoneme has merged with *n*- (< **n*-) in almost all the languages (including Middle and Modern Tamil). Some relic forms after merger are retained in Malayāḷam, Koḍagu, Tuḷu and Havyaka Kannaḍa (Subrahmanyam 1983: 375–6). Burrow (1946: 603–16) has discussed this problem in great detail, followed by Krishnamurti (1961: §§1.25–32, pp. 13–17), Emeneau (1970a), Zvelebil (1970b) and Subrahmanyam (1983). Burrow gives 12 Tamil examples for **ñā*-, of which in 5 cases Malayāḷam has *ñ*- but Tamil has *n*-, e.g. Ta. *nāṟu* 'young plant': Ma. *ñāṟu*; he cites 18 cases of Ta. *ña*- corresponding to *ña*-, *ñe*- in Malayāḷam and suggests that original *a* and *e* merged with *e* after *ñ* in Old Tamil. Then he gives examples of alternation of *na-/ne-* in Kannaḍa and Telugu and derives these from an original *ñ*- which no language preserves. He contrasts these with etymologies pointing to unchanged **na*- or **ne*- (607–8). From Burrow's treatment of the problem we note three facts: (1) neutralization of contrast between *ă* and *ĕ* after **ñ*-; (2) because of neutralization, the varying vowel qualities occurring after *n*- (as *na-/ne-*) do not necessarily indicate the original qualities of vowels before such neutralization occurred in Proto-Dravidian, if such a stage really existed; and (3) that the merger of **ñ*- with **n*- started very early in Proto-South Dravidian and was accomplished in SD II by the time it branched off. In South Dravidian I the merger was completed in Kannaḍa; while the change was still in progress, Tuḷu split first, followed by Pre-Tamil from which Koḍagu and then Malayāḷam split later. Therefore, all these languages show the retention of **ñ*- in different degrees. In Central Dravidian and North Dravidian, we do not know when PD **ñ*- merged with the reflexes derived from **n*-. Where there is *ñ*- in Ta. Ma. and Ø- in the other languages, it is possible that **ñ*- is secondary in Ta. Ma. (<**y*-) (see for examples Krishnamurti 1961: §1.31, p. 17), e.g. Ta. *ñaṇṭu* : Te. *eṇḍri* 'crab' (also Ø in Ka. Go. and all Central Dravidian languages).

The merger is described by the following rule:

Rule 17. *Palatal nasal reduction*

PD **ñ* > **n*/ #__ $V_1(V_1 = \breve{\bar{a}}\ \breve{\bar{e}})$

DEDR has 37 etymologies listed under *ñ-* (2901–2937). A re-examination of these shows that both Tamil and Malayāḷam provide evidence for *ñ- > n-* and also variation between *ā̆* and *ē̆*, during the historic period, Ta. *ñā-*, *ñi-*: Ma. *nā-*, *ni-* [2918, 2921, 2922], Ta. *nā-*: Ma. *ñā-* [2906, 2909, 2911, 2914], Ta. *ne-* : Ma. *ñe-* [2925, 2928, 2929, 2933, 2934, 2935], Ta. *na-* : Ma. *ña-/na-* [2903, 2905], Ta. *no-* : Ma. *ño-* [2936]. Beside these there are other correspondences: Ta. *ña-/ñe-* : Ma. *ña-/na-* [2904], Ta. *ñā-* : Ma. *ñā-* [2908, 2910, 2912, 2913, 2915, 2919, 2920]; there is one case where Ta. *ñā-*: Ma. *ñē-* [2917]. Shanmugam (1971b: 37–8) gives illustrations for the merger of *ñ-* with *n-* in Pre-Tamil.

When we are dealing with this problem, we need to consider the period (pre-ninth century CE) when Tamil and Malayāḷam have to be taken as dialects of the same language, rather than as two independent languages. In that case, it appears that the vocalic variation *ā̆* and *ē̆* is shared by both of them as also the replacement of *ñ* by *n*. It appears in Proto-Dravidian **ñ* was probably followed by all the vowels, but during the historical period we find mainly *ā̆*, *ē̆*, *i* and *ō̆*, but not *ī* and *ū̆*; this distribution seems phonologically defective and unmotivated. It could be that **ñ-* was frozen midway of the change (after its merger with **n-* was completed before the other vowels) in a few South Dravidian I languages. What is difficult to ascertain is if the vowel qualities were distinct in some subgroups, mainly South Dravidian II and Central Dravidian, when **ñ-* coalesced with *n-* in these languages.

Notice, Ta. Ma. *ñā-*: *nā-* in other languages in 2906, 2909, 2914, 2918, but Ta. Ma. **ñā-* : *nē-* in other languages in 2908, 2910–2913, 2915, 2919, 2920; Ta. *ñā-*, Ma. *ñē-* all others *nā-/nē-* (2907). In some South Dravidian II languages the vowel is represented as *ō-* before retroflex consonants, suggesting a change of *ē- > ō-* through retraction.

(68) PD **ñāṇ/ñēṇ* 'string, cord'. SD I: Ta. Ma. *ñāṇ*, Ta. *nāṇ*, To. *nȫṇ*, Tu. Ka. *nēṇu*; Te. *nānu* 'a necklace', Go. *nōṇe*, Kui *nōṇu*, Kuvi *nōṇo* 'rope' [2908].

(69) PD **ñāṯu* 'to emit smell' > SD I: Ta. *ñāṟu*, *nāṟu*, Ma. *nāṟuka* 'to stink', Ko. *nār* 'to smell bad', Koḍ. *nār*, Tu. *nād-uni* v.i., Ka. *nāṟu*; CD: Pa. *ned-* (*nett-*) 'to smell' [2918].

(70) PD **ñēnṯu* 'time, day'. SD I: Ta. *ñānṟu*, *nānṟu*, Ma. *ñānnu*; SD II: Te. *nē̆ḍu* 'today', Go. *nēnḍ*, Koṇḍa *nēnṟu*, Kuvi *nēcu*, *ninju*, Pe. *nēnjeṅ*, Manḍa *nēnj(e)* 'today' [2920].

The question is, if (68) and (70) point to PD **ē* and (69) to PD **ā*, how does one explain the different qualities of vowels in South Dravidian I and South Dravidian II? There is one precious etymology that Burrow has ignored and the other writers have also not considered. Malayāḷam has **ñān/ñan-* 'I' corresponding to *nān/nan-* in South Dravidian I, *nēn/nan-*, *nā-* beside *nān/nā-* in South Dravidian II. I have explained this problem elsewhere (section 6.4.1.1). It shows that the domain of variation between low and mid front vowels is mainly South Dravidian I and South Dravidian II. They are distinguished in Central Dravidian and North Dravidian. Our tentative conclusion is that the pre-merger qualities of the vowels after *_ñ_ are preserved in the languages outside South Dravidian I and South Dravidian II, for the simple reason that they do not show variation between _ā̆_ and _ē̆_. Therefore, the merger of one set of vowels with the other and the consequent neutralization of their qualities must have taken place at the stage of Proto-South Dravidian.

4.5.4 _**Initial consonants: glides or semivowels**_

4.5.4.1 *w-

It may be recalled that /*w/ occurs only before unrounded vowels in Proto-Dravidian. It remains unchanged in all languages, except in Kannaḍa of SD I and in all members of the North Dravidian subgroup. Kuṛux and Malto of ND are surrounded by the Bihari languages, in which OIA *_v-_ > _b-_ around the eighth century CE (Masica 1991: 202–3). But the same feature (PD *_w-_ > _b-_) is found in Brahui also in native vocabulary, although, in its present habitat, it is in contact with Indo-Aryan languages (Sindhi, Lahnda etc.) in which the sound change *_v-_ to _b-_ had not taken place. This is, therefore, one of the pieces of evidence to say that Brahui was spoken in Northern India along with Kuṛux and Malto before the speakers migrated northwest to their present habitat. Elfenbein (1987: 229) says that Brahuis 'emigrated to their present habitat 1000 years ago . . . ', but he does not give linguistic arguments. In South Dravidian I Kannaḍa also changed a word-initial _w_ to _b_ as attested by the inscriptions with effect from the seventh century CE (_TVB_: 27, also fn. 40, p.127, Gai 1946: 15, 16). Forms with _b-_ increase with time, but items with _v-_ also occur in inscriptions till the twelfth century. Pampa Bhārata, the first literary work in Kannaḍa, has mainly _b-_ for *_w-_; only three words are recorded in it with _v-_. In verb and noun compound words beginning with _v-_ are retained still in spelling, e.g. _eḷa-vāẓe_ 'young plantain', _key-vīsu_ 'to wave a hand' (Ramachandra Rao 1972: 11, 92, 158). The change was extended to some non-initial positions in later Kannaḍa, e.g. _obbanu_ 'one man' (<*_or-banu_ <* _or_(_u_)-_wanu_), _ib-baru_ 'two persons' (< *_ir-baru_ <*_iru-waru_). This sound change does not seem to arise from any contact situation. The isogloss of this change also extends to Koḍagu, Tuḷu, Baḍaga and different Kuṟumba dialects. Even Telugu has some words with _b-_ borrowed from Kannaḍa from early time, e.g. _baḍalu_ 'to be tired': Ka. _baẓal_ (_TVB_: 27).

Rule 18. _Bilabial glide to voiced stop or Glide fortition_

a. *_w_ > _b_/#__ (Ka. Koḍ. Tu. Baḍaga, Kuṟumba)
b. *_w_ > _b_/#__ (ND: Kuṛ.–Malto, Brahui)

There is no contrast between bilabial [w] and the labio-dental [v] in any of the Dravidian languages, at any stage. PD *_w-_ occurs only before low and front vowels /a ā i ī e ē/.

The non-occurrence of labial (rounded) vowels distinctively after /w/ in Proto-Dravidian perhaps hints at its phonetic value of being a bilabial. A _w_-onglide occurs with words beginning with rounded vowels in all southern languages as a phonetic phenomenon. I prefer to use /w/ in my reconstructions for Proto-Dravidian and also for Telugu. Several authors write <v> instead but they do not mean that the sound that they are representing is a labio-dental. The choice seems to be purely arbitrary.

(71) PD *_waH-_, *_waH-r_ 'to come'. SD I: Ta. _varu-_ (_va-nt-_, _vā-_, _vār-_), _varavu_ 'coming', _vāri_ 'income', Ma. _varuka_ (_va-nn-_, _vār-_, _vā-_), Ko. _vār-_ (_va-d-_, _vā-_), To. _pōr-_ (_po-d-_, _pa-_), Koḍ. _bar-_ (_ba-nd-_, _bā-_, _bapp-_), Tu. _bar-pini_, Baḍaga _bā_ (_ba-nd-_, _bar-_, _bapp-_), Ka. _bar-_, _bār-_ (_ba-nd-_, _bā-_); SD II: Te. _wa-cc-_ (_rā-_), Go. _vai-_, _vāy-_ (_vā-t-_, _var-_), Koṇḍa _vā-_ (_vā-t-_, _ra-_), Kui, Kuvi, Pe. Manḍa _vā-_ (_vā-t-_): CD: Kol. _var-_ (_vatt-_, _va-_, _vā-_), Nk. _var-/va-_ (_vatt-_), Pa. _ver-_ (_ve-ñ-_ < *_we-nj-_ <_we-nd-_ <_war-nd-_; _a_ > _e_ before an alveolar in Parji), Oll. _var-_ (_vad-_), Gad. _vār-_ (_vadd-_); ND: Kuṛ. Malt. _bar-_, Br. _bann-ing_ (_bar-ba-_) [5270].

This verb is irregular. To explain the unexplained length in imperatives and negatives, I have reconstructed a laryngeal *_H_ for Proto-Dravidian (see Krishnamurti 1997b:153). Also see ety. (14), (61), (87) and (99).

Rule 18b is a shared innovation among the three North Dravidian languages. This change is likely to have occurred under the influence of the Magadhan languages of eastern India (Bengal and Bihar). In that case how can we justify the position of Brahui being the first branch of Proto-Dravidian, as claimed by some writers? Sindhi, Lahanda and Jaṭki (Western Indo-Aryan) are the neighbouring NIA languages of Brahui which did not change OIA *_v-_ to _b-_. Elfenbein (1987) thinks that Brahuis moved westward from the Kuṛux–Malto area about eight hundred years ago. Since Brahui shares other sound changes with Kuṛux–Malto, to say that it independently developed Rule 18b needs stronger arguments. Brahui has preserved _b-_ even where Kuṛ.–Malto have lost it, e.g. *_wil_ 'bow': Br. _bil_ [5422].

4.5.4.2 *y-

Only Early Tamil preserves PD *_y_ but it occurred only before _ā_ in about thirty words. It appears that *_y-_ loss started in Tamil quite early, e.g. _yāṟu_/_āṟu_ 'river' (Shanmugam 1971b: 36–7), but many forms still retained it in the Cankam texts.[8] South Dravidian I

8 Shanmugam (1971b: 36) says that there were 5 occurrences of loss of _y-_ in Sangam texts and still there occur 25 instances of _yā_. In the case Ta. _āḷ_ :Te. _ēlu_, a ninth-century inscription shows *_yāḷ_ although it was not preserved in any classical text.

and Central Dravidian languages usually show -*ā* after **y*- and South Dravidian II and North Dravidian languages -*ē* (Burrow 1946a: 599). It appears that contrast between *ā̆* and *ē̆* was neutralized after **y* in Proto-Dravidian.

Rule 19. *Initial glide loss*

**y* > Ø/#__*Ā̆*

Burrow (1946) dealt with this sound change at length. He showed several cases of alternation of *a*/*e* and *ā*/*ē* among words even when Old Tamil does not have a **y*-, e.g. Ta. Ma. Ka. Tu. *āḷ* 'to rule, govern': Te. *ēlu*. I reconstructed **yāḷ* (*TVB*: 90) which later turned up in a ninth-century Tamil inscription (Shanmugam 1971b: 37); similarly, Ta. Ma. Ka. *aẓu* 'to cry': Te. *ēḍcu* also looks to PSD **yāẓ* not attested anywhere. The verb 'to say' has an aberrant comparative phonology requiring the reconstruction of four variants **an-*/**en-*/**in-*/**ān-*. Previously, we thought that it derived from PD **yan-*, but this would not explain the *in-* and *ān*-forms. A better explanation is provided by a laryngeal in the root as **aHn-* (Krishnamurti 1997b). As in the case of **ñ-*, the Proto-Dravidian vowel following **y-* has to be an archiphoneme //Ā̆// representing the neutralization of *ā̆* and *ē̆*.

Even Early Tamil shows *ā*/*ē* variation. T. P. Meenakshisunaran (1968: §3, p. 228) gave examples of forms with *ē-* derived from **yā-* before those with *ā-*, e.g. *ētu* < *yātu* 'what?', *ēẓil* < *yāẓ* 'harp' etc. *DEDR* gives 13 entries (5149–5161).

(72) PD **yĀṭu* 'goat, sheep'. SD I: Ta. *yāṭu*, *āṭu*, Ma. *āṭu*, Ko. *āṛ*, To. *ōḍ*, Koḍ. *āḍï*, Tu. *ēḍï*; SD II: Te. *ēṭa* 'ram', Go. *ēṭi*, Kui–Kuvi *ōḍa*; ND: Kuṛ. *ēṛā* 'she-goat', Malt. *ēṛe*, Br. *hēṭ*|| > Skt. *ēḍa-*, *ēḍī-*, *ēḍaka-* [5152].

In one case there is an alternation of *sā-*/*yā-*/*tā-*/*Ø-* which leads us to posit a **c-* >(**h-*) >**y-* in Pre-Dravidian:

(73) PD ?*cām-p-* > *yām-p* 'tortoise'. SD I: Ta. *yāmai*, *āmai*, Ko. *ēmb*, Koḍ. *āme*, Tu. *ēme*, Ka. *āme*, *āve*, *ēme*, *ēve*; SD II: Te. *tā̃b-ēlu*, Go. **sēm-* > *hēm-ul*, *sam-el*, *yām-ōl*, Koṇḍa *tāmb-el*(*i*), Kui *sēmbi*, Kuvi *hēmbi*, *tāmb-eli*, Pe. *hām-aṇ* [5155].

It appears that the merger of **ñ-* with *n-* and **y-* > *Ø* are typologically motivated sound changes because of their asymmetrical distribution when compared to the other word-initial consonants. I have argued elsewhere that typologically motivated sound changes tend to be more regular than others and also more sweeping geographically. While there is no language that preserves **y-*, the number of languages that still retain **ñ-* seems to be very small (Malayāḷam, Koḍagu and Tuḷu with defective distribution in the last two).

4.5.5 *Medial consonants: obstruents*

Based on his study of Tamil, Caldwell (1956: 138–9) proposed the 'law of convertibility of surds and sonants' as representing 'the Dravidian phonetic system', i.e. surds word-initially and in gemination and sonants between vowels and in postnasal position. Krishnamurti (*TVB*: §§1.74–8) reviewed the history of the discussion on intervocalic obstruents obtaining at the mid century (Jules Bloch, P. S. Subrahmanya Sastri, Alfred Master, S. K. Chatterji) and concluded as follows: (1) On comparative grounds even Proto-Dravidian had lenis obstruents in intervocalic position and voiced ones in post-nasal position. Alfred Master (1937–9) mentioned the 'spirantization' of **-p-*, **-c-* as -**w-*, **-y-* in Ancient Tamil. He has also shown proof of *-t-* being pronounced *-d-* in Early Tamil. Krishnamurti (*TVB*: 31–2) has added comparative evidence of **-k-* [-g-] and **-c-* (> *-s-* >*-y-*) being weakened and lost in compensatory lengthening of V_1 in (C)V_1__-V_2- sequences in many Dravidian languages: *tō-l* < **tok-al* [3559, see ety. (31)], **kē-mpu* < **key-a-mpu* < **kic-a-mpu* [2004, see ety. (7)]. Here, vowel-lengthening goes to the Proto-Dravidian or Proto-South Dravidian stage. Intervocalic *-*ṯ*- has two realizations [-ḏ-] and [-ṟ-] in postnasal and intervocalic positions, perhaps dialectally in Proto-Dravidian.

It is not possible to find consistently shared innovations in the case of intervocalic obstruents. Therefore, they are depicted as patterns in figure 4.3. The most common reflex is shown in bold-face (see Krishnamurti 1998a).

4.5.5.1 *-p- = *-w-

Actually there is no item with **-p-* since it already became **-w-* in Proto-Dravidian. Wherever there is an alternation between root final *-p* and *-w-*, we can set up **-p*, through internal reconstruction, since it would contrast with unchanged *-w*/*-w-*.

(74) PD **kap(p)-* ~ **kaw-*V- 'to cover, overspread'. SD I: Ta. *kappu, kavi*, Ma. *kappukua, kaviyuka*; *kamiccal* 'inundation', Ko. *kavc-*, To. *kofy-* (*kofs-*), Tu. *kabiyuni* 'to besiege, surround', Ka. *kappu* 'to cover', *kavi* 'to cover', *kavicu* 'cause to come upon'; SD II: Te. *kappu* 'to cover', *kaviyu* 'to pounce upon, attack', *kamiyu* id.; Koṇḍa *kap-* 'clouds to overcast sky', Kuvi *kaph-* 'to outflank'; CD: Pa. *kapp-*; ND: Kuṛ. *khap-*, *kapp-* 'to cover', Malt. *kap-* 'to touch, meddle' [1221, 1225].

We notice the weakening of *-p-* to *-w-* in South Dravidian I and South Dravidian II languages. Also notice *-w-* sporadically becomes *-m-* in some languages, Malayāḷam and Telugu here. Also see ety. (10) **cup-* / **cuw-ar* > *up-*/*uw-ar* in South Dravidian I and South Dravidian II; **kep-* 'to say, speak' ~*kew*-V- 'ear' [1955, 1977a, c]; here, Tu. *keppu, kepputana* 'deafness' vs. Ta. Ma. *ceviṭu*, Ko. *kevṛ*, To. *kyūḍ*, Ka. *keppu*,

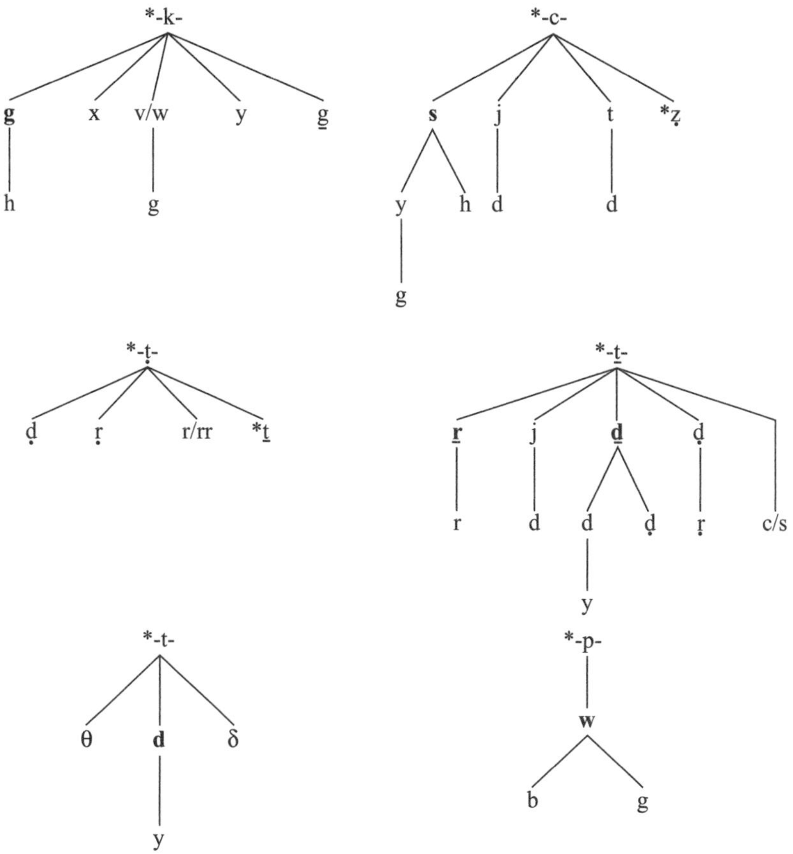

Figure 4.3 Reflexes of Proto-Dravidian intervocalic stops

kivaḍu; *keppu* 'a deaf man'; Te. *cewuḍu* 'deafness' (Gondi and Kolami have words borrowed from Telugu). I consider 1955 and 1977 related following their semantic and formal similarity and the pattern of noun–verb relationship in other body parts, e.g. **kay* 'hand': **key* 'to do', Te. *winu* 'to hear' : *wīnu* 'ear'.

4.5.5.2 *-t- [-d-]

Intervocalic *-t-* is represented as *-d-* in all languages that developed contrast between *-t-* and *-d-*; To. has θ. In Toda *-y* + *t* → *s*, *kwïy-* (*kwïs-*), cf. Ta. *koy-* (*koy-t-*) 'to cut'. Kuṛux and Malto also have *-th-* [ð] (Emeneau 1970a: §34, Mahapatra 1979: 27–8). In Modern Telugu intervocalic *-d-* in allegro becomes *-y-* or *-Ø-*, e.g. *caduwu-tū* → *caw-tū-*

'reading', *sampādincu* 'to earn' → *sampāyincu*. Some dialects of Gondi have *-dd-* after a short vowel.

(75) PD **met*-Vẓ 'brain', Ko. *medl*, Ka. *miduḷ*, *meduḷ*: SD II: Te. *medaḍu*, Go. *medur*, *maddur*; CD: Kol. Nk. *mitik*, Pa. *medek*, Gad. *medik*; ND: Kuṛ. *meddō*, Malt. *medo* [5062].

4.5.5.3 *-t̲- [-d̲-/-r̲-]

This phoneme patterns with stops in gemination and in postnasal position. In intervocalic position South Dravidian I and South Dravidian II represent this phoneme by a phone, transliterated as [-r̲-], which is phonetically a voiced alveolar trill contrasting with the flap *-r-* in all the literary languages. Toda in South Dravidian I and Koṇḍa in South Dravidian II preserve the contrast between *-r̲-* and *-r-*. The Mar̲ia dialect of Gondi has a uvular [r] written as [r̥] corresponding to South Dravidian *-r̲-* and it contrasts with *-r-*.[9] Several of the Nilgiri languages (Kota, Toda, Iruḷa, Kur̲umba) preserve the contrast of the three coronal consonants of Proto-South Dravidian, namely *t*: *t̲*: *ṭ* which they have inherited from Pre-Tamil, particularly in the postnasal position and gemination. The rest of the languages have merged *-r̲-* (<**t̲*) with *-r-*. The Kui–Kuvi–Pengo–Manḍa sub-branch of South Dravidian II developed [-r̲-] later to an affricate *-j-*. In the Central Dravidian languages the [-d̲-] variant has spread, although some etymologies show reflexes of [-r̲-], probably through dialect mixture. Tuḷu of South Dravidian I also represents this phoneme as *-j-/-d-* and sometimes *-r-*; Kuṛ.–Malto have -s-, *-r-*, *-ṛ-* and Brahui *-r-*,*-rr-*. (For a survey of the views of earlier scholars on **t̲* see *TVB*: §1.103–7, fn. 56; for details about reflexes Subrahmanyam 1983: 343–50.)

(76) PD **kut̲*-V- 'thigh'. SD I: Ta. *kur̲aṅku*, Ma. *kur̲aku*, *kur̲avu*, Ko. *korg*; SD II: Te. *kur̲uwu*, Go. *kurki*, *kohki* (< **kuR-kk-*; *r̲* becomes *R*, voiceless alveolar trill, before a voiceless stop), Koṇḍa *kur̲gu* (pl *kuRku*), Kui *kuju* (pl *kuska*), *kujugu*, Kuvi *kudgu*; CD: Kol. *kudug* (obl *kudg-*), Pa. *kudu* (pl *kudul*), NE *kuḍu*, Oll. *kuyug* (pl *kuygul*); ND: Kuṛ. *xosgā* 'leg, thigh', Malto *qosge* [1840].

(77) PD **āt̲*- 'to become cool, (fire, lamp) to be extinguished, to dry up'. SD I : Ta. Ma. *ār̲u* v.i., *ār̲r̲u* v.t., Ko. *ār-* v.i., *āt-* v.t., To. *ōr̲-* v.i., *ōt̲-* v.t., Koḍ. *ār-* v.i., *āt-* v.t., Tu. *āruni*, *ājuni*, Ka. *ār̲u* v.i., *ār̲isu* v.t.; SD II: Te. *ār̲u* v.i., *ārcu*, *ārpu* v.t., Go. *ār-*, (Mar̲ia dial.) *ār̥-*, Koṇḍa *ār̲-*, Kui *āj-* v.i., *ās-* v.t., Kuvi *āy-*; ND: Kuṛ. *arta'-* 'to spread out in the sun for drying' [404].

[9] Burrow and Bhattacharya (1960: 76) say, 'The treatment of original r̲ in the Hill-Mar̲ia dialect sets this dialect apart from all the rest of Gondi. Here original r̲ has been changed into a guttural fricative, which was usually transcribed <u>gh</u> or g in such transcriptions as we have come across, but which we, for etymological convenience, have transcribed r̥.'

Also study ety. (4a), (9), (22), (47a) and (67). Two points must be noted: (a) South-Central Dravidian (South Dravidian II) shares with South Dravidian I the common innovation of showing the [*-ṟ-] allophone whereas the reflexes in the Central Dravidian languages look to [*-ḏ-]. This supports our separating South Dravidian II from Central Dravidian and making it a closer sister of South Dravidian I; (b) in Modern Tamil, Kannaḍa and Telugu the difference between the two *r*'s is lost totally, but this is not a shared innovation. The phonetic proximity between *ṟ* and *r* must have typologically triggered this change, which is quite regular. Even in literary Telugu and Kannaḍa, the merger started first in closed syllables and spread to the intervocalic position (*TVB*: §1.103, particularly fn. 60).

There are some etymologies in which South Dravidian I and other subgroups have **ṭ*, but South Dravidian II has **ṯ*. It appears that *-*ṭ* merged with *-*ṯ* in South Dravidian II and the sound change discontinued after a few etyma were affected:[10]

(78) PD **pā-ṭ-* 'to sing'. SD I: Ta. Ma. *pāṭu* 'to sing, chant', *pā* 'verse', *pāṭṭu* n 'song', Ko. *pāṛv-* (*pāṛd-*), To. *pōṛ-* v, *pōṭ* 'song', Koḍ. *pāḍ-* v, *pāṭï* n; CD: Kol. *pāḍ-*, Nk. *pāṛ-*, Pa. *pāḍ-*, l. Gad. *pār-* v, *pāṭe* n; ND: Kuṛ. *pāṛ-* 'to sing', Malt. *pāṛ-* 'to bewail'; SD II: Te. *pāḍu* v, *pāṭa* n, Go. *pār-*, *wār-*; (Maṛia dial) *pāṛ̥-* (*ṛ̥*<**ṯ*); Koṇḍa *pāṟ-* 'to sing', *pāṭa* 'song' probably lw from Telugu; Kuvi *pāc-* (<**pāṯṯ-*) [4065].

One can consider **pā-* as the root with *-*ṭ* and *-*ṯ* as formatives at a deeper chronological layer. Telugu goes with South Dravidian I in this respect because of its geographical and cultural proximity to the literary languages of South India.[11] Other items include SD I **noṭ-V-* 'to wash', CD **noḍ-*, ND *nōḍ-* > SD II **noṯ-*: Go. *norr-*, (Maṛia dial) *noṛ̥-* (*noht-*), Koṇḍa *noṟ-* (*noRt-*), Kui *nog-*, Kuvi *nor-* (-*h*-), Pe. *noz-*, *nuz-* (*nost-*), Maṇḍa *nuy-* [3783]; similarly, **nāṭu* 'country, place' >**nāṯ* (SD II, except Te.) 'village', cf. Go. *nāṛ̥-* (Maṛia dial), Koṇḍa *nāṟu*, Kui *nāju* [3638], Kuvi *nāyu* (pl *nāska*) [3638], **ōṭ-*:**oṭ-V* 'to break', SD II: Go. (dial) *ōṛ-*, *ōr-*, v.i., *ōh-* v.t., Kui *ōj-* v.i., *oh-* v.t., Kuvi *ōy-* v.i., *ōh-* v.t., Pe. *ōh-* (*ōst-*) [946], **kōṭu* 'horn', SD II: Go. *kōṛ̥u*, *kōr* (pl *kōhk*) 'horn', Kui *kōju* (*kōska*)

10 Burrow and Bhattacharya (1960: 76–7) have indirectly indicated the merger of **ṭ* with **ṯ* in Gondi, while talking about ṛ̥ of Maṛia Gondi. 'This sound invariably corresponds to an original Gondi alveolar ṟ (which itself represented either Primitive Dravidian *ṟ* or -*ḍ*-).' They have made reference to the difference between *r* representing original *ṟ* and that representing original -*ḍ*-, for instance (Tr.) '*nār* "village" obl. *nāṭ-* with -*ṭ*- representing original -*ṭṭ*-' (1960: 77).

11 Old Telugu has several verbs with allomorphic alternation between *ḍ* and *ṟ*, e.g. *paḍu* v.i.'to suffer': *paṟucu* v.t. 'to make to suffer', *ceḍu* 'to perish': *ceṟucu* 'to kill', similarly *āḍu* 'to shake', *ōḍu* 'be defeated', *kūḍu* 'to join' have transitives *ār-cu*, *ōr-cu*, *kūr-cu*. These indicate that the alternation between **ṭ*/**ṯ* originated at the Proto-South Dravidian II stage and spread further in the languages through lexical diffusion (see *TVB*: 37, 45–6). There is one item in which only Telugu shows -*ṟ*- corresponding to **ṭ* in the other languages: **kaṭ-V-* 'to bite', Te. *kaṟacu* [1124]. *DEDR* puts the Telugu form under 1390 Ta. *kaṟi* 'to chew', but semantically 1124 is more normal.

[2200]. The *h*-forms in Gondi–Kui–Kuvi–Pengo–Maṇḍa come from **ṯṯ* or voiceless **ṯ* [P, i.e. a voiceless alveolar trill [R]. The merger is in some cases confined to one or two South-Central Dravidian (SD II) languages, e.g. PD **iṭ*-V- 'to put, place' > Koṇḍa *iḍ-* 'to put', *iṟ-* 'to serve', Pe. *iṭ-* 'to put', *iz-* 'to serve'; all other languages show reflexes of **ṭ* only [442], PD **cūṭ-/*cuṭ*-V- 'to be hot, to burn', SD II: Go. *surr-/hurr-*, *or̥-*'to cook', Koṇḍa *suṟ-* (*suR-*), 'to roast', Kui *sug-*, Kuvi *hūr-*, Pe. *huz-* (*hust-*): ND Kuṛ. Malt. *kuṛ-* [2654].

In contrast to these there are quite a few items in which the reflexes of **ṯ* and **ṭ* are kept apart in SD II (see ety. (9), (17) and (76)).

4.5.5.4 -*ṭ- [-ḍ-]

In South Dravidian I this is represented as *-ṭ-* [*-ḍ-*] in Ta. Ma., in Ko. and To. *-ṛ-/-ḍ-*, in Koḍ. Tu. Ka. *-ḍ-*; in SCD (SD II): Te. *-ḍ-* [-ṛ-], Go. *-r*, *-rr*, Koṇḍa, Kuvi, Pe. Maṇḍa *-ṛ*, Kui *-ḍ*, C] *ṛ*; CD: Kol. (dial) *-ḍ-/-ṛ-*, Nk. *-ṛ-*, Pa. *-ḍ-*, Oll. Gad. *-r*, *-rr*; ND: Kuṛ. Malt. *-ṛ-*, Br. *-ṛ*, *-r*, *-rr* (*TVB*: §§1.82–6, Emeneau 1970a: 64–5, Subrahmanyam 1983: §24, pp. 335–40). In the case of Toda–Kota the conditioning factors are not known. Here I have excluded the words in which **ṭ* merged with **ṯ* in South Dravidian II (see the previous section).

(79) PD **kūṭu* 'nest, receptacle'. SD I: Ta. Ma. *kūṭu*, Ko. *gūṛ*, To. *kūḍ*, Koḍ. *gūḍï*, Tu. *gūḍu*, Ka. *gūḍu*; SD II: Te. *gūḍu*, Go. *gūḍa*, Koṇḍa *gūṛu*, Kuvi *kūḍa*; CD: Pa. *gūḍa*, Oll. *gūḍe*, Gad. *gūḍu* [1883].

There is doubt if the merger of **ṭ* with **ṯ* was initiated in Proto-South Dravidian itself, because South Dravidian I also has a similar alternation in a few lexical items, e.g. Ta. *iṭu* 'to hit against, collide' [443]: Ta. *iṟu* 'to break, snap' [520], Ta. *keṭu* 'to perish' [1942]: Ta. *ceṟu*, *ceṟi* 'to kill, destroy' [1981] (see fn. 11).

4.5.5.5 *-c- [-s-]

In *TVB* (§§1.112–18) three lines of development of **-c-* have been indicated, namely (a) *-c-* >*-t-* [-d-] (sporadic merger with a dental stop); (b) *-s-* > *-y-* > *-g-/-w-*; (c) *-s-* > *-h-* > *Ø*. Besides these, there also seems to have been an alternation between **-c* and **-ẓ* in Proto-Dravidian itself, so that we get reflexes for both the Proto-Dravidian phonemes. Of the above (c) is still an ongoing sound change in Gondi–Kui–Kuvi–Pengo–Maṇḍa. Evidence for (a) and (b) is seen without a clear geographical division in different subgroups. It has already been suggested that, where South Dravidian I lost **c-*, it was likely to have passed through intermediate changes as in (c), although indirect evidence is available for this assumption (see fn. 4 above). The weakening of **-c-* is not found in North Dravidian.

(80) PD **pacc-* /**pac-*V- 'green/yellow'. SD I: Ta. *pacu* adj 'green, greenish yellow', *pai* 'greenness', v.i. 'to become green', *paccai* 'greenness'; Ma. *pacu, pai, paim-* 'fresh, tender, green', *pacca* 'greenness', Ko. *pac*, To. *poč* 'green', Koḍ. *pacce*, Tu. *pacca, paji* 'green', *pasɛ* 'moisture': SD II: Te. *pasi* 'young, tender', *pasimi* 'yellowness', *pasiḍi* 'gold', *pacca* 'green, yellow', *pairu* 'green crop', Go. *pahna* 'green, unripe', Koṇḍa *pasi* 'green, tender', *pasiŋ* 'turmeric', Pe. *pazi* 'fresh' [3812].

(81) PD **uc*-V- 'to breathe': SD I: Ta. *uy-* 'to live', *uyal* 'living', *uyir* v.i.'to revive', *uyirppu* n. 'breath', Ma. *uyir, ucir* 'life, breath', *uyirkka* 'to live', Ko. *ucr* 'life', To. *ūr, usir* 'life', Koḍ. *usïrï* 'breath', Tu. *usuru, usulu* 'breath, life'; SD II: Te. *usuru* 'life', *ūrcu* 'to sigh, breathe', *ūrpu* 'breath, sigh', Koṇḍa *usur* 'life, breath'; ND : Kuṛ. *ujj-* 'to take life', *ujjta-* 'to revive', Malt. *uj-* 'to live', n. 'life', Br. *ust* 'heart, mind' [645].

In ety. (31), we notice *-c->-t-* [-d-] in South Dravidian I: Koḍ. *peda*, Tu. *pudarï*, Koraga *podari, hudari*; CD: Pa. Oll. Gad. *pidir* 'name'; for *-c-* >*-y-* >*-g-*, see Te. *pagulu* 'to break', *bigiyu* 'to be tightened', *mugiyu* 'to end', *vagacu* 'to consider' in which *-g-* < *-y-* (*TVB*: §§1.79, pp. 33–4). This change characterizes all South Dravidian I languages also, cf. Ta. Ma. *paku* 'to break, be separate', Tu. *pagiyuni*, etc. all from **pay*-V- [3808]. Where Proto-Dravidian had **-c-*, it is in most cases preserved by Kannaḍa to a much larger extent than any other South Dravidian I language. In Middle Tamil we notice secondary *-s-* from an underlying *-y-*, perhaps a case of hyperstandardization. The direction of change was *-c-* [-s-] > *-y-* and not the reverse, e.g. Literary Ta. *kayiṟu* 'rope': Maturai Ta. *kacaru, kacuru, kaciru* (Zvelebil 1970b: 112). We can therefore rely on the contrasts of *-s-* and *-y-* in Kannaḍa as representing the Proto-South Dravidian contrasts. There are several examples suggesting a Proto-Dravidian alternation between **-c-* and **-ẓ-*, e.g. **pic*-V- : **piẓ*-V- 'to squeeze' [4135, 4183], **mac*-V-: **maẓ*-V- 'to delay, be dull' [4627, 4750] (see *TVB* §§1.117–18).

4.5.5.6 *-k- [-g-]

This phoneme is represented as *-g-* in most of the languages. Exceptions are: Tamil and Malayāḷam write *-k-*, phonetically realized as *-g-* in Malayāḷam, but as [ɣ] or [h] in modern dialects of spoken Tamil. Sri Lanka Tamil dialects have [x]. Toda has /x/ phonetically [ɣ], Te. *-g-/-w-*, Go. Kuvi *-y-*. In Central Dravidian Parji has /v/ and /y/ in different dialects corresponding to South Dravidian *-g-*; in North Dravidian, Kuṛ.*-x-* and Malt. g̱ [voiced uvular fricative], Br. ḵẖ [x].

(82) PD **pok-ay* 'smoke'. SD I: Ta. *pukai*, Ma. *puka*, Ko. *peg*, To. *pax*, Koḍ. *poge*, Tu. *pugɛ, pogɛ*, Ka. *poge*; SD II: Te. *poga, pova*, Go. *pogo, poyo*, Koṇḍa *pogo*, Kui *pōkaṛi*, Kuvi *bōyi*; CD: Kol. Nk. *pog*, Oll. *pog*, Gad. *pōgu* [4240].

(83) PD **pok*-V- 'imperial pigeon'. SD I: Ma. *pokiṇa*, *pokaṇa*, *pōṇa*; SD II: Go. *pōnāṛ*; Kuvi *pōlgu* 'green pigeon'; CD: Kol. *pōl*, Pa. *pōnal*; ND: Kuṛ. *poxa*, Malt. *poge* [4454].

It has been already explained that -*k*- behaves like the semivowels -*y*- and -*w*- in producing compensatory lengthening of V_1 through syllable contraction, e.g. **tok-al* >*tō-l* 'skin' (ety. (28); also see (7), (8), (10), (27), (29), (30) and (31)).

4.5.6 *Non-initial consonants: nasals*

4.5.6.1 *-m-/ *-m

In disyllabic stems ending in *-*n*, Old Tamil developed alternative stems in -*m*. Comparatively -*n* forms are more widely distributed: **maran* 'tree', Ta. *maram*, *maraṉ*, Ma. *maram*. South Dravidian II, Central Dravidian and North Dravidian forms point to an original *-*n*, see ety. (35), [4711a], **koḷan* 'tank': Ta. Ma. *kuḷam*, Te. *kolanu*, Kui *glūnju* [1828]. Therefore *-*n* can be taken to represent Proto-Dravidian and the -*m* forms developed in free variation to -*n* forms in some SD I languages. In Old Kannaḍa also final -*n*/-*m* are both represented by an *anuswāra* <ṃ> which was phonemically -*m*/-*n* when followed by a vowel. Middle and Modern Kannaḍa lost the final <ṃ> and the same tendency is found in Tuḷu and Koḍagu (Subrahmanyam 1983: 386–7). Intervocalic -*m*- sporadically alternates with -*w*- in several languages.

(84) PD **cam*-V- 'to form, to be made'. SD I: Ta. Ma. *camai* v.i. 'to be made, to mature, to get ready', v.t. 'to acquire', *cavaraṇai* 'preparedness', Ma. *camayuka*, v.i., *camekka*, v.t., Ka. *same*, *save* 'to be made ready', *samaṟu*, *savaṟu* 'to make proper', *savaraṇe* 'making ready', SD II: Te. *sama-kaṭṭu* 'to be ready' (perhaps lw from Kannaḍa), *savar-incu* 'to trim'; Kol. *savaril*- 'to make oneself ready' (perhaps lw from Te.) [2342]. PD **nām-*/ **nam*-V- 'to be emaciated': Ta. *nāmpu*, Ka. *nāmbu*; Te. *nawayau* [3648], also Ka. *name*/*nave* 'become thin', Tu. *nameyuni* 'to wear away' [3598] (see *TVB*: §§1.98, 1.111).

In Modern Telugu a new sound change has commenced by merging -*m*- with -*w*- in a few lexical items in the younger generation of speakers, *māmiḍi* > *māwiḍi* 'mango', *manamaḍu* > *manawaḍu* 'grandson', etc.

4.5.6.2 *-n-/ *-n

Intervocalic *-*n*- (an alveolar nasal) remains unchanged in all languages. Finally it merges with *-*m* in South Dravidian I (see above). There are instances of -*n* alternating with -*l* in Dravidian.

(85) PD **cal-*/ **can*- 'to go, (time) to pass'. SD: Ta. *cel*- (*ceṉṟ*- [<**cel-nt*-]), Ma. *celka*, Ko. *cal*- (*cad*-), To. *sal*- (*sad*-), Ka. *sal*- (*sand*-), Tu. *salluni*,

> *sanduni*: SD II: Te. *can(u)*- (*caṇ-ṭ-*) 'to go, to be fit', *cellu* 'to pass, as time, be current, to be suitable', *calupu* v.t. 'to pass time, to do', Go. *son-*, *sond-*, *han-*, *hand-* 'to go', Koṇḍa *son-* (*soR-*), *solp-* 'to pass time', Kui *sal-* (*sas-*), Kuvi *hal-* (*hacc-*), Pe. Manḍa *hal-* (*hac-*); CD: Nk. *ca-* (*caṇḍ-*), Pa. *cen-* (*cend-*), Oll. *sen-* (*sey-*, *senḍ-*), Gad. *cen-* (*cey-*); ND: Kuṛ. *calr-* 'to continue, go on' [2781].

Here the *n*-stem seems to have arisen from restructuring on the basis of the past stem. It is not certain if it goes back to the Proto-Dravidian stage. Krishnamurti (*TVB*: §1.96) has also dealt with **n*/**ṯ* alternation at a reconstructed stage, e.g. Te. *mānu* 'to heal': Ta. *māṟu*, Te. *kan-* 'to bring forth young', *kandu* 'infant': Ka. *kaṟu* 'young child', *kandu* 'calf': CD: *kar* 'sapling'; ND: Br. *xan-* 'to give birth to' [1411].

4.5.6.3 *-ṇ- / *-ṇ

South Dravidian I preserves intervocalic -*ṇ*. South Dravidian II: Early Telugu inscriptions (up to the ninth century CE) preserved the contrast between -*ṇ*- and -*n*-, e.g. *paṇi* 'command, work', *koṇi* 'having taken' vs. *ani* 'having said', and the merger seems to have been completed by the eleventh century CE (*TVB*: §1.82). Although -*ṇ* merged with -*n*, certain paradigms of verbs ending in -*n*(<*-*ṇ*) show in sandhi a change of a dental to a retroflex, e.g. *kaṇ-ṭi-ni* 'I saw', but *kan-i* 'having seen';[12] Koṇḍa–Kui–Kuvi–Pengo–Manḍa also preserve morphophonemic *ṇ*, e.g. *uṇ-* (past *uṭ-*). Koṇḍa has retained the contrast between *n* and *ṇ* even at the lexical level. In Central Dravidian Ollari preserves the contrast of *n* and *ṇ*, while the other members show merger. North Dravidian languages have completely merged *ṇ* with *n*.

There is no evidence to reconstruct *-*ñ*-/ -*ñ* for Proto-Dravidian.

4.5.7 *Non-initial consonants: other sonorants*

4.5.7.1 *Liquids* *-r, -ẓ, *-l, *-ḷ

4.5.7.1.1 *-r-/*-r Alveolar and retroflex phonemes did not occur word-initially in Proto-Dravidian. /r/ has remained unchanged in most of the languages. One exception is Toda in which it has several reflexes *r*, *š*, *ṣ*, *Ø*, the conditioning factors of which are not known. In several items V_1r-V_2 contract to $\bar{V}_1$, e.g. To. *ūṇ* 'pith' : Ta. *uram* 'heart of tree' [*DED* 558], To. *tūḷ-* (*tūḍ-*) 'to roll up' : Ta. *curuḷ* 'to roll up' [*DED* 2211] etc. In most such cases V_1 happens to be a non-low vowel. In closed Pre-Toda syllables

[12] The past-tense allomorph is *-ti-* (<**-tt-i-*) elsewhere, e.g. *pō-ti-ni* 'I went'. If we take the underlying root as *kan-*, there is no phonetic motivation to descriptively derive *t* → *ṭ*/#*kan*+___. If we take the underlying *-n* as *-ṇ*, then the sandhi rule becomes normal. After alveolar *-n* ending stems like *an-* 'to say', the tense suffix became **ṯṯ-i* which later merged with *ṭṭ-i*, e.g. **an-tti* >**an-ṯṯi* > **an-ṭṭi* > *an-ṭi*. These two paradigms have structurally merged, obscuring the different historical routes. Therefore, the surface solution is to say the *t* → *ṭ* operates after (C)V*n*- roots to derive the correct forms.

_-r-_ preceding a stop consonant was lost, To. _ïfoθ_ : Ta. _iru-vatu_ 'twenty' [474], _teg-_ 'to fasten a loin cloth': Ta. _ceruku_ [2778]. Before a non-apical obstruent (i.e. _p t k_), _*r_ > _š_, e.g. To. _ašky_ 'rice' (<_*ar-kki_) : Ta. _arici_ [215]], To. _ešt_ 'bull' (<_*er-tt-_): Ta. _erutu_, Ko. _et_, Ka. _ettu_ [815]. PSD _*r_ > _ṣ_ in Toda following a front vowel and before a voiceless non-apical obstruent, To. _peṣk_ 'flying fox' (<_*ver-kk-_) : Ta. _veruku_ 'tom-cat' [5490]. In the majority of cases PD _*r_ remains in Toda, e.g. To. _ïr_ 'female buffalo': Ta. _erumai_ [816], _pī̈r_ 'quarrel': Ta. _pōr_ [4540]. Some of the South Dravidian II languages have [ṛ] corresponding to _*r_. Brahui has _-r_/_-rr_; it is lost in inflection before a consonant, e.g. _marr-_ 'to obey' [4722], but _baf-_, _bass-_ 'to come' (in inflection) from _waru-w-_, _war-cc-_. In Kannaḍa and Telugu root-final _-r_ gets assimilated to the following stop consonant(s), voiceless or voiced, e.g. Te. _wiccu_ 'to blossom, to open, burst', _wiri_ 'flower', _wirugu_ 'to break', Ka. _biccu_, _bircu_ id. [5411] (for further details see _TVB_: § 1.101, p. 44, §§1.173–85, pp. 74–9; Emeneau 1970a: 90–1, 1994: 49–70, Subrahmanyam 1983: 393–403).

4.5.7.1.2 _*-ẓ-_/_*-ẓ_ The liquids _r_ and _ẓ_ are never geminated in Proto-Dravidian or in older descendant languages. The phoneme _*-ẓ_, which was apparently pronounced as a retroflex approximant (frictionless continuant), survives in some regional and social dialects of Tamil and in Malayāḷam. In several modern dialects of Tamil and in the rest of the languages it has merged with many other phonemes including Ø. Since no clear isoglosses enclosing subgroups are discernible, it appears that the phoneme survived until recent times in most of the languages. It was retained in the early records of literary languages and a separate symbol was employed for it in early Telugu and Kannaḍa inscriptions. The reflexes are as follows: SD I: Mdn Ta. (social dialects) _ẓ_, _ḷ_, _y_, Ma. _ẓ_, Ko. _y_, _r_, _Ø_, To. _š_, _ṣ_, _w_, _ḍ_, _r_, _y_, _ḷ_, _Ø_, Iruḷa. _ḷ_, Koḍ. _y_, _ḷ_, _Ø_; Tu. _ḷ_ (Brahmin dial.), _r_ (Common dial), OKa. _ẓ_, Middle and Mdn Ka. _ḷ_, _r_; SD II: Early Inscriptional Te. _ẓ_, Old and Later Te. _ḍ_, _r_, Go.–Koṇḍa–Kui–Kuvi–Pe.–Manḍa _ṛ_; CD: Kol. Nk. _r_, Nk. (Ch.) _y_, _Ø_, Pa., Oll. _r_, Gad. _ḍ_; ND: Kuṛ.–Malt. _Ø_, _r_, _ḍ_; Br. _r_, _rr_, _Ø_. Some of the languages have clearly definable conditions of split, e.g. Ka. _-r_[C, _ḷ_ elsewhere, Telugu C]_r_-, _ḍ_ elsewhere, etc. The only subgroup that has a regular development is South Dravidian II (other than Telugu) which has _ṛ_ as the dominant reflex. In South Dravidian I, the widely shared reflex is _-ḷ_ (see Krishnamurti 1958b, _TVB_: §1.124, 2001a: 42–75, Burrow 1968a, Emeneau 1957b: 51–7, 1970a: 98–9).

(86) PD _*uẓ-u_ 'to plough, dig up'. SD I: Ta. _uẓu_, Ma. _uẓu_, Ko. _ug-_ (_uṛt-_), To. _uṣf-_ (_uṣt-_), Koḍ. _ūḷ-_ (_upp-_, _utt-_), Tu. _ūḍuni_; SD II: Te. _dunnu_ (<_*uẓ-n-_) v.t., _dukki_ (<_*ḍukk-_ <_*uẓ-kk-_) n. 'ploughing, tillage', Go. _uṛ-_, Koṇḍa–Kui–Kuvi–Pe.–Manḍa _ṛū-_ (_ṛū-t-_); CD: Kol. Nk. _ur-_, Pa. _uṛ-_, Gad. _ūḍ-_; ND: _uy-_ (_uss-_) 'to plough', Malt. _us-_ 'to turn up as pigs do' [688].

In South Dravidian II by metathesis and vowel contraction *ẓ comes to be in initial position as in the above case **ẓū-* < **uẓ-u-*. In Telugu the resultant initial *ẓ-* becomes *ḍ-*, which subsequently merged with *d-* (< **t-*), e.g. *ḍig(g)u*/*ḍigu* > *digu* 'to descend' (< **iẓ-g-*) (see *TVB*: §§1.124–9, pp. 52–5). It appears that this Proto-Dravidian phoneme has the least stability among liquids. The fact that it has merged with several existing phonemes and is eliminated from the inventory of most of the languages hints at two factors. First, it was a highly marked segment both in its phonetic properties and also in its status as a phoneme; second, there was some kind of typological pressure to eliminate it from the normal system.

4.5.7.1.3 *-l-/*-l In South Dravidian I Kota changes *-li* to *-j*, **puli* 'tiger' > Ko. *puj*, **eli* 'rat' > Ko. *eyj*. Toda has *-s̱* for **-l*. In Tuḷu, *-l-* becomes *-r-* intervocalically in many words irregularly, e.g. **talay* 'head' >Tu. *tarɛ*, but **malay* 'forest' > Tu. *malɛ* (Kekunnaya 1994: 58–9). In Kui described by Winfield **-l*>*-ḍ* (rather unusual!), but in C] position *-l*; other dialects of Kui show *-l*. Brahui has two lateral phonemes, voiced /l/ and voiceless /ɬ / (written as <*l̲h̲*>in Bray 1909) corresponding to both **-l* and **-ḷ*, e.g. **pāl* 'milk' > Br. *pāɬ* and **tēḷ* 'scorpion' > Br. *tēɬ*; the conditions of split in Brahui are not clear. The remaining languages represent **l* as an alveolar lateral. It has been pointed out that **l* and **ṟ* alternate in Proto-Dravidian (see ety. (1), (2), (4a), (13), (14), (24) and (56)).

4.5.7.1.4 *-ḷ-/*-ḷ All South Dravidian I languages preserve the contrast between alveolar and retroflex laterals /l ḷ/. Toda develops *-ḷ* into a voiceless retroflex lateral (in some environments), Tuḷu merges *-ḷ* with *-l* in the North Common dialect, elsewhere it is preserved. In South Dravidian II, in Telugu it merged with *-l* since the tenth century. In Gondi, Koṇḍa *ḷ* > *ṛ*, *l* (in different dialects); in Kui *-ḷ* merges with *-l* (<*-*l*) and splits as C] *l* and elsewhere *-ḍ* ~ *-l* (regionally); Kuvi–Pengo–Manḍa have *-ṛ*. In Central Dravidian Naikṛi preserves *-ḷ* after non-front vowels, but it has *-l* after the front vowels; the rest of the languages have *-l*. In ND **-ḷ* merges with **-l* in Kuṛux and Malto; in Brahui **-ḷ* merged with **-l* which then split into *-l* and *-ɬ* under conditions not yet clear.

(87) PD **kaḷan* 'open place, threshing floor'. SD I: Ta. *kaḷam*, *kaḷan̲*, Ma. *kaḷam*, Ko. *kaḷm*, To. *koɬn̲* (obl *koɬt-*), Koḍ. Tu. *kaḷa*, Ka. *kaḷa*, *kaṇa* 'threshing floor, battle floor'; SD II: Te. *kalanu*, Go. *kalam*, *kaṛā*, Koṇḍa *kalam*, *kaṛan*, Kui *klai*, Kuvi *kṛānu*, Manḍa *kāṛa*; CD: Kol. *kalave*, Nkṛ. *kaḷave*, Nk.(Ch.) *kalay*, Pa. *kali*, Oll. *kalin*; ND: Kuṛ. *xall-* 'field', *khalī* 'threshing floor', Malt. *qalu* 'field on the hills' [1376].

In a typologically driven change **ṇ* and **ḷ* tended to merge with the alveolar **l***n* in all languages outside the South Dravidian I group; this could be due to contact with

Indo-Aryan languages which lack such contrast. But it must be noted that the merger is not a shared innovation in these subgroups.

4.5.7.2 *Semivowels* *w, *y, *H

4.5.7.2.1 *-w-/*-w Intervocalic *-w-* is derived from root-final **-p* followed by formative suffixes in most cases, e.g. **cup-*: **cuw-ar* (ety. 10). Other instances of *-w-* show alternation with *-m-* and *-k-* in many languages (see *TVB*: §1.111 a, b, c). There are very few roots in Dravidian with an underlying *-w*, followed by formative suffixes, reconstructable to PD **-w-*. I consider **kew-i* 'ear' related to **kep-* 'to say' (see ety. (18)). Several items that show *-w-* also seem to derive it from an older *-k-* (see ety. (27)), **tē-* 'to belch' (<**tew-V-* < *tek-V-* [3451, 3453]). In *nīṟu, niw-uṟu* 'ashes'only Telugu preserves the *-w-* form. In To. and Br. *-f-* corresponds to *-w-* not necessarily of the root syllable. In Middle Kannaḍa *-w-* of the suffix syllable became *-b-*, e.g. *iru-war* 'two persons' > *ir-war* > *irbar* > *ibbaru*. Br. *bar-if-* 'to cause to come', cf. Ta. *varu-vi-*.

4.5.7.2.2 *-y-/ *-y Both intervocalic and root-final *-y* alternate in Proto-Dravidian itself with *-c-*. However, there are still etymologies in which all the languages show only *-y-*. The following is a good example of PD **-y-*:

(88) PD **wāy*/**way*-V 'open space'. SD I: Ta. Ma. *vayal*, Koḍ. *bēlï*, Ka. *bayal*(*u*), Tu. *bayilï*; SD II: Te. *bayalu* (lw < Ka.), *wēwili* 'field', Go. *vāvur*, *vāya*, Kuvi *bayalu*; CD: Kol. *vēgaḍ*, Nk. (Ch.) *vāyur*, *vāvur*, Pa. *vāya* [5258].

There are more cases of *-y-* < *-c-*, e.g. PD **pic-ar* >**piy-ar*/*pey-ar* > *pēr* 'name' (ety. (31)), PD **kac-* ~ **kay-* 'bitter' (ety. (42)), PD **pac-* ~ **pay-* 'yellow-green' (ety. (80)). There is a large number of etymologies requiring a final **-y*, PD **kay* 'hand' (ety. (41)), PD **key* 'to do' (ety. (49)), **kāy* 'to be hot' (ety. (52)), **ney* 'oil' (ety. (43)). In most of the languages the loss of *-y* produces compensatory lengthening of a preceding non-low vowel, **ciy-*/*cī-* 'to give' (ety. (45)).

4.5.7.2.3 *-H My recent researches showed that Proto-Dravidian had a laryngeal /H/, which patterned with semivowels [−syll, −cons] (Krishnamurti 1997b). It survived in a few lexical items in early Tamil as a restricted phoneme called *āytam* [aːydam]. It occurred as a root-final segment before a voiceless stop in the deictic forms such as *aḥ-tu* 'that' (neut sg), *iḥ-tu* 'this' (neut sg), *paḥ-tu* 'ten'; *-tu* is a neut sg suffix in these three forms and the roots end in *-ḥ*. The properties of *āytam*, as described by Tolkāppiyam, were: (i) it occurred after a short vowel and before a stop (voiceless), and its place of articulation is like that of the stop (Subrahmanya Sastri 1934: 66). In other words [ḥ] assimilates to the following voiceless stop. There is /pattu/ beside /paḥtu/, but the forms /attu/ and /ittu/ are not attested. There are other constructions like Ta. *ap-poẓutu* 'that time, then', *ip-poẕutu* 'this time, now', Te. *appuḍu* 'then', *ippuḍu* 'now', attested in early literary texts. In addition, all subgroups have *ā* and *ī* as remote and proximate demonstrative adjectives which also go back to PD **ā*, **ī* ; they are free forms which occur in noun phrases before other nouns bound syntactically as determiners, but not morphologically. It appears that what is called *āytam* in Tamil was an /h/ type of sound, which lengthened the preceding vowel, when the output is a free form or assimilated to a following voiceless stop in fused compounds; thirdly, it is lost if the following segment is phonetically voiced in the environment of [V which was not an enunciative vowel. Thus we have three developments *ā*, *ī*; *aḥ*-, *iḥ*-; or *a*-, *i*-; the last in the pronouns *a-tu* and *i-tu* also reconstructable to Proto-Dravidian. Similarly, *paḥ*- with -*ḥ* assimilated in *pat-tu* has a variant *pā*- in OTa. *oṉ-pā-ṉ* 'nine' (−1, +10 = 9), but *pat-iṉ*- (adjectival form of *pattu*). Tolkāppiyam had all four, *iru-paḥtu* 'twenty', *eẕu-patu* 'seventy', *oṉ-pāṉ* 'nine', *pati-iṉ-oṉṟu* 'eleven'. There are other lexical items (about half a dozen) in which *āytam* occurred in Old Tamil with cognates in the other languages with length of the preceding vowel or gemination of the following voiceless stop. Apparently the *āytam* was fast going out of use and it was preserved in some relic forms like the above.

The Old Tamil *āytam* apparently was a reflex of a PD **H* (laryngeal) which seemed to have had a much wider distribution in Proto-Dravidian but survived in a few frozen forms in Early Tamil. As far as the three lexical items are concerned there is no doubt that an *h*-like element must be responsible for the phonological processes. The remote and proximate forms in Kuvi–Gondi in South Dravidian II and Kuṛux.–Malto in North Dravidian have a *h*- freely varying with zero in deictic forms, Go. *had/ad* 'that', *hid/id* 'this', *hav/av* 'those', *hiv/iv 'these'*; Pengo and Kuvi also have *h*- forms in the demonstrative bases. Kuṛ. *asan/hasan* 'there', *iyyā/hiyyā* 'in this place', have the sporadic retention of PD **h*. Medieval Kannaḍa had *ahaṅge/hāṅge* 'that manner', *ihaṅge/hīṅge* 'this manner' in which the source of -*h* is not known. It could well be a surviving remnant of a Proto-Dravidian laryngeal. It surfaced in written records after /h/ became phonemic in Kannaḍa after the sound change *p*- > *h*- which started in the tenth century and was completed by the fourteenth century.[13] The numeral 'ten' has aspirated variants in Kannaḍa and Telugu from early times, Te. *ēṃbhadi* 'fifty' (eighth century; B. Radhakrishna 1971: 249), Ka. *ombhattu* 'nine', *tombhattu* 'ninety' (AD 869, SII xi, Part 1, No. 13). The aspiration of the allomorphs of 'ten' continues into the modern languages, Te. *mupphay* 'thirty', *nalabhay* 'forty', *ēbhay* 'fifty'.

There are several words and grammatical forms showing the same phonological processes reminiscent of the behaviour of a laryngeal, but the /ḥ/ would not surface, since it was not phonemic in any of the early stages of the literary languages (except for Early

[13] The /h/ in the forms cited for Kannaḍa could not be traced to an older **p*-. The laryngeal articulation could be recognized after /h/ started contrasting with /p/ in Medieval Kannaḍa.

Tamil for a brief period). Its effects are, however, seen in the neighbouring phonemes. The attractive candidates for proposing a laryngeal are (i) the root of the number word 'three' _*muH-/mū-_; (ii) eight irregular verbs with aberrant phonology, namely _*caH-_ 'to die', _*taH-r-_ 'to bring', _*waH-r-_ 'to come', _*aHn-_ 'to say', _*tiHn-_ 'to eat', _*uHṇ-_ 'to eat, drink', _*weHn-_ 'to hear', _*kaHṇ-_ 'to see'. In all these, the free forms (imperatives, e.g. _wā_, _tā_ and derived nouns, _tīn_, _ūṇ_) have long vowels and the bound forms in inflection have short (sometimes long) vowels, a result, it can be claimed, of the loss of the laryngeal before a voiced consonant. The replacement of _H_ by _y_ later explains all the qualitative changes in vowels; (iii) twenty-one verbs and derived nouns which are related by a quantitative change in the vowels, i.e. long vowels in free forms (nouns) and short vowels in inflected verbs, e.g. _*keṭu_ 'to perish': _*kēṭu_ 'evil'; (iv) personal pronouns in which the nominatives (free forms) have long vowels and the oblique stems (bound forms) have short vowels, _*yān/ *yan-_ 'I', etc; (v) the negative morpheme in Proto-Dravidian _*-aHa-_ on the basis of _-ā-_, _-ay-_, _-a-_, _-Ø-_, _-wa-_, _ʔ-_, _ʔ_V- in different subgroups (see for details Krishnamurti 1997b: §§4–5). Only a few examples involving the laryngeal are given here:

(89/48) PD _*cah-_ 'to die'. SD I: Ta. _cā-_ (_cāv-_, _cett-_ <_*ca-tt-_) v.i., Ma. _cā-_ (_catt-_), with _-y_<_*-H_, To. _soy-_ (_soyt-_), Ko. _cāv_ 'death', Koḍ. _cāvï/cāḷ-_ (_cāv-_, _catt-_) 'to die', _cāvu_ 'corpse', Ka. _sāy-_ (_satt-_) v.i., _sāvu_ n., Tu. _sai-pini_, _tai-pini_ v.i., _sāvu_, _tāvu_ n.; SD II: Te. _ca-cc-_ (<_caH-cc-_) v.i., _cāwu_ n., Go. _sai-_, _sāy-_, _sā-_, _hā-_, Koṇḍa, Kui _sā-_ (_sāt-_), Kuvi _hai-_ (_hāt-_), Pe. Manḍa _hā-_ (_hāt-_); CD _*cay-/ *cāy_: Pa. _cay-_ (_ca-ñ-_ <_*cay-nj-_<_*cay-nd-_), Oll. _say-_, Gad. _cay-_; ND: _*caH-_ >_*ceH-_ >_*keH-_: Kuṛ. _khē-_, _kē-_ (_kecc-_), Malt. _key-_ (_kec-_), Br. _kah-_ (_kask-_, neg. _kas-_) 'to die', _kas-if-_ 'to kill' [2425].

Variations in vowel length and quality, the appearance of _-y_ in many languages and the preservation of _-h_ in Brahui support the setting up of a laryngeal /H/ in the root in Proto-Dravidian. Also see _*aHn-_ 'to say', _*waH-r-_ 'to come' (ety. (5), (72)). For more examples see Krishnamurti (1997b). For the negative morph at the Proto-Dravidian stage, I reconstructed _*-aHaH_ which would develop to _-āy/-ay_ (<_*-āH_<_**-aH-aH_); the occurrence of _-āy_ in Malayāḷam and _-ay_ in Tuḷu and Parji are thus explained. Loss of _-y_ before a consonant is common in Dravidian. The resultant short _-a-_ is lost in some languages either after long vowel stems or in the unaccented position in verb conjugation, e.g. Te. $rā + a + ka \rightarrow rā\text{-}ka$. SCD (SD II) _-wa_ (>_-ʔa-_) from -_*HaH_ is also explainable by the rule $*H \rightarrow w/\_\_+a$ which is needed, anyway, to explain PD _*aw-anṯu_ 'he', _*aw-ar_ 'they (persons)', _aw-ay_ 'they (non-persons)' and PSD I _*aw-aḷ_ 'she'.

There is now reasonable evidence to believe that South Dravidian I lost PD _*c-_ through the intermediate stages of _*s-_ and _h-_ and the missing phonetic links were not recorded because the laryngeal articulation ceased to operate in most of the literary languages by the early CE. Some islands had remained which gave the evidence of _h-_ in deictic bases. But loanwords from Dravidian into Sanskrit and Prakrits show evidence of *-s-* and *-h-* in *kaṭāha-* 'heifer', *kalaha-* 'strife, quarrel', *tulasī-* 'basil plant', *sarāhaya-* 'a snake' (the last one a folk etymology because of *-haya* 'horse' from Dravidian **saraha-* <**saras-*) (see section 4.5.1.3, fn. 5 above).

4.5.7.3 *Initial apicals through metathesis and vowel contraction*

Non-nasal apical consonants (**ṯ* [r̠], **ṭ* [ḍ], *l*, *ḷ*, *r*, *ḻ*),[14] which did not occur word-initially in Proto-Dravidian, shifted to the initial position in the languages of South-Central Dravidian (South Dravidian II) by a phonological change. In radical syllables which had $V_1R\text{-}V_1\text{-}$, R (R = non-nasal apical consonant) comes to the initial position by this sound change. If the Proto-Dravidian base was $(C_1)V_1C_2\text{-}V_2\text{-}$ this sound change has resulted in creating consonant clusters (with R as the second member) which were also not allowed in Proto-Dravidian. A recent discussion of this sound change occurs in Krishnamurti (1978a) within the framework of lexical diffusion. Earlier discussion with bibliographical references occurs in Krishnamurti (1961: 51–7), Emeneau (1970a: 33–6), Zvelebil (1970b) and Subrahmanyam (1983: §16, pp. 223–48).

Rule 20. *Apical displacement (Proto-South Dravidian II)*

a. $V_1R\text{-}V_2\text{-} > R\bar{V}_1\text{-}\ (V_1 = V_2, \text{ or } V_2 = [+\text{low}])$

a′. $V_1R\text{-}V_2\text{-}(CC)\text{-} > RV_1\text{-}\emptyset\text{-}CC\text{-}\ (V_2 = [+\text{high}] \text{ and } V_1 \neq V_2)$

b. $C_1V_1R\text{-}V_2\text{-} > C_1R\bar{V}_1\text{-}\ (V_1 = V_2, \text{ or } V_2 = [+\text{low}])$

b′. $(C_1)V_1R\text{-}V_2\text{-}CC\text{-} > (C_1)RV_1\text{-}\emptyset\text{-}CC\text{-}\ (V_2 = [+\text{high}] \text{ and } V_1 \neq V_2)$

Rules 20a, a′ shift medial apicals to word-initial position with compensatory lengthening of the root vowel (V_1) in 20a. Rules 20b, b′ create consonant clusters with an apical R as the second member. Rules 20a, b have been treated in section 4.3.3 under vowels. After V_1R- metathesize to $RV_1\text{-}V_2$, V_1 and V_2 contract to produce a long V_1 by Rules 20a, b. Here both the vowels are of the same quality, or V_2 is a low vowel *-a*, while V_1 can be **i*/**e*, **u*/**o* or **a*. It may be recalled that Proto-Dravidian **i *u* merged with **e *o*, respectively, before [*C-*a* in Proto-South Dravidian, the undivided stage of South Dravidian I and South Dravidian II (see section 4.4.2, Rule 4a, b). Rules 20a′, b′ suggest loss of V_2 and simple metathesis of V_1R to RV_1. Here the root and suffix vowels ($V_1\text{-}V_2$) are not of the same quality and V_2 is a high vowel /i u/; mid vowels /e o/ do not occur as V_2.

These changes were inherited at the undivided stage of Proto-South Dravidian II and they continued into the modern languages even after successive breaks. Consequently, the segments represented by C,R, V_1, and V_2 are different at different stages. In Telugu in the case of Rules 20a, b, R is any apical consonant specified above. But for Rules 20a′, b′,

14 Retroflex nasal [ṇ] also did not occur word-initially, but it is not involved in this sound change.

C_1 has to be one of /p t k b d g m s w/ and R is /ṯ [ṟ] r ẓ/; the retroflex stop and laterals /ḍ l ḷ/ are excluded as R. For the remaining five languages of this subgroup Rules 20a, a′ are the same. But in the case of 20b, b′, C_1 adds *n* to the consonants specified for Telugu, and R includes all apicals including the laterals and *ḍ*. The change is generalized by enlarging the environments. The consonant clusters formed by Rules 20 b, b′ got simplified later by the following rules:

Rule 21. *Initial cluster simplification*

a. CR- > C-/#__ (Telugu)

b. CR- > R-/#__ (Gondi–Koṇḍa–Kui–Kuvi–Pengo–Manḍa)

Gondi has evidence of the operation of Rules 20a and a′; it has indirect evidence of Rules 20b and b′ having operated in some dialects, because there are examples which resulted from the application of Rule 21b for which the input is 20b and b′. Koṇḍa also has examples like Gondi for Rules 20a and a′ and 21b which presuppose that at one time it also had 20b and b′. Rule 21b operates where C_1 is /n w s/.

Old and Middle Telugu has evidence of all the rules that are applicable. In Modern Telugu, Gondi and Koṇḍa, the above rules have ceased to operate. But in the subgroup Kui–Kuvi–Pengo–Manḍa the sound changes, which apparently have had a history of over 2,500 years, are still in progress. This is evident from the fact that free variation between unchanged and changed forms is attested in the dialects of each of these (see Krishnamurti 1978a: §2.5, p.10). The reflexes of non-nasal apicals after the operation of the sound changes are given in Krishnamurti 1978a: table 10.1. Only Telugu data are given below:

	#__	#C__
-*ṯ- [-ṟ-]	ṟ- (>r-)	r-
-*ṭ- [-ḍ-]	ḍ- (>d-)	—
-*r-	r-	r-
-*ẓ-	ẓ- (>ḍ- >d-)	ẓ- (>r-)
-*l-	l-	—
-*ḷ-	l-	—

Word-initially, Early Telugu kept the three-way contrast *ṟ*: *ḍ* : *r*. In Middle and Modern Telugu, *ṟ*- merged with *r*- (<**r*) and *ḍ*- with *d*- (<**t*-). In the postconsonantal position, both *ṟ* and *ẓ* merged with *r* (<**r*). By Rule 21a, C*r*- became C- with the loss of *r*-.

The following examples illustrate the rules with special reference to the developments of medial apicals after they have shifted to the initial syllable:

(90) PD **kōẓ-/*koẓ-*V- 'young, tender, fresh'. SD I: Ta. *koẓuntu* 'tender, young', *kuẓantai* 'infant', *kuẓai* 'to sprout' (<**koẓ*-V-), Ma. *koẓunnu* 'tender shoot', To. *kwïẓ*, 'twig', Ka. *koṇasu* 'young one of wild beasts', Tu. *korɛ* 'weak,

small', Koraga *korayi*, *kori* 'husband'; SD II: Te. *koḍuku* 'son', *kōḍ-alu* 'daughter-in-law', *krotta*, *kro-* 'new' (<**koẓ-tt*), Mdn Te. *kotta* 'new', Go. *koṛs-* 'to sprout', *koṛi-āṛ* 'daughter-in law, younger brother's wife', Koṇḍa *koṛo* 'child', *koṛya*, *koṛesi* 'daughter-in-law', Kui *kōṛu* 'new shoot', *koṛgi* 'fresh, new', *kuṛa*, *kṛua*, *kṛuha* 'husband', Kuvi *kuṛia* 'daughter-in-law', *kṛōgi* 'young, immature', Pe. *kṛogi* 'fresh', *koṛiy gāṛ* 'son's wife', Manḍa *kuṛiya gāṛ* id.; CD: Kol. *koral*, Nk. *koraḷ* 'daughter-in-law, bride', Pa. *koṛ* 'very young', *koṛc-* 'to sprout', *koṛol* 'bride', Oll. *koṛal* 'son's wife', Gad. *koḍus-*, *koḍc-* 'to sprout'; ND: *xōr-* 'to shoot out new leaves', *korrā* 'fresh', Malt. *qōro* 'infant', Br. *xarr-* 'to sprout', *xarruni* 'greenness, wife' [2149].[15]

In South Dravidian I Kannaḍa has no cognate with *-ḷ* but *-l/-ṇ* alternate in Old Kannaḍa. Tuḷu, Koraga have *-r* for *-ẓ* as expected. In South Dravidian II *-*ẓ* is represented by *-ṛ* whether in intervocalic or postconsonantal position. North Dravidian has *-r* for **ẓ*.

(91) PD **īr/ir-V-* 'two'. SD I: Ta. *iraṇṭu* 'two' (>Middle and Mdn Ta. *reṇṭu*), *īr-/iru-* adj *raṇṭu*; *īr-/iru* adj, Ko. *ir-* adj, To. *ēḍ* 'two', *ï-*, *īr-* adj, Ir. *raṇḍu*, *reṇḍu*, Koḍ. *daṇḍï* 'two', *īr-/iru-* adj, Ka. *eraḍu* 'two', *iru-* adj: SD II: Te. *reṇḍu* 'two', *īr/iru-* adj, Go. *ranḍ* 'two', *rahk rahk* 'two each', *ir-* adj, Koṇḍa *ruṇḍi* 'two', *ri-* adj, *riʔer* 'two men', *rineṇḍ* 'two days', Kui *rīṇḍe* 'two', *rī-* adj, Kuvi *riṇḍi* 'two', *rīari* 'two men', Pe. *riṇḍek* 'two women', *riṇḍaŋ* 'two things', *rikar* 'two men', Manḍa *ri* 'two', *rikar* 'two men'; CD: Kol. *indiŋ* 'two things', *īral* 'two women', Nk. (Ch.) *erṇḍi* 'two things', *ir-* adj, Pa. *irḍu* 'two things', Oll. *inḍi*, Gad. *iḍḍig* 'two'; ND: Kuṛ. *ē*^{n}*ḍ* 'two', *irb-* 'two persons', Malt. *iwr* (<**irw-*) 'two persons', Br. *iraṭ* 'two', *irā* adj [474].

In South Dravidian I, we notice a recent trend of short vowel loss before alveolar *r-* (aphaeresis) in a few lexical items: Tamil, Malayāḷam, Kannaḍa, Koḍagu and Iruḷa show such forms. Te. *reṇḍu* was perhaps from an older unattested **rēṇḍu* (<**er-aṇḍ-*) with shortening of *rē-* to *re-* before a consonant cluster. The other South Dravidian II (SD II) languages had **rīṇḍ-* from **ir-i-nḍ* / **ir-u-ṇḍ* with shortening of *ī* to *i* before a consonant cluster in some of the languages. In the case of Koṇḍa *ruṇḍi* (<**riṇḍi*), the front vowel is retracted because of the following retroflex consonant-cluster. In North Dravidian Kuṛux *ē* is a little puzzling, since it does not derive from Proto-South Dravidian **eraṇḍ-*.

15 Note that this etymology has interesting semantic extensions reflected in the whole family, namely to sprout > (a) fresh, tender, young > (b1) new, immature > (b2) child, bride (kinship terms: wife, husband, son, daughter, daughter-in-law, brother's wife, etc.). Central India is rich in the shift to kinship terms. Telugu here has both *-ḍ-* and C]*r-*, i.e. *koḍuku* 'son', *kōḍalu* 'daughter-in-law', *krotta* 'new' with simplification of *kr-* to *k-* in Modern Telugu.

It must be an independent and sporadic vowel change. All languages preserve the root syllable *īr/ir*-V-. This etymology supports the assumption that metathesis took place at the undivided stage of these languages. Also note ety. (32), (33), (34), (35) and (38), which provide evidence of the operation of the above rules. In the whole subgroup (minus Telugu) the sound change included, among the initial consonants, the nasal *n*- and among the members of R, the retroflex stop **ḍ* and the lateral phonemes **l*, **ḷ*., e.g.

(92) PD **kaṭ-ac-* 'male of a domestic animal'. SD I: Ta. *kaṭā*, *kaṭavu*, *kiṭā* 'male of sheep, goat, bull', Ma. *kaṭā*, *kiṭā*, *kaṭacci*, Ko. *kaṛc*, Koḍ. *kaḍïci*, Ka. *kaḍasu*, Tu. *gaḍasu*; SD II: Go. *kāṛā*, Koṇḍa (dial.) *gṛālu*, Kui *grāḍu*, *ḍrāḍu*, *kṛai* 'young female buffalo', Kuvi *ḍālu*; ND: Kuṛ. *kaṛā* 'young male buffalo', *kaṛī* 'young female buffalo' (the final vowels are gender markers), Br. *xarās* 'bull' [1123]; also section 4.5.1.3, fn. 5.

Note the sporadic change of *g*- >*ḍ*- in Kui. Also notice the loss of the initial member of the cluster in Kuvi. Similarly **caracc-/*carancc-* 'snake' >Te. *trā̃cu, tācu* 'cobra', Go. *taras*, *taranj*, Koṇḍa *saras*, *srāsu*, Kui *srāsu*, *srācu*, Kuvi *rācu*, Pe. *rāc*, Manḍa *trehe* [2359].

(93) PSD II **nela-nj-* >**nlēnj-* >*lēnj-* 'moon' : Go. *nelenj-*, *lenj-*, Kui *ḍānju* (*ā* <**ē*), Kuvi *lēnju*, Pe. Manḍa *lēnj-*; SD I **nel-aH-* <**nel-ac-*: Ta. Ma. *nil-ā*, *nil-avu*, Koḍ. *nelaci*; CD **nel-iŋ-*: Pa. *neliñ* (pl. *nelñil*), Oll. *neliŋ*, Gad. *nelā* (pl. *nelŋīl*) [3754].

(94) PD **tiṯ*-V- 'to open'. SD I: Ta. *tiṟa* (*tiṟant-*) 'to open (as a door, one's eyes)' Ma. *tuṟakka*, Ko. *terv-* (*terd-*), To. *teṟ-* (*teṟθ-*), Koḍ. *tora* (*torand-*), Tu. *jappuni* 'to open', *terapu* 'space'; SD II: Te. *teṟacu* 'to open', Go. *tarī-*, *terr-*, *teṟ-*, Koṇḍa *ṟe-* (dial. *teṟe-*) 'to open', Kui *dāpa* (*dāt-*; *ā* <**ē*), Kuvi *de-*, Pe. Manḍa *jē-* (<**ṟē-*); ND: Kuṛ. *tisg-* 'to open', Malt. *tisg-* 'to lift the latch' [3259].

In a quantitative study (Krishnamurti 1978a: 9), it was shown that only 16 per cent of the eligible lexical items were affected by the above changes in Gondi, 21 per cent in Koṇḍa, but 72 per cent in Kui, 61 per cent in Kuvi, 63 per cent in Pengo and 65 per cent in Manḍa. The sound changes spread through the mechanism of lexical diffusion. Telugu was not included in the study because it has a much larger lexicon than the other non-literary languages and would not have a parity for comparison. The sound changes have ceased to operate in two of the seven languages, namely Telugu and Gondi. But in Koṇḍa dialectally consonant clusters are formed, e.g. *maran* 'tree' (Araku dialect): *mrānu* (Sova dialect). In the remaining four languages the sound changes are still ongoing.

There has been discussion of the phonetic mechanism underlying apical displacement. It is crucial to note that this sound change occurs in polysyllabic stems and not in monosyllables. The formative syllable can be -V_2, V_2-P, V_2-L, V_2-NP, V_2-PP etc. (see figure 4.1). I explained the mechanism as follows:[16]

> Stage II: The second syllable, being heavy (i.e. CVC as opposed to light CV), carried stress only when V_1 and V_2 were of the same quality or when V_2 was [+low]. The sequences V_1 and V_2 were:
>
> *(C) V_1C -V_2 . . .
>
> | | |
> |---|---|
> | i | i |
> | u | u |
> | a | a |
> | i/e | a |
> | u/o | a |
>
> When the consonant between V_1 and V_2 was R (a liquid, a phonetic continuant ([ṟ] ←/*ṯ/), or a flap *r*, *ṛ* (<**r*, **ẓ*, **l*, **ḷ*)), V_1 tended to become weaker in articulation, being closely followed by more prominent V_2 across a lighter consonant. This led to the lengthening of V_2 and the loss of V_1, producing initial apicals and consonant clusters followed by a long vowel which was identical with V_1 in quality. There is evidence that, before this happened, e$a and o$a also became *e$e and *o$o, respectively. Consequently, **moẓ-ang-* >**mo.z-ong* >**mẓō-ng-* 'to roar . . .
>
> Where the qualities of V_1 and V_2 were not identical in quality, V_2 tended to be weakened and lost, bringing the root-final consonant R into contact with the suffix consonant, e.g. **miẓ-u-ng* > **miẓ-ng-* 'to swallow'. The vowel sequences were:
>
> *(C) V_1C -V_2..
>
> | | |
> |---|---|
> | i | u |
> | e | u/i |
> | a | u/i |
> | u | i |
> | o | u/i |
>
> Presumably, *i merged with u in V_2 position. The loss of *u in the second syllable is a much older tendency, found in all subgroups of the Dravidian

[16] During my fieldwork on the Koṇḍa language, I noticed that the dialect of my informant in the Araku valley did not have initial consonant clusters, but he regularly stressed the second syllable when the first syllable was short, e.g. *sarás* 'snake', *marán* 'tree', *peṛélzinàd* 'it is exploding'. When I visited the Sova village to the northwest, I found the speakers there pronounced these forms with initial clusters, *srāsu*, *mrānu*, *pṛēlzinad*. This gave me the insight that it was a single jump from stressed second syllable to vowel lengthening of the syllable and loss of the first syllable. Also notice *peṛél-* where the second syllable (originally **a*) became *e* before 'apical displacement' (see Krishnamurti 1969a: 23).

> family. Therefore it appears that vowel lengthening operated in the environments that preserved V_2.
>
> Stage III: The outputs of Stage II with patterns like (C)VR-C . . . were subjected to assimilation in Subgroup I (i.e. SD I), but to metathesis in Subgroup 2 (i.e. SD II). The function of metathesis was to preserve the root syllable from threatened assimilation of the final consonant. Therefore *(C)VR-C . . . > (C)RV-C . . . .
>
> Stage IV: During this stage, the consonant clusters formed through the earlier processes were again simplified by loss of R in Telugu (see Krishnamurti 1961, §1.145) and loss of C in the other languages of Subgroup 2 (SD II). The rules of apical displacement must have started at least two thousand years ago, and are still going on in some of the languages of this subgroup, particularly in Kui. (Krishnamurti 1978a: Appendix, pp. 18–19)

Kolami and Parji of Central Dravidian borrowed forms which had undergone metathesis in Early Telugu. These forms still show word-initial *ḍ*- that Telugu merged with *d*- later, indicating the early chronology of their borrowing, e.g. Te. *duwwu* 'tiger' (<**ḍuww*- <**ẓu-ww*- <**uẓ-(u)-w*-), > lw Kol. (Kinwaṭ dial) *ḍū*-, Pa. *ḍū*- (pl *ḍuvul*). SD I: Ta. *uẓuvai* 'tiger', SD II: Go. *ḍū*, *ḍuwwal*, *ḍuwāl* 'panther' [692]. Te. *ḍig*(g) *u* > *digu* 'to descend, get down', Go. *ḍig*-, Koṇḍa *ḍig*-: Kol. *ḍig*-, *ḍigg*-, *dig*-, Nk. (Ch.) *ḍig*-, but Pa. *iṛv*-, Oll. *iṛg*-, Gad. *iḍg*-; SD I: Ta. Ma. *iẓi*, Ka. *iḷi* [502]. But the Central Dravidian languages have not borrowed any items with consonant clusters; by this evidence we believe that these forms have not resulted from a shared innovation but from borrowing.

There is an extension of the above rules to a few cases even where C_2 is not an apical consonant (in one or two languages of this subgroup), e.g. Te. *adi* (noml) 'she, it' : *dān-i*- (obl; <**ad-an*-), *idi* 'this one' (n-m sg), *dīni*- (obl; <**id-an*-), *ēdi* 'which one?': *dēni*- (obl; <**ed-an*-); Koṇḍa *adi* (noml) 'that woman or thing': *dani*- (obl), *idi* (noml) 'this woman or thing' : *deni*- (obl; <**id-an*-), so also in the plural Te. *awi* : *wāni*, *iwi* : *wīni*, *ēwi*: *wēni*-, etc. Koṇḍa also has *avi*: *wani*, *ivi*:*veni*, etc. Similarly corresponding to Te. *wā̃ḍu*: *wāni*- 'that man', *wī̃ḍu* : *wīni*- 'this man', *ewā̃ḍu* : *ewani*-/*wēni*- 'which man?', Koṇḍa has *wānṟu*: *wani*, *wēnṟu* : *weni*-, *ayenṟu* : *ayeni*-. The first two are from PD **awanḏu*/*awanṟu*, **iwanḏu*/*iwanṟu*. Note that Telugu kept the distal and proximal difference by maintaining the vowel qualities also in the metathesized forms. The developments in Koṇḍa were normal since C*e*- of the proximal forms from **i*C-*a* would not make them homophonous with the interrogative forms, as would have happened in Telugu. The interrogative forms in Koṇḍa are not part of the deictic paradigm as in Telugu.[17]

[17] In Koṇḍa the interrogative root is *ay*-: *ay-en*-/*ay-enṟu* 'which man?' *ay-ed* 'which woman/thing?', *ay-er* 'who? (m and f)', *ay-ev* 'which? (non-pers)'.

In Classical Telugu the verb *an-* 'to say' has metathesized doublets *an-an* ~*ñā-n* 'to say', *ana-ka* ~ *nā-ka* 'without saying', *anaw-ũḍu* ~ *nā-wũḍu* 'after saying'. No other language has metathesized forms involving *-n* as C_2. There is one case with a metathesized *-m-* and one with *-g-* as C_2 in South Dravidian II (excluding Telugu):

(95) PD **mak-anṯu* 'male', **mak-aḷ* 'female'. SD I: Ta. *makaṉ* 'son' (>*māṉ*, *mōṉ*), *makaḷ* 'daughter', *makkaḷ* 'children', Ma. *makan*, *mōn* 'son', *mōḷ* 'daughter', *makkaḷ* 'children', Ko. *mog* 'child, wife', To. *mox* 'child, son, male, daughter', Koḍ. *mōvėⁿ* 'son', *mōva* 'daughter', *makka* 'children', Ka. *maga*, *magan* 'son, male', *magaḷ* 'daughter', *makkaḷ* 'children', Tu. *mage*, *mōnu* 'son', *magaḷu* 'daughter', *makkaḷ* 'children'; SD II: Te. *maganṟu* 'son' (inscr), *maga*, *moga* 'male', *magãḍu* 'husband, brave person', *maguwa* 'woman', Go. *miyāṛ* 'daughter', Koṇḍa *maga koṛo* 'male child', *gāṛu*, *gālu* 'daughter', Pe. Manḍa *gāṛ* (< **mgāḷ*), Manḍa *nā-mgāṛ* 'my daughter'; ND: Malt. *maqe* 'boy', *maqi* 'girl' [4616].

This change is restricted to Koṇḍa, Pengo and Manḍa. Another form involving *-m-* is Koṇḍa *mūl* (*mūṭ-*) 'to urinate', *mūlku* 'urine', Kui *mūl-* (*mūṭ-*), Kuvi *mūṇk-* v., *mrūka*, *mṇūka* n., Pe. *mūṇku*, Manḍa *mūṇke* n. The Central Dravidian and North Dravidian languages provide evidence for the reconstruction of **um(b)-uḷ* v.; South Dravidian I has forms beginning with *m-* in modern dialects: Ta. *mōḷ* v., Ma. *moḷḷu* n., Ko. *moḷ* n., Ir. *maḷ* 'to urinate' [644]. This is a very intriguing etymology.

4.5.8 ***Consonant groups -CC, -C-CC***

Only three kinds of consonant groups occurred in postvocalic position in Proto-Dravidian, namely geminates (of obstruents and some non-obstruents) and clusters of homorganic nasal + stop, homorganic nasal + geminate stop. A single voiceless stop occurring in postvocalic position (i.e. C_2 of $(C_1)VC_2$-) in any of the Dravidian languages can be traced back to a geminate stop in Proto-Dravidian. If it was a single stop, it would appear in all languages as a lenis consonant. The Kui–Kuvi–Pengo–Manḍa subgroup does not contrast between single and double consonants. The Nilgiri languages which lose the final enunciative vowel also do not show the contrast between P and PP.

4.5.8.1 -PP

In most of the languages, other than Tamil and Malayāḷam, a geminate stop is retained after a Proto-Dravidian short vowel, but it is simplified to P after a long vowel, e.g. Te. Ka. *āḍu* 'to play', *āṭa* 'game', Ko. *āṛ-* v.i., *āṭ-* v.t.,To. *ōḍ-* v.i., *ōṭ-* v.t., Koḍ. *āḍ-* v.i., *āṭ-* v.t.: Ta. Ma. *āṭu* v.i. 'to play', *āṭṭu* v.t., *āṭṭ-am* (<**āṭ* + *tam*) 'game, dance' [347]. In most of the languages, the contrast of single vs. double stop developed into voiced vs. voiceless, particularly in the environment of V̄].

4.5.8.1.1 *-pp

(96) PD **kupp*-V 'heap', SD I: Ta. *kupp-ai*, *kupp-am*, *kupp-al* 'heap', Ma. *kuppa*, Ko. *kip* 'rubbish', To. *kïp* id., Koḍ. *kuppï* 'heap of dung', Ka. *kuppe*, *guppe* 'heap', *kuppu* 'to heap up', Tu. *kuppɛ*, *guppɛ*, *kippɛ*; SD II: Te. *kuppa*, Go. *kupa*, *kuppa*, Koṇḍa *kupa*, Kui, Pe. Manḍa *kupa*, Kuvi *kūpa*, *kuppa*; CD: Kol. *kupp kal-* 'to gather', Pa. *kuppa* 'stack', *koppa* 'hillock', Oll. *kuppā* 'heap'; ND: Kuṛ. *xop-* 'to form into a pile', Malt. *qop-* 'to heap up' [1731a].

Also see ety. (74) and (100) (for South Dravidian I). Here, the Proto-Dravidian root could be **kup-* with a derivational suffix *-ay* which is also reconstructable for the whole family.

4.5.8.1.2 *-tt[18]

(97) PD **pitt-* 'to fart'. SD II: Te. *pittu* 'to fart', Go. *pitt-/pīt-* v., *pītu* n., Koṇḍa *pīt-* v.i., *pītu* n., Kui, Kuvi, Pe. Manḍa *pīt-*; ND: Kuṛ. Malt. *pīt-* [4167].

It is interesting to note that this has no cognates in South Dravidian I and Central Dravidian. It could be related to PD **piy/*pī* 'excrement' [4210] or **pi-n/* **pi-ṯ* 'back, buttocks' [4205] (*TVB*: §1.194, p. 82), represented in all subgroups.

4.5.8.1.3 *-ṯṯ

(98) PD **waṯṯ-/waṯ-*V- 'to dry up'. SD I: Ta. *vaṟṟu* 'to evaporate', Ma. *vaṟṟuka*, Ko. *vat-*, Koḍ. *batt-*, Ka. *battu*, *baccu*, Tu. *battelï* 'leanness'; SD II: Te. *waṭṭu* 'to dry up', Go. *vatt-*, Koṇḍa *vaR-*, Kui *vas-*, Pe. Ma. *vac-*: CD: Kol. *vat-*, Pa. *vett-*, *veṭṭ-* 'to wither', *vetip-* (*vetit-*) v.t. 'to dry up something', Oll. *vaṭ-*, Gad. *vaṭṭ-* v.i., *vaṭp-* v.t. 'to dry up in sun'; ND: Kuṛ. *batt-* 'liquids decrease by evaporation', Malt. *bat-* '(water) to dry up', Br. *bārring* 'to become dry', *bārif-* 'to make dry' [5320].

Most of the languages of South Dravidian also preserve the forms traceable to the root **waṯ-*V-. Note that **ṯṯ* merges with a dental *-*tt* in Modern Tamil, Kannaḍa, Tuḷu, Koḍagu, Gondi, Kolami, Parji (dialectally) and Kuṛux–Malto; it merges with **ṭṭ* in Telugu, dialectally in Parji, Ollari and Gadaba. It is preserved distinctively as a voiceless alveolar trill

[18] The past-tense suffiix *-tt-* is not considered here. Following a root ending in *-y* or a front vowel, the tense allomorph *-tt-* becomes *-cc-* in Modern Tamil, Malayāḷam, Koḍagu, Kota and Toda (see Subrahmanyam 1983: §26.5.1, pp. 366–70).

/R/ contrasting with /ṟ/ in Koṇḍa; in the other members of the subgroup it merges with a palatal or sibilant *c*/*s*. The last one seems to be the only shared innovation. The gradual elimination of **ṯ* in most of the languages has led the six-point stop system to become five-point like most of the languages in the Indian area. Also study ety. (16) and (77).

4.5.8.1.4 *-ṭṭ

(99) PD **koṭ-*∼ *koṭṭ-*/*koṭ*-V 'to beat'. SD I: Ta. Ma. *koṭṭu* 'to tap, to beat, hammer, pound', Ta. *koṭu* 'to thrash', Ko. *koṭk-*, To. *kwïṭk-*, Koḍ. *koṭṭ-* 'to tap', Ka. *koṭṭ-aṇa* n. 'beating the husks of paddy', Tu. *koḍapuni* 'to hammer', Te. *koṭṭ-* v.t., Go. *koṭ-* 'cut with axe, strike with horn', *kohk-* 'to pound', Pe. *koṭ-* 'to thresh with flail'; CD : Pa. *koṭṭ-*, Oll. *koṭ-*; ND: Kuṛ. *xoṭṭ-* 'to smash', *xoṭr-* 'to be broken', Malt. *qoṭ-* 'to break', *qoṭr-* 'to be broken' [2063].

Some of the languages show *-ḍ-* (<**-ṭ-*) which alternated with **ṭṭ* when followed by a derivational suffix beginning with a vowel.

4.5.8.1.5 *-cc

(100) PD **mucc-*∼**muc*-V-∼**muy-* 'to cover'. SD I: Ta. *muccu* 'to cover', Ko. *muc-*, To. *müc-*, Koḍ. *mucc-*, Ka. *muccu*, Tu. *muccuni*; Te. *muccu* 'to close' (archaic), Go. *mucc-*, *muc-* 'to cover', Koṇḍa, Kui *mus-* 'to cover', Kuvi *muh-*, *muc-*, Pe. Manḍa *muc-*; CD: Nk. *mus-*, Nk.(Ch.) *muc-*; ND: Kuṛ. *mucc-* 'to close door', *mus*^{u}*g-* 'to wrap up', Malt. *muc-* 'to close', *musg-* 'to pack up', Br. *must* 'shut, closed' [4915].

Notice again the alternation between *c* and *s* (geminate and single) in several languages. There is an etymologically related set requiring PD **muy*/**mūy* presupposing the weakening of *-c* to *-s* and -**y* in Proto-Dravidian itself. *DEDR* lists this group under the same etymology (also see *TVB*: §1.193, p. 82).

4.5.8.1.6 *-kk-

(101) PD **wekk-* 'to hiccup'. SD I: Ta. *vikku* 'to hiccup', n. 'hiccup', Ma. *vikkuka*, v.i., *vikku* n. 'impediment in speech', *vikkam* 'stammering', To. *pïk-* 'to cough', Ka. *bikku* 'to pant, sob, hiccup', n. 'hiccup', Tu. *bikkuni* 'hold one's breath', *bikkï* n. 'holding one's breath, sob': SD II: Te. *vekku*, *vegacu* 'to hiccup', *vekk-ili* 'hiccup', Kui *vek-* 'to cough', Kuvi *vek-* 'to choke when drinking or eating'; CD: Kol. *veksi* 'hiccup'; ND: Kuṛ. *bekkh-* 'to be choked', Malt. *beq-* [5383].

As stated earlier, Proto-Dravidian stop geminates occur root-finally (with enunciative *-u*) where the root is also a free form or when it is followed by derivational suffixes beginning with vowels. If a formative suffix follows there is no gemination, e.g. see ety. (99)–(101).

4.5.8.2 -PP < -R-P, -BB < -R-B

There occur in some languages of South Dravidian I, South Dravidian II and Central Dravidian double voiceless and voiced stops which have resulted from assimilation of a root-final consonant (non-nasal sonorant), **r*, * *ṟ*, **l*, **ḷ*, **ẓ* with a stop which is part of the derivative suffix. These are originally trisyllabic bases of the type $(C_1)V_1C_2$-V_2-PP/-NP, preserved in Tamil and Malayāḷam. In such cases V_2 (= *u*) is lost and C_2 is regressively assimilated to the following P or B. The resulting disyllabic forms are found largely in Telugu and Kannaḍa (and also Tuḷu and Koḍagu through contact with Kannaḍa). The South Dravidian II and Central Dravidian languages which also attest to the loss of V_2 generally preserve the unassimilated clusters. Examples: Te. *ippa Bassia longifolia*, Kol. *ippa*, Ka. *ippe*, Tu. *ippe*; *irippe* 'the olive tree', Koṇḍa *ipa* (*maran*): Pa. *irup*, *irpa*, Gad. *irpa*, Go. *iru*, *irup*, *iṛup*, *hirp*; Kui, Kuvi *irpi*; Ta. *iruppai* 'mahua tree', Ma. *iruppa* [485]. A good case for voiced stop gemination is Te. *taggu* 'to decrease', Ka. *taggu*, *targu*, *taẓgu* 'to be, become low', *tāẓ* 'being low', Tu. *tagguni* 'to be humble', *tāruni* 'to sink in', Ko. *tag*, To. *tog*. These forms presuppose an underlying **taẓ-unk-* from PD **tāẓ* 'to fall, be low'; cf. Ta. Ma. *tāẓ*, To. *tōy*, Ka. *tāẓ*, *tāḷ* 'to be low, decrease, decay', Br. *daṛ-* 'to go down' [3178]. (For further discussion with examples, see *TVB* §§1.173–1.185, pp. 74–9.) The loss of a high vowel in a heavy syllable, i.e. *ip$pa* < *ir$pa* <*ir$ppa-*<*ir$up$pa-* seems to be a typological feature of most of the languages (outside Tamil and Malayāḷam) to promote the favourite stem types, (C)$\bar{V}$C-, or (C)VCC-. It is not a shared innovation.

4.5.8.3 *Gemination of sonorants*

PD **r* and **ẓ* do not geminate in any language. Although doubling of the other sonorants like nasals *m*, *n*, *ṇ*, laterals *l*, *ḷ*, semivowels *w*, *y* is found in different languages, there is no evidence for their reconstruction in Proto-Dravidian. There are only a few cases of single vs. double contrast in the case of the two laterals **l* and **ḷ* (see Emeneau 1970a: 94–5). Emeneau cites **nelli Phyllanthus emblica*; this occurs with gemination in Tamil, Malayāḷam, Koḍagu, Kannaḍa, Tuḷu, Telugu and Parji *nelli*, but Koṇḍa *neli*, Kui *neḍi* [3755]. For **ḷḷ*, Emeneau gives PD **piḷḷay* 'child', which occurs with a double consonant in Tamil, Malayāḷam, Koḍagu, Kannaḍa, Tuḷu, Telugu, Kolami, Naiki, Gondi, Kuvi, Kuṛux and Brahui. Koṇḍa and Malto have a single *-l-*. This can be taken as a clear case of PD **ḷḷ* (also see *TVB*: §§1.198–1.202; Subrahmanyam 1983: §§34–5).

4.5.8.4 **-NP*

Following open-syllabled roots $(C_1)V_2$-, or stems that already had the first layer of formatives -V_2 as in the type $(C_1)V_1C_2$-V_2-, a series of morphs occurred with grammatical alternation, namely -NP and -NPP in the case of verbs in which -NP signalled intransitive + non-past/past and -NPP, the corresponding transitive + non-past/past. Even within Proto-Dravidian, the tense meaning was lost first in most of the area and the morphs signalled only voice, which continued in Tamil–Malayāḷam–Koḍagu of South Dravidian I and the Koṇḍa–Kui–Kuvi–Pengo–Manḍa group of South Dravidian II. Both the voice and tense meanings survive in the conjugation of certain verbs in Tamil–Malayāḷam–Koḍagu (Krishnamurti 1997a). This problem will be discussed in detail in section 7.3. In the case of nouns -NP signals a substantive and -NPP an adjective.

It happens that in several cases the etymological boundary is between N and P (see figure 4.1), i.e. the root is a $(C_1)VC_2$- type where C_2 is N. In that case, the following formative is -P. There is no way to separate this group from the former except through comparison of cognates.

In trisyllabic stems reconstructed for Proto-Dravidian, the vowel of the second syllable ($V_2 = u$) is lost leading to the assimilation of C_2 (usually **ẓ, *l, *ḷ*) with the following nasal in many languages of South Dravidian. I have dealt with the above types in detail in *TVB*: §§1.160–1.172. Except for Tamil and Malayāḷam, most other languages lose the nasal after a long vowel, i.e. $\bar{V}$] NB > $\bar{V}$]B and the sequence -NP [NB] is preserved after a short vowel. Kota loses the nasal after a long vowel but retains it after a short vowel. Toda regularly loses the preconsonantal nasal irrespective of the length of the preceding vowel. In Malayāḷam where NP stands for **-nk*, **-ñc*, **-nt* there is progressive assimilation as *-ṅṅ*, *-ññ* and *-nn* suggesting that the postnasal stops were voiced allophonically at an earlier stage. The alveolar sequence **-ṉṯ* also produces a dental geminate suggesting an earlier merger of **-ṉṯ* with **-nt*. The retroflex and labial sequences (*-ṇḍ*, *-mb*) are not assimilated. Assimilation was attested in the inscriptions even by the tenth century. The alveolar sequence becoming /nn/ was attested in the eleventh and twelfth centuries. The sequence /nt/ is always assimilated when it is a past-tense marker. Formative /nt/ shows assimilation after (C)VC-V and not after the radical vowel, i.e. (C)$\bar{V}$-, (C)V-. In the case of velar and palatal sequences assimilation after the radical vowel is much less frequent than after the formative vowel. About 75 per cent of the velar sequences and 50 per cent of the palatal sequences show progressive assimilation. In compounds there is no nasal assimilation, if the nasal and stop are separated by a word boundary, e.g *muẓaṅ-kāl* 'knee', *muẓaṅ-kai* 'elbow'. The assimilation is said to be a sound change still in progress (Subrahmanyam 1983: §22.5, pp. 309–12, V. I. Subramoniam 1972, N. Kumaraswami Raja 1980). In the case of Old Telugu after a long vowel, the preconsonantal nasal was replaced by nasalization of the preceding vowel; the nasalized vowels became oral in Middle and Modern Telugu, e.g. PSD **ūnku* 'to swing' > OTe. *ū̃gu* > Mdn. Te. *ūgu*.

4.5.8.4.1 -mp [mb] Kannaḍa loses the nasal after a long vowel, but retains the sequence *-mb* after a short vowel. Koḍagu and Tuḷu retain *-mb*. In Telugu and the other languages of South Dravidian II and in the Central Dravidian languages, there was progressive assimilation of _-mb_ to _-mm_ after a short vowel and _-m_ after a long vowel. A similar change occurs optionally in Tuḷu also after a short vowel, but they could as well be independent changes. In North Dravidian the sequence is retained, but there are no clear etymologies.

(102) PD *_nampu_ (<*_nay-mp-_) 'to long for, trust'. SD I: Ta. _nampu_, Ma. _nampuka_, Ko. _namb-_, To. _nob_, Koḍ. _namb-_, Tu. _nambuni_, _nammuni_; SD II: Te. _nammu_, Koṇḍa _nami-_, Kui _nam-_, Kuvi _namm-/nam-_ [3600]. Cf. Ta. _naya_ 'to desire', _naccu_ 'to be agreeable', Te. _nayamu_ 'good', _naccu_ 'to be agreeable' etc. [3602, 3576].

(103) PD *_pāmpu_ 'snake'. SD I: Ta. _pāmpu_ n. adj _pāppu_, Ma. _pāmpu_, Ko. _pāb_, To. _pōb_, Koḍ. _pāmbï_, Ka. _pāvu_, _hāvu_, Tu. _hāvu_ (<lw. Ka.); SD II: Te. _pāmu_ n., _pāpa-_ adj; CD: Kol., Nk. Nk. (Ch.) _pām_ (lw < Te.), Pa. Oll. _bām_, Gad. _bāmu_, _bāmb_ [4085]. Te. _nōmu_ 'a religious vow' is from *_nōn-pu_, cf. Ta. _nōṉ_ 'to practise austerities', Ta. Ma. _nōṉpu_, _nōmpu_ 'ceremonial fasting', Ka. _nōn_ v., _nōmpu_ n., Tu. _nōmbu_ 'fasting' [3800].

4.5.8.4.2 *-nt [nd]

(104/46) PD *_cīntu_ 'date palm', *_cīntt-_ adj. SD I: Ta. _īntu_, _īñcu_ 'date-palm, Phoenix farnifera'_, _īccam paṉai_ 'wild date-palm', Ma. _īntal_, Ka. _īcal_, Tu. _īñcilï_, _īcilï_ (<*_īntt-_), _īndï_ 'sago-palm'; SD II:Te. _ī̃ta_, _ī̃du_, Go. _sīndi_, _hīndi_, _īndi_, Koṇḍa _sītel_, Kui _sīta_, Kuvi _sīndi_; CD: Pa. _cīnd_, Gad. _sīndi_; ND: Kuṛ. _kī̃dā_ 'palm tree'. || Skt. _hintāḷa_ 'marshy date tree', Pkt. _sindī_ 'date palm' [2617, _CDIAL_ 14093].

This is an important etymology for two reasons: (i) When Proto-Dravidian *_c-_ was lost in the southern group (SD I), it passed through two intermediate stages *_s-_ and *_h-_; both these stages are preserved in Pkt. and Skt. loanwords; *_ntt_ changes to *_ncc-_ following a palatal vowel in the languages which show a palatal. Tamil and Malayāḷam lose the nasal before a geminated stop (see section 4.5.8.5). (ii) It attests the change of Proto-Dravidian *_c-_ to _k-_ in North Dravidian.

In some of the languages, trisyllabic bases become disyllabic with the loss of _-u-_ before _-nt-_:[19]

(105) PD *_maruntu_ 'medicine', adj *_maruntt-_. SD I: Ta. _maruntu_ n., adj _marutt-_, _maruttaṉ_ 'physician', Ma. _marunnu_, Ko. _mad_, To. _mad_, Koḍ. _maddï_, Ka.

[19] The past-tense *_-nt-_ is also found in SD I languages and in Central Dravidian (see Emeneau 1967, Subrahmanyam 1983: §26.5). This sequence is palatalized to _-nj-_ after front vowels in South Dravidian I. In Central Dravidian Parji also independently palatalizes _-nd-_ to _-nj-_ but this is a recent development.

mardu, *maddu*,Tu. *mardï*; SD II: Te. *ma-ndu* 'medicine', Go. *mat*, *matu*, *matta*; CD: Pa. *merud* (pl *merdul*), Oll. *mardil*, Gad. *marid*; ND: Kuṛ. *mandar*, Malt. *mandru* [4719].

In **cīntu* 'to blow the nose' which is from **cīm-t-* based on comparative evidence; the root is preserved in Ka. *sīn-*, Tu. *sīmpï* 'to blow the nose', Kor. *cīmpu* [2618].

4.5.8.4.3 *-nṯ- [nḏ/nṟ] See ety. (3) **en-ṯu* 'sun', (4b) **nin-ṯ-* 'to be full', (70) **ñēnṯu* 'time, day'. In a large number of etymologies it seems that **-nṯ* arises in sandhi by combining a root-final alveolar nasal with a following dental formative suffix. In this sequence the voiced alveolar stop **ḏ/*ṟ* merges with a dental, a retroflex or a palatal stop. Merger with a palatal voiced stop occurs in Kui–Kuvi–Pengo–Manḍa, which is a shared innovation. PD **nṯ* represented as OTa. *-nṟ* becomes *ṇṇ* in Modern Tamil (*oṇṇï* 'one' from older *onṟu*); in Malayāḷam it develops to a dental geminate *-nn-* (apparently through an intermediate merger stage of *-nd-*); Kota and Toda preserve *ḏ* with the loss of the nasal; in Old Telugu it was recorded as *-nṟ* in inscriptions and merged with *-ṇḍ* later; Gondi has merged it with a dental or retroflex in different dialects; in Central Dravidian, Parji (dialectally) and Gadaba represent this as *-ṇḍ*. In Kannaḍa, Koḍagu, Kolami, Naiki and Kuṛux–Malto, **ḏ* merges with a voiced dental stop *-d*. In the Kui–Manḍa subgroup and in Tuḷu, **-nṟ* merges with *-nj*. Except for the Kui–Manḍa subgroup, none of the above developments can be called a shared innovation. This means that the cluster was preserved until all the subgroups were split into independent languages and the phoneme got eliminated through mergers later, owing to the typological pressure of converting the six-point stop system to a five-point one like the other languages in the area.

(106) PD **on-ṯu* 'one'. SD I: Ta. *onṟu* (>*oṇṇu*), Ma. *onnu*, Ko. *oḏ*, *-onḏ*, To. *wïḏ*, Koḍ. *ondï*, Ka. *ondu*, Tu. *oñji*: SD II: Te. *oṇḍu*, Go. *uṇḍī*, *undī*, Koṇḍa *unṟi*; ND: Kuṛ. *ōn*, *ōnd*, Malt. *-ond*, Br. *asiṭ* [990d].

4.5.8.4.4 *-ṇṭ [ṇḍ]

(107) PD **kaṇ-ṭ*V 'warrior'. SD I: Ta. *kaṇṭaṉ* 'warrior, husband', *kaṇ-avaṉ* 'husband', Ma. *kaṇṭan* 'the male, of a cat', *kaṇavan* 'husband', Ko. *gaṇḍ* 'male', To. *koḍṇ* 'Baḍaga husband', Koḍ. *kaṇḍë* 'male (of dogs and other animals)', Ka. *gaṇḍu* 'bravery', *gaṇḍa* 'strong person, husband', Tu. *gaṇḍu* 'male, stout', *kaṇḍaṇi* 'husband'; SD II: Te. *gaṇḍu* 'bravery', *gaṇḍu-billi* 'male cat'; CD: Nk. *gaṛek* 'man, male'; ND: Malto *geṇḍa* 'male' ||>Skt. *gaṇḍa-*, *gaṇḍira-* 'hero' [1173].

See ety. (91) for **ṇṭ* in the second syllable.

(108) PD **piṇṭ-* <***piẓ-nt-* 'to squeeze'. SD I: Ta. *piṇṭi* 'what is squeezed', Koḍ. *puṇḍ-*, Ka. *piṇḍu*, *hiṇḍu* 'to squeeze out', Tu. *purñcuni*, *pureñcuni* 'to

squeeze, as a lemon', puṇḍiyuni, 'to wring a wet garment', piṇḍ, puṇḍi 'oilcake'; SD II: Te. piṇḍu 'to squeeze, milk, wring', piṇḍi 'oilcake'; CD: Kol. pinḍ-, pīṇḍ-, Nk. pīṇḍ- [4183].

Languages belonging to all subgroups also have cognates for the same meaning from *piẓi [4183]. It must be admitted that there are hardly any cases where -ṇṭ is a primary suffix, i.e. where it is not derived from sandhi between the root final *ṇ with a following -t (P-suffix), or from *-ẓ + nt- >-ṇ-ṭ-. Other cases include *paṇṭu 'fruit' <*paẓ-nt- [4004], uṇṭu 'to be' <*uḷ-nt- [697].

4.5.8.4.5 *-ñc [ñj]

(109) PD *tuñc- 'to sleep'. SD I: Ta. Ma. tuñcu (cf. tuyil 'to sleep', n. 'sleep'): SD II: Go. sunj-, hunj-, unj-, Koṇḍa sunz-, sus-, Kui sunj-, Kuvi hūnj-, Pe. Manḍa hunj-; CD: Pa. tuñ-, cuñ- 'to sleep', tuñ-ip- 'to put to sleep', Oll. tuñ-, tuyŋg-, Gad. tuŋ-; ND: ?Br. tūl- 'to sit' [3291].

If *tuy- was the underlying root (past:*tuy-nt-) we need to posit palatalization for Proto-Dravidian itself as in *tu(y)-ñc- plausibly from *cu(y)-ñc- <*cuy-ntt-. There are long vowel forms which look to *cuy-/*tuy- as the ultimate root: To. tüs̲, Gad. (P) tuyŋg-, Kui sūs-, Br. tūl-. By putting all these in the same group, *DEDR* seems to suggest this. There is another related group of etyma, *uy-al, *tuy-al 'to wave, swing', ū-nku 'to swing', [731, 3376b], *tū-nku 'to shake, swing, sleep' [3376a], ultimately traceable to the root *cuy- on account of t-/Ø- alternation. Other forms include *añcu 'to fear' [55], *nañcu 'poison', nañcc- adj [3580], *neñcu 'heart, core' [3736].

4.5.8.4.6 *-nk [ng] This sequence can be primary derivable from PD *-nk or from a combination of root-final -ṇ or -m with a following stop suffix *-k.

(110) PD *ponku 'to boil'. SD I: Ta. poṅku 'to boil, bubble up', Ma. poṅṅuka, Ko. pog- 'to boil over', poŋg- 'to increase', To. pïg-, Koḍ. poŋŋ-, Tu. boṅguni 'to be distended', pongaḍε 'proud flesh'; SD II: Te. pongu 'to boil', n. 'boiling, joy, pride', Go. pōŋ- 'to swell', Koṇḍa poŋi- 'to swell up', Kuvi poŋg- 'to swell'; CD: Kol. poŋg- 'to boil over', Nk. poŋg- 'to expand'; ND: Kuṛ. pūx- 'to swell, as rice in water', pokpokr- 'to puff out', Malt. pogole- 'to swell', poŋgj- 'to be increased', pūgr- 'to be swollen' [4469].

Note that Malayāḷam and Koḍagu show progressive assimilation of *nk to ṅṅ, suggesting that [ŋg] as an intermediate stage was part of the PSD phonetic state.

From the foregoing description the *-NP sequence is preserved in most of the languages as -NB after a radical short vowel. Kota optionally and Toda regularly drop the nasal but retain the voiced stop even after a radical short vowel.

4.5.8.5 **-NPP*

Kumaraswami Raja published a paper and then a short monograph (1969a, b), showing the necessity to reconstruct a sequence of *-NPP for Proto-Dravidian on the basis of the correspondences in table 4.8, originally observed in the major literary languages.

Table 4.8. *Correspondences of Proto-Dravidian * NP and *NPP in Tamil–Malayāḷam and Telugu–Kannaḍa*

Proto-Dravidian	Tamil–Malayāḷam	Telugu–Kannaḍa
a. *NP	NP [NB]	NB/V__ B/$\bar{V}^{n}$__ (Telugu) B/$\bar{V}$ __ (Kannaḍa)
b. *PP	PP	PP/V__ P/$\bar{V}$ __
c. *NPP	PP	NP/V__

In Tamil and Malayāḷam *NP and *PP remain unchanged irrespective of the length of the preceding vowel. In Kannaḍa and Telugu, which developed contrastive voicing from the earliest known period, *NP, *PP occurred as NB, PP after short vowels. Only after long vowels Kannaḍa and Telugu had different developments. But correspondence (c) is not taken care of by (a) and (b). There are cognates in which Tamil and Malayāḷam show PP and Telugu and Kannaḍa show NP (contrasting with NB from PD *NP), e.g.

(111) PD **tōṇ-ṭṭ-am* 'garden' from **tōṇṭu* 'to dig'. SD I: Ta. Ma. *tōṇṭu* 'to dig', *tōṭṭam* (<**tōṇṭ* + *tam*) 'garden', Ko. *tōḍ-* v., *tōṭm-* n., To. *twī̄ṛ-* v., *twī̄ṭm-* n., Koḍ. *tōḍ-* v., *tōṭa* n., Ka. *tōḍu* 'to dig, take water out of a well', *tōṇṭa*, *tōṭa* 'garden',Tu. *tōḍuni* v., *tōṭa* n.: SD II: Te. *tō̃ḍu* (> Mdn Te. *tōḍu*) 'to draw water up, to scoop out', *tō̃ṭa* (> Mdn Te. *tōṭa*) 'fenced garden', Koṇḍa *ṭōṇṭa* 'garden'; CD: Pa. *ṭō̃ḍ-* 'to draw water from well', Gad. *tōnḍ-* 'to bale out water' [3549].

This example clearly shows that a voiceless *-ṭ* after a nasal, i.e. in *-ṇ]ṭ*, must be derived from a geminate *-ṭṭ* of Proto-Dravidian. Tamil, Malayāḷam, Kota, Toda, Koḍagu and Tuḷu do not show a nasal before a voiceless single *-ṭ*, which meant that they had lost the nasal, but retained the geminate, represented as *-ṭṭ* in Tamil and Malayāḷam and as *-ṭ* in the others. It appears that Koḍagu and Tuḷu borrowed the form from Kannaḍa after it had lost *ṇ* before *ṭ*. Old Telugu and Old Kannaḍa preserved the nasal + a single voiceless stop. In other words, in the languages which had already developed voiced–voiceless contrast in stops, PD *NP: *NPP developed into NB: NP (Kannaḍa–Telugu in the above example);

in the languages which had not developed the voicing contrast (particularly Tamil and Malayāḷam) the original differentiation of single vs. double stop remained and the pre-consonantal nasal was lost. Note that no language preserves the sequence *-NPP, since phonotactically it is not permitted in any of the descendant languages. Kumaraswami Raja proposes the following correspondences (~ = nasalization of the preceding vowel):

***-nkk:** Ko. (*ŋ*)*k*, Ka. Tu. (*ṅ*)*k*; Te. *ṅk*/~*k*; Kol. Nk. (*ŋ*)*k*, Oll. ~*k*; Kuṛ. *ŋkh*, *ŋk*, ~*x*, *kk*, Malt. (*n*)*q*, (*n*)*k*, Br. *nk*; the remaining languages have no nasal.

***-ñcc:** Ko. Ka. Tu. (*n*)*c*; Te. *nc* /~*c*, Go. *nc*; Kol. *ns*; Kuṛ. ~*c*, Br. *nc*; the rest *cc*, *c* or *s*.

***-ṇṭṭ:** Ko. Ka. Koḍ. Tu. (*ṇ*)*ṭ*; Te. Go. (*ṇ*)*ṭ*; Kol. Nk. Pa. Gad. (*ṇ*)*ṭ*; Kuṛ. (*ṇ*)*ṭ*; the rest *ṭṭ* or *ṭ*.

***-ntt:** Ka. *nt*, *c*, *s*, Tu. *nt*/*ñc*, ~*t*/~*c*, *t*/*c*; Kol. Gad. *nt*; Kuṛ. ~*t*. The others have no evidence of a nasal.

***-ṉṯṯ:** Ko. *nṯ*, *ṯ*, Ka. Tu. (*n*)*t*; Te. ~*t*/~ *ṭ*/*ṭ*; Kuṛ. ~*t*; the rest of the languages have *ṯṯ*, *ṭ* or *t*.

***-mpp**: Ka. Tu. (*m*)*p*; Te. (*m*)*p*/~*p*; Kol. (*m*)*p*; Kuṛ. (*m*)*p*/~*p*.

In all the correspondences, Tamil and Malayāḷam always have geminates with the loss of the nasal. Phonetically NP is an impossible cluster in Tamil and Malayāḷam. It appears that Kota must have split from Pre-Tamil before it lost the nasal, hence it attests to the presence of NP clusters. Toda must have branched from Pre-Tamil after the loss of *N; therefore, there is no single case of a nasal before a voiceless stop in Toda. In the remaining South Dravidian languages, Kannaḍa and Tuḷu show NP sequences regularly; Koḍagu also shows nasals occasionally. In South Dravidian II Telugu preserves the nasal before a voiceless stop at some point in its history, followed occasionally by Gondi. The rest of the languages have lost the nasal before a voiceless stop. In Central Dravidian most languages show the NP cluster contrasting with NB. In North Dravidian Kuṛux and Brahui preserve the nasal before voicelss stops. As in the case of NP, the etymological boundary may also fall between the root-final N followed by geminate stop suffix (PP).

(112) PD **aṇ-ṭṭ-* 'to adhere, stick'. SD I: Ta. Ma. *aṭṭu* v.t. 'to join, stick', Ka. *aṇṭu* 'to stick, adhere to', *aṇke*, *aṇpu* 'smearing', Tu. *aṇṭuni* v.i. 'to stick', v.t. 'to attract', *aṇṭï* 'gum'; SD II: Te. *aṇṭu* v.i., Pe. *anḍ-* 'to adhere', Kuvi *aṭ-* 'to get stuck'; CD: Kol. *aṇṭ-* 'to stick', *aṭ-*, Nk. *aṭṭ-* [96].

(113) PD **kalanku* v.i. 'to stir', **kalankku* v.t. 'to agitate, stir'. SD I: Ta. *kalaṅku* v.i., *kalakku* v.t., Ma. *kalaṅṅuka* v.i., *kalakkuka*, v.t., Ko. *kalg-* v.i., *kalk-* v.t., To. *kalx-* v.i., *kalk-* v.t., Koḍ. *kalaŋg-* v.i., *kalak-* v.t., Ka. *kalaṅku*, *kalaku* v.t. 'to agitate, perturb', *kalaḍu* 'to be shaken', Tu. *kalaṅkuni* v.i. 'to be turbid', *kalaṅkï* 'turbidness'; SD II: Te. *kala*^{n}*gu* 'to be stirred up', *kala*^{n}*cu*

v.t., *kala*^{n}*ka* n.'confusion, turbidness', Kui *glahp-* (*glaht-*) 'to confound'; ND: Kuṛ. *xalx-* 'to disturb, make muddy', Malt. *qalg̣-* 'to disturb, as water' [1303].

Note that NP: NPP of the second syllable originally represented an intransitive–transitive difference in South Dravidian I and II. It is preserved in Tamil, Malayāḷam and some of the Nilgiri languages in South Dravidian I; in Kannaḍa the transitive is a relic form not matched by a corresponding intransitive; in Tuḷu the form with the suffix traceable to NPP gives intransitive meaning. In South Dravidian II Kui–Kuvi–Pengo–Manḍa generally retain the NB–NP alternation to signal intransitive–transitive difference. North Dravidian has also lost the original alternation but retains the formal difference.

4.6 Conclusion

I have classified the sound changes into shared innovations and typologically motivated changes, which behave differently in subgrouping languages. This is a proposal that I am making for historical linguists to consider.

4.6.1 *Shared innovations*

4.6.1.1 *South Dravidian*

There are two clear phonological innovations shared by all members of the two subgroups of South Dravidian, South Dravidian I and South Dravidian II : (i) The merger of Proto-Dravidian high vowels **i* **u* with **e* **o* in Proto-South Dravidian in the environment [C-*a* (see Rule 4a, c, section 4.4.2). The etymologies attesting the origin of long vowels *ē* and *ō* from PD **i*/**e*C-*a*, **u*/**o*C-*a* in the two subgroups show clearly that the developments in Central Dravidian and North Dravidian are different (see Rule 2 in section 4.3.2.1 followed by ety. (7), (8), (10); Rule 4 in section 4.4.2.2 and Rule 6 in section 4.4.3 and ety. (31), (32), (34), (36); see also Krishnamurti 1980: 502–3). (ii) The loss of **c* through two intermediate stages of *s* and *h*, initially and medially in South Dravidian I. This change is also shared by South-Central Dravidian (South Dravidian II) where *s-* >*h-* is found in many of the languages dialectally. In Gondi *h-* >*Ø-* is an ongoing change which is completed in the southern dialect of Koya. Kui–Kuvi–Pengo–Manḍa show the rule of *s* > *h* spreading dialectally. I have proposed that the South Dravidian I change had also gone through similar intermediate stages although they were not directly attested in any of the languages. However, there is ample indirect evidence of Sanskrit and Prakrit borrowings from Dravidian with *s* and *h* attesting to these stages (see Rule 13, section 4.5.1.3, fn. 5; see ety. (10), (24), (45), (46/104). The formative suffix *-ā* in Old Tamil is also shown to have developed from a prehistoric **-aha* <**-asa* through contraction. (iii) The apical displacement rules by which medial apicals came to word-initial position characterized South Dravidian II as a shared innovation (Rule 20, section 4.5.7.3, ety. (90)–(94)). But we also notice a similar, if not an identical, rule now spreading in South Dravidian I in a few lexical items by which the medial apicals come to the initial position by loss of a word-initial short vowel (see section 4.4.4.6). There is no evidence of this as a genetic phenomenon either in Central or in North Dravidian. (iv) In both these subgroups PD *ṯ is represented by ṟ in intervocalic position (sections 4.5.5.3, 4.5.8.4.3). This distinguishes South Dravidian subgroups from Central Dravidian, where it remains a stop [*d̠]. Telugu goes with South Dravidian I in merging ṟ with *r* in all positions. This is a typologically motivated change in all the languages with independently recorded histories and not a shared innovation.

South Dravidian II has two exclusive isoglosses: (i) The replacement of *ẓ by ṛ occurs in all except Telugu where it is replaced by ḍ; (ii) the replacement of *ḷ *ṇ by *l n* regularly in Telugu and by *l*/ṛ (dialectally) and ṇ/*n*, respectively, in the other members of South Dravidian II. Kui–Kuvi–Pengo–Manḍa replace PSD *ṯ [ṟ], *nṯ [nṟ], *ṯṯ [*R* = voiceless alveolar trill] by palatal affricates *j*, *nj* or *s* the corresponding voiceless consonant (instead of *c*) (see section 4.5.8.1.3).

Within South Dravidian I, there are isoglosses enclosing smaller subgroups. Tamil and Malayāḷam have three shared innovations, (i) PSD *e, *o[C-a> i, u[C-a (Rule 4b, c, section 4.4.2, ety.(22)–(26)), (ii) the palatalization rule (Rule 14b, section 4.4.1.4, ety.(37), (38), (49)–(51)), and (iii) the uniform loss of N from PD *NPP clusters (section 4.5.8.5., ety. (111)–(113)).

Centralized vowels occur in Toda, Koḍagu and Kuṟumba, but not in Kota. I have proposed that the phonetic basis of this, namely retracted tongue position before retroflex consonants, was an inherited feature from Pre-Tamil (section 4.4.4.2) and it is not an areal feature of the Nilgiri languages, since Kota and Baḍaga do not have it. We must still examine if there is strong morphological evidence for putting Toda and Kota as branches from a single node.

One clear isogloss encloses Kannaḍa, Koḍagu, Kuṟumba and Tuḷu, i.e. *w- > b- (Rule 18a, section 4.5.4.1, ety. (14), (71), (88), (101)). A rule rounding front vowels after labial consonants is found in Tuḷu and Koḍagu, see Rules 8b (section 4.4.4.3) and 9 (section 4.4.4.5). Kannaḍa change *p- >h- >Ø-* (Rule 12) is found in Baḍaga only as a shared innovation, according to some scholars (section 4.5.1.1, ety. (16), (17), (29), (31), (82)). It is found in many of the neighbouring languages, Koḍagu, Tuḷu, Kuṟumba, Kota etc. through contact and borrowing.

4.6.1.2 *Central Dravidian*

It is important to know that the changes shared by South Dravidian I and South Dravidian II are not shared by Central Dravidian. That is why South Dravidian II which was originally grouped with Central Dravidian has been separated from it in my writings from 1974 onwards. A shared innovation of Central Dravidian languages is the treatment of **ṯ* [d̠] intervocalically. It is represented by *-d-* in Kolami, Naiki and Parji and by *-y-* (<*-d-*) in Ollari and Gadaba. The NE dialect of Parji shows it as a retroflex stop *-ḍ-*. Kolami and Naiki also show *-r-* which look like borrowings from Telugu. The treatment of a single **ṯ* as [ṟ] in the intervocalic position is a shared phonetic phenomenon of Proto-South Dravidian (section 4.5.5.3). The Central Dravidian languages represent this as a stop [d] in all positions.

(114) PD **kēṯ*/ **keṯ*-V- 'to winnow', **kēṯṯ*- n. 'winnowing basket'. South Dravidian I : Ta. *cēṭṭai* 'winnowing basket' (lw <Te.), Ma. *cēṟuka* v., Ko. *kēr-* v., To. *kȫṟ-* v., Ka. *kēṟu* v.; SD II: Te. *cerugu* (<**ceṟ-ugu*) v.t., *cēṭa* 'winnowing basket' (<**cēṯṯa-* <**kēṯṯ-*), ND: Kuṛ. *kẽ̄s-*, Malt. *kēs-* : CD: Kol. Nk. *kēd-* v., *kēt-* n. 'winnowing basket', Pa. *kēd-*, *kēḍ-* v., *kēti*, *kēṭi* n., Oll. *kēy* v., *kēti*, *kēṭin* n., Gad. *kēy* v., *kēṭen* n. [2019].

The other South Dravidian II languages do not have the verb (Pengo has a doubtful verb *jēc-* 'to winnow'), but have the derived noun borrowed from Pre-Telugu after palatalization in the form **cēṯṯ*-V: Go. *sēti*, *hēti*, Koṇḍa *sēRi*, Kui *sēsi*, Kuvi Pe. Maṇḍa *hēci* 'winnowing basket'. The absence of a verb corresponding to the derived noun and the fact that 'winnowing baskets' made by Telugus are used in South Dravidian II tribal areas supports early borrowing of the Pre-Telugu word into this subgroup. Also note that Tamil has a noun borrowed from Telugu and no verb; the other South Dravidian I languages also have no derived noun. Only the Central Dravidian languages have both the verb and the noun with different phonology.[20]

An isogloss which binds a subgroup of Central Dravidian is the loss of word-initial *n-*; this is found in the whole subgroup in two items, e.g. **īn*/**in-* 'you' (<**nīn*/**nin-*), but it is regular in the case of Kolami–Naiki (Suvarchala 1992: 20). We cannot attribute this to this subgroup since *n-* loss is sporadically found in other languages also (see *TVB*: §1.218–220, pp. 91–2).

4.6.1.3 *North Dravidian*

The shared innovations are **k* becoming *x*/*q* before all vowels except the high front ones (Rule 15, section 4.5.1.4) and the velarization of PD **c* before high vowels (Rule 13c, section 4.5.1.3, ety. (46) ff.). Another shared innovation is **w-* >*b-* perhaps under the influence of the neighbouring Eastern Indo-Aryan languages (Rule 18b). This sound change has implications for the original home of Brahui. Western Indo-Aryan (Kashmiri, Sindhi, Lahanda, Panjabi, Gujarati, Marathi) did not share the East IA change of **v-* > *b-*.

[20] Zvelebil has treated the forms with *s*/*h* in South-Central Dravidian as a case of irregular palatalization (1970b: 117–18). 'This replacement seems however irregular and dependent upon some additional factors...' (118).

This makes it likely that the speakers of Brahui left east India where they were with Kuṛux–Malto till after the operation of this sound change around the eighth century AD. Many scholars think that Brahui is the first column of speakers left behind when the Proto-Dravidian speakers entered India from the northwest. This is highly speculative, since Brahui does not preserve any archaic features. The oldest Dravidian features in phonology and grammar are preserved in the southern group of languages.

4.6.2 *Changes with typological goals*

A number of sound changes have occurred or are occurring in contiguous languages at different times, producing a final result, which, if we looked back after many years, would give the impression that they were shared innovations. These are different from the sound changes discussed in section 4.6.1 in several respects: (1) they do not have a fixed, definable time frame, except that they are all post-Proto-Dravidian; (2) there is evidence that they have been occurring in different languages at different times; some are on-going; (3) they cut across the subgroups set up on the basis of shared innovations; (4) it seems possible that their spread can be defined in terms of broad geographical regions. For these reasons they are considered typologically motivated sound changes, since each of these can be shown to have affected the phonological systems of the concerned languages in creating greater internal symmetry and cohesion (see Krishnamurti 1998a: 75–8).

1. Proto-Dravidian root-final *-*ay*, developed to -*ey* and then to *ē̆* and *ī̆* in almost all South-Central Dravidian, Central Dravidian and North Dravidian languages (section 4.4.7). This change (monophthongization) has eliminated diphthongs in most of the languages.

2. PD **y*- is lost in all languages except Old Tamil; Modern Tamil and Malayāḷam also do not have it. The vowel following **y* was *Ā̆ representing neutralization of *ā̆* and *ē̆*. This vowel was represented as *e*/*ā* in South Dravidian I, as *ē*/*ā* in South-Central Dravidian, as *a*/*ā* in Central Dravidian and as *e*/*ē* in North Dravidian. Similarly PD **ñ*- merged with *n*- in all languages except in Malayāḷam (with some relics in Koḍagu and Tuḷu) which have retained some items with **ñ* and not all. There are a few lexical items with **ñ* followed by *i* and *ō̆*, and not by the other vowels, *ī* and *ū̆* (see Rule 17 and section 4.5.3.3). The restricted distribution of these phonemes, compared with the other consonants that occur initially in Proto-Dravidian, and their low functional load must have been the typological factors leading to their eventual elimination through merger in most of the languages.

3. PD **ẓ* is the most characteristic of Proto-Dravidian phonemes which is not found in many languages of the world. It is a retroflex frictionless continuant (approximant). It is lost in all languages consequent on splits and mergers during the historic times, except in some regional and social dialects of Tamil and Malayāḷam. In Parji of Central Dravidian, it developed to *ṛ* distinctively. It merges in different languages with *ḍ ṛ l ḷ c*

r y š ṣ Ø. No clear isoglosses seem possible except for a subgroup of South Dravidian II, i.e. Koṇḍa–Gondi–Kui–Kuvi–Pengo–Manḍa in which it developed to *ṛ* (see section 4.5.7.1.3).

4. PD **ṇ* **ḷ* (retroflex sonorants) became deretroflexed as dental/alveolar *n l* in South Dravidian II, Central Dravidian and North Dravidian. These phonemes are, however, internally reconstructable in certain languages of South-Central Dravidian and Central Dravidian. All South Dravidian I languages preserve them. Retroflex **ḷ* is allophonically preserved in Naikṛi after non-front vowels; before front vowels **l* and **ḷ* merged into /l/; **ṇ* is preserved in Koṇḍa. The merger of the two retroflex sonorants with alveolars is still an ongoing change, and it is a sweeping one too. The languages in which the changes have occurred during the recent past border on Indo-Aryan languages which have only *l* and *n* (except Marathi which probably has retroflex *ḷ* and *ṇ* being a geographical neighbour of Kannaḍa which preserves the contrast between *l*:*ḷ* and *n*: *ṇ*) (see sections 4.5.7.1d, 4.5.6).

5. PD /*ṯ *ṯṯ *nṯ/ are preserved only in Toda, Iruḷa and Kuṟumba, and to some extent as /ṯṯ/ and /nḏ/ in Malayāḷam in South Dravidian I; they are preserved as /ṟ R nṟ/ in Koṇḍa of South Dravidian II. PD * *ṯ* [ṟ] merged with the flap /r/ in all the literary languages and in others that inherited the [ṟ] allophone in South Dravidian I. In South Dravidian II in the subgroup Kui–Kuvi–Pengo–Manḍa, it merged with *j*; so also, *-*nḏ* became -*nj* and **ṯṯ* [R] merged with *c/s*. In Central Dravidian **ṯ* [ḏ] merged with /d/. In the languages of all subgroups (except some Nilgiri languages and the subgroup of South Dravidian II mentioned above), the sequences /ṯṯ nṯ/ have merged with dental /tt nd/ or retroflex / ṭṭ ṇḍ/. Some of these changes are datable within the literary languages. No common historical stage can be postulated. These chains of sound changes have led to the six-point stop system becoming five-point as it is in most of the languages of the Indian linguistic area (see sections 4.5.5.3, 4.5.8.1.3, 4.5.8.4.3).

6. Two syllable types have become normalized in all languages except Tamil and Malayāḷam, namely (C)VCCV or (C)V̄CV. A number of phonological changes have occurred leading to this typological goal. Such a shift is also evidenced in Indo-Aryan (Krishnamurti 1991a). PP >P, NP >B/#(C)V̄__is part of this strategy. Loss of a high vowel /i u/ in the medial (unaccented) syllable has led to the creation of disyllabic forms from underlying trisyllabic ones, e.g.**mar-u-ntu* 'medicine': Te. *mandu*, Ka. *maddu*, *mardu*, Pa. *merd*- (<**mar-nt*-).

7. Consequent on changes in canonical shapes, obstruent voicing became phonemic in almost all the languages except Tamil, Malayāḷam and Toda, as follows:

PD	*P-	*-P-	*-PP-	*-NP-	*-NPP- >
post-PD	?	-B-	-P-	-NB-	-NP-

The initial position is filled by secondary voicing and through borrowings from Indo-Aryan. The older single vs. double contrast became voiced vs. voiceless (see general comments in sections 4.5.1, 4.5.2, 4.5.5, 4.5.8.1, 4.5.8.4, 4.5.8.5).

4.6.2.1 *Observations*

(a) Most of the historically identifiable shared innovations have exceptions. The typologically motivated ones are extremely regular.

(b) It is likely that shared innovations generally spread through lexical diffusion. Typologically triggered sound changes show the Neogrammarian regularity and they are exceptionless. It is not clear if they imply a different mechanism.

(c) What are the consequences of recognizing two types of sound change for the comparative method and reconstruction?

What is proposed here is that certain sound changes are motivated or caused by system-internal pressures and such changes tend to be very regular compared to those which are caused by sporadic shifts in the speech habits of speakers. For instance, in Dravidian, the palatalization of a velar before palatal vowels is one such, although it is phonetically conditioned and quite common in the languages of the world. There is nothing system-internal to initiate this change, although it may have brought about changes in the distribution of certain phonemes. In contrast to this, the replacement of *-ṯ- [-ṟ-/-ḏ-] by *r/d/j*, of **ṯṯ* by *tt/t* ~ *ṭṭ/ṭ*~ *c/s* and of *nṯ* [nḏ/nṟ] by *nd/ṇḍ/nj* in different languages is typologically motivated. Hence, its spread has been sweeping and there are hardly any exceptions after its operation (for further discussion, see Krishnamurti 1998a).

This proposal must be examined seriously by historical linguists.

5

Word formation: roots, stems, formatives, derivational suffixes and nominal compounds

5.1 Structure of roots and formatives

It is beyond doubt that Proto-Dravidian roots (verbal and nominal) were all monosyllabic with the canonical shape $(C)\breve{\bar{V}}(C)$ (see section 4.2). As Caldwell has already mentioned (1956: 206ff.):

> We find in these languages groups of related words, the first syllables of which are nearly or wholly identical, whilst their second syllables are different in each instance, and in consequence of this difference produce the required degree of diversity in the signification of each member of the group.

Regarding the elements that follow the root, Caldwell says:

> The specialising particle, which was probably a separable suffix, formative, or postposition at first, has become by degrees a component part of the word; and this word, so compounded, constitutes the base to which all formatives, properly so called, and all inflexional particles are appended. (1956: 206)

Caldwell recognized the underlying root of a family of words as the invariable element; he calls the variable elements, mainly of the -L/-VL type (see section 4.2), 'particles of specialization'. The stems formed by the addition of these enter into inflection as verbs or nouns, etc. The so-called 'specialising particles' diversify the meaning of the root but no clear meaning can be assigned to each of them. He also calls them 'formative additions' (1956: 203).

Caldwell divides roots into those which occur either as verbs or as nouns, and nouns, which cannot be derived from any underlying verbs, e.g. **kāl* 'leg', **kal* 'stone' (1956: 196). Suffixes of NP: NPP type (see section 4.2), which signal intransitive–transitive meaning, were 'signs of verbal nouns', according to Caldwell (1956: 196). The vowels, which occurred between the roots and these 'clashing consonants', were inserted 'euphonically' (1956: 196). In our terminology, he considers V_2 as an epenthetic vowel.

He gives examples both from verb stems and noun stems that have what we now consider *-V-L, *-V-NP, and *-V-NPP. Caldwell also calls attention to a parallel phonological process in Tamil, i.e. gemination of the final obstruent in forming transitive verbs from intransitive, and in forming adjectives out of nouns, e.g. Ta. *tir-u-ntu* v.i. 'to change', *tir-u-ttu* v.t. 'to correct, rectify' (<*tir-u-ntt-); *mar-u-ntu* 'medicine', adj. *mar-u-ttu* (<*mar-u-ntt-). Caldwell has not given any supporting arguments for considering the formatives, i.e. L, P, NP, PP and NPP, as 'signs of verbal nouns which secondarily became verbs' (198). Actually it appears that the opposite is the fact. There is more justification to treat the formatives as original tense and voice suffixes, which later lost the tense meaning first, but retained transitivity. In some languages even the latter meaning is lost and they have become simple formatives without any grammatical and semantic content. Caldwell, following Gundert, further tried to derive some of the -VL suffixes from independent roots like *il 'house', *uḷ 'to be', but this was a mere guess and not supported by comparative evidence (see Krishnamurti 1961: §2.32, p.145). He also thought that it was 'euphony only that determined which of the consonants *g*, *ś*, *ḍ*, *d*, or *b* should be affixed as a formative to any particular verb or noun'. Even this is speculation as can be seen from below.

Table 5.1. *Canonical shapes and number of root morphs in Proto-Dravidian*

Canonical form of the root	Number of root morphs
1. V̆- (5 short vowels)	= 5
2. V̆C (5 short vowels × 16 consonants[1])	= 80
3. CV̆ - (6 consonants[2] × 5 short vowels)	30
(3 consonants[3] × 3 short vowels)	9 = 39
4. CV̆C (39 × 16 consonants)	= 624
Total	= 748
5. 1–4 with long vowels	= 748
Grand total	= 1,496

The total number of possible (not necessarily actual) and reconstructible roots for Proto-Dravidian would be 1,496 on the basis of morpheme structure conditions, dictated by the phonotactics described in section 4.2 as per the details given in table 5.1.

Any chosen Proto-Dravidian root, therefore, has to be one or the other of this total number.

1 All consonants except *ñ*.

2 *p*, *t*, *c*, *k*, *m*, *n*.

3 *y*, *ñ*, *w* occur only before unrounded vowels /i e a/. We are still not certain about the total distribution of the laryngeal *H in Proto-Dravidian.

5.2 Variability of formative suffixes[4]

A Dravidian Etymological Dictionary of 1984 [*DEDR*] has scores of entries, which lead us to reconstruct primary roots as well as extended stems for Proto-Dravidian (mainly of verbs but also of nouns), e.g.[5]

(1) a. **tir-a-y* (*-p-/-mp*, *-nt-*) v.i. 'to roll'; (*-pp-/-mpp-*, *-ntt-*) v.t. 'to roll up'; n. 'wave, screen', **tir-a-nku* v.i. 'be curled up', **tir-a-nkku* v.t. 'to shrivel' [3244].

b. **tir-a-ḷ* (*-p-*, *-ṇṭ-*) v.i. 'to become round', (*-pp-*, *-ṇṭṭ-*) v.t. [3245].

c. **tir-i-* (*-p-*, *-nt-*) v.i. 'to turn'; (*-pp-*, *-ntt-*) v.t. 'to turn'; **tir-uku* v.i., **tir-u-kku* v.t. 'to twist'; **tir-u-mpu* v.i., **tir-u-mppu* v.t. 'to twist, turn' [3246].

d. *tir-u-ntu* v.i. 'to be corrected, be repaired'; **tir-u-nttu* v.t. 'to correct, rectify' [3251].

The Proto-Dravidian root obviously must be **tir-*, meaning 'turn, roll, twist, change shape' → 'correct', etc. The formatives occur in two layers. The first layer is V = *i*, *a*, *u*; and the second layer, either a sonorant (L) as in *y*, *ḷ*; or a simple or geminated stop ± homorganic nasal: P as in **ku*; PP as in **kku*; NP as in **nku*, **ntu*, **mpu*; NPP as in **nkku*, **nttu*, **mppu*. The bound root **tir-* patterns with autonomous roots like **key* 'to do', **wil* 'to sell', **cal* 'to go', etc. which enter into inflection without any formative being added.

It is well known that the pairs of suffixes **k* : **kk*, **nk* : **nkk*, **nt* : **ntt*, **mp* : **mpp* synchronically encode an intransitive:transitive distinction in both South Dravidian I and South Dravidian II. But why should there be so many series of suffixes fulfilling the same function? And how do sets of related forms such as those in (1) above arise? These are the problems that I want to address in this chapter.

The morphophonemic changes that the roots and suffixes undergo when followed by different formatives have been discussed in section 4.3.

Through comparison of the cognates of (C)V̄C-type stems involving suffixes in L or P within reconstructed Proto-Dravidian, it is possible, in some cases, to identify an underlying root of the type *(C)V̄-. For instance, the stems **kā-y-*/**kā-*, **kā-nku* (v.i.) : **kā-nkku* (v.t.), **kā-ntu* (v.i.) : **kā-nttu* (v.t.), **kā-mpu* (v.t.) : *kā-mppu* 'be(come) hot, burn, to dry up, etc' [1458], and **kā-ḷ* 'to burn, flame' [1500] could possibly be related to words meaning 'black, burnt, etc.', such as **kā-r* : **kar*-V- 'be scorched, burnt black, black' [1278], with **kā-* as the ultimate root and the semantic development 'burn' → 'burn black' → 'black colour' → 'coal', etc.

[4] What follows is a summary of my recent paper on formative suffixes (see Krishnamurti 1997a).

[5] The suffixes in parentheses refer to non-past and past markers, respectively. The numbers in square brackets refer to the entries in *DEDR*.

5.3 Primary derivative suffixes as earlier inflectional suffixes: the hypothesis

Based on a critical study of many etymologies of the type (1) above, I venture to propose that primary derivative suffixes arose through the incorporation of inflectional suffixes into the stem, and that this development took place in several stages, largely within Proto-Dravidian.

At a very early stage within Proto-Dravidian, sonorant suffixes of the L type (*l*, *ḷ*, *r*, *ẓ*, *w*, *y*) were added to (C)V̄- or (C)VC-V-stems to form extended intransitive/middle-voice stems. This assumption is based on the observation that verb stems ending in sonorant suffixes tend to be intransitive in the descendant languages. Forms with these suffixes are preserved intact in the literary languages of the south, namely Tamil, Malayāḷam, Kannaḍa and Telugu. At a later period, -L, -V-L lost their identity as grammatical elements and became incorporated into the preceding stems, as in (1a, b) above (Krishnamurti 1961: 146–7; Emeneau 1975: 2–3).[6]

Proto-Dravidian also had a very early stage in which P suffixes were added to primary roots, and later to extended stems with -L and -V-L. Only a subgroup of South Dravidian consisting of Tamil, Malayāḷam, Koḍagu, Toda, Kota and Baḍaga preserves this stage of development in verb conjugation, e.g. Ta. *aẓ-i* (*-v-*, *-nt-*) v.i. 'to perish', *aẓ-i* (*-pp-*, *-tt-*) 'to destroy' [277]; compare this with *aẓ-u-ku* 'to rot', *aẓ-u-nku* 'to be spoiled' [284]. These P-suffixes signal both tense and voice. Dental vs. non-dental indicates past vs. non-past; simple (N)P signals intransitive, and geminate (N)PP, transitive:

(2)		Non-past		Past
	Intransitive	**p*	**k*	**t*
		**mp*	**nk*	**nt*
	Transitive	**pp*	**kk*	**tt*
		**mpp*	**nkk*	**ntt*

The non-past paradigms include present, future, aorist (habitual), infinitive, imperative, negative, etc. Within the non-past, there must have been a morphological contrast between the labial and velar series, but the contrast tended to be blurred later.

The next stage was the incorporation of tense/voice suffixes into the preceding stems, with loss of tense meaning but preservation of the voice distinction. The latter is

[6] I made this observation by comparing -(V)L-suffixes of Telugu verbal bases with those of the other Dravidian languages. I pointed out that the use of *-r-* as an intransitive reflexive marker occurs synchronically in Kuṛux (*kam-* 'to make': *kam-r-* 'to be made') reflecting the Proto-South Dravidian situation. Since such a construction also occurs in Malto, Emeneau proposed the reconstruction of *-r-* as intransitive marker in Proto-Dravidian and suggested that it was incorporated into verb stems in all Dravidian languages except in Kuṛux and Malto (1975: 2–3; for Malto, see also Mahapatra 1979: 144–52). I have not gone beyond this point in investigating the *V-L-suffixes of Proto-Dravidian.

preserved mostly in disyllabic and trisyllabic stems, with NP: (N)PP indicating an intransitive:transitive alternation in most of South Dravidian. Traces of this alternation are found in Kannaḍa and Tuḷu.[7] South Central Dravidian also preserves this stage, with the exception of Telugu and Gondi; and some traces exist in all other subgroups and languages (Subrahmanyam 1971: 52–4). As a consequence of this change, the contrast *NP: *NPP (or its reflexes NP: PP, (N)B: (N)P, etc.) has come to signal only an intransitive:transitive distinction.

The languages which have lost the paired intransitives and transitives of the above type have added the reflexes of _*-tt_ or _*-pp_ as transitive–causative markers, e.g. Te. _jaru-gu_ 'to slide' : _jaru-pu_ 'to move', _tiru-gu_ v.i.'to revolve': _tri-ppu_ v.t.'to revolve'. It is certain that these were already in use for certain stems in Proto-Dravidian before the emergence of innovative pairs of intransitive–transitive markers.

Since several languages across subgroups show the additive morphemes _-pp_, _-tt_ (> _-cc_ following a front vowel or _-y_) as transitivizers, they need to be reconstructed for Proto-Dravidian (sections 7.3.1–.2). Some of the intransitive bases to which these are added reflect simple Proto-Dravidian roots such as _*mēy-_ (_-pp-_) 'to graze', _*kāy-_ (_-pp-/ -tt-_) 'to burn', _*tiHn-_(_-tt-_) 'to eat', _*uHṇ-_(_-tt-_) 'to drink' etc. suggesting the antiquity of the additive morphemes. After the final split into subgroups, it is likely that their use was extended to most of the verb stems in the languages that had lost the (N)P:(N)PP pattern marking intransitive:transitive. Another factor contributing to the extensive use of the additive elements is their structural parallelism (_-mp-p-_ > _-pp_, _nt-t-_ > _-tt_) to the final –CCV of paired intransitive–transitive sets which had originally a much wider grammatical function; e.g. Old Tamil _naṭa-_ (past intr. _nata-nt-_, past tr. _nata-tt-_ < _*naṭa-nt-t-_), Mdn Ta. _naṭa-_ v.i. 'to walk' : _nata-tt-_ v.t. 'to make someone walk' (only additive without tense meaning).

A final, analytic, stage is found in all South Dravidian literary languages. New transitive stems are derived by the addition of different auxiliary verbs to non-finite forms of the main verb, as in Te. _wirugu_ v.i. 'to break'; _wiraga goṭṭ-_ v.t. 'to break or snap' (< _wirag-an-_ (inf) + _koṭṭ_ 'to beat'). In some cases, the older suffixal structures coexist with the final analytic stage, but with semantic differences; cf. Mdn Te. _kāl-cu_ 'to light (a cigarette), to burn' beside _kāla beṭṭ-_ 'to burn something down'.

[7] _DEDR_ 169: Ta. _am-u-nku_ v.i. 'to sink, be pressed down, crushed'; _am-ukku_ (< _*am-unkk_) v.t. 'to crush'; Ka. _am-ugu_, _av-ugu_ v.i. 'to yield to pressure'; _av-uṅku_ (beside _am-uku_ etc.) v. t. 'to press or hold firmly'; Tu. _av-uṅk-uni_, _av-ump-uni_ 'to press down'. Tuḷu here offers evidence for _*nkk_ and _*mpp_ of Proto-Dravidian with loss of the tense contrast. _DEDR_ 240: Ta. _al-aṅku_ v.i. 'to be, shaken, etc.', _al-akku_ v.t. 'to cause to move, shake', Tu. _al-aṅk-uni_ v.t. 'to agitate, wave'; _al-aṅg-uni_ has both intransitive and transitive meanings; _DEDR_ 524: Ta. _iṟuku_ v.i. 'to become tight', _iṟukku_ v.t. 'to tighten'; Ka. _iṟuṅku_ v.t. 'to compress' (also _iṟaṅku_, _iṟiṅku_ presupposing PSD _*iṟunkk-_ v.t.); so also _DEDR_ 3246: Ka. _tirumpu_ v.t. 'to cause to go round'.

I assume that the first two developments took place at various stages within Proto-Dravidian, with each successive stage having a wider spread – lexical and areal – than the earlier one, but with all the three stages still synchronically coexisting. Typologically we notice a progression from synthetic to analytic in this scenario. Note also that extended stems of two or three syllables are more numerous than monosyllabic roots in the later stages of Proto-Dravidian.

The next question is to find empirical support for the above proposal and to find missing links in the morphological development of extended stems.

5.4 Case studies

The most transparent etymology which gives immediate evidence for how formatives came into existence is that of PD **o* 'to be appropriate, to suit' [924]:

(3) SD I: Ta. *o* (*-pp-*, *-tt-*) 'to be suited, appropriate', *oppu* (*-iṉ-*) 'to agree, assent', n. 'consent, uniformity', *opp-am* 'comparison', *oppu-mai* 'likeness', *ovvu* 'to be like, congruous', Ma. *okku-ka* 'to be like', *ott-a* 'equal, consistent', *opp-am* 'equality, harmony', Koḍ. *o* (*-pp-*, *-tt-*) 'to be suitable', *otta-* (*-aṇḍ-*) 'to consent', To. *up-* (*-y-*) 'to be pleased, to agree', Ko. *op-* (*-y-*) 'to be acceptable', Ka. *oppu* 'to agree with', *oppa* 'fitness', *opp-ike* 'agreeing', *ommu* 'to concur', Tu. *oppiyuni* 'to agree to', *ottoṇï* 'to agree', *ombuni* 'to be suitable';
SD II: Te. *oppu* 'to suit, be agreeable', n. 'fitness, beauty', *oppa-g-incu* 'to entrust', *oppu-dala* 'assent', *-yokka* genitive suffix meaning 'belonging to', *ommu* 'to suit', *ovvu* 'to agree', Go. *app-* (< *opp-*) 'to be pleasing', Koṇḍa *op-* (*op-t-*) 'to agree', Kuvi *ōp-* (*-it-*) 'to agree, consent';
CD: Kol. *ovvol* 'good', Pa. *op-ip-* (*op-it-*) 'to give in charge, hand over';
ND: Kuṛ. *okk-* 'to fit in well, agree with'.

One can see that the extended stems *o-pp-*, *o-tt-*, *o-mp-*, *o-kk-*, *o-ww-*, etc. have arisen from a monosyllabic root **o-* which still occurs in Tamil and Koḍagu. The similarity between the stem extensions and tense morphs is striking.

The etymologies of three frequently used verbs, namely **ā-* 'to be, happen, become', **pō* 'to go' [4572] and **uḷ* 'to be' [697], bear ample evidence to how extended stems with original inflectional morphs have gradually evolved as formatives, having lost their grammatical meaning:

5.4.1 *ā *'to be' [333]*

(4) a. **ā-*: Ta. *ā* (past stem *ān-*, *āyi-*) 'to be, happen', *ā* (*-pp-*, *-tt-*) v.t. 'to cause, bring about'; *ā* n. 'becoming', *ā-m* (<**ā*+*um*) 'yes'; Tu. *ā-pini* (2neu sg

past *āṇḍu*); OTe. *ā* (in *āyen*/*ayyen* 3 past suffix *-en* with inserted glide *y*) id.; Go. *ay-* (irregular, 3sg imperfective *ānd*; some forms from *ā*), most dialects have *ā* 'to be'; Koṇḍa, Kui, Kuvi, Pengo, Manḍa *ā* (*ā-t-*) id.

b. **āku* v.i.: **ākku* v.t.: Ta. *āku* (*āku-v-*, *āk-i*) v.i., *ākku* (*ākk-i-*) 'to make', *ākk-am* n. 'creation' (transitive noun), *āk-a* inf 'completely'; Ma. *āku-ka* v.i., *ākku-ka* v.t., *ākk-i-kka* (< **ākku-wi-kka-* caus inf of tr with loss of *-w-*) 'to cause to make'; Ko. *āg* v.i. (*āy-*/*ān-*; some forms from *ā-*); *āk-* v.t.; To. *ōx* (*ōy-*, *ōn-*, *ō*) v.i., *ōk-* (*ōky-*) v.t.; Ka. *āgu* (*ān-*, *āy* etc.); Koḍ. *āg-* (irreg *āy-*, *ān-*, *ā*) v.i., *āk* (*āk-i*) v.t.; Te. *agu*, *awu* (*ay-i* ppl, *ay-na* adj); Nk. *akk-* 'to make'.

c. **ā-p-* v.i. 'to become': **ā-pp-* v.t. 'to make, etc.': Kui *āva-* (*ā-t-*) 'to become', *āp-ka* (*āp-ki*) plural action stem; Kol. *āp-* (*āp-t-*) 'to keep in a place'; Nk. *āp-* 'to keep'. Cf. Ta. *ā-*(*pp-*) 'to cause, bring about'.

d. **ān-*/*an-* v.i.: Tu. (2neu sg past *āṇḍu*); Kol. *an-* (irreg, past *anḍ-*, imper *ān-*) 'to be in place'; Nk. *anḍ* 'to be'; Br. *anning* (*an-*, *as-*, *a-*) 'to be'.

Note that both *ā-* and *āku-* are used as inflectional bases in Old Tamil (PN), as in *āk-iṉ-* 'if' beside *ā-*(*y*)*iṉ* id., *āk-um* '(subj) will become' : *ā-m* id. (Subramoniam 1962). The last two forms are also given by Tolkāppiyam (first century AD or BC). It can therefore be concluded that *ā-* is not simply a contraction of *āku-* (Israel 1973: 235).[8]

As for the putative suffixes in (4b–d), note that the Old Tamil classics use *-k-* beside *-t-* in aorist, i.e. non-past, constructions (Israel 1973: 145, 193ff.), as in *uṇ-k-um* 'we drink', *kaṇ-ṭ-um* 'we see', *varu-t-um* 'we come' from the roots *uṇ-* 'to drink', *kāṇ-* 'to see' and *varu* 'to come'. (The suffix *-um* when not following *-k-* or *-t-* is said to simultaneously mark habitual tense and person. In Malayāḷam, the sufixes *-um* and *-kkum* similarly occur as non-past aorist markers.) Further, **-p-* [-w-] occurs as a future-tense marker added to *āku-* in OTa. *āku-pa*/*-va* 'they will become' (Israel 1973: 235). That is, it too marks a non-past structure. Finally the base form in (4d) corresponds to the past stem of the South Dravidian languages.

Given this evidence, we can interpret the data in (4) as follows. Set (a) naturally contains the original, unmodified root. Set (b) is based on an extended stem *ā-k-* of set (a), which incorporates an old non-past suffix *-k-* (intransitive) : *-kk-* (transitive). This set shows variation between **ā* and **āk* in inflection. Set (c) is based on another non-past stem of *ā*, viz. *ā-p-* [*ā-w-*] : *ā-pp-*. Set (d) is based on the past stem of set (a), namely *ān-*. All the four sets can be derived from the following reconstructed system of early Proto-Dravidian.

[8] The infinitive *āka* is ambiguous, since it can be analysed either as *ā-ka* or as *āk-a*. Classical Tamil also has the simple infinitive *ā* < *ā-a* with loss of the short *a* (Agesthialingom 1979: 94).

(5)		Non-past		Past
	Intransitive	**ā-k-*	**ā-p-*	**ā-(i)n-*
	Transitive	**ā-kk-*	**ā-pp-*	**ā-tt-*

As we have seen, the formations in *-k(k)-* and *-p(p)-*, as well as the one in *-(i)n-*, have become generalized verb stems, losing their tense distinctions. In set (c), however, **-pp-* (> *-p-*) has retained traces of its voice distinction by serving as a transitive marker in some of the languages. Only the suffix *-tt-* is retained as an inflectional morpheme in South Central Dravidian.

Further support for the reconstructed formations in (5) comes from the distribution of forms in the various subgroups of Dravidian; cf. (6). None of the extended forms is limited to just one subgroup, a fact which precludes the assumption that they originated in the various descendant subgroups. The geographical distribution, combined with the data in (4), further suggests that the incorporation of suffixes into the stem began within Proto-Dravidian, for, again, the use of extended forms with loss of their original tense and/or voice distinctions cuts across the different descendant subgroups.

(6)		
	a. **ā*	SD, SCD
	b. **āk-* :*ākk-*	SD; Nk. of CD
	c. **āp-* : **āpp-*	Ta. of SD; Te., Kui of SCD; Kol., Nk. of CD
	d. **ān*	Tu. of SD; Go. of SCD; Kol., Nk. of CD; Brahui of ND

5.4.2 *pō *'to go' [4572]*

A structural parallel to **ā* in Proto-Dravidian is found in **pō* beside **pōku* 'to go' attested only in South Dravidian and South Central Dravidian.

(7) a. **pō* : Ta. *pō* (non-past: *pōv-/pōkuv-/pōtuv-*, past: *pōn-/pōyin-*; neg *pōk-*); Ma. *pōka*; Koḍ. *pō* (*pōp-*, *pōk-*, *pōc-*, *pōy-*); Ka. *pō*, *pō-li*, *pō-lu* 'state of going, ruin'; Te. *pō* (*pō-yi*).

b. **pō-k-* : **pō-kk-*: Ta. *pōku* (future: *pōku-v-*, neg. *pōk-*), *pōk-ai* n. (intr) 'departure'; *pōkku* (*pōkk-i-*) 'to cause to go, send'; *pōkk-am* n. (tr) 'causing to go; exit, way'; Ma. *pōka* (inf, interpreted as *-ka*, but historically *-k + a*), *pōk-al* n. 'going', *pōkkuka* v.t. 'to make to go, remove', *pōkk-al* n. 'removing'; Ko. *ōg* (*ōy-/ōn-*, also *ō* based on **pō*), *ōk-c* 'to cause to go', *pōk-* (*pōk-y-*) 'to spend time'; To. *pī̈x* (*pī̈-*); Ka. *pōgu*, *hōgu*; Koḍ. *pōk-*; Te. *pōwu* (*-w-* < *-g-*), non-past neg *pō-*, *pōw-* (intr), *pōka* n. 'going, departure'; Koṇḍa, Pe. *pōk* (*-t-*) 'to send'; Maṇḍa *pūk-* (*-t-*) id.

These forms illustrate the way the stems of set (b) were remade from the root of set (a) by incorporating the non-past suffixes *k:kk* into the stem in the intransitive and transitive respectively. Interestingly, there is a greater regularity in the inflection of the extended stem than that of the original root **pō-*. Also notice the occurrence of *pōku* in the NON-PAST intransitive paradigm of Old Tamil as *pōku-v-*, neg. *pōk-*, as opposed to *pō* in PAST *pō-y-in*, *pō-n*. This distribution preserves a trace of *-ku-* as a non-past (aorist, optative) marker, even though the suffix generally has lost its meaning. Koṇḍa, Kui and Pengo of South Central Dravidian retain only the transitive forms of the derived stem. Telugu shows both South Dravidian and South Central Dravidian features.

5.4.3 *uḷ *'to be, have'* : *uṇṭu (< *uḷ-ntu) *'is, are' [697]*

The form **uḷ* is attested in Ta. Ma. *uḷ*; Ko. *oḷ*; Ka. *uḷ*, *oḷ* 'to be, to have'; Koḍ. *uḷḷ-*; Kui *lohpa* (*loh-t-*) 'to remain'; the form **uṇṭu* is reflected in Ta. *uṇṭu* 'is, are' (existence), *uṇmai* 'truth'; Ma. *uṇṭu* 'there is, exists'; Ko. *oḍo* (3neu of **oḷ*); To. *wïḷd-* 'to exist' (3rd pers *wïḍ-i*); Ka. *uṇṭu* (3neu) 'that is, that exists', n. 'existence'; Koḍ. *uṇḍï* (3rd pers *uḷḷ-*); Tu. *uṇḍu* (3neu sg of *uḷḷ*, pres tense); Te. *uṇḍu* 'to exist, live, dwell', *uṇḍu(nu)* fin verb 'he, she, it, they (neu) are', *uṇḍ-r-u* 'they (hum) are', where *-ḍ-* is a sandhi variant of the aorist suffix *-d-* (an alternative form occurs later as *uṇḍu-du-ru* where *uṇḍu* is entirely treated as a root); Br. *uṭ* (pres 1sg), *us* (pres 2sg), *un* (1pl), *ure* (2pl), *ur* (3pl) related irregularly to the root *anning* 'to be'.

Since both South Dravidian, South Central Dravidian and Brahui of North Dravidian inherit reflexes of **uṇṭu*, the form must be reconstructed for Proto-Dravidian, as an inflected form of the root **uḷ*. Now, Tolkāppiyam analyses **uṇṭu* (< **uḷ-ntu*) as containing *-tu-*, a non-past marker. But in terms of Proto-Dravidian morphophonemics the morph should have the form **ntu* to yield *uṇ-ṭu* < **uḷ* + *ntu*; and this **-ntu-* is clearly different from the past-tense marker *-tu-*. (Ka. *uṇṭu* is derivable from **uṇ-ṭṭu*, in which case the underlying sequence is interpretable as *t* (non-past) + *tu* (neu sg). In Old Kannaḍa the form is used in the neuter singular and plural (cf. Ramachandra Rao 1972: 257).[9]

Moreover, the form *uṇ-ṭu* is nowhere used in the past tense. The incorporated suffix **-ntu-* must therefore be the same aorist marker that is retained in Old Tamil (*-t-*) and also in Literary Telugu (*-d-*). In Old Tamil it occurs with only a limited number of verbs in the first plural and the second singular and plural (Glazov 1968: 106). It expresses an indefinite present–future meaning, as in *varu-t-i* (KT 91.14) 'you come', *āṭu-t-um* (Cil.9.63) 'we will bathe ourselves'.

The use of **uṇṭu* differs from these other structures with **-ntu-* in two significant ways: (i) it is used as a third person in almost all the Dravidian languages, and (ii) it is not limited to Old Tamil and Literary Telugu but is found in all the subgroups of

[9] Another etymology similar to **uṇṭu* is **wēṇṭu* [*DEDR* 5528] from **wēḷ-ntu*/**wēṇ-tu* which has cognates for the composite form in most of the languages of South Dravidian and Central Dravidian, and Telugu of South Central Dravidian. Here **(n)tu* is a non-past morpheme of Proto-Dravidian.

Dravidian. The latter fact permits us to consider it an inheritance from Proto-Dravidian. Now, its third-person use is in complementary distribution with the first- and second-person use of non-past **-ntu-* in Old Tamil and Literary Telugu. It therefore provides the 'missing link' that permits us to reconstruct a complete Proto-Dravidian paradigm for forms containing the suffix **-ntu-* and thus permits us to show that the Old Tamil and Literary Telugu forms are not just regional innovations.[10]

Notice finally that the Telugu verb *uṇḍu* occurs in both past and non-past paradigms (*uṇḍ-i-ri* 'they (3hum) were', *uṇḍu-du-ru* 'they are/will be'), thereby losing the original signification of *ḍ* < **nt* as a non-past marker. (The only exception is the third-person human plural *uṇ-ḍ-ru* 'they are' of Classical Telugu, which is now archaic.) Here, then, we find the same phenomenon of 'tense loss' as with incorporated markers such as *-*k*(*k*)- discussed in sections 5.4.1–2.

5.4.4 *Incorporation of tense–voice suffixes as stem formatives*

In all the South Dravidian languages, except Kannaḍa, there is a verbal conjugation (*Tamil Lexicon* Class IV) in which tense and voice are combined in the same morphs. Roots which generally end in *i*, *u*, *y* (incl *ay*), *r* and *ẓ* belong to this class. The conjugation is characterized by the following original suffixes:

(8)

	Non-past		Past	
	Intr	Tr	Intr	Tr
Aorist	(*k*)-*um*	*kk-um*	*nt*	*tt*
Future	*p* [-w-]	*pp*		

In the following discussion we will see how these tense–voice suffixes were incorporated to form extended stems in different South Dravidian, South Central and Central Dravidian languages. Let us begin with an examination of reflexes of the verb **iẓ-i* 'to descend' [502].

(9)

	Non-past		Past	
	Intr	Tr	Intr	Tr
Ta.	*iẓi-v-*	*iẓi-pp-*	*iẓi-nt-*	*iẓi-tt-* (> *iẓi-cc-*)
Ma.	*iẓi-v-*	*iẓi-pp-*	*iẓi-ññ-*	*iẓi-cc-*
Koḍ.	*ïḷi-v-*	*ïḷi-p-* (dial. *ï̄p-*)	*ïḷi-nj-*	(*ïḷïp-i-*)
To.	*īx-* (< **iẓ-g-*)	*īk-* (< **iẓ-kk-*)	(*īx-y-*)	(*īk-y-*)
Ka.	*iḷi-v-*	*iḷi-p-*	*iḷi-d-*	*iḷi-s-i*
Pa.	*iṛ-v-* (< **iṛ*-g)	*iṛ-k-ip-*		*iṛ-k-it-*

10 An alternative analysis of *uṇ-ṭu* as containing the third singular neuter suffix *-tu* must be rejected, since it would not permit us to account for its tense meaning (present–future) and since the attested forms are not confined to the neuter singular.

Oll.Gad.	*iṛ-g-*	*iṛig-p-*		*iṛig-t-*
Te.	*ḍiggu/ḍigu* (< **iẓ-g*)	*ḍi-mp-*	[*ḍindu*] (arch.)	*ḍi-nc-*
Kui	*dī-v-*	*dī-p-*	*dī-t-*	*dī-p-t-*
Koṇḍa	*ḍi-g-*	*ḍi-p-*	(*ḍig-it-*)	*ḍi-p-t-*
PD	**iẓi-(m)p-* /*-(n)k-*	**iẓi-mpp-*	**iẓi-nt-*	**iẓi-ntt-*

Note that in the non-past there is evidence for both a labial and a velar suffix as seen in Toda, Kannaḍa (*iẓaku* v.t.), Parji, Gadaba, Telugu and Koṇḍa. The Toda stem is remade in the intransitive and transitive by incorporating the erstwhile non-past morphs **k*: **kk* (or **nk*: **nkk*). So also in Parji and Ollari *iṛv-*/*iṛg-* have become the basic stems without any tense meaning attached to their *v*/*g*. In Parji the intransitive:transitive alternation is retained as *g*:*k*, whereas it is only signalled by suffixation in Ollari. In Kui, too, the *-v-* : *-p-* alternation signifies intransitive and transitive in the non-past (infinitive).

The Telugu forms are diagnostic for the reconstruction of the proto-suffixes. A new verbal base *ḍindu* (< **iẓ-nd-*; cf. Ta. *iẓi-nt-*) v.i. 'to sink, fall, droop, die' is created incorporating the Proto-Dravidian intransitive past tense morph *-nt-* (Krishnamurti 1961: 52). The intransitive form *ḍiggu*/*ḍigu* is from **ẓi-gg-* < **iẓ-g-* (see Krishnamurti 1961: §1.124; 52, 53) through metathesis, gemination of the voiced stop after (C)V-, and subsequent degemination. The comparison with Parji, Ollari and Toda shows an underlying velar *g* (< *-k-*) which was apparently a non-past marker. There are two transitive forms in Telugu: *ḍi-nc-*, which occurs as a base before past-tense suffixes and *ḍi-mp-*, which occurs before non-past suffixes in Classical Telugu. Owing to the retention of the nasal, these forms are traceable to PD **iẓ* (*i*)*-ncc-* (< **iẓi-ntt-*) for the past tense base and **iẓ* (*i*)*-mpp-* for the non-past base.

Tamil, Malayāḷam and Koḍagu attest the past-tense form *iẓi-cc-* from *iẓi-tt-*. The nasal of **ntt* (transitive past, corresponding to **nt* intransitive past) is lost here in accordance with normal sound change (see section 5.3 above). The Telugu suffix retains the original alternation of **nt* : **ntt*. Again, *ḍi-mp-* (< **iẓi-mpp-*) 'to make one dismount' presupposes an intransitive **-mp* as opposed to transitive **-mpp* in the non-past. This piece of evidence allows us to reconstruct **mp* beside **p* as non-past intransitive marker within Proto-Dravidian; however, while we have evidence for **k* there is none for **nk* in the intransitive non-past.

I propose that **nk* and **mp* were incorporated into stems as (derivative) voice suffixes carrying intransitive meaning at a deeper chronological stratum of Proto-Dravidian. The morphs **p* and **k* must have replaced **mp* and **nk* respectively in all non-past environments. Note that Old Kannaḍa (Pampa Bharata; cf. Ramachandra Rao 1972: Index) has *iḷi-s-* and *iḷi-p-* as past and non-past bases requiring underlying *iẓi-cc-*, *iẓi-pp-* as found in the Tamil–Koḍagu subgroup (with *-cc-* > *-c-* > *-s-*; *-pp-* > *-p-* in Kannaḍa). This illustration shows that the tense/voice conjugation, which is still retained intact in the Tamil–Koḍagu subgroup of South Dravidian, is reconstructible for Proto-Dravidian. In the other members of South Dravidian, Central Dravidian and South Central Dravidian, these morphemes have lost their tense meaning, becoming mere formative suffixes. The erstwhile tense marking can, however, be reconstructed from the distribution of these morphemes in verb paradigms as illustrated above.

The past suffix *-ttu* and the non-past suffix *-ppu*, when delinked from their unlikely looking relatives *-nt* (past intr) and *-p*, *-mp-* (non-past intr), have come to be segmented as pure transitive markers which have become additive morphemes in a later chronological stratum of Proto-Dravidian.[11] Cf. Ta. *iẓi-ttu* (*iẓi-tt-i*), *iẓi-ccu* 'to lower'; *iẓi-vu*, *iẓi-pu* n. 'inferiority' (intr), *iẓi-ppu* n. 'contemptuous treatment' (tr).

The above discussion leads us to set up the following reconstructions within Proto-Dravidian.

(10)

Non-past		Past	
Intr	Tr	Intr	Tr
**iẓi-p-* : **iẓi-mp-*	**iẓi-pp-* : **iẓi-mpp-*	**iẓi-nt-*	**iẓi-ntt-*
**iẓi-k-* : **iẓ-nk-*	**iẓi-kk-* : **iẓi-nkk-*		

In this particular example evidence is lacking for the suffix *nk:nkk*, but such evidence is found in various other etymologies where the suffix is seen to have been completely incorporated into the base in early Proto-Dravidian. Consider for instance **wir-i-* 'to extend, open, split, crack, burst' [5411]. The data in (11a) present a similar picture to those in (10); but as (11b) shows, for this stem, some languages presuppose a velar non-past suffix, instead of a labial.

(11)

		Non-past		Past	
		Intr	Tr	Intr	Tr
a.	Ta.	*viri-v-*	*viri-pp-*	*viri-nt-*	*viri-tt-*
	Ma.	*viri-v-*	*viri-pp-*	*viri-ññ*	*viri-cc-*
	Koḍ.	*biri-v-*	*biri-p-*	*biri-ñj-*	*biri-c-*
	To.			*pir-s-*	*pir-c-*
				(< *piry* + θ-)	(< *piry* + *t*-)
	Ka.	*biri-v-*		*biri-d-*	

[11] As stated earlier (section 5.3), I am not ruling out the other possibility of **-tt*, **-pp* being also original and ancient.

b.	Te.	_viru-**gu**_			
	Kui	_vri**nga**_	_vripka_ (<*_vrik-pa_)	_vring-i_	_vrik-t-_
		vrī-va		_vrī-t-_	

The Kui forms presuppose the non-past forms *_wiri-nk_ : *_wiri-nkk_ beside the original root *_wiri-_ (with non-past _-w-_) in _vrī-va_. However, as shown by _vring-i_ (past intr), the velar suffix has been incorporated into the stem. The nominal suffixes also exhibit variation, e.g. Te. _wiriwi_ 'abundance'; Ta. _virivu_ n. 'expansion', _virippu_ n. 'opening out'; Ma. _viriccal_ (< *_viri-tt-al_) n. 'split'. Such nominals are based on underlying tense/voice suffixes.

On the basis of the above discussion, we can also provide a morphological account for the Proto-Dravidian reconstructions of extended stems derived from the root *_tir-_ 'to turn, twist' etc. (section 5.2 above); cf. (12).

(12) Proto-Dravidian root: *_tir-_:

a. With vowel suffixes: *_tir-i-_ [3246], _tir-a-_, _tir-u-_

b. With -L suffixes: *_tir-a-ḷ_, *_tir-a-y_ [3245, 3244]

c. With stop suffixes:

Nonpast		Past	
Intr	Tr	Intr	Tr
*_tir-u-ku_ [3251]:	*_tir-u-kku_ [3246]	*_tir-u-ntu_ :	*_tir-u-nttu_ [3257]
*_tir-a-nku_ :	*_tir-a-nkku_ [3244]		
*_tir-u-mpu_ :	*_tir-u-mppu_ [3246, 3258]		

5.4.5 _**Examples incorporating past *-nt- in the stem**_

There are, in addition, several examples of fresh verbal bases in different Dravidian languages, formed by incorporating the Proto-Dravidian past-tense morph *_nt_. Subrahmanyam (1971: 204–6) cites the following examples:

(13) a. PD *_iru-_ (*_iru-nt-_ past intr) 'to exist, to be' [480]: Kui _rīnd-_ 'to be stable, steady' (earlier: Emeneau 1967a: 391).

b. PD *_nōy_ (*_nōy-nt-_) 'to pain' [3793]: Kuṛ. Malt. _nunj-_ 'to pain'.

c. PSDr *_pāy_ (*_pāy-nt-_) 'to spring, leap' [4087]: Kui _pānj-_ 'to fly, leap'.

d. PD *_piẓi_ (*_piẓi-nt-_) 'to squeeze, press' [4183]: Ka. _piṇḍu_, _hiṇḍu_; Koḍ. _puṇḍ-_; Tu. _puṇḍiyuni_; Te. _piṇḍu_; Kol., Nk. _piṇḍ-_ 'to squeeze, wring' : Ta. Ma. Ka. _piẓi_. Kui, Koṇḍa and North Dravidian also have forms from *_piẓi_. Tu. _purñcuni_, _pureñcuni_ 'to squeeze' are from *_piẓ(i)-ntt-_ and *_pi-ẓ-ay-ntt-_, respectively. Note a restricted Proto-Dravidian sandhi rule *_ẓ_ + _nt_ →* _ṇṭ_.

e. PSD **kuṟay* (**kuṟay-nt-* : **kuṟay-ntt-*) 'to be reduced in size' [1851]: Kota *kornj* v.i., *korc* v.t.; PSD **piri* (**piri + nt* : **piri-ntt*) 'to separate' [4176]: Kota *pirnj* v.i., *pirc-* v.t.

f. **paẓ*-V- (*paẓ*-V-*nt-*) 'to ripen' [4004] (not included in Subrahmanyam's list): Te. *paṇḍu* 'to ripen, mature', n. 'fruit'; Kol. Nk. *paṇḍ-* 'to become ripe'; Pa. *paṇḍ* 'a plant matures'; Go. *paṇḍ-*, Koṇḍa *paṇḍ-* 'to ripen'; Kuvi *paṇḍu* 'ripe fruit' (< **paẓ* (*u*)-*nt-*, past intransitive stem); Tu. *parnduni* 'to ripen', *parndï* 'ripe fruit'; Pa. *paṛñ-* 'to ripen'; Oll. *paṛng-* 'to become grey (of hair)'. Tamil, Malayāḷam etc. have *paẓu*; cf. Malto *pān-*, Kuṛ. *pān* (*pañjā*) 'to ripen', *pañjka* 'fruits'. PD **paẓ-i-/-u-* with non-past **-nk-*, past **-nt-* would explain all the items in this etymology.

5.4.6 *Further discussion*

Let us at this point take stock of our findings so far, amplifying them with a few additional comments.

(i) The verb conjugation with inflectional morphemes signalling both tense and voice is an ancient one, still preserved in the Tamil–Koḍagu subgroup of South Dravidian.

(ii) The non-past intransitive morphs **-nk*, **-mp* lost their inflectional value and became incorporated as mere voice markers in early Proto-Dravidian.

(iii) In the Tamil–Koḍagu subgroup the loss of N in NPP led to its merger with PP in the non-past as in (14).[12]

(14)

Proto-Dravidian		Tamil–Koḍagu subgroup	
Non-past		Non-past	
Intr	Tr	Intr	Tr
**p*	**pp*	*p*	*pp*
**mp*	**mpp*	—	*pp*
**k*	**kk*	*k*	*kk*
**nk*	**nkk*	—	*kk*

The merger of **mpp* with *pp* and of **nkk* with *kk* must have led to the analogical replacement of the intransitive suffixes **mp* and **nk* by *p* and *k*, respectively, in South Dravidian (Tamil–Koḍagu subgroup). This did not happen in the case of **nt* because the past suffix **t* had a very low functional yield (only nine Old Tamil verbs take it in their past tense), whereas **nt* had a much higher frequency, and transitive formation by geminating the final consonant of the tense marker affected the past allomorph **-nt-* in many more cases than **t* in the Tamil–Koḍagu subgroup.

12 Emeneau (1967a: 366, 388–90) and Subrahmanyam (1971: 95–9) consider the system an innovation within South Dravidian.

(iv) Palatalization of a dental stop (single or double) after *y/i is witnessed in many languages, requiring its reconstruction for the Tamil–Koḍagu subgroup, for Pre-Parji, and for Proto-South Central Dravidian (see the next section), and also perhaps for Kuṛux–Malto. Apparently, the sound change was developing dialectally within Proto-Dravidian itself.

5.4.7 *Past *-c incorporation in Telugu*

Many Old Telugu verbs ending in *-cu* do not have corresponding palatal formatives in other language groups, e.g. *ēḍ-cu* 'to weep', *naḍa-cu* 'to walk', *nil-ucu* 'to stand', *maṟa-cu* 'to forget'. In the conjugation of these verbs, the formative *-cu* occurs in the past inflection (also in the durative) alternating with *w* in the non-past, as in *nil*(*i*)*-ci* 'having stood', *nil*(*a*)*-w-an* (inf.) 'to stand'.

I have shown elsewhere (Krishnamurti 1961: §§2.84–7, 162–3; §§2.43–2, 45, 14–15.2) that the *c* was incorporated into the base from an old past suffix *-*cci* which occurs as past participle morph in the other South Central Dravidian languages (§§7.4.1.5, 7. 7. 1. 2). Similarly *cēyu* 'to do' : *cē-si* 'having done' has a *-si* traceable to *-*ci*. Because of the wider occurrence of *-i* as past participle suffix in verbs like *win-i* 'having heard', *kaṭṭ-i* 'having built' etc. which goes back to PD *-*i*, *-*c-* and *-*cc-* have been reanalysed as parts of the stems; hence **cē-si* → *cēs-i*, **nil-ci* → *nilc-i*. The *-w-* variant is a reflex of Proto-Dravidian non-past *-*p-* [*-w-*]. I further have shown that a similar incorporation of the *c* of **ci* into the verb bases can be suspected in many other languages of South Central and North Dravidian (165). Note that Kuṛux–Malto and Brahui retain a Proto-Dravidian suffix **cc* as past-tense marker, which does not result from palatalization of **tt* (165), e.g. Te. *pāṟu*, *paṟ-acu* 'to flee': Malto *par-ce* 'to run away' [4020; cf. 3963].

In some cases, where Old Telugu *-cu*/*-ncu* were used as transitive markers (alternating with non-past *-pu*/*-mpu*) they could be traced back to the palatalized past suffix *-*tt*/ *-*ntt* following a front vowel or *y* as in *ḍi-nc*/*ḍi-mp-* 'to lower', *kā̃cu* /*kā̃pu* (< **kāy-ntt*/**kāy-mpp*) 'boil'. Later on, *-cu* was generalized as a transitive marker and extended to stems of different underlying structure, e.g. *kālu* intr 'to burn' : *kāl-cu* tr 'to burn'. The non-past marker *-pu*/*-mpu* was analogically replaced in entire paradigms by the original past-transitive marker converted into a transitive suffix with the loss of tense meaning.

5.4.8 *Additive *-tt and *-pp as transitive–causative markers*

Something similar must have happened in the languages of South Dravidian I. The past and non-past transitive markers of stems of Tamil Class IV verbs, reconstructible as *-(*n*)*tt-* and *-(*m*)*pp-*, must have occurred in syntactic contexts where they could be interpreted as mere transitive markers added to the corresponding intransitive stems. Thus R. Kothandaraman identifies three types of Old Tamil stems derived from the conjugation in **nt* : **ntt*, and these stems reflect three Pre-Tamil stages of change in their syntactic functions; cf. (15). In Type I both sets of forms are used as past participles, in their original intransitive–transitive function. In Type II the first form functions as a past participle in intransitive, while the second one has become a new verbal base to which *-ttu* is added as a transitive marker, having lost its tense meaning. A new past participle is formed from this form, as in *vāẓ-tt-i* from Ta. *vāẓ-ttu* 'to felicitate, bless', tr of *vāẓ*. This development helps to explain how **tt* and **pp* came to develop into transitive suffixes within Proto-Dravidian. In Type III, Pre-Tamil or Proto-South Dravidian totally lost the inflectional meaning of **nt* : **(n)tt*, and the stem was remade retaining only the voice difference. This last type is apparently the latest stage in the evolution of formatives, still within Proto-Dravidian in the case of certain forms.

(15)

		Tamil	
		Past intr	Past tr
Type I	**mēy* 'graze'	*mēy-ntu*	*mēy-ttu* [5093]
Type II	**wāẓ* 'live, flourish'	*vāẓ-ntu*	*vāẓ-ttu* (only tr) 'to felicitate, bless' [5372]
Type III	**tir-* 'be changed'	*tiru-ntu*	*tiru-ttu* (formatives mark only intr–tr)
		(*tirunt-i*) 'be changed'	(*tirutt-i-*) [3251] 'to rectify'

Extended stems with **nk* : **nkk*, **mp* : **mpp* must, then, go back to a much deeper chronological stratum within Proto-Dravidian, since none of the descendant languages preserves **(n)k* : **(n)kk* in the non-past. Telugu provides indirect evidence for **mpp* (non-past tr) presupposing a corresponding **mp* (non-past intr). Therefore, wherever these suffixes are found in extended stems their history is to be traced by extending the logic or parallel developments of the dental series.

Alveolar and retroflex series, wherever they occur (cf. Ta. *curuḷ* 'to curl up', past *curuṇṭ* (v.i.) : *curuṭṭ* (v.t.) < **curuḷ-nt-* : **curuḷ-ntt*), are to be taken as sandhi variants of the dental suffix. Note that *curuṭṭu* belongs to Type II above; it acts as a remade stem only in the transitive.

There is no evidence to set up an independent palatal series of (*c*) : *ñc* : *ñcc* as formatives for Proto-Dravidian since this series is derivable through palatalization of dentals following front vowels – a widely inherited dialectal change within Proto-Dravidian.

We have noticed that, when the tense signification is lost, **tt* and **pp* came to be interpreted as mere transitive suffixes within Proto-Dravidian. Tamil generally has *pp* after roots of Class IV ending in *i* and *y*, and *tt* after others. Other languages have generalized one or the other through a combination of phonological and morphological criteria. What is interesting is that **tt*, **pp*, **kk* in derived nouns carry transitive meanings, while

**t/nt*, **k/nk* and **p/mp* carry intransitive meanings. Consider the following examples, e.g. Ta. *aẓi* (*-v-*, *-nt-*) 'to perish', (*-pp-*, *-tt-*) 'to destroy' → Verbal nouns: *aẓi-mpu* 'evil deed', *aẓi-vu* 'destruction' (intr.), *aẓi-ppu* 'destruction' (tr.); Ma. *aẓi-yuka* 'to be expended, etc.' → *aẓivu* (intr.) 'expense', *aẓi-cc-al* (tr.) 'expenditure'; Inscr. Te. *ẓaccu* (< **aẓi-cc-* < **aẓi-ntt-*, **aẓi-mpp-*) v.t. 'to destroy' → *ḍa-pp-i* 'destruction' [277]; Ta. *aṟi* 'to know' → *aṟi-vi* (intr.) 'knowledge', *aṟivai* 'wisdom' [314] (see section 4.5.8.5).

No Dravidian language preserves PD *NPP as such, but Kumaraswami Raja (1969b) has conclusively shown that such a reconstruction is warranted by the correspondence NP:PP in different Dravidian languages, such as Ka. *eṇṭu* 'eight': Ta., Ma. *eṭṭu* (< **eṇ-ṭṭu*), Ko. *eṭ*, To. *öṭ*, Kod. *ëṭṭ* [847]. The NP sequences are generally attested in Telugu and Kannaḍa and occasionally in North Dravidian, where voiced and voiceless stops contrast after homorganic nasal; cf. e.g. Ka. *tirumpu* 'to cause to go round' : Ta. Ma. *tiruppu* id. (< **tir-umpp-*); Te. *peṇṭi* 'female of animal' : Ta. *peṭṭai*, Ma. *peṭṭa* (< **peṇ-ṭṭ-ay*). The solution provided by Kumaraswami Raja has a far-reaching effect on our understanding of a number of problems of comparative Dravidian morphology.

5.5 Earlier studies on stem formatives

After Caldwell there was not any serious study for a long time on how stem formatives evolved in Dravidian. Krishnamurti has given the comparative distribution of -V-L, -V-(N)P, and V-(N)PP among different subgroups. He proposed that disyllabic stems in -V + liquid *r*, *l*, *ḷ* tend to be mostly intransitive thereby giving these an erstwhile grammatical function still preserved synchronically in Kuṛux and Malto (see section 5.3). He also suggested that a former past morph **-ci*/**-cci* got incorporated into certain stems through reanalysis as formative **c*/**cc* + past *i*. Emeneau ([1967b/1994: 99–100) considered that *NP : *NPP found in SD I minus Kannaḍa and Tuḷu was an innovation in South Dravidian. But I have given arguments why this type of inflection must be a retention and not an innovation (Krishnamurti 1994a: xxi). The main argument was that it was unusual for innovating a combination of such complex grammatical features as tense and voice in the same markers rather than losing one of these at a time by a process of simplification. One set of languages has retained voice and lost tense, i.e. most of SD I and the Kui–Manḍa subgroup of SD II. Loss of both these categories occurs in Kannaḍa, Tuḷu and Telugu, which have a number of lexical items without matching intransitive–transitive pairs. The progression of change was tense–voice > voice > Ø (Krishnamurti 1994a: xxiv).

In another article, Emeneau (1975, repr. 1994) discusses at length the formation of plural action stems in Kui–Kuvi with *-k-*, *-p-*, *-v-*, *-b-* and reconstructs this phenomenon back to Proto-Dravidian and treats it as a retention in Kui–Kuvi, etc. I gave reasons to treat these as only relics of Proto-Dravidian non-past markers that have acquired a new meaning in a subgroup consisting of Kui–Kuvi, with traces in Koṇḍa–Pengo–Manḍa

(Krishnamurti 1994a: xxii–xxiv, [1997a: §7.2] 2001: 302–4). Winfield (1928) classifies verbs into four conjugations in terms of the augment they take in the formation of the present participle, namely 1st: *-k*, 2nd *-pa*, 3rd *-v*, 4th *-b*. When the same augments are added uniformly to all bases, they denote plural action, but are inflected like Class 1. This transition provides the clue for these consonantal elements (which derive from Proto-Dravidian non-past markers) signalling a plural action in Kui and being frequentative markers in the other members of this subgroup.

5.6 Stem formatives in nouns

If all instances of *-(V)-NP, *-(V)-NPP added to verbal roots originally referred to tense and voice, which meanings they had lost in the course of evolution, how can we interpret nouns which cannot be traced to any extant verbs, e.g. **mar-u-ntu* 'medicine'? Disyllabic and trisyllabic nouns of this kind can mostly be related to verbs, and we also showed the meaning of transitivity surviving in derived nouns. Since the incorporation of the tense–voice morphs into the stem was a process which was going on in the Proto language from an indefinite period, the absence of formal marking between verbal and nominal bases could lead to the formation of certain nominal stems from other nouns following the same phonological pattern, e.g. *mar-u-ntu* from *mar-am* 'tree'. The best we can do at this point is to call it a 'phonological analogy'. While going through the *DEDR* one does not come across a large number of such underivable stems of two or three syllables. What is proposed here is that, at the level of roots, both nouns and verbs are distinct grammatically, but with identical phonological structure, e.g. **pal* 'tooth', **pāl* 'milk', **kal* 'stone', **kāl* 'leg'; in some cases, it appears that the noun and verb are semantically and phonologically related **kaṇ* 'eye': **kāṇ* [*kaHṇ*] 'to see', **kay* 'hand', **key* 'to do', etc. This kind of pattern equivalence between nominal and verbal stems of different sizes is the basis of what I am calling 'phonological analogy', which must have given rise to forms like *mar-u-ntu* 'medicine' at a deeper chronological stratum within Proto-Dravidian. The absence of a large number of such nominal stems of two or three syllables with *-NP, *-NPP as the final syllable, not related to any extant verbs, is the basis of the authenticity of the above arguments.

The process of gemination of a final P (P → PP) had two functions in Proto-Dravidian: (i) it formed the transitive stem; (ii) it also derived a nominal stem from adverbs or adjectives. Consequently, we find the transitive stems to have an identical phonological structure to derived nominals in a considerable number of cases. It is this coincidence in structure that led Caldwell to say that NP: PP (our *P: *PP, *NP: *NPP) originally marked nouns and secondarily they became verbal. The opposite is the truth, which is borne out by the following arguments and examples.

(i) Intransitives ending with NP do not function as nominals, but transitive-like stems function also like nominals.

(ii) The intransitive nominals are derived by adding noun-forming suffixes to intransitive verb stems, whereas the transitive stems can occur as nominals without further additions.

(iii) The transitive stems can also take other noun-forming affixes. In that case, it is a parallel process of noun-formation by adding derivative morphs to transitive stems.

(iv) That the transitive stems look identical to nominal stems is a structural coincidence and not a semantic or grammatical shift. Primarily the stems are verbal.

5.7 Phonological changes in Proto-Dravidian roots[13]

A proto-Dravidian root can be either free or bound. Free roots can be free forms or words; in the case of verbs, most verb roots may also occur without any additions as minimal utterances in the imperative sg. The degree of freedom from high to low is indicated by the canonical forms as (C)V̄C< (C)VC < (C)V̄ <(C)V-; the last one is always bound (see *TVB*: §2.113, 2.114; pp. 173–4). Numerically roots which are free forms are many more than the bound ones (see section 5.1).

The syllable structure of the Proto-Dravidian roots and stems is best preserved in Early Tamil, and to some extent in Malayāḷam, a west coast dialect of Tamil which became an independent language by about the ninth century. The reconstructed roots undergo a number of changes, which have been treated under different headings in chapter 4. Some alternations go to Proto-Dravidian itself, namely consonantal changes in section 4.3; contraction of $(C_1)V_1C_2\text{-}V_3$ > $(C)\bar{V}_1$-, e.g. *pey-ar* > *pē-r* 'name', **kic-ampu* > **kiy-ampu* > *kī-mpu*/*kē-mpu* 'a yam' in section 4.3.2.1; a long root vowel becoming short, when followed by a formative V (=V_2), **īr-*/ **ir*-V- 'two' (adj), in section 4.3.2.2. These need not be repeated here.

There is a set of sound changes that introduced quantitative changes in the root syllable in different subgroups and individual languages. These have been described both comparatively and typologically by Krishnamurti earlier (1955). I summarize the findings as follows:

1. $(C)V_1$*y*/*w*/*k*-V_2 > $(C)\bar{V}_1$-. This is the same as the Proto-Dravidian rule mentioned above, except that it continues into the historical period of individual languages. It is therefore (see Krishnamurti 1955:§8) not reconstructed for a distant past, but for a much later time frame, e.g. Te. *ūr-cu* 'to breathe', *ūr-pu* 'breath' < **uy-r-cc-*, **uy-ir-pp-*; the older stage has *-c-* [645]; only Telugu shows contraction. Toda has contraction of syllables with the loss of a liquid **r* or **ẓ*.

2. Loss of a semivowel *y*/*w* as C_2 can lead to compensatory lengthening of the preceding vowel when followed by *-NP/-NPP. In other words, a root of (C)VC- type

[13] Caldwell maintained that 'stability in the root-vowels is the rule, and change is the exception' (1956: 217). He did point out some of the changes which have been handled in recent years either by morphophonemic changes within Proto-Dravidian or by positing a laryngeal.

becomes (C)V̄, e.g. Te. *tū̃gu* (< **tuy-nk-*), Ta. *tū-ṅku*, Ma. *tū-ṅṅuka*, Ka. *tū-gu*, Tu. *tū-ṅkuni* [3376a,b]; in some cases the root-final *-y* is lost without compensatory lengthening, Te. *bo-nku* 'to lie' (< **poy-nkk-*), Ta. Ma. *poy* 'to lie', *po-kkam* 'falsehood' (<**poy-nkk-am*) [4531, 4559 no need to put in two entries; **poy-* is from older **poc-*] (see Krishnamurti 1955: §§16,17).

3. PD *V*y*/*V̄*y* are both represented as V̄*y* in Old Telugu in the case of both verbs and nouns. In other words, contrast of length is lost before *-y* in root syllables in Telugu (Krishnamurti 1955: §14, fn. 20, Subrahmanyam 1970a).

4. Metathesis and vowel contraction led to disyllabic and trisyllabic bases becoming monosyllabic and disyllabic, respectively, in SD II languages (see section 4.4.3), **mar-an* > *mrā-n* in Old Telugu, Koṇḍa, Kui–Kuvi (see ety. 35), Te. *kro-tta* <**koẓ-utt-*V [2149] (see section 4.5.7.3). (Krishnamurti 1955: §§18–20, *TVB*: §§1.121–59.)

5. In PD trisyllabic stems, V_2 is lost, leading to three developments: (i) assimilation of the root-final liquid to a following -PP/-B. This change will give rise to disyllabic stems, e.g. Te. *ceppu* 'sandal' (<**cer-pp-* < **ker-pp-*); cf. Ta. *cer-uppu*, Ma. *cerippu*, Ko. *kevr* (<**ker-v-*), To. *kerf*; CD: Kol. Nk. *kerri*, Nk. (Ch.) *kerri*, *kerig*; ND: Kuṛ. *kharpā*.; Gondi and Parji borrowed the word from Pre-Telugu before assimilation of the consonants: Go. *serpum*, *sarpum*, etc. Pa. *cerup*, *cerpu* [1963]. The syllable reduction with the loss of the unaccented vowel runs through all subgroups [1963]. Depending on the pre-assimilation stage, Telugu and Kannaḍa developed geminate voiced stops also as a result of this change, Te. *taggu* 'to be reduced', Ka. *taggu*, *targu*, *taẓgu* id. (<**taẓ-u-nk-*, with loss of *-u-*, *-n-*, and voicing of *k* to *g*); cf. Ta. Ma. *tāẓ* 'to be lowered' [3178], see section 4.5.8.3 (for a detailed treatment, see Krishnamurti 1955:§§7–10, *TVB* §§1.173–85); (ii) metathesis of (C)VL- to (C)LV- in SD II languages, Te. *brungu* 'to be immersed' (<**mẓu-ng-* <**muẓ-ng-* <**muẓ-u-nk-*), Kui *bṛuḍga* id. [4993]; (iii) loss of the root-final liquid, cf. Ta. *muṅku*, Ma. *muṅṅuka* 'to sink, plunge' (< **muẓ-nk-* <**muẓ-u-nk-*), Kol. Nk. *muŋg-*, Kui, Pe. Manḍa *munj-* [4993].

6. Some grammatical classes have alternation between short and long vowels: (i) verbal roots have short vowels and derived nouns have long vowels, e.g. **keṭ-u* v.i. 'to perish, to be spoiled': **kēṭu* 'damage, evil' [1942]; (ii) in personal pronouns the nominatives have long vowels, but the oblique stems have short vowels, e.g. **tān* /**tan-* 'self'; (iii) several irregular verbs have such length alternation: **war-*/ **wā-* 'to come', **tar-*/ **tā-* 'to give to the 1st or 2nd person' etc. Caldwell mentioned some of these but could not provide any solution (Caldwell 1956: 210–17). Until recently, multiple reconstruction of roots was the solution adopted by Dravidian comparativists. Recently Krishnamurti explained all such irregular alternations in terms of a reconstructed laryngeal **H* (see Krishnamurti 1997b; for a summary see section 4.5.7.2.3). A laryngeal **H* was lost and it simultaneously lengthened a preceding vowel when the output was a free form, but was lost systematically when the output was a bound form, thus PD ***taHn* > **tān*/*tan-* nom/obl, ***keHṭ-u* > **kēṭ-u*/ **keṭ-u-* n./v., ***waH-r-* > **wā*/ **wa-* imper./past. Early Tamil

preserved a few relics of a PD laryngeal in deictic bases: *aḥ-* 'remote', *iḥ-* 'proximate', the number word 'ten' *paḥ-tu* and about half a dozen lexical items of which three have cognates with lengthened vowels (see Krishnamurti 1997d: 147–50).

5.8 Derivational suffixes

Each of the Dravidian languages has a stock of noun-forming and verb-forming affixes, which will be dealt with in the respective chapters. Derivational suffixes which are reconstructible are not many and are given below.

5.8.1 *Deverbal nominals*

(a) By adding **-ay* to monosyllabic verb roots, **wil* 'to sell': **wil-ay* 'price' [5221: SD I and Te.], Ta. *vila-ai*, Ma. *vil-a*, Ka. *bel-e*, Te. *wel-a* 'price'; **kaṭṭ-* 'to tie, bind': **kaṭṭ-ay* 'dam' [1147: SD I, SD II, CD, ND]; Ta. *naku* 'to laugh': *nak-ai* n., Ka. *nagu* 'to laugh': *nag-e* 'laughter' [3569].

(b) By geminating the final stop of the root in disyllabic stems or the formative of stems of two or more syllables, e.g. root-final stop: **āṭu* 'to play': **āṭṭ-u* 'playing, a game' [347], **añcu* 'to fear': *accu* (<**añcc-*) n. 'fear' [55]; also by adding *-am* to the stem with the final stop doubled: *āṭṭ-am* 'game, dancing', *acc-am* (< **añcc-am*) n. 'fear' (Ta.–Ma.).

(c) By adding *-al* to the verb root: Ta. Ma. Ko. *añc-al* n. 'fear' (see (b)); **keṭ-u* 'to perish' : **keṭ-al* 'evil' (SD I); **kūṭu* v.i. 'to join', *kūṭṭu* 'to join' v.t., n. 'mixture' (see (a)): *kūṭ-al* 'joining (intr.)', *kūṭṭ-al* 'uniting' (tr.), also **kūṭṭ-am* 'union', see (SD I and Te.) [1882]; **enku* 'to remain, be left over', + *al* → **enk-al* 'left-over food': Ta. *eñcu* 'to remain', *eñc-al* 'defect', *eccam* (< **eñcc-am*), Ma. *ecc-il*, Ka. *enj-al*, Koḍ. *ecci* (*l*-loss); SD II: Te. *eng-ili* n. 'left-over food', Pe. Kuṛ. Malt. have verbs derived from **enk-* [14] [780].

(d) By adding **-t-al/*-tt-al* which consists of two noun-forming elements **-t/-tt* + *al*; also similarly **-t-am*. These are added to roots ending **-ṭ*, e.g. **ōṭu* v.i. 'to run', **ōṭṭu* v.t. 'to make to run': Ta. *ōṭṭu*, *ōṭ-ṭ-am* 'running' (<**ōṭ* + *t-*, *ōṭ* + *t-am*) (SD I and II). An agentive noun is derived by adding *-i* to transitive stems, e.g. *ōṭṭ-i* 'captain of a ship' (Ta. Ma.); Ka. *kūḍu* 'to join': *kūṭ-am* 'union' (< **kūṭ-t-am*), *pāḍu* 'to sing': *pāṭ-am* 'song'.

(e) By geminating the post-nasal stop of a formative in stems of two or more syllables. Some languages lose the preconsonantal nasal (PP < *NPP) and others degeminate the voiceless stop (NP < *NPP); Ta. *may-aṅku* 'to be confused': *may-akku*, *may-akk-am* 'confusion' (<**may-an-kk-*), Ta. *añcu* 'to fear' : *accu* 'fear' (<**añcc-*) (SD I and Te.).

(f) By lengthening the root-vowel, sometimes in combination with other processes, e.g. **keṭu* 'to perish, be spoiled': **keṭ-ṭa*, **kēṭu*, **keṭ-al*, **keṭu-ti* 'ruin, loss, damage' (mainly SD I and Te.).

[14] Koṇḍa has unexpected palatalization of the verb, *enz-* 'to be left over', *es-* v.t. 'to leave or save food'.

(g) *-am* added to an intransitive or transitive verb stem, **cōṭ-* 'to run', **cōṭ-am* 'boat' [2861] > Ta. Ma. *ōṭ-am*, Ka. Tu. *ōḍ-a*, SD II: Te. *ōḍ-a*; (>lw Go. Pa. *ōḍ-a*).[15] Ka. *sōl* 'to be defeated': *sōl-am* 'defeat'.

(h) Multiple noun formatives: *am + t + am → antam*, *opp-antam* 'agreement, contract' from *oppu* 'to agree', in Ta. Ma. Ka. Te. *opp-andam* id. Note that *oppu* is a reanalysed stem from the root **o-* incorporating the non-past morph *-pp*, which occurs in all subgroups as such [924]. It also functions as a nominal stem *o-ppu* 'uniformity, suitability'; with the addition of *-am*, *opp-am* 'comparison, likeness' (SD I and Te.). With a different non-past suffix incorporated: *o-kk-* (cf. Ma. *okkuka* 'to be like', Kuṛ. *okk-* 'to tally, agree with'), **okk-al* 'relatives, kinsmen' (SD I) [925]. Another complex noun formative is **t + al + ay →* **talay*, cf. Te. *oppu-dala* 'agreement', Ka. *tavu* 'to decrease': *tavu-dale* 'destruction' (see section 5.6 (3)).

(i) *-(*i*)*kay*. Ka. *bēy* 'to burn': *bē-ge* 'fire, flame', *paṇṇu* 'to make': *paṇṇ-ige* 'decoration', *tuḍu* 'to wear'(< **toḍu*) : *toḍ-ige* 'ornament to wear'

(j) *-(*i*)*kk-ay*: Ka. *alasu* 'to be weary': *alas-ike* 'weariness', *ir-* 'to be': *ir-ke* 'an abode', *agal* 'to be separated': *agal-ke* 'separation'; Te. *kōru* 'to wish' : *kōr-*(*i*)*ke* 'a wish', *pūnu* 'to undertake', *pūn-*(*i*)*ke*, *pūn-*(*i*)*ki* 'perseverance', *manu* 'to live': *man-iki* 'living'.

5.8.2 *Deadjectival nominals*

(k) *-*may*. Ta. *pēr*/*per-u* adj 'big', *peru-mai* 'abundance', Ka. *per-me* 'increase, greatness', *hem-me* 'pride, insolence'; Te. *pēr-mi* 'greatness, superiority' [4411].

5.9 Compounds

Here we deal only with reconstructible compounds, sequences of at least two roots, which function as words in Proto-Dravidian, or at least in one of the subgroups. Consequently, compound-like constructions, which are not attested by at least two languages, have been eliminated. All the items are taken from *DEDR*. Several of these present problems of analysis, both phonological and semantic. However, we can still see the patterns that were established in the family before the individual languages emerged and enlarged the inventory.

Emeneau, in an unpublished paper,[16] has discussed two items: 5496b *weṇṇey* 'butter' (**weḷ* + **ney*, lit. 'white ghee/oil') and 4460a **po*C-*kuẓ*-V 'navel' ('hollow of stomach'), of which the second member is 1818 **kūẓ*/**kuẓ*-V 'pit, hollow', and the first part has been identified as 4460b **poṭ-* 'navel'.[17] He has also dealt with six items mainly confined to individual languages.

[15] cf. Skt. *hoḍa* 'boat, rafter'. Note Skt. *h-* preserves the intermediate stage in the sound change *c-* > **s-* > *h-* > ø [1039]. The other 'run' word in [1041] is cognate with the other two.

[16] I am indebted to Professor Emeneau for loaning me a copy of the paper entitled 'Some Dravidian noun compounds'.

[17] Most languages point to a reconstruction with two voiced stops or at least one, **boḍ-*/**moḍ-*; only Malayāḷam shows *p-*. If the first part should mean 'stomach', 4494 **poṭṭV* 'stomach' would

The patterns are analysed below into constituents, in terms of their parts of speech and their likely meaning relationships, treating the linear constituents as x and y.

5.9.1 *Verb + verb*

(Doing x + doing y): there are not many of this type.[18]

Ta. Ma. *ār-āy* 'to investigate', *ār-āycci* 'research', Ka. *ār-ay*, Te. *ār-ayu*, *ar-ayu*, Koṇḍa *rey-* 'to search' [**ār* 'to become full', 368 + **āy* 'to search', 363].

5.9.2 *Noun + noun*

This construction is quite common. The first N stands in an attributive relation to the second, e.g. 'the fly of honey, honey-bee', 'water from eyes, tears', 'God's/King's residence, temple/palace', etc. The underlying case relations are set out in terms of the meaning relationship between the two constituents, x and y.

(i) xy = y lives on x or y causes x

3268b: Ta. *tēṉ-ī* 'honey-bee', Koḍ. *tēm-puḷu*;[19] Te. *tē̃ṭ-i* 'honey-bee', Kuṛ. *tīn-ī* 'bee', Malt. *tēn-i* 'honey, bee' [**tēn*/**tīn* 'honey' 3268a, **ī* 'fly' 533; lit. 'honey-fly'].

(ii) xy = y comes out of x (x = source, y = object produced)

1159b: Ta. Ma. *kaṇ-ṇīr*, Ko. *kaṇīr*, To. *keṇīr*, Ka. *kaṇ-ṇīr*, Tu. *kaṇṇi-nīr*, Te. *kan-nīru*, Go. *kan-nīr*, *kanḍ-ēr*, *kān-ēr*, Koṇḍa *kaṇ-er(u)*, Pe. *kaṇ-er*,[20] Kui *kanḍ-ru*, Kuvi *kanḍ-ru*, Br. *xaṛīnk* [**kaṇ* 'eye' 1159a, **nīr* 'water' 3690a; lit. 'eye-water'].

2402b: SD II: Go. *saṛāpī*, *haṛap*, *aṛpi* 'cowdung', Koṇḍa *saṛapi*, *rāpi*, Kuvi, Pe. Manḍa *ṛāpi*; CD: Nk. *sanap*, Pa. *caṛpi*, Oll. *saṛpi*, Gad. *saḍpi*; 2402a SD II: Koṇḍa *ṛānu* 'ox', dial. *saṛa* id., Kuvi *sṛahnu kōḍi* 'bullock'; cf. Gad. *saṛit* 'bullock' [*?*caṭ-a* 'bullock' + **pī* 'excrement' 4210].

2625: Ta. *īr*, *īrppi*, Ka. *īpi*, *sīr*, *īr*; Te. *īpi* n., *īrcu* v.t., Go. *sīr*, *hīr*, *īr*, Kui *sīr-eni* 'comb', Kuvi *hīru* 'nit', Pe. Manḍa *hīr*; Kuṛ. *cīr* [**cīr* 'nits', + **pī* 'eggs laid by, excrement' SD I and Te.].

3408: Ta. *teṅku*, *teṅkam*, *tēṅ-kāy* 'coconut', Ma. *tēṅ-ṅā*, *teṅṅaṅ-kāyi* 'coconut', To. *tö-goy*, Ka. *teṅ-gāy*, Tu. *teṅ-gï* 'coconut tree'; Te. *ṭeṅ-kāya* 'coconut (palm)' [cf. 3449: **teṉ* 'south' + **kāy* 'fruit', lit. 'fruit-from-south tree'].

fit better. Te. *pokk-ili* also presents a problem because **ẓ* becomes *ḍ* and not *l* intervocalically in Telugu.

18 Actually the verb compounds or compound verbs are separately discussed in the chapter on the verb.

19 *puḷu* is not a cognate; this is given only to support the identification of **ī* as another word and not a suffix.

20 It appears that *-er* in some of the SD II languages is from PD **yāṯ* 'water' > SD II *ēṟu* which replaced **nīr*.

(iii) xy = y belongs to x (x = owner/resident, y = place)

2177: Ta. Ma. *kōy-il* 'palace, temple', *kōv-il* 'temple', *kō*, *kōṉ* 'emperor, king'; Te. *kōv-ila*, *kōv-ela* 'temple' [**kō* 'King/God' 2177, **il* 'house' 494; lit. 'King's/God's place'].
2215: Ka. *kōnēri*, *kōnēru*; Te. *kōnēṟu* 'a square tank with steps on four sides, a temple tank' [?God's-tank; cf. **yāṯ*-V 'tank' 5159].

(iv) xy = y is called x (x = proper noun, y = common noun)

2607: Ta. *cī-kkāy*, Ma. *cīkka-kkāyi*, Ka. *sī-ge*, Te. *sī-kāya*, *cīki-rēni* 'soapnut tree'.

(v) xy = object y has quality x (y is head and x attribute)

4035: Ta. *paṉi* 'dew', Ta. *paṉ-ṉīr* 'rosewater', Ma. *pani-nīr* id., Ka. *pan-nīr*, Koḍ. *pan-nīrï*, Tu. *pan-nīrï* 'perfumed water, rosewater': 'dew water' > 'rose water', Ka. *pan-nīr*; Te. *pan-nīru* 'rose water' [**pan*-V 'dew, coldness', **nīr* 'water' 3690a].

(vii) xy = y has x (the meaning of x is not clear; could it mean 'bent'?)[21]

4990: Ta. *muẓam* 'cubit', Ta. Ma. *muẓaṅ-kāl* 'knee', *muzaṅ-kai* 'elbow', Ko. *mo-gay* 'elbow', *mo-gāl* 'knee', Ka. *moẓa-kāl* 'knee', *moẓa key* 'elbow', *moḷa* 'cubit', Koḍ. *moḷa-kay* 'elbow', Tu. *muraṅ-gè*, *moraṅ-gè* 'cubit'; SD II; Te. *mūra* 'cubit', *mrō̃ceyyi*, *mrō̃ kālu*, *mō̃kar-illu* 'to bend'; CD: Kol. *mov-ka*, *mō-ki* 'elbow'; ND: Kuṛ. *mū̃kā* 'knee', Malt. *mū-ke* 'knee' (loss of final *-l* in ND).

5.9.3 *Adjective + noun*

The first element is a descriptive adjective qualifying a following noun head:
5312: Te. *karu-wali* 'soft breeze', *wali* 'chill, cold', 5312:**waḷ-i* 'wind' [SDI, SD II, CD; the meaning of *karu-* is not clear].
3184: Ta. *tāẓ-vaṭam* 'necklace of beads or pearls', Ma. *tāẓ-vaṭam*, *tā-vaṭam*, Ka. *tā-vaḍa*, Te. *tā-waṭam*, *tā-waḷam* 'necklace of lotus beads, rosary' [*tāẓ* 'low' > 'hanging' 3178 and *vaṭam* 'string' SD I and Te. Go. 5220].
3758: Ta. *neru-nal*, *neru-nai*, *neṉ-ṉal* 'yesterday', Ka. *nin-ne*, Koḍ. *nin-nāndï*, Te. *nin-na*, Go. *nin-nē* (obl. *nin-nēṭ*), Koṇḍa *i-ʔen* (*i-ʔeR-*), dial. *i-nen*, Manḍa *ineliŋ*; **neṟ*- > **nṟe*- > *ṟe*-: Kui *riīsi*, Kuvi *reʔe*, *reʔeni*; Br. *darō* [cf. Ma. *in-nāḷe*, To. *ï-nēṟ*, Ko. *nēr* (obl. *nēṭ*-)].[22]

21 In the following example, the first constituent is likely to be **moẓ*-V- 'to bend' [5123]; the 'cubit' meaning must be later, because of the following **kay* 'hand', but that meaning would not go with **kāl* 'leg'.

22 Kui–Kuvi indicate the first constituent as **niṯ*-V 'to be complete, full' [3682], but Ta. *neru-* does not phonologically match, although **nēr-*/ *ner*-V- [3672] looks better. The forms with **nin-*/**in-* require **nin-ṯ-* 'to be full' which *DEDR* connects to **niṯ-* [3682]. These etymologies need further examination.

5020b: Ta. *mun̠-nāḷ* 'yesterday', Ka. *mon-ne* 'day before yesterday', Te. *mon-na*, Go. *mun-ne*, *mon-ne*, Koṇḍa *mu-ʔe* (*mu-ʔeR-*) 'day after tomorrow', Pe. ? *mayhiŋ* id., Manḍa *maʔhiŋ*, Kui *maisi* 'a future day' [4615].
4411: Ta. *perum-puli* 'tiger', Te. *pedda puli*, *be-bbuli* 'big tiger', Kol. *per-pul*, Oll. *ber-pul*, Gad. *ber-bullū* [*pēr/*per-V + *puli* 'tiger' 4307; in Telugu 'a cheetah' is called *ciruta puli* 'small tiger'].
4954: Ta. *mutu* 'old', *mūtt-appan̠* 'father's father', Ma. *mūtta-* 'old, grown', *mūtt-appan* 'father's elder brother, father's father', Ka. *muttu* 'advanced age', *mutta-* 'aged', Koḍ. *mutt-ajjë* 'great-grandfather', *mut-tāy* 'great-grandmother', Te. *mut-tāta* 'great-grand-father', *mutt-awwa* 'great-grandmother'.
4106. Ta. *pākkan̠*, Ka. *bāvuga*; Te. *bāvuru-billi*, Go. *bakoval*, Pe. *boyka*, Kui *bāoḍi*, *bāoli*, Kuvi *bā̃uli* (Is.) 'wild cat' [Te. also *bāvurumanu*]; Nk. *bagale*, Pa. *bāvki*. This group sounds foreign and needs further investigation.
4337: Ta. *pun̠-cey* 'land fit for dry cultivation', Ma. *puñ-ca-kkaṇṭam* 'field under irrigation', Ka.? *puṇaji*, Tu. *puñ-ca-kaṇḍa* 'a very good rice field', Te. *pun-ja* 'land for dry cultivation' as opposed to *nan-ja*.[23] Cf. Ta. *pun̠am* 'upland fit for dry cultivation'.
4654: Te. *maḍ-iwēlu* 'washerman', Ka. *maḍi-vāḷa*, *maḍi-vāḷi* 'washerman/woman', Koḍ. *maḍi-vāḷë* 'washerman', Tu. *maḍḍ-ele* 'washerman' [*maṭi 'ceremonial purity' 4654 and *wēl-ay* 'work' 5540 (SD I)].
4813: Te. *mēna-māma* 'maternal uncle', *mēn-atta* 'paternal aunt'(see 4813 and 53b in Appendix); Te. *mēna-* 'connected through a man's sister or woman's brother, cross-', *mēna-gōḍalu* 'niece', Nk. *meonak* 'cross-cousin', Koṇḍa *mēṇa'en* (Burrow and Bhattacharya) 'father's sister's son', Pe. *mēṇa ṭonḍen* 'male cross-cousin', Kuvi *mehṇ-attayi* 'female cross-cousin' || *CDIAL* 10341 *maithuna-* 'copulation', *DNM mehuṇaya-* 'father's sister's son', *mehuṇia-* 'mother's brother's son', *-iā-* 'mother's brother's daughter'.
2539: Ta. *cemmal* 'water', Tu. *simma* 'cold', *temma* 'cold, cough', Te. *cemma, camaru, cemaṭa*; *temm-era* 'cold breeze'; 810: Ka. *eral* 'breeze, wind'.

5.9.4 *Verb + noun*

There is a small class of constructions with a verb as a modifier of a following noun head:
2882: Ta. *cōmpu* 'to be idle', *cōmp-ēr̠i*, *cōm-ār̠i* 'an idler', Ka. Tu.Te. *sōmāri* (the second element is not clear, but it means 'a male person').
3246: Ta. *tiri* 'to turn, revolve', Ka. *tiragaṇi/e* 'turning, a wheel for raising water'; Te. *tirugali* 'a hand-mill' [the second element is **kal* 'stone' 1298].

[23] A plausible etymology for Te. *nan-je* is **nal/nan* 'good' [3610] and *cey* 'field' from **key* [1958]. It follows that *pun-je* is from **pul-/pun-* 'small, bad' [4301] and *cey* 'field'.

5372: Ta. *vāval, vavvāl, vauvā* 'bat', Ma. *vāval, vavvāl*, Ka. *bāval(i), bāvul(i)*, Koḍ. *bāali*, Tu. *bāvali*; Te. ?*bāvuru pilli* 'a wild cat', Kol. *velape*, Kuvi *bāpla*; cf. Ta. *vavvu* 'to snatch', *vau(vu)* 'to seize, snatch, steal', Ma. *vavvāyi, vavvāli* 'fox', Te. *bāwu-konu* 'to gobble up'.[24]

5.9.5 *Compounds with doubtful composition*

?2274: Ta. *ak-kuḷ, caṅkam* 'armpit', *ak-kuḷu* 'to tickle', Ka. *cak-kala-guḷi* 'tickling another', *ak-kaḷike* 'tickling', Koḍ. *kak-kuḷi* id.; Te. *canka* 'armpit', *cakkili gili* 'tickling'; Kuṛ. *caŋgr-* 'to itch'. The second element is **kuẓi* 'pit', but the first is not clear.[25]

3971: Ka. *pari-yāṇa, pari-vāṇa, hari-vāṇa, ari-vāṇa* 'a plate-like vessel of metal', Tu. *harivāṇa*; cf. Ta. *aruvāṇam* 'copper tray', Te. (*h*)*ari-vāṇam* (lw < Late Ka.).

[24] The second element *āl* looks like an archaic word, ?**yāl*, meaning 'an animal', cf. Te. *tōḍ-ēlu* 'wolf', *tā̃b-ēlu* 'a tortoise', *kund-ēlu* 'hare'.

[25] Another parallel etymology discussed by Emeneau (see fn. 16 above) is 1234 To. *komkwïṛ*, Ka. *kavuṅ-kuẓ, kaṅ-kuẓ, koṅ-kuẓ* 'armpit', Tu. *kaṅ-kuḷa*, Go. *kakri*, Pa. *kav-kor, kav-koḍ* 'armpit'. Emeneau suggests **kam*-V/*kav*- 'smelling' [1334] and **kuẓ-i* 'pit'. It appears that Te. *kawung-ili* 'embrace' does not belong to this set. It is likely to be related to Te. *kaw-iyu* 'to cover completely' from **kap*- [1221].

6

Nominals: nouns, pronouns, numerals and time and place adverbs

6.1 Introduction

Nominals in Dravidian are a morphosyntactic class of words, which are inflected for case. Nominals consist of four subclasses: nouns, pronouns, numerals and adverbs of time and place. All but the adverbs are distinguished for gender and number, besides being inflected for case. Adverbs of time and place are morphologically nominal, since they carry case suffixes, but syntactically they function as adverbs, i.e. modifiers of the verb.

Noun stems can be simple, complex or compound. Simple stems are identical with the roots, e.g. **kāl* 'leg', **ūr* 'village'. Complex stems result from the addition of derivational morphemes to verbal, adjectival, or nominal roots, e.g. **wil-ay* 'price' from **wil* 'to sell' (see section 5.8.1a), **weḷḷ-ay*, **weḷ-u-ppu*, **weṇ-may* 'whiteness' from **weḷ* / **weṇ* 'white' [5496]. Compound stems consist of a minimum of two roots of which the head is a noun and the satellite a noun, an adjective or a verb, e.g. **kaṇ-ṇīr* 'tear' (N + N), lit. 'eye-water' [1159b], **kiṯṯ-eli* 'a mouse' (adj + N) (lit. 'small rat') [1594].

6.2 Gender and number: identification and definition

Gender is a system of classifying 'nouns' (other than time and place adverbs) in terms of certain semantic and formal properties, supported by their grammatical behaviour. In Dravidian, gender is distinguished in terms of the semantic categories [± human], [± male human],[1] and marginally [± animate]. In all Dravidian languages [− animate]

[1] Traditional grammars have recognized the importance of the category of [± human] in gender distinction. They called *uyar-tiṇai* 'high class' [+ high] vs. *aḥ-ṟiṇai* (← *al* + *tiṇai*) 'low class' [− high] (Tolkāppiyam, col: 2); correspondingly, *mahat* [+ high] and *amahat* [− high] in Telugu (Āndhraśabdaciṃtāmaṇi). [+ high] represented [+ human] and [− high], [− human]. In Old Tamil [+ high] split into two in the singular [+ male human], [− male human] and in the plural [+ human]; [− high] represented [− human] both in the singular and in the plural. It meant non-human animate and inanimate. In Telugu *mahat* [+ high] meant [+ male human] in the singular, but [+human] in the plural; *amahat* [− high] meant a 'woman or a non-human' in the singular, but in the plural it meant [− human]. Gods, male and female, are fitted into the human class; therefore, the choice of 'superior' vs. 'inferior' as opposed to 'human' vs. 'non-human'. These categories correctly represent the grammatical situation of these languages as can be seen from the following discussion (see Bloch 1954: 5–8, Israel 1973: 15–32 for details of Tamil).

(things) and [− human, + animate] (plants, animals, birds, etc.) are combined into one category called the neuter gender, in the singular or plural, as the case may be.

Gender distinction in Dravidian is expressed in substantives (basic and derived), the third personal (demonstrative and interrogative) pronouns, and numerals used either as adjectives or as predicates in equative sentences, e.g. OTe. *reṇḍu*[1] *bomma-lu*[2] 'two[1] dolls[2]', *iru-wuru*[1] *tammu-lu*[2] 'two[1] younger brothers[2]' (attributive use), *bomma-lu*[1] *reṇḍu*[2] 'the dolls[1] (are) two[2]' (predicative use). In most of the languages, finite verbs and nominal predicates copy the gender of subject nouns, which govern them. Adjectives do not carry any marker of agreement with the head noun in gender and number. Not every language has all the types of gender marking, e.g. Malayāḷam has lost the agreement feature in verbs, but the demonstrative pronouns retain the difference, e.g. *vannu* 'he, she, it, they [± human] came'.

Only some subclasses of nouns carry overt gender marking in any language. Thus, in Modern Telugu *moguḍu* 'husband' (gender marked by *-ḍu*), *anna* 'elder brother' (gender unmarked) are m sg, *pustaka-m* 'book' (*-m* is gender marker), *amma* 'mother' are non-m sg. Where the gender is not formally marked, it is expressed in the finite verbs, e.g. *anna*[1] *wacc-ǣ-ḍu*[2] 'the elder brother[1] came[2]', *amma*[1] *wacc-in-di*[2] 'mother[1] came[2]' (*-ḍu* and *-di* signal gender). Tolkāppiyam gives examples with identical subjects but with different agreement in finite verbs (Israel 1973: 24), e.g. *kōtai vantāṉ* 'Kotai (a man's name) came', *kōtai vandāḷ* 'Kotai (a woman's name) came', *kōtai vandadu* 'Kotai (an animal's name) came'. Overt marking of gender is found mostly among nouns, which are [+ human] following a universal pattern. 'There is a hierarchy determining overt gender marking in languages with semantic gender assignment: human > animal > other animate > other' (Aikhenvald 1996 MS: 10).

Numerals qualifying a noun marked [+ human] incorporate a human classifier, which is absent when they are used attributively to non-human nouns, e.g. Te. *mugguru*[1] *manuṣulu*[2] 'three persons', but *mūḍu*[1] *pustakālu*[2] 'three[1] books[2]'. The demonstrative pronouns reflect the basic contrasts of gender and number in different Dravidian languages. Gender and number are interrelated categories and have to be treated as a single system.

There are two numbers in Dravidian, singular and plural. The singular is unmarked in nouns. In personal and demonstrative pronouns it is possible to segment a marker for the singular, which is replaced by a plural morph in the plural. In Proto-Dravidian, a distinction was made between [+ high] and [− high] in plural marking. The feature [+ high] in South Dravidian I (and Telugu) and North Dravidian meant [+ human] (men, women, men and women), but in South Dravidian II (without Telugu) and Central Dravidian it meant [+ male hum], which could extend to mixed groups (men, men and women) but not to an exclusive group of women. The reconstructed morphemes are *-V*r* for [+ high], **-nk*(*k*), -Vḷ or a combination of these two as **-nk*(*k*)Vḷ for [−high]. All subgroups inherit -V*r*, but there is no clear-cut subgrouping in the case of the marker for [– human] plural. But we notice, in most of the languages, a gradual generalization of the [–human] plural for both classes of nouns. The original [+ human] suffix *-V*r* has very restricted use in modern literary languages also.

The languages of South Dravidian I have **-kkaḷ*, South Dravidian II (other than Telugu) and Brahui have **-nk*(*k*), Tuḷu of South Dravidian I and Central Dravidian have *V*ḷ* or **-nkk*-V*ḷ*. Telugu has *-V*ḷ*, but there are a few lexical items with **-nkk-aḷ* as plural which were reanalysed as stem *-nkk* and plural -V*ḷ*, e.g. Te.*mrānu* sg 'tree', *mrā*^{n}*ku-lu* pl 'trees' (< PD **maram-kkaḷ*).

6.2.1 ***Gender–number contrasts based on demonstrative pronouns***

Gender contrasts are presented below in each of the languages and also in some dialects, in terms of the demonstrative pronouns; for illustration, only the forms derived from the remote demonstrative root PD **aH*, which is the unmarked demonstrative, are taken.[2] It must be noted that gender and number are distinguished in Dravidian only in the third person. The first and second persons carry only a number distinction, unlike Modern Indo-Aryan in which male and female speakers and addressees have gender marking on the verb.

In table 6.1. each row has cells and each cell represents a semantic space occupied by one form. The maximum possible number of cells is six. If there is only one form occupying the space of two or three cells, its meaning also correspondingly expands to include those meanings. Thus in Telugu and the other South-Central Dravidian languages *adi* (corresponding to PD **atu*) means 'she, it' because it occupies the semantic space of 'she' (human female) and that of 'it' (non-human animate and inanimate).

6.2.2 ***Gender subsystems***

There are several subsystems of gender in different languages and subgroups and there is no total unanimity among scholars on the reconstruction of the category of gender for Proto-Dravidian. There are three dominant types of gender–number distinction in Dravidian, and each has been separately claimed to represent the Proto-Dravidian system, according to some scholars.

Type I in table 6.2 represented the proto-stage of South Dravidian I (Tamil, Malayāḷam, Koḍagu, Kuṟumba, Iruḷa, Toda, Kota, Kannaḍa and possibly Tuḷu), with five formal and semantic contrasts. In the plural the derivative of **awar* meant 'they' (men, men and women, or women).

[2] The reconstructions for the proximate demonstrative are **iw-anṯu*, **iw-aḷ*, **i-tu*, **iw-ar*, **iw-ay*. Here, the laryngeal **H* becomes *w* before *-a*, and is lost before a phonetic voiced stop [d] (see Krishnamurti 1997b).

Table 6.1. *Semantic and formal contrasts in the third-person demonstrative pronouns in different Dravidian languages*

Gloss	1 'he' (human)	2 'she' (human)	3 'it' (non-human)	4 'they' (human male)	5 'they' (human female)	6 'they' (non-human)
Proto	**awanṯu*	**awaḷ*	**atu*	**awar*	—	**away*
1. Ta.	*avaṉ*	*avaḷ*	*atu*	*avar*		*avai*
(Kāṇ.)	*ave*^{n}	*ava*	*adu*	*avru*		*adu*
(Eruk.)			*adu*			*ay*
2. Ma.	*avan*	*avaḷ*	*atu*	*avar*		*avai*
3. Koḍ.	*avën*	*ava*	*adï*	*ayŋga*		*adï*
4. Kuṟumba	*ava*^{n}	*ava*	*adu*	*avaru*		*adu*
5. Iruḷa	*ave ~ aven*	*ava ~ avaḷ*	*adu, adi*	*avaru*		*ave*
6. Toda			*aθ*			*aθām*
7. Kota	*avn*	*avḷ*	*ad*	*avr*		*ad*
8. Kannaḍa	*avaM, avanu*	*avaḷ*	*adu*	*avaru*		*avu*
(Gowda, S Havyaka)	*ãvã*		*adi*			*avu*
(Hālakki)	*avənu*	*avəḷu*	*adu*	*averu*		
9. Tuḷu	*āye*	*āḷï*	*avu*	*ākuḷu*		*aykuḷu*
				ārï		*avu*
10. Te.	*wā*^{n}*ḍu*		*adi*	*wāru*		*awi*
11. Go.	*ōr, ōṛ*		*ad*	*ōṛ/ōṛk*		*av*
(Koya)	*ōṇḍ*		*addu*	*ōr*		*avvu*
12. Kui	*aʔanju*		*ʔāri*	*āru*		*āvi*
13. Kuvi	*āasi*		*ādi*	*āri*	*āti*	
14. Koṇḍa	*vāṉru*		*adi*	*vār*		*avi*
15. Pengo	*avan*	*adel*	*adi*	*avar*	*avek*	*avaŋ*
16. Kol.	*am/amd*		*ad*	*avr*		*adav*
17. Naik.	*avnd*		*ad*	*avr*		*adav*
18. Pa.	*ōd/ōḍ*		*ad*	*ōr*		*av*
19. Oll.	*ōṇḍ*		*ad*	*ōr*		*av*
20. Gad.	*ōṇḍ*		*ad*	*ōr*		*av*
21. Kur.	*ās*		*ād*	*ār/abṛar*		*abṛā*
22.Malt.	*āh*		*āth*	*ār*		*āth*
23. Br.			*ōd*			*ōfk*

From this inherited type, some members have innovated certain changes which are idiosyncratic: the Kāṇikkāra dialect of Tamil, Koḍagu, Kuṟumba and Kota have replaced non-human plural **away* by the singular form **atu*. Two non-standard Kannaḍa dialects, Gowda and Southern Havyaka, have replaced **awaḷ* by **atu*, as found in South Dravidian II and Central Dravidian, or it could be a retention of the Proto-Dravidian system (see below). Hālakki Kannaḍa, on the other hand, extends the meaning of **awar*

Table 6.2. *Gender and number in South Dravidian I*

Type I		Singular		Plural	
Proto-form	**awan*[3]	**awaḷ*	**atu*	**awar*	**away*
Meaning	[he] (hum m)	[she] (hum f)	[it] (non-hum)	[they] (hum)	[they] (non-hum)

to non-human category also, replacing **away* (an unexpected change). Toda and the Erukala dialect of Tamil have lost gender distinction and preserved only the number distinction of singular and plural, i.e. Er. *atu*, To. *aθ* 'he, she, it', Er. *ay*, To. *aθām* 'they' (hum and non-hum).[4] Koḍagu hum pl *ayŋga* (< **aw*(V)-*nkaḷ*) is an independent innovation (analogical, based on the 1pl), which replaced the derivative of **awar* (see table 6.1).

Table 6.3. *Gender and number in South Dravidian SD II minus Telugu and Central Dravidian*

Type II		Singular	Plural	
Proto-form	**awanṯu*	**atu*	**awar*	**away*
Meaning	[he] (hum m)	[she, it] (hum f and non-hum)	[they] (hum [men])	[they] (hum f and non-hum)

Type II with two contrasts in the singular and two in the plural is found in all South Dravidian II languages except Telugu (Gondi, Koṇḍa, Kui, Kuvi, Pengo, Manḍa) and in all Central Dravidian languages (Kolami, Naiki, Parji, Ollari, Gadaba). What is important to note is that the semantic range of **awar* 'they' encompasses 'men' or 'men and women', but not an exclusive group of 'women' as in the case of South Dravidian I. Both in form and in meaning the singular and plural are symmetrical, singular male human vs. others, plural male human vs. others, except that the male human form may also signal mixed groups of 'men and women' in plural. Deviations from this type are explainable: Pengo has a six-way contrast, *avan* 'he', *adel* 'she', *adi* 'it', *avar* 'they (men, men and women)', *avek* 'they (women)', *avaŋ* 'they' (non-human and inanimate); *adel* consists of *ad* (3n-m sg) plus *-el* derived from **āḷ* 'woman' (cf. **aw-aḷ* of South

[3] PD **awanṯu* lost the final syllable in South Dravidian I as a shared innovation, because all members of this subgroup have *avan* as the 3m sg. Only Kannaḍa human plural forms like *magand-ir* 'sons' are relics preserving the original stem-final *-nṯ* which synchronically is treated as part of the suffix (see fn. 9).

[4] Such a loss of gender must have independently taken place in Brahui of North Dravidian also.

Dravidian I); *avek* is an innovation formed by adding a 'female human' derivative suffix *-k* used in noun morphology to the inherited non-human *ave* (< **away*); *avaŋ* is similarly innovated by adding a common plural suffix *-ŋ* to the base *ava-* .(cf. Pengo *gaṛce-k* 'girls', *kōḍi-ŋ* 'cows').[5]

Table 6.4. *Gender and number in Telugu and North Dravidian*

Type III		Singular	Plural	
Proto-form	**awanṯu*	**atu*	**awar*	**away*
Meaning	[he]	[she, it]	[they]	[they]
	(hum m)	(hum f and non-hum)	(hum)	(non-hum)

This type is found in Telugu[6] of South Dravidian II and in Kuṛux and Malto of North Dravidian. Although there are only four contrasts, two in the singular and two in the plural, the meaning of **awar* 'men, men and women, women' and of **away* 'they (non-hum)' is like that of Type I. In the singular, the contrasts are like those of Type II. Malto created a covert distinction between the feminine and neuter in certain cases, e.g. *ade-n* 'her', but *adi-n* 'it (acc)'; similarly *ade-t: adi-t* (instr), *ade-nte: adi-nte* (abl), *ade-no: adi-no* (loc). This contrast is not found in genitive *adi-ki* and dative *adi-k* (Mahapatra 1979: 77). Telugu has created separate lexical forms to denote a woman, e.g. *āme*, *āviḍa* 'that woman', but the agreement in finite verbs is the same non-masculine suffix *-di*.

Now the question is which of these three types represents Proto-Dravidian.

6.2.3 *Reconstruction of Proto-Dravidian gender*

Emeneau (1955b: §10.17) followed by Subrahmanyam (1969: §§6, 9; 1976) and Shanmugam (1971a: 123) consider Type III to represent Proto-Dravidian since it is found in languages from different subgroups and the system is skewed. Jules Bloch (1954: 5–7) and Krishnamurti (1961, §4.30, 1975b: 334–46) consider Type II to be the original from which Types I and III can be derived as typologically motivated innovations. Burrow and Bhattacharya (1953: §12) consider the South Dravidian system (Type I) as proto. I do not see any reason to change my earlier stand that Type II represents

[5] Burrow and Bhattacharya have drawn attention to this innovation (1970: 24–5). They say that the 'feminine' is distinguished from the neuter 'in the plural of verbs, and in the plural of adjectives and pronouns, by the use of the termination *-k*, contrasting with neuter *-ŋ*' (1970: 24).

[6] Corbett (1991: 153), while discussing gender overlap ('she' is non-masculine in the singular but human in plural) in Modern Telugu, speaks of 'three controller genders' and 'two target genders', perhaps correlating with semantic and grammatical contrasts. Thus 'feminine' and 'neuter' are controller genders but the use of *-di* in verbal agreement for *adi* 'she, it' is taken as a non-masculine target gender.

Proto-Dravidian. The arguments given in detail in Krishnamurti 1975a are summarized here:

1. It would be much simpler to motivate innovations which resulted in Types I and III from II than the reverse. The innovation in South Dravidian I (Type I) is the creation of a feminine singular category in **awaḷ* by adding the derivative suffix *-*aḷ* to the underlying root **aw-*, a process also found in noun morphology, e.g. **mak-anṯu* 'son', **mak-aḷ* 'daughter' [4616]. In the case of plural the difference is one of semantic extension of 'men' > 'men and women' > 'women', because of **awar* being the natural choice to represent mixed groups of 'men and women'. We can even say that the first part in semantic extension took place within Proto-Dravidian itself (see Krishnamurti 1975a: §12). The later shift in Types I and III is the use of **awar* to mean exclusive group(s) of women. This last change did not take place in Central Dravidian and South Central Dravidian.[7] On the contrary, it would be difficult to motivate a change in South-Central Dravidian (South Dravidian II) and Central Dravidian from Types I or III to II, i.e. splitting the meaning of 'men and women' by assigning 'women' to the non-human group signalled by **away*. What could be the linguistic or sociological contexts in which such a semantic shift would be induced? Therefore, Type II is a plausible candidate to represent the Proto-Dravidian gender system.

2. The creation of **awaḷ* in South Dravidian I has restricted the meaning of **atu* to non-human animate and inanimate in the singular. Similarly the extension of **awar* to human has restricted the meaning of **away* in South Dravidian I (plus Telugu) and North Dravidian to non-human animate and inanimate.

3. Telugu, being a major literary Dravidian language, has a great deal of give and take with the other literary languages of South Dravidian, Tamil and Kannaḍa. This explains why it was influenced by the semantic shift of the other literary South Dravidian languages in the case of [+ high] plural, while retaining the inherited system in the singular. A similar shift independently in Kuṛux–Malto only shows the naturalness of the semantic change involved.

4. South-Central Dravidian (South Dravidian II) and Central Dravidian are genetically distinct subgroups and their sharing a common gender system would show that it is a shared retention and not a shared innovation. Note that PD **awanṯu* (nominative, **awan* oblique) is preserved in South Dravidian II, Central Dravidian and North Dravidian,

[7] There are independent and isolated innovations in different languages involving the 'human female' subcategory. Note *avek* 'they (women)' was innovated only by Pengo in South Dravidian II (table 6.1). In Gadaba the finite verb suffix for m pl, *-ar*, is found in some sentences as agreeing with subject nouns meaning 'women', instead of the expected *-av*; Texts II: 98. *āsmaskil uṇkun kēdar*, 99. *ōr pāṭel pārdar*, 98. 'Women will do planting of seedlings', 99. 'They will sing songs' (Bhaskararao 1980: 75, 83, also cf. 15). In Malto the accusative case inflection is *ad-in* 'her', but *ad-en* 'it' (acc) from the same pronoun *ād* 'she, it' (Mahapatra 1979: 13). These illustrate the naturalness of the grammatical change in question.

being a retention. But South Dravidian I has lost *-ṯu of the nominative and analogically restructured the nominative as **awan* on the oblique (cf. a similar independent change in Pengo). In Koṇḍa also, a similar loss of the final syllable occurs in finite verbs, when they are not followed by a vowel; e.g. *vānṟu kitan* 'he did', but *vānṟu kitanṟ-a?* 'Did he do?'[8]

5. In derivational morphology *-*ar* is the plural of *-*anṯ* 3m sg. It would then make sense to consider *-*ar* to originally mean 'men' before it extended to 'persons'.

6. The only argument in favour of Type III being the proto is that it is shared by members of diverse subgroups, Telugu of South Dravidian II and Kuṛux–Malto of North Dravidian. As a general principle this is fine, but it cannot be applied as a rule of thumb. In that case, the lack of gender in Toda and Brahui should be considered proto since they are from widely separated branches of the family. Item (4) above uses the same argument as well as many others to consider Type II as reflecting the Proto-Dravidian situation. (For further elaboration, see Krishnamurti 1975a.)

6.2.4 *Gender-number marking in finite verbs*

The pronominal suffixes in finite verbs, which agree with subject NPs, are closely related in form to the demonstrative pronouns and are reconstructible for Proto-Dravidian, i.e. *-*anṯ* m sg (> *-*an* in South Dravidian I), -V*r* m pl or hum pl, *-*at* n–m sg ; in the case of non-masculine plural, the widely distributed reconstruction is *-*aw* in South Dravidian I, South Dravidian II and Central Dravidian. There are, however, several exceptions to the proto system. The number of contrasts in verb concord is sometimes less, but never more, than the number of contrasts specified by the demonstrative pronouns.

Within South Dravidian I, the Kāṇikkāra and Erukala dialects of Tamil, Modern Malayāḷam, Koḍagu, Kuṟumba and Toda have lost gender distinction in the verb system either by a total loss of agreement features in personal suffixes (as in Modern Malayāḷam) or by extending the distribution of the non-human singular suffix, as in Koḍagu, and Toda. In Kuṟumba and Kota, the third neuter singular is extended to the plural also. In Kuṟumba *-ad* occurs in the singular for 'he, she, it' and for the neuter plural 'they'; *-o* occurs corresponding to *V*r* with the loss of *-r*.

In South-Central Dravidian, Gondi and Pengo have extended the velar suffix *-*kk*, *-*nk* of non-person plural to verbs, taken from the noun morphology. Pengo, which has a six-way distinction in subject pronouns, has a five-way distinction in verb agreement, with one morpheme *-at* for feminine singular and non-human singular, true to the subgroup trait. All other South-Central Dravidian and Central Dravidian languages have a four-way contrast in verb agreement corresponding to subject pronouns.

[8] The independent developments in Koṇḍa and Pengo point to the naturalness of the loss of the final unaccented syllable in a free form.

Kuṛux and Malto use the same form for the singular and plural non-human, as is the case with Later Tamil and Kota (Subrahmanyam 1971: 401–2). Brahui, which has retained only number and lost all gender distinction, preserves the traces of Proto-Dravidian contrasts in form in pronouns and in verb agreement, e.g. *ōd* 'he, she, it', *ōfk* 'they' (< **at* and **aw*(*a*) + *kk*); in the verbs *ē*, *as*, *ār*(*a*), *ur* occur in the singular and *ir*, *ēr*, *ira*, *or*, *ur*, *as* in the plural. It is apparent that these can be traced to PD *-*anṯ*, *-V*r* on formal grounds. It therefore appears that Brahui originally had a four-way contrast of gender–number as in the other two North Dravidian languages.

6.2.5 *Gender-number marking in nominal derivation*

The determination of gender in Dravidian is mostly based on meaning and not on form as the preceding description shows. There are, however, certain derivational morphemes, which may denote either lexical (sex) or grammatical gender. But true grammatical gender is expressed by the anaphoric use of pronouns, or by numeral or verbal agreement. The markers are *-*an-ṯ*/*-*wan-ṯ* (male or masculine singular in Proto-Dravidian), *-*aḷ*, *-*i* (female or feminine singular in South Dravidian, South-Central Dravidian, North Dravidian), *-*ar*/*-*war* (masculine plural/human: Proto-Dravidian); *-(*n*)*k*(*k*)*a* (South-Central Dravidian, Brahui), *-*ḷ* (Central Dravidian, Telugu, Tuḷu), or a combination of the two as *-(*n*)*k*(*k*)*aḷ* (common or originally non-human plural: South Dravidian, Central Dravidian, Tuḷu). Cardinal, elicited numerals have neuter (non-person) concord, but, when they classify persons, the derivative suffix *-*war* is added to the numeral root morpheme, e.g. Tamil *mūnṟu* 'three things', but *mū-var* 'three persons'. The common plural form, *-*nkk*V*ḷ*, has progressively replaced the human plural and it appears to be a trend already prevalent in the pre-divided stage of Proto-Dravidian. Even in Caṅkam Tamil we note the use of *-kaḷ* added to *-ar* as a plural marker, e.g. *arac-ar-kaḷ* 'kings' (Kalittokai 25:3) (see Rajam 1992: 272).

The gender–number marking (lexical in some and grammatical in others) is illustrated below for most of the languages (largely based on Shanmugam 1971a: 30–103, Zvelebil 1977: 12–16).

South Dravidian: *-*an*/*-*wan*, *-*aḷ*, *-*i*; *-*ar*/*-*war*, *-*k*(*k*)*aḷ*.

1. Tamil: *kaḷ-vaṉ* 'thief', *kaḷ-vi* 'a female thief', *mak-aṉ* 'son', *mak-aḷ* 'daughter', *tōẓ-i* 'a female friend', *kaḷ-var* 'thieves', *kēḷ-ir* 'relatives', *ai-var-kaḷ* 'five persons' (*-kaḷ* added to *-var*, Classical Tamil); *yāṇṭu-kaḷ* 'years', *maraṅ-kaḷ* 'trees', the use of *-kaḷ* to denote plural neuter is extremely rare in Tamil. Modern Tamil loses the final *-ḷ*, *maran-ka* 'trees', *pasu-kka* 'cows' etc.
2. Malayāḷam: *taṭṭ-an* 'goldsmith', *mak-aḷ* 'daughter', *kora-tt-i* 'a Korava woman', *īẓa-var* 'toddy-tappers', *iru-var* 'two persons', *aṭṭu-kaḷ* 'leeches', *maraṅ-ṅaḷ* 'trees', *paśu-kkaḷ* 'cows'.

3. Kota: *kurḍ-n* 'blind man', *kaḷ-i* 'female thief', *av-r* 'those persons', *āḷ-gūḷ* 'people', *nāy-gūḷ* 'dogs', *marm-gūḷ* 'trees'.
4. Toda: *koḷ-ṇ* 'thief', *toḷx-t-y* 'woman of goldsmith caste', *mīm-i* 'mother-in-law', *mox-ām* 'boys', *pūf-ām* 'flowers'.
5. Koḍagu: *kaḷḷ-ën* 'male thief', *kaḷḷ-i* 'female thief', *kaḷḷa-(r)* 'thieves', *mū-vë* 'three persons', *tōḷën-ga(ḷ)* 'wolves', *aṇṇa-ṅga(ḷ)* 'elder brothers'. [Koḍagu loses word-final liquids.]
6. Kannaḍa: *aras-an* 'king', *mag-an* 'son', *aras-i* 'queen', *mag-aḷ* 'daughter', *pola-ti* 'an outcaste woman' (see section 6.2.6 below for *-t*), *aras-ar* 'kings', *kaḷḷ-ar* 'thieves', *magan-dir*[9] 'sons', *tāy-vir* 'mothers', *mane-gaḷ* 'houses', *gorav-ar-kaḷ* 'masters' (the last in an inscription of the ninth century; see Gai 1946: 28), *nāy-guḷu* 'dogs'.
7. Tuḷu: *kurḍ-e* 'blind man', *kurḍ-i* 'blind woman', *ajj-erï* 'grandfathers', *ir-verï* 'two persons', *pili-kḷu* 'tigers', *pū-kuḷu* 'flowers'; *arasu-ḷu* 'kings', *pucce-ḷu* 'cats'.[10]

South-Central Dravidian: **-an-ṯ*/ **-wan-ṯ*, **-aḷ*, **-i*; *-Vr, *-(*n*)*k*(*k*)V. Here, the derived female forms do not represent the feminine gender. A female human plural **-si-kk* has developed as an innovation in all these languages, except Telugu.

8. Telugu: *tammu-ṇḍu* 'younger brother', *kōḍ-alu* 'daughter-in-law', *iru-wuru* 'two persons', *rāju-lu* 'kings', *tōṭa-lu* 'gardens'. An older *-(*n*)*kkaḷ* reanalysed as -(*n*)*kk*- and -V*ḷ* can be detected in certain forms like *mrānu* 'tree': *mrā*^{n}*-kulu* 'trees', *goḍugu* 'umbrella' : *goḍugu-lu* 'umbrellas' (< PD **maram*, **koṭ*-V-); (*-lu* plural from *-*ḷ*V is an exception in this subgroup.)
9. Gondi: *tott-ōr* 'ancestor' (*-ōr* < **ōṟ* < **awaṟ* < **awa-nṟu*), *sēlāṟ* (pl *sēlā-hk*) 'younger sister' (from **sēl-āḷ-sk*), *pēṟ-ī* 'girl', *kanḍ-īr* 'boys', *mar-k* 'sons', *kaṭ-k* 'eyes', *mārē-ng* 'plumes', *piṭṭē-ng* 'birds'.
10. Koṇḍa: *kaṭka-yen* 'miserly person', *kaṇ-i* 'blind woman', *ana-si-r* 'older brothers', *rās-ku* 'kings', *noṟes-ku* 'tigers', *bīb-si-k* 'elder sisters', *kome-ŋ* 'branches', *ṟēto-ŋ*, 'crabs'.

[9] This particular plural form belongs to a small class preserved in Early Kannaḍa in an inscription of the eighth century (Gai 1946: 28) where the historically correct analysis was *magand-ir* (< **mak-anṯ-*). But by reanalysing it on the presumption that the stem was *magan-*, the grammarians treated *-dir* as the plural suffix. There were also in Old Kannaḍa *avand-ir* 'those persons', *ivand-ir* 'these persons' in which the stems reflect Proto-Dravidian **awanṯ-* and **iwanṯ-* (Ramachandra Rao 1972: 54). In Middle and Modern Kannaḍa, *-ndru* has become a productive human plural suffix, added to kinship terms (see Krishnamurti 1975a: 340, Kushalappa Gowda 1972: 218).

[10] The use of *-ḷu* as a plural marker in the last two examples is found only in Tuḷu in South Dravidian I. This was one of the reasons to class Tuḷu with Central Dravidian earlier. Later in this chapter it is argued that *-*ḷ* is a retention of a Proto-Dravidian plural sign in Telugu, Tuḷu and the Central Dravidian languages.

11. Kui: *tōṛ-enju* 'friend' (*-nj* < **-nṯ*), *gah-ali* (pl *gah-al-ska*) 'sweeper woman', *dāda-ru* 'elder brothers', *tōṛe-ŋga* 'male friends', *kōr-ka* 'buffaloes', *kōḍi-ŋga* 'cows'.
12. Kuvi: *kūt-ka* (*kūndu* sg) 'mushrooms', *kōma-ŋga* 'branches', *seppu-ŋa* 'shoes'.
13. Pengo: *ṭoṇḍ-en* 'brother', *toṛnd-el* 'sister', *ṭoṇḍ-ar* 'brothers', *ā-cku* 'women', *kogle-k* 'women', *kōḍi-ŋ* 'cows'.
14. Manḍa: *nā-mga-hke* (< **nā-magaḷ-ska*) 'my daughters', *hūlpand-el* 'a beautiful woman', *kaṛd-er* 'boys', *kan-ke* 'eyes', *pṛē-ke* 'bones', *tūku-ŋ* 'feathers' (Burrow 1976: 42–3).

Central Dravidian: **-an-ṯ*, **-aḷ*, *-V*r*, *-*ḷ*, *-(*k*)*k*V*ḷ*; innovated: **-cil*, **-til*.

15. Kolami: *tōr-en* (with loss of final *-d*, cf. Parji) 'younger brother', *komm-al* 'daughter', *mās-ur* 'men', *doŋga-l* 'thieves', *gār-sil* 'hail stones', *ella-gul* 'houses'.
16. Parji: *tol-ed* (obl. *tol-en*) 'brother' (*-ed* < **-eḏ* < **-aḏ* < **-an- ḏ*), *kēt-al* 'widow', *tol-er* 'brothers', *mayi-l* 'husbands', *tulla-kul* 'weavers', *puṛut-il* 'insects', *vār-til* 'roots', *ēnu-cil* 'elephants'.
17. Ollari: *maggi-inḍ* 'man', *koṛ-al* 'son's wife', *il-er* 'bridegrooms', *ki-l* 'hands', *gar-sil* 'hail stones', *sir-kil* 'buffalos', *aya-sil* 'wives', *kanīr-til* 'tears', *ile-v* 'brides'.

North Dravidian: **-an-ṯ*/**-wan-ṯ*, **-i*, *-V*r*/*-*w*V*r*; **-kk* (the last only in Brahui).

18. Kuṛux: *āl-as* 'man', *āl-i* 'woman', *āl-ar* 'men' (neu pl *guṭhī* is apparently not Dravidian, e.g. *man guṭhī* 'trees').
19. Malto: *maq-e* 'son', *qal-we* 'thief', *maq-i* 'girl', *mal-er* 'men'.
20. Brahui: *bā-k* 'mouths', *puṭ-āk* 'hairs'.

6.2.6 ***Reconstruction of gender–number suffixes***

The suffixes that can be reconstructed for Proto-Dravidian are *-anṯ* for masculine singular (in derivation, male human singular), *-aḷ*, *-i* for feminine or female human singular and -V*r* for [+ high] plural (either male human or simply human plural, depending on the language and subgroup). Within Proto-Dravidian itself it appears that **-anṯ* / **-wanṯ* and **-ar*/*-*w*V*r* occurred as allomorphs of masculine singular and masculine plural, respectively. Kuṛux *xal-b-as* 'thief', *xal-b* 'theft' and Malto *qal-we* 'theft' would lead us to relate *w-*/*b-* to the **w* of **-wanṯ* (see Shanmugam 1971a: 107–8). But, alternatively, -**w* could be an abstract noun-forming suffix derived from PD **-way* also (see section 5.8), to which the gender marker *-as* (< **-anṯ*) was added. In any case, I think that these allomorphs **-anṯ* ~ **-wanṯ* go to Proto-Dravidian; the second allomorph was due to reanalysing *w-* as part of the suffix, separating *a-*, *i-*, *u-* as the deictic roots. I have identified the deictic roots as **aH-*, **iH-*, **uH-* and proposed a rule **H* → *w*/__ + *a*, by which **aw-anṯu*, **iw-anṯu* and **uw-anṯu*, **aw-ar*, **aw-ay*, etc. were derived. This rule was extended to environments of following semivowels also in Early Tamil: *aw-yāṉai* 'that elephant' (see section 4.5.7.2 c; Krishnamurti 1997b). The laryngeal was assimilated to a following voiceless stop or was dropped before voiced stops: **aH + kaṭal →* *ak-kaṭal* 'that sea', **aH-t ∼ *aH-tu → att- ∼ a-tu* [*adu*]. When it was not bound, **aH* was contracted to **ā* in all subgroups. These developments explain how the analogical restructuring of **-waṉṯ* and **-war* could go to the late stages of Proto-Dravidian itself.

South Dravidian I had two clear shared innovations: (i) The loss of **ṯ* in nominative singular (see fn. 3 above) and (ii) the creation of *awaḷ* as feminine singular. The final **ṯ* (perhaps a nominative marker) is preserved in all other subgroups – South Dravidian II, Central Dravidian and North Dravidian. Certain other consonants occur before the gender suffixes, which have to be taken as stem formatives and not part of the gender markers, e.g. **-kk-anṯu* in Ta. *mutu-kk-aṉ*, Te. *muduk-ā̃ḍu*, Pa. Oll. *mutt-ak*; **-tt-anṯu/*-tt-i* in Ta. Ma. *oru-tt-an* 'one man', *oru-tt-i* 'one woman', beside *oru-vaṉ*, has cognates in Te. *ōr-ti* 'one woman', Kuṛ. *or-ot*, Malt. *or-te* 'one man'. With the loss of the gender marker, it could be that the stem formatives took over the function of marking gender in Parji, Gadaba, Kuṛux and Malto.

The feminine suffix **-aḷ/*-āḷ* is found in South Dravidian I and South Dravidian II and Central Dravidian as part of their derivational morphology in several items denoting a female person, e.g. **mak-aḷ* 'daughter' (South Dravidian I, South Dravidian II) [4616], **kōẓ-āḷ* 'daughter-in law' (South Dravidian II and Central Dravidian) [2149]. An innovation of Central Dravidian is to create three sets of derived nouns by adding gender suffixes to numerals one to three (see numerals in this chapter).

There were two plural suffixes in Proto-Dravidian, -V*r* for [+ high] also called the epicene plural and **-(n)kk*V, **ḷ* and *(n)kk*V*ḷ* for [– high], neuter or non-human plural. The latter one became generalized as the normal plural suffix in different languages. There is no dispute about the reconstruction of the first. The 3 hum pl suffix -V*r* occurred as plural marker of masculine/human nouns in all literary languages in their earlier stages, but it was gradually replaced by the neuter plural which came to be known as the common plural. Examples: Ta. *kēḷ-ir* 'relatives', Ka. *kaḷḷ-īr* 'thieves', Te. *allu-ru* 'sons-in-law'. In the modern languages, the demonstrative pronouns still show *-ar*, Ta. Ma. *av-ar*, Ka. *avru*, Te. *wāru* (for the other languages see table 6.1). The agreement marker in the finite verbs is also retained as -V*r*, Ta. *avaru pōrāru* 'They are going' (3 pol sg), Te. *wāḷḷu weḷtāru* 'They will go', *wāru weḷtāru* 'He (pol) will go'. The -V*r* is also retained in the plural of human numerals, Ta. *iruvar* 'two persons', Ka. *ibbaru* id., OTe. *iruwuru*, Mdn Te. *mu-gguru* 'three persons' from earlier *mū-guru* < *mū-wuru*. The languages of South Dravidian II and Central Dravidian also preserve the [+ high] plural marker in numerals and finite verbs, Koṇḍa *riʔer* 'two persons', *vār vātar* 'they came'.

The neuter plural *-(*n*)*kaḷ* used in South Dravidian I was considered a combination of two suffixes *-(*n*)*kk*V and *-*ḷ* by Jules Bloch (1954: 10). He says, 'The guttural alone is common to the whole family.' Even by the Early Caṅkam period -*kaḷ* was becoming a common plural, e.g. *arac-ar-kaḷ* 'kings'. The variant *-(*n*)*kk* occurs in South Dravidian II and Brahui; *-*ḷ* occurs as one of the plurals in Central Dravidian and Tuḷu. Telugu has generalized *-*ḷ*. All languages of South Dravidian I and Central Dravidian have reflexes of *-(*k*)*kaḷ*. The suffix shared by South Dravidian II and Brahui must be a retention and not a shared innovation; so also, *-*ḷ* must be a retention because it is shared by Telugu, Tuḷu and Central Dravidian. The combination of these two into *-(*n*)*kk*V*ḷ* must be an innovation in South Dravidian I and Central Dravidian, representing a shared isogloss.

6.2.7 ***Conclusion***

From a synchronic and diachronic study of gender–number in Dravidian, the following general observations can be made:

1. Reduction in gender–number distinctions tends to be a typologically motivated and not a genetically inherited change; therefore, it does not serve always as a strong basis of subgrouping.
2. The number of gender–number contrasts in governed positions (e.g. finite verbs) is never larger than in governing positions (Subject NPs).
3. Category simplification (neutralization) takes place more often in governed positions than in governing positions.
4. In neutralization, there are cases of suspension of (a) both number and gender (Malayāḷam in verbs) or (b) suspension of gender but retention of number (Kannaḍa dialects, Gowda and Southern Havyaka in verbs, Toda and Brahui in pronouns), but no language retains gender alone totally suspending number (also see Greenberg 1963: 95, Universals 36 and 37).
5. In neutralization, it is more often the unmarked categories (singular in number and non-masculine in gender) that extend their ranges of usage than the marked ones. Thus non-masculine **atu* (sg) replaces **away* (pl), and these two replace masculine **awaṉṯu* and **awar*, respectively, and not vice versa. There is one exception to this statement in the Hālakki dialect of Kannaḍa (see table 6.1, Kannaḍa).
6. In gender–number reconstruction, contrasts in subject pronouns are more basic and primary than agreement features in verbs.

6.3 **Cases**

Case relations in Dravidian are expressed either by bound morphemes or by grammaticalized nouns or verbs, called postpositions. We will begin with case markers, which are reconstructible, and then deal with postpositions of individual languages. The nominative case is unmarked. The noun is used in its elicitation form in the nominative singular; in the plural it is the noun with the plural suffix. A final consonant or syllable found in the nominative is sometimes missing in non-nominative cases, e.g. Ta. *mara-m*/*mara-n̲* 'tree': Ta. *mara-tt-ai* 'tree' (acc), *mara-tt-in-* (gen) 'of a tree', Ka. *mara* 'tree', *mara-da-* 'of a tree'. Here, one can technically consider *-m* as the nominative singular, but it does not make the analysis any simpler. The plural forms retain the final *-m*: Ta. *maraṅ-kaḷ* (nom pl) 'trees', *maraṅ-kaḷ-ai* (acc pl) 'trees'. Therefore, it would be much simpler to propose Ø marking in the nominative and posit loss or addition of any element to the stem when it occurs with other cases.

The demonstrative and interrogative masculine forms based on the deictic roots as well as certain masculine nouns end in **-nṯu* in nominative singular in Proto-Dravidian, e.g. **awa-nṯu* 'he', **maka-nṯu* 'son'. The oblique stem occurs without the final **-ṯu* in all the languages. It is, therefore, technically correct to consider **-ṯu* as nominative singular which is replaced by **-r* in the plural. In the languages of South Dravidian I, the final **-ṯu* was lost as a shared innovation in the nominative singular, i.e. the nominative was restructured on the analogy of the oblique base ending in *-n*, e.g **awan-*. With the exception of these two cases, the nominative case does not carry any marking.

6.3.1 *The oblique stem*

The non-nominative cases are called the oblique cases. Some noun stems add certain suffixes or augments to form the oblique stem. These elements were called 'inflectional increments' by Caldwell. It is difficult to predict or define the phonological or semantic properties of stems that have different forms between the nominative and the oblique cases. The 'inflectional increments' are called *cāriyai* ('signs, markers') by Tolkāppiyam and *upavibhakti* (co-cases) in traditional Telugu grammars. In modern descriptions they are called 'empty morphs', 'link morphs' or 'augments'. Their function is to make the stem eligible to receive case markers. I call them augments, which is a neutral term. They have no semantic content. But in several languages, the oblique stem is identical in form with the genitive case form, which is used as an attribute to a following noun. In Telugu, an oblique stem can either take a case suffix or syntactically function as an adnominal, e.g. *kannu* 'eye', obl *kaṇ-ṭi*, with case marking *kaṇṭi-ki* 'to the eye', *kaṇṭi-tō* 'with the eye'; syntactically, *kaṇṭi*^{1} *pāpa*^{2} 'the pupil^2 of the eye^1'. The following augments can be reconstructed for individual subgroups or the whole family, as the case may be.

6.3.1.1 *-tt-

South Dravidian I The most widely represented augment is **-tt-* which occurred in Pre-Tamil after nouns of (C)VCV*m*/*n̲* type. It replaces the final nasal. The reflexes of this can be found in Tamil, Malayāḷam, Iruḷa, Koḍagu, Toda and Kota. Kannaḍa and Tuḷu have *-d-* correspondingly:

Old Tamil: Neuter nouns ending in *-a*] *m* replace *-m* by *-tt-* as an augment, e.g. *mara-m*/*-ṉ* 'tree': *mara-tt-* in all cases, except the sociative *-oṭu* in Old Tamil, *mara-ttu-kku* 'to a tree', *mara-tt-il* 'in a tree', but *kālam-oṭu* 'with time' (Shanmugam 1971a: 201–3). Also stems of three morae (C)V̄CV/(C)VCVCV, in which the final syllable is *-ṭu*/*-ṟu*, add the augment *-tt-*, *kāṭu* 'forest': *kāṭṭ-il* 'in the forest' (< **kāṭ-tt-*), *kaḷiṟu* 'male elephant', *kaḷiṟṟ-oṭu* 'with a male elephant'. These two types are further generalized in Modern Tamil; even loanwords ending in *-m* like Skt. *dūram* 'distance' and Eng. *sisṭem* (system) replace the final *-m* by *-tt-* before case suffixes. Modern Tamil also has the obliques of stems ending in *-ṭu* and *-ru* (< *ṟu*) as *kāṭṭ-*, *ātt-* (< *āṟṟ*), respectively (Schiffman 1999: 25–6). Note that Old Tamil *ṯṯ* becomes *tt* in Modern Tamil.

Malayāḷam has a parallel pattern; neuter nouns ending in *-am* and stems in final *-ṭu*/*-ṯu* add *-tt* as augment. Final *-m*/*-n* is dropped and sandhi will result in the gemination of retroflex and alveolar voiceless stops as in Tamil, *mara-tt-āl* (instr), *kāṭṭ-āl* 'by the forest', *cōṟṟ-il* 'in the rice'. Modern Malayāḷam obligatorily takes two augments *-tt-* and *-in-* in dative and genitive cases, *mara-tt-in* 'of the tree' (Asher and Kumari 1997: 191–4).

Iruḷa has *-tt-* for stems ending in *-am*, *mara-tt-e* 'tree' (acc), *kelaca-t-ke* 'for work' (dat); *-tt-* is also extended to human nouns, e.g. *rāman-itt-i* 'in Raman', *avaḷ-itt-i* 'in her' (Perialwar 1978b: 7–9).

Koḍagu adds *-t-* after nouns ending in *-am*, e.g. *maram* 'tree': *mara-t-na*/ *mara-tï-na* (acc), *mara-t-iñji* (abl), *mara-t-lï* (loc).

Toda has *-t-* as oblique marker which replaces a stem-final nasal (*-n*, *-ṇ*, *-m*), e.g. *mēṇ* 'tree': *mēṇ-t-k* 'to a tree', *neln-* 'ground': *nelt-*, *īrm-* 'dampness': *īrt-*; also in the class of forms that had an underlying *-ṭ*/*-ṯ*, *kwī̄ṛ* 'horn': *kwī̄ṭ-*, *āṟ* 'way, road': *āṯ-*. The same marker is extended to other classes, *nes̱of* 'moonlight': *nes̱ot-*; *-t*, *-d*, *-θ* are all added to stems in the genitive case (Emeneau 1984: 70–6).

Kota has *-t* in inherited stems in final *-m*, *-ṛ*, *-r*, e.g. *mar-m* 'tree': *mar-t-n* 'tree' (acc), *mol-m* 'hare': *molm-t-k* 'to the hare', **nāṛ-t-* → *nāṭ-* 'country', **vēr-t-* → *vēṯ-* 'root'.

Kannaḍa has *-d-*, perhaps a weakened variant of *-tt-* in the class of neuter stems ending in *-am*, *mara-d-a* (gen) 'of the tree', *mara-d-inda* (instr–abl) 'by the tree', in genitive, instrumental–ablative and locative cases. Baḍaga also has *-d* in *a*-ending stems, *mara-d-ō* 'in the tree', *hāva-d-enda* 'by the snake'.

Tuḷu has *-ta* and *-da* as genitive markers in complementary classes of stems, e.g. *pū-ta* 'flower' (gen), *kañji-da* 'calf' (gen); the ablative case marker is given as *-ttï*. It is not clear if the dental element is to be interpreted as an augment or part of the case suffixes. Note that it recurs in two cases. Correspondingly, the neuter demonstrative nouns have *-ta* and *-tɨ*, *ay-t-a* 'that' (gen), *ay-tɨ* (abl). After human nouns the genitive is *-na*, which shows that *-a* can be treated as the genitive suffix and *-t-* and *-n-* as augments (Bhat 1967: 85–7). Koraga has *-tt*/*-t* in non-human stems in all three dialects, e.g. *mara-tt-a* (acc), *erdï* 'ox': *erdï-ta-* (Bhat 1971: 7, 2, 40).

South Dravidian II Telugu has *-t-i* (< **-tt-i*) as oblique-genitive marker[11] in stems of three morae ending in **-ṭu* [-ḍu] and **-ṯu* [-ṟu], *nāḍu* 'country': *nāṭi-*, *ēṟu* 'river, stream': *ēṭi-ki* 'to the river'; disyllabic stems in final V̄*yi*/V̆*ṟu* replace the final syllable by *-ti*, e.g. *cēyi* 'hand': *cē-ti-*, *paṟu* (also spelt *paṟṟu*) 'village name suffix, low land': **paṟ-ti*/*par-ti*. These processes and forms also continue in Modern Telugu, except for the merger of OTe. *ṟ* with *r* (< **r*).

In Gondi, singular nouns of the non-human category in final *-a* or a sonorant consonant *-n*, *-r*, *-ṛ*, *-m* take the *-t* augment, *lōn* ~ *rōn* 'house' (< **ḷōn*/*ṛōn* < **oḷ-an*): *rō-t-āl* 'from the house', *mara(n)* 'tree': *mara-t-*, *nār* 'village': **nār-t-* → *nāṭ-[ē* 'in the village' (here *r* is from Pre-Gondi **ṟ*). Monosyllabic stems in final liquids and semivowels add *-d* as the oblique marker, e.g. *kay* 'hand: *kay-d-*, *kāl* 'leg': *kāl-d-ē* 'with the leg', *nēl* 'field': *nēd-*. There are distributional differences between dialects (Rao 1987b: 139–48).

In Koṇḍa non-masculine stems ending in vowels or nasals take *-di* as the oblique formative, e.g. *ayli* 'girl': *ayli-di-ŋ* (acc–dat), *guṟam* 'horse': *guṟam-di-ŋ* (acc–dat.). This suffix can be interpreted as a sequence of *-d-* (weakened form of *-tt-*) plus *-i* (the genitive marker). In a few irregular stems an underlying *-d-* or *-t-* as augment is needed to explain the locative forms, e.g. *ilu* 'house': *inṟo (< *il-n-d-o)* 'in the house', *nāṟu* 'village': *nāṭo* (< *nāṭ-ṭo*< **nāṭ-t-o*) 'in the village'.[12] There are a few exceptions to this with a zero oblique suffix, *goṛeli* 'axe': *goṛeli-ŋ* (acc–dat). a few loanwords in final *-m* take *-ti* instead, *dēsem* 'country': *dēsem-ti-* (obl–gen). For details, see Krishnamurti 1969a: 248–53.

Kui has the augment *-tin-* (< **tt-i* + *n*, a sequence of three augments) in neuter stems of the type, (C)V̄C, e.g. *kōru* 'buffalo': *kōru-tin-gi* (dat), *kōr-ka* (pl): *kōrka-tin-gi* (dat). 'The genitive is the same as the inflectional base' (Winfield 1928: 24, 28).

In Kuvi *-ta-* occurs as the oblique marker in non-human nouns in the singular and plural before the dative suffix, e.g. *ilu* 'house': *ilu-ta-ki* (dat), *ilka-ta-ki* (pl dat); *-t-* occurs in singular nouns before accusative and locative cases, e.g. *ilu-t-i* 'house' (acc), *ilu-t-a* (loc). In a different dialect, owing to prehistoric sandhi, some stems have irregular obliques in the locative, e.g. *ilu* 'house': *ijo-* (loc), *nāyu* 'village': *nājo-* (loc). The genitive is *-t-i* (Israel: 1979: 61–4; see the Koṇḍa forms above).

In Pengo and Maṇḍa *-t-* is added as an augment to non-human nouns, Pe. *mar* 'tree': *ma(r)-t-iŋ* (acc), *ma(r)-t-o* (loc), *ma(r)-t-i* (gen), *mar-(t)-aŋ* (instr–loc); in the plural *key-ku-t-aŋ* 'from the hands'; with sandhi in *nāz* 'village': *nāṭ-i* (gen), *nāṭ-iŋ* (acc–dat), *nāṭ-o* (loc); the *-d-* variant occurs in monosyllabic stems which do not end in voiceless consonants, e.g. *kāl* 'leg': *kāl-di* (gen), *kāl-d-iŋ* (acc–dat). Maṇḍa has *vay-ti-k*

[11] Actually this is a combination of two augments, *tt* + *i*. For *-i* see below.

[12] It appears that the change of PD **-ṭ-* > *-ṟ-* in South Dravidian II must be a recent change in the nominative after the paradigm was formed on the *ṭ*-ending base (see section 4.5.5.3–4).

'mouth' (acc–dat); a variant of *-t-* is *-d-* in *key* 'hand': *key-d-aŋ* (inst–abl) (Burrow and Bhattacharya 1970: §§63–7).

Central Dravidian Kolami has only four stems that take the oblique marker *-t-*, *nal: naṭ-*, *siḍ: siṭ-*, *ul: uṭ-* (all meaning 'day'), *vēgaḍ* 'field': *vēgaṭ-* (Emeneau 1955b/1961: 61).

Naiki (Chanda) uses *-t-* in some non-masculine nouns in some of the cases (genitive, locative, ablative) in the singular, *kī* 'hand': *kī-t-un* (loc), *ūr* 'village': *ūr-t-a* (gen).

In Parji, *-t-* occurs as an augment in the case of certain neuter nouns before ablative, genitive and locative cases, *mer* 'tree': *mer-t-o* (gen), *mer-t-i* (loc), *juve* 'well' : *juve-t-are* 'from the well'.

Ollari has a trace of this suffix in a few neuter words, e.g. *polub-t-un* 'in the village', *kī-t-in* 'in the hand'; it has a variant in *-ṭ-* but we do not know the conditions, *mar-ṭe-vēr* 'root of the tree'.

Gadaba has *-t-* in some singular stems, *tōṭa* 'garden': *tōṭa-t-in* (loc), *polub-t-un* 'in the village'.

North Dravidian Only Brahui in North Dravidian has anything similar to PD **-tt-* in its genitive, *xarās-tā* 'of the bull'; in the other oblique cases there is an augment *-t-* before the case suffixes in the plural: dat–acc sg *xarās-e* '(to) the bull', pl *xarās-t-e* '(to) the bulls', abl sg *xarās-ān* 'from the bull', *xarās-te-ān* 'from the bulls' (Bray 1909: 43).

Summary The foregoing distribution justifies the reconstruction of **-tt-* as an oblique marker in substantives of certain inanimate subclasses of stems. For South Dravidian I, we can include in these two clear subclasses: *-m*/*-n* ending (*mara-m* 'tree') neuter nouns and those that end in *-ṭu*/*-ṯu* preceded by a (C)V̄ or (C)VCV-. Kannaḍa regularly and Koṇḍa partially changed *-tt-* > *-t-* [-d-]. The classes of stems taking the augment *-tt-* are retained intact in South Dravidian I. In South Dravidian II and Central Dravidian these subclasses are expanded to include other stems but still the grammatical category of gender is identical. In South Dravidian II, *-tt-* is combined with other augments to form complex augments, **tt* + **i* (Telugu, Koṇḍa), **tt* + **i* + **n* (Kui). Pengo and Maṇḍa use *-ti* as a genitive marker, *-t-* oblique, *-i-* genitive. Telugu, Koṇḍa, and Kui have adopted the genitive base as the oblique stem, hence its double function. There are several less pervasive oblique markers, discussed below.

6.3.1.2 *-an/*-in; *-n*V*

South Dravidian I In Old Tamil *-aṉ* occurred with demonstrative pronouns, quantifiers and numerals; *-iṉ* after disyllabic and trisyllabic stems ending in *a ā u ū ē ai* in the instrumental, dative and occasionally sociative cases. The stem ending in *-in* by itself was genitive, which could be used syntactically as an adnominal.

Ta. *atu* 'that one': *at-aṉ-ai* (acc) 'that', *at-aṉ-āl* (instr) 'by that', *āṟu* 'six': *āṟ-aṟ-ku* (dat) 'to six' (*ṉ* → *ṟ*/__[+ stop, − voice]); *eẓutt-iṟ-ku* 'to letter', *kaṉav-iṉ-āl* 'by dream'. In classical texts there were usages without the augments also, e.g. *kal* 'stone': *kaṟ-ku* 'to stone', *kaṇṇu* 'eye': *kaṇṇ-āl* 'by the eye'.

Malayāḷam had *-an* as an augment of demonstratives in early inscriptions. Sometimes *-in* was used, instead, e.g. *iranṭu* 'two: *iranṭ-in-āl* 'by twos', *itu* 'this one': *it-in-ukku* 'to this'. Otherwise, *-in* had the same distribution as *-iṉ* of Old Tamil. Stems that take *-tt-* add *-in-* also in dative and genitive, (dat) *mara-tt-in-nə* 'to the tree', (gen) *mara-tt-in-ḏe* 'of the tree' (Asher and Kumari 1997: 191–4).

In Iruḷa *-(a)n* occurs as augment with animate nouns including the personal pronouns before instrumental, e.g. *nā* 'I': *nan-an-āle* 'by me', *nām* 'we': *nam-an-āle* 'by us', *piḷḷe* 'child': *piḷḷe-n-āle* 'by the child'. In Koḍagu *-ïn*/*-n* are used as augments after neuter demonstrative pronouns in accusative, dative and genitive cases, *ad-ïn-a* (acc), *ad-ïn-gu* (dat), *ad-ïn-ḏu* (gen). They also occur after many neuter nouns of one or two syllables in accusative, instrumental and ablative cases, e.g. *ūr* 'village': *ūr-n-*, *baṭṭe* 'road': *baṭṭe-n-*. Numerals take *-ān-*, e.g. *eṭṭu* 'eight': *eṭṭ-ān-a* 'eight' (acc), *eṭṭ-āṉ-ḍa* (gen).

Kota has *-n* after neuter demonstratives, *ad-n-k* 'to that' (dat), *ad-n-l* 'in that' (loc), *ed-n-l-tr* (abl) 'from what?' Toda adds *-n* in adnominal use of some noun stems, *pāw* 'river': *a*[1] *pāw-n*[2] *bȫr*[3] 'the name[3] of that[1] river[2]'.

In Kannaḍa *-aṟ*, a sandhi variant of *-an* (see Tamil above), became generalized as the oblique marker of neuter demonstratives in the singular and plural and in numerals, *ad-ar-ke* (*r* ← *ṟ*/__*k*; dat) 'to that', *ad-aṟ-im* (instr) 'by that', *eraḍu* 'two': *eraḍ-aṟ-oḷage* (loc) 'in two'. In Pampa Bhārata, this occurs with the plural demonstrative forms, *av-aṟ-*, *iv-aṟ-* in dative and instrumental–ablative. The augment *-in*/*-i* occurs more widely after consonant-final stems in all cases except the accusative, *magaḷ-in-ge* 'to the daughter', *dēvar-i* (*n*)*-ge* 'to the gods'. Baḍaga has *-n-* after the third neuter demonstratives, *ad-n-a* (acc, gen).

In Tuḷu *-n* occurs as an augment after human nouns and after stems ending in *-e*, *guru-n-a* (gen) 'of a Guru', *kudke-n-a* 'of a fox', *magaḷ* 'daughter': *magaḷ-n-a* (also *kudk-a* and *magaḷ-a*, which establish *-a* as the genitive suffix). Koraga has *-n-* for human nouns in genitive, *appe-n-a* 'of mother'.

South Dravidian II Telugu has *-an-i* (a sequence of two augments) as oblique augment in demonstrative neuter forms, in the singular and plural, before metathesis took place, e.g. *adi* 'that': *dān-i-*< **ad-an-i*, *idi* 'this': *dīn-i-* < **id-an-i*, *ēdi* 'which?': *dēn-i-* < **ed-an-i*; so also the plurals, e.g. *awi* 'they' *wān-i-* < **aw-an-i*, etc.[13] Stems ending in neuter

[13] Curiously, spoken Telugu has in the plural *wāṭ-i* < **aw-aṯṯ-i* with the augment **-aṯṯ* which compares better with Classical Tamil augment *-aṟṟ-* in the neuter plural demonstratives (see 6.3.1.3). It appears that Old Telugu normalized the augment used in the singular, while spoken Telugu

singular *-mu* take *-na-* as oblique marker, *gur̲r̲amu* 'horse': *gur̲r̲amu-na-ku*/*gur̲r̲ā-na-ku* 'to the horse'. Masculine singular nouns ending *-ṇḍu* in the nominative replace it by *-ni*, *magaṇḍu* 'husband': *maga-ni-ki* 'to the husband'. These *-na*/*-ni* do not seem to be historically related to **-an*/**-in*.

Gondi has *-n* as an augment after masculine nouns ending in a vowel, *marri* 'son': *marrī-n-*, *muriyal* 'father': *muriya-n-*, *tammur* 'younger brother': *tammu-n-*. This feature is found in all dialects. The augment *-n* is also used after the plural suffix *-k* or *-ø* of some non-masculine as well as masculine nouns, e.g. *kaṛ-k* 'eyes': *kaṛ-k-n-gagā* 'in the eyes', *mark* 'sons': *mark-n-*. Female human nouns that end in a vowel or the derivative suffix *-al*, or any of the consonants *-r*, *-ṛ*, *-ḍ*, replace the stem-final consonant by the augment *-n*, e.g. *tange* 'elder sister': *tange-n-*, but *yāyal* 'mother': *yāya-n-*, *sēlāṛ* 'sister': *sēlā-n*. Some other Gondi dialects add *-t*, e.g. *sēlāṛ-t-*, which apparently was the original condition. The addition of *-n* instead in female human nouns must be a recent innovation in the northern and central dialects (see Rao 1987b: 146–8).

Koṇḍa attests an underlying *-an-i* (two suffixes *-an* + *-i*) in the neuter demonstrative forms, which have undergone phonological changes, partly similar to those in Telugu, *adi* 'that': *da-ni*, *idi* 'this': *de-ni*, *avi* 'they': *va-ni*, *ivi* 'these': *ve-ni*.[14] The masculine plural ending *-r* takes *-i* as the oblique formative and those ending in common plural in *-k* or *-ŋ* take *-a* as the oblique marker.

Kui has masculine nouns ending in *-nju* in the singular and *-ru* in the plural, e.g. *nega-nju* 'good man', *nega-ru* 'good men'; the obliques are formed by adding *-i* to *negan-* and *negar-* as *negan-i-* and *negar-i-* to which the other case suffixes are added (note that *-ju* corresponds to PD **-ṯu* which occurs only in the nominative singular, see section 6.3). In the case of nouns meaning female human, the oblique augment is clearly *-n*/*-ni*, e.g. *aja* 'mother': *aja-ni* (gen), *aja-n-gi* (dat), *aja-ni-i* (acc); pl *aja-ska* 'mothers', *aja-ska-ni* (gen), *aja-ska-n-gi* (dat). Even 'neuter plurals that end in *-nga* are declined like masculine nouns' (Winfield 1928: 25–30). Here also, we notice an extension of human inflectional increment to non-human classes.

Kuvi has *-n*/*-na* as augment of nouns referring to humans, e.g. *aya* 'woman': *aya-ni-ki* (dat), *aya-n-i* (gen); in plural the variant is *-ṇ*, *aya-ska-ṇ-i* (acc pl).

In Pengo *-n* occurs in the genitive plural of non-human nouns ending in *-ku*, e.g. *key-ku* 'hands': *key-ku-n-i* (gen). Manḍa also has *-n-* in the oblique-genitive, e.g. *kiy-ni*[1] *neter*[2] 'blood[2] of hand[1]', *mar-ni*[1] *ākeŋ*[2] 'leaves[2] of the tree[1]'.

from the earliest times has preserved the inherited contrast in the augments. This is one class of exception to the metathesis rules which involve mainly coronal consonants (section 4.5.7.3).

[14] It is not clear if the metathesized forms are a shared innovation with Telugu or borrowings from Early Telugu. The sequence **id-an-* should have become **ed-an* and **dēn-* in Early Telugu. But the vowel is *ī* in *dīn-*, perhaps to avoid homonymy with the interrogative *dēn-* from *ēdi* + *an*. But Koṇḍa has the correct quality of the vowel in the obliques of *idi* and *iwi*, since the interrogative forms are different, i.e. *ayen* 'who?', *ayed* 'which?'

Central Dravidian Kolami has no instances of an oblique with *-n*. Naiki (Chanda) has *-n* in animate nouns in some of the cases, e.g. *tōlel* 'brother': *tōle-n-un* (acc.), *bāy* 'woman': *bāy-n-un* (acc); it also occurs in genitive, *pul-ne*[1] *tala*[2] 'head[2] of tiger[1]'.

Parji has *-n* as oblique marker of some stems in ablative and genitive cases, e.g. *kici-n-a* 'of fire', *kici-n-ar* 'from fire'. Ollari has examples of *-n-* in genitive, *kor-n-e*[1] *cenḍi*[2] 'cock's[1] comb[2]'.

Gadaba has *-n*/*-in*/*-un* as a genitive marker, *-n* after a vowel and *-in* ~*-un* after a consonant, e.g. *māre-n-* 'tree', *verg-in* 'cat', *polb-un* 'village'. Here the V before *-n* is conditioned by the preceding vowel.

North Dravidian In Kuṛux *-in*/*-i* occurs after non-masculine singular demonstrative stems before all cases, *ād* 'it': *ād-i-ge* (dat), *ād-in-tī* (abl).

There is no evidence of an oblique marker involving *-n* in the other North Dravidian languages.

Summary On the basis of comparative evidence, *-*an* can be reconstructed for South Dravidian I and South Dravidian II, particularly with respect to non-masculine demonstratives in the singular, **at-u*, **it-u*, **yāt-u*. Data from Tamil, Malayāḷam, Koḍagu, Kota, Baḍaga and Kannaḍa (here, *aṟ-* rather than *-an*) of South Dravidian I and Telugu and Koṇḍa of South Dravidian II support this reconstruction. In some members the augment has extended distribution: Iruḷa has shifted *-an* to personal pronouns. The variant *-in* occurs clearly in South Dravidian I, Tamil and Malayāḷam, with a different distribution from that of *-an*, but *-an* and *-in* have become free variants in some of the languages, e.g. Malayāḷam, Koḍagu and Kannaḍa.

In South Dravidian II, the augments *na-*/*ni-* occur in some of the members typically with animate (generally human) nouns as distinguished from *-*tt* which occurs predominantly with non-human/inanimate nouns. This occurs in Telugu and Gondi (with masculine nouns), and Kui–Kuvi (with feminine nouns). Modern Kannaḍa, Tuḷu and Koraga of South Dravidian I and Naiki of Central Dravidian also seem to follow this pattern with a morpheme of the shape *-n*V. The reflexes of *-*in* also occur with other classes of stems, not semantically so definable.

The other Central Dravidian languages do not show this trend, but they have the -*n*V morph occurring in the genitive forms in Parji, Ollari and Gadaba. It is possible to reconstruct *-*n*V as another oblique marker. North Dravidian (other than Kuṛux) has lost both *-V*n* and **n*V-.

6.3.1.3 *-an-t̲t̲-/*-in-t̲t̲-

Tamil, Malayāḷam and Telugu give evidence of this complex augment. In Early Tamil *-aṟṟu* occurs after plural neuter demonstrative roots *av-*, *iv-*; also after interrogative and indefinite pronouns, *yā-* '(an interrogative root)', and *pala-* 'many', *cila-* 'few', e.g. *av-aṟṟ-uḷ* 'in them', *iv-aṟṟ-oṭu* 'with these', *pala-v-aṟṟ-ai* 'many things' (acc). Malayāḷam has parallel uses of *-aṟṟ-*, e.g. *av-aṟṟ-in-/avai(y)-iṟṟ-in/avai(y)-iṟ-in* (dat). Shanmugam (1971a: 241) considers that Old Kannaḍa *-aṟ-* is related to this morph rather than to **-an*, by simplification of the geminate to a single consonant.

Only Telugu has anything to compare with *-aṯṯ-* in the spoken forms, *awi* 'those (non-human)': *wā-ṭi-* (< **aw-aṯṯ-i*), *iwi* 'these (non-human)': *wīṭ-i-* (< **iw-aṯṯ-i*), *ēwi* 'which ones? (non-human)': *wē-ṭi-* (< **ew-aṯṯ-i*), respectively. Koya, a dialect of Gondi, has *vā-ṇṭi-* requiring a proto-form **aw-anṯṯ-i*. This looks like a borrowing from Early (preliterary) Telugu because of the retention of the pregeminate nasal.

Telugu also has *-iṇṭi-* (< **in-ṯṯ-i*) as a complex oblique marker with number words, definite and indefinite, e.g. *reṇḍu* 'two': *reṇḍ-iṇṭi-* (obl/gen), *mūḍu* 'three': *mūḍ-iṇṭi-* 'three' (obl/gen), *anni* 'that many (non-hum)': *ann(i)-iṇṭi-*, etc. This is a combination *in* + *tt* + *i* → *in-ṯṯ-i*. From this it appears, on comparative grounds, that Old Tamil *aṯṯ-* is a combination of *an* + *ṯṯ-* with the loss of *n* before a geminate (PP < *NPP is a regular rule in Tamil–Malayāḷam). For further details, see section 6.5 below.

6.3.1.4 *-a/*-i

The vowels **-a* and **-i* occur as oblique markers in South Dravidian II and North Dravidian. Therefore, they are reconstructible for Proto-Dravidian. In South Dravidian I *-a* occurs as oblique marker with personal pronouns in dative, e.g. Ta. *eṉ-a-kku* 'to me', *niṉ-a-kku* 'to you'. Tuḷu has *-e-* as oblique maker after plural nouns, *maro-kuḷ-e* (obl–gen) 'trees', *maro-kuḷ-e-gï* 'to trees'. Kannaḍa also has *-a* in personal pronouns, *nann-a* 'my', *nan-a-ge* 'to me', etc.

Telugu adds *-a* to the common plural in *-lu* to form the oblique stem, which also signals the genitive case at the syntactic level, *bomma-lu* 'dolls': *bommal-a* (obl–gen), *rāju* 'king', *rāju-lu* 'kings': *rājul-a-* (obl–gen), *rāju-l-a-nu* 'kings' (acc). The vowel *-i* is added to human plural nouns ending in *-ru* and demonstrative pronouns, *wā̃ḍu* 'he': *wān-i*, *wāru* 'they' (hum): *wār-i* (obl–gen): *wār-i-ki* (dat), *wār-i māṭalu* 'their words' (gen). *-i* is also added as an oblique marker to a class of nouns of three morae each, ending in a sonorant, V̄] *n, r, l*, e.g. *ūru* 'village: *ūr-i*, *kālu* 'leg': *kāl-i*, *cēnu* 'field': *cēn-i*. It is not certain if this is derivable from **-in* with the loss of final *-n*, but there is no internal evidence for such a loss.

In Koṇḍa *-a-* and *-i-* have similar distribution, *-a-* after the common plural nouns and *-i* after the masculine plural, *-ru*, e.g. *ayli-k* 'girls': *aylik-a-* (obl–gen), *ayli-k-a-ŋ* 'girls' (acc–dat), *buba-r* 'parents'; *bubar-i* (obl–gen). *-i* occurs in the oblique–genitive forms of *van-i* 'that man', *ven-i* 'this man', *ayen-i* 'which man?' Kui has *-i* as oblique marker after masculine nouns in the singular and plural, e.g. *neganju* 'a good man': *negan-i* (obl–gen), *ābaru* 'fathers': *ābar-i* (obl–gen). In most cases, the oblique stem also functions as an adnominal or in the genitive case.

Kuṛux adds *-ā-* as an augment in the case of personal pronouns in the dative case, e.g. *nīm* 'you (pl)': *nīm-ā-ge* 'to you'. In Brahui, monosyllabic nouns take the augment *a-* before the sociative and genitive cases, e.g. *mār* 'son': *mār-a-to* 'with son', *bā* 'mouth': *bā-a-nā*; *-e-* occurs as the oblique-genitive marker after all personal pronouns (except the 2pl) before ablative, instrumental and locative cases, e.g. *nan* 'we': *nan-e-ān* (abl), *nan-e-at* (instr).

It is hard to interpret Tuḷu *-e* and Brahui *-e* comparatively. In any case, they are not apparently related, since Tuḷu *-e* corresponds to PD **-ay* for which there is evidence. **-i* can be reconstructed for South Dravidian II.

6.3.1.5 *Summary*

Looking at the permutations and combinations of the different augments, it appears tempting to interpret these in terms of minimal constituents, **i*, **a*, **n*, **tt*. The inflectional increments (which in most cases are also markers of the genitive case) can be generated by combining these in different sequences:

1. *-a-*: SD I (in personal pronouns), SD II: Telugu, Koṇḍa; ND: Kuṛux, Brahui
2. *-n-*: Koḍagu in SD I; Gondi in SD II; Central Dravidian
3. *-tt-*: SD I (Kannaḍa has a weakened variant *-d-*); Gondi, Pengo, Manḍa; Central Dravidian; Brahui
4. *-i-*: SD II
5. *-a-n-*: SD I, SD II: Telugu, Koṇḍa
6. *-n-a-*, *-n-i-*: Telugu
7. *-tt-a-*: Tuḷu (also genitive), Kuvi
8. *-tt-i-*: SD II: Telugu, Koṇḍa, Kui, also Pengo and Manḍa in genitive
9. *-i-n-*: SD I
10. *-n-ṯṯ-*: Telugu, Koṇḍa, Pengo, Manḍa
11. *-a-n-ṯṯ-*: Tamil, Malayāḷam (with loss of nasal as **aṯṯ-* in *av-aṟṟ-*), Telugu **-aṭ-i*: *wāṭ-i* obl of *awi* 'they (non-hum)'
12. *-n-ṯṯ-i-*: SD II in some restricted classes of stems, Te. *illu: iṇṭi* (< **il + n-ṯṯ + i*), Koṇḍa *ilu: inṟ-o* (< ** il-n-do*) (loc).
13. *-i-n-ṯṯ-i-*: Telugu *-iṇṭi-* in numerals etc.

All possible sequences can be generated by the following schema that I proposed in 1980 in a paper (see Krishnamurti 1985: 221):

	**tt*	**n*	**n + tt → n-ṯṯ*	**tt-V-n*
**i*	**i-tt*, **tt-i*	**i-n*, **n-i*	**-i-n-ṯṯ*, **n-ṯṯ-i*	**tt-i-n*
**a*	**a-tt*, **tt-a*	**a-n*, **n-a*	**-a-n-ṯṯ*, **n-ṯṯ-a*	**tt-a-n*

It is not possible to recover the criteria underlying the use of different augments in Proto-Dravidian. It can be done for some augments in certain subgroups, like *-an* in the case of neuter demonstrative singular stems, shared by Tamil and Telugu (**at-an-*, **it-an-* etc.);

similarly *-tt-* occurs with non-personal nouns ending in *-n*, **mara-n* 'tree' :**mara-tt-*. In any case the criteria are definitely not phonological. Ta. *-a-ṟṟ-* (*av-aṟṟ-ai* 'them' neu) and Te. *-i-ṇṭ-i* (*āṟ-iṇṭi-ki* 'to six') can best be explained by positing loss of a nasal in **-a-n-ṯṯ* in Tamil and Malayāḷam and with retention of a nasal and with change of the vowel (**-i-n-ṯṯ-i*) in Telugu.

6.3.2 ***Case markers***

The case markers that can be clearly reconstructed for Proto-Dravidian are the accusative, dative and genitive. The other cases do occur in all languages but the markers are restricted to subgroups or individual languages. The distribution of case markers is sometimes determined by the gender of the noun [± animate], [± human], etc. and sometimes by phonological criteria, such as consonant-ending/vowel-ending. For data I have generally followed Shanmugam (1971a) but I have independently checked his data and analysis for individual languages and added material where necessary, from the source publications. Paradigms from selected languages of each subgroup are given in a following section to facilitate comparison. Members of a paradigm with case markers which are not reconstructible are given in parentheses.

The syntax of cases will be dealt with in chapter 9.

6.3.2.1 *Accusative case*

(i) * -ay

South Dravidian I This morph is found clearly in a subgroup of South Dravidian I, namely Tamil, Malayāḷam, Koḍagu, Iruḷa, Kuṟumba. Traces of its retention are found in Kui–Kuvi (somewhat uncertain) and in Brahui. It is therefore reconstructible for Proto-Dravidian.

Old Tamil: *-ai* is the accusative marker, obligatorily used with [+animate] nouns (Shanmugam 1971a: 256), e.g. *vēẕatt-ai kaṇṭāy* 'you see the elephant'. It is optionally dropped after personal pronouns in Old Tamil: *niṟ*[1] *kaṇṭ-iciṉ-ōr-ē*[2] 'those who saw[2] you[1]'. In Modern Tamil *-ai* becomes *-e* and it is obligatory with animate nouns, e.g. *enn-e* 'me'; with inanimate nouns the use of an accusative is a sign of definiteness that the speaker intends to convey, *maram* 'tree': *mara-tt-e* 'the tree' (acc).

Malayāḷam: *-ai* occurred in early inscriptions. It was replaced by *-e* in records from the tenth century, e.g. *ñān*[1] *avan-e*[2] *aṭiccu*[3] 'I[1] beat[3] him[2]'. With non-human nouns its use was optional.

Iruḷa accusative case markers are *-e*/*-ne*, *-ne* after stems ending in *-e*, *-e* elsewhere, e.g. *vēle-ne* 'work', *pëde-ne* 'daughter', *avan-e* 'him', *giḍa-tt-e* 'plant' (Perialwar 1978b: 9–10).

Koḍagu: *-a* (< *-ai*) occurs after stems in a final liquid, *avaḷ-a* 'her' (acc); *-na* occurs elsewhere, *mara-t-n-a* 'tree' (acc), *mēji-n-a* 'table' (acc).

In Ālu Kuṟumba, the accusative case marker is *-na*, *uli-na* 'tiger' (acc) following vowel-ending stems. The marker is optional with inanimate nouns.

South Dravidian II Kui: the accusative suffix is *-i* used in the case of human nouns, e.g. *mrīeni-i* 'son' (acc): its use is optional in the case of non-personal nouns, *mrahnu-tin-i* 'tree' (acc).

Kuvi: *-i* in *mṛeha-ʔ-i* 'man' (acc), *kaḍḍa- t-i* 'river'(acc); optional in [−human] nouns, e.g. *hiccu*^{1} *ḍupdu*^{2} 'put out^{2} the fire^{1}'.

North Dravidian Brahui: *-e* marks the accusative case, which appears to have been derived from **ay*, e.g. *dā shar-e* 'this village' (acc), *musi huchch-e* 'three camels' (acc). This is also used in a dative sense.

(ii) *-Vn

This morph is attested in all major subgroups.

South Dravidian I Toda: *-n* is the marker for accusative; it is represented as *-ṇ* after stems in final retroflexes, e.g. *ōḷ-ṇ* 'man' (acc), *kūx-n paṯ* 'catch the girl'; *nïm-n* 'you' (acc).[15]

Kota: *-n* occurs as the accusative marker, obligatorily with animate nouns and optionally with non-animate ones, *kaḷ-n* 'thief', *pujgūḷ-n* 'tigers'; *ūn mar-t-n/marm-n erckō* 'he cut down the tree'. In non-initial syllables the V of -V*n* is lost in Toda and Kota.

Kannaḍa: *-aM*, *-an*, *-ān*, *-ā* occurred in the inscriptions. The long-vowel forms occurred in earlier records, e.g. *biẓidōn-ā* 'the one who has fallen' (acc), *kōṭe-y-an* 'fort' (acc), *kayy-an* 'hand' (acc). Its use is optional after non-human nouns,[16] e.g. *karṇaN-aM* → *karṇan-am* 'Karṇa' (acc), *kajjaM-aM* → *kajjam-am* 'work' (acc) (Ramachandra Rao: 58–9). In Modern Kannaḍa *-annu* is the accusative marker, obligatorily used in human nouns or as a marker of definiteness in the case of non-human and inanimate nouns (Sridhar 1990: 160–1).

Baḍaga: the final nasal is lost (?) and the accusative morph looks deceptively like a reflex of **-ay*, but it is not so, since Baḍaga is closer to Kannaḍa than to Pre-Tamil, e.g. *adu-n-a* 'that', *mara-v-a* 'tree'.

Tuḷu: *-nu*/*-nï* and *-anu* mark the accusative, e.g. *kañji-nï koṇola* 'take away the calf', *en-anu* 'me', *in-anu* 'you'.

15 The marker is seldom lost after human nouns, but it is optional after non-human nouns. After a noun phrase involving an attribute to the noun head the accusative is always expressed (Emeneau 1984: 76–8).

16 For the phonemic interpretation of the morphophonemes *N*, *M*, see fn. 20.

South Dravidian II Telugu: *-nu*/*-ni*, alternating with *-n*, are complementary morphs marking accusative, obligatorily with animate nouns, but optionally with non-animate ones, *pāṟa-nu* 'Brahmin' (acc; inscriptional), *āli-n*(*i*) 'wife', *bhārya-n*(*u*) 'wife' (acc); *wāri-n*(*i*) 'them'. The final vowel was optional in poetic language, but not so in Modern Telugu. The final vowel of the case morph is harmonized to the vowel in the preceding syllable. In Old Telugu, sometimes the marker is dropped in poetic language in the case of personal pronouns, *nin-* 'you' (acc), alternatively *ninn-u*(*n*), *nin-un*, etc.

Gondi: *-n* after long vowels, *-ūn* after consonants, e.g. *bayyē-n* 'mother', *kōndā-t-ūn* 'ox' (acc), *tarās-ūn* 'snake' (acc). In the Koya dialect it is *-ini*/*-in* (Tyler 1969: 53), e.g. *meṭṭā-t-ini* 'mountain' (acc).

Koṇḍa: in Koṇḍa, Pengo and Manḍa, the accusative and dative cases are represented by the same marker, *-ŋ*/*-ŋi* in Koṇḍa obligatorily after human nouns, e.g. *aya guruye-ŋ osinar* 'they are bringing the Guru', *na-ŋi* 'me'; *ṟēto*[1] *ṛista*[2] 'I will release[2] the crab[1]'.

Pengo: *-aŋ* after plural stems and *-iŋ* elsewhere, e.g. *key-di-ŋ* 'hand', *keyku-k-aŋ* [?] 'hands' (acc), *nekuṛ-ti-ŋ* 'dog' (acc).

Central Dravidian The whole subgroup shares two features in the marking of accusative case: (i) *-n* occurs after vowel-ending stems and -V*n* after consonant-ending stems; (ii) the use of the accusative marker is optional in the case of inanimate nouns.

Kolami: *-n*∼*-un*, *-n* after any stem in a final vowel, liquid or semivowel, and *-un* elesewhere, e.g. *ella-n* 'house' (acc), *kōlavan-un* 'a Kolami man' (acc).

Naikṛi (wrongly claimed to be a dialect of Kolami) has the same marker for the accusative and dative, e.g. *-ŋ*/*-ūŋ*, e.g. *pul-ūŋ* 'tiger' (acc), *ellā-ŋ* 'to the house', *an-ūŋ* 'me, to me' (Thomasiah 1986: 95)

Naiki (Chanda): *-n* ∼ *-un*/*-on*, e.g. *kōnda-n* 'bull' (acc), *pul-un* 'tiger' (acc); optional use in neuter nouns, e.g. *kokke*[1] *īv*[2] *ilupti*[3] 'you[2] tore[3] the cloth[1]'.

Parji: *-n*∼*-in* (freely varying with *-i* before some stems) (Burrow and Bhattacharya 1953: 21), e.g. *ēnu-n*[2] *kaṭṭen*[1] 'I tied[2] an elephant[1]', *pall-in*[1] *petten*[2] 'I picked[2] a fruit[1]', *koṛol-in*[1] *ciur*[2] 'give[2] the bride[1]'. Optional use in inanimate nouns, *nīr*[1] *ender*[2] 'bring[2] water[1]'.

Ollari: *-n* ∼ *-in*, e.g. *māl-in* 'daughter', *ḍurka-n* 'panther' (acc). Bhattacharya (1957: 21) says that these morphs freely vary with *-ŋ*/*-iŋ* which are accusative–dative. Inanimate nouns take the marker optionally, *ān*[1] *kis*[2] *siṭṭon*[3] 'I[1] put out[3] the fire[2]'.

North Dravidian Kuṛux: *-an* after non-human nouns ending in a consonant, *-n* after such nouns ending in a vowel, and *-in* elsewhere. The personal pronouns also have the same distribution, e.g *xess-an*[1] *cā̃xālagd -as*[2] 'he is sowing[2] rice[1]', *ā*[1] *aḍḍō-n*[2] *ērā*[3] 'see[3] that[1] ox[2]'. The accusative is sometimes used for dative, perhaps under the influence of surrounding Indo-Aryan (Shanmugam 1971a: 355).

Malto: the case suffix is *-n*/*-in* in most cases; after stems ending in *-du*, the final syllable is replaced by *-a*/*-an*, e.g. *male-n* 'to the man', *maler-in* 'to the men'; *ṭūḍ-a*/*ṭūḍ-an* 'to the tiger'.

Summary Of the two case suffixes which can be reconstructed for Proto-Dravidian, **-ay* and *-V*n*, we notice that the languages derived from Pre-Tamil (Tamil, Malayāḷam, Koḍagu, Iruḷa, Kuṟumba) have a shared innovation in the loss of *-V*n*, while the other South Dravidian I languages have lost **-ay*. This innovation provides us evidence to show that Toda–Kota must have split off from Pre-Tamil prior to the other Pre-Tamil descendants. The loss of *-V*n* in Pre-Tamil can be attributed to a period after Toda–Kota branched off and before the palatalization rule set in Pre-Tamil, i.e. ca. third century BCE. By that time Koḍagu–Iruḷa–Kuṟumba must also have separated from Pre-Tamil as another sub-branch. Zvelebil (1972c) suggests a revised stemma for this subgroup based on the retention of **-ay* as accusative. It is doubtful if its retention can be invoked in setting up isoglosses for subgrouping.

The allomorph **-ay* is independently preserved in Brahui. Its seeming retention in the other languages like Parji, Kui–Kuvi may be misleading, indicating the possibility of loss of final *-n* in all allomorphs.

Most languages show that the accusative is optional in the case of noun stems carrying the gender features [−animate] or [−human] which probably defined the original distribution of the two allomorphs in Proto-Dravidian. The representation of the accusative and dative by the same marker is typically found in languages which are surrounded by New Indo-Aryan, in which there is a single marker for both these cases (Masica 1991: §10.4).

6.3.2.2 *Dative case*

A geminate velar consonant **-kk-* is the core of the dative suffix. A preceding nasal is needed to account for the developments in some of the languages, so **-nkk*. The geminate may be weakened to *-k-* [g] in some languages. It is used for a wide range of meanings as goal, indirect object (listener, recipient), purpose, comparison, cause, location in time and place, etc. It also occurs in a genitive sense to denote adnominal relationship (in kinship), possession (with stative predicates), direction, etc.

South Dravidian I Tamil: *-kku* occurs in classical poetry, e.g. *iravalar-kku*[1] *īyum*[2] (Pat. 81.23) 'will give[2] to the poor[1]', *pāvai-kku*[1] *pū*[2] *kkoytu*[3] (PN 11.4) 'having plucked[3] the flowers[2] for the doll[1]'. Adnominal (genitive) uses: *nampikku*[1] *makaṉ*[2] 'son[2] of Nampi[1]', *eṉa-kku*[1] *vīṭu*[2] 'my[1] house[2]', *ūr-kku*[1] *kuṇakku*[2] 'east of[2] the village[1]' (Shanmugam 1971a: 264–7). Stative use in Modern Tamil, e.g. *avar-ukku tamiẓ teriyum-aa?* 'Does he know Tamil?'

Malayāḷam: *-kku* is the widely used morpheme in dative, e.g. *kōyil-kku* 'to the temple', *tēvar-kku*[1] *kuṭutta*[2] *bhūmi*[3] 'land[3] given[2] to Devan[1]'. (A variant of *-kku* is *-inu*, which is used after numerals and some abstract nouns. Its origin needs to be explored, e.g. *ūṇ-inu*[1] *kātirukunnu*[2] '(someone) is waiting[2] for food[1]'.)

Kota and Toda: the suffix is *-k*, e.g. Ko. *peḍ-k* 'to wife', *en-k* 'to me', *mar-t-k* 'to tree', *pāb-k* 'to the snake'; To. *nïn-k* 'to you', *kōtfoy-k* 'to wife'.

In Iruḷa, the dative is marked by *-(u)kku* and *-kke* which are morphologically conditioned, e.g. *nin-ukku* 'to you', *bāvi-kke* 'to well', *paḷḷikuḍa-kke* 'to school' (Perialwar 1978b: 17–18). The Purposive (Perialwar 1978b: 18–19) seems to be a variant of dative marked by *-kk/-kkāyi*, e.g. *telya-kku* 'for oil', *tingudu-kkāyi* 'for eating'. Zvelebil (1973: 19) gives *-kke* (after non-front vowels), *-kkye* (after front vowels) and *-ke* after consonants, *cōḷa-kke* 'for maize', *cemi-kkye* 'for the ear'.

Ālu Kuṟumba has *-gu* for dative without any change, *kūcu-gu* 'to the child', *uli-gu* 'to the tiger'.

Koḍagu: the allomorphs are *-gï* after stems ending in a nasal and *-kï* elsewhere, e.g. *avën-gï*[1] *koḍïte*[2] 'I gave[2] him[1]', *ava-kï* 'to her', *pattu*[1] *gaṇḍa-kï*[2] 'at[2] 10[1] o'clock[2]'.

Kannaḍa: *-(k)ke* occurs as dative marker after stems ending in *-a* and after pronouns which take *-ar* as the augment, and *-(g)ge* elsewhere (Ramachandra Rao 1972: 59–60), e.g. *nagara-kke* 'to the town', *id-ar-kke* 'to this', *mane-ge* 'to the house', *ālaya-ke* 'to the temple', *avanu*[1] *kaṣṭa-kke*[2]*sikkidanu*[3] 'he[1] is caught[3] in (lit. to) difficulties[2]', *nahuṣaṅ-ge*[1] *magan*[2] *yayāti*[3] 'Yayati[3], son[2] of Nahusha[1]'. In Modern Kannaḍa the dative markers are *-ge/-ige* and *-kke*.

Baḍaga: *-ga* is the dative suffix, e.g. *adu-ga* 'to that', *avaka-ga* 'to them', *mane-ga* 'to/for the house'.

Tuḷu: the markers are *-ku/-kï/-gï* with morphological complementation, e.g. *kay-kï* 'to the hand', *en-kï* 'to me', *jōkuḷa-gï* 'to the children', *kañji-gï*[1] *koḷḷa*[2] 'give[2] to the calf[1]', *vyāpāroṅ-ku* 'for business', *eṅ-ku*[1]*mage*[2] 'my[1] son[2]'.

South Dravidian II Telugu: *-ki(n)/-ku(n)* are the markers: *-kin* after stems ending in *-i*, and *-ku(n)* elsewhere, e.g. *tammul-a-ku(n)* 'to the younger brothers', *wān-i-ki(n)* 'to him', *āme-ku(n)* 'to her', *pani-ki* 'for work', *mūḍugaṇṭal-a-ku* 'at 3 o'clock', *nāku*[1] *talli*[2] 'my[1] mother[2]'. In Modern Telugu the final *-n* is uniformly dropped.

Gondi: *-k* is the normal suffix. In the Koya dialect *-ku/-ki/-iki* are the markers of dative, *annā-n-k* 'to the elder brother', *pel-di-ki* 'for marriage', *lōhk-in-ki*[1] *gaḍḍi*[2] *kōysi*[3] 'having cut[3] the grass[2] for (thatching) houses[1]'.

Koṇḍa: the suffix *-ŋ/-ŋi* used for accusative and dative seems to have been derived by combining the accusative *-n* with dative *-k*, i.e. /ng/, e.g. *baŋa-di-ŋ* 'because of hunger', *būḍ-di-ŋ*[1] *sona*[2] 'I will go[2] for bathing[1]', *dokri*[1] *ḍokre-ŋ*[2] *veRtad*[3] 'the old woman[1] said[3] to the old man[2]', *onṭi*[1] *ganṭa-di-ŋ*[2] 'at[1] 1o'clock[2]'.

Kui: *-gi* is the marker of dative after stems in a final *-n*, *-ki* is used elsewhere, e.g. *āba-ki* 'to father', *aja-n-gi* 'to mother', *kōḍi-tin-gi*[1] *tinba*[2] *sīmu*[3] 'give[3] (food) to eat[2] to the cows[1]'.

Kuvi: the dative marker is uniformly *-ki*, e.g. *mṛeha-ki* 'to the man', *aya-na-ki* 'to the woman', *karata-ki* 'because of heat'.

Pengo: has the same morpheme *-aŋ/-iŋ* for accusative and dative as Koṇḍa, e.g. *ōḍa-ti-ŋ*[1] *rinḍan*[2] *komon*[3] 'a goat has (to the goat[1], there are) two[2] horns[3]', *āha-t-iŋ*[1] *hunjavatan*[2] 'he did not sleep[2] out (because) of greed[1]', *puni-t-iŋ*[1] *vaḍu*[2] 'come[2] on the full-moon day[1]'.

Central Dravidian Kolami: *-ŋ* after stems ending in a vowel, *-uŋ* elsewhere, e.g. *ella-ŋ* 'to the house', *avar-uŋ* 'to them'.

Naiki (Chanda): the dative marker looks like a semantic extension of the accusative, e.g. *avn-un*[1] *ān*[2] *entar*[3] 'I[1] will tell[2] him[3]', *īr-un sē* 'go for water'.

Parji: in the northern dialect *-g/-ug* and in the southern dialect *-ŋ/-uŋ*, e.g. *maḍi-g/ maḍi-ŋ* 'for the axe', *ēnu-g/ ēnu-ŋ* 'for the elephant', *pāp-ug/pāp-uŋ* 'for the child'. Dative uses include the indirect object, purpose, cause, etc.; e.g. *cēpid-ug* 'for the broom', *nuṛñil-ug* 'because of mosquitoes'.

Ollari: the dative markers are *-ŋ/-iŋ/-uŋ*, e.g. *an-uŋ* 'to me', *sūr-uŋ* 'for selling', *aṭ-uŋ* 'for beating'.

Gadaba: the accusative–dative are marked by *-n/-un/-in*, e.g. *gonḍsa-n* (spelt *goṇsa-n* by the author) 'squirrel' (acc), *vars-in* 'paddy', *elb-un* 'white ant'. The accusative–dative is said to be identical with the oblique–genitive (Bhaskararao 1980: 20–1).

North Dravidian Kuṛux: the dative is *-gē*, e.g. *ēn*[1] *ās-gē*[2]*ci-ck-an*[3] 'I[1] gave[3] him[2]', *eŋgā-gē*[1] *dhibā*[2] *malī*[3] 'to me[1] there is no[3] money[2]'.

Malto: the suffixes are *-k/-ik* occurring after vowel-ending and consonant-ending stems, respectively, e.g. *male-k* 'to a man', *mal-er-ik* 'to men' (Mahapatra 1979: 68–70).

Brahui: the accusative *-e* is also used as dative, e.g. *shar-e xuṛk* 'near to the town'.

Summary For Central Dravidian we need to reconstruct **-ng* (< PD **-nk*). Naiki seems to have lost the original dative suffix and extended semantically the accusative for dative meanings. In South Dravidian II Koṇḍa and Pengo innovated a morpheme for accusative and dative traceable to **-n-g*. The remaining South Dravidian I and II languages require **-kk*V which is weakened to *-k*V [-gV] in some members, Koḍagu, Kannaḍa, Baḍaga and Tuḷu in South Dravidian I and Kui in South Dravidian II. In North Dravidian, only Kuṛux and Malto require a velar in reconstruction **-k*V. On comparative grounds we can reconstruct for Proto-Dravidian **-nk* alternating with **-nkk* with the loss of nasal in many of the languages of South Dravidian I and South Dravidian II. One also needs to look at the possible influence of NIA dative, which is predominantly represented by a velar consonant.

The use of *-V*n* reconstructed for accusative is noticed to have been extended to dative meaning in some of the languages, e.g. OTa. *viẕav-iṉ*[1] *celvam*[2] 'we will go[2] to the festival[1]', Ma. *celav-inu* 'to the expenditure', Kuṛ. *ēn*[1] *īs-in*[2] ... *ānkan*[3] 'I[1] told[3] him[2]'. The other languages use the dative case suffix with verbs meaning 'to go, come' or 'to say, speak'. Shanmugam (1971a: 379) assumes that locative **-in* is used in a dative sense here, but this proposal is doubtful. It is possible that the Proto-Dravidian accusative *-V*n* survives in Tamil–Malayāḷam only in these cases and not as a marker of direct object. The extension of the accusative to dative in Naiki and Kuṛux could be under the influence of their Indo-Aryan neighbours.

6.3.2.3 *Genitive case*

The augments added to form oblique stems in many languages also signal the genitive case. In other words, the oblique stem may optionally function as an adjective when it qualifies a noun head, e.g. Te. *iṇṭi-* obl of *illu* 'house'. It is a morphological construction when followed by case markers, e.g. *iṇṭi-ki* 'to the house', but it has a syntactic function (i.e. becomes a genitive stem) when followed by another noun, e.g. *iṇṭi pedda* 'head of the house'. Several languages have postpositions meaning 'belonging to' to denote a periphrastic genitive. This is at least true of South Dravidian I and II.

South Dravidian I Tamil: Classical Tamil has *-a* and *-atu*/*-ātu* in genitive, e.g. *maratt-a*[1] *kōṭu*[2] (KT 99.4) 'branch[2] of a tree[1]', *niṉṉ-a*[1] *kaṇṇi*[2] (PN 45.3) 'your[1] garland[2]', *vēntaṉ-atu*[1] *toẕilē*[2] 'the duty[2] of the king[1]' (Aiṅk. 451), *taṉ-ātu*[1] *ūr*[2] (Cil. 2.8.3) 'his[1] village[2]'. The augments *-aṉ* and *-iṉ* are also used as markers of genitive, e.g. *at-aṉ niṟam* 'its chest' (Kali 52: 3–4), *palav-iṉ*[1] *ciṉai*[2] 'branch of[2] a jack fruit tree[1]'.

The postpositional noun *uṭai* 'wealth, possession' and its adnominal form *uṭaiya* 'belonging to' are used more frequently in later Tamil (Modern Tamil also *ōḍe*) as genitive markers, e.g. *avar-uṭai*[1] *nāṭu*[2] 'his[1] country[2]', *tamm-uṭaiya*[1] *taṇṇaḷi*[2] 'his[1] kindness[2]'. Malayāḷam has the derivatives of *uṭai*, *uṭaiya* in genitive.

Iruḷa marks the genitive by *-a* (after personal pronouns) or *-ttu* (elsewhere), e.g. *nan-a* 'my', *mara-ttu*[1] *pammu*[2] 'fruit of tree' (Perialwar 1978b: 24–5). Zvelebil (1973: 19) lists *-tu*, *-ttu*, *-te*, *-ṭe* as 'possessive' case markers, but does not give their distribution.

Kota: the genitive suffix is *-d* apparently related to OTa. *-atu*, e.g. *en-d* 'my', *cāym-d* 'God's', *mar-t-d* 'of tree'.

Toda: the augments *-n* (< *-V*n*), *-t*, *-d-*, *-θ* are used in a possessive sense (for distributional statements, see Emeneau 1984: 75–6). *-d* (< **at*-V) is used, *en*^{1} *ok-n*^{2} *ōṭ*^{3} 'my^{1} elder sister's^{2} husband^{3}', *koṟ-d*^{1} *kōl*^{2} 'calf's^{1} leg^{2}'.

Kannaḍa: the genitive is expressed by *-a*/*-ā* and the augment *-da*, e.g. *avar-ā*^{1} *magaḷu*^{2} 'his (pol)^{1} daughter^{2}', *aśvamēdha-da*^{1} *phala*^{2} 'the fruit of^{2} the horse-sacrifice^{1}'. In Old Kannaḍa *atu* (? < **-att-*) was also used in genitive, *en-atu*^{1} *śauryam*^{2} 'my^{1} valour^{2}'.

Baḍaga: *-a* is the genitive suffix, e.g. *aman-a* 'his', *avkar-a* 'their'.

Tuḷu: *-a* is the genitive suffix added to stems with the augments *-t*/*-d*/*-n*, e.g. *kay-t-a* 'of hand', *kañji-d-a* 'of calf', *āya-n-a* 'his'.

South Dravidian II Telugu: Old Telugu has *-du*/*-adu* in the genitive, e.g. *nī-du*^{1} *karuṇa*^{2} 'your^{1} mercy^{2}'. All oblique stems in the singular may also carry genitive meaning when followed by noun heads. In the plural *-a* is added to plural suffix as an augment before case suffixes. The oblique stem also functions as an adnominal form, *bomma-l-a*^{1} *koluwu*^{2} 'show^{2} of dolls^{1}'.

Gondi: the genitive suffixes are *-nā*/*-vā*/*-ā*, e.g. *nāṭ-nā* 'of the village', *mī-vā* 'your (pl)', *kallē-n-ā* 'of thief', *kuhī-t-ā* 'of well'. In the Koya dialect, the genitive suffix is *-a* or *-i*, e.g. *mald-a* 'of peacock', *tappē-n-i* 'father's' (Tyler 1969; Shanmugam 1971a: 321–2).

Koṇḍa: the oblique suffixes *-ti*/*-di*/*-Ri*, *-a* and *-i* also function as genitive suffixes (Krishnamurti 1969a: 252), e.g. *kusa-di*^{1} *ēṟu*^{2} 'boiled water^{2} of vegetables^{1}', *goṟo-ti*^{1} *koṇḍa dēvuṇ(ḍ)*^{2} 'the Koṇḍa God^{2} of hills^{1}', *vank-a*^{1} *āram*^{2} 'their^{1}(n-m pl) food^{2}', *anar-i*^{1} *nāṭo*^{2} 'elder brothers'^{1} village^{2}'. The only non-augment type of genitive is *-ṇi* which occurs with some stems, *rās-k-a- ṇi* 'belonging to kings', *nāṭo-ṇi* 'of the village'. Here, there is a semantic fusion between possession and location.

Kui: the oblique stem is used in the genitive, *mṛehe-n-i* 'of man', *aja-n-i* 'of mother'.

Kuvi: *-i* is the genitive sign added to the oblique stems in final *-t* or *-n*, e.g. *mṛeha-t-i* 'of man', *aya-n-i* 'of woman', *kaḍḍa-ŋa-t-i* 'of rivers'.

Pengo: the genitive marker is *-i*, *dēs-t-i*^{1} *rāja*^{2} 'the king^{2} of the country^{1}', *kāl-d-i*^{1} *pṛēn*^{2} 'bone^{2} of leg^{1}'.

Central Dravidian Kolami: *-e* after *n*-ending stems and *-ne* elsewhere represent the genitive case, e.g. *ann-e* 'my', *kis-ne* 'of fire'.

Naikṛi has *-ē*/*-nē* as genitive markers, *avan-ē* 'his', *sup-nē īr* 'salt water'; Naiki (Chanda): *-e*/*-ne* mark the genitive case, e.g. *pul-ne*^{1} *tala*^{2} 'head^{2} of tiger^{1}', *ummel-e* 'of mosquito'; *-ta*/*-ṭa* also mean 'pertaining to', *am-e*^{1} *ūr-ta*^{2} *ōp*^{3} 'god^{3} of our^{1} village^{2}' (see section 6.3.1.1).

Parji: the genitive markers are *-n*/*-in* and *-ta*/*-to* of which *-t* represents the augment, e.g. *kōc-in* 'king's', *tāte-n* 'of father', *mer-t-o evul* 'leaves of the tree', *polub-t-a*[1] *pāv*[2] 'village[1] path[2]'.

Ollari: *-n*/*-in* in phonological complementation represent the genitive; these are said to be in free variation with *-ŋ*/*-iŋ*, e.g. *sēpal-in* 'girl's', *ayal-iŋ*[1] *garnḍa*[2] 'wife's[1] cloth[2]', *ī*[1] *kōnde-ŋ*[2] *kōrgul*[3] 'this[1] cow's[2] horns[3]'; *-ne* is also used as the genitive marker, e.g. *kor-ne cenḍi* 'cock's comb'.

North Dravidian Kuṛux: several suffixes are said to mark the genitive, *-gahi*, *-hi*, *-ta*, *-ā*, *-ntā*, according to different authors, e.g. *āl-gahi* 'of the man' (*LSI*), *ālas-hi*[1] *kitāb*[2] 'man's[1] book[2]', *pūp-ta*[1]*raŋ*[2] 'colour[2] of the flower[1]', *padda-ntā*[1] *pāb*[2] 'road[2] of the village[1]' (Shanmugam 1971a: 358–9).

Malto: the genitive marker *-ki* appears to have been borrowed from Hindi/Bengali, e.g. *male-ki* 'of the man', *maqe-ki ṭeḍuð* 'the boy's hand'. There is agreement between the genitive case and the head noun, e.g. *taŋgade-ki-ð*[1] *pel-ð*[2] *barca-ð*[3] 'the son's[1] wife[2] came[3]'. This feature of agreement also suggests Indo-Aryan influence.

Brahui: *-t-ā*, *-n-ā* mark the genitive of which *-t*/*-n* are oblique augments; hence *-ā* is the genitive marker, e.g. *kharās-tā* 'of the bull', *tē-nā*[1] *hullī*[2] 'your[1] horse[2]'.

Summary (i) The suffix *a*/*ā* has wider distribution in the family, e.g. SD I: Tamil, Kannaḍa, Baḍaga, Tuḷu; South Dravidian II: Telugu, Gondi, Koṇḍa; North Dravidian: Kuṛux, Brahui. In some of the languages, the suffix follows the augments *-t*/*-n*. (ii) The suffix *-in* as genitive occurs in South Dravidian I: Tamil, Toda and CD: Parji, Ollari, Gadaba. (iii) *-atu*/*-tu* occurs in South Dravidian I: Tamil, Kota, Toda; South Dravidian II: Old Telugu, mostly in the case of forming the genitives of personal pronouns. (iv) The suffix *-i*, which is not likely to be related to *-in*, is found in human nouns in South Dravidian II: Telugu, Koṇḍa, Gondi and Pengo.

(i) and (ii) can be reconstructed for Proto-Dravidian; (iii) was probably an innovation in Proto-South-Dravidian. (iv) is reconstructible for South Dravidian II.

6.3.2.4 *Instrumental–sociative*

The instrumental has two meanings: the instrumental meaning, i.e. 'by means of (an instrument)' or the sociative,[17] i.e. 'in company with', or 'possessing a state like happiness, anger etc.' In some languages, both the meanings are expressed by the same marker, but in others, by different markers.

[17] Other designations of this case are comitative, associative. There is an element of universality in the instrumental being used in both the meanings, 'instrument' and 'in company with', cf. Te. *-tō* English *with*, Hindi *-se* and Sanskrit *saha*.

The instrumental case is marked by Ta. *-āṉ/-āl*,[18] Ma. *-āl*, Ko. To. *-āl/-ār*; e.g. Ta. *vill-iṉ-āl* 'with the bow', *kai-y-āṉ* 'by hand', Ma. *rōga-tt-āl* 'because of/by disease', Ir. *-āle*, *nan-an-āle* 'by me' (only with human nouns or pronouns), Ko. *em-āl* 'by us', *kaṇ-ār* 'by the eye'. Kannaḍa has *-iM*, *-in*, *-inda* following the oblique formatives -Ø or *-d*, *naya-d-iM* 'with politeness', *iv-aṟ-iM* 'from these things', *adhikāra-d-inda* 'with authority' (soc), *kōl-inda* 'by a stick', *ivand-ir-inda* 'from these persons'.

Ta. *oṭu*, *ōṭu*, *uṭaṉ* 'with, in the company of' are used as the markers of sociative (comitative) case, e.g. OTa. *ivaḷ-ōṭu*[1] *vāẓiya*[2] 'may you prosper[2] with this woman[1]' (Pat. 21:37–8), *kāl-oṭu* 'with the wind' (Naṟṟ 2:9), *evvam-oṭu* 'with distress', *kiḷai-uṭaṉ* 'with relatives'. Ma. *ōṭe*: *vastraŋŋaḷ-ōṭe* 'with clothes'; Toda has *-wïṛ* 'with' for sociative, e.g. *kurb-wïṛ* 'with Kurumbas'. Kannaḍa has *-oḍane* as a sociative marker. The Tuḷu markers *-ḍa*, *-ṭa*, *-aṭa* may be related to PSD **oṭ*-V: *nin-aṭa* 'with you', *kañji-ḍa* 'with the calf' (soc), but the vowel quality poses a problem.

In South Dravidian II, Old Telugu had *-an* in instrumental sense, e.g. *kōl*(*a*)*-an* 'by an arrow'. The postpositions *-tō*, *-tōn*, *tōḍ-an* are used in instrumental and sociative meanings, *cēt-an* 'by means of ' (lit. 'by the hand') used for a noun meaning a 'human instrument' or the causee Agent occurring as a complement of true causative or passive verbs; Modern Telugu uses the latter two. Examples: *katti-tō*(*n*) 'with a knife' (instr), *sīta- tō* 'with Sita' (soc), *Sugrīwuḍu Rāmuni -cēta Wālini camp-inc-enu* 'Sugriva caused Wali to be killed by Rama', *Wāli Rāmuni-cēta campa -baḍenu* 'Wali was killed by Rama'. In Gondi *-ē* is the instrumental–locative marker, e.g. *kay-d-ē* 'with the hand', *rūsī-n-ē* 'with knives'. In some of the dialects it is *-e*/*-i*. In many dialects *-al* (< **-āl*) is used as instrumental–ablative, *curi-t-al* 'by knife', *rō-t-al* 'from home'. Koṇḍa has *-aṇḍ* as instrumental–ablative, e.g. *guṇḍu-d-aṇḍ* 'by a bullet', *āgasam-d-aṇḍ* 'from the sky'. For sociative, Koṇḍa uses the postposition *-vale*, *nā vale* 'with me'. Kui uses *-ke*/*-ge* in sociative meaning, e.g. *aja-n-ge* 'with the mother', *mā-ke* 'with us'. A postposition *-tole* is used in Kuvi for instrumental, e.g. *hēpor-tole* 'with broom'. In Pengo the instrumental is marked by the postpositions *-hudaŋ*, *-lahaŋ*, *-hoke*, e.g. *nāli-hudaŋ* 'with a gun', *ṭeŋgiya-hoke* 'with an axe'.

None of the suffixes provides the basis for reconstruction of an instrumental in South Dravidian II. It is not certain if OTe. *-an* (instr–loc) and Koṇḍa *-aṇḍ* are related to Pre-Tamil *-ān/-āl*.

Among the Central Dravidian languages Kolami has *-aḍ*/*-naḍ*, *-inn-aḍ* 'by you', *gollin-aḍ* 'with the bow'. Naiki (Chanda) has *-la*/*-le* for instrumental–ablative, e.g. *suri-la* 'with a knife'; *-t-al* and *-aṛ* are the other markers of ablative, e.g. *por-t-al* 'from top', *id-aṛ* 'from here'. For sociative, a postposition *-nokon* is used: *tōle-nokon* 'with father'. Parji

[18] In Old Tamil *-āṉ* is said to have both genitive and locative meanings.

instrumental–sociative is marked by *-oḍ*/*-noḍ* which is cognate with Kolami *-aḍ*/*-naḍ* and Naiki *-aṛ*. Tuḷu instrumental *-ḍa* seems closer to these than any other; Pa. *cēpid-oḍ* 'with a broom', *ōn-oḍ* 'with him', *inn-oḍ* 'with you'. Ollari has *-nāl* for instrumental–sociative, e.g. *koṭal-nāl* 'with a spade', *kuse-nāl* 'with vegetables'. For Central Dravidian it appears we can reconstruct *-aḍ* ~ *-naḍ* as instrumental–sociative. Ollari *-nāl* corresponds to OTa. *-āl*.

Kuṛux and Malto have non-native instrumental markers: Kuṛ. *-trī*/*-trū* 'through', e.g. *eŋg-trī* 'by me', Malt. *-t*/*-et*/*-it*, e.g. *maler-it* 'by men', *man-et* 'by the tree', *male-t* 'by the man', *kīṛ-et* 'because of hunger'. Brahui instrumental is marked by *-aṭ*, *dū-aṭ* 'by hand'; *-to*/*-ton* are used in instrumental–sociative meanings, and look very much like Te. *-tō(n)*, e.g. *nā mārā-to* 'with your son', *nā īlum-ton* 'with your brother', *laṭṭa-to* 'with the stick'. *-tō(n)* can be reconstructed for Proto-Dravidian in view of their occurrence in Telugu and Brahui in both the meanings of the instrumental case, i.e. instrumental and sociative.

Pre-Tamil *-āl*/*-āṉ* looks related to Ollari *-nāl*. SD I (Tamil–Malayāḷam–Kota–Kannaḍa–Baḍaga) sociative *-*oṭu*/*-*ōṭu*, Tuḷu instrumental *-ḍa*/*-ṭa*, and CD *-aḍ*/*-oḍ* are said to be related (Shanmugam 1971a: 376–7).

6.3.2.5 *Ablative*

In most of the languages the ablative of motion is rendered by postpositions meaning 'having stayed (in a place)'. In several languages the instrumental and ablative or the locative and ablative have identical markers. A review will show that the case meaning was present in Proto-Dravidian but not an exclusive marker.

Old Tamil used *-iṉ* for ablative, comparative and instrumental, e.g. *malai-y-iṉ* 'from the hill', *vaṇṭ-iṉ* 'like the bee', *vaḷi-y-iṉ* 'by the air', *kaṇṇ-iṉ nōkki* 'having seen with the eyes'. In Kannaḍa *-im*/*-in*/*-inda* are instrumental–ablative, *kere̱y-im* 'from the lake'. Baḍaga ablative is *-enda*, e.g. *aman-enda* 'from him'. Tuḷu ablative markers are *-ttï*/*-ntu*, e.g. *kanḍo-ntu* 'from the field'.

In South Dravidian II, Telugu has only a postposition for ablative. Gondi has *-al* for instrumental–ablative traceable to PD *-*āl*. Koṇḍa instrumental–ablative is *-aṇḍ*, *ḍuḍu-d-aṇḍ* 'by a stick', *āgasam-d-aṇḍ* 'from the sky'. There is another kind of ablative in *-ŋ* added to the oblique–genitive stems of certain 'place' nouns marked by *-ṇi*, *abe-ṇi-ŋ* 'from there', *inṟo-ṇi-ŋ* 'from the house' (Krishnamurti 1969a: 257–8). The only bound form in Kui is *-ṭi* for ablative 'motion from', *kui-ṭi* 'from above', *lai-ṭi* 'from inside' etc. Kuvi also has *-ṭi* with [−human] nouns, *ilu-ṭi* 'from house', *ilk-a-ṭi* 'from houses' (Israel 1979: 70–1). Pengo instrumental–ablative is marked by *-aŋ*, *kāl-d-aŋ* 'with foot', *joyl-t-aŋ* 'from the jail' (Burrow and Bhattacharya 1970: 39).

Kolami uses the instrumental *-aḍ/-naḍ* in some cases, e.g. *ind- aḍ* 'from here'. In Naiki (Chanda) the instrumental–ablative is marked by *-la*, *suri-la* 'with a knife', *aŋgaṛ-la* 'from the market'; *-aṛ* and *-tal* (?*t-al*) are also used as ablative markers with place nouns, *ad-aṛ* 'from there', *por-t-al* 'from the top'. Parji has several suffixes for the ablative, *-i*, *-ug/-uŋ*, *-ar/-are*, e.g. *mer-t-i* 'from the tree', *kon-t-ug*, *kon-t-ar* 'from the mountain', *juvi-t-are* 'from the well'. Ollari has *-uŋ* for ablative, *mar-ṭ-uŋ* 'from the tree'. In Gadaba, the ablative marker *-uṭ* follows the augment *-k*, e.g. *ule-k-uṭ* 'from the house', *māre-k-uṭ* 'from the tree' (Suvarchala 1992: 87–90).[19]

In Kuṛux *-tī* expresses instrumental–ablative, e.g. *parta-tī* 'from the mountain', *Rancin-tī* 'from Ranchi'. This is also used in comparison, e.g. *ās*[1] *eŋgan tī* [2] *kōh'ā taldas*[3] 'he[1] is greater[3] than I[2]'. Malto ablative is marked by *-nte* after human nouns ending in a vowel, *-inte* after those ending in a consonant, and *-te* elsewhere, e.g. *male-nte* 'from a man', *maler-inte* 'from men'. Like Kuṛux, *-tī* is also used as another marker of the ablative. In Brahui, the ablative suffix is *-ān*, *tug̲h-ān* 'from sleep'; it is also used to mark instrumental and comparative cases.

Gondi *-al*, Naiki (Chanda) *-al* and Brahui *-ān* marking ablative appear to be related to SD I *-āl/-ān* instrumental. Even Koṇḍa *-aṇḍ* seems to belong to this set. There seems to be syncretism in the use of three case markers, instrumental, ablative and locative. SD I *-in*, Parji *-t-i*, Kuṛux–Malto *t-ī* used for ablative seem to be basically Proto-Dravidian locative suffixes.

6.3.2.6 *Locative*

Only some of the languages have a locative case marker. Most languages use different postpositions meaning 'place, direction'. Even where a primary case suffix is used, it is also found in other case meanings. There are no exclusive, non-overlapping locative case markers.

Old Tamil has *-il/-iṉ* as locative signs occurring with inanimate nouns and pronouns, *maruk-iṉ* 'in the street', *irav-iṉ* 'at night', *cilamp-il* 'in the mountain'; *-ttu* has a locative meaning with certain place and weather words, *nilam* 'ground': *nila-ttu* 'on the ground' (Shanmugam 1971a:273). Malayāḷam also has *il*, e.g. *avaḷ-il* 'in her'. Kota has *-l* and Toda *-s̲/-z*, related to pre-Tamil **-il*, e.g. Ko. *marm-t-l* 'in the tree', Toda has *-s̲* (< **-l*) with variants in *š, ž, ṣ, ẓ*, e.g. *ïr- s̲* 'among the buffaloes'. Koḍagu locative marker is *-lï*, e.g. *mane-lï*, *tōṭa-t-lï*.

In Tuḷu the locative suffix is marked by *-ṭï/-ṭu* or *-ḍï/-ḍï*, e.g. *pū-ṭï* 'in the flower', *kañji-ḍï* 'on the calf'. In Old Tamil *uṭaṉ* was used as one of the postpositions in locative meaning, e.g. *cilam-uṭaṉ* 'in the hill' (Shanmugam 1971a: 276).

[19] Suvarchala separates *-t* and *-k* as augments in Parji and Gadaba, respectively. The authors of the descriptive grammars have not proposed this segmentation.

Old Telugu had a homophonous marker for both instrumental and locative, namely *-a(n)*, *cēt-an* 'in hand', *iṇṭ-an* 'in the house'. Modern Telugu uses this form only in some limited expressions like *poddu-n-a(n)* 'in the morning', *kind-a* 'below', *mīd-a* 'above', *paḍama-ṭ-a(n)* 'in the west', in which the case suffix got incorporated into the lexeme of the stem. Gondi *-te*/*-de* is used both for instrumental and locative, e.g. *nāṭ-e* 'in the village'. In Koṇḍa *-to*/*-do* (→ *-ṟo*) marks the locative after some place nouns, e.g. *nāṭ-o* (← *nāṭ-to*), *-tu*/*-du*/*-Ru* in others, e.g. *gaḍa-du* 'in the river'; in the case of plural oblique stems in final *-a*, the locative is marked by *-ŋ*, *paṇku-ŋ-a-ŋ* 'on the stones'. In Kui *-a* occurs as the locative marker, e.g. *paheri-a* 'in the road'. Burrow and Bhattacharya (1961: 128) noticed *-ta* in the dialects that they studied, e.g. *neppi-ta* 'on the shoulder'. Kuvi locative is *-ta*, e.g. *kaḍḍa-ta* 'in the river'; *-to* is also used, e.g. *nāyu* 'village': *nāṭ-o* 'in the village'. Pengo marks the locative by *-to*, e.g. *guḍi-to* 'in the hut'; after plural nouns the locative is *-aŋ*, ?*key-(ku-)k-aŋ* 'in the hands'. Except Telugu, the other South-Central languages mark the locative by a dental stop followed by a vowel, *-a*/*-e* or *-u*/*-o*.

In the Central Dravidian languages the locative can be derived from PD *-V*n*, e.g. Nk. (Ch.) *kuḍḍ-in* 'on the wall', Oll. *ki-t-in* 'on the hand', Gad. *māre-t-in* 'in a tree'; *-un* is found in some stems, e.g. Nk. (Ch.) *ūr-un* 'in the village', Oll. *soṛ-t-un* 'in the field', Gad. *polub-t-un* 'into the village'. Kolami has *-t* in locative, comparable to Ta. *-ttu* and Koṇḍa *-tu*/*-du*, e.g. *ella-t* 'in the house', *ūr-t* 'into the village' (Suvarchala 1992: 96–8). Parji has several markers for the locative, *-i*, *-ti*, *-el* and the postpositions *ka*/*kan*, e.g. *ī polub-t-i* 'in this village', *meram-el* 'in the jungle', *vāye-k-el* 'in the field'.

Kuṛux and Malto use *-nū* for the locative, e.g. Kuṛ. *eḍpa-nū* 'in the house', Malt. *ālar-nū* 'in/among men'. Mahapatra (1979: 73) gives *-no*/*-ino* as the locative marker in Malto, e.g. *man-no* 'in the tree', *maler-ino* 'in the people'. Brahui has two sets of markers: *-āṭĭ̄*, *āi* (dialectally *-ā*) and *-is*/*-isk*/*-ik* not apparently related to those in the other two languages, *shahr-āṭī* 'in the town', *xarās-ā* 'on the bull'. The second set means 'near, in the vicinity of, etc.', e.g. *mash-is* 'near the hill'.

The markers **-il*/**-in* account for South Dravidian I and Central Dravidian markers. Hence they can be reconstructed for Proto-Dravidian. Malto *-ino*/*-no* and Kuṛ.–Malt. *-nū* may be related with the loss of the first vowel to this; then the reconstruction goes to Proto-Dravidian. Old Telugu *-an* for instrumental–locative has already been compared with SD I **-ān*/**-āl*. Perhaps Parji *-el* (in which Pre-Parji *a* became *e* before PD **l*, see section 4.4.5) is also cognate with this. In Kannaḍa *-in* has an ablative meaning, while the locative is expressed by a postposition. On the basis of Ta.–Ma. *-ttu* used in the locative and SD II *-tu*/*-du*, we can reconstruct *-*tt*V as another locative suffix. In the locative case there is an abundance of postpositions used by all the languages.

6.3.3 *Postpositions*

Postpositions are historically independent words, which perform the function of case markers. They are sometimes added to stems already inflected with bound case markers. Alternatively they occur after the oblique stems of nouns in the place of bound cases. Some of the nominal postpositions also have oblique forms to which case signs can be added. It is not possible to reconstruct most of the postpositions for Proto-Dravidian but the semantic categories represented by them seem to be a shared feature of many of the languages, like 'near, above, below, front, back, up to (space and time), because of, for the purpose of, compared to', etc. Some of these are in the process of becoming grammaticalized, i.e. they have lost their autonomous status as words. Some are frozen words, which are not used elsewhere with the same meaning. Both Dravidian and Indo-Aryan have several such postpositions.

South Dravidian I Tamil: *koṇṭu* 'having taken' (past participle of *koḷ* 'to take') was used in the Instrumental meaning in Old Tamil, e.g. *kōl*[1] *koṇṭu*[2] *puṭaikkum*[3] '(some one) will beat[3] with[2] (lit. holding) the stick[1]'. For ablative Old Tamil has *niṉṟu* 'having stood', *iruntu* 'having been', e.g. *nīr niṉṟu* 'from water', *kālai-iruntu* 'from morning'. In the ablative the verbal participles *niṉṟu* 'having stayed' (← *nil* + *ntu*, *nil* 'to stand'), *iruntu* 'having been' (ppl of *iru* to be), e.g. *nīr niṉṟu* 'from water', *kālai iruntu* 'from morning'. The postposition *uṭai* 'possession' [*DEDR* 593] is more common as a genitive marker with animate nouns and pronouns than the bound markers, e.g. *avar-uṭai* 'their', *pari-y-uṭai* 'of horse'. Many postpositions were used in Old Tamil in the locative case, *kaṇ*, *kāl*, *akam* 'inside', *uḷ/oḷ* 'inside' [*DEDR* 698], *pāl*, *kaṭai* 'place', *vaẕi*, *mutal* 'beginning', *talai* '?space', *mēl* 'above', *varai* 'up to (place)', *vayiṉ* 'with', etc. (Shanmugam 1971a: 274–8).

Spoken Tamil (Schiffman 1999: 29–44) uses a number of postpositions (grammaticalized, inflected nouns or verbs), e.g. *kiṭṭe* in a dative sense for human possession, *en-kiṭṭe*[1]*paṇam*[2]*irukku*[3] 'I have money' (lit. 'in my possession[1], there is[3] money[2]'); it has an ablative meaning when followed by *irundu*. The postpositions *sēndu* 'together with', *mūlam* 'through', *vare* 'up to, until' occur with nouns in the nominative; *kūḍe* 'along with', *mēle* 'above', *pakkam* 'near', *kīẕe* 'below', *aṇḍe* 'near' occur with nominative or genitive; *āha* 'on behalf of ', *aḍiyle* 'at the bottom of', *edire* 'opposite', *mēle* 'above', *uḷḷe* 'inside of', etc. occur with nouns in the dative, e.g. *vīṭṭukku edire* 'opposite the house'; *sēttu* 'together', *pāttu* 'at, towards', *tavira* 'except for, besides', etc. occur with stems inflected in the accusative, *enne tavira* 'besides me'.

Malayāḷam has *koṇṭu* as instrumental (*arici-koṇṭu* 'with rice') and *il niṉṟu*, later *il ninnu*, as ablative postpositions. The latter have developed into *-innu*, *-īnnu* and *-nnu* through grammaticalization, e.g. *viruttiy-il niṉṟu* 'from the land', *mēl-īnnu* 'from above', *vīṭṭ-iy-nnu* 'from the house'; *kūṭe* is used as comitative postposition.

ĀKu. *-iddu* is from *irdu* 'having been'. Kota markers *-tr*/*-ltr* are apparently not derived from the above, e.g. *ayk-tr* 'from there', *pay-ltr* 'from the house'. Purposive *-kāṛy* of obscure origin is a postposition, e.g. Ko. *nāym-t-kāṛy* 'for justice'. Toda ablative *-nid̠* is derived from **-nin̠ṯu*; it also has *-s̠n* whose origin is not known, e.g. *kwïg-s̠n* 'from the plains'. Locative *-kiz*/*-giz* are postpositions.

Koḍagu: the postpositions *oṇḍï* (cf. Ta.–Ma. *koṇ-ṭu*) 'having taken' and *kay-ñja* (< **kay-ind-a*) 'by hand' are used in the instrumental meaning, e.g. *kat-tin-oṇḍï* 'with a knife', *nāḍa-kayñja* 'by me' (cf. Te, *cĕ̄ta* 'by hand'). In the sociative meaning *jotëli*, *kūḍa* and *pakka* are used as postpositions, e.g. *aveṇḍa kūḍa* 'with him'; in the ablative the postpositions are *iñji* (< **irnj- < irundu*) and *kayñja*, e.g. *nann iñji* 'from me', *mara-t-iñji* 'from the tree', *nāḍa kayñja* 'from me' (lit.'from my hand'). Locative *-alli* which is apparently borrowed from Kannaḍa is a grammaticalized postposition, meaning 'in'.

Kannaḍa: clearly the locative *uḷ/oḷ*, *oḷage* and *alli* are postpositions, *puyyal-oḷ* 'in distress', *enn-alli* 'with me'. The locative postposition is also used in instrumental and causative meanings.

Tuḷu: the ablative case markers, *-ntu* and *-ḍḍï* look like truncated words of unknown identity, *kaṇḍo-ntu* 'from the field', *mara-ḍḍï* 'from the tree'.

South Dravidian II Telugu: two non-finite verbs, *kūrc-i* (*kūr-cu* 'to put together' tr of *kūḍu* 'to meet'), *gur̠inc-i* (*gur̠incu* 'to aim at', a frozen verb) 'having regard to, concerning, about', are added to inflected accusative nouns, *ā rāju-nu gūrci/gur̠inc-i wiṇṭini* 'I heard about that king'. These occur both in Old and Modern Standard Telugu. The causee agent is marked by the instrumental postposition *cēt-an*, *cē-(a)n* 'by' (the instrumental of *cē(yi)* 'hand'), the sociative–instrumental is marked by *tō-(n)*, *tōḍ-an* (*tōḍu* 'company'), *katti-tō* 'with a knife', *sīta-tō* 'with Sita', Three postpositions are used with dative meanings, namely OTe. *kai* 'for' (← *ku* + *ayi* 'having been for'), OTe. *kor̠a-ku* 'for the purpose of ' (*kor̠a* 'purpose, work'), OTe. *poṇṭe* (< SD **por-u-ṇṭ-*) 'for the purpose of', cf. Ta. *poruṭṭu* 'for the sake of', *poruḷ* 'thing, matter' [*DEDR* 4544], Mdn Te. *kōsam/kōsaram* 'for the sake of' (perhaps from dat. *ku* + *ōsara* < Skt. *avasara-* 'pupose'). In the ablative *uṇḍ-i* (ppl of *uṇḍu* 'to be') is added to the accusative in *-n*; consequently, by reanalysis, *nuṇḍi* became the grammaticalized postposition meaning 'from'. Modern Telugu uses *nunci/ninci* (ppl *uncu* 'to keep', tr of *uṇḍu* 'to be') but interpreted as an intransitive, e.g. *āme ūri-ninci waccindi* 'she came from the village' (literally, 'being in the village, she came'). Old Telugu also used *kōlen* 'for'. Another widely used postposition in the sense of 'because' was *walana(n)* > *walna(n)* > *walla* from *walanu* 'possibility, skill', e.g. *nā walla* 'because of me'; others include *dāka(n)* 'up to, until' > Mdn Te. *dākā* : *iṇṭidākā* 'up to the house', *ninnaṭi-dākā* 'until yesterday'.

The genitive was marked by a postposition of obscure origin, *-yokka*, in learned speech and in commentaries on Sanskrit texts, but not in poetic compositions. This could be related to PD **o* 'to join, unite' which had an infinitive *-okka* in Tamil and Malayāḷam. This is also a case of a frozen, inflected verb. It is not also used in Modern spoken Telugu and is considered unidiomatic in writing. In the locative, Old Telugu has *andu* 'that place', *-lō(n)*, *-lōpala(n)* 'inside', of which the last two continue in Modern Telugu. Several words of direction are also used, namely *mundu* 'front', *wenaka* 'back', *daggara* 'near', *mīd-a*, *pai-na* 'above', *kind-a*, *diguwa-na*, *aḍugu-na* 'below, at the bottom'. The comparative postposition is *-kaṇṭe* (said to be dative *ku* + *aṇṭē* 'to' + 'if one says') both in Old and in Modern Telugu, e.g. *wāḍu nā-kaṇṭe poḍugu* 'he is taller than me' (lit. 'he-I obl more than- tall').

Sometimes more than one postposition can be used, e.g. *iṇṭ(i) lō-nunci* 'from inside the house', *ceṭṭu daggar-i-ki* 'near (to) the tree' (also see Mahadeva Sastri 1969: 166–70).

Gondi: *-aggā* 'with' occurs after human nouns, *vōn aggā* 'with him'. The Koya dialect uses *tōṇṭe* 'with' for instrumental-sociative, e.g. *goḍḍel-tōṇṭe* 'with an axe', *nā-tōṇṭe* 'with me'. Tyler (1969: 54–5) calls this a suffix and not a postposition, although it looks like a clear borrowing from Early Telugu oblique of *tōḍu* (perhaps originally **tōṇḍu*), namely *tōṭi*. He gives a list of fifteen postpositions, e.g. *porro* 'on', *perke* 'after', *pakka* 'beside', *kunci/nunci* 'from', etc.

Koṇḍa: the postpositions include *vale* 'in company with', *vandiŋ* 'for the purpose of', *daka* 'until' (< lw Telugu), *loʔi* 'inside', *ban* 'place', *musku* 'above', *aḍgi* 'below', etc. (Krishnamurti 1969a: 261).

Kui: *-ṛahi* marks the instrumental, *heni-ṛahi* 'with a razor'. Winfield lists (1928: 24–5) a number of postpositions for dative, ablative and locative, classified as (a) location (locative case meanings), (b) motion (to and from), and (c) association (with, by means of) etc. Examples: *tani* 'in', *lai* 'below', *sōṛi* 'near'; *ṛai* 'from', *bahata-ngi* 'motion to' (humans); *tangi* 'for', *tingi* 'because of', *rohe* 'together with', *ṛai* 'with' (instrumental).

Kuvi: the postpositions include *taṇa* 'at' (loc), *taṇa -ṭi* 'from place' (abl), *tole/tale* 'in company with' (soc), and seventeen forms in the locative, e.g. *ḍagre* 'near', *dari* 'near', *tāleṇi* 'below', two for 'limitative', *epe* 'up to, until', and three for comparative, e.g. *kihā* 'than', *lehē* 'like' (Israel 1979: 73–6).

Pengo: the list includes *lahaŋ*, *hudaŋ*, *hoke* in instrumental meaning, *saŋ* as a sociative marker. The ablative is marked by *nāṭaŋ* 'since', also used as instrumental with some nouns, *hombā nāṭaŋ* 'since Monday', *kīsaŋ nāṭaŋ* 'with tusks'. For dative, *kāji* and *bisre* 'for the sake of" are used. Six postpositions are given for the locative, e.g. *tāke*, *bitre*, *mīgo*, *hāgi*, etc. *ēzuŋ tāke* 'into the water', *mar jopi* 'on to the tree', *mar hāgi* 'underneath a tree' (Burrow and Bhattacharya 1970: 41–3).

Central Dravidian Kolami: in the ablative meaning *-tanaṭ*, *-nattaḍ*, *-naḍ* 'from, through' are used, e.g. *ūr tanaṭ* 'from the village'. In the dative *-nadaŋ*/*-adaŋ* 'to, near' are used, e.g. *amn-adaŋ* 'his possession'.

Naikṛi uses *-lāḍ* and *-tanāṭ* for the ablative, *ellā tanāṭ* 'from the house', *phoy lāḍ* 'from above'.

Naiki (Chanda): for the sociative meaning, *-nokon* is used: *tōle-nokon* 'with father', *maye-nokon* 'with mother'. In the locative *-lopun* occurs, e.g. *īr-lopun* 'inside water'.

Parji: in the locative the postposition *-kan*/*-ka* (cf. OTa. *kaṉ*) occurs after the genitive of a noun, followed by the ablative suffix *-ṭi*/*-ṭa*, e.g. *murtal-in-kanṭa* 'from (the place of) the old woman', *mer-to-ka* 'on to the tree'.

Ollari: *-payiṭ*/*-payṭi* is added to the inflected dative, e.g. *ayal-iŋ payiṭ* 'for (the sake of) mother', *kōndel-iŋ payiṭ* 'for the cows'. *-pelṭuŋ* is used in the ablative meaning, e.g. *mar-in-pelṭuŋ* 'from the tree' (Bhattacharya 1957: 22).

Gadaba: the list includes *aṭer* 'away from', *aḍgun* 'below', *kakel* 'near', *tanḍrel* 'inside', *kana* 'than', *ḍāŋka* 'till' etc. (Bhaskararao 1980: 60–1).

North Dravidian Kuṛux: the instrumental suffixes look like postpositions, i.e. *-trī*/*-trū* and the adverb *lēkē*. So does the genitive *gahi* 'possession'.

Malto: the sociative is marked by *-gusan*/*-ganē*, *ālar-guṭṭhiar-gusan* 'with men'.

Brahui: it is not certain how to distinguish case suffixes from postpositions morphologically.

Of the locative, postposition 'inside' [**uḷ*, **uḷ-a-* 698] can be reconstructed for Proto-South Dravidian because it occurs in Kannaḍa in SD I and Telugu, Gondi, Kui–Kuvi of South Dravidian II. Many of the native words used as postpositions can be reconstructed for Proto-Dravidian like the words meaning 'above, high' [**mē*, **mē-l* 5086] and 'below' [**kīẓ* 1619]. I have not attempted it for all the postpositions.

6.4 Pronouns

Pronouns anaphorically refer to nouns and can be substituted for them. They are a subclass of nominals since they are distinguished for number and/or gender and carry case markers. Pronouns are divided into three subclasses: (1) personal pronouns, (2) demonstrative pronouns and (3) interrogative pronouns. Personal pronouns occur in first and second persons and in the reflexive. These are distinguished only for number and not for gender. Demonstrative and interrogative pronouns are distinguished for number as well as gender. Etymologically also there are differences between these subclasses. The demonstrative pronouns are derived from deictic roots meaning 'this, that, yonder', while the interrogative pronouns are derived from the interrogative root, meaning 'what?' or 'who?' The personal pronouns are primary forms and are not derived from other roots.

Table 6.5a. *First-person-singular pronouns in the nominative and oblique*

Group I: First-person-singular 'I' [*DEDR* 5160]	Nominative	Oblique
Proto-Dravidian	**yaH-n*/ **yā-n*	**yan-*
Ta.	*yāṉ*	*eṉ-*
Ma.	—	*en-*
To.	*ōn*	*en-*
Ko.	*ān*	*en-*, *e-*
Koḍ.	—	*en-*
Ka.	*āN*[20]	*en-*
Tu. (dial)	*yānï*, *ēnï* (dial)	*en-*
Te.	*ēnu*	—
Go. (dial)	*anā*, *annā*, *ana*	—
Kui	*ānu*	—
Pe.	*ān(eŋ)*	—
Manḍa	*ān*	—
Kol.	*ān*	*an-*
Nk.	*ān*	*an-*
Pa.	*ān*	*an-*
Oll.	*ān*	*an-*
Gad.	*ān*	*an-*
Kuṛ.	*ēn*	*eŋg-*
Malto	*ēn*	*eŋg-*
Br.	*ī*	(?) *kan-*

Morphologically all pronouns carry case markers and postpositions. Interrogative and demonstrative pronouns are used syntactically in correlative constructions of the type, 'whoever asked . . . he' (section 9.3.2.3).

6.4.1 *Personal pronouns*

The personal pronouns pose interesting phonological and morphological problems in Dravidian. We will start with the cognates of the pronouns in the first person in different Dravidian languages.

6.4.1.1 *The first person*

Tables 6.5a–e give the forms of the first person in the nominative and oblique divided into phonologically coherent groups.

[20] In Kannaḍa, morphophonemic//N, M// are phonemically /m/ finally, but /n/ and /m/ respectively in gemination. Intervocalically N = /n/, M = /m/ or /v/. Apparently PD **n* fell together with **m* in Early Kannaḍa in the utterance-final position, but the contrast is preserved elsewhere, see Ramachandra Rao (1972: §§2.7, p. 38).

Table 6.5b. *Alternative forms of the first person singular*

Group II	Nominative	Oblique
Proto-South Dravidian	**ñān-*	**ñan-*, **ñā-*
Ta.	*nān* (> Mdn *nã̄*)	—
Ma.	*ñān* (dial *nān*)[21]	—
Kod.	*nānï*, *nā*	*nan-*, *nā-*
Ka.	*nā*N	*nan-*
Te.	*nēnu*; *nānu* (mdn regional substandard)	*nan-*, *nā-*
Go. (dial)	*na(n)nă̄*, *nan*	*nā-*
Konda	*nān*	*nā-*
Kui (BB)	*nānu*	*nan-*, *nā-*
Kuvi	*nānū* (F), *nānu* (S)	*nā-*
Pe.	—	*naŋg*, *nā-*

It is clear that Groups I and II are not etymologically related. Group I is derived from Proto-Dravidian **yān*/**yan-*[22] and Group II, which is confined only to South Dravidian I and South Dravidian II, requires us to reconstruct **ñān*/**ñan-* at the Proto-South Dravidian stage. We will see below what led to the creation of a second form in the singular in Proto-South Dravidian. I discussed the problems of the personal pronouns in great detail in an article in 1968 (reprinted with a postscript in Krishnamurti 2001a: 76–98), which continue to be discussed by Dravidianists. It is well established that the vowels **ă̄*/ **ĕ̄* alternate after the reconstructed palatal consonants **y* and **ñ*. The presence of **ñ-* in Malayāḷam and the alternation of the vowels in Telugu are sufficient to posit **ñ-* in Proto-South Dravidian for Group II. Also notice that the oblique is formed by shortening the long vowel of the nominative in both Group I and Group II. Additionally, in Group II there is a second oblique normally used in non-accusative cases. It is formed by dropping the final consonant of the nominative.

There are no serious phonological problems. There was neutralization of contrast between **ă̄* and **ĕ̄* in Proto-Dravidian after **y* leading to an alternation between these two vowels in different languages. South Dravidian I has *ā-*/*e-* (nominative/oblique),

[21] A. C. Sekhar (1953: 88–9) quotes one instance of Ma. *nān* in a tenth-century inscription and suggests, in agreement with Ramaswami Aiyar, that '*ñān* may have been a west coast archaism'. In old and modern Malayāḷam *ñān* is the standard form of the 1sg; only *ñān* (but not *nān*) occurs in *Rāmacaritam*, the earliest literary work in Malayāḷam (c. twelfth century AD); see George (1956: 159).

[22] My recent research supports the positing of a laryngeal **H* in the personal pronoun in Early Proto-Dravidian as **yaHn*/**yan-*, where *aH* becomes *ā* in Proto-Dravidian when the outcome is a free form; the laryngeal is lost, when the outcome is a bound form like **yan-*. Since this proposal is still to be discussed by Dravidian scholars I am giving only the traditional reconstructions in this chapter.

Table 6.5c. *First-person-plural pronouns in the nominative and oblique*

Group III: First-person-plural 'we' (exclusive, unless otherwise specified) [*DEDR* 5154]	Nominative	Oblique
Proto-Dravidian	**yaH-m*/ **yā-m*	**yam-*
Ta.	*yām*; *yāṅ-kaḷ*[24]	*em-*
Ma.	—	*eṅ-ṅal-*
To.	*em*	*em-*
	om (incl)	*om-* (incl)
Ko.	*ām*	*em-*
		am- (incl)
Kod.	*eŋ-ga*	*eŋ-ga-*
Ka.	āM	*em-*
Tu. (dial)	*yāṅ-kuḷï*, *eṅ-kuḷï*	*yaṅ-kuḷe-*, *eṅ-kuḷe-*
Te.	*ēmu*	—
Go.	*amm-ă̄ṭ*, *amm-oṭ*, *amm-ok*	—
Kui	*āmu*	—
Pe.	*āp(eŋ)*	—
Manḍa	*ām*	—
Kol.	*ām*	*am-*
Nk.(Ch.)	*ām*	*am-*
Pa.	*ām*	*am-*
Oll.	*ām*	*am-*
Gad.	*ām*	*am-*
Kuṛ.	*ēm*	*em-*
Malto	*ēm*	*em-*

Central Dravidian *ā-/a-* and North Dravidian *ē-/e-*. Tuḷu and Telugu have *ē-*, while the other South Dravidian II languages have *ā-* in the nominative. Old Tamil preserved the PD **y-* but it was replaced by *Ø-* in Later Tamil and all other languages.[23] Toda *ō-* corresponds to Ta. *ā-*. What is important to note is that the South Dravidian II languages have no phonologically related oblique forms in Group I. The oblique bases of these languages have initial *n-* (see Group II).

Table 6.5c gives the plural forms. There were in Proto-Dravidian two plurals in the first person, one including the person addressed, called the inclusive plural, and the other excluding the person addressed, called the exclusive plural. Table 6.5c mainly refers to forms of the first person exclusive, but there was already confusion between the exclusive

[23] The Tuḷu non-Brahmin dialect has *yānï*, which appears to be a recent development by lowering the vowel in *(y)ēnï*. There are no other cases of retention of PD **y-* in Tuḷu to support the assumption that this was a retention.

[24] 'The double plurals *nāṅkaḷ* and *yāṅkaḷ* are found as early as the Cīvakacintāmaṇi period' (Subbaiya 1923: 1).

Table 6.5d. *Alternative forms of the first person plural (exclusive)*

Group IV	Nominative	Oblique
Ta.	*nāṅ-kaḷ* (Mdn *nāṅ-kal-kaḷ*)	—
Ma.	*ñāṅ-ṅaḷ*	*ñaṅ-ṅaḷ-*
Kod.	*naŋ-ga*	*naŋ-ga-*
Te.	*nēmu, mēmu*	*mamm-, mā-*
Go. (dial)	*mamm- ăṭ, mā-ṭ,* *mām-aṭ, mamm-oṭ,* *mamo-o,* *mar-at, mamm-*a, *mā-m*	 *mā-*
Koṇḍa	*māp*	*mā-*
Kui (BB)	*māmu*	*ma-*
Kuvi	*māmbū* (F), *māmbu* (S) *mārrō* (F), *māro* (S)	 *mā-*
Pe.	—	*maŋg-, mā-*

Table 6.5e. *The first-person-plural (inclusive) forms*

Group V: First-person-plural 'we' (inclusive, unless otherwise specified) [*DEDR* 3647]	Nominative	Oblique
Ta.	*nām*	*nam(m)-*
Ma.	*nām*	*nam(m)*
Ka.	*nā*M (*nām, nāvu*)	*nam(m)-*
Tu.	*nama*	*nama-*
Te.	*manamu*	*mana-* (? < *nam-a-*)
[Go.	*namoṭ* (excl)	*mā-*]
Kol.	*nēnḍ*	*nēnḍ-*
Nk.	*nēnḍ/nēm*	*nēnḍ-*
Kuṛ.	*nām*	*nām-, naŋ-g-*
Malto	*nām*	*nam-*
[Br.	*nan* (incl and excl)	*nan-*]

and inclusive plurals. The forms in Group III which are derivable from **yām*/ **yam-* denote the first person exclusive. Note that the oblique is formed uniformly by replacing the long vowel of the nominative by a corresponding short vowel (with expected variation following **y*).

The forms in Group IV and Group V are obviously related. Group V forms represent the inclusive plural but no language shows **ñ-*; however, the alternation of *ā/ē* (see Te. *nēmu, mēmu* and *nē-* forms in Kolami and Naiki) suggest an original **ñ-*. Actually Malayāḷam preserves the *ñ-* forms in Group IV although the meaning is 'we (exclusive)'. It is clear that the distinction between the inclusive and exclusive forms got disturbed mainly in the case of forms with a nasal initial. The question is how does Group IV mean 'we (exclusive)' and Group V 'we (inclusive)'? In the literary languages also the distinction between the 'inclusive' and 'exclusive' got blurred from early times. I made the following proposal to account for all irregularities including the *m*-initial forms in the languages of South Dravidian II.

In Proto-Dravidian there was one singular form **yān*/**yan-* 'I' and two plural forms, **yām*/ **yam-* 'we (exclusive)' and **ñām*/**ñam-* 'we (inclusive)'. These are preserved intact in Central Dravidian (Kolami–Parji etc.) and North Dravidian (Kuṛux–Malto). In Proto-South Dravidian, the parent of South Dravidian I and II, a second singular **ñān*/*ñan-* was analogically created through back formation from the second plural **ñām*/ *ñam-*. Only these languages show *n-* forms beside the initial zero forms inherited from Proto-Dravidian **yān*/**yan-*. The formal rivalry between the two sets of forms, not supported by a functional (semantic/grammatical) difference, has further led to a number of changes:

(a) Note formal mismatch between the nominative and oblique forms (see the gaps represented by dashes for Groups I to IV). Such a mismatch is confined to those languages that have inherited the innovative singular in *n-* beside the normal form in *Ø-*.

(b) The presence of two singulars (with no meaning difference) and two plurals (with meaning difference) has weakened the original meaning contrast between the two plural forms. The addition of *-kaḷ* to the inclusive/exclusive plural **ñām*/**yām* (see Groups III and IV) to mean an exclusive was a shared feature of Tamil–Malayāḷam–Iruḷa– Kuṟumba–Koḍagu of South Dravidian I. Kannaḍa had lost the inclusive–exclusive distinction when one set got normalized as *nān: nām* replacing **ān*/**ām*. In South Dravidian II, the inherited plural **nām*/**nēm*, which later developed to *mām-*/*mēm*, being restructured on the analogy of the oblique **mā-*, meant only 'we (exclusive)' (see (c) below).

(c) In the above groups one notices that the singular–plural difference is signalled by the final consonants, *-n* for singular and *-m* for plural. But when the languages of Proto-South Dravidian II innovated a second oblique (in cases other than nominative and accusative) with the loss of the final consonant, i.e. **ñān* ≫ **ñā-* > **nā-*, **ñām* ≫ **ñā-*> **nā-*, the singular–plural contrast was lost. It was restored by a morphological change of substituting *m-* for *n-* initially in the oblique plural of all these languages uniformly. Note that all languages of South Dravidian II have *nā-* as the oblique stem for the nominative *nān*/*nēn* in the singular ('I'), and *mā-* as the oblique stem in the plural ('we') corresponding to the nominative **nām*/**nēm*. Later, the nominatives got restructured on the basis of the oblique stems; consequently we notice variation between *n-* and *m-* stems in the nominative of the plural (study Groups IV and V).

(d) Different languages of South Dravidian II have independently restored the inclusive plural, not related to the inherited set, by morphological innovation, e.g. Te. *mana-mu*

Table 6.6a *Second-person-singular pronouns in the nominative and oblique*

Group I: Second-person-singular 'thou' (*DEDR* 3684)	Nominative	Oblique
Ta.	*nī*	*nin̲(n̲)-*
Ma.	*nī*	*nin(n)-*
To.	*nī*	*nïn-*
Ko.	*nī*	*nin-/ni-/di-*
Kod.	*nīnï, nī*	*nin-, nī-*
Ka.	*nīN, nīn(u)*	*nin(n)-*
Tu.	*ī*	*nin-, in-*
Te.	*nīwu, īwu*	*nin-, nī-*
Go.	—	*nī-*
Koṇḍa	*nīnu*	*niŋ-, nī-*
Kui	*īnu* (W)	*nī-*
	nīnu (BB)	*nin-, nī-*
Kuvi	*nīnū* (F), *nīnu* (S)	*nī-*
Pe.	*ēn(eŋ)*	*niŋgeŋ-* (acc–dat), *nī-*
Kol.	*nīv*	*in-*
Nk.(Ch.)	*nīv, īv*	*in-*
Pa.	*īn*	*in-*
Oll.	*īn*	*in-*
Gad.	*īn*	*in(n)-*
Kuṛ.	*nīn*	*niŋg-*
Malto	*nīn*	*niŋg-*
Br.	*nī*	*ne-, n-*

(?< **nama-*), Go. *aplō* (lw < Marathi), Koṇḍa *mā-ṭ* (contrasting with exclusive *mā-p*; *-ṭ* occurs as plural suffix in Gondi but of obscure origin), Kui *āju*, Pe. *ās/āh* (< ?*āṯ*-V-).

A detailed discussion of the arguments and counter arguments relating to the above issues with a critical review occurs in Krishnamurti 1968: 189–205, 2001a: 76–98 (see particularly the postscript).

6.4.1.2 *The second person*

Group I in table 6.6a derives from the reconstruction **nīn/*nin-*. The loss of final *-n* in the nominative is a shared innovation of a subgroup of South Dravidian I (Tamil, Malayāḷam, Koḍagu, Toda, Kota and Tuḷu); that there was a final *-n* is attested by its presence in the oblique form. The initial *n-* is lost in all Central Dravidian both in the nominative and in the oblique as a shared innovation. The loss is also found sporadically in Tuḷu, Telugu and Pengo. The final *-n* is replaced by *-wu* in Early Telugu, but the oblique is *nin-*. Kolami–Naiki have apparently borrowed the nominative forms from

Table 6.6b *Second-person-plural forms*

Group IIA: Second-person-plural 'you' (*DEDR* 3688)	Nominative	Oblique
Ta.	*nīm, nīṅ-kaḷ, nīr, nīyir, nīvir*	—
Ma.	*niṅ-ṇal*	*niṅ-ṅal-*
To.	*nïm*	*nïm-*
Ko.	*nīm*	*nim-*
Kod.	*niŋ-ga*	*niŋ-ga-*
Ka.	*nīM (nīm, nīvu), nīṅ-gaḷ*	*nim(m)-*
Tu. (dial)	*nī-kuḷï, in-kuḷu, īru*	*ni-kuḷe-, in-kuḷe-, īre-*
Te.	**nīr, īru*	—
Go. (dial)	*nim-aṭ, nim-eṭ; im-eṭ, imm-ăṭ*	—
Kui	*īr, nīm* (BB)	*nim-*
Pengo	*ēp(eŋ)*	—
Manḍa	*īm*	—
Kol.	*nīr*	*im-*
Nk.	*nīr*	*im-*
Nk. (Ch.)	*īm*	*im-*
Oll.	*īm*	*im-*
Gad.	*īm*	*imm-*
Kuṛ.	*nīm*	*nim-*
Malt.	*nīm*	*nim-*

Early Telugu, hence Kol. Nk. *nīv/īv*, but note the oblique is the regular *-in* like the other Central Dravidian languages.

As in the case of the first person, there are two ways of forming the obliques: (a) by shortening the long vowel of the nominative, a feature of the whole family, i.e. *nin*; (b) by dropping the final consonant of the nominative, i.e. *nī*; the latter is an innovation of South Dravidian II, which has both types of obliques, the (a) type in the accusative and the (b) type in all other cases.[25] The vowel *ē* instead of *ī* in Pengo in the second person is aberrant and cannot be explained now.

The second-person-plural forms (table 6.6b) in Group IIA are derivable from PD **nīm/*nim-* with the following subsequent changes: (a) addition of the common plural **-kaḷ* to the plural form as an alternative to the basic form, perhaps as a polite expression in South Dravidian I; (b) the regular dropping of initial *n-* in Central Dravidian, and in variant forms in Tuḷu, Telugu, Kui and Pengo, as a parallel development to their singulars; (c) the mismatch between the nominative and oblique in Kolami–Naiki can be explained only by invoking borrowing from Early Telugu in the form **nīr*. Actually

[25] Koḍagu of South Dravidian I is unique in independently developing the (b) type of oblique in the first and second person singular in dative and genitive, e.g. dat: *nā-kï* 'to me', *nī-kï* 'to you' (Ebert 1996: 31–2).

Table 6.6c *Plural forms in South Dravidian II*

Group IIC	Nominative	Oblique
Te.	*mī-ru*	*mimm-*, *mī*
Go.	*mim-eṭ*, *mīṭ*	*mī-*
Koṇḍa	*mī-ru*	*miŋ-*, *mī-*
Kui	*mī-mu* (BB)	*mī*
Kuvi	*mī-mbū*(F), *mī-mbu*(S)	*mī-*
Pengo	—	*miŋg*, *mī-*

Table 6.6d *Tamil and Brahui bound plural stems*

Group IID	Nominative	Oblique
Ta.	(Old) –	*num-*; (Mdn) *um-*, *uṅ-kaḷ*
Br.	*num*	*num-*

this form provides a missing link in Telugu prehistory. But notice the oblique is *im-* from which we can predict that the nominative *$\bar{\imath}$*m* was replaced by borrowed *nīr*, as it happened in the singular in these two languages; (d) the replacement of the inherited plural marker *-m* by *-r* (the plural human suffix in the third person) in Old Tamil, Tuḷu and in Telugu, Koṇḍa, Kui and Kuvi is a shared innovation of these two subgroups, not found in Central Dravidian; (e) Gondi treats **nim-* as a singular and adds a plural suffix-*aṭ* to form the plural.

Table 6.6c shows that the languages of South-Central Dravidian (SD II) have innovated oblique *mī-* (≪ **nī* ≪ **nīm*) by a morphological change to restore the singular–plural distinction as in the case of the first person plural. The oblique is uniformly *mī-* in all languages of South Dravidian II, which indicates its primacy over the nominative forms with wide variability. Later the initial *m-* was analogically extended to the nominatives. Consequently we find in Telugu **nīru*, *īru*, *mīru* (the last in Mdn Te.), Gondi *im-*, *nim-*, *mim-* plus plural *-aṭ*, also *mī-ṭ*, Koṇḍa–Kui–Kuvi *mīru* beside *mīm-* (≪**nīm*).

Table 6.6d: the oblique of **nīm* should be normally **nim* or with loss of *n-* **im*; but Old Tamil shows *num-*/*um-* instead, explained as involving a vocalic change *i* > *u* when followed by *-m* in this particular item (Bloch 1954: 32). Brahui also has *num-* in the nominative and oblique. Since no other language in the family shows this development, we can consider these as independent changes.

Table 6.6e illustrates a unique development in pre-Gondi. The plural stem came to be treated as singular and a plural morph -V*ṭ* was added to it to make it a plural. A similar

Table 6.6e *Gondi plural stems (construed as singular)*[26]

Group IIe: Second-person-singular 'thou' (*DED* 3684)	Nominative	Oblique
Go. (dial)	*nimā, nim(m)a, nim-aṭ, nim-eṭ; ima, immā, imm-ā̆ṭ, im-eṭ*	*nī-*

Table 6.7a. *Reflexive pronoun singular*

Language	Nominative	Oblique
Proto-Dravidian	**tān*	**tan-/*taṉṉ-*
Ta.	*tāṉ*	*taṉ-*
Ma.	*tān*	*tan-*
Ko.	*tān*	*tan-*
To.	*tōn*	*tan-*
Koḍ.	*tānï*	*tan-*
Ka.	*tān*	*tan-*
Tu.	*tānï*	*tan-*
Te.	*tānu*	*tan-*
Go.	*tān, tanā, tannā, tānā*	*tan-*
Kui	*tān*	*tāṛan-*
Kuvi	*tānu*	*tan-*
Kol.	**tān*	*tan-/tann-*
Pa.	*tān*	*tan-*
Oll.	*tān*	*tan-*
Kuṛ.	*tān*	*taŋg-*
Malt.	*tān*	*taŋg-*
Br.	*tēn*	*tēn-*

development is also witnessed in the case of *(m)amm-Vṭ* 'we'. It would be worthwhile to investigate if there was any sociolinguistic circumstance that led to these unique formations.

6.4.1.3 *The reflexive pronoun*

The reflexive pronoun actually refers to the third person singular and plural (which some Tamil scholars have called 'the fourth person'). It cannot be used for the first and second persons anaphorically, except in specialized cases (see section 9.3.4.2,

[26] The plural becoming singular is attested in many European languages including English, in which 'thou' (2sg) is replaced by 'you' (2pl). In non-standard varieties of English a new grammatical plural is innovated as 'you-all' or 'you-se'. (I thank Comrie and Dixon for these comments independently communicated to me.)

Table 6.7b. *Reflexive pronoun plural*

Language	Nominative	Oblique
Proto-Dravidian	**tām*	**tam-*
Ta.	*tām, tāṅ-kaḷ, tam-ar*	*tam-, tamm-*
Ma.	*tām, tāṅ-kaḷ, taṅ-ṅaḷ, tam-ar*	*tam-, tamm-*
Ko.	*tām*	*tam-*
To.	*tam*	*tam-*
Koḍ.	*taŋga*	*taŋga-*
Ka.	*tām, tāvu, tam-ar, tav-ar*	*tam-, tamm-*
Te.	*tāmu, tā-ru, tam-aru*	*tama-*
Go.	*tammā, tamm-aṭ*	
Kui	*tā-ru* (m), *tāi* (neu)	*tāṛan-*
Kuvi	*tāmbu, tambū*	*tam-*
Kol.	**tām*	*tam-*
Pa.	*tām*	*tam-*
Oll.	*tām*	*tam-*
Kuṛ.	*tām*	*tam-*
Malt.	*tām, tāmi*	*tam-*

example (33) with comment). However, it is included here on morphological grounds, i.e. like the personal pronouns; it is not distinguished for gender but carries number and is inflected for case. The reconstructions **tān*/**tan-* (sg) 'he, she, it . . . self', **tām*/**tam-* 'they (pl, all genders) . . . selves' do not present any problems. In South Dravidian I the singular form is used as an emphatic clitic as well as a reflexive pronoun.

There are two other plural forms: Tamil–Malayāḷam add the common plural suffix *-kaḷ* to the plural stem as in the case of the other personal pronouns; there is another plural form replacing the inherited plural marker *-m* by the human plural suffix *-ru, tā-ru* in Telugu and Kui. Another polite plural by adding *-ar* to the plural stem **tām* occurs in SD I and in Telugu. In Telugu the form *tam-aru* is employed in the second person singular implying a higher degree of politeness than what is conveyed by the normal plural *mī-ru* 'you (pl)'.

6.4.2 *Demonstrative and interrogative pronouns*

These are etymologically and morphologically different from the other personal pronouns. They are derived from deictic bases which I reconstruct with a laryngeal in Proto-Dravidian, **aH* 'that' (distal), **iH* 'this' (proximal) and **uH* (intermediate). The interrogative pronouns are derived from **yaH(aH)* 'which?' The demonstrative and interrogative pronouns carry gender and number and are inflected for case. Not only the demonstrative pronouns but also the time ('now, then, when') and place adverbs ('here, there, where') are derived from deictic and interrogative bases. These last two are devoid of number and gender but are inflected for case. For historical details of **H* in deictic bases, see section 4.5.7.2.3.

The third-personal demonstrative pronouns derived from the deictic root **aH* have been treated in the discussion on gender–number (see section 6.2). The following is a list of pronouns other than those denoting 'he, she, it, they' (human and neuter) derived from the deictic and interrogative bases. Most of them are morphological complexes denoting 'place, time and manner'. They are syntactically adverbial but are morphologically treated as a subclass of nominals since they can be inflected with cases/postpositions. Many of them can be reconstructed for Proto-Dravidian. Sources for the following: *DEDR* (1984) and for Old Tamil Rajam (1992).

6.4.2.1 *PD* *aH/ *ā *'that (remote)' [1],* *iH/ *ī *'this (proximate)' [410]*

South Dravidian I Tamil: *a-/ā* adj 'that', *av-aṇ, a-ṅku, a-mpar, ā-ṉ, ā-ṇku, ā-ṇṭu/ ā-ṇṭ-ai* 'there', *ā-ṅku* 'that manner', *ap-pōḻu/ap-poḻutu* 'then, that time', *at-tuṇai* 'that much', *a-ṉṟu, a-ṉṟ-ai* 'that day', *a-ṉai* 'of that nature', *a-ṉai-ttu* 'that much', *a-mpar* 'yonder'; *i-/ ī* adj 'this', *iv-aṇ, i-ṅku, ī-nku, ī-ṇṭu/ī-ṇṭ-ai, ī-ṉ* 'here, this place', *i-mpar* 'here, this world', *ip-poḻutu* 'now, this time', *it-taṉai* 'so much', *i-ṉai* 'of this nature', *i-nṟu* 'today', *i-ṉi* 'now', *i-ṉṉa* 'such as this'.

Malayāḷam: *a-/ ā* adj, *a-ṅṅu* 'there', *a-nai-tt-um* 'so much', *a-nnu* 'that day', *ap-poḻutu* 'that time, then'; *i-/ī* adj 'this', *i-ṅṅu* 'in this direction', *it-taram* 'this kind', *innu* 'today', *ip-paṭi* 'thus', *ip-pōḷ* 'this time, now'.

Kota: *a-/ay-* adj, *a-nta* 'so great', *a-nā-* 'such'; *i-/ī* adj 'this place', *i-nta* 'so great', *i-nm* (obl *i-nt-*) 'like this', *i-nt-al* 'so many as this', *i-nḏy* 'today'.

Toda: *a-* adj, *a-ḏ* 'on that day', *a-t* 'that many', *ā-n-k* 'to that place'; *i-* adj 'this', *i-ṯ* 'in this direction', *ï-t* 'this many', *ï-ḏ* 'today', *i-l* 'in this place', *ī-n-k* 'to this place'.

Koḍagu: *a-/ā* adj, *a-lli* 'there', *ak-ka* 'then', *at-tï* 'to that side'; *i-/ī* adj, *i-lli* 'here', *ik-ka* 'now', *it-tï* 'to this side', *i-ntë* 'of this kind', *i-ndï* 'today'.

Kannaḍa: *a-/ā* adj, *a-nittu* 'that much', *ā-ce* 'that side, beyond', *ā-su* 'that much', *at-tal* 'on that side', *ah-aṅge, hā-ṅge, hā-ge* 'that manner', *a-lli* 'there', *ak-ka* 'then'; *i-/ī* adj, *i-nittu* 'so much as this', *i-su/ī-su* 'so much as this', *it-tal* 'on this side', *ih-aṅge/hī-ṅge* 'in this manner', *ik-ka* 'now', *i-lli* 'here', *i-ndu* 'today', *i-nu* 'the current time'.

Tuḷu: *a-/ā* adj, *ā-mbe* 'there', *ā-tï* 'so much', *a-ḷta* 'of that place', *a-ḷtï* 'thence', *ā-pe* 'yonder', *ā-ni* 'then'; *i-/ī* adj, *mūḷu* (< **i-mbuḷ*) 'here', *ī-tï* 'this much', *i-ñca* 'thus', *it-tɛ* 'now', *i-ni, i-nne* 'today'.

South Dravidian II Telugu: *a-/ā* adj, *ak-kaḍa* 'there', *ap-puḍu* 'then', *ac-caṭu, a-ndu* 'there', *a-nta* 'that much', *a-nni* 'that many', *a-ṭṭu* 'that manner', *ā-wala/aw-wala* 'that side', *a-ṭu* 'that side'; *i-/ ī* adj, *ik-kaḍa* 'here', *ip-puḍu* 'now', *ic-caṭu, i-ndu* 'here', *i-nta* 'this much', *i-nni* 'this many', *i-ṭṭu* 'this manner', *ī-wala/iw-wala* 'this side', *i-ṭu* 'this side'.

Gondi: *a-ggā/ha-ggā* 'there', *ap-pōṛ* 'then', *ā-han* (< **ā-ṯṯ-*) 'thus', *an-nēṭ* 'that day'; *i-ggā* 'here', *i-ŋgā* 'now', *i-hin, ī-hun* (< **ī-ṯṯ-*) 'like this', *hī-kē* 'here', *hī-pē* 'with this'.

Koṇḍa: *ay-a* adj 'that', *a-tal* 'that side', *a-be* 'there', *ā-Ru* 'that manner', *na-so* 'that much', *na-ni* 'that sort of'; *iya/yā* 'this', *i-tal* 'this side', *i-be* 'here', *ī-Ru* 'this manner', *iy-el/ē-l* 'now', *ni-so* 'this much', *ni-ni* 'this sort of' [the source of the *n-* forms is not clear].

Kui: *a-/ā* adj, *ā-mba/a-mba* 'there', *ā-ne* 'in that direction', *ase/āse* 'so much'; *i-/ī* adj, *i-mba* 'here', *i-ne* 'this side', *i-se/ī-se* 'this much', *ī-soṛi* 'so many'.

Kuvi: *ā* adj, *a-mba* 'there'; *ī* adj, *i-mba* 'here', *i-c(c)eka, i-cura/ic-cōra* 'so much, so many', *ī-yona* 'this year'.

Pengo: *ā, āy, a-nda* adj, *a-ce, a-ceke* 'that big', *a-be, ha-be, a-mbe* 'there', *a-n*i 'over there'; *ī, i-nda* adj, *i-ce, iceke* (neu pl *i-ciŋ, i-coŋ*) 'so big, so many, so much', *i-be, i-ni* 'here', *i-leŋ* 'so, in this way', *iy-onḍiŋ* 'this year'.

Manḍa: *ī* adj, *i-cek* 'this much', *i-ni, ī-ba* 'here' [*a-* forms not given in *DEDR*].

Central Dravidian Kolami: *a-naŋ* 'in that way', *ap-puḍ, ā-puḍ* 'then', *at-tin* 'there', *at-tek* 'that much'; *ī* adj, *it-tan* 'man of this place', *it-tin* 'here', *it-te* 'this much', *i-nḍi* 'now', *i-nḍeḍ, i-neṛ* 'today'.

Naiki: *a-tan* 'there', *at-te* 'that much', *a-sen* 'like that (person)', *ay-el* 'that direction'; *ī* adj, *i-naŋ* 'in this manner', *it-tin* 'here', *it-tek* 'so much', *i-nḍi* 'now', *i-ndaṛ* 'today'.

Naiki (Ch.): *ac-cir* 'day before yesterday', *a-tan* 'there', *at-te* 'that much'; *i-tak, i-tan* 'here', *it-te* 'this much', *i-ndi, i-nḍi* 'now', *ī̆-sen* 'in this manner', *iy-el* 'in this direction', *i-phuṛ* 'now', *iy-ānḍ* 'this year', *i-nen* 'today'.

Parji: *ā* adj, *at* 'in that direction', *a-na, a-ni* 'there', *ā-ta* 'like that', *ā-te*(*n*) 'so, in that way'; *ī* adj., *i-t-/it-tu* 'in this direction', *i-ni* 'here', *ī-ta* 'like this', *ī-te*(*n*) 'this way', *iy-aḍ* 'this year', *i-ne*(*n*) 'today'.

Ollari: *ā, āy* adj, *ā-l* 'there', *ā-cin* 'that day', *a-paṛ* 'like that'; *ī* adj, *i-nḍi* 'now', *i-t, īl* 'here', *i-ne*(*n*) 'today'.

Gadaba: *a-, ay-* adj, *a-ṭen* 'that way', *a-paḍ* 'that way', *a-puḍ* 'then', *a-man, a-l* (*lu*) 'there', *ay-nes* 'that day'; *i, iy* adj, *i-nen* 'today', *i-paḍ* 'in this fashion', *i-maṭuk* 'from here, from now', *i-man* 'here', *iy-ānḍ* 'this year', *i-l* (*lu*) 'here'.

North Dravidian Kuṛux: *a-/ ā* adj, *a-dā, ah-āy* 'there', *anti* 'then', *a-san/ha-san, a-yyā/ha-yyā* 'there', *an-nū* 'in that way'; *ī* adj, *i-dā, i-san/hi-san* 'here', *i-yyā/hi-yyā* 'over here', *ī -ge* 'therefore', *in-nū* 'in this direction', *in-nā* 'today'.

Malto: *ā* adj, *a-nde* 'then, thus', *a-no* 'there', *ā-ṇy* 'thus', *ā-ṭi* 'that place, spot'; *ī* adj, *ih-in, i-nda, i-ṉhi* 'here', *ī-nki, ī-nle* 'thus', *i-ne* 'today'.

Brahui: *ī* a base declined for case, to which the suffix enclitic pronouns are added; ?*ai-nō, a-nnō* 'today'.

Note that the laryngeal **H* lengthens the preceding vowel, hence **ā, *ī*, or assimilated to the following stop, or lost before voiced consonants. The *h* sound (> *y*) found in some of the languages presumably indicates the retention of the laryngeal, or its later development into a semivowel.

6.4.2.2 *PD* *uH *'yonder, not too distant' [557]*

Not all subgroups show evidence of the intermediate distance form.

South Dravidian I Ta. *u-/uvv-* adj 'of intermediate distance from speaker', *uv-an̠, uv-aḷ, uv-ar, u-tu, uv-ai* 'that man, that woman, those persons, that thing, those things (respectively)', *unta* adj, *u-ṅku/ū-ṅku* 'yonder', *up-pāl* 'the side near the person addressed', *u-mpar* adv 'yonder, aloft', *uv-aṇ* 'upper place', *uv-aṇ-ai* 'height'. Ma. (no forms are reported), Ko. *ū-n, ū-ḷ, ū-r* 'he, she, they (near the speaker)'; Ka. *ū* adj, *uv-a/ū-ta, uv-aḷ/ū-ke, uv-ar, ud-u, uv-u* 'this man, woman, these persons, this thing, these things (intermediate)', *u-nitu* 'so much as this', *u-ntu* 'this manner', *u-nne* 'this time', *u-lli* 'this place', Tu. *u-ndu, u-nde-kuḷu* 'this thing, these things'.

South Dravidian II Te. *u-lla* 'over there, nearer the speaker' (Classical); Koṇḍa *u-nda* (imper sg), *u-ndaṭ* (pl) 'take this', *u-nzar* 'take (sacrificial offering to Gods/dead elders)', Kuvi *ū/hū* adj, *ū-asi/hūv-asi, ū-ari/hūv-ari, ū-di/hū-di, ū-ati/hūv-ati, hū-aska* 'that male, those males, that female or thing, those females or things', *ū-ceka* 'so much', *ū-mba/hū-mbaa* 'there'.

Central Dravidian Pa. *ū-d, ū-r* 'this male, these males', *ut* 'in that direction'.

North Dravidian Kuṛ. *hū* adj, *hū-s, hū-r/hu-bṛar, hū-d/hu-bṛā* 'this man, these persons, this female or thing, these females or things', *hu-dā, hui-yyā, hu-san* 'there (close to you)', *hu-nnū* 'by that way', Malt. *u-thi* 'look there'.

The long vowel in the root syllable, gemination of the consonant in the morph following the deictic root and the *h*-forms in Kuvi and Kuṛux – all relate to the underlying laryngeal as part of the Proto-Dravidian root.

6.4.2.3 *PD* *yAH/*yĀH[27] *Interrogative root underlying words meaning 'who, which, what, etc.'*

The vowel following **y* represents neutralization *a* and *e* (see section 4.5.4.2), hence it is indicated by *A*. There is greater variation in the development of interrogatives in different languages.

[27] The reason for reconstructing *A* and *Ā* before the laryngeal **H* is to account for variation between *ew-/ēw* ~ *āw* in which /w/ is a reflex of PD **H*, in several languages (see mainly South Dravidian I languages).

South Dravidian I Tamil: *yā* adj 'what', *yāv-an̠/ēv-an̠*, *yāv-aḷ*, *yā-r/yā-var* (> *ā-r/ āv-ar*), *yā-tu/yāv-atu* (>*ē-tu*), *yāv-ai* (also later forms still within Old Tamil *ev-an̠*, *ev-aḷ*, *ev-ar*, *e-tu*, *ev-ai*) 'which man, woman, persons, thing, things (respectively)', *e-n̠n̠-a/ē-n̠* 'what, why, how', *yā-ṅku*, *yā-ṇṭu/yā-ṇṭ-ai* 'where', also *e-ṅku* id., *et-tuṇai* 'how much, many', *ep-poẓutu* 'what time', *e-n̠r̠u* 'when', *e-n̠ai* 'of what nature, how many'.

Malayāḷam: *yāv-an/ēv-an*, *yā-vaḷ/ēv-aḷ*, *yāv-ar/ēv-ar/yā-r/ā-r*, *yā-tu/ē-tu* 'which man, woman, people, thing', *e-ṅṅu* 'where', *et-tira* 'how much', *ep-pōḷ* 'when', *ep-pur̠am* 'which side'.

Kota: *e-/ey-* adj, *ev-n*, *ev-ḷ*, *ev-r*, *e-d/ē-d/e-n* 'which man, woman, persons, thing, things', *ey-k* (dat) 'whither', *ey-tr* abl 'whence', *ey-ōn*, *ey-ōḷ*, *ey-ōr*, *ey-d* 'man, woman, persons, thing from where', *e-ṯ* 'which direction', *e-nt-k* (dat) 'to what extent', *e-ntal* 'how many', *e-ntā* 'how great'.

Toda: *e-/ē* adj, *ē-θ* 'which person or thing', pl *ē-θ-ām; ē-l* 'where', *ē-ḏ/e-ḏ* 'why', *e-t* 'how many', *in-* 'what, why'.

Kannaḍa: *yā*, *ā*, *ē*, *e-* adj, *yā*, *yāv-a*, *ā*, *āv-a*, *dāv-a*, *ē* 'what, which', *yā-r*, *ā-r*, *dā-ru* 'who', *yāv-anu*, *āv-aM* 'which man', *yāv-aḷu*, *āv-aḷ* 'which woman', *āv-udu* 'what', *e-nitu/e-nittu* 'how much', *ē-su* 'how much, many', *e-lli* 'where', *eh-eṅge/hē-ṅge* 'how', *hē-ge* id.

Koḍagu: *ā-rï*, *dā-rï* 'who', *ēv-ė*^{n}, *ēv-a*, *ēv-u*, *ē-dï* 'which man, woman, thing/things', *e-nnï* 'what', *e-lli* 'where', *ek-ka* 'when', *e-ndï* 'which day', *ec-cë* 'how many'.

Tuḷu: *ē-rï* 'who', *dā*, *dāv-a* 'what', *dāy-e* 'why', *ē-ni*, *ē-pa*, *ē-po* 'when', *ē-tï* 'how much', *e-ñca* 'how', *ō-ḷu*, *o-ḷpa* 'where'.

South Dravidian II Telugu: *ē-wāḍu/e-w(w)aḍu* 'which man', *ē-wāru/e-w(w)aru* 'which persons', *e-w(w)ate* 'which female person', *ē-di*, *ē-mi(ṭi)* 'what, which one (n-m)', *ep-puḍu* 'when', *ek-kaḍa* 'where', *e-ndaru* 'how many persons', *e-nta* 'how much', *e-nni* 'how many' (non-hum), *e-ndu-ku* (dat) 'why', *e-ṭṭulu* 'how', *ē-lāgu* 'which manner, how', etc.

Gondi: *bō-r* (obl *bō-n-*) (< **wō-r̠* < **wō-nr̠-* < **wē-nr̠-* < **ew-anr̠*) 'who', ?*bap-pōṛ* 'when'. There are many *b-* forms which require an older ** w-*.

Koṇḍa: *ay-e* adj 'which, what', *ay-en/ey-en* 'which man', *ay-ed/ ey-ed* 'which woman or thing', *ini* 'what', *ini-k-an* 'who', *e-mbe* 'where', *e-so* 'how much', *e-soṛ* 'how many', *e-seŋ* 'when', *e-sti vale* 'whenever, when', *ē-nr̠u* 'who' (Sova dial).

Kui: *an-* (dial *in-*) 'what', *an-i* adj, *in-aki* 'why', *e-st-* 'which', *e-se* 'how much', *e-soni/e-soṛi* 'how many', *e-mbe* 'where'.

Kuvi: *in-i* adj, *en-a* 'what', *e-cura*, *e-ccōra* 'how many', *e-cela*, *e-cceka* (dial) 'when', *i-mbi* 'where'.

Pengo: *in-en* (pl *iner*) 'who', *in-a* 'what', *in-ak-an* 'who', *in-ak-a* (neu) 'what', *e-ce/e-ce-k* 'how much', *e-ca-k-an* 'how big (m)', *ime* 'where'.

Maṇḍa: *am-nan*, *in-an* 'who (m sg)', *am-d-el*/*in-d-el* 'who (f sg)', *am-d-i*/*in-d-i* 'which (neu sg)', *in-a* 'what', *e-ceŋ* 'when', *e-ce*(*k*) 'how much'.

Central Dravidian Kolami: *ē* adj (rarely used), *e-md*/*ē-n*/*ē-nd*, *ē-r*, *e-d*, *e-dav*/*ē-v* 'which man, men, woman or thing, women or things (respectively)', *e-naŋ* 'how', *ette* 'how much', *et-tin* 'where', *ē-puḍ*/*ep-puḍ* 'when'.

Naiki: *ē-n* 'who (m)', *ē-d* 'which woman or thing', *ē-v* id. (pl), *et-tin* 'where', *e-punḍ*/*e-phuṛ* 'when'.

Naiki (Ch.): *ē-n* (obl *ē-r-*), *ē-d* 'who (m), which one (f, neu)', *et-te* 'how much', *e-sen* 'how', *ē-l* 'which direction'.

Parji: *ē-d* (obl *ē-r-*) 'who', *ā-ro* adj. 'which', *ē-di* (obl *ē-ri-*) 'anybody', *e-te*(*n*) 'how', *e-ñot* 'how much'.

Ollari: *ēy-inḍ* (sg), *ēy-ir* (pl) 'who (m)', *e-ṭen* 'how', *ē-ṭ* 'where', *e-sel* 'when', *ē-net* 'how much'.

Gadaba: *ey-inḍ* (sg), *ey-ir* (pl) 'who (m)', *ē-di* (sg), *ē-vi* (pl) 'which, who (n-m)', *e-cel*, *ē-l* 'where', *e-ṭen* 'in which manner'.

North Dravidian Kuṛux: [*nē* 'who'], *endr* (sg) 'what', *e-kd-as*, *e-kd-ā* 'which man, which woman/thing', *e-kā* adj, *e-kāge* 'when', *e-kayyā* 'where'.

Malto: [*nēreh*, *nērith*/*nēth*, *nērer*], *indru* 'which man, woman, persons, thing', *ik* adj, *ike*(*h*), *iker*, *ikī*(*th*), *ikīr*, *iku*(*th*), 'which man, men, woman, women, thing (respectively)', *ikni* 'how', *ikon* 'how much'.

Brahui: *dēr*, *dē* 'who'(sg/pl), *ant* 'what', *arā*, *arāfk* 'which (sg/pl)', *arā* adj, *at* 'how many', *axa* 'how much', *ama*, *amar* 'how', *amarī* 'what manner'.

In addition to **yAH*/**yĀH*, there seems to be another Proto-Dravidian root **yAn* which also denotes the interrogative in several subgroups; specially study the forms that have *en-*/*an-*/*in-* in Tamil, Malayāḷam, Koḍagu, Kannaḍa, Telugu and all languages of South Dravidian II, Kolami in Central Dravidian and Kuṛux–Malto in North Dravidian. In terms of word structure, it would seem that the root has a final *-n* here, rather than positing loss of *H* before an *n*-suffix. In that case there would have been a long vowel resulting from the loss of a laryngeal **H*. Therefore, this must be taken as an independent reconstruction.

6.5 Numerals

Numerals are morphologically a subclass of nominals in that they are distinguished for number and gender and inflected for case. The cardinal numerals (the citation forms) are all non-masculine/non-human (neuter) in gender, e.g. Te. *nālugu* 'four' (cardinal, citation form), *nālugu bomma-lu* 'four dolls', *nālugu āwulu* 'four cows'. Separate classifiers or human plural suffixes are used when they qualify words denoting human beings: Te.

nalu-guru manuṣu-lu 'four persons'. Etymologically, the cardinals of one to five, eight to ten are morphological complexes involving an adjectival root and a marker of 'neuter' gender represented by **-tu/*-ku*. The number words for 'six', 'seven' and 'hundred' have a zero neuter morph, which is replaced by a human classifier when they occur as attributes to noun heads which are [+ human]. Cardinals can be used as nouns or adjectives of nouns denoting non-persons. To denote persons the numeral stem is followed by a human plural suffix *-(*w*)V*r* or a classifier meaning 'people'.[28] The numeral 'one' has more than one root in Proto-Dravidian.

The literary languages have basic numerals for 'one' to 'ten' and 'hundred', and compounds for 'eleven' to 'ninety-nine', and 101 to 999. Only Telugu has a native number word for 'thousand', i.e. *wēyi*. Tamil and the other South Dravidian I languages have borrowed all numbers, a thousand and higher, from Indo-Aryan.[29] All languages of South Dravidian I preserve the basic number words. Only Telugu in South Dravidian II retains all basic number words and also a basic word for 'thousand'. The tribal languages of Central and Northern India have borrowed many number words and the method of reckoning from the neighbouring Indo-Aryan and/or Munda languages.

The Dravidian method of reckoning is decimal, since compounds (of basic number words) are used for expressions from 'eleven' and anything higher, involving the processes of addition or multiplication. To indicate addition a higher number occurs as the first constituent of a compound and a lower number as the second; in multiplication the first constituent is a smaller number and the second a higher number; e.g. Mdn Te. *padi* 'ten', *padak-oṇḍu* 'eleven' $(10 + 1)$, *padih-ēḍu* 'seventeen' $(10 + 7)$, but *ira-way* 'twenty' (2×10), *ira-way okaṭi* 'twenty-one' $((2 \times 10) + 1)$. The same principle applies to all higher numbers such as *pan-dhommidi*[1] *wandala*[2] *ēbhay*[3] 'nineteen[1] hundred[2] fifty[3]' $(((10 + 9) \times 100) + 50)$. Panikkar (1969) has proposed complicated formulas for the Dravidian system of counting, but they are all explainable in terms of the above simple position-based processes, which he also recognizes.[30] Kuṛux and Malto deviate from the decimal system of counting, because of the influence of the neighbouring Munda language, Santali, which uses *kōṛi/kuṛī* 'score' as a basic number. Malto uses native

28 Modern Tamil uses *pēr* 'name' as a classifier denoting 'persons' added to the basic (non-human) numeral, e.g. *raṇṭu pēr vantāṅka* 'two persons came'. Modern Telugu uses *mandi* 'persons' from 'eight' onwards.

29 Ta. Ma. *āyiram*, Ko. *cāvrm*, To. *sȫfer*, Koḍ. *āirë/āira*, Ka. *sāvira/sāsira*, Tu. *sāvira/sāra* 'thousand'. All from Skt. *sahásra-* [*DEDR*, Appendix 11].

30 'Whether a given sequence is derived by multiplication or by summation can be easily inferred by observing the values of its constituents. In multiplications, the linear arrangements of the constituents will be from the lowest to the highest, i.e. the values of the constituents will be in an increasing order, while in summation the order will be decreasing. If both increasing and decreasing orders are found in sequence, then it is one of multiplication and summation' (Panikkar 1969: 213). I have arrived at the principles independently.

words in bound form only, e.g. *kōṛi-ond ēke* 'one-score-one'(lit. 20-1-1), *kōṛi-ond dūye* 'one score two'(lit. 20-1-2) (Mahapatra 1979: 119–22). Kuṛux uses native words 'one' to 'four' attributively, *ort mukkā* 'one woman', *ẽ̄ṛ aḍḍō* 'two oxen', but *kurī-ẽ̄ṛ* or *duī kuṛī* 'lit., 20-2 or 2-20 = 40' (Grignard 1924a: 30–1). The Brahui system of counting is taken from Balochi, e.g. *yanz-da* 'one-ten = 11', *sēnz-da* 'three-ten = 13' etc. (Sabir 1995: 7). Some dialects of Kui–Kuvi also use the system of multiplying by twenties, e.g. Kui *oṛiŋ gōṛi* '7 × 20 = 140' [910].

All Dravidian languages preserve the first two numbers 'one' and 'two'. Non-literary languages of central and north India have borrowed numerals from the neighbouring literary languages of the same family or another family with which they are in greater contact. Malto, Kuvi and Kui (Winfields's) have borrowed all numerals 'three + (three and everything higher)', Brahui 'four +', Kuṛux, Koṇḍa, Ollari, Gadaba 'five +', Kolami, and different dialects of Gondi 'six +', Parji 'seven +', and finally Kui (Letchmajee 1902, Friend-Pereira 1909) 'eight +' (Emeneau 1957a; repr. 1967b: §12).

The Central Dravidian languages have introduced a tripartite gender system in the first four numerals in derivational morphology, like 'two men, two women, two things (non-persons)', although in other respects there are only two genders (masculine: non-masculine) in these languages. Similar innovations to separate the 'female person' from the non-person category occur as isolated innovations in Pengo and Malto, and in the plural marking of several of the languages of South Dravidian II and Central Dravidian, independently, attesting to the naturalness of such an innovation. It may be noted that in Proto-South Dravidian I a feminine gender category was innovated both in the demonstrative pronouns and in verb agreement. In the following the basic numerals are given, first the adjectival form followed by the cardinal, which is derived from the adjectival root. In numeral 'one' the cardinal form and the adjectival root are etymologically different; hence they are given as separate groups.

6.5.1 *'one'*

(a) *PD* *on- *adj 'one',* *on-ṯu n. *'one thing' [990 (c)]*

SD I: OTa. *oṉṟu*, *oṟṟ-ai* 'one, one of the pair' (< **onṯṯ-ay*), Mdn Ta. *oṇṇï* 'one thing', *oṭṭ-ai* 'one of a pair', Ma. *onnu*, *oṟṟa* 'one, single', Ko. *oḏ*, To.*wïḏ*, Koḍ. *ondï*, Ka. *ondu*, Tu. *oñji* (for the root **on-* see section 6.5.10b).[31]

SD II: Te. *oṇḍu* 'one (neu)', *oṇṭi* adj 'single', *oṇṭ-ari* 'a single person, lone', Go. *unḍī̆*, *undī*, *onḍ*, Koṇḍa *unṟi*.

ND: Kuṛ. *ōn*, *ōnd* 'one whole', Malt. *-ond* 'one thing'.

[31] Rajam (1992: 443–7) calls the adjectival roots 'oblique stems'. This is not correct since she has used 'oblique' to denote stems to which case suffixes are added in non-nominative cases. All cardinal forms occur also as adjectivals in Classical Tamil. No ordinals are used in Old Tamil.

There is a verb **on-ṯu* 'to be united' in several languages. Note the absence of cognates in Central Dravidian for 'one' (a) and (b). The reconstruction given under Old Tamil is needed to explain Ta. *-ṟṟ-/-ṭṭ* and Te.*-ṇṭ-*.

(b) *PD* *ōr/or-*V adj [990 (a)]*

SD I: Ta. *ōr/or-u* adj 'one', *oruv-aṉ*, *oru-tt-aṉ* 'one male person', *oru-tt-i* 'one female person', *ōr-mai* 'unity', Ma. *ōr/oru* 'one', *oruv-an/oru-tt-an* 'one person', Ko. *ōr/or/o-* 'one', To. *wïr* adj, also *oš/o*, Koḍ. *ōr/orï* adj, Ka. *ōr/or(u)* id. *oru-vaN* (> *or-ba* > *obba*) 'one man', Tu. *oru/or-* adj, *or-ti* 'one woman'.

SD II: Te. *oṇḍ-oru-lu* 'each other', Go. *oror* 'one', *or-pan* 'one place', Koṇḍa *or-en(ṟu)* 'one person', *or neṇḍ* 'one day', *or-su* 'once', Kui *ro* adj 'one', *ro-ʔanju* 'one man', *ro-ṇḍe/ro-ṇḍi* 'one woman or thing', Kuvi *rō* 'one', *ro-ʔesi* 'one man', *ro-ndi* 'one woman or thing', Pe. *ro*, *ro-nje* 'one', *ro-k-an* 'one man', *ro-nj-el* 'one woman'.

ND: Kuṛ. *or^{o}t* 'one man or woman', Malt. *ort* adj 'one' (of persons), *orte* 'one man', *orti* 'one woman', Br. *asi* adj 'one', *asiṭ* 'one entity'.

The Brahui form phonologically goes better with 'one'(a), see numeral 'three'. There are verbs with the root **or*-V meaning 'to be united, to be together, etc.' in Tamil, Malayāḷam, Kannaḍa and Telugu. A subgroup of South Dravidian II (Kui–Kuvi–Pengo–Manḍa), which lacks cognates to 'one'(a), has innovated a cardinal on the root in 'one'(b).

(c) *PD* *o-kk *adj [990 (b)]*[32]

This underlies forms meaning 'one man, woman, thing'. The ultimate root seems to be **o* 'to be united' [924].

[SD I: Ta. Ma. Koḍ. *okka* 'together', Ma. *okkuka* 'to be together'.]

SD II: Te. *ok(k)a* adj 'one', *ok(k)ā̃ḍu*, *ok(k)arū̃ḍu* 'one man', *ok(k)ate* 'one woman', *ok(k)aṭi* 'one thing', Go. *ōkā* 'one each' (lw from Te.).

CD: Kol. *ok* adj, *okkon* 'one man', *okkod* 'one woman or thing', Nk. Nk. (Ch.) *okko*, *okkod*, Pa. *ok* adj 'one', *okur* 'one man', *okal* 'one woman', *okut/okti* 'one thing', Oll. *ukur* (m), *ukuṭ/okuṭ* 'one woman or thing', Gad. *ukkur* (m), *okal* (f), *ukuṭ* (neu).

The adoption of a non-numeral root as a numeral is an innovation in Central Dravidian with the isogloss also engulfing Telugu (perhaps because of geographical contiguity) which has two cardinal words for 'one' in classical texts. Modern Telugu has dropped the OTe. *oṇḍu* 'one' but has regularized the *okk-* form.

32 It is doubtful if (a) (b) and (c) are phonologically related, but *DEDR* gives them all under one entry on the basis of meaning. It is distantly possible that in Pre-Dravidian there was an ultimate root **o* 'to be united' which occurs as the underlying form of (c). In that case, the other reconstructions also go to Proto-Dravidian involving different formatives.

6.5.2 ***'two'***

PD **īr/ir*-V adj 'two', **ir-aṇ-ṭu* n (non-hum, neu) [474].

SD I: Ta. Ma. *īr/iru-* adj, *iraṇṭu* (>*raṇṭu*), Ma. *īr/iru* adj., *raṇḍu*, Ir. *raṇḍu*, *reṇḍu*, Ko.*ir-/i-*, *eyḏ*, To. *īr/i-/ï-* adj, *ēḍ*, Koḍ. *īr/iru-*, *daṇḍï*, but *pann-eraṇḍï* 'twelve', Ka. *Ir/iru*, *eraḍu*, Tu. *ir-*, *raḍḍï*.

SDII: Te. *īr/iru-*, *reṇḍu*, Go.ir-, *ranḍ(u)*, *riʔ-/ri-*, Koṇḍa *ruṇḍi*, Kui *rī*, *rīnḍe*, *rīnḍi*, Kuvi *rī*, *rindi*, Pe. *ri*, *rinḍ-ek* 'two women', *rinḍ-aŋ* 'two things' (neu).

CD: Kol. *īr-*, *indiŋ* 'two things', *iddar* 'two men' (< lw Te.), *īr-al* 'two women', Nk. *ir-*, *indiŋg*, *iddar*, *iraḷ*, Nk. (Ch.) *ir-*, *eronḍi*, *iroṭ-er*, *ira*, Pa.*ir-*, *irḍu*, *irul*, *iral*, Oll. *ir-*, *inḍi*, *irul*, *iral*, Gad. *ir-*, *iḍḍig*, *iruvul*, *iral* (same meanings as in Kolami).

ND: Kuṛ. *irb* 'two persons', *ē̃ṛ*, *ēṇḍ*, Malt. *-ist*, Br. *irā*.

The full form with two formatives (*-aṇ* and *-tu*) is reconstructible for Proto-Dravidian, compare Ta. *iraṇṭu*, Ka. *eraḍu* with Kuṛ. *ēṇḍ*. The Kota form *eyḏ*, according to Emeneau, has *ḏ* instead of *ḍ* (1957a; repr. 1967b: §4) on the analogy of the numerals *oḏ* (<**on-ṯu*) 'one' and *mūnḏ* (< **mūnṯu*) 'three'. In the Koṇḍa–Manḍa subgroup of South Dravidian II, the cardinals seem to be derivable from **iruṇḍ-* and not **iraṇḍ-* (>**er-aṇḍ-*); in the latter case these languages would have shown *e-* instead of *i-*. Note that in Kui–Kuvi–Pengo–Manḍa the cardinal 'one' is derived from the adjectival root **ōr/or*-V and not from **onṯu* like the other members of the subgroups, i.e. Telugu–Gondi–Koṇḍa. The *-nḍ* suffix is analogically extended to the numeral one in Kui *ronḍe*, Kui *ronde* (doubtful transcription) 'one' from **or-ṇḍ-*.

6.5.3 ***'three'***

PD **muH-/ *mū-* adj, **mū-nṯu* n (non-hum) [5052].

SD I: Ta. *mū-/muC-* adj (*mūv-ar* 'three persons', *mup-patu* 'thirty'), *mūṉṟu* (> Mdn *mūṇu*), Ma. *mū-/muC-*, *mūnnu*, Ko. *mū-/mu-*, *mūnḍ*, To. *mū-/mu-*, *mūḏ*, Koḍ. *mū-/muC-*, *mūndï*, Tu. *mū-/mu-*, *mūji*, Ka. *mū-/muC-*, *mūṟu*.

SD II: Te. *mū-/muC-*, *mū̃ḍu*, Go. *mū-/muy-*, *mŭnḍ*, Koṇḍa *muʔ-*, *mūnṟi*, Kui *mū-/muʔ-*, *mūnji*.

CD: Kol. *muy-*, *mūndiŋ*, Nk. *muC-/muy-*, *mūndiŋ*, Nk. (Ch.) *muy-*, *mūndi*, Pa. *mū-/muy-*, *mū̃duk*, Oll. *mūnḍ*, Gad. *muy-*, *mūḍug*.

ND: Kuṛ. *mūnd* 'three things', *nubb* 'three persons', Br. adj *musi*; *musika* 'three times'.

A Proto-Dravidian laryngeal is responsible for lengthening the vowel in **mū-*, for substituting a *y* in Central Dravidian languages (*muy-*), and for gemination of the following consonant, e.g. Ta. *mup-patu* 'thirty', Te. *mup-padi* 'thirty', *mun-nūṟu* 'three hundred'. Note that most languages of Central Dravidian have added another neuter suffix -*ŋ* to the cardinal numerals two to four, thereby construing the cardinal as an adjectival form, see Kolami, Naiki, Parji and Gadaba.

6.5.4 ***'four'***

PD **nāl*/ **nal*-V- adj, *nāl*, **nāl-nk*(*k*)V / **nān-k(k)*V n (non-hum) [3655].

SD I: Ta. *nāl-*/*nal*-V- adj, *nāl*, *nāṉ-ku*, *nāl-ku*, Mdn Ta. *nālu*, Ma. *nāl*/*nal*-V-, *nāl*, *nāṅ-ku*, *nān*, Ko. *nāl*/*nār*/*nā*- adj, *nān-g*, To. *nō*- adj, *nōn-g*, Kod. *nā*-, *nal*-, *nālï*, Ka. *nāl*/*nal*-V-/*nāl(u)*/*nā*-, *nāl*-(*u*)*ku*, *nā-ku*, Tu. *nāl*/*nal*-V- adj, *nālï* n.

SD II: Te. *nalu*- adj, *nāl*-(*u*)*gu* n, Go. *nāl-uŋ*(*g*)- (neu), *nāl-vir*/-*vur* 'four men', Koṇḍa *nāl-gi* (n-m), *nāl-ʔer* 'four men/persons', Kui *nā̆l-gi* 'four', *nāl-ur* 'four men'.

CD: Kol. Nk. *nāl*/*nall*-, *nāl-iŋ*, Nk.(Ch.) *nāli* 'four' (n-m), *nal-gur* (m), Pa. adj, *nālu*(*k*) 'four things', *nel-vir* 'four men', Gad. *nlagur* 'four men' (?lw < Te.).

ND: Kuṛ. *nāx* 'four things', *naib* 'four (indefinite)'.

6.5.5 ***'five'***

PD **cay-m-* adj, **cay-m-tu* n (non-hum) [2826].

SD I: Ta. *ai*(*m*)- adj, *ain-tu* (> Mdn Ta. *a-ñcu*) 'five (non-human)', *aim-patu* 'fifty', *ai-var* 'five persons'; Ma. *ai-*/*am*- adj, *a-ñcu*, *am-patu* 'fifty', Ko. *ay*- adj, *anj*, To. *oy*- adj, *üz*, Koḍ. *ay-*/*ayy*-, *aym*- adj, *añji* n, Tu. *ai*- adj, *ainï* 'five'.

SD II: Te. *ēn*-/ *ē̃*-/*ē*- adj, *aidu* 'five' (neu), Go. *sey-*/*sī-*/*hay*- adj, *saiyuŋg*-, *sīyuŋ*, *hayuŋ*, *ayŋ* n (neu), *say-uṟ*/*hay-vur*/*hay-ur*/*ayvur*/*ey-vur* 'five' (m), Kui *sē*- adj, *sēŋgi*/*siŋgi* 'five'(n-m).

CD: Kol. *ayd* n (lw < Te.), *sē-gur* 'five persons', Nk. (Ch.) *sē-ndi* 'five' (n-m), Pa. *cey-*/*cē*- adj, *cē̃-duk* 'five things', *cē-vir* 'five men', *cey-al* 'five women'.

There are no cognates in North Dravidian; also none recorded in Ollari–Gadaba of Central Dravidian.

6.5.6 ***'six'***

PD **caṯ*-V- adj, **cāṯ-u* n 'six' [2485].

SD I: Ta. *aṟu*- adj, *āṟu* 'six', *aṟu-var* 'six persons', Ma. *aṟu*- adj, *āṟu*, Ko. *ar*- adj, *ār*, To. *aṟ*- adj, *ōṟ*, Koḍ. *aru*- adj, *ārï*, Ka. *aṟu*- adj, *āṟu*, Tu. *aji*- adj, *āji*.

SD II: Te. *aṟu-* (> Mdn *aru*) adj, *āṟu* (> Mdn *āru*), Go. (dial) *sāruŋg, hāruŋg, ārū* n (n-m), *sār-vur/hār-vur/ḁ̄ṟ-vur* 'six men', Kui *sāja-* adj/n, *sajgi* n 'six' (Letchmajee 1902, Friend-Pereira 1909).

CD: Nk.(Ch.) *sādi* 'six'.

6.5.7 ***'seven'***

PD **eẓ-*V adj, **ēẓ*/**eẓ-*V n 'seven' (n-m) [910].

SD I: Ta. Ma. *eẓ-*V- adj, *ēẓu* n, *eẓu-var* 'seven persons', Ko. *eḷ-/e-* adj, *ēy/ēg* n, To. *ȫ* adj in some cpds, *öw* n, Koḍ. *ëḷï-* adj, *ë̄ḷï* n.'seven', Ka. *eḷu-* adj, *ēẓ/ēḷ* n., *ēẓ-var* 'seven persons', Tu. *ēḷ/eḷ-* adj, *ēḷï, ēḷverï* 'seven persons';

SD II: Te. *ēḍu, ḍe-* adj, *ēḍu* (n-m), *ēḍu-guru* 'seven persons', *ḍeb-badi* 'seventy', Go. *ēṟuŋ(g)* 'seven', *ēṟ-vir* 'seven men', Kui ?*oḍgi, oḍ, oḍgi* 'seven'.

CD: Kol. *ēḍ/ēṟ, eḍ-gur* 'seven persons' (lw < Te.).

6.5.8 ***'eight'***

PD **eṇ* adj, **eṇ-ṭṭu* n [783].

SD I: Ta. *eṇ-* in *eṇ-patu* '8 × 10 = 80', *eṇ-var* 'eight persons', *eṭṭu* 'eight' n, Ma. *eṇ-, eṭṭu*, Koḍ. *ëm-badï* 'eighty', *ëṭṭï* 'eight', Ka. *eṇ-, eṇṭu* (< * *eṇ- ṭṭ-*), Tu. *eṇ-ma* 'eight', *eṇ-pa* 'eighty'.

SD II: OTe. *en-* in *enu-badi* 'eighty', *en*(*i*)-*midi* 'eight', Go. *aṟmur* 'eight' (* *e-* > *a*, **ṇ* > *ṟ*);

CD: *enumidi* 'eight' (lw < Te.), *en-māṭar* 'eight persons'.

In Telugu *-midi*, a modified form of *padi* 'ten', seems to have been added on the analogy of *tommidi* (< *toṇ-padi* 'one less ten') 'nine'. Note that the gender marker *-ṭu* (<-**tu*) is confined only to South Dravidian I. The origin of *-ma* in Tuḷu is not clear, unless it is the first part of the reanalysed human plural (*-mar*< *-*war*).

6.5.9 ***'nine'***

PD **toḷ*/**toṇ* adj [3532].

SD I: Ta.*toḷ-/toṇ-* 'nine or $^{9}/_{10}$', *toṇ-ṭu* 'nine', Ta. Ma. *toṇ-ṇūṟu* '$^{9}/_{10}$ of 100 = 90', *toḷḷ-āyiram* '$^{9}/_{10}$ of 1000 = 900', Ko. *tom-battu* '9 ×10 = 90', Koḍ. *tom-badï*, Ka. *tom-b*(*h*)*attu*, Tu. *soṇ-pa* id.

SD II: Te. *tom-badi* 'ninety', *tom-maṇḍru* 'nine persons', but *tom-midi* '$^{9}/_{10}$ of 10 = 9'. Go. *tomidi* 'nine', *tomabai* 'ninety'.

CD: Kol. *tomdi* 'nine'.

The Kolami and Gondi forms are loanwords from neighbouring Telugu. In Telugu both the meanings as attested in Tamil must have been prevalent, requiring their reconstruction for Proto-South Dravidian. However, **toṇ* 'nine' as a basic numeral is more widely distributed in South Dravidian I and South Dravidian II. Also see *oṉ-pat*V 'one less ten' in section 6.5.10.

6.5.10 (a) ***'ten'***

PD **paH-* adj, **paH-tu* n, *pat-in-* in cpds [3918].

SD I: Ta. *paḥ-* adj, *paḥ-tu/pat-tu*, *paḥ-pattu* '10 × 10 = 100', *patt oṉ-patu* 'nineteen', *pat-iṉ-/padi-/paṉṉ-* 'ten in cpds eleven to eighteen', e.g. *patin-oṉṟu* 'eleven', *paṉṉ-iraṇṭu* 'twelve', *pati-nāṉku* 'fourteen' etc., *pat-iṉ mar* 'ten persons', Ma. *pattu* 'ten', in cpds *pat-in-*, *patin-mar* 'ten persons', Ko. *pat-* 'ten', *pad-/padn-/pan-/-vat/-bat/-at* in numeral cpds, To. *pot* 'ten', in cpds *pon-/-poθ/ -foθ/-boθ/ -oθ*, Koḍ. *pattï* 'ten', in cpds *patt-/padïn-/padi-/pann-/-padï/-vadï/-badï*, Ka. *pattu*, in cpds as first member *padin-/padi-/pann-/payin-*, as second member *-pattu/-vattu/-battu*, Tu. *pattï*, in cpds as first member *patt-/padï-/padïn-*, as second member *-pa/-va*.

SD II: Te. *padi* 'ten', as first member in cpds *padu-/pad-un-/pan-*, as second member *-padi/-badi/-wadi*, Mdn Te. first member *padak-/pann-/pada-/padh-/padih-/padah-/pan-*, as second member *-phai/-bhai/-wai*, Go. *pad*, *padi* (lw < Te.).

CD: Kol. *padi* (lw < Te.).

(b) ***'ten' minus***

SD I: **on-pat*V 'one less 10 = 9', Ta. *oṉpatu*, Ma. *ompatu*, Ko. *onbād*, To. *wïnboθ*, Koḍ. *ombay*, Ka. *om-battu*, Tu. *ormba*.

SD II: Go. *un-mā* 'nine'.

This seems to be a construction confined to South Dravidian I. The etymology of the Gondi form is not clear. The first part **on-* must be the root underlying **on-ṯu* 'one'. The minus value attributed to the first lower number by position (only before 'ten' in this case) is an innovation of South Dravidian I on the basis of a similar meaning in the case of **toḷ-* /**toṇ-* (see section 6.5.9). Telugu *pad-i* as a cardinal seems to be a reanalysed form from the composite numeral involving *-in* with loss of final.

It is interesting to note that OTa. *paḥtu* is one of the few words that preserved a Proto-Dravidian laryngeal **H* as a voiceless glottal continuant. The peculiar phonological changes of the root as *patt-/pat-*V as the first member of a compound, and *-pay/-pă̆* as the second member of a compound, are attributed to this phenomenon.

6.5.11 *'hundred'*

PD **nūṯ* (obl and in cpds *nūṯ-ṯ-*) 'hundred' [3729]

SD I: Ta. Ma. *nūṟu* 'hundred', *nūṟṟu-var* 'a hundred people', Ko. *nūr*, To. *nūṛ*, Koḍ. *nūrï* (obl *nūiṭ-*), Ka. *nūṟu* 'hundred', *nūr-var* 'a hundred persons', Tu. *nūdu* (obl *nūta-*).

SD II: OTe. *nūṟu* (obl *nūṭi-*, in cpds. *nūṭa-*), Mdn Te. *nūru* (obl. *nūṭ-*); Go. *nūr* (pl *nuhk*), apparently an early borrowing from Telugu.

The languages of South Dravidian I have borrowed the word for 'thousand' from Prakrit **sāsira* (< *sahasira-* < Skt. *sahásra-*): Ta. Ma. *āyiram*, Koḍ. *āirë* (for loss of **s-* see section 4.5.1.3), Ko. *cāvrm*, To. *sōfer*, Ka. *sāvira*, *sāsira*, Tu. *sāvira*, *sāra* [*DEDR*, Appendix 11]. Numerals higher than a thousand, like *lakṣa* 'hundred thousand' and *kōṭi* 'a crore, 100 lakhs', are borrowed into all the literary languages from Sanskrit.

Case suffixes are added to numerals either directly in some cases or to their oblique bases, treated partly in section 6.3.1. Tamil has oblique markers in *-aṉ/-iṉ*, *-att-*, or *-u* occurring after numerals (Andronov 1969: 97–8); *āyiram* (obl *āyira-tt-*) is treated like *maram* 'tree'. Telugu adds a complex oblique suffix *-iṇ-ṭ-i* with all numerals from 'two' onwards, *reṇḍ-i(ṇ)ṭi-ki*, *nūr-iṇṭi-ki* 'to two', 'to one hundred', etc.

6.5.12 *Ordinals*

Ordinals are formed by adding an adjectival suffix derived from the verbs **ā* 'to be' or **aHn-* 'to say', to the cardinals, e.g *-ām* in Tamil–Malayāḷam (*raṇṭ-ām* 'second'). OTe. *agu/awu* 'to become', hab adj *agu-/awu-*, OTe. *āṟ-awu* 'sixth', *muppadi-(y)-awu* 'thirtieth'. In modern Telugu the suffix *-ō* (< *-awa-*, <*awu*) is added to cardinals to make them attributive, e.g. *mūḍ-ō* 'third', *mupphayy-ō* 'thirtieth'. Old and Modern Kannaḍa add *-aneya* (*-nē* in fast speech), *eṇṭ-aneya* 'eighth'.

6.6 Quantifiers

Non-numeral quantifiers include expressions such as 'some, many, all' in different genders: SD I **kil-a* 'few, some' [1571]; PD **pal-*V- 'many' [3987]. Cognates occur for the last item in South Dravidian I, Telugu and Malto: Ta. *pal-avu* (neu), *pal-ar* 'many persons', Ka. *pal-a*, *pal-avu* 'several', *pal-ar*, *pal-a-var* 'several persons', Te. *palu-wuru* id., Malto (as a verb) *pal-war-* 'to be multiplied'; PD **ell-*V 'all' [844]. Cognates occur in South Dravidian I, Telugu, Kuvi of South Dravidian II: Ta. *ell-ām* 'all, whole', *ella-var-um/ell-ār-um* 'all persons', Ka. *ella* 'all, everything', *ell-ar-um* 'all persons', Te. *ella* 'all', *ella-(wā)r-u(n)* 'all persons', Kuvi *ele ʔe* 'whole'; *-um/-un* is an 'additive' particle (Emeneau 1974a: 107–8). Other expressions include **ko-ñcc-* 'small, little' [2047]: Ta. *ko-ccai*, *ko-ccu* 'small, mean', *ko-ñcam* 'little', Ma. *ko-ccu*, *ko-ñcam*, Ka. *ko-nca*, *ko-nce* 'a little, inferior', Te. *koncem(u)* id.; Kuvi *koceka* 'little'; cf. Pa. *koyyal* 'lean'. There are indefinite quantifiers like Te. *konni* 'some' (neu), *kondaru* 'some people', *konta* 'some quantity', but clear cognates are not available.[33]

6.7 Pronominalized nouns

Nouns and adjectives (descriptive and verb derived) can be used as predicates in equative sentences. They carry gender–number–person suffixes in agreement with the subject noun phrase just like the finite verbs. These are called by different names, 'appellative verbs or conjugated nouns' (Caldwell 1956: 477–81, attributed to Beschi as the first user, p. 478), 'pronominalized nouns' (Bloch 1954), 'personal nouns' (Andronov 1969: 122–5), 'derived pronominals' (Krishnamurti 1969a: 246–8) and 'predicative nouns' (Varadarajan cited by Israel 1973: 167–8). Tolkāppiyam calls them *viṉai-k-kuṟippu* 'verbal signs'. The tense is said to be 'covert' in these forms as opposed to regular verbs (Israel 1973: 162).

I give examples from Telugu using the forms *manci-wāḍu* 'a good man', *manci-di* 'a good woman', which are derived from the adjective *manci* 'good' in the third person as the basic form:

3m sg	*wāḍu manci-wāḍu* 'he (is) a good man'
3n-m sg	*āme manci-di* 'she (is) a good woman'
3hum pl	*wāḷḷu manci-wāḷḷu* 'they (are) good persons'
2sg	*nuwwu manci-wāḍ-i-wi* 'you (are) a good man' (addressee: man)
	nuwwu manci-dān-i-wi 'you (are) a good woman' (addressee: woman)
2pl	*mīru manci-wāḷḷu* 'you are good persons'
1sg	*nēnu manciwāṇṇi* (← *wāḍ-i-ni*) 'I am a good man'
	nēnu mancidānni (← *dān-i-ni*) 'I am a good woman'
1pl (excl)	*mēm (u) manciwāḷḷ-am* 'we are good persons'
1pl (incl)	*manam manciwāaḷḷam* 'we are good persons'

(*wāḍu* 'he' + *lu*→ *wāḷḷu*; *-lu* is pl suffix)

Notice that the third-person form is the base of the other persons. The oblique stems of *wāḍu* and *adi* are *wāḍ-i* and *dā-ni-* to which the personal suffixes are added: 2sg *-wu*, 2pl = 3pl *-ru*, 1sg *-ni*, 1pl *-am*. Even a Sanskrit noun like *kawi* 'poet', *kaw-ulu* 'poets' can be 'conjugated' similarly, *kawi-ni*, *kawu-l-am* (1sg/pl), *kawi-wi*, *kawu-lu* (2sg/pl), *kawi*, *kawu-lu* (3sg/pl). A woman may optionally be referred to as *kawayitri* 'poet-ess'. Nominalized verbs with tenses can also fit into these constructions, e.g. *wacc-ina-wāḍu/-di* 'the man/woman who came', *wacc-ē-wāḍu/-di* 'the man/woman who comes',

[33] *DEDR* gives some cognates in 2101 like Tuḷu *kondra* 'some, little', Kui *gonde* 'some', but they do not fit into the paradigmatic series as in Telugu, *anni-inni-enni-konni*, *anta-inta-enta-konta*, *andaru-indaru-endaru-kondaru* etc.

rāni-wāḍu/-*di* 'the man/woman who does not come' etc. In other persons, it is possible to say *nēnu waccina-wāṇṇi* 'I was the comer' etc. These constructions occur in Old as well as Modern Telugu. In Telugu even the first and second persons indicate gender in derived nominals, since the inflected form is taken from the third person, which distinguishes gender.

Old Tamil included two kinds of structures under *viṉai-k-kuṟippu*, predicative nouns carrying personal suffixes and defective verbs, which do not carry tense markers, e.g. 3m sg *all-aṉ* 'he is not', 3f sg *all-aḷ*, 3hum pl *all-ar*, 3neu sg *aṉṟu*, 3neu pl *all-a* (Israel 1973: 170–4). The personal suffixes are added to nouns in Old Tamil (Zvelebil 1977: 49), e.g. *nal* 'good':

1sg	-*ĕ̄n*	*nall-ēṉ* 'I am a good person'
1pl	-*ĕ̄m*, -*ă̄m*, -*ōm*	*nall-ēm*
2sg	-*ai*, -*āy*, -*ōy*	*nall-āy*
2pl	-*īr*	*nall-īr*
3m sg	-*ă̄ṉ*, -*ōṉ*	*nall-āṉ*
3f sg	-*ă̄ḷ*, -*ōḷ*	*nall-āḷ*
3neu sg	-(*t*)*tu*	*nan-ṟu*
3hum pl	-*ă̄r*, -*ōr*	*nall-ār*
3neu pl	-*a*	*nall-a*

In Tamil the forms occurring with the first- and second-person morphs can also be inflected with case suffixes, but not so in Kannaḍa and Telugu, e.g. *pāvi-ēṉ-ai* (acc)-*p-paṇi koṇṭāy* 'you have taken me, the sinful one, for service' (Zvelebil 1977: 49), *vallēṉ-ai* 'I (acc) who am strong' (Andronov 1969: 124). Jules Bloch (1954: 45) also cites examples with pronominalized forms based on verbs with tense signification, *pōnēn-ai aḍittān* 'he hit me who was going'. Literary Kannaḍa has pronominalized forms attested in Pampa Bhārata, e.g. *peṇḍati-y-en* 'I am the wife', *makkaḷ-evu* 'you are the children', *gōvan-ay* 'you are the cowherd', *balayutar-ir* 'you are the persons with strength' (Ramachandra Rao 1972: §7.2, p. 150).

In South Dravidian II these constructions are common, e.g. in Koṇḍa (Krishnamurti 1969a: 246–8) we have the following paradigm: *nān peri-k-a* 'I am (a) great (one)', *māp peri-k-ap* 'we (excl) are great', *māṭ peri-k-aṭ* 'we (incl) are great', *nīn*(*u*) *peri-k-i* 'you are great', *mīr peri-k-ider* 'you (pl) are great'. Like Telugu and unlike Tamil, nouns derived from tensed verbal adjectives also have derived pronominals of this kind, e.g. *visir* 'to throw': *visir-ti-k-a* 'I was the thrower' etc. We find pronominalized constructions with numeral adjectives also, *māp riʔep* 'we two' (excl), *māṭ riʔeṭ* 'we two' (incl),[34] *riʔider* 'you two' (Krishnamurti 1969a: 247–8). Kui has *ānu kūent-enu* 'I am Kui', *ām kūingan-amu* 'we are Kuis'. In Gondi similar constructions occur, e.g. *immā*[1] *bōn-ī*[2] 'who art[2]

34 Compare Te. *mēm/manam iddar-am* 'we two . . . (excl/incl)'.

thou[1]?', *imm-aṭ*[1] *bōr-īṭ*[2] 'who are[2] you (pl)[1]?', *amm-aṭ*[1] *vartal-ōr-ām*[2] 'we[1] are the guests[2]'(Bloch 1954: 37).

In Kuṛux there are forms of the type *ēn kūṛux-an* 'I am a Kuṛux man', *ēn kūṛux-nin* 'I am a Kuṛux woman', *nīn ek-ā ort-ī* 'who art thou?', *ēm Rancintam* 'we are the Ranchi ones' (Bloch 1954: 38; Hahn 1911: 73–5). Since the construction of pronominalized nouns occurs in South Dravidian I, South Dravidian II and North Dravidian, it can be reconstructed for Proto-Dravidian.

6.8 Conclusion

In this chapter we find morphological evidence in support of the subgrouping of the Dravidian languages adopted in this book. There are two exclusive innovations supporting the common descent of South Dravidian I and South Dravidian II from Proto-South Dravidian, namely (i) the back-formation of **ñān* 'I' from **ñām* 'we' (inclusive)', on the basis of the principle of proportional analogy **yān: *yām :: ? : *ñām*. Note that none of the members of Central Dravidian and North Dravidian has any first-person form beginning with *n-*. The fact that there were two rival singular forms derived from **yān*/**yan-* and **ñān*/**ñan-*, without any semantic difference, has led to many phonological and morphological readjustments in the languages of South Dravidian I and South Dravidian II (section 6.4.1.1). (ii) Another exclusive innovation is the replacement of the plural suffix *-m* by human plural suffix -V*r* in the nominative as a doublet in the second person and reflexive plural, i.e. *nī-m* ≫ *nī-r*/*nī-y-ir*/*nī-w-ir*, *tā-m* ≫ *tā-r*/*tam-ar*. The obliques, which are bound forms, remain stable as *nim-, tam-*, respectively (section 6.4.1.2).

Two clear innovations set off South Dravidian I from South Dravidian II and other subgroups: (i) the creation of a singular feminine gender (illustrated by **aw-aḷ* 'that woman'), and (ii) the loss of the final syllable **-ṯu* in nominative masculine singular, i.e. South Dravidian I **awan* < PD **awan-ṯu* 'that man' (section 6.2.6). Within South Dravidian I, another shared innovation is the addition of *-kaḷ*, a common plural suffix, to the plurals of the first- and second-personal pronouns in Tamil, Malayāḷam, Koḍagu, Old Kannaḍa (in the 2pl) and Tuḷu (see table 6.4c); Toda and Kota lack this feature.

All languages of South Dravidian II have oblique stems **nā-* (1sg), **mā-* (1pl), **nī-* (2sg), **mī-* (2pl). These are explained as arising from a process of dropping the final consonants of the nominative stems and other consequent changes, i.e. shifting the plural marker to the initial position in **mā* and **mī* (section 6.4.1.1) and analogically replacing the initial *n-* by *m-* in the nominatives. These changes have affected only the languages of South Dravidian II. Some scholars have tried to explain these as arising from metathesis, i.e. **an-a-*/**e-na-* > *nā*, **am-a*/**em-a-* > *mā-*,**in-a-* > *nī-*, **im-a-* > *mī-*, but there is no other case to support metathesis or aphaeresis involving alveolar and bilabial nasals in South Dravidian II; these scholars have not addressed that problem

(Burrow 1946a: 597, fn.4, Shanmugam 1971a, Subrahmanyam 1970b, G. U. Rao 1987b, Zvelebil 1990a).

In the use of cases, a subgroup within South Dravidian I is clearly demarcated by an exclusive innovation of loss of the accusative -V*n* and the use of *-ay*. These languages are closely related or are offsprings of Pre-Tamil, namely Old Tamil, Malayāḷam, Koḍagu, Iruḷa and Kuṟumba, but excluding Toda and Kota (section 6.3.2.1; mainly see discussion at the end of this section). This shows that Toda and Kota separated before this innovation took place.

In the case of numerals, the Central Dravidian languages stand alone by an innovation of numeral 'one' from the root *okk-* (section 6.5.1). The isogloss encloses the neighbouring Telugu and Gondi, which have other derived forms also. Alternatively, the innovation could have arisen in Early Telugu and been borrowed at an undivided stage of Central Dravidian languages, over one thousand years ago. This is a plausible inference, because Telugu has a productive use of the derivatives of **okk-* (section 6.5.1c, and not a, b); secondly there is a good deal of evidence of the Central Dravidian languages borrowing from Early Telugu or Pre-Telugu. Notice the borrowing of **nī r* 'you (pl)' from Pre-Telugu by Kolami and Naiki, which alone retain the evidence of such a Pre-Telugu form. The inherited nominative *īm* was replaced by *nīr*, but the oblique remains as *im-* (section 6.4.1.2).

Appendix: Paradigms of nominal declension

Paradigms are given only from those languages whose descriptive grammars cite them. I have not made any attempt to construct the paradigms from descriptive accounts.

South Dravidian I

1a. Old Tamil (Lehmann 1998: 80)

	malar 'flower'
Nom	*malar*
Acc	*malar-ai*
Soc–Instr	*malar-ōṭu, malar-oṭu, malar-āṉ, malar-āl*
Dat	*malar-kku*
Equative-Abl	*malar-iṉ*
Loc	*malar-il, malar-kāṇ etc.*
Gen	*malar-atu*

The case markers are the same irrespective of the gender features of the nominal stems unlike in Modern Tamil. Lehmann means comparative ('like etc.') by equative. This suffix *-in* does not continue in Modern Tamil.

1b. Modern Tamil (Asher 1982: 103)

	payyaṉ 'boy'	*maram* 'tree'
Nom	*payyaṉ*	*maram*
Acc	*payyaṉ-e*	*mara-tt-e*
Dat	*payyaṉ-ukku*	*mara-tt-ukku*
Instr	*payyaṉ-āle*	*mara-tt-āle*
Com	*payyaṉ-ōṭe*	*mara-tt-ōṭe*
Loc	*payyaṉ-kiṭṭe*	*mar-tt-ile*
Abl	*payyaṉ-kiṭṭ-eruntu*	*mara-tt-il-eruntu*
Gen	*payaṉ (ōṭa)*	*mara-ttu*

The difference between the two nouns in the locative and ablative arises from the difference in the feature of [± animate].

2. Malayāḷam (Asher and Kumari 1997: 191–4)

Case	Marker	Stems 'son'	'daughter'	'boy'	'tree'
Nom	ø	*makan*	*makaḷ*	*kuṭṭikaḷ*	*maram*
Acc	*-e*	*makan-e*	*makaḷ-e*	*kuṭṭilaḷ-e*	*maratt-e*
Dat	*-kkə/-(n)ə*	*makan-nə*	*makaḷ-kkə*	*kuṭṭikaḷ-kkə*	*maratt-iṉ-ṉə/-nə*
Soc	*-ōṭə*	*makan-ōṭə*	*makaḷ-ōṭə*	*kuṭṭikaḷ-oṭə*	*mara-tt-ōṭə*
Loc	*-il*	*makan-il*	*makaḷ-il*	*kuṭṭikaḷ-il*	*mara-tt-il*
Instr	*-āl*	*makan-āl*	*makaḷ-āl*	*kuṭṭikaḷ-āl*	*mar-tt-āl*
Gen	*-uṭe/-ṟe*	*makan-ṟe*	*makaḷ-uṭe*	*kuṭṭikaḷ-uṭe*	*mara-tt-inṟe*

3. *Koḍagu* (Ebert 1996: 30–1)

	akkë 'elder sister'	*mōva* 'daughter'	*mūḍi* 'girl'	*mane* 'house'	*mara* 'tree'
Singular					
Nom	*akkë*	*mōva*	*mūḍi*	*mane*	*mara*
Dat	*akkën-gï*	*mōva-kï*	*mṭḍi-kï*	*mane-kï*	*mara-kï*
Acc	*akkën-a*	*mōvaḷ-a*	*mūḍi-na*	*mane-na*	*maratï-na*
Gen	*akkën-ḍa*	*mōva-ḍa*	*mūḍi-ra*	*mane-ra*	*maratï-ra*
Loc	–	–	–	*mane-lï*	*maratï-lï*
Abl	–	–	–	*mane-nja*	*maratï-nja*
Plural					
Nom	*akkën-ga*	*mōle-ya*	*mūḍi-ya*		
Dat	*akkën-ga-kï*	*mōle-ya-kï*	*mūḍi-ya-kï*		
Acc	*akkën-gaḷ-a*	*mōle-yaḷ-a*	*mūḍi-yaḷ-a*		
Gen	*akkën-ga-ḍa*	*mōle-ya-ḍa*	*mūḍi-ya-ḍa*		

4. *Kannaḍa* (Steever 1998 based on Sridhar 1990)

	mara 'tree'	*mane* 'house'	*huḍuga* 'boy'
Singular			
Nom	*mara*	*mane*	*huḍuga*
Obl	*mara-d-*	*mane-*	*huḍuga-n-*
Acc	*marav-annu*	*maney-annu*	*huḍuga-n-annu*
Dat	*mara-kke*	*mane-ge*	*huḍuga-n-ige*
Gen	*mara-d-a*	*maney-a*	*huḍuga-n-a*
Loc	*mara-d-alli*	*maney-alli*	*huḍuga-n-alli*
Abl	*mara-d-inda*	*maney-inda*	*huḍugan-inda*
Plural			
Nom	*mara-gaḷu*	*mane-gaḷu*	*huḍuga-ru*
Acc	*mara-gaḷ-annu*	*mane-gaḷ-annu*	*huḍuga-r-annu*
Dat	*mara-gaḷ-ige*	*mane-gaḷ-ige*	*huḍuga-r-ige*
Gen	*mara-gaḷ-a*	*mane-gaḷ-a*	*huḍuga-r-a*
Loc	*mara-gaḷ-alli*	*mane-gaḷ-alli*	*huḍuga-r-alli*
Abl	*mara-gaḷ-inda*	*mane-gaḷ-inda*	*huḍuga-r-inda*

5. Tuḷu (Bhat 1998: 164)

	mara 'tree'	*mage* 'son'	*kallï* 'stone'	*pū* 'flower'
Singular				
Nom	*mara*	*mage*	*kallï*	*pū*
Acc	*mara-nï*	*maga-nï*	*kallï-nï*	*pū-nu*
Dat	*mara-kï*	*maga-kï*	*kallï-gï*	*pū-ku*
Abl	*mara-ḍdï*	*maga-ḍdï*	*kallï-ḍdï*	*pū-ḍdu*
Loc 1	*mara-ṭï*	*maga-tï*	*kallï-ḍï*	*pū-ṭu*
Loc 2	*mara-ṭɛ*	–	*kallï-ḍɛ*	*pū-ṭɛ*
Soc	*mara-ṭa*	*maga-ṭa*	*kallï-ḍa*	*pū-ṭa*
Gen	*mara-ta*	*maga-na*	*kallï-da*	*pū-ta*
Plural				
Nom	*mara-kulu*	*maga-llu*	*kallu-lu*	*pū-kulu*
Acc	*mara-kul-e-nï*	*maga-ll-e-nï*	*kallï-l-enï*	*pū-kul-e-nï*
Dat	*mara-kul-e-gï*	*maga-ll-e-kï*	*kallï-l-e-gï*	*pū-kul-e-gï*
Abl	*mara-kul-e-ḍdï*	*maga-ll-e-ḍdï*	*kallï-l-e-ḍdï*	*pū-kul-e-ḍdï*
Loc 1	*mara-kul-e-ḍï*	*maga-ll-e-ḍï*	*kallï-l-e-ḍï*	*pū-kul-e-ḍï*
Loc 2	*mara-kul-e-ḍɛ*	–	*kallï-l-e-ḍɛ*	*pū-kul-e-ḍɛ*
Soc	*mara-kul-e-da*	*maga-ll-e-ḍa*	*kallï-l-e-ḍa*	*pū-kul-e-ḍa*
Gen	*mara-kul-e-na*	*maga-ll-e-na*	*kallï-l-e-na*	*pū-kul-e-na*

In the plural *-e* is the oblique marker uniformly.

South Dravidian II

6. Modern Telugu (Krishnamurti and Gwynn 1985)

	bomma 'doll'	*tammuḍu* 'younger brother'	*illu* 'house'
Singular			
Nom	*bomma*	*tammuḍu*	*illu*
Obl–Gen	*bomma -ø*	*tammuḍ-i*	*iṇ-ṭi*
Acc	*bomm-ø/-nu*	*tammu-ṇṇi*	*iṇ-ṭi-ni*
		(← tammuḍi-ni)	
Dat	*bomma-ku*	*tammuḍ-i-ki*	*iṇ-ṭi-ki*
Instr–Soc	*bomma-tō*	*tammuḍ-i-tō*	*iṇ-ṭi-tō*
Abl	*bomma-ninci*	*tammuṇ-nunci/-ninci*	*iṇ-ṭi-nunci/-ninci*
Loc	*bomma-lō*	*tammuḷ-lō*	*iṇ-ṭ(i)-lō*
		(← tammuḍ-i-lō)	
Plural	*bomma-lu*	*tammuḷ-ḷu*	*iṇḍ-ḷu/iḷ-ḷu*
	'dolls'	*'younger brothers'*	*'houses'*
Nom	*bomma-lu*	*tammuḷ-ḷu*	*iṇḍ-ḷu/iḷ-ḷu*
Obl–Gen	*bomma-l-a*	*tammuḷ-ḷ-a*	*iṇḍ-ḷ-a/iḷ-ḷ-a*
Acc	*bommalu/*	*tammuḷ-ḷ-a-nu*	*iṇḍ-ḷu/iḷ-ḷu (or)*
	bomma-l-(a)-nu		*iṇḍ-ḷ-a-nu/iḷ-ḷ-a-nu*
Dat	*bomma-l-a-ku*	*tammuḷ-ḷ-a-ku*	*iṇḍ-ḷ-a-ku/iḷ-ḷ-a-ku*
Instr–Soc	*bomma-l-a-tō*	*tammuḷ-ḷ-a-tō*	*iṇḍ-ḷ-a-tō/iḷ-ḷ-a-tō*
Abl	*bomma-l-a-nunci*	*tammuḷ-ḷ-a-nunci*	*iṇḍ-ḷ-a-nunci/iḷ-ḷ-a-nunci*
Loc	*bomma-l-(a)-lō*	*tammuḷ-ḷ-a-lō*	*iṇḍ-ḷ-a-lō/iḷ-ḷ-a-lō*

7. Koṇḍa (Krishnamurti 1969a: 261–4)

Stem	Oblique	Acc–Dat	Instr–Abl	Loc
kiyu 'hand'	*kiyu-di*	*kiyu-di-ŋ*	*kiyu-d-aṇḍ*	*kī-du*
nāṟu 'village'	*nāṟu-di*	*nāṟu-di-ŋ*	*nāṟ-d-aṇḍ*	*nā-ṭo*
sālam 'cavw'	*sālam-ti*	*sālam-ti-ŋ*	*sālam-t-aṇḍ*	*sālam-i*

In the plural the use of instrumental–ablative is rare.

8. Kui (Winfield 1928: 25–8)

	āba 'father'	*aja* 'mother'	*kōru* 'buffalo'
Singular			
Nom	*āba*	*aja*	*kōru*
Gen	*āba*	*aja-ni*	*kōru*
Acc	*āba-i*	*aja-ni-i*	*kōru-tin-i*
Dat	*āba-ki*	*aja-n-gi*	*kōru tin-gi*
Ass	*āba-ke*	*aja-n-ge*	–
Abl	*āba* +	*aja-ni* +	*kōru* +
Plural			
Nom	*āba-ru*	*aja-ska*	*kōr-ka*
Gen	*āba-r-i*	*aja-ska-ni*	*kōr-ka*
Acc	*āba-r-i-i*	*aja-ska-ni-i*	*kōr-ka-tin-i*
Dat	*āba-r-i-ki*	*aja-ska-n-gi*	*kōr-ka-tin-gi*
Assoc	*āba-r-i-ke*	*aja-ska-n-ge*	–
Abl	*āba-r-i* +	*aja-ska-ni* +	*kōr-ka* +

Winfield gives a long list of postpositions that occur in the ablative. The appropriate one is to be chosen in declension.

Central Dravidian

9. Ollari (Bhattacharya 1957: 25)

	aba 'father'		*ēnig* 'elephant'	
	Singular	Plural	Singular	Plural
Nom	*aba*	*aba-r*	*ēnig*	*ēng-il*
Acc	*aba-n/-ŋ*	*aba-r-an/-aŋ*	*ēng-in*	*ēng-il-in*
Instr	*aba-nāl*	*aba-r-nāl*	*ēnig-nāl*	*ēng-il-nāl*
Dat	*aba-payiṭ*	*aba-r-payiṭ*	*ēnig-payiṭ*	*ēng-il-payiṭ*
Abl	*aba-ṭuŋ*	*aba-r-ṭuŋ*	*ēnig-ṭuŋ*	*ēng-il-ṭuŋ*
Gen	*aba-n*	*aba-r-in*	*ēng-in*	*ēng-il-in*
Loc	*aba-tun*	*aba-r-tun*	*ēnig-tin*	*ēng-il-tin*

North Dravidian
10. Kuṛux (Hahn 1911: 15)

Masculine: *āl, ālas* 'man'

	Singular	Plural
Nom	*āl, āl-as*	*āl-ar*
Gen	*āl, āl-as gahi*	*āl-ar gahi*
Dat	*āl, āl-as-gē*	*āl-ar-gē*
Acc	*āl-an, āl-as-in*	*āl-ar-in*
Abl	*āl-tī, āl-as-tī*	*āl-ar-tī, āl-ar-intī*
Instr	*āl-trī, āl-as-trī*	*āl-ar-trī, āl-ar-trū*
Loc	*āl-nū, āl-as-nū*	*āl-ar-nū*

Feminine: *mukkā* 'woman'

	Singular	Plural
Nom	*mukkā*	*mukka-r*
Gen	*mukkā gahi*	*mukka-r gahi*
Dat	*mukkā-gē*	*mukka-r-gē*
Acc	*mukka-n*	*mukka-r-in*
Abl	*mukka-n-tī*	*mukka-r-tī, mukka-r-in-tī*
Instr	*mukkā-trī, -trū*	*mukka-r-trī, mukka-r-trū*
Loc	*mukkā-nū*	*mukka-r-nū*

Neuter: *allā* 'dog'

	Singular	Plural
Nom	*allā*	*allā guṭhi*
Gen	*allā gahi*	*allā guṭhi gahi*
Dat	*allā-gē*	*allā guṭhi-gē*
Acc	*alla-n*	*allā guṭhi-in*
Abl	*allā-tī, alla-n-tī*	*allā guṭhi-tī, -in-tī*
Instr	*allā-trī, -trū*	*allā guṭhi-trī, -trū*
Loc	*allā-nū*	*allā guṭhi-nū*

11. Brahui (Bray 1909: 43)

xarās 'bull'

	Singular	Plural
Nom	*xarās*	*xarās-k*
Gen	*xarās-n-ā*	*xarās-t-ā*
Dat–Acc	*xarās-e*	*xarās-te*
Abl	*xarās-ān*	*xarās-te-ān*
Instr	*xarās-aṭ*	*xarās-te-aṭ*
Conj	*xarās-to*	*xarās-te-to*
Loc	*xarās-ṭī* 'in . . .'	*xarās-tē-ṭī*
	xarās-āi 'on . . .'	*xarās-te-āi*

7

The verb

7.1 Introduction

It has been pointed out that Dravidian roots are monosyllabic, of eight canonical forms, which can be conflated into the formula (C)V̄̆(C), i.e. V, CV, VC, CVC; V̄, CV̄, V̄C, CV̄C. In terms of the phonotactics of Dravidian, a total of 1,496 roots can be reconstructed for Proto-Dravidian (section 5.1). These may be optionally followed by formative suffixes of the type -V, -VC, -VCC, or -VCCC. The details can be captured by the diagram in figure 7.1.

A Dravidian root, of whatever part of speech, may be:

(a) An open syllable, i.e. V, CV, V̄, CV̄ followed either by a Ø formative or one of the formatives of the shape L (sonorant), stop (P), geminate stop (PP), nasal + homorganic stop (NP), or a nasal + a geminate homorganic stop (NPP), e.g. **o-* 'to suit' [924], **ā-* 'to be, become' [333], **po-* 'to perforate' [4452], *po-k-/po-t-* 'to make a hole' [4348], **pū* n. 'flower', v.i. 'to flower' [4348], **kā*/**kā-n*/**kā-ṭu* 'forest' [1418, 1438].

(b) A closed syllable, i.e. VC, CVC, V̄C, or CV̄C without further accretions, e.g. **oy* 'to carry' [984], **key* 'to do', **āṭ-u* 'to dance' [347], **kāl* 'leg' [1479]. There is reason to believe that there are some roots of (C)VCC- type contrasting with (C)VC- which prosodically belong to this slot. Some of the roots of V̄̆C and CV̄̆C type may have been originally open-syllabled roots like (a) with the final consonant being historically a formative (cf. *DEDR* 4452, 4348, and 1418, 1438 above). The etymological boundary in such forms would be V̄̆-C, CV̄̆-C.

(c) The closed syllable roots with a short vowel[1] may be further extended by formatives in two layers: V_2 = /i u a/. It is not possible to assign any meaning to these vowels, but they are detachable on structural and etymological grounds; V_2 may be followed by the above suffixes, i.e. L, P, PP, NP, NPP as a second layer, e.g. **naṭ-a* 'to walk' [3582], **par-a* 'to spread' [3949], **pēr*/**per*-V- 'big' [4411], **mar-a-n* 'tree', *al-a-nk-* 'to shake', etc.

(d) There is one class of exceptions to (c) indicated in the last row, i.e. some nasal-ending roots may be followed by P or PP. In other words, in such stems the etymological

[1] A (C)V̄C type root becomes (C)VC when a vowel formative follows (see section 4.3.3.2).

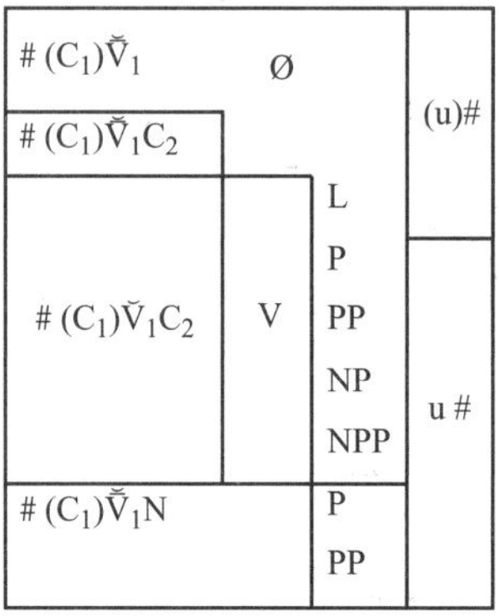

Figure 7.1 Structure of Proto-Dravidian roots and stems (same as 4.1)

boundary is N-P, N-PP where N belongs to $\breve{\bar{V}}_1$ of the root, e.g *en-ṯ- 'sun' [869], *eṇ-ṭṭ- 'eight' [784], *wēṇ-ṭu 'to wish' [5528].

If the base ends in a P it is followed by a non-morphemic *-u obligatorily. However, this is optional if the last segment is a sonorant (L). The number of possible roots (primary and extended) increases as we proceed from open-syllable roots to closed syllables, i.e. (C)$\breve{\bar{V}}$C > (C)$\breve{\bar{V}}$ and monosyllabic to disyllabic (C)VC-V- > (C)VC- (see section 5.1). Actually the roots of the (C)V- type are rare, e.g. PD *o-: Ta. *o-* (*-pp-*, *-tt-*) [924]; most other languages have cognates with incorporated suffixes (see section 5.4.). A root in Dravidian can be morphosyntactically a noun or a verb or an adjective, e.g. *ā 'to become' [333], *ā 'cow' [334], *ī 'fly' [533], *pī 'excrement' [4210], *pū n. 'flower', v. 'to flower' [4348], *pēr/*per-V- 'big' [4411], *pō 'to go' [4572], *nī 'to abandon' [3685], *mā 'animal, beast, deer' [4780], *nō 'to suffer' [3793], *nū 'sesame seed' [3720]. From the canonical structure we cannot predict the part of speech of a given root. It has been demonstrated with adequate evidence that, in disyllabic and trisyllabic stems with extended formative suffixes, these suffixes (-V-L, -V-P, -V-NP, -V-PP, -V-NPP) were originally markers of tense and voice in Early Proto-Dravidian. They gradually lost the tense meaning first and later the voice meaning, thereby becoming mere formatives (see chapter 5).

7.2 The verbal base

Synchronically, a verbal base (root with or without formatives) is said to be identified by its form in the imperative singular (Caldwell 1956: 446), e.g. *wā* 'come', *koy* 'cut' in most languages. This is not always true, Telugu and Koṇḍa *rā* (< *wrā- < *war-a-) 'come' is a suppletive in imperative singular and plural: Te. *rā* imper. 2sg, *rā-ṇḍi* 2pl,

Koṇḍa *ra-ʔa* 2sg, *ra-du* 2pl. A verb in Dravidian is inflected for tense/aspect/mood and carries a verbal base as its nucleus. A verbal base in Dravidian may be simple, complex or compound. A simple base is identical to the monosyllabic verb root $(C_1)\breve{\bar{V}}(C_2)$, or a disyllabic one extended with a short vowel $(C_1)V_1C_2$-V_2 in which -V_2 does not contribute to the root meaning, e.g. **ā* 'to be, become' [333], **key* 'to make' [1957], **cal* 'to go' [2781], **man* 'to be' [4778], **wāẓ* 'to flourish' [5372], **par-a* 'to spread' [3949], **iẓ-i* 'to descend' [502]; a complex base has a root and a formative suffix, encoding voice, transitivity or causation, e.g. **aṭ-a-nku* 'to be subdued, hidden': **aṭ-a-nkk* 'to control, hide' [63], **key-pi-* 'to cause one to do'; a compound base has more than one root with the final constituent as a verb, e.g. **akam* 'inside': Ta. *aka-ppaṭu* 'to be included', Te. *aga-paḍu* 'to be seen, to fall in the visual field' [7].

Morphologically a verb may be finite or non-finite. A finite verb has the structure stem + tense-mode + (g)np (gender–number–person) marker, which normally agrees with the head of the subject noun phrase (NP), Ta. *nāṉ cey-t-ēṉ* 'I did', Koṇḍa *vāṉṟu ki-t-an* 'he did'. Historically some descendant languages have lost the agreement features, either partially or fully, like Modern Malayāḷam, or neutralized all gender–number contrasts in the third person, like Toda and Brahui. A non-finite verb has two components, the verb base + tense/aspect, e.g. Ta. *cey-tu* 'having done', Koṇḍa *ki-zi* id., perfective participle or gerund in both the languages; syntactically, it heads a subordinate clause. In unmarked word order the verb, finite or non-finite, occupies the end position of the clause.

7.3 Intransitive, transitive and causative stems

A simple verb may be inherently intransitive (**ā-* 'to be') or transitive (**ciy-* 'to give') depending on its meaning and its relationship with the complement phrases in a given clause. I suggested in section 5.3 (earlier *TVB*: §2.38, pp. 145–6) that 'sonorant suffixes of the R type (*l, ḷ, r, ẓ, w, y*) were added to $(C)\breve{\bar{V}}$- or (C)VC-V-stems to form extended intransitive/middle-voice stems'. Synchronically, a transitive verb is changed to intransitive/middle voice in Kuṛux and Malto by adding *-r*, e.g. Kuṛ. *kam-* 'to make': *kam-r-* 'to be made', Malt. *ey-* 'to bind': *ey-r-* 'to bind oneself'. This seems to be a relic of a Proto-Dravidian usage, since it is not found in any of the neighbouring Indo-Aryan and Munda languages. Note that most verbs ending in formative -(V) *l*/-(V) *r* in South Dravidian I and South Dravidian II tend to be intransitive.

Three complementary modes of forming transitive–causative stems were quite ancient: (1) by the addition of **-tt* to monosyllabic roots that end in an apical stop or nasal /ṯ n ṭ ṇ/, and of **-pp* to roots ending in final **-i* or **-y* (the Proto-Dravidian conditions are not all recoverable). In Central Dravidian both these suffixes got generalized as causative markers; (2) by the addition of a causative morph *-pi-* ~ *-wi-* ~ *-ppi-* to a transitive verb stem, simple or complex; (3) a complementary type to these is represented by roots of $(C_1)\bar{V}C_2$ type, where C_2 is a liquid sonorant, or a disyllabic root of the type (C) VCV- or (C) VCV-*y*. A subset of these stems formed transitives by geminating the final stop of the tense suffixes. In other words, tense and voice were a composite category in this class of stems. Paradigms of this type survive intact in a subgroup of South Dravidian, namely Tamil–Malayāḷam–Koḍagu–Iruḷa–Toda and Kota (see section 5.4.4); (4) a fourth type, mainly confined to South Dravidian (SD I and SD II), is the formation of transitive stems by geminating the final P of the formative syllable in disyllabic or trisyllabic bases. The final P here is interpreted as part of an erstwhile tense–voice morpheme, which got incorporated into the base by (3) and lost its tense meaning but retained only the voice distinction (see section 5.3; earlier Krishnamurti 1997a).

7.3.1 *Transitive–causative stems by the addition of* *-tt

This pattern is preserved intact in South Dravidian I. Isolated members of the other subgroups bear evidence to PD **-tt*, but they use different additive morphemes.

(1) PD **kūṭu* v.i./tr. 'to be joined, meet'/v.t. **kūṭ-ṭu* (< **kūṭ-tt-*) 'to unite, put together' [1882].
SD I: Ta. Ma. *kūṭu/kūṭṭu*, Ko. To. *kūṛ-/kūṭ-*, Koḍ. *kūḍ-/kūṭ-*, Ka. *kūḍu* v.i., *kūṭa* 'joining, connexion' (derived by adding *-a* to the transitive base **kūṭṭ-*), Tu. *kūḍuni* v.i., *kūṭuni*, *kūṇṭuni* v.t. 'to mix', *kūṭa* n. 'mixture';
SD II: Te. *kūḍu* v.i., but *kūḍ-ali* 'junction', but *kūṭ-ami* 'joining, assembly'.

The other South Dravidian II languages, as well as those of Central Dravidian and North Dravidian, have only the intransitive form.

(2) PD **uHṇ/*ūṇ* 'to eat, drink', *ūṭṭ-* (< **uHṇ-tt-*) 'to give to eat or drink' [600].
SD I: Ta. *uṇ-* v.i./v.t., *ūṭṭu-* v.t., *ūṇ* n 'food', *ūṭṭ-am* 'food' (based on the caus. stem), Ma. *uṇṇuka/ūṭṭuka*, Koḍ. *uṇ*, Ko. *uṇ-/ūṭ-*, To. *uṇ-*, Ko. To. *ūṇ* 'food', Ka. *uṇ-/ūḍu* v., *ūṭa* 'a meal', Tu. *uṇpini* v., *ūṭa* 'a meal';
SD II: Te. *ūṭu* 'cattle to drink water completely', Go. *uṇḍ-* 'to drink', *uht-* 'make to drink', Koṇḍa *uṇ-* 'to drink', *ūṭ-pis-* 'cause to drink', Kui *uṇba-/ūṭpa-*, Kuvi *un-* ~ *unn-* ~ *ūnd-/ūṭ-*, Pe. *uṇ-/ūtpa-*, Manḍa *uṇba-/ūṛpa-*;
CD: Kol. Nk. *un-/ūr-t-*, Pa. *un-/unṭ-ip-*;
ND: Kuṛ. *ōn-* 'to drink, eat', *ōn-d-nā/on-ta' ānā* 'to give a meal'; *ōnkā* 'thirst'; Malt. *ōn-* 'to drink, to be coloured', *on-d-* 'to drink, to dye'.

The causative suffix *-tt-* is retained in South Dravidian I and South Dravidian II with the exception of Kannaḍa and Tuḷu in South Dravidian I and Telugu and Gondi in South Dravidian II. Traces of a dental suffix are found in Gondi, Parji and Kuṛux–Malto, justifying its reconstruction for Proto-Dravidian. In Kuṛux, a distinction is made between a transitive with one Agent and a causative with two Agents, e.g. *co'onā* 'to rise': *cō-d-nā/ cō-da' ānā* 'to raise': *cō-d-ta' ānā* 'to order one to raise' (Grignard 1924a: 96–7). It appears the same marker is used both as a transitive and as a causative. It occurs twice in double-agent causatives. However, the first variant cited has only *-d-* to express transitive meaning. Hahn gives *-d-* as an alternative suffix used in forming causative verbs (also see Hahn 1911: 65). Malto adds *-d* or *-tar* to form transitive-causatives, *īl-* 'to stand': *il-d-* 'to erect', *pūn-* 'to wear a necklace': *pūn-d-* 'to make one wear a necklace', *kud-* 'to work': *kud-tar-* 'to make to work'. A second causative is formed by adding *-tita*/*-tite* to a transitive, e.g. *ey-* 'to bind': *ey-tar-* v.t. 'to bind': *ey-tar-tita* 'to cause to be bound by someone' (Mahapatra 1979: 150–2).

(3) PD **tiHn-* 'to eat': **tīn-t̲t̲-* 'to feed' [3263].
SD I: Ta. *tin̲/tīr̲r̲u* 'to eat/to feed', *tīni* 'food', Ma. *tinnuka/tīr̲r̲uka*, *tīn* n., Koḍ. *tinn-/tīt*, Ko. *tin/tīṭ*;
SD II: Go. *tin-/tih-* ~ *tiht-*, Koṇḍa *tin-/tīR-pis-*, Kui *tinba-/tīspa-*, Kuvi *tinj-/tīss-*, Pe. *tin-/tīc-pa-* (PD **t̲t̲* > Koṇḍa *-R*, Kui–Kuvi–Pengo–Manḍa *-c-/-s-*, Go. *-h*; section 4.5.8.1.3).
CD: Kol. Nk. *tin-* 'to eat', Pa. *tin-* 'to eat', *ti-tt-ip-* (< **tin-t̲t̲-* + *ip-*) 'to cause to eat', Oll. Gad. *tin-* 'to eat';
ND: Kuṛ.-Malt. *tin-d-* 'to feed', Kuṛ. *tī'ni kēyu* 'right hand' (lit. 'eating hand'; this meaning is also found in the languages of South Dravidian II and Central Dravidian [3263b]).

The long-vowel form, owing to a lost laryngeal, occurs in the causative and in a free form, noun or adjective. Koṇḍa and Parji have added a causative suffix *-pis*, *-ip* to a transitive form obtained through (4) above; *-pa* in Kui–Pengo is a frequentative suffix. Since all groups retain evidence of a dental used as a causative marker, it can be reconstructed for Proto-Dravidian. Again Kannaḍa and Tuḷu of South Dravidian I, Telugu of South Dravidian II, and several languages of Central Dravidian have lost the forms with **-tt* as a transitive–causative marker.

(4) PD **māt̲-* v.i. 'to be changed, altered', **māt̲t̲-* (< **māt̲-tt-*) v.t. 'to change, alter' [4834].
SD I: Ta. Ma. *mār̲u/mār̲r̲u* v.i./v.t., *mār̲r̲-am* n. 'diversity, reply, word', Ma. *mār̲r̲-am* 'change, barter, diversity, reply, word', Ko. *mār̲-/māt-*, *mānt* 'word, language', To. *mōr̲-/mōt-* ~ *mōt̲-*, Koḍ. *mār-* 'to sell', *māt-* 'to change', Ka. *mār̲u* 'to be changed, to sell, to oppose, be hostile', *mātu* 'word' (based on the transitive stem), Tu. *māruni* 'to dispose of', *mārtɛ* 'selling, bargain';
SD II: Te. *mār̲u* v.i. 'to change, to be exchanged', *māṭa-* 'word', Koṇḍa *mār̲-* 'to barter, exchange', Kui–Kuvi *māsk-* (< *māR-k-*) 'to exchange'.

There are no transitive forms inherited from the proto-stage in Kannaḍa, Tuḷu, Telugu and the other South Dravidian II languages, but the noun form in Kannaḍa and Telugu is based on the transitive stem. No cognates are reported from Central Dravidian.

(5) PD *$p\bar{u}ṇ$ 'to put on, wear, be yoked', *$p\bar{u}ṇ$-ṭṭ- (< **pūṇ-tt-) 'to put on, yoke' [4361].

SD I: Ta. *pūṇ-/pūṭṭ-* v.i./v.t., Ta. *pūṭṭ-ai* 'cord for fastening bullocks', Ko. *pūṛ-/pūṭ-*, To. *pūḷ-/pūṭ-*, Ka. *pūṇ-* 'to fix as an arrow, to begin, vow, etc.', *pūḍu* (< **pūṇ-ḍ-* with loss of nasal) 'to join, tie, yoke, bring about, begin, etc.', Tu. *pūḷ* 'to wear', *pūṭ* 'to tie around someone's neck' (*DVM*: 81);

SD II: Te. *pūnu* 'to undertake', *pūn-cu* 'to yoke', Go. *puh-* 'to yoke', *puh-t-* 'to yoke the plough', Koṇḍa *pūṭ-* 'to yoke the bullocks', Kui *pūnḍ-* 'to meet', *pūṛ-pa-/pūṭ-pa* 'to yoke', Kuvi *pūṭ-* id., Pe. *pūṭ-* id;

CD: Gad. *pūndu* n. 'yoke' (lw < Te. dial);

ND: *pun-d-* 'to yoke', *pūn* n. 'necklace', Malt. *pūn-* 'to put on one's neck', *pun-d-* 'to put on another's neck', *pūnu* 'necklace'.

Kannaḍa and Tuḷu also have a dental suffix as transitivizer. Telugu adds *-c*, *pūn-cu* in transitive. The rest of the South Dravidian II languages retain the suffix. Central Dravidian lacks the transitivizing suffix. North Dravidian has the weakened form *-d* < *-tt* and is crucial for reconstructing *-tt* in Proto-Dravidian.

7.3.2 *Transitive–causative stems by the addition of* *-pp

The transitive–causative *-pp* as an additive has been used by Kannaḍa and Tuḷu of South Dravidian I, Telugu (extensively) and other members (partially) of South Dravidian II, all languages of Central Dravidian and perhaps Brahui of North Dravidian.

SD I: Ka. (Inscriptional) *tiri* 'to go round': *tiri-pu* 'to cause to go round', *muḍi* 'to be finished': *muḍi-pu* 'to finish', Tu. *oḷi* 'to remain': *oḷi-pu* 'to preserve', *bigi* 'to become tight': *bigi-pu* 'to tighten', *uri* 'to burn': *uri-pu* v.t. 'to burn', *oḍe* (< **oṭ-ay*) 'to break': *oḍe-pu* v.t. 'to break';

SD II: Te. Some trisyllabic and disyllabic stems ending in *-gu*, *-cu* or *-yu* replace the last syllable by *-pu* in forming transitives, *jaru-gu* v.i. 'to move': *jaru-pu* v.t. 'to move', *tiru-gu* 'to revolve, wander': *tri-ppu* v.t., *teli-yu* 'to know': *telu-pu* 'to inform', *mē-yu* 'to graze': *mē-pu* 'to graze cattle' (in the last two the *-y* is lost before *-pu*). There are some original monosyllabic roots in Old Telugu that have transitive–causative stems by adding *-pu*, e.g. *can(u)* '(time) to pass': *calu-pu* 'to pass time', *kon(u)* 'to take' occurs as reflexive auxiliary: *kolu-pu* 'to cause to take', *wīḍ-konu* 'to leave': *wīḍ-kolu-pu* 'to cause to leave' (for further details see *TVB* 194–9). Gondi in the South Bastar dialect has *-p* as a transitive marker, e.g. *kās-* 'to boil': *kā-p-* v.t. 'to boil', *nil-* 'to stand': *nil-p-* 'to erect' (G. U. Rao, 1987b: 208–9). Koṇḍa has additive *-p* (beside NP ~ PP type), *nil-* 'to stand': *nil-p-* 'make stand', *mēy-* 'to graze': *mē-p-* 'cause to graze', *sā-* 'to die': *sa-p-* 'to kill'. Kui *e-* 'arrive': *e-p-* 'cause to arrive', *sā-* 'die': *sā-p* 'kill', *jā-* 'to descend': *jā-p-* 'cause to descend' (Winfield 1928: 139–40). Pengo *hō-* 'to go out': *ho-p-*, *rī-* 'to be torn': *ri-p-* 'to tear';

CD: Kolami has *-ap/-ip/-p* as transitive markers, e.g. *negay* 'to fly': *nega -p-* 'cause to fly', *ḍāṭ-* 'to cross': *ḍāṭ-ip-* 'to make to cross', *tīr-* 'to be finished': *tīr-p-* v.t. 'to finish'; Nk. has *-up/-ip/-p*, e.g. *il-* 'to stand': *il-up-* 'cause to stand', *kāy-* 'to be hot': *kā-p-* 'to heat'; Parji has *-p* added before the normal transitive-causative suffix *-ip/-it* for some stems, e.g. *muy-* 'to be covered': *muy-p-ip-/-it-* ' to cover', *narc-* 'to be afraid': *nar-p-ip/-it-* 'to frighten'; Oll. *iṛg-* 'to descend': *iṛig-p/-t*, *aṛ-* 'to cry': *aṛ-p-/-t-* 'make to cry'; Gad. *ag-* 'be torn': *ak-p-* 'to tear', *tōṇḍ-* 'to appear': *tōḍ-p-* 'to show', *sen* 'to go': *soy-p-* 'to send'. It is clear that the Central Dravidian languages form transitives by the addition of *-p/-t* (< PD **-pp/*-tt*).

ND: Brahui has *-if/-f* as a causative marker, e.g. *bin-* 'to hear': *bin-if-*, *kah-* 'to die': *kas-f-if.*

It is not certain if the Central Dravidian and North Dravidian labial has to be related to *-pp-* in Proto-Dravidian causative *-ppi-/-wi-* or to the additive morph *-pp* which needs to be reconstructed for Proto-Dravidian in view of its occurrence in South Dravidian I, South Dravidian II and Central Dravidian.

7.3.3 *Causative stems by the addition of* ***-pi- ~ -wi- ~ -ppi-**

The causative *-pi-* [-wi-] ~ *-ppi-* is attested in Tamil-Brahmi inscriptions of the second century BCE, e.g. *koṭupitōn* (= /koṭu-ppi-tt-ōṉ/) 'he caused (something) to be given', *aṟupita-* (= /aṟu-ppi-tta/) rel. ppl 'that caused to be cut' (Mahadevan 1971: 90–1). This causative is also found in South Dravidian II and in Brahui. See the following stages of its development.

The Proto-Dravidian causative suffix is **-pi-* (allomorphs **-wi-*, **-pi-*, and **-ppi-*), which is generally added to transitive stems requiring a second-agent subject in the sentence (Meenakshisundaran 1965: 111); cf. e.g. *amma kēṭ-pi-kk-um* '(The word) "amma" will make someone listen' (Tolk. 761). The causative morpheme in Old Telugu has two alternants, *-i-nc-/-pi-nc-* before past suffixes and *-i-mp-/-pi-mp-* before non-past suffixes, e.g.

Past participle: *cēy-i-nc-i* 'having caused (something) to be done', *naḍa-pi-nc-i* 'having caused somebody to walk'

Past finite: *cēy-i-nc-en(u)* '(3sg subj) caused (it) to be done', *naḍa-pi-nc-en(u)* '(3sg subj) caused one to walk'

Past adjective: *cēy-i-nc-ina* 'that which was caused to be done', *naḍa-pi-nc-ina* 'that which was caused to walk'

Negative: *cēy-i-mp-a-* (+ personal affixes) 'Someone will not cause it to be done', *naḍa-pi-mp-a-* (+ personal affixes) 'Someone will not cause one to walk'

Infinitive: *cēy-i-mp-aN* 'to cause (it) to be done', *naḍa-pi-mp-aN* 'to cause one to walk'

Imperative: *cēy-i-mp-umu* (2sg) '(you sg) cause it to be done', *naḍa-pi-mp-umu* '(you sg) cause one to walk'; *cēy-i-mp-ũ-ḍu* (2pl) '(you pl) cause it to be done', *naḍa-pi-mp-ũ-ḍu* 'you (pl) cause one to walk'

Comparison of the Telugu causative stems with Old Tamil inflectional stems permits reconstruction of Proto-Dravidian causative stems as follows:

PD **key* 'to do': Ta. *cey*, Te. *cēyu*

	Old Tamil	Old Telugu	Proto-Dravidian
past:	*cey-vi-tt-*	*cēy-i-nc-*	**key-pi-ntt-*
	naṭa-ppi-tt-	*naḍa-pi-nc-*	**naṭa-ppi-ntt-*
non-past:	*cey-vi-pp-*	*cēy-i-mp-*	**key-pi-mpp-*
	naṭa-ppi-pp-	*naḍa-pi-mp-*	**naṭa-ppi-mpp-*

It is obvious that Old Telugu *-i-/-pi-* correspond to Old Tamil causative *-vi-/-ppi-* with the loss of *-v-* in Telugu; the following *-nc-/-mp-* then correspond to Tamil and Proto-Dravidian past and non-past morphs. Telugu preserves the *N of *NPP of Proto-Dravidian, lost in Tamil.

The Telugu causative *-i-nc-/-pi-nc-* must be explained as a reanalysed causative morph incorporating the proto-past-tense suffix with palatalization of **-i-ntt* to **-i-ncc*; the alternating **-i-mpp* was the original non-past suffix, which accounts for Telugu non-past *i-mp/-pi-mp*. In both cases, PP is simplified to P, but the nasal (N) of the proto-sequence *NPP is retained. Although the tense meanings were lost, the distribution of the allomorphs between past and non-past are reminiscent of their original distribution. Kannaḍa of South Dravidian I and a number of South Central Dravidian languages use the derivatives of **-icc*/**-ipp* and **-picc*/**-pipp* as causative–transitive suffixes.

Old Kannaḍa had *-isu* as a causative–transitive suffix alternating with *-ipu* just like Telugu. The suffix *-isu* occurred in past-tense formations like *kiḍ-is-i* 'having made to ruin', while *-ipu* occurred in future paradigms (Ramachandra Rao 1972: 147, 317).

kiḍu	'to be spoiled'	*kiḍ-isu* (caus):	*kiḍ-ip-ar* 'they will spoil'
karagu	'to be melted'	*karag-isu* (caus):	*karag-ip-en* 'I will melt'
āḷ	'to rule'	*āḷ-isu* (caus):	*āḷ-ip-avu* 'we will cause to rule'
gel	'to win'	*gel-isu* (caus):	*gel-ip-am* 'we will cause to win'

The evidence of Old Kannaḍa supports the origin of *-isu/-ipu* from underlying tense-based causative morphs, although *-isu* was generalized, replacing *-ipu* in later Kannaḍa.

Similarly, in Middle and Modern Telugu *-incu* has been analogically extended to all environments. The morphs Te. *-incu* and Ka. *-isu*, besides being causative markers, are also added productively to intransitive bases to form transitives, e.g. Te. *āḍu-* 'to shake, play': *āḍ-incu-* 'to make one to shake, play', Ka. *āḍu-*: *āḍ-isu* id.

Derivatives of **-i-ncc-/*-pi-ncc-* (< **-wi-ntt/*-ppi-ntt-*) are found in several other languages . In South Central Dravidian, the distribution has come to be phonologically conditioned. In Adilabad Gondi, *-ūs*, *-pūs* are frequently used as transitive–causative morphs, as in *kar-ūs-* 'to teach', *muṟ-ūs-* 'to immerse', *aṭṭ-ūs* 'to cause to cook' (Subrahmanyam 1968a: 5). Koya has *-is* as causative marker in such forms as *ūḍ-* 'to see': *ūḍ-is* 'to make see', *ninḍ-* 'to fill': *ninḍ-is* 'to make full' (Tyler 1969: 80). It is possible to reconstruct **-pis* as a causative marker for Proto-Gondi (see Rao 1987b: 203, table 9). The use of *-is/-pis/-bis* is quite productive in Koṇḍa, e.g. *kaṭ-* 'to bite': *kaṭ-is-/kaṭ-pis-* 'to cause to bite'; *uRk-* 'to run': *uRk-is* 'to make run'; *ki-* 'to do': *ki-bis* 'to cause to do' (Krishnamurti 1969a: 274–6).

The above evidence points to the palatalization of *(*n*)*tt* to *(*n*)*cc* following a front vowel in a large number of South and South Central Dravidian languages. The development of this morpheme actually provides us with an isogloss separating the languages of South Dravidian I and South Dravidian II from Central Dravidian (Parji, Kolami, Naiki, Ollari and Gadaba) and North Dravidian.

7.3.4 *Transitive-causative stems with the addition of* *-cc

Toda and Kota of South Dravidian I have causative *-c* where it is not the result of palatalization of **-tt*, e.g. To. Ko. *nil-c-* 'to make to stand' [3043], *tīr-c-* 'to finish' [2683], To. *köṟ-c-*, Ko. *keṟ-c-* 'to kill' [1614]. In Old Kannaḍa *-cu* occurs as a transitivizer after stems ending /i e l ḷ r ẓ/, e.g. *agal-* 'to be separated': *agal-cu* 'to separate', *tīr-* 'to be finished': *tīr-cu* 'to finish', v.t. (*DVM*: 20–1, Ramachandra Rao 1972: 146); *-isu* (< **-wi-ncc-*) got generalized as a transitive–causative marker in Kannaḍa from the earliest times, *māḍi-is-ida* adj 'that caused to be done' (Gai 1946: 76–8). Both Old Kannaḍa and Old Telugu had parallel usages of *-isu* and *-incu*, respectively, because they were also used as verbalizers with Sanskrit nouns, Ka. *sādh-isu* 'to accomplish', Te. *sādh-incu* id. It has already been pointed out that corresponding to Old Telugu *-inc/-imp* Kannaḍa has *-isu/-ipu* in past and non-past paradigms. Telugu has employed *-cu* and *-ncu* as transitive markers, not to be mistaken with *-incu*, e.g. *kālu* 'to burn': *kāl-cu*, *digu* 'to get down': *di-ncu* 'to make one get down'. The transitive markers *-cu/-ncu* alternate with *-pu/-mpu* before non-past suffixes just like *-inc* ~ *-imp*. We are, therefore, led to believe these were constructed analogically from the transitive–causative *-i-nc*. This is a matter belonging to the Pre-Telugu stage. Subrahmanyam (1971: 88) considers the *-c/-p* alternation an innovation in Telugu, but does not explain the purpose of such an innovation and also fails to explain a parallel alternation in Old Kannaḍa also in *-isu/-ipu*. This alternation is different from the *-c*/*-w* alternation in Telugu where I proved that *-c* is a past marker and *-w* a non-past marker, e.g. *pili-ci* 'having called'; *piluw-aka* 'not calling' (section 5.4.7). Gondi has *-s* as a transitive–causative marker in some of the dialects (Western Gondi), e.g. *hūṛ-* 'to see': *hūṛ-s-* 'to show'; in many forms it is followed by another transitive suffix of the shape -V*s*/-V*h* (*-ih*/*-eh*/*-ah*/*-uh*), *kī-s-ih-*/*kī-s-ah-*/*kī-s-uh-* 'cause someone to do', which appears to be the causative *-is* from *-i-cc* (<**-i-ncc-*). There is, thus, justification to reconstruct **-cc* as another transitive–causative suffix which is retained by fewer languages than the reflexes of **-tt* and **-pp*. After the front vowels and *-y*, **-tt* got palatalized and merged with PD **-cc* (transitive marker) in South Dravidian I; particularly, Middle Tamil, Malayāḷam, Toda, Kota and Kannaḍa data support this observation.

7.3.5 ***Transitive–causatives combined with tense markers***

I showed cases (section 5.4.4) where both tense and voice were combined in a subgroup of South Dravidian I. There is a class of monosyllabic and disyllabic verbs, which still belong to this inflectional class in this subgroup, e.g.

(6) PD **tir*-V- (non-past: *tir*-V-*p-* ~ *tir*-V-*mp-*/*tir*-V-*k-* ~ *tir*-V-*nk-*, past: *tir*-V-*nt-*) v.i. 'to turn, revolve, vary', (non-past: *tir*-V-*pp-* ~ *tir*-V-*mpp-*/*tir*-V-*kk* ~ *tir*-V-*nk*k, past: *tir*-V-*ntt-*) v.t. 'to turn, twist, change' [3246].

SD I: Ta. *tiri* (*-v-*, *-nt-*) v.i., (*-pp-*, *-tt-*) v.t., Ma. *tiriyuka* v.i./*tirikka* v.t., Ko. *tiry-* (*tir-c*) v.i., *tirc-* (*tir-c-*) v.t., To. *tïry-* (*tïrc-*) v.t., Koḍ. *tir-* (*tir-i-*) v.i., Ka. *tiri* v.i., Tu. *tiri* n. 'wick of a lamp';

SD II: Te. *tiri* n., *tiriyu* 'to wander for alms', Go. *tiri* v.i., *tirī-t-* v.t., Koṇḍa *tiri* v.i., *tiris-* v.t.

From the above type, trisyllabic stems were created incorporating the tense–voice morphs with loss of tense meaning:

a. With the non-past velar suffix incorporated [3246, 3244]:

SD I: Ta. *tir-u-ku* 'to twist', n. 'bend, curve', *tir-u-kku* v.t. 'to twist', n. 'twist, send', *tir-a-nku* 'to be wrinkled, be curled up as hair', *tir-a-kku* ?v.i. 'to be crumpled', *tir-a-nk-al* 'being shrivelled up',[2] Ma. *tir-u-kuka*/*tir-u-kkuka* (both have transitive meaning), n. *tir-u-kkal* 'plaiting of hair', Ko. *tirg-* v.i. 'to turn', *tirk-* v.t. 'to turn', *tirgan* n. 'wheel', To. *tïrx-* v.i., *tïrk-* v.t., *tïrk* n. 'a turn in road', Koḍ. *tirïg-* v.i. 'to go about, wander', *tirïk-* v.t. 'to turn', *teraŋg-* v.i. '(thing) moves, shifts', *terak-* 'to shift without lifting', Ka. *tirugu* v.i. 'to turn around', *tiruvu* v.i. 'to turn as head', *tirag-aṇe*

[2] The second item is given in another entry by *DEDR* 3244.

'that which turns, a wheel for raising water', Tu. *tiṅg-uni* v.i., *tiṅgaṇε* n. 'hinge' (no morphologically derived transitives in Kannaḍa and Tuḷu);

SD II: Te. *tirugu* v.i., n. 'twist', but *trikku* n. 'twist' (no morphologically related causative);

CD: Kol. Nk. *tirg-* 'to turn, wander', *tip-/tipp-* v.t. (lw < Te.), Pa. *tirk-* v.i. 'to writhe'.

ND: Br. *trikking* 'to wither up, change colour' [3244].

b. With non-past labial suffix incorporated:

SD I: Ta. *tir-u-mpu* v.i. 'to turn, turn back, be changed', *tir-u-ppu* v.t. 'to turn, to cause to return', Ma. *tirumpuka* v.i. 'to turn round', *tirippuka* v.t., To. *tïrb-* v.t. 'to twist as cane', *tïrp-* 'to turn key', Ka. *tirumpu* (< **tir-u-mpp-*) 'to cause to go round', *tiripu, tirupu* id., *tirupu* n. 'a screw', *tirupa* n. 'wandering for alms', Tu. *tirpuni* 'to twirl round';

SD II: Te. *tri-ppu* v.t. (matched as transitive of *tir-ugu*), 'to turn, revolve', *tiri-p-emu* 'begging, alms' (collected going from house to house), Koṇḍa *tirp-* v.t. of *tirvi-* 'to turn back, come round', *terb-* v.i. 'to coil round', *terp-* 'to roll up', Kui *trēba* 'to wander about', *trehpa* 'to cause to wander', Kuvi *termp-* 'to roll', *treph-* v.t. 'to involve', Manḍa *trīmb-* 'to go round';

ND: Kuṛ. *ter*^{e}*m-* (*tirmy-*) 'to roll something oneself'.

c. With the past marker *-nt-/-ntt-* incorporated [3251]:

SD I: Ta. *tir-u-ntu* v.i. 'to be changed, corrected', v.t. *tiruttu* v.t. 'to repair, rectify', Ma. *tiruttuka* v.t. 'to mend, correct', Ta. Ma. *tiruttam* n. 'correction, correctness', Ko. *tirt-* 'to change one's frame of mind', To. *tïd-* 'to correct, make straight', Koḍ. *tidd-* (lw < Ka.) 'to twist and clean (moustaches)', Ka. *tiddu, tirdu* 'to make straight, to correct' (< *tir-t-* < *tir*-V-*tt-*), Tu. *tirduni* 'to correct, mend';

SD II: Te. *diddu* 'to correct, set right' (perhaps lw < Ka. before *t-* became *d-*).

d. With -V-L suffixes added to the root **tir-* [3245]:

SD I: Ta. *tir-aḷ* (*tir-aḷ-v-, tir-a-ṇṭ-*) 'to become round', *tiraṭṭu* (< *tiraḷ-ttu*) v.t. 'to make round balls of rice', *tiraḷ-ai, tiraṇ-ai* 'a ball', *tir-ai* (*-v-, -nt-*) v.i. 'to be heaped up, coagulate', (*-pp-, -tt-*) v.t. 'to cause to gather', *tirai-yal* 'roll of betel', Ma. *tiraḷuka* v.i., *tiraṭṭuka* v.t. 'to ball up', *tirayuka* 'to coagulate, (milk) balls itself', *tirekkuka* v.t. 'to roll up betel', Ko. *terṇ* (*terḍ-*) 'to become round', *terṭ-* (*terṭy-*) 'to make round', *terv-* (*terd-*) 'to roll up', Ka. *teraḷu* 'to ball itself', *teraṭu* 'to make round';

SD II: ? Te. *teralu* 'to abound, increase'.

The derivatives of *tir- are cited in *DEDR* under four entries, which are phonologically related, namely 3244, 3245, 3246, 3251. Earlier, Krishnamurti (1997a) has given adequate evidence to show that disyllabic and trisyllabic stems with -NP/-NPP arose in Proto-Dravidian from Pre-Dravidian paradigms in which these suffixes stood as markers of tense and voice. This particular inflectional type is preserved only in the subgroup Tamil–Malayāḷam–Koḍagu–Kota–Toda as is evident from the above groups of etyma. These suffixes first lost their tense meaning and became markers of transitivity, apparently within Proto-Dravidian itself. This pattern is widespread in South Dravidian I and South Dravidian II. Kannaḍa–Tuḷu of South Dravidian I and Telugu–Gondi of South Dravidian II have lost the paired stems with NP/NPP related as intransitive/transitive, since the meaning of voice is also lost in them. However, Kannaḍa–Tuḷu have some archaic forms of the *NPP stage, cf. Ka. *tirumpu* tr. from **tirumpp-* without the matching intransitive **tiruwu* (<**tirumpu*). The loss of paired transitives and/or intransitives in Kannaḍa, Tuḷu and Telugu (and other languages that have partially lost them) is compensated by extending the usage of the less marked mode of attaching to the root a transitive–causative marker, derived from *-*tt*, *-*pp* or the causative *-*pi*. The past intransitive *-nt-* and transitive *-ntt-* became palatalized to *-nc-*/*-ncc-* in many languages of South Dravidian I including Middle Tamil and Malayāḷam, Ta. *kāy-* v.i., *kāycc-* v.t. (< *kāy-tt-* < **kāy-ntt-*) 'to boil, cook, heat', Ma. *kāyuka* v.i., *kāccu-ka* v.t., Ko. *kāy-* v.i., *kāc-* v.t., To. *kōy-* v.i., *kōc-* v.t., Koḍ. *kāy-* v.i., *kāc-* v.t. 'to boil', Ka. *kāy* v.i., *kāysu*/*kāsu* v.t., but not in Tuḷu. Forms of this type may have provided the basis for setting up *-c*/*-cc* as a transitive marker through reanalysis. There is a possibility of *-c* being an independent transitive marker surviving in these two languages of South Dravidian I: Ko. *kal-*, To. *kał* 'to learn': Ko. To. *kal-c-* 'to teach', *nil-* 'to stand': *nil-c-* 'to make stand' might have been constructed in this manner.

The languages which have lost the paired intransitive–transitive markers have resorted to additive morphemes to fulfill the same function, e.g. Te. *tirugu* has lost **tiru(k)ku*, but the transitive is *trippu* (<**tir-pp-*), which lost its paired intransitive **tirumbu* (which would have become *tirumu* in Old Telugu). The cognates under (a)–(c) show how paired intransitives and transitives with incorporated tense–voice morphs are represented in most of the languages of South Dravidian I and South Dravidian II (minus Telugu). Telugu and Kannaḍa, being close geographic neighbours with shared literary and cultural history, have deviated from this pattern. They use the additive transitivizers *-cu* and *-pu* beside the transitive–causative markers *-incu*/*-isu*. All Central Dravidian languages have lost these paired stems. In Parji the causative is formed by the addition of *-ip*/*-it* to the root, e.g. *ūŋg-* v.i. 'to swing': *ūk-ip*/*-it*, *ōḍ-* 'to be broken': *ōṭ-ip*/*-it* 'to break'. Burrow and Bhattacharya (1953: 46–7) say that herein is an original intransitive–transitive pair signalled by *-ŋg*/*-k*, *-ḍ*/*-ṭ*, etc. alternation, to which the causative morphs *-ip*/*-it* are added. There are also examples where voiceless stops do not occur when the causative marker is added, e.g. *vaŋg-ip/-it* 'to cause to bend', *panḍ-ip-/-it* 'to cause to be tired', etc. (46). The loss of paired intransitive–transitive stems may be taken as a shared innovation of Central Dravidian. The North Dravidian languages have preserved some traces of the paired intransitive–transitive stems.

7.3.6 *Paired intransitives and transitive stems with -(N)P/-(N)PP alternation*

Only some typical reconstructions with distribution in terms of subgroups are given here with references to *DEDR* entry numbers. Although Kannaḍa has lost this type it has some archaic pairs illustrating its occurrence in Early Kannaḍa or Pre-Kannaḍa, e.g. *aḍagu* 'to be humbled': *aḍaku* 'to humble', *amugu* 'to yield to pressure': *avuku* 'to press firmly' (*DVM*: 21, 51). In South Dravidian II Telugu and Gondi are to be excluded in the case of forming paired transitives, but the Kui–Kuvi–Pengo–Manḍa subgroup preserves it as a productive type.

(1) PD **aṭ-a-nk-*/**aṭ-a-nkk-* v.i.'to be compressed, be hidden', 'to press down, hide' [63].

South Dravidian I, South Dravidian II; the Central Dravidian forms with initial *ḍ-* are apparently borrowings from Telugu in which **aḍ-a-* > *ḍā-* was an old change. There are cognates from North Dravidian: Kuṛ. *aṛk-* 'to knead', Malt. *aṛg-* 'to press down', *aṛk-* 'to thrust'.

(2) PD **kal-a-nk-*/**kal-a-nkk-* 'to be agitated'/'to agitate, disturb' [240].

South Dravidian I (Tamil, Malayāḷam, Kota, Toda, Koḍagu, Kannaḍa, Tuḷu). Old Kannaḍa has *kalaṅku* (< **kalankk-*) as an archaic transitive form; South Dravidian II (Telugu: intransitive only); Central Dravidian: none; North Dravidian: Kuṛ. *xalax-* 'to disturb, make muddy', Malt. *qalg-* 'to disturb as water', *qalgr-* 'to be disturbed'

(3) PD **ā-* 'to be', **ā-ku* 'to be, become', **ā-kku* 'to cause to be, to make' [333].

South Dravidian I and South Dravidian II. The Central Dravidian and North Dravidian languages have taken a secondary base **ā-n-* formed as the past stem of PD **ā* (see section 5.4.1 d).

(4) PD **tū-nk-*/**tū-nkk-* v.i./tr. 'to swing' [3376].

South Dravidian I (all), South Dravidian II: Te. *tū̃gu* 'to swing, doze' (only the intransitive form; the transitive is *tū̃cu* 'to weigh'), Koṇḍa, Kui–Kuvi, Pengo, Manḍa; Central Dravidian: none; North Dravidian has evidence of a velar suffix in derived nouns, Kuṛ.

tungul, Malt. *tumgle*, Br. *tugh* 'dream, sleep'. The paired forms are in South Dravidian I and South Dravidian II.

It is not generally possible to find cognates for paired transitive–intransitives outside South Dravidian I and South Dravidian II, but that the pattern was prevalent in Proto-Dravidian before its breakup can be seen from the above examples, particularly the rare ones in Kuṛux–Malto. From comparative data, it appears that the incorporation of the velar suffixes was perhaps the oldest stage in Proto-Dravidian; the process then spread to the other sets and mainly got restricted to South Dravidian I and South Dravidian II.

7.3.7 *Summary*

I have identified three main patterns of forming transitive–causative stems: (1) by adding **-tt* (section 7.3.1), **-pp* (section 7.3.2) and **-cc* (section 7.3.4) to complementary classes of monosyllabic and disyllabic roots of (C)V̆̄(C) in Proto-Dravidian; (2) by geminating the final stop of the formative suffix -P/-NP which originally represented both tense and voice in disyllabic and trisyllabic stems (section 7.3.5):

	Non-past	Past
Intransitive	**-k/-p*, **-nk/-mp*	**-t/-nt*
Transitive	**-kk/-pp*, **-nkk/-mpp*	**-tt/-ntt*

The velar, labial and palatal series of type (1) presumably occurred in lexical or grammatical complementation in Proto-Dravidian, which is not recoverable. In type (2), by a sound change *-NPP > *-PP, most languages in South Dravidian have merged the geminated equivalents of pre-nasalized stops with geminate oral stops. In chapter 5 (see section 5.4.4) I have argued that the above are preserved as a relic conjugation in the languages derived from Pre-Tamil (Proto-(Tamil–Malayāḷam–Koḍagu–Iruḷa–Toda–Kota)). I also suggested that the loss of tense and retention of voice has led to *NP ~ *NPP representing voice change (intransitive → transitive) in South Dravidian I and South Dravidian II, e.g. **tū-nk-* v.i. 'to swing' → **tū-nkk* v.t. 'to swing' [3376], **tir-u-nt-* 'to be turned, changed' → **tir-u-ntt-* 'to turn, change' [3251]. This type is mainly found in South Dravidian I and South Dravidian II, but traces of it are also noticed in the other subgroups, requiring us to reconstruct it for the late stages of Proto-Dravidian, before it split into subgroups (sections 5.4.4–5.4.5). (3) A complementary to types (1) and (2) is the use of the additive morpheme **-ppi* ~ **-pi* [wi] added to transitive stems to form double-agent causatives (A_1 causes A_2 to act on Object). Incorporating erstwhile tense morphs *-(p)pi-ntt* (> **-(p)pi-ncc-* ~ **-(p)pi-cc*) past and **-(p)pi-mpp-* (> **-(p)pi-mp-* ~ **-(p)pi-pp-*) non-past, the resultant markers account for the causative markers in Kannaḍa of South Dravidian I and all members of South Dravidian II. This isogloss of double-causative marking thus establishes the undivided stage of South Dravidian I and South Dravidian II (sections 7.3.3–6).

The loss of paired intransitive–transitive stems may be taken as a shared innovation of the languages of the Central Dravidian group, although traces are embedded redundantly in such pairs as Pa. *ūŋg-* v.i. 'to swing': v.t. *ūk-ip*/*-it-* (see section 7.3.5). They are preserved only in a few archaic forms in Kannaḍa and Tuḷu of South Dravidian I, and Kuṛux–Malto of North Dravidian, but totally lost in Telugu of South Dravidian II.

7.4 Tense

There are two tenses reconstructible for Proto-Dravidian, i.e. past and non-past. Non-past includes the habitual (present/aorist/indefinite/generic) and future. Some languages have also developed a separate present tense. Perfective, durative, infinitive, concessive, conditional etc. represent aspects associated with the past or non-past tense markers. Some of these are traditionally considered moods, but there is always a tense marker historically traceable in their formation, usually the past or non-past without necessarily referring to time. A number of modal auxiliaries are added to the non-finite form of a verb to express modes such as ability–inability, probability, prohibition, permission, obligation, etc. The modes are normally expressed by a limited number of auxiliary verbs, added to the finite or non-finite form of the primary verb. The nucleus of the verb (the main meaning carrier) also has some auxiliaries (called vectors/operators/co-verbs, etc.) added to the primary root, covering such semantic categories as transitive, causative, reflexive–reciprocal and benefactive. Complex stems are a part of the lexical representation of extended forms of the main verb. Almost any verb (simple, complex or compound) can take any modal auxiliary (hence, grammatical), but only some operators modify the meaning of the primary verb. Finite and non-finite verbs have both affirmative and negative inflection. A finite verb is the head of the main clause, and a non-finite verb, the head of a subordinate clause. Morphologically the finite verb, in most cases, carries an agreement marker with the subject phrase in gender–number–person.

7.4.1 *Past markers*

The past-tense markers are *-t-*/*-tt-*, *-nt-* (v.i.) ~ *-nt-t-* (v.t.), *-i-* ~ *-in-*, *-cc-*, *-kk-* which could have occurred in complementary environments in Proto-Dravidian, but these are not fully recoverable, owing to some subgroups analogically regularizing one or more of the original allomorphs. There is complementation with some overlap between *-t-* and *-tt-* in different subgroups. In South Dravidian I and South Dravidian II, the past stem is the same in finite verb inflection (past tense) and in the formation of the past verbal adjective (relative participle) and the gerund (perfective participle). Some languages of Central Dravidian and South Dravidian II have the gerund formed by the addition of *-(*c*)*ci* not used in the finite forms. But the palatal affricate does occur as a past marker in Old Tamil, Toda–Kota of South Dravidian I, Telugu of South Dravidian II and in North Dravidian; it is, therefore, reconstructed as a past allomorph of Proto-Dravidian. Therefore, **-cc-i* can be taken as a sequence of two past allomorphs **-cc* and **-i*.

7.4.1.1 *-t-

In South Dravidian I and Central Dravidian and *-tt- in South Dravidian II and North Dravidian. This occurs clearly after monosyllabic roots ending in an alveolar or retroflex nasal, e.g.

(1) PD *tiHn- (tin-ṯ-/tin-ṯṯ-) 'to eat' [3263].[3] (See section 7.2.1 (3).)
SD I past *tin-ṯ-: Ta. tiṉ- (tiṉ-ṟ-), Ma. tin- (tin-n-), Ko. tin- (tiḏ-), To. tïn- (tïḏ-), Koḍ. tinn- (tin-d-), Ka. tin(nu)- (tin-d-), Tu. tin- (tin-d-/tin-t-);
SD II past *tin-ṯṯ-: OTe. tin- (tin-ṭ- < tin-ṭṭ- < *tin-ṯṯ-); *ti-ṯṯ- with the loss of the root-final nasal: Go. tin- (ti-tt-), Koṇḍa tin- (tiR-), Kui tin- (ti-s-), Kuvi tin- (ti-c-), Pe. tin- (ti-c-/ci-c-), Manḍa tin- (ti-c-);
CD past *tin-ṯ-: Kol. Nk. (Ch.), Pa. tin- (tin-d-), Oll. tin- (tin-ḍ-), Gad. tin- (tiy-).

We note that South Dravidian I and Central Dravidian require a past-tense marker -t- and South Dravidian II requires -tt-. This is true of the other (C)Vn- roots, **aHn- > *ān-/*a(y)n- > *e(y)n- > *i(y)n- [868] 'to say': SD I *en-ṯ-/an-ṯ-/in-ṯ-; CD: en-ṯ-; SD II *an-ṯṯ-/*in-ṯṯ-; ND: ān- (see Krishnamurti 1997b/2001a: 333).

(2) PD *uHṇ- (uṇ-ṭ-/uṇ-ṭṭ-) 'to eat, drink' [600]. (See section 7.3.1 (2).)
SD I: Ta. Ma. uṇ- (uṇ-ṭ-), Ko. To. uṇ- (uḍ-), Koḍ. uṇ- (uṇ-ḍ-), Ka. uṇṇu (uṇ-ḍ-), Tu. uṇ (uṇ-ḍ- past; uṇ-ṭ- perfect);
SD II: Go.–Koṇḍa–Kui–Pe. uṇ- (uṭ-); Manḍa un- (uc-; probably on the analogy of tic past stem of tin-: tic-);
CD: Kol. un- (un-d-), Nk.–Pa.–Oll.–Gad. un- (un-ḍ-);
ND: Kuṛ. ōn- (oṇ-ḍ-), Malt. ōn- (on-ḍ-) 'to drink'.

Derived nouns and the causative stem in South Dravidian I, South Dravidian II require the reconstruction of *ūṇ-; this and the long vowel in North Dravidian are explained as arising from a Proto-Dravidian laryngeal *H within the root, i.e. *uHṇ-. In Malto -t-, -y-, -Ø are the allomorphs before different personal morphs in the past tense. Under the aspectual system the perfective (past) aspect is expressed by -t-/-c- (Mahapatra 1979: 163–9). In Kuṛux, the past-tense marker -k- is added to onḍ- (onḍ-k-an 'I drank') and not to the root ōn-; here, the stem alternant seems to have incorporated a historically older past morph.

7.4.1.2 *-tt-

Actually *t ~ *tt can be taken as morpheme alternants without clearly defined distribution. In Tamil there are bases consisting of two short syllables, of which the second

[3] PD *tiHn- shows a long vowel, i.e. ī from iH in the case of the derived noun and in the formation of the causative; the laryngeal is lost in non-causative inflection (Krishnamurti 1997b; 2001a: 333).

is *-ṭu*/*-ṟu*, which form the past stem by geminating the final stop, e.g. *keṭu-* 'to perish': *keṭṭ-*, *peṟu* 'to get': *peṟṟ-*. In traditional descriptions these are shown to have *-t-* past and not *-tt-*, but comparatively, both South Dravidian II and Central Dravidian independently support the past marker as **-tt-* in these cases. The voiceless geminate in all languages is explained better by this reconstruction.

(3) PD **iṭ-u* (*iṭṭ-*) 'to put, place' [442]

SD I: Ta. Ma. *iṭu* (*iṭṭ-*), Koḍ. *ïḍ-* (*ïṭṭ-*), Ko. *iḍ-* (*iṭ-*), To. *ïḍ-* (*ïṭ-*), Ka. *iḍu* (*iṭṭ-*) (Tuḷu past is different);

SD II: Koṇḍa *iḍ-* (*iḍ-t-*), *iṭ-ki-* 'to put on, wear', *iṟ-* (*iR-t-*) 'to serve food', Kui *iṭ-a* (*iṭi-*), Pe. *iṭ-* (*iṭ-t-*), *iz-* (*is-t-*) 'to put in, as salt', Manḍa *iṭ-*. Note that Proto-Dravidian **-ṭ-* has merged with **-ṯ-* in South Dravidian II (section 4.5.5.3, see ety. (78)); Te. *iḍu* and Go. *irr-* do not have past stems like the others.

CD: Kol. *īḍ-* (*iṭṭ-*), Nk. (Ch.) *iṛ-* (*iṭṭ-*), Pa. *iḍ-* (*iṭṭ-*), Gad. *ir-* (*iṭṭ-*).

The languages of North Dravidian have no cognates for this verb.

(4) PD **caH-* (*ca-tt-*) 'to die'. **caH* > cā- ~ *cay-*/*cey-* > **key-* (ND) [2426]. (See Krishnamurti 1997b/2001a: 331.)

SD I: Ta. *cā-* (*cett-*), Ma. *cāka* (*ca-tt-*), Koḍ. *cā-* (*ca-tt-*), To. *soy-* (*so-t-*), Ka. *sāy* (*sa-tt*), Tu. *saipini* 'to die';

SD II: Koṇḍa *sā-* (*sā-t-*), Kui *sāva* (*sā-t-*), Kuvi–Pengo–Manḍa *hā-* (*hā-t-*);

CD: Pa. *cay-* (*ca-ñ-*), Oll. *say-* (*sa-d-*);

ND: Kuṛ. *khē'-* (*ke-cc-*), Malt. *key-* (*ke-cc-*), Br. *kah-* (*kask-*).

Tuḷu of South Dravidian I, Telugu of South Dravidian II, the remaining Central Dravidian languages and the languages of North Dravidian follow different routes in past formation. Only Gondi has replaced this root by a borrowed word.

(5) PD **kā-* (*kā-tt-*) 'to protect, guard' [1416].

SD I: Ta. *kā-* (*kā-tt-*), Ma. *kākkuka* (*kā-tt-*), Koḍ. *kā-* (*kā-t-*), Ko. *kā-v-* (*kā-t-*), To. *kō-f-* (*kō-t-*), Ka. *kā-* (*kā-d-*); Tu. *kā-puni* 'to watch';

SD II: Te. *kā-cu* v.t., *kā-pu* n., Koṇḍa *kā-pu* n., Kui *kā-p-a* (*kā-t-*), 'to wait for', Kuvi–Pe.–Manḍa *kā-* (*kā-t-*) 'to watch, wait';

CD: Kol.–Nk. *kay-* (*kay-t-*) 'to herd cattle', Pa. Oll. *kā-p-* (*kā-t-*) 'to wait';

ND: *xā-p-* 'to protect, guard', Malt. *qā-p-* 'to watch, wait for', Br. *xwā-f-* 'to graze'.

The past *-tt-* is supported by South Dravidian I, South Dravidian II and Central Dravidian languages. Again, Kannaḍa–Tuḷu of South Dravidian I, Telugu–Gondi of

South Dravidian II and North Dravidian have adopted a different way of forming the past. We can clearly see that the inflected non-past stem has become the base in many languages (see Kota–Tuḷu, Kui, Parji–Ollari and all North Dravidian languages).

It has been pointed out that there was a class of verbs which combined tense and voice. Such verbs formed past transitive from *-*nt-t*- which lost the nasal in several South Dravidian languages and became identical with the additive past -*tt*-:

(6) PSD **kaẓi* (-*nt*-) v.i. 'time to pass, become spent, ruined', (-*nt-t*-) v.t. 'to spend/waste time, void excreta, reject' [1356].

SD I: Ta. *kaẓi* (-*nt*-/-*tt*-) v.i/v.t., Middle Ta. *kaẓi-cc*- (< *kaẓi-tt*-) past, *kaẓi-cc-al* n. 'diarrhoea', Ma. *kaẓiyuka* v.i., *kaẓikka* v.t., To. *koḍy*- (*koḍ-s*-) 'time to pass', *koḍc*- (*koḍ-č*)[4] 'chase out of sight', Koḍ. *kayy*- (*kay-ñj*-) v.i. 'time passes', *kay*- (*kay-c*-) v.t. 'to pass time'. In this subgroup of South Dravidian I the past suffix -*tt*- got palatalized to -*cc*-. Kannaḍa and Tuḷu have cognates but the past markers are different.

SD II: Koṇḍa *kaṛs*- (*kaṛs-t*-) 'to defecate', Kui *kṛahpa*- (*kṛah-t*-), Kuvi *gṛah*- (*gṛah-t*-), Pe. *kṛac*- (-*c*-), Manḍa *gṛah*-.

The uninflected stem in South Dravidian II looks like the past stem of South Dravidian I incorporating the palatalized past suffix.

7.4.1.3 *-nt-

In South Dravidian I, -*nt*- is the past-tense marker of mostly monosyllabic or disyllabic roots ending in /u i y r ẓ/. It happens that most of them are intransitive. The corresponding transitive forms have *-*nt-t*- (> -*tt*- in SD I). It also occurs in Pre-Tamil descendants (Malayāḷam–Koḍagu–Kota–Toda) in a special class of stems (Arden's seventh conjugation, *Tamil Lexicon*'s twelfth conjugation), in which the past is marked by -*nt*- and the non-past by -*pp*-. Most of these bases (some seventy) are disyllabic ending in -*a*. This class of verbs contrasts with the former class in which -*nt*- and -*v*- stand for past and non-past in the intransitive and -*tt*- and -*pp*- for the transitive, respectively. In Middle Tamil, Malayāḷam, Koḍagu, Toda and Kota, following a front high vowel *i* or *y*, the past markers -*nt*- and -*tt*- were palatalized to -*ñc*- (Ta. *ñj*, Ma. *ññ*, Koḍ. *ñj*, Ko. *c*, To. *s*) and -*cc*-, respectively.

Kannaḍa preserves -*nd*- in six verbs following the (C)V- allomorph of the root, *nō*- 'to suffer': *no-nd*-, *bar*- 'to come': *ba-nd*-, *tar*- 'to bring': *ta-nd*-, *mī*- 'to bathe': *mi-nd*/*mī-d*, *bē*- 'to be hot': *be-nd*-; after other monosyllabic bases, the past is -*d*- (*DVM*: 198ff.).

[4] In Toda Stem I corresponds to the intransitive stem in Tamil and Stem 2 corresponds to the past stem of the transitive. Thus Ta. *kaẓi* = To. *koḍy*-, Ta. *kaẓi-cc*- = To. *koḍc*-. The sandhi rules account for the past stems of Toda, $t + y \rightarrow s$, $c + i \rightarrow \check{c}$.

Parallels are noticed in Central Dravidian (mainly Parji and Gadaba), e.g. Pa. *ver-* (*ve-ñ-* < **we-nj-*), Oll. *var-* (*va-n-*). Even where South Dravidian I languages do not have *-nt-*, Parji–Ollari–Gadaba had a past *-nd-*, Pa. *koy-* (*ko-ñ-*) 'to cut, reap'. These roots in Old Tamil had *-t-* as past marker, *cey-* (*cey-t-*) 'to do', but Modern spoken Tamil has *sey-* (*se-ñj*) presupposing a past form with *-nd-* (*sey-nd-*).

In actual conjugation, the past-tense morph *-nt-* is mainly confined to South Dravidian I; there is, however, evidence of the incorporation of *-nd-* as a stem formative in several languages (see section 5.4.5). It can, therefore, be reconstructed for Proto-Dravidian.

(7) PSD **iru* (*iru-nt-*) 'to exist, live, belong to (with dative subject)' [480].
SD I: Ta. *iru* (*iru-nt-*) v.i., *iru-ttu* 'to cause to sit', Ma. *iri* (*iru-nn-*) 'to remain, to sit', *iru-ttuka* 'to seat', To. *ïr-* (*ïθ-*), Koḍ. *ir-* (*i-ñj-* < **ir-nd-*), Ka. *ir-* (*ird-/-idd*), Tu. *ippuni* (*itt-*);
SD II: Kui *rīnda* (*rīnd-i*) 'to be stable', *rīspa* (*rīs-t-*) 'to set in position'.

Notice that Kui has incorporated a Proto-South Dravidian past morph as a stem formative and also has a corresponding transitive which falls into the class of NP (v.i.), NPP (v.t.) with loss of tense meaning.

(8) PD **cal-* (*can-ṯ-* < **cal-nt-*) 'to go, pass, occur' [2781].
SD I: Ta. *cel* (*ceṉ-ṟ-*), *cel-uttu* 'to cause to go', Ma. *cel-ka* (*cenn-*) v.i., *cel-uttuka* v.t., Ko. *cal-* (*cad-*). To. *sal-* (*sad-*), Ka. *sal-* (*sa-nd-*), Tu. *sall-uni* 'to be valid, fit', *sand-uni* 'to pass as time';
SD II: Te. *canu* (*caṇ-ṭ-*), Go. *son-*, *sond-*, *hon-* (*hott-*), *han-* (*hat-*), Koṇḍa *son-* (*soR-* < **soṯṯ-* < **son-ṯṯ-*); Kui *sal-* (*sas-*), Kuvi *hal-* (*hacc-*), Pe.–Manḍa *hal-* (*hac-*);
CD: Nk. *ca-* (*caṇḍ-*), Pa. *cen-* (*cen-d-*), Oll. *sen-* (*sey-*, *senḍ-*).

South Dravidian I clearly has *-nt-* suffix. Tu. *sand-*, Go. *sond-* point to the restructuring of past stem as the normal base. South Dravidian II has *-tt-* as past and Central Dravidian *-d-*; Ollari–Gadaba *-yy-* forms point to an analogical extension of the *key-* 'to do' paradigm to other monosyllabic verbs. The rounding of the root vowel (*a* > *o*) is an idiosyncratic change in Gondi–Koṇḍa for which we do not know any reason at present.

(9) PD **waH-r* (imp. *wā-*, past *wa-nt-* < **war-nt-*) 'to come, to happen' [5270].
SD I: Ta. *var-u* (*vā* imp sg; past *va-nt-*, inf *var-a-*) v.i., *var-u-ttu* v.t. 'to cause to come', Ma. *var-uka* (imp *vā-*, past *va-nn-*) v.i., *var-u-ttuka* v.t., Ko. *vār-* (*vā-*, *va-d-*), To. *pōr-* (*po-d-*), Koḍ. *bar-* (*bā-*, *ba-nd-*), Ka. *bar-* (*bā-*, *ba-nd-*), Tu. *barpini* 'to come';
SD II: Te. *wacc-* (imp *rā-* < **wrā-* < **war-ā*), past *wa-cci-*; earlier past marker *-cci* got incorporated into the basic stem through reanalysis, see

TVB:162–3); Go. *wāy-* (imp *war-ā*, past *wā-t-*), Koṇḍa *wā-* (imp sg *rʔa-*, past *wā-t-*), Kui–Kuvi–Pe.–Manḍa *vā-* (*vā-t-*);

CD: Kol. *var-* (imp *vā-*, past *va-tt-*), Nk. (Ch.) *var-/va-* (*va-t-*), Pa. *ver-* (*ve-ñ-* < *ve-ñj-* < *ver-nd-* < *var-nd-*; radical *a* becomes *e* before an alveolar in Pre-Parji, see section 4.4.5), Oll. *var-* (*vad-*, *van-*), Gad. *vār-* (imp *vā-*, *var-*, past *va-dd-/va-nn-*);

ND: Kuṛ.-Malt. *bar-* 'to arrive', Br. *banning* (imp. *ba*, past *bass-*).

South Dravidian I and Parji of Central Dravidian agree in having *-nt-* as a past marker. The other Central Dravidian languages have analogically restructured their past forms with either *-d-* or *-tt-* as the marker. South Dravidian II (except Telugu) has regularized *-t-* (<**-tt-*) as the past marker. North Dravidian has regularized *-cc-* as the past-tense marker.

(10) PD **kāy* (*-nt-*) v.i. 'to grow hot', (*-nt-t-*) v.t. 'to boil, heat' [1458].

SD I: Ta. *kāy* (*-nt-/-tt-* ~ *-cc-*) v.i./v.t.; also *kāy-ttu/kāy-ccu* v.t. 'to boil, ignite', also *kā-ntu* v.i. (with an erstwhile past marker *-nt-* incorporated into the stem, following the loss of root-final *-y*, as expected); Ma. *kāy-uka* v.i., *kāy-kka/kāy-cc-uka* v.t.; *kā-nt-uka* 'to be hot', Ko. *kāy* (*kāc-*) v.i., *kāc-* (*kāc-*) v.t., To. *kōy-* (*kōs-*) v.i., *kōc-* (*kōč-*) v.t., Koḍ. *kāy-* (*kā-ñj-*) v.i., *kā-c-* (*kā-c-i*) v.t., Ka. *kāy-* (*kāy-d-/kā-d-*), Tu. *kāy-uni* v.i.;

SD II: Te. *kāyu* (*kās-i*) 'to shine', Go. *kās-* v.i., *kās-is/-ih-* v.t., Koṇḍa *kāy-* (*kāy-it-*) 'to warm oneself at fireplace'; (restructured stems occur: *kā-mb-* v.i., *kā-p-* v.t.), Kui *kāg-*, Kuvi *kāy-* v.i.; (restructured bases: *kā-nd-* v.i., *kā-t-* v.t.), Pe. Manḍa *kāy-* v.i., Manḍa also *kā-nd-* '(sun) to be hot';

CD: Nk. (Ch.) *kāy* 'to be hot', Pa. *kā-p-ip-* (past *-p-it*) v.t., Oll. *kāy-p-* (*kāy-t-*) v.t., Gad *kāy-kil* 'fever';

ND: Kuṛ. *xāy-* 'to dry up', *xai-d-* v.t., Malt. *qāy-/qeyr-* 'to be boiled'.

Although only South Dravidian I has evidence of *-nt-* as past marker, the fact that South Dravidian I and South Dravidian II have a restructured verb *kā-ntu* (see Tamil, Malayāḷam, Pengo, Manḍa) shows that its use was much more extensive at an earlier stage of Proto-Dravidian.

7.4.1.4 *-i- ~ *-in-[5]

These suffixes occur generally after disyllabic and trisyllabic stems of three or more morae, ending in an obstruent, i.e. -P, -PP, NP followed by the non-morphemic *-u*. The

[5] Tolkāppiyam says that *-i* occurs as the past marker after verb stems ending in /u i ai ṇ r l ḷ/, citing verbal adjectives ending in *-iya/-iṉa*, e.g. *peyar-iya*, *coll-iya*, *aruḷ-iya*. After the final short vowel *-u*, *-iṉa* occurs, *ōṯṯ-iṉa* (Israel 1973: 33–5).

reflexes of these are lost in Gondi and Pengo of South Dravidian II, Kolami–Naiki of Central Dravidian and Brahui of North Dravidian (*DVM*: §2.26, pp. 214ff.).

Old Tamil has *-iṉ-* as past marker in finite verbs of the above canonical structure, e.g. *vāṅk-iṉ-ēṉ* 'I bought', but *vāṅk-i* 'having bought' (perfective participle). This is true of all verbs ending in two consonants (-PP, -NP, *-ḷḷu*, *-ṇṇu*) following a short vowel, or of $(C_1)\bar{V}C_2/(C_1)VC_2VC_3V$ where the final consonant, C_2/C_3, is a stop or *-v-*. Kota has *-y-* corresponding to Pre-Tamil *-i-* as a perfective marker, e.g. *namb-* 'to believe': *namb -y-*, *amk-* 'to press': *amk-y-*. Toda also has *-y-* in the corresponding position, *nob-* 'to believe': *nob-y-*; Koḍagu has *-i* just like Tamil–Malayāḷam. In Kannaḍa *-i* is combined with a dental suffix in denoting the past tense in finite verbs, *mād-id-anu* 'he did', but *-i-* occurs as perfective marker, e.g. *māḍ-i* 'having done'. Tuḷu has *-y* as the past marker of immediate past of some classes of verbs, e.g. *pari-* 'to drink': *pari-y-*. In the distant past *-t-* is the tense marker, e.g. *pari-t-*.

In South Dravidian II, Old Telugu has *-(i)ti-* in past finite verbs except in the third person; e.g. Te. 1sg *cepp-iti-ni* 'I said', 1pl *cepp-iti-mi* 'we said', 2sg *cepp-iti-wi* 'you said', 2pl *cepp-iti-ri* 'you said (pl)', 3sg and inanimate pl *-e-*, *cepp-e-nu* 'he/she/it/they (neu) said', 3h pl *cepp-i-ri*. It seems that *-ti* was the original past (cf. *win-ṭi-ni* 'I heard') and the *-i-* preceding *-ti* could be epenthetic. Pure *-i-/-iy-* occurs in the 3sg *-e-n*(< *iy-an*; *-an* 3m sg) in which the gender–number morph got obscured because of sandhi and hence was generalized as the 3sg and inanimate plural. The perfective participle is formed by adding *-i*, e.g. *cepp-i* 'having said'. A number of stems ending in *-c* and *-s* in Telugu, like *pilucu* 'to call', have finite and non-finite forms like *pili-ci* 'having called', *pili-c-en* 'he/she/it called', *cēyu* 'to do': *cē-si* 'having done', etc. In these, historically final *-ci* and *-si* were the original past markers. The wider use of *-i* as past participle marker has led to a reanalysis of these constructions by treating *-c*/*-s* as part of the stem (*TVB*: §2.85). Gondi and Koṇḍa also have **-ci* as the perfective marker in synchronic grammars, e.g. Go. *son-jī* 'having gone', *kī-sī* 'having done', Koṇḍa *son-si*, *ki-zi* id. Koṇḍa has *-it* as past marker (*i* + *t*) in finite verbs, broadly after stems ending in an obstruent, *tōṟ-* 'to appear': *tōṟ-it-an* 'he appeared'. In Pengo the participle is formed by adding *-si*/*-zi*/*-hi*, *uṇ-zi* 'having drunk', *kūk-si* 'having called', *ta-hi* 'having brought', *nil-ci* 'having stood' (cf. Koṇḍa *ta-si*, *nil-si*). Kui also has *-it-* as past marker in finite verbs after stems ending in an obstruent; the past participle suffix is *-sa*/*-ja* (after nasal or vowel-ending stems, *-a* elsewhere). Kuvi has *-it* ~ *-t* as past markers, e.g. *ajj-* 'to fear': *ajj-it-*. The perfective participle is formed by adding *-ca*/*-ja*/*-sa*/*-ha*, e.g. *ven-ja* 'having heard'.

Parji has *-i-* ~ *-ci* as a marker of the gerund, *cen-i* 'having gone', *ver-i* 'having come', but *nil-ci* 'having stood'. Ollari has *-i* alternating with *-si*/*-zi* in forming the past participle, e.g. *sūṛ-i* 'having seen', *uṇ-zi* 'having drunk'. In Gadaba *-i* occurs in the perfective particple as an alternant of *-ji* ~ *-ci*, e.g. *in-ji* 'having said', but *vār-i* 'having come'. The finite verbs in the past do not use the vowel *-i*, but *-n* occurs in Class 6, e.g. *vār* 'to come': past stem *va-n-o-*, *kē-* 'to do': *ke-no-*. This *-n* can be related to the morph-complex *-in* of South Dravidian I. Kolami and Naiki do not have anything comparable involving *-i*.

Malto has *-y-* as a past marker in the third person; in other environments *-t-* occurs in the past, e.g. *amb-* 'to leave': *amb-y-ah* (3m sg), *amb-y-ad* (3f sg), *amb-y-ar* (3hum pl), but *amb-t-an* (1sg). Malto also uses *-y-* as a completive marker, e.g. in the past it occurs with the past tense morph *-t-/-c-* and in non-past with *-d-/-n-*, *amb-iy-t-an* 'I left off' (Mahapatra 1979: 163–74). Droese uses *-i* as perfective marker, *onḍ-i* 'having drunk'.

South Dravidian I and South Dravidian II use *-in-/-i-* as markers of the past tense/aspect in finite and non-finite verbs; *-i-* occurs in combination with past *-tt-* in several of the South Dravidian II languages. In Central Dravidian and North Dravidian it is found only in non-finite verbs denoting past/perfective aspect. It appears that the dental suffix has spread at the expense of this form.

7.4.1.5 *-cc-

In early literary Tamil *-iciṉ-* occurs as a redundant marker of past in a special class of finite verbs, e.g. *eṉṟ-iciṉ* 'I said', *vant-iciṉ* 'I came', *peṟṟ-iciṉ* 'she obtained'. There is no (g)np marker, but the inflected forms occurred in 1sg, 3sg, or 2 imperative sg. Pronominalized nouns based on these forms occurred in the third person in all genders and numbers, e.g. *pirint-iciṉ-ōḷ* 'she who separated', *kaṇṭ-iciṉ-ōr* 'those that saw'. This form is interpreted as a sequence of two past allomorphs *-cc and *-in* (*DVM*: §2.27). Emeneau (1957b: §§39–56) surveys the past-tense markers in the whole family and proposes that Toda and Kota, along with the relic usage of Tamil, have also inherited the palatal/sibilant as a past marker, To. 1sg *pī-š-pen* 'I went', Ko. *vad-c-ē* 'I came'.

Telugu has a *-cu* as the final syllable of bases of three morae, e.g. *pilucu* 'to call', *teṟacu* 'to open', *ēḍcu* 'to cry', *īḍcu* 'to drag' and the past forms are *pilic-e-nu* 'he called', *pilic-i* 'having called', etc. Cognates from the other languages in South Dravidian lack this stem-final syllable, Ta. *viḷi, teṟa, aḻu, iḻu*, respectively. I interpreted *-cu* in these forms as a consequence of the incorporation of an original past marker *-c(c)i* which occurs synchronically in South Dravidian II and Central Dravidian (*TVB*: §§2.84–90). The alternation of *-y/-s* in tri-moraic bases that end in *-yu*, e.g. *orayu* 'to rub': *oras-i* 'having rubbed', *cēyu* 'to do': *cēs-i* 'having done', etc. has also been explained as resulting from incorporating the past allomorph *-si* (following the loss of *-y*, *ora-si* < *oray-ci-*), retained intact in the other South Dravidian II languages (*TVB*: §§2.39–50). In some cases Kannaḍa, Tuḷu and even Tamil–Malayāḷam have cognates with -V*cu* as a formative, where Telugu has -V*yu*, e.g. Te. *enayu* v.i./v.t. 'to mix, mingle': Ta. *iṇ-ai* 'to join', Ma. *in-ayuka*, Ka. *eṇ-asu* 'to add together'; Te. *al-ayu* 'to be tired': Ta. *al-acu*,

Ma. *al-asuka*, Ka. *al-asu*, Tu. *al-asuni*, Malto *al-esi* 'sweat, heat' (see Emeneau 1957b: §48). Following the general trend in Dravidian of reanalysing former tense markers as formatives, adequately illustrated earlier, it could be that there was a widely used palatal suffix as the past allomorph in the whole family and that it got incorporated into the stem as a formative, later weakened to *-y-* in South Dravidian I (for *-c-* [-s-] > *-y*/*-Ø*, see section 4.5.1.3). I have also cited more examples of South Dravidian II and North Dravidian languages incorporating **-cc* as a formative, e.g. Te. *paṟ-acu* 'to flee': Malt. *par-c-*, Te. *kaḍ-acu* 'to cross, time to pass': Kui *grās-* (*TVB*: §2.89–90). While discussing the distribution of *-i*, I gave examples for the occurrence of *-cc*V as a gerund in the other languages of South Dravidian II.

Even in Central Dravidian several verb stems end in *-c*/*-s*, not found in the other subgroups, Kol. -Nk. *ars-*, Pa. *narc-*, Oll. *nars-*, Gad. *narc-* 'to fear': Nk. *ari*, Pa. Oll. Gad. *nar* n. 'fear' [3605] (see *DVM*: 223–4). These cases are covered by the same argument as above.

Kuṛux–Malto–Brahui synchronically employ *-cc* as a past marker extensively, sometimes with another past marker *-k*, or other times all by itself, e.g. Type VI verbs take *-c-* past in the 3sg *rah-* 'to be': *rah-c-as* 'he was'; in the 1sg/pl and 2sg/pl the stem is *rah-ck-*. Verbs representing 'the historical past' take *-c-*/*-j-* as past marker, e.g. Kuṛ. *khe-* 'to die': *ke-cc-*, *ciʔ-* 'to give': *ci-cc-*, *man-* 'to become': *man-j-*, *bar-* 'to come': *bar-c-*; Malt. *key-* 'to die': *ke-c-*, *ci-* 'to give': *ci-c-*, *bar-* 'to come': *bar-c-*; Brahui has *-ss-* correspondingly, *man-* 'to become': *mass-*, *bann-* 'to come': *bass-*.

7.4.1.5.1 *Possible relationship between* *-in *and* *-cin Meenakshisundaran (1965: 84–5) says that Tolkāppiyam takes *-ciṉ* as the basic form of the suffix, treated as an 'expletive' of the second person, although 'he also states that this expletive can be used in the other persons' (cites Tolk. 759–60). Meenakshisundaran suggests that *-iciṉ* with the loss of *-c-* in Pre-Tamil would give rise to *-iin*. 'This will give us *-in* the past tense sign, as found in Tamil' (1965: 85). He also traces the long *-ii* occurring as past participle marker in Cankam Tamil to *-iin* derived from *-iciṉ*. In any case it is quite tempting to find some relationship between the past *-in-* and the relic usage of **-cin-* with the loss of *c-*. The past markers *-ci(n)* ~ *-i(n)* (in South Dravidian II and Central Dravidian) could have lost the final *-n* which could be quite normal. We cannot presently resolve the question whether *-cc-* and *-in* are independent past markers, and whether *-cc-in* is a combination of both. There is more evidence to consider it as a morphological complex, because Kuṛux and Malto, which do not lose **c-*, have a reflex of past **-i*.

7.4.1.6 *-kk-

Tamil has four disyllabic roots ending in *-ku*, *puku* 'to enter' [4238], *naku* 'to laugh' [3569], *taku* 'to fit' [3005], *toku* 'to aggregate, assemble' [3476], whose past stems are *pukk-*, *nakk-*, *takk-* and *tokk-*. Ramaswami Aiyar (1938: 750) puts these with stems of the type in (C)V*ṭu*/-*ṯu* and says that their past stems are formed by gemination of the root-final stop. He suggests that the gemination may have been the result of 'sandhi action of the past suffix'. Subrahmanyam (1971: 103), following this suggestion, derives gemination in *naku*, etc. also by sandhi of $k + t$, which is neither phonologically motivated nor possible in Dravidian. In South Dravidian, only Koraga, a minor tribal language adjacent to Tuḷu, forms the past by the addition of *-k*. The Onti dialect uses *-k-*/*-kk-*/*-g-* as past markers, e.g. *kuṭṭu* 'to beat': 1sg *kuṭṭu-g-e*, 1pl *kuṭṭu-g-a*, 2sg *kuṭṭu-g-a*, 2pl *kuṭṭu-g-erï*, 3m sg *kuṭṭu-g-i*, 3f/neu sg *kuṭṭu-g-u*, 3m/f pl *kuṭṭu-g-erï*; in Tappu also the past suffix is *-g-*; the 3f/neu sg suffix is *-ïdï* instead of *-u*; in the Mudu dialect, again, the difference is only in the personal suffixes, 1sg/pl *-e*/*-u*, 2sg/pl *-a*/*-rï*, 3mf sg *-i*, fn *-ïdï*, mf pl *-rï*. The past suffix is *-k-* after monosyllabic bases, e.g. *ī* 'to give': *ī-k-e* 'I gave'; it is *-kk-* after stems in final *i* or *e*, e.g. *negi-kk-i* 'he said', but *jēkï-g-e* 'I washed' (Bhat 1971). In my opinion this is an innovation in Koraga of giving a past meaning to a non-past suffix just like Kota, which uses *-p-* (<**-pp*), a non-past marker, as a past marker. Note that the non-past marker in Koraga is *-n-* which derives from **-n*.

ND: Kuṛux uses *-k-*/*-ʔ-* as the past marker in finite verbs in the first and second persons, *es-* 'to break': 1sg *es-k-an*, 1pl *es-k-am*, 1pl (inc) *es-k-at*, 2sg *es-k-ai*, 2pl *es-k-ar*, 3m sg *esʔas* 'he broke', 3f sg *esʔā*, 3m/f pl *esʔar* (Hahn 1911: 45). Some verbs have *-ck-* (combination of two past markers $c + k$) as the past marker, *raʔ-ck-an* 'I remained', etc. (Hahn 1911: 50). Brahui also has *-k-* as the past marker beside *-s-*/*-ss-* in different classes of stems (Emeneau 1962d: 23).

7.4.1.7 *Summary*

Four sets of allomorphs surface as markers of the past tense in Dravidian: (1) *-t-* ~ *-tt-* ~ *-nt-*, (2) *-i-* ~ *-in-*, *-cc-in*, (3) *-cc-*, (4) *-kk-*. The last one, *-kk-*, occurs only in North Dravidian[6] and is geographically complementary to groups (1) and (2). In Kuṛux–Malto some conjugations show either (3) or (4), but some complex morphs involve both (3) and (4). One of the isoglosses binding North Dravidian from others is the loss of the dental group (1) as past marker in most items while generalizing (3) and (4).

Following broadly the distribution of these in Old Tamil texts, we can say that in South Dravidian I *-t-* and *-tt-* occur in complementary environments, *-t-* after monosyllabic roots with a short radical vowel ending in /n ṇ r ẓ y/; since /r ẓ/ do not occur root-finally, they have to be followed by the vowel *-u*, e.g. *tin-* 'to eat', *uṇ-* 'to drink', *cey-* 'to do',

[6] Ramaswami Aiyar (1938) says that the gemination of the final stop in four disyllabic roots (see section 7.4.1.6), *puku-* (*puk-k-*) 'to enter', etc. derives gemination as a result of sandhi of final *-k* with the past *-t* (**-kt-* > *-kk-*), but phonologically this is an impossible type in Dravidian. *DVM*: 103 endorses this view. I have explained that the use of a velar stop for past in Koraga is an innovation which has nothing to do with the ND *-kk-* (section 7.4.1.6).

aẓ-u- 'to weep'; *-tt-* occurs as a past tense marker after disyllabic roots ending in an apical stop /ṯ ṭ/. Strong verbs of (C)VCV/(C)V̄C-type take *-kk-* before the infinitive suffix *-a* (section 7.4.1.2); *-nt-* occurs as a past marker in other overlapping classes and also as a portmanteau morph representing past and intransitive, with *nt-t-* representing the corresponding transitive (section 7.4.1.3). In South Dravidian II languages *-tt-* got generalized as the past-tense marker (see examples in section 7.4.1.2) and also in Kolami and Naiki of Central Dravidian.

The suffixes *i* ~ *in* (2) could have been in phonological complementation to the other groups. Broadly, they occurred after disyllabic and trisyllabic bases of three to five morae ending in an underlying stop followed by the non-morphemic *-u* (section 7.4.1.4). There is doubt whether the perfective participle *-*cci-* in South Dravidian II and Parji–Ollari–Gadaba of Central Dravidian is a sequence of two past morphs, **cc* and **i* with the loss of final *-n*. We need to consider if this sequence, in turn, could be related to Classical Tamil *-iciṉ* (see section 7.4.1.5).

7.4.2 ***Non-past markers***

Several markers come under this category, not all of which are reconstructable. They have overlapping time reference like the future tense, the present-future, the future-habitual, the aorist or habitual (generic) tense, the present tense, etc., besides non-finite forms like the durative, infinitive, purposive, permissive, etc. in which the time reference is not to the past. The non-past marked by *-k(k)-* or *-p(p)-* [-w-, -pp-] is reconstructable. Different languages have followed independent strategies in forming the present tense.

7.4.2.1 *-(m)p-[-w-] ~ *-(m)pp-, *-(n)k- ~ *-(n)kk-

I posited earlier (chapter 5) the above as non-past markers in intransitive and transitive verbs. Evidence for *-mp-/-mpp-* is taken from the tense morphs following the causative *-*p(p)i-* preserved in the alternation *-i-nc-* (past)/*-i-mp-* (non-past) in Old Telugu. After the loss of tense meaning, *-mp-/-mpp-* as well as *-nk-/-nkk-* became simply the intransitive–transitive markers as in Ta. *tir-u-mpu/tir-u-ppu* 'be turned/ turn' [3246], *kala-nku/kal-a-kku* 'be agitated/agitate' [1303] (see sections 5.4.4, 7.3.3).

There are conjugation classes in Old Tamil in which *-v-* occurred after the so-called weak (= regular) verbs and *-pp-* after 'strong verbs' as markers of the future tense, e.g. *cey-* 'to do': *cey-v-*, *naṭa* 'to walk': *naṭa-pp-*. The distribution of *-v-/-pp-* also corresponds to the distribution of the infinitive markers *-k-/-kk-*, e.g. *ceyy-a* 'to do', *niṟ-ka* 'to stand', but *naṭa-kk-a* 'to walk'. In Caṅkam Tamil *-pp-* freely varied with *-kk-* in the formation of infinitives, *kā-pp-a/kā-kk-a* 'to protect'. Malayāḷam has *-kk-* as the infinitive marker in the so-called 'strong' verbs, e.g. *kēḷ-kk-uka* 'to hear', but *var-uka* 'to come' (*DVM*: 423–5). We need to consider the velars here actually as markers of non-past. These distributional aspects are found systematically in South Dravidian I mainly in the Pre-Tamil descendants (Malayāḷam, Koḍaga, Iruḷa, Kuṟumba, Toda, Kota); Kannaḍa and Tuḷu also attest these suffixes. Most members of South Dravidian II bear witness to an erstwhile use of a labial as non-past marker. In Brahui *-p-* (<*-pp-*) occurs in negative non-past regularly.

South Dravidian I: OTa. has *-um* in 3sg (mfn) and 3neu pl, e.g. *ceyy-um* 'he, she, it, they (neu) will do'. Alternatively, we find *cey-v-āṉ* (3m sg), *cey-v-āḷ* (3f sg), *ceyy-um* (3neu sg/pl), beside the first and second persons (sg/pl) with the tense morph *-p-/-pp-*; *-um* is here considered a tense marker rather than a fusion of different personal signs. (We can posit *-w-* in **cey-w-um*, and say that **-w-* is lost in sandhi before a labial vowel; note where the following vowel is not a labial, **-w-* appears, e.g. the human plural is Ta. *cey-v-ār*.) Secondly, there is a pair of extended future markers in Old Tamil involving both the velar and labial suffixes, *-kuv-/-kkuv-*, e.g. *cey-v-ēṉ/cey-kuv-ēṉ* 'I will do', *koṭu-kkuv-ēṉ/koṭu-pp-ēṉ* 'I will give'. We also find *-k-/-kk-* as a future marker in the first person in Classical Tamil, e.g. *varu-ku* 'I will come', *varu-k-am* 'we will come', *urai-kk-ō* 'I will tell' (Tolk.1181.2). A non-past verbal participle is formed by adding *-pu* to a base, e.g. *eṉṉai nōkku-pu* 'looking at me' (KT 1.3–4). Glazov (1968: 103–9) calls this 'the adverbial participle of present-future aorist'. There is another construction in Old Tamil with *-p-* as future marker in the 3pl, e.g. *eṉ-p-a* 'they speak' (Tolk.1), *cey-pa* 'they [± hum] will do' (KT 42.16).

Old Malayāḷam had personal suffixes following non-past *-v-* ~ *-m-/-pp-* corresponding to Middle Tamil *-v-/-pp-*. But the personal suffixes were lost gradually by the fourteenth century and the aorist tense replaced the future tense of Middle Tamil. Tamil *-um* (aorist) became *-ū*; so we have *-v-ū/-m-ū* (the latter following a root-final nasal) and, *-pp-ū* corresponding to OTa. *-v-um/-pp-um*; these are used as aoristic in Malayāḷam, *avan-ē var-ū* 'he will only come'.[7] Unlike the Tamil *-um* forms, the aorist forms in *-ū* occurred in all third-personal forms including the human plural. By the fifteenth century *-um* had spread to all persons and denotes aoristic-future (Ramaswami Aiyar 1936: 67–9).

Koḍagu has *-v-/-pp-* as non-past markers, e.g. *key-v-i* 'I will work', *key-v-a* 'we will work', 2sg *key-v-iya*, 2pl *key-v-ira*, 3sg/pl *key-v-a* (with neutralization of gender and number).

Kota has *-kv-/-gv-* as future markers corresponding to Classical Tamil *-kuv-/-kkuv-*, e.g. *va-* 'to come': 1sg *va-kv-ēn* 'I will come', 1pl (excl) *va-kv-ēm*, (incl) *va-kv-ōm*, 2sg *va-kv-i*, 2pl *va-kv-im*, 3sg/pl *va-kv-ō/ va-kōk-ō/va-kug-ō*.

Toda future is formed by adding *-k-* to the root: *kiy-k-in* 'I will do'.

Kannaḍa has a system parallel to Tamil; the present-future is formed by *-v-/-pp-* before personal suffixes, e.g. *kuḍu* 'to give', 1sg *kuḍu-v-eN* 'I will give', 1pl *kuḍu-v-eM*,

7 Ramaswami Aiyar says that *-ū* is not from *-um*, because there are usages like *-v-ū/-pp-ū* and *-um* never occurred after the non-past markers. He thinks that it is *-v-atu* (3neu sg) which becomes *-vū* (1936: 73).

2sg *kuḍu-v-ay/-e/-i*, 2pl *kuḍu-v-ir*, 3m sg *kuḍu-v-aM/-oM*, 3f sg *kuḍu-v-aḷ/-oḷ*, 3h pl *kuḍu-v-ar/-or*, 3neu sg *kuḍu-v-udu/-adu*, 3neu pl *kuḍu-v-uvu/-avu*.

Tuḷu dialects have two types of forms that have a bilabial; (1) present future *-puv-/ -p-/-b-*, e.g. *kal-* 'to learn': *kal-puv-ɛ* 'I learn', but 3neu sg *kal-p-uṇḍu*; *-p* also occurs after some monosyllabic and disyllabic verbs, e.g. *paṇ-* 'to tell': *paṇ-p-*, *ā-* 'to become': *ā-p-*. Bases of three morae take *-b*, *tāṅgï-* 'to support': *tāṅgï-b-*. The future tense has *-p/-v/-b*; *-b* after nasal-ending stems, *-p-* and *-v-* are morphologically conditioned, e.g. *kā-* 'to wait': *kā-p-*, *paṇ-* 'to tell': *paṇ-b-/paṇ-v-/pam-b-* (dial), *tū-* 'to see': *tū-v-*. A sample paradigm: *kal-* 'to learn': 1sg *kal-p-ɛ*, 1pl *kal-p-a*, 2sg *kal-p-a*, 2pl *kal-p-arï*, 3m sg *kal-p-e*, f *kal-p-alï*, 3h pl *kal-p-erï*, 3neu sg *kal-p-u*, 3neu pl *kal-p-a*.

South Dravidian II: Telugu has nothing comparable beyond the *-mpu* variant in non-past paradigms in the causative, e.g. *cēs-/cēy-* 'to do', *cēy-inc-* 'cause to do': *cēy-imp-umu/-ũḍu* 'make somebody do it' (imp 2sg/pl), *cēy-imp-aN* (inf), etc. Another possible trace of an older non-past **-w-* can be detected in the non-past paradigms of certain bases ending in *-cu*, e.g. *nil(u)-cu* 'to stand': *nil(i)-ci* 'having stood', *nil(i)-c-enu* '3sg/3neu pl stood', but *nil(a)-w-aN* inf 'to stand', *nilu-w-umu* (imp 2sg), *nila-w-aka* 'not standing', etc. Here *-c-*, a part of an original past marker, is reanalysed as part of the base, but it occurs in the past paradigms only. In the non-past *-w-* replaces *-c-* (see *TVB*: §§2.84–6).

Gondi (Adilabad dialect) has *-k-* as future marker in the first and second persons complementary to *-ān-*, which occurs in the 3sg and pl, e.g. *aṭṭ-* 'to cook': 1sg *aṭ-k-ā*, 1pl (excl) *aṭ-k-ōm*, (incl) *aṭ-k-āṭ*, 2sg *aṭ-k-ī*, 2pl *aṭ-k-īṭ*, 3m sg *aṭṭ-ān-ūr*, 3m pl *aṭṭ-ān-īr*, etc.

Koṇḍa has Stem + *-pu/-bu* in non-finite verbs meaning 'as soon as, at the time of', *koṟu kere-pu* 'as soon as the cock crows', *man-bu* 'while staying'.

In Kui *-ki/-pi* is added to form the present participle, e.g. first conjugation *aḍ-a* 'to join': *aṭ-k-i*, second conjugation *aṭp-a* 'to join': *aṭ-p-i*; third conjugation has a *-v-* augment which is retained after a front vowel, but is lost elsewhere, before *-ki* is added, *gi-v-a* 'to do': *gip-ki*, but *sāva* 'to die': *sāva-i*; the fourth conjugation has the augment *-b* and the present tense is formed by adding *-i* to it, *sal-b-a* 'to go': *sal-b-i*. I consider the augments, which appear in the present participle, as the relics of the erstwhile non-past markers (for detailed discussion, see Krishnamurti 1994a: xxii–xxiii). The plural action stems are identical with the ones that have a velar or labial augment, but they are inflected like the first conjugation.

Kuvi also has *-k/-p* as 'plural action' suffixes added to verbs to denote frequentative meaning, e.g. *kac-* 'to bite': *kas-ki-*, *tīh-* 'to feed': *tīs-p-* 'to feed frequently'. There is a 'motion suffix' *-k-/-g-* in both Kui and Kuvi but it does not occur with plural action stems, e.g. *kā-ka-mu* 'go and watch' (Israel 1979: §5.24, 151–5). There is also the use of *-pi-/-vi-* added to a base to form the stem of the 'habitual mood', e.g. *pay-* 'to beat': *pay-vi-*, *hī-* 'to give': *hī-vi-*, *taʔ-* 'to bring': *ta-pi-* (Israel 1979: 174–5).

In Pengo Burrow and Bhattacharya call these intensive–frequentative bases, corresponding to 'plural action' bases of Kui–Kuvi. These are formed by adding *-pa*/*-ba* or *-ka*, e.g. **ūṭ-* 'to give to drink': *ūṭ-pa-*, *tūb-* 'to blow': *tūb-ba-*, *kat-* 'to cut': *kat-ka-*. Some bases occur only with the frequentative suffixes, *ī-ba* 'to bathe', *īt-pa-* v.t. 'to bathe somebody'. Motion bases are not formed from intensive bases. They are mutually exclusive (Burrow and Bhattacharya 1970: 82–7).

The above facts indicate that the use of *-p*/*-k* suffixes with several allomorphs to denote intensive–frequentative ('plural action') meaning or that of 'motion' is an innovation in Kui–Kuvi–Pengo–Manḍa and to some extent in Koṇḍa by assigning a meaning to non-past markers which have lost their original signification. Particularly Kui continues to use these in one non-past inflection, i.e. the present participle.

Central Dravidian: Kolami forms a 'future gerund' (actually an inceptive mood meaning 'about to [action] . . . ') by adding *-ak* to verb roots, e.g. *tin-ak* 'about to eat', and a future-habitual adjective in *-eka*, e.g. *tin-eka* 'that eat(s)/will eat'. Naiki (Ch.) has durative in *-eka-*, e.g. *ser-eka* 'going'. The imperative (?) in Parji is formed with *-ek-* in 1sg and all 3n-m sg/pl, e.g. *cūṛ-ek-en* 'let me see', etc. The *-k-* suffix in all these seemingly cognate grammatical markers has a non-past reference and can be related to PD **-k-/-kk-*. Parji has *-k-/-p-* in different dialects before the present-tense suffix *-m-*, e.g. *kā-k-m-en* (northern dialect), *kā-p-m-en* (southern dialect). Most verbs have *-t* in past and *-p* in non-past as augments. This alternation is also true of Ollari and Gadaba.

North Dravidian: Brahui has *-ik*/*-a* in 3sg present in both affirmative and negative forms, e.g. *bin-ik-Ø* '(3 subj) hears', *bim-p-a-kØ* '(3 subj) does not hear'. We may suspect a reflex of Proto-Dravidian velar non-past *-kk-* here.

7.4.2.2 *-t*V*-

The reflexes of a dental stop as non-past marker occur in South Dravidian I, South Dravidian II and Central Dravidian. There is variation in different languages in its time reference, aorist, present–future, future, habitual, etc.

South Dravidian I: in Caṅkam Tamil *-tu-/-ttu-* occurs as a marker of an 'indefinite present–future tense' before the 1pl, 2sg and pl, e.g. *varu-t-i* 'you (sg) come' (KT 91.14), *vēṇṭu-t-ir* 'you (pl) will wish', *iru-tt-um-ō* 'shall we be?' (KT 75.19). The personal morphs, following the non-past *-v-/-pp-*, are different from the above (Glazov 1968: 106). This *-t-* behaves differently in sandhi from the past marker *-t-*, *cēṟi* (< *cel* + *ti*) 'you (sg) go': *ceṟṟ-āy* (*cel* + *tt-*) 'you (sg) went'. It is the possible effects of homonymy between these two types of *-t-* that may have led to the dropping of *-t-* in the aorist tense.

South Dravidian II: Old Telugu has *-du-* as aorist (present–future) marker in 1sg/pl 2sg/pl 3h pl in complementation with *-unu*, used uniformly for 3sg (m, n-m, neu sg and neu pl), *pāḍu* 'to sing': *pāḍu-du-nu* (1sg), *pāḍu-du-mu* (1pl), *pāḍu-du-wu* (2sg), *pāḍu-du-ru* (2pl), *pāḍ-unu* 'he, she, it, they (n-h) sing', *pāḍu-du-ru* 'they (h) sing'. *-eda-* also occurs as a free variant of *-du-*, but it referred to the present time more frequently than the *-du-* forms. Both these have become obsolete in Modern Standard Telugu, except in one verb of cognition, *erugu* 'to know', e.g. *erugu-du-nu/-mu/-wu/-ru* 'I/we/you (sg/pl) know', and rarely in the subjunctive mood, e.g. *nēn-ē ī pani cēddunu* (← *cēs-du-nu*) 'I myself would have done this job'. The hortative in Old Telugu also had the non-past marker *-du-* before 1pl (incl) suffix *-amu* and this construction survives in Modern Telugu, e.g. OTe. *cēyu-d-amu* 'let us do', Modern Te. *cēd-d-ām* (← *cēs-d-ām*).

Central Dravidian: Kolami has *-at-* as a marker of present–future in the first and second persons alternating with -Ø in the third person, *sī-* 'to give': *sī-at-un* (1sg), *sī-an* (3m sg). It has a morphological complex *-d-at-* as a future marker in the Wardha dialect in the first and second persons, alternating with *-d-* in the third person, e.g. *sī-d-at-un/-um* (1sg/pl), *sī-d-an* (3m sg). The durative has the same tense marker but the personal suffixes are slightly different, *sī-d-un/-um* (1sg/pl); in the other persons *-n-* replaces *-d-*. The present–future in the Naiki of Chanda is *-t-*, e.g. *an-* 'to be': *an-t-an* 'I am/will be'. *-at-/-d-/-Ø-* are the markers of the future tense, e.g. *kak-* 'to do': *kak-at-un* (1sg), *kak-d-an* (3m sg)/*kak-Ø-an* (3n-m sg).

In Parji, the future-tense marker after *-n* final stems is *-d-*, e.g. *tin-d-an* 'I will eat'; in the northwestern dialects, *-d-* is replaced by *-r-*, *cūṛ-r-an* 'I will see'. The non-past negative in some members of the paradigm is marked by *-d-* alternating with *-n-/-m-/-r-/-t-/-y-*, e.g. *cūṛ-a-d-a* (3m sg).

In Ollari the present–future is consistently marked by *-d-*, e.g. *vanḍ-* 'to cook': *vanḍ-d-an* 'I cook', *var-* 'to come': *va-d-an* 'I come'. In Gadaba, the non-past markers are *-d-/-t-/-y-*, e.g. *pōr-* 'to ask': *pōr-t-an* (1sg). The non-past marker is *-d-* after consonant ending bases, *kar-* 'to drop': *kar-d-an* (1sg). The progressive/durative is marked by *-id-/-ud-*, e.g. *āḍ-* 'to weep': *āḍ-id-an* (1sg) (Suvarchala 1992: 130–58).

North Dravidian: Kuṛux has *-d-* as the present-tense marker before all persons except the third plural in male speech. In female speech it is replaced by -ʔ- in the first person, e.g. *es-* 'to break', male speech/female speech: *es-d-an/es-ʔ-ēn* (1sg), *es-d-am/es-ʔ-ēm* (1pl excl), *es-d-at* (1pl incl), *es-d-ay/is-d-i* (2sg), *es-d-ar/es-d-ay* (2pl), *es-d-as* (3m sg), *is-ʔ-i* (3n-m sg), *es-n-ar/es-n-ay* (3h pl).

The above data from all the subgroups go to prove that Proto-Dravidian had **-t-* as aorist (present–future/non-past) marker in verbs, but it has gone out of use because of the dental stop **-t-/-tt-* [-d-/-t-] occurring more widely as a past-tense marker. The geminated *-tt-* [*-t-*] has remained more stable as a past marker, seen from the earlier treatment.

7.4.2.3 *-um

Caldwell (1956: 513–19) suggests that an impersonal 'aoristic future' is formed by adding *-um* to stems ending in *-k-/-kk-* (apparently non-past suffixes). This form is used only in the third person and does not carry (gender)–number–person markers. Both *-um* and the other non-past markers are all reconstructible for Proto-Dravidian. This is found in South Dravidian I, South Dravidian II and Central Dravidian. Therefore, it needs to be reconstructed for Proto-Dravidian. It is interpreted as a tense marker involving person marking also, a kind of portmanteau morph. Glazov considers it only as the marker of an indefinite tense.

South Dravidian I: in Old Tamil *-um* occurs after *-kk-* in the case of 'strong verbs', e.g. *naṭa-kk-um* 'he, she, it, they (neu) walk'; otherwise, it occurs after a simple verbal base, e.g. *ceyy-um* '(subject) does'. We can take *-kk-* here as the non-past marker (which is represented by Ø after the so-called weak verbs like *cey-* 'to do'). In that case, it does stand as a marker of neutralized gender–number in the third person. In later Tamil it further got restricted only to the third non-human singular and plural. Andronov (1969: 135) considers *-m-* as a future marker, e.g. *eṉ-* 'to say': *eṉ-m-*; this is interpreted by Subrahmanyam (1971: 248) as a variant of *-um* in predicative (pronominalized) nouns, e.g. *eṉ-m-ar* 'those who say'. In Old Malayāḷam the *-um* forms occurred first in all members of the third person, but its usage got extended to all persons in Modern Malayāḷam.

The velar suffixes *-g-/-k-* (< *-k-/-kk-*) occur before the third-personal *-um* in Old and Medieval Kannaḍa in the aorist, *āḷ-g-um* 'he, she, it, they will rule' (*DVM*: 258); *ā-* 'to become': *a-kk-um* 'he, she, it or they will become', *bar-* 'to come', *bar-k-um* '. . . will come', *ār-* 'to be satisfied': *ār-g-um* '. . . will be satisfied' (Ramachandra Rao 1972: 137). Kannaḍa has extended the use of the velar to all bases, thereby clearly putting *-um* in the slot of agreement markers.

Tuḷu has *-u-* for future in the third singular e.g. *par-u* 'it will drink', *bar-u* 'it will come', *tin-u* 'it will eat'; here *-u* corresponds to *-um* in Tamil, *paruk-um*, *var-um*, *tiṉṉ-um*, respectively.

South Dravidian II: Old Telugu uses *-un(u)* as the aorist (called *taddharmakālam-* by Telugu grammarians) marker in the third singular (mfn) and third neuter plural almost parallel to the distribution of *-um* in Old Tamil. The aorist adjective is also marked by *-u(n)*, *cēyu-pani* 'the work one does', *cēyun-atā̃ḍu* 'the man who does'. In Modern Telugu *-unu* usage is restricted to a limited semantic subclass of verbs (denoting cognition, motion), *telus-u(n)* '(dat subj) it is known', *dēwuḍ(u) erug-u(n)* 'God (nom subject) knows', Infinitive + *wacc-u(n)*, *rā-wacc-u(n)* '(subj) may come', etc.

Central Dravidian: Parji present-tense marker *-m-* can be said to have developed from PD **-um*, e.g. *ver-* 'to come': *ver-m-en* 'I come', except that *-m-* occurs in all persons. Parji has restricted the time reference to 'present' and to habitual (all tenses). The occurrence of personal morphs, after verbal adjectives ending in *-um*, is found in Old Tamil itself, *ceyy-um-ōṉ* 'he who does', *tin-m-ār* 'those who eat'. These pronominalized nouns set the stage for converting such forms into finite verbs. Such derived nominals are also found in Kannaḍa and Telugu.

7.4.2.4 *-*n*-

South Dravidian I: Old Tamil is said to have -*un*/-*n*- used as adjectival formatives, followed by personal suffixes in deriving predicative nouns in the third human plural, e.g. *ceppu-n-ar* 'those who tell', *varu-n-ar* 'those who come', *tuṟakk-un-ar* 'those who renounce', *ī-n-ar* 'those who give' etc. This -*n*- is said to be a dental, contrasting with an alveolar -*ṉ*- which occurs in Old Tamil only in non-initial positions. Subrahmanyam (1971: 322) thinks that this is not a variant pronunciation of -*um*/-*m*, although the distribution of this -*un*/-*n* is similar to that of -*um*/-*m* (notice it occurs after -*kk*- in strong verbs). Note that in Telugu -*un*, -*n* corresponds to OTa. -*um*/-*m*.

South Dravidian II: Koṇḍa has -*n*- as non-past (future-habitual) marker in finite and non-finite verbs, *ki-n-an* 'he does/will do', *ki-n-i* adj 'the one doing'. A morphological complex -*zi-n*-, used as present continuous, includes the perfective participle -*zi*- plus the non-past -*n*-, e.g. *son-sin-an* 'he is going'. -*n*- is represented by -Ø- after -*n*/-*ṇ* ending bases, *man-Ø-an* 'he will be', *uṇ-Ø-an* 'he will drink'. Pengo future is marked by -*n*- and it corresponds in every respect to Koṇḍa -*n*-, e.g. *huṛ*- 'to see': *huṛ-n*-, *in*- 'to say': *in-Ø*-; non-past adjective *huṛ-n-i*. In Kui -*d*- and -*n*- occur as future markers in complementary distribution, e.g. *kō*- 'to reap': *kō-Ø-i* (1sg), *kō-n-amu* (1pl excl), *kō-n-asu* (1pl incl), *kō-d-i* (2sg), *kō-d-eru* (2pl), *kō-n-enju* (3m sg), *kō-n-eru* (3m pl), *kō-n-e* (3n-m sg), *kō-n-u* (3n-m pl). In stems of Conjugation I, an epenthetic vowel -*i* is added before -*d*-/-*n*-. Kuvi also has parallel distribution of -*d*-/-*n*- as future markers, *hī*- 'to give': *hī-d-i* (2sg), *hī-n-esi* (3m sg). In both Kui and Kuvi -*d*- undergoes certain sandhi changes following -*n*-/-*ṇ*-/-*l*-.

Central Dravidian: Kolami has a durative paradigm in which -*d*- occurs in the first person and -*n*- in others, e.g. *sī*- 'to give': *sī-d-un* (1sg), *sī-d-um* (1pl), *sī-n-iv* (2sg) etc. In Adilabad Kolami -*n*- occurs in a hortative in all persons, *vēl-n-am* 'let us ask'.

North Dravidian: in Kuṛux -*d*- and -*n*- occur complementarily as present-tense markers, 3h pl *es-n-ar* 'they break' (male speech)/*es-n-ay* (female speech). Malto also has -*n*-/-*i*- for present tense; -*n*- occurs in the third human plural, elsewhere -*i*-, e.g. *band*- 'to draw': *band-n-er* (3h pl).

7.5 Pronominal suffixes (gender–number–person markers)

Finite verbs tend to carry agreement markers with the subject NP (occurring in the nominative) in gender–number–person (gnp). In particular constructions some of these categories may be neutralized or collapsed into fewer, like -*um* agreeing with some members of the third person (see section 7.4.2.3). In Toda and Brahui which have lost gender in the third person, the agreement is only in number (sg/pl) of the subject NP. Malayāḷam lost the personal suffixes of finite verbs around the fourteenth century. One can see phonological resemblance between the personal/demonstrative pronouns and the gnp markers in most cases. Table 7.1 presents pronominal suffixes, based on Subrahmanyam

Table 7.1. *Pronominal suffixes (gender–number–person markers) in finite verbs in South Dravidian I ('–' indicates that the form is non-existent)*

Person	Ta. (Old)	Ma. (Old)	Koḍ	Ir.	Ko.	To.	Ka.	Tu.	Koraga
1sg	*ē̆ṉ, aṉ, al*	*ēn, an*	*ë, i*	*e/en*	*ē(n)*	*en, in, n*	*eM, enu, e*	*ɛ/o/a*	*e*
1pl (excl)	*ē̆m, ā̆m, um/ōm*	*ōm*	*i, a*	*ēm, am*	*ēm*	*em, im, m*	*eM, evu*	*o, a*	*a*
1pl (incl)	–	–	–	*o/om*	*ō(m)*	*um*	–	–	–
2sg	*ī̆, ā̆y, ōy*	*āy, ā*	*iya*	*a/aḷ*	*ī*	*y, i*	*ay, e, i*	*a*	*a*
2pl	*ir, īr(kaḷ)*	*īr*	*ira*	*iri/ir iy*	*īm, īr*	*ts* (sib)	*ir, iri*	*arï*	*erï*
3m sg	*ā̆ṉ, ōṉ*	*ān*	*a, ëtï*	*e/en*	*ān*	*t, u, č, k*	*aM, oM, anu, a*	*e*	*i*
3f sg	*ā̆ḷ, ōḷ*	*āḷ*		*a/aḷ*	*āḷ*		*aḷ(u), āḷ*	*-aḷï/olu*	–
3neu sg	*(a)tu*	*atu*		*ud(u)*	*d*		*udu, du, itu, tu*	*nï, uṇï, ṇḍï uṇḍï*	*ḍï, u*
3h pl	*ar, ār(kaḷ), a*	*ār*		*ar(u) ār*	*ār*		*ar(u), ār, or*	*erï*	*erï*
3neu pl	*a*	*a, ava, ana*		*ina/ inaḷ*	–		*uvu, avu*	*o, a*	–

(1971: 399–402), Rajam (1992: chs. 26, 27; for Classical Tamil), Suvarchala (1992: 189–201, for Central Dravidian) and Rao (1987b: 134–42 for Proto-Gonḍi).

7.5.1 *South Dravidian I*

The reconstructions of the personal suffixes are: 1sg **-V̄̆n*, 1pl **-V̄̆m*, 2sg **-ī̆*, **-ā̆y*, 2pl **-ī̆r* (replacing older **-īm*), 3m sg **-an* (< **an-ṯ-*), 3f sg **-ā̆ḷ*, 3h pl **-ā̆r*, 3neu sg **atu*, 3neu pl **-a(w)*. These are the final syllables or -VC of the nominative forms of the personal and demonstrative pronouns, except in the second person. The 1sg/pl **-V̄̆n/*-V̄̆m* correspond to the first-person pronouns **yān/*yām/*ñām*. The qualitative variation is due to the neutralization of *ā̆/ē̆* following **y*. The variation in vowel quantity is due to the unaccented position of personal suffixes as final constituents of the verb. In Caṅkam Tamil the first singular marker **al* occurred after the non-past suffixes only and is of obscure origin. The commentators of Tolkāppiyam suggested that *-ē̆m* was the agreement marker of exclusive plural and *-ā̆m* that of inclusive plural. Toda and Telugu support *-ā̆m* as the pronominal suffix of the first plural inclusive. Koraga is closest to Tuḷu in personal suffixes, although it has no separate marking for feminine singular unlike Tuḷu. The second person singular seems to have had two nominative bases **(n)ī(n)* and *ā̆y of which the former occurs in all Dravidian languages, ā̆y occurs only as an agreement marker in South Dravidian I,[8] Koṇḍa–Kui–Kuvi–Pengo–Manḍa (*-i* < *-ay*) of South Dravidian II and in Kuṛux–Malto of North Dravidian. Since the agreement marker bears resemblance to nominative forms of pronouns, it is reasonable to think that the nominative requiring *-ā̆y* as an agreement marker must have been lost in Proto-Dravidian itself. Another change at the Proto-South Dravidian stage was the replacement of the second-person-plural *-īm* by *-īr*, retaining the second-person root vowel, but replacing the plural marker *-m* by the third-person-human-plural *-r*. The alternative forms in Kota *īm-/īr-* represent either retention of *-īm* or a late analogical restoration of *-m*. The third-personal suffixes bear the expected resemblance to the nominative forms in South Dravidian I.

The personal suffixes listed under Malayāḷam occurred in older texts and they were not very different from those of Middle Tamil. Līlātilakam, a Malayāḷam grammar of the fourteenth century, observes that 'low castes in Malabar do say *vandān, irundān*'[9] (Ramaswami Aiyar 1936: 54). Inscriptions of the thirteenth and fourteenth centuries already have forms without personal suffixes, e.g. *cē-vi-ccu* (< *cey-vicc-* < OTa. *cey-vitt* + personal suffixes 'subject cause(s) something to be done by another agent'). Eẓuttaccan (sixteenth century) used forms both with and without personal suffixes. The ones used were the first person singular in past and non-past, masculine and feminine third person (singular and plural) in the past; the second person singular past and present were much less used. The ones that were dropped include *-ōm* (1pl), *-īr* (2pl), *-ana/-a* (3neu pl) (Ramaswami Aiyar 1936: 38). In Iruḷa *-e/-en* etc. are phonologically conditioned, *-e* finally and *-en* before a vowel.

The Iruḷa second singular has *-aḷ* which is puzzling, since it looks identical with the feminine singular suffix *-aḷ*. The non-human plural has also *-ḷ* in *-inaḷ*. The authors of Iruḷa grammars have not thrown any light on this point.[10] Koḍagu, Tuḷu and Koraga have no suffix-final nasals in 1sg, 1pl and 3m sg.

7.5.2 **South Dravidian II**

The reconstructions for South Dravidian II are 1sg *-V*n*, 1pl (excl) *-V*m*. The first person plural inclusive has *-*aṯṯ*, developing to *-ṭ* in Gondi, *-s* in Kui-Pengo and *-h*(< *-s*) in

[8] In Old Tamil *-i* occurred as agreement marker of 2sg only after future stems in *-t/-tt*, and *-ay*, elsewhere (*DVM*: 410).

[9] These meant 'he came, he was' in Tamil. This observation means that the colloquial speech was more like literary Tamil, while the literary dialect of Malayāḷam innovated loss of personal suffixes. Since Malayāḷam is the only language in South Dravidian I which had lost all personal suffixes in finite verbs, it would be interesting to study the sociolinguistic factors which promoted such a loss.

[10] Perialwar (1978b) differs from Zvelebil (1973) only on the form of two personal endings, 3m sg *-an*, 3h pl *-ār* (89). Both of them give *-a/-aḷ* as the 2sg and *-ina/-inaḷ* as the 3neu pl.

Table 7.2. *Pronominal suffixes (gender–number–person markers) in finite verbs in South Dravidian II*

	Te.	PGo.	Koṇḍa	Kui	Kuvi	Pengo	Manḍa
1sg	*nu, ni*	*an/n*	*a*	*enu, e, i*	*ni, i, e*^{n}	*aŋ*	*u, i*
1pl (excl)	*mu, mi,*	*am/m*	*ap*	*amu, ami*	*ami, omi*	*ap*	*uŋ*
1pl (incl)	*amu*	*aṭa*	*aṭ*	*asu*	*ohi, o*	*as*	–
2sg	*wu, wi*	*in*	*i, id*[V	*i*	*i*	*ay*	*i*
2pl	*ru, ri*	*ir/iṭ*	*ider*	*eru*	*eri*	*ader, ider*	*ir*
3m sg	*(ṉ)ḍu*	*onṟ/nṟ*	*an, anṟ*	*enju*	*esi*	*an*	*un*
3m/h pl	*ru, ri*	*or/r*	*ar*	*eru*	*eri*	*ar*	*ir*
3non-m sg	*du, di*	*e/u*	*ad*	*e*	*e*	*at*	*i, in*
3n-m pl	*wu, wi*	*aŋ/uŋ*	*e*	*u, o*	*u, o*	(f) *ik*, (n) *iŋ*	*iŋ*

Kuvi. The inclusive plural pronoun in Kui in the nominative is *āju* (< **āṯ-*), Pengo *ās-/āh-* (< **āṯṯ-*), with which **-aṯṯ* as a personal marker agrees. Koṇḍa normally preserves **-ṯṯ* as *-R*, but in this case it shows similarity with the Gondi form. The first inclusive agreement marker -V*t* in Ollari of Central Dravidian and Kuṛux of North Dravidian do appear to be related. There is no clue to its origin except that it is a native form more widely represented in the subgroup Gondi–Koṇḍa–Kui–Kuvi–Pengo–Manḍa and was restored to bring out in the verbal system the initial loss of a contrast between inclusive and exclusive plurals.

The second singular is **i* (< **-ay*) and the plural **-ir* (< **-īr*). Telugu *-wu*/*-wi* is an independent development, representing the final syllable of the nominative form *nīwu* 'you (sg)'. Pengo *-ay* is a retention of Proto-Dravidian second-person-singular agreement marker and *-i* in Koṇḍa–Kui–Kuvi is an expected phonological equivalent. The second plural in Gondi is generally *-ir* but many dialects also have *-iṭ* alternating with *-ir*. The nominative plural forms have *-aṭ*/*-eṭ* suffix added to the plural base *nim-*/*im-*; so also the first person plural exclusive and inclusive have several variants constructed similarly, e.g. *am-oṭ* 'we (excl)', *mar-aṭ* 'we (incl)'. Even then the origin of *-ṭ* in the second person needs to be explored. The fact that *-ir* is the marker of second person plural in the whole subgroup shows that the replacement of **nīm* by **nīr* was a shared innovation at the Proto-Dravidian stage, reflected in the personal suffixes of both South Dravidian and Central Dravidian.

The masculine third person singular and plural are **-anḏ* and **-ar*, represented in all languages. Koṇḍa and Pengo show *-an* in the environment [Ø ~ *-anṟ*/*-anj* in the environment [V (*-an* finally but *-anṟ* in Koṇḍa and *-anj* in Pengo when followed

Table 7.3. *Pronominal suffixes (gender–number–person markers) in finite verbs in Central Dravidian*

	Kolami (W)	Nk./Nk.(Ch.)	Parji	Ollari	Gadaba
1sg	*un, n, an*	*un, n, an*	*on, en, an, n, in*	*an, on, en, n*	*an, on, en, n*
1pl (excl)	*um, am, m*	*um, am, m*	*am, um, om, m*	*am, em, om, m*	*am, em, om, m*
1pl (incl)	*am*	–	?Imp. *ar* Pot. *umur*	*at, t*	
2sg	*iv, v*	*i*	*ot, at, ut, t*	*aṭ, oṭ, eṭ, ṭ*	*aṭ, oṭ, eṭ, ṭ*
2pl	*ir, r*	*ir*	*or, ur, ar, r*	*ar, er, or, r*	*er, or, ar, r*
3m sg	*an, en, n, nd*	*an, en, n*	*ed/od, ad, id, d*	*aṇḍ, eṇḍ, oṇḍ, ṇḍ*	*aṇḍ, eṇḍ, oṇḍ, ṇḍ*
3m pl	*ar, er*	*ar, er, r*	*ar, or, er, ir, r*	*ar, er, or, r*	*ar, er, or, r*
3n-m sg	*a(d), d, un, in*	*d, un, an*	*o, a, u, ø*	*a, eṭe, e, d, ø*	*a, eṭe, e, (a)d*
3n-m pl	*av, ev*	*e, a*	*av, ev, uv, v*	*av, ev, eṭev*	*?er, ev, av, v, eṭev*

by a vowel). This means that the final consonant *-*ṯ* was lost in these two languages in the free forms. There is more variation in the non-masculine third-person-singular *-*at* and pl *-*aw*. The singular *-*ad* is represented in Telugu, Koṇḍa and Pengo. Telugu non-masculine plural -*wu*/-*wi* is a reflex of the pronoun *awi* (< *aw-ay*). Gondi and Pengo -V*ŋ* is based on the neuter plural suffix, found in noun morphology. Pengo has further innovated a separate marker for female human plural -*ik* taken from derivational morphology, a feature not shared by the other members of the subgroup.

7.5.3 **Central Dravidian**

The reconstructions for first person singular and plural are the same as in South Dravidian I and II, i.e. *-V*n* and *-V*m*; similarly the masculine third singular and plural remain *-*anḏ* and *-V*r*. There is greater uniformity in the non-masculine third singular and plural reflecting broadly the initial/final syllables of the nominatives, PCD *ad, *aw (< PD *at-V, *aw-ay*). Kolami borrowed from Pre-Telugu the second singular and plural *nīw*(*u*) and **nīr* (> later in Te. *mīru*) as well as the personal markers *-V*w* and -V*r*. Ollari first plural inclusive -*at* and the second singular -V*t*/-V*ṭ* (< *-V*ṯṯ*) look parallel to Gondi redundant plural -*ṭ* and the South Dravidian II first plural inclusive marker derived from *-*aṯṯ*.

Table 7.4. *Pronominal suffixes (gender–number–person markers) in finite verbs in North Dravidian*

	Kuṛux	Malto	Brahui
1sg	*n*	*in, en, on*	*iv, ēv, v, r*
1pl (excl)	*m*	*im, em, om*	*in, n*
1pl (incl)	*at, t*	–	–
2sg	*ay, y,* (f) *ai,* (n) *i*	(m) *ne, e, ene, o* (f/n) *ni, i, eni*	*is, ēs, s*
2pl	*ar, r* (f) *ai* (n) *i*	*er, or*	*ire, ēre, re*
3m sg	*as, s*	*ah, ih, eh, oh*	*e, ik, ak*
3n-m sg	*ī,* (n) *ī (d/t)*	*aθ, iθ, eθ, oθ*	
3h pl	*ar, r* (f) *ai*	*er, ar, or*	*ir, ēr, as, os*
3n-h pl	–	–	

7.5.4 *North Dravidian*

The reconstructions for Proto-Dravidian are: 1sg/pl *-V*n*/*-V*m*, 1pl (incl) *-V*t̲t̲*, 2sg/pl **-ay* ~ **-i*/**-ir*, 3m sg/pl *-V*nt̲*/*-V*r*, 3n-m sg *-V*d*. Note that Brahui has lost gender distinction but the contrasts survive but indifferently as *-as*/*-os* (< **-ant̲*), *-ir*, *-ēr* (< *V*r*), *-e* (< *-V*d*); the neuter plural is -V*k* in noun morphology which is used as one of the singular markers.

7.5.5 *Summary*

The personal suffixes reflect the gender contrasts of the subject pronouns in the third person. -V*r* in the third plural represents [+human]; in South Dravidian II, other than Telugu, and Central Dravidian, -V*r* refers to subject words meaning 'men or men and women', but not an exclusive group of women. The non-masculine (neuter) plural stands for 'they' (non-men). This semantic extension is therefore reconstructable for Proto-Dravidian. Through a later innovation, following natural circumstances, South Dravidian I, Telugu and Kuṛux–Malto extended it to an exclusive group of women also and restricted the meaning of neuter plural to non-human categories.

7.6 Finite verbs in the past and non-past

Morphologically most finite verbs have three constituents, stem + tense/mood + pronominal suffix, of which the last agrees with the subject noun phrase in (gender-) number-person. Steever (1988: 111–14) defines finiteness as a syntactic property. Gender occurs only in the third person. Some finite verbs may not carry agreement markers, but those that carry tense and agreement markers are always finite. In the light of the description and distribution of tense and person markers, some sample paradigms of finite verbs are given below.

7.6.1 South Dravidian I

1a. *Old Tamil: past* Following the past stem and before the personal suffixes, Old Tamil optionally uses certain 'empty markers' called *cāriyai* (*-aṉ*/*-iṉ*)[11] which have no parallels in the other Dravidian languages. The diversity of personal morphs indicates a mixture of several chronological layers as well as regional varieties in the poetic dialects of Early Tamil. Where the verb stems have morphophonemic changes in inflection, the roots are cited separately.

1sg *kāṇ-* 'to see': *kaṇṭ-aṉ-aṉ* 'I saw', *maṟa-nt-iciṉ yāṉ* 'I forgot', *toṭu-tt-eṉ* 'I got hold of', *eṭu-tt-ēṉ* 'I acquired', *var-* 'to come': *va-nt-ēṉ* 'I came', *tōṉṟ-iy-ēṉ* 'I appeared'

1pl *kaṭi-nt-aṉ-am* 'we avoided' (with *-aṉ* as an empty marker), *vēṇṭ-iṉ-am* 'we wished', *kāv-iṉ-em* 'we lifted (the pots) by hanging', *vē-ṭṭ-ēm* (← *vēḷ-tt-ēm*) 'we desired'

2sg *va-nt-atai* 'you arrived' (here both *at-* and *-ai* appear to be the 2 person markers); *va-nt-aṉ-ai* 'you came' (with *-aṉ* as an empty marker), *āṉṟ-iciṉ nī* 'you stop . . . ', *niṉai-iṉ-ai* 'you thought', *va-nt-ōy* 'you came'

2pl *o-tt-aṉ-ir* 'you were agreeable', *koḷ-* 'to receive': *ko-ṇṭ-ir* 'you received', *uḷḷ-iṉ-ir* 'you thought of', *eṉ cey-t-īr* 'what did you do?'

3m sg *cey-t-aṉ-aṉ* 'he did', *tīr-tt-aṉ-aṉ* 'he removed, cured', *tāṅk-iṉ-aṉ* 'he held up', **kōḷ-paṭu* 'to be caught': *kōṭ-paṭṭ-ām* 'we were caught', *koṇ-ṭ-āṉ* 'he took hold', *ceṉṟ-iciṉ-ōṉ* 'he left'

3f sg *koṇṭ-aṉ-aḷ* 'she took', *toṭaṅk-iṉ-aḷ* 'she started', *pōy-iṉ-āḷ* 'she went'

3h pl/hon sg *maṟa-nt-aṉ-ar* 'he (hon) forgot', *cey-t-ōr* 'he/they did', *koṭu-tt-ōr* 'they gave away'

3neu sg *cel-* 'to go': *ceṉṟ-atu* (< **cel-nt-atu*) 'it left', *curuṅk-in-ṟu* 'they dwindled'

3neu pl *cey-t-a* 'they (neu) did'

1b. *Old Tamil: non-past*

1sg *kāṇ-p-al/kāṇ-kuv-al* 'I see', *varu-v-al* 'I shall come', *kara-pp-aṉ* 'I will hide', *malai*[1] *akaẓ-kkuv-aṉ*[2] 'I will dig[2] the mountains[1]', *kaṭal*[1] *tūr-kkuv-aṉ*[2] 'I will fill up[2] the ocean[1]', *maṟa-pp-eṉ-ō* 'will I forget?', *uva-pp-ē-ṉ* 'I shall rejoice', *aṟi-v-ēṉ* 'I realize'

1pl *kāṇ-k-am/kāṇ-kuv-am* 'we will look at', *cel-v-ām* 'we will/let us go', *nāṇ*[1] *niṟu-pp-ām*[2] 'we will contain[2] our shame[1]', *āku-t-um* 'we are becoming', *varu-t-um* 'we are coming', *amai-k-um* 'we agree with', *cel-*

[11] The examples are all from Caṅkam Classics, cited from Rajam (1992: 585–603).

'to go': *cē-ṟ-um* 'we shall go' (< *cel-t-*), *cel-v-ēm* 'we are going', *aṟi-vi-pp-ēm* 'we will make (somebody) know', *tīr-kkuv-ōm* 'we will cure'

2sg *eṉ-p-ā* 'you are saying', *tuṟa-pp-āy* 'you are renouncing (her)', *pō-kuv-āy* 'you are going', *iṟa-tt-i* 'you are departing', *añcu-t-i* 'you are afraid of', *pōku-t-i* 'you are leaving', *ā-v-ai* 'you are/will be', *cey-kuv-ai* 'you make'

2pl *aṟi-t-ir* 'you know', *eṇṇu-t-ir* 'you are thinking', *maruḷ-t-īr* 'you are confused', *eṉ-p-īr* 'you are asking'

3m sg *varu-kuv-aṉ/varu-v-aṉ* 'he will come', *yāṇṭu*[1] *oḷi-pp-āṉ*[2] 'where[1] is he hiding[2]?', *aracum*[1] *cell-um*[2] 'even the king[1] will go[2]'

3f sg *eṉ-p-aḷ* 'she says', *varuntu-v-aḷ* 'she is grieving', *cel-v-āḷ* 'she will leave', *ivaḷum*[1] *tēmp-um*[2] 'even she[1] is sobbing[2]'

3h pl *ā-p-a/āku-p-a* 'they will belong', *kāṇ-p-ar* 'they will see', *maṟa-pp-ar* 'he (hon) will forget', *koṭu-kkuv-ar* 'they will give'

3neu sg *vē-v-atu* 'it will heat up', *mīṉ vazaṅk-un-tu* (< *-um-tu*) 'the fish move about', *ulakam*[1] *viya-kk-um*[2] 'the world[1] admires[2]'

3neu pl *kaṇṇum*[1] *paṭu-kuv-a*[2] 'eyes[1] will close[2]', *kaṇṇum*[1] *civa-kk-um*[2] 'the eyes[1] are turning red[2]'

2a. *Modern Tamil: past (Schiffman 1999: 65–71)*

pār 'to see', *iru* 'to be located', *sāppiḍu* 'to eat', *vāngu* 'to buy, fetch', *paḍi* 'to read', *oḍe* (v.i./v.t.) 'to break'

1sg *pā-tt-ēn, iru-nd-ēn, sāppi-ṭṭ-ēn, vāng-in-ēn, paḍi-cc-ēn, oḍe-cc-ēn*

1pl *pā-ttō-m, iru-nd-ōm, sāppi-ṭṭ-ōm, vāng-in-ōm, paḍi-cc-ōm, oḍe-cc-ōm*

2sg *pā-tt-ē, iru-nd-ē, sāppi-ṭṭ-ē, vāng-in-ē, paḍi-cc-ē, oḍe-cc-ē*

2pl *pā-tt-īnga, iru-nd-īnga, sāppi-ṭṭ-īnga, vāng-in-īnga, paḍi-cc-īnga, oḍe-cc-īnga*

3m sg *pā-tt-ān, iru-nd-ān, sāpp-ṭṭ-ān, vāng-in-ān, paḍi-cc-ān, oḍe-cc-ān*

3f sg *pā-tt-ā, iru-nd-ā, sāppi-ṭṭ-ā, vāng-in-ā, paḍi-cc-ā, oḍe-cc-ā*

3h pl/hon sg (mf) *pā-tt-āru, iru-nd-āru, sāppi-ṭṭ-āru, vāng-in-āru, paḍi-cc-āru, oḍe-cc-ānga*

3neu sg *pā-tt-adu, iru-nd-adu, sāppi-ṭṭ-adu, vāng-in-adu, paḍi-cc-adu, oḍe-cc-adu* (v.t.), *oḍe-nj-adu* (v.i.)

2b. *Modern Tamil: future*

1sg *pā-pp-ēn, iru-pp-ēn, sāppiḍu-v-ēn, vāngu-v-ēn, paḍi-pp-ēn, oḍe-pp-ēn*

1pl *pā-pp-ōm, iru-pp-ōm, sāppiḍu-v-ōm, vāngu-v-ōm, paḍi-pp-ōm, oḍe-pp-ōm*

2sg *pā-pp-ē, iru-pp-ē, sāppiḍu-v-ē, vāngu-v-ē, paḍi-pp-ē, oḍe-pp-ē*

2pl *pā-pp-īnga, iru-pp-īnga, sāppiḍu-v-īnga, vāngu-v-īnga, paḍi-pp-īnga, oḍe-pp-īnga*
3m sg *pā-pp-ān, iru-pp-ān, sāppiḍu-v-ān, vāngu-v-ān, paḍi-pp-ān, oḍe-pp-ān*
3f sg *pā-pp-ā, iru-pp-ā, sāppiḍu-v-ā, vāngu-v-ā, paḍi-pp-ā, oḍe-pp-ā*
3h pl/hon sg (mf) *pā-pp-ānga, iru-pp-āru, sāppiḍu-v-āru, vāngu-v-āru, paḍi-pp-ānga, oḍe-pp-ānga*
3neu sg *pā-kk-um, iru-kk-um, sāppiḍu-um, vāng-um, paḍi-kk-um, oḍe-kk-um* (v.t.), *oḍey-um* (v.i.)

The conjugations of Modern Spoken Tamil are much simpler and systematic. Compared to Old Tamil, the phonological changes include (a) representing the voiced stops distinctly, (b) loss of stem final *r* before geminate consonants, *pā(r)-tt-/-pp-*, (c) palatalization of a dental following a front vowel or *y*, e.g. *oḍe-nj-* (< *oṭay-nt-*), *paḍi-cc-* (< **paṭi-tt-*) etc., (d) stem-final *-e* < *-ai*. Morphological changes include (e) the replacement of human plural -V*r* in the second and third persons by *-nga* < **-m-kaḷ*, (f) restricting the OTa. aorist *-um* to the third neuter singular, and (g) the Old Tamil non-past markers have become regular future-tense markers.

3. *Iruḷa: past and non-past* The past is marked by *-t(t)-/-ṭ(ṭ)-, -nd-/-nḏ-/-ṇḍ-, -in-/-n-* and non-past by *-kk-/-g-* (Zvelebil 1973: 22–3), *muḍi-* 'to finish': *muḍi-tt-e, muḍi-kk -e* (1sg), *iru-* 'to sit': *iru-nd-e, iru-kk-e, kā-* 'to guard': *kā-tt-e, kā-kk-e, nil-* 'to stand': *ni-nḏ-e, ni-kk-e*; *tin-* 'to eat': *tin-ḏ-e, tin-g-e, pō-* 'to go': *pō-n-e, pō-g-e*. The distribution of *-kk-, -g-* corresponds to strong and weak verbs of Tamil. Also there is no palatalization of the past *-tt-* in Iruḷa unlike in Middle Tamil, Malayāḷam and Koḍagu. The paradigm of *var-* 'to come' in non-past is given below; the second example occurs when followed by a vowel (Zvelebil 1973: 26):

1sg *var (u)-g-e* 'I come', *var(u)-g-en-o*? 'do I come?'
1pl (excl) *var(u)-g-amu/var(u)-g-ēmu, . . . m-o*?
1pl (incl) *var(u)-g-o, var(u)-g-om-o*?
2sg *var(u)-g-a, var(u)-g-aḷ-o*?
2pl *var(u)-g-iri, var(u)-g-iriy-o*?
3m sg *var(u)-g-e, var(u)-g-en-o*?
3f sg *var(u)-g-a, var(u)-g-aḷ-o*?
3h pl *var(u)-g-aru/var(u)-g-āru, . . . r-o*?
3neu sg *var(u)-g-udu, . . . d-o*?
3neu pl *var(u)-g-ina, var(u)-g-inaḷ-o*?

4. *Kota: past and non-past* There seems to be a reversal in the semantics of past and non-past suffixes in Kota. The past stem formed the regular base to which a non-past

suffix -*p*-/-*k*- is added before the personal suffixes in forming the past finite verb, e.g. *vā*- (*va-d*-) 'to come' (the first paradigm is the regular past and the second past irrealis). In historical terms, the ascribing of a past meaning to an original non-past suffix -*p*- is an innovation in Kota. The suffix -*c*- in the second past is an original past-tense marker. But note that *vad*- (< *va-nd*-) itself is a past stem historically.

1sg *vad-p-ē(n)* 'I came', *vad-c-ē* 'I would have come'
1pl (excl) *vad-p-ēm*, *vad-c-ēm*
(incl) *vad-p-ōm*, *vad-c-ōm*
2sg *vad-p-ī*, *vad-c-ī*
2pl *vad-p-im*, *vad-c-īm*/-*īr*
3 (sg/pl) *vad-k-ō*;
3m sg *vad-c-ān(ē)*
3f sg *vad-c-āḷ(ē)*
3h pl *vad-c-ār(ē)*
3neu sg/pl *vad-c-ad(ē)*

5. *Toda: past and non-past* Past and non-past, e.g. *pï: x*- (*pī*-) 'to go', *pōr*- (*pod*-) 'to come'. S[2] given in parentheses is the past stem, which forms the basis of both past and non-past tenses (Emeneau 1984: 114, 130–1).

1sg *pī-š-p-en* 'I went', *pod-š-p-en* 'I came'; *pī-p-en* 'I will go', *pod-p-en* 'I will come'
1pl (excl) *pī-š-p-em*, *pod-š-p-em*; *pī-p-em*, *pod-p-em*
(incl) *pī-š-p-um*, *pod-š-p-um*; *pī-p-um*, *pod-p-um*
2sg *pī-š-p-y*, *pod-š-p-y*; *pī-p-y*, *pod-p-y*
2pl *pī-š*, *pod-š*; *pī-t-š*, *pod-t-š*
3sg pl *pī-č*, *pod-š*; *pī-t*, *pod-t*

6. *Koḍagu: past and non-past* Stems of Cl. I *ōd*- (*ōd-i*) 'to read', Cl. II *āy*- (*ā-ñj*-) 'to choose', *mara*- (*mara-nd*-) 'to forget', Cl. III *kë̄ḷ*- (*kë̄ṭṭ*-) 'to ask', *oraḍ*- (*oraṭ*-) 'to answer' (Ebert 1996: 10–13, 18).

1sg *ōd-ïn-ë*, *ā-nj-ë*, *mara-nd-ë*, *kë̄-ṭ-ë*, *ora-ṭ-ë*; *ōdu-v-i*, *ay-uv-i*, *mara-p-i*, *kë̄-p-i*, *oraḍ-uv-i*;
1pl *ōdï-c-i*, *ā-nj-atï*, *mara-nd-atï*, *kë̄-ṭ-atï*, *ora-ṭ-atï*; *ōd-uv-a*, *ay-uv-a*, *mara-p-a*, *kë̄-p-a*, *oraḍ-uv-a*;
2sg *ōd-i-ya*, *ā-nj-iya*, *mara-nd-iya*, *kë̄-ṭ-iya*, *ora-ṭ-iya*; *ōd-uv-iya*, *ay-uv-iya*, *mara-p-iya*, *kë̄-p-iya*, *oraḍ-uv-iya*
2pl *ōd-i-ra*, *ā-nj-ira*, *mara-nd-ira*, *kë̄-ṭ-ira*, *ora-ṭ-ira*; *ōd-uv-ira*, *ay-uv-ira*, *mara-p-ira*, *kë̄-p-ira*, *oraḍ-uv-ira*;
3sg/pl = 1pl structurally.

The first person plural and the third-personal forms in the singular and plural are totally identical. Apparently there is neutralization of gender and number in the third person, e.g. *ōdï-c-i* 'we, he/she /it /they read (past)', *ōd-uv-a* 'we, he/she/it/they will read'.

7a. *Old Kannaḍa*

Past *-t-/-d-/id-/-nd-*, non-past *-v-*.

1sg *ir-* 'to be': *ir-d-eN* 'I was', *tōṟu* 'to show': *tōṟ-id-eN* 'I showed', *iḍ-* 'to hit': *iṭ-ṭ-eN* 'I hit', *peṟu-* 'to obtain': *pet-t-eN* 'I obtained', *keḍu-* 'to perish': *keṭ-ṭ-eN* 'I was ruined', **koḍu-/kuḍu-* 'to give': *koṭ-ṭ-eN* 'I gave': similarly, *bāẓ-d-eN* 'I lived', *i-tt-eN* 'I gave', *tōṟu-v-eN/tōr-p-eN* 'I will show', *ī-v-eN* 'I will give', *māḍu-* 'to do': *māḍu-v-eN/māẓ-p-eN* 'I will perform'.

1pl *ba-nd-evu* 'we came', *pēḷ-d-evu* 'we spoke', *pēḷ-v-evu* 'we will speak'.

2sg *māṇ-d-e* 'you (sg) stopped', *sa-tt-e* 'you died', *māḍ-id-ai* 'you did', *ba-nd-ai* 'you came', *koṭ-ṭ-ai* 'you gave', *tōṟu-v-ai* 'you are showing', *nuḍu-v-ai* 'you are talking'.

2pl *māḍ-id-ir* 'you did', *aṟi-v-ir* 'you will know', *bar-p-ir* 'you will come'.

3m sg *baẓal-d-aN* 'he became tired', *uguẓ-d-aN* 'he spat', *aẓi-v-aN* 'he will destroy'.

3f sg *ir-d-aḷ* 'she was', *pet-t-aḷ* 'she gave birth to', *meṭṭu-v-aḷ* 'she will step on'.

3h pl *aṟi-d-ar* 'they knew', *ba-nd-ar* 'they came', *kiḍu-v-ar* 'they will perish'.

3neu sg *ba-nd-udu* 'it came', *bar-p-udu* 'it will come', *kuḍu-v-udu* 'it will give'.

3neu pl *aẓ-tu-vu* 'they cried', *suṭ-ṭu-vu* 'they burnt', *bar-p-uvu* 'they will come'.

7b. *Modern Kannaḍa (Sridhar 1990: 219–27)* *māḍu-* 'to do, make', *kollu-* 'to kill'. In colloquial Kannaḍa the Old Kannaḍa non-past markers *-v-/-p-* have been, by and large, replaced by the present-tense marker *-utt-* to denote present, habitual and future (Sridhar 1990: 219–20).

1sg *māḍ-id-e(nu)* 'I did', *ko-nd-e(nu)* 'I killed'; *māḍ-utt-ēne/-īni* 'I do/ will do'

1pl *māḍ-id-evu, ko-nd-evu, māḍ-utt-ēve/-īvi*

2sg *māḍ-id-e/-i, ko-nd-e, māḍ-utt-iye/-īya/māḍu-v-e*

2pl *māḍ-id-iri, ko-nd-iri, māḍ-utt-iri/-īra*

3m sg *māḍ-id-a(nu), ko-nd-a(nu), māḍ-utt-āne/māḍu-v-anu*

3f sg *māḍ-id-aḷu, ko-nd-aḷu, māḍ-utt-āḷe/māḍu-v-aḷu*

3h pl *māḍ-id-aru, ko-nd-aru, māḍ-utt-āre/māḍu-v-aru*

3neu sg *māḍ-i-tu, ko-nd-itu, māḍ-utt-ade/māḍ-at-te* (?)

3neu pl *māḍ-id-avu, ko-nd-avu, māḍu-tt-ave/māḍu-v-vu*

8. *Tuḷu: past and non-past* The past markers are -*Ø*- in the neuter third singular, otherwise -*id*/-*d*/-*ḍ*, -*t*, -*y*, e.g. *tin*- 'to eat': *tin-d-ɛ* 'I ate', *tinn-ï* 'it ate', *kēṇ*- 'to ask': *kēṇ-ḍ-ɛ* 'I asked', *kēṇ-ï* 'it asked'; *kal* 'to learn' (Common dialect), *kaṭï* 'to tie' (Brahmin dialect). The present-future (habitual) markers are -*v*-/-*b*-, -*p* with phonological and morphological conditioning, e.g. *pō*- 'to go': *pō-p-ɛ* 'I go', *kaṇḍu* 'to steal': *kaṇḍu-p-e* 'he steals', *aḍapu*/*dappu* 'to plough': *aḍapu-v-e*/*dappu-v-e* 'he ploughs'. Also cf. Kekunnaya (1994: 85–99). The past paradigms of *kal*- 'to learn', *kaṭ*- 'to tie':

1sg *kal-t-ɛ*, *kaṭ-y-ɛ*
1pl *kal-t-a*, *kaṭ-y-o*
2sg *kal-t-a*, *kaṭ-y-a*
2pl *kal-t-arï*, *kaṭ-y-arï*
3m sg *kal-t-e*, *kaṭ-y-e*
3f sg *kal-t-alï*, *kaṭ-y-aḷï*
3h pl *kal-t-erï*, *kaṭ-y-erï*
3neu sg *kal-t-iṇḍï*, *kaṭ-ø-ṇi*
3neu pl *kal-t-a*, *kaṭ-y-o*

9. *Koraga: past and non-past* The past markers in different dialects are -*k*-/-*kk*-/-*g*-, non-past marker -*n*-. The personal suffixes are separated by hyphens in the examples in table 7.5: *kuṭṭu*- 'to beat' (Onti dialect), *kaṭṭï*- 'to tie' (Tappu dialect), *ojji*- 'to say' (Mudu dialect); paradigms in past and simple non-past (Bhat 1971).

We notice traces of South Dravidian I suffixes mainly in the second plural, third human plural and third neuter singular. The second singular -*a* could be derived from South Dravidian I -*ay*. The first singular and plural have lost the final consonants of the original -*en*, -*am*. So has the third masculine singular with vowel-raising, -*an* > -*en* > -*in* > -*i*, -*ar* > -*er*; Koraga past -*k*-/-*g*- may appear to be like that of North Dravidian, but there are no other features that it shares with North Dravidian. It appears that the non-past

Table 7.5. *Past and non-past finite verbs in Koraga dialects*

Onti		Tappu		Mudu	
past	non-past	past	non-past	past	non-past
1sg *kuṭṭu-g-e*	*kuṭṭu-n-e*	*kaṭṭï-g-e*	*kaṭ-ṇ-e*	*ojji-g-e*	*ojji-n-e*
1pl *kaṭṭu-g-a*	*kuṭṭu-n-a*	*kaṭṭï-g-a*	*kaṭ-ṇ-e*	*ojju-g-u*	*ojju-n-u*
2sg *kaṭṭu-g-a*	*kaṭṭu-n-a*	*kaṭṭï-g-a*	*kaṭ-ṇ-a*	*ojji-g-a*	*ojji-n-a*
2pl *kaṭṭu-g-erï*	*kaṭṭu-n-erï*	*kaṭṭï-g-erï*	*kaṭ-ṇ-erï*	*ojji-g-rï*	*ojji-n-rï*
3m sg *kaṭṭu-g-i*	*kuṭṭu-n-i*	*kaṭṭï-g-i*	*kaṭ-ṇ-i*	*ojji-g-i*	*ojji-n-i*
3h pl *kaṭṭu-g-erï*	*kaṭṭu-n-erï*	*kaṭṭï-g-erï*	*kaṭ-ṇ-erï*	*ojji-g-rï*	*ojji-n-rï*
3fneu sg *kaṭṭu-g-u*	*kaṭṭu-n-ḍï*	*kaṭṭï-g-ïdï*	*kaṭṭï-n-dï*	*ojji-g-ïdï*	*ojji-n-dï*

velar has assumed a past meaning in this language, in the same manner that in Kota past negative paradigm *-p* (non-past marker) is used as a past-tense sign. The non-past *-n-* has its source in South Dravidian I. In most respects, Koraga seems to be closer to Tuḷu common dialect than to any other member of South Dravidian I.

7.6.2 *South Dravidian II*

10a. *Old Telugu: past and non-past* The past is marked by *-e-/-iye-*, *-iti-* ~ *-ti-* ~ *-ṭi-* and non-past by *-Ø-*, *-eda-/-du-* ~ *-tu-* before personal suffixes. Examples of *waṇḍu-* 'to cook', *an-* 'to say', *cūc-/cū-* 'to see' are:

Past

1sg *waṇḍ-iti-ni* 'I cooked', *aṇ-ṭi-ni* 'I said', *cūc-iti-ni* 'I saw' (in poetry sometimes the final *-ni* can be changed to *-n* or completely dropped)

1pl *waṇḍ-iti-mi* , *aṇ-ṭi-mi*, *cūc-iti-mi*

2sg *waṇḍ-iti-wi*, *aṇ-ṭi-wi*, *cūc-iti-wi*

2pl *waṇḍ-iti-ri*, *aṇ-ṭi-ri*, *cūc-iti-ri*

3m sg *waṇḍ-e-nu* 'he, she, it (n-h) cooked', *an-e-nu*/*an-iy-enu* 'he, she, it, they (n-h) said', *cūc-e-nu* 'he, she, it, they (n-h) saw'.

3hpl *waṇḍ-i-ri* 'they (h) cooked', *an-i-ri* 'they (h) said', *cūc-i-ri* 'they (h) saw'.

Non-past

1sg *waṇḍ-udu-nu*/*waṇḍ-eda-nu* 'I cook', *an-du-nu*/*an-eda-nu* 'I say', *cū-tu-nu*/*cūc-eda-nu* 'I see'

1pl *waṇḍ-udu-mu*/*waṇḍ-eda-mu*, *an-du-mu*/*an-eda-mu*, *cū-tu-mu*/*cūc-eda-mu*

1pl hortative 1sg *waṇḍu-da-mu* 'let us cook', *an-da-mu* 'let us say', *cū-ta-mu* 'let us see'

2sg *waṇḍu-du-wu*/*waṇḍ-eda-wu*, *an-du-wu*/*an-eda-wu*, *cū-tu-wu*/*cūc-eda-wu*

2pl *waṇḍu-du-ru*/*waṇḍ-eda-ru*, *an-du-ru* ~ *aṇ-ḍ-ru*/*an-eda-ru*, *cū-tu-ru*/*cūc-eda-ru*

3sg/n-h pl *waṇḍ-unu* 'he/she/it/they (n-h) cook', *an-unu* 'he/she/it/they (n-h) say', *cūc-unu* 'he/she/it/they (n-h) see'.

3h pl *waṇḍ-udu-ru*/*waṇḍ-eda-ru*, *an-du-ru* ~ *aṇ-ḍ-ru*/*an-eda-ru*, *cū-tu-ru*/*cūc-eda-ru*

The past-tense morpheme was -$V_1 t V_2$- of which the -V_1- part is predictable. The past suffix is **-tt-i*, presumably a sequence of two past markers. After a root-final alveolar/retroflex nasal, *-t-* becomes *-ṭ-*. In Old Telugu in the third person there was neutralization of both gender and number yielding a peculiar opposition like human plural vs. others (m sg, n-m sg, n-h pl) vs. human plural both in the past and non-past.

This feature is found only with *-um* in Old Tamil also but it was extended to the past tense in Old Telugu. The past marker in the third singular and neuter plural was apparently *-iya-* which later became *-e-*.[12]

In the non-past, the second and third persons plural are totally identical. The non-past marker *-t-* belongs to Proto-Dravidian. It appears that *-du-/-eda-* were not totally synonymous. The *-eda-* forms were mostly in the present tense and the *-du-* forms in habitual–future. However, this was an innovation in the Telugu literary language, which was not successfully carried out. Both these non-past markers have become archaic in Modern Telugu, which has *-t-un-* for the durative (present-progressive), *-t-* for the habitual–future and -ǣ-for the past.

10b. *Modern Telugu: past and non-past* The past and non-past of Modern Telugu are not directly related to corresponding markers of Literary Telugu. The past marker -ǣ- is likely to have been derived from *-inā-* (past *-in-*, *-ā-* presumably a part of the personal suffix) with the loss of *-n-*. The non-past *-t-* was already in colloquial use in the twelfth century but it entered the literary dialect only after the sixteenth century.

Past

1sg *waṇḍ-ǣ-nu* 'I cooked', *an-nā-nu* 'I said', *cūs-ǣ-nu* 'I saw'

1pl *waṇḍ-ǣ-m(u)* 'we cooked', *an-nā-m(u)* 'we said', *cūs-ǣ-m(u)* 'we saw'

2sg *waṇḍ-ǣ-w(u)* 'you (sg) cooked', *an-nā-w(u)* 'you (sg) said', *cūs -ǣ-vu* 'you (sg) saw'

2pl *waṇḍ-ǣ-ru* 'you (pl) cooked', *an-nā-ru* 'you (pl) said', *cūs -ǣ-ru* 'you (pl) saw'

3m sg *waṇḍ-ǣ-ḍu* 'he cooked', *an-nā-ḍu* 'he said', *cūs -ǣ-ḍu* 'he saw'

3h pl *waṇḍ-ǣ-ru* 'they (h) cooked', *an-nā-ru* 'they (h) said', *cūs -ǣ-nu* 'they (h) saw'

3neu sg *waṇḍ-in-di* 'she/it cooked', *an-na-di* 'she/it said', *cūs-in-di* 'she/it saw'

3neu pl *waṇḍ-ǣ-y(i)* 'they (n-h) cooked', *an-nā-y(i)* 'they (n-h) said', *cūs -ǣ-y* 'they (n-h) saw'

Non-past (habitual–future)

1sg *waṇḍu-t-ānu* 'I cook/will cook', *aṇ-ṭ-ānu* 'I cook/will cook', *cūs-t-ānu* 'I see/will see'

1pl *waṇḍu-t-ām(u)*, *aṇ-ṭ-ām(u)*, *cūs-t-ām(u)*

2sg *waṇḍu-t-āw(u)*, *aṇ-ṭ-āw(u)*, *cūs-t-āw(u)*

[12] This alternation is found in older and later forms of a number of nouns ending in *-e*: *kann-iya* > *kann-e* 'maid', *paḷḷ-iya-mu* > *paḷḷ-e-mu* 'a metal plate', *wiḍ-iya-mu* > *wiḍ-emu* 'betel leaf and betel-nut preparation'.

2pl *waṇḍu-t-āru, aṇ-ṭ-āru, cūs-t-āru*
3m sg *waṇḍu-t-āḍu, aṇ-ṭ-āḍu, cūs-t-āḍu*
3h pl *waṇḍu-t-āru, aṇ-ṭ-āru, cūs-t-āru*
3n-m sg *waṇḍu-tun-di, aṇ-ṭun-di, cūs-tun-di*
3neu pl *waṇḍu-t-āy, aṇ-ṭ-āy, cūs-t-āy*

Both the past and non-past markers can be traced to Proto-Dravidian sources: Te. -ǣ-/ -*in*- to PD *-*in*-/*-*iy*- and -*t*- to Proto-Dravidian non-past *-*t*-/-*tt*-, followed by *-*ā* which is part of the personal suffix. The non-past -*t*- is also involved in the formation of the periphrastic durative, which will be described later.

11. *Gondi: past and non-past* Rao (1987b: §4.2.3) reconstructs the following paradigm for the simple indicative past for Gondi dialects, e.g. *tin*- (*ti-tt*-) 'to eat'. The past stem is derived from **tin-t̠t̠*- with the loss of -*n*. Except Telugu all languages of South Dravidian II lose the root-final *-*n* before *-*t̠t̠*.

1sg *ti-tt-an*, 1pl *ti-tt-om*, 2sg *ti-tt-i*(*n*), 2pl *ti-tt-ir*, 3m sg *ti-tt-or̠*, 3m pl *ti-tt-or*, 3n-m sg *ti-tt-u*, 3n-m pl *ti-tt-u-ŋ*.

The non-past (also called present-future) is marked by -*nt*-/-*int*-/-*t*- in different dialects, e.g. *tin*- 'to eat', *wā*- 'to come': *tin-t-on* 'I eat/am eating', *wā-t-an* 'I come/am coming' (South Bastar), *tin-t-on, wā-nt-on* (Adilabad), *tin-da-t-o-na, wāy-i-t-o-na* (Western/ Northern) (Rao 1987: 220). Rao reconstructs forms like **tinda-t-an* for simple non-past, in which -*da*- got dropped in the Adilabad dialect. Still, the contrast between past and non-past is maintained as *ti-tt-an* vs. *tin-t-an*. It appears that the dental is presumably related to non-past -*t*-/-*tt*- found in South Dravidian I and Telugu. The origin of the allomorphs -*ant*-/-*int*-/-*nt*- needs to be examined. In the dialects in which *wā-t-an* is non-past, the past is *wa-tt-an*.

The future in Gondi is signalled by -*k*-/-*kk*-/-*ak*-, -*an*-/-*ar*-/-*al*- (Rao 1987b: 226–8), e.g. *tin*- 'to eat', *doh*- 'to tie', *wā*- 'to come':

Western	North Bastar
1sg *tin-da-k-a*	*tind*(*a*)-*k-a*(*n*)
1pl (excl) *tin-da-k-om*	*tind*(*a*)-*k-om*
1pl (incl) *tin-da-k-aṭ*	–
2sg *tin-da-k-i*	*tind*(*a*)-*k-i*(*n*)
2pl *tin-da-k-iṭ*	*tind*(*a*)-*k-iṭ*
3m sg *tin-d-an-ul*	*tinda-n-or*
3m pl *tin-d-an-ur*	*tinda-n-ur*
3n-m sg *tin-d-al-Ø*	*tind-yar-Ø*
3n-m pl *tin-d-an-uŋ*	*tind-an-uŋ*

In verb stems of (C)V̄- type, the dental suffix is not attested, *sī-k-a* 'I will give', *wā-i-ka* 'I will come', *hūr-k-a* 'I will see'. There is also a past habitual conjugation in Gondi

Table 7.6. *Tense markers in Gondi dialects (based on Rao 1987b: 233)*

Dialect	Non-past	Past	Habitual past	Future
Western	*t*	*tt*	*nd*	*k, an/al*
Northern	*t*	*tt*	*nd*	*k, an/al/ar*
South-Bastar	*it*	*tt*	*nd*	*k*
South-Bastar (S)	*t*	*tt*	*n*	*k*
South-East	*it*	*tt*	?	*k/kk*
Central	*int*	*tt*	*nd*	*k, an/al*
North-Bastar	*int*	*tt*	*nd*	*k, n, ar*
Hill-Maria	*int*	*tt*	*nd*	*k, n, aR*
Adilabad	*ant*	*tt*	*(a)nd*	*k, n, ar*
Southern	*ant*	*tt*	*nd*	*k, an/ar*

Table 7.7. *Past and non-past finite verbs in Koṇḍa*

Person	Past	Non-past
1sg	*ḍig-it-a, ki-t-a, mū-ṭ-a, i-R-a*	*ḍig-n-a, ki-n-a, mū-ṇ-a, in-Ø-a*
1pl (excl)	*ḍig-it-ap, ki-t-ap, mū-ṭ-ap, i-R-ap*	*ḍig-n-ap, ki-n-ap, mū-ṇ-ap, in-Ø-ap*
1pl (incl)	*ḍig-it-aṭ, ki-t-aṭ, mū-ṭ-aṭ, i-R-aṭ*	*dig-n-aṭ, ki-n-aṭ, mū-ṇ-aṭ, in-Ø-aṭ*
2sg	*ḍig-it-i(d), ki-t-i(d), mū-ṭ-i(d), i-R-i(d)*	*ḍig-n-i(d), ki-n-i(d), mū-ṇ-i(d), in-Ø-i(d)*
2pl	*ḍig-it-ider, ki-t-ider, mū-ṭ-ider, i-R-ider*	*ḍig-n-ider, ki-n-ider, mū-ṇ-ider, in-Ø-ider*
3m sg	*ḍig-it-an, ki-t-an, mū-ṭ-an, i-R-an*	*ḍig-n-an, ki-n-an, mū-ṇ-an, in-Ø-an*
3m pl	*ḍig-it-ar, ki-t-ar, mū-ṭ-ar, i-R-ar*	*ḍig-n-ar, ki-n-ar, mū-ṇ-ar, in-Ø-ar*
3n-m sg	*ḍig-it-ad, ki-t-ad, mū-ṭ-ad, i-R-ad*	*ḍig-n-ad, ki-n-ad, mū-ṇ-ad, in-Ø-ad*
3n-m pl	*ḍig-it-e, ki-t-e, mū-ṭ-e, i-R-e*	*ḍig-n-e, ki-n-e, mū-ṇ-e, in-Ø-e*

formed by the addition of *-nd-*/-V*nd-* to the stem only in some dialects. Rao (1987b: 230–3) reconstructs -V*nt-* as the non-past suffix, with loss of V and *n* in different dialects resulting in *-t-* as the non-past marker in some dialects. He also reconstructs -V*k-* as the future suffix in Proto-Gondi and gives a comparative table of different tense markers in different dialects, shown here as table 7.6.

12. *Koṇḍa: past and non-past* The past marker is *-t-* with its sandhi variants (*-it-*, *-ṭ-*, *-R-*) and the non-past marker is *-n-* with its sandhi variants (*-ṇ-*, *-Ø-*), e.g. past: *ḍig-* (*ḍig-it-*) 'to get down', *ki-* (*ki-t-*) 'to do', *mūl-* (*mūṭ-*) 'to urinate', *in-* (*iR-*) 'to say'; non-past: *ḍig-n-*, *ki-n-*, *mūṇ-*, *in-Ø-*.

Koṇḍa has another finite verb paradigm, durative (past and non-past), formed by *-sin-*/ *-zin-*, which is a combination of perfective marker *-si-*/*-zi-* and the non-past-tense marker *-n-*. Such constructions with complex tenses/aspects are discussed below (section 7.12).

13. *Kui: past and non-past* The past-tense allomorphs are *-t-*/*-it-*/*-d-* with sandhi variants *-ṭ-*, *-s-* and the future-tense allomorphs are *-d-*/*-n-* in morphological

Table 7.8. *Past and non-past conjugations in Kui*

Person	Past	Non-past (future tense)	Hortative
1sg	*kō-t-e*	*kō-Ø-i*	*tāk-ak-anu* 'let me walk'
1pl (excl)	*kō-t-amu*	*kō-n-amu*	*tāk-ak-amu*
1pl (incl)	*kō-t-asu*	*kō-n-asu*	*tāk-ak-asu*
2sg	*kō-t-i*	*kō-d-i*	*tāk-ak-ati*
2pl	*kō-t-eru*	*kō-d-eru*	*tāk-ak-ateru*
3m sg	*kō-t-enju*	*kō-n-enju*	*tāk-ak-anju*
3m pl	*kō-t-eru*	*kō-n-eru*	*tāk-ak-aru*
3n-m sg	*kō-t-e*	*kō-n-e*	*tāk-ak-ari*
3n-m pl	*kō-t-u*	*kō-n-u*	*tāk-ak-ai*

Table 7.9. *Past and non-past finite verbs in Kuvi*

Person	Past	Non-past (future tense)	Non-past (permissive)
1sg	*hī-t-eʔe*	*hī-ʔ-i*	*vā-p-eʔe* 'I may come'
1pl (excl)	*hī-t-omi*	*hī-n-omi*	–
1pl (incl)	–	–	–
2sg	*hī-t-i*	*hī-d-i*	–
2pl	*hī-t-eri*	*hī-d-eri*	–
3m sg	*hī-t-esi*	*hī-n-esi*	*vā-p-esi* 'he may come/let him come'
3m pl	*hī-t-eri*	*hī-n-eri*	*vā-p-eri* 'they may come, let them come'
3n-m sg	*hī-t-e*	*hī-n-e*	*vā-pu* 'she or it may come/let her or it come'
3n-m pl	*hī-t-u*	*hī-n-u*	*vā-p-e* 'they may come/let them come'

complementation (*-d-* in the second person and *-n-* elsewhere). Some typical conjugations, e.g. *kō-* 'to reap', *tāk-* 'to walk', are shown in table 7.8.

It is interesting that both *-d-* and *-n-* occur as non-past markers in complementation; *-k-/-ak-* in the Hortative is to be traced to Proto-Dravidian non-past **-kk-* which is also found in the present participle *-ki-*, e.g. *aṭ-ki* 'joining' from *aḍ-* 'to join'.

14. *Kuvi: past and non-past* The past markers are *-t-* with its sandhi variants *-it-*, *-cc-*, *-s-/-h-*, e.g. *ve-cc-* (< **wen-ṯṯ-* 'hear' past) after *n*-ending stems which lose *-n*; the non-past (future-tense) markers are *-d-* and *-n-* as in Kui. The permissive/hortative is formed by adding *-ap-* (*-mb-* in some conjugations) which clearly seem to be related to or even derived from Proto-Dravidian non-past **-mp-/-mpp-* [-mb-/-mp-] adapted for the paradigms in table 7.9; e.g. *hī-* 'to give', *vā-* 'to come'.

15. *Pengo: past and non-past* The past marker is *-t-* with its sandhi variants (*-ṭ-*, *-c-*) and the non-past (future) is marked by *-n-* and its sandhi variants (*-ṇ-*, *-Ø-*), e.g. *huṛ-* 'to see'.

Table 7.10. *Past and non-past finite verbs in Pengo*

Person	Past	Non-past (future tense)	Non-past (present)
1sg	*huṛ-t-aŋ*	*huṛ-n-aŋ*	*huṛ-n-aŋg-a*
1pl (excl)	*huṛ-t-ap*	*huṛ-n-ap*	*huṛ-n-ap-a*
1pl (incl)	*huṛ-t-as*	*huṛ-n-as*	*huṛ-n-ah-a*
2sg	*huṛ-t-ay*	*huṛ-n-ay*	*huṛ-n-ay-a*
2pl	*huṛ-t-ader*	*huṛ-n-ader/-ider*	*huṛ-n-ader-a*
3m sg	*huṛ-t-an*	*huṛ-n-an*	*huṛ-n-an-a*
3m pl	*huṛ-t-ar*	*huṛ-n-ar*	*huṛ-n-ar-a*
3n-m sg	*huṛ-t-at*	*huṛ-n-at*	*huṛ-n-at-a*
3n-m pl	f *huṛ-t-ik*, n *huṛ-t-iŋ*	f *huṛ-n-ik*, n *huṛe-niŋ*	f *huṛ-n-ik-a*, n *huṛ-n-iŋg-a*

Table 7.11. *Past and non-past finite verbs in Manḍa*

Person	Past	Non-past (future tense)	Non-past (present)
1sg	*kṛak-t-u*	*kṛag-Ø-i*	*kṛag-Ø-i-ba*
1pl (excl)	*kṛak-t-uŋ*	*kṛag-d-uŋ*	*kṛag-d-uŋ-ba*
1pl (incl)	–	–	–
2sg	*kṛak-t-i*	*kṛag-d-i*	*kṛag-d-i-ba*
2pl	*kṛak-t-ir*	*kṛag-d-ir*	*kṛag-d-ir-ba*
3m sg	*kṛak-t-un*	*kṛag-n-un*	*kṛag-n-un-ba*
3m pl	*kṛak-t-ir*	*kṛag-n-ir*	*kṛag-n-ir-ba*
3n-m sg	*kṛag-Ø-i*	*kṛag-Ø-in*	*kṛag-Ø-in-ba*
3n-m pl	*kṛak-t-iŋ*	*kṛag-n-iŋ*	*kṛag-n-iŋ-ba*

The split of the non-past into future and present is an exclusive innovation of Pengo. The future is also used as habitual. The present tense is created out of the future construction by a simple addition of *-a* at the end. There are two morphophonemic changes: the final *-ŋ* of the first person singular, when followed by a vowel, is realized as /ŋg/. Historically, the addition of *-g* to *-n* (whereby *-n* became *-ŋ*) is also a feature exclusively found in Pengo. The final /s/ becomes /h/ intervocalically in the first person plural inclusive.

16. *Manḍa: past and non-past (Burrow 1976)* The personal terminations of Manḍa are different from those of Pengo. The past marker *-t-* has sandhi variants similar to Pengo (Burrow 1976: 48), e.g. *in-* 'to say': *ic-* (< **iR-* < *in-t̲t̲-* with loss of *-n* and change of *-t̲t̲* to voiceless trill *-R*), *vanj-* 'to cook': *vanc-* (< **vanr̲-*:**vant̲t̲-*). The non-past (future) marker is *-n-/-d-*; as in Pengo a present tense is created by the addition of *-ba* at the end of each member of the non-past paradigm; e.g. *kṛag-* 'to buy'. It is not

Table 7.12. *Past and non-past finite verbs in Kolami*

Person	Past	Non-past (present–future)	Non-past (future)	Non-past (durative)
1sg	*sī-t-an*	*sī-at-un*	*sī-dat-un*	*sī-d-un*
1pl (excl)	*sī-t-am*	*sī-at-um*	*sī-dat-um*	*sī-d-um*
1pl (incl)	–	–	–	–
2sg	*sī-t-iv*	*sī-at-iv*	*sī-dat-iv*	*sī-n-iv*
2pl	*sī-t-ir*	*sī-at-ir*	*sī-dat-ir*	*sī-n-ir*
3m sg	*sī-t-en/-end*	*sī-Ø-an*	*sī-Ø-an*	*sī-n-en*
3m pl	*sī-t-er*	*sī-Ø-ar*	*sī-Ø-ar*	*sī-n-er*
3n-m sg	*sī-t-in/-un*	*sī-Ø-a(d)*	*sī-Ø-a(d)*	*sī-Ø-un*
3n-m pl	*sī-t-ev*	*sī-Ø-av*	*sī-Ø-av*	*sī-n-ev*

Table 7.13. *Past and non-past finite verbs in Naiki*

Person	Past	Non-past (present)	Non-past (future)	Non-past (Hortative)
1sg	*sī-t-ān*	*udd-eŋt-ān*	*sī-sāt-un*	
1pl (excl)	*sī-t-ām*	*udd-eŋt-ām*	*sī-sāt-ūm*	*sī-nār*
1pl (incl)				'let us give'
2sg	*sī-t-ī*	*udd-eŋt-ī*	*sī-sāt-ī*	
2pl	*sī-t-īr*	*udd-eŋt-īr*	*sī-sāt-īr*	
3m sg	*sī-t-ēn*	*udd-eŋt-ēn*	*sī-sā-n*	
3m pl	*sī-t-ēr*	*udd-eŋt-ēr*	*sī-sā-r*	
3n-m sg	*sī-t-īn*	*udd-eŋt-īn*	*sī-sā-d*	
3n-m pl	*sī-t-ēv*	*udd-eŋt-ēv*	*sī-sā-v*	

stated if the tense suffix is zero in the first singular and third non-masculine singular in non-past paradigms.

7.6.3 *Central Dravidian*

The suffixes *-d-/-n-* which mark non-past (future) in South Dravidian II have a durative meaning in Kolami. The present tense is marked by *-at-/-Ø-* in Kolami.

17. *Kolami: past and non-past* The past-tense marker is *-t-*, with a variant *-d-* after six stems ending in *-n*, *-r-*, *-l*, *tin-* 'to eat': past *tin-d-*; *-t-* has sandhi variants *-ṭ-/-d-/-ḍ-*. The non-past is split into three subtypes of tenses, present–future (or habitual) with the marker *-at-* (*-a-* + past-tense *-t-*), future *-dat-* which seems to be a combination of non-past *-d-* and past *-t-* with an intervening vowel *-a-*, and finally *-d-/-n-* marking durative. The last named suffixes are markers of non-past in South Dravidian II, e.g. *tin-* 'to eat': *tin-d-*, *sī-* 'to give': past *sī-t-*, present–future *sī-at-*, future *sī-dat-* and durative *sī-d-*.

18. *Naiki/Naikṛi: past and non-past (Thomasiah 1986)* The past-tense marker is *-t-*/*-d-* (*-d* after *n*-final stems, *-t* elsewhere) with sandhi variants *-ṭ-* (after final *-ḍ*, *-ḷ* + *t*, *-r* + *t*), *-ḍ-* after root-final *-n*. The future tense is marked by *-sā-* (in the third person) and *-sāt-* elsewhere. Its origin is obscure. The hortative is said to be formed by a composite suffix *-nār-* (Thomasiah 1986: 128), but it appears to be analysable into non-past *-n-* and the personal suffix *-ār* which includes *-r-*, bearing similarity to the second person plural *-īr*. The infinitive is formed by adding *-eŋ-*; it seems that *-eŋ-t-* consists of the infinitive plus the non-past *-t-*, *-sāt-* and the present tense by *-eŋt-*, e.g. *sī-* 'to give', *udd-* 'to sit'.

Naiki (Chanda) has similar paradigms, e.g. *kak-* 'to do': 1sg *kak-t-an*, 1pl *kak-t-am*, 2sg *kak-t-i*, 2pl *kak-t-ir*, 3m sg *kak-t-en*, 3m pl *kak-t-er*, 3n-m sg *kak-t-un*, 3n-m pl *kak-t-e*. The difference between the two dialects seems to be mainly in the third-person non-masculine suffixes. The present–future is marked by *-t-* in irregular and *-el-*/*-l-* in regular verbs, *an-* 'to be', 1sg *an-t-an* etc. The third non-masculine singular is *an-t-un*/*an-l-en*, and the plural is *an-t-e*/*an-l-e*. Forms with *-ent-* are said to be more common, e.g. *ēnd-* 'to dance': *ēnd-ent-am* 'we dance', *kak-ent-i* 'you (sg) are doing'. The future is marked by *-at-* (with variants *-d-* in the third masculine singular and plural and third non-masculine plural, and *-an-* in the third non-masculine singular), e.g. 1sg *kak-at-un*, 1pl *kak-at-um*, 2sg *kak-at-i*, 2pl *kak-at-ir*, 3m sg *kak-d-an*, 3m pl *kak-d-ar*, 3n-m sg *kak-Ø-an*, 3n-m pl *kak-d-a*. Future *-d-* has a variant *-ḍ-* after stems ending in *-ḍ* (*DVM*: 169–70, 287–8, Suvarchala 1992: 133–5).

19. *Parji: past and non-past* The past tense is marked by *-t-* (*kud-* 'to cut': *kut-t-*) and its sandhi variants *-d-* (*cen-* 'to go': *cen-d-*) and *-ṭ-* (e.g. *iḍ-* 'to put': *iṭṭ-*). In the southern and northwestern dialects *-t-* is preceded by the vowels *-a* and *-o*/*-e* respectively; these vowels are apparently epenthetic. In the northwestern dialects they copy the quality of the following vowel in the personal suffixes. There is evidence to believe that the Proto-Parji epenthetic vowel here was *-u-* (see Krishnamurti 1978b/2001a: 197–8), e.g. *cūṛ-* 'to see', *ver-* 'to come'.

Burrow and Bhattacharya (1953: 52–4) call the first cited paradigm extended past. In the northeastern dialect, the past tense is marked by zero, an unusual phenomenon in the Dravidian languages. It seems possible that there could have been a past marker represented by a vowel (from PD *-*i*), which was lost in sandhi before the vowel of the personal suffixes.

Another set of past suffixes include *-ñ-* (< *-nj-* < *-nd-*) after roots ending in *-r* or *-y*/*-i*, *ver-* 'to come': *ve-ñ-*, *koy-* 'to reap': *ko-ñ-*. A few have *-n-* as past marker, e.g. *aṛ-* 'to weep': *aṛ-n-*. The non-past (present) *-m-* (with dialect variants *-am-*/*-um-*/*-om-*) has already been traced to Proto-Dravidian non-past *-*um* (section 7.4.2.3). The origin of the future marker *-r-* (*-ur*) and its dialect variant *-iy-* is not clear. After *n*-final stems

Table 7.14. *Past and non-past finite verbs in Parji*

Person	Past (south)	Past (northeast)	Non-past: future (northwest)	Non-past: present (northeast)
1sg	*cūṛ-at-en*	*cūṛ-Ø-en*	*cūṛ-r-an*	*ver-m-en*
1pl (excl)				*ver-m-om*
1pl (incl)	*cūṛ-at-om*	*cūṛ-Ø-om*	*cūṛ-r-am*	
2sg	*cūṛ-at-ot*	*cūṛ-Ø-ot*	*cūṛ-r-at*	*ver-m-ot*
2pl	*cūṛ-at-or*	*cūṛ-Ø-or*	*cūṛ-r-ar*	*ver-m-or*
3m sg	*cūṛ-at-ed*	*cūṛ-Ø-ed*	*cūṛ-r-ad*	*ver-m-ed*
3m pl	*cūṛ-at-er*	*cūṛ-Ø-er*	*cūṛ-r-ar*	*ver-m-er*
3n-m sg	*cūṛ-at-a*	*cūṛ-Ø-oto*	*cūṛ-r-a*	*ver-m-o*
3n-m pl	*cūṛ-at-ov*	*cūṛ-Ø-ov*	*cūṛ-r-av*	*ver-m-ov*

Table 7.15. *Past and non-past finite verbs in Ollari*

Person	Past: *sūṛ-* 'to see'	Past: *man-* 'to be'	Non-past: present–future *vanḍ-* 'to cook'	Non-past: present–future; *sī-* 'to give'
1sg	*sūṛ-Ø-en*	*ma-ṭ-on*	*vanḍ-d-an*	*sī-d-an*
1pl (excl)	*sūṛ-Ø-em*	*ma-ṭ-om*	*vanḍ-d-am*	*sī-d-am*
1pl (incl)				
2sg	*sūṛ-Ø-eṭ*	*ma-ṭ-oṭ*	*vanḍ-d-aṭ*	*sī-d-aṭ*
2pl	*sūṛ-Ø-er*	*ma-ṭ-or*	*vanḍ-d-ar*	*sī-d-ar*
3m sg	*sūṛ-Ø-enḍ*	*ma-ṭ-onḍ*	*vanḍ-d-anḍ*	*sī-d-anḍ*
3m pl	*sūṛ-Ø-er*	*ma-ṭ-or*	*vanḍ-d-ar*	*sī-d-ar*
3n-m sg	*sūṛ-Ø-eṭe*	*ma-ṭ-e*	*vanḍ-d-a*	*sī-d-a*
3n-m pl	*sūṛ-Ø-eṭe-v*	*ma-ṭ-ev*	*vanḍ-d-av*	*sī-d-av*

the future marker is *-d-* which can be traced to Proto-Dravidian non-past **-t*. A large class of transitive stems in *-p/-t* 'use the *t-* stem to form the future as well as the past, e.g. from *pay-p-/pay-t-* 'to divide', etc., the future paradigm is 1sg *pay-t-an* etc. The contrast is maintained in *n*-final stems, e.g. *ven-* 'to hear': past *ve-tt-* (< **wen-ṯṯ-*), future *ven-d-* (< **wen-t-*) (Burrow and Bhattacharya 1953: 55).

20. *Ollari: past and non-past* The past tense is indicated by *-Ø-* as in Parji with perhaps the loss of the reflex of an original past suffix derived from PD **i*. Another past allomorph is *-n-*. The inherited past *-t-* occurs in another set of verbs with its sandhi variants *-ṭ-*, *-ḍ-*, e.g. *man* 'to be': *maṭ-* (< **man-ṯṯ-*), *un-* 'to drink': *unḍ-* (< **uṇ-ṭ-*), *kā-* 'to watch': *kā-t-*. The present–future is marked by *-d-* (variants *-y-/-t-*).

Bhattacharya (1957: 30–7) put the 'union vowel' (*o/e*) in the tense slot. However, it would be more appropriate to treat this as part of the personal suffix, because it occurs even when there is a distinctive marker of tense (see columns 2–4 in table 7.15). Ollari

Table 7.16. *Past and non-past finite verbs in Gadaba*

Person	Past: *ēnd-* 'to play'	Past: *in-* 'to say'	Non-past: *kar-* 'to drop'	Non-past: *pōr-p-/pōr-t-* 'to ask'
1sg	*ēnd-Ø-en*	*iṇ-ṭ-on*	*kar-d-an*	*pōr-t-an*
1pl (excl)	*ēnd-Ø-em*	*iṇ-ṭ-om*	*kar-d-am*	*pōr-t-am*
1pl (incl)				
2sg	*ēnd-Ø-eṭ*	*iṇ-ṭ-oṭ*	*kar-d-aṭ*	*pōr-t-aṭ*
2pl	*ēnd-Ø-er*	*iṇ-ṭ-or*	*kar-d-ar*	*pōr-t-ar*
3m sg	*ēnd-Ø-enḍ*	*iṇ-ṭ-oṇḍ*	*kar-d-aṇḍ*	*pōr-t-aṇḍ*
3m pl	*ēnd-Ø-er*	*iṇ-ṭ-or*	*kar-d-ar*	*pōr-t-ar*
3n-m sg	*ēnd-Ø-eṭe*	*iṇ-ṭ-e*	*kar-d-a(d)*	*pōr-t-a(d)*
3n-m pl	*ēnd-Ø-eṭev*	*iṇ-ṭ-ev*	*kar-d-av*	*pōr-t-av*

also has *-n-* as the past marker in some verbs like Parji. The present–future is marked by *-y-* in the case of stems ending in *-n*, e.g. *man-* 'to be' (past: *ma-ṭ-*; non-past *ma-y-*); *-t-* is used as non-past marker of transitive–causative stems in *-p/-t*, *kā-t-an* 'I will watch'. This is homophonous with the past-tense form but the contrast is introduced in the vowel of the personal suffix.

21. *Konḍekor Gadaba: past and non-past* Bhaskararao (1980: 42–8) also treats the vowels *e/o* as past markers in all cases. This analysis puts the inherited past marker *-t-* and its variants as morphophonemic changes of stems, e.g. *in-* 'to say': past *in-ṭ-* in 1sg *in-ṭ-on*, analysed by Bhaskararao as *inṭ-o-n*, thus making the epenthetic vowel the past marker as has been done by Bhattacharya. We reject this analysis. The non-past marker is *-d-* (variants *-y-* and *-t-*). Again, here the author considers *-d-* alternating with *-a-* in different classes.

There is also a progressive (durative) paradigm, which is formed by adding *-id-/-ud-* to a stem. Again we notice that the marker is clearly the non-past with an additional contrast introduced by vocalism, e.g. *āḍ-* 'to weep', 1sg *āḍ-id-an*, etc. But with bases that have a labial vowel or a labial or velar consonant in the stem the preceding vowel is *u*, e.g. *uḍv-* 'to comb': 1sg *uḍv-ud-an*, etc., *kāp-/kāt-* 'to guard': 1sg (?) *kā-kud-an* etc.

7.6.4 North Dravidian

22. *Kuṛux: past and non-past* The past markers are *-k-/-ø-*, *-ck-/-c-*, *-jk-/-j-* morphologically conditioned. Mid vowels alternate with high vowels and /a/ with /ə/ before tense suffixes in some conjugation classes. Stem alternations like *on-/onḍ-* and *kuḍ-/kuṭ-* suggest the incorporation of an inherited past suffix being reduced to a stem alternation. In some classes of verbs the general past is marked by *-k-* and the immediate past by

Table 7.17. *Past and non-past finite verbs in Kuṛux*

Person	Past: *nulx-* 'to swallow'	Past: *baʔ-* 'to say'	Non-past: present *esʔ-* 'to break'	Non-past: future *esʔ-* 'to break'
1sg	*nulx-k-an*	*bā-ck-an*	*es-d-an*	*esʔ-o-n*
1pl (excl)	*nulx-k-am*	*bā-ck-am*	*es-d-am*	*esʔ-o-m*
1pl (incl)	*nulx-k-at*	*bā-ck-at*	*es-d-at*	*esʔ-o-t*
2m sg	*nulx-k-ay*	*bā-ck-ay*	*es-d-ay*	*esʔ-o-y*
2f sg	*nulx-k-i*	*bā-ck-i*	*is-d-i*	–
2pl	*nulx-k-ar*	*bā-ck-ar*	*es-d-ar*	*esʔ-o-r*
3m sg	*nulx-Ø-as*	*bā-c-as*	*es-d-as*	*esʔ-o-s*
3m pl	*nulx-Ø-ar*	*bā-c-ar*	*es-n-ar*	*esʔ-o-r*
3n-m sg/pl	*nulx-Ø-a*	*bā-c-a*	*isʔ-ø-i*	*esʔ-o-Ø*

Table 7.18. *Past and non-past finite verbs in Malto*

Person	Past	Past (Droese) *band-* 'to draw'	Non-past: present	Non-past: future
1sg	*amb-t-an*	*band-ek-en*	*amb-Ø-in*	*amb-Ø-an*
1pl (excl)	*amb-t-am*	*band-ek-em*	*amb-d-am*	*amba-n-am*
1pl (incl)	*amb-t-ey*	*band-ek-et*	*amb-d-ey*	*amb-Ø-ey*
2m sg	*amb-t-e*	*band-ek-e*	*amb-d-e*	*ambe-n-e*
2f sg	*amb-t-i*	*band-ek-i*	*amb-d-i*	*ambe-n-i*
2pl	*amb-t-ar*	*band-ek-er*	*amb-d-ar*	*amba-n-ar*
3m sg	*amb-y-ah*	*band-ø-ah*	*amb-d-ah*	*amba-n-ah*
3m pl	*amb-y-ar*	*band-ek-er*	*amb-n-ar*	*amba-n-ar*
3f n sg	*amb-y-að*	*band-ø-ath*	*amb-Ø-ið*	*ambe-n-ið*

-ac-k- (apparently a combination of two past morphs adapted to an idiosyncratic function). The present tense is marked by *-d-/-n-* and the future by *-o-*.

In the use of present tense, there are different forms when women speak among themselves in 1sg *es-ʔ-ēn*, 1pl (excl) *es-ʔ-ēm*, 2sg *is-d-i*, 2pl *es-d-ay*, and 3hum pl *es-n-ay*. This is an Indo-Aryan feature introduced into native morphology.

23. *Malto: past and non-past (Mahapatra 1979: 163–8; Droese 1884: 50–4)* The past tense is marked by *-t-/-y-* and the non-past by *-d-/-n-/-Ø-*. Droese notes the past markers as *-c-*, *-y-*, *-j-*, *-ḍ-*, *-t-*, *-s-* and *-q-*, e.g. *coy-* 'to rise': *cō-c-*, *kōḍ-* 'to drink': *kōḍ-y-*, *ōn-* 'to drink': *on-ḍ-*, *men-* 'to be': *men-j-*, *bar-* 'to come': *bar-c-*, *qoy-* 'to reap': *qo-s-*, *an̲h-* 'to beat': *a-t-*, *cog-* 'to set loose': *co-q-*. These are followed by *-(e)k-* in the first and second persons. These markers are derivable from PD **-cc-*, **-tt-*, **-i-* and **-kk-*. Mahapatra gives only *-t-* as the past tense marker, e.g. *amb-* 'to leave'. Subrahmanyam (1971: 300–1), following Droese, gives the present-tense markers as *-i-/-in-* and the

future markers as *-e-*/*-en-*. Mahapatra's analysis is better in including the vowel as part of stem alternation rather than that of the tense suffix.

24. *Brahui: past and non-past* The past markers are *-ā-*, *-ē-*, *-k-*/*-g-* and *-is-*/*-s-*/*-ss-* of which the last two are native and inherited from Proto-Dravidian. 'The past stem appears in four tenses, which are essentially periphrastic constructions with the present and past of the verb *anning* "to be"' (Emeneau 1962d: 22), e.g. *tix-* 'to place': 1sg *tix-ā-ṭ*, 1pl *tix-ā-n*, 2sg *tix-ā-s*, 2pl *tix-ā-re*, 3sg *tix-ā-Ø*, 3pl *tix-ā-r*. A sample conjugation of a verb taking a velar past, e.g. *kun-* 'to eat': 1sg *kun-g-uṭ*, 1pl *kun-g-un*, 2sg *kun-g-us*, 2pl *kun-g-ure*, 3sg *kun-g-Ø*, 3pl *kun-g-ur*. Note that gender distinction is lost in Brahui. *-s*/*-us* are added to the past stem to form the pluperfect, e.g. 1sg *tix-ā-s-uṭ*, *kun-g-us-uṭ*; the perfect is formed by *-n*/*-un* in the same way.

7.7 **Non-finite verbs: past-stem based**

Non-finite verbs are called participles in traditional grammars. Syntactically, a non-finite verb is the head of a subordinate clause; morphologically, it lacks the agreement markers in (g)np, which most (but not all) finite verbs have. All non-finite verbs are based on either the past or the non-past stem. They denote different aspects, moods and modes. The past-stem-based non-finite verbs are the gerund, the conditional and concessive forms and the past relative participle. The non-finite verbs based on the non-past are the non-past (durative or continuous, present, future, habitual) participle and the infinitive. Even the finite forms of the imperative and optative 'moods' carry non-past markers. In the following the morphology of each of the non-finite verbs is given in the affirmative and negative inflection and the proto-forms are proposed, where possible.

7.7.1 ***Past or perfective participle***

This is called by different names including 'the gerund', 'past adverb', 'past participle', 'adverbial participle' etc. all with the meaning 'having . . . ed'. It denotes the completion of an action or state before the commencement of the action or state denoted by the main verb, e.g. Mdn Te. *annam*[1] *tin-i*[2] *paḍukoṇ-ṭā-ḍu*[3]/*paḍukon-nā-ḍu*[3] 'having eaten[2] the meal[1], (he) sleeps/(he) slept[3]'. It has a number of uses, which will be discussed in syntax.

7.7.1.1 *South Dravidian I*

1. Tamil: the gerund markers are those that form the past stem + *-u* (the so-called enunciative vowel). A gerund is an independent word and not a bound form, i.e. *-tu*/*-ttu*/*-ntu*, and its sandhi variants, *-ṭu* ~ *-ṟu*/*-ṭṭu* ~ *-ṟṟu*/*-ntu* ~ *-ṇṭu* ~ *-ṉṟu*, etc., e.g. *uḻu-* 'to plough': *uḻu-tu* 'having ploughed', *nīḷ-* 'to be long, to extend': *nī-ṭu* (< **nīḷ* + *tu*) 'having been long (ref. time)', *uṇ-* 'to eat or drink': *uṇ-ṭu* 'having drunk', *tiṉ-* 'to eat':

tiṉ-ṟu 'having eaten'; _pār-_ 'to see': _pār-ttu_ 'having seen', _kēḷ-_ 'to hear': _kē-ṭṭu_ (< _*kēḷ-ttu_) 'having heard', _kal-_ 'to learn': _kaṟṟu_ (< _*kaṯ-ṯu_ < _*kal-tt-_) 'having learnt'; _akaẓ-_ 'to dig': _akaẓ-ntu_ 'having dug', _kol-_ 'to destroy': _koṉ-ṟu_ (< _*kol-nt-_) 'having destroyed', _vekuḷ-_ 'to be enraged': _veku-ṇṭu_ (< _vekuḷ-nt-_) 'having been enraged/roused'. Another set of markers in ancient Tamil is _-i_ which derives from PD _*-i_, and several others, which are peculiar to Classical Tamil, namely _-īi_, _-āa_, _-ūu_, and _-pu_. We are not sure of the phonetics of the extra long vowels or vowel sequences not allowed by Dravidian phonotactics. They are considered simple vowels, lengthened rhetorically, and therefore not phonemic, like 'truly' in English. Meenakshisundaran says that OTa. _-iin-_ can be taken to derive from _-iciṉ-_ with the loss of _-c-_ (_-isin-_ > _-ihin-_ > _-iin-_) (see section 7.3.1.5.1). In Gondi–Koṇḍa the past participial suffix is _*-ci-_ but in Kui–Kuvi it is _*-ca-_. It is not certain if Old Tamil vowel sequences are to be traced to _*-aha-_, _*-uhu-_ and _*-ihi-_ with Ø < _-h-_ < _-c-_ and with identical vowels before and after. In any case, such an ancient phenomenon as double nuclei in Old Tamil writings requires a satisfactory historical and comparative explanation and solution. The examples cited from Ramaswami Aiyar (1938: 759–60) are _toẓ-āa_, beside _toẓu-tu_ (PN) 'having worshipped', _iṭ-ūu_, beside _iṭṭu_ 'having placed' (PN), _tar-īi_, beside _ta-ntu_ 'having given' (KT).

2. Malayāḷam: the perfective participle is formed by adding _-u_ to the past stem, _van-nu_ (< _*va-ndu_) 'having come', _cey-tu_ 'having done', _kaṇ-ṭu_ 'having seen'. This contrasts with the finite verb only in the final vowel, _vannə_ '(subject) came'.

4. Kota: the past stem takes _-ṯ_ in forming the past participle. This appears to be a generalization of the _-ṯ-_ allomorph (which occurs after _-n_ final stems) of the past stem, _va-d-ṯ_ 'having come', _iḏ-ṯ_ 'having said', _tin-kc-ṯ_ 'having fed'.

5. Toda: here also the past participle is not identical with the past stem but is formed by adding a sibilant to the past stem, e.g. _pič_ 'having gone' (past stem _pī-_), _poz_ 'having come' (past stem _pod-_).

6. Kodagu: the past participial marker is _-tï_ /_-itï_ added to the past stem, e.g. _bar-_ 'to come': _ba-nd-itï_ 'having come', _māḍu-_ 'to make': _māḍ-i-tï_.

7. Kannaḍa: like Tamil the past stem ending in _-tu_ or _-i_ is also the perfective participle, e.g. _kēḷ-_ 'to hear': _kēḷ-du_ 'having heard', _bar-_ 'to come': _ba-ndu_ 'having come', _āḍu-_ 'to dance': _āḍ-i_ 'having danced' etc.

8. Tuḷu: the perfective participle is formed by adding _-tï/-dï_, sometimes both, to the verb stem, _kal-_ 'to learn': _kal-tï_ /_kal-tï dï_ 'having learned', _tū-_ 'to see': _tū-dï_ 'having seen', _bar-_ 'to come': _bat-tï_ /_bat-tï dï_ 'having come'.

7.7.1.2 _South Dravidian II_

In this subgroup the perfective participle is not identical to the past-tense stem as in South Dravidian I, but to a sequence of Proto-Dravidian past _*-cc_ and _*-i_, another past morph (section 7.4.1.5). The vowel is _-a_ in three languages. It is likely that _*-cc-i_ was the original marker and some of the languages replaced the vowel by *-a* owing to vowel harmony with the stem vowel.

9. Telugu: the perfective participle is formed by adding *-i*, e.g. *peṭṭu-* 'to put': *peṭṭ-i* 'having put', *winu-* 'to hear': *win-i*, etc. Historically, some verbs originally had *-ci*/*-si* as the past marker leading to *-c*/*-w* or *-s*/*-y* alternation in paradigms between the past and non-past, *pilucu-* 'to call': *pili-ci* 'having called', *pila-w-aN* inf 'to call', *cēyu* 'to do': *cē-si* 'having done': *cēy-aN* inf 'to do'. But these stems are reanalysed with *-i* as past and the alternations were attributed to the stems before past and non-past suffixes (see *TVB*: 162–4).

10. Gondi: in Gondi *-ci*/*-ji*/*-si* are phonologically conditioned allomorphs used as markers of the perfective participle, e.g. *toh-* 'to show': *toh-ci* 'having shown', *son-* 'to go': *son-ji* 'having gone', *sūṛ-* 'to see': *sūṛ-si* 'having seen'. The southern dialects, bordering on Telugu, also have the *-i* variant, e.g. *ūḍ-* 'to see': *ūḍ-i* 'having seen' (southeastern dialect).

11. Koṇḍa: the perfective participle is marked by *-zi*/*-si*/*-i* which occur in complementary environments, e.g. *toR-* 'to tie': *toR-si-* 'having tied', *piṇḍ-* 'to carry': *piṇḍ-zi* 'having carried', *as-* 'to hold': *as-i* 'having held'.

12. Kui: the perfective markers are *-sa*/*-ja*/*-a* again in complementation (partially phonological and partially morphological), *ā-* 'to become': *ā-ja* 'having become', *tin-* 'to eat': *tin-ja* 'having eaten'. *-i* occurs alternatively in a limited number of verbs instead of *-a*, *āj-a*/*āj-i* 'having cooled'.

13. Kuvi has similar morphs with similar distribution, i.e. *-sa*/*-ha*/*-a*, *-ca*/*-ja* (dial), e.g. *hī-* 'to give': *hī-ha* 'having given', *tōs-* 'to show': *tōs-sa* 'having shown', *ve-* 'to beat': *ve-ca* 'having beaten', *ven-* 'to hear': *ven-ja* 'having heard'; *pāy-* 'to beat': *pāy-a* 'having beaten'.

14. Pengo: the gerund markers are *-si*/*-zi*/*-hi*/*-i*; Burrow and Bhattacharya also give *-ci*/*-ji* as variants, but it is not certain if *c*/*s* and *j*/*z* contrast in the same dialect, e.g. *as-* 'to seize': *as-si* 'having seized', *kūk-* 'to call': *kūk-ci*/*-si*/*-hi* 'having called' (apparently in different dialects), *kā -* 'to watch': *kā-hi* 'having watched', *vā-* 'to come': *vā-zi* 'having come', *koy-* 'to cut': *koy-ji* 'having cut'. A variant with the *-a* vowel also occurs rarely, e.g. *ta-* 'to bring', *ta-ha vā-* 'get it and come, bring it'.

7.7.1.3 *Central Dravidian*

15. Kolami: the gerund marker is *-ūt* in the Adilabad dialect and *-t* in Wardha; an alternative mode is by adding *-na* to the past stem in *-t*, *sī-t-na* 'having given'; Adilabad *siyy-ūt* 'having given'.

16. Naiki (Chanda): the perfective participle is formed by adding *-un* to the past stem in *-t*, *pak-t-un* 'having beaten', *tin-d-un* 'having eaten'.

17. Parji: like the languages of South Dravidian II and unlike Kolami–Naiki, the perfective participle is formed by adding *-ci*/*-i*; *-ci* occurs after verb stems with final alternants *-t*/*-p* in past and non-past conjugations, elsewhere *-i* is used, e.g. *ver-i* 'having come', *cen-i* 'having gone', *nilp-*/*nilt-* 'to stand': *nil-ci*, *kāp-*/*kāt-* 'to wait': *kā-ci* 'having waited'.

18. Ollari: just like in Parji, the perfective markers are *-si*/*-zi*/*-i*, e.g. *sūṛ-i* 'having seen', *kar-si* 'having crossed', *uṇ-zi* 'having drunk'.

19. Gadaba: there are three alternants *-ji*/*-ci*/*-i*, *-ji* after *n*-final roots (Class 5, exception *pun-*), *-ci* after roots with final *-p*/*-t* alternation, e.g. *goyalp-* 'to rinse': *goyal-ci*, and *-i* elsewhere, *vār-* 'to come': *vār-i* 'having come'. Bhaskararao (1980: 47–8) calls this 'the incompletive suffix'.

7.7.1.4 *North Dravidian*

There is no perfective marker in these languages, which can be traced to Proto-Dravidian sources. The perfective participle is formed by adding *-ār* in Kuṛux, which Subrahmanyam (1971: 222) thinks to be a borrowing of Hindi *-kar* (*jā-* 'to go': *jākar* 'having gone'), e.g. *ci-* 'to give': *ci-ār* 'having given'. In Malto one of the two markers is definitely native, *-i* and *-le*, *onḍ-i* or *onḍ-le* 'having drunk'. Brahui has no non-finite perfective participle.

7.7.1.5 *Summary*

Since **-ci*/*-cci* has reflexes in South Dravidian II and three languages of Central Dravidian, it can be reconstructed for Proto-Dravidian. It appears to be a sequence of two past morphs **cc* and **-in* with the final consonant lost in the proto-stage itself, since the gerund is a free form occurring before pause syntactically. Alternatively, **-cci* can be taken as an innovation in South Dravidian II, since it is present in all the languages, with the isogloss enclosing areally (through structural diffusion) some languages of Central Dravidian, namely, Parji–Ollari–Gadaba, but not Kolami–Naiki (see feature 26 in table 11.1c). The whole sequence **-cc-in* corresponds with the relic sequence *-icin̲* used in Early Tamil as an extended form of the past finite verbs (see section 7.3.1.5.1).

7.7.2 *Past adjective or the past relative participle*

In most languages the past adjective is reconstructible. It is normally formed by adding an adjectival suffix to the past stem, e.g. Ta. *va-nt-a*, Te. *wacc-in-a* 'the one who/which came'. This participle is the main instrument of the relative clause (in the absence of correlative pronouns). For instance, constructions like 'Sita, who sang a song' or 'the song, which Sita sang' are rendered like 'the-song-sung-Sita', 'Sita-sung-song' by converting the fiinite verb into a relative participle which is placed before the noun head (subject, object, instrument etc.).

7.7.2.1 *Distribution in different subgroups*

South Dravidian I In Old Tamil the adjectival suffix *-a* is added to the past stem, e.g. *iṭu-* 'to place', past stem *iṭ-ṭ-*: *iṭ-ṭ-a* 'that placed', *nōkku* 'to see': *nōkk-iṉ-a*/*-iy-a* 'that seen', *or-īy-a* 'that disengaged'. Malayāḷam follows a similar process, e.g. *cey-* 'to do': *cey-t-a* 'that done', *eẓutu-* 'to write': *eẓut-iy-a* 'that written'. Kota and Toda have innovated independent formatives in relative participles. Koḍagu adds *-ë* to the past stem, e.g. *māḍu-* 'to make': *māḍ-in-ë*/*-iy-ë* 'that made', *bar-* 'to come': *ba-nd-ë* 'the one who/which came'. Kannaḍa forms the relative participle by the addition of *-a* to the past stem, e.g. *bar-* 'to come': *ba-nd-a* 'the one who/which came', *kēḷ-* 'to hear': *kēḷ-d-a* 'that heard', *māḍu-* 'to make': *māḍ-id-a* 'that made'. Tuḷu forms the past relative participle by adding *-i*/*-ī* or *-ina*/ *-na* in different social and regional dialects, e.g. *bar-* 'to come': *ba-tt-i*/*ba-tt-ī*/*bat-na* (South and North Brahmin and South Common), *batt-in-a* (North Common), *ā-* 'to become' *āy-i*/*ā-n-a* (South Brahmin and Common), *ā-t-ī* (North Brahmin and Common) (Kekunnaya 1994: 111–12). Tuḷu makes a distinction between the distant past (inherited past) and the immediate past (perfect tense). There are adjectives formed on both past and perfect stems. The perfective is innovated in Tuḷu, e.g. *tin-* 'to eat': *tin-d-i* 'the one who ate/that which is/was eaten', *tin-t-i* 'that had (been) eaten', *pō-* 'to go': *pō-y-i* 'that went', *pō-t-i* 'that had gone', *kal-* 'to learn': *kal-t-i* 'that learnt', *kal-tïd-i* 'that had learnt'.

South Dravidian II Telugu forms the past relative participle by the addition of *-in-a*, which consists of the past *-in-* and the adjectival *-a*, *ceppu* 'to say': *cepp-in-a* 'the one who told/that told'. In some disyllabic verbs, the final consonant is doubled in the past adjective as a free variant of the *-ina* form, *ceḍu-* 'to perish': *ceḍ-ina*/*ceḍḍ-a* 'that perished', *tagu-* 'to fit': *tag-ina*/*tagg-a* 'that which fitted'. In Gondi, the past adjective is formed by the addition of *-ā*/*-a* to the past stem, e.g. *ki-* 'to do': *ki-t-ā* 'done', *uḍ-t-a* 'that ploughed' (Koya dialect), *kās-* 'to boil': *kās-t-a ēr* 'boiled water'. Koṇḍa–Kui–Kuvi–Pengo–Manḍa add *-i* to the past stem, e.g. Koṇḍa *sā-* 'to die': *sā-t-i* 'the dead . . . ', *gūr-* 'to sleep': *gūr-it-i* 'the one that slept'; Kui *pū-* 'to blossom': *pū-t-i* 'the blossomed', *tin-* 'to eat', past stem *tis-*: *tis-i* 'the one that ate/was eaten'; Kuvi *pāy-* 'to beat': *pāy-it-i* 'that beat/was beaten'; Pe. *niŋ-* 'to rise': *niŋ-t-i* 'that rose', *ēnd-* 'to dance': *ēnd-t-i* 'that danced'; Manḍa *hen-ti*[1] *āk-iŋ*[2] 'leaves[2] that changed colour[1]'.

Central Dravidian Kolami and Naiki add *-a* to the past stem in forming the relative participle, e.g. Kol. *ār-* 'to dry': *ār-t-a* 'that dried', *tin-* 'to eat': *tin-d-a* 'the one that ate/was eaten'; Naiki *arup-* 'to cut': *arup-t-a* 'the one cut'. In Parji, Ollari and Gadaba, there do not seem to be relative participles formed on the past stem. There are, however, forms based on non-past stems. In Gadaba the non-past relative participle is formed by adding *-dan* to the verb stem, e.g. *ūḍ-* 'to plough': *ūḍ-dan* 'that which is ploughed'. There is another relative participle suffix, *-te* for human and *-o* for non-human. It appears that in one allomorph *-t* is a past marker, e.g. *aḍg-* 'to dig': *aḍig-t-enḍ* 'the man who dug', *aḍg-o-nḍ-i* 'the woman who dug'.

North Dravidian In Kuṛux, the past adjective is formed by adding *-ā* to the the past stem, *kundr-* 'to be born': *kundr-k-ā* 'that born', *un-* 'to drink': *unkh-k-ā* 'that drank/drunk'. There is nothing comparable in Brahui. Malto forms the participle by adding *-pe* of obscure origin, e.g. *dary-* 'to draw': *dary-pe* 'that drawn'.

Summary The suffix *-a* is found in South Dravidian I, Telugu and Gondi of South Dravidian II, Kolami and Naiki of Central Dravidian and Kuṛux of North Dravidian. The suffix *-i* is found in Tuḷu of South Dravidian I and in a subgroup of South Dravidian II, i.e. Koṇḍa–Kui–Kuvi–Pengo–Manḍa. It appears that both **a* and **i* can be reconstructed for Proto-Dravidian as adjectival markers, also found more extensively as genitive suffixes in nominal inflection.

7.7.3 ***Conditional and concessive forms***

The conditional forms meaning 'if (subject) does/did' and the concessive forms meaning 'even if (subject) does/did' are rendered as non-finite verbs in most Dravidian languages. Such constructions are based on the past stem in some languages; in others they are based on non-past stems or formed with suffixes added to the basic stem. The meaning does not necessarily denote the time of action. In any case, these constructions are not traceable to Proto-Dravidian.

South Dravidian I Old Tamil adds *-iṉ* to the bare stem in the case of weak verbs and to the non-past stem in *-kk/-pp* in the case of strong verbs; the concessive is formed by adding the conjunctive particle *-um* to the conditional form, e.g. *kāṇ-iṉ* 'if one sees', *nī-kk-iṉ/nī-pp-iṉ* 'if one removes', *iru-pp-iṉ* 'if one stays'; concessive *tōṉṟu-* 'to see': *tōṉṟ-iṉ-um* 'even if one sees . . . ' In Later Tamil the conditional form is based on the past stem by the addition of *-āl/-ēl*, e.g. *kāṇ-* 'to see': *kaṇ-ṭ-āl* 'if one saw', *uṇ-* 'to eat': *uṇ-ṭ-ēl* 'if one ate'. The concessive is formed by adding *-um* to the conditional, e.g. *kaṇ-ṭ-āl-um* 'even if one saw'. In Old Malayāḷam *-il/-kil* are added in forming the conditional; in Modern Malayāḷam just as in Tamil the conditional is formed by adding *-āl* to the past stem, e.g. OMa. *var-il/varu-kil* 'if one comes', Mdn Ma. *cey-t-āl* 'if one did'. The concessive is formed by adding *-um* to the conditional form. Kota adds *-mēl* to the past stem in forming the conditional *va-d-mēl* 'if one came'. In Koḍagu, *ēngi* is added to the past stem to form the conditional, e.g. *ba-nd-ēngi* 'if one came'. Subrahmanyam (1971: 131) considers this morpheme as a complex consisting of the verb *en-* 'to say' plus the conditional morph *-kil* found also in Malayāḷam. Koḍagu loses the final *-l*, but the length of the vowel is unexplained. Kannaḍa has a totally different conditional marker *-are*, concessive marker *ar-ū*. Old Kannaḍa has *-oḍe* instead, added to the past stem and *-are* in Modern Kannaḍa, e.g. *bare-* 'to write': *bare-d-are* 'if one wrote', *bare-d-arū* 'even if one wrote', *pēḷ-* 'to speak': *pēḷ-d-oḍe* 'if one spoke'. Tuḷu adds *-ḍa* to finite verbs in forming the conditional, e.g. *kal-* 'to learn': *kal-t-e* 'he learnt', *kal-t-e-ḍa* 'if he learnt'.

South Dravidian II In Old (Literary) Telugu the conditional was formed by adding *-in-an*, which was homophonous with the concessive. It appears that *-in* was the original conditional suffix, which compares well with South Dravidian I *-in*; the conjunctive *-an* was added to it to derive a concessive meaning originally, but it also came to be interpreted as a conditional with bleaching of the meaning of the suffix *-an*. In Modern Telugu the concessive is *-inā*, which can be derived from older *-in-an* by the loss of *-n* and lengthening of the preceding vowel. In Middle Telugu inscriptions, we have *in-ānu* as an intermediate stage of the concessive form, before the loss of final *-nu*, which reflects a conflict between pronunciation and writing. In Early Modern Telugu the conditional is represented by *-itē/-tē/-ṭē* which is totally unrelated to *-in* or *-inan*. It is said that this has resulted from a wrong analysis of verbs in the second singular followed by *-ēni* 'if' a conditional particle, e.g. *cēsiti(wi)* + *ēni* 'if you had done' → *cēsitēni* → *cēsitē(n)*. With *n*-final roots the suffix is *-ṭē*, e.g. *an-* 'to say': *aṇ-ṭē(ni)* 'if you said'. The meaning got generalized to all subjects. In Gondi, the conditional suffix is *-ēke/-eke* added to the past or non-past stem, e.g. *vā-* 'to come': *vā-t-ēke* 'if one came'. The past conditional is used mainly in forming the subjunctive mood (contrafactual condition, e.g. 'if you came, I would have given you' etc.). The concessive is expressed by the addition of *-tēr-/gir*, *vā-t-ēk(e)tēr* 'if one came'. Koṇḍa adds *-iŋa* to the past stem to form the conditional, e.g. *vā-* 'to come': *vā-t-iŋa* 'if one came'; the concessive is formed by the addition of a conjunctive suffix *-ba*, *vā-t-iŋa ba* 'even if one came'. The suffix *-iŋa* probably has an underlying *-in* followed by *-ga*, although we cannot attribute any meaning to the latter element (section 7.6.2 (15)). Kui adds *-eka* to the past stem to form the conditional, e.g. *tāk-* 'to walk': *tāk-it-eka* 'if (one) walked/walks'; the emphatic particle *-ve* is added to the conditional to form the concessive, e.g. *sah-* 'to beat': *sah-t-eka-ve* 'even if (one) beat/beats'. In Kuvi, the conditional marker is *-ihi* added to the past stem, e.g. *tōs-* 'to show': *tōs-t-ihe* 'If (I) beat (him)'. In Pengo the conditional marker is *-is* added to the past stem, e.g. *vā-* 'to come': *vā-t-is* 'if (one) comes'. Note that Pengo *-is* and Kuvi *-ihi* are cognate.

Central Dravidian In Kolami (Wardha dialect) the conditional marker is *-te* added to the future finite form. This is clearly a borrowing from Telugu, but used differently. In the Adilabad dialect the marker is *-tē-*, again reminiscent of borrowing from Modern Telugu (*-tē-* see above), e.g. *kak-* 'to do': *kak-tē* 'if (one) does/did'. Naiki adds *-te* to the past or future finite verb, e.g. *si-* 'to give': *si-t-an* 'I gave', *si-t-an-te* 'if/when I gave'. This is also a clear case of borrowing from Telugu, but it is interesting that a bound form is borrowed and added innovatively to a free form. Parji has a different process. It adds (a) *-oḍ* or *-oḍ-el*, e.g. *tōnd-* 'to appear': *ili*[1] *tōnd-oḍ*[2] 'if[2] a bear[1] appears[2]'; or (b) *-ek*, e.g. *var-* 'to come': *vāni*[1] *var-ek*[2] 'if[2] rain[1] comes[2]'; or (c) *-em*, e.g. *men-* 'to be': *netta*[1] *pāp*[2] *men-em*[3] 'when[3] the dog[1] is[3] a baby[2] . . . ' Ollari adds *-koṛ-en/-goṛ-en* to the base, e.g. *sī-* 'to give': *sī koṛ-en* 'if one gives', *un-* 'to drink': *un-goṛ-en* 'if one drinks'. I wonder if the conditional morph *-en* is added to the reflexive *-koṛ* here. Gadaba has two allomorphs *-oṭ/-goṭ* which are added to the basic stem to form the conditional, e.g. *anuyp-/anuyk-* 'to kill': *anuyk-oṭ* 'if one kills', *tin-* 'to eat': *tin-goṭ* 'if one eats'.

In North Dravidian there are no non-finite verbs used in conditional and concessive meanings.

Summary It is not possible to reconstruct a marker for conditional in Proto-Dravidian. The distribution of relevant markers is as follows:

(1) *-iṉ*: Old Tamil (added to basic or the non-past stem)
(2) *-il*: Old Tamil, Malayāḷam (basic stem or non-past)
(3) *-āl*: Middle and Modern Tamil, Malayāḷam (added to the past stem)
(4) *-ēl*: Middle and Modern Tamil (added to the past stem)
(5) *-ēn-kil*: Koḍagu (added to the past stem)
(6) *-oḍe*: Old Kannaḍa (added to the past stem)
(7) *-are*: Modern Kannaḍa (added to the past stem)
(8) *-ḍa*: Tuḷu (added to the past stem)
(9) *-ēn(i)*: Old Telugu (added to the past stem or any free form including a finite verb); *-tē*: Modern Telugu by metanalysis of the second singular finite verb ending in *-ti* (*wi*) + *ē*(*ni*) → *tē*(*n*); *-ēni*(*n*) 'if' is a clitic which can be added to any free form in a sentence. But *-tē* ~ *-ṭē/-itē* is a grammaticalized bound form which is added to the stem variant in the past tense, *cūc-* 'to see': *cūs-tē* 'if one sees'; Kolami–Naikṛi have borrowed the suffix *-tē* from Middle Telugu. Note the construction in the other Central Dravidian languages is different.

(10) *-is*/*-ih*: Pengo–Kuvi
(11) *-ēk*/*-ek*: Gondi, Kui, also Parji
(12) *-iŋa*: Koṇḍa
(13) *-em*: Parji
(14) *-kor̤-en*: Ollari
(15) *-oṭ*/*-goṭ*: Gadaba

It may be possible to reconstruct *-in*/*-il* for Pre-Tamil on the basis of (1), (2); (12), (13) and the second morph of (14) seem to be distantly derived from or related to **-in* although the vowel *-e* in (13) and (14) and the velar element in (12) are bothersome. Again (3)–(5) and (9) reconstruct to **-ēl*/*-ēn*; *-em*/*-en* of (13) and (14) are perhaps also related to this set. OTe. *-ēn-* appears to be the conditional form of an archaic stem *-ēn* (< **ay-m-* 'to be') with the the suffix **-in*. In any case the variety and diversity of forms indicate its origin after the split of different branches of Proto-Dravidian.

7.8 Non-finite verbs: non-past-stem based

The non-past stem is the base of several non-finite verbs like the non-past participle (durative, present, present–future, future–habitual, etc. contrasting with the past participle), non-past relative participle (verbal adjective) and the infinitive. The imperative verb also has a non-past stem incorporation because all imperatives intrinsically refer to non-past time.

7.8.1 *South Dravidian I*

The literary dialect of Tamil has a non-finite verb with *-pu* as a suffix, e.g. *tāẓ-* 'to fall': *tāẓ-pu* 'on falling' (when something falls); *iṭu-* 'to place': *iṭu-pu* 'on placing something'. Note that Koṇḍa of South Dravidian II has exactly the same construction and, therefore, **-pu* is reconstructable for Proto-South Dravidian. The consonant *-p* must be a reflex of the non-past **-pp*. The present relative participle is formed by adding *-a* to the present tense stem in *-kiṟ-*/*-kinṟ-* 'the one who/which is doing'/' . . . is done', e.g. *pār-* 'to see': *pār-kkiṟ-a*/*pār-kkinṟ-a* 'that which sees/is seen'. Another non-past relative participle is formed by adding the aorist marker *-um*/*-kk-um*, e.g. *eẓu-* 'to rise': *eẓ-um* 'the one who/which rises/will rise', *pār-* 'to see': *pār-kk-um* 'that which sees/will see'.

In Malayāḷam the future adjective is formed by adding *-um*, e.g. *aṟi-* 'to know': *aṟi-y-um* 'one who/which knows'.

In Kota, the present participle is formed by adding *-r* to the past stem in *-t* (S_2; see Emeneau 1994: 87–92), *nō-* 'to see': *nō-č-r* 'seeing', *org-* 'to sleep': *org-y-r* 'sleeping'. (*-r*- seems to correspond to *-kiṟ-* of Tamil.) The non-past adjective is also unique, formed by adding *-vd*/*-bd*, e.g. *tin-* 'to eat': *tin-bd* 'that is/will be eaten'. In Toda, the non-past adjective is formed by adding *-θ* to the verb stem, e.g. *naṛ-* 'to walk': *naṛ-θ* 'that which walks'.

In Koḍagu, the non-past adjective is formed by adding *-v-ë/-pp-ë* to the basic verb stem. Apparently, the consonantal element is the non-past-tense marker followed by an adjectival suffix, *māḍu-* 'to make': *māḍu-v-ë* 'that which does', *ba-* 'to come': *ba-pp-ë* 'that which comes'.

The Kannaḍa present participle is formed by adding the present-tense marker, i.e. *-ut(t)um*, e.g. *aḷu-* 'to weep': *aḷ-utum* 'weeping', *bar-* 'to come': *bar-uttum* 'coming'. The non-past adjective is formed by adding the adjectival suffix *-a* to the non-past stem, e.g. *āḷ-* 'to rule': *āḷ-v-a* 'that rules/will rule', *en-* 'to say': *en-ba* 'that which says/will say'.

In Tuḷu, the present participle marker is *-ontu/-ondu* (different social dialects) added to the past verb stem of two classes of verbs and to the bare stem in two other classes, e.g. *kal-* 'to learn': *kal-t-ontu/-ondu* 'learning', *tū-* 'to see': *tūv-ontu/-ondu* 'seeing'. The non-past adjective is formed by adding an adjective marker *-i* to the present–future stem of the verb, *kal-p-i/kal-pub-i* 'that which learns/will learn'. Subrahmanyam (1971: 261) thinks that *-ontu* is the perfective participle of the reflexive verb, which is added to the past stem of a basic verb to form the 'present adverb'. This process is found also in Tamil and Malayāḷam.

7.8.2 ***South Dravidian II***

The Old Telugu durative participle is formed by adding *-cun*, which has no corresponding form in any other language. There is a phonological possibility that it could be related to *-cin* (*-c* + *-in*) found in Classical Tamil; alternatively OTe. *-cu* could be the source of Ka. *-t(t)u*, the present participial marker. One of the variants of the non-past adjectives is formed by the marker *-u(n)*, e.g. *win-* 'to hear': *win-u(n)* *ata*^{n}*ḍu* 'the man who listens'. This is reconstructible to PD **-um/-un*. There is another marker *-uḍu(n)/-wuḍu(n)* in Old Telugu which meant 'after, on... Ving etc.', e.g. *an-* 'to say': *an-uḍu(n)* 'as soon as one says/has said'. The other markers of relative adjectives in non-past are *-eḍi/-eḍu* (> Mdn Te. *-ē*), e.g. *cēyu-/cēs-* 'to do': *cēs-edi/-eḍu* 'the one who does': Mdn Te. *cēs-ē* id.

The Gondi durative participle is formed by adding *-cēr/-jēr/-sēr* which occur in complementation, e.g. *toh-* 'to show': *toh-cēr* 'showing', *un-* 'to drink': *un-jēr* 'drinking', *vār-* 'to sing': *vār-sēr* 'singing'. The non-past adjective is formed by adding *-vāl* to the verb stem, *veh-* 'to tell': *veh-vāl māynāl* 'the person that tells'. This suffix is considered a nominal formative. The non-past conditional is formed on the non-past stem by adding the conditional marker *-ēkē*, e.g. *aṭ-* 'to cook': *aṭ-n-ēkē* 'if one cooks/while cooking'.

In Koṇḍa *-pu* marks the simultaneative, e.g. *koRku*^{1} *ker-pu*^{2} 'when/as^{2} the cocks^{1} crow^{2}'; it has an alternant *-bu* after stems ending in a nasal, e.g. *man-* 'to be': *man-bu* 'while staying'. The durative aspect in the finite verb is formed by adding the non-past *-n* to the perfective marker *-si-/-zi-*, e.g. *ki-* 'to do': *ki-zin-a* 'I am/was doing'. The durative conditional is formed by adding *-iŋ* to the durative stem in *-zin-/-sin-*, e.g. *ki-zin-iŋ* 'as one is/was doing'. The non-past adjective marker is *-i* added to the non-past stem in *-n*, e.g. *gūr-* 'to sleep': *gūr-n-i* 'that which sleeps'; the non-past marker is dropped after stems ending in *-n* or *-ṇ*, *uṇ-Ø-i* 'that which eats/will eat'.

In Kui the present (durative) participle is formed by adding *-ki/-pi* ~ *-bi/-ji* occurring in complementation. These are related to Proto-Dravidian non-past **-kk/ *-pp* and the perfective marker **-(c)ci*, e.g. *aj-* 'to fear': *as-ki* 'fearing', *ār-* 'to call': *ār-pi* 'calling', *tin-* 'to eat': *tin-ji* 'eating', *in-* 'to say': *in-ji* 'saying'. The non-past adjective is formed by adding the adjectival suffix *-i* to the non-past base in *-in/-n*, e.g. *ēnd-* 'to dance': *ēnd-in-i* 'that which dances/will dance', *kō-* 'to reap': *kō-ni* 'that which reaps/will reap'.

Kuvi present (durative) participle is formed by the addition of *-ci/-ji/-si/-hi* corresponding to the perfective participle of Gondi and Koṇḍa, e.g. *hī-* 'to give': *hī-hi* 'giving', *ve-* 'to beat': *vec-ci* 'beating', *ven-* 'to listen': *ven-ji* 'listening'. The non-past adjective is formed by adding *-i* to the non-past stem in *-in/-n*, e.g. *pāy-* 'to beat': *pāy-in-i* 'that which beats/will beat'. The non-past adjective in Pengo is formed by adding the adjectival suffix *-i* to the non-past stem in *-n*, e.g. *koṛ-* 'to buy': *koṛ-n-i* 'one who buys/will buy'. This is entirely similar to the form in Koṇḍa.

7.8.3 *Central Dravidian*

In Kolami the present participle is formed by adding *-san*, e.g. *ōl* 'to see': *ōl-san* 'eating'; the future participle is formed by adding *-ak*, *ōl-ak* 'about to see'; the durative adjective is formed by adding *-a*, e.g. *tin-* 'to eat': *tin-a* 'the one(s) who is/are eating'; the future adjective is formed by adding *-eka*, *var-* 'to come': *var-eka* 'that which comes/will come'. Predicative nouns can be formed by adding *-r-* followed by personal suffixes, e.g. *kalk-eka-r-an* 'I am the man who does' etc. Naiki (Chanda) forms the non-past participle by adding *-eka*, e.g. *ser-* 'to go': *ser-eka* 'going'.

In Parji the non-past participle is formed by adding *-oḍ/-ek/-em* with slightly different meanings, e.g. *men-* 'to live': *men-oḍ* 'while living/if (one) lives', *ver-* 'to come': *ver-ek* 'on coming home', *men-em* 'when (one) is living'. The habitual adjective is formed by adding the adjectival suffix *-an* to the future stem in *-r-/-d-/-t-/-iy-*, e.g. *ven-* 'to hear': *ven-d-an* 'one that hears', *cok-* 'to climb': *cok-r-an* 'the one that climbs', *vīt-* 'to sow': *vīt-iy-an* 'the one that sows'. Predicative nouns are formed by adding the third-personal suffixes (not the first and second) to these, e.g. *ci-* 'to give': *ci-r-an-ed* 'the man who gives'.

Ollari non-past participle is formed by adding *-iŋ/-uŋ*, e.g. *un-* 'to drink': *un-uŋ* 'while drinking', *val-* 'to fly': *val-iŋ* 'while flying'. The habitual adjective is formed by adding the adjectival suffix *-an* to a non-past (habitual) stem, e.g. *sī-* 'to give': *sī-d-an* 'one who gives/will give', *pun-* 'to know': *pu-y-an* 'one who knows/will know'.

7.8.4 *North Dravidian*

In Kuṛux the present participle is formed by adding *-nū*/*-num* to the verb stem, e.g. *es-* 'to break': *es-nū* 'breaking', *es-nū*/*es-num* 'breaking'; a particle *-ti*(*m*) may be added optionally. Another construction meaning 'on V-ing' is formed by adding *-ā*, followed by *-xane*(*m*), e.g. *esʔ-ā xane*(*m*) 'on breaking, in the act of breaking'. Another participle meaning 'till, up to' is formed by adding *-tʔā*/*-tʔaa*, e.g. *bij-* 'to dawn': *bij-tʔā*/*-tʔaa* 'till day-break'. The non-past adjective is formed by adding *-ū*/*-ō*, e.g. *es-* 'to break': *is-ū* 'that breaks/will break'; before *biri* 'time', it is *-ō*, e.g. *ōn-* 'to eat': *ōn-ō biri* 'eating time'. In Malto the present participial suffix is *-e* ~ *-i*/*-ne*, *-le* whose distribution is not clear, e.g. *band-* 'to draw': *band-ne*/*-le*/*-e*/*-i* 'drawing'. The suffix *-no* is added to the verb stem to mean 'while V-ing', e.g. *agr-* 'to mount': *agr-no* 'while mounting'. The present adjective is formed by adding *-u*, e.g. *baj-* 'to strike': *baj-u* 'that which strikes'.

In Brahui, the present participle formative is -(*i*)*sa*, e.g. *bis-* 'to bake': *bis-isa* 'baking', *kar-* 'to do': *kar-isa* 'doing'. The present adjective is formed by adding *-ok*, e.g. *bin-* 'to hear': *bin-ok* 'one who hears', *pār-* 'to say': *pār-ok* 'one who says'.

7.8.5 *Summary*

There is great diversity in the formation of non-past non-finite verbs, but one can see the underlying non-past stem (with **-pp-* ~ *-w-*/**-kk*/**-t* ~ [-d- ~ -r-]), which is reconstructable for most of the languages. It appears that there is a phonological thread connecting OTa. *-ciṉ-*, Te. *-cun*, Koṇḍa *-c-in-* and Kolami *-san*. Again the adjectival suffixes *-ūn*/*-ōn* of Kuṛux derive from PD **-um*, the aorist marker (section 7.4.2.3). It appears that different subgroups and languages have innovated constructions based mostly on the native stock of morphs marking the non-past. The verbal adjective is formed by adding to the tensed stem the adjectival suffix **-a*/**-i* in different subgroups.

7.9 Non-finite verbs: the infinitive[13]

The infinitive occupies a special status among the non-finite verbs, since it is reconstructable for Proto-Dravidian as **-ǎn*. It has many syntactic functions, most of which are shared irrespective of its morphological makeup. It is clearly built on the non-past stem formed with **-pp*/ **-kk* at least in some classes of verbs. Anne David (1999: 31) gives the following as the functions of the Dravidian infinitive:

> (1) as complements to verbs that convey a desiderative, modal, aspectual or manipulative sense; (2) as complements to NPs; (3) in adverbial clauses

[13] Data for the uses of the infinitive for many of the Dravidian languages is taken from Anne David's excellent unpublished PhD dissertation 'A Comparative Study of Dravidian Infinitives' (Department of Linguistics, Chicago University 1999). I am indebted to her for sending me a complimentary copy of the dissertation. To distinguish the infinitive meaning from the root meaning, glosses for the roots are given without 'to' in the following examples.

of purpose, causation or simultaneity; (4) as finite verbs with a modal sense of imperative, optative or obligative; and (5) in periphrastic constructions to convey negation or future tense . . . These are all uses that occur in at least three or four subgroups; within the individual languages not all of them may be found, and there are other uses not mentioned here that are peculiar to a very few or even to only one language.

7.9.1 *South Dravidian I*

In Old Tamil the infinitive is formed by adding *-a* to the weak verbs or *-pp-a*/*-kk-a* to the strong verbs; *-pp-* is more common than *-kk-*. Apparently the consonantal element is a marker of the non-past tense, e.g. *cey-* 'do': *ceyy-a* 'to do', *kā-* 'protect': *kā-pp-a*/*kā-kk-a* 'to protect'. The suffixes *-pāṉ*/*-vāṉ* occur as infinitive markers in later Caṅkam classics, *kāṇ-* 'see': *kāṇ-pāṉ* 'to see', *koḷ-* 'take': *koḷ-vāṉ* 'to take'. Here *-āṉ* is the infinitive marker with *-p*/*-v* signalling non-past. Derived nouns in *-al* are sometimes used in the same way as infinitives but as purposive nominals, e.g. *cey-* 'to do': *cey-aṟ-ku* 'for doing'. In Modern Tamil the infinitive suffixes *-a*/*-kk-a* occur in complementary verb classes, e.g. *var-* 'come': *var-a vēṇṭum* '(one) must come', *paṭi-* 'to read': *paṭikk-a ārampi-tt-ān* 'he started to read'. Here, *-kk* is historically the non-past marker, which appears only in the strong verb class. But the infinitive co-occurs with the main verb in any tense and is synchronically treated as neutral in tense.

In Old Malayāḷam the infinitive is formed by adding *-ān* to the non-past stem in *-m*/*-pp*/*-uv-*/*-v* corresponding to Old Tamil *-pāṉ*/*-vāṉ*, e.g. *kāṇ-m-ān* 'to see', *koṭu-pp-ān* 'to give', *cey-v-ān* 'to do'. Modern Malayāḷam *-ān* as an infinitive suffix preceded by *-kk* in the case of strong verbs, e.g. *avan*[1] *var-ān*[2] *paṟaññu*[3] 'he[1] was asked[2] to come[3]', *ñān*[1] *uṇṇ-ān*[2] *vannu*[3] 'I[1] came[3] to eat[2]' (David 1999: 64–5).

Iruḷa infinitive markers are *-a*/*-ka*/*-ga* in complementary verb classes, *pō-* 'go': *pō-ga* 'to go', *eḍu-* 'take': *eḍu-kka* 'to take'. Toda has no infinitive by the addition of a derivative of **-an*/*-ān*. Subrahmanyam (1971: 426) says that Kota infinitives are formed by *-l* or *-lk*; *-l* is a marker of a verbal noun and *-k* the dative suffix 'for verb-ing', e.g. *nōṛ-* 'to see': *nōṛ-lk ilā* '(subject) will not see'.

Old Kannaḍa infinitive in *-al* is clearly a verbal noun which has an overlapping usage with the true infinitive in *-a*, e.g. *nuḍi-al-ke*[1] *bandam*[2] 'he came[2] to speak/for speaking[1]'. Compare this with *upadravam*[1] *māḍ-a*[2] *bēḍa*[3] 'do not[3] make[2] trouble[1]'.

7.9.2 *South Dravidian II*

In Old as well as Modern Telugu, the infinitive suffix is *-an*, added to the basic verb stem, the main meaning carrier; it can also occur as a finite verb without any (g)np marker in the optative mood; as a non-finite verb, it can be followed either by modal auxiliaries or by voice modifiers (see section 7.15.2); or, it can function as a verbal noun, particularly in Old Telugu as a complement to the finite verb, before the latter got converted to a grammaticalized modal auxiliary. Some of these will be discussed in chapter 9; e.g. (inscr) *ēḷ-* 'to rule': *Dhanañjayuṇḍu*[1] *rēnāṇḍu*[2] *ēḷ-an*[3] 'as[3] Dhananjaya[1] ruled over[3] Rēnāṇḍu[2]', *nī*[1] *vāncchа*[2] *pāḍugānu*[3] 'may[3] your[1] desire[2] perish[3]!'; *kāc* 'to protect'; *kāv-an-gala* adj [protect-inf-able-adj] 'one who can protect', *cēyu-* 'to do': *cēy-an un-n-a* [do-inf-be-past-adj] 'one about to do', *cēy-a(n)-bōwu* [do-inf-go-adj] 'that about to do', *cēy-a(n)waccu* [do-inf-come-Ø (g)np] 'one may do', *cēy-a(n) walayu* [do-inf-need-Ø(g)np] 'one needs to do'; in these the infinitive is a complement to the main verb expressed by *walayu*, *waccu*, etc. Later, these elements have become the auxiliaries, meaning 'one must go', 'one may do', etc. These usages continue into Modern Telugu as modal auxiliaries (see Krishnamurti and Gwynn 1985: 212ff.). *-kān*, the infinitive of *aw-* 'to be, become', can be optionally added to the infinitive in *-an*, e.g. *cēy-an* 'to do': *cēy-a(n)-gān* 'as one does/did'. As a nominal the *-an* form occurred in Old Telugu in such constructions as *cēy-an*[1] *ārambhincenu*[2] 'he/she started[2] doing[1] (it)'. In Modern Telugu, here the infinitive is replaced by an action nominal in *-aṭam/-aḍam*, *ceyy-aḍam ārambhinc-ǣ-ḍu* [do-nominal suff. begin-past-he] 'he started doing (it)'.

The Gondi infinitive marker is *-ānā* taken from Indo-Aryan. The infinitive is used as an imperative in the obligative mode, as in Hindi, e.g. *kharal*[1] *wadk-ānā*[2] '(one) must speak[2] truth[1]'. In the Adilabad dialect *-ā* is the infinitive formative, e.g.

tind-ā[1]	*par-ō-n*[2]
[eat-inf	be-able-neg-1sg]
'I cannot[2] eat[1]'	

In the Koya dialect the infinitive is *-a* as in Telugu, *ūḍ-* 'see': *ūḍ-a* 'to see'; the Abhuj Maṛia dialect has *-ā* or *-ī* in complementary environments. It appears that these do not contrast with their corresponding short vowels (David 1999: 117), e.g. *kīy-* 'do': *kīy-ā* 'to do', *targ-* 'climb': *targ-ī* 'to climb'. There are also verbs with *-ānā* (borrowed from Hindi) functioning both verbally and nominally, e.g.

nāk	*hand-ānā*	*āyintā*
we (dat)	go-noml	become
'we have to go'		

In Kui the infinitive is formed adding *-a* to a non-past stem ending in *-Ø/-p/-b/-v*, which Winfield calls semi-formatives (David 1999: 120), e.g. *iṭ-a* 'to place', *vē-pa* 'to strike', *kās-pa* 'to heat', *ā-va* 'to become', *sī-va* 'to give', *in-ba* 'to say', *sōl-ba* 'to enter'. *-a* occurs with 'strong' verbs and the other markers with 'weak' verbs. Kuvi has two groups of suffixes {*-ali*, *-sali*, *-cali*, *-hali*, *-jali*}. The first consonant seems to be a marker of the past. In the dialect that Joy Reddy (1979) has analysed , the infinitive markers are similar but for a change in the vowel quality{*-eli*, *-ali*, *-heli*, *-jeli*}, e.g. *koḍ-* 'to buy': *ēvasi*[1] *hēru*[2] *koḍ-ali*[3] *vā-t-esi*[4] 'he[1] came[4] to buy[3] a pair of oxen[2]' (Israel 1979: 204).

There is another set of markers *-ayi*/*-nayi* which are considered action noun formatives (David 1999: 127), e.g. *han-* 'to go': *han-n-ayi* 'going' (*-n-* non-past marker), *ha-c-ayi* 'the act of having gone'. The suffix *-al* of Kuvi can be compared with South Dravidian I nominal *-al* (cf. Kannaḍa above).

Koṇḍa, Pengo and Manḍa have a different way of forming the infinitive of a verb which is not traceable to Proto-Dravidian. In Koṇḍa (Krishnamurti 1969a: 279–83) the infinitive markers are {*-eŋ* ~ *-teŋ* ~ *-deŋ* ~ *-ḍeŋ* ~ *-ṟeŋ*} all in complementary distribution, generally phonologically, but partially also morphologically. The infinitive is used as a finite verb in the obligative mode (perhaps under the influence of Indo-Aryan), or as a non-finite verb or as a nominal derived from the verb. Examples:

> *iḍzi*[1] *ṛis-teŋ*[2] '(he) should put it (the book) down[1] and leave it[2]' (as obligative finite verb)
>
> *ibe*[1]*manṟeŋ*[2] *āʔed*[3] 'staying[2] here[1] is not possible[3]' (nominal subject)
>
> *anasi*[1] *uṇḍeŋ*[2] *bastan*[3] 'the elder brother[1] sat[3] to eat[2]' (finite verb complement)

There are other kinds of uses, which will be discussed under syntax.

Pengo has *-eŋ*/*-teŋ*/*-deŋ*/*-ḍeŋ* (also *-ceŋ*/*-jeŋ* in some types of sandhi) as the infinitive markers with partly phonological and partly morphological complementation, e.g. *ki-* 'do': *ki-deŋ* 'to do', *ah-* 'seize': *as-teŋ* 'to seize', *uṇ-* 'to drink': *uṇ-ḍeŋ*, *vanj-* 'cook': *vanj-eŋ* 'to cook', *uj-* 'suck': *uj-jeŋ* 'to suck'. The uses of the infinitive are comparable to those of Koṇḍa. Manḍa forms the infinitive of a verb by adding *-teg*/*-deg* to the verb stem, e.g. *ki-deg* 'to do', *un-jeg* 'to eat'. Clearly we can see that *-teg* is derived from *-*teng-* by the loss of nasal. Note that the infinitive suffix occurs seemingly after another infinitive suffix *-ka*/*-ga* (cf. Kui) added to the verb stem (David 1999: 136–7), e.g.

> *gṛah-ka-deg*[1] *hac-un*[2] 'he went[2] to defecate[1]'
>
> *ān*[1] *kūliŋ*[2] *vīd-ga-deg*[3] *hal-i-ba*[3] 'I[1] am going[3] to sow[3] rice[2]'

Only Telugu, Kui, Kuvi and to some extent Manḍa show a formative element signalling non-past before the infinitive suffix. Pengo and Manḍa use *-pa*, corresponding to Koṇḍa *-pu* as a marker of simultaneous action, e.g. Pe. *kos kṛe-pa* 'as the cock crows', Manḍa *kuy ār-pa* 'as the cock crows', Koṇḍa *koRku kere-pu* 'as the cocks crow'. These seem to be relic uses of an inherited infinitive analysable as non-past *-p* plus infinitive *-a*/*-u* (see section 7.8.1).

7.9.3 *Central Dravidian*

Kolami has *-eŋ*/*-eŋk*/*-eŋg* as infinitive markers in mutual complementation (in some contexts in free variation), e.g. *kor-* 'bring': *kor-eŋ* 'to bring', *ser-* 'go': *ser-eŋ* 'to go', *tin-* 'eat': *tin-eŋk tōd* 'do not eat', *sī-* 'give': *sī-eŋg* 'to give'. In Naiki of Chanda, the infinitive suffix is *-en*, *tin-en* 'to eat', *kicc-en* 'to pinch'; Naikṛi also has *-eŋ* as the infinitive marker.[14]

In Parji the infinitive suffix is *-r-an* followed by the dative case suffix, *-ug* in the Northwest dialect, e.g. *cum-* 'seize': *cum-ran-ug* 'for seizing', *ver-* 'to come': *ver-ran-ug* 'to come'. In the case of stems with an alternating *-p/-t*, the infinitive is formed by replacing the alternating formatives by -V*k*, e.g. *nil-p-/nil-t-* 'stand': *nil-uk* 'to stand', *et-ip-/-et-it-* 'lift': *et-ik* 'to lift up'. In the Southern dialect, the infinitive is marked by *-ay-uŋ* in the general class of verbs and only two examples are given; in the case of stems with final *-p/-t*, the infinitive *-uŋ* is added to the stem in final *-p* non-past stem, e.g. *eti-p-uŋ* 'to raise'; *-u/-uŋ* are widely used infinitive suffixes, e.g. *ōd*[1] *verci-l*[2] *koy-u*[3] *cend-ed*[4] 'he[1] went[4] to harvest (cut)[3] rice[2]'. The infinitive is also used as a nominal, e.g. *cay-u*[1] *erko*[2] *ki*[3] *pīy-u*[4] *erko*[5] '(either) dying[1] be[2] or[3] living[4] be[5]' ('Let there be dying or living').

Ollari infinitive markers are *-iŋ/-uŋ*, e.g. *ēnd-iŋ*[1] *sūṛ-uŋ*[2] *se-y-a*[3] 'she (? went) will go[3] to see[2] the dance[1]', *ān*[1] *variŋ*[2] *mey-en*[3] 'I[1] forgot[3] to come[2]'. The Kondekor Gadaba has, correspondingly, *-in/-un* (the vowel is predictable by the quality of the vowel of the verb stem) to form the infinitive, *kuy-* 'cut': *kuy-un* 'to cut', *in-* 'to say': *in-in* 'to say': *unn-un*[1] *ōḍ-en*[2] 'I was able[2] to eat[1]'.

7.9.4 *North Dravidian*

In Kuṛux, besides *-nā*, which is borrowed from Hindi, there is also *-ā* added to the verb root, according to Hahn, e.g. *er-* 'break': *er-ā* 'to break'; *es-nā* 'to break' is more normal. Vesper gives *-a* as the marker, e.g. *nan-* 'do': *nan-a* 'to do' (cited by David 1999: 158–9). The Malto infinitive marker is *-e*, e.g. *bar-* 'come': *bar-e* 'to come'. It appears that *-ot(i)* is the more common infinitive suffix (*-e* and *-po* are said to be nominalizing suffixes), *aṛs-* 'reach': *aṛs-oti* 'to reach'.

Brahui adds *-ing* to form the verbal noun and also the infinitive, e.g. *bin-ing* 'to hear', *tix-ing* 'to place', *sill-ing* 'to wash', etc. When compared to the other Dravidian languages they also seem to function like infinitives (David 1999: 165–8).

7.9.5 *Summary*

There is diversity in the formation of the infinitives. Anne David set up twenty-three different suffix groups on the basis of what she calls 'virtual similarity'. I am comparing below only those which lead to reconstruction either at the Proto-Dravidian level or at the level of subgroups. There are two elements for comparison: (a) the formative

[14] Thomasiah (1986: 134) writes *-ēŋ* , e.g. *tin-ēŋ* 'to eat', but there is no contrast between short and long vowels in non-radical syllables.

Table 7.19a. *Infinitive markers in South Dravidian I*

Language	Infinitive marker	Formative preceding
Old Tamil	*-a*	*-(k)k-/-(p)p-/Ø*
	-āṉ, -ākku (< **āṉ-kk-*)	*-p-/-v-, -p-*
Old Malayāḷam	*-a*	*-kk-/ø*
	-e/-ē	
	-ān	*-m/-pp/-v*
Iruḷa	*-ākku*	*-k/-g*
Koḍagu	*-ë* (+*kï*)	*-v/-p*
Kota	*-l, -lk*	
Old Kannaḍa	*-al* (+*ke*)	
Tuḷu	*-alka/-akka*	

Table 7.19b. *Infinitive markers in South Dravidian II*

Old Telugu	*-aN*	*Ø, -w, -mp*
Modern Telugu	*-a(n)*	*-w/Ø*
Gondi	*-a/-ā, ī, -lē* (dial)	
Koṇḍa	*-teŋ/-deŋ/-ḍeŋ/-ṟeŋ/-eŋ;*	
Kui	*-a(n)*	*-Ø/-p/-v/-b*
Kuvi	*-ali* ~ *-eli*	*-s/-c/-j/-h*
Pengo	*-teŋ/-deŋ; -u*	
Manḍa	*-teg/-deg*	

preceding the infinitive; (b) the infinitive marker. The formative, wherever it occurs, is clearly a non-past marker. We can isolate the infinitive suffixes with and without preceding non-past markers (also see David 1999: ch. VI), as in table 7.19a, b.

Tamil, Malayāḷam and Iruḷa treat *-a* and *-ān* as infinitive markers added to a non-past stem in final *-pp/-kk*. Subrahmanyam considers *-pp/-kk* as mere formatives of strong verbs and not as non-past markers (1971: 440). The final *-kk* following *-ān* (*ākk-* < **ān-kk-*) seems to be the dative marker following the nominal use of the infinitive. It is not clear if *-a* and *-ān* are related in these three languages. There is some phonological difficulty in this assumption. The infinitive *-a* geminates a following stop across a morph boundary, e.g. OTa. *niṟ-ka ppāṭ-in-āṉ* 'he sang (of you) so it (your fame) would stay' (David 1999: 190). This would not happen if the morph were *-an*.

Koḍagu, Kota, Kannaḍa and Tuḷu have *-al* as the infinitive and nominal marker, which is followed by the dative *-kk*. At this point, I do not think that *-an* and *-al* are variants. For South Dravidian I we reconstruct **-ān* and **-al* as infinitive–nominal markers. Besides we have also to set up **-a* as an infinitive marker.

Table 7.19c. *Infinitive markers in Central Dravidian*

Kolami	*-eŋ(g)*	
Naikṛi	*-eŋ*	
Naiki (Chanda)	*-en*	
Parji	*-uŋ*	*-p*
	-u/*-ug*/*-(u)k* (NW)	
Ollari	*-u*/*-uŋ*/*-iŋ*	
Gadaba	*-un*/*-in*	

Te. *-aN* and Kui *-a*(*n*) are probably related to SD I *-ān*, found in a subgroup. In Kui *-an* occurs before the emphatic particle *-e*, elsewhere *-a*. It is likely that SD I *-ān* > SD II *-an* in the unaccented position. Note that the infinitive follows a non-past stem in Telugu and Kui as in the case of *-ān* in South Dravidian I. A comparison of forms in the three languages is revealing (see *DVM*: 438–9), e.g. Kui *ār-p-a* 'to call', OTa. *ār-pp-a*, OTe. *ār-w-a*, Kui *nil-p-a* 'to stand', OTa. *niṟ-p-a*, OTe. *nil-(u)w-a*. Here Kui *-p-*/ OTa. *-pp-* and OTe. *-w-* historically represent a non-past morph.

In Modern Telugu, dialectally, *-an* tends to be replaced by *-a*, e.g. *ceyy-an-ē lēdu*/*ceyy-(a)-ē lēdu* '(one) did not do'. In complex verb formation, we need to posit an underlying *-an* as the infinitive marker in Modern Telugu: (a) /k c t p/ become /g j d b/ following infinitive *-n*; (b) the infinitive *-n* is lost before a consonant (Krishnamurti and Gwynn 1985: 211–12).

Kuvi *-ali*/*-eli* is traceable to the noun formative *-al* of the other subgroup of South Dravidian I. The third group of suffixes is *-en*/*-en-g* preceded presumably by the non-past **-t*; evidence for these is found in Koṇḍa–Pengo–Manḍa. Again the velar element *-g* could be treated as the dative suffix which got generalized throughout. The basis for separating **-t* as the non-past marker is based on the use of *-en*/*en-g* in Central Dravidian and Brahui.

Parji (Northwestern dialect) *-k* in the infinitive is also a non-past marker, but it takes over the function of the infinitive also, e.g. *paru-k* 'to spread': OTa. *para-kk-a*; the other dialects have *-p* instead.

These languages support a reconstruction *-V*n-g*, where the V has three qualities *-e*/*-u*/*-i* followed by apparently the dative marker **-k*(*k*). We can go to a further level of abstraction and set up *-V*n* as the infinitive marker with -*V getting realized as *-a* in South Dravidian I and in a subgroup of South Dravidian II and becoming a high or mid vowel in another subgroup of South Dravidian II, Central Dravidian and North Dravidian.

Kuṛux *-ā* supports an underlying **-ān*/*-an*; Brahui *-ing* again falls in line with the PD *-V*n* followed by the velar suffix denoting dative and the V being realized as a front

Table 7.19d. *Infinitive markers in North Dravidian*

Kuṛux	*-ā*
Malto	*-oti*
Brahui	*-ing*

high vowel, since short *-e* (probably the underlying one) had to become either a high vowel or a low vowel *-a*.

For Proto-Dravidian we can set up *-V*n* as the infinitive marker, with the value of V changing from one set of languages to another, which do not clearly correspond to the present subgrouping. The weakest part of the argument is our inability to explain a wide variation in the quality of the suffix vowel, except that it occurred in the unaccented (non-radical) syllable. An alternative solution is to set up two different morphs for PD, i.e. **-ān* and **-en*, which presumably occurred in complementation (perhaps lexical) and one of these got generalized in one group of languages and the other in the other group. Note that both allomorphs overlap in South Dravidian II and North Dravidian.

7.10 Negation in finite and non-finite verbs

In Dravidian there is a negative conjugation of the verb mainly in the non-past or with zero time reference. Here, there is no tense marker co-occurring with the negative suffix in the non-past and the negative marker **-aH-* fills the slot of a tense marker, i.e. Stem + negative marker + person. The negative allomorphs occurring in inflected verbs have abnormal phonology and are, therefore, of uncertain origin. The notion of a zero negative in Dravidian is a myth.

7.10.1 *South Dravidian I*

All languages have markers in the third neuter in negative finite verbs (tenseless) and certain non-finite verbs like the adjectival (relative participles) and adverbial (gerund) forms. In several languages the negative is signalled by a zero, when followed by personal suffixes beginning with vowels. The list of allomorphs is *-ā-/ -āy-/-ay-/-a-/-Ø-*. I tried to derive all these from PD **-āH-/*-aH-aH-* (Krishnamurti 1997b/2001a: 337–40) involving one or two laryngeals with the following developments. Straightforwardly we get *-ā-* through contraction, ***aHaH- > *-āH > -āy*. In Malayāḷam and Kota *-āy* and in Tuḷu *-ay* occur as clear negative markers, and nobody has explained the source of *-y* in these allomorphs, so far. When followed by a consonant, *-āy- > -ā*, or it loses the final *-y*, which is phonologically normal in Dravidian; hence, *-ā-tu* in the 3neu sg in Tamil, Malayāḷam, Kota and Toda. In unaccented position a long *-ā-* can become short *-a-*, as is found in Kannaḍa and Tuḷu. The origin of -Ø- is explained below. First let us look at the conjugations in different languages.

In Old Tamil-Ø- and *-ā-* functioned as negative allomorphs in non-past conjugation in complementary environments, -Ø- before personal suffixes beginning with a vowel and *-ā-* before a consonant or zero; e.g. *kāṇ-* 'to see:

1sg *kāṇ-Ø-ēṉ* 'I do not see'
1pl *kāṇ-Ø-ēm/-ōm* 'we do not see'
2sg *kāṇ-Ø-āy* 'you (sg) do not see'
2pl *kāṇ-Ø-īrkaḷ* 'you (pl) do not see'
3m sg *kāṇ-Ø-āṉ* 'he does not see'
3f sg *kāṇ-Ø-āḷ* 'she does not see'
3h pl *kāṇ-Ø-ār(kaḷ)* 'they (h) do not see'
3neu sg *kāṇ-ā-tu* 'it does not see'
3n pl *kāṇ-ā-Ø* 'they (n-h) do not see'

I have reconstructed the negative morpheme as **aH* (for some languages **aH-aH*) for Proto-South Dravidian. Phonologically this would account for the above developments in Old Tamil: **H* [h] being non-phonemic in South Dravidian at some stage, it was lost, leaving a short *-a-* which was also lost before another vowel (of personal suffix) in sandhi resulting in *-Ø-* as the negative marker. Before a consonant or in the final position *-aH-* contracted to long *-ā-*. In Modern Tamil the negative suffix overtly survives only in the third neuter singular, e.g. *ceyy-ā-tu* 'it will not do', *teriy-ā-tu* 'it is not known'. In Old Tamil the negative of a perfective participle or gerund is formed by adding *-ā/-ā-tu/ -ā-mal* to the verb stem, e.g. *cey-* 'to do': *ceyy-ā/ceyy-ātu/ceyy-āmal* 'without doing', *tīr-* 'to end': *tīr-ā/tīr-ātu/tīr-āmal* 'without ending'. The negative adjective is formed by simply adding the negative marker *-ā* to the verb base, e.g. *muṟai*[1] *ceyy-ā*[2] *maṉṉavaṉ*[3] 'the king[3] who does not do[2] justice[1]'. Alternatively, the adjectival suffix *-a* is added to the negative participle in *-ā-tu* (negative + 3neu sg) as *-āt-a*, e.g. *ceyy-āt-a* 'that does/did not do'. The negative abstract noun is formed by adding the nominalizing formative *-mai* to the negative stem, e.g. *ceyy-ā-mai* 'not doing', *aṟi-* 'to know': *aṟiy-ā-mai* 'not knowing'.

Old Malayāḷam texts have a few forms similar to Tamil with -Ø- negative filling the tense slot in non-past conjugations, e.g. *oẕiy-Ø-ēn* 'I will not exclude myself'. However, these are few and are generally considered remnants of a period when Tamil and Malayāḷam were the dialects of the same language. Literary Malayāḷam has independent negative verbs in different tenses, present, past and future. For instance, a past negative construction was like *var-ā-ññ-u* (< *var-āy-ñju* < *var-āy-ntu*, root + neg *-āy-* + past *-ntu*, with no personal suffix) '(subject) did not come', *koṭ-ā-ññ-ān* (< *koṭ-āy-nt-ān* with a personal suffix) 'he did not give'; future negative, e.g. *var-āy-um* 'subj will not come', *pār-āy-um* 'they will not see'. There are also negative adjectives of the type, *kāṇ-ā-ññ-a* past neg adj, with *-a* as adj suffix (< **kāṇ-āy-ñj-a* < **kāṇ-āy-nd-a*) 'that did not see'. Note that the final *-y* of the negative allomorph is lost before a consonant. The other negative non-finite forms include *kāṇ-āte* adv 'without seeing', *kāṇ-āy-ka* neg (verbal noun) 'not seeing'. The negative verbal noun was formed by adding *-ka* to the negative stem, e.g. *ceyy-āy-ka* 'not doing'. It is important to notice *-āy-* as the negative marker here with *-ā-* as a variant, after the loss of the final *-y*. This is independently derivable from ***aH-aH* > ***āH* > *-āy*.

Kota also has both zero forms (Stem + Ø neg + person) and those with *-āy-* as negative markers, e.g. *tin-* 'to eat': 1sg *tin-Ø-ē(n)* 'I do not eat', 1pl (excl) *tin-Ø-ēm*, (incl) *tin-Ø-ōm*, 2sg *tin-Ø-ī*, 2pl *tin-Ø-īm*, 3sg/pl *tin-Ø-kō*. Another construction has Stem + *āy* + tense + person similar to Malayāḷam, e.g. *vār-āy-p-ēn* 'I was not coming', *vār-āy-kv-ēn* 'I do/will not come'.[15] Here *-p-* is used as past marker (an innovation in Kota) and *-kv-* (OTa. *-kkuv-*) as the non-past marker. The independent attestation of *-āy-* in two languages supports the reconstruction ***aH-aH* as the Pre-Tamil negative marker, beside **aH* which is adequate to explain Tamil data; *-āy-* also occurs in negative verbal nouns formed with the suffix *-vd*, *tin-āy-vd* 'not eating'.

Toda *tin-ōθ* 'without eating' corresponds to Ta. *tin-ātu* adv. In finite verbs, the suffix is *-Ø-*, e.g. *kïy-Ø-ini* 'I do/did not do'.

Koḍagu *keyy-a-Ø* '(subject) will not do', *cuḍ-at-ë* neg adj 'that not burn (all tenses)', *keyy-ate* adv 'without working'.

Kannaḍa *nōḍ-Ø-e(nu)* 'I do not see', *nōḍ-a-du* 'it does not see', *nōḍ-ad-a* adj 'that... not see (all tenses)', *nōḍ-ade* adv 'without seeing'. The inscriptional forms of an earlier era had *-āde* (*DVM*: 347–8). The shortening of *-ād* to *-ad* is possible in the unaccented position.

Tuḷu has *-ay-/-a-* as negative markers in which the final *-y* has apparently developed out of an older laryngeal **H* in **aH*/**āH*, e.g. *kēṇ-* 'to hear': 1sg *kēṇ-ay-ɛ* 'I do not hear', 1pl *kēṇ-ay-ã*, 2sg *kēṇ-ay-a*, 2pl *kēṇ-ay-arï*, 3m sg *kēṇ-ay-e*, 3f sg *kēṇ-ay-aḷï*, 3hum pl *kēṇ-ay-erï*, 3neu sg *kēṇ-a-nḍï/-ṇï*, 3neu pl *kēṇ-ay-a*. The negative adjective and adverb are compound constructions involving the auxiliary *-ji/-ri* which seem to be related to SD **il* < **cil*. The negative adverb is formed by adding *-antɛ/-ande*, e.g. *bar-antɛ/bar-ande* 'without coming'. The negative adjective is formed by replacing the final vowel by *-i*, e.g. *pō-* 'to go': *pōv-ant-i/pōc-and-i* 'that which... not go' (all tenses).

15 Emeneau (1944: 28, cited in *DVM*: 342, fn.4), Andronov (1976c) and Steever (1993: 127–8) consider Kota *ā-y-* here as the past stem (Emeneau's S^2) of *āg-* 'to be, become', used as an auxiliary. The past stem (S^2) is said to be the base for forming the tenses, past and present–future. Hence, *vār-āy-p-ē(n)* 'I was not coming' with the past *-p-* and *vār-āy-kv-ē(n)* 'I do/will not come' with present–future *-kv-*. In that case there would be no negative marker (also see *DVM*: 342–3 and fn.4). Andronov (1976c) says that the inflected *āy-* verb is added to the negative adjective *vār-ā*. It appears to me that *-āy-* is the negative marker here and is comparable to the one in Malayāḷam.

The above data show that in South Dravidian I the negative suffix occurring in finite verb inflection had at least five allomorphs *āy*/*ay*∼*ā*/*a*∼*Ø*. The verbal adjective and adverb have presumably incorporated an erstwhile past allomorph **t*∼**tt* with neutralized tense meaning. In *-āy-*/*-ay-* the *-y* element is not a glide created in sandhi (contrary to Subrahmanyam's suggestion in 1971: 348, fn.), because its occurrence is not predictable in terms of the preceding and following segments, vowels or consonants. To account for *ā*/*a* and also the *y* element, we need to set up for Proto-South Dravidian **aH* (or more legitimately **āH*) as the negative marker.

7.10.2 *South Dravidian II*

The South-Central Dravidian data are examined below.

Telugu (Old and Modern), e.g. *cepp-* 'to tell': 1sg *cepp-a-nu* 'I do not tell'. There is no change before other personal suffixes; *cepp-a-ni* adj 'that . . . not told' (all tenses), *cepp-aka* adv 'without telling'. In Modern Telugu another auxiliary *uṇḍ-an* (inf of *uṇḍu* 'to be') is added to the negative adverb in *-aka*, e.g. *ceppa-ak-uṇḍ-ā* 'without telling'. It is to be explored if *-k-* in *-aka-* is a reflex of an old laryngeal. The negative abstract noun is formed by adding *-a-mi* (< **-aH-may*), *cepp-a-mi* 'not telling'.

In Gondi the negative marker is **-w-* before personal suffixes beginning with a front vowel, and *-Ø-* before a rounded vowel *-o* (*-wo* < *-wa*), e.g. *tin-* 'to eat':1sg *tin*(*n*)*-Ø-on* (< **tin-w-on* < **tin-w-an*, with loss of *-w-* before a labial vowel), 'I do not eat', 1pl *tin*(*n*)*-Ø-om*, 2sg *tin-w-i*/*-in*, 2pl *tin-w-iṭ*/*-ir*, 3m sg *tin*(*n*)*-Ø-ol*/*-or*/*-o̱r*/*-on*/*-onḍ*, 3m pl *tin*(*n*)*-Ø-or*/*-oṛ*, 3n-m sg *tin*(*n*)*-Ø-o*/*-oye*, 3n-m pl *tin*(*n*)*-Ø-oŋ*/*-oku*. The negative adverb, e.g. *sūṛ-vāk* 'without seeing', and the negative conditional, e.g. *veh-v-ēkē* 'if one does/will not tell' have *-v-* in Gondi dialects as the negative marker.

Koṇḍa negative marker in verb inflection is /ʔ/. In the Guṛi dialect of Koṇḍa /v/ occurs instead, which should have been the primary form of negation, e.g. 1sg *ki-ʔe* 'I will not do' (Guṛi dialect *ki-v-e* etc.), 1pl (excl) *ki-ʔ-ep*, 1pl (incl) *kiʔeṭ*, 2sg *ki-ʔi*, 2pl *ki-ʔ-ider*, 3m sg *ki-ʔ-en*, 3m pl *ki-ʔ-er*, 3n-m sg *ki-ʔ-ed*, 3n-m pl *ki-ʔ-u*. In all non-finite forms involving the negative, negation is indicated by *-ʔ-*, e.g. *ki-ʔ-i* (non-past adj), *ki-ʔi-t-i* (past adj), *ki-ʔ-eṇḍa* (neg adv) 'without doing'.

Kui has almost the same type of conjugation as Koṇḍa with *-ʔ-* occurring as a negative marker in non-past, e.g. *tin-* 'to eat': 1sg *tin-ʔenu* 'I do not eat', 1pl (excl) *tin-ʔ-amu*, 1pl (incl) *tin-ʔ-asu*, 2sg *tin-ʔ-ai*, 2pl *tin-ʔ-eru*, 3m sg *tin-ʔ-enju*, 3m pl *tin-ʔ-eru*, 3n-m sg *tin-ʔ-e*, 3n-m pl *tin-ʔ-o*. In the negative past (which will be discussed later), the marker is *-ʔa-*, e.g. 1sg *tin-ʔa-t-enu* (stem-neg-past suff-pers) 'I did not eat', *tin-ʔa-n-i* (non-past neg adj), *tin-ʔa-t-i* (past neg adj). The negative adverb is formed by adding *-arnge*/*-araa*, e.g. *sūṛ-* 'to see': *sūṛ-arange*/*-araa* 'not having seen'.

Kuvi has parallel constructions, except that *-a-* is replaced by *-o-* owing to the influence of Oriya, e.g. *pāy-* 'to beat': 1sg *pāy-ʔo-Ø*, 1pl (excl) *pāy-ʔo-mi*, 1pl (incl) *pāy-ʔo-hi* 'you do not beat', 2sg *pāy-ʔo-di*, 2pl *pāy-ʔo-der*i, 3m sg *pāy-ʔo-si*, 3m pl *pāy-ʔo-ri*, 3n-m sg *pāy-ʔ-e*, 3n-m pl *pāy-ʔ-u*. The negative past is like *pāy-ʔa-t-i* 'you did not beat', *pāy-ʔa* (non-past neg adj), *pāy-ʔa-t-i* (past neg adj) and *pāy ʔa-naha* 'not having beaten' (neg adv), and the negative verbal noun, *pāy-ʔa-tay*i 'not beating'.

Pengo non-past negative inflection has *-u-* (*-vu-*) as the negative marker, but when followed by an unrounded vowel, *-v-* surfaces, e.g. *huṛ-* 'to see': 1sg *huṛ-u-ŋ* (< **huṛ-vu-ŋ*) 'I do not see', 1pl (excl) *huṛ-u-p*, 1pl (incl) *huṛ-u-s*, 2sg *huṛ-u-y*, 2pl *huṛ-u-der*, 3m sg *huṛ-u-n,* 3m pl *huṛ-u-r*, 3n-m sg *huṛ-u-t*, 3n-m pl *huṛ-u-ŋ*. After vowel-ending roots the second person singular is realized as *-vi-*, e.g. *o-* 'to take': *o-v-i* 'you will not take'. The past negative has forms like *huṛ-va-t-aŋ* 'I did not see,' and the negative adjective *huṛ-v-i* (non-past), *huṛ-vi-t-i* (past). The negative adverb has a complex *-va-daŋ* added to the stem, *ta-va-daŋ* 'without bringing'.

For South-Central Dravidian (other than Telugu), we need to reconstruct **-wa-* as the basic negative morpheme. In Koṇḍa–Kui–Kuvi **-w-* became a glottal stop *-ʔ-*, and the following vowel has vanished in Koṇḍa and Kui, but is preserved in different shapes in Gondi, Kuvi and Pengo. It appears that we can reconstruct **-Ha-* (a part of **aH-aH*) as the negative morpheme for Proto-South-Central Dravidian with **H* developing into **-w* in prevocalic position.

7.10.3 *Central Dravidian*

The data from Central Dravidian can be explained in terms of PD **-aH-* as the negative marker. The reflex of **-H-* is lost except in Parji where *-ay-* is derived from an older *-aH-*. Kol. *sī-e-n* 'I do not give', *sī-e-t-an* 'I did not give'. It has several negative non-finite verbs by adding the inflected forms of *tōt-* in negation, e.g. present durative participle and the negative of *tōt-*, e.g. *vātōten* 'I am not coming/will not come'; the past durative negative is formed by present participle + past negative forms of *tōt-*, e.g. *anuŋ*[1] *vessa*[2] *vā tottin*[3] 'fever[2] would not have come[3] to me[1]'; the perfective negative is formed by adding the negative forms of *tōten* to the perfective participle, *ān adn tin-t tottantiri* 'although I had not eaten'; the future negative is formed by adding the negative forms of *tōt-* to the future participle, e.g. *varak tōten* 'I will not come'; the negative participle is formed by adding *sel-* (< ?* < *cil-* 'to be not') to the verb stem, *tin-sel* 'not having eaten' (*DVM*: 366–7); the negative adjective is formed by simply adding the negative marker *-e* to the stem, *tin-e* 'not eating/eaten' (neg adj in all tenses).

Pa. *cūṛ-a-n-a* 'I do not see' (the final *-a-* is idiosyncratically a copy of the neg.*-a-* repeated after the personal suffix), *cūṛ-ay-Ø-a* (3n-m sg) 'it does not see' (note *-ay-* instead of *-a-*), *cūṛ-a* (non-past neg adj), *cūṛ-aka* (adv) 'without seeing', Oll. *sūṛ-a-n* 'I will not see', *sūṛ-a* 'that . . . not see' (all tenses), *sūṛ-a kerin* (adv) 'without seeing'.

The Ollari past negative is formed by adding the past-tense forms of the archaic verb **uḷ-* to the negative participle, e.g. *man-* 'to be': *man-(a) uṭon* 'I did not stay'; the past negative durative is formed by adding the past-tense form of *man-* 'to be' with a main verb in the non-past negative, e.g. *īl-* to fall': *īl-a-n-i ma-ṭ-on* 'I was not falling'. The negative participle is formed by adding the negative marker to the verb stem, e.g. *pun-* 'to know': *pun-a* 'not knowing'. The present, perfective and future are formed periphrastically by adding the negative inflected forms of *man-* 'to be' in past and non-past to the participles of the present, past or future, e.g. *sūṛ-i manan* 'I have not seen', *sūṛ-i man-uṭon* 'I had not seen'.

7.10.4 *North Dravidian*

Among the North Dravidian languages Kuṛux and Malto have no negative inflectional suffix. Brahui has *a*/*Ø* in negative verbs, preceded by a tense-marking consonant. Br. *tix-p-a-r* 'I do not place', *tix-t-avaṭ* 'I did not place' (past stem followed by the negative present form of the substantive verb *affaṭ* → *avaṭ* 'I am not').

7.10.5 *Summary*

Subrahmanyam (1971: §4.22–4) reconstructs **-ā-* for Proto-Dravidian. He says it was preserved only in the third neuter in South Dravidian and in the other persons it became a zero; its shortened form *-a-* occurred in Telugu, Tuḷu, Central Dravidian and Brahui. He does not explain the widely distributed allomorphs *-āy-*/*-ay-* and also how *-ā-* could be totally lost in most of the inflectional forms. For South-Central Dravidian, he reconstructs **-vā-* (because some Gondi dialects have a long vowel) and says, 'At present it is difficult to explain the additional *v* in the suffix' (1971: 387). Alfred Master (1947: 146) cites a 1935 article of Jules Bloch (*BSL* no.107, p.35), in which Bloch suggested that the negative suffix *-a-* 'was preceded prehistorically by an ill-determined consonantal element, possibly guttural, laryngeal or glottal'. It is not clear why Bloch suggested this 'element' preceded rather than followed **-a-*. He must have thought so because of the developments in South-Central Dravidian and Brahui. He guessed correctly that Kui 'glottal stop should be the remnant of an old consonantal articulation' (Bloch 1954: 67).

Taking the total scenario into account, we can reconstruct **-aHa-* (or **-aHaH-* > *-āy-*/*-ay-*) for Early Proto-Dravidian or Pre-Dravidian which developed into a long grade *-ā-* (by contraction), a short grade **-a-* by loss of **H* and the zero grade by the loss of this vowel before personal suffixes beginning with vowels. In some of the languages (Malayāḷam, Kota, Tuḷu and Parji) the morpheme-final **H* was further softened into a semivowel *-y*/*-w*. These developments explain the entire data of South Dravidian, Tuḷu and Central Dravidian, Telugu of South-Central Dravidian and Brahui of North Dravidian. Telugu, being geographically close to the South Dravidian literary languages, had followed the southern pattern by selecting *-a-* in negative inflection.

How can we relate the Proto-South-Central Dravidian reconstruction **-wa-* to PD **-aHa*(*H*)*-*? Three possibilities are suggested: (a) the South-Central Dravidian **-wa-* was an independent innovation not related to PD *-*aHa*(*H*)-; (b) Early PD *-*aHa*(*H*)- split into *-*āH*- in Proto-South Dravidian and to *-*Ha*(*H*)- in Proto-South-Central Dravidian, as an innovation that separated these two branches, by a process of contraction and truncation (reducing the morpheme size with loss of -*a*- in unaccented positions). Then, the other subgroups (Central Dravidian and North Dravidian) require minimally a proto-form *-*aH*- which must have developed on the same lines as SD -*aH*- > *-*aØ*- > -*Ø*[V-; (c) the Proto-Dravidian suffix remained **aHa*(*H*)- in all subgroups except Proto-South-Central Dravidian, either in its full form as *-*aHa*(*H*)- or its contracted form as *-*āH*-, because both these could lead to *-*āy*-/*-*ay*- > -*ā*-/-*a*- > -*Ø*-. In that case, only South-Central Dravidian innovated *-*Ha*(*H*)- by a rule of truncation; *-*H*- developed to *-*w*- originally in intervocalic or prevocalic position, later generalized to all positions; a further change of *-*wa*- > -*ʔa*- occurred in Koṇḍa–Kui–Kuvi as a shared isogloss. Koṇḍa–Kui further reduced it to -*ʔ*- in non-past paradigms, but the trace of the vowel is preserved in the past negative, e.g. Koṇḍa *ki-ʔ-en* 'he does/will not do', *ki-ʔe-t-an* 'he did not do', *ki-ʔi-t-i* 'you (sg) did not do'. Alternative (a) is ruled out because of the widespread phonetic, semantic and grammatical similarity of the relevant allomorphs in different subgroups. Alternative (b) is less likely, because the developments of the reconstructed morpheme have to be replicated in different subgroups independently. Therefore, alternative (c) seems closer to the truth. I believe that the process of contraction *-*aHa*(*H*)- > *-*āH*- is not as atypical a sound change as truncation *-*aHa*(*H*)- to *-*Ha*(*H*)-. Therefore, only Proto-South-Central Dravidian could have innovated the latter type of change. In any case, the involvement of a laryngeal **H* in negative verb inflection, as already guessed by Jules Bloch over sixty years ago, would account for the data better than any of the earlier explanations.

7.10.6 *Negation by verbs* ***al- *and* *cil-** *etc.*

A peculiarity of the Dravidian languages is the use of a basic verb meaning 'not to be', **cil*-, which is found in all subgroups. It occurs both as the main verb and as an auxiliary. In South Dravidian I it became *il*- (through earlier *hil*- and *sil*-). Another verb *al*- 'to be not so-and-so' occurs mainly in Old Tamil and some other languages of South Dravidian I with approximately the same meaning.

7.10.6.1 *South Dravidian I*

In Old Tamil the inflected forms of *al*- 'to be not' are added to verb stems to express negation in non-past; the inflected forms of *il*- 'to be not' (< **cil*-) are added to the past participle or the past participial noun to express past negative. In later Caṅkam texts there are also usages of adding the *al*- forms to bare (untensed) verbal stems, e.g. *cel*- 'to go': *cell-al-am* 'we will not go', *koḷ*- 'to receive': *koḷḷ-al-ir* 'you (pl) will not receive', *nill-al-a<u>n</u>* 'he will not stand'. These forms appear as though they fit into the pattern: stem + tense + (g)np; in that case, we need to treat -*al*- as negative-cum-tense marker like -*a*-, but this argument is not sustainable, since the finite forms of *al* also occur after other finite verbs in Old Tamil texts, e.g. *kalank-iṉ-ēṉ*[1] *all-ø-ēṉ*[2] [I was disturbed[1], not[2]] 'I was not disturbed', *cel-v-ēm*[1] *all-Ø-ēm*[2] ' we will[1] not[2] go[1]'. Steever (1988: 42–4) proposes that forms like *cell-al-am* have resulted from the telescoping of two finite verbs, i.e. *cel-v-ēm all-ēm*. Something of the kind has happened in South-Central Dravidian but we are not sure if this is also replicated in South Dravidian I. Note that the inflected *al-* is also added to pronominalized nouns, e.g. *peṇṭ-ir-ēm*[1] *all-Ø-ēm*[2] 'we are not[2] women[1]'. The inflected forms of *il-*, in addition to past participles, are also used with pronominalized nouns, e.g. *va-nt(u)il-ār* 'they (h) did not come', *aṟi-nt(u) il-ir* 'you did not know'. Verbal nouns are also followed by inflected *il-* forms, e.g. *aṟi-nt-at(u) il-ēṉ* (lit. 'knowing (past)-not-I') 'I did not know'. In Modern Tamil *illai* 'it is not' is added to the infinitive or the noun formed on the past participle to express past negative, e.g. *var-* 'to come': *var-a (v) illai*, *va-nt-atu illai* '(one) did not come'. Negation in the non-past is rendered by adding *illai* to the nominalized verbs in non-past, e.g. *varu-kiṟ-atu illai* [come-dur suffix-3neu sg not] '(one) does not come', *varu-v-atu illai* [come-non-past-3neu sg not] '(one) will not come'.

In Malayāḷam *illa* 'it is not' is added to the non-finite verbs (past and present participles and the infinitive) to express negation in different tenses, e.g. *cey-tu illa* '(one) did not do', *ceyy-unn(u) illa* '(one) is not doing', *ceyy-uka*/*ceyy-(a) illa* '(one) will not do'.

The Koḍagu past negative is formed by adding *ïle* to the past stem of a verb, e.g. *ba-nd-ïle* '(one) did not come'. A past perfect negative was innovated by adding *ille* to a stem with double past marking, e.g. *ba-nd-it(i) ille* '(one) has not come'. The non-past negative is formed by adding *-ïle* to the non-past stem, e.g. *ba-pp-ïle* '(one) does/will not come', *tin-* 'to eat': *tim-b-ïle* '(one) does/will not eat'.

In Kota *ilā* is added to the past stem to form negative past, e.g. *avn*[1] *kekn*[2] *keč-ilā*[3] 'he[1] did not do[3] the work[2]'.

In Kannaḍa the past and non-past negatives are formed by adding *illa* to the infinitive or the nominal of a verb, e.g. *nōḍu-* 'to see': *nōḍ-al illa* 'one did not see', *nōḍu-v-ad(u) illa* 'one does/will not see'.

Tuḷu deviates from the other South Dravidian I languages. Negative suffixes *-ji*/*-ri* (different social dialects) are added to tensed stems in distant past, immediate past and present–future to express negation; the personal suffixes follow in forming negative finite verbs, e.g. *kal-* 'to learn': immediate past: *kal-tï-j-i* (1sg) 'I did not study', distant past: *kal-tï-dï-j-i* 'I did not study', present–future: *kal-pu-j-i* 'I am not studying/will not study'. The personal suffixes are: 1sg/pl *-i*/*-a*, 2sg/pl *-a*/*-arï*, 3m sg *-e*, 3f sg *-alï*, 3h pl *-erï*, 3neu sg/pl *-i*/*-a*. The past conditional form was innovated by combining the past and non-past markers, e.g. *kal-tïdï-v-ay-e* (root-past$_1$-past$_2$-non-past-neg-3m sg) 'he would not have learnt', *ba-ttïdï-v-ay-e* 'he would not have come'. Here, *-ay-* is the negative marker.

Summary: in all languages (except Tuḷu), negation with tense is expressed by an inherited grammatical template: {tensed stem or tensed nominal + *illai*}. Here *illai* is to be interpreted as a uniform marker of negation meaning 'not', although technically it is neuter singular of the irregular verb, *il-* < **cil-* 'not to be'.

7.10.6.2 *South Dravidian II*

In Telugu the negative verb root *lē-* 'to be not' (< **il-a-* < **cil-a*) occurs both as the main verb and as auxiliary. As a main verb, the personal suffixes are added to the root with Ø tense marking, 1sg *lē-nu* 'I am/was not', 1pl *lē-mu*, 2sg *lē-wu*, 2pl *lē-ru*, 3m sg *lē*^{n}*-ḍu*, 3hum pl *lē-ru*, 3n-m sg *lē-du*, 3n-h pl *lē-wu*. The paradigm of *lē-* occurring after an infinitive has a modal meaning (capabilitative), e.g. OTe. *cēyu-*/ Mdn Te. *cēs-* 'to do': *cēy-a*(*n*) *lē-nu* 'I cannot do' etc. (see section 7.15.2(9)viib). The past negative in Middle and Modern Telugu is formed by adding the 3neu sg form of *lē-* (i.e. *lē-du*) to the infinitive, e.g. *cēy-a*(*n*) *lē-du* '(one) did not do' corresponding to Ta. *var-a v-illai* which has the same structure. In Old Telugu the negative past was formed by two serial verbs (see section 7.13). The present negative in Modern Telugu is formed by adding *lē-du* to an action nominal in *-aṭam*/*-aḍam*, e.g. *cēy-aṭam*/*-aḍam lēdu* (lit. doing-not-it) 'one is not doing' (in all numbers and genders).

Some Gondi dialects use a structure similar to Telugu to form the past negative, e.g. *ūḍ-* 'to see': *ūḍ-*(*a*) *ill-ā-na* 'I did not see' (Koya dialect: *DVM*: 356).

Koṇḍa has *sile* 'it is not' occurring as the main verb and not as an auxiliary. There are also other non-past finite verbs with (g)np suffixes, 3m sg *sil-en* 'he is not', 3m pl *sil-er*, 3neu sg *sil-ed*/*-e*, 3neu pl *sil-u*.

Kui has periphrastic constructions with the inflected negative verb *siḍ-* 'to be not' added to present and perfective participles, e.g. *tāk-* 'to walk', *tāk-ai* 'walking' (present participle): *tāk-ai siḍ-enu* 'I am not walking' (present negative), *tāk-ai siḍ-at-enu* [lit. walking-not-past suff.-I] 'I was not walking' (imperfect negative), *tāk-a siḍ-enu* [lit. having walked-not-I] 'I have not walked' (perfective negative), *tāk-a siḍ-at-enu* 'I had not walked' (pluperfect negative). Notice that these distinctions are brought about by using the present and past participles of the main verb and the non-past and past inflection of the negative verb, **sil-* 'not to be'. Kuvi also follows the same mode.

In Kuvi *hil-* (< **sil-*) 'to be not' is used both as a main verb and as an auxiliary in the formation of non-past negatives, e.g. *pāy-* 'to beat': *nānu pāy-i hil-ʔ-o* [lit. I-having beaten not-I] 'I am not beating' (present negative), *nānu pāy-i hilʔatʔe* [lit. I-having beaten not-past-I] 'I was not beating'. Also the perfect and pluperfect negatives are made by adding the non-past and past *hil-* to the perfective participle as in Kui, e.g. *nānu pāy-a hil-ʔo*/*hil-ʔa-t-ʔe* 'I have/had not beaten'.

7.10.6.3 *Central and North Dravidian*

The derivatives of **cil* are used with negative inflection as the main verb. This will make the meaning of **cil-* 'to be'. This is true of North Dravidian also. It appears that the use of inflected **cil* as an auxiliary is an innovation in Proto-South Dravidian, another feature that binds South Dravidian I and South Dravidian II as a major branch of Proto-Dravidian.

7.11 Other simple finite verbs (affirmative and negative)

7.11.1 *Imperative singular and plural*

All Dravidian languages have finite verb forms in the imperative mood. There is no particular marker for the imperative. The verb consists of the stem + the second person singular and plural. Some languages show evidence of the imperative stem being identical with the stem in non-past finite verbs. In most of the languages the imperative singular is -Ø-, i.e. the singular form is identical with the bare stem without a person–number marker. One set of the second-person suffixes in the imperative mood is different from the one found in tensed finite verbs. The negative imperative is formed by putting the marker of negation in the tense slot, i.e. between the stem and the person marker.

7.11.1.1 *South Dravidian I*

1. Tamil: in Old Tamil, there are several modes of forming the imperative singular, i.e. *-Ø/-āy/-m* ~ *-mm* (generally followed by a clitic *-ō/-ē*) / *-ti/ -mati*, e.g. (a) *kēḷ-Ø* 'hear, ask!', *pāṭu* 'sing!'; (b) *cell-āy* 'go!', (c) *uṇ-m* 'eat!', *uḷḷu-m-ō* 'think!', *cey-mm-ē* 'do!', (d) *teri-ti* 'know!', (e) *karai-mati* 'call!'. The forms under (c) are occasionally used in the hortative plural also, e.g. *vaik-am*[1] *va-mm-ō*[2] 'let us stay[1] and come[2]'. The imperative second plural is formed by adding to the stem *-miṉ* or *-īr*, e.g. *cēr-miṉ* 'reach!', *cell-īr* 'go!'. In Modern Tamil the second singular (informal) is close to the verb base and not identical with it in all cases, e.g. *ceyy-i* 'do!', *paṭi* 'read!', *pō* 'go!'; *-um* and in plural *-uṅ-kaḷ* are used in the imperative second plural or honorific singular, e.g. *vār-um* 'come!', *koṭ-uṅkaḷ* (coll. *koṭ-ungō*) 'give!'

The negative imperative or prohibitive is formed by adding the negative suffix *-ā-* to the verb stem followed by 2sg *-ti*; e.g. *nill-ā-ti* 'do not stand!', *pōk-ā-ti* 'do not go!'; the 2pl *-miṉ/-ir* are added to the negative particle *-al-* which is suffixed to the verb stem, e.g. *koll-aṉ-miṉ* 'don't kill!' (*l* → *n*/__*m*), *nill-al-ir* 'don't stand!' Another type of prohibitive second person plural is formed with the personal suffix *-īm* added to negative [nominal] in *-ātu*, e.g. *cell-āt-īm* 'do not go!' ModernTamil has a corresponding usage, e.g. *coll-ā-ti-ṅkaḷ* 'do not tell!'

2. Malayāḷam: the second singular is *-Ø/-āy* in Old Malayāḷam; the second plural is formed by adding *-vin/-ppin/-min* (*-ppin* after strong verbs and *-min* after nasal final stems), e.g. 2sg *cey*, pl *cey-vin* 'do!', sg *naṭa/naṭakku* 'walk!', pl *naṭa-pp-in* 'walk!', *kāṇ-min* 'see!' Modern Malayāḷam adds *-u* (formal) and *-ə* (informal) as imperative signs both in the singular and the plural. A polite imperative is formed by adding the infinitive markers *-ka/-kka* in finite forms, *pāṭu-ka* 'sing!', *paṟa-kka* 'tell!' The aorist *-ū* (< *-um*) form added to non-past stems is used in the imperative, e.g. *koḷ-v-ū* 'take!', *kēḷ-p-ū* 'hear!' The prohibitive is formed by adding *-ka* in the singular, and *-vin* in the

plural, to the negative stem formed by the suffix *-āy-*, e.g. *ceyy-āy-ka* '(one) should not do', *nill-āy-vin* 'do not stand!'

3. Kota: the imperative second singular is *-Ø* and the second plural *-m*, e.g. *tin-*, *tin-m* 'eat! (sg, pl)'. The prohibitive singular is formed by adding to the verb stem *-ād-ī*, pl *-ād-īm*, *vār-ād-ī*, *vār-ād-īm* 'don't come! (sg/pl)'.

4. Toda: the imperative singular is *-Ø*, plural *-s̱*, e.g. *nil*, *nil-s̱* 'stand! (sg pl)'. The prohibitive is formed by adding *-oṭi* to the past stem, *pod-oṭi* 'don't come! (sg/pl)'.

5. Koḍagu: the imperative singular is *-Ø* and the plural *-ri* (<*-iri*, 2 pl suffix), e.g. *bā* 'come! (sg)', *bā-ri* 'come! (pl)'. The prohibitive singular and plural are formed by adding the negative marker and the personal suffixes to the verb stem, i.e. *-a-te* (sg), *-a-ti* (pl), *tar-a-te* 'do not give! (sg)', *tar-a-ti* 'do not give! (pl)'.

6. Kannaḍa: the second singular is *-Ø* and the plural *-i*/*-im*/*-ir*/ *-(i)ri*, e.g. *māḍu* 'do! (sg)', *māḍ-i*/*-im*/*-(i)ri* 'do! (pl)'. The prohibitive is formed by adding the negative particle *-al* to the stem with a Ø suffix for person in the singular; *-im* is added in the plural, e.g. *nōḍ-al* 'do not see!(sg)', *nōḍ-al-im* 'do not see! (pl)'. In Modern Kannaḍa, the prohibitive is expressed by a periphrastic construction, *nōḍa bēḍa* 'you need not see' (infinitive of *nōḍu* + the negative imperative of *bēḍu* 'is needed'; further see non-finite verbs, below).

7. Tuḷu: the second-person-singular suffix is *-Ø*/*-la* and the plural *-i*/*-le*, e.g. *uṇu*/*uṇ-la* 'eat! (sg)', *jekkī*/*jek-la* 'wash! (sg)', *kalp-i*/*kalpu-le* 'learn! (pl)', *ba-le* 'come! (pl)'. The prohibitive is formed by adding *-aḍ-* to the verbal base followed by 2sg *-a* and 2pl *-e*.

Summary: except for Tuḷu, the remaining South Dravidian I languages have the singular formed by *-Ø* or *-āy*, the second-singular suffix of finite verbs. The plural is formed by a variant of *-*w-in* (non-past marker plus the plural suffix **-im*/*-ir*). Malayāḷam preserves evidence of the non-past in *-vin*/*-min-*/*-pin*/*-ppin*. In Proto-Dravidian there is neutralization of final *-n*/*-m* (**maram*/*maran* 'tree') which explains how *-in* can be related to the second-plural suffix *-im*; *-ir* is the alternative suffix. The replacement of *-īm* by *-īr* (2pl) as a personal suffix must have been a Proto-South Dravidian phenomenon, but the imperatives have relics of the replaced morph in some of the Pre-Tamil descendants (see Old Tamil, Malayāḷam, Kota); Toda has *-s̱* in the second plural, corresponding to Tamil *-l*, presumably a reflex of the negative particle *-al* which has acquired a number meaning in Toda. The Tuḷu *-l*-V represents the negative particle *-al-* followed by the personal suffixes which are shortened to a point where they do not bear resemblance to those of any other South Dravidian I language.

7.11.1.2 *South Dravidian II*

8. Telugu: in Old Telugu the second-person-singular suffixes are *-Ø*/*-mu*/*-mmu* (the last after short-vowel-ending monosyllabic roots) and the second plural *-ṇḍu* after stems which end in non-morphemic *-u*. Alternatively, *-u* can be analysed as part of these suffixes; e.g. *cepp-u*(*mu*) 'tell! (sg)', *cepp-uṇḍu*/*-uḍu* 'tell! (pl)'. The imperatives can

be followed by address clitics *-ā/-ī*. In Modern Telugu, the singular is *-u* and plural *-aṇḍi*. When the singular form is followed by a vowel (generally of the complementizer *-an-* 'to say'), *u* is replaced by *-am*. In other words the underlying *-um* surfaces in some phonological contexts even in Modern Telugu. The simple prohibitive is formed by the negative marker *-ak-* between the verb stem and the personal suffix, *cepp-ak-umu* 'don't tell! (sg)', *cepp-ak-uṇḍu/-ūḍu* 'don't tell! (pl)'; in Modern Telugu *cepp-ak-u*, *cepp-ak-aṇḍi*, respectively. Imperatives in monosyllabic bases are *ra-mmu* 'come! (sg)', *ra-ṇḍu* 'come! (pl)': Mdn Te. *rā* (sg), *ra-ṇḍi* (pl). The corresponding negative imperatives are *rā-k-umu*, *rā-k-uṇḍu*: Mdn Te. *rā-k-u*, *rā-k-aṇḍi*.

9. Gondi: in the singular the imperative is *-m-* after stems ending in a long vowel (C)V̄-, *-Ø-* after stems ending in *-n*, and *-ā-* elsewhere; the plural suffix is *-ṭ*, e.g. *sī-* 'to give': *sī-m*, *sī-m-ṭ* 'give!' (sg/pl)', *tin-* 'to eat': *tin-* (sg), *tin-Ø-ṭ* (pl), *var-ā*: *vara-ā-ṭ* 'come! (sg/pl)'. In the Koya dialect the imperative *-mu/-mmu* occurs in the singular for stems of the (C)V̄(C) type; the plural suffix *-ṭ* is added in the plural. For other stems the sg is *-a* or *-u*, e.g. *uḍ-* 'to plough': 2sg *uḍ-mu*, 2pl *uḍ-mū-ṭu*; *tinn-* 'to eat': 2sg *tinn-u*, 2pl *tinn-ū-ṭu*. The prohibitive is formed by adding *-mā* in 2sg, *-mā-ṭ* in 2pl, e.g. *vāy-* 'to come': *vāy-mā* 'don't come! (sg)', *vāy-mā-ṭ* 'don't come ! (pl)'.

10. Koṇḍa: the imperative second singular is marked by *-ʔa* and the second plural by *-du* with its sandhi variants (*-tu/-ṟu/-ḍu* phonologically conditioned): *vā-/ra-* 'to come': *raʔa* (sg), *ra-du* (pl), *nil-* 'to stand': *nilʔa* (sg), *nin-ṟu* (pl), *veR-* 'to tell': *veR-ʔa* (sg), *veR-tu* (pl), *uṇ-* 'to drink': *uṇʔa* (sg), *uṇ-ḍu* (pl). Irregular verbs *ta-* 'to bring' and *sī-* 'to give' have suppletive variants, *si-da* 'give me'(object 1sg), *si-da-ṭ* (object 1pl); *siʔa* 'give to the 3sg': *si-du* 'give to the 3pl'.

11. Kui: The second-singular suffix is *-mu* (*-amu/-umu*) and second plural is *-du* and its sandhi variants (*-ṇḍu*, *-nju*) and *-aṭu*, e.g. *tin-* 'to eat': *tin-umu* (sg), *tin-ju* (< **tin-ṟu*), *uṇ-* 'to drink': *uṇ-umu* (sg), *uṇ-ḍu* (pl), *kō-* 'to reap': *kō-mu* (sg), *kō-du* (pl), *lāk-* 'to sacrifice': *lāk-amu* (sg), *lāk-aṭu* (pl). The prohibitive is formed by adding to the verb stem the negative suffix *-ʔa-* before the second singular *-Ø* and second plural *-ṭu*, e.g. *kō-ʔa-Ø* 'do not reap' (sg), *kō -ʔa-ṭu* (pl).

12. Kuvi: the second-singular marker is *-amu/-mu* and the second plural *-adu/-du*, *hī-* 'to give', *hī-mu/hīy-a-mu* (sg), *hī-du/hīy-a-du*, *ven-* 'to listen': *ven-a-mu* (sg), *ven-ju* (pl). The prohibitive has three slots: stem + *ʔa* (neg marker) + 2sg *-ni*, 2pl *-du*, e.g. *hī-ʔa-ni* 'don't give! (sg)', *hī-ʔa-du* (pl).

13. Pengo: the suffixes are 2sg *-a/-am*, pl *-aṭ*, e.g. *hiy-* 'to give' : *hiy-a* (sg), *hiy-aṭ* (pl), *ṛu-* 'to plough': *ṛuv-a* (sg), *ṛuv-aṭ* (pl). Certain clitics *-de/-ṟe* are added in the singular, e.g. *kiy-am-de* 'do!' (sg). The prohibitive singular is *-ma* and the plural *-ma-ṭ*, just as in Koṇḍa.

Summary: for South Dravidian II, we can reconstruct *-V*m* for sg *-*d*V for plural. While the singular is found in all members of the subgroup (except Koṇḍa in which *-m* occurs in the prohibitive only), the plural is found in Telugu (the suffix -V*ṇḍu* presupposes an older *-*ṉḏu*), Koṇḍa, Kui and Kuvi. The other set of suffixes, *-*wa* (in which -*w*- becomes a glottal stop in Koṇḍa, Kui and Kuvi) in the singular and -V*ṭṭ* in the plural, is apparently different in origin, found in Gondi (including the Koya dialect), Koṇḍa (in the prohibitive), Kui and Pengo. Note the absence of a glottal stop and the presence of a glide in the corresponding position. Kui has both the sets of suffixes. The Telugu suffix cannot be derived from -*um* + -*ṭu* (*DVM*: 495), because a voiceless -*ṭ* goes back to -*ṭṭ* and would have remained a voiceless -*ṭ* in Telugu as -(*u*)*mṭu* and not -(*u*)*ṇḍu*. Note that Gondi has a second-plural suffix in -V*ṭ* in the personal pronouns and in the verbs (also in Koṇḍa first-person inclusive -*aṭ*). The -V*ṭ* is more widespread in the imperative verbs only and not simple finite verbs in the indicative mood.

7.11.1.3 *Central Dravidian*

14. Kolami: the imperative suffixes are singular -Ø, plural -*r*/-*ur*. In the prohibitive the negative in -*ne*- is followed by -*m* in the singular and -*r*/-*ḍ* in the plural, e.g. *tin*- 'to eat': *tin* (sg), *tin-ur* (pl). The prohibitive: *tin-ne-m* (sg) 'do not eat!', *tin-ne-ḍ*/-*r* (pl). Naiki has the same prohibitive structure as Kolami. Here, the personal suffix -*m* compares well with imperative singular *-V*m* of South Dravidian II.

15. Parji, Ollari: the imperative singular is -Ø and the plural -*ur*. The prohibitive has base + (*e*)*m* + person -*en* (sg), -*or* (pl). An epenthetic vowel -*e* occurs before-*m*, e.g. *cūṛ*- 'to see': *cūṛ* (sg), *cūṛ-ur* (pl); the prohibitive *cūṛ-em-en* 'do not see!' (sg), *cūṛ-em-or* 'do not see!' (pl). Ollari imperative has -V*ṭ* in the sg and -V*r* in the pl, *nagu-p*- 'to make one laugh': *nagup-uṭ* (sg), *nagup-ur* (pl). The prohibitive is marked by -*men*, e.g. *sūṛ-men* 'do not see!' The imperative plural is similar to the one in other finite verbs. The singular in the prohibitive has -*m*, derivable from PD *-V*m*.

7.11.1.4 *North Dravidian*

16. Kuṛux: the imperative suffix is -*ā* in the singular and plural added to the verb stem. When the addressee is a woman or non-human, it is replaced by -*ai*. When women speak among themselves, it is -*ē*, e.g. *es*- 'to break': *nīn*/*nīm es ʔā* 'you (sg/pl) break', f neu *esʔai*; women among themselves, *esʔē*. In polite imperative -*kē* is used instead. Here, -*k*- appears to be the non-past marker with a new connotation, e.g. *barʔā* 'come', *bar-kē* 'come, if you please'. So also -*kō*/-*koʔe* are used as 'a kind of mild imperative', the former when addressing boys and the latter in addressing girls. Hahn compares these forms with Mundari polite imperative -*ko*-, e.g. *senkome* 'please go' (Hahn 1911: 54–5). The prohibitive is expressed by prefixing *ambā* (f *ambai*, *ambē*) to the verb, apparently a non-Dravidian construction, *ās ambas bardas nekkā* 'he shall not come'.

17. Malto: the imperative markers are -*a* (non-future) and -*ke* (future) both in the singular and plural, e.g. *amb*- 'to leave': *amb-a*, *amb-ke*. The prohibitive is formed by

adding *-m-* to the stem to which the personal suffixes are added, *ambo-m-a/-Ø* (non-future), *ambo-ma-ke* (future) (Mahapatra 1979: 174). Note that *-ke* has a tense meaning in Malto and politeness meaning in Kuṛux, but it does seem to correspond to Proto-Dravidian non-past **-kk-*. I cannot make any decision about Mundari *-ko-* in *senkome*, cited by Hahn above.

18. Brahui: the suffix is *-Ø/-a/-e* in the singular. A 'strengthened imperative' is formed by *-ak*. The plural is *-bo/-ibo*, e.g. *bin-* 'to hear': *bin* (sg), *bin-bo* (pl), *bin-ak* (extended imperative). The prohibitive consists of the verbal base + *-pa-/-fa-* (neg) + *-Ø* (sg)/*-bo* (pl), e.g. *bis-* 'to bake': *bis-pa-bo* 'do not bake', *ba-* 'to come' : *ba-fa-bo* 'do not come'. It appears that *-p-/-f-* is a reflex of non-past and *-a-* is the true negative sign in these constructions.

7.11.2 ***The optative mood***

The optative mood refers to a wish or curse by subjects in all persons (he/she/it/they/you sg, pl) including (but not normally) even the first person (speaker), i.e. the optative may refer to the second- or third-person subject. All literary languages and some non-literary languages have such constructions.

7.11.2.1 *South Dravidian I*

1. Tamil: in Old Tamil the optative is expressed by the suffixes *-ka* or *-iya* added to the verbal stem with the subject stated separately, e.g. *vāẓ-* 'to flourish': *vāẓ-ka* or *vāẓ-iya* 'may (the subject) flourish!' With the strong verbs the suffix is *-kka*, e.g. *oẓi-kka* 'may (one) destroy!' An alternative usage is that of the optative of *āku* 'to be', i.e. *āku-ka* after a finite verb, e.g. *ceytēṉ ā-ka* 'may I do!' Another mechanism is the use of derived nominals in *-al/-tal* as optative predicates, e.g. *aṟi-* 'to know': *aṟi-tal* 'may (one) know!', *cey-al* 'may one do!' The negative optative verb consists of three constituents, the stem + neg particle *-aṟ* + optative *-ka*, e.g. *cell-* 'to go': *cell-aṟ-ka* 'may (one) not go', *vār-aṟ-ka* 'may (one) not come'.[16] Another construction is by the addition of the negative particle *-il* followed by the optative *-iyar*, e.g. *kāṇ-* 'to see': *kāṇ-il-iyar* 'may (one) not see!'

2. Malayāḷam: the construction corresponding to Old Tamil optative is used as a polite imperative in Malayāḷam, e.g. *aṟi-* 'to know': *aṟika* 'please know', *col-* 'to say': *coll-uka* 'please say', *paṟa-* 'to tell': *paṟa-kka* 'please tell'.

3. Toda: the optative suffix is *-mo*, e.g. *kïy-* 'to do': *kïy-mo* 'let (one) do', *naṛ-* 'to walk' : *naṛ-mo* 'let (one) walk'. This suffix looks similar to the South Dravidian II imperative singular, -V*m*.

4. Kannaḍa: the suffixes *-ge/-ke* mark the optative added to the verb stem, e.g. *kāṇ-* 'to see': *kāṇ-ge* 'may (one) see', *bar-* 'to come': *bar-ke* 'may (one) come!' In Modern Kannaḍa the suffix is *-ali*, *kāṇ-ali* 'may (one) see', *bar-ali* 'may (one) come!'

[16] The sandhi rule *ṉ* → *ṟ*/_*k* indicates that *-ka* was probably voiceless and doubled as *-kk*.

5. Tuḷu: the optative is expressed by the suffix *-oḍï*, e.g. *kalp-* 'to learn': *kalp-oḍï* 'may (one) learn'. This suffix seems to be related to the obligative *-oḍu*, *pōv-oḍu* '(one) must go'.

7.11.2.2 *South Dravidian II*

6. Telugu: the optative is expressed in Old Telugu by *-eḍun*/*-eḍin* or *-tan*/*-tam* added to a verb stem, e.g. *mīku*[1] *śubhambu*[2] *kali-ge ḍunu*[3]/*kalugu-tanu*[3] 'may[3] good things[2] happen[3] to you[1]'. The optative of the verb *agu-* 'to be', i.e. *kā-ka*, can occur after a finite verb in the optative mood, e.g. *tirigi puṭṭu-du-wu gā-ka* 'may you be reborn'.

7. Koṇḍa: the optative is formed by adding the optative suffix *-i-*/*-pi-* to the verb stem before personal suffixes, mainly of the third person; there is one case in the second singular, e.g. *gumeṇḍ paṇḍ-i-d* 'may the pumpkin grow', *uṇzi son-i-r* 'let them eat and go', *mā anar ibe ēṟu iyba-pi-r* 'let my elder brothers bathe here'. These constructions are called Desiderative-Permissive by Krishnamurti (1969a: 282).

The optative suffix *-ka*/*-kka* in Tamil, Malayāḷam, Kannaḍa and Telugu appears to be a combination of non-past *-k*/*-kk* and the infinitive *-a*.

7.12 Durative or progressive (in present/past) in some languages of South Dravidian

The verbs expressing the Durative (continuous action) in Tamil, Kannaḍa, Tuḷu of South Dravidian I and Telugu and Koṇḍa of South Dravidian II are apparently independent innovations which do not reconstruct to Proto-South Dravidian.

7.12.1 *South Dravidian I*

It is said that in Middle Tamil (post-Caṅkam) *-kiṉṟ-* /*-kiṟ-* emerged as the suffixes used to express the present continuous, illustrated by the following paradigm, e.g. *cey-* 'to do':

1sg *cey-ki(ṉ)ṟ-ēṉ*	1pl *cey-ki(ṉ)ṟ-ōm*
2sg *cey-ki(ṉ)ṟ-āy*	2pl *cey-ki(ṉ)ṟ-īr(-kaḷ)*
3m sg *cey-ki(ṉ)ṟ-āṉ* }	3h pl *cey-ki(ṉ)ṟ-ār(-kaḷ)*
3f sg *cey-ki(ṉ)ṟ-āḷ* }	
3neu sg *cey-k(ṉ)ṟ-atu*	3neu pl *cey-k(ṉ)ṟ-aṉa*

The present adjective (relative participle) is formed by adding *-a* to the form ending in *-ki (n)ṟ-*, e.g. *cey-ki(ṉ)ṟ-a-* 'that is doing/done'. In Colloquial Tamil, the marker is *-r-*/*-kr-*, *cey-r-ẽ* 'I am doing', *pā-kr-ẽ* 'I am seeing'. In some Caṅkam classics the suffix sequence *-(k) iṟ-p-* occurs as an alternative marker of the future tense, e.g. *kara-* 'to conceal': *kara-kkiṟ-p-eṉ* 'I will conceal', *kāṇ-kiṟ-p-ār* 'they will see'. Native grammarians consider the underlying morph to be *-kil-*/*-kiṉ-*. Middle and Modern Tamil present continuous (durative) *-kiṉṟ-/-kiṟ-* is related to this (*DVM*: 244–5). If *kil-* 'to be able' is taken to be the underlying morph, then the structure of this finite verb is different from others, i.e. VSt + Aux (*kil* + tense *-nt-*) + (g)np. The only problem is that the filler of the slot 'tense' should then be the non-past *-t-* and not the past *-nt-*.

The Malayāḷam present-tense marker *-unn-* is derived from older *-inṟ-* (<*-kiṉṟ-*) which occurred as present-tense suffix around the tenth century (*DVM*: 249); the relative participle is formed by adding the adjectival *-a* to *-unn*, e.g. Ma. *vāẓ-kinṟ-a* > *vāẓ-unn-a* 'that is living'.

Kannaḍa has a periphrastic present tense formed by adding to the past stem the inflected future finite verb of the auxiliary *ā-* 'to be': *kēḷ-* 'to hear': *kēḷ-d-a-p(p)-em* 'we will hear', which later became *kēḷ-d-a-h-em*. In Modern Kannaḍa such forms have undergone a semantic change expressing 'uncertainty /possibility' with future reference, e.g. *id-d-(h)-ēnu* 'I may be'. Here older *-ah-* is lost. In Modern Kannaḍa the present-tense finite verb is formed by adding *-utt-* to the stem followed by (g)np suffixes, e.g. 1sg *māḍ-ut(t)-ēne* 'I am doing', 1pl *māḍ-ut(t)-ēve*, 2sg *māḍ-ut(t)-i/ī*, 2pl *māḍ-ut(t)-īri*, 3m sg *māḍ-ut(t)-āne*, 3f sg *māḍ-ut(t)-āḷe*, 3h pl *māḍ-ut(t)-āre*, 3neu sg *māḍ-ut(t)-ade*, 3neu pl *māḍ-ut(t)-ave/-āve*. The present participle is formed by adding *-ut(t)u/-ut(t)ā* to the verb stem, e.g. *māḍ-ut(t)ā* 'doing'. In Old and Medieval Kannaḍa it was formed by adding *-ut(t)um*, e.g. *nagu-* 'to laugh': *nag-ut(t)um* 'laughing', *aḷ-* 'to weep': *aḷ-u(t)tum* 'weeping'.

Tuḷu has present–future and future tenses; the former is an innovation because it is based on two non-past morphs, whereas the future is formed with one morph, e.g. *kal-* 'to learn': *kal-pu-v-ɛ* 'I am learning' as opposed to future *kal-p-e* 'I will learn'. The present participle is formed by adding *-ontu/-ondu* to the past stem, e.g. *kal-t-ontu /-ondu* (Brahmin and Common dialects) 'learning', *tin-* 'to eat': *tin-d-ontu/tin-d-ondu* 'eating'. The non-past adjective is formed by adding the tense marker *-pub-/-p-* in different social dialects followed by the adjectival suffix *-i*, e.g. *kal-pub-i/-p-i* (Class I stems) 'the one who learns'; with others only *-p-/-b-*, e.g. *tū-* 'to see': *tū-p-i* 'that which sees/will see'. Another non-finite verb to express simultaneous action is *-naga*, whose origin is obscure, e.g. *kalpu-naga* 'while learning', *kēṇ-* 'to ask': *kēṇ-ṇaga* 'while asking'.

7.12.2 *South Dravidian II*

Old Telugu has *-cu (n)* as the present participle marker, *cēyu-* 'to do': *cēyu-cu (n)* 'doing'. The durative verb is formed by adding to this the inflected forms of the verb *un-* 'to be' followed by the past-tense marker *-n-* and (g)np suffixes. Here the past-tense suffix has both present and past meanings, e.g. *cēyu-c-un-n-a-* adj [do-durative-be-past-adj] 'the one doing in the past or present'. With the addition of demonstrative suffixes, we derive *cēyu-c-un-n-a-wā̃ḍu* 'the man who is/was/has been doing' etc. At a later period these became finite verbs like *cēyu-c-un-n-ā̃ḍu* 'he is/was/has been doing'. In Modern Telugu *-tū* is the marker of the present participle and the durative verb is formed by adding to the verb stem the non-past marker *-t-* followed by the inflection of *un-* 'to be', *cēs-* 'to do': *cēs-tū* 'doing': *cēs-t-un-n-āḍu* 'he is/was/has been doing'.

In Koṇḍa {*-sin-* ~ *-zin-*} marks the durative aspect in finite and non-finite verbs. This is a morph complex consisting of *-si*/*-zi*, the perfective participle marker, plus the non-past-tense marker *-n-*, e.g. *ven-* 'to listen': *ven-zin-an* 'he is listening', *ven-zin-i* adj 'the one hearing', *ven-zin-iŋ* 'as one is/was listening', etc. The present continuous in Kui is formed by adding the future-tense paradigm of the verb *man-* 'to be' to the present participle in *-pi*, e.g. *ḍēs-* 'to build': *ḍēs-pi man-Ø-amu* 'we are building', *ṛū-* 'to plough': *ṛū-i* (loss of *-v-* < *-p-*) *ma-Ø-i* (loss of *-n*) 'I am ploughing'. The present participle is formed by adding to the stem *-pi*/*-bi*/*-ki* with sandhi variants. The consonants *p* ~ *b*/*k* encode the non-past, e.g. *aḍ-* 'to join': *aṭ-ki* 'joining', *dī-* 'to fall down': *dīp-ki* 'falling down', *ār-* 'to call': *ār-pi* 'calling', *jel-* 'to pull': *jel-bi* 'pulling'; in some classes of verbs the present-participle marker is *-ai*, e.g. *tāk-* 'to walk': *tāk-ai* 'walking'; *-ji* occurs after some monosyllabic ones, *tin-* 'to eat': *tin-ji* 'eating', *sal-* 'to go': *sa-ji* 'going'. In Kuvi also the present tense is formed periphrastically by adding an inflected auxiliary *man-* 'to be' in the future tense to the present participle of the main verb ending in *-ci*/*-ji*/*-si*/*-hi*, e.g. *tōs-* 'to show': *tōs-si manjaʔi*/*maʔi* 'I am showing'. Note that the non-finite verbs ending in **-ci*/ **-cci* mean perfective or past participles in Telugu, Gondi and Koṇḍa unlike in Kui–Kuvi. The formation of the present tense in Pengo is idiosyncratic. It adds *-a* at the end of the future-tense finite form to convert it into the present tense, e.g. *huṛ-* 'to see': *huṛ-n-an* 'he will see': *huṛ-n-an-a* 'he is seeing'. This is apparently a recent innovation by introducing an element of contrast, although in a slot that does not refer to tense/aspect.

7.12.3 *Central Dravidian*

Kolami present–future marker *-s*/*-sat*/*-at* seems to have an element comparable to **-ci* plus the non-past **-tt*. Naiki also has *-at-* as a future marker. The present-tense *-m-* in Parji is traceable to PD **-um*.

7.12.4 *Summary*

Jules Bloch (1954: 77) considered OTa. *ki(n)ṟ-* as a verb meaning 'to be'. Andronov considers *kiṉṟ-* as the past stem of the root *kil-* 'to be able'; alternatively, he thinks that *k-*/*kk-* are non-past markers followed by the past stem of *il-* 'to be' (cited and supported by *DVM*: 309–10). There is no evidence to support *kiṟ-* or *il-* as verbs meaning 'to be'. Ta. and SD I *il-* is from PD **cil-* which means 'to be not' and not 'to be'. Tamil, Malayāḷam and Tuḷu have no present participles; the meaning is conveyed by the past participle of the reflexive auxiliary *koḷ-* 'to take', i.e. *koṇṭu* added to the past participle of the main verb, e.g. Ta. *kaṟṟu-k-koṇṭu* 'learning' from *kal-* 'to learn', past stem **kal +tt-*. The Tuḷu present participle *kal-t-ontu/-ondu* seems to have the same kind of structure.

It appears that Ka. *-ut(t)um-* and Te. *-cun* could be related, in which case the palatal has to be older.[17] It is also tempting to compare OTe. *-cun* with Koṇḍa *-si-n-/-zi-n-* with exactly the same meaning with a possible change of the front high vowel to the back one. The only problem is that *-ci-n-* consists of two morphs, the perfective participle **-ci* plus non-past **-n*; Telugu does not inherit the non-past *-n* like the other members of South Dravidian II. Steever (1993: 91) argues that Koṇḍa durative verbs in *-si-n-/-zi-n-* are derived by the Compound Contraction Rule from *ki-zi ma-n-an* → *ki-zin-an*, but Koṇḍa also has *kizi manan* 'he has been doing' (perfect continuous) contrasting with *kizinan* 'he is doing' (present continuous). In the case of the other pairs of finite verbs, which Steever (1993: chs. 3, 4) has illustrated to have contracted into single finite verbs, the older and later structures do not survive synchronically in the same language. We must therefore take *-sin-/-zin-* as a complex morpheme innovated by Koṇḍa. Ka. *-ut(t)um* and Mdn Te. *-tū* (durative markers) are apparently cognates.

7.13 Serial verbs

A peculiarity of Dravidian morphology and syntax is the existence in some clauses of two finite verbs, called serial verbs. Steever (1993: 78–9) defines a serial verb 'as a complex form in which two or more formally finite verb forms enter into construction. Both the main and auxiliary verbs in these constructions are inflected for tense and subject-verb agreement in contrast to the typical Dravidian compound verb, in which one form at most can be formally finite.' These are reconstructible for Proto-Dravidian as structural templates, filled in by synonymous, and not necessarily cognate, morphemes. Telugu, a member of South Dravidian II and a literary language, has a past negative of the following structure, Vst^1-Neg-(g)np followed by Vst^2-past tense-(g)np. Vst^2 is the verb *ā-* 'to be' used as an auxiliary and Vst^1 is any verb, e.g. *ceppu-* 'to tell':

1sg *cepp-a-n(u) ay-ti-ni* (lit. I do not tell, I was), 'I did not tell'
1pl *ceppa-m(u) ay-ti-mi* 'we did not tell'
2sg *cepp-a-w(u) ay-ti-wi* 'you (sg) did not tell'
2pl *cepp-a-r(u) ay-ti-ri* 'you (pl) did not tell'
3m sg *cepp-a-ḍ(u) ayy-e(n)* 'he did not tell'
3n-m sg *cepp-a-d(u) ayy-e(n)* 'she/it did not tell'
3h pl *cepp-a-r(u) ay-i-ri* 'they (h) did not tell' etc.

Note that both the verbs are finite and they constitute a single predication. They cannot be separated by other words or clitics and, therefore, are a single construction/compound

[17] *c* (affricate) > *t* (dental) is more natural as an unconditioned sound change than *t* > *c*.

word and not a sequence of two words. Such constructions occur in Old Telugu and Muria Gondi (Steever 1993: 113–15).

In the other South Dravidian II languages, similar finite verbs got telescoped into a single finite verb. Steever (1993: ch. 4) has shown that similar finite verbs underlay the emergence of single finite verbs in the past negative in South Dravidian II and Central Dravidian languages, by a set of systematic historical changes, e.g. Koṇḍa: *ki-ʔe-n* 'he does/will not do' + *ā-t-an* 'he was' → *ki-ʔe-t-an* 'he did not do'. The last consonant of the negative personal suffix *-n* and the first syllable of the auxiliary verb *ā-* 'to be' are lost. Steever has derived such synthetic past negative finite verbs from two analytic verbs which were like those in Telugu, by a set of rules which he calls 'Compound Verb Contraction': (1) the word boundary between the two verbs becomes a morpheme boundary, (2) affix truncation leaves only the first vowel of the personal suffix, i.e. *-e* of *-en* (3m sg), *-i* of *-ider* (2pl) of the first verb, (3) shortening of the first long vowel of the auxiliary verb, i.e. *ā-t-an* becomes **a-t-an*, (4) vowel cluster simplification, i.e *-e* + *a-* becomes *-e*. For deriving the correct forms he has used these rules sometimes in different order. It is clear that vowel shortening and vowel cluster simplification can be dispensed with. Instead of the shortening of the first vowel of the auxiliary verb, we need a rule of loss of the first syllable of the auxiliary; this rule will also apply to the auxiliary verb which begins with a consonant, i.e. *ma-n-an* in Pengo and Kolami in which *ma-* is lost. On the other hand, the vowel cluster simplification rule should normally result in Dravidian in the second vowel surviving and the first vowel being lost. In the cases illustrated by Steever, it is the preceding vowel that survives and the succeeding vowel that goes. In terms of 'Compound Verb Contraction' Steever has succeeded in explaining synthetic verbs like the present perfect in Pengo and the past negative in Koṇḍa and some of the Central Dravidian languages. By extending the pattern he was able to explain the verbs in Kui–Kuvi which include *-ta-* ~ *-tar-* /*-da-* ~ *-dar-*/*-a-* ~ *-ar-* as the 'transition particle' in clauses with transitive verbs incorporating such particles to encode direct objects. This pattern is also witnessed in some other South Dravidian II languages.

Of all South Dravidian II languages, only Koṇḍa seems to have several types of serial verbs which were treated as 'compound verbs' by Krishnamurti (1969a: 304–12). The coordinate compound verbs have two or more underlying finite or non-finite verbs, e.g. *vā-t-an* 'he came' + *suṟ-t-an* 'he saw' → *vā-t-a suṟ-t-an* 'he came and saw', *maR-t-iŋ* 'after turning back' + *bēs-t-iŋ* 'after looking back' → *maR-t-i bēs-t-iŋ* 'as one turned and looked back'. I stated clearly the rules underlying such formations. The coordinated stems should have the same tense and person inflection in the finite and the same marker in the non-finite. When the two verbs come together, only the first vowel of the marker following the tense sign remains and the rest of the segments are lost: *vand-it-ider* 'you were tired' + *vā-t-ider* 'you came' → *vand-it-i vā-t-ider* 'you came tired' (also see *maR-t-i bēs-t-iŋ* above).

There are also Subordinate Compounds in which the first stem is the main verb and the second a member of a closed set of auxiliaries. These encode intensity and aspectual contrasts, e.g. *ek-t-an* 'he climbed' + *ṛis-t-an* 'he left it' → *ek-t-a ṛis-t-an* 'he climbed up it'. Here *ṛis-* is used as an auxiliary verb to signal 'completion of action'. In the formation of aspectual compounds the second stem is *man-* 'to be', *gūr-it-an* 'he slept' + *ma-R-an* 'he was' → *gūr-it-a ma-R-an* 'he had slept'.

7.13.1 *South Dravidian I*

Old Tamil had *va-nt-ēṉ* 'I came' beside *va-nt-aṉ-eṉ* which were considered free variants, the second involving an empty marker *-aṉ-* following the past stem, called *cāriyai* in traditional Tamil grammars. Steever (1993: 98–9) considers this the perfect-tense form meaning 'I have come' and relates *-aṉ-* to the auxiliary verb **man-n-en* (as in **va-nt-en *man-n-en*) without evidence for such a non-past finite form. In the absence of comparative data from any other member of South Dravidian I, this proposal remains unsubstantiated.

Also Rules of Degemination, Affix Truncation and *ma-* Deletion (note only *m-* is deleted here) leading to **man-n-en* → **ma-n-en* → *-a-n-en*. Old Tamil also had serial verbs with the negative verb *al-* as the auxiliary, e.g. *va-nt-ēṉ all-ēṉ* [come-past-I, be not-I] 'I did not come' beside forms that have *-al-* alone as the negative marker, e.g. *kēḷ-al-am* 'we will not listen'. The latter, according to me, is a straightforward negative verb of the structure Vst-neg marker-(g)np. But again, Steever takes such constructions as the result of a sequence of two verbs, of which the main verb is said to lose the tense and person markers followed by the negative verb **al-am*. Again, this kind of 'affix truncation' of the main verb is unparalleled in the languages of South Dravidian I, and hence suspicious.

7.13.2 *South Dravidian II*

a. *Koṇḍa (negative past derivation), e.g.* ki- *'to do'* Note that the rules deriving the composite form from two finite verbs are quite simple and systematic. They include (1) replace the word-boundary between the two finite verbs with a morpheme boundary (compound verb contraction); (2) truncate the personal suffix of the main verb to the first vowel (or loss of all segments except the first one = vowel); (3) drop the first syllable of the auxiliary verb. Note that the personal endings of the resultant past negative are the allomorphs, which occur in non-negative verbs. This feature proves that there is contraction of a negative non-past with a past verb 'to be' in the affirmative.

b. *Pengo (present-perfect derivation)* The present-perfect tense in Pengo has three different realizations, which are said to be free-variants: (1) (Vst-Pst-PE) + *na*, (2) (Vst-Pst-PE) + non-Pst-PE, (3) Vst-Pst-non-Pst-PE. The first two types apparently

Table 7.20a. *Historical derivation of Koṇḍa negative past*

Negative	non-past	+	past of *ā-* 'to be'	>	Negative past
1sg	*ki-ʔ-e*	+	*(ā)-t-a*	>	*ki-ʔ-e-t-a* 'I did not do'
1pl excl	*ki-ʔ-e(p*	+	*ā)-t-ap*	>	*ki-ʔ-e-t-ap* 'we did not do'
1pl incl	*ki-ʔ-e(ṭ*	+	*ā)-t-aṭ*	>	*ki-ʔ-e-t-aṭ* 'we (incl) did not do'
2sg	*ki-ʔ-i*	+	*(ā)-t-i*	>	*ki-ʔ-it-i* 'you (sg) did not do'
2pl	*ki-ʔ-i(der*	+	*ā)-t-ider*	>	*ki-ʔ-it-ider* 'you (pl) did not do'
3m sg	*ki-ʔ-e(n*	+	*ā)-t-an*	>	*ki-ʔ-et-an* 'he did not do'
3m pl	*ki-ʔ-e(r*	+	*ā)-t-ar*	>	*ki-ʔ-et-ar* 'they (men)* did not do'
3n-m sg	*ki-ʔ-e(d*	+	*ā)-t-ad*	>	*ki-ʔ-et-ad* 'she/it did not do'
3n-m pl	*ki-ʔ-u*	+	*ā)-t-e*	>	*ki-ʔ-ut-e* 'they (n-m) did not do'

*also 'human' in appropriate linguistic contexts.

Table 7.20b. *Historical derivation of Pengo present perfect*

Reconstruction of Pre-Pengo paradigm			Pengo present-perfect tense	
1sg	**huṛ-t-aŋ man-n-aŋ*	>	1sg	*huṛ-t-a(ŋ maØ)-n-aŋ*
1pl excl	**huṛ-t-ap man-n-ap*	>	1pl excl	*huṛ-t-a(p maØ)-n-ap*
1pl incl	**huṛ-t-as man-n-as*	>	1pl incl	*huṛ-t-a(s maØ)-n-as*
2sg	**huṛ-t-ay man-n-ay*	>	2sg	*huṛ-t-a(y maØ)-n-ay*
2pl	**huṛ-t-ader man-n-ader*	>	2pl	*huṛ-t-a(der maØ)-n-ader*
3m sg	**huṛ-t-an man-n-an*	>	3m sg	*huṛ-t-a(n maØ)-n-an*
3m pl	**huṛ-t-ar man-n-ar*	>	3m pl	*huṛ-t-a(r maØ)-n-ar*
3n-m sg	**huṛ-t-at man-n-at*	>	3n-m sg	*huṛ-t-a(t maØ)-n-at*
3f pl	**huṛ-t-ik man-n-ik*	>	3f pl	*huṛ-t-i(k maØ)-n-ik*
3n pl	**huṛ-t-iŋ man-n-iŋ*	>	3n pl	*huṛ-t-i(ŋ maØ)-n-iŋ*

have the truncated non-past paradigm added to the past-finite verb; the last variant is more synthetic since it has a complex tense morph (Pst-non-Pst) followed by personal ending. The last one conforms better to the word-formation rule of Dravidian. All these three variants are derived by Steever (1993: ch. 3) from two underlying serial verbs, the past finite followed by the non-past finite with the base *man-* 'to be'. The template in table 7.20b is comparable to that of Koṇḍa past negative, although different auxiliaries are used, *huṛ-* 'to see', *man-* 'to be'.

As in the case of Koṇḍa the rules operate as follows: (1) replace word boundary by a morpheme boundary (leading to contraction of two verbs into one); (2) a morphophonemic rule drops the final *-n* of the root *man-* before another *-n* (non-past marker); (3) drop all segments of the personal ending except the first vowel in the first verb; (4) drop the first syllable of the auxiliary. As a consequence of the application of these rules, the resultant present perfect has a complex tense marker *-t*V*-n* which fits the word-formation rule of Dravidian. Steever (1993: 81–2) derives the other variant paradigms of Pengo by applying the rules in different order.

c. *Gondi–Kui–Kuvi etc.* Koṇḍa also has a present/past perfect or progressive construction involving *man-* 'to be' as the auxiliary, e.g. *gūrita manan* 'he is sleeping' < *gūr-it-an* 'he slept' and *man-Ø-an* 'he is', with affix truncation of the first verb, *veyu*[1] *kāk-t-a(r)*[2] *ma-R-ar*[3] '(their) mouths[1] remained[3] open(ed)[2]'. In such compound constructions involving *man-* we do not find the deletion of the first syllable of the auxiliary *man-* 'to be'.[18] There are instances of deletion of *man-/ma-* in Kui, Kuvi and Gondi (Steever 1991: 91–3). It was noticed by Winfield (1928: 89) in Kui in the formation of the present progressive as an allegro variant of the uncontracted construction, e.g. *gip-ki manji* → *gip-ki-nji* 'you are doing' (present participle *gip-ki* + *man-j-i* 'you are'), *ta-sa man-Ø-eru* → *ta-sa-n-eru* 'they have brought'. This form corresponds to Koṇḍa present perfect *ta-si man-Ø-ar* 'they have brought', and it also contrasts with *ta-sin-ar* 'they are bringing'. In Kuvi *man-* and its past stem *mac-* lose the root vowel in contraction, e.g. *kug-a ma-c-i* → *kuga-m-c-i* 'you had sat down', *kug-a man-Ø-e* → *kug-a-mn-e* 'she has sat down'. In the Koya dialect of Gondi the present participle of a verb is combined with an inflected form of *min-* 'to be' and is contracted to a single word, e.g. *ūḍ-ōr min-n-iri* → *ūḍ-ō-n-iri* 'you are seeing' (*ūḍ-* 'to see').

7.13.3 *Central Dravidian*

Parji present perfect/progressive is also formed by serial verbs, i.e. the past finite + the non-past (future) finite without any contraction, e.g. *ve-ñ-ot mẽ-d-at* 'you have come', *veṛka e-ñ-er mẽ -d-ar* (lit. pleasure become-past-3pl be-future-3pl) 'they have become happy'. These forms exactly match 'morpheme for morpheme' the reconstructed Pengo present perfect (Steever 1993: 87).[19] Parji, in addition, uses the same form also as a present progressive.

7.13.4 *North Dravidian*

Parallel constructions have been cited by Steever (1993: 93–6) from Kuṛux and Old Tamil to show that serial verb constructions go back to Proto-Dravidian. In Kuṛux Proto-Dravidian **man-* is replaced by a borrowed copular verb *raʔ-* 'to be' (Hin *rahnā*) in the formation of present- and past-perfect tenses, e.g. *ēn*[1] *es-k-an*[2] *raʔ-ck-an*[3] 'I[1] had

[18] I have reservations in accepting the hypothesis of Steever (1993: 91) that the Koṇḍa durative marker *-zi-n-/-si-n-* is the result of *ma-* deletion. It could simply be the result of adding the non-past marker *-n* to the perfective marker *-zi/-si*, e.g. *ki-zi* 'having done', *ki-zin-an* 'he is doing'.

[19] Note that Pre-Parji *a* becomes *e* before an alveolar consonant (see section 4.4.5).

broken (it)[2, 3] (lit. I[1] broke[2], I remained[3]), *coc-k-ar*[1] *ra-c-ar*[2] 'they had dressed as men' (lit. they dressed as men[1] (they) remained[2]). Steever (1993: 95–6) has shown that in locative meaning *manna* 'to be' was replaced by borrowed *raʔ-*, but it remained in other contexts.

7.13.5 *Summary*

Serial verbs, i.e. two finite verbs of which the first is the main and the second the auxiliary, can be reconstructed for Proto-Dravidian. There is evidence of the existence of such verbs in Old Tamil, Old Telugu and other South Dravidian II languages, besides Parji of Central Dravidian and Kuṛux of North Dravidian. In some of the languages of South Dravidian II the serial verbs contract into one finite verb with the auxiliary suffering compression. It is not certain if any language of South Dravidian I had such synthetic finite verbs.

7.14 Compound verb stems

Compound verb stems have the main verb as head of the construction. These are lexical compounds for which it is not possible to state rules. The frequent ones are $N + V^1$ and $V^1 + V^2$. In both the cases V^1 is the main verb; V^2 is a member of a closed set while V^1 is a member of an open set (any verb stem). Examples are given below from the literary languages.

In Classical Tamil both the above types are found. I have taken here only those compounds in which V^1 is not inflected, e.g. *eḥku* 'to pull, comb (cotton)' + *uṟu* 'to feel' → *eḥk-uṟu-* 'to feel the pull', *aṟi* 'to know' + *kil* 'to be able' → *aṟi-kil* 'to be able to know', *tar-* 'to bring': *taru-kil-* 'to be able to bring', *kaṭi* 'to guard' + *koḷ* 'to take hold of' → *kaṭi-koḷ-* 'to undertake to guard', *puku* 'to enter' + *tar* 'to bring' → *puku-tar-* 'to make an entry into', *pō* 'to go' + *tar* 'to bring' → *pō-ttar-* 'to bring back', *atir* 'to vibrate' + *paṭu* 'to befall, suffer' → *atir-paṭu-* 'vibrate violently' (Rajam 1992: 501–20). In the foregoing examples, Rajam says that V^1 has the 'force' of a verbal noun, which does not seem to be correct on comparative grounds, cf. the verbs with *tar-* as V^2 in Kannaḍa and Telugu. There are several examples of N + Vtype, e.g. *al* 'darkness' + *ār-* 'to be full' → *all-ār-* 'be full of darkness', *melku* 'cud' + *iṭu* 'put' → *melk-iṭu-* 'drop or let out cud', *kātal* 'love' + *cey* 'to make' → *kātal-cey-* 'to love'.

In literary Kannaḍa 'root compounds' (Ramachandra Rao 1972: 152ff.) consist of two-verb roots ($V^1 + V^2$) in which V^2 is *sal-* 'to go', *tar-* 'to bring', *ēẓ-* 'to rise' etc., e.g. *taṟi-* 'to cut': *taṟi-sal* 'to determine clearly', **ey-* 'to go': *ey-tar* 'to approach, reach', *oge-* 'to emerge': *oge-tar-* 'to be born', *naḍe-* 'to walk': *naḍe-tar-* 'to approach', *pō-* 'to go': *pō-tar-* 'to come', **jīr-* '?to call': *jīr-ēẓ-* 'to scream, cry', *pāṟ-* 'to run': *pāṟ-ēẓ-* 'to leap'. It is difficult to define, from available source materials, how the meaning of the second verb modifies the meaning of the first. These have tended to become idioms in the course of time. Note that *tar-/tār-* 'to bring' occurs as the second member of verb compounds in literary Tamil and Telugu also.

In compounds of the type N + V, the function of the verb is to incorporate the noun in the VP by verbalizing it. The frequently used set of verbs in Old Kannaḍa are *koḷ-/goḷ-* 'to take', *key-/gey-* 'to make', *pōgu-* 'to go', *āḍu-* 'to move', *paḍu-* 'to get, obtain, suffer', *āgu-* 'to become', *kuḍu-* 'to give', *biḍu-/viḍu-* 'to leave, abandon', *iḍu-* 'to put' etc.; e.g. *aḍi* 'feet': *aḍi-goḷ-* 'to take to one's heels', *kene* 'cream': *kene-goḷ-* 'to form into cream', *arasu* 'king': *arasu-gey-* 'to rule', *bijayam* (< Skt. *vijaya-*) 'victory': *bijayam-gey-* 'to grace, go/come with dignity', *uḍi* 'piece': *uḍi-vōgu-* 'to go to pieces', **all-* 'shaking'; *all-āḍu-* 'to shake, tremble', *kaṭṭu* 'tying': *kaṭṭu-vaḍu* 'to be imprisoned', *tale* 'head': *tale-vaḍu-* 'to confront, attack', *bāy* 'mouth': *bāy-viḍu* 'to cry in pain'. It appears most of these are idiomatic expressions, in which the meaning of the constitute is not derivable from the meanings of the constituents.

Literary Telugu used a wealth of compound verbs consisting of $V^1 + V^2$ or N + V, almost comparable to the Kannaḍa compounds. One of the V^2 following the main verb is *-tencu-/tēru-* 'to bring', cognate with Ka. Ta. *tā-/tar-/tār-* 'to give to 1/2 pers, to bring'. It is added to verbs of motion, e.g. *canu* 'to go': *canu-dencu* 'to come', *arugu-* 'to go': *arugu-dencu* 'to come', *naḍacu* 'to walk': *naḍa-tencu* 'to walk toward the speaker', *negayu* 'to jump': *negayu-dencu* 'to rise toward'. Here it appears that the addition of *tencu-/tē-/tēr-* means 'motion toward the speaker'. A similar semantic shift is also found in Kannaḍa in *pō-* 'to go': *pō-tar-* 'to come'. *-konu* 'take', a reflexive auxiliary, is added to some roots to form idiomatic compounds, e.g. *paḍu-* 'to fall': *paḍu-konu* 'to lie down', *anu-* 'to say': *anu-konu* 'to think'. As a reflexive auxiliary it is added to the perfective participle of V^1, *ceppu* 'to tell': *ceppi-konu* 'to appeal', *teṟacu* 'to open': *teṟac-i konu* '(something) to open on its own'. In Modern Telugu the perfective participle is obscured because of vowel harmony, e.g. *cepp-u kon-* 'to appeal', *teruc-u-kon-* v.i. 'to open'.

N + V compounds are more numerous with *konu* 'to take', *cēyu* 'to do', *āḍu*¹ 'to move', *āḍu*² 'to speak', *āḍu*³ 'to play', *paḍu* (tr *paṟucu*) 'to occur, suffer', *pōwu* 'to go', *āru* 'to be full' etc. in the verb position. Examples: *cē-* 'hand': *cē-konu* 'to take, accept', *tala* 'head': *tala-konu* 'to attack', *weli* 'outside': *welu-waḍu* 'to come out': *welu-war-incu* 'to pull out', *daya* 'mercy': *daya-cēyu-* 'to be merciful' > 'to come/to grant', *paṭṭamu* 'anointing': *paṭṭamu-gaṭṭu* 'to anoint', **mēl* 'above, up': *mēl-konu* 'to wake up', **aga-* 'visual field, inside': *aga-paḍu* 'to appear', *māṭa* 'word': *māṭ-āḍu* 'to speak', *pōru* 'fight': *pōr-āḍu* 'to fight', *impu* 'sweetness': *imp-āru* 'to be full of sweetness' etc.

In Modern Telugu there are practically no $V^1 + V^2$ compounds where both are simple roots; [20] but many N + V compounds exist and new ones are created. Since for some of

[20] The only exception is *anu-kon-* 'to think'. A number of reflexive stems have lost the grammatical marking of the main verb, so they appear to be sequences of two verb roots, e.g. *terucu-kon-* '(door) to open itself', *āḍu-kon-* 'to play for oneself'.

these compounds both the meaning and the grammatical category of the first constituent are not synchronically available, traditional Telugu grammarians have given such idiomatic verb compounds a new name, *śabdapallawa* 'new shoots of words'; they are defined as 'sequences with unpredictable meanings in which a verb root is added to elements that are not necessarily verb roots',[21] meaning thereby nouns and some obscure elements. Old and Modern Telugu *sama-kūḍu-* 'to accrue', *nalla-baḍu-* 'to blacken', *nidra-pō-* 'to go to sleep', *aga-paḍu* 'to appear' belong to N + V type although the meanings of *sama-*, *aga-* are not synchronically transparent.

Kui has compound stems of the N + V type where the verb is an auxiliary *man-* 'to exist', *ā-* 'to be', *sī-* 'to give', *in-* 'to say', *is-* 'to cause to say', etc.; e.g. *kari in-* 'to be healed', *kari is-* 'to heal' (idiomatic), *reha āva* 'to be joyful' (Winfield 1928: 123–7).

Koṇḍa has both coordinate and subordinate verb compounds but in all cases V^1 is also inflected. I have not come across any compound stems with uninflected V^1. There are N + V^1 compounds where V^1 is a member of a finite set, including *ā-* 'to be', *ki-* 'to make', *si-* 'to give', *son-* 'to go', *sō-* 'to come out', *ṛey-* 'to beat, strike', e.g. *kōpam ā-* 'to become angry' (*kōpam* 'anger'), *gazibizi ā-* 'to be confused' (*gazibizi* 'confusion'), *gōla ki-* 'to scold' (*gōla* 'scolding'), *saṛa si-* 'to sprinkle cowdung solution' (*saṛa* 'cowdung solution'), *tevgu son-* 'to become blunt (sharpness to go)', *mūRi sō-* 'nose to run' (*mūRi* 'running nose'), *piṟu ṛey-* 'to rain heavily' (*piṟu* 'rain') (Krishnamurti 1969a: 312–13).

Pengo has compound stems with *ā-* 'to be' and *ki-* 'to do' added generally to Indo-Aryan nominal stems to form intransitive or transitive bases respectively, e.g. *janom ā-* 'to be born', *janom ki-* 'to give birth to' (Burrow and Bhattacharya 1970: 106–7).

Compound verb stems are described for few languages of Central Dravidian. Bhaskararao (1980: 26–7) mentions 'composite bases' of two kinds: first, reflexive/reciprocal bases and conjunct verbal bases. The second kind are illustrated by N + V^1 combinations, e.g. *vā-*'to come': *kayar vā-* 'to get angry' (*kayar* 'anger'), *kē-* 'to do': *gōsa-kē* 'to make noise' (*gōsa* 'noise'); he gives usages with other verbalizers, namely *bēp-* 'to get a feeling', *aṭ-* 'to beat, strike', *man-* 'to exist', *puc-* 'to take out', *sūḍ-* 'to perceive' (*ruci-sūḍ-* 'to taste' < lw Te. *ruci cūḍ-* 'lit. taste-to see' = 'to get a taste'), *ēr-* 'to become': *arg-ēr* 'to be digested', *opp-ēr-* 'to agree'. The last verb is the most productive in forming N + V compounds.

In North Dravidian, for Kuṛux Hahn (1911: 70–3) gives many examples of $V^1 + V^2$ and N + V compounds. $V^1 + V^2$: with V^1 uninflected, e.g. *es xac-*, with V^1 inflected, e.g. *esā xac-* 'to do breaking' (*ēn īd-in esā xackan* 'I have done breaking of this'). He calls such verbs 'completives'; some are 'intensives' like *esā capnā-* 'to break quickly'. In some others, the second verb is a modal auxiliary, treated elsewhere in this chapter.

21 *Bālawyākaraṇamu*, Kriyāparicchedamu (chapter on the verb), Sūtram 118.

Hahn calls the N + V^1 type compounds 'nominals', 'though in reality they are rather idiomatic phrases' (1911: 70). The verbs illustrated are *ēx-* 'to cool', *ēr-* 'to see', *man-* 'to exist', *kōr-* 'to enter', *amb-* 'to leave', *okk-*, *lad-*, *pac-*, *kaʔa-*, *khār-* etc.: *cokh man-* 'to pass by', *nāṛī kōr-* (lit. fire to enter) 'to have fever', *nāṛī amb-* 'fever to leave', *aḍḍā ēr-* 'to look out for an opportunity' etc.

Malto (Mahapatra 1979: 186–91) has both V^1 + V^2 and N + V types of compound verb stems. V^2 is a closed set of ten verbs, *et-* 'to get down', *oŋ-* 'to wash', *bar-* 'to come', *ēk-* 'to go', *kud-* 'to do', *kaṭ-* 'to pass', *tey-* 'to send', *urq-* 'to come out', *ondr-* 'to bring', *oy-* 'to take'. Mahapatra says that S^2 (S = Stem) modifies the meaning of S^1, *ok-et-y-ah* 'he sat down', *ok-* 'to sit'. Noun–verb compounds have V^1 as *man-* 'to be', *nan-* 'to do', *kor-* 'to enter', *gaṛar-* 'to become', *lag-* 'to feel'; e.g. *berbad nan-* 'to cause destruction', *gobol nan-* 'to occupy', *īksi kor-* 'jealousy enters', *kīṛe lag-* 'to feel hungry', etc. There is another class that is called balance verbs: 'a few verb roots which occur as balance words with other verbs', e.g. *piṭa baja* 'beat + kill' → 'beating severely', *naḍa pāṛa* 'dance + sing' → 'enjoying thoroughly'. It is not clear if these are nominals or compound verbs.

7.15 Complex predicates and auxiliaries

Complex predicates consist of one main verb (principal meaning carrrier) and one or more auxiliaries. Auxiliaries have two grammatical roles: (i) they may occur as main verbs when they retain their full lexical meaning, or (ii) they may follow main verbs to represent various grammatical relations with modified semantic structure. The number of such auxiliaries is finite in each language and it is not possibile to reconstruct all of them for Proto-Dravidian or one of the subgroups, unequivocally. Cross-linguistically we notice parallelisms in the selection of certain verbs as auxiliaries (mainly those meaning 'be, go, come, leave, take, give', etc.).

Combinations of an uninflected main verb and an auxiliary are treated as lexical compounds (section 7.14, see A1 in figure 7.2). A1.1 are root compounds which occur in the older stages of the literary languages, in which the uninflected V^1 is followed by a limited number of auxiliary verbs V^2 which modify the valency of V^1. A1.2 are a special class of stems in South Dravidian II languages (mainly in Kui–Kuvi–Pengo with traces in Telugu–Gondi and Koṇḍa) in which the main verb V^1 + **taH-* 'give to the 1/2 pers' inherited from Proto-South Dravidian has reduced the auxiliary to a suffix as a marker of direct or indirect object when it denotes the first or second person. Although the construction is reconstructible, it has taken a new grammatical and phonological shape in South Dravidian II.

In Dravidian languages auxiliaries occur after an inflected main verb (infinitive or past/non-past participle). Functionally such auxiliaries belong to two subclasses:

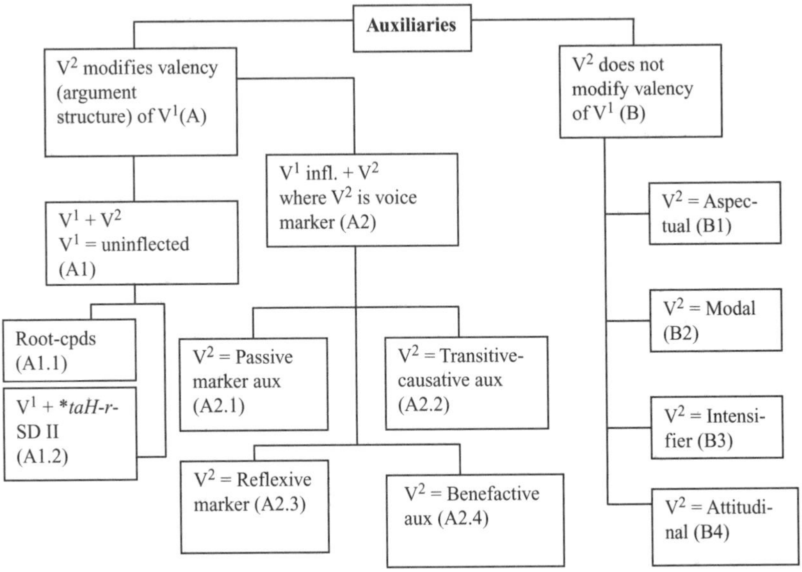

Figure 7.2 Functional classification of auxiliary verbs

(1) those that change the argument structure (valency) of the main verb, and (2) those that preserve the valency but express other grammatical relations like aspect, intensity, mood, mode etc. The valency-changing auxiliaries have co-occurrence restrictions with the main verb and modify its lexical structure and meaning. There are no such restrictions on valency-preserving auxiliaries, since they occur with any main verb, simple, complex, or compound. Figure 7.2 presents a functional subclassification of the auxiliaries.

7.15.1 *South Dravidian I*

It will be clear from the following descriptions that we can reconstruct for Proto-South-Dravidian I some valency-changing auxiliaries, i.e. Vinf + *paṭu-* 'experience, suffer' for passive, Vppl + *koḷ-* 'take' for reflexive, Vppl + *koṭu-* 'to give' for benefactive, Vinf + *vai-* 'throw', *cey-* 'do' for causative; similarly, some valency-preserving auxiliaries, mainly the aspectual and modal ones, can also be reconstructed, i.e. Vppl + *iru* for perfective, Vppl + *viṭu-* 'leave' for 'completive', Vppl + *pō-* 'go' for 'exhaustive', Vinf + *kūṭu-* 'to join, suit' and *varu-/vār-* 'come' for various shades of meaning such as 'may/may not', 'propriety/impropriety', **vēḷ-* 'to wish, desire', *vēṇṭu-* 'be needed' for desiderative/permissive/obligative/prohibitive etc.

Except for Kota, Tuḷu and Koraga which might have lost these, the rest of the members of South Dravidian I have not only inherited these auxiliaries, but also added some more either individually or in smaller subgroups. Sometimes we notice only the sharing of the semantic category and not the actual cognates, e.g. in Tamil and some others closer to it, there is Vppl + *pār-* 'see' (attemptive), but Kannaḍa has Vppl + *nōḍu* 'see' for the same modal meaning 'try to'.

1. Tamil: Tolkāppiyam does not mention auxiliary verbs but uses nine of them in the text (Tinnappan 1980): inf + *paṭu-* in passive, e.g. *coll-a.p-paṭu* 'it was said', verbal noun in *-al* + *vēṇṭ-um* as obligative, e.g. *mikut-al vēṇṭ-um* 'must be doubled', *vēṇṭ-ā* neg obligative, Vppl + *koḷ* as reflexive, e.g. *teri-* 'to know': *terintu koṇṭu* 'having known (by oneself)', Vppl + *koṭu-* 'to give' in benefactive, Vppl + *iru-* 'to be' to denote past perfect, Vinf + *kūṭ-ā* 'does not suit' in prohibitive etc.

Caṅkam Tamil is said to have fifteen auxiliaries (Srinivasan 1980) of which *tā-/taru-* 'to give to 1/2 pers' has the highest frequency. This seems to be a valency-changing auxiliary (A), but we are not clear how it modifies the meaning of the main verb. Rajam (1992: 501–20) considers all non-first stems (S^2, S^3) as non-auxiliary and treats such combinations as compound stems (see section 7.14). Examples: *ta-ntu* + *iṭu* → *ta-nt-iṭu* 'to bring and leave', *iṟai-koṇ-ṭu* + *iru* (*iṟai* 'to sit', *koḷ-* refl, *iru-* 'to be') 'to remain sitting' (here the last two stems are auxiliaries). The other V^2 are *ī-* 'to give', *kil-* 'to be able', *koḷ-* 'to take' (used reflexively): *eṭu-ttu koḷ-* 'to draw toward oneself', *taku-* 'to suit', *paṭu-* 'to feel' (*atir-paṭu-* 'to vibrate'), *peṟu-* 'to experience, obtain', *var(u)-* 'to come', *viṭu-* 'to leave' (*niṉṟu-viṭu-* 'to stay together with', *nil-* 'to stand'). It seems that the second stems (V^2) were in a transitional stage between being a member of a compound verb (in which V^1 and V^2 retain their lexical status) and being grammaticalized auxiliaries; particularly examine the usages of *iru-* and *viṭu-*. Middle Tamil (inscriptional AD 900–1050) uses several auxiliaries, i.e. *vēṇṭum, kaṭavu* for obligatory mode, *iru-*, *nil-* for the perfective, *-koḷ* for reflexive, *kuṭu-* (< *koṭu-*) for benefactive, *vay-*, *cey-* for causative, *paṭu-*, *peṟu-* for passive, etc. (Karthikeyan 1980).

Modern Tamil employs some thirty-five auxiliaries; not all these derive from Old Tamil (Agesthialingom and Srinivasa Varma 1980, Asher 1985, Lehmann 1989, Schiffman 1999; most of the sentences below are cited from Lehmann 1989).

(A) Valency changing with inflected main verb followed by an auxiliary (A2):

(A2.1) Passive: inf of V_1 + *paṭu-* 'to suffer'

(ia) *vēṭ-aṉ*[1] *māṉ-ai*[2] *kkoṉ-ṟ-āṉ*[3]
[hunter deer-acc kill-past-3m-sg]
'the hunter[1] killed[3] the deer[2]' (Agentive)

(ib) *māṉ*[1] *vēṭ-an-āl*[2] *koll-a-ppaṭ-ṭ-a-tu*[3]
[deer hunter-by kill-inf-aux-past-3neu-sg]
'the deer[1] was killed[3] by the hunter[2]'

The passive is rarely used in conversational Tamil but it is not so rare in formal written Tamil (Asher 1985: 152).

(A2.2) Causative: the main verb is changed into a causative when any of the auxiliaries *vai-* ‘put’, *cey-/paṇṇu-* ‘make’ is added to the infinitive stem of the main verb:

(iia) *kumār*[1] *va-nt-āṉ*[2] ‘Kumar[1] came[2]’
(iib) *rājā*[1] *kumār-ai*[2] *var-a*[3] *vai-tt-āṉ*[4] ‘Raja[1] made[4] Kumar (acc)[2] (to) come[3]’

(A2.3) Reflexive: V^1 perfective participle + V^2*koḷ-* ‘take’

(iii) *uṉ*[1] *caṭṭ-ai.*[2] *k kazaṭṭ-i*[3]*.k koḷ*[4] ‘take off[3,4] your[1] shirt[2]’

(A2.4) Benefactive: the auxiliary *vai-* ‘put’ is added to the perfective/past participle of an intransitive verb in a benefactive sense, e.g. *tiṟa-* (*tiṟa-nt-*) ‘to be open’: *tiṟa-ntu vai-* ‘to keep open’; *koṭu-* ‘give’ is added instead, if the beneficiary is another person and not oneself.

(iv) *katav-ai*[1] *tiṟa-ntu*[2] *vai*[3] ‘keep[3] the door[1] open[2]’
(v) *rājā*[1] *kumār-ukku*[2]*.k katav-ai*[3] *tiṟa-ntu*[4] *koṭu-tt-āṉ*[5] ‘Raja[1] kept[5] the door[3] open[4] for Kumar[2]’

(B) Valency preserving: V^1 is inflected and the V^2 (auxiliary) only specifies the intention of the speaker in relation to action of V^1 (mode), but the valency of the main verb remains unchanged.

(B1) Aspectual: the present/past/future perfect is formed by adding the inflected verb *iru-* ‘to be’ to the past/perfective participle of the main verb. The sequence *koṇṭu* + *iru-* is added to express the progressive aspect in the present, past or future; by adding *viṭu-* to the past/perfective participle, the perfective aspect ‘thoroughly, definitely’ is expressed:

(vi) *kumār*[1] *ippōtu*[2] *vant(u) iru-kkiṟ-āṉ*[3] ‘Kumar[1] has come[3] now[2]’
(vii) *āṟu*[1] *maṇikku*[2]*.k kumār*[3] *paṭittu-koṇ-ṭu iru-nt-āṉ*[4] ‘at[2] six[1] o’clock[2] Kumar[3] was reading[4]’
(viii) *kumār*[1] *kūṭṭa-tt-il*[2] *pēc-i.k koṇ-ṭu iru-pp-āṉ*[3] ‘Kumar[1] will be speaking[3] at the meeting[2]’ (*kūṭṭ-am* ‘meeting’, *pēcu-* ‘to speak’)
(ix) *kumār*[1] *nēṟṟu*[2] *va-ntu viṭ-ṭ-āṉ*[3] ‘Kumar[1] came[2] yesterday[3]’ (also implies ‘unexpectedly’)
(x) *kūppiṭu*[1] *viṭu-v-āṉ*[2] ‘(he) will[1] (definitely[2]) call[1]’

Other aspectual auxiliaries include *āku-* ‘to become’ (perfective participle + *āy-ṟṟu* 3neu sg) to express completion of ‘affective’ verbs (Lehmann 1989: 210–11).

(xi) *pālkāraṉ*[1] *va-ntu*[2] *āyiṟṟu*[3] ‘the milkman[1] has come’[23] (having come-it happened)

(B2) Modal auxiliaries: these auxiliaries have defective morphology and peculiar morphophonemic changes. One set occurs only in the third neuter singular: V^1 inf + *vēṇṭ-um* 'is needed' (Obligative), V^1 inf + *vēṇṭ-ām* 'not needed' (negative obligation); *pō-* 'go', *vā-* 'come', *iru-* 'be', *pār-* 'see' is the other group (Lehmann 1989: 211–18):

(xii) *kumār*[1] *vīṭṭu-kku*[2] *pōk-a vēṇṭ-um*[3] 'Kumar[1] must go[3] home[2]'

(xiii) *nī*[1] *iṉi-mēl*[2] *inta*[3] *marunt-ai*[4]*.c.cāppiṭ-a*[5] *vēṇṭ-ām*[6] 'you[1] don't need [6] to take (ingest)[5] this[3] medicine[4] from now on[2]'

The other modal auxiliaries include inf + *kūṭ-um*/*kūṭ-ātu* (for possibility, obligation, desideration and permission and their negative counterparts; *kūṭu-* 'to join'), inf + *muṭi-y-um*/*muṭi-y-ātu* (possibility/impossibility), inf + *pō-* 'go'/*varu-* 'come' (intention, prediction), inf + *iru* (intention to perform an action), inf + *pār-* 'to see' (trying an action).

(B4) Attitudinal auxiliaries include V^1 ppl + *taḷḷu-* 'to push' (chain action both in positive and negative; *ūtu-* 'to blow/smoke'), Vppl + *kiṭa-* 'to lie' (durative), Vppl + *kiẓi-* 'to tear' (speaker's negative attitude), e.g.

(xiv) *kumār*[1] *cikareṭ*[2] *ūt-i*[3]*.t taḷḷu-kiṟ-āṉ*[4] 'Kumar[1] smokes[3] one cigarette[2] after another[3,4]'

(xv) *kumār amerikāv-ukku pōy-i kiẓi-pp-āṉ* 'Kumar will not be able to go to America'

(B3) Intransitive verbs representing a sudden change of state take *pō-* as aux following the Vppl; also *tīr-* is added to a Vppl to express an effective involvement of a subject in an emotional state/activity:

(xvi) *pāṉai*[1] *uṭai-ntu*[2] *pōy-i-ṟṟu*[3] 'the pot[1] got broken[2] off[3]' (lit. broke and went off)

(xvii) *avaḷ aẓu-tu tīr-tt-āḷ* 'she cried herself out'

There is difference of opinion among Tamil scholars regarding the auxiliaries which are exclusively attitudinal.

2. Malayāḷam has eighteen auxiliary verbs, according to E. V. N. Namboodiri (1980), and twenty, according to Somasekharan Nair (1980), many of which have cognates in Tamil lexically and grammatically: Vppl + *iri-* 'sit' present/past perfect depending on the tense of the aux, e.g. *vann-irikkunnu* 'he has come', *vann-irunnu* 'he had come', Vppl + *pō-* 'go' denotes 'thoroughly, unfortunately', e.g. *paẓam*[1] *cīññu-pōyi*[2] 'the fruit[1] was (completely) rotten[2]'; following a non-past verb, *pō-* denotes 'about to', *ñān vīẓān pōyi* 'I was about to fall', Vppl + *kūṭ-ā* denotes prohibition, V non-past ppl + *kūṭ-um* expresses willingness, V^1(past/non-past) + *koḷ-* denotes 'humility, responsibility', etc., Vppl + *kaḷa-* means 'completion, surprise', e.g. *ñān*[1]*vyākaraṇam*[2]*maṟannu-kaḷaññu*[3] 'I[1] forgot[3] the grammar[2] completely[3]', Vppl + *koṭu* (indirect object in 3 pers) + *tar*

(indirect object in 1/2 pers) mean 'benefactive' or doing an action for another's benefit, Vppl + *viṭu-* completion of an action, e.g. *avan-e*[1] *śikṣiccu*[2] *viṭṭu*[3] '(someone) punished[2] him[1] (and closed the matter[3])'.

3. Koḍagu: fewer auxiliaries are reported in published literature (Balakrishnan 1977, 1980; Ebert 1996). Vinf + *aṇḍ* is used in obligative mode, e.g. *nānï māḍ-aṇḍ-u* 'I must do', *avën ōd-aṇḍ-a* 'he must not read', prohibitive by adding *āg-a* (neg imp of the verb *āgu-* 'to be') to the infinitive, e.g. *avë*^{n} *naḍapëk āg-a* 'he should not walk' (lit. he-walking-not be). There are three auxiliaries which express different aspects: *irï-*, inflected for past and non-past tenses, is added to the perfective participle, to denote the perfect aspect in past or non-past, e.g. *nānï māḍ(i)-ir-uvi* 'I will be doing', *naṅga tand (u)-irï-t-ëtï* 'we have given'. Ebert (1996: 28) says 'the specifier *ïr-* conveys the notion of doing something to the end', e.g. *nari nāy-na kond-ïrtï* 'the tiger killed the dog'. The 'completive' aspect is expressed by the auxiliary *-iḍ* added to the past participle, e.g. *ayṇga māḍ-(i)-iṭ-ëtï* 'they have done it'. The reflexive is formed by Vppl + *-oḷ* (< **koḷ-*), e.g. *nīṅga nind(ï)-oḷ-i* 'you (pl) stand there'. Balakrishnan calls these 'perfective' and 'completive' moods. The auxiliary *pō-* 'go' is added to the Vppl to indicate 'that something disappears or has some negative consequences' (Ebert 1996: 28), *avë*^{n} *cattï-pōcc-i* 'he died'. The past form of *ā-/āc-*'be, become' is added to Vppl to indicate 'that an action was terminated with a positive outcome', e.g. *ava-ḍa uṇḍ-it-āc-i* 'she has eaten her meal (she is satiated)' (Ebert 1996: 27–30).

4. Iruḷa: the auxiliaries are part of its inheritance from Pre-Tamil. The ones discussed by Perialwar (1980) and Zvelebil (1973, 1980) are: Vppl + *iru* for present or past perfective, *tin-ṟ-iru-kk-e* [eat-past ppl be-non-past-pers suff] 'I have eaten', *pā-tt-iru-nd-ēmu* [see-past be-past-pers suff] 'we had seen', *van-nd-uru-ku-du* (note *uru-ku* for *iru-kku*) 'it has come' (Zvelebil 1980: 35). In fast speech the above verbs are pronounced *tin-ṟ-ukke* and *pātt-undēmu*. The others include Vppl + *veyi* 'to keep' (OTa. *vai-*), + *kāṭṭu* 'show', + *viḍu* 'to leave' (definitive), + *muḍi* (completive) (these three occur with transitive main verbs); Vppl (v.i.) + *pō-* 'go', *pō-cu* (past 3neu sg), e.g. *kamcu*[1] *kīndu*[2] *pōcu*[3] 'the shirt[1] is torn[2] off[3]' (?accidental), Vppl (v.i./tr.) + *ā-* 'be', *ā-cu* (past 3neu sg), e.g. *adu vand-ācu* 'it has come', *nī nīru kuḍitt(u)-ācu* 'you drank the water' (?finality). The auxiliaries *kol-/ko-/on-* 'get' are added to Vppl in reflexive and reciprocal meanings, e.g. *tin-d-oṇḍ-e* 'I ate myself', Vppl + *koṇḍ-iru* is used for 'durative' [?corresponding to Kannaḍa *avaru pāḍ-i koṇ-ḍ-iru-kk-āru* 'they are/were singing'] (durative aspect; in fast speech *-oṇḍ-ri-*, e.g. *cē-d-oṇḍ-ri-nd-e* 'I was doing'), + *tole*, e.g. *nī pōyi tole* 'you (sg) go away' (contempt). Modal auxiliaries include Vppl + *muḍi* (past/non-past inflection) denoting 'ability/inability', Vnon-past in *-g-* adds *-oṇu* (variant of *vēṇu/vēṇḍu*) 'is needed', *nīm-ō*[1] *avan-ō*[2] *var-g-oṇu*[3] 'either you[1] or he[2] should come[3]', inf + *vēṇḍu* (obligatory), *vēṇḍ-a* (prohibitive), e.g. *nī pōg-a vēṇḍ-a* 'do not go' (2sg).

5. Toda uses 'aspectual auxiliaries' added to the past stem, S^2 of the main verb. Three of them have phonological changes in inflection: S^2-*ïḍ-* (*-ïṭ-*) the 'preservative'

auxiliary has a past *ïṣ*-(<-*ïṭṣ*-), the 'completive' auxiliary S^2-*fïḍ*- (-*fïṭ*-) is related to *pïṛ*- (*pïṭ*-) 'to leave', corresponding to Ta. *viṭu*- (*viṭṭ*-), and the 'perfective continuative' is from S^2-*ïr*- (*ïθ*-) 'to sit, remain'. Some eight other auxiliaries are written as separate words, including 'reflexive-durative' *kwïḷ*-, *kwïḍ*- (Ta. *koḷ*-), 'continuative' *pï̄x*- 'to go' (Ta. *pō*-), etc. (Emeneau 1984: §VII.8).

6. Kota: the verbal auxiliaries are: V^1 + *āko* 'may', + *ākē* 'can', e.g. *gey-ākō* 'may do', *ug-ākē* 'can plough', V^{1}inf + *āg* 'to be', e.g. *koṛlk-āykō* 'gave' (lit. giving-was); the others are *ik*-, *oḷ*- vā-, *ōṛ*- added to the past stem of the main verb. The usages show that some of these meant aspects, present/past durative, but the author does not specify how the auxiliaries are used. Two others mentioned are -*ōg* 'to go', *ār* 'to be able', added to the verbal noun. The Kota auxiliaries do not seem to compare well with those of Toda or the other languages, which have several auxiliary verbs inherited from Proto-South Dravidian I (G. Subbiah 1980).

7. Kannaḍa: literary Kannaḍa uses several auxiliaries with approximately the same meanings as Tamil and Malayāḷam. Vinf in -*al* + *tīr*- 'be possible', + *āṟ* 'be able', *mecc-al āṟ-en* 'I cannot like', + *āgu*- 'suit' (prohibitive), e.g. *pōg-al āg-a-du* '(one) should not go', + *ī* 'to give' (permissive), *ir-al ī-v-en-e*? 'am I going to allow it to happen?', + *bār-a-du* 'does not come' (neg potential) *gel-al bār-a-du* '(one) cannot win', + *vēẓ-kum* 'is desired'/+ *vēḍ-a* 'not desired' (desiderative/neg desiderative) *nil-a vēẓ-kum* 'it must stand (permanently)', *ir-al vēḍ-a* 'should not remain'. There are several auxiliaries which occur after the past/perfective participle (ppl): Vppl + *ā*- 'to be', e.g. *kond-a-pp-an* 'he will kill' (having-killed-he-will-be), *keṭṭ*(*u*)-*a-pu-du* 'it will be spoiled' [the special meanings are not clarified by the author]. The aux -*ir*- 'be' is added to the present/past/negative participles or the infinitive in -*al* to express durative action, e.g. *nurgu*- 'to crush', present participle *nurg-utt*-, *nurgutt-ire* 'while being crushed', *ese-du ir-k-um* 'it continues to shine', *kuḍ-al* 'give' (inf), *kuḍ-al-ir-p-an* 'he will certainly give'. The passive is formed by adding the auxiliary *paḍu* to Vinf, e.g. *pēẓ-al-paḍu*- 'to be told' (Ramachandra Rao 1980).

Modern Kannaḍa (Sridhar 1990: §2.1.3.3) adds the inflected forms of *ir*- 'to be' to the main verb (perfective participle) to form the present/past/future perfective, e.g. *hōg*-(*i*)-*id-d-a* (< *-*ir-d-a*) 'he had gone', *hōgi iru-tt-āne* 'he will have gone'. The other auxiliaries include *koḷ*- 'take' (reflexive) and *koḍu*- 'give' (benefactive) (both valency changing), *biḍu*- 'leave' (finality, completion), *hōgu*- (unintended action), *nōḍu*- 'see' (attemptive), *hāku*- 'put' (exhaustive action) (for examples, see Sridhar 1990: 232–3). The potential and negative potential is formed by Vinf + *bahudu* 'possible', *balla* (3m sg) 'can do', and *āgu* 'become, happen' (240–1).

8. Tuḷu: there are certain suffixes (some of which appear to be grammaticalized auxiliaries) to express different aspects and modes (Bhat 1967: 50–70). Reflexives are formed by the addition of -*oṇu* (<* *koṇ*-), e.g. *koy*- 'pluck': *koyy-oṇu* 'pluck for oneself', *bare*- 'write': *bare-voṇu* 'write for oneself'; after bases ending in -*pu*, the suffix is -*toṇu*,

e.g. *kaḍ-pu* 'cut' : *kaḍ-t-oṇu* 'cut oneself' (*-t-* is historically an old past-tense marker), corresponding to *koḷ-* being added to Vppl in the other South Dravidian I languages. The 'completive' is formed by adding *-t-rï/-tt-rï/-d-rï/-ḍ-rï/-rï* to the verbal bases of different classes (Bhat 1967: 51), *mī-* 'bathe': *mī-trï* 'bathe away', *tin-* 'eat': *tin-drï* 'eat away'. Here also the dental could be a remnant of a past marker. The perfective is a tense in Tuḷu, unlike the other South Dravidian I languages, formed by a suffix {*t/tïd/d*} as opposed to the past {*y/t/d* ~ *ḍ*}, and not by means of an auxiliary.

7.15.2 *South Dravidian II*

The auxiliaries *paṭu-* 'experience' (passive), *way-* 'throw' (transitivizer), *koḷ-* 'take' (reflexive), *pō-* 'go' (completive following Vppl, inceptive following Vinf), **ciy-* 'give' (permissive following Vinf) can be traced to Proto-Dravidian or Proto-South Dravidian. The auxiliary **taH-r-* 'give to 1/2 pers' is one of the oldest auxiliaries, shared by both South Dravidian I and South Dravidian II in compound stems (A1 in figure 7.2 above), but it got incorporated into V^1 as a suffix marking a direct or indirect object in the first or second person in South Dravidian II languages. In some others, synonyms and not cognates occur, e.g. *man-* 'be' (SD I *ir-*) in forming compound tenses or aspects. Unfortunately some of the descriptions of South Dravidian II and Central Dravidian languages are inadequate to make further generalizations.

9. Telugu: there are nearly twenty verbs used both as main verbs and as auxiliaries in the earliest literary work by Nannaya (AD 1040). The auxiliaries may precede or follow the main verb, although the frequency of auxiliaries following the main verb is much higher; besides, other words may be inserted between the main verb and the auxiliary, e.g. *cepp-an*^{1} *ēla*^{2} *walas-e*^{3} [tell-inf^1 why^2 be needed-past-3sg^3] 'why^2 (did) one need^3 to tell^1?' These two factors mean that the auxiliaries at that stage of evolution of Telugu have not been fully grammaticalized elements. Half of them do not continue in modern Telugu (the meaning of the independent verb is given first, followed by its meaning as an auxiliary in the parentheses): Vinf + *agu-* 'be, become' (be possible), Vinf + *ōḍu-* 'to fear'(hesitate), Vinf + *ōpu-* 'to tolerate' (be capable), Vinf + *kanu-/kāncu-* 'see' (attempt, be able), Vinf + *canu-* 'go' (be just), Vinf + *tagu-* 'to suit' (be proper), Vinf + *toḍãgu-* 'attempt' (begin), Vinf + *nērcu-* 'learn a skill' (can manage/cannot manage), Vinf + *pūnu* 'be tied to yoke' (make effort), Vinf + *cālu* 'be sufficient' (be able), Vinf + *walacu*/neg. *oll-* 'love, like' (want to/not want to) (see Ushadevi 1980).

In Modern Telugu, the valency changing auxiliaries (A) in figure 7.2 are:

(A1) Compound lexical items in which V^1 is uninflected and V^2 is an auxiliary; these are treated in section 7.14.

(A2) In these the V^1 is inflected and the auxiliary V^2 changes the valency of the V^1.

(A2.1) Passive: Vinf + *paḍu-*, e.g. *cēs-* 'do': *cēy-a-baḍu-* 'to be done', *cacc-* 'die', *ca-mpu-* 'to kill': *camp-a-baḍu-* 'be killed' (ia) *rāwaṇuḍu*[1] *cacc-ǣ-ḍu*[2] 'Ravana[1] died[2]'

(ib) *rāwaṇuḍu*[1] *rāmuḍ-i-cēta*[2] *camp-a-baḍḍāḍu*[3] 'Ravana[1] was killed[3] by Rama[2]'

(A2.2) Transitivizers: there are nearly 100 change-of-state and change-of-position verbs (V^1) which are mostly intransitive. The infinitive stems of these are followed by a limited number of auxiliaries, which convert them into transitive stems: *koṭṭ-* 'to beat', *peṭṭ-* 'to put', *wēs-* 'to throw', *tīs-* 'to remove', e.g. *wirugu-* v.i. 'to break': *wirag-a-goṭṭ-* v.t. 'to break', *āru-* 'to dry': *ār-a-beṭṭ-* 'to (lay something to) dry', *paḍu-* v.i. 'to fall': *paḍ-a-goṭṭ-* v.t. 'to fell', *paḍ-a-wēs-* 'to throw away', *wiḍu-* 'to be separate': *wiḍ-a-dīs-* 'to separate' (for a complete list of such verbs with auxiliaries, see Krishnamurti 1993, Appendix 2). I proposed that *koṭṭ-* occurs in the case of verbs representing a sudden change of state or position, and *peṭṭ-* in the case of a gradual change of state verbs:

(iia) *māmiḍi*[1] *paḷḷu*[2] *rāl-i-pōy-ǣ-y*[3] 'the mango[1] fruit[2] fell off[3]' (on their own)

(iib) *wāḍu*[1] *māmiḍi*[2] *paḷḷu*[3] *rāl-a-goṭṭ-ǣ-ḍu*[4] 'he$_1$ felled[4] the mango[2] fruit[3]'

(A2.3) Reflexive: Vppl + *kon-* 'take', e.g. *cēs-* 'to do' : //cēs-i-kon-// → /cēs-u-kon-/ 'to do something for oneself', *wiraga-goṭṭ-u-kon-* 'to break (a body part) by oneself':

(iii) *wāḍu*[1] *kālu*[2] *wirag-a-goṭṭ-u-konnāḍu*[3] 'he[1] broke[3] (his) leg[2]'

The underlying forms of V^1 had a perfective participle marker *-i* which became *-u* (*cēs-i-kon-* → *cēs-u-kon-*) through vowel harmony of the rounded vowel in the following syllable.

(A2.4) Benefactive: Vppl + *peṭṭ-* 'put', e.g. *rās-* 'to write'; *rās-i-peṭṭ-* 'to write for the benefit of another person(s)', *waṇḍu-* 'to cook': *waṇḍ-i-peṭṭ-* 'to cook for others':

(iv) *mā āwiḍa*[1] *rōjū*[2] *padimandiki*[3] *annam*[4] *waṇḍ-i peḍu-tun-di*[5] 'my wife[1] daily[2] cooks[5] food[4] for ten persons[3]'

(A2.5) Permissive: Vinf + *icc-* 'give', e.g. *ceyy-an-icc-* 'to let (somebody) do', *weḷḷ-an-icc-* 'to let (somebody) go', *uṇḍu-* 'to stay': *uṇḍ-an-icc-* 'to let (one) stay':

(v) *nannu*[1] *mī iṇṭ-(i)-lō*[2] *padi*[3]*-rōju-lu*[4] *uṇḍ-an-iww-aṇḍi*[5] 'please let (permit)[5] me[1] to stay[5] in your house[2] for ten[3] days[4]'

Since there are co-occurrence restrictions in the above combinations of V^1 and V^2 (except in the case of A2.5 which will be discussed later), all such collocations are treated as a lexical expansion of the main verb, i.e. V^1. These can be followed by auxiliaries which do not change the argument structure of the stem to which they are affixed (B). The main subclasses in Telugu are:

(B1) Aspectual: the durative is formed by adding the inflected verb *un-* 'to be' to the non-past participle, e.g. *cēs-t(u)* + *un-nā-ḍu* 'he/is/was/has been doing'. The inflected verb *un-nā-ḍu* 'he is/was/has been' is the only one in Telugu which has an aspectual and non-tense meaning, both in finite and non-finite forms; the durative in the present/past and perfect is, therefore, formed by adding it to the non-past stem of any main verb. Telugu does not have present or past perfect like some of the South Dravidian I languages in the finite form like **cēs-i un-nā-ḍu* 'he has/had done', but it does occur in the contra-factual conditional form/perfective irrealis, e.g. *cēs-i uṇ-ṭē* 'if (one) has/had done . . .'

(vi) *mīr-ē*[1] *īpani*[2] *cēs-i uṇṭē*[3] *bāg-uṇḍ-ē-di*[4] 'had[3] you yourself[1] done[3] this job[2], it would have been good[4]'

(B2) Modal auxiliaries: Vinf + *kala*-(g)np 'be'/*lē*-(g)np 'not be' (potential/neg potential), Vinf + *kalugu*- (potential, same as Vinf + *kala*-), Vinf + *pō*- 'go' (inceptive, 'about to V'), Vinf + *lē-ka pō*- (negative potential–perfective), Vinf + *waccu* 'it comes' (probabilitative–permissive, 'allowed to, permitted to'), Vinf + *kūḍ-a-du* 'does not suit' (negative probabilitative–permissive; 'not allowed to V'), Vinf + *-wāli/-āli* (< OTe. *walay-un* 'is needed' got grammaticalized as an auxiliary verb and then as a mere bound morpheme) (obligative; 'should/must'), Vinf + *oddu* (< **wal-a-du* 'it is not needed') (prohibitive; 'should not, must not'). Examples:

(viia) *nēnu kāru naḍap-a gala-nu* 'I can drive a car' (potential)
(viib) *nēnu kāru naḍap-a lē-nu* 'I cannot drive a car'(neg potential)
(viii) *ceṭṭu*[1] *kinda*[2] *paḍ-a bō-t-unnadi*[3] 'the tree[1] is about to fall[3] down[2]' (inceptive)
(ixa) *mīru rēpu nannu kalaw-a waccu* 'you may meet me tomorrow'
(ixb) *nuwwu sigareṭlu tāg-a gūḍ-a-du* 'you should not smoke cigarettes'
(xa) *nēnu rēpu āfīsuku weḷḷ-āli* 'I must go to the office tomorrow'
(xb) *nuwwu jwaramtō āfīsuku weḷḷ-a waddu* 'you must not go to the office with fever'

In examples (ixa)–(xb) the finite verb agreement shows third neuter singular, but the subject NP can be in any gender–number–person. Also note that these forms have no non-finite verbs, unlike the others which occur both in finite and non-finite forms.

(B3) Intensifier auxiliaries: Vppl + *pō*- 'to go' (intensified action). Here the main verbs are intransitive and denote change-of-state, e.g. *cacc*- 'to die':

(xi) *wāḍu*[1] *haṭhāttu-gā*[2] *cacc-i pōy-ǣ-ḍu*[3] 'he[1] died (away)[3] suddenly[2]'

Another type is Vppl + *pō-/ wēs*- 'throw' where the main verb is transitive, e.g. *tin*- 'to eat':

(xii) *annam*[1] *antā*[2] *wāḍ-ē*[3] *tin-i-pōy-ǣ-ḍu/wēs-ǣ-ḍu*[4] 'he himself[3] ate up[4] all[2] the food[1]' (completely, exhaustively)

What is given under (A2.5) should properly belong to (B2) modal auxiliaries, because any verb can carry the permissive mode and there are no co-occurrence restrictions between V^1 and V^2. But the permissive complex stems can take other modal auxiliaries, thus behaving like those of A2, e.g.

(xiii) *nēnu*[1] *ninnu*[2] *ṭikkeṭṭu*[3] *lēk-uṇḍā*[4] *sinimā-ku*[5] *weḷḷ-an-iww-a-gala-nu*[6] ‘I[1] can let[6] you[2] go[6] to the cinema[5] without[4] a ticket[3]’

Its ambivalent status is because of this overlap. Modern Telugu uses several auxiliaries under Attitudinal (B4), such as *cacc-* ‘die’, *ēḍuc-* ‘weep’, added to Vppl to denote contempt, disgust, etc.

(xiv) *tondaragā nijam cepp-i ēḍu* ‘tell the truth quickly’ (disgust)
(xv) *ā sangati ēd-ō tondaragā cepp-i cāwu* ‘tell that matter quickly’ (extreme impatience)

10. Koṇḍa has reflexive complex predicates (A.2.3) formed by adding a suffix *-ay* to V^1, followed by the auxiliary *ā-* ‘become’ with finite or non-finite inflection as V^2, e.g. *ḍūs-* ‘comb’: *ḍūs-ay ā-* ‘comb oneself’, *pas-* ‘scratch’: *pas-ay ā-* ‘scratch oneself’; the reciprocal predicates are formed by adding *-as* to the V^1 followed by inflected *ā-* ‘become’, e.g. *kat-* ‘cut’: *kat-as ā-* ‘to cut each other’. We are not certain if *-ay* and *-as* are derivational suffixes which change the verb into an abstract noun first, followed by the auxiliary. In that case, they do not belong here. Two other sets of complex predicates are the Aspectual (B1) and Intensive (B3):

(B1) Aspectual: V^1 may be inflected (finite/non-finite) for past, non-past or perfective *-zi*, followed by *man-* ‘be’ as V^2 for different aspects as per the chart below:

V^1	V^2(*man-* ‘become’)	Grammatical name
past (*-t-*)	past	past perfect
non-past (*-n-*)	non-past	present perfect
perfective (*-zi-*)	durative	non-past durative
	past	past durative

Examples (Krishnamurti 1969a: 304–12):

naŋi[1] *kāp-ki-t-a*[2] *ma-R-ar*[3] ‘(they) were[3] waiting[2] for me[1]’ (past perfect)
ḍāŋ-it-a[1] *man-an*[2] ‘he has[2] hidden[1] (himself)’ (present perfect)
nān[1] *iḍ-n-a*[2] *man-zin-a*[3] ‘I[1] shall[3] (continue to) keep[2] (them with me)’ (non-past durative)
ven-zi ma-R-an ‘(he) was listening’

(B3) Intensive complex predicates: V^2 is a member of a closed set of verbs such as *son-* ‘go’, *ṛis-* ‘leave’, *si-* ‘give’, *ta-* ‘bring’, *o-* ‘carry’, *pok-* ‘discard’ etc. added to V^1 in expressing various shades of meanings, which I have lumped into one class as ‘Intensive’

(Krishnamurti 1969a: 306–7); (V^1 is underlined), e.g.

Past: *sā-t-a so-R-ar* 'they were dead and gone'
ek-t-a ṛis-t-a 'I climbed up it'
si-t-a pok-t-an 'he gave it away'
sō-n-a so-n-a 'I will get out'
vīs-i ta-t-an 'he has finished them off'
tō̱r-is-n-a sī-n-a 'I will show you clearly'

It must be noted that some of the above are serial verbs, where two finite verbs occur together as a single predicate and certain morphophonemic changes take place in the first verb of the series (see section 7.13).

11. Kui does not have an elaborate auxiliary system like Koṇḍa, but certain verbs do occur as auxiliaries, e.g. *man-* 'be present, exist', *ā-* 'become', *sā-* 'die', *sī-* 'give', *duh-* '?may, might' (Winfield 1928: 123–8). Examples:

(i) *āmu ē iḍu tani man-ji manamu*
[we that-house-in having stayed-be-non-past-1pl]
'we are lodging in that house' (present durative)

(ii) *ē kṛāḍi-tini vī-va ā-n-e*
[that-tiger-acc shoot-inf be-non-past-3neu-sg]
(lit. there will be a shooting that tiger)
'that tiger must be shot' (obligative)

(iii) *īnu*[1] *vrīs-ki*[2] *duh-umu*[3]
[you sg write-pres pl keep-imp-sg]
'you[1] go on[3] writing[2]' (pres dur in imper mood)[22]

(iv) *ānu nī sinḍa oska jī-a-t-e*
[I your cloth sew-pres pl give-trans prtcl-past-1sg]
'I sewed your cloth for you' (benefactive)

In (iv) a 'transition particle' *-a-/-ar-* (~ *-ta-/-tar-*), denoting first- or second-person object, is inserted in the auxiliary after the root and before the tense morph. This particle is comparatively traced to the Proto-Dravidian verb **taH-/*taH-r-* (pos and neg) 'give to 1/2 pers'. The reduction of the auxiliary into an object agreement marker is an innovation of the South Dravidian II languages, mainly Kui–Kuvi–Pengo–Manḍa with traces in Telugu and Koṇḍa.[23] The transition particle can be embedded before the tense morph

[22] Winfield says 'Any tense and mood of duhpa may be used with the present verbal participle of the main verb to express continued action' (1928: 126).

[23] In Koṇḍa *si-* 'give' has two imperatives, *si-ʔa* 'give' (3sg), *si-du* 'give' (3pl). as opposed to *si-da* 'give me/us' (imper 2sg), *si-da-ṭ* 'give me/us' (imper 2pl) (Krishnamurti 1969a: 261; also the remarks of Burrow in the Foreword xvi). Old and Modern Telugu has a form derived from the same root, i.e. *in-da-(mu)* 'here, take this', addressing a second person.

either in the main verb or in the auxiliary (Winfield 1928: 101–11). Steever (1993: ch. 2) has convincingly argued for this shift having taken place in Proto-South Dravidian II, building on the insights provided by Emeneau's 1945 article and the observation of Burrow and Bhattacharya (1961: 131). We have already seen in section 7.14 that Old Tamil, Old Kannaḍa and Old Telugu have reconstructable root compounds with **tā-/tar-*V (< PD **taH-/taH-r-*) as V^2.

The use of *man-* in non-past and past as an auxiliary also generates durative and perfective forms in the present and past, e.g. *sīp-ki man-j-ai-i* 'I am giving you', *sīp-ki manj-a-t-e* 'I was giving you', *sīa manj-a-t-e* 'I have given to you', *sīa manj-a-t-e* 'I had given to you'. Therefore, the use of *man-* is parallel to its use in Koṇḍa as an aspectual marker, but for the 'transition particle'.

12. Kuvi: Vinf + *ā-* 'become' in non-past marks Obligative (B2), Vinf + *hī-* 'give' is Permissive (B2), e.g.

(i) *īkokasi*[1] *oso*[2] *tinj-aliā-n-e*[3] 'this boy[1] must take (eat)[3] the medicine[2]' (lit. to-eat shall-be)

(ii) *ēvaṇaʔi*[1] *mīyali*[2] *hī-mu*[3] ' allow[3] him[1] to bathe[2]'

In Kuvi the durative and perfective participles are formed by adding to the stem {*ci/si/ji/hi/i*} and {*ca/sa/ja/ha/a*}. The auxiliary *man-* is added (in finite or non-finite inflection) to these participles of V^1 to form 'compound tenses' (Israel 1979: 178–81), i.e. different aspects in the past and non-past, e.g. *ki-hi ma-c-eʔẽ* 'I was doing' (past durative), *ki-hi man-esi* 'he is doing' (non-past durative), *ki-ha maceri* 'they had done' (past perfect), *ta-ca mane* 'she has brought' (present perfect). The reflexive is formed by adding *koḍ-* (< **koḷ-* 'take') to the perfective form of V^1, e.g. *nānu*[1] *paya*[2] *koḍiʔí*[3] 'I[1] beat (having beaten)[2] myself[3]'.These formations are comparable to those in Koṇḍa and Kui.

13. Pengo: parallel to Kui, Pengo also has compound stems with PD **taH-* incorporated as an auxiliary, but it behaves like a suffix, rather than as an auxiliary verb. It is included in the main verb with different allomorphs {t/d/ta/da}when the object of the main verb is the first or second person. Burrow and Bhattacharya (1970: 7–9) call this a 'special base', e.g. *kūk-* 'call': *kūk-ta-*, *kēr-* 'sing': *kēr-da-*, etc. The tense suffixes and (g)np markers are added to these special bases, e.g. *huṛ-da-t-aŋ* 'I saw (object)'. The underlying morph **taH-* was actually an auxiliary which retains its identity in South Dravidian I (see section 7.14), but is reduced to a bound morph in South Dravidian II languages. In figure 7.2 this is included under A1.2, since V^1 is uninflected and as a special class confined to South Dravidian II languages, e.g. *ēzuŋ*[1] *hop-ta-t-at*[2] '(she) brought out[2] water[1]'.

Pengo has causatives formed by adding *ki-* 'do' as auxiliary to the 'verbal root enlarged by the suffix *-i*' (Burrow and Bhattacharya 1970: 102–3), e.g. *uh-* 'pound': *uh-i ki-* 'cause to pound', *ven-* 'hear', *ven-ba-* (intensive–frequentative base) 'ask': *ven-bi ki-* 'cause to ask', *por-* 'wear': *por-i ki-* 'wrap a garment around another'. The reflexive is formed by adding a suffix *-iya* to the verb root followed by the auxiliary *ā-* 'be', e.g. *ī-ba* 'bathe': *īb-iya ā-* 'bathe oneself'. The status of *-iya*, which seems to be similar to Koṇḍa *-ay*, is not clear. It may be a deverbal nominal. Several bases add *ā-* 'become' and *ki-* 'do' to derive intransitive and transitive complex stems, e.g. *jama ā-* 'be assembled', *jama ki-* 'bring together'. Here the stem is an Indo-Aryan noun.

The imperfect durative is formed by Vppl + *man-* (past), e.g. 1sg *huṛ-ji ma-c-aŋ* 'I was seeing' (lit. seeing/having seen, I was), 2sg *huṛ-ji ma-c-ay*, 3msg *huṛ-ji ma-c-an*. It is also used to express pluperfect (past perfect), e.g. *il*[1] *rōs-teŋ*[2] *vā-zi ma-c-an*[3] '(he) had come[3] to build[2] the house[1]'(Burrow and Bhattacharya 1970: 70–1).

7.15.3 *Central Dravidian*

14. Parji: the inflected auxiliary *man-* 'be', in the present tense (future in form), occurs after the past finite verb (V^1) to denote the present perfect/durative, e.g. *nil-t-en mĕd-an* 'I am standing', *pāp cājen mĕd-an* 'I have done evil'. Secondly, the past tense of the verb *man-* is added to Vppl to denote past perfect/durative, e.g. *cen-i mettom* 'we had gone', *netta maḍi mēdu* 'the dog was sleeping' (Burrow and Bhattacharya 1953: 58).

15. Ollari: Vppl + *man-* {*man-/maṭ-/may-*} accounts for the present and past perfect aspects, e.g. *ver-i may-a* 'it has come', *soy-si may-an* 'I have sent', *sen-zi maṭ-on* 'I had gone'. The negative form of the auxiliary is used to negate the perfect aspect, e.g. *sūṛi manan* 'I have not seen', *sen-zi man-u-ṭon* 'I had not gone' (Bhattacharya 1957: 44–5).

16. Gadaba: under 'post-verbals' some modal auxiliaries have been incompletely dealt with in Bhaskararao (1980: 56–7). These occur after Vinf. Some are recognizably known auxiliaries, e.g. *sen-* 'go' is added in forming the inceptive: *ēnd-in sey-on* 'I am going to play', *sī-* 'give' is added to form the permissive, e.g. *nag-in sin-on* 'I allowed (one) to laugh', *ir-* (*iṭṭ-*) 'keep' is also said to form 'permissive': *nag-in iṭṭ-on* 'I allowed (one) to laugh', *āḍ-in irr-an* 'I will not allow (one) to weep'.

7.15.4 *North Dravidian*

North Dravidian has inherited some Proto-Dravidian auxiliaries **ā-* 'be, become', **uḷ-/uṇ-* and **man-* 'stay, be' (all in Brahui). Kuṛux and Malto replaced the 'be' verbs by a Hindi counterpart *raʔ-* (< *rah-*) 'be'. Malto auxiliary *tey-* corresponds to PD **taH-* and Kuṛ. *ci-* in permissive is an inheritance from PD **ciy-* 'give' which occurs in the other subgroups also.

17. Kuṛux: Grignard (1924a: 68–70, 219–26) discusses 'compound tenses' formed by the use of the auxiliary *raʔ-*'be' (borrowed from IA, but corresponding to *ir-* of South Dravidian I and *man-* of South Dravidian II) inflected in the past or non-past, but added to the past-tense form of V^1, e.g. *kecckas rahcas* 'he had died/he was dead/he was dying' (past perfect/durative), *kerkas raʔos* 'he will have gone/he will be gone/he will be going' (non-past perfect/durative). The durative aspect is said to be exceptional.

Kuṛux has sequences of two verbs called 'compound verbs' in which the first gives 'the general meaning' and the second 'the special meaning' (Hahn 1911: 72–3), e.g. *es-* 'break': *es/esā xac-nā/cukr-nā* 'to have done breaking', *baro/barā xac-nā/-cukr-nā* 'to have done coming'. These are called 'completives': *vā* 'come'+ *ci-* 'give', e.g. *tiḍar ciʔi-nā* 'throw down', *barā cap-nā* 'come quickly' (intensive), *barā ciʔi-nā* 'allow to come', *onā ciʔi-nā* 'allow to eat' (permissive). V^2 *oṇg-* 'be able to' is added to V^1 to form the potential modal and *pol-* 'be unable to' is added to form the negative potential. Desideratives are formed by adding *bedd-* 'seek' or *ṭuk-* 'to desire'. The inceptive is formed by adding *helr-* 'begin', e.g. *kālā helr-nā* 'begin to go'. The durative aspect is denoted by adding to Vppl the auxiliary verb *raʔ-a-nā* 'be, stay' or *kaʔ-nā* 'go', e.g. *nīn ijjkām raʔā* 'remain standing', *ās urb manjkas kāʔadas* 'he continues to become rich'.

18. Malto: V^2 in Malto may be any one of the following: *et-* 'get down' (abrupt termination of action), *oŋ-* 'finish' (completive), *bar-* 'come' (action oriented toward speaker), *ēk-* 'go' (continuation/durative), *kud-* 'do' (exaggeration of an action), *kaṭ-* 'pass' (?surpassing an action, with V^1 like *beg-* 'jump', *caṛqr-* 'miss'), *tey-* 'send' (expediting an action with V^1 like *mēnd-* 'light fire', *oy-* 'take', etc.), *urq-* 'come out' (forcing an action with V^1 like *murg-* 'drag', *band-* 'pull', etc), *ondr-* 'bring' (initiate an action away from speaker with V^1 like *lap-* 'eat', *ceḍ-* 'carry', etc.), *oy-* 'take' (initiate an action towards the speaker with V^1 same as for *ondr-*). Most of this description is not very helpful, particularly to judge any changes in the valency of V^1 without illustrations from texts (Mahapatra 1979: 186–8).

Das (1973: 70–2) describes some compound verbs with V^2 auxiliaries: Vppl + *ḍoke* 'remain, stay' (durative), e.g. *bande ḍok-in* 'I am pulling'; Vppl + *oŋge* 'make an end', *qace* 'remove', *oje* 'posses' (perfective aspect), e.g. *maqer boŋg(e) oŋgrar* 'the boys had run'; Vppl + *naqe* 'act to one another' (reciprocal), *baj-* 'beat': *bajr naqe* 'beat one another'; Vpast + *siŋge* 'do often' (frequentative), e.g. *ahi*[1] *teho*[2] *a maqen*[3] *posc siŋgyaθ*[4] 'his[1] mother[2] used to support[4] the child[3]'; Vpast + *koḍe* 'do away with', *moḍye* 'trample' (intensive), *darc koḍe* 'seize upon', *cape moḍe* 'trample down'.

19. Brahui: the 'substantive verb' is {*un/uṭ/us/ur*} 'be' and there is an auxiliary {*mann/ma/mar*} 'become' which are said to be in complementation when they occur as main verbs. As an auxiliary an inflected *ur-* 'be' is added to the past stem of V^1 to form perfective and durative aspects, e.g. *xalk uṭa* 'I was striking', *bass uṭa* 'I was coming' *xalkus uṭ* 'I had struck', *bassus uṭ* 'I had come'. The perfective is formed by adding the 'perfective formative' *-un* followed by 'the present of the substantive verb', e.g. *xalk-un uṭ* 'I have struck', *bass-un uṭ* 'I have come'. According to Elfenbein (1987: 218), some of these forms are based on the Baloch aspectual system. Still the final verb *-uṭ* has a Dravidian source.

8

Adjectives, adverbs and clitics

8.1 Introduction

In this chapter I treat certain parts of speech which are identified mainly syntactically, namely adjectives, adverbs and clitics. There are a few words which are basic adjectives and adverbs, e.g. in adjectives the three deictic bases *ā* 'that', *ī* 'this' and *ē* 'what?' occur only in attributive position before noun heads. There are also certain suffixes, which derive adjectives from nominals (nouns, pronouns, numerals etc.) and verbs (the relative participles), but all adjectives are identified as a class only by their syntactic function as qualifiers of noun heads. The exclusive basic adverbs that I can think of are reduplicated expressions, which function as manner adverbials, e.g. Te. *gaṇṭa*[1] *gaṇagaṇa*[2] *mōgindi*[3] 'the bell[1] rang[3] *gaṇa gaṇa*[2]', *wāḍu*[1] *gaḍagaḍa*[2] *māṭlāḍatāḍu*[3] 'he[1] speaks[3] fast[2]'. Clitics are indeclinable. They are syntactic affixes, which can be added to any autonomous unit, i.e. word, phrase, clause, with various shades of meaning, e.g. **ā*, added to declarative sentences to convert them into 'yes–no' questions, **ē* (also **tān* 'self' in Tamil), an emphatic particle meaning 'only', and **ō* to express doubt or 'either–or' relationship, etc. Each language has created a host of such clitics, beside the inherited ones. These three parts of speech will be treated comparatively below.

8.2 Adjectives

Adjectives, like the other major parts of speech, nouns and verbs, can be defined in terms of certain universal semantic types and certain language-specific morpho-syntactic properties. Dixon (1982: 1–62) sets up seven semantic types to make up adjectives as a word class: (1) dimension (big–small), (2) colour (black–white), (3) age (old–young), (4) value (good–bad), (5) physical property (hard–soft), (6) human propensity (kind–cruel), (7) speed (fast–slow). Even languages with a minor class of adjectives show the oppositions found in the first four types. Dixon includes 'taste' (sweet–sour) under physical property. The Dravidian languages have adjectives, which belong to the semantic types (1) to (5). Those of (6) are mainly nominal and (7) adverbial. Words which are basic adjectives belong to two classes, namely limiting adjectives (quantitative adjectives involving numerals etc.) and descriptive (covered by the above semantic types). Both these are reconstructible for Proto-Dravidian. Derived adjectives such as genitive stems of nouns and relative participles in different tenses are syntactically modifiers of noun heads, and they have been treated in the chapters on nominals (chapter 6) and the verb (chapter 7). Bhat (1994) makes a vehement plea for adjectives as a distinct category on a par with nouns and verbs, despite the fact that, in some languages, there is categorial neutralization, adjective–noun and adjective–verb. He shows several semantic and morphosyntactic properties distinguishing adjectives from nouns, with which the former are identified in Dravidian. These include: (a) semantic distinctiveness of denoting a property as opposed to an object (noun) or action (verb); and adding quantification (degree) to the property; (b) being subordinate to the head noun and therefore not being eligible to shift to the position of focus or topicalization in a sentence; (c) clitics cannot be added to an adjectival phrase; (d) adjectives do not carry agreement features with the head noun and do not allow echo formation like independent phrases[1] (features of Dravidian) (Bhat 1994: 18–41).

Caldwell (1956: 308–18) devoted ten pages to treating adjectives. He said, 'Dravidian adjectives, properly so called . . . are nouns of quality or relation, which acquire the signification of adjectives merely by being prefixed to substantive nouns without declensional change.' The example that Caldwell gives is Ta. *poṉ* 'gold', which is a noun root. It is true that all nominals inflected for the oblique–genitive function as adjectival; also in nominal compounds of $N^1 + N^2$, the first noun stands in an attributive position to the following noun head, e.g. *poṉmuṭi* 'a gold crown'. But not all adjectives are of these derived types. Andronov thinks that there is greater justification for setting up 'adjectives' as a part of speech in Modern Tamil, but not so in Old Tamil. He cites Pope and Jules Bloch denying the existence of adjectives as a word class. Burrow, Emeneau, Master and Zvelebil do not subscribe to this view (Andronov 1972b: 167–9). According to Andronov bound adjectives such as *perum-*, *pēr-*, *peru-* cannot be regarded as words, since they are not free forms; e.g. *peru-vilai* 'big price', *perum-pāvi* 'big sinner', *pēr-utavi* 'big help' (1972b: 170). Since these are adjectival roots, pure and simple, and do not behave like nominal or verbal forms, I consider them a separate part of speech, 'adjectives'. Tolkāppiyam does not mention adjectives. The traditional name of an adjective in Tamil is *peyar-aṭai* 'that which is adjacent to the noun' (Rajam 1992: 435, fn. 1). In the traditional grammars of Telugu, Kannaḍa and Malayāḷam, the Sanskrit word (*nāma*) *viśēṣaṇa-* 'the qualifier one

[1] An echo word is a word coined to imitate a natural word in a language. It begins with *gi-/gī-* replacing the first (C)V̌- of the word of which it is an echo and repeating the remaining part of the word, e.g. Te. *illu* 'house', *kāru* 'car'. An echo word follows the model, e.g. *illu gillu* 'house etc.', *kāru gīru* 'car etc.'. There is an air of trivializing the meaning of the main word by using an echo word next to it. In an adjective + noun combination, an echo word can be created for the whole combination and not for the adjective alone, e.g. Te. *kotta* adj 'new': *kotta kāru, gitta kāru* 'a new car etc.', but not **kotta gitta kāru*.

(of a noun)', as opposed to *viśeṣya-* 'the qualified one (noun)', is used. In Steever (1998a) 'adjectives', as a part of speech, are discussed only for three languages, Telugu, Koṇḍa and Gondi.

Adjectives in Dravidian do not agree with the noun head in gender and number as they do in Indo-Aryan. The only exception is in the case of quantitative adjectives, which agree with the noun head in number and gender, and this is a Proto-Dravidian feature, e.g. Te. *mūḍu ceṭ-lu* 'three trees': *mu-gguru manuṣulu* 'three persons', *enni ceṭlu* 'how many trees?': *endaru manuṣulu* 'how many people?' The cardinal number *mūḍu* and the indefinite interrogative *enni* agree with neuter nouns; the human classifiers *-guru* (*-wuru* <*-waru* <**-war*) and *-daru* are added to the adjectival roots **mū-* and **en-* to form adjectives/nouns denoting humans. Adjectives can occur as predicates by adding pronominal suffixes in agreement with the subject NP, e.g. Ta. *avaṉ*[1] *nallavaṉ*[2] 'he[1] is a good man[2]', Te. *wāḍu manciwāḍu* 'he is a good man' (Ta. *nalla-*, Te. *manci-* 'good'). A clitic cannot be added to an adjectival phrase or a relative clause, since these are not autonomous constituents of a sentence without a noun head (see section 8.4).

Like the other word classes, adjectives are simple, complex, or compound. Simple adjectives are adjectival roots with appropriate morphophonemic variants in some cases (see section 8.2.1). Complex adjectives result from derivational processes from other adjectives, nouns or verbs, e.g. Ta. *per-iya* (*pēr-/peru-*) adj 'big', *palam-āṉa* 'strong' (lit. strong-the one that was). Compound adjectives are generally the reduplicated ones in certain contexts, with emphasis or intensity added to the basic meaning, e.g. OTe. *ī(y)ā*[1] *dēśambu*[2] *anan*[3] *ēla*[4]? 'why[4] say[3] this or that[1] country[2]?' Mdn Te. *pedda pedda*[1] *iḷḷu*[2] 'big, big[1] houses[2]' (= very big houses).

8.2.1 *Basic adjectives in Proto-Dravidian*

All subgroups preserve basic adjectives in at least three subclasses: (a) descriptive, (b) demonstrative (deictic bases), (c) quantitative, i.e. both definite like 'two, three' and indefinite like 'some, many, how many?' (b) and (c) are called 'limiting' adjectives. All these can be reconstructed for Proto-Dravidian. By derivational processes adjectival roots may give rise to other adjectives, adverbs, nouns or verbs. It is possible that some of the daughter languages have preserved only the derived stems and not the underlying adjectives. The fact that there are over thirty roots, which are syntactically adjectival in Proto-Dravidian, is the justification for setting up adjectives as a part of speech. Several of these survive in the descendant languages.

Demonstrative and interrogative bases

(1) **aH* 'that' (see section 6.4.2.1) [1]

(2) **iH* 'this' (see section 6.4.2.1) [410]

(3) **uH* 'yonder' (see section 6.4.2.2) [557]

(4) **yaH/*yāH* 'which' (see section 6.4.2.3) [5151]

The long-vowel forms **ā*, **ī* occur in all subgroups as demonstrative adjectives.

Colour

(5) **kār/ *kar*-V 'black'. SD I: Ta. *karu* adj, *kar*, *kār-i*, *karu-mai* 'blackness', Ma. *kār*, *kari*, *karu* 'black', Ko. *kār*, *kar*, To. *ka-*, *kax*, *kaxt*, Koḍ. *kari* 'black', Ka. *kār*, *kare* 'blackness', Tu. *kāri*, *kariya* 'black'; SD II: Te. *kāru*, *kari* 'black', Go. *kāryal*, *kari* 'black'; CD: Kol. *kāri* 'black', Nk. (Ch.) *karan/karen* 'black', Pa. *ker-/kerv-* v.i. 'burn', Gad. *karid* v.i. 'burn away as rice'. Most languages also have verb forms based on **kar*-V- 'to burn' derived from the adjectival root [1278a, c].

(6a) **kem-* 'red'. SD I: Ta. *cem-*, *cey- cē-* 'red', Ma. *ce-*, *cem-*, *cēya*, Ko. *ken*, *kep*, *kēt*, To. *kö-/ke-*, Koḍ. *kem-*, Ka. *kem-*, Tu *kem-*, *keñca* 'red'; SD II: Te. *cem-* 'red' in cpds; CD: Pa. *key* 'red'; ND: Kuṛ. *xẽso* 'red, blood', Malt. *qēso*, Br. *xīs-un* [1931].

(6b) PSD **eṯ*-V 'red': SD I Ta. *eṟ-uẓ* 'a hill tree with red flowers'; SD II: Te. *eṟ(ṟ)a/eṟ(ṟ)a-ni* 'red', *eṟ-upu* 'redness', Go. *erra* 'red' (lw < Te.), Koṇḍa *eṟa*, *eṟa-ni* 'red'; CD: Kol. (Kinwaṭ) *eroṟi* 'red' (?lw < Te.).

(7) **pacc-/*pac*-V- 'green, yellow'. SD I: Ta. *pacu* 'green, yellow', v.i. 'be green', *paccai* 'greenness, freshness', Ma. *pacu*, *pai*, *pai-m* adj, Ko. *pac*, To. *poč* 'green', Koḍ. *pacce* 'green', Ka. *pacce*, *pasi*, *pasu* 'greenness', Tu. *pacca* 'green'; SD II: Te. *pacca* 'green, yellow', *pacci* 'raw', *pasi* 'young, tender', *pasupu* 'turmeric', Go. *pahna* 'green', Koṇḍa *pasi* 'green', *pasiŋ* 'turmeric', Pengo *pazi* 'fresh'; CD: Kol. *pasuḍi* 'yellow', Nk. *pasap* 'turmeric', Pa. *pay* 'green', Gad. *pay* id. [3821].

(8) **weḷ/*weṇ* 'white'. SD I: Ta. *veḷ* 'white, pure, shining', *veṇ-mai* 'whiteness', Ma. *veḷi*, *veḷivu*, *veṇmai* 'whiteness', Ko. *veḷ*, To. *pöɫ* 'white', Koḍ. *boḷi* 'light', *boḷïtë* 'white', Ka. *beḷ*, *beḷa*, *beḷ(u)pu* 'whiteness', *beḷagu* n. 'light, lamp', Tu. *boḷï* 'white'; SD II: Te. *velũgu* v.i. 'shine', *vella* 'white', Go. *weṛci* 'light', Kui *lōngi* 'white', Kuvi, Pengo, Manḍa *ṛinj-* 'be white'; CD: Kol. *veluŋ* n. 'light' (lw < Te.), Pa. *vil* 'white', *vil-i/vil-g* 'be white', Oll. *viled* 'white'; ND: Kuṛ. *billī* 'light', *bilc-* 'v.i. 'shine', Malt. *bilbilr-* 'shine',?Br. *tūbē* 'moon' [5496a, b].

Position (direction)

(9) **teṉ* 'southern'. SD I: Ta. *teṉ* 'south, southern', Ma. *ten*, Ka. *teṅ-gāli* 'south wind', Koḍ. *tekkï*, *tëkkï* 'south', Tu. *tenkāyi* '?south, southern'; SD II:

Te. *temm-era* (<**temb-eral* 'south wind') 'southern breeze', *ṭen-kāyi* 'coconut' [3449].

(10) **waṭ-a* 'northern'. SD I: Ta. *vaṭa* 'northern', *vaṭakku* 'north', Ma. *vaṭa*, *vaṭakku* 'north, northern', Koḍ. *baḍakï* 'north', Ka. *baḍa*, *baḍagu* 'north', Tu. *baḍakāyi* 'north, northern'; SD II: Te. *vaḍaku* 'northern' [5218].

(11) **pin/ *piṯ-* adj/adv/n 'back, end in place or time, afterwards'. SD I: Ta. *piṉ* adj id., *piṉṉ-aṉ* 'younger brother', *piṉṉ-i* 'mother's younger sister', *piṉ-ṟu* v.i. 'retreat'; Ma. *pin* 'behind, after', *pinnē* 'after', Ko. *pin* 'again, other', To. *pïn* 'afterwards', Ka. *pin*, *pim*, *him* 'behind', *piṅ-gu* 'go back', *pin-te* 'the back part', *piṟ-e* 'buttock', *pin-cu* 'be behind', Tu. *pira* 'behind', *pirapa* 'back'; SD II: Te. *pinn-i* 'mother's younger sister', *piṟ(ṟ)a* 'buttock', *pinna* adj 'younger in kinship', Go. *pirne* 'two days after tomorrow', Koṇḍa *pina* 'young, small', *piṟa* 'buttock'; CD: *pena* 'in addition', Nk. (Ch.) *pinne(n)* 'day after tomorrow', Pa. *piŋ-ge* id., Gad. *pirral*, *piral* 'buttocks'; ND: Kuṛ. *pisā* 'afterwards', *pisnā* 'next year', Malt. *pisi* 'below' [4205].

(12) **mun* adj 'prior, before, front'. SD I: Ta. *muṉ* 'front, previous', *muṉ-ṉāḷ* 'yesterday', *muṉ-ai* 'war front', Ma. *mun*, Ko. *mun*, *mu-*, To. *mun*, Ka. *mun* 'that which is before, preceding in space', *mundu* 'front', *mun-cu* 'go before', *mon-ne* 'day before yesterday', Tu. *munè* 'point, end'; SD II: Te. *mun-i* 'first, former, front', *munu-pu*, *munnu* 'olden times', *mon-a* 'war-front, end', *mun-du* 'front', *monna* 'day before yesterday', Go. *monne* id., *munnē* 'before', Kuvi *munu* 'point of needle'; CD: Pa. *muna vanda* 'fore-finger', *mona* 'tip', Gad. *muŋgal* 'in front'; ND: *mund* 'first', Malt. *mundi* 'formerly', Br. *mōn* 'front' [5020 a, b].

Age

(13) **paẓ-a* 'old, used' (mainly referring to objects). SD I: Ta. *paẓa* adj, *paẓa-mai* 'oldness', Ma. *paẓa* adj, *paẓama* n, Ko. *pay-/pa-* adj, To. *pāw/pā-* adj, Koḍ. *paḷe* adj, OKa. *paẓa*, *paẓe* adj, Tu. *para*, *paratï* adj; SD II: OTe. *prā̃-*, *prā̃ta* (>Mdn Te. *pāta*) adj, Go. *paṛna*, Koṇḍa *paṛay* adj, Kui *pṛāḍi*, Kuvi *prāʔi*, Pe. *pṛān*, Maṇḍa *pṛān(ca)* adj; ND: Kuṛ *paccā* 'old', Malt *pace* id. [3999].

(14) **puc-*V/**put-*V- 'new'. SD I: Ta. *putu*, *put-iya* 'new', *putta-putiya* 'brand new', Ma. *putu* 'new, fresh', Ko. *pud*, To. *puθ*, *puθn* 'new', Koḍ. *pudïyë* 'new' (masc), Ka. *posa*, *hosa* 'new, fresh', Tu. *posa*; SD II: Go. *puhnā* 'new', Koṇḍa *pūni*, Kui *pūni* 'new, fresh', Kuvi *pūn*, *puʔni*, Pe. *pūn*, Maṇḍa *pūn*; CD: Nk. (Ch.) *puni*, Pa. *pun*, Gad. *punc*; ND: Kuṛ. *punā*, Malt. *pune*, Br. *pūs-kun* [4275].

It is clear that in South Dravidian II **c* > *t* in all except in Kannaḍa and Tuḷu; in South Dravidian II, Central Dravidian and North Dravidian the root-final **-c* became -s >*-h* > *-Ø* with the compensatory lengthening of the preceding vowel, followed by an adjectival suffix -(V)*n*; note particularly Go *-h*, Kuvi *-ʔ* and Br. -s [4275]. South Dravidian II, Central Dravidian and Kuṛux–Malto require a reconstruction involving the addition of an adjectival suffix *-ani* to the root **puy-* < **puc-*.

(15) **mutt-/*mut-*V 'old, ancient'. SD I: Ta. *mutu* adj 'old', *mutu-mai* 'antiquity', *mutt-eyil* 'ancient fortress', Ma. *mutu* 'old, prior, ripe', Ko. *mud*, To. *muθ*, *muθy* 'old', Koḍ. *mudi* adj 'old', Ka. *muttu*, *mudi* 'old age', Tu. *mudi*, *mudu* adj; SD II: Te. *mudi* adj, Go. *muy-tor*, *mudi-yal* 'old man'; CD: Nk. *mudgan* 'husband', Pa. Gad. *mutt-ak* 'old man'. ND: Br. *mutkun* 'old' [4954].

(16) **kōẓ/*koẓ*-V 'new, young, tender'. SD I: Ta. *kuẓa* adj 'young', *koẓu-mai* 'freshness, beauty', Ka. *koḍa* 'tender age', Tu. *koré* 'weak, small'; SD II: OTe. *kro-*, *krotta* 'new', Mdn Te. *kotta*, Go. *koṛs-* 'to sprout', Kui *koṛgi* 'newly sprouted, green', Kuvi *kṛōgi* 'young', Pe. *kṛogi* 'fresh, new (of leaves)', Manḍa *kṛugi* id.; CD: Pa. *koṛ* 'very young', *koṛc-* 'to sprout', Gad. *koṛuŋ* 'young shoot'; ND: Kuṛ. *xōr-* 'to shoot out new leaves', Malt. *qōroce* 'to sprout', Br. *xarring* 'to sprout'. Words meaning 'young man/woman, son/daughter-in-law, husband', etc. are derived in South Dravidian from this adjective in several languages [2149].

(17) **eḷ*-V 'young, tender'. SD I : Ta. *iḷa*, *iḷai* 'young, tender', *iḷai* 'youth', Ma. *iḷa* adj, Ko. *eḷ*, To. *eḷ*, Koḍagu *ëḷeë* n 'youth', Ka. *eḷ*, *eḷa*, *eḷe* 'tenderness, youth', *eḷadu* 'that is tender', Tu. *eḷatï*, *eḷe* adj, *lattï* id. (dial); SD II: Te. *lē-*, *lẽ̄ta* 'young', tender', Go. *raiyō/leyor* n. 'adult boy', *raiyā/leyā* n. 'young girl', Kui *lāvenju* 'grownup boy', *lāʔa* 'grownup girl', Kuvi *rāʔa/lāʔa* 'young woman, virgin'; CD: Kol. Nk. *lēŋga* 'calf', Pa. *iled* 'young man', *ile* 'young woman', Oll. *ilenḍ* 'bridegroom', *ile* 'bride', *iled* 'grownup girl'; ND: ? Br. *īlum* 'brother', *īṛ* 'sister' [513].

Dimension (shape and size)

(18) **pēr/per-*V 'big'. SD I: Ta. *pēr*, *per-u*, *per-um*, *per-iya* adj 'great, large, big', *peru-mai* n 'bigness', Ma. *pēr*, *per-u*, *per-iya* 'great, large', Ko. *pe-* 'big', To. *pe-* adj, Koḍ. *perï*, *perï-m* adj, Ka. *pēr*, *per* adj/n, *per-me* n 'increase', Tu. *per-i*, *per-iya* adj; SD II: Te. *pēr-*, *pedda-* (< **per-da-*) adj, *pēr-mi* n 'greatness', Go. *per-mā*, *ber-iya* adj 'great', Konḍa *peri*, *per* adj, *piri-* 'to grow', Kui *pēr-(eṛi)* 'a large (rat)', *prē-nḍa* 'father's elder brother', Kuvi *bir-* v.i. 'grow', Manḍa *pē-mba* 'father's elder brother'; CD: Kol. *pera-*, *per* 'big', Nk. (Ch.) *phar* 'big, elder', Pa. *berto* 'big',

per- 'big', *peru* 'much', Oll. *per-/ber-* 'big', *ber-pul* 'tiger', Gad. *ber-bullū* id.; ND: Br. *pir-ing* 'to swell' [4411].

(19) **kīṯ- /*kiṯ-V* 'small'. SD I: Ta. *cīṟ-/ciṟu, ciṟṟu* 'small', Ma. *ciṟṟu*, Ko. *kir*, To. *kïṟ*, Koḍ. *kïrke*, Ka. *kiṟi/u*, Tu. *kigga*; SD II: Te. *ciṟu*, Go. *kiṛk-* 'very thin'; CD: Kol. Nk. ?*kīke* 'boy' [1594].

(20) **kuṯ-V* 'short'. SD I: Ta. *kuṟu, kuṟṟ-uyir* 'half-dead', Ma. *kuṟu*, Ko. *kurg-* 'become small', To. *kuṟx-* id., Ka. *kuṟu*, Tu. *kuru*; SD II: Te. *kuṟu-, kuṟuca-* 'short, dwarfish', Go. *kurrā*, Koṇḍa *kuṟi*, Pengo *guhu, guspa* 'short' [1851].

Physical property (including sensations involving the eyes/tongue/skin etc.)

(21) **in-* adj/n 'sweet'. SD I: Ta. *iṉ-* adj/n, *iṉ-pu/iṉ-p-am* 'sweetness, delight', *iṉ-i* 'be sweet', Ma. *iniya* 'sweet', *ini-tu* 'a sweet thing', Ka. *in, im-pu, im-bu* 'sweetness', Tu. *im-pu* 'agreeableness'; SD II: Te. *in-cu* 'be agreeable', *im-pu, im-mu* (<**im-bu*; note the underlying root **in* is an adjective) 'pleasantness'; ND: Kuṛ. *embā* 'pleasant to taste', Malt. *embe* 'sweet', Br. *han-ēn* 'sweet' [530a, b].

(22) **puḷ-* adj 'sour'. SD I: Ta. *pu-ḷ-i* 'turn sour', *puḷ-i-ccal* 'acidity', *puḷ-i-ppu* 'sourness', Ma. *puḷ-i* 'sourness', v 'turn sour', Ko. *puḷy* adj 'sour', To. *püḷy*, Koḍ. *puḷ-i* adj, Ka. *puḷ-i/-u* n 'sourness', *puṇ-ise* 'tamarind', Tu. *puḷ-i-(pu)* 'acidity', *puṇ-i-kè* 'tamarind'; SD II: Te. *pul-i, pulla-(ni)* 'sour', *pul-u-pu* 'sourness', *pul-iyu* v.i. 'turn sour', Go. *pulla, puḷḷa* 'sour', Koṇḍa *pula* 'sour soup', Kuvi *pulla* adj; CD: Kol. *pulle* adj, Pa. *pul, pul-di, pull-aṭ* adj, Gad. *pullā* 'sour' [4322].

(23) **wal* 'strong', **wal-a kay* 'right hand'. SD I: Ta. *val* adj 'strong', *vall-ai* 'strength', *vallu* 'be able', *vala-kkai* 'right hand'; Ma. *val, valu, valiya* adj, *vallu-ka* v.i., Ko. *val*, To. *paṣ*, Koḍ. *bala* 'power, strength', Ka. *bal, bali* vb 'grow strong', *bala key* 'right hand', Tu. *balu* 'great'; SD II: Te. *vali* 'big, large', *vala*^{n}*ti* 'competent person', *vala-* 'right' (<'strong'), Go. *wallē* 'much, very'; CD: Pa. *vela key* 'right hand', Gad. *valan* 'thick, stout'; ND: Malto *balehne* 'large', Br. *balun* 'big, large, elder' [5276].

(24) **taṇ* adj 'cool, cold'. SD I: Ta. *taṇ* adj. *taṇ-ṇīr* 'cold water', *taṇṇ-am, taṇ-pu* 'coldness', Ma. *taṇ* adj, *taṇ-u-ppu* n 'coldness', *taṇ-ikka* v.i. 'cool', Ko. *taṇīr* 'cold water', To. *to(ṇ)-* adj 'cool', Koḍ. *taṇ-i* v.i., *taṇ-ï, taṇ-ïpï* 'coolness', Ka. *taṇ* adj/n, *taṇ-asu* n 'coldness', Tu. *taṇu* adj/n 'coolness, cold', *taṇṇi* adj; SD II: Te. *tan-iyu* 'be satisfied', ?*taḍi* 'wet', Go. *daṛeŋg-* 'be cold'; ND: Kuṛ. *cai*^{n}*-nā* 'get wet'.||> Pkt. *taṇṇāya* 'damp', **thaṇḍā-* 'cold' are considered early borrowings from Dravidian. *CDIAL* 13676(2) [3045].

Value

(25) PSD **nal* 'good, beautiful'. SD I: Ta. *nal, nalla* adj, *nal-am* n 'goodness', *nalku* 'to rejoice', Ma. *nal* adj, *nalam* 'goodness', Ko. *nal-* adj, To. *naṣ, naṣθ* 'beauty', Koḍ. *nallë* adj, Ka. *nal* 'goodness', Tu. *nali, nalï* 'good, cheap'; SD II: Te. *naluwu* 'beauty', Go. (M) *nelā* 'good' [3610].

Numerals As mentioned in section 6.5, cardinals of 'one' to 'five' and 'eight' to 'ten' are morphological complexes involving an adjectival root and a marker of a neuter gender represented by **-tu*/**-ku*. In the following I am citing the adjectival part with cross-references to fuller etymologies in section 6.5.

(26) **ōr*/**or*-V 'one' (see section 6.5.1 (b)) [990a].
(27) **īr*/*ir*-V 'two' (see section 6.5.2) [474].
(28) **muH-* 'three' (see section 6.5.3) [5052].
(29) **nāl*/**nal*-V- 'four' (see section 6.5.4) [3655].
(30) **cay-m-* 'five' (see section 6.5.5) [2826].
(31) **eṇ-* 'eight' (see section 6.5.8) [783].
(32) **toḷ-*/**toṇ-* 'nine' (see section 6.5.9) [3532].
(33) **paH-* 'ten'(see section 6.5.10) [3918].

The foregoing list covers most of the basic adjectives that are reconstructible for Proto-Dravidian or for one of the subgroups.

Note that among the descriptive adjectives South Dravidian I and South Dravidian II have cognates in all cases; Central Dravidian has no cognates for as many as eight adjectives, namely two denoting 'position' (9), (10), one 'age' (13), two 'dimension' (19), (20), two 'physical property' (21), (24), and one 'value' (25). North Dravidian also has no cognates for eight adjectives: (5) (7) representing 'colour', (9), (10) 'position', (19), (20) 'dimension', (22) 'physical property' and (25) 'value'. This provides additional support to the subgrouping adopted here.

8.2.2 *Basic and derived adjectives in modern languages*[2]

South Dravidian I

1. In Classical Tamil many basic adjectives occur as noun modifiers without any change or suffixation, e.g. <u>*tol*</u> *kuṭi* '<u>established</u> clan', <u>*karum*</u> *pukai* '<u>black</u> smoke', <u>*veḷ*</u> *aruvi* '<u>white</u> waterfall', <u>*irum*</u> *kuyil* '<u>dark</u> cuckoo', <u>*vaṭa*</u> *malai* '<u>northern</u> mountain', <u>*mū*</u> *eyil* '<u>three</u> fortresses', <u>*perum*</u> *kal* '<u>big</u> rock', <u>*ciru*</u> *mīṉ* '<u>small</u> fish', <u>*mutu*</u> *cuvar* '<u>old</u> wall', <u>*iṉ*</u> *kālai* '<u>pleasant</u> morning', etc. Nearly fifty such basic adjectives have been cited by Rajam (1992: 434–42), including deictic and some numeral bases, but excluding

[2] Adjectives in the examples and their glosses are underlined where necessary.

verbal participles for Classical Tamil. The adjectives, like nouns, could also be used predicatively in Old Tamil, e.g. *nallōr*[1] *yārkoḷ*[2] 'who are[2] (these) good people[1]?' *iru-v-ām iṭaiyē* 'between the two of us' etc.

In Modern Tamil there are some high frequency adjectives that cannot be derived from noun or verb roots, e.g. *nalla* 'good', *periya* 'big', *cinna* 'small', *putu* 'new', *paẓaya* 'old'; also a few basic colour terms are derived from adjectival roots, namely *karuppu* 'black', *cevappu* 'red', *veḷḷa* 'white', *pacce* 'green' (Asher 1985: 186–7). Two adjectivalizing suffixes *-āṉa* 'that which is/was' (historically the past relative participle of *āku* 'become') and *-uḷḷa* 'that which has' (the relative participle of the verb **uḷ* 'be, exist') are added to nouns to derive adjectives in reduced relative clauses, e.g. *aẓaku* 'beauty': *aẓak-āṉa* 'beautiful', *ganam-uḷḷa*[1] *kaṇṇāṭi*[2] 'thick[1] mirror[2]' (lit. weight-having glass). When the basic adjectives are used predicatively, (pro)nominalizing suffixes *-atu*/*-cu* (3n sg) or *-avan*/*-avaḷ*/*-avar* (3m sg, f sg, h pl), etc. are added, e.g. *avan*[1] *vīṭu*[2] *peri-cu*[3]/*cinn-atu*[3] 'his[1] house[2] (is) big[3]/small[3]', *avan periy-avan* 'he is a big man' (see section 9.2.4).

2. In Malayāḷam 'inherent adjectives', most of which carry the adjectivalizing suffix *-ya*/*-iya* include *nalla* 'good', *ceṟ-iya* 'small', *val-iya* 'big', *per-iya* 'big', *kuṟ-iya* 'short', *put-iya* 'new', *paẓa-ya* 'old', *eḷ-iya* 'humble', *iḷa-ya* 'young' (Asher and Kumari 1997: 349–60). Abstract nouns, and other nouns both uninflected and inflected, add *-āya* and *-uḷḷa* (relative participles of *ākuka* 'become' and *uṇṭə* 'to exist, have', respectively), *prasiddham* (< Skt.) 'famous': *prasiddham-āya*[1] *cikilsa*[2] 'famous[1] (medical) treatment[2]', *miṭukkə* 'cleverness': *miṭukk-uḷḷa*[1] *kuṭṭi*[2] 'child[2] who has cleverness[1]' (a clever boy), *kāṭṭ-il uḷḷa*[1] *maraŋŋaḷ*[2] 'trees[2] in the forest[1]'. These can be treated as reduced relative clauses (see section 9.3.2).[3] When adjectives are used predicatively, they are nominalized by the addition of appropriate gnp suffixes (see section 6.7), e.g. *kuṭṭi*[1] *nalla-van*[2] *āṇə*[3] 'the boy[1] is[3] good (one)[2]'.

Although the available grammars do not include demonstrative–interrogative and numeral roots under basic adjectives, they are used as such in both Tamil and Malayāḷam.

3. Basic adjectives in Old Kannaḍa consist of: (a) demonstrative and interrogative roots *ā* 'that', *ī* 'this' and *āva* 'which?' (b) about forty-seven qualitative adjectives, e.g. *oḷ* ~ *oḷḷ* 'good': *oḷ-nuḍi* 'good word', *oḷḷ-āne* 'good elephant', *taṇ* ~ *taṇṇ-* 'cool': *taṇ-buẓil* 'cool grove', *taṇṇ-elar* 'cool breeze' etc., and (c) nine numeral adjectives, e.g. *or* ~ *ōr* 'one': *or-vāgam* 'one part', *ōr-aḍi* 'one foot', *ay* 'five': *ay-nūṟu* 'five hundred'. Most of these are traceable to Proto-Dravidian sources.

Several subclasses have been identified among the derived adjectives: (a) Adj + *ya* → Adj, e.g. *ini-ya* 'sweet': *ini-ya kavite* 'sweet poetry'; (b) N (body part, abstract noun) + *ili* ('not possessing that') → *nāṇ* 'shame': *nāṇ-ili* 'shameless', *pallu* 'tooth': *pall-ili*

[3] Thanks to Sanford B. Steever for suggesting this aspect of analysis.

'toothless'; (c) a numeral + *aneya* → Ordinal, e.g. *āṟu* 'six': *āṟ-aneya* 'sixth'; (d) bound adjectives of the shape C_1V_1*tta-* preceding certain nouns of C_1V_2CV or C_1V_2CVC shape, e.g. *tudi* 'end': *tutta-tudi* 'the very end', *modal* 'first': *motta-modal* 'the very first' etc.; (e) bound adjectival roots which occur attributively to the following noun heads only in compounds, e.g. *naṭṭ-iruḷ* 'midnight' (cf. *naḍu* 'middle'), *pin-gōḷ* 'the rear of army' (cf. *pin-du* 'back side', see PD **pin* section 8.2.1), *kīẓ-il* 'lower house' (*keẓ-a-gu* 'below', Proto-Dravidian root **kīẓ* 'below'; *il* 'house'); (f) some nouns are used attributively to the following noun head, e.g. *alar-ambu* 'flower arrow' (*alar* 'flower', *ambu* 'arrow') in *karmadhāraya* (Adj + N) compounds; (g) a noun is adjectivalized by the addition of *-ina*/*-ṇa*/*-da* (genitive suffixes) before other noun heads, e.g. *mutt-ina*[1] *tuḍige*[2] 'an ornament[2] of pearls[1]' (*muttu* 'pearl'); (h) verbal adjectives or relative participles formed by addition of *-a* to tensed stems, e.g. *nō-* v.i. 'be wounded', past stem *no-nd-*, relative participle *no-nd-a* : *no-nd-a simga* 'a wounded lion', non-past relative participle in *pāḍuv-a*[1] *tumbi*[2] 'a singing[1] bee[2]', negative non-past relative participle in *aṟiy-ad-a*[1] *vidde*[2] 'unknown/unlearnt[1] skill[2]' (Ramachandra Rao 1972: 160–8; the examples are from a tenth-century literary work, Pampa Bhārata).

Modern Kannaḍa has both attributive and predicative uses of adjectives, e.g. *cikka* 'small', *doḍḍa* 'big', *tuṇṭa* 'naughty': *cikka huḍuga* 'small boy', *tuṇṭa huḍuga* 'a naughty boy' (adjectival use); *avanu cikk-avanu* 'he is a small man', *avaru tuṇṭa-ru* 'they are naughty' (predicative usage). Note that an adjective is nominalized when it occurs predicatively (Sridhar 1990: 248–50).

4. In Koḍagu, the adjectives are treated as a subclass of nominals (Ebert 1996: 34–5). Adjectives carry a suffix *-ë*/*-iyë*, e.g. *cer-iyë* 'small', *nall-ë* 'good', *per-iyë* 'older', *eḷ-iyë* 'younger'. Adjectival use: *nall-ë nīrï* 'good water'. Predicative use: *nīru nall-adï* 'the water is good'. Balakrishnan (1977: 173–81) treats adjectives as a separate part of speech. He gives many examples of basic and derived adjectives, e.g. *arme* 'rare', *aynï* 'true', *kïrï* 'small', *perï* 'big', etc., beside deictic and interrogative roots *ā*/*ī*/*ē*, numeral adjectives like *ōr-āṇḍï* 'one year', bound ones in compounds like *kem-maṇṇï* 'red soil' (*kem-* 'red'), are all treated under basic adjectives. Under derived he treats several adjectivalizing suffixes added to other adjectives, adverbs, nouns and verbs, e.g. *a-në* 'that type of', *ëḷ-eyë* 'young', *akka-të* 'of that time', *bala-tï* 'right', *paṇḍē-të* 'old', relative participles like *baddë*[1] *bāke*[2] 'lived[1] life[2]'.

5. Emeneau's *Toda Grammar and Texts* (1984: 109–14) has a small chapter on adjectives. He says the adjectives do not take case suffixes like nouns (110). Among the subclasses, numeral adjectives like *oḏ* 'one', demonstrative and interrogative roots like *i* 'this', *a*/*ay* 'that, those', *ē*/*ēy*[4] 'which?' are listed. Among descriptive adjectives, *per*/*pe* 'big', *kïṟ* 'small': *kïṟ xūx* 'small girl', *kuṟ* 'short', *kuṟ monsn* 'small man', *pöṫ* 'white':

[4] Note that the *-y* in two of these cases is the reflex of an older laryngeal **H*.

pöṭ ïr ‘white buffalo’, etc. In all, eighteen such adjectives used attributively have been identified. These are all traceable to adjectival roots of Proto-Dravidian listed in section 8.2.1 above. An adjective may occur predicatively with a nominalizer suffix, e.g. *pul*[1] *počïyi*[2] ‘the grass[1] is green[2]’; attributive usage in *poč es̱* ‘green leaves’, etc.

Data on Iruḷa, Tuḷu and Koraga adjectives are not available from published sources. Ālu Kur̠umba data do not throw any new light on the problem of adjectives.

South Dravidian II

6. Telugu is said to have four subclasses of adjectives (Krishnamurti and Gwynn 1985: 116–28): (i) basic, (ii) derived, (iii) positional and (iv) bound. Basic adjectives, which occur only as attributes to head nouns, consist of the demonstrative and interrogative roots, *ā* ‘that’, *ī* ‘this’, *ē* ‘what’, beside *oka* ‘one’, *prati* (< Skt.) ‘each’, *ceri* ‘each (of two persons or things)’ used attributively before cardinals ‘one’ to ‘ten’, or rounded numbers: *ceri*[1] *mūḍu*[2] ‘three[2] each[1]’, *ceri*[1] *iraway*[2] ‘twenty[2] each[1]’; *ara* ‘half’ is more frequently used as an adjective than as a noun.

Derived adjectives: (a) all nominals in genitive–oblique are used attributively to following noun heads, e.g. *illu* ‘house’, *iṇṭi*- gen: *iṇṭi kappu* ‘roof of the house’, *nēnu* ‘I’: *nā pēru* ‘my name’, *paṇḍ-lu* ‘fruit’: *paṇḍl-a buṭṭa* ‘a basket of fruit’; (b) adjectives/nouns denoting size/shape add *-āṭi* to make them attributes to noun heads, e.g. *poḍugu* adj/n ‘tall, tallness, length’: *poḍug-āṭi* ‘long’, *lāwu* ‘stout, stoutness’: *lāw-āṭi*. ‘stout, fat’; (c) abstract noun + *ayna-* (past relative participle of *aw-* ‘become’), e.g. *andam* ‘beauty’: *andam-ayna pilla* ‘a beautiful girl’, *teliwi* ‘intelligence’: *teliw-ayna maniṣi* ‘an intelligent person’ etc. This suffix can be added to those of (b) also or any other nominal to convert it into an adjectival phrase; (d) attribute + head compounds are formed from a closed set of neuter singular nouns ending in *-m(u)* by replacing it with *-pu*, e.g. *gurram* ‘horse’: *gurra-pu baṇḍi* ‘horse-drawn cart’, *pallam* ‘low land’: *palla-pu nēla* ‘low-lying land/irrigated land’; in one case the final *-mu* is replaced by *-pa*, *inumu* ‘iron’ : *ina-pa kaḍḍī* ‘an iron bar’;[5] (e) numerals take *-ō* to make them ordinals, e.g. *reṇḍu* ‘two’: *reṇḍ-ō* ‘second’; (f) a few nouns denoting measures add *-eḍu* (Old Te. *-ẽḍu* > Modern Te. *-eḍu*) to convert them into adjectives, *mūra* ‘cubit’: *mūr-eḍu* ‘a cubit of…’, *cēra* ‘palm’; *cēr-eḍu* ‘palmful’ etc.; (g) adverbs of manner derived from deictic and interrogative bases add *-ṭi* to derive adjectives, *alā* ‘that manner’: *alā-ṭi* ‘such a’; the adverbs *aṭu* ‘that side/way’, *iṭu* ‘this side/way’ and *eṭu* ‘which side/way’ add *-waṇṭi* to form derived adjectives, *aṭuwaṇṭi* (*goppa*) *maniṣi* ‘that kind of (great) person’.

Positional adjectives are nouns in the nominative, which precede a head noun attributively. These are used differently from the oblique–genitives. All cardinals (number

[5] In Old Telugu two other words *pāmu* ‘snake’ and *nāmu* ‘stubble of millet left in the field after harvesting’ also had adjectival forms *pā̃pa-* and *nā̃pa-*, respectively (derived from **pām-pp-* and **nām-pp-*), e.g. *pā̃pa-r̠ēḍu* ‘king of snakes’, *nā̃pa-cēnu* ‘a field with only stumps after harvesting’.

words) can occur as adjectives when they qualify a following noun, e.g. *renḍu pustakālu* 'two books', *iddaru manuṣulu* 'two persons'. Some of these are lexical compounds (specific + generic), e.g. *cintaceṭṭu* 'tamarind tree', *māmiḍi-panḍu* 'mango fruit', *gulābi-mogga* 'rose-bud'. There is a class of descriptive adjectives, which may also be used as nouns, but they occur more frequently as adjectives, e.g. *pedda* 'big', *cinna* 'young' *manci* 'good', *ceḍḍa* 'bad', *ekkuwa* 'much', *takkuwa* 'little', *anta* 'that much', *inta* 'this much', *enta* 'how much'. A preadjectival qualifier is *cālā* 'very', *cālā pedda* 'very big'; words like *ekkuwa* 'excess, much' are used both attributively and predicatively without change, e.g. *wāḍiki*[1] *ekkuwa*[2] *pani*[3] *ceppǣnu*[4] '(I) gave (told)[4] him[1] much[2] work[3]' (adjectival use), *wāḍiki pani ekkuwa ayindi* [he-to work excess become-past-3n sg] 'his work has become excessive' (nominal use).

Bound adjectives are a class of stems of CVCCV or CVCVCV, which become adjectival by the addition of *-ni*/*-ṭi*, abstract nouns by the addition of *-na*, and adverbs by the addition of *-gā*. These are mostly terms of colour, taste and density, e.g. *tella-* 'white': *tella-ṭi*/*tella-ni* 'white, whitish', *tella-na* 'whiteness', *tella-gā* 'being white'; *tella-* is used in an idiomatic compound, e.g. *tellawāḍu* 'whiteman' vs. *tella-ṭ i wāḍu* 'a fair-complexioned man'. Some of the other bound adjectival stems are *nalla-* 'black', *erra-* 'red', *pacca-* 'green-yellow', *tiyya-* 'sweet', *pulla-* 'sour', *metta-* 'soft', *nunna-* 'smooth', *sanna-* 'thin, fine', *cakka-* 'nice', *palaca-* 'thin', *cikka-* 'thick' etc.

Abstract nouns in final *-na* and others, which do not necessarily belong to the above set, occur predicatively in verbless sentences without the addition of pronominal suffixes, e.g. *atanu cāla poḍugu* 'he (is) quite tall', *ā cokkā telupu/tella-na* 'that shirt (is) white', *āwu pālu palaca-na* 'cow's milk (is) thin', *nāku*[1] *ī ūru*[2] *kotta*[3] 'this town[2] (is) new[3] to me[1]'; alternatively, with the copula, the adverbial form is used, e.g. *atanu cāla poḍugu-gā uṇ-ṭā-ḍu* [he much tall-being be-hab-3m sg] 'he is quite tall' etc. 'Sentences of this type are frequently used in a generic sense, i.e. when one speaks of qualities of objects as habitual or timeless properties' (Krishnamurti and Gwynn 1985: 126).

A restricted class of adjectives and nominals denoting 'time' and 'place' (syntactically adverbs) take a bound adjective of two syllables C^1V^1*ṭṭa-*, of which C^1 and V^1 are the same as the first CV of the qualified word, adding 'intensity' to the meaning of the underlying form, e.g. *ciwara* 'end' : *ciṭṭa-ciwara* 'the very end', *modalu* 'beginning': *moṭṭa-modalu* 'the very/real beginning', *naḍi* (adj) 'middle'; *naṭṭa-naḍi* 'the exact middle' etc. Note that these are not a productive type (new formations are not possible) and there is only one word beginning with a vowel in this class.

Qualitative adjectives can be reduplicated to add extra emphasis to the head noun or when a plurality of objects or persons are referred to, e.g. *pedda pedda iṇḍlu* 'very big houses', *goppa goppa-wāḷḷu* 'very very great persons', *cinna cinna rāḷḷu* 'very small stones/pebbles'. The morphology of adjectives derived from verbs, i.e. relative participles, has been dealt with elsewhere (see sections 7.7.2, 7.8.1).

7. In Gondi (Abhujmaṛia dialect: Natarajan 1985: 145–52), demonstrative pronouns are also used as adjectives, unlike in the other members of South Dravidian II, e.g. *ad nār* 'that village', *aw nāhk* 'those villages'. While cardinals occur as attributes to non-masculine nouns, a human classifier is added to underlying roots, when human nouns occur as heads, e.g. *reṇḍ pillāŋ* 'two girls', but *iru-wir pēkōr* 'two boys', *hay-ŋ lōh-k* 'five houses': *ay-wir pēkōr* 'five boys'. This feature of gender agreement between human and non-human categories is also found in the other Dravidian languages and is not a consequence of IA influence, cf. Te. *reṇḍ(u) iḷḷu* 'two houses', but *iddaru pillau* 'two children'.

Most of the descriptive adjectives are loanwords from Hindi or Marathi, e.g. *calāk* 'wise', *bariyā* 'big'; *punā* 'new' is native. Derived adjectives add the genitive suffix *-tā* to nominal or adjectival stems, *kās* 'hot': *kās-tā ēr* 'hot water'. Also adverbs and post-positions can be adjectivalized by adding *-tā*, e.g. *pirnē* 'last year': *pirnē-tā musu*r 'last year's rain', *lōpā* 'inside': *lōpā-tā* 'the object inside'. There are nominal compounds, in which the first uninflected noun functions as an attribute, e.g. *markā marā* (cf. Koṇḍa *maRka maran*) 'mango tree'. Owing to the influence of Hindi, both borrowed and native adjectives agree with the following noun in gender and number, e.g. *kāriyāl pēkāl* 'black boy' (native): *pāndrī āncāṛ* 'white woman' (*-āl* m sg and *-ī* f sg; gender agreement), *ḍengā marā* 'tall tree': *ḍengāl mānkāl* 'tall man', *punā lōn* 'new house': *punāŋ lōhk* 'new houses' (native; number agreement). This is a case of Hindi influence on Gondi who are bilingual in their native language and a nearby dominant Hindi/Marathi language.

8. Koṇḍa (Krishnamurti 1969a: 265–71) basic adjectives comprise (a) demonstrative and interrogative bases such as *aya* 'that', *yā* 'this' and *aye* 'what?'; (b) some twenty-three descriptive adjectives, e.g. *moga* 'male', *izri* 'small', *peri* 'big', *negi* 'good', *seʔi* 'bad', *vaRi* 'mere' etc.; (c) bound adjectives include (i) numeral adjectives of 'one' to 'three', *or*/*oko* 'one', *ri* 'two', *mu* 'three', as in *or neṇḍ* 'one day', *ri neṇḍ* 'two days', *mu neṇḍ* 'three days' etc., and (ii) the first members of certain 'frozen' compounds, e.g. *bānz raza* 'barren king', *sir naruṇ*(*ḍ*) 'frail human' etc. Complex adjectives are derived from other adjectives, nouns or verbs. Derived from other adjectives: (d) *na-ni* 'that sort of', *na-so* 'that much', *ni-ni* 'this sort of', *ni-so* 'this much', *e-so* 'how much' are derived from bound allomorphs of demonstrative and interrogative roots, i.e. *na-*, *ni-*, *e-*; (e) addition of the adjectival suffix *-ni or -ti*/*-di* to descriptive adjectives, e.g. **e̱ra-* 'red': *e̱ra-ni* 'red', **ves-*: *ves-ni* 'hot', etc. *mis-* 'superior': *mis-ti* 'high', *viḍi* 'separate': *viḍi-di* id.; (f) nominal stems in genitive–oblique formed by the addition of $\{$*-ti* $\sim$ *-di* $\sim$ *-Ri*$\}$ or *-i*, *-ṇi*, e.g. *go̱ro-ti*[1] *koṇḍa dēwuṇ*[2] 'the Koṇḍa god[2] of the hills[1]', *van-i*[1] *sokeŋ*[2] *pāteŋ*[3] 'his[1] shirts[2] and dhoti[3]', *em*(*b*)*e-ṇi* 'of which place' (*embe* 'where'), *ruṇḍi*[1] *kālk-a*[2] *muv-eŋ*[3] 'the bells[3] of[2] two[1] legs[2]'. In the case of personal pronouns, possessive pronouns like *nā* 'my', *nī* 'your' are used adjectivally: (g) a small class of

nouns denoting measure become adjectival by adding a suffix *-eṇḍ*, e.g. *kuṇḍa* 'pot': *kuṇḍ-eṇḍ ēṟu* 'a potful of water', *muṭi* 'a closed fist': *muṭ-eṇḍ iska* 'a handful of sand' (cf. Telugu: (f)); (h) in endocentric compounds, many nouns function as qualifiers of the following noun heads, e.g. *yā*^{1} *panṟi*^{2} *kaṇḍa*^{3} 'this^{1} pig's^{2} flesh^{3}', *seṟu*^{1} *gopu*^{2} 'tank^{1}-bound^{2}'; (i) cardinals (non-masculine) or those with the masculine classifier may be used as attributes to the following noun heads, e.g. *unṟi*^{1} *māṭa*^{2} 'one^{1} word^{2}', *āṟu*^{1} *bōde-k*^{2} 'six^{1} young women^{2}', *riʔ-er*^{1} *maṟisi-r*^{2} 'two sons'. (j) The morphology of relative adjectives derived from tensed stems has been dealt with elsewhere (see sections 7.7.2, 7.8.1).

Compound adjectives are mostly iterative descriptive adjectives, e.g. *kogri* 'small': *kogri kogri pāseŋ* 'very small pieces of waist cloth', *ḍagṟu* 'nearby': *ḍagṟu ḍagṟu poṭi-ŋ* 'the birds (acc) very nearby'. Descriptive adjectives can be used predicatively by adding a formative *-k-* followed by the personal suffixes, e.g. *negi* 'good': 1sg *negi-k-a* 'I am a good person', 1pl (excl) *negi-k-ap* 'we (excl) are good', 1pl (incl) *negi-k-aṭ* 'we (incl) are good' etc. (see section 6.7).

9. Kui (Winfield 1928: 33–5) has a few basic adjectives, but several subclasses of derived adjectives like the other members of South Dravidian II. Basic adjectives: *kogi/kogeri* 'small', *negi* 'good', *pṛāḍi* 'old', *pūni* 'new', e.g. *kogeri iḍu* 'a small house'. Winfield gives only one or two examples each of derived adjectives: (a) *vaḍi vīra* 'stony earth' (the noun *vaḍi* 'stone', becomes an adjective by position), (b) *lāven-i ḍeli* 'youthful days' (the first word is the genitive of *lāvenju* 'young man'), *uṇba siḍru* 'drinking water/ water to drink' (infinitive as an adjectival). For relative participles see sections 7.7.2, 7.8.1. The numerals for 'one' and 'two' have bound adjectives, e.g. cardinal *ronḍe* 'one': adjectival *or-*, *rīnḍe* 'two': adj *rī-*.

10. Kuvi (Israel 1979: 127–30) adjectives are simple, complex or compound. The simple adjectives comprise descriptive, demonstrative, interrogative and numeral adjectives. Forty-one basic descriptive adjectives have been identified by Israel; some of these are traceable to Proto-Dravidian or Proto-South Dravidian sources, e.g. *kṛōgi* 'young' (<* *koẓ-uw*), *puʔuni* 'new', *peni* 'cold' (< SD II **pin-i* ?< PD **pan-i* [4035]); demonstrative: *ē* 'that', *ī* 'this', *ū* 'that (over there)'; interrogative: *amini/emini* 'which', *āni/ēni* 'what', e.g. *amini ilu* 'which house', *emini kokasi* 'which boy'; numeral: *rō* 'one', *rī* 'two' etc. Derived adjectives may be derived from other adjectives, nouns or verbs, e.g. *i-* 'this': *i-cayi/i-ceka* 'this much', *e-* 'that': *e-cayi* 'that much'; from nouns: all oblique–genitive stems are used adjectivally, e.g. *kaḍa* 'river', *ēyu* 'water': *kaḍa-ti ēyu* 'river-water', *nā tanji* 'my father'. Relative participles derived from verbs have been treated in sections 7.7.2, 7.8.1. In endocentric constructions many nominals in the nominative occur adjectivally to the following noun heads, e.g. *leli mrānu* 'tamarind tree'. There are several compound adjectives, mainly the reduplicated ones, e.g. *gaḍu* 'plenty'; *gaḍu gaḍu* 'plentiful', *ici-ici* 'very small' etc.

11. Pengo (Burrow and Bhattacharya 1970: 44–57) has over twenty basic adjectives, several of which are native, e.g. *kariya* 'salty', *kṛogi* 'fresh', *nekri* 'good', *pazi* 'green', *pūn* 'new', *pṛān* 'old', *vari* 'empty' etc. When they are used predicatively, they take a formative *-k-* followed by personal suffixes, e.g. *andel*[1] *haru-k-adel*[2] 'that woman[1] is small[2]', *nā*[1] *il*[2] *pṛān-a-k-a*[3] 'my[1] house[2] is old[3]'. Pronominalized adjectives may also be used as subject NPs, e.g. *gaja* 'big': *gaja-k-an*[1] *vā-t-an*[2] 'the big man[1] came[2]'. Demonstrative adjectives are *ī* 'this', *ā*, *ē* 'that' and interrogative is *ina* 'what', e.g. *ī poṭiŋ* 'these birds', *ā injo* 'in that house', *ē kogle* 'that woman', *ina tōr* 'what name?' Some adjectives add *-ṭi* to derive other adjectives (cf. Telugu above) both in their attributive and predicative use, e.g. *haru* 'small': *haru-ṭi hazi* 'a small road', *ī nāguṛ gaja-ṭi* 'this river is big'. This suffix is also added to adjectives borrowed from Oriya, e.g. *gūṛa-ṭi* 'round'. Some adjectivals are based on relative participles, e.g. *ke-* 'to be bitter': *ke-ni karla* 'a bitter gourd' (*-ni-* non-past relative adjective suffix). Numeral adjectives are derived from numeral roots, e.g. *ro-* 'one', *ronje* 'one thing' (cardinal), e.g. *ro bopa* 'one lad', *ri-* 'two': *rinḍaŋ* 'two' (cardinal), e.g. *ri kaṇku* 'two eyes', the human plural form is *ri-y-ar* 'two people' (cf. Koṇḍa *riʔer*, OTe. *ir(u)-wuru* < PSD **iru-war*). From 'three' onwards, Oriya numerals are used and the human classifier *jaṇ* is also borrowed with them, *daha jaṇ* 'ten persons'.

Central Dravidian

12. For Kolami Emeneau (1955b: 31–3) includes demonstrative, numeral and descriptive adjectives under monomorphemic (basic) type, e.g. *ā* 'that', *ī* 'this': *ī ēḍ* 'this year', *ok* 'one': *ok siḍ* 'one day', *pulle* 'sour', *telmi* 'white', *doo* 'big'. Derived adjectives include (a) tensed verb stems as relative participles, e.g. *tin-a* 'that which is eating', *tind-a* 'that which ate', *tin-ek-a* 'that which will eat' etc.; the negative adjective ends in *-e*, *tin-e* 'that which does/did/will not eat'. (b) Those derived from noun stems take *-ta*, e.g. *kis* 'fire': *kis-ta* 'of fire', *mut* 'before': *mut-ta sāl* 'next year'. Here, *-t-* is said to belong to the oblique stem and *-a* is the genitive suffix. The oblique–genitive is *-e* following the plural suffix, e.g. *puvu-l* 'flowers': *puvu-l-e ār* 'flower garland'. This suffix occurs also in the case of personal pronouns in the allomorph *-ne*, *ān* 'I': *ann-e* 'my', *īn* 'you': *inn-e* 'your'; *-ne* occurs frequently with other stems also, e.g. *bāma-* 'Brahmin': *bāma-ne* 'of Brahmin', **tām* 'they': *tam-ne* 'their own'. Emeneau points out that his data are inadequate for a finer analysis (1955b: 31).

13. Naiki of Chanda (Bhattacharya 1961: 95), unlike the other members of the subgroup, uses demonstrative pronouns (with gender–number suffixes) instead of deictic roots as demonstrative adjectives also, e.g. *id nīr* 'this water', *ad bāyko* 'that woman', *ōn kīken* 'that boy', *īn pōrakun* 'to this boy'. The genitive suffix *-ta* and the adjectivalizer *-n* are used in forming derived adjectives from other adjectives or nouns, e.g. *rān-ta āte* [forest-of dog] 'wild dog', *madge-ta saṭṭ* [mango-of tree] 'mango tree'; *kara-n kokke* 'black saree'. Two other endings *-ṭ* and *-ek* are also used, e.g. *amba-ṭ* 'sour', *tika-ṭ*

'pungent'. Descriptive adjectives are used without change both attributively and predicatively, e.g. *puni apaṛ* 'new house' (adjectival use), *amme*[1] *apaṛ*[2] *puni*[3] *anlen*[4] 'our[1] house[2] is[4] new[3]' (predicative use).

14. Parji (Burrow and Bhattacharya 1953: 32–5) has basic adjectives traceable to Proto-Dravidian, e.g. *pun* 'new', *vil* 'white', *key* 'red', *pay* 'green', *koṛ* 'young', *pul* 'sour', etc.: *pun ole* 'new house', *vil pū* 'white flower', *key cōra* 'dark red pot', *pay meram* 'green grass', *koṛpāp* 'young baby', *pul cāva* 'sour gruel'. When used predicatively these take personal suffixes, 1sg *pun-en* 'I am new', 1pl *pun-om* 'we are new'; also in full sentences like *ān vil-en āy* 'I am white'. The derived nominals may also occur in non-predicate position as in *pun-ed*[1] *ve-ñ-ed*[2] 'the new man[1] has come[2]'. Some adjectives occur with a derivational suffix *-to*, e.g. *ber-to* 'big' (<**per*-V-), which the authors identify with the genitive *-to* as in *polub-to* 'of village'. A number of derived adjectives end in *-a*, e.g. *ṭiṭṭ-a* 'straight', *tirr-a* 'sweet', *pull-a* 'sour' etc. They take personal suffixes when they are nominalized, e.g. *koṛey-a* 'lame': *koṛey-a-l* 'a lame man', *koṛe-y-a-ṭ* 'a lame woman', but *koṛeya vẽ̄did* 'a lame god'. Parji has borrowed many uninflected as well as inflected adjectives from the neighbouring Halbi, an Indo-Aryan language, e.g. *naŋgal* 'naked', *koyli* 'black' etc. Parji is shifting to the Indo-Aryan type of inflecting the adjectives to agree with the noun head, e.g. *geya-l manja* 'a simple-minded man' (*-l* is m sg suffix), *tirra-ṭ medi* 'sweet mango' (*-ṭ* marks non-masculine singular). The demonstrative adjectives (1953: 39–42) are *ā* 'that': *ā meri* 'that tree', *ī* 'this': *ī meri* 'this tree'; the interrogative adjective is *āro* 'which' in *āro polub* 'which village?', but *āra manja* 'which man?' The shorter radical numerals are used attributively (1953: 36–8), although Burrow and Bhattacharya do not treat these under Adjectives, e.g. *ok mīn* 'one fish', *ir vōkal* 'two years', *īr-er* 'two yokes of bullocks'. Also examine fused forms *o-poṭ* 'one time', *ir-oṭ* 'twice', *mu-poṭ* 'three times', *nel-poṭ* 'four times', *cem-boṭ* 'five times', *a-poṭ* 'that time', *i-poṭ* 'this time'. The morphology of the relative participles has been dealt with elsewhere (sections 7.7.2, 7.8.3, 7.10.3).

15. Ollari (Bhattacharya 1957: 27–9) basic adjectives of native stock include (a) demonstratives *ī* 'this', *ā*/*āy* 'that' and interrogative *ēy* 'which' and (b) a few descriptive adjectives, e.g. *kareya* 'salty', *pun* 'new', *per*/*ber* 'big' etc. The descriptive ones are also used predicatively, e.g. *ī*[1] *sēpakil*[2] *niyaṭ-or*[3] *mayar*[4] 'these[1] boys[2] are[4] good ones[3]' (*niya* 'good', *-ṭ* adjectival formative). Verbal and nominal stems are converted to adjectives by adding *-onḍi*, e.g. *pāp* n 'young one': *pāp-onḍi* 'young, small'.

16. Gadaba adjectives may be simple or derived, but no details are given in the grammar (Bhaskararao 1980). In the vocabulary we find the following adjectives listed: *a*/*ay* 'that', *i*/*iy* 'this', *ēkami* 'as a whole', *ō* 'one', *kīṭṭe* 'of below', *koppen* 'full, satisfied' (*eran* 'red', *gīral* 'striped', *guḍḍi* 'blind', *gullan* 'hollow', *cevṭi* 'deaf', *tellan* 'white', *paccan* 'yellow', *pullan* 'sour'; all these are lws < Te.), *golt-eḍ* 'two palmfuls joined', *jēn-eḍ* 'span long', *ḍebra* 'left', *tayoni* 'a little, a few', *tiron* 'sweet', *niya* 'good'. We are not sure which of these are basic and which are derived. Apparently those that end

in *-en*/*-an*/*-on* and *-eḍ* are derived since they look similar to the Telugu suffixes *-ani* and *-ẽḍu* (see (6) above).

North Dravidian

17. Kuṛux, according to Hahn (1911: 18–20), has adjectives which can 'mostly' be used as nouns also, e.g. *mechā* 'high, height', *xẽso* 'blood, red colour' etc. Verbal adjectives or relative participles are formed (a) by putting an infinitive before the head noun, e.g. *ōn-nā* 'to eat': *ōn-nā ālō* 'eatable things' and (b) by placing the past or non-past participle before a qualified noun, e.g. *ān-kā kathā* 'a spoken word', *kec-kā ālar* 'dead people', *īr-ū ālas* 'the man who sees', *pār-ū pellō* 'the girl who sings'. Nouns with the genitive marker *-ntā* function as adjectivals and qualify the following nouns, e.g. *eṛpa-ntā*[1] *nēgcār*[2] 'home[1] custom[2]', *pūrba-ntā*[1] *ālar*[2] 'oriental[1] (east-of) men[2]'. Out of fifty-four descriptive adjectives listed by Hahn (1911: 20), the following are identified as native: *mechā* 'high', *punnā* 'new', *paccā* 'old', *xarxā* 'bitter', *tīnī* 'sweet', *panjkā* 'ripe', *pokkō* 'swollen', *porcō* 'half-boiled', *sannī* 'small', *tinḍī* 'firm'. Degrees of comparison are rendered through postpositions.

Grignard (1924a: 41–3, 183–91) gives *ī*, *hū*, *ā* as the three demonstrative adjectives, proximate, intermediate and remote. The intermediate *hū* is traceable to PD **uH*, preserved in some languages of South Dravidian I, and again in North Dravidian. Several adjectives are indeclinable, but a few carry gender agreement with the qualified noun (masculine/feminine), apparently a feature borrowed from the neighbouring Hindi, e.g. *algā*/*algī* m/f 'redundant' (borrowed adjective), *ort*/*urtī* m/f 'one' (native), *otxā*/*utxī* m/f 'alone' (native) etc. When used predicatively, adjectives carry gnp markers. When a numeral is used attributively, it adds *-goṭā* (with several allomorphs), if the following noun is neuter, or *-jhan*, if it denotes humans, e.g. *mūnd oṭā ekhō* 'three cows'; in some cases an inherited classifier *-ar* (humans) is used, *ā*[1] *mūnd-ar*[2] *eksan*[3] *ker-ar*[4]? 'where[3] are those[1] three men[2] gone[4]?' Note that *mūnd* 'three' is a native numeral.

18. Malto adjectives (Mahapatra 1979: 110–40) occur without any change in the attributive position, but when used predicatively, they add personal suffixes, e.g. *bēḍo maleh* 'big man', *bēḍo gaṛið* 'big cart', *bēḍo puḍað* 'big belly'; *ēn bēḍo-n* 'I am big', *āh bēḍo-h* 'he is big' etc. Simple (monomorphemic) adjectives drop a final *e* when used attributively, e.g. *pūne* 'new': *pūn daṛið* 'new cloth'. Adjectives are reduplicated for emphasis, *labo* 'good': *lab labo* 'very good'; some do not lose the final vowel, e.g. *moṭa* 'fat': *moṭa moṭa* 'very fat'. Demonstrative and interrogative adjectives (underlined) are a subset of simple adjectives, e.g. *ī kolme* 'this pen', *ā maleh* 'that man', *ik maleh* 'which man?' *indr jāti* 'what caste?', *ī nond* 'this much', *ā nond* 'that much', *ēn nond* 'how much?'

Derived adjectives are formed from other adjectives, nouns, verbs or adverbs. The formative *-o* is added to nominal or verbal bases to form adjectives, e.g. *bālke* 'turmeric':

bālk-o 'yellow', *qēs-du* 'blood': *qēs-o* 'red'; *alkr-* 'to open': *alkr-o* 'open', *pac-* 'become old': *pac-o* 'old'; some bases add *-ro*/*-sro* to form adjectives, e.g. *oṛmẹ* 'ash': *oṛm-ro* 'ash coloured', *am-du* 'water': *am-sro* 'watery', *qāy* 'to dry': *qāy-ro* 'dried', *kit-* 'to rot': *kit-ro* 'rotten'.

Under the influence of Indo-Aryan some adjectives qualifying human nouns are distinguished for gender, e.g. *bobe* m: *bobi* f 'dumb', *lela* m: *leli* f 'foolish'. There are other mechanisms of distinguishing gender, i.e. by adding *-tāwe* m: *-tāni* f, e.g. *pesa* 'money': *pesa-tāwe* m: *pesatāni* f 'moneyed'. There are several adjective-forming suffixes added to nominal/adjectival stems (both native and borrowed), e.g. *-te* in *meca* 'up': *mec-te tebṛe* 'upper lip' (native), *-to* in *male* 'man': *mal-to* 'masculine' (native), *-balo* in *kukdu* 'head': *kuk-balo* 'headless', *-lāgo* in *tise* 'sour': *tis-lāgo* 'somewhat sour' etc. Many nouns function as attributes to other nouns in endocentric compounds without any change, e.g. *male* 'man': *mal kukdu* 'man's head', *baṛe* 'banyan tree': *baṛ ceya* 'shade of the banyan tree'. Genitive forms of personal pronouns occur attributively to noun heads, e.g. *ē* 'I': *eŋ-muṛse* 'my husband', *nām* 'we (incl)': *nam desi* 'our country'. The relative participles derived from verb stems have been treated elsewhere. The past participle is formed by adding *-pe* to the base, and the habitual by adding *-po*. Here the element *-p* in the past is not genetically accountable, unless the non-past *-p* has assumed this meaning, e.g. *kuṛp(e)*^{1} *cete*^{2} 'baked^{1} fish^{2}', *cuypo*^{1} *daṛi*^{2} 'cloth^{2} for weaving^{1}'. The present participle *-u* can be connected to PD *-um* (see section 7.4.2.3), *cōy-u*^{1} *boḍa*^{2} 'snake^{2} that flies^{1}'.

In numeral phrases Malto uses classifiers extensively. Under 'three' the order is classifier + number + noun; above 'three', number + classifier + noun. These must have entered Malto from Tibeto-Burman through the route of Bengali etc. (see Emeneau 1956, Bhattacharya 1975), e.g. *jen* (with live referents): *tīni jen maler* 'three-classifier-men', *ḍaṛa* (for long, large objects): *tīni ḍaṛa māsdu* 'three-classifier-bamboos', *kaṭi* (long, small objects): *tīni kaṭi cabi* 'three-classifier-keys', *panda* (long, flexible objects): *tīni panda pāwdu* 'three-classifier-roads', *paṛa* (long fruit, like bananas), *paṭa* (flat, broad objects, like clouds etc.), *kanḍa* (flat, broad cotton objects, like pants etc.), *kukdu* (round, heavy objects, like the head etc.). For further details see Mahapatra (1979: 121–40).

19. Brahui adjectives, according to Bray (1909: 61–9), are monosyllabic or disyllabic, but most of them seem to have been borrowed from Balochi. The few identifiable Dravidian adjectives occur with an ending *-un*/*-kun*, e.g. *bal-un* 'strong', *pūs-kun* 'new', *mut-kun* 'old', *bār-un* 'dry', *bās-un* 'hot', *xīs-un* 'red', *ma-un* 'black' etc. *-ēn* is a Balochi suffix as in *kub-ēn* 'heavy' (Elfenbein 1998: 398); it is sometimes added to inherited adjectival stems also, e.g. *xar-ēn* 'bitter', *han-ēn* 'sweet'. An adjective may be used without further suffixation as a predicate, e.g. *dā*^{1} *zāifa ɣāk*^{2} *ush-kun*^{3} *o*^{4} 'these^{1} women^{2} are^{4} slender^{3}'. Adjectives must take a definite or indefinite marker, when used attributively;

the indefinite marker is -*ō*, e.g. *asi*[1] *chaṭṭ-ō*[2] *mār-as*[3] ‘a[1] lazy[2] lad[3]’. The definite marker is -*ā*/-*angā* added to a monosyllabic adjective, e.g. *zēb-ā*[1] *masiṛ*[2] ‘the pretty[1] girl[2]’, *kub-angā*[1] *paxīr*[2] ‘the hump-backed[1] beggar[2]’. The suffix -*tir* is added to the adjective to form the comparative degree, e.g. *shar* ‘good’: *shar-tir* ‘better’. This is a ‘modern adaptation from without’ (perhaps Balochi) (Bray 1909: 68), but the positive form itself is used in the ablative case to express degrees of comparison, like the other Dravidian languages.

8.3 Adverbs

Caldwell (1956: 553–4) says, ‘properly speaking, the Dravidian languages have no adverbs at all; every word that is used as an adverb in the Dravidian languages is either a verbal theme, or the infinitive or the gerund of the verb; and illustrations of the manner in which those words acquire an adverbial force will be found in the ordinary grammars of each of the Dravidian dialects’. He does recognize iterative adverbs, as in ‘*maḍa-maḍa (v)endru iḍi viṛundadu*, Tam. it thundered terribly, literally, the thunderbolt fell, saying *maḍa-maḍa*’ (554; *ṛ* = *ẓ*).

There are few, if any, monomorphemic forms which function only as adverbs. Adverbs are mainly a derived class of words drawn from different parts of speech: (a) uninflected or inflected nominals denoting time and place and those inflected with postpositions/cases, denoting location, cause, purpose etc., e.g. Te. *a-ppuḍu* ‘then’, *i-kkaḍa* ‘here’, *aydu gaṇṭal-a-ku* ‘at five o’ clock’, *rēpu* ‘tomorrow’, *andu-kōsam* ‘for that purpose’ etc.; (b) non-finite verbs, like the durative and perfective participles, the infinitive of purpose (also their reduplicated ones), conditional and concessive forms (which head subordinate clauses), which refer to manner, e.g. Te. *cūsi cūsi* ‘having seen for a long time’, *tini tini* ‘having eaten for a long time’, Te. *cūḍa cūḍa* (in poetry) ‘as one keeps observing’ etc.; (c) manner adverbials formed by adding to nouns of quality or adjectives the infinitive of the verb **ā* ‘to be’ (*āk-a* in Tamil, -*gā* in Telugu), Ta. *vēkam-āka*, Te. *wēgam-gā* [speed-so as to be] ‘speedily’; Ta. *putuc-āka* , Te. *kotta(di)-gā* ‘being (a) new (thing)’; and (d) by adding the manner particle to deictic bases, e.g. Te. *a-lā* ‘in that manner’, *i-lā* ‘in this manner’, *e-lā* ‘how, in which manner?’

Many Dravidian languages use onomatopoetic words without any suffixation as manner adverbials. Perhaps these can be called the basic forms of adverbs, since they cannot be used as any other part of speech without additional markers, e.g. Te. *nuwwu*[1] *gaḍagaḍa*[2] *māṭl-āḍu-tā-wu*[3] [you advbl speak-non-past-2sg] ‘you[1] speak[2] too fast[3]’. In this sentence *gaḍagaḍa* is used as a manner adverbial, but only in reduplicated form; the constituent root **gaḍa* cannot be used instead. An adverb can be verbalized by the addition of -*l*-*āḍu* in *gaḍagaḍa-l-āḍu* ‘to shiver (in fear)’. -*āḍu* is a verb meaning ‘to act’, and the preceding -*l* has to be interpreted as the plural suffix -*lu*, although *gaḍagaḍa-lu* does not occur as a noun elsewhere. The plural could be analogical on the basis of such expressions as *māṭa-lu* 'words' + *āḍu* → *māṭ-l-āḍu* 'to speak', *debba-lu* 'beatings' + *āḍu* → *debba-l-āḍu* 'to fight' etc.

8.3.1 *Adverbs in modern languages*

Adverbs of time, place, quantity and manner are mostly derived from demonstrative or interrogative bases, which are, therefore, classed as complex or derived adverbs. Except for manner adverbs, most of these complex forms are morphologically nominal. Several of them are reconstructable for Proto-Dravidian or some subgroups. Among the descendant languages, there is overlap in assigning different meaning to contrasting forms, e.g. PD **ap-pōẓ* 'that time, then' (Tamil, Malayāḷam, Telugu, Gondi, Kolami, Naiki and Parji), PSD **a-mp*V- 'there' (Tamil, Tuḷu, Koṇḍa–Kui–Kuvi–Pengo–Manḍa), PD * *ā̆-n*(V)*k-/-t-* ∼ *-tt-* 'that place/time/much/many/manner' (different languages), PD **a-l*(*l*)- 'that place', PD * *ā̆-ṯṯ-* 'that place, manner' (Telugu, Gondi, Koṇḍa, Brahui), PD **a-n*V 'there, then' (Tamil, Gondi, Malto). Derivatives from the other bases PD **iH-* 'this', **uH* 'yonder', **yaH-* 'what', more or less, generally follow the above pattern. However, because of such overlap both in form and in meaning, some items derived from one demonstrative root may not have parallels with those of the other demonstrative root. A good instance is PD **i-nṯu* 'today, now' (Tamil, Malayāḷam, Kota, Toda, Koḍagu, Kannaḍa and Tuḷu of South Dravidian I, Kolami, Naiki, Parji, Ollari and Gadaba of Central Dravidian, Kuṛux, Malto and Brahui of North Dravidian), but **a-nṯu* 'that day, then' has cognates only in Old Tamil, Kota, Toda and Kannaḍa of South Dravidian I, but not in others. This would give us the impression that the former was a basic adverb in those languages, which do not have other matching deictic forms.

It is possible to reconstruct some time and place words, outside these paradigms, e.g. PSD **ñānṯu* 'today' (South Dravidian I and II) [2920], *nēram* 'time, sun' (South Dravidian I, Brahui) [3774], **niṯu-nay* 'yesterday' (South Dravidian I and II and Brahui) [3758], *elli* 'tomorrow' (Tuḷu, Telugu, Brahui), PSD **kaṭay* 'end, place' in Te. *a-kkaḍa* 'that place' etc. These forms are nominal and not examples of basic adverbs. We are left with expressives (onomatopoetic expressions and reduplicatives) as the only examples of exclusive adverbs. Emeneau and Hart (1993) have given many instances of these with cognates to make out a case for initial voiced stops at a reconstructed stage for some of these, e.g. reduplicative *dabadaba* 'running fast' [3069] (with cognates in South Dravidian I and South Dravidian II, mostly with a word-initial voiced stop, not allowed in Proto-Dravidian), also onomatopoetic *dabukku-na* 'haste, falling sound etc.'. Syntactically these are treated as nominal complements of the verb 'to say', i.e. OTa. *enṟu* (> Modern Tamil *-nu*), Te. *an-i* etc. Therefore, the status of expressives as basic adverbs in Dravidian is doubtful, although some languages like Telugu can use them without the inflected verb 'say'. We, therefore, conclude that adverbs are not an independent part of speech in Dravidian.

Since the morphology and syntax of adverbs are covered in different chapters, only a brief account of adverbs, basic and derived, from major languages is given below, excluding adverbial nouns denoting time and place derived from demonstrative and interrogative bases.

8.3.1.1 *South Dravidian I*

In Classical Tamil (Rajam 1992: 897–907), *val* 'fast' in *val eyti* 'having reached fast' was considered the only basic adverb. The infinitives *āk-a* (<*āku* 'be' + *a*) and *eṉ-a* (<*eṉ-* 'say' + *a*) are added to nominal or adjectival stems to derive adverbs: *iṉitu* 'sweetness' + *āka* → *iṉit-āka* 'sweetly', *mel* 'gentle' + *eṉa* → *mell-eṉa* 'gently'. Iterative expressions like *melmel-a-* 'softly', *kiṇkiṇ-i* 'jingling' are used adverbially; traditional grammarians had not treated them as a separate class of words, but called them *iraṭṭai-k-kiḷavi* 'double words' (Rajam 1992: 927–32).

Simple adverbs in Modern Tamil (Lehmann 1989: 135–46) are said to include *iṉṉ-um* 'still', *miṇṭ-um* 'again', *mella* 'slowly', *iṉi-mēl* (now-above) 'hereafter' etc. The author says that these are primarily used as adverbs and are 'not decomposable', a questionable claim. A number of postpositions are also said to function as adverbials, *kīḻ-ē* 'down', *piṉṉ-ē* 'behind', *muṉṉ-ē* 'in front' etc. These are nominals with the clitic *-ē*. The derived adverbs include the nominals of time and place derived from demonstrative and interrogative bases, e.g. *i-p-paṭi* 'this way', *a-p-paṭi* 'that way', *e-p-paṭi* 'which way'. A productive mechanism of forming adverbs is by adding *-āka* (< *āk-a*) or *āy* to nouns or adjectives, e.g. *oru mātam*[1] *oru nimiṣam-āk-a*[2] *pōy-iṟ-ṟu*[3] 'one month[1] passed[3] like a minute[2]'. Comparison of adverbs is rendered by using the postposition *viṭa* 'than' with the phrase representing the standard of comparison, e.g. (Asher 1985: 194) colloquial Tamil:

onne	*viṭa*	*ava*	*vēkam-ā*	*pēcu-v-ā*
[you-acc	than	she	speed-advl	speak-fut-3f-sg]

'she speaks faster than you'

Modern Malayāḷam adds *-āyi* (perfective participle of *ā-* 'become') to nouns and adjectives to form adverbs, e.g. *avan*[1] *viśadam-āyi*[2] *paṟaññu*[3] 'he[1] spoke[3] in detail[2]' (lit. clarity-becoming). In addition to time and place nominals derived from deictic and interrogative roots, many other words or postpositions denoting location such as *mēle* 'up', *tāḻe* 'down' and time words like *nāḷe* 'tomorrow' etc. are used as modifiers of verbs. Besides, there is a small class of manner adverbials like *melle* 'softly', *uṟakke* 'loudly', which function as adverbs (Asher and Kumari 1997: 109–16).

For Classical Kannaḍa (Ramachandra Rao 1972: 172–81), nearly twenty items have been cited as basic adverbs, some of which have cognates in Old Telugu as adverbs, e.g. *karam* 'excessively', e.g. *karam*[1] *oppidan*[2] 'he adorned[1] very much[2]'. Among derived adverbs, many adjectives add *-ane/-age* to form adverbs, *mell-ane*[1] *pattu*[2] *viḍisi*[3] 'having loosened[3] the hold[2] slowly[1]'. A large number of expressive adverbs with reduplicated roots were used in classical texts for both abstract and concrete ideas, some of which are onomatopoetic, e.g. *malamala maṟug-i* 'having grieved very much', *pana pana paniye* 'trickling down drop by drop'; some non-iterative, expressive adverbs also occur, e.g. *bhōmk-ane kaṇḍ-an* 'he saw suddenly'.

Like the other major languages, Modern Kannaḍa has a productive morphological mechanism of forming adverbs by adding *āg-i* 'having been' to certain nouns and adjectives, native as well as borrowed, e.g. *jōr-āgi* 'loudly', *spaṣṭav-āgi* 'clearly', *hosat-āgi* 'newly'. There is a class of manner adverbs which are onomatopoetic, *dhaga dhaga* (*-ne*) '(burn) *dhaga dhaga*', *ciṭṭa-ne* 'shrill-ly', *thaṭṭa-ne* 'suddenly'. Many postpositions denote 'place' and form heads of adverbial phrases, e.g. *mēle* 'above'; *pakka* 'side', *keḷage* 'below' etc. (Sridhar 1990: 254–6, 280–1).

8.3.1.2 *South Dravidian II*

In Old and Modern Telugu, the time and place words derived from demonstrative and interrogative bases are morphologically nominal, but syntactically adverbial, as is true of the other Dravidian languages: *a-ppuḍu* 'then', *i-ppuḍu* 'now', *e-ppuḍu* 'when', *a-kkḍa* 'there', *i-kkaḍa* 'here', *e-kkaḍa* 'where?', etc. Under basic adverbs, there are some items that do not seem to be derived from other parts of speech, e.g. OTe. *negi-*(*n*) 'splendidly', *arthi-*(*n*) 'with pleasure' (*-n* is locative–instrumental suffix), *kaḍu-*(*n*) 'much', *maṟi* (> Mdn Te. *mari*) 'again', OTe. *inka/īka*[6] (> Mdn Te. *inka/iha*) 'now, hereafter', *niruḍu* 'last year', *taruwāta*(*n*) (considered the locative of **taruwāyi*, which does not occur) 'next', *pimmaṭa* 'after' (see Mahadeva Sastri 1969: 255–6, Ranganathacharyulu 1987: 184–7, Montgomery 1963: 13–14). At least some of these cannot be descriptively derived from other word classes.

The most productive mechanism is by adding *-gā* (suppletive infinitive of *aw-* 'to be') to nouns and adjectives, *calla-gā* 'coolly', *tondara-gā* 'quickly', *pedda-gā* 'loudly'. Expressive adverbs occur extensively in both Old and Modern Telugu: OTe. *all-alla-na* 'slowly', *waḍa waḍa waḍanku-cu* 'shivering from cold', Mdn Te. *gabagaba naḍuc-* 'walk fast', *wela wela pō-* 'grow pale' etc. Besides these, there are one-word expressive adverbs ending in *-na* like *gabhālu-na* 'suddenly', *cappu-na* 'immediately', *ṭhappu-na* 'making the noise *ṭhap*' etc. In Modern Telugu, the manner adverbs *a-lā* 'that manner', *i-lā* 'this manner', *e-lā* 'which manner' have fused elements with deictic roots which make them behave like basic adverbs (*-lā* occurs always bound). The following

[6] *DEDR* 410(c) cites this as derived from proximal **iH* (my reconstruction) with cognates from Tamil, Malayāḷam, Kota, Toda, Kannaḍa, Koḍagu of South Dravidian I, Gondi, Kui of South Dravidian II and Kolami of Central Dravidian. Note that most of the languages have no corresponding forms derived from distal **aH*.

forms can be cited under compound adverbs, *ippuḍ-ippuḍ-ē* 'only now' (*ippuḍu* 'now', *-ē* emphatic clitic 'only'), *ēṭ-ēṭ-ā* 'year after year', *ūr-ūr-ā* 'in every village' (*-ā* locative suffix from older *-an*), *metta-metta-gā* 'very smoothly' (Krishnamurti and Gwynn 1985: 269–79).

Koṇḍa (Krishnamurti 1969a: 314–19) has several basic adverbs representing time and manner, e.g. *ēl* 'now', *ādvat* 'after', *maṟi* 'then, again', *velaru* 'all day long'; *aŋa* 'separately', *edgara* 'absolutely', *eski* 'speedily', *gadem* 'suddenly' etc. Complex adverbs include adjectives and nouns that carry the markers *-aŋa*/*-ŋa* and *-eṇḍa*, e.g. *eṟa-ŋa* 'reddishly', *gopa-ŋa* 'largely' (*-ŋa* < Te. *-ngā*), *negi* adj 'nice': *neg-eṇḍa* 'nicely'. Some reduplicated expressives function as manner adverbs, like *gudu-gudu* 'with great energy', *baṟa baṟa* 'sound of downpour', *ḍubku ḍabku* 'noise of rain drops on dried leaves'. Some expressives with adverbial *-na* occur, e.g. *galgal-na* 'jingling', *liṭ-na* 'suddenly' etc. Certain suffixes or particles are added to nouns, adjectives and verbs to form adverbs, e.g. *-laka* 'at the rate of': *uRku laka* 'one each', *mūRku laka* 'three each', *-lakeṇḍa* 'like, as if' in *mī-lakeṇḍa* 'like you', *-ban* 'place', *nī-ban* 'at your place', *vizeri-ban* 'near all people', *embe-ban* 'at which place?' etc.

Pengo (Burrow and Bhattacharya 1970: 57–9) manner adverbs from demonstrative bases are *i-leŋ* 'in this manner', *a-leŋ*/*e-leŋ* 'in that manner'; the interrogative one is *in-es* 'how?' There are time and place adverbs as in the other languages of Dravidian. Onomatopoetic expressions like *buga-buga* 'sound of a peacock', *nona-nona* 'sound of a bee' are used adverbially followed by the verb *in-* 'say'.

Kuvi (Israel 1979: 212–15) has adverbs classified as simple, complex and compound. Some twenty items are given as basic adverbs, which are mostly borrowed items denoting manner: *dīre* 'slowly' (< Oll. *dhīre*), *ṛapa* 'completely' etc. Manner adverbs derived from the demonstrative bases are *i-le(ki)* 'in this way', *e-le(ki)* 'in that way', *ū-leki* 'in that way (far)'. Complex adverbs are derived by adding *-ʔe* to nominal and adjectival stems, e.g. *sato* 'truth': *sat-eʔe* 'truly', *peni* 'cold': *peni-ʔe* 'coldly', *nehi* 'good': *nehi-ʔe* 'nicely' etc. One set of compound verbs are iterative and onomatopoetic, e.g. *pica pica* 'one by one', *lidi lidi* 'softly' etc. Even non-expressive adverbials are reduplicated to express 'intensity of meaning', *begi* 'quickly': *begi begi* 'very fast' etc.

8.3.1.3 *Central Dravidian*

Adverbs, as a separate part of speech, are not found in Kolami (Emeneau 1955b). For Naikṛi under simple (monomorphemic) adverbs are given certain doubtful items denoting time, place, quantity and manner (Thomasiah 1986: 147–50), e.g. *iṇḍi* 'now', *lōpā(ḷ)* 'in', *niṇḍā* 'full', *ollākē* 'slowly' are given; the underlined items are loanwords from Telugu. Manner adverbs from demonstrative and interrogative roots are *a-nāŋ* 'in that manner', *i-nāŋ* 'in this manner', and *e-nāŋ* 'which manner'. Te. *lāg-ā*, Pe. *-leŋ*, Kuvi *-leki* and Naikṛi *-nāŋ* appear to be related as cognates. Under compound adverbs are cited certain onomatopoetic words like *gaṭ-gaṭ* 'drinking quickly', *than-than* 'rapidly' as manner adverbials; also reduplicated ones occur, e.g. *disā-misā* 'approximately', *ghāy-ghāy* 'soon', etc. In Naiki (Chanda) (Bhattacharya 1961: 95), *-el* occurs as place suffix, e.g. *ay-el* 'in that direction', *iy-el* 'in this direction', *ēl* 'which way, where'. The time adverbs include some unanalysable ones, e.g. *ine*(*n*) 'today', *indi* 'now', *vēgen* 'tomorrow', *pinne* 'day after tomorrow'. The manner adverbials are *is-en* 'in this manner', *es-en* 'how'. One example of a reduplicated adverbial is available, *haru-haru* 'slowly'.

Parji (Burrow and Bhattacharya 1953: 68) has both deictic and non-deictic adverbs. The manner adverbs are *at-ni* 'that way', *it-ni* 'this way', and *et-ni* 'in what way'. There are several non-deictic ones, e.g. *ine* 'today', *ori* 'yesterday', *tolli* 'tomorrow', *piŋge*, *pidne* (dial) 'the day after tomorrow', *kiṛi* 'below', *mari* 'again', etc. Non-productive morphological complexes functioning as adverbs include *nirḍi* 'last year' (cf. Te. *niruḍu*), *piraḍ* 'next year', *okec* 'once' etc. The ones borrowed from Halbi, an Indo-Aryan language, are *murle* 'completely', *jaṭke* 'quickly' etc.

Ollari (Bhattacharya 1957: 29) has a place suffix *-el* (cf. *-el* in Naiki, Chanda above) occurring in *dig-el* 'in the direction of' (< Skt. *dik-*), *pak-el* 'near' (< Oll. *pak-* 'side' < Skt. *pakṣa-*); *-ken* is a quantifier suffix found in *sane-ken* 'after a little while', *olo-ken* [ɔlɔken] 'a little', *mul-ken* 'much, many', apparently borrowed from Oṛiya.

Gadaba (Bhaskararao 1980: 60–8, under different headings) place adverbs have suffixes *-el*, *-an*/*-un*, e.g. *kak-el* 'near', *mund-el* 'in front of', *taṇḍr-el* 'inside', *pak-an* 'near', *aḍg-un* 'below', *kos-an* 'at the end of', etc. A number of heads of adverbial phrases are listed by Bhaskararao (1980: 60), who calls them adverbial postpositions, e.g. *ḍāŋka* 'till' (OTe. *dā̃k-an* > Mdn Te. *dāk-ā*), and case suffixes like *-kanna* 'than' (< Te), *-nuṇḍi* 'because of': *sēpal nuṇḍi* 'because of children' (< Te. *-nuṇḍi* 'from'). Manner adverbials from demonstrative and interrogative bases are *i-paḍ* 'in this fashion', *a-paḍ* 'in that fashion', *e-ṭen* 'in which fashion'; the forms *iy-nes* 'this day', *ay-nes* 'that day' and *ey-nes* 'which day'.[7] Reduplicated numerals and non-finite verbs function as manner adverbials, e.g. *iḍig-iḍig* 'in twos', *apuḍ-apuḍ* 'then itself', *senji-ginji* 'having gone a long distance'. Onomatopoetic adverbs are also reduplicated: *kis-kis* 'monkey's sound', *par-par* 'sound of tearing', etc.

8.3.1.4 *North Dravidian*

Kuṛux has a number of adverbs of time, place, quantity and manner, some native, but most of them borrowed from Indo-Aryan or Munda. The suffixes *-tā*/*-ntā* are added to time or place adverbs meaning 'at, of', and *-tī* is added to denote 'from', e.g. *akkun* 'just now': *akkun-tā* 'at the present moment', *akkun-tī* 'from this moment', *mund* 'before': *mund-tī*

[7] The *y*-element in the demonstrative roots is most likely traceable to an older laryngeal *H. Such relics are attested in Toda–Kota, Ollari, Koṇḍa and Kuṛux–Malto.

'beforehand'; *-m* is added as an adverbial suffix, *nelā* 'tomorrow': *nel-am* id. Another native adverb is *innā* 'today'. Adverbs of place: *isan*/*hisan* 'here', *asan*/*hasan*/*husan* 'there', *eksan* 'where', *iyyā*/*hiyyā* 'in this place', *ayyā*/*hayyā*[8] 'in that place', *ekayyā* 'in what place'. Adverbs of manner include morphological infinitives and gerundives, beside some onomatopoetic words, e.g. *huḍuṛ huḍuṛ* '*dinā tōknar* 'they stamp the ground violently (in dancing)'. Quantitative adverbs include *jokk-jokk, batre-batre* 'to a certain extent', *ongh-on* 'once', *pār-ē̃ṛ* 'twice', *pār-mund* 'three times', *pār-nāx* 'four times' with native numerals coming in the second position; but in *pā̃c dhā̃ō̃* 'five times' the numeral occurs as the first member.

For Malto Droese (1884: 88–100) cites several time, place and manner adverbs: *ā dine* 'on that day', *ī dine* 'in these days' (*ā* and *ī* are demonstrative adjectives), *akohi* 'recently', *aneke* 'now', *mundi* 'formerly', *ā baje* 'on that side', *ano* 'there', *ino* 'here', *ikeno* 'where', *pisi* 'below', *aneke* 'now', *ik-onno* 'when', *ine* 'today', *ine-tente* 'from today', *ule* 'inside', *ānki* 'that way', *ik-ni* 'how', *īnki* 'this way'.

Mahapatra (1979: 192–5) illustrates simple, complex and compound adverbs with examples. Simple: *ina* 'today', *inor* 'now', *ikni* 'how' etc.; complex: *dina* + *ond* → *din-ond* 'one day', *ī-no* 'this side', *ā-no* 'that side' etc.; compound stems: *ī kaṛa* 'this time', *ā kaṛa* 'at that time', *ī bēr* 'this day', *ā bēr* 'that day' etc. The manner adverbs include *bāg* 'fortunately', *cīg* 'silently', *sewre* 'completely' etc. Onomatopoetic ones include *giṛ-giṛ-re* 'hurriedly', *bor-bor-re* 'noisily' etc.

In Brahui (Bray 1909: 21–19) time, place and manner adverbials are nominals, derived from demonstrative and interrogative bases, but most of them are loanwords from Balochi and Indo-Aryan. A few native items are detected in *darō* 'yesterday', *mulxudo* 'the day before yesterday' (Dravidian part is underlined), *ēlō-dē* 'the next day' (*ēlō* 'the other'), *annā*[9] 'still', *dā-hun* 'thus', *o-hun* 'that manner (mediate)', *ē-hun* 'that manner' (remote), *o-ng(ī)* 'that direction (mediate)', *ē-ngī* 'that direction' (remote), *arā-ngī* 'which direction'.

8.4 **Clitics**

Clitics are a class of syntactic affixes, which can be attached to any autonomous constituent of a sentence – word, phrase or clause. Clitics are not added to adjectival phrases or clauses. The meaning of a clitic depends on the unit of the sentence to which it is attached. A sentence can be grammatical without any clitic. Clitics are not bound to a

[8] Here, the optional *h-* element is a reflex of the Proto-Dravidian laryngeal **H* lost in other languages.

[9] Andronov (1980: 90 fn43) compares this with Ta. *iṉṉum* 'yet, still, more', Ma. *ini*, Kota *in*, To. *īnm*, Ka. *inu, innu, innum*, Koḍagu *innū* 'still other', Te. *inka* 'now, hereafter', Kolami *in*. *DEDR* 410 derives all these forms from the deictic root **i*-/**ī*-. The proximate base in Brahui is *dā*-, a loanword from Pashto.

particular morphological class of words or part of speech, and that distinguishes them from morphologically bound suffixes.

Only four clitics can be reconstructed for Proto-Dravidian: **-um* conjunctive, **-ē* emphatic, **-ā* interrogative and **-ō* dubitative–alternative. Different modern languages have evolved other clitics, between five and twelve, which are not discussed below.

8.4.1 *-um *co-ordinating*

Modern Tamil (Lehmann 1989: 150–63) uses *-um* in several meanings depending on the items with which it co-occurs: (a) 'also', (b) 'totality', (c) 'any/none', when added to interrogative words, depending on the positive or negative governing verb, (d) 'and', when added to each of the coordinating phrases, (e) 'even, although', when added to a conditional phrase. Examples:

(a) *rājā nēṟṟ-um va-nt-āṉ* 'Raja came yesterday also'; *kumār-um va-nt-āṉ* 'Kumar also came'

(b) *mūṉṟu peṇpiḷḷai-kaḷ-um va-nt-ār-kaḷ* 'all the three girls came'

(c) *kumār eṅkē.y-um pōk-a.v-illai* 'Kumar didn't go anywhere' (*eṅke* 'where') *yār-um varu-v-ār-kaḷ* 'Everyone will come' (*yār* 'who' 3hum pl)

(d) *kumār-um rājāv-um va-nt-ār-kaḷ* 'Kumar and Raja came'

(e) *kumār*[1] *va-nt-āl-um*[2], *nāṉ*[3] *avaṉ-iṭam*[4] *pēc-a māṭṭ-ēṉ*[5] 'Even if[2] Kumar[1] comes[2], I[3] won't talk[5] with him[4]'

Malayāḷam (Asher and Kumari 1997: §1.3) is expected to have all the usages of *-um* found in Tamil, but the available descriptions do not treat all the details. Some of them are illustrated: the usage of 'also': *avan roṭṭi tinnu; veḷḷavum kuṭiccu* 'he ate the bread; he drank water also'; the usage of 'and' in *rāghavan-um kumār-um vannu* 'Raghavan and Kumar came'; the usage of question word 'when' + *-um* = 'always' in *avar eppōẓ-um vāyiccu-koṇṭ-irukk-unnu* [they always read-prog-pres] 'they are always reading'.

Koḍagu (Balakrishnan 1977: 207–10, Ebert 1996: 37–8) uses *-u*/*-ū* in different meanings, 'also', 'and' (added to coordinated constituents), 'even though', e.g. *mōvaḷ-ū bātï* 'the daughter also came', *nān-ū nā-ḍa akkë-nū*… 'I and my elder sister', *avën band-ū prayōjna ille* 'although he came, there was no use at all', *alli avaḷ-ū pāḍici* 'she also sang there'.

Old Kannaḍa uses *-um* (variant *-am*) with the meaning 'and' added to coordinated noun or verb phrases, *iḍ-ut-um*… *ār-ut-um*… *nung-ut-um* 'hitting, shouting and swallowing', *tāy-um tande.y-um* 'mother and father'; *-um* added to a single phrase/word, meaning 'even, also', e.g. *nuḍiyey-um* 'even after saying', *ad-um* 'that also'; a complex clitic *-ān-um* 'even', e.g. *ār-* 'who': *ār-ānum* 'whosoever', *ēnu* 'what': *ēn-ānum* 'whatsoever' (usages from Pampa Bhārata of the tenth century; B. Ramachandra Rao 1972: 182–9).

Modern Kannaḍa *-ū /-nū* correspond to OKa. *-um*; for the usage meaning 'and', e.g. *narahari.y-ū sōmasēkhara-nū pēṭege hōdaru* 'Narahari and Somasekhar went to the market'; for the usage of a question word like *ēnu* 'what' + *ū* = 'anything', e.g. *viji ēn-ū koḷḷal-illa* 'Viji has not bought anything' (Sridhar 1990: 102, 104).

In South Dravidian I, Toda has all the usages found in Tamil. Kota has most of them but in one usage it replaces *-m* by *-dan* (cf. Ta. *tāṉ* 'self').

Telugu has all the five usages with *-um* > *ū* for *u*-ending words; for others lengthening of any word-final vowel, e.g. 'also': *wāḍikī*[1] *ī sangati*[2] *telusu*[3] [he-dat-cl this-matter be-known-3neu sg] 'he also[1] knows[3] this matter[2]', 'and': *ill-ū wākil-ī* 'the house and the gate', non-finite verb *win-i* 'having heard' + cl = 'even after listening (to what is said)...': *wāḍu win-ī māṭl-āḍ-a lēdu* 'he didn't speak, even having heard...', question word *ewaru* 'who' + cl → *ewar-ū* with a negative verb 'nobody': *nā*[1] *peḷḷiki*[2] *ewar-ū*[3] *rālēdu*[4] 'nobody came [3,4] [anyone[3] did not come[4]] to[2] my[1] wedding[2]', numeral + cl: *iddar-ū debba tinnāru* 'they both got hurt',

Among North Dravidian, Kuṛux has *-im/-um~-m* in usage (c), e.g. *eksa' ānum/ānim* 'anywhere, everywhere, somewhere' (see section 8.4.4.1). Brahui has *-(h)um* in two meanings 'also, and' following nominals, e.g. *ī hum duzzī kattanuṭ* 'I too have committed theft' (Bray 1909: 229, Emeneau 1980b: 213).

Among the remaining languages of South Dravidian II and Central Dravidian, several of the usages occur in different combinations but with different morphological markers (for details, see Emeneau 1980b: 213–16).

8.4.1.1 *Convergence between Indo-Aryan and Dravidian*

Emeneau (1980b: 197–249) gives a detailed account of the usage of **-um* in Dravidian and compares it with Sanskrit *-api* (< IE **epi*) which has parallels in Indo-European as a verbal prefix. Its usage as an enclitic particle in Sanskrit, from Old Indic to the classical period, reflects transfer of the usages of the derivatives of **-um* in Dravidian to *-api*; this phenomenon heralds a new aspect of convergence between Indo-Aryan and Dravidian. He attributes five meanings to *-api*, which were progressively acquired by Sanskrit and transmitted to Middle and New Indo-Aryan. The meanings are: (a) 'also', (b) 'and', (c) 'even if, even though' (Skt. *yady-api ... tathā 'pi*), (d) 'totalizing' or 'summing' following a numeral of members of a numbered group, (e) added to an interrogative pronoun, an indefinite meaning results, 'whoever, someone, anyone', e.g. *katham* 'how': *katham api* 'anyway, by any means'. He says usages (a) and (b) were Vedic; (c) was Vedic and Classical; (d) and (e) were Classical and they continued into Middle Indic and New Indic with different markers and with some disintegration of the original semantic structure (1980b: 197–200). Emeneau surveys in detail the usages of **-um* (its derivatives as well as substitutes) in different Dravidian languages and concludes, 'None of the Sanskrit structure is inherited straightforwardly from Indo-European or from Indo-Iranian . . . The Sanskrit usages are essentially a calque of Dravidian **-um* by Sanskrit *api*' (1980b: 217–18).

8.4.2 *-ē *emphatic*

This clitic adds emphasis to the meaning of any constituent of a clause to which it is attached, broadly meaning 'only'.

In Modern Tamil it is used in addition to *tān̲* 'self' which is an innovation in Proto-South Dravidian I. Modern Tamil usages include the following: *avarkaḷ*[1] *en̲n̲-ai.y-ē̲*[2] *kūppiṭu-kir̲-ārkaḷ*[3] 'they[1] are calling[3] me only/just me[2]', *kumār nēr̲r̲u iṅkē va-nt-ān̲-ē̲* 'Kumar did come here yesterday'. A special usage is the addition of *-ē̲* to an infinitive before a negative finite verb, e.g. *kumār*[1] *var-a.v-ē̲*[2] *var-a-māṭṭ-ān̲*[3] [Kumar come-inf come-inf-not 3m sg] 'Kumar[1] will[3] definitely[2] not come[3]'. It also relativizes a clause and embeds it in the matrix clause, e.g. *nān̲*[1] *nēr̲r̲u*[2] *pār-tt-ēn̲-ē̲*[3] *anta.p paṭam*[4] *nan̲r̲-āka*[5] *iru-nt-atu*[6] '(the one[2]*)* I[1] saw[2] yesterday[2], that movie[4] was[6] nice[5]'.

Malayāḷam (Asher and Kumari 1997: §1.11) adds *-ē* and *-tanne* to any major constituent of a sentence as emphatic particles, e.g. *rāman ippōẓ-ē var-unnuḷḷū* 'Raman is coming only now', *ñān-ē var-ām* 'I shall come', *avan karaŋŋu-koṇṭ-ē irunnu* [he cry-prog-emph be-past] 'he was continuously crying'.

Koḍagu expresses emphasis by adding *-ē* to any autonomous constituent of a sentence, e.g. *avaḷ-ē bātï* 'she came herself', *nānï nāḷe.y-ē pōpi* 'I will go only tomorrow'.

In Classical Kannaḍa, *-e*/*-ē* can be added to nouns, verbs or adverbs, e.g. *namb-en* 'I will not believe': *namb-en-e̲* 'I will certainly not believe', *en-ge.y-e̲* [I-to-emph] 'for me only', *ādam-e̲* 'only excessively'. Modern Kannaḍa (Sridhar 1990: §1.11) continues the usage of *-ē* in addition to *tān-ē* as emphatic clitics, e.g. *rāman-ē banda* 'Rama himself came', *avanu kared-ē karī-t-āne* [he call-ppl-emph call-non-past-3m sg] 'he will definitely call'. Adding the clitic to the first member of a reduplicated verb is an idiomatic usage of emphasis in Dravidian, which is not easily translatable into English. Also cf. Te. *wāḍu pilw-an-ē pilus-tā-ḍu* [he call-inf-emph call-future-3m-sg] 'he will certainly call'. Note that in Kannaḍa the first repeated verb is the perfective participle and not infinitive as in Telugu.

Telugu (Krishnamurti and Gwynn 1985: 280–3) uses *-ē* as an emphatic marker both at the sentence level and at the constituent level, e.g. *adi nā pustakam-e̲* 'that is certainly my book', *ad-ē nā pustakam* 'that is my book', *āme*[1] *nā-tō*[2] *ā sangati*[3] *cepp-an-e̲ lēdu*[4] 'she[1] did not at all speak[4] with me[2] (about) that matter[3]'; *cepp-a-lēdu* [tell-inf be-not-3neu-sg] is a compound verb meaning '(one) did not tell'. (Any subject may occur in the sentence and the third neuter singular neutralizes all agreement contrasts.) The only grammatical element which can be inserted within such a compound is a clitic. A more emphatic way is to repeat the infinitive followed by *-ē* before the finite verb, i.e. *cepp-an-ē cepp-a-lē-du* (see the Kannaḍa example above).

Gondi (Abhujmaria dialect; Natarajan 1985: 228) uses *-ē* as an emphatic clitic, e.g. *māṭ-ē̲ u-ṭṭ-ōm* 'we only/ourselves drank', *nanā pun-ō-n-ē̲* 'I do not know at all'. Koṇḍa also has *-e* ~ *-ne* as an emphatic clitic, e.g. *ḍokra*[1] *nāṭo-ne*[2] *man-zin-an*[3] 'the old man[1] was staying[3] in the village only[2]', *daniŋ-e o-n-a* 'I will carry that one only'. There is no evidence of emphatic *-e*/*-ʔe* in Kui, Pengo and Manḍa. But in Kuvi (Israel 1979: 224–5) some examples of the usage of this clitic are cited, e.g. *ī kama*[1] *ēvasiʔ-e*[2] *ki-n-esi*[3] 'only he[2] will do[3] this work[1]', *ēdi-ʔe* 'she herself', etc.

Among the Central Dravidian languages Naikṛi (Thomasiah 1986: 156) has *-ī*, called an emphatic clitic, e.g. *ān-ī̲* 'I myself', *an-ūŋ-ī̲* 'me alone'. The quality of the vowel makes it a phonological problem. Parji and Ollari grammars do not treat particles or clitics as a part of speech. Gadaba (Bhaskararao 1980: 61) cites two examples of *-i* being an emphatic particle, *ōṇ* (= *ōnḍ*)[1] *vagoṭ -i*[2] *īn*[3] *vā*[4] 'you[3] come[4] only if he[1] comes'.

In Malto *-i* is cited as a particle meaning 'certainly', e.g. *ēn ēk-an-i* 'I shall go certainly'. There is no evidence of PD **-ē* emphatic in North Dravidian. On the basis of **-ē* > *-ē* South Dravidian I and South Dravidian II, we can reconstruct **-ē* as an emphatic clitic for Proto-South Dravidian. Central Dravidian *-i* and Malto *-i* (if they are taken as cognates) would enable us to reconstruct this clitic for Proto-Dravidian. It is very likely that *-i* represents Indo-Aryan/Hindi *-hī* (emphatic) with *h*-loss. Since clitics are important elements of discourse, it is quite possible that borrowed ones from the neighbouring dominant Indo-Aryan languages have replaced the native ones. This is clearly true of the interrogative clitic below.

8.4.3 **-ā interrogative*

This is added to a declarative sentence or to any free constituent of a clause to elicit a 'yes' or 'no' answer. The question marker is underlined. Examples:

Tamil

(1) *kumār*[1] *nēr̲r̲u*[2] *rājā.v-ai*[3] *aṭi-tt-ān̲*[4] 'Kumar[1] beat[4] Raja[3] yesterday[2]'

a. *kumār*[1] *nēr̲r̲u*[2] *rājā.v-ai-ā̲*[3] *aṭi-tt-ān̲*[4] 'was it Raja[3] (acc Q) that Kumar[1] beat[4] yesterday[2]?'

b. *kumār*[1] *nēr̲r̲-ā̲*[2] *rājā.v-ai*[3] *aṭi-tt-ān̲*[4] 'was it yesterday[2] (Q) that Kumar[1] beat[4] Raja[3]?'

c. *kumār-ā̲*[1] *nēr̲r̲u*[2] *rājā.v-ai*[3] *aṭi-tt-ān̲*[4] 'was it Kumar[1] (Q) that beat[4] Raja[3] yesterday[2]?'

Kannaḍa In Classical Kannaḍa, in addition to *-a*/*-ā*, *-e*/*-ē* and *-o*/*-ō* were also used as question markers, e.g. *mared-a* 'did you forget?', *kuḍuv-ā* 'will you give?'; *kaṇḍir-e* 'did you see?' *āyt-ē* 'did it happen?'; *illey-ō* 'does it not exist?'

(2)a. *nimm-a[1] tāyi[2] āfis-ige[3] hōg-idd-ār-ā̠[4]* 'has[4] your[1] mother[2] gone[4] to the office[3]?'

The yes–no question clitic has the form *-nā* following a constituent ending in a vowel, e.g.

b. *nenne-nā̠[1] avanu[2] pustaka[3] koṇiddu[4]?* 'was it yesterday[1] that he[2] bought[4] the book[3]?'

Toda, Koḍagu and Tuḷu also use *-ā* as a marker of yes–no questions (Emeneau 1984: 132, Balakrishnan 1977: 206, Bhat 1998: 170). Koḍagu also has variants in *-la* and *-na*, e.g.

Koḍagu

(3) *māḍaṅga-na̠?* 'shall we do?'

Tuḷu

(4) *yānï baroḍ-ā̠* 'shall I come?'

Malayāḷam uses *-ō* (with positive forms) and *-ē* (with negative forms) as markers of neutral yes–no questions. No examples for *-ā* as question marker are given.

Telugu

(5)a. *idi mī ill-ā̠* 'is this your house?'
   b. *id-ǣ mī illu?* 'is this your house?'

Konḍa

(6) *niṇi[1] lōku[2] manar-a̠[3] sile-na̠[4]?* [you-to[1] folks[2] be-hum pl-Q[3] be-not-Q[4]] 'do[3] you[1] have[3] any folks[2] or not[4]?'

Gondi, Kui–Kuvi–Pengo–Manḍa use *-ki* of Indo-Aryan origin to frame questions requiring yes–no answers.

Kolami

(7) *amd vatt-en-a* 'has he come?'

Naikṛi

(8)a. *sīnār-ā* 'will we give?', *tīsātīy-ā* 'will you eat?'

Naikṛi also has *-kī* as an interrogative particle, e.g.

b. *vānā vāsād-kī tōy?* 'will the rain come or not?'

Gadaba

(9) *ōṇḍ*^{1} *ay kōs-un*^{2} *cēdel*^{3} *si-n-oṇḍ-ā*^{4} 'did^{4} he^{1} give^{4} a porcupine^{3} to that king^{2}?'

Since South Dravidian I, South Dravidian II and Central Dravidian have evidence of interrogative *-ā*, it can be reconstructed for Proto-Dravidian. Several languages in central and north India have replaced it by a borrowed clitic *-ki* from Indo-Aryan.

8.4.4 * *-ō* ***dubitative–alternative***

PD *-*ō* has several complementary functions. As a sentential clitic it makes the proposition doubtful. Added to two or more coordinating NPs, it means 'either . . . or'. Added to an interrogative word, it has an indefinite meaning. It also marks the first of two correlative clauses. All these usages are retained in the literary languages.

Tamil (Lehmann 1989: 154–6)

(1)a. *kumār*^{1} *eppōtu*^{2} *varuvāṉ*^{3}*-ō*^{4} 'I wonder^{4} when^{2} Kumar^{1} will come^{3}'

b. *nēṟṟu*^{1} *yār-ō*^{2} *uṅkaḷ-ai*^{3}*.k kūppiṭṭāṉ*^{4} 'someone^{2} called^{4} you^{3} yesterday^{1}' (*yār* 'who')

c. *kumār-ō rājā.v-ō varu.v-ārkaḷ* 'Kumar or Raja will come'

d. *evaṉ*^{1} *nēṟṟu*^{2} *va-nt-āṉ-ō*^{3} *avaṉ*^{4} *eṉ*^{5} *tampi*^{6} '(the one) who^{1} came^{3} yesterday^{2}, he^{4} (was) my^{5} younger brother^{6}'

Malayāḷam (Asher and Kumari 1997: 139–41, 146–8)

(2) *ñān*^{1} *cōṟ-ō*^{2} *cappāttiy-ō*^{3} *kaẓikkām*^{4} 'I^{1}'ll take^{4} either rice^{2} or chapatti^{3}'

Kannaḍa (Ramachandra Rao 1972: 186, Sridhar 1990: 259–61) Literary Kannaḍa has the usage of *-o*/*-ō* to express doubt, to convert an interrogative into an indefinite pronoun, and to express 'either-or' coordination (example (3) is from Old Kannaḍa and (4a–c) from Modern Kannaḍa):

(3) *kār-o*^{1} *mēṇ*^{2} *kāḷarakkasan-ō*^{3} 'is it a dark cloud^{1} or^{2} a black demon^{3}?'

(4)a. *yār-ō*^{1} *baruttiddāre*^{2} 'somebody^{1} is coming^{2}' (*yār* 'who')

b. *surēṣa-nō*^{1} *vāṇi-yō*^{2} *baruttāre*^{3} 'either Suresh^{1} or Vani^{2} will come^{3}'

c. *ninage*^{1} *ēnu*^{2} *bēk-ō*^{3} *togō*^{4} [you-to what be-needed-non-past-clitic take-2sg] 'take^{4} whatever^{2} you^{1} want^{3}'

For Koḍagu only single words are given, e.g. *dār-ō* 'who?' (in doubt), *nīn-ō* 'you?' (in doubt).

Telugu (Krishnamurti and Gwynn 1985: 289–93) All uses of *-ō* in Modern Telugu were already there in the inscriptional and literary varieties beginning from the seventh century. Only examples from Modern Telugu are given:

(5)a. *ewar-ō*^{1} *wacc-ǣ-ru*^{2} 'somebody^{1} has come^{2}'

b. *āyana*^{1} *mana*^{2} *ūru*^{3} *enduku*^{4} *wacc-ǣ-ḍ*^{5} *-ō*^{6}*!* 'I wonder ^{6} why^{4} he^{1} came^{5} to our^{2} village^{3}!'

c. *nēnu enn-ō dēśālu cūsǣ-nu* 'I have seen many countries' (*enni* 'how many?')

d. *ewaru*^{1} *mundu*^{2} *wastār-ō*^{3} *wāḷḷu*^{4} *gelustāru*^{5} 'whoever^{1} come^{3} first^{2}, (they^{4}) will win^{5}'

e. *mā wāḍu*^{1} *amerkā-nunci*^{2} *rēp-ō*^{3} *elluṇḍ (i)-ō*^{4} *was-tā-ḍu*^{5} 'our boy^{1} will come^{5} from America^{2} tomorrow^{3} or the day after tomorrow^{4}'

Gondi Subrahmanyam (1968: 77) gives only one example of *-ō* as a clitic of uncertainty, e.g. *bōr* 'who': *bōr-ō* 'somebody' (Adilabad dialect). There is also another 'free form' *behē*, which expresses uncertainty, e.g. *vōr*^{1} *vātōr*^{2} *behē*^{3} 'he^{1} came^{2}, didn't he^{3}?'

Koṇḍa (Krishnamurti 1969a: 329) Examples are available for the addition of the clitic *-ō* with interrogative words to form indefinite pronouns. I treated this as a separate morpheme from *-o/-no,* which occurs as a coordinating conjunction expressing uncertainty. It is clear that they are one and the same.

(6)a. *ayer-o*^{1} *gor̠on*^{2} *katki-zin-ar*^{3} 'some people^{1} were cutting^{3} (the trees in) the forest^{2}'

b. *ri-neṇḍ-e*^{1} *soRad-o*^{2} *mu-neṇḍ-e*^{3} *soRad-o*^{4} . . . 'maybe two days^{1} had passed^{2} or three days^{3} had passed^{4} . . . '

The remaining South Dravidian II languages, Kui–Kuvi–Pengo–Manḍa, do not have any form that is comparable. Kui *-ve . . . -ve* and Kuvi *-va . . . -va* are coordinating conjunctions, but they do seem to be related to the clitic *-ō*. Their source has to be investigated.

Among the Central Dravidian languages, only Naikṛi has a clitic *-ō*, which is illustrated with finite verbs meaning 'doubt', e.g. *seddēn-ō* 'whether he has gone', *vattēn-ō* 'whether he has come . . . ' When added to interrogative words, they become indefinite pronouns, e.g. *ēr-ō* m pl 'some one', *ēd-ō* neu sg 'something' (Thomasiah 1986: 155, 158). Gadaba uses *ēm-ō* (lw < Te. *ēmi* 'what' + *-ō*) to express doubt, when attached to a finite verb (Bhaskararao 1980: 61).

None of the North Dravidian languages has retained this clitic. As in the case of other clitics, it has been replaced by borrowed substitutes for expressing the same ideas.

9

Syntax

9.1 Introduction[1]

The unmarked order of constituents in a sentence is Subject–Object–Verb (SOV) in the Dravidian languages. A number of other features seem to flow from this dominant pattern: adjectives (including possessive nominals) precede noun heads, adverbs precede the verbs that they modify, complements precede the matrix clauses, auxiliaries follow the main verb, and postpositions rather than prepositions follow nominals. Dravidian languages have the nominative–accusative pattern with subject–predicate agreement, and not the absolutive–ergative.[2] A sentence in Dravidian may be simple, complex or compound.[3]

9.2 Simple sentences

A simple sentence is represented by two grammatical constituents, Subject + Predicate. The subject is either a Noun Phrase (NP) with the head noun in the nominative case, or a Postpositional Phrase (PP) with the head noun in the dative case (see discussion in

[1] Most of the available descriptions of the non-literary languages do not deal with syntax. Even for the literary languages, we do not have any study of syntax of the language of the classical texts. Therefore, it is not easy to make a systematic study of comparative syntax and make statements applying the comparative method. Secondly, there has not been any significant study of comparative syntax in Dravidian. Most research during the last century concentrated on comparative phonology and some aspects of morphology. Steever's work (1988, 1993) represents the beginning of research on some aspects of comparative morphosyntax in Dravidian. These limitations have to be borne in mind by readers while studying this chapter. I have, therefore, limited my illustrations to the four literary languages, representing South Dravidian I and II. Occasionally I have referred to the other languages, wherever possible. I have also not attempted reconstruction of Proto-Dravidian patterns, as I did in the other chapters.

[2] 'A language is said to show ergative characteristics if, at some level, S (intransitive subject) is treated in the same way as O (transitive object), and differently from A (transitive subject)' (Dixon 1987: 2).

[3] The illustrative sentences are taken from published sources, except for Telugu, from Krishnamurti (1969a), Bhaskararao (1980), Steever (1988, 1998: including chapters by different authors), Lehmann (1989), Krishnamurti and Gwynn (1985), Sridhar (1990), Asher and Kumari (1997) and others cited in appropriate places.

section 9.2.5). The latter type is called the dative subject. The Predicate is represented either by a Verb Phrase (VP) or a NP. Both these may have PPs as complements or adjuncts. Sentences that have NP predicates are generally equative. The four types are illustrated below, taking (to the extent possible) one language from each subgroup:

(1) NP + VP

a. Ta. *avaṉ va-nt-āṉ*
[he come-past-3m-sg]
'he (informal) came'

b. Te. *wāḍu wacc-ǣ-ḍu*
[he come-past-3m-sg]
'he (informal) came'

c. Pa. *tolen-kul verrar*
[brother-pl come-past-3m-pl]
'the brothers came'

d. Kuṛ. *tam-bas ke-cc-as*
[he-gen-father die-past-3m-sg]
'his father died'

(2) NP + NP

a. Ta. *avar eṉ āciriyar*
[he-hon I-poss teacher-hon]
'he (polite) is my teacher'

b. Te. *wāru mā guruwu-gāru*
[he-hon we-gen teacher-hon]
'he (polite) is my teacher'

c. Kol. *inne-t pēr tān-ed*
[you-sg-gen name-nom what-nom]
'what is your name?'[4]

d. Malt. *āh eŋki baya-h*
[he-nom my brother-nom-3m-sg]
'he (is) my brother'

(3) PP_{dat} + VP

a. Ta. *avaṉukku kōpam va-nt-atu*
[he-dat anger come-past-3n-sg]
'he got angry'

b. Te. *wāḍiki kōpam wacc-in-di*
[he-dat anger come-past-3n-sg]
'he got angry'

[4] This usage is from Adilabad dialect. The Wardha dialect has a copula *anda* 'is' added to the NP + NP sentences owing to Marathi influence (Subrahmanyam 1998: 323).

c. Kol. *an-uŋ karu va-tt-in*
[I-dat hunger come-past-1sg]
'I am hungry'

d. Br. *bandaɤ-as-ē irā mār assur*
[man-one-dat/acc two son(s) be-past-3pl]
'a man had two sons'

(4) PP_{dat} + NP

a. Ta. *avan̲-ukku oru makan̲*
[he-dat one son]
'he has a son'

b. Te. *wāḍ-i-ki oka koḍuku*
[he-dat one son]
'he has a son'

c. Pa. *ōn-uŋ sat-jan cind-ul*
[he-dat seven-people-class children]
'he has seven children'

d. Malt. *sardare-k ēna goṭu gāydu*
[chief-dat how many cow(s)-nom]
'how many cows does the chief have?'

The presence of the four patterns in all four subgroups allows them to be reconstructed for Proto-Dravidian. The Brahui sentence in (3) should normally belong to (4) but a copula is used under the influence of the surrounding Indo-Aryan.[5]

There is agreement in gnp between the subject NP and the predicate NP in (2) as in the case of verbal predications, i.e. NP + VP in (1).[6] In South Dravidian (SD I and SD II), for equative sentences, even the first- and second-person subjects have agreement in the predicate NP, not only in number and person, but also in gender. The verb in NP + VP shows agreement only in number and person and not in gender, when the subject is in the first or second person. These are discussed, in detail, under pronominalized nouns in section 6.7 and the pattern is reconstructible for Proto-Dravidian. Examples:

(5) a. OTa. *yām . . . ōr . . . uyir-am*
[we . . . one . . . breath-1pl]
'we (are) of one breath'

b. OTa. *nām nāṭṭ-ōm*
[we town-adj-1pl]
'we (are) town-folk' (*nāṭu* 'town, country')

[5] Brahui also has NP predicates, e.g. *numā šahraṭī aṭ urā/ō* [your village-loc how-many houses-nom] 'how many houses (are there) in your village?' However, verbal predicates are preferred (Elfenbein 1998: 410–11).

[6] See section 7.5.1 for discussion on the loss of personal suffixes in Middle and Modern Malayāḷam.

c. MTe. *nēnu manci-wāṇṇi* (←*wāḍ-i-ni*)
[I good-man-obl-1sg]
'I am a good man'

d. MTe. *nēnu manci-dānni* (←*dān-i-ni*)
[I good-she-obl-1sg]
'I am a good woman'

The 2m sg is (*nuwwu*) *manci-wāḍ-i-wi* 'you are a good man', 2f sg (*nuwwu*) *manci-dān-i-wi* 'you are a good woman', 2pl *mīru manic-wāḷḷu* 'you (pl) are good persons', 3m sg *wāḍu manic-wāḍu* 'he is a good man', 3h pl *wāḷḷu manci-wāḷḷu* 'they are good persons', 3non-m sg *āme/adi maici-di* 'she/it is a good one', 3neu pl *awi manci-wi* 'they (non-hum) are good ones'. Modern Tamil has lost the corresponding constructions.

In equative sentences with NP predicates there is no reference to tense and aspect. Therefore, the implied time reference is either 'generic', i.e. a feature habitually ascribed without reference to a particular time, as in (6), or it refers to the time of the utterance, as in (7) and (8), e.g.

(6) Te. *himālayālu*[1] *anni*[2] *parwatāl-a-kannā*[3] *cālā*[4] *ettu*[5]
[Himalayas all mountains-obl-than much height]
'Himalayas[1] (are) much[4] higher[5] than[3] all[2] the mountains[3]' (generic use)

(7) Te. *rāmayya-ku mugguru pillalu*
[Ramayya-dat three-classifier children]
'Ramayya has three children' (present time)

(8) Te. *āme tella-ni telupu*
[she white-adj whiteness]
'she is very fair' (lit. she is white as whiteness)

When an abstract noun occurs as the predicate NP, gnp agreement with the subject NP is suspended as in (6) and (8).

9.2.1 *Sentence types based on the declarative*

With a slight modification, we can relate interrogative and imperative sentences to declarative, illustrated in this section. Imperative sentences require the imperative singular and plural finite verbs, instead of the tensed finite verbs of declarative sentences; these have been discussed in section 7.11.1. There are two kinds of interrogative sentences: (i) those that require a yes–no answer are formed by adding the interrogative clitic *-*ā* (-*ē*, -*ō* in some languages) to the whole clause or to the constituent that is questioned (see section 8.4.3), and (ii) those intended to elicit information are framed by replacing any constituent NP or AdvP by a corresponding question word, e.g.

(9) a. Ta. *kumār enṟu-kku varu-v-āṉ*
[Kumar what-day-dat come-fut-3m-sg]
'which day will Kumar come?'
b. Ka. *nimma hesaru ēnu*
[you-hon-obl name what]
'what is your name?'
c. Te. *mī ku enta-mandi pillalu*
[you-dat how-hum-class child-pl]
'how many children do you have?'
d. Koṇḍa *nīnu embe soRi mani*
[you-sg where go-past-2sg be-non-past-2sg]
'where have you gone?'
e. Ga. *ī kor ēyr-ne*
[this fowl who-gen]
'whose fowl is this?'
f. Malto *ēkā āl-as bar-c-as*
[which man come-past-3m-sg]
'which man came?'
g. *ēkā āl-ī bar-c-a*
[which woman come-past-3f-sg]
'which woman came?'

Note that the question word occurs in the same position within the clause where the anticipated answer occurs, e.g. for (9c) an answer could be *māku mugguru pillau* 'we have three children'; *enta-mandi* 'how many' and *mu-gguru* 'three (persons)' occur in the same position of the respective clauses. Negative sentences occur with a negative finite verb, substituting for the affirmative finite verb in non-past or past (see section 7.10).

9.2.2 *Core and peripheral arguments*

The finite verb is an obligatory constituent of a verb-final sentence. Since the personal ending encodes information about the subject, it is possible to use a finite verb, even without specifying the subject. A sentence like Te. *pani*[1] *antā*[2] *cēs-ǣ-ḍu*[3] [work whole do-past-3m sg] '(he) did[3] the whole[2] work[1]' is well-formed, even without a subject argument. Similarly, there are no complements that are obligatory, as in English, like the direct object argument with a transitive verb, e.g. Te. *ewaru an-n-āru*? 'who said?' is a well-formed sentence even without the direct object. The criteria used to distinguish a complement from an adjunct in terms of core and peripheral arguments are not adequate for Dravidian (see Matthews 1996 [1981]: 123–45, Dixon and Aikhenvald 2000: 2–4).

An intransitive clause has S (= Subject) as the core argument. A transitive clause is said to have two core arguments: A (subject) and O (object). It is possible also to have non-normal (non-canonical) case marking of both intransitive and transitive clauses in Dravidian when the subject is marked for dative and not nominative (see Aikhenvald et al. 2001: viii). Both intransitive and transitive clauses may have the subject either in the nominative or in the dative case, e.g. intransitive clause: Te. *wāḍu weḻḻ-ǣ-ḍu* 'he went' (subject in nominative), Te. *wāḍ-i-ki kōpam-gā undi* [he-dat anger-advl be-3neu-sg] 'he is angry'(subject in the dative). Transitive clause: *wāḍu*^{1} *annam*^{2} *tin-n-āḍu*^{3} [he food-acc eat-past-3m-sg] 'he^{1} ate^{3} a meal^{2}' (subject in the nominative and object in the accusative); Te. *wāḍ-i-ki udyōgam dorik-in-di* [he-obl-dat job be-found-past-3neu-sg] 'he found a job' (lit. to-him a-job was-found). This can be interpreted as a transitive sentence with the subject in the dative and the object in the nominative. In such sentences the object NP is also a core argument, since non-mention of the object in the sentence produces an ungrammatical sentence like **wāḍ-i-ki dorik-in-di* 'to him (it) was found'. Similarly, predicates like 'see, know, like' have the subject NP in the dative (as a PP) and the object NP in the nominative; e.g. Te. *nāku ayskrīm iṣṭam* [I-dat ice-cream likeable] 'I like ice-cream', Te. *mīku kāfī kāwāl-ǣ*? [you-dat coffee be-wanted-Q] 'do you want coffee?' Dixon and Aikhenvald (2000: 3) set up SE (= extension to core) as core arguments for such intransitive clauses. A transitive clause has A (subject of a transitive verb) and O (object) as core arguments, sometimes including E (recipient, beneficiary), when the verb is ditransitive ('give, tell' etc). Non-canonical marking of the logical subject by dative and of object by nominative have to be accommodated for both S and AO clauses (for further examples of dative subject, see section 9.2.5.4 (B)).

9.2.3 ***Free word order, shift of focus by clefting***

Because of rich nominal and verbal morphology expressing grammatical relations (with case marking in nominals and gnp marking in verbs), the grammatical burden on word order is reduced in Dravidian. Therefore, it is possible to change the unmarked word order of constituents, keeping the verb in the final position, without any erosion to the semantic structure of the sentence (Krishnamurti and Gwynn 1985: 16–31, Lehmann 1989: 176–80, 368–70)

(10) a. Ta. *nē<u>r</u><u>r</u>u*^{1} *mantiri-avarkaḷ*^{2} *kuẓaint-ai.kku*^{3}*-p.paric-ai*^{4} *k.koṭu-ttār*^{5}
[yesterday minister-hon-pl child-dat prize-acc give-past-3hon-pl]
'yesterday^{1}, the minister^{2} gave^{5} the child^{3} a prize^{4}'

The adverb (*nē<u>r</u><u>r</u>u*^{1}), the subject NP (*mantiri-avarkaḷ*^{2}) and the two PPs (indirect object *kuẓaint-ai-kku*^{3} and direct object *paric-ai*^{4}) can be shifted to any position in the sentence, keeping the finite verb (*koṭu-tt-ār*^{5}) in the sentence-final position. Any of the phrases can be focussed by (i) nominalizing the finite verb, and (ii) shifting the focussed phrase to the final (predicate) position; alternatively, if any clitic (emphatic *-tāṉ* or *-ē*) is added to any of the constituents, that constituent receives focus without being shifted to the predicate position or disturbing the nominalized finite verb. The resultant sentence with the nominalized verb behaves like an equative sentence.

b. Ta. *nēṟṟu*[1] *kuẓaint-ai.kku*[2]*-p. paric-ai*[3] *k.koṭu-tt-atu*[4] – *mantiri.y-avarkaḷ*[5]
'yesterday[1], (it was) the minister[5] (who) gave[4] the child[2] a prize[3]'

c. Ta. *nēṟṟu*[1] *mantiri.y-avarkaḷ*[2] *paric-ai*[3] *k.koṭu-tt-atu*[4] – *kuẓaint-ai.kku*[5]
'yesterday[1], (it was) to the child[5] (that) the minister[3] gave[4] a prize[3]'

d. Ta. *nēṟṟu*[1] *mantiri.y-avarkaḷ*[2] *kuẓaint-ai.kku*[3] *k.koṭu-tt-atu*[4] – *paric-ai*[5]
'yesterday[1], (it was) a prize[5] (that) the minister[3] gave[4] to the child[3]'

e. Ta. *mantiri.y-avarkaḷ*[1] *kuẓaint-ai.kku*[2]*-p. paric-ai*[3] *k.koṭu-tt-atu*[4] – *nēṟṟu*[5]
'it was yesterday[5], that the minister[1] gave[4] the child[2] a prize[3]'

If any clitic like the emphatic particle *-tāṉ* is added to any of the constituents, the nominalized finite verb need not be shifted from the sentence-final position:

f. Ta. *nēṟṟu*[1] *mantiri.y-avarkaḷ- tāṉ*[2] *kuẓaint-ai.kku*[3]*-p. paric-ai*[4] *koṭu-tt-atu*
[yesterday minister-hon-pl-emph child-dat prize-acc give-past-3n-sg-nom]
'yesterday[1], it was the minister[2] who gave[5] the child[3] a prize[4]'

Malayāḷam (Asher and Kumari 1997: 181–2) has a similar usage of clefting for emphasis, but instead of an emphatic clitic the verb *āṇə* 'be-present' is added to the constituent focussed. The nominalized finite verb is not shifted from the sentence-final position.

(11) a. Ma. *rāman innale kṛṣṇaṉ-ṉə raṇṭə pustakam koṭuttu*
[Raman yesterday Krishnan-dat two book(s)-acc give-past]
'Raman gave Krishnan two books yesterday'

b. Ma. *rāman-āṇə innale kṛṣṇa-ṉṉə raṇṭə pustakam koṭutt-atə*
[Raman-it is yesterday Krishnan-to two books give-past-3neusg]
'it was Raman that gave two books to Krishnan yesterday'

Similarly, different constituents can be emphasized by adding *āṇə*, as in *innale-āṇə* 'it was only yesterday . . . ', *kṛṣṇaṉ-ṉ-āṇə* 'it was to Krishnan . . . ', *raṇṭə pustakam-āṇə* 'it was two books that. . . .'

In Kannaḍa (Sridhar 1990: 139–40) the finite verb is nominalized by adding *-adu* in the place of the personal suffix and by shifting the focused constituent to the final position as is done in Tamil, e.g.

(12) a. Ka. *tārā*[1] *nenne*[2] *barōḍa-kke*[3] *hō-d-aḷu*[4]
[Tara yesterday Baroda-to go-past-3f-sg]
'Tara[1] went[4] to Baroda[3] yesterday[2]'
b. Ka. *nenne*[1] *barōḍa-kke*[2] *hō-da-ddu*[3] – *tārā*[4]
[yesterday Baroda-dat go-past-3neu-sg Tara]
'it was Tara that went to Baroda yesterday'

Telugu (Krishnamurti and Gwynn 1985: 31–6), a member of South Dravidian II, also has such cleft constructions as a means of shift of focus/emphasis within a sentence, e.g.

(13) a. Te. *rāmu*[1] *ninna*[2] *kamalaku*[3] *pustakam*[4] *icc-ǣ-ḍu*[5]
[Ramu yesterday Kamala-dat book give-past-3m-sg]
'Ramu[1] gave[5] a book[4] to Kamala[3] yesterday[2]'
b. Te. *ninna*[1] *kamalaku*[2] *pustakam*[3] *icc-in-di*[4] – *rāmu*[5]
[yesterday Kamala-dat book-acc give-past-3neu-sg – Ramu]
'it was Ramu that gave a book to Kamala yesterday'
c. Te. *rāmu*[1] *ninna*[2] *pustakam*[3] *icc-in-di*[4] – *kamalaku*[5]
[Ramu yesterday book-acc give-past-3neu-sg – Kamla-dat]
'it was to Kamala[5] that Ramu[1] gave[4] the book[3] yesterday[2]'
d. Te. *rāmu*[1] *ninna*[2] *pustakam*[3] *icc-in-di*[4] – *kamalaku*[5] *kādu*[6]
[Ramu yesterday book-acc give-past-3neu-sg – Kamala-to be-not-3neu-sg]
'it was (not)[6] to Kamala[5] that Ramu[1] gave[4] the book[3] yesterday[2]'

Similarly, the object NP *pustakam* and the AdvP *ninna* can also be brought into focus position. Note that (13b, c) are verbless equative sentences, which can be negated by adding *kādu* 'it is not' at the end of the sentences as in (13d). The position of the nominalized verb need not be shifted to the penultimate position, if a clitic is added to any of the constituents as in Tamil, e.g.

e. Te. *rāmu*[1] *ninna*[2] *kamalak-ā*[3] *pustakam*[4] *icc-in-di*[5]
'was it to Kamala[3] that Ramu[1] gave[5] the book[4] yesterday[2]?'

Since members of two subgroups SD I and SD II have formation of cleft sentences as a means of focussing individual constituents in a sentence, this phenomenon could be taken as an inherited one, which is either lost or not reported from the other subgroups. The function of nominalizing the finite verb seems to be to enable any of the arguments to occupy the focus position without involving agreement. The sentence therefore becomes equational and not verbal.

An important question is whether free word order in the Dravidian languages is clause-bounded or not. Mohanan and Mohanan (1994: 161) argue with illustrations from Hindi and Malayāḷam that 'dependent' words of an embedded clause can be interspersed with 'dependent' words in the main clause. They say that scrambling need not be clause-bounded. Another claim is about the canonical word order for SOV languages as 'subject < adjunct < secondary object < object < predicate' (Mohanan and Mohanan 1994: 170, fn 6ii). While the positions of the subject and predicate are fixed, it is not certain if the order proposed for the other constituents is canonical in Dravidian. Very often a time/place adverbial precedes the subject. The so-called unmarked constituent order and the principles governing topicalization in discourse have to be investigated together to find a solution. In Telugu it is found that direct objects of the verbs in the subordinate clause and main clause cannot be shifted away from their governing verbs in scrambling, e.g.

f. Te. *ninna amma* [*pilla-l(a)-ni naww-inc-aṭāni-ki*] *oka katha cepp-in-di*
[yesterday mother children-acc laugh-caus-noml-dat one story tell-past-3fn-sg]
'yesterday, mother told a story to make the children laugh'

f′. Te. **amma nawwincaṭāniki ninna oka katha pillalni ceppindi*
[mother laugh-caus-noml-dat yesterday one story boy-acc tell-past-3fn-sg]

In (13f′) both the direct objects are shifted away from their respective governing verbs, *nawwincaṭāniki . . . pillalni, oka katha . . . ceppindi*, and placing them together in a wrong order is what makes the sentence ungrammatical. If the direct objects from the main clause and the subordinate clause remain next to their respective verbs the sentence remains grammatical. This particular phenomenon may indicate a closer cohesion between transitive verbs and direct objects, which is not true of the other complement phrases with respect to predicates.

9.2.4 *Noun phrase*

A noun phrase has a noun as head, optionally preceded by one or more modifiers. The order of such modifiers within an adjectival phrase (AdjP) is Determiner + Quantifier + Descriptive Adjective + Noun (Head). Even among the descriptive adjectives it is possible to set up an order on a semantic basis, e.g. value + age + colour + dimension etc.; alternatively, 'dimension' may immediately follow 'age' and precede 'colour'. There may be as many as six adjectives modifying the head noun, although normally the number does not exceed one or two. Examples:

(14) a. Ta. *anta*^{1} *mūṉṟu*^{2} *periya*^{3} *peṭṭi*^{4} 'those^{1} three^{2} big^{3} boxes^{4}'
b. Ma. *ā*^{1} *kaṟutta*^{2} *valiya*^{3} *pucca*^{4} 'that^{1} big^{3} black^{2} cat^{4}', *paẓaya*^{1} *valiya*^{2} *nīla*^{3} *kōṭṭə*^{4}, 'old^{1} big^{2} blue^{3} coat^{4}'

c. Ka. *ā*^{1} *eraḍu*^{2} *doḍḍa*^{3} *maysūru*^{4} *mallige*^{5} *hūv-ina*^{6} *hāra-gaḷu*^{7} 'those^{1} two^{2} big^{3} Mysore^{4} jasmine^{5} flower-gen^{6} garland pl^{7}'

d. Te. *ā*^{1} *reṇḍu*^{2} *manci*^{3} *kotta*^{4} *tellaṭi*^{5} *pedda*^{6} *pustakālu*^{7} 'those^{1} two^{2} good^{3} new^{4} white^{5} big^{6} books^{7}'

e. Koṇḍa *ruṇḍi*^{1} *muṭiŋ*^{2} *pūlu*^{3} 'two^{1} fistfuls^{2} of flowers^{3}', *unṟi*^{1} *kota*^{2} *kilpa*^{3} 'one^{1} new^{2} comb^{3}'

Possessive adjectives also occur as modifiers as in (14c) above. One or more relative clauses may also occur as a common type of noun modifier within a NP, e.g.

(15) a. Te. *idi*^{1} *pustakam*^{2} 'this^{1} (is) a book^{2}'

b. Te. *idi*^{1} *nā*^{2} *pustakam*^{3} 'this^{1} (is) my^{2} book^{3}'

c. Te. *idi*^{1} *nēnu*^{2} *rāsina*^{3} *pustakam*^{4} 'this^{1} (is) a book^{4} that I^{2} wrote^{3}'

d. Te. *idi*^{1} *nēnu*^{2} *rāsina*^{3} *moṭṭa-modaṭi*^{4} *pustakam*^{5} 'this^{1} (is) the very first^{4} book^{4} that I^{2} wrote^{3}'

nēnu rās-ina pustakam [I write-past-adj book-nom] 'the book I wrote' is a relativization of *nēnu pustakam rās-ǣ-nu* 'I wrote a book.' A NP with an embedded relative clause as a modifier in a nominal predication (15d), in terms of a tree structure, would be:

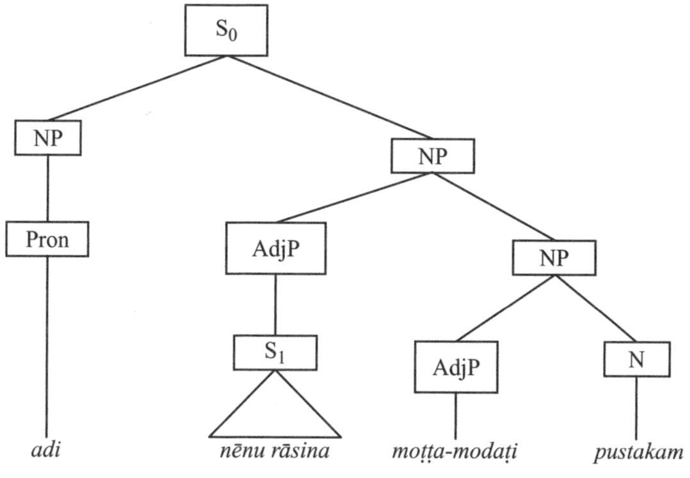

A clause can be transformed into a NP by replacing the finite verb with a verbal noun (see sections 9.3.2.2, 9.3.3.3). Alternatively, the tense and personal suffixes are replaced by a nominal suffix, for instance, *-aṭam*/*-aḍam* in Telugu (section 9.3.2.5):

(16) a. Te. *mīru eppuḍu amerikā-nunci tirig-i wacc-ǣ-ru?*
[you-pl. when America-from return-ppl come-past-2pl]
'when did you return from America?'

b. Te. *mīru amerikā-nunci tirig-i rāw-aṭam eppuḍu*?
[you-pl America-from return-ppl come-noml when]
'when (was/would be) your returning from America?'

Although (16b) could be synonymous with (16a), there is no explicit time reference in it; it can refer to either future time or past time, depending on the discourse context. (16b) is a nominal predication and an equative sentence, whereas (16a) is a verbal predication with explicit tense marking. Alternatively, a tense-based nominal may replace a finite verb as in (13) above.

9.2.5 *Postpositional phrase (PP)*

A postpositional phrase consists of NP + case/postpositional marking. A PP occurs as a complement to the main verb in the predicate phrase. According to some scholars (Steever 1988, Lehmann 1989: 177) there is no VP with a direct object and the main verb as immediate constituents in Dravidian, as there is in English. The VP, according to them, is the main verb, followed by auxiliaries, which carry tense and gnp markers.[7] In the descriptive grammars of Tamil (Lehmann 1989), Malayāḷam (Asher and Kumari 1997), and Kannaḍa (Sridhar 1990), NPs followed by postpositions and cases are treated differently. For instance, they consider a NP in the nominative as the subject, but NPs inflected with non-nominative cases, which function as complements to predicates, are also treated simply as NPs. Only NPs inflected with postpositions are treated as PPs. Some postpositions are said to occur after the nominative of the head noun of a NP, where they are in free variation with case markers, e.g. Ma. *tī koṇṭə* [fire take-ppl] 'with fire' is in free variation with *tīy-in-āl*, in which *-āl* is the instrumental case marker (Asher and Kumari 1997: 210), e.g.:

(17) a. Ma. *kaḷḷakkār tī koṇṭə kuṭil naśippiccu*
[bandit-pl fire-take-ppl hut-acc destroy-past]
'the bandits destroyed the hut with fire'
b. Ma. *kaḷḷakkār tīi-in-āl kuṭil naśippiccu*
[bandit-pl fire-instr hut-acc destroy-past]
'the bandits destroyed the hut with fire'

Case markers are suffixes and bound morphemes, whereas postpositions are grammaticalized words (nominal or verbal). Some of these are frozen only as postpositions

[7] This claim needs to be examined in the light of sentence (13f, f′) above. In a complex sentence there seems to be a constraint on the relative distance between a transitive verb and its direct object in scrambling. The finite verb governing a PP representing a direct object argument can be relativized without exception. But it is not true of other arguments within a predicate phrase (see discussion in section 9.3.2.1 below).

(morphologically not different from bound suffixes), while others may also occur as independent words, in some contexts. Postpositions carry meanings similar to those of case suffixes like 'in, on, into, below, above, behind, before, up to, from the place etc.' I do not distinguish cases from postpositions functionally for the following reasons:

1. The range of meanings specified by prepositions in an analytical language like English is partly expressed by case markers and partly by postpositions in Dravidian.

2. Postpositions are grammaticalized nouns or verbs, which relate NPs to the main verb, in the same way that prepositions do in English (for details of postpositions see section 6.3.3).

3. Functionally postpositions and cases are the same, though morphologically they can be distinguished into different subclasses: (i) N (= head noun) + case/postposition (with partial or full free variation), (ii) N + case, (iii) N + postposition, (iv) N + case + postposition, (v) N + postposition + case, but all these sequences have the function of converting a NP into a complement to the head of the VP (main verb). These are illustrated from Telugu, e.g. *bomma* 'doll, picture'; the oblique is marked by -*Ø* for this stem:

(18) (i) *bomma-ku* [doll-obl-dat] 'for the doll', *bomma kōsam* [doll-obl pp] 'for the sake of the doll'

The case marker and the postposition can freely vary in some contexts;

(ii) *bomma-nu* [doll-obl-acc] 'doll' (direct object)
(iii) *bomma walla* [doll-obl-pp] 'by reason of the doll'
(iv) *bomma-nu gurinci* [doll-obl-acc pp] 'about the doll' (lit. 'having aimed at the doll', but the postposition is frozen and the literal meaning is not transparent)
(v) *bomma kind-i-ki* [doll-obl bottom-obl-dat] 'below the doll' (*kinda* 'bottom')

4. Some case markers and postpositions have the same underlying root etymologically. Thus, the locative case marker -*uḷ* 'inside' is used as a postposition in Tamil, Malayāḷam and Kannaḍa; but in Telugu -*lō* is used as a case marker as well as a postposition, e.g. *in-ṭi-lō* 'in the house': *lō-* and *lō-pala* 'inside' are also used as postpositions, to which a case suffix can be added, e.g. *iṇ-ṭi-lō-ki*/ *iṇ-ṭi lōpal-i-ki* [house-obl inside-obl-dat] 'into the house'.

5. Some Dravidian languages use a bound case marker for the ablative (meaning 'source'), while others use a postposition instead (see section 6.3.2.5). Old Tamil used a case suffix -*iṉ*, e.g. *malai.y-iṉ* 'from the hill', while Modern Tamil uses two postpositions: *niṉṟu* 'having stood' = 'from' (ppl of *nil-* 'stay, stand'), *iruntu* [be-perf-participle] 'having been (in a place)' = 'from', e.g. *kālai iruntu* 'from morning'. Malayāḷam uses -*il-iruntu* 'having been in a place', e.g. *kōyil-il-iruntu* [temple-from] 'from the temple',

and *ninnə* (< OTa. *niṉ-ṟu*) 'from', e.g. *vīṭṭ-il ninnə* [house-in stay-ppl] 'from the house'; Kannaḍa uses the case marker *-inda* for ablative, e.g. *mara-d-inda* [tree-obl-from] 'from the tree'. It also uses the postposition *kaḍe.y-inda* 'from the side of' in the place of the case marker *-inda*. Such alternation between case suffixes and postpositions within a language and across languages indicates their functional unity. Secondly, certain postpositions have been totally grammaticalized and lost their original historical connection to words such as Ma. *ninnə*, and Modern Telugu ablative *-nunci* (see section 9.2.5.5). Both formally and functionally they are no different from case suffixes.

6. In terms of syntax, there is no difference in the role the NP (part of PP) has with respect to the predicate, whether it is followed by a case suffix or a postposition.

All these arguments support the stand taken here that PPs are complements/adjuncts to the predicate phrase and represent NPs inflected with either case suffixes or postpositions, irrespective of their surface morphological differences.

A NP, which occurs in the nominative without any case marking, functions as the subject of a sentence with a nominal or verbal predicate. Any verb – intransitive, transitive and causative – may occur as the head of the predicate phrase. When the predicate denotes a stative verb (like, want, have etc.) or a psychosomatic state (hunger, anger, disgust etc.) and not action, the subject referring to the experiencer is in the dative case, which is a PP. The surface subject that occurs in the nominative within the PP is not the subject of the sentence. PPs, which carry non-nominative cases/postpositions, are treated below.

9.2.5.1 *PP in accusative*

(NP + accusative case; see section 6.3.2.1.) The direct object of a transitive verb carries obligatorily the accusative case marker, if the head noun of the NP denotes an animate being (for further details see section 6.3.2.1); otherwise, the accusative is marked by *-Ø*:[8]

(19) a. Ta. *kumār iṭli cāppi-ṭṭ-āṉ*
Kumar idly-accØ eat-past-3m-sg]
'Kumar ate idly'

b. Ma. *avan kuṭṭi-y-e aṭiccu*
[he child-acc beat-past]
'he beat the child'

c. Ka. *rāma āfisu-nalli chatri biṭṭu-biṭṭa*
[Rama office-loc umbrella-accØ leave-past-3m-sg]
'Rama left the umbrella in the office'

[8] Lehmann (1989: 27–30) says that even with inanimate nouns the case is marked (*-ai* in Tamil) if the speaker intends to refer to the object with definiteness. But several speakers deny that 'accusative' is a definiteness marker in Tamil. A similar observation is made for Kannaḍa by Sridhar (1990: 160–1), but it is not in evidence in Telugu.

d. Te. *pillawāṇṇi wāḷḷ-a nānna koṭṭ-æ̅-ḍu*
[boy-m-sg-acc they-gen-father beat-past-3m-sg]
'their (his) father beat the boy'

9.2.5.2 *PP in instrumental*

Verbs requiring (i.e. semantically permitting) the use of an instrument such as 'strike, beat, kill, cut, sweep, weigh, make', etc. take an argument NP denoting an instrument marked [– animate] with which the action is accomplished. Both case markers and postpositions are used for this purpose (see section 6.3.2.4). In some languages the instrumental case includes 'cause' also. In Telugu causative verbs require the causee Agent to be marked by the postposition *-cēta* 'by the hand of', 'by means of'. The main verb in the passive voice requires the Agent argument to be marked by instrumental *-āl* in Tamil and by *-cēta* in Telugu (for the use of passive auxiliaries, see sections 7.15.1 (1), 7.15.2 (9)),

(20) a. Ta. *kumār katti.y-āl paẓa-tt-ai veṭṭ-iṉ-āṉ*
[Kumar knife-instr fruit-obl-acc cut-past-3msg]
'Kumar cut the fruit with a knife'

b. Ta. *kumār maṇṇ-āl pāṉai.c cey-t-āṉ*
[Kumar clay-instr pot-accØ do-past-3m-sg]
'Kumar made a pot with clay'

c. Ma. (see (16a, b) above)

d. Ka. *śaŋkara kōl-in-inda jhari.y-annu ettida*
[Shankara stick-instr centipede-acc lift-past-3m-sg]
'Shankara lifted the centipede with a stick'

e. Te. *kamala kalam-tō parīkṣa rās-in-di*
[Kamla pen-instr examination-accØ write-past-3f-sg]
'Kamala wrote the examination with a pen'

f. Te. *nēnu rāmu-cēta kāru kaḍig-inc-æ̅-nu*
[I Ramu-instr car-accØ wash-caus-past-1sg]
'I had the car washed by Ramu'/ 'I caused the car to be washed by Ramu'

g. Ta. *kumār appā.v-āl aṭikka-p.paṭṭ-ān*
[Kumar father-by beat-inf-suffer-past-3m-sg]
'Kumar was beaten by his father'

h. Te. *rāmu rawḍīl-a-cēta koṭṭ-a-baḍ-ḍ-āḍu*
[Ramu rowdies-obl-instr beat-inf-suffer-past-3m-sg]
'Ramu was beaten by rowdies/hooligans'

Note that Tamil uses a case suffix in (20g) and Telugu uses a postposition for the same function.

9.2.5.3 *PP in comitative/sociative*

Some languages use the instrumental marker for 'with, together with' required by verbs denoting 'movement, speech, reciprocity' such as 'go, run, speak, fight, play' etc.

Tamil uses the case suffix *-ōṭu* or the postposition *-uṭan̠* in some contexts. Tamil: *man̠aivi.y-ōṭu*/*-uṭan̠* 'with wife' (verb: 'come'), *caṭṭai*^{1}*-y-ōṭu pan̠iyan*^{2} 'an undershirt^{2} with a shirt^{1}' (verb: 'buy'), 'smile with love', 'shout with anger' etc. include a comitative case/postposition.

In Malayāḷam the postposition *kūṭe* 'together' (< PD **kūṭu* 'to join') is added to the oblique–genitive stem of head noun of a NP, *accan̠r̠e kūṭe* 'with father' with the finite verb 'go'. The suffix *-ōṭe* occurs in such phrases as *vrttikeṭṭa*^{1} *vastraŋ-ŋaḷ*^{2}*-ōṭe*^{3} 'with^{3} dirty^{1} clothes^{2}' (verb: 'come'), *vrttikeṭṭa*^{1} *kai-kaḷ*^{2}*-ōṭe*^{3} 'with^{3} dirty^{1} hands^{2}' (verb: 'eat') etc.

In Kannaḍa three postpositions are used: *jote*, *oḍane*, *kūḍa* 'with', e.g. *nimma śrīmati.y-oḍane* 'with your wife' (verb: 'come for dinner').

Telugu uses the same marker *-tō* for both instrumental and comitative, e.g. *sīta-tō* 'with Sita' ('Rama went to a forest'), *ḍabbu-tō* 'with money' ('a burglar ran away'). A NP denoting a psychosomatic state may take the case marker *-tō* when the predicate is a copula or any verb expressing animate feelings, e.g. *ākali-tō* 'with hunger' (verb: 'be, cry', etc.), *kōpam-tō* 'with anger', *prēma-tō* 'with love' (verb: 'be, look at, kiss'), *viyatnām-tō* 'with Vietnam' (verb: 'fight'), *nā-tō* 'with me' (verb: 'speak'), etc.

9.2.5.4 *PP in dative*

9.2.5.4.1 *As complement to predicate* The morphological distribution of the dative case marker **-kku* in different languages and subgroups has been discussed in section 6.3.2.2. The functions of dative PP include (i) goal (with verbs of motion), (ii) indirect object (with 'give, tell' etc.), (iii) a point in time or duration of time, (iv) purpose, (v) recipient of a benefit (with 'give, send' etc.), (vi) distributive, (vii) reference point (comparing distance between places), (viii) cause, (ix) possessive. All literary languages have usages for most of these. Examples are given for a few functions from each language:

(21) a. Ta. *kumār ūr-ukku pō-n̠ān̠* (goal)
[Kumar village-dat go-past-3m-sg]
'Kumar went to the village'

b. Ta. *kumār aintu maṇi-kku varu-v-ān̠* (point in time)
[Kumar five hour-dat come-fut-3m-sg]
'Kumar will come at 5 o'clock'

c. Ta. *matrāsu-kku nūr̠u mail-il pāṇṭiccēri* (point of reference)
[Madras-dat hundred mile-loc Pondicherry]
'Pondicherry is one hundred miles from Madras'

d. Ka. *avara tande-tāyi tīrthayātre-ge hōg-(i) idd-āre* (purpose)
[they-gen father-mother pilgrimage-dat go-n-past-perf-3h- pl]
'their parents have gone on a pilgrimage'

e. Ka, *avaḷu rāman-ige ondu sveṭar koṇḍaḷu* (benefactive)
[she Rama-dat one sweater buy-past-3f-sg]
'she bought a sweater for Rama'

f. Te. *ā ceṭṭu gāli-ki paḍ-i-pōy-in-di* (cause)
[that tree wind-dat fall-ppl-go-past-3neu-sg]
'that tree fell due to wind'

g. Te. *rāmu kamla-ku bharta* (possessive)
[Ramu Kamala-dat husband]
'Ramu is Kamala's husband'

h. Te. *maniṣi-ki oka rūpāyi coppu-na iwwu* (distributive)
[person-dat one rupee rate-at give-2imper-sg]
'give each person a rupee'

i. Koṇḍa *atek vani-ŋ salva si-t-an* (indirect object)
[Atek he-obl-dat/acc breakfast give-past-3m-sg]
'Atek gave him breakfast'

For the benefactive, Kannaḍa uses a postposition *-ōskara* added to the dative *-ge* (NP + *g-ōskara*); for the corresponding function, Telugu uses *kōsam* as a single morpheme (the dative *-ku* is inseparable); the etymology of these postpositions is obscure. For expressing the comparative degree, Tamil uses the dative suffix, while Telugu uses a postposition *-kaṇṭe*/*-kanna*, e.g.

j. Ta. *atu-kku itu mōcam* (comparative)
[that-dat this deceit/evil]
'this is worse than that'

k. Te. *dā-ni-kaṇṭe idi anyāyam* (comparative)
[that one-obl-than this-one unfair]
'this is more unfair than that'

9.2.5.4.2 *As dative subject* A special feature of the Dravidian languages (also shared by Indo-Aryan though as an areal feature) is the use of the postpositional phrase in the dative as the subject of intransitive and transitive clauses, denoting 'possessor of experience' with stative predicates of a psychosomatic nature, like knowledge, hunger, anger, cold, fever etc. For many dative-subject predications, 'verbs are morphologically defective' both in Tamil and in Telugu. This topic needs fuller treatment in syntax along with justification for treating such phrases as subject arguments (Lehmann 1989: 184–93, Krishnamurti 1994c):

(22) a. Ta. *Kumār-ukku vayiṟṟ-ai.p paci-kkiṟ-atu*
[Kumar-dat stomach-acc feel-hungry-pres-3neu-sg]
'Kumar feels hungry for food'
b. Ta. *Kumārukku taṉṉ-ai.p puri.y-a.v-illai*
[Kumar-dat self-acc understand-inf-be-not-3neu-pl]
'Kumar did not understand himself'
c. Ma. *avaḷ-kkə dāh-ikk-unnu* (experience: dative subject)
[she-dat thirst be-pres]
'she is thirsty'
d. Ma. *enikkə imglīṣ aṟiyām* (cognition)
[I-dat English know]
'I know English'
e. Te. *Rāmu-ku talanoppi wacc-i, paḍukon-nā-ḍu*
[Ramu-to head-ache come-ppl, (he) lie down-past-3m-sg]
'Ramu had a head-ache and lay down'
f. Te. *Rāmuku tana-sangati tana-k-ē teliy-a-du*
[Ramu-dat self-gen-matter self-dat-emph know-neg-3neu-sg]
'Ramu does not know himself (his own affair)'

The reflexive **tān/tan*-V 'self' normally requires a nominative subject as its antecedent in a complex sentence. But in (22b,d,f) the reflexive refers to the person signalled by the dative PP, thereby suggesting that it is the subject argument. Secondly, the subject of the main clause (where it is marked [+ human]) and of the subordinate clause headed by a perfective participle should be coreferential and identical; (22e) shows that the subjects of both the clauses refer to the same, though one is in the dative and the other, the deleted subject in the main clause, if specified, would have been in the nominative.

9.2.5.5 *PP in ablative*

The modern literary languages do not have a case marker for 'source'; instead they use postpositions. Modern Tamil adds *iru-ntu* 'having been' (the perfective participle of the verb *iru-* 'be') to the NP in the locative, e.g. *maram* 'tree', *mara-tt-il* [tree-obl-loc] 'on the tree', *mara-tt-il-iruntu* 'from (above) the tree'. It is added directly to adverbs of place, *aṅk-iruntu* [there-from] 'from there'. Malayāḷam adds the postposition *-ninnə* (< OTa. *nin-ṟu* < *nil-ntu*; *nil-*'to stand') 'having stood/stayed' to the locative PP, e.g. *rāman-il ninnə* 'from Raman'. Kannaḍa *-inda* is a case suffix for the instrumental–ablative directly added to the complement NP, e.g. *rēvati.y-inda* 'from Revati'; it is also used with the adverb *kaḍe* 'side, direction', as in *dhārwāḍ kaḍe.y-inda* 'from Dharwar'. Old Telugu uses *-n-uṇḍ-i* 'having been' (*uṇḍu-* 'be'), the *-n* being a remnant of a locative suffix added to the preceding NP, e.g. *iṇṭ-an uṇḍ-i* [house-in having been] 'from the house' ← *iṇṭ-an* 'in the house' + *uṇḍ-i* 'having been'. Note that this is the semantic equivalent of Ta. NP loc. + *iru-ntu*. In Modern Telugu the postposition has dialect variants *-nuṇḍi* (Telangana districts) *-n-unc-i* (> *-n-inci*) (coastal districts and modern standard). The coastal forms have been grammaticalized to a point where they have totally lost any historical connection to the older form and meaning.[9]

This PP is used with verbs of motion ('go, come') to refer to one or more from a group (verb: 'choose, select'), or to a range from one point to the other in time and place (several verbs like 'wait, burn, rain, etc.'). Examples:

(23) a. Ta. *kumār maratt-il-iruntu viẓu-nt-āṉ*
[Kumar tree-loc-be-ppl fall-past-3m-sg]
'Kumar fell from the tree'

b. Ma. *enikkə paṇam bāŋk-il ninnə kiṭṭ-i*
[I-dat money bank-loc from get-past]
'I got money from the bank'

c. Ka. *kall-in-inda eṇṇe tege.y-alu sādhyav-ē?*
[stone-obl-abl oil-acc take-inf possible-Q]
'Is it possible to extract oil from stone?'

d. Te. *reṇḍu gaṇṭal-a-nunci wāna kurus-t-un-n-adi*
[two hour-pl-obl-abl rain rain-n-past-be-past-3neu-sg]
'it has been raining for two hours'

9.2.5.6 *PP in locative*

A number of postpositions refer to location like Te. *mīda*, *pai-na* 'above', *kinda* 'below', *mundu* 'in front', *wenaka* 'back', *pakka* 'side', *lō-pala* 'inside' etc. The other literary languages have corresponding forms. These occur after the genitive–oblique base, to which case signs are added. These, in turn, are treated as nouns of place and can take case markers, e.g. *illu* 'house': obl *iṇṭi-*; with postpositions: *iṇṭi-mīda/mundu/wenaka/pakka/lōpala/daggara*, etc. 'on or above/ behind/in front of/at the back of/on the side of/inside/ near the house'. When the postpositions are inflected, we get *iṇṭi-mīd-i-nunci* 'from above the house', *iṇṭi-wenaka-guṇḍā* 'through the back of the house,' *iṇṭi-mundu-nunci* 'from the front of the house', *iṇṭi-daggar-i-ki* 'to near the house', *iṇṭi-lōpal-i-nunci* 'from inside the house' etc. Several modifiers may precede these. As syntactic constituents, these are no different from sequences of NP + case such as *iṇṭi-nunci* 'from the house', *iṇṭi-ki* etc. Those that still function as free lexical items denoting place and time can be treated as adverbials with case inflection.

9 *uncu* 'to let stay, keep' is the transitive of *uṇḍu* 'to be', but semantically, there is no reason why a transitive should replace an intransitive in an ablative sense. The process of grammaticalization of loc + *uṇḍi* was complete by 1000 CE, since the restructured *-nuṇḍi* already came to stay in Old Telugu itself.

For the general locative case, Tamil uses the case suffix *-il* and the postposition *-iṭam* 'place' (for animate nouns). The Malayāḷam locative suffix is *-il*. Both Tamil and Malayāḷam have a number of words denoting 'location', 'direction', 'extent' added as postpositions to NPs or PPs, e.g. Ta. *varai* 'until, up to': *vīṭu varai* 'up to the house', *aintu maṇi varai* 'up to five o'clock', *pakkam, kiṭṭa* 'near': *vīṭṭu pakkam* [house-obl near] 'near the house', Ma. *tāze* 'below', *pin̲n̲e* 'behind', *tekkə* 'south' etc. When a NP or a PP is followed by one of these words, they become adverbial phrases. Examples for the locative:

(24) a. Ta. *kuruvi mara-tt-il uṭkār-kir̲-atu*
[bird tree-obl-loc sit-pres-3neu-sg]
'a bird is sitting on the tree'
b. Ta. *Kumār appā.v-iṭam va-nt-ān̲*
[Kumar father-loc come-past-3m-sg]
'Kumar came to (his) father'
c. Ma. *ñān mēṣa.y-uṭe mīte irunnu*
[I table-gen upon (pp) sit-past]
'I sat on the table'
d. Ka. *beŋguḷūr-in-alli mane-gaḷ-a bele jāsti*
[Bangalore-loc house-pl-gen price high]
'the price of houses in Bangalore is high'
e. Te. *wāḷḷu ippuḍu amerikā-lō un-n-āru*
[they (hum) now America-in be-non-past-are]
'they are now in America'
f. Koṇḍa *kuṟka-d zāva bāṭa ki-t-an*
[bowl-loc food serving do-past-3m-sg]
'he served food in the bowl'

9.2.6 *Adjectival phrases*

Adjectival phrases occur only as modifiers of noun heads. There is a precedence hierarchy among different types of descriptive adjectives within an adjectival phrase, as illustrated in section 9.2.4, and earlier in section 8.2.2. Demonstrative/possessive and numeral adjectives may precede descriptive adjectives within an adjectival phrase. A relative clause may precede an adjectival phrase, illustrated in (15d): Te. *idi* [[*nēnu rāsina*] [*moṭṭamodaṭi*] *pustakam*]] is a nominal predication, NP + NP with an embedded relative clause as part of the AdjP within the predicate NP. The internal structure of this sentence has been illustrated in a tree structure in section 9.2.4.

The structure of a Tamil adjectival phrase is similar to that of the other Dravidian languages. Examples: *nalla peru tōḷ* [nice-3neu pl big shoulder] 'big nice shoulders'

(Naṟṟ 13–15); the order of the adjectives follows the same order as stated for Telugu. A relative participle can be a part of the expanded adjectival phrase (see sections 8.2.2, 9.3.2.1).

The adjectival phrase in Malayāḷam is said to have three constituents: (i) a pure adjective, (ii) a noun with an adjectival suffix or, in the case of Sanskrit nouns, by dropping the final *-m*, *vidēśam* 'foreign'→ *vidēśa-*, (iii) a relative clause. Details of these have been discussed in sections 8.2.2 and 9.3.2.1. Kannaḍa has the same model as the other Dravidian languages, for which, see sections 8.2.2 and 9.3.2.1.

Telugu uses the adverb *cālā* 'much, very' and Kannaḍa *bahaḷa* 'very', Malayāḷam *vaḷare* 'very' as modifiers of descriptive adjectives, e.g. Te. *cālā goppa wyakti*, 'a very great individual', Ma. *vaḷare miṭukku uḷḷa* 'very bright' (having much brightness).

9.2.7 *Adverbial phrase (AdvP)*

An adverbial phrase has an adverb as head preceded by modifiers. Morphological adverbs as a part of speech have already been dealt with in section 8.3. Most adverbs are said to be nominals of time and place. Extended nominals of this kind are syntactically adverbial, e.g. Te. *sruṣṭi*[1] *modaṭi*[2] *nunci*[3] *ippaṭi*[4] *wara-ku*[5] [creation beginning-obl-from now-obl-till] 'from[3] the beginning[2] of creation[1] till[5] now[4]' would be an example of a time adverbial phrase. The only modifiers of adverbs are other adjectives like Te. *cālā* 'very': *cālā*[1] *tondara-gā*[2] 'very[1] fast[2]'. There are some distributive phrases consisting of interrogative words with the clitic *-ō* meaning 'any time, place . . . ', followed by *oka* 'one' + the demonstrative adverbial word meaning 'time, place', e.g. *eppuḍ(u)-ō oka-(a)ppuṭu* 'sometime' (lit. 'any time-one time'), *ekkaḍ(a)-ō oka cōṭa* 'at some place'. Also note reduplicated time and place adverbs with specialized meanings, *appuḍ(u)-appuḍu* 'now and then', *akkaḍ(a)-akkaḍa* 'here and there'. A relative clause can be embedded within an adverbial phrase as its modifier, giving rise to an adverbial clause, e.g. Te. *nēnu mimmal-ni cūsina-appaṭi-nunci* [I you-hon-acc see-past-adj time-obl-abl] 'from the time I saw you . . . ' The adverbializing suffix *-gā* may be used with any NP to convert it into an adverbial phrase, e.g. *tondara* 'speed': *tondara-gā* 'quickly', *picciwāḍu* 'a mad man': *picciwāḍu-gā* 'as a mad man', *ī kampenīki mēnējaru-gā* [this company-dat manager-advl] 'as a manager of this company', *nālug(u)-aydu ēḷḷu-gā* [four-five years-advl] 'for four or five years'.

Tamil also has nominals denoting place and time which are syntactically adverbial. Nouns followed by the infinitive *āk-a* (*āku* 'be') are quite frequently used for a variety of adverbial functions, namely manner: *āttiram-āka* 'angrily'; comparative role: *appāv-āka* 'like father'; *paittiyakāran-āka* 'like a madman', *nimiṣam-āka* 'like a minute'; time location: *cāyaṅkālam-āka* 'in the evening'; purpose: *vēlai-āka* 'for work'; duration: *varuṣam-āka* 'for a year'; distributive: *oṉṟu oṉṟu-āka*. Time and place adverbial phrases include quantifiers such as *anta muẓu vīṭu* 'that whole house', *caṟṟu nēram* 'a little time' etc.

Malayāḷam adverbial phrases, like Tamil, are nominals followed by *āyi* (ppl of *ā* 'be'), e.g. *bhamgi* 'beautiful': *bhamgi.y-āyi* 'beautifully'. Modifiers of adverbs include *vaḷare, adhikam* 'much': *vaḷare vēgam* 'very fast'.

In Modern Kannaḍa *bahaḷa* 'very' is an adverbial modifier, e.g. *bahaḷa bēga* 'very fast'. Adverbial phrases include a comparative degree, *ellariginta*[1] *heccu*[2] *nīṭu-āgi*[3] [all-hpl-dat-comp much neat-advl] 'more[2] neatly[3] than all others[1]'.

9.3 Complex sentences

A complex sentence consists of one main clause (matrix clause) and one or more subordinate clauses to its left. There are several strategies of forming complex sentences in Dravidian: (i) by embedding clauses headed by non-finite verbs; (ii) by embedding a relative clause, changing the finite verb into a verbal adjective/relative participle, and shifting the head NP to its immediate right; (iii) by embedding an action clause, changing the finite verb into an action nominal; (iv) by embedding adverbial clauses headed by time or place Adverbial Phrases (AdvP); and (v) by embedding a variety of clauses with finite verbs, by means of complementizers, like *-ō* and non-finite forms of the verb meaning 'say' (PD * *aHn-*). If more than one subordinate clause is embedded, they are adjoined by pauses or conjunctive particles.

9.3.1 *Non-finite verb clauses*

The non-finite clauses are headed by perfective participle, conditional, concessive and infinitive verbs. The subordinate clause(s) are enclosed in square brackets.

9.3.1.1 *Perfective participle*[10] *clause*

(25) a. OTa. *an̲n̲ai* [... *en̲ mukam nōkk-i*] [*nak-ūu*] ... *peyar-nt-ōḷ*
[mother ... my face look-ppl laugh-ppl go-past-3f-sg]
'mother looked at my face, laughed, and went away'

b. Ta. *kumār* [*iṅkē va-ntu*] *en̲n̲ai kūppiṭṭ-ān̲*
[Kumar-nom here-emph come-ppl I-acc call-past-3m-sg]
'Kumar came here and called me'

c. Ma. *avan* [*kuḷicciṭṭə*] *ūṇə kaẓiccu*
[he bathe-ppl meal eat-past]
'he, having bathed, ate the meal'

[10] This is also called conjunctive participle, adverbial participle, gerund, converb etc. with different markers (section 7.7.1). It means 'having completed the action specified by the verb to which the marker is attached'. Traditionally it is called 'past participle', but it can be governed by a finite verb in the past, future or present in the matrix clause. What it means is that the action is completed before the beginning of the action specified by the governing main verb. I have, therefore, decided to give it an aspectual name rather than a tense name as 'perfective' and not 'past'.

d. Ka. *mantrigaḷu* [*mēja-nnu kuṭṭi kuṭṭi*] *bhāṣaṇa māḍidaru*
[minister-hon table-acc pound-ppl pound-ppl speech make-past-3hon]
'the Minister spoke, frequently pounding on the desk' [lit. having pounded, having pounded]

e. [*gāliwāna wacc-i*] *illu paḍipō-in-di*
[storm come-ppl house fall-past-3neu-sg]
'Because of the rain the house fell down'

These usages show a variety of meanings, all of which go back to the reconstructed stage, i.e. sequencing two or more actions in time (25a,b,c); denoting manner of the action denoted by the main verb (25d); the subordinate clause in (25e) stands in a causal relationship to the action expressed by the main clause. In the case of (25a–d) the subject NPs of the main clause and the subordinate clause, marked [+ human], have to be coreferential and identical, but not in (25e), where the semantic relationship is different; 'storm' is the subject of the subordinate clause and 'the house' is the subject of the main clause. There are other time-related symmetrical clauses, where the constraint of coreferential subject is not applicable, as in (21f, g). All these are shared by all Dravidian languages and the type is reconstructible for Proto-Dravidian. There are still other uses of the clause headed by a perfective participle (some idiosyncratic to some languages), details of which can be found in Krishnamurti and Gwynn (1985: 188–95, 340–2) and Lehmann (1989: 265–78), e.g.

f. Te. *rātri weḷḷ-ipōy-i pagalu wacc-in-di*
[night go-ppl, day come-past-3neu-sg]
'the night having passed, day broke'

g. *maẓai pey-tu, veyil aṭi-ttu, vāṉavil tōṉṟ-i.y-atu*
[rain-nom pour-ppl, sunshine-nom beat-ppl, rainbow-nom appear-past-3neu-sg]
'it rained, the sun shone, and a rainbow appeared'

9.3.1.2 *Conditional and concessive clause*

The formation of the conditional verb 'if... verb' is discussed in section 7.7.3. The conditional clause, in some contexts, may focus on the time of action, i.e. 'when I opened the letter... ', instead of 'if I opened the letter... ' The concessive is derived by adding the derivatives of the conjunctive particle **-um*/ **-am* to the conditional verb (section 8.4.1).

(26) a. Ta. [*kumār va-nt-āl*] *nāṉ uṉṉai kūppiṭu-v-ēṉ*
[Kumar-come-past-cond I he-acc call-fut-1sg]
'if Kumar comes, I will call him' (conditional)

b. Ta. [*kumār iṅkē va-ntu iru-nt-āl*] *nāṉ uṉṉai kūppiṭṭu iru-pp-ēṉ*
[Kumar here come-ppl be-past-cond I he-acc call-past-ppl be-fut-1sg]
'if Kumar had come, I would have called you' (contra-factual)

c. Ta. [*nāṉ eṉṉa coṉ-ṉ-āl-um*] *kumārukku āṭcēpam* (concessive)
[I what(ever) say-past-cond-conc Kumar-dat objection]
'whatever I say, Kumar (has) objections'

d. Ma. [*nī vann-āl-ē*] *ñān pōkū*
[you come-cond-emph I go-fut]
'I go only if you come'

e. Ma. *ñān* [*paṭicc-āl-um*] *pass ā-v-illa*
[I read-past-cond-conc pass be-fut-neg]
'even if I study, I will not pass'

f. Ka. *mīna* [*lāṭari.y-alli gedd-are*] *nin-a-ge swīṭ koḍ-is-utt-ēne*
[Meena lottery-in win-past-cond you-dat sweets give-caus-fut-1sg]
'if Meena wins the lottery, I will buy you sweets'

g. Te. [*wāna-lu kuris-tē*] *paṇṭalu paṇḍu-t-āyi*
[rain-pl rain-past-cond crop-pl grow-hab-3neu-pl]
'if rains fall (rain), crops will grow'

h. Te. [*nēnu wacc-inā*] *āyana rāḍu*
[I come-past-conc he come-neg-3m-sg]
'even if I come, he will not come'

In the above usages, although the conditional form is built on the past stem of the verb, there is no specific reference to the past time in any of the languages. The conditional and concessive forms are morphologically related in Tamil, Malayāḷam and Kannaḍa, but not in Telugu. The history of this problem has been discussed in section 7.7.3.

9.3.1.3 *Infinitive clauses*

A comparative study of the morphology of the infinitive is discussed in section 7.9.1. Infinitive clauses serve as complements to noun phrases, verbs representing speech acts and modal, aspectual and desiderative meanings. The major languages of South Dravidian I preserve several of the usages at the syntactic level, which got grammaticalized as compound verbs in Telugu (see section 7.15.2 (9)). Only a few typical usages are cited below. For further details, see Krishnamurti and Gwynn (1985: 211–29), Lehmann (1989: 257–65), David (1999).

(27) a. Ta. *rājā* [*kumār-ai.k kuṭi-kk-a*] *kaṭṭayapaṭ-ṭ-āṉ*
[Raja-nom Kumar-acc drink-inf force-past-3m-sg]
'Raja forced Kumar to drink'

b. Ta. [[*kumār varu-kiṟ-ēṉ*] *eṉ-ṟu coll-a*] *nāṉ kēṭ-ṭ-ēṉ*
[Kumar come-pres-1sg say-ppl tell-inf I hear-past-1sg]
'I heard Kumar say, "I am coming"'

c. Ta. [*kumār coll-a*] *nāṉ cey-t-ēṉ*
[Kumar say-inf I do-past-1sg]
'I did what Kumar said'

d. Ta. [*ōṭ-a ōṭ-a*] *nāṉ avaṉ-ai viraṭṭ-iṉ-ēṉ*
[run-inf run-inf I he-acc scare-past-1sg]
'I scared him (so that) he ran away'

e. Ma. *avan* [*uṇṇ-ān*] *pōyi*
[he eat-inf go-past]
'he went to eat'

f. Ma. *enikkə* [*cila sādhanaŋŋaḷ vāŋŋān*] *uṇṭɛ*
[I-dat some thing-pl buy-inf be-pres]
'I have some things to buy'

g. Ka. *mīna vyāyāma kalasal-ikke basavannaguḍi-ge hōg-utt-āḷe*
[Meena exercise-acc teach-inf-dat Basavannagudi-dat go-pres-3f-sg]
'Meena goes to Basavannagudi to teach (for teaching) exercise'

h. Te. [*mīru ā sangati nāt-ō ceppan*] *akkara lē-du*
[you-hon that matter-Øacc I-com tell-inf need be-not-3neu-sg]
'there is no need for you to tell me this matter'

i. Te. *āyana*[1] *eppuḍū*[2] *mā ūru*[3] *rā-n-ē*[4] *rā-ḍu*[5]
[he never our-town come-inf-emph come-not-3m-sg]
'he[1] is sure not to come[4,5] to our town[3] anytime[2]'

In Kannaḍa the infinitive is a nominal formed by adding *-al* and the resultant form takes case suffixes as in (27g). Telugu also uses a nominalized verb *nērp-aḍam* 'teaching' = Ka. *kalas*(*u*)*-al* and not an infinitive *nērp-an* (inf) 'to teach', corresponding to (27g):

j. Te. *mīna wyāyāmam nērpaḍā-ni-ki basavannaguḍi weḷ-tun-di*
[Meena exercise teach-noml-obl-dat Basavannagudi-dat go-non-past-3f-sg]
'Meena goes to Basavannagudi to teach exercise'

Corresponding to Tamil and Malayāḷam usages (27a–f), Old Telugu used infinitives, but in Modern Telugu, some of these (27a, c, e, f) can be rendered by nominalized verbs, and some others by an extended infinitive, i.e. infinitive followed by the adverbial suffix *-gā*, e.g. *ceppa-gā* 'as one says/said' with focus on the time of action. Thus for (27b):

k. [$_{\text{INF}}$ [$_{\text{S}}$ *kumār was-tā-nu* $_{\text{S}}$] *ani ceppa-gā* $_{\text{INF}}$] *nēnu win-n-ānu*
[Kumar come-fut-3m-sg say-ppl tell-ing-advl I hear-past-1sg]
'I heard Kumar saying, "I will come"'

9.3.2 *Noun clauses*

The noun clause is the most versatile in its occurrence and frequency in the Dravidian languages, because many other clauses feed into the structure of a noun clause. They are: (i) a postpositional clause has an underlying noun clause plus case/postposition added to the head noun; (ii) adverbial clauses of time and place have almost the same kind of internal structure as the noun clause, except for change in the head nominals; (iii) any finite clause (= a clause with a finite verb) can be embedded as NP in another clause, by means of a clitic or a participle derived from the verb meaning 'say', i.e. Ta. *eṉ-ṟu*, Ka. *en-du*, Te. *an-i* 'having said, so', Ta. *enn-um*, Ka. *ennu-v-a/em-ba*, Te. *an-ē* (non-past relative participle) 'said, called, such', used as a complementizer; (iv) relative clauses (participial and co-relative) modify NPs in creating noun clauses; (v) action noun clauses are formed by nominalizing the verb with or without tense marking. All these types are present in all the literary languages. First we start with noun clauses built on the relative clause.

9.3.2.1 *Relative clauses*

In the place of correlative pronouns, all Dravidian languages change tensed finite verbs into adjectivals (relative participles) by replacing the personal suffixes with adjectival markers *-a* or *-i* (section 7.7.2). 'A simple sentence can be changed into a relative clause by replacing its finite verb by a relative participle (or verbal adjective) in the corresponding tense-mode and shifting the noun that it qualifies as head of the construction. The whole clause with the noun head then becomes a noun clause and can be embedded in the place of a noun phrase (NP) in the matrix sentence as its subject, direct object of the finite verb, predicate complement, or as an adverbial of Time/Place' (Krishnamurti and Gwynn 1985: 343). All relative clauses occur as complements to NPs to their left. The relativized VP is shifted to the left of the NP that it modifies and the resulting noun clause is then embedded in the matrix sentence. Not all NPs can be head of relative clauses. Those that occur in nominative, accusative and instrumental cases, with respect to their predicates, can be shifted as heads of relative clauses. A noun related to the verb in dative as goal can be relativized and not the one as 'purpose'; the NP in comitative case cannot be relativized. Let us examine the following sentences:

(28) a. Ta. $[_{\text{PP}}[_{\text{NP}}[_{\text{S}}[_{\text{AdjP}}$ *nēṟṟu iṅkē va-nt-a* $_{\text{AdjP}}][_{\text{NP}}$ *anta paiyaṉ* $_{\text{NP}}]_{\text{S}}]_{\text{NP}}]$*-ai* $_{\text{PP}}]$
(subordinate clause) [yesterday here come-past-adj that boy-acc]
nāṉ iṉṟu pār-tt-ēṉ (main clause) [I-nom today see-past-1sg]
'today I saw the boy (acc), who came here yesterday...'

b. Ta. $[_{\text{NP}}[_{\text{AdjP}}$ *kumār-ai kaṭitta* $_{\text{AdjP}}]$ *nāy* $_{\text{NP}}]$ . . .
[Kumar-acc bite-past-adj dog]
'the dog which bit Kumar . . . '

c. Ma. *avane kuttiya katti*
[he-acc stab-past-adj knife]
'the knife that someone stabbed him with'

d. Ma. *pūcca kiṭakunna cākə*
[cat lie-pres-adj sack . . .]
'the sack on which the cat lies . . . '

e. Ka. *hinde gōḍaun iruva aŋgaḍi*
[behind warehouse be-non-past-adj shop]
'the shop which has a warehouse at the back'

f. Te. *pulini camp-in-a maniṣi*
[tiger-acc kill-past-adj person]
'the person who killed the tiger'

g. Te. *puli camp-in-a maniṣi*
[tiger-nom kill-past-adj man]
'the person whom the tiger killed'

h. Te. *annam tin-ē balla*
[food eat-hab-adj table]
'the table on which one eats' (dining table)

i. Te. *annam tin-ē kancam*
[food eat-hab-adj plate]
'the plate in which one eats'

j. Te. *annam tin-ē ceyyi*
[food eat-hab-adj hand]
'the hand with which one eats'

The above examples show that clauses in which NPs stand in certain case relationships with the predicate alone will become heads of relative clauses, namely nominative in (28a, g), accusative in (28b, f), instrumental in (28c, j), locative in (28d) denoting 'on', (28e) 'at the back', (28h) 'on', (28i) 'in'. Dative case qualifies in the meaning of 'goal', 'recipient', but not 'purpose'; comitative meaning also blocks relativization, e.g.

k. Te. *bāwi-nunci nīḷḷu tōḍutāru* ⇒ *nīḷḷu tōḍ-ēbāwi*
[well-abl water-Øacc draw-hab-3h-pl] ⇒ [water-acc draw-hab-adj well]
'(they) draw water from the well' ⇒ 'the well from which water is drawn'

l. Te. *rāmu kamala-ku appu icc-ǣ-ḍu* ⇒ *rāmu appu icc-in-a kamala*
[Ramu Kamala-to loan give-past-3m-sg] [Ramu loan give-past-adj Kamala]
'Ramu gave a loan to Kamala' ⇒ 'Kamala to whom Ramu gave a loan'

m. Te. *rāmu mandukōsam weḷḷ-ǣ-ḍu* ⇒ **rāmu weḷḷ-in-a mandu*
[Ramu medicine-for go-past-m-sg] [Ramu go-past-adj medicine . . .]
'Ramu went for medicine' ⇒ *'the medicine Ramu went for . . . '

n. Te. *rāmu kamala-tō sinimā cūs-ǣ-ḍu* ⇒ * *rāmu sinimā cūs-in-a kamala*
[Ramu Kamala-with cinema-acc see-past-3m-sg] [Ramu cinema see-past-adj Kamala . . .]
'Ramu saw a movie with Kamala'⇒*'Kamala, Ramu saw a movie with . . . '

Tamil, Malayāḷam and Kannaḍa also cannot relativize NPs governed by the dative case meaning 'purpose', the instrumental case meaning 'cause', and the sociative case with verbs of 'motion' (Krishnamurti and Gwynn 1985: 247–8, Lehmann 1989: section 4.40 citing earlier writers; Asher and Kumari 1997: 58–67, Sridhar 1990: 57–67).

9.3.2.2 *Pronominalized relative clauses*

(i) A relative clause, instead of taking a NP as head that it modifies, may add to the relative participle a pronominal suffix, appropriate to the replaced NP in number and gender, from the third-person demonstratives, and the resultant clause has the privileges of a NP to be embedded in a matrix clause. (ii) A neutral type of relativization with the third neuter singular being added to the relative participle is different from the above, because it is used when one of the constituents of a sentence needs to be shifted to the predicate position as a focussed element; the resultant sentence becomes the subject NP in nominal predication. This has been illustrated in section 9.2.4 (10)–(13). Examples for (i):

(29) a. Ta. *nā̱n nē̱ṟṟu pār-tt-a paiya̱n* ⇒ *nā̱n nē̱ṟṟu pār-tt-ava̱n* (see 28a)
[I yesterday see-past adj boy] [I yesterday see-past-adj-he]
'the boy I saw yesterday' ⇒ 'he whom I saw yesterday'

b. Ma. [*nī paṟañña-tə*] *śari āṇə*
[you say-past-noml right be-pres]
'what you said is right'

c. Te. *kamala ninna pāḍ-in-a pāṭa* ⇒ *kamala ninna pāḍ-in-adi*
[Kamala yesterday sing-past-adj song] [Kamala yesterday sing-past-adj-it]
'the song Kamala sang yesterday . . . ' ⇒ 'that which Kamala sang yesterday'

The replacement of a relative participle + noun head (more correctly NP) by a nominalized verb is called a 'headless relative clause' in Malayāḷam (Asher and Kumari 1997: 57–8); *vann-avan* 'the man who came', *vann-avaḷ* 'the woman who came', *vann-avar* 'the persons who came' are given as examples. It is safe to consider these as a type of noun clause, since the other constituents of the clause are not affected by this replacement as in (29a, b).

9.3.2.3 *Factive clauses*

Another way of forming a noun clause is to use an abstract nominal meaning 'fact' as head under NP, corresponding broadly to English 'the fact that . . . ' In Telugu *-aṭṭu/-aṭlu*, a bound abstract noun meaning 'that matter, fact, thus', is added to the tensed verbal adjective. Correspondingly, in Modern Tamil, *ceyti* 'news', *uṉ-mai* 'fact' are used as NPs, e.g.

(30) a. Te. *nāku* $_{NP}$[$_S$[*mī pēru inta-ku mundu win-n-(a)*]$_S$ *-aṭṭu*]$_{NP}$ *jnāpakam lēdu*
[I-dat you-poss name now-dat before hear-past-fact memory be not-3n-sg]
'I do not remember having heard your name before'

b. Ta. $_{NP}$[$_S$[*mantiri nēṟṟu va-nt-a*]$_S$ *ceyti*]$_{NP}$
[minister yesterday come-past-adj news]
'the news that the minister came yesterday'

The factive noun clause in *-aṭṭu* can be changed into a manner adverbial clause by the addition of *-gā*. Note that *-gā* can be added to adjectives or nouns to adverbialize them (see section 8.3.1.2), e.g.

c. *āme* [*nidra pō-tunn(a)-aṭṭu(gā)*] *naṭinc-in-di*
[she sleep-go-dur- adj-noml-advl pretend-past-3f-sg]
'she pretended she was sleeping'

In Modern Telugu, there is another noun clause, which can be treated as a subtype of the factive noun clause. In this a limited set of abstract nouns meaning 'thought', 'idea', 'habit', 'intention', responsibility', 'possibility', 'necessity' occurs as head NP of the relative clause (Krishnamurti and Gwynn 1985: 354–5). I have not come across matching illustrations from the other literary languages, e.g.

d. Te. *wāḍ-i-ki* [*uttaram cadiw-ē ālocana*] *taṭṭ-a lēdu*
[he-dat letter-Øacc read-hab-adj thought occur-inf-be-not-3neu-sg]
'the thought of reading the letter did not occur to him'

9.3.2.4 *Correlative relative clause*

Many Dravidian scholars think that correlative relative clauses occur in Dravidian through diffusion from Indo-Aryan (Krishnamurti and Gwynn 1985: 361, Sridhar 1990: 47, Asher and Kumari 1997: 53). Steever (1988: 33) vehemently rejects this notion, because all literary Dravidian languages have them from the beginning of literature and this phenomenon is reconstructible for Proto-Dravidian. Secondly, reduplication of interrogative (correlative) and demonstrative (relative) pronouns (quantification) is extensively found in Dravidian, which is an indigenous feature and not borrowed from Indo-Aryan. Thirdly, a language may have more than one grammatical strategy, i.e. there is nothing unusual in Dravidian languages having both the correlative and participial constructions. All these grounds, according to Steever, warrant the construction to be native. It is true that correlative constructions occur in classical texts (Lehmann 1998: 94, see (31a) below), but they are not favoured in spoken varieties of modern standard languages, except for rhetorical purposes. Secondly, there is no specific set of correlative pronouns in Dravidian as there is in Indo-Aryan (Hindi *jo . . . vo*, *jab . . . tab*, etc.). This is, however, not a strong ground to deny the existence of correlative constructions in Dravidian, because languages like English also use question words in similar contexts, e.g. 'the man, who . . . ', 'the book, which . . . '

A correlative construction has two related clauses with finite verbs. The first relative clause has an interrogative word as a correlative pronoun. It is adjoined to the main clause, which begins with a corresponding demonstrative pronoun, by a complementizer *-ō* in modern languages. Examples:

(31) a. OTa. [*e-vaẓi nall-avar āṭ-avar*] *a-vaẓi nallai* . . . (PN 183)
[which-place good-3m-pl men-3m-pl that-place good-2sg]
(lit.) 'at which place men are the good ones, at that place you are good'

b. Ta. [*uṅkaḷ-ukku evvaḷavu vēṇṭ-um-ō*] *avvaḷuvu nāṉ taru-kiṟ-ēṉ.*
[you-pl-dat how-much want-fut-3neu-sg-comp that-much I give-pres-1sg]
'how much you want, that much I will give you'

c. Ma. [*ēt-oruvan drōham ceyy-unnuvō*] *avan pāpi ākunnu*
[which-one-m-sg evil-acc do-pres he sinner become-pres]
'he who does evil becomes a sinner'

d. Ka. [*yāva huḍuga nimm-a kai-kuluk-id-an-ō*] *ā huḍuga nann-a geḷeya*
[which boy you-gen hand-shake-past-3m-sg-comp that boy I-gen friend]
'the boy who shook hands with you is my friend'

e. Te. [*ēdi kāwāl(i)-ō*] *adi paṭṭu-ku-pō*
[what be-wanted-comp that take-refl go-imp 2sg]
'take away what you want'

9.3.2.5 *Action clause*

Any simple sentence can be changed into a noun clause by adding a nominal derivational suffix to the verb stem (simple, complex or compound) replacing tense-mode and personal morphemes. The resulting clause can be embedded in another clause either as its subject NP or as a predicate complement (PP) with appropriate case marking. Unlike the clauses in section 9.3.2.2, these do not carry any tense sign and therefore can be used with any time reference based on pragmatic context. Old Telugu added *-ṭa* (*cēyu-ṭa* 'doing', *tinu-ṭa* 'eating', *ālōcincu-ṭa* 'thinking', etc.). Modern Telugu adds *-aṭam*/*-aḍam* (dial), instead. The resulting verb is inflected with cases/postpositions like any neuter noun ending in *-m*, e.g. *cepp-aṭam* '(the action of) telling': *cepp-aṭāni-ki* 'for telling', *cepp-aṭam-walla* 'because of telling', *cepp-aṭam-lō* 'in telling'. In Telugu, this is a frequently used noun clause denoting action, without any other part of the clause being disturbed. Its versatility is owing to the fact that the infinitive has lost its nominal function in Telugu and, therefore, Telugu uses the action clause, where Tamil, Malayāḷam and Kannaḍa would prefer to use an infinitive clause, e.g.

(32) a. Te. *wāḍu tin-aṭāni-ki weḷḷ-ǣ-ḍu*
[he eat-noml-dat go-past-3m-sg]
'he went to eat (for eating)'

corresponding to (26e) of

Ma. *avan [uṇṇ-ān] pōyi*
[he eat-inf go-past]
'he went to eat'

For corresponding untensed action nouns, Tamil uses *-al*, e.g. *cey-* 'do': *cey-al* 'doing', or *-tal*/*-ttal* and Kannaḍa uses *-al* (which represents a merger of the infinitive and the nominalizing suffix), and Malayāḷam uses many derivational suffixes, namely *-avə*, *-al*, *-ppə*, *-tta*, *-ttam* (Asher and Kumari 1997: 41–2). Apparently these are not much favoured in usage (Lehmann 1989: 300–1):

b. Ka. [*mīna bombāyi-ge hōg-alu*] *nirākaris-id-aḷu*
[Meena Bombay-to go-inf/noml refuse-past-3f-sg]
'Meena refused to go to Bombay'

Corresponding to the Kannaḍa infinitive *hōg-alu* 'to go', Telugu uses an action nominal with dative *pōw-aṭāni-ki* 'for going'.

c. Ma. [*ī pāṭ-atte koy-ttə*] *nāḷe āṇə*
[this field-loc-adj harvest-noml tomorrow be-pres]
'harvesting of this field is tomorrow'

d. Te. [*nuwwu inta śrama paḍaṭam*] *nāku iṣṭam lēdu*
[you such trouble-take-noml I-dat liking be-not-3neu-sg]
'you – taking so much trouble – I do not like'

e. Te. *wāḷḷu* [*mammal-ni peṇḍli-ki pilaw-aṭāni-ki*] *wacc-ǣ-ru*
[they we-acc marriage-dat call-noml-dat come-past-3h-pl]
'they came to invite us to the wedding.'

f. Te. [*raylu rāwaṭam-tōn-ē*] *nāku ceppaṇḍi*
[train come-noml-with-emph I-dat tell-imp-pl]
'please tell me as soon as the train comes (with the coming of the train)'
g. Te. *wāna kuraw-aṭam inkā āg-a-lēdu*
[rain rain-noml still cease-inf- be-not-3neu-sg]
'it has not stopped raining still'

Note that the action nominal refers to habitual tense in (32d), to the past tense in (32e), to future in (32f) and to present durative in (32g).

9.3.3 *Finite predicate clauses*

Except for correlative relative clauses discussed in section 9.3.2.4, we have mainly dealt with subordinate clauses with non-finite verbs or verb-derived nominals, which do not complete a predication. In all such cases, there is only one finite verb in a complex sentence and one or more non-finite verbs. When a clause with a finite verb has to be embedded in another clause, or adjoined to the main clause, a complementizer clitic or a clitic-like verb is used.

9.3.3.1 *Embedding by clitic* -ō

In section 8.4.4 it has been shown that in South Dravidian I and II, the clitic *-ō* is added to a correlative clause to join it to the main clause. All literary languages and some non-literary languages adopt this strategy. The question-word interrogative clauses add *-ō* to be attached to the matrix clause. The *-ō* clitic also embeds a conditional sentence with a past-tense verb in all the literary languages.

(33) a. Te. [*wāḍu eppuḍu was-tā-ḍ-ō*] *nāku teliyadu*
[he when come-hab-3m-sg I-dat know-neg-3neu-sg]
'I do not know when he will come.'
b. Te. [*nuwwu ī sangati ewarik*(*i*)*-annā ceppāw*(*u*)*-ō*], *campēs-tā-nu*
[you this matter anybody-dat tell-past-2sg-comp (I) kill-fut-1sg]
'if you tell this to anybody, I will kill you'
c. Ta. [*nī aẓu-t-āy-ō*] *u͟n͟n͟ai aṭippē͟n͟*
[you cry-past-2sg-comp you-acc beat-fut-1sg]
'if you cry, I will beat you'
d. Ka. [*nāḷe.y-oḷage bāḍige kaṭṭ-id-ir-ō*] *sari, illad-iddāre...*
[tomorrow-within rent pay-past-2pl-comp, fine; if not...]
'if you pay up the rent by tomorrow, OK, if not . . . '

Sentence (33a) has a noun clause embedded as the direct object of the verb 'know'; in (33b,c,d) the complementizer *-ō* converts the first finite clause into a conditional clause and it is replaceable by a corresponding non-finite clause with a conditional verb (see section 9.3.1.2). The semantic and grammatical differences between the two types of conditions need to be investigated.

9.3.3.2 *Embedding by verb* *aHn- *'say'*

The perfective, conditional, concessive and relative (adjectival) participles of the verb 'say' are used as complementizers in embedding a variety of finite clauses in matrix clauses. Clauses with finite predications are attached to the main clause as the direct object complement of the verb 'say'. The most commonly used one is the perfective participle Ta. *e<u>n</u>-<u>r</u>u*, Ma. *en-nə*, Ka. *en-du/an-ta*, Te. *an-i* 'having said' in reporting speech acts as a quotative complementizer. The finite verbs in the matrix clause may be one of 'know, think, hear, ask, speak' etc. This mechanism is found in all subgroups and is reconstructible for Proto-Dravidian, e.g.

(34) a. Ta. [*kumār e-p.pōtu varu-v-ā<u>n</u>*] *e<u>n</u>-<u>r</u>u kēṭ-ṭ-ār-kaḷ*
[Kumar when come-fut-3m-sg say-ppl ask-past-3h-pl]
'they asked (me) when Kumar would come'

b. Ta. [*ava<u>n</u> var-a vēṇṭ-um*] *e<u>nr</u>-āl nāḷai var-al-ām*
[he come-inf want-fut-3neu-sg say-cond tomorrow come-noml-fut-3neu-sg]
'if he wants to come, he may come tomorrow'

c. Ma.[*ñā<u>n</u> var-ām*] *ennə rāma<u>n</u> pa<u>r</u>aññu*
[I come-fut-mod say-ppl Raman say-past]
'Raman said, "I will come"'

d. Ma. [*avan varum*] *enn-āl-um avaḷ kūṭe varilla*
[he come-fut say-conc she along with come-neg]
'even if he comes, she will not come' (lit. 'he comes, even if one says . . . ')

e. Ka. [*ayskrīm tinn-a bēku*] *endu/anta annis-utt-ade*
[ice cream eat-inf want say-ppl feel-non-past-3neu-sg]
'(I) feel like eating ice cream' (lit. ice cream–want to eat–so it strikes)

f. Te. *nuwwu nātō* [*rēpu wastānu*] *ani ceppǣwu*
[you I-obl-com tomorrow come-hb-1sg say-pp say-past-2sg]
'you said to me, "I will come tomorrow"'

g. Te. [*jailu-nunci elā tappincukō-ṭam-ā*] *ani wāḍi ālōcana*
[jail-from how escape-noml-Q say-ppl he-gen thinking]
'his idea is how to escape from the jail'

h. Te. *nāku* [*amerikā weḷḷ-āli*] *ani undi*
[I-dat America go-must say-ppl-comp be-3neu-sg]
'I would like to go to America'

i. Kol. [*nīv sā-t-iv*] *ena ān ar-t-an*
[you-sg go-pres-2sg say-ppl I weep-past-1sg]
'I wept thinking that you are leaving'

The non-finite forms of the verb 'say' have a variety of usages. The perfective participle is mainly used as a quotative marker as in (34a, c, f); note that the quoted clause is in direct speech. The distinction between direct and indirect reporting is subtle in Dravidian. The difference is observed in the different use of subject pronouns in embedded and main clauses, at least in Telugu (see Krishnamurti and Gwynn 1985: 363–8):

j. Te. *rāmu* [*nēnu rēpu weḷtānu*] *ani kamalatō cepp-ǣ-ḍu*
[Ramu I tomorrow come-fut-1sg say-comp Kamala-com tell-past-3m-sg]
'Ramu said to Kamala, "I will go tomorrow"'
j′. — [*tānu*————————] —
'Ramu said to Kamala that he would go tomorrow'

Instead of *nēnu* 'I' in (34j), the reflexive pronoun *tānu* 'self' is used in (34j′) co-indexed with the third-person subject in the higher sentence, suggesting indirect reporting.[11] Still the verb agreement of the quoted clause is in the first person singular. Another strategy is in the case of reporting imperative sentences (see Krishnamurti and Gwynn 1985: 366–7).[12] (34g) shows that the subordinate clause can be a complement to a head noun meaning 'idea, thought' etc. in the main clause; in (34i) *en-* means 'thinking' which is reporting a 'thought' and not 'speech'; (34e,h) illustrate the use of the subordinate clause as a desiderative complement to the main clause, literally meaning 'I must eat ice cream, so (saying/thinking), it is to me', 'I must go to America, so it is to me.' The conditional and concessive forms of 'say' mark the subordinate clauses, as grammaticalized conditional and concessive markers added to these clauses without the lexical meaning of 'say'. The verb 'be' is also used in the same way, Ta. *āṉ-āl* 'if', *āṉ-āl-um* 'even if…'; Telugu adds *ay-itē* 'if', *ay-inā* 'even if' to factive clauses in *-aṭṭu* (section 9.3.2.3).

9.3.4 *Adverbial clauses*

Adverbs of time and place are morphologically nominals, since they can be inflected for case, although they are devoid of gender and number. There are three types of adverbial

[11] The reflexive pronoun *tānu* (<**tān*) anaphorically refers only to the third person and not to the first or second person. Note that although the subject of direct report is in the first person in the embedded clause, it is replaced in indirect report by *tānu* 'self' because it refers to the antecedent subject of the matrix clause which is in the third person. If the matrix subject is in the first person, it cannot be replaced by *tānu* (Rama Rao 1968).

[12] Parallel mechanisms must be available in the other major Dravidian languages although I have not come across these in available grammars.

clauses: (i) a relative clause with an Adverbial Phrase of time or place, with an inflected or uninflected adverb as head, (ii) a noun clause (NP) or a postpositional (PP) clause, followed by postpositions denoting time and place, and (iii) an embedded AdvP with a manner adverbial as head; these include non-finite verbal participles, which modify the predicate as manner adverbials, e.g.

(35) a. Te. $_{\text{AdvP}}$[$_{\text{AdjP}}$[*atanu upanyāsam cebu-tun-na*]$_{\text{AdjP}}$ *mūḍu gaṇṭa-l-ū*]$_{\text{AdvP}}$ *wāna kuris-in-di*
[he lecture speak-dur-adj three hour-pl-conj prcl rain rain-past-3neu-sg]
'it rained during the three hours he was lecturing'

b. Te. $_{\text{AdvP}}$[$_{\text{AdjP}}$[*āyana pani cēs-ē*]$_{\text{AdjP}}$ *cōṭ-i-ki*]$_{\text{AdvP}}$ *nēn-ē weḻ-ǣ-nu*
[he work do-hab adj place-obl-dat I-emph go-past-1sg]
'I myself went to the place where he works'

c. Te. [*rāmu weḻ-in*(*a*)*-appaṭi-nunci*] *kamala-ku oṇṭ*(*i*)*lō bāgā lēdu*
[Ramu go-past-adj time-obl-abl Kamala-dat body-obl-loc well-adv be-not-3neu-sg]
'Since the time Ramu left, Kamala has not been feeling well'

d. Te. *nāku telis-in-*(*a*)*-anta wara-ku* . . .
[I-dat know-past-quan up to . . .]
'as far as I know . . . '

e. Te. *nēnu rāw-aṭāni-ki mundu* . . .
[I come-noml-obl-dat before . . .]
'before my coming . . . '

f. Te. *wāḍu* [*parigettu-koṇ-ṭū tondara-gā*] *wacc-ǣ-ḍu*
[he run-refl-dur quick-adv come-past-3m-sg]
'he came running fast'

g. Ta. [*maẓai pey-t-atu-kku appuṟam*] *payir naṉṟāka vaḷar-nt-adu*
[rain-nom fall-past-noml-dat after crops goodness-adv grow-past-3neu-sg]
'After it rained/rains, the crops grew/grow well'

h. Ma. *nī var-um-pōḷ enta koṇṭu var-um*
[you come-fut-time what bring-fut]
'when you come, what will you bring?'

i. Ma. *niŋŋaḷ jōli tīrkkunnatə vare* . . .
[you-hon work finish-pres-noml until . . .]
'until you finish the work . . . '

j. Ka. *railu biḍu-v-a samaya-kke* . . .
[train leave-fut-adj time-dat. . .]
'by the time the train leaves. . . '

k. Ka. *ī haḷḷige baruvadakke munce . . .*
[this village-dat come-nonpast-noml-dat before . . .]
'before you came to this village . . . '

l. Ka. *syāmnna [ēd-uttā] ba-nd-a*
[Shymanna pant-nonpast-pp come-past-3m-sg]
'Shymanna came panting'

9.4 Compound sentences (coordination)

Two or more autonomous units (words, phrases, clauses) of equal grammatical status and rank from two or more underlying clauses can be conjoined together within one sentence, called a compound sentence. The relationship of conjoining can be additive ('and'), alternative ('or'), or adversative ('but'). At the word level, conjoining by 'and' relationship produces *dvandva* compounds, e.g. Te. *talli-daṇḍrulu* 'mother and father', *annā-dammulu* 'elder and younger brother', *akkā-celleḷḷu* 'elder and younger sisters'. These are lexical compounds not always derivable by syntactic processes. Therefore, such compounds are not discussed in this section. We will restrict our attention to coordination of phrases and clauses.

9.4.1 *'And' coordination*

Any of the phrases NP, PP, AdvP or the predicate phrase may be coordinated as long as the other phrases remain the same. Tamil and Malayāḷam add *-um*, the conjunctive particle, to each of the phrases coordinated. Kannaḍa uses *-ū* and Telugu lengthens the final vowels of the coordinated phrases (see section 8.4.1 for the distribution of the conjunctive morpheme). Examples:

(36) a. Ta. *[eṉ [makan-um makaḷ-um] appuṟam varu-v-ārkaḷ*
[I-obl son-conj daughter-conj later come-fut-3h-pl]
'my son and daughter will come later'

b. Ma. *sīta [innale.y-um] rādha [inn-um] kālējil cēr-nnu*
[Sita yesterday-conj Radha today-conj college-loc join-past]
'Sita joined the college yesterday and Radha did so today'

c. Ka. *avaru [haṇav-annu vaḍeve.y-annu] byānkin-alli iṭṭidd-āre*
[he-hon money-conj jewellery-conj bank-loc keep-pr-pf -3h-pl]
'he has kept money and jewellery in the bank'

d. Te. *āmeku oka [maga-pillawāḍū oka āḍa-pilla]*
[she-dat one boy-child one girl-child]
'she has a boy and a girl'

Sentence (36a) is an example of coordinating two subject NPs, namely *eṉ makaṉ* 'my son' and *eṉ makaḷ* 'my daughter', while the AdvP *appuṟam* 'afterwards' and the VP remain lexically the same. The only difference is in the agreement suffix in the VP, which is plural as opposed to two singular predicates in the underlying structures, namely *makaṉ . . . varu-v-aṉ* and *mak-aḷ varu-v-aḷ*. Sentence (36b) illustrates the coordination of the time adverbials, *innale* 'yesterday' and *inne* 'today', as well as the subjects of the sentence. It seems to be a case of clause coordination with time adverbials focussed. Sentence (36c) exemplifies the coordination of two PPs (NPs + accusative) in otherwise the same clause. Sentence (36d) is a nominal predication with a dative subject, in which the predicate NPs, *oka moga-pillawāḍu* 'one boy' and *oka āḍa-pilla* 'one girl', are coordinated both by a combination of vowel length and by intonation.

9.4.2 *'Or' coordination*

The most common coordinator is the clitic *-ō* which is added to each of the coordinated words, phrases or clauses, see section 8.4.4. Tamil (1c), Malayāḷam (2a), Kannaḍa (4b) and Telugu (5f) as illustrations of phrase coordination. Clause coordination is illustrated by a sentence from Koṇḍa (6b). Tamil uses other coordinators also, namely *illai-eṉṟāl, allatu, -āvatu* 'if not'; adjectival phrases and finite clauses can be coordinated only by *illai-eṉṟāl* or *allatu* in Tamil, e.g. [*periya allatu ciṟiya*] *vīṭu* 'big or small house'. Malayāḷam uses *-ill-eŋkil/ -all-eŋkil* 'if not, or else'; the choice of the negative morpheme *-ill* or *-all* depends on whether the alternation is between verbs or nouns. Kannaḍa uses *athavā* 'or else', borrowed from Sanskrit, or *illa/illavē* 'if not' but only once between the coordinated phrases or clauses. Sometimes both the strategies are used redundantly. Telugu uses *ay-inā* 'even if be' or *annā* 'even if said' in the place of *ō . . . ō* after each of the coordinated phrases. If two interrogative clauses are coordinated each of them carries the interrogative marker *-ā*. Some more examples of clause coordination:

(37) a. Ta. [*kumār varu-v-āṉ*] *illaieṉṟāl / allatu* [*rājā varu-v-āṉ*]
[Kumar come-fut-3m-sg or/or Raja come-fut-3m-sg]
'Either Kumar will come or Raja will come'

b. Ma. *avan* [*varika.y-ō sandēśam ayakkuka.y-ō*] *cey-t-illa*
[he come-inf-coor message send-inf-coor do-past-neg]
'He neither came nor sent any message'

c. Ka. [*rūpa baruttaḷ*]-*ō* [*avaḷ-a gaṇḍa baruttān*]-*ō gott*(*u*)-*illa*
[Rupa come-pres-f-sg-coor she-gen husband] [come-pres-m-sg-coor know-neg]
'(I/we) do not know if Rupa will come or her husband will come'

d. Te. *āyana ninna ūḷḷō unnār-ā lēr-ā*
[he yesterday town-loc be-past-3m-pl-Q be-not-Q]
'was he in town or not yesterday?'

Sentence (37a) illustrates the coordination of two finite clauses in 'either/or' relationship; (37b) coordinates two infinitive clauses; (37c) shows coordination of two finite clauses by *ō . . . ō* and also *illa*, redundantly; (37d) coordinates two finite interrogative clauses by repeating them with the question clitic, one after the other with deletion of identical elements from the second clause, i.e. dropping the parts in the parentheses (*āyana ninna ūḻḻō*) *lēr-ā*. The coordination of interrogative clauses follows the same strategy in the other languages also.

9.4.3 *'But' coordination*

Tamil uses the coordinator *ān̠-āl* between the conjoined phrases or clauses. Even adjective phrases and clauses can be coordinated. Malayāḷam uses *eŋ-kil-um* as the coordinator. As in Tamil, adjectives can be coordinated by *ennāl*. Kannaḍa uses *ādare* to coordinate only clauses; 'but' coordination is not possible between phrases, according to Sridhar (1990: 102). Telugu 'but' coordination is accomplished by placing *kāni/gāni* between coordinated clauses. When the same coordinator is added to coordinate phrases one after each, they mean 'either . . . or'. Adjectival clauses, in general, cannot be coordinated in Telugu, as happens in Tamil and Malayāḷam in this case.

(38) a. Ta. *idu [kumār koṭu-tt-a] ān̠āl [eẓut-āt-a] kaṭitam*
[this-one Kumar give-past-adj but-coor write-neg-adj letter]
'this is the letter Kumar gave, but did not write'
b. Ta. *avan̠ [vantān̠] ān̠āl [on̠rum coll-a.v-illai]*
[he come-past-3m-sg but anything say-inf-be not-3neu-pl]
'he came, but did not say anything'
c. Ma. *avan [kuḻḻan] eŋkilum [sundaran] āṇə*
[he short-m but beautiful-m be-pres]
'he is short but beautiful'
d. Ma. *[naracca] ennāl [putiya] jīns*
[faded but new jeans]
'faded but new jeans'
e. Ka. *nanna hattira [dāra ide] ādare [sūji illa]*
[I-poss near thread is but needle be-not]
'I have thread with me but no needle'
f. Te. *[rāmu bāgā sampāyis-tā-ḍu] gāni [paysā-kūḍā kharcu-peṭṭ-a-ḍu]*
[Ramu well earn-hab-3m-sg but penny-too spend-neg-3m-sg]
'Ramu earns well, but does not spend even a penny'

Telugu uses some other clause coordinators like *kābaṭṭi*, *kanuka/ganuka* 'therefore' to join a causal clause with the main clause. There are a few other coordinator-like elements used in Telugu, which need to be studied comparatively, e.g. *telisī-teliyaka* 'knowingly and unknowingly' (adverbial modifying the verb 'tell'), *ānī-ānakuṇḍā* 'leaning and not leaning' (adverbial with the VP 'sit on a chair-arm'), *waccī-rāni* 'acquired and not acquired' (adjectival modifying the noun *telugu*). These are apparently coordinated perfective participles (because of lengthening of the vowels of coordinated phrases) in the affirmative and negative, but they have become idiomatic and cannot be derived from underlying clauses[13] (see Krishnamurti and Gwynn 1985: 336–9).

9.5 Minor sentences

The properties of minor sentences are: '(1) They do not have a subject and predicate as required by simple, complex or compound sentences; (2) they are self-contained autonomous expressions which are used either as whole utterances, or in conjunction with other minor or regular sentences in discourse; (3) when minor sentences precede or follow other sentences, the former do not influence or are influenced by the latter' (Krishnamurti and Gwynn 1985: 299). Minor sentences include vocatives or address terms, sometimes combined with pre-vocative politeness clitics, greetings, interjections and other short utterances, which convey the purport of the accompanying discourse. We will start with examples from Telugu:

(39I) Interjections

a. *ayyō* 'alas!', *pāpam* 'mercy', *abbā* 'ouch', *bhēṣ* 'excellent', *are are* 'hey' (in wonder) etc. *chī chī* 'terrible!' (disapproval). These may be followed by short sentences.

(39II) Address terms

b. *or-ēy/ēm-rā/ōri* (male addressee, with zero-degree politeness)
c. *os-ēy/ēm-ē/ōsi* (female addressee, same as b in politeness)
d. *ēm-ōy* (male addressee, with first-degree politeness)
e. *ēm-ayya/amma* (male/female addressee, second-degree politeness)
f. *ēm-aṇḍi* (male/female addressee with third- or highest-degree of politeness)
g. *nānnā* 'father', *ammā* 'mother', *tātā* 'grandfather' etc. all kinship address terms
h. *śāstri/śarma/ḍākṭaru/subbārāwu* + *gāru* (marker of third-degree politeness) with each address term outside the immediate family.

(39II b–f) occur as conversation openers, sometimes before address terms as pre-vocatives. The clitics of politeness can also occur after any autonomous unit of a clause,

[13] For example, *telisī-teliyaka* means 'with half knowledge' which cannot be derived from two underlying clauses, in which one would mean 'knowingly' and the other 'not knowing'. Then, these have to be taken as compound words at the morphological level.

e.g. *cūśǣr(u)-aṇḍī* 'have you seen?' *ewar-ōy wacc-in-di* 'who has come?' (addressing a male with first-degree politeness). For an explanation of degrees of politeness, see Krishnamurti and Gwynn 1985: 301–3.

(39III) Greetings and other short expressions
- i. *namaskāram-aṇḍi/-ayya/-amma* 'hello' (polite salutation)
- j. *awnu* 'yes', *kādu* 'no', *mancidi* 'fine', *alān-ā* 'is that so?' (*-aṇḍi/-amma/-ayya/-ōy/-rā* after each, depending on addressee's status)
- k. *sarē* 'O K' (*-aṇḍi/-amma/-ayya/-ōy/-rā* with final *-n* before clitics beginning with vowels)
- l. *idugō* 'here', *adugō* 'there' (pointing out or handing in something; with politeness clitics as above)

For further details, see Krishnamurti and Gwynn (1985: 299–306).

The examples given for Tamil (Asher 1985: 100–11, 119–20) are given in different sections. These include:

(40)
- a. *evvaḷavu ruciyāna halvā* [how much tasty halva] 'what a tasty *halvā*!'
- b. *appaṭi.y-ā* 'is that so?'
- c. Vocative in the case of names ending in *-an* is *-ā*, e.g. *rāman*: voc *rāmā*; all stems in final vowel lengthen that vowel, *tampi* 'younger brother': voc *tampī*, *cuntaram* (proper noun): *cuntarō̃*
- d. Interjections: *appā/ammā* (pain), *appāṭiyō* (fear), *ayyō* (sorrow), *ōkō* (surprise), *cī cī* (disapproval), *pāvam* (sorrow and sympathy), *pramātam* (appreciation and wonder). The last word is borrowed from Sanskrit where it means 'danger, unintended fault'

Malayāḷam (Asher and Kumari 1997: 186–7, 223–4, 449–50) has the same classification:

(41)
- a. Greetings include *namaskāram* (general), *salām alaikkum* (Moslems) 'salutation'.
- b. Vocatives: male names in final *-an* replace it by *-ā*, *-m* ending female names double the final *-m*, all vowel-final names lengthen the vowel and other consonantal-final words add *-ē* in address, e.g. *mādhavan*: *mādhav-ā*, *kamala-m*: *kamala-mm*, *makkaḷ* 'children (one's own)': *makkaḷ-ē*, *rāṇi*: *rāṇ-ī* (proper noun). Pre-vocatives include *hē*, *allayō* 'hello' (polite), *ēṭā/ēṭī* m/f 'hello' (familiar).
- c. Interjections: *ate* 'yes', *ayyaṭā* (contempt), *ayyō/ayyayyō* (grief, sympathy), *āvō* (doubt), *ohō* 'is that so?', *chī* (disgust), *bhēṣ* (appreciation).

Kannaḍa (Sridhar 1990: 149–51) follows a similar pattern.

(42) a. Vocatives: the final vowel of a common noun or a proper noun is lengthened, e.g. *huḍugā* 'boy', *huḍugī* 'girl', *aṇṇā* 'dad', *ammā* 'mother, madam'; *ēnrī* 'hello' (polite, to draw one's attention).
b. Interjections: *ayyō* (pain, pity), *abbā* (incredulity, shock), *che* (mild disapproval), *thū* (disgust), *ēnu* 'what a . . . !'
c. Greetings: *namaskāra*, *kṣēmav-ā* 'how do you do?'
d. Short utterances: *haudu* 'yes', *hū* 'OK', *illa* 'no'.

A comparison of the four languages shows that several of the minor sentence types are shared: (i) lengthening of the final vowel of the word in addressing; (ii) using the terms for 'mother' (*amma*) and father (*ayya*, *abba*) followed by *-ā/-ō* in expressing pity, grief, etc.; (iii) the use of interrogative stem *ēm* followed by clitics in expressing different degrees of politeness; (iv) the use of /h/ in *ōho*, *āha* in expressing wonder, amazement etc.; (v) the use of /c/ or /ch/ followed by front high or non-high vowels (*chā*/*chī*/*che*) usually reduplicated in expressing disgust, disapproval. Items (i) to (iii) can be reconstructed as shared patterns from Proto-South Dravidian. The last two could be recent innovations, which have diffused across languages. They are also found in Indo-Aryan.

9.6 Sentence negation

Morphologically negation is expressed in verbal conjugation in Dravidian. This topic has been dealt with in section 7.10.1–5. Besides, there is a negative verb **cil* reconstructible for Proto-Dravidian (see section 7.10.6). This verb is used as an auxiliary with non-finite verbs to denote sentence negation. In South Dravidian I there is another negative verb *al-*, which is used in negating nominal predications.

In the modern languages of South Dravidian I, nominal predications are negated by *alla* 'not be so-and so' (identity negation) and verbal predications by *illai* 'not be, not (do)' (existential negation). Telugu and the other South Dravidian II languages have no counterpart to *alla*. Instead, they use the negative form of the verb **ā* 'to be' to negate identity (Te. *kā-du*, Koṇḍa *āʔed*). For verbal predications, in existential meaning, Telugu uses *lē-* 'be not' which corresponds to *il-* of South Dravidian I, both from PD **cil-* with the loss of *c-* in South Dravidian I, but retained in South Dravidian II with the exception of Telugu. Let us look at sentence negation in Tamil:

(43) a. Ta. *kumār vakkīl illai*/*alla*
[Kumar lawyer be-not-3neu-pl]
'Kumar is not a lawyer' (identity negation)
b. Ta. *ānantan ūrle ill-ai*
[Anandan town-loc be-not-3neu-sg]
'Anandan is not in town' (existential negation)

c. Ta. *pey uṇ-ṭu*
[ghost exist-3neu-sg]
'ghosts exist'

c′. Ta. *pey ill-ai*
[ghost not-exist-3neu-sg]
'ghosts do not exist'

d. Ta. *kumār kōvil-ukku.p pō-ṉ-atu illai*
[Kumar temple-dat go-past-noml be not-past-3neu-sg]
'Kumar has never gone to a temple'

e. Ta. *ravi nēṟṟu/nāḷai var-a.v ill-ai*
[Ravi yesterday/tomorrow come-inf not-3neu-pl]
'Ravi did not come yesterday/will not come tomorrow'

f. Ta. *kumār var-āt-atu nall-atu alla*
[Kumar come-neg-noml nice-3neu-sg be-not 3neu-pl]
'Kumar not coming was not nice'

The negative verbs *il-* 'be not' (to negate existential, locative, copula usages) and *al-* (to negate copula usage) are not inflected for tense but marked only for third neuter plural as *ill-ai*, *all-a*, but agree with both singular and/or plural subjects. In equative sentences, both the verbs occur as predicates in free variation (43a). In formal Tamil *alla* is used to negate nominal predications and *illai* for the rest, as in (43f) (Asher 1985: 77). This distinction is lost in colloquial speech. In sentences with a locative PP as complement (43b) only *illai* occurs. Sentence (43d) has a nominalized finite verb in the subject NP and (43e) refers to an action and not a state. In both cases *illai* is used. Sentences (43c, c′) have an existential predicate and *illai* is used to negate it. As an auxiliary *illai* occurs after a main verb in the infinitive in verbal predications (43e) for negating an action done in the past or non-past.

Malayāḷam uses *alla* to negate a nominal predication with the copula *āṇə* and *illa* a verbal predication with the copula *uṇṭə*. All other verbal predications add *illa* to the finite verb to negate it.

(44) a. *rāman ḍākṭar āṇə*
[Raman doctor be-pres]
'Raman is a doctor'

a′. *rāman ḍākṭar alla*
[Raman doctor neg]
'Raman is not a doctor'

b. *kuṭṭi vīṭṭ-il uṇ-ṭə*
[child house-loc be-pres]
'the child is at home'

b′. *kuṭṭi vīṭṭ-il illa*
[child house-loc not]
'the child is not at home'

c. *avan paṭiccu*
[he study-past]
'he studied'

c′. *avan paṭicc(u)-illa*
[he study-past not]
'he did not study'

d. *avan var-um*
[he come-fut]
'he will come'

d′. *avan varuka.y-illa/ var-illa*
[he come-inf neg]
'he will not come'

e. *avan innale vann-illa*
[he yesterday come-past-neg]
'he didn't come yesterday'

f. *avan-alla innale vann-atə*
[he-neg yesterday come-noml-neg]
'it was not he that came yesterday'

The past negative is formed by simply adding the negative verb *illa* to the past finite verb (44c, c′). This is also true of the present tense. To denote future negative *illa* is added to the infinitive (44d, d′). Sentence (44e) is like (44c′), but (44f) is a cleft sentence with a nominalized verb. The phrase negated in a nominal predication has *alla* added to it and not *illa*.

Kannaḍa follows the same pattern in the distribution of *alla* to negate nominal predication and *illa* to negate verbal or existential predicates.

(45) a. *sarōja ḍākṭaru alla*
[Saroja doctor neg]
'Saroja is not a doctor'

b. *sarōja ōd-id-du kādambari alla*
[Saroja read-past-nom novel neg]
'what Saroja read is/was not a novel'

c. *nīnu avar-a mane-ge hōg-a kūḍ-a-du*
[you they-gen house-dat go-inf proh]
'you should not go to their house'

d. *doḍḍ-avar-ige eduru āḍ-a bār-a-du*
[old-persons-dat opposite speak-inf-proh]
'one must not talk back to elders'

e. *nāḷe.y-inda kelasakke bar-a bēḍa*
[tomorrow-abl job-dat come-inf-neg]
'don't come to work from tomorrow'

f. *anil kālēji-ge hōgal/houvadu illa*
[Anil college-dat go-inf/non-past noml neg]
'Anil did/does not go to college'

Sentences (45a, b) are negatives of nominal predications, hence *alla* is the negative marker; (45f) has *illa*, being a verbal predication. Sentences (45c, d, e) relate to the usage of negative modals with different auxiliaries added to the infinitive of the main verb: *kūḍ-a-du* 'it does not suit' is the third neuter singular negative of the verb *kūḍu-* 'to suit', *bār-a-du* 'it does not come' is the third neuter singular negative of the verb *bar-/ bār-* 'come'. Both these verbs occur after the infinitive and are totally grammaticalized as though they are uninflected prohibitive markers. In (45e) *bēḍa* 'is not needed' is the opposite of *bēku* 'is needed', both historically related to **wē-ṇṭ-ā-tu,* **wēḷ-kk-um*, from PD **wēḷ-* (*wē-ṇṭ-*) 'to desire'.

Telugu has a negative verb derived from *lē-*'is/was not' (< **il-a* < **cil-a-*) inflected for gender, number and person as a finite verb; it is used to negate verbal predications. Nominal predications are negated by *kā-du* (3neu sg), suppletively related to **aw-* 'to be'.

(46) a. *śarma-gāru ḍākṭaru kādu*
[Sarma-hon doctor be-not]
'Mr Sarma is not a doctor'

b. *akkaḍa nilabaḍḍa-di śarma-gāru kādu*
[there stand-past-noml Sarma-hon not]
'the person standing there is/was not Mr Sarma'

c. *śarma-gāru ūḷ-ḷō lē-ru*
[Sarma-hon town-in be-not-3h-pl]
'Mr Sarma is not in town'

d. *nēnu sinimāku rāw-aṭam-lēdu*
[I cinema-dat come-noml not]
'I am not coming to the movie'

e. *ninna mā iṇṭi-ki ḍākṭaru-gāru rā-lēdu*
[yesterday our house-dat doctor-hon come-inf-not]
'the doctor did not come to our house yesterday'

f. *mīru peddagā māṭlāḍ-a gūḍadu*
[you-pl loudly speak-inf proh]
'you should not speak loudly'

g. *sigareṭ-lu tāg-a waddu*
[cigarette-pl smoke-inf-proh]
'don't smoke cigarettes'

Sentences (46a, b) are nominal predications and hence they carry *kādu* as the negative verb. (46c) is a verbal predication with a PP in locative and therefore it takes *lēru*. Note that this verb agrees with the subject NP in gender, number and person. The negative verb *lē-du*, without subject agreement, is added to an action nominal of the main verb to form durative negative and to the infinitive to form past negative (46d, e). In sentence (46f) the infinitive of the main verb is followed by *kūḍ-a-du* (see Kannaḍa) as a prohibitive marker. In (46g) an imperative prohibitive is formed by adding *waddu* (historically from *wal-a-du* '(it) is not needed').

In both South Dravidian I and II we notice parallel processes in negation by using different verbs to distinguish between nominal and verbal predications. The remaining types of negation are formed as part of verb conjugation in both the subgroups.

9.7 Reflexivity and reciprocality

If two NPs are coreferential within the same clause, one of them uses a variable reflexive pronoun or some other strategy. There are three devices to express reflexivity in Dravidian: (i) by replacing one of the coreferential NPs with the correct personal pronoun with appropriate case marking; (ii) by using a reflexive pronoun *tān/tan*-V 'self' if the coreferential phrase is in the third person; (iii) by marking the verb with a reflexive auxiliary, derived from PD *koḷ-/koṇ-* 'take'; (iv) a combination of the use of (i) or (ii) with (iii) as required by the selected verb. The emphatic clitic *-ē* or *-tān* (the latter optionally in Tamil and Malayāḷam) may occur in combination with any of the above or sometimes even independently to denote reflexivity. In reciprocal usage, a clause has two NPs or PPs, both denoting referents participating in a reciprocal activity denoted by the predicate. One of these phrases (which we may call the Reflexive Phrase) has the structure 'one-person/persons/thing/things + postposition followed by one-person/persons/thing/things + postposition'. This phrase modifies the predicate.

(47) a. Ta. *nāṉ eṉṉ-ai maṟa-ntu viṭṭēṉ* (Reflexive)
[I I-acc forget-ppl leave-past-1sg]
'I forgot myself'

b. Ta. *avaḷ taṉṉ-ai kaṇṇāṭi.y-il pārttu koṇ-t-āḷ* (Reflexive)
[she she-acc mirrior-loc see-ppl take-past-1f-sg]
'she looked at herself in the mirror'

c. Ta. *kumār taṉa-kk-uḷḷ-ē ciri-ttu.k-koṇ-ṭ-āṉ* (Reflexive)
[Kumār he-dat-inside laugh-ppl-hold-past-3m-sg]
'Kumar laughed within himself'

d. Ta. *avarkaḷ oruvar-iṭam oruvar pēc-iṉ-ārkaḷ* (Reciprocal)
[they one-person-loc one-person talk-past-3h-pl]
'they talked to each other'

e. Ta. *kumār-um rājā.v-um oruvar-ai oruvar pār-tt-ārkaḷ* (Reciprocal)
[Kumar-cl Raja-cl one-person-acc one-person see-past-3h-pl]
'Kumar and Raja looked at each other'

f. Ma. *ñāṉ-ē cey-t-āl praśnam tīr-um* (Reflexive)
[I-emph do-(past)-cond problem end-fut]
'if I do it myself the problem will be solved'

g. Ma. *avan svantam talay-il aṭi-ccu* (Reflexive)
[he self head-loc beat-past]
'he beat his own head'

h. Ma. *nī-tanne atə ceytu koḷḷu* (Reflexive)
[you-emph that do-past-take-imp-sg]
'do it yourself'

i. Ma. *avar oruvan maṟṟavan-ōṭə samsāriccu* (Reciprocal)
[he one-m-sg other-m-sg-soc speak-past]
'they spoke with each other'

The above sentences illustrate reflexivity and reciprocality in Tamil and Malayāḷam. In sentence (47a) the object argument is expressed by the first person in accusative coreferring to the subject pronoun *nāṉ* 'I'. In (47f, h) in Malayāḷam the emphatic markers *-ē*, *-tanne* added to the subject NP also mark reflexivity. The Sanskrit word *svantam* 'one's own' is used in Malayāḷam as a reflexive pronoun in (47g). In Tamil in sentences (47b, c) the reflexive pronoun *tāṉ/taṉ-* occurs coindexed with the third-person subjects *avaḷ* 'she' and *kumār* 'Kumar', respectively. Sentences (47b, c, h) illustrate the use of a reflexive auxiliary *koḷ-* in addition to the reflexive pronoun. In these cases, to obtain the meaning of self-benefaction the use of the auxiliary is obligatory.

Reciprocality is expressed by a Reciprocal Phrase 'one [±hum] . . . one [±hum]' as shown in (47d, e). In the place of the second constituent of the phrase Malayāḷam uses a different lexical item meaning 'another person' (47i). It is important to note that the entire string has to be treated as a single phrase (NP or PP), since it does not allow scrambling of the words within the string and interspersing them with words of other phrases.

(48) a. Ka. *rāma tanna makkaḷ-ige cākalēṭu koḍis-id-a* (Reflexive)
[Rama refl-poss children-dat chocolate give-past-3m-sg]
'Rama gave chocolates to his children'

b. Ka. *ravi baṭṭe oge-du koṇ-ḍ-a* (Reflexive)
[Ravi clothes wash-ppl refl-past-3m-sg]
'Ravi washed (his) clothes himself (his own sake)'

c. Ka. *bāgilu hāk-i koṇḍ-it-u* (Reflexive)
[door shut-ppl refl-past-3n-sg]
'the door closed itself'

d. Ka. *bassu kāru ond-akk-ondu ḍikki hoḍe-d-avu* (Reciprocal)
[bus car one-dat-one collision hit-past-3n-pl]
'the bus and the car collided with each other'

e. Ka. *obba-bbar-inda aydu rūpāyi togō* (Reciprocal)
[one-one-h-instr five rupee take-imp]
'take five rupees from each person'

In (48a) the reflexive possessive *tanna-* 'his', which is a modifier of an indirect object in a Postpositional Phrase, is coindexed with the antecedent subject NP *rāma.* Sentence (48b) illustrates the use of the reflexive auxiliary. Sentence (48c) is a case of the reflexive auxiliary converting a transitive verb into anti-passive with an inanimate subject NP. Sentence (48d) exemplifies the use of a Reciprocal Phrase with participant referents being [−hum]; in (48e), the ablative PP with the head nominal marked [+ hum], is a Distributive Phrase, used reflexively in discourse, but it has no antecedent NP within the sentence.

Telugu of South Dravidian II also has parallel strategies for both reflexivity and reciprocality. First study the illustrative sentences.

(49) a. Te. *parīkṣa tapp-ina-andu-ku nēnu nann-ē tiṭṭu kon-n-ānu* (Reflexive)
[exam fail-past-adj-noml-dat I I-acc-emph accuse refl-past-1sg]
'I accused myself for failing (in) the examination'

b. Te. *ninnu nīw-ē pogaḍu kon-n-āwu-ṭa* (Reflexive)
[you-acc you-nom-emph praise refl-past-2sg-evid]
'it seems you praised youself'

c. Te. *rāmu tana ātmakatha rāsu-kon-n-āḍu* (Reflexive)
[Ramu self-poss own-story write-refl-past-3m-sg]
'Ramu wrote his autobiography'

d. Te. *kamala [rāmu tana-nu prēmis-tunn-āḍu] an-i anukon-n-adi* (Reflexive)
[Kamala Ramu refl-acc love-dur-3m-sg say-ppl think-past-3f-sg]
'Kamala thought that Ramu is/was loving her'

e. Te. *āyana oka-r-i-ni okar-i-ki paricayam cēs-ǣ-ḍu* (Reciprocal)
[he one-h-acc one-h-dat introduction do-past-3m-sg]
'he introduced (us/them) each other (one to the other)'

f. Te. *mīru okk-okkaru wanda rūpāyalu candā-lu iww-āli* (Reciprocal)
[you-pl one-one-h hundred rupees donation-pl give-must]
'you must all give 100 rupees each (as) donation'

In (49a, b) the personal pronouns themselves have occurred as reflexives, marked by the emphatic *-ē*, and the reflexive auxiliary *kon-* also occurs. In (49c) the reflexive pronoun *tan-a* in the direct object PP is coindexed with the referent of the subject NP, also reinforced by a reflexive verb. Note that in Telugu *kon-* 'take' and *peṭṭ-* 'place', when used as auxiliaries, are mutually complementary, functioning as self-benefactive and non-self-benefactive auxiliaries, respectively, e.g *rāsu kon-* 'write for oneself' vs. *rāsi peṭṭ-* 'write for others', *waṇḍu kon-* 'cook for oneself' vs *waṇḍi peṭṭ-* 'cook for others'.[14] In sentence (49d), the reflexive pronoun in the embedded sentence is coindexed with the subject NP in the matrix sentence, i.e. *kamala*. Sentence 49(e) is an example of the use of a reciprocal compound. If the first constituent is not marked for any oblique case, the whole string becomes a Distributive compound meaning 'each one'.

Strategies of reflexivity (i) through the repetition of personal pronouns in first and second persons and the use of **tān* 'self' a reflexive pronoun for third-person animate, and/or (ii) adding a reflexive auxiliary to the main verb are the shared features of all South Dravidian languages and can be reconstructed for Proto-South Dravidian. The second strategy is also shared by members of the other subgroups and can be reconstructed for Proto-Dravidian, although see section 7.15.

9.8 **Anaphora**

The absence of stringent conditions on word order, combined with case marking on complement NPs and (gender)–number–person marking on the verb, allows deletion of NP arguments, without ambiguity, as a common type of anaphora in discourse, in any continuous narration, or conversation, either in speech or in writing. The missing arguments can be retrieved from pragmatic or discourse contexts. Thus in a Telugu dialogue, note the deletion of all phrases except the ones questioned, in answers:

A: *mīru ekkaḍi-nunci wastunnāru* 'where are you coming from?'
B: *iṇṭi-nunci* 'from home'
A: *ekkaḍiki weḷtunnāru* 'where are you going?'
B. *sinimā-ku* 'to a movie'
A: *aytē, wīḍ(u)-ewaḍu* 'then, who is this boy?'
B: *mā reṇḍō wāḍu* 'our second boy'

14 The auxiliaries *kon-* and *peṭṭ-* are added to the perfective participle of the main verb, marked by *-i* as *rās-i, waṇḍ-i* etc., but the final vowel is changed to *-u* when followed by *kon-* through vowel harmony; note that it is retained before *peṭṭ-*. In spoken Telugu *kon-i* is grammaticalized into *-ku*, which looks like a mere suffix.

All literary Dravidian languages follow the same pattern (Asher 1985: 79–84, Asher and Kumari 1997: 156–7, Sridhar 1990: 115–17, Lehmann 1989: 365–8).

(50) a. Ta. *avar-kaḷ aṭi-pp-ār-kaḷ*
[they-h beat-fut-3h-pl]
'they will beat' (object not stated: me/us, him/her, them, somebody)
b. Ma. *eppō vannu*
[when come-past]
'when did (you/he/she/it/they) come?'
c. Ka. *nenne ravi manege hōg-idd-e*
[yesterday Ravi house-to go-past-1sg]
'yesterday (I) went to Ravi's home' (the subject NP is inferred from the predicate)

A demonstrative pronoun (he/she/it) anaphorically refers to the NP in the preceding clause(s) in the third person. The reflexive pronoun derived from PD **tān/tan-* is used anaphorically for a NP or PP with the head nominal in the third person. Both the governing NP and the reflexive **tān* have to be within the same clause or they have to be coreferential if they are in different clauses. (The subordinate clauses are enclosed in square brackets.)

(51) a. Te. [*rāmu*$_i$ *āfīsu-ku was-tē*] *atan-i-ni*$_i$ *nā daggar-i-ki tīsu-ku-rā*
[Ramu office-dat come-if/when he-acc I-obl presence-dat bring-refl-come-imp]
'when Ramu comes to the office, bring him to me'
b. Te. *kamala*$_i$ [*rāmu*$_j$ *tana-ni*$_i$ *prēmis-tunn-āḍu*] [*an-i*] *anukon-na-di*
[Kamala Ramu she-acc love- dur-3m-sg say-ppl-comp think-past-3f-sg]
'Kamala thought that Ramu is/was loving her'
c. Te. *rādha-ki*$_i$ *tānu*$_i$ *anda-gatte-nu ani telusu*
[Radha-dat she beautiful-female-1sg say-ppl-comp know-hab]
'Radha knows that she is a beautiful woman'
d. Te. *gōpāl*$_i$ [*rāmu*$_j$ *tana-ni*$_j$ *tānu*$_j$ *poguḍu kon-nā-ḍu*] [*ani*] *anukon-n-āḍu*
[Gopal Ramu self-acc self-nom praise-refl-past-3m-sg say-ppl-comp think-past-3m-sg]
'Gopal thought that Ramu praised himself'

Sentence (51a) is what somebody said to somebody. Neither the speaker nor the addressee is specified in the sentence; *nā daggariki* 'to my presence' has the first-person anaphora in *nā-* 'my'. The second person is deleted since that fact is recoverable from the imperative sentence. The demonstrative pronoun *atani-ni* 'him' is coreferential with the subject NP, which occurs in the preceding subordinate clause. If the NP and the reflexive pronoun exchange positions with the same case marking, there will not be any change in meaning, although, in unmarked constituent order, the anaphoric pronoun relates to a preceding NP. In (51b) the reflexive *tana-ni* in the subordinate clause is coindexed with the subject NP, Kamala, in the higher clause. Sentence (51c) has a dative subjective and an irregular verb as predicate. In a simple sentence the reflexive *tānu* always refers to the preceding subject NP. But in a complex sentence there are some constraints on coindexing the reflexive *tānu*. The underlying object clause in (51c) is *nēnu anda-gatte-nu* 'I am a beautiful woman', in which *nēnu* 'I' is replaced by reflexive *tānu* 'self' because the subject of the main clause 'Radha' is in the third person. It is also grammatical to say [*tānu andagatte*] *ani* with NP predicate in the third person instead of first person. In (51d) the reflexive pronoun is reduplicated as an appositive phrase with one member in the nominative and the other marked for a non-nominative case. The reduplicated reflexive refers to the NP within the same clause only. Also note that the verb in the subordinate clause has a reflexive auxiliary (see Subbarao and Lalitha Murthy 2000 for a comprehensive treatment of the phenomenon of anaphora in Telugu).

e. Ta. *kamalā* $_{i}$ [*avaṉ* $_{j}$ *taṉṉ-ai* $_{ij}$ *veṟu-kkiṟ-āṉ*] *eṉ-ṟu niṉai-tt-āḷ*
[Kamala he self-acc hate-pres-3m-sg say-ppl-comp think-past-3f-sg]
'Kamala thought that he hated her/himself'

f. Ma. [*tannōṭa*$_{i}$ *ār-um*$_{j}$ *paṟaññ-illa*] *ennə kamalam*$_{i}$ *āvalāti paṟaññu*
[self-soc anyone say-past-not comp Kamala complain-past]
'Kamala complained that nobody told her'

g. Ka. *sadasyaru*$_{i}$ [*rāma.n-annu tamma*$_{i}$ *pratinidhi*] *y-āg-i cunāyis-id-aru*
[members Rama-acc refl-pl-poss representative-advl elect-past-3h-pl]
'the members elected Rama as their representative'

In (51e) the reflexive is said to ambiguously refer either to *avaṉ* (subject NP of the subordinate clause) or to *kamalā* (subject NP of the main clause) in Tamil (Lehmann 1989: 366). In Telugu in sentences of this type the reflexive only relates to the subject in the matrix and not to that of the subordinate clause. Sentence (51f) in Malayāḷam is a straightforward case of the reflexive *tann-* referring to the subject NP of the matrix clause, *kamalam* 'Kamala', and not to the subject NP of the subordinate clause, *yār-um* 'any one'. In (51g) the embedded clause is a nominal predication *rāma tamma pratinidhi* 'Rama is their representative'. It is linked to the main clause by an adverbial particle *āg-i* 'being, as'; *tamma* 'their', as expected, anaphorically relates to the subject NP in the matrix sentence, *sadasyaru* 'members'.

9.9 Conclusion

The four major Dravidian languages mainly treated in this chapter belong to two sub-groups, South Dravidian I and South Dravidian II. All of them have the same patterns of forming nominal and verbal predications. Malayāḷam is the only member which has innovated the use of a copular verb *āṇə* as predicate in NP–NP type of clauses. In the formation of phrases, complex and compound sentences, and minor sentences etc. all these languages adopt practically the same principles and strategies. Therefore, they definitely go back to an undivided stage of these two branches, namely Proto-South Dravidian. Future research should focus on comparing these patterns with those in other subgroups to find out if they can be reconstructed for Proto-Dravidian.

10

Lexicon

10.1 **Introduction**

The Dravidian lexicon may be divided into native and borrowed. I have drawn on the native lexicon to reconstruct Proto-Dravidian culture in section 1.2.2, based on *DEDR* (1984). The vocabulary is classified into semantic and functional categories like material culture, social organization (including kinship terms), flora and fauna, weather and water resources etc. A wide spectrum of native lexicon is thereby covered. Since the contact of Dravidian with Indo-Aryan goes back to c. 1500 BCE, a number of Dravidian words found their way into Indo-Aryan at all stages, Old, Middle and Modern. Southworth (1995: 264) estimates that 88 lexical items were borrowed into Sanskrit from Dravidian from the Proto-Indo-Iranian period down to Classical. Some aspects of this process have been described in chapter 1 (section 1.7). We find that NIA exhibits more of structural borrowing and less of lexical borrowing from Dravidian. This has been explained as a function of the absorption of a Dravidian substratum into Indo-Aryan from the earliest stages of contact, which gradually affected its grammatical structure over three millennia.

10.2 **Indo-Aryan loanwords in South Dravidian I and II**

The four languages of South Dravidian, after their separation from Proto-South Dravidian, developed their own writing systems (see chapter 3) and became vehicles of literature at different periods, Tamil from the early Christian era, Malayāḷam (an off-shoot of Tamil) from the twelfth century, Kannaḍa from the eighth century and Telugu from the eleventh. Inscriptional records are available in all these languages several centuries earlier than poetic compositions. Although we do not know when these languages came to be exposed to Sanskrit grammar and literature, traces of borrowing from Sanskrit, Pali and Prakrits are found in the literary texts even from the time of Tolkāppiyam (c. late BCE). Apparently some words from Sanskrit were borrowed at a common undivided stage of Tamil and Kannaḍa, i.e. Proto-South Dravidian I, perhaps two or three centuries before Tamil literary texts were composed. This would place the branching off of these to about the fifth century BCE. Contact of these languages with Sanskrit should be placed around that time or slightly earlier. The separation of South Dravidian I and South

Dravidian II (of which Telugu is an offshoot) must have preceded this (the break-up of SD I) by at least three or four centuries, because of atypical shared innovations in SD II, not found in SD I, namely initial apicals and consonant clusters through metathesis and vowel contraction, distinct oblique stems in personal pronouns (section 6.4.1.1–2), different non-animate plural suffix **-nk(k)-* (section 6.2.6), generalization of **-tt-* as past marker (section 7.4.1.2) etc. It is, therefore, not possible for Tamil–Kannaḍa and Telugu to have borrowed from Sanskrit at a common undivided stage. Most probably Telugu borrowed from Sanskrit and Prakrits (Middle Indic) independently. A good example is the word for the numeral 'thousand':

(1) Skt. *sahásra-*, Pkt *sahasira-* > Ta. Ma. *āyiram*, Ko. *cāvrm*, To. *sōfer*, Ka. *sāvira*, *sāsir(a)*, Koḍ. *āirë*, Tu. *sāvira* [*DEDR* Appendix 11].

It appears that Toda and Kota borrowed the item from Kannaḍa, while Koḍagu borrowed it from Malayāḷam. The initial sibilant remains in Kannaḍa, while Tamil and Malayāḷam merge it with *Ø-* (see section 4.5.1.3). Telugu has a native item *wēyi* here and not a borrowed one from Indo-Aryan. This points to the fact that Telugu did not share a common stage of borrowing from Sanskrit with Early Tamil and Kannaḍa. Since the formation of the Prakrits already showed tendencies of a Dravidian substratum (see Bloch 1930), items borrowed from Middle Indic into the literary Dravidian languages already were close to the Dravidian phonological system and would thus give the impression that they were shared borrowings; one such item is Ka. *āma* (< *āwa-*), Tu. *āve*, Te. *āwamu* [< Skt. *āpāka-* 'potter's kiln'; *DEDR* Appendix 12].

In 1962 Emeneau and Burrow published a monograph, *Dravidian Borrowings from Indo-Aryan* (*DBIA*), with 337 entries as a Supplement (actually a Complement) to *DED* (1961). The *DEDR* has an Appendix of 61 items, which is a Supplement to *DBIA*. In the introduction, the authors (1962: 1) say:

> The Dravidian languages at all periods in the record show borrowings from Sanskrit, and there is a tendency for all four of the literary languages in the south to make literary use of the total Sanskrit lexicon indiscriminately, a tendency, seen at its most extreme in Kittel's lexicon of Kannaḍa. The present volume does not record such wholesale borrowing. An attempt has been made to restrict the items to those that have a wide popular, as well as literary, usage. Criteria that are used to determine this are extensions of meaning or far-reaching phonetic changes, or both. Another criterion that has been followed is the penetration of Indo-Aryan words into the non-literary languages of the south (through the intermediacy of the literary languages, of course), whether or not special meaning developments are found.

The items include not only the historically oldest assimilated loans from Middle Indic sources in South Dravidian I, like [55] *ēṇi* 'ladder' (**heṇi-*< Pkt. *seṇi* < Skt. *śreṇi-*),[1] but also some recently borrowed Sanskrit words, which are assimilated later in popular usage with occasional semantic shifts, e.g. [1]:

(2) Skt. *ahaṃ-kāra-* 'pride, haughtiness' > Ta. *akaṅkāram* n. *āṅkāri-* v.i. 'be arrogant', Ma. *ahaṃ-kāram/āṅ-kāram* n, Ka. *ahaṃ-kāra* n, Tu. *ahaṅ-kāra, āṅkāra-* 'self-consciousness', *āṅkariyuni* 'be proud, arrogant', Te. *aham-kāram, ā̃karamu* n. 'pride, arrogance'.

Items such as [3] *akrama-* 'confusion' (→ 'injustice' in Dravidian), [8] *atiśaya-* 'pre-eminence' (→ 'surprise'), Te. *atiśayam-* 'arrogance', [9] *adr̥ṣṭa-* 'invisible, destiny' (→ 'luck'), [24] *avasara-* 'time, opportuity' (→ 'urgency, need'), *udyoga-* 'act of undertaking' (→ 'employment'), [97] *kāla-* 'time', [94] *kārya-* 'action', [92] *kāraṇa-* 'cause' etc. are found, because they also occur in non-literary languages and some have semantic shift in the literary languages.

Some items which are given as loans are perhaps native, since they occur in classical literary texts: [75] Ta. *kapilai, kavalai* 'waterlift', Ka. *kapile, kavile*; Te. *kapila* 'water-lift' occurs in Tikkana's Mahābhārata of the thirteenth century and is not likely to have been borrowed from Hindi *kapi* 'pulley'. Also included in the list are some which came from sources other than Indo-Aryan, e.g. [328] Ta. *vāttu* 'duck, goose', Ma. *bāttu*, Ka. Te. *bātu*, Tu. *battu* is traced to Hindi *bat-*, *batak* 'duck' (<Pers.). This word is traced historically to Portuguese *pato* 'gander'(Kapp 1998: 21), and is attested in a sixteenth-century literary work in Telugu (see below). The Portuguese initial *p-* must have sounded close to a voiced stop which explains *p-* > *b-* as also found in Malayāḷam, Kannaḍa and Telugu. Tamil changes *b-* to *v-*.

The loanwords found in classical texts are traditionally classified into two categories: *tadbhava-* (derived from Prakrits and not directly from Sanskrit; lit. 'derived from that') and *tatsama-* (unassimilated loanwords from Sanskrit; lit. 'same as that'). The earlier stratum shows assimilated loanwords (*tadbhava-*) mostly taken from Pali and Prakrits and some directly from Sanskrit but with phonological changes that suit Dravidian. The spread of Jainism and Buddhism during the early centuries of the CE must have been responsible for the spread of learning Pali and Prakrits in the Dravidian south. There are Prakrit names in the cave inscriptions written in Tamil–Brahmi, c. second century BCE (Meenakshisundaran 1965: 171; Mahadevan 1971: 99).

Tolkāppiyam, an early treatise on Tamil grammar and poetics, already shows several Sanskrit terms like Ta. *ulakam* (< Skt. *loka-*) 'world', *kālam* (< Skt. *kāla-*) 'tense,

[1] Te. *niccena* 'ladder' is derived from Pkt. *nisseṇi* < Skt. *niś-śreṇi-* 'ladder'. This again supports the independent access of Telugu to Sanskrit and Prakrit borrowing. It appears that South Dravidian I innovated the meaning 'ladder' for *ēṇi*, since Skt. *śreṇi* and Pkt. *seṇi* mean 'line, row' and not 'ladder'.

time', *uvamai* (< Skt. *upamā*) 'simile', *kāmam* 'love' (< Skt. *kāma-*). Besides, there are some concepts borrowed and calqued in Tamil, e.g. *tokai* 'compound' (lit. 'combination') from Skt. *samāsa-*, *vēṟṟ-u-mai* 'case' (lit. 'division, separation') from Skt. *vibhakti-* from *vi-bhaj-* 'divide', etc. The Caṅkam anthologies, considered the earliest of Tamil literature, belong broadly to the second century BCE to the third century CE. Even Sanskrit proper names occur extensively, like *kaṅkai* (< *gaṅgā-*) 'Ganges', *yavaṉar* (< Skt. *yavana-*) 'Greeks', beside assimilated loans like *kaṇṇaṉ* (< Pkt. *kaṇha-* < Skt. *kr̥ṣṇa-* 'epic name'). Texts of Middle Tamil literature (300–600 CE) are flooded with borrowed words from Sanskrit and Middle Indic. Vaidyanathan (1982) has identified 764 items in selected literary texts of this period (300–600 CE). A number of them have Prakrit sources, e.g. Ta. *māṇikka-* < Pkt. *māṇikka-* < Skt. *māṇikya-* 'ruby', Ta. *amuta-* < Pkt. *amuta-* < Skt. *amr̥ta-* 'nectar', but many more are taken from Sanskrit as adapted *tatsamas* with different phonological changes, e.g. Ta. *amirtam-* < Skt. *amr̥ta-* 'nectar', Ta. *mētai* < Skt. *mēdhā* 'wisdom', *iravi-* < Skt. *ravi-* 'son', etc. South India became the centre of Sanskrit study and several poets and rhetoricians like Daṇḍin hailed from the south. The popularity of the Sanskrit epics, the Rāmāyaṇa and the Mahābhārata and the spread of Vaiṣṇavism and Saivism in the south led to a greater exposure of the literati to Sanskrit learning. While native personal names are found in the cave inscriptions, the names of kings of the Cōḷa and Cālukya dynasties are all Sanskritic, such as Kulōttuṅga-, Nr̥patuṅga-, Rajarāja-.

Of all the four literary languages Malayāḷam has absorbed Sanskrit more than any other language. It developed a special style called *Maṇipravāḷa*, in which inflected Malayāḷam words are interspersed with inflected Sanskrit words like stringing corals (*pravāḷa*: Sanskrit) and diamonds (*maṇi*: Keraḷabhāṣā or Malayāḷam) together in a necklace. Most literary works from Rāmacaritam (twelfth century CE) to Eẓutaccan's Mahābhāratam (seventeenth century) were composed in this style, which facilitated the absorption of an enormous amount of Sanskrit vocabulary into Malayāḷam (Gopalakrishnan 1985, Sukumara Pillai 1985, Prabodhachandran Nayar 1985, Gopinathan Pillai 1985: 31–98).

Pampa's Vikramārjuna Vijayam alias Samasta Bhārata, the first major literary work of Kannaḍa (tenth century CE), and the Āndhra-Māhābhārata of Telugu by Nannaya (eleventh century CE) show extensive importation of Sanskrit words and compounds into these languages. This tradition is followed by all successive writers in any standard poetic work. As a consequence of extensive borrowing of the *tatsama* element from Sanskrit, the phonological inventories of Malayāḷam, Kannaḍa and Telugu have been enlarged by the addition of ten aspirated stops /ph th ch ṭh kh bh dh jh ḍh gh/, fricative /h/, and two sibilants /ś ṣ/. Vocalic *r̥ l̥* of Sanskrit have been added to the alphabet and in spelling Sanskrit words in writing, although they were pronounced [ri~ru] and [lu], respectively. Voiced stops became phonemic in these languages through internal changes as well as through borrowed vocabulary from Indo-Aryan.

The *tadbhava* loanwords, which follow native phonology, represent an earlier chronological stratum of borrowing in all literary languages, e.g.

(3) Ma. *bōy*, Ka. *bōya*, *bōyi*, Tu. *bōyi*, *bōvi*, Te. *bōya*, *bōyaḍu* (m sg), *bōyeta* (f sg) 'palanquin bearer, fisherman', Go. *pōī* 'male of fisherman caste' [*DEDR* Appendix 51; Skt. *bhōgin-*, Pkt. *bhōi-* 'headman of a village'; *CDIAL* 9623; Emeneau 1980e: 315–25].

Deaspiration of *bh-* to *b-* in most of the languages and devoicing in Gondi are significant aspects of assimilation.

(4) Ta. *toṉṉai*, Ka. Te. *donne*, Tu. *donnɛ* 'leaf-cup', Gad. *dona*, Go. *ḍona*, Koṇḍa *done*, Kui *ḍono*, Kuvi *dunnō* 'leaf-cup' [*DEDR* Appendix 45; from Skt. *droṇa-*; *CDIAL* 6641].

Simplification of initial consonant cluster is an aspect of assimilation to Dravidian.

10.3 Phonological principles governing loanwords from Indo-Aryan

The following is a selected list of items drawn from *DBIA* (1962). The number in square brackets refers to the entry in *DBIA*.

(5) Skt. *agni* 'fire' > Pali, Pkt. *aggi* > SD I: Ta. *akki*, Ma. *akki*, Koḍ. *agg-* v.t. 'fire consumes', Tu. *aggi*; SD II: Te. *aggi* [5].

(6) Skt. *ārdra*(*ka*)- 'fresh ginger' > Pkt. *alla-*, *allaa* > SD I: Ta. *allam*, Ka. *alla*; SD II: Te. *allamu*, Kuvi *alomi* id. [22].

(7) Skt. *ājñā-* 'order, command' > Pkt. *āṇā* > SD I: Ta. *āṇai* 'command, oath', Ma. *āṇa*, Ka. *āṇe*; Koḍ. *āṇe ïḍ-* 'to curse', Tu. *āṇe* 'oath'; with the verb *iṭu*/*iḍu* 'put', it means 'to swear' in all; SD II: Te. *āna* 'command', *āna-beṭṭu* 'adjure' [32].

(8) Skt. *avalagna-* 'hanging down from' > Pkt. *olagga-* 'to do service', *olaggā* 'attendance' > SD I: Ta. *ōlakkam* 'assembly of state', Ma. *ōlakkam* 'splendour, majesty', Ka. *ōlaga-* 'service, homage, assembly', Tu. *ōlaga*/*-e* 'royal assembly'; SD II: Te. *ōlagamu* 'court held by a king' [63].

(9) Skt. *gr̥dhra-* 'vulture' > Pali, Pkt. *gaddha-* > SD II: Te. *gradda* (>*gadda*), Go (Koya) *gadda*; CD: Kol. Nk. Pa. *gadda* (perhaps lws from Te.) [83].

(10) Skt. *kamsa-* 'bell-metal, brass, vessel made of metal' > SD I: Ta. *kañcam* 'bell metal, drinking vessel', *kañcakāraṉ* 'brazier', To. *koc* 'brass', Ka. *kañcu*, *kañca* 'brass, vessel made of bell-metal', *kañcagāṟa* 'brazier', Tu. *kañci*, *kañcu* 'bell metal', *kañcigāre* 'brazier'; SD II: Te. *kancu* 'brass', *kancam* 'plate made of any metal', *kancara* 'brazier' [67].

(11) Skt. *kāṣṭha-* > Pkt. *kaṭṭha-* 'piece of wood' > SD I: Ta. *kaṭṭai* 'firewood, log', Ko. *kaṭ*, To. *kaṭy*, Ka. *kaṭṭige* 'timber, stick', Tu. *kaṭṭige* 'fuel,

firewood'; SD II: Te. *kaṭṭiya*, *kaṭṭe* 'fuel, stick', Go. *kaṭīā*, *kaṭiya*, *kaṭṭe* (dial). The Dravidian forms presuppose Skt. **kāṣṭh-ikā-* with a diminutive suffix and Pkt. **kaṭṭh-iā* [68].

(12) Skt. *śrēṣṭhin-* 'person of authority, head of a guild'> Pali Pkt. *seṭṭi-* 'merchant'. Ta. *ceṭṭi* 'Vaiśya caste man', *ceṭṭicci* f, *eṭṭi* 'title of distinction conferred on persons of the Vaiśya caste', Ma. *ceṭṭi* m, *ceṭṭicci* f id.; *ceṭṭyān*, *eṭṭiyān* 'one of the foreign merchant classes', To. *siṭy* 'man of Chetti caste (Tamilaian)', Ka. *seṭṭi* 'merchant, banker'; SD II: Te. *seṭṭi* 'merchant' [175].

(13) Skt. *bhojana-* 'eating, meal' > Pkt. *bhoaṇa*, *bhoṇa* > SD I: Ta. *pōṉakam*, *pōṉam* 'food, boiled rice', Ka. *bōna* 'cooked food', Tu. *bōna*; SD II: Te. *bōnamu* 'food, boiled rice' [281].

(14) Skt. *maryādā-* 'frontier, limit, custom, propriety' > SD I: Ta. *mariyātai*, *maruvāti* 'limit, courtesy, customs', Ma. *mar(i)yāda* (written with *d*, not *t*) id., Ko. *marvādy*, *marādy* 'respect', Koḍ. *mariyādi* 'custom, honour, respect', To. *marso θy* 'respect', Ka. *mar(i)yāde* 'limit, propriety, custom, respect', Tu. *mar(i)yādi/a* 'custom, usage, respect'; SD II: Te. *mar(i)yāda* 'respect, custom' [289].

In the above groups, except for (10) and (14), all loanwords recorded for Dravidian are phonologically closer to Pali and Prakrit forms than to Sanskrit. There is no doubt that these entered the Dravidian languages from Pali/Prakrits, which were the spoken forms of Middle Indic. It means that *tadbhav*-ization had already taken place in Prakrits, because of the Dravidian substrate among Prakrit speakers, and that facilitated borrowing into the surviving Dravidian speech communities. Item (14) from Sanskrit does not offer any phonetic problem in Dravidian; therefore, it is taken almost as a *tatsama*. Item (10) has *-ms-* (nasal stop + sibilant) in Sanskrit which is not allowed by Dravidian phonotactics, hence it is assimilated to nasal + affricate *-nc-* [ñc] as expected. Another important aspect to be noted from the above list (as the authors of *DBIA* have already mentioned) is that the non-literary languages had borrowed these items from the neighbouring literary languages, because borrowing from Indo-Aryan happened, in the initial stages, only in literate speech communities.

The phonological changes found in the major literary languages in the formation of *tadbhavas* (irrespective of chronological routing) are as follows:

(15) (i) deaspiration of stops and loss of /h/;
(ii) *ś ṣ* > *s/c*; loss of Pkt *s-* in early loanwords; *ṣ* > *ẓ*, *ṭ* [ḍ] in Tamil and Malayāḷam;
(iii) assimilation of heterogeneous clusters of consonants or vowel insertion between such consonants;

(iv) simplification of word-initial clusters by loss of a consonant or by splitting them by inserting a vowel (anaptyxis or *svarabhakti*);
(v) developing a prothetic vowel before word-initial *r* and *l*;
(vi) shortening of non-initial long vowels; also those before -CC, irrespective of position;
(vii) replacement of Skt. *r̥* (a vocalic segment) by V/*r*V/V*r*;
(viii) devoicing of word-initial voiced stops (mainly in Tamil–Malayāḷam) and voicing or lenition of intervocalic single voiceless stops, i.e. /g s ḍ d w/ ← Skt. /k c ṭ t p/;
(ix) replacement of Sanskrit diphthongs *āi āu* by *ay aw*;
(x) replacement of Sanskrit word initial *y*- by *j*-, perhaps through Prakrits.

Several of these can be detected in items (3) to (14) listed above. Some more examples are given under each language to show how the above principles apply to loanwords, irrespective of the intermediate stages; roman numbers in brackets after the entry refer to those under (15). Examples:

(16) Tamil
ñāṉam 'knowledge' < Skt. *jñāna*- (iv)
cūttiram 'aphorism' < Skt. *sūtra*- (iii)
irutu 'season' < Skt. *r̥tu*- (vii)
virutti- 'growth' < *vr̥ddhi*- (i, vii)
urōma- 'hair' < Skt. *rōma*- (v)
tōcam [tosam] 'fault' < *dōṣa*- (ii, viii)
ceṭṭi 'foreman of a guild' < *śrēṣṭhin*- (i, ii, iii, iv)
ulakam 'world' < Skt. *loka*- (v)
aracaṉ 'king' < Skt. *rājan*- (v)
tiraviyam 'substance' < Skt. *dravya*- (iv, viii)

(17) Malayāḷam (Gopalakrishnan 1985: 31–50)
kētam 'affliction' < Skt. *khēda*- (i)
kakanam 'sky' < *gaganam* (viii)
ñānam 'knowledge' < Skt. *jñāna*- (iv)
caci < Skt. *śaśi* 'moon' (ii)
tavam 'penance' < Skt. *tapas*- (viii)
uruvam 'form' < Skt. *rūpa*- (v)
iṭavam 'name of a monkey' < Skt. *r̥ṣabha*- (i, ii, vii)
puruvam 'eyebrow' < Skt. *bhrū*- (i, iv, viii)
uma < Skt. *umā*- (vi)
ēṇi 'ladder' < Pkt. *sēṇi*-< Skt. *śrēṇi*- (ii, iv)
aran < Skt. *hara*- (i)

catti 'lance' < *śakti* (iii)
cakkira 'wheel' < Skt. *cakra-* (iii)

(18) Kannaḍa (Ramachandra Rao 1972)
akkaram 'letter' < Skt. *akṣara-* (iii)
arasu 'king' < Skt. *rājan-* (v)
āgasam 'sky' < Skt. *ākāśa-* (vi, viii)
kappura- 'camphor' < Skt. *karpūra-* (iii, vi)
kabba- 'a poetical work' < Skt. *kāvya-* (iii)
kanci 'a place name' < Skt. *kāñci-* (vi)
katturi 'musk' < Skt. *kastūri* (iii, viii)
kara 'sharp' < Skt. *khara-* (i)
kavila- 'brown coloured cow' < Skt. *kapilā-* (viii)
kajjam 'work, business' (< Pkt. *kajja-*) < Skt. *kārya-* (iii, x)
jaḍe- 'matted hair' < Skt. *jaṭā-* (viii)
javvana- 'youth' < Skt. *yāuvana-* (ix, x)
dese 'direction' < Skt. *diśā-* (ii)
diṭṭi 'look' < Skt. *dṛṣṭi-* (iii, vii)
pasādam 'free gift' < Skt. *prasāda-* (iv)
bannam 'ruin, destruction' < Skt. *bhagna-* (i, iii)

(19) Telugu
akkaramu 'letter' < Skt. *akṣara-* (iii)
aradamu 'chariot' < Skt. *ratha-* (i, v, viii)
ākasamu 'sky' < *ākāśa-* (ii, vi)
kata 'story' < Skt. *katha-* (i)
kappuramu 'camphor' < Skt. *karpūra-* (iii, vi)
garuwamu 'arrogance' < Skt. *garva-* (iii)
kanci 'a place name in Tamil Nadu' < Skt. *kāñci-* (vi)
kawila 'brown-coloured cow' < Skt. *kapilā-* (vi, viii)
batti 'devotion' < Skt. *bhakti-* (i, iii)
ceṭṭi/*seṭṭi* 'a merchant' < Skt. *śrēṣṭhin-* (i, ii, iii, iv, vi)
diṣṭi 'evil eye' < Skt. *dṛṣṭi-* (vii)
jawwanamu 'youth' < Skt *yāuvana-* (ix, x)
uṅkuwa 'fee' < Skt. *śulka-* (ii – with change of *-lk* to *ṅk*)

Among the *tadbhavas*, those which had lost the word-initial sibilant (through an intermediate stage of **h-*), e.g. *ēṇi* 'ladder', *āyiram* 'thousand', etc. and also words that have a prothetic vowel before Skt. *r-* and *l-*, e.g. *aracaṉ*, *arasu* 'king', belong to the earliest stratum. All literary languages have developed word-initial *r*, *l* through later borrowing or through internal changes, e.g. Ta. *ranṭu* 'two' by the time of Middle Tamil. The rest of the changes are prompted by the phonological structure of the Dravidian languages, namely deaspiration, intervocalic stop lenition/voicing, assimilation of consonant clusters. Their application in different languages independently would also give the same output. Hence, we cannot set up a common stage of borrowing involving these changes in all cases. Even by the earliest literary period of Kannaḍa and Telugu (8–10 CE) the *tatsama* stage came with more scholars adopting unassimilated words into the poetic dialect. Perhaps the speech of the uneducated masses still converted the words that they needed to use as *tadbhavas*.

10.4 Loanwords from Perso-Arabic sources

During the six centuries of Moghul rule of north India and over three centuries of the Bahmani Sultans of Deccan (fourteenth to eighteenth centuries), the major languages of south India borrowed a number of words of Persian (the state language) and Arabic (the religious language) origin. From the fifteenth century onwards these words found their way into South Dravidian through Dakkhini Urdu. Village officials dealing with land records used many administrative terms relating to land revenue and legislation, which have become part of the common language, e.g. Te. *gumāstā* 'clerk', *sistu* 'cess', *tahasīl* 'land tax', *kāyitam* 'paper', *dastāwēz* 'document', *cirunāmā* 'address', *rājī* 'compromise', *munasabu* 'munisiff, a village administrator', *jillā* 'district', *tālūkā* 'town, a subdivision of a zilā', etc. The *Tamil Lexicon* has recorded more than a thousand Urdu words (Meenakshisundaran 1965: 188).

10.5 Loanwords from western languages: Portuguese and English

The Portuguese was the first western nation to come to India (early sixteenth century) and it 'was the mediator of terms for products, artefacts and institutions of pre-industrial Europe' (Masica 1991: 73). The hot chillies and tobacco were brought to India by the Portuguese. The number of words taken from Portuguese is no more than one hundred in any of the modern languages but they represent many commonly used items like 'soap', 'towel', 'key', 'cabbage' etc. which continue in usage even now. The terms cited for Tamil are: *paṟanki* (< *Franco*) 'a Frenchman, a foreigner', Ta. *vāttu* 'duck', *cā* 'tea', *alamāri* 'almairah', *cāvi* 'key', *mēcai* 'table', *pēṣk-ar* (< Port. *fiscal*) 'cashier' (final *-ar*, h pl hon suffix), *āyā* 'dry nurse', *koyyā* 'Guava tree and fruit'. Kapp (1998) has traced Portuguese as the source of a number of Telugu and Kannaḍa words and several of these are used in the modern standard languages, e.g.

(20) Words borrowed from Portuguese

Portuguese	Telugu	Kannaḍa	Gloss
aia 'dry nurse'	*āyā*	–	'baby sitter'
armário 'cupboard'	*almara*	*almāri/u*	'wardrobe'
camisa 'shirt'	*kamīju*	*kamisu*	'shirt'

chave 'key'	*cavi/cevi*	*chavi/sāvi*	'key'
estirar 'stretch out'	*istrī*	*istri /istari*	'ironing of clothes'
hospital 'hospital'	*āspatri*	*āspatri*	'hospital'
meia(s) 'sock(s)'	*mē-jōḍu/jōḷḷu*	*mē-jōḍu*	'pair of socks' (*jōḍu* 'pair')
mesa 'table'	*mējā*	*mēju*	'table'
mestre 'master'	*mēstrī*	*mēstre/i*	'foreman'
pena 'writing pen'	*pēnā*	*pēnu*	'pen'
pipa 'a barrel, cask'	*pīpā*	*pīpe*	'a drum'
toalha 'towel'	*tuw(w)āla*	*tuvāl*	'a towel'
sabão 'soap'	*sabbu*	*sab(b)u*	'soap'
pato 'duck'	*bātu*	*bātu*	'duck'

All the above words are still in vogue in modern standard languages. Unlike English words which can be easily detected, the Portuguese loans have lost traces of their historical origin and they are considered native Telugu and Kannaḍa words, even by educated people. The earliest usage of a Portuguese word in Telugu is *bātu(wu)* 'duck' in a sixteenth-century poem Āmuktamālyada (1:65) by Kr̥ṣṇadeva Rāya who ruled both Andhra and Karnataka states during the early sixteenth century.

Loanwords from English progressively got established from the beginning of the nineteenth century and each of the major languages has hundreds of them, many assimilated into the native fold. Each language has also borrowed independently and adjusted them to the native phonological system. In borrowing English loanwords, certain features are shared by the four major languages (see Krishnamurti 1998c: 190–201): (i) English alveolar /t/ is replaced by Dravidian retroflex /ṭ/; (ii) English /v w/ are replaced by Dravidian /w/; (iii) spelling pronunciation is rampant, creating double consonants like /bʌṭṭʌr/ for Eng. *butter*, etc.; (iv) a [y] onglide is added to words beginning with a front vowel and [w] onglide to words beginning with a back rounded vowel, e.g. Eng. *ink* [iŋk] → SD [yiŋk], E. *ooze* [u:z] → SD [wūz].

Words used by most people, understood even by the uneducated, include items such as *office, coffee, telephone, road, school, radio, television, college, cinema, bank, police, post, stamp, station, money order, card, cover* etc. Both code-switching and code-mixing are extensively prevalent when two or more people who are educated in English meet and talk. There is more bilingualism in English now than when the British left in 1947. For more details, see Krishnamurti (1998c: 308–17).

10.6 Neologisms

The four major literary languages are spoken by over 95 per cent of the total population of the Dravidian speakers (220 million). Three of these languages have modern standard varieties for writing and formal communication. The standard varieties are based on the educated speech of a cultural centre in each case: for Kannaḍa, the Bangalore–Mysore area, for Telugu, the central coastal districts (Gunturu, Krishna, East and West Godavari) and for Malayāḷam the Tiruvananthapuram–Cochin area, which corresponds to the old feudatory state of Travancore–Cochin. Although there was a *Paccamalayāḷam* movement like the 'pure Tamil movement', it has had no impact on modern creative writers. In Medieval Telugu also there was an attempt to write poems in native Telugu (*accatelugu*), but it did not develop into a cultural movement. Malayāḷam goes a step beyond the other two major languages and uses inflected Sanskrit words and phrases in modern writings and discourse, e.g. *svayam eva* 'spontaneously', *svapne'pi* 'even in a dream', *kim api* 'how much' (Gopalakrishnan 1985: 47). This style in speech is undoubtedly a consequence of the spread of *Maṇipravāḷa* as a favoured mode of writing in Keraḷa for several centuries (Sukumara Pillai 1985).

Tamil has a diglossic situation:[2] the written and formal spoken forms are based on an older literary dialect (see Ferguson 1964: 435, Krishnamurti 1998c: 141–64), not on any modern regional variety. This is not always a pure literary variety but tends to have the phonology and morphophonemics of the classical language. In Tamil, 'in the first quarter of the twentieth century, a purist movement arose . . . it is against the use of foreign, especially Sanskrit words' (Meenakshisundaran 1965: 175). The purist movement was part of a cultural Renaissance against the rise of Brahmins and Brahminism with whom the spread of Sanskrit was associated. Around 1900 CE, it was estimated that about 45–50 per cent of the vocabulary in Tamil was Sanskritic. 'The influence of Sanskrit within the last fifty years has been reduced to about 20% of the vocabulary' (Zvelebil 1975 citing a political scientist's estimate).

As evidence of lexical modernization in Tamil, the following forms of native origin have replaced Sanskrit terms, so far in use, cited by Zvelebil (1975):

(21)	Adapted Sanskrit term	Tamil equivalent (current)
	parīkṣai (Skt. *parīkṣā-*)	→ *tērvu* 'examination'
	cinēkitaṉ (Skt. *snēhita-*)	→ *tōẓan* 'friend'
	pustakam (Skt. *pustaka-*)	→ *nūl* 'book'
	carvakalācālai (Skt. *sarvakalāśālā-*)	→ *pal-kalai.k-kaẓakam* 'university, an assembly of many faculties'
	pāṣācāstiram (Skt. *bhāṣāśāstra-*)	→ *moẓi-iyal* 'science of language, linguistics' etc.

[2] I am using 'diglossia' in the original sense in which it was used by Ferguson and not in its later usage by several writers for stylistic differences of any kind to be found in any literate speech community. For a detailed discussion of this phenomenon, see Britto (1986).

Zvelebil (1975: 439) endorses these attempts at nativization of general and technical terms and says that they 'often increase efficiency, economy and precision of the language'. Other linguists may consider this reform as an unnecessary interference with the normal growth of a language through time-honoured processes of borrowing. Much time would be wasted if assimilated English loanwords like *radio*, *telephone*, *station* etc. were to be replaced by newly coined native terms, which have to be learnt afresh by everybody. The other languages do not have any trace of this trend, which means that speakers of these languages consider borrowing as a natural corollary of growth.

10.6.1 *Language of news media*

In 1978 a seminar was held at Osmania University on the modernization of Indian languages in news media and a publication was brought out with adequate case material from nine major Indian languages (Krishnamurti and Mukherji 1984). Telugu, Kannaḍa and Tamil were included in the study. It was noticed that there were eight processes underlying new coinages in different languages, based on English models. These have developed independently in each language (see Krishnamurti 1984; 1998: 227–48). They are: (i) total borrowing as *tatsamas* (with phonetic adaptation); (ii) loan blends, i.e. partial borrowing combining native and non-native constituents; (iii) loan translation or calquing; (iv) 'adaptive coining', i.e. coining a new expression with native or Sanskritic elements which strike the native writers as the best translation of a given expression in English; (v) paraphrasing; (vi) assigning a new meaning to some traditional expressions; (vii) extending the meaning of existing words (loan shift) by using an old word in a new context, or creating translation equivalents within the native stock; (viii) totally coining new terms within the cultural matrix of native speakers after assimilating a non-native concept into native consciousness. A few examples, mainly from the major literary languages, will illustrate these processes.

(22)(I) Loanwords

English	Telugu	Kannaḍa	Tamil
bank	*byānku* [bæŋku]	*byānku* [bæŋku]	*bēnk*
hotel	*hōṭal*	*hōṭēlu*	*ōṭṭal*
police	*pōlīsu*	*pōlīs*	*pōlīs*

(II) Loan blends

writ petition	*riṭ darakhāstu* [Eng. + Pers.][3]	*riṭ arjī* [Eng. + Pers.]	–
World Bank	*prapanca byānku* [Skt. + Eng.]	*wiśva byānku* [Skt. + Eng.]	*ulaku vanki* [Ta. + Eng.]

[3] Here the Persian originals have been taken through the route of Dakkhini (Urdu of south India).

small-scale industry	Te. *cinna-tarhā-pariśrama* [Te. small-Ur. type-Skt. industry]
state lottery	Ka. *rājya lāṭarī* [Skt. state-Eng. lottery]

(III) Loan translations

English	Telugu	Kannaḍa	Tamil
black money	*nalla dhanam* [Te. + Skt.]	*kappu haṇa* [Ka. + Ka.]	*karuppu paṇam* [Ta. + Ta.]
black market	*nalla bajāru* [Te. + Ur.]	*kāḷa sante* [Skt. + Ka.]	–

(IV) Adaptive coining

English	Telugu	Kannaḍa	Tamil
agitation	*āndōḷaṇa* [Skt.]	*āndōḷaṇa* [Skt.]	–
agriculture	*sēdyam* [Te.]	*kṛṣi* [Skt.]	*makasūl* [Ur.]
transport	*rawāṇā* [Ur.]	*sārige* [Ka.]	*pōkkuvaruttu* [Ta.]

self^1-sufficiency^2	Te. *swayam*^{1} *samruddhi*^{2} [Skt. + Skt.]
in^1-patient^2	Ka. *oḷa*^{1} *rōgi*^{2} [Ka. + Skt.]
cross^1-examination^2	Ta. *kar̲ukku*^{1} *visāriṇai*^{2} [Ta. + Skt.]
inquiry^1 committee^2	Ka. *tanikhī*^{1} *samiti*^{2}[Ur. + Skt.]

The difference between (iii) and (iv) is subtle; (iii) is a literal translation of the model, word by word; (iv) is also a translation but not literal; each language has a way of considering what would be the best way of rendering the model in such a way that it would sound natural in the language concerned. Note that the resource language for coining can be native or any other language which has become nativized like Sanskrit or Urdu.

(V) Paraphrasing

'non-aligned' : Te. *ē* *rājya-kūṭāni-kī* *cend-a-ni*
[whichever nation-group-dat belong-neg-adj]
'not belonging to any groups of nations'

(VI) Semantic reinterpretation

Some established Sanskrit expressions are given a new context and meaning, e.g.

radio	Te. *ākāśa-wāṇi* [Skt. + Skt.], Ta. *vān̲-oli* [Ta. + Ta.] 'sky-voice' (originally 'an invisible voice from the sky foreboding future events')
fuel	Te. *indhanam* (originally 'dry wood used in sacrificial fire')
missile	Ka. *brahmāstra* ('Brahma's arrow', epic meaning 'an arrow which never fails to destroy the target, a powerful weapon')

(VII) Loan-shifts

Using established words in new contexts:

New meaning	Traditional meaning
reserve (of funds)	Te. *nilawa* ‘saving’(lit. ‘that which is stationary’)
industry	Ka. *kai-gārike* ‘hand-work’
seniority	Ka. *jyeṣṭhate* ‘elderliness’
aim	Ta. *kuṟi* ‘aim to shoot at’

(VIII) Idiomatic translation or creative coining

smuggled goods	Te. *donga saruku* [stolen goods]
black-marketing	Te. *donga wyāpāram* [thief business]
injection	Te. *sūdi mandu*, Ka. *cuccu maddu* [needle medicine]
television	Ta. *paṭa rēḍiyō* [picture radio]

The foregoing examples give a fair idea of the way the major languages are building different registers for modern communication.

10.7 Structured semantic fields

Proto-Dravidian had only four basic terms for colour, white, black, red, yellow–green (see section 8.2.1: items 5–8). Among kinship terms there are expressions for ‘man, woman, father, mother, daughter, son, younger and elder brother, younger and elder sister’ (see section 1.2.2.3). The remaining are restricted to certain languages or subgroups. In modern languages, many new combinations have been innovated for other kin relations, particularly for the second ascending generation (grandfather, grandmother) or the second descending generation (grandson, granddaughter), for parallel and cross-cousins and their parents etc. These have been discussed in section 1.2.2.3. A brief survey of body parts is stated below. Only words denoting the following are reconstructable for Proto-Dravidian.

(23) Reconstructed words for body-parts

body	**may-(mt)-* SD I, II, > **mē-nd-* SD II, CD, ND [5099]; **oṭal* SD I and SD II; also means ‘chest, stomach’ [585].
bone	**el-*V*-mp/-nk* SD I; Te. [839], **peẓ-an*, SD II [4418] ‘bone, stone of fruit’.
breast	**mul-ay* SD I [4985], Te. *cannu*; **pāl* ‘milk’; SD II (Go. Koṇḍa); CD (Pa.) ‘woman’s breast’ [4096]; the semantic shift is witnessed only in some languages of central India.
ear	**kewi* SD I, SD II, CD, ND[1977a]; **kir-*V- Tu. of SD I and Kui–Kuvi of SD II [1977b].
eye	**kaṇ* SD I, SD II, CD, ND [1159a].
finger	**wir-al* SD I, Te.; *wir-and /-anj* SD II, CD [5409].

foot	**aṭ*-V, SD I, **aṭ*-V-*k*- SD II 'foot, bottom, base', CD [72].
hand	**kay* [2023] SD I, SD II, CD, ND 'hand, arm' [2019].
head	**talay* 'head, hair, top' SD I, SD II, ND; also 'honeycomb' Pa., Nk., Go. [3103].
heart	**kuṇṭi* 'heart, kidney' SD I, SD II, CD, ND [1693].
intestines	**kuṭ-al* SD I [1652], **piẓ-ul* CD, Go. [4193].
knee	**moẓ*-V- 'joint', *moẓ-am kāl/-kay* 'knee, elbow' SD I, SD II, CD, ND [4990].
leg	**kāl* SD I, SD II, CD, ?Brahui *trikkal* 'tripod'; 'leg/foot' [1479].
mouth	**wāy* 'mouth (edge, beak, mouth of vessel, aperture, blade of sword)' SD I, SD II, CD, ND [5352].
liver	**taẓ*-V-*nk/-nkk* SD II, SD II (except Telugu), Tu. and CD [3120], **ir*-V*l/w* SD I [546].
nail	**ukir* 'finger nail, toe-nail' SD I, **gōr*/ **kōr* SD II, CD, Br.; **or-kk*- Kuṛ.–Malt. [561].
navel	**boṭ*-V- SD I, SD II, ND [4460b], **pok-kuẓ*-V- SD I, SD II, CD [4460a].
neck/throat	**kaẓ-u-tt*- SD I, *kaẓ-nt*(*t*)- Tu., CD, SD II [1366]; *ku-nt-/ntt-* ~ *ko-nt-/ntt-* 'throat, voice, tone' SD I, SD II [1718].
nose	**mū-nk*(*k*)*u* SD I, SD II, CD, *mū-nc*- ND 'nose, beak' [5024]
skin	**tokk-*/**tokal*/ **tōl* SD I, SD II, CD [3559].
skull	**puṯ*-V 'gourd shell, skull' SD I, SD II, CD [4332].
stomach	**poṭṭ-/poṭ*-V- 'belly, stomach, pregnancy, intestines' SD I, SD II, CD, ND [4494]; **wac*-V*ṯ* SD I, SD II [5259], *wac*-V-(*kk*) Koṇḍa–Kui–Kuvi–Pe.–Maṇḍa; *was*-V*r*-, *way-nc*- Tu. [5259].
tendon, nerve	**ñar-ampu* 'tendon' ('nerve, sinew, vein, pulse') SD I, SD II, CD [2903].
thigh	**kuṯ-u-k/u-w* SD I, SD II, CD, ND 'thigh (of human or animal)', **kuṯ-a-nk/-nkk* SD I [1840].
tongue	**nā-l*, *nā-l-k(k)* SD I, SD II, *nā-nk*- (<***nāl-nk-k*) CD [3633].
tooth	**pal* SD I, SD II, CD, ND; by extension 'harrow' in Ta. Te. [3986a].

A comparative listing of basic vocabulary is not attempted here, since many Proto-Dravidian reconstructions occur in different places throughout this volume: kinship terms (chapter 1), personal pronouns (chapter 6), numerals (chapter 6), body parts (above) and basic verbs and adjectives (chapters 7 and 8) and many widely represented etymologies under comparative phonology (chapter 4).

There is one other aspect of interest in the Dravidian lexicon, i.e. expressives, which include onomatopoetic expressions, echo words and lexical reduplicatives. There is overlap among these three categories. All of these are found in the literary languages from the time of early records and need to be considered as a heritage of Proto-Dravidian.

10.8 Strategies of expressives

10.8.1 *Onomatopoetic expressions or ideophones*

Emeneau (1969a: 274–99; repr. 1980a: 250–93) has discussed this phenomenon in comparison with Indo-Aryan counterparts. Abbi (1992) has dealt with 'reduplication' as a cover term for 'expressives, echo-words, grammatical and lexical reduplicatives' comprehensively for the whole of South Asia. Apparently, the phenomenon of onomatopoeia is found in many language families and is not an areal feature of South Asia alone. However, the phonological and morphological aspects for each family are unique. In Dravidian Emeneau proposes two types of onomatopoeia, namely non-reduplicated and reduplicated. The non-reduplicated ones generally have the structure (C)VCVCC-/CVC-V̄C- with the second syllable longer than the first which is not a favoured type of lexeme in non-ideophones. Both the types can be verbalized with an inflected form of the verb **aHn-* 'say' (> *ān/an-/en-/in-*).

(24) Non-reduplicated

A. Telugu

(i) Adverbials marked by *-na*, e.g. *digg-ana* 'suddenly' (OTe.), *gabhāl(u)-na* 'urgently', *dabukku-na* 'suddenly', *bhaḷḷu-na* 'coming of dawn', *bhōru-na* 'weeping loudly', *guṭukku-na* 'swallowing fast', *gammu-na* 'silently', *pheḍēl-na* 'cracking up', *gappu-na* 'fire flashing', *cappu-na* 'quickly', *ṭhappu-na* 'sounding thap' etc.

(ii) With *-an* 'say': *curukku-m-an* 'a body part burns with a heated object suddenly', *thaḷukku-m-an* 'flash like lightning' etc.

B. Kota

(i) With the verb *-in* 'say', e.g. *daṇak in-* 'become limp with fatigue', *kuḷak in-* 'body feels cool'.

(ii) With an adverbial marker *-n*, e.g. *burak-n* 'suddenly', *diḍak-n* 'in a flash', *dabak-n* 'with noise of falling', *paṭār-n* 'with noise of breaking'.

(iii) With -V̄*l*: *daḍ-āl* 'with a sudden jerk', *car-īl* 'with the noise of snake's motion'.

The reduplicated ones are more numerous and widely represented. Several of these can be reconstructed for Proto-Dravidian. A few examples from *DEDR*:

(25) PD **kala-kala-* > SD I: Ta. *kalakala* (*-pp-*, *-tt-*) 'rustle, tinkle, rattle', *kalakalam* 'chirping of birds', *kaḷakaḷ*(*a*)-*eṉ-al* [sound-say-noml] 'tinkling', Ma. *kaḷakaḷa* 'confused noise', Ka. *kalakala* 'buzz of a crowd', *galagala*/*gaḷagaḷa* 'rattling, clinking', Tu. *kalakala* 'hum', *galagala* 'noise of bracelets etc.'; SD II: Te. *kalakala* 'confused noise, buzz of a crowd', *kalakala-l-āḍu* 'to shine forth, glow on face', *galagala-l-āḍu* v.i 'sound of bracelets, metal ornaments, coins, etc.', Go. *kalla* 'uproar, commotion', Kuvi *kālori ā-* 'to shout'; CD: Nk. (Ch.) *kalla* 'noise'; ND: *qal-qal-tre* 'shake water or cowries'| Skt. *kala-* 'soft melodious sound'; *CDIAL* 2914 [1302].

Note that there is a meaning difference between *kalakala* and *galagala* in Telugu and Kannaḍa.

(26) **tapa-tapa* or?**daba-daba* 'imitating walking fast' > SD I: Ta. *tapukk-eṉ* '[*tapukk*-say], rashness, haste', Ko. *dabāl in-* 'noise of falling from height', Ka. *tapp-ane* 'suddenly', *dabakk-ane* 'noise of heavy body falling', *dabb-ane* 'suddenly', Tu. *dabakka* 'suddenly', *dabadaba* 'palpitation of heart': SD II: Te. *dabbu-na* 'suddenly', *dabadaba* 'walking fast', Go. *topne* 'quickly', Kuvi *toppe*, *tobbe* 'quickly', Pe. *tapp in-ji* [*tapp* say-ppl] 'suddenly'| *CDIAL* 6170 with **dab-* [3069].

Emeneau (1969a: Appendix) has cited 43 entries from *DED* (1961) and compared the Dravidian cognates with comparable entries in Indo-Aryan from Turner (1966) and could find parallels in almost all cases. He suggests that R̥gvedic *budbuda-* 'bubble' could be the earliest loanword based on PD **buḍabuḍa-* (1980b: 282–3), disputed by Hock (1996: 29, 39–40). Emeneau says, 'It is probable that in reconstructed PDr. no isolated word should begin with a voiced stop, except for some members of the onomatopoetic class' (1980b: 287–8). Emeneau and Kausalya Hart (1993) have pursued this question further, taking data from Modern Tamil in which many of the onomatopoetic expressions are rendered with voiced initial stops, although in script they are represented voiceless. They suggest on the basis of comparative evidence that 'in expressive items there are phonetic developments different from those that are regarded as regular for the language that is being treated' (Emeneau and Hart 1993: 83). They examine a total of 76 entries from *DEDR* (1984) and propose 24 items out of these as probably beginning with voiced stops.

10.8.2 ***Echo words and intensives***

In echo-word formation, reduplication occurs partially and not fully, and the echo word is not onomatopoeic. For any base word of any part of speech, beginning with either a vowel or a consonant with variable vowel length, i.e. (C)V/(C)V̄-, an echo word is formed replacing this syllable by *gi-/gī-* respectively (the vowel length in the echo word corresponds to the vowel length of the model word); the rest of the model is repeated after *gi-/gī*. The echo word means 'that and the like, or that etc.', e.g. Te. *illu gillu* 'house, etc.', *puli gili* 'tiger, etc.'. In other words, for a given word of the structure (C)V̆̄X, there can be an echo word of the structure *gĭ̄*X where X = that part of the word excluding the initial (C)V̆̄. The echo word need not occur immediately after the model word, but can be coordinated with it in a compound sentence, e.g.

(27) Te. *wāḍ-i-ki illu lē-du, gillu lēdu*
[he-obl-dat house be not-3neu-sg , such a thing be not-3neu-sg]
'he has no house and nothing of that sort'

This pattern is available in Tamil, Malayāḷam and Kannaḍa definitely. It is reported for some tribal languages also (for Toda, see Emeneau 1938, for Ālu Kuṟumba, see Kapp 1985; a short bibliography occurs in this last reference). This pattern can be reconstructed for Proto-South Dravidian with a voiced stop as part of the first syllable of the echo word.

Intensives are a restricted set involving a model and a partly reduplicated component, which intensifies the meaning of the model word. Here the model is a nominal or adjectival and the reduplicated part becomes a morphological extension of the base word and is not separable from it, as in the case of echo words. Emeneau (1987a) discusses this phenomenon and cites twenty-five examples drawn from *DEDR* (1984). Intensives are mainly found in the four major literary languages and therefore the construction is reconstructable for Proto-South Dravidian. However, it is not a productive type like onomatopoeic expressives, which are an open set admitting possible new formations. First the examples may be examined. $C_1V_1C_2C_2$*a*- is the reduplicated part added before the model in Tamil and Kannaḍa; in Telugu C_1V_1*ṭṭa*- is added. $C_1V_1C_2$- are identical with #CVC- of the base word (also see section 8.3.1).

(28) a. Ta. *putta(m)-putiya* 'brand new' (*putu, putiya* 'new') [4275].
b. Ka. *tutta-tudi/tuṭṭa-tudi* 'the very end', Te. *tuṭṭa-tudi* id. (*tudi* 'end') [3314]
c. Ka. *motta-modalu* 'the very beginning', Te. *moṭṭa-modalu* id. (*modalu* 'beginning') [4950].
d. Ta. *veṟṟa-veṟitu* 'absolute worthlessness' (*veṟi-tu* 'uselessness', *veṟu* 'empty') [5513].

e. Ta. *naṭṭa-naṭu* 'the very middle', Ka. *naṭṭa-naḍuve* id., Te. *naṭṭa-naḍi* adj 'the very central' (Ta. *naṭu*, Ka. *naḍu*, Te. *naḍi* 'middle, centre') [3584].

The principle is that Tamil and Kannaḍa geminate the C_2 of the base word in each case and Telugu uses C_1V_1*ṭṭa-* in all cases. Three cases from Tamil and Kannaḍa also show C_1V_1*ṭṭa-* as in Telugu irrespective of C_2 of the model word. Ta. *paṭṭa-ppakal*, Ma. *paṭṭā-pakal*, Te. *paṭṭa-pagalu* 'broad daylight' (*pagal(u)* 'day'). In all cases, the resultant reduplicated morpheme functions as a bound adjective of the model. Tamil has cases where C_2 is not a stop; it can be a nasal /n ṇ/, or a lateral /ḷ/. This pattern is not found in Kannaḍa and Telugu.

Another intensive with partial reduplication is found in one interjection in all major languages, e.g. Te. *ayyō* 'alas' : *ayy-ayyō* (denotes greater intensity of sympathy). Tamil, Malayāḷam and Kannaḍa also have the same pair of expressions. We cannot explain the last one by sandhi since a long vowel + short vowel will not result in the loss of the long vowel. It is a case of partial reduplication of the model $V_1C_1C_1$- by dropping the final vowel. Old Telugu has another interjection *ōhō* (surprise) → *ōh-ōhō* (denotes more surprise) with reduplication of $\#\overline{V}_1C_1$-.

Another type of expressive is the reduplication of words of different parts of speech in distributive or intensive meanings, e.g. Te. nouns: *illu* 'house': *ill-illu* 'every house', *iṇṭi-ki* [house-obl-dat] 'to a house'; *iṇṭ-iṇṭi-ki* 'to each house'; pronouns: interrogative, *ewaru* 'who': *ewar-ewaru* 'who particularly?' (distributive); numerals: *iddaru* 'two persons': *iddar-iddaru* 'two each, by twos'; demonstrative adverbs: *akkaḍa* 'there': *akkaḍ-akkaḍa* 'here and there', *appuḍu* 'then': *appuḍ-appuḍu* 'now and then'; adjectives: *pedda* 'big': *pedda-pedda* 'very big', *cinna* 'small' : *cinna-cinna* 'very small'; adverbs: *tondara* noml 'quickness', *tondara-gā* 'quickly': *tondara-tondara-gā* 'very fast'; verbs: *tin-* 'eat', *tin-i* [eat-ppl] 'having eaten': *tin-i tin-i* 'having eaten a lot'; OTe. *cuc-/cūḍ-* 'see', *cūḍ-an* [see-inf] 'to see': *cūḍ-a-cūḍ-a* 'as one keeps seeing'.

These patterns are found in all Dravidian languages. Particularly the reduplication of inflected verbs, like the gerund, is a very ancient feature in Dravidian occurring in early texts of the literary languages. It is also found in Indo-Aryan in the post-Ṛgvedic period. Hock (1996: 18, fn.1) says, 'Non-verbal iteration is found to varying degrees in many early Indo-European languages, but verbal iteration (of the type Skt. *utplutya utplutya* 'continually jumping up') first appears in late Vedic.' The extensive use of reduplicated verbs in Modern Indo-Aryan and other languages in South Asia is illustrated by Abbi (1992: 31–54). The variety of uses between Indo-Aryan and Dravidian is striking. Diachronically, this is a feature that goes back to Proto-Dravidian and must have spread to Middle and Modern Indic by diffusion. Examples from different Dravidian languages occur in earlier chapters under different parts of speech.

11

Conclusion: a summary and overview

11.1 Introduction

A summary of conclusions from different chapters, which throw light on the subgrouping of the Dravidian languages adopted here, will be presented with a short review of earlier work on this topic. I will briefly speculate on the probable date of Proto-Dravidian. I have left out several questions like the original home of the Dravidians and whether they were the same people who ruled the Indus valley around 2500 BCE. The Proto-Dravidian culture that I have reconstructed, based on comparative vocabulary in section 1.2.2, must help archaeologists and linguistic archaeologists to sort out this problem. I have hinted at the future direction for research in Dravidian studies, comparative and typological.

11.2 Earlier attempts at subgrouping the Dravidian languages

Serious attempts at the subgrouping of the Dravidian languages proceeded hand in hand with the study of a number of new languages, mainly in central India, namely Kolami, Parji, Naiki, Ollari, Gadaba, Koṇḍa, Pengo etc. during 1950–75. Earlier, L. V. Ramaswami Aiyar, E. H. Tuttle and T. Burrow (till 1950) placed Telugu in South Dravidian (our South Dravidian I). I have noted that Telugu is genetically closer to its northern neighbours, Gondi, Koṇḍa, Kui, Kuvi, to which Pengo and Manḍa were added later. Burrow and Bhattacharya (1953: xi) have pointed out the close relationship among Parji, Ollari, Gadaba, Kolami and Naiki. They also speak of 'many signs of special connection between Gondi–Koṇḍa and Kui–Kuvi'. In *TVB* (ch. 4: 236–74), I argued for placing Telugu genetically as a close sister of Gondi–Koṇḍa–Kui–Kuvi, but its geographical and cultural contact with the other literary languages of south India was responsible for the diffusion of some of the features of South Dravidian I to Telugu, e.g. loss of PD $^{*}c > s > h > \emptyset$, and having 'he', 'she/it' in the singular (in common with the other Central Dravidian languages) and 'they' (human plural) and 'they' (non-human plural) in common with South Dravidian I in gender. Consequently, Central Dravidian has emerged as another branch of Proto-Dravidian with two sub-branches, Telugu–Kuvi on the one hand and Kolami–Gadaba, on the other. This scenario was accepted by all

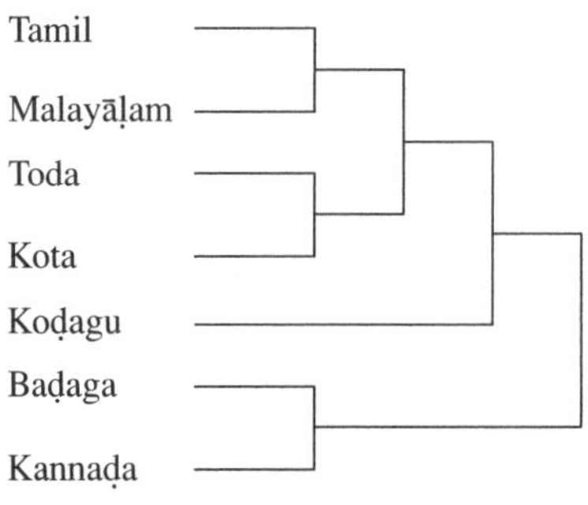

Figure 11.1 Subgrouping of South Dravidian by Emeneau (1967b)

Dravidian scholars until the mid 1970s (see my first review article on Dravidian studies in Krishnamurti 1969b/2001a: 114–16).

In the case of the South Dravidian languages Emeneau (1967b/1994) has proposed a subgrouping (differently configured) as in figure 11.1. Emeneau set up two intermediate stages: Proto-Toda–Kota node connecting Proto-Tamil–Malayāḷam node, which is brought out by the diagram. I have given morphological arguments to place Koḍagu closer to Tamil–Malayāḷam than to Toda–Kota. Three other languages have since been studied, namely Iruḷa, Kuṟumba (with several dialects) and Koraga. The position of Tuḷu in the Southern group still has difficulties, although it seems to be part of South Dravidian I, perhaps the very first to branch from it. Koraga is close to Tuḷu. Iruḷa and Kuṟumba are closer to Tamil–Malayāḷam (see section 4.4.4.2).

North Dravidian consisting of Kuṛux, Malto and Brahui has not presented any problems, with Kuṛux–Malto being one branch and Brahui the other.

11.2.1 *Studies in lexicostatistics*

Andronov (1964c) attempted a glottochronological study based on Swadesh's 100-word list with cognates from major and known Dravidian languages. He puts the modern standard varieties of Tamil–Malayāḷam, Kannaḍa and Telugu in the Southern group. He put Kolami–Parji and Gondi as another subgroup, which he designated Central Dravidian. He has all the three languages from North Dravidian. The procedure suffers from several shortcomings and inadequacies. Except for the literary languages, vocabularies of the remaining ones are not comprehensive. It is difficult to decide if a cognate has failed to be recorded or it has not existed, in several cases. The basic word list has been questioned by many scholars for decades. For instance, the first item 'all' has different lexical representations between human/non-human, e.g. Telugu *antā*, given in the list, refers to

[± human], but *annī* or *allā* is only [−human], e.g.

atanu[1]	*cepp-in-di*[2]	*allā*[3]	*cēs-ǣ-ḍu*[4]
[he	speak-past-noml	all	do-past-3m-sg]

'he[1] did[4] all[3] that has been said[2] (by/to him)'

If Andronov chose *allā*, it would have been a case of retaining a cognate (*ellā* in Ta. Ma. Ka.), but he chose *antā* and noted it as a case of loss of a cognate. Again, for item 31 'foot', he cited Telugu *pādamu*, a learned borrowing from Sanskrit, although *aḍugu*, a cognate with Ta. Ma. Ka. *aḍi*, is the one widely used in Modern Telugu. By his lexicostatistic study he worked out the time distance between pairs of languages. The closest sisters, Tamil–Malayāḷam with a retention rate 73 per cent of cognates, are said to have been separated by 1,043 years, i.e. the tenth century AD, which is, in any case, the known historical date. The greatest time depth is between Telugu and Brahui, with 16 per cent retention of cognates indicating a distance of 6,075 years or 4100 BC. What is surprising is that every language is separated from Brahui by over 5,000 years including its closest sisters Kuṛux (by 5,505 years) and Malto (5,874)! Kuṛux and Malto are shown to be closer to Tamil (4,596 and 4,872 years, respectively) than to Brahui (Andronov 1964c: 184). The fact of the matter is that Brahui has retained only 15 per cent of native lexical items and the influence of Balochi has been immense, despite its contact with Balochi being only for 1,000 years (Elfenbein 1987: 219, 229). We still do not have a measure of how fast borrowed words replace native items. The misleading time depth is caused by loss of many cognates in Brahui because of heavy borrowing from Balochi and Indo-Aryan. However, in terms of shared phonological and morphological innovations, it could not have been separated for more than a thousand years or so from Kuṛux–Malto. Further, the Brahui specialist, Elfenbein, says, '. . . the estimate by "glottochronological" methods that Brahui separated from the rest *ca*. 3000 BC, is perhaps not to be taken too seriously' (1987: 229). This is enough for Andronov's glottochronology.

There are two other lexicostatistical studies by Kameswari (1969) and Namboodiri (1976) that I reviewed in 1980 (see Krishnamurti 1985/2001a: 256–7). There is wide variation in the dates of separation of individual languages by the two authors, which I pointed out as evidence for the unreliability of the technique employed; for instance, 'Tamil and Telugu diverged around 400 BC to AD 400 (Kameswari), 11th century BC (Namboodiri)' (Krishnamurti 1985/2001a: 256).

11.2.2 *Other proposals*

Krishnamurti (1969b/2001a: 114–17, 1985/2001a: 255–7) has surveyed the earlier views on subgrouping and the reasons for revisions at each stage. In *TVB* (ch. 4), he proposed three branches: South Dravidian (treated as South Dravidian I in this volume), Central

Dravidian consisting of two subgroups, Telugu–Gondi–Koṇḍa–Kui–Kuvi–Pengo–Manḍa and Kolami–Naiki–Parji–Ollari–Gadaba; North Dravidian has the same members, Kuṛux–Malto–Brahui. This proposal was widely accepted by the Dravidian scholars and adopted for about three decades. In the mid 1970s, he found new evidence to separate the Telugu–Manḍa subgroup from Central Dravidian and designated it as another branch of South Dravidian, called South Dravidian II or South-Central Dravidian, changing the erstwhile South Dravidian to South Dravidian I (see Postscripts of chapters 4 and 8 of Krishnamurti 2001a). This revision is widely accepted now, and it is followed in this book for which exhaustive evidence is presented below in section 11.3.

Southworth (1976) discusses in detail the subgrouping of the Dravidian languages with three isogloss maps and makes some useful suggestions. Basing his assumption on McAlpin's hypothesis of Dravidian and Elamite being sisters of one parent language, Proto-Elamo-Dravidian (which McAlpin has failed to establish), Southworth thinks that 'Dravidian speakers moved from somewhere near Mesopotamia to South Asia, possibly sometime in the third millennium BC' (1976: 131). Southworth sets up seven subgroups for Dravidian besides the North Dravidian, namely (1) Kolami–Naiki–Parji–Gadaba, (2) Kui–Kuvi–Koṇḍa–Pengo–Manḍa, (3) Gondi–Telugu, (4) Tuḷu, (5) Kannaḍa, (6) Toda–Kota, (7) Tamil-Malayāḷam (1976: 131).

11.3 The subgrouping adopted in this book

The subgrouping adopted in this book is that Proto-Dravidian has three main branches. The first branch is Proto-South Dravidian which split into South Dravidian I and South Dravidian II (also called South Central Dravidian); the second is Central Dravidian and the third North Dravidian (see section 1.4). This is the one which most Dravidian scholars follow currently (figure 11.2a; also see Krishnamurti 2001a: 381, fig. 21.1). It is also possible to set up an original binary division of Proto-Dravidian into Proto-North Dravidian and Proto-South and Central Dravidian (see figure 11.2b). There is lean evidence to set up a common stage of South and Central Dravidian, but generally a binary division of a speech community is more likely than a ternary. A subsequent split leads to the two branches Proto-South Dravidian and Proto-Central Dravidian. The former splits into South Dravidian I and II.

In tables 11.1a–d, features from comparative phonology, morphology and syntax are given a '+' sign indicating innovation and a '−' sign indicating retention within the specified subgroup or a part of it. A '0' sign says that the feature is either not registered or not relevant in the specified subgroup. Discussion follows each table and isogloss maps are presented at the end of the section.

Out of the nine features listed in table 11.1a, F1a, 2 and 3a support a common stage of Proto-South Dravidian. Features 3c and 4 are exclusive innovations of South Dravidian II.

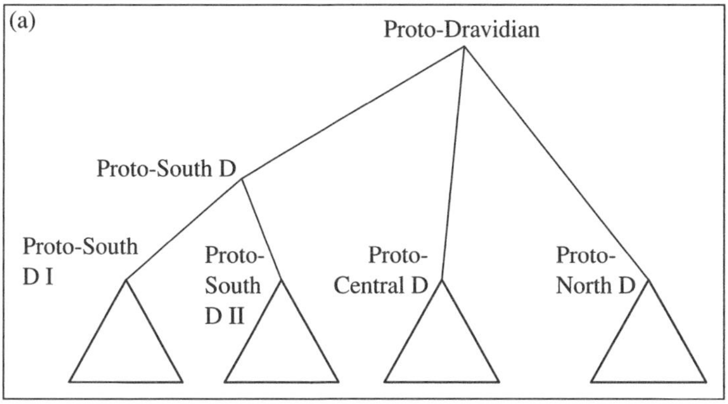

Figure 11.2a Proto-Dravidian with main branches (alternative 1)

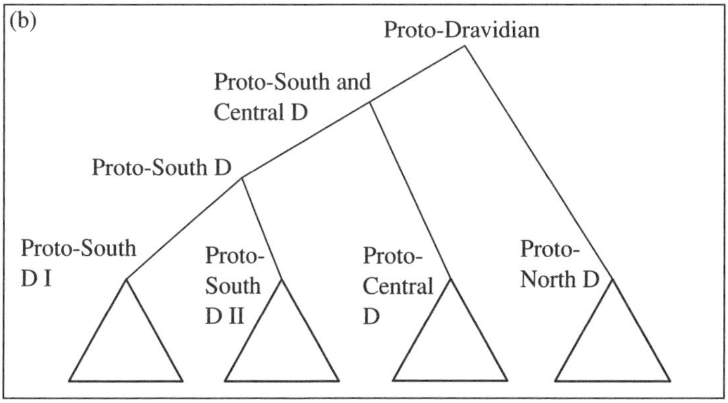

Figure 11.2b Proto-Dravidian with main branches (alternative 2)

Only F3b is an innovation restricted to Central Dravidian; F8b and 9 characterize North Dravidian. F1b, 5 and 8a, on the one hand, and 6 on the other, demarcate smaller subgroups within South Dravidian I and South Dravidian II, respectively. There are other minor sound changes without a clear clue to subgrouping like **w* > *b* in Middle Kannaḍa which has spread by diffusion to Kuṟumba, Koḍagu, Tuḷu and Baḍaga; a similar sound change has independently taken place in North Dravidian, presumably under the influence of Eastern Indo-Aryan (section 4.5.4.1). This sound change is also shared by Brahui and is one of the arguments to say that Brahui had not separated from Kuṛux and Malto until around the eighth century CE. Another sound change which probably involved diffusion as an important factor from Indo-Aryan is the deretroflexion of **ṇ* **ḷ* to *n l* in several languages of South Dravidian II, Central Dravidian and North Dravidian

Table 11.1a *Subgrouping supported by phonological features*

Feature(s) = F	SD I	SD II	CD	ND	Reference/ remarks
1a. PD *i *u > PSD *e *o /__+a	+	+	–	–	section 4.4.2
1b. PSD *e *o > *i *u/__+a	+ Ta. Ma.	–	0	0	section 4.4.2.2 (1)
2. PD *c > *s > *h > Ø/#__	+	+	–	–	section 4.5.1.3.2
3a. PD *ṯ > ṟ/V__V, > ḏ~ṟ/ *Vn__	+	+		+	section 4.5.5.3
3b. PD *ṯ > ḏ/V__V, *n__			+		section 4.5.5.3 (?retention)
3c. PSD *ṯ > PSD II ḍ/V_V	–	+	–	–	section 4.5.5.3 sporadic
4. Apical displacement	–	+	–	–	sections 4.4.3, 4.5.7.3
5. (C)ē-/ō- > (C)ā-	0	+ Kui–Kuvi	0	0	section 4.4.2.2
6. Centralized vowels ë ö	+ Ir. To. Kuṟ. Koḍ	0	0	0	section 4.4.4.2
7. PD *n- > Ø-			+ Kol. Nk.		section 4.5.3.2 Regular in CD; sporadic in SD
8a. PD *k > c/#__V[–Back]C [–Retroflex]	+ Ta. Ma.	–	–	–	section 4.5.1.4
8b. PD *k > x/# __ V	–	–	–	+	V = all except high front vowels; section 4.5.1.4
9. PD *c > k/#__V	–	–	–	+	V = non-low vowels; section 4.5.1.3

(sections 4.5.6–7) as it is in many Indo-Aryan languages of central and northern India. Another sound change exclusively innovated by Kannaḍa and inherited by Baḍaga, considered a dialect of Kannaḍa that split off in about the sixteenth century CE, is **p- > h- > Ø* (section 4.5.1.1).

Among the nine morphological innovations in nominals listed in table 11.1b, there are two that establish South Dravidian I and South Dravidian II as closer sisters, derived from a common undivided stage, see F10 and 11. F12, 14 and 15 are clear innovations in South Dravidian I, not shared by South Dravidian II; similarly, F13 is a shared innovation in South Dravidian II. There are two features which are exclusive to Central Dravidian, namely F16 and 17. There can be a question of how Telugu happens to have a numeral derived from **okk-* beside the regular items *oṇḍu* 'one' (n-msg), *or-u^{n}ḍu* 'one man', *ōr-ti* 'one woman'. The last two have become archaic, since Modern Telugu has only

Table 11.1b *Subgrouping supported by morphological features of nominals*

Feature(s) = F	SD I	SD II	CD	ND	Reference/ remarks
10. **ñān*/*ñan*- 'I' beside **yān*/*yan*- 'I'	+	+	–	–	section 6.4.1.1; the root vowel: archiphoneme **ă*/*ĕ*
11. 2pl pronoun **nī-m* > **nī-r*	+	+	–	–	section 6.4.1.2
12. Addition of *-*kaḷ* to the 1pl 2pl pronouns, e.g. **yām-kaḷ* 'we'	+ Ta. Ma. Koḍ. Kuṟ. Ka. Kor. Tu.	–	–	–	section 6.4.1.1
13. 1sg obl.**nā*-, 2sg obl **nī*-; 1pl obl. **mā*-, 2pl obl **mī*-	–	+	–	–	sections 6.4.1.1–2
14. Creation of **aw-aḷ* etc. 3f sg	+	–	–	–	sections 6.2.2–3, 6.2.6
15. Loss of **ṯ* in 3m sg **aw-anṯ*, **iw-anṯ* 'he'	+	–	–	–	sections 6.2.2–3, 6.2.6
16. Numerals 1–4 + derivational markers for m sg, f sg, neu sg	–	–	+	–	sections 6.5, 6.5.1
17. *okk*- 'one'	–	–(+ Te.)	+	–	section 6.5.1: 'one' (c)
18. Loss of –V*n* as accusative marker	Ta. Ma. Ir Koḍ. Kuṟ.	–	–	–	section 6.3.2.1

o(*k*)*ka*- 'one' and its derivatives, *ok*(*k*)*a-ḍu* 'one man', *ok*(*k*)*a-te* 'one woman', *ok* (*ka*)-*ṭi* 'one thing'. It is possible that the Central Dravidian innovation might have spread to Telugu through diffusion at some prehistoric time, although, normally, the direction of borrowing is from Telugu to the Central Dravidian languages. A more plausible alternative is that the doublet was created in Pre-Telugu and spread to Central Dravidian at an undivided stage of the latter. There is evidence of several prehistoric borrowings from Telugu to Kolami–Naiki, e.g. **nīr* 'you (pl)' replaced Pre-Kolami **īm*, since the oblique remains *im*-. This borrowing provides a valuable missing link in the prehistory of Telugu, because inscriptions and literary records only show *mīru* which replaced **nī-ru* (<< **nī-m*) in Pre-Telugu (see Krishnamurti 2001a: 96–7). F18 is the absence of -V*n* as accusative marker in Tamil, Malayāḷam, Iruḷa, Kuṟumba and Koḍagu which I consider off-shoots from a stage of Pre-Tamil after Toda–Kota had split off in South Dravidian I. This subgroup within South Dravidian I is supported by other isoglosses, e.g. see F6 above and discussion in section 4.4.4.2.

Out of the thirteen features identified under verbs in table 11.1c, F19, 21 and 31 support the undivided stage of South Dravidian I and South Dravidian II; I have proposed that

Table 11.1c *Subgrouping supported by morphological features of verbs*

Feature(s) = F	SD I	SD II	CD	ND	Reference/ remarks
19. Causative + past *-*(p)pi-ntt-* > *-*(p)pi-nc-*/ *-*(p)pi-c-*	+ Ta. Ma. Ka	+	–	–	sections 7.3.3–6
20. Tense–voice marking NP ~ NPP	+ Ta. Ma. Koḍ. To. Ko.	–	0	0	sections 5.4.4, 7.3.6–7
21. Paired intr/tr: NP vs. NPP	+	+	–	–	section 7.3.6
22. Loss of past-tense marker *-*kk*	+	+	+	–	section 7.4.1.6
23. Loss of past marker with a dental *-*t* or *-*tt*	–	–	–	+	section 7.4.1.1
24. Generalization of *-*tt* as past marker	–	+	(+) Kol. –Nk.	0	section 7.4.1.2
25. Non-past -*um* loss	–	–	–	+	section 7.4.2.3
26. Perfective participle *-*cci*	0	+	+ Pa. Oll. Gad	0	sections 7.7.1.2
27. -V*t*/*ṭ* as 2sg in finite verbs	–	–	+ Pa, Oll Gad	–	section 7.5.3
28. Past relative participle: past + *i*	–	+	–	–	-*a* in SD I, CD and ND; section 7.7.2.1
29. **cil* > (**sil* > *hil*) > **il* 'to be not'	+	+ (Te.)	–	–	section 7.10.6
30. Compound verb contraction	–	+ (–Te.)	–	–	Exception Telugu; sections 7.13, 7.13.2
31. Use of **taH-r* 'give to 1/2 pers' as auxiliary	+	+	0	0	section 7.14

Table 11.1d *Subgrouping supported by morphosyntactic features of adjectives, adverbs, clitics and syntax*

Feature(s) = F	SD I	SD II	CD	ND	Reference/remarks
32. Loss of several basic adjectives	–	–	+	+	CD and ND lost 8 each; section 8.2
33. Adverb **ñānṯu* 'today' lost	–	–	+	+	section 8.3
34. Loss of interrogative particles -*ē*, -*ō*	–	+	+	+	generalization of -*ā* in SD II, CD, ND; section 8.4.3
35. Use of *tān* 'self' as an emphatic particle; alternatively -*ē*	+	–	–	–	section 8.4.2
36. copular verb **ir-* 'be' substituting **man-*	+	–	–	–	The retention is **man-* 'to be'; section 7.15.1.ff.

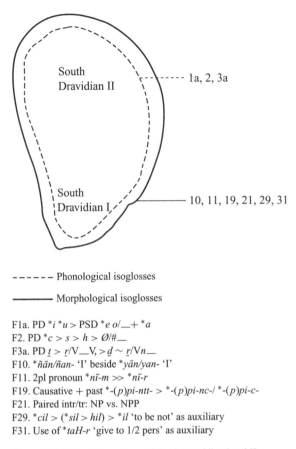

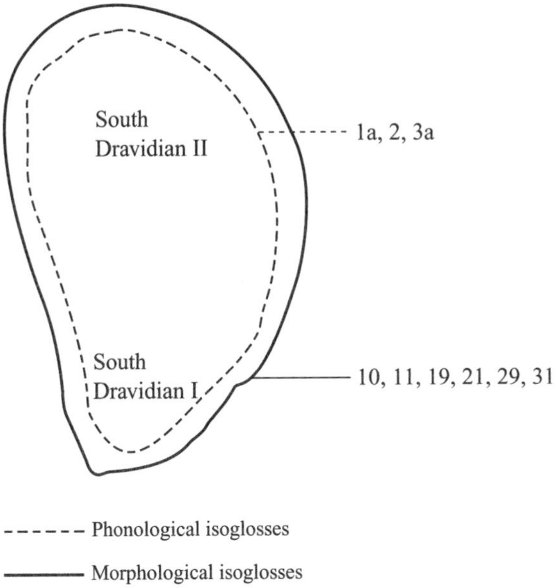

F1a. PD *i *u > PSD *e o/__+ *a
F2. PD *c > s > h > Ø/#__
F3a. PD ṯ > ṟ/V__V, > ḏ ~ ṟ/Vn__
F10. *ñān/ñan- 'I' beside *yān/yan- 'I'
F11. 2pl pronoun *nī-m >> *nī-r
F19. Causative + past *-(p)pi-ntt- > *-(p)pi-nc-/ *-(p)pi-c-
F21. Paired intr/tr: NP vs. NPP
F29. *cil > (*sil > hil) > *il 'to be not' as auxiliary
F31. Use of *taH-r 'give to 1/2 pers' as auxiliary

Figure 11.3 Shared innovations of South Dravidian I and II

F31 was a retention in South Dravidian; even then, it shows the togetherness of these two subgroups since the feature is lost (not attested) in Central and North Dravidian. In other words, retention supported by solid geographical contiguity could be taken as a positive factor in subgrouping. Note F20 represents retention in a geographically close-knit subgroup, which is established by other shared innovations. South Dravidian I has *il- 'to be not' derived from *cil- (again a phonological feature), and Telugu, by diffusion, shares this feature in lē- (< *il-a-) 'to be not' with loss of c-. through the intermediate stages of *h- <*s-. The generalization of *-tt- as the past marker (F24) distinguishes South Dravidian II, with the isogloss also spreading into some languages of Central Dravidian. F30 is typically noticed in South Dravidian II, with the exception of Telugu. It establishes Koṇḍa–Kui–Kuvi–Pengo–Manḍa as a minor subgroup within South Dravidian II.

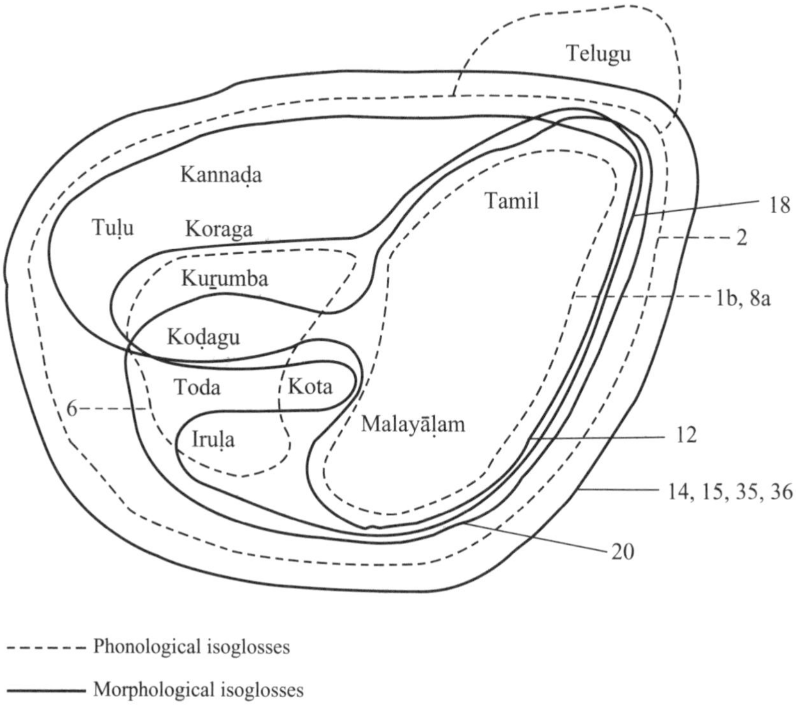

F1b. PSD *e *o > *i *u/__+a
F2. PD *c > Ø- (through *s- > *h- not attested directly)
F6. Centralized vowels in root syllables
F8a. PD *k > c-/#__V [–Back], C [–Retroflex]
F12. Addition of *-*kaḷ* (n-hpl suff) optionally to 1pl and 2pl
F14. Creation of **aw-aḷ* etc. 3f sg
F15. Loss of **ṯ* in 3m sg **aw-anṯ*, **iw-anṯ* 'he'
F18. Loss of -V*n* as accusative marker
F20. Tense–voice marking by final
NP ~ NPP
F35. Use of *tān* 'self' as an emphatic particle; alternatively -*ē*
F36. copular verb **ir-* 'be' replacing **man-*

Figure 11.4 South Dravidian I (with the isogloss of F2 overlapping into Telugu)

There is no exclusive feature demarcating Central Dravidian but Kolami–Naiki and Parji–Ollari–Gadaba emerge as minor subgroups in terms of F24 and 27.

The loss of a dental (F23) and the generalization of *-*kk* (F22) as the past marker, and the loss of non-past *-*um* (F26), distinguish North Dravidian from others.

The five features listed in table 11.1d give partial evidence for the established subgroups. The use of **tān* as an emphatic marker in addition to the normal **ē* is an

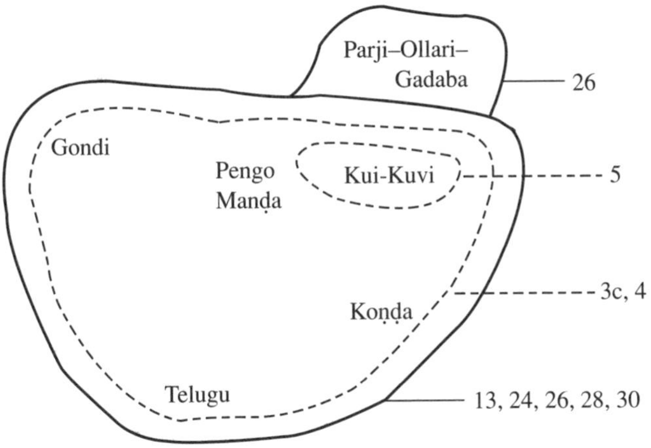

------- Phonological isoglosses

——— Morphological isoglosses

F3c. PSD *ṯ > PSD II ḍ/V_V
F4. Apical displacement
F5. (C)*ē-/ō-* > (C)*ā-*
F13. 1sg obl **nā-*, 1pl obl **mā-*
2sg obl *nī-*, 2pl obl **mī-*
F24. Generalization of **-tt* as past marker
F26. Perfective participle **-cci* ~ **-ci*
F28. Past relative participle: past marker + *i*
F30. Compound verb contraction

Figure 11.5 South Dravidian II (with the isogloss of F26 overlapping into Parji–Ollari–Gadaba of Central Dravidian)

innovation of South Dravidian I (F35). All but South Dravidian I show only *-ā* as an interrogative clitic for 'yes–no' responses (F34). The loss of several basic adjectives in Central Dravidian and North Dravidian (but different lexical items) shows that they are independent branches (F32). Similarly, the Proto-Dravidian adverb **ñānṯu* 'today' is retained in South Dravidian I and South Dravidian II (F33), but lost in Central Dravidian and North Dravidian. A very good feature is the replacement of **man-* 'be' by *ir-* in South Dravidian I as a copular verb (F36).

Summary There are several exclusive isoglosses supporting Proto-South Dravidian and the two branches from it. There are also definite features setting off North Dravidian from the rest. There are relatively fewer shared innovations by Central Dravidian, the definite ones being F3b, 16, 17 and 32. The fact that Central Dravidian does not share

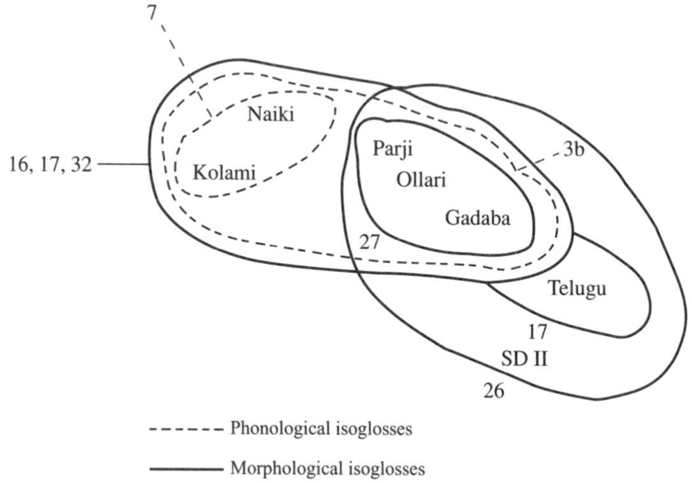

F3b. PD *$\underline{t}$ > $\underline{d}$/V__V, *n*__ (could be interpreted as a retention)
F7. PCD **n*- > Ø-
F16. Numerals 1–4 + derivational markers for msg, fsg, neusg
F17. *okk*- 'one'
F26. Perfective participle *-cci* ~ *-ci*
F27. *-Vt/ṭ* as 2sg in finite verbs
F32. Loss of several (8) basic adjectives

Figure 11.6 Central Dravidian

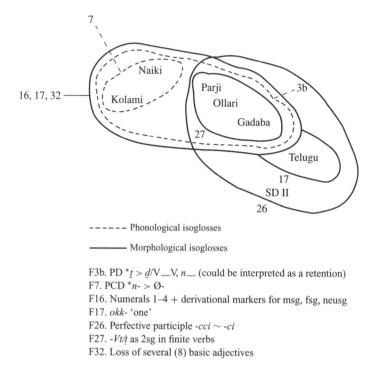

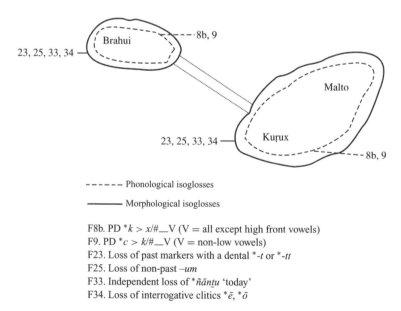

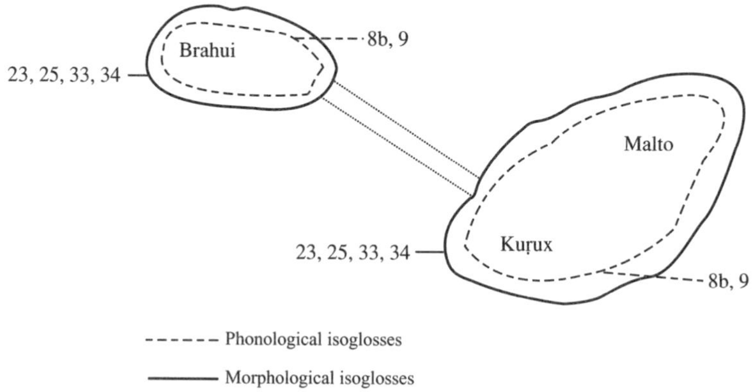

F8b. PD **k* > *x*/#__V (V = all except high front vowels)
F9. PD **c* > *k*/#__V (V = non-low vowels)
F23. Loss of past markers with a dental *-*t* or *-*tt*
F25. Loss of non-past *–um*
F33. Independent loss of **ñāṉṯu* 'today'
F34. Loss of interrogative clitics **ē*, **ō*

Figure 11.7 North Dravidian

any of the specific innovations attributed to South Dravidian and North Dravidian puts it as a group by itself. Being surrounded by South Dravidian II languages, either Kolami–Naiki or Parji–Ollari–Gadaba sometimes share their features spread through borrowing and diffusion.

The major shared innovations are depicted in figures 11.3 to 11.7 keyed to the numbered features listed in the above tables.

11.4 The antiquity of Proto-Dravidian and formation of South Dravidian I and II

I have not addressed this problem so far because definite archeological and scriptural evidence is lacking. In section 1.2.2.9, I maintained that the speakers of the Dravidian languages were native to India. This meant that they had not entered India from the northwest during the recent past (second or third millennium), as proposed by some scholars. But, in view of the theory that modern humans spread out of Africa between 60,000 and 70,000 years ago to all corners of the world (section 1.2.1; Cavalli-Sforza 2000: 92), the Dravidian speakers might have entered India at some very distant past. On cultural grounds, I have suggested the probability of the Indus civilization being Proto-Dravidian. If later researches prove this to be correct, we, then, have a tentative date of Proto-Dravidian around the early part of the third millennium. Even otherwise, a date closer to that is needed to account for all later developments. We are still not certain which form of Dravidian the R̥gvedic Aryans came across around 1500 BC. It could be some ancient form of Dravidian, but certainly not Proto-North Dravidian. While many Dravidian speakers got assimilated into the Aryan society progressively, the ones who resisted were slowly pushed toward the periphery of the Indo-Gangetic plain and many had moved toward east and south even by the end of the second millennium. A reference in *Aitareyabrāhmaṇa* (7:3:18; ca. seventh century BCE) that the Aryan sage Viśwāmitra cursed his fifty older, disobedient sons to live as hunter-gatherers with the names *andhra, śabara, puṇḍra, pulinda* and *mūtiba* already registers the names of two tribes, one speaking a Dravidian language, i.e. *andhra* (Andhra), and the other *śabara* (Savara), a Munda language. Bharata's *Nāṭyaśāstra* 'The Science of Dramaturgy'[1] of the fourth century BCE mentions certain tribal speeches as *vibhāṣā* as opposed to Sanskrit and Prakrits. Mention of *dramila-* '(Pre-)Tamil' and *āndhra-* '(Pre-)Telugu' occur here. We can, therefore, infer that the split of South Dravidian I (with Pre-Tamil as the dominant language) and of South Dravidian II (with Pre-Telugu as the dominant language) could precede the period of *Aitareyabrāhmaṇa* by at least four or five centuries, i.e. around

[1] 'śakār(a)-ābhīra-caṇḍāla-śabara-dramil(a)-āndhra-jāḥ| hīne vanecarāṇāṃ ca vibhāṣā nāṭake smr̥tāḥ' (17:50). People called *śakār*(a)-, *ābhīra-, caṇḍāla-, śabara-, dramil(a)-, āndhra-* and other inferior forest dwellers speak 'dialects' or *vibhāṣā* which need to be considered in plays.

the eleventh century BCE. Note that it would take a long time for major differences in phonology and morphology to develop between South Dravidian I and II (see F4, 10, 13–15, 18, 25, 28, 35, 36). We notice that the split of the other major branches could have been somewhat before or after this point in prehistory.

The split of Pre-Tamil from the rest (presumably Tuḷu–Koraga, Kannaḍa) could be placed around the sixth century BCE; the other descendants branched off from Pre-Tamil before the palatalization rule occurred (section 4.5.1.4) in Early Tamil (ca. third century BCE); all literary texts were composed in Tamil after that period. On linguistic grounds, then, between the sixth and the third century BCE, successive splits of Pre-Tamil had occurred, first Toda–Kota, Koḍagu (perhaps Kuṟumba), then Iruḷa, all prehistoric; the split of Malayāḷam has come about during the historic period, i.e. ninth to thirteenth century CE. We notice shared innovations in Toda–Koḍagu–Kuṟumba–Irula (F6) and in Tamil–Malayāḷam and this cluster (F18, 20).

There is no knowing when South Dravidian II split off into the present languages, but we notice smaller clusters of one or two members (Gondi, Koṇḍa, Kui–Kuvi, Pengo–Manḍa) which I would posit between the fifth and thirteenth century CE. The North Dravidian branch must have split from Proto-Dravidian when one column of Dravidian speakers moved toward the south crossing the Vindhya mountains in the post-R̥gvedic period, i.e. thirteenth to tenth century BCE. Central Dravidian then broke off, around between the tenth and eighth century BCE. These dates are tentative based on relative chronology and not on lexicostatistics.

11.5 **Desiderata**

A comprehensive bibliography of linguistic publications is now available for both comparative Dravidian and the major literary languages, thanks to the efforts of the renowned librarian L. S. Ramaiah (1994–2001). The decipherment of the Indus seals would throw light on whether this civilization had any relationship to Proto-Dravidian, but this branch of knowledge is still in the hazy zone of speculation. Efforts should be made to discover new languages in central India covering the Daṇḍakāraṇya area, the mountainous terrain connecting Madhya Pradesh, Andhra Pradesh and Orissa. A more systematic study and analysis of Gondi dialects is a desideratum. A Manḍa grammar, with texts and a lexicon, said to be under preparation for over fifteen years, is urgently needed. Modern descriptions of the dialects of Kui, Kuvi, Malto, Kuṛux and Brahui with texts are called for. Our study of the comparative morphology and syntax of Dravidian is still in its infancy. Much work needs to be done on comparative syntax. More specific studies are called for to determine the place of Tuḷu, Koraga, Kuṟumba (several dialects) and Iruḷa in relation to each other and also in relation to the major languages of South Dravidian I. The monumental *DEDR* needs to be revised every twenty years, and the next revision should be around 2004. It is now possible to add reconstruction of root morphemes under each entry. Since not much is known of the Munda languages, the areas of convergence between Dravidian and Munda need exploration. Any new information on the genetic relationship of Dravidian with language families outside South Asia should be welcome. It is hoped that this humble effort will inspire young scholars to take up unsolved issues in comparative and historical Dravidian for further research.

BIBLIOGRAPHY

Aalto, Pentti. 1971. The alleged affinity of Dravidian and Finno-Ugrian. In Asher (ed.), 1: 262–6.

Abbi, Anvita. 1992. *Reduplication in South Asian Languages: an Areal, Typological and Historical Study*. New Delhi: Allied Publishers Limited.

Agesthialingom, S. 1979. *A Grammar of Old Tamil, with Special Reference to Patiṟṟuppattu*. Annamalainagar: Annamalai University.

1980a. Auxiliaries and main verbs. In Agesthialingom and Srinvasa Varma (eds.), 1–32.

1980b. First person markers from Old to Middle Tamil. In Vaidyanathan (ed.), 1: 68–104.

Agesthialingom, S. and Kumaraswami Raja, N. (eds.). 1969. *Dravidian Linguistics (Seminar Papers)*. Annamalainagar: Annamalai University.

Agesthialingom, S. and Kushalappa Gowda, K. (eds.). 1976. *Dravidian Case System*. Annamalainagar: Annamalai University.

Agesthialingom, S. and Sakthivel, S. (eds.). 1973. *A Bibliography of Dravidian Linguistics*. Annamalainagar: Annamalai University.

Agesthialingom, S. and Shanmugam, S.V. (eds.). 1972. *Proceedings of the Seminar on Dravidian Linguistics III*. Annamalainagar: Annamalai University.

Agesthialingom, S. and Srinvasa Varma, G. (eds.). 1980. *Auxiliaries in Dravidian (Seminar Papers)*. Annamalainagar: Annamalai University.

Agesthialingom, S. and Subrahmanyam, P. S. (eds.). 1976. *Dravidian Linguistics V*. Annamalainagar: Annamalai University.

Aikhenvald, A. Y. 1996. Gender and noun class. In C. Lehmann (ed.), *Handbuch der Morfologie*. Berlin: Mouton de Gruyter (forthcoming).

Aikhenvald, Alexandra Y., Dixon, R. M. W. and Onishi, Masayoshi (eds.). 2001. *Non-Canonical Marking of Subjects and Objects*. Amsterdam and Philadelphia: John Benjamins Publishing Company.

Aitareyabrāhmaṇam. 1987. Varanasi: Choukhamba Sanskrit Sansthan.

Ananda Vasudevan, C. P. 1973. Dravidian-Greek connections. *IJDL* 2: 180–6.

Ananthanarayana, H. S. 1970. Prakrits and Dravidian languages. *Proceedings of the Seminar on Prakrit Studies*, 65–75. Baroda.

Anavaratvinayakam Pillai, S. 1923. *Dravidian Studies III: The Sanskritic Element in the Vocabularies of the Dravidian Languages*. Madras: Superintendent, Government Press.

Andres, Susie. 1978. A Description of Muria Gondi Phonology and Morphology. PhD Dissertation, Department of Linguistics, Deccan College, Poona.

Andrewskutty, A. P. 1975. Pronouns and reflexives in Malayāḷam. *IJDL* 4.1: 44–82.

Andronov, M. S. 1961. New evidence of possible linguistic ties between the Deccan and the Urals. *Dr. R.P. Sethu Pillai Silver Jubilee Commemoration Volume*, 137–40. Madras.

1963. Dravidian languages. *AO* 31: 177–97.

1964a. Materials for a bibliography of Dravidian linguistics. *TC* 11: 3–50.

1964b. On the typological similarity of New Indo-Aryan and Dravidian. *IL* 25: 119–25.
1964c. Lexicostatistic analysis of the chronology of disintegration of Proto-Dravidian. *IIJ* 8: 170–86.
1965. *The Tamil Language.* Moscow: Nauka Publishing House.
1969. *A Standard Grammar of Modern and Classical Tamil.* Madras: New Century Book House Pvt. Ltd.
1970. *Dravidian Languages.* Moscow: Nauka Publishing House.
1971. Comparative studies on the nature of Dravido-Uralian parallels (A peep into the pre-history of language families). In Asher (ed.), 1: 267–77.
1972a. Notes on Brahui. *JTS* 1.1: 1–6.
1972b. Notes on the nature and origin of the adjective in Tamil. In Agesthialingom and Shanmugam (eds.), 167–78.
1975a. Dravidian pronouns: a comparative study. *JTS* 7: 14–18, 8: 18–32.
1975b. Observations on accent in Tamil. In Schiffman and Eastman (eds.), 3–10.
1976a. Case suffixes in Dravidian: a comparative study. *Anthropos* 71.5–6: 726–37.
1976b. Dravidian numerals: an etymological study. *IJDL* 5.1: 5–15.
1976c. The negative in Dravidian: a comparative study. *JTS* 10: 1–12.
1977a. Pronominal suffixes in Dravidian: a comparative study. *IJDL* 6.1: 97–114.
1977b. Hypercorrection in Dravidian. *IL* 38.4: 221–6.
1978. *Sravnitelnaya grammatika Dravidiskikh yazykov* (*A Comparative Grammar of the Dravidian Languages*). Moscow: Institute of Oriental Studies, Academy of Sciences, USSR.
1979. Verbals in Dravidian: a comparative study. *IJDL* 8: 52–70.
1980. *The Brahui Language.* Moscow: Nauka Publishing House.
Annamalai, E. 1968. Onomatopoetic resistance to sound change in Dravidian. In Krishnamurti (ed.), 15–19.
Annamalai, E. and Steever, S. B. 1998. Modern Tamil. In Steever (ed.), 100–28.
Annapurnamma, R. 1980. Auxiliary verbs in Old and Modern Telugu. In Agesthialingom and Srinvasa Varma (eds.), 387–414.
Apparao, P. S. R. 1959. *Nāṭyaśāstramu.* (Original Sanskrit translated into Telugu.) Secunderabad: Andhra Pradesh Nāṭyasanghamu.
Arden, A. H. 1934. *A Progressive Grammar of Common Tamil,* 4th edn revised by A. C. Clayton, with an appendix on Tamil phonetics by J. R. Firth. Madras: Christian Literature Society.
1976. *A Progressive Grammar of the Tamil Language* (5th printing). Madras: Christian Literature Society.
Asher, Ronald E. (ed.). 1971. *Proceedings of the Second International Conference-Seminar of Tamil Studies,* vol. 1. Madras: International Association of Tamil Research.
1982. *Tamil* (Lingua Descriptive Studies 7). Amsterdam: North-Holland.
1985. *Tamil* (Croom Helm Descriptive Grammars). London: Croom Helm. [Repr. of Asher 1982.]
Asher, Ronald E. and Kumari, T. C. 1997. *Malayalam.* London and New York: Routledge.
Austerlitz, R. 1971. Long-range comparisons of Tamil and Dravidian with other language families in Eurasia. In Asher (ed.), 1: 254–61.
Balakrishnan, R. 1976. *Phonology of Kodagu with Vocabulary.* Annamalainagar: Annamalai University.
1977. *A Grammar of Kodagu.* Annamalainagar: Annamalai University.
1980. Auxiliary verbs in Kodagu. In Agesthialingom and Srinvasa Varma (eds.), 519–24.
Banerjee, Muralydhar. 1931. *Deśīnāmamālā of Hemchandra, Part I: Text with Readings, Introduction and Index of Words.* Calcutta: University of Calcutta.
Basham, A. L. 1979. Aryan and non-Aryan in South Asia. In Deshpande and Hook (eds.), 1–9.

Beames, John. 1966. *A Comparative Grammar of the Modern Aryan Languages of India: Hindi, Panjabi, Sindhi, Gujarati, Marathi, Oriya, and Bengali.* (Originally published 1872–79.) Delhi: Munshiram Manoharlal.

Bhaskararao, P. 1980. *Koṇekor Gadaba: a Dravidian Language*. Poona: Deccan College Postgraduate and Research Institute.

Bhat, D. N. S. 1967. *Descriptive Analysis of Tuḷu*. Poona: Deccan College Postgraduate and Research Institute.

1971. *The Koraga Language*. Poona: Deccan College Postgraduate and Research Institute.

1978. *Pronominalization*. Poona: Deccan College.

1994. *The Adjectival Category.* Amsterdam and Philadelphia: John Benjamins Publishing Company.

1998. Tuḷu. In Steever (ed.), 158–77.

Bhat, M. M. 1951. A study of cases in Dravidian languages. *Proceedings and Transactions of the All India Oriental Conference: Thirteenth Session*, 173–6. Nagpur: Nagpur University.

Bhattacharya, S. 1957. *Ollari, a Dravidian Speech.* New Delhi: Department of Anthropology (Memoir No. 3), Government of India.

1961. Naiki of Chanda. *IIJ* 5: 85–117.

1975. Linguistic convergence in the Dravido-Munda culture areas, *IJDL* 4.2: 199–214.

Bloch, Jules. 1919. The intervocalic consonants in Tamil (translated from French with additions by J. D. Anderson). *IA* 48: 191–5.

1930. Some problems of Indo-Aryan philology: Indo-Aryan and Dravidian. *BSO(A)S* 5: 719–56.

1934. *L'Indo-Aryen du veda aux temps modernes,* 321–31. Paris: Adrien Maisonneuve.

1935. La forme negative du verbe dravidien. *BSL* 36: 155–62.

1946. *Structure grammaticale des langues dravidiennes*. Paris: Adrien Maisonneuve.

1954. *The Grammatical Structure of Dravidian Languages* (translated by R. G. Harshe into English from French). Poona: Deccan College Post Graduate and Research Institute.

Bomhard, Allan R. and Kerns, John C. 1994. *The Nostratic Macrofamily: a Study in Distant Linguistic Relationship* (Trends in Linguistics, Studies and Monographs 74). Berlin and New York: Mouton de Gruyter.

Bouda, K. 1953. Dravidisch und Uralaltaisch. *Ural-Altaische Jahrbücher* (Wiesbaden) 25: 161–73.

1956. Dravidian and Uralaltaic. *Lingua* 5: 129–44.

Bray, Denys De S. 1909. *The Brahui Language,* Part 1. Calcutta: Superintendent, Government Printing, India.

1934. *The Brahui Language.* Part II: *The Brahui Problem.* Part III: *Etymological Vocabulary.* Delhi: Manager of Publications.

Breton, Roland J-L. 1997. *Atlas of the Languages and Ethnic Communities of South Asia.* Walnut Creek, London, New Delhi: Alta Mira.

Brigel, J. 1872. *A Grammar of the Tuḷu Language*. Mangalore: Bäsel Mission Press and Tract Depository.

Bright, W. 1966. Dravidian metaphony. *Language* 42: 311–22.

1975. The Dravidian enunciative vowel. In Schiffman and Eastman (eds.), 11–46. [Revised in Bright 1990: 86–117.]

1990. *Language Variation in South Asia*. New York and Oxford: Oxford University Press.

(ed.) 1992. *International Encyclopedia of Linguistics.* New York, Oxford: Oxford University Press.

1996. Kannaḍa and Telugu writing systems. In Daniels and Bright (eds.), 413–19.

1998. The Dravidian scripts. In Steever (ed.), 40–71.

Britto, Francis. 1986. *Diglossia: a Study of the Theory with Application to Tamil.* Washington, DC: Georgetown University Press.

Brown, Charles Philip. 1852. *A Dictionary, Telugu and English. Madras.* 1905. 2nd edn. Revised and enlarged by M. Venkata Ratnam, W. H. Campbell and K. Veeresalingam. Madras: Christian Literature Society. [1966. 1st edn reprinted by A. P. Sahitya Akademi, Hyderabad.]

Burnell, A. C. 1968 (enlarged and improved reissue of 1st edn of 1878). *Elements of South Indian Palaeography (from the Fourth to the Seventeenth Century A.D. being An Introduction to the Study of South-Indian Inscriptions and Mss).* Varanasi, Delhi: Indological Book House.

Burrow, T. 1938. Dravidian studies I: Initial voiced stops. *BSOS* 9: 711–22.

1940. Dravidian studies II: Notes on the interchange of short o e with i u in South Dravidian. *BSOS* 10: 289–97.

1943. Dravidian studies III: The developments of initial *k*- in Dravidian. *BSOAS* 11.1: 122–39.

1944. Dravidian studies IV: The body in Dravidian and Uralian. *BSOAS* 11.2: 328–56.

1945. Some Dravidian words in Sanskrit. *TPS* 79–10.

1946a. Dravidian studies V: Initial *y*- and *ñ*- in Dravidian. *BSOAS* 11.3: 595–616.

1946b. Loan words in Sanskrit. *TPS* 1–30.

1947. Dravidian studies VI: The loss of initial *c/s* in South Dravidian. *BSOAS* 12.1: 132–47.

1948. Dravidian studies VII: Further Dravidian words in Sanskrit. *BSOAS* 12.2: 365–96.

1955. *The Sanskrit Language.* London: Faber and Faber.

1960. Sanskrit and the Pre-Aryan tribes and languages. *Indo-Asian Culture* 8: 333–56.

1968a. The treatment of primitive Dravidian *ṟ* in Kuṟux and Malto. In Krishnamurti (ed.), 62–9.

1968b. *Collected Papers on Dravidian Linguistics.* Annamalainagar: Annamalai University.

1971. Spontaneous cerebrals in Sanskrit. *BSOAS* 34: 538–59.

1972. A reconstruction of Fortunatov's law. *BSOAS* 35.3: 531–45.

1976. A sketch of Maṇḍa grammar in comparison with Pengo. In Agesthialingom and Subrahmanyam (eds.), 39–56.

1983. Notes on some Dravidian words in Sanskrit. *IJDL* 12.1: 8–14.

Burrow, T. and Bhattacharya, S. 1953. *The Parji Language.* Hertford.

1960. A vocabulary of the Gondi dialects. *Journal of the Asiatic Society* 2: 73–251.

1961. Some notes on the Kui dialect as spoken by the Kuṭṭia Kandhs of north-east Koraput. *IIJ* 5: 118–35.

1963. Notes on Kuvi with a short vocabulary. *IIJ* 6: 231–89.

1970. *The Pengo Language.* Oxford: Clarendon Press.

Burrow, T. and Emeneau, M. B. 1961. *A Dravidian Etymological Dictionary* [*DED*]. Oxford: Clarendon Press.

1968. *A Dravidian Etymological Dictionary – Supplement* [*DEDS*]. Oxford: Clarendon Press.

1972. Dravidian etymological notes [DEN]. *JAOS* 92: 397–418, 475–91.

1984 (2nd edn). *A Dravidian Etymological Dictionary* [*DEDR*]. Oxford: Clarendon Press.

Butt, Miriam, King, Tracy Holloway, and Ramchand, Gillian (eds.). 1994. *Theoretical Perspectives on Word Order in South Asian Languages.* Stanford: Center for the Study of Language and Information.

Caldwell, Robert. 1956/61 (1856 1st edn, 1875 2nd edn, 1913 3rd edn revised and edited by J. L. Wyatt and T. Ramakrishna Pillai; reprinted). *A Comparative Grammar of the Dravidian or South-Indian Family of Languages.* Madras: University of Madras.

Campbell, Lyle. 1998. Nostratic: a personal assessment. In Salmons and Joseph (eds.), 107–52.

1999. Nostratic and linguistic palaeontology in methodological perspective. In Renfrew and Nettle (eds.), 179–230.

Cavalli-Sforza, L. L. 2000. *Genes, Peoples and Languages* (translated by Mark Seielstad). New York: North Point Press.

Cavalli-Sforza, L. L., Menozzi, P. and Piazza, A. 1994. *The History and Geography of Human Genes.* Princeton: Princeton University Press.

Census of India 1991. 1997. Series 1-India, Paper 1 of 1997 Language: India and States (Table C-7). New Delhi: Registrar General and Census Commissioner, India.

Chatterji, S. K. 1926. *The Origin and Development of the Bengali Language.* 3 volumes. Calcutta: University Press. [Repr. 1970. London: George Allen and Unwin.]

1957. Indian philology. *TC* 6: 195–225.

Chidambaranatha Chettiar, A. 1945. The Dravidian neuter and plural. *IL* 9: 1–6.

Cole, R. A. 1867. *An Elementary Grammar of the Coorg Language*. Bangalore: Wesleyan Press.

Collins, Mark (ed.). 1974 (repr). On the octaval system of reckoning in India. In *Dravidic Studies IV*, 169–211. Madras: University of Madras.

Comrie, Bernard. 1995a (repr. 1998). *Tense.* Cambridge: Cambridge University Press.

1995b. Focus in Malayāḷam. *Journal of the Asian and African Studies*, nos. 48, 49: 577–603.

1998. *Aspect.* Cambridge: Cambridge University Press.

Corbett, Greville. 1991. *Gender.* Cambridge: Cambridge University Press.

Dani, Ahmad Hasan. 1963. *Indian Palaeography.* Oxford: Clarendon Press.

Daniels, Peter and Bright, William O. (eds.). 1996. *The World's Writing Systems.* London: Oxford University Press.

Das, Sisir Kumar. 1973. *Structure of Malto.* Annamalainagar: Annamalai University.

David, Anne. 1999. A Comparative Study of Dravidian Infinitives. PhD Dissertation, Department of Linguistics, Chicago University.

Dawson, James. 1870. Gondi words and phrases. *JASB* 39: 108ff., 172ff.

Deshpande, Madhav M. 1979a. Genesis of Rgvedic retroflexion: a historical and sociolinguistic investigation. In Deshpande and Hook (eds.), 235–315.

1979b. *Sociolinguistic Attitudes in India: an Historical Reconstruction.* Ann Arbor: Karoma Publishers, Inc.

Deshpande, Madhav M. and Hook, Peter Edwin (eds.). 1979. *Aryan and Non-Aryan in India.* Ann Arbor: University of Michigan, Center for South and Southeast Asian Studies.

Diffloth, G. 1968. The Iruḷa Language: a Close Relative of Tamil. PhD dissertation, University of California at Los Angeles. [Xerox copy, University Microfilms, Ann Arbor, Michigan, 1976.]

Dixon, R. M. W. (ed.). 1987. *Studies in Ergativity.* Amsterdam: Elsevier Science Publishers B.V.

1982. *Where Have all the Adjectives Gone? and Other Essays in Semantics and Syntax.* Berlin: Mouton Publishers.

Dixon, R. M. W. and Aikhenvald, Alexandra Y. (eds.). 2000. *Changing Valency: Case Studies in Transitivity.* Cambridge: Cambridge University Press.

Dolgopolsky, Aaron B. 1986. A probabilistic hypothesis concerning the oldest relationships among the language families of Northern Eurasia. In Shevoroshkin et al. (eds.), 27–50.

1998. *The Nostratic Macrofamily and Linguistic Paleontology.* (With an introduction by Colin Renfrew.) Cambridge: McDonald Institute for Archaeological Research.

Driberg, J. G. and Harrison, H. J. 1849. *Narrative of Second Visit to the Gonds of the Nerbudda Territory with a Grammar and Vocabulary of their Language.* Calcutta.

Droese, Ernest. 1884. *Introduction to the Malto Language.* Agra: Secundra Orphanage Press.

Ebert, Karen. 1996. *Koḍava.* Munich and Newcastle: Lincom Europa.

Ekka, Francis. 1972. Remarks on the treatment of PDr **o:* in Kuṛux and Malto. *IJDL* 1.2: 19–28.

Elfenbein, J. 1982. Notes on Balochi-Brahui linguistic commensality. *TPS* 77–98.

1983a. The Brahui problem again. *IIJ* 25: 103–32.

1983b. A Brahui supplementary vocabulary. *IIJ* 25: 191–209.

1987. A periplus of the 'Brahui problem'. *Indo-Iranica* (fascicule 2). 215–33.

1997. Brahui phonology. In Alan Kaye (ed.), *Phonologies of Asia and Africa*, 797–811. Winona Lake, Indiana: Eisenbrauns.

1998. Brahui. In Steever (ed.), 388–414.

Ellis, Francis Whyte. 1816. Note to the Introduction of A. D. Campbell's *A Grammar of the Teloogoo Language,* 154–5. Madras [Repr. with an editorial note by N. Venkata Rao in *Annals of Oriental Research of the University of Madras* 12: 1–35. Madras: University of Madras.]

Emeneau, M. B. 1938. Echowords in Toda. *New Indian Antiquary* 1: 109–17. [Repr. in Emeneau 1967b: 37–45.]

1944–6. *Kota Texts* (in 4 volumes). UCPL 2. Berkeley and Los Angeles: University of California Press.

1945. The Dravidian verbs 'come' and 'give'. *Language* 21: 184–213.

1953a. The Dravidian kinship terms. *Language* 29: 339–53.

1954. Linguistic pre-history of India. *PAPS* 98: 282–92. [Repr. 1956. *TC* 5: 30–55 and in Emeneau 1980b: 105–25.]

1955a. India and linguistics. *JAOS* 75: 145–53.

1955b. *Kolami, a Dravidian Language.* UCPL 12. Berkeley: University of California Press. [Repr. 1961 by Annamalai University, Annamalainagar.]

1956. India as a linguistic area. *Language* 32: 3–16.

1957a. Numerals in comparative linguistics (with special reference to Dravidian). *Bulletin of the Institute of History and Philology*, Academia Sinica (Taipei). 29: 1–10.

1957b. Toda, a Dravidian language. *TPS* 15–66.

1961a. Brahui demonstrative pronouns. *Journal of the Asiatic Society* 3.1–5. [Repr. in Emeneau 1994: 17–22.]

1961b. North Dravidian velar stops. In *Te. Po. Mī.Maṇiviẓā Malar* (Studies Presented to Professor T. P. Meenakshisundaran), 371–88. [Repr. in Emeneau 1994: 1–15]

1962a. Bilingualism and structural borrowing. *PAPS* 106: 430–42.

1962b. Dravidian and Indian linguistics. Berkeley: Center for South Asian Studies, UC (Mimeographed).

1962c. New Brahui etymologies. In *Indological Studies in Honor of W. Norman Brown* (American Oriental Series 47), 59–69. [Repr. in Emeneau 1994: 23–34.]

1962d. *Brahui and Dravidian Comparative Grammar.* UCPL 27. Berkeley: University of California Press.

1964. Linguistic desiderata in Baluchistan. in *Indo-Iranica (Mélanges présentés à George Morgenstierne à l'occasion de son soixante-dixième anniversaire)*, 73–7. Wiesbaden: Otto Harrasowitz.

1965. *India and Historical Grammar.* Annamalainagar: Annamalai University.

1966 (pub. 1968). Some South Dravidian noun formatives. *IL* 27: 21–30. [Repr. in Emeneau 1994: 163–70.]

1967a. The South Dravidian languages. *JAOS* 87: 365–413.

1967b. *Dravidian Linguistics, Ethnology and Folktales: Collected Papers.* Annamalainagar: Annamalai University.

1969a. Onomatopoetics in the Indian linguistic area. *Language* 45: 274–99.

1969b. Kota vowel shift. *JTS* 1: 21–34. [Repr. in Emeneau 1994: 175–82.]

1970a. *Dravidian Comparative Phonology: a Sketch.* Annamalainagar: Annamalai University.

1970b. Koḍagu vowels. *JAOS* 90: 145–58. [Repr. in Emeneau 1994: 183–201.]

1971a. Dravidian and Indo-Aryan: the Indian linguistic area. In Sjoberg (ed.), 33–68.

1971b. Koḍagu and Brahui developments of Proto-Dravidian -*ṛ*-. *IIJ* 13.3: 176–98. [Repr. in Emeneau 1994: 203–22.]

1973. Review of Kamil V. Zvelebil, *Comparative Dravidian Phonology* (1970). *Linguistics* 107: 77–82.

1974a. Review of Martin Pfeiffer, *Elements of Kuṛux Historical Phonology* (1972). *Language* 50: 755–8.

1974b. The Indian linguistic area revisited. *IJDL* 3.1: 92–134.

1975. Studies in Dravidian verb stem formation. *JAOS* 95: 1–24. [Repr. in Emeneau 1994: 223–63.]
1978. Towards an onomastics of South Asia. *JAOS* 98: 113–30.
1979. Toda vowels in non-initial syllables. *BSOAS* 42: 225–34. [Repr. in Emeneau 1994: 275–86.]
1980a. Indian demonstrative bases: a revision. *Proceedings of the Sixth Annual Meeting of the Berkeley Linguistic Society*, 20–7. [Repr. in Emeneau 1994: 307–15.]
1980b. *Language and Linguistic Area* (Selected and Introduced by Anwar S. Dil). Stanford: Stanford University Press.
1980c. Brahui laterals from Proto-Dravidian *ṟ. *JAOS* 100: 311–12. [Repr. in Emeneau 1994: 303–6.]
1980d. Brahui laterals from Proto-Dravidian. In Bhakti P. Mallik (ed.), *Suniti Kumar Chatterji Commemoration Volume*, 101–5. Burdwan: University of Burdwan.
1980e. Sanskrit *bhōgin-* 'wealth' → 'village headman; fisherman, palanquin bearer'. In K. Klar, M. Langdon and S. Silver (eds.), *American and Indo-European Studies: Papers in Honor of Madison S. Beeler*, 315–25. The Hague: Mouton.
1983. Demonstrative pronominal bases in the Indian linguistic area. *IJDL* 12.1: 1–7.
1984. *Toda Grammar and Texts.* Philadelphia: American Philosophical Society.
1987a. Some notes on Dravidian intensives. In George Cardona and Norman H. Zide (eds.), *Festschrift for Henry Hoenigswald: on the Occasion of his 70th Birthday,* 109–13. Tübingen: Gunter Narr Verlag. [Repr. in Emeneau 1994: 323–7.]
1987b. The right hand is the 'eating hand': an Indian areal linguistic inquiry. In *Dimensions in Social Life: Essays in Honor of David Mandelbaum*, 263–73. [Repr. in Emeneau 1994: 329–34.]
1988. Proto-Dravidian *c* and its developments. *JAOS* 108: 239–68.
1989. The languages of the Nilgiris. In Hockings (ed.), 133–42.
1991. Brahui personal pronouns: 1st singular and reflexive. In Lakshmi Bai and Ramakrishna Reddy (eds.), 1–12.
1992. Foreword to Hockings and Pilot-Raichoor (eds.), vii–x.
1994. *Dravidian Studies: Selected Papers.* Delhi: Motilal Banarsi Dass.
1995. The palatalizing rule in Tamil-Malayāḷam and Telugu. *JAOS* 115.3: 401–9.
1997a. Brahui etymologies and phonetic developments: new items. *BSOAS* 60.3: 440–7.
1997b. Linguistics and botany in the Nilgiris. In Hockings (ed.), 74–105.
2000. Some Dravidian noun compounds. (MS.).
Emeneau, M. B. and Burrow, T. 1962. *Dravidian Borrowings from Indo-Aryan.* UCPL 26. Berkeley: University of California Press.
Emeneau, M. B. and Hart, Kausalya. 1993. Tamil expressives with initial voiced stops. *BSOAS* 56: 75–86.
Erdosy, George (ed.). 1995. *The Indo-Aryans of Ancient South Asia: Language, Material Culture and Ethnicity.* Berlin and New York: Walter de Gruyter.
Fairservis, Walter A. Jr. 1983. The script of the Indus Valley civilization. *Scientific American* 248.3: 44–52.
1986. The Harappan civilization according to its writing: a model for the decipherment of the script. *Tamil Civilization* 4: 103–80.
1992. *The Harappan Civilization and its Writing.* New York: E. J. Brill.
Ferguson, Charles A. 1964. Diglossia. In Dell Hymes (ed.), *Language, Education and Society,* 429–39. New York: Harper and Row.
Firth, J. R. 1934 (4th edn). Appendix to A. H. Arden. *A Progressive Grammar of Common Tamil.* Madras: Christian Literature Society.

Fitzgerald, A. G. 1913. *Kūviṅga Bassa: the Kondh Language as Spoken by the Parjas of the Madras Presidency*. Calcutta: Catholic Orphan Press.

Friend-Pereira, J. E. 1909. *A Grammar of the Kui Language*. Calcutta.

Fürer-Haimendorf, C.von. 1954. When, how and from where did the Dravidians come to India? *Indo-Asian Culture* 2.3: 238–47.

Gai, G. S. 1946. *Historical Grammar of Old Kannaḍa* (based entirely on the Kannaḍa inscriptions of the 8th, 9th and 10th centuries AD). Poona: Deccan College.

Garman, Michael. 1986. An approach to Dravidian derivational morphology. *IJDL Working Papers in Linguistics* 2.1: 47–67.

George, K. M. 1956. *Rāmacaritam and the Study of Early Malayāḷam*. Kottayam: The National Book Stall.

Gildea, Spike (ed.). 2000. *Reconstructing Grammar: Comparative Linguistics and Grammaticalization*. Amsterdam and Philadelphia: John Benjamins Publishing Company.

Glazov, Yuri. 1968. Non-past tense morphemes in ancient Tamil. In Krishnamurti (ed.), 103–9.

Godavarma, K. 1941–2. A study of personal pronouns in the South Dravidian languages. *New Indian Antiquary* 4: 201–20.

Gopalakrishnan, N. 1985. Sanskrit impact on Malayāḷam. In Prabhakara Variar (ed.), 31–54.

Gopinatha Pillai, N. R. 1985. Standardization of poetical language. In Prabhakara Variar (ed.), 91–8.

Greenberg, Joseph H. (ed.). 1963. *Universals of Language*. Cambridge, Mass.: MIT Press.

2000. *Indo-European and its Closest Relatives: the Eurasiatic Language Family*. Stanford: Stanford University Press.

Grierson, G. A. 1906. *Linguistic Survey of India*, vol. IV (*Muṇḍā and Dravidian Languages*), Sten Konow (ed.). [Repr. 1967. Delhi: Motilal Banarsidass.]

Grignard, A. 1924a. *A Grammar of the Oraon Language*. Calcutta: Catholic Orphan Press.

1924b. *An Oraon–English Dictionary*. Calcutta and Vienna.

Gundert, H. 1872. *A Malayāḷam and English Dictionary*. Mangalore: Basel Mission Press.

Gurov, Nikita. 2000. Spisok Kuipera Substratnaya lesika 'Rigvedy': Protsessy yazykovoi interferentsii v Yuznnoi Azii 2-1 tys. do n.e. In *Protsessy yazykovoi interferentsii v Yuznnoi Azii na rubezhe 3-go tysyacheletiya*, 25–37. Moscow. [F. B. J. Kuiper's list of substratum vocabulary in the Rigveda: processes of language interference in South Asia in the 2nd – 1st millennia BCE. In *Processes of Language Interference in South Asia in the 2nd – 1st Millennia BCE*, 25–37.] Moscow.

Gwynn, J. P. L. (assisted by J. V. Sastry). 1991. *A Telugu–English Dictionary*. Delhi: Oxford University Press.

Hahn, F. 1903. *Kurukh (Orāõ^{n})–English Dictionary*, Part I. Calcutta: Bengal Secretariat Press.

1911. *Kurukh Grammar*. Calcutta: Bengal Secretariat Press.

Haridas Bhat, K. S. and Upadhyaya, U. P. 1988–97. *Tuḷu Lexicon* (in 6 volumes). Udupi: Rashtrakavi Govinda Pai Samshodhan Kendra, M G M. College.

Heesterman, J. C., Schokker, G. H., and Subramoniam, V. I. (eds.). 1968. *Pratidānam: Indian, Iranian, and Indo-European Studies, Presented to Franciscus Bernardus Jacobus Kuiper on his Sixtieth Birthday* (Janua Linguarum Series Major 34). The Hague, Paris: Mouton.

Herring, H. 1994. Great German Dravidologists. *IJDL* 23.2: 53–66.

Hislop, Stephen. 1866. *Papers Relating to the Aboriginal Tribes of the Central Provinces*. Edited with notes and preface by R. Temple. Nagpore.

Hock, Hans H. 1975. Substratum influence on (Rig-Vedic) Sanskrit? *Studies in Linguistic Sciences* 5: 76–125.

1982. The Sanskrit quotative: a historical and comparative study. *Studies in Linguistic Sciences* 12: 39–85.

1996. Pre-Ṛgvedic convergence between Indo-Aryan and Dravidian? A survey of the issues and controversies. In Jan E. M. Houben (ed.), *Ideology and Status of Sanskrit: Contribution to the History of the Sanskrit Language*, 17–58. Leiden: E. J. Brill.

Hockings, Paul (ed.) 1989. *Blue Mountains (The Ethnography and Biogeography of a South Indian Region on the Nilgiri Hills)*. Delhi: Oxford University Press.

(ed.) 1997. *Blue Mountains Revisited (Cultural Studies on the Nilgiri Hills)*. Delhi: Oxford University Press.

Hockings, Paul and Pilot-Raichoor, Christiane. 1992. *A Badaga-English Dictionary* (Trends in Linguistics, Documentation 8). Berlin and New York: Mouton de Gruyter.

India 2001: a Reference Annual. 2001. Compiled and edited by Research, Reference and Training Division, Publication Division. New Delhi: Government of India, Ministry of Information and Broadcasting.

International Encyclopedia of Linguistics, *see* Bright (1992).

Israel, M. 1971. The so-called inflexional increments in Tamil with special reference to Tholkaappiyam. In Asher (ed.), 319–28.

1973. *The Treatment of Morphology in Tolkāppiyam*. Madurai: Madurai University.

1977. Demonstratives in Kuubi, Kuui and Kuuvi. *IJDL* 5.2: 223–32.

1979. *A Grammar of the Kuvi Language*. Tiruvananthapuram: International School of Dravidian Linguistics.

James, Gregory. 1991. *Tamil Lexicography* (Lexicographica: Series Maior 40). Tübingen: Max Niemeyer.

Jhungare, Indira Y. 1985. Topic prominence in Indo-Aryan and Dravidian. *IJDL* 14: 181–98.

Joseph, P. M. 1989. The word *Draviḍa*. *IJDL* 18.2: 134–42.

Joy Reddy. 1979. *Kuwi Grammar*. Mysore: Central Institute of Indian Languages.

Kameswari, T. M. 1969. The chronology of Dravidian languages – a lexico-statistic analysis. In Agesthialingom and Kumaraswami Raja (eds.), 269–74.

Kapp, Dieter B. 1978. Pālu Kuṟumba riddles: specimens of a South Dravidian tribal language. *BSOAS* 41: 3. 512–22.

1984a. *Ālu Kuṟumba Nāyaⁿ (Die Sprache der Ālu-Kuṟumba Nāyaⁿ: Grammatik, Texte, Wörterbuch)*. Wiesbaden: Otto Harrassowitz.

1984b. Ālu Kuṟumba riddles. *BSOAS* 47.2: 302–23.

1985. Echo-word formation in Ālu Kuṟumba. *IJDL* 14.1: 35–55.

1987. Centralized vowels in Ālu Kuṟumba. *JAOS* 107.3: 409–26.

1998. Dravidian borrowings from Portuguese (Kannaḍa and Telugu). *PILC Journal of Dravidic Studies* 8.1: 13–32.

Karthikeyan, G. 1980. Analysis of auxiliaries in Tamil inscriptions (from 900 to 1050 AD). In Agesthialingom and Srinvasa Varma (eds.), 157–66.

Kedilaye, A. S. 1968. Gender in Dravidian. In Agesthialingom and Kumaraswami Raja (eds.), 169–76.

Kekunnaya, Padmanabha. 1994. *A Comparative Study of Tuḷu Dialects*. Udupi: Rashtrakavi Govinda Pai Research Centre.

Kittel, F. 1873. Notes concerning numerals in the ancient Dravidian. *IA* 2: 24–5, 124–5.

1894. *A Kannaḍa-English Dictionary*. Mangalore: Bäsel Mission Press. Revised and enlarged by M. Mariappa Bhat. 1968–71. Madras University. [Repr. 1983. New Delhi: Asian Educational Services.]

Klaiman, M. H. 1986. Semantic parameters and South Asian linguistic area. In Krishnamurti et al. (eds.), 179–94.

1987. Bengali syntax: possible Dravidian influences. *IJDL* 6: 303–17.

Koskinen, K. 1996. Taamarai 'lotus' and the name Tamiẓ. *IJDL* 25.2: 141–2.

Kothandaraman, P. 1985. Velar datives in Dravidian. *ISDL Working Papers in Applied Linguistics* 1: 115–20.

Kothandaraman, Pon. 1980. Auxiliaries in Tamil. In Agesthialingom and Srinvasa Varma (eds.), 45–58.

Kothandaraman, R. [No date]. Functional shift in finite constructions in Tamil. MS.

Krishnamurti, Bh. 1955. The history of vowel-length in Telugu verbal bases. *JAOS* 75: 237–52. [Repr. as 'Alternations in vowel length in Telugu verbal bases: A comparative study', with a postscript in Krishnamurti 2001a: ch. 1, 1–28.]

1958a. Alternations *i/e* and *u/o* in South Dravidian. *Language* 34: 458–68. [Repr. with a postscript in Krishnamurti 2001a: ch. 2, 29–41.]

1958b. Proto-Dravidian *ẓ*. *IL: Turner Jubilee Volume-1* 19: 259–93. [Repr. with a postscript in Krishnamurti 2001a: ch. 3, 42–75.]

1961. *Telugu Verbal Bases: a Comparative and Descriptive Study.* UCPL 24. Berkeley and Los Angeles: University of California Press.

1963. Review of T. Burrow and M. B. Emeneau, *A Dravidian Etymological Dictionary. Language* 39: 556–64.

(ed.). 1968a. *Studies in Indian Linguistics: M. B. Emeneau Ṣa ṣṭip ūrti Volume*. Poona and Annamalainagar: Centres of Advanced Study.

1968b. Dravidian personal pronouns. In Krishnamurti, 1968a: 189–205. [Repr. with a postscript in Krishnamurti 2001a: ch. 4, 76–98.]

1969a. *Koṇḍa or Kūbi a Dravidian Language.* Hyderabad: Tribal Cultural Research and Training Institute.

1969b. Comparative Dravidian linguistics. *Current Trends in Linguistics,* vol. 5 (South Asian Linguistics), 309–30. The Hague: Mouton and Co. [Repr. as 'Comparative Dravidian studies', in Krishnamurti 2001a: ch. 5, 99–120.]

1969c. Dravidian nasals in Brahui. In Agesthialingom and Kumaraswami Raja (eds.), 65–74. [Repr. in Krishnamurti 2001a: ch. 6, 121–6.]

1971. Some observations on the Tamil phonology of the 12th and 13th centuries. In Asher (ed.), 356–61. [Repr. in Krishnamurti 2001a: ch. 7, 127–32.]

1975a. Gender and number in Proto-Dravidian. *IJDL* 4: 328–50. 1976. [Repr. with a postscript in Krishnamurti 2001a: ch. 8, 133–53.]

1975b. Review of M. B. Emeneau, *Dravidian Comparative Phonology: a Sketch. JAOS* 95: 312–13.

1976. Review of Kamil Zvelebil, *Comparative Dravidian Phonology*. *Lingua* 39: 139–53.

1978a. Areal and lexical diffusion of sound change: evidence from Dravidian. *Language* 54: 1–20. [Repr. in Krishnamurti 2001a: ch. 10, 162–82.]

1978b. On diachronic and synchronic rules in phonology: the case of Parji. *IL* 39: 252–76. [Repr. in Krishnamurti 2001a: ch. 11, 183–203.]

1980. A vowel-lowering rule in Kui-Kuvi. In *Proceedings of the Sixth Annual Meeting of the Berkeley Linguistic Society*, 495–506. Berkeley: University of California. [Repr. in Krishnamurti 2001a: ch. 12, 204–12.]

1983. (With Lincoln Moses and Douglas Danforth) Unchanged cognates as a criterion in linguistic sub-grouping. *Language* 59: 541–68. [Repr. in Krishnamurti 2001a: ch. 13, 213–42.]

1984. Modernization of South Indian languages: lexical innovations in newspaper language. In Bh. Krishnamurti and Aditi Mukherjee (eds.), 96–114. [Repr. in Krishnamurti 1998c: 227–48.]

1985. An overview of comparative Dravidian studies since *Current Trends* (1969). In Veneeta Z. Acson and Richard L. Leed (eds.), *For Gordon Fairbanks*, 212–31. Honolulu: University of Hawaii Press. [Repr. in Krishnamurti 2001a: ch. 14, 243–60.]

1989. (With G. U. Rao) A problem of reconstruction in Gondi: interaction between phonological and morphological processes. *Osmania Papers in Linguistics,* 1–21 (1987 volume). [Repr. in Krishnamurti 2001a: ch. 15, 261–72.]

1991a. The emergence of the syllable types of stems (C)VCC(V) and (C)$\bar{\text{V}}$C(V) in Indo-Aryan and Dravidian: conspiracy or convergence? In William G. Boltz and Michael C. Shapiro (eds.), *Studies in the Historical Phonology of Asian Languages* (Current Issues in Linguistic Theory 77), Amsterdam: John Benjamins B. V. [Repr. in Krishnamurti 2001a: ch. 16, 273–83.]
1991b. Dravidian lexicography. *Wörterbucher, Dictionaries, Dictionnaires (An International Encyclopedia of Lexicography)*, 2521–34. Berlin: Walter de Gruyter.
1992a. Dravidian languages. *International Encyclopedia of Linguistics* 1: 373–6. Oxford and New York: Oxford University Press.
1993. Complex predicates in Telugu. In Manindra K. Verma (ed.), *Complex Predicates in South Asian Languages*, 135–56. New Delhi: Manohar; also printed in *Bulletin of the Deccan College Post-Graduate and Research Institute* (Professor S. M. Katre Felicitation volume), vols. 51–2: 313–28. Poona: Deccan College.
1994a. 'Introduction' to Emeneau 1994: xv–xxvii.
1994b. Indian Names: Dravidian. In L. Zgusta (ed.), *Namen Forschung, Proper Name Studies, Les noms propres,* 665–71. Berlin: Walter de Gruyter and Co.
1994c. Stative expressions in Indian languages: some semantic and syntactic aspects. *Osmania Papers in Linguistics* 16/17: 39–71 (H. S. Ananthanarayana Festschrift).
1997a. The origin and evolution of primary derivative suffixes in Dravidian. In Hans Henrich Hock (ed.), *Historical, Indo-European and Lexicographical Studies (A Festschrift for Ladislav Zgusta on the Occasion of his 70th Birthday)*, 87–116. Berlin: Mouton de Gruyter. [Repr. in Krishnamurti 2001a: ch. 17, 284–306.]
1997b. Proto-Dravidian laryngeal **H* revisited. *PILC Journal of Dravidic Studies* 7.2: 145–65. Pondicherry: Pondicherry Institute of Linguistics and Culture. [Repr. as 'Evidence for a laryngeal *H* in Proto-Dravidian' in Krishnamurti 2001a: ch. 19, 323–44.]
1997c. Le genre et le nombre en dravidien. In Mary-Annie Morel (ed.), *Faits de langues*, 71–6. Revue de Linguistique 10 (Les langues d'Asie du sud). Paris: Ophrys.
1998a. Patterns of sound change in Dravidian. In Rajendra Singh (ed.), *The Yearbook of South Asian Languages and Linguistics*, 63–79. New Delhi: Sage Publications India Pvt. Ltd. [Repr. in Krishnamurti 2001a: ch. 18, 307–22.]
1998b. Regularity of sound change through lexical diffusion. *Language Variation and Change* 10.2: 193–222. [Repr. in Krishnamurti 2001a: ch. 20, 345–69.]
1998c. *Language, Education and Society.* New Delhi: Sage Publications.
1998d. Telugu. In Steever (ed.), 202–40.
2001a. *Comparative Dravidian Linguistics: Current Perspectives.* Oxford: Oxford University Press.
2001b. Landmarks in comparative Dravidian studies. In Krishnamurti 2001a: ch. 21, 370–82.
Krishnamurti, Bh. and Benham, Brett. 1998. Koṇḍa. In Steever (ed.), 241–69.
Krishnamurti, Bh. and Gwynn, J. P. L. 1985. *A Grammar of Modern Telugu*. Delhi: Oxford University Press.
Krishnamurti, Bh., Masica, Colin P. and Sinha, Anjani, K. (eds.). 1986. *South Asian Languages: Structure, Convergence and Diglossia.* Delhi: Motilal Banarsidass.
Krishnamurti, Bh. and Mukherjee, Aditi (eds.). 1984. *Modernization of Indian Languages in New Media*. Hyderabad: Osmania University. (Department of Linguistics, Publication No. 4).
Kuiper, F. B. J. 1967. The genesis of a linguistic area. *IIJ* 10: 81–102.
1991. *Aryans in the Rigveda.* Amsterdam: Rodopi B. V.
Kumaraswami Raja, N. 1969a. Post-nasal plosives in Telugu. In Agesthialingom and Kumaraswami Raja (eds.), 75–84.
1969b. *Post-nasal Voiceless Plosives in Dravidian* (Department of Linguistics Publication no. 18). Annamalainagar: Annamalai University.

1975. A note on kuṟṟiyal ukaram. *JTS* 8: 1–7.
1980. Geminate dental/alveolar nasal in Malayāḷam: a historical study. *JTS* 17: 15–26.
Kushalappa Gowda, K. 1972. *A Grammar of Kannaḍa (Based on the Inscriptions of Coorg, South Kanara and North Kanara Districts 1000–1400A.D.)*. Annamalainagar: Annamalai University.
Lahovary, Nicolas. 1963. *Dravidian Origins and the West: Newly Discovered Ties with the Ancient Cultures and Languages*. Bombay: Orient Longmans.
Lakshmi Bai, B. and Ramakrishna Reddy, B. (eds.). 1991. *Studies in Dravidian and General Linguistics: a Festschrift for Bh. Krishnamurti*. Osmania University Publications in Linguistics no. 6. Hyderabad: Osmania University, Department of Linguistics.
Lehmann, Thomas. 1989. *A Grammar of Modern Tamil*. Pondicherry: Pondicherry Institute of Language and Culture.
1991. Grammatik des Alttamil: Morphologische und Syntaktische Analyse der Cankam-Tamil des Dichters Kāpilar. PhD Dissertation, University of Heidelberg.
1998. Old Tamil. In Steever (ed.), 75–99.
Letchmajee, Lingum. 1902 (2nd edn). *An Introduction to the Grammar of the Kui or Kandh Language*. Calcutta.
Lind, A. A. 1913. *A Manual of Mardia Gondi* (cited by Burrow and Bhattacharya 1960).
Lisker, L. and Krishnamurti, Bh. 1991. Lexical stress in a 'stressless' language: judgments by Telugu- and English-speaking linguists. *Proceedings of the XII International Congress of Phonetic Sciences* (Université de Provence), 2: 90–3.
Lust, Barbara C., Wali, Kashi, Gair, James W. and Subbarao, K. V. (eds.). 2000. *Lexical Anaphors and Pronouns in Selected South Asian Languages*. Berlin: Mouton de Gruyter.
Mahadeva Sastri, K. 1969. *Historical Grammar of Telugu (with Special Reference to Old Telugu 200 BC to 1000 AD)*. Tirupati: Sri Venkateswara University.
Mahadevan, Iravatam. 1971. Tamil-Brahmi inscriptions of the Sangam age. In Asher (ed.), 73–106.
1977. *The Indus Script: Texts, Concordances, and Tables*. New Delhi: Archeological Survey of India.
Mahapatra, B. P. 1979. *Malto: an Ethno-Semantic Study*. Mysore: Central Institute of Indian Languages.
Mallory, J. P. 1989. *In Search of Indo-Europeans: Language, Archaeology and Myth*. London: Thomas and Hudson.
Männer, A. 1886. *Tuḷu-English Dictionary*. Mangalore. [Repr. 1983 New Delhi: Asian Educational Services.]
Marlow, Elli Johanna Pudas. 1974. More on the Uralo-Dravidian Relationship: a Comparison of Dravidian Etymological Vocabularies. PhD Dissertation, University of Texas at Austin.
Masica, Colin Paul. 1976. *Defining a Linguistic Area: South Asia*. Chicago: Chicago University Press.
1991. *The Indo-Aryan Languages*. Cambridge: Cambridge University Press.
Master, Alfred. 1937–9. Intervocalic plosives in Early Tamil. *BSOAS* 9: 1003–8.
1946. The zero negative in Dravidian. *TPS* 137–55.
1947. Indo-Aryan and Dravidian. *BSOAS* 11: 297–307.
1948. Indo-Aryan and Dravidian III. *BSOAS* 12: 340–64.
Matthews, P. H. 1996 (2nd edn). *Syntax*. Cambridge: Cambridge University Press.
McAlpin, David W. 1974. Towards Proto-Elamo-Dravidian. *Language* 50: 89–101.
1975. Elamite and Dravidian: further evidence of relationship. *Current Anthropology* 16: 105–15.
1979. Linguistic pre-history: the Dravidian situation. In Deshpande and Hook (eds.), 175–89.

1981. *Proto-Elamo-Dravidian: the Evidence and its Implications.* Philadelphia: American Philosophical Society.
Meenakshisundaran, T. P. 1965. *A Historical Grammar of Tamil.* Poona: Deccan College.
1968. The phoneme *y* in ancient Tamil. In Krishnamurti (ed.), 226–30.
Menges, K. H. 1964. Altaijisch und Dravidisch. *Orbis* 13: 66–103.
Menges, Karl H. 1969. The Dravido-Altaic relationship. *JTS* 1.1: 35–39.
1977. Dravidian and Altaic. *Anthropos* 72: 129–79.
Mitchell, A. N. 1942. *A Grammar of Maria Gondi as Spoken by the Bison Horn or Dandami Marias of Bastar Sate.* Jagdalpur.
Mohanan, K. P. 1996. Malayalam writing. In Daniels and Bright (eds.), 420–5.
Mohanan, K. P. and Mohanan, T. 1994. Issues in word order. In Butt et al. (eds.), 91–118.
Mohanty, P. 1994. Plural markers in Kui and Kuvi: a reconstruction. *IJDL* 24.2: 67–76.
Montgomery, Stephen E. 1963. The Telugu Adverb. MA Dissertation, University of Texas, Austin.
Moseley, Christopher and Asher, R. E. (Gen. eds.). 1994. *Atlas of the World's Languages.* London and New York: Routledge.
Moss, Clement F. 1950. *An Introduction to the Grammar of the Gondi Language.* Jabbalpore: Mission Press.
Namboodiri, E. V. N. 1976. *Glottochronology (as applied to four Dravidian languages).* Trivandrum: Sangma.
1980. Auxiliaries in Malayalam. In Agesthialingom and Srinvasa Varma (eds.), 261–90.
Natarajan, G. V. 1985. *Abujhmaria Grammar.* Mysore: Central Institute of Indian Languages.
Ohno, Susumu. 1980. *Sound Correspondences between Tamil and Japanese.* Tokyo: Gakshuin University.
1983. A study of the relationship between Tamil and Japanese. *IJDL* 12.2: 366–96.
Panikkar, G. K. 1969. Dravidian numeral constructions. In Agesthialingom and Kumaraswami Raja (eds.), 203–17.
Parpola, Asko. 1994. *Deciphering the Indus Script.* Cambridge: Cambridge University Press.
Perialwar, R. 1978a. *Irula Phonology with Vocabulary.* Annamalainagar: Annamalai University.
1978b. *A Grammar of the Irula Language.* Annamalainagar: Annamalai University.
1980. Auxiliaries in Irula. In Agesthialingom and Srinvasa Varma (eds.), 509–18.
Pfeiffer, Martin. 1972. *Elements of Kuṟux Historical Phonology.* Leiden: E. J. Brill.
Pilot-Raichoor, Christiane. 1997. Badaga and its relations with neighbouring languages. In Hockings (ed.), 136–47.
Possehl, Gregory L. 1996. *Indus Age: the Writing System.* New Delhi: Oxford University Press and IBH Publishing Co. Pvt. Ltd.
Prabhakara Variar, K. M. (ed.). 1985. *History of Malayalam Language.* Madras: University of Madras.
Prabhoo, Lalita R. 1980. Dative case in Indo-Aryan and Dravidian: contact and interference in the Indian subcontinent. *IJDL* 9.2: 253–73.
Prabodhachandran Nayar, V. R. 1985. Language of the Pāṭṭu literature. In Prabhakara Variar (ed.), 81–9.
Radhakrishna, Budaraju. 1971. *Early Telugu Inscriptions (upto 1100 A.D. with Texts, Glossary and Brief Linguistic History).* Hyderabad: A. P. Sahitya Akademi.
Rajam, V. S. 1992. *A Reference Grammar of Classical Tamil Poetry.* Philadelphia: American Philosophical Society.
Ramachandra Rao, B. 1972. *A Descriptive Grammar of Pampa Bhārata.* Mysore: University of Mysore.
1980. Auxiliaries in literary Kannaḍa. In Agesthialingom and Srinvasa Varma (eds.), 453–68.
Ramachandra, Tirumala. 1993. *Mana-lipi puṭṭuprūwōttarālu* (Our Script, its Origin and Evolution, in Telugu, 3rd edn.). Hyderabad: Vishalandhra Publishing House.

Ramaiah, L. S. 1994–2000. *An International Bibliography of Dravidian Languages and Linguistics.* Madras: T. R. Publications Private Ltd. (1994. Vol. 1: *General and Comparative Dravidian Languages and Linguistics*; 1995. Vol. 2: *Tamil Language and Linguistics*; 1998. Vol. 3: *Telugu Language and Linguistics*; 2001: Vol. 5: *Malayāḷam Language and Linguistics*; Forthcoming: Vol. 4: *Kannaḍa Language and Linguistics*; Vol. 6: *Non-Literary Dravidian Languages and Linguistics.*)

Rama Rao, C. 1968. Direct and indirect reports: a hypothesis concerning the universals. *Pakha Sanjam* 1: 14–21.

Ramaswami Aiyar, L. V. 1936. *The Evolution of Malayalam Morphology*. Ernakulam: Cochin Government Press.

1937. The history of the Tamil-Malayalam alveolar plosive. *Journal of Ramavarma Research Institute* 5: 29–45, 83–106; 6: 7–30, 91–108; 7: 71–81, 102–17.

1938. The morphology of the Old Tamil verb. *Anthropos* 33: 747–81.

Ranganathacharyulu, K. K. 1987. *A Historical Grammar of Inscriptional Telugu* (*1401 AD to 1900 AD*). Hyderabad: Department of Linguistics, Osmania University.

Rao, G. U. 1987a. The development of personal pronouns in modern Gondi. *Studies in the Linguistic Sciences* 17.1: 35–50.

1987b. A Comparative Study of the Gondi Dialects (with Special Reference to Phonology and Morphology). PhD Dissertation in Linguistics, Osmania University, Hyderabad.

Renfrew, Colin and Nettle, Daniel (eds.). 1999. *Nostratic: Examining a Linguistic Macrofamily.* Cambridge: McDonald Institute for Archaeological Research, University of Cambridge.

Renfrew, Colin, McMahon, April and Trask, Larry (eds.). 2000. *Time Depth in Historical Linguistics.* Cambridge: McDonald Institute for Archaeological Research, University of Cambridge.

Sabir, Abdul Razzak. 1995. Morphological similarities in Brahui and Balochi languages. *IJDL* 24.1: 1–8.

Salmons, Joseph C. and Joseph, Brian D. (eds.). 1998. *Nostratic: Sifting the Evidence.* Amsterdam and Philadelphia: John Benjamins Publishing Company.

Sambasiva Rao, Gali. 1973. On Proto-Dravidian morphophonemics. *IJDL* 2.2: 217–42.

1977. Dravidian alternations. *IL* 38.2: 86–94.

Sankaran, C. R. 1939. Reconstruction of proto-Dravidian pronouns. *BDCRI* 1.1: 96–105.

Sapir, Edward. 1921. *Language.* New York: Harcourt, Brace and World, Inc.

Schiffman, Harold F. 1999. *A Reference Grammar of Spoken Tamil.* Cambridge: Cambridge University Press.

2000. Deverbal nominal derivation in Tamil. MS. 1–6.

Schiffman, Harold F. and Carol M. Eastman (eds.). 1975. *Dravidian Phonological Systems.* Seattle, Washington: Institute for Comparative and Foreign Area Studies, University of Washington.

Schrader, Friedrich Otto. 1937. On the Uralian element in the Dravida and Muṇḍā languages. *BSOAS* 8: 751–62.

Schultze, F. V. P. 1911. *A Grammar of the Kuvi Language.* Madras: Graves, Cookson and Co.

1913. *Vocabulary of the Kuvi-Kond Language.* Madras.

Sekhar, A. C. 1953. *Evolution of Malayalam.* Poona: Deccan College.

Sengupta, Sunil. 1974. Problems of numeral classifiers in Dravidian languages. *IJL* 1: 89–101.

Sethumadhava Rao, 1950. *A Grammar of the Kolami Language.* Hyderabad.

Shalev, Michael, Ladefoged, Peter and Bhaskararao, Peri. 1994. Phonetics of Toda. *PILC Journal of Dravidic Studies* 4.1: 19–56.

Shanmugam Pillai, M. 1971. Cases in Tamil, primary and secondary. *Proceedings of the First All India Conference of Linguists*, 229–34. Poona: Deccan College.

Shanmugam, S. V. 1969. The gender and number categories in Dravidian. *Journal of Annamalai University* 26: 79–100.
1971a. *Dravidian Nouns: a Comparative Study.* Annamalainagar: Annamalai University.
1971b. Some problems of Old Tamil phonology. *IIJ* 13: 31–43.
1972a. Gender and number sub-categorization in Dravidian. In Agesthialingom and Shanmugam (eds.), 383–97.
1972b. Dental and alveolar nasals in Dravidian. *BSOAS* 35: 74–84.
Shevoroshkin, Vitalij V. and Markey, T. L. (ed. and trans.). 1986. *Typology Relationship and Time* (A Collection of Papers on Language Change and Relationship by Soviet Linguists). Ann Arbor: Karoma Publishers, Inc.
Singh, Mona. 1994. Thematic roles, word order, and definiteness. In Butt et al. (eds.), 217–35.
Sjoberg, Andrée F. (ed.). 1971a. *Symposium on Dravidian Civilization.* Austin: Center for Asian Studies, University of Texas at Austin.
1971b. Who are the Dravidians? The present state of knowledge. In Sjoberg (ed.), 1–31.
1990. The Dravidian contribution to the development of Indian civilization: a call for reassessment. In *Comparative Civilizations Review* 23: 40–74.
1992. The impact of the Dravidian on Indo-Aryan: an overview. In Edgar C. Polomé and Werner Winter (eds.), *Reconstructing Languages and Cultures*, 507–29. (Trends in Linguistics, Studies and Monographs 58). Berlin and New York: Mouton de Gruyter.
Smith, Ian. 1991. Interpreting conflicting isoglosses: historical relationships among the Gondi dialects. In Lakshmi Bai and Ramakrishna Reddy (eds.), 27–38.
Somasekharan Nair, P. 1980. Auxiliaries in Malayāḷam dialects. In Agesthialingom and Srinvasa Varma (eds.), 291–304.
Somayaji, G. J. 1947. *āndhrabhāṣāwikāsamu* (Evolution of the Telugu Language). Visakhapatnam: The author, Maharanipeta.
South Indian Inscriptions. 1892–1983. Madras: Archeological Survey of India. (Currently available with) New Delhi: Navrang.
Southworth, Franklin C. 1976. On subgroups in Dravidian. *IJDL* 5.1: 114–37.
1979. Lexical evidence for early contacts between Indo-Aryan and Dravidian. In Deshpande and Hook (eds.), 191–234.
1995. Reconstructing social context from language: Indo-Aryan and Dravidian pre-history. In Erdosy (ed.), 258–77.
1998. On the origin of the word *tamiẓ*. *IJDL* 27.1: 129–32.
Sreekantaiya, T. N. 1935. The mutation of i, u, e and o in Kannaḍa. *Proceedings and Transactions of the Eighth All India Oriental Conference*, 769–800.
Sridhar, S. N. 1990. *Kannada.* London and New York: Routledge.
Srinivasan, R. 1980. Auxiliary verbs in Sangam literature. In Agesthialingom and Srinvasa Varma (eds.), 231–60.
Steever, Sanford B. 1988. *The Serial Verb Formation in the Dravidian Languages.* Delhi: Motilal Banarsidass.
1991. Exceptions to case-marking and the grammar of complementation in Dravidian. In Lakshmi Bai and Ramakrishna Reddy (eds.), 198–214.
1993. *Analysis to Synthesis*. Oxford: New York and London.
1996.Tamil writing system. In Daniels and Bright (eds.), 426–30.
(ed.). 1998a. *The Dravidian Languages*. London and New York: Routledge.
1998b. Kannada. In Steever 1998a: 129–57.
1998c. Malto. In Steever 1998a: 357–87.
Subbaiya, K. V. 1909–11. A primer of Dravidian phonology. *IA* 38: 159–70, 166–221.
1923. The history of first personal pronouns in various Dravidian languages. In *Dravidic Studies II*. Madras: Superintendent, Government Press.

1974. The pronouns and pronominal terminations of the first person in Dravidian. In Mark Collins (ed.). *Dravidic Studies II*, 17–79. Madras: Madras University Press.

Subbarao, K. V. and Lalitha Murthy, B. 2000. Lexical anaphors and pronouns in Telugu. In Lust et al. (eds.), 217–72.

Subbiah, G. 1980. Auxiliaries in Kota. In Agesthialingom and Srinvasa Varma (eds.), 497–508.

Subrahmanya Sastri, P. S. 1934. *History of Grammatical Theories in Tamil.* Madras: Journal of Oriental Research.

1947. *A Comparative Grammar of the Tamil Language.* Tiruvadi, Tanjore Dist.

Subrahmanyam, P. S. 1964. Two problems in Parji verb forms. *IL* 25: 47–55.

1965. The intransitive and transitive suffixes of Kui. *JAOS* 85: 551–65.

1967–8. The personal pronouns in Dravidian. *Bulletin of the Deccan College* 28: 112–26.

1968a. *A Descriptive Grammar of Gondi*. Annamalainagar: Annamalai University.

1968b. The position of Tuḷu in Dravidian. *IL* 29: 47–66.

1969a-i. The Central Dravidian languages. In Agesthialingom and Kumaraswami Raja (eds.), 107–34.

1969a-ii. The Central Dravidian languages. *JAOS* 89: 739–50.

1969b. The gender and number categories in Dravidian. *Journal of Annamalai University* 26: 79–100.

1970a. Long vowels before *y* in Telugu bases. *IL* 31: 69–73.

1970b. The personal pronouns in Dravidian. *Bulletin of the Deccan College Research Institute* [1967–68], 28.3–4: 1–16.

1971. *Dravidian Verb Morphology: a Comparative Study.* Annamalainagar: Annamalai University.

1973. Notes on Dravidian etymological notes. *IL* 34: 138–46.

1975. Quantitative variation in Dravidian. *IL* 36: 11–15.

1976a. A review of 'Gender and number in Proto-Dravidian', by Bh. Krishnamurti. *IJDL* 5.1: 138–43.

1976b. The Toda developments of Proto-Dravidian **a* **ā*, **l* and **ḷ*. In Agesthialingom and Subrahmanyam (eds.), 87–120.

1977a. Proto-Dravidian **r* in Toda. *IL* 38: 1–5.

1977b. The Toda reflexes of PDr. **l* and. **ḷ* *JAOS* 97: 178–81.

1977c. Dravidian alternations: a critique. *IL* 38: 227–33.

1980. Modal auxiliaries in Telugu. In Agesthialingom and Srinvasa Varma (eds.), 327–48.

1983. *Dravidian Comparative Phonology*. Annamalainagar: Annamalai University.

1988. Comparative Dravidian studies from 1980. *IJDL* 17.1: 59–91.

1991. Tense formation in Kota-Toda: a comparative study. In Lakshmi Bai and Ramakrishna Reddy (eds.), 49–72.

1993. The personal pronouns in Dravidian. *PILC Journal of Dravidic Studies* 3.1: 27–52.

1998. Kolami. In Steever (ed.), 301–27.

Subramanian, P. R. (ed.). 1992. *Dictionary of Contemporary Tamil (Tamil-Tamil-English).* Chennai: Cre-A.

Subramoniam, V. I. 1962. *Index of Puṟanāṉūṟu.* Trivandrum: University of Kerala.

1968. A problem in the reconstruction of Proto-Dravidian nasal phonemes. In Heesterman et al. (eds.), 344–7.

1972. Rules of nasal assimilation in Malayāḷam. *IJDL* 11.11: 137–43.

Sukumara Pillai, K. 1985. The language of Maṇipravāḷa literature. In Prabhakara Variar (ed.), 55–79.

Sumati, S. 1982. Comparative Phonology of the South-Central Dravidian Languages. MPhil. Dissertation, Department of Linguistics, Osmania University, Hyderabad.

Suvarchala, B. 1984. Central Dravidian Comparative Phonology. MPhil. Dissertation, Osmania University, Hyderabad.

1992. *Central Dravidian Comparative Morphology.* New Delhi: Navrang.

Tamil Lexicon, vols. 1–6. 1924–39. Madras: University of Madras.

Thapar, Romila. 2000. The Rgveda: encapsulating social change. In K. N. Panikkar, T. J. Byres and Utsa Patnaik (eds.), *The Making of History*, 11–40. Delhi: Tulika.

Thomasiah, K. 1986. Naikṛi Dialect of Kolami: Descriptive and Comparative Study. Unpublished PhD thesis, Annamalai University, Annamalainagar.

Thomason, Sarah Grey and Kaufman, Terrence. 1988. *Language Contact, Creolization, and Genetic Linguistics.* Berkeley and Los Angeles: University of California Press.

Tinnappan, S. P. 1980. Auxiliary verbs in Tolkāppiyam. In Agesthialingom and Srinivasa Varma (eds.), 45–58.

Trautmann, Thomas R. 1981. *Dravidian Kinship* (Cambridge Studies in Social Anthropology 36). Cambridge: Cambridge University Press.

Trench, C. J. Chenevix. 1919. *A Grammar of Gondi as Spoken in the Betul District, Central Provinces, India.* Vol. I *Grammar.* Madras: Superintendent, Government Press.

1923. Vol. II. *Gondi Vocabulary and Texts.* Madras: Superintendent, Government Press.

Turner, R. L. 1966. *A Comparative Dictionary of the Indo-Aryan Languages [CDIAL].* 3 vols. London: Oxford University Press.

1967. Geminates after long vowels in Indo-Aryan. *BSOAS* 30.1: 73–82. Repr. in *Collected Papers 1912–73*, 405–15. 1975. London: Oxford University Press.

Tuttle, E. H. 1927. Dravidian 1 and 2. *American Journal of Philology* 48: 267–72.

1928. I, we and you. *American Journal of Philology* 49: 334–42.

1930. *Dravidian Developments* (Language Monographs, no. 5). Philadelphia: Linguistic Society of America.

1940. Dravidian gender words. *BSOAS* 4: 769–78.

Tyler, Stephen A. 1968. Dravidian and Uralian: the lexical evidence. *Language* 44.4: 798–812.

1969. *Koya: an Outline Grammar, Gommu Dialect.* UCPL 54. Berkeley and Los Angeles: University of California Press.

Ushadevi, A. 1980. Auxiliary verbs in Nannaya. In Agesthialingom and Srinvasa Varma (eds.), 415–52.

Vachek, Jaroslav. 1978. The problem of the genetic relationship of the Mangolian and Dravidian languages. *AO* 46: 141–51.

1981. The Dravido-Altaic relationship: lexical and sound correspondences. *Proceedings of the 5th International Conference-Seminar of Tamil Studies,* vol.1: 159–70. Madras: International Association of Tamil Research.

1983. Dravido-Altaic: the Mongolian and Dravidian verbal bases. *JTS* 23: 1–16.

1985. The Mongolian and Dravidian verb phrase: its patterns and the underlying verb forms. In Jaromir Vochala (ed.), *Asian and African Linguistic Studies* 11: 26–45. Prague: Univrszita Karlova.

1987. The Dravido-Altaic relationship (some views and future prospects). *AO* 55: 139–49 (Bibliography at the end).

Vaidyanathan, S. 1980. *Studies in Dravidian Linguistics,* vol. 1. *Pakha Sanjam* 10 (special issue). Patiala: Department of Anthropological Linguistics, Punjabi University.

1982. *Studies in Dravidian Linguistics,* vol. 2. *Pakha Sanjam* 15 (special issue). Patiala: Department of Anthropological Linguistics, Punjabi University.

Venkatarama Aiyar, C. P. 1974 (repr.). The demonstrative bases. In Mark Collins (ed.), *Dravidic Studies I,* 1–15. Madras: University of Madras.

Williamson, H. 1890. *Gond Grammar and Vocabulary.* London.

Winfield, W. 1928. *A Grammar of the Kui Language*. Calcutta: Asiatic Society of Bengal.

Winslow, Miron. 1862. *A Comprehensive Tamil and English Dictionary of High and Low Tamil.* Madras. [Repr. 1987. New Delhi: Asian Educational Services].
Zvelebil, K. V. 1955. The present state of Dravidian philology. *TC* 4: 53–7.
1956. One hundred years of Dravidian comparative philology. *AO* 24: 599–609.
1961. Dravidian philology, general linguistics and early history of India. In *Dr. R. P. Sethu Pillai Silver Jubilee Commemoration Volume*, 127–34. Madras.
1962. Personal pronouns in Tamil and Dravidian. *IIJ* 6: 65–9.
1964. *Tamil in 550 A.D.: an Interpretation of Early Inscriptional Tamil*. Prague: Publishing House of the Czechoslovak Academy of Sciences.
1967. On morphophonemic rules of Dravidian bases. *Linguistics* 32: 87–95.
1970a. From Proto-South Dravidian to Old Tamil and Malayalam. *AO* 38: 45–67. [Repr. in Asher 1971: 1: 54–72.
1970b. *Comparative Dravidian Phonology*. The Hague: Mouton.
1971a. Irula vowels. *IIJ* 13: 113–22.
1971b. Review of T. Burrow and M. B. Emeneau, *A Dravidian Etymological Dictionary (supplement)* (1968). *IIJ* 13.2: 152–4.
1972a. Initial plosives in Dravidian. *Lingua* 30: 216–26.
1972b. The descent of the Dravidians. *IJDL* 1: 57–63.
1972c. Dravidian case-suffixes: attempt at a reconstruction. *JAOS* 92: 272–76.
1973. *The Irula Language*. Wiesbaden: Otto Harrassowitz.
1975. Word-borrowing and word-making in modern South Asian languages: Tamil. In *South Asian Digest of Modern Writing* IV: 86–97.
1977. *A Sketch of Comparative Dravidian Morphology* (part I). Mouton: The Hague.
1979. *The Irula (ĕṟla) Language,* part II. Wiesbaden: Otto Harrassowitz.
1980. A plea for Nilgiri areal studies. *IJDL* 9: 1–22.
1982a. Beṭṭa Kuṟumba: first report on a tribal language. *JAOS* 102: 523–7.
1982b. *The Irula (ĕṟla) Language,* part III: *Irula Lore, Texts and Translations*. Wiesbaden: Otto Harrassowitz.
1988. Jēnu Kuṟumba. Brief report on a 'tribal' language of the Nilgiri area. *JAOS* 108: 197–301.
1990a. *Dravidian Linguistics: an Introduction.* Pondicherry: Pondicherry Institute of Linguistics and Culture.
1990b. The language of the Sholegas, Nilgiri area, South India. *JAOS* 110.2: 417–33.
1997. Language list for Dravidian. *AO* 65: 175–90.
1999. The Dravidian perspective. In Renfrew and Nettle (eds.), 359–65.
Zvelebil, K. V. and Zgusta, L. 1961. Review of four works by N. Lahovary. *AO* 29: 127–30.

INDEX OF RECONSTRUCTIONS WITH GLOSSES

Asterisks are not marked since all the items listed below occur with asterisks in the book. They are all reconstructed forms and must be deemed to carry an asterisk each, if cited anywhere else. All reconstructions, unless otherwise stated, are to be taken as representing Proto-Dravidian (PD); reconstructions done at the level of subgroups are indicated by subgroup name: SD I, SD II, CD or ND, as the case may be. The order of entries follows Indic Roman, adapted to Dravidian, i.e. <a ā i ī u ū e ē o ō, k, c ñ, ṭ ṇ, ṯ, t n, p m, y r l w, ḷ ẓ H>. Lexical items (roots, stems, words, compounds) and grammatical morphs (suffixes which are bound) are listed separately. The numbers in square brackets refer to entry numbers in *DEDR*, followed by the page number(s) of this book. New abbreviations V = a vowel; Vb = main verb in complex stems, indicated by V in the book.

A. Lexical items

akam 'inside', *aka-ppaṭu* 'to be included' [7], 279.
akaẓ-tt-ay 'moat' [11], 8
akka- 'elder sister' [23], 10
añc- 'to fear', *añc-al*, *añc-c*(*-am*), n. 'fear' SD I, Te. [55], 199
aṭ-a-nk- 'be compressed, hidden', *aṭ-a-nkk-* v.t. 'to control, hide' PSD [63], 107, 279, 289
aṭ-a-ppay 'betel pouch' [64], 16
aṭ-ay-kkāy 'areca nut' SD I [88], 9
aṭ-V 'foot, bottom, base' SD I, *aṭ*-V*k*- SD II, CD [72], 484
aṭṭu 'pancake' [76], 10
aṇ-ṭṭ- 'to adhere, stick' [96], 172
aṇṇa- 'elder brother' [131], 10
aṯ-V- 'to know' [314], 14
aṯṯ-/āṯṯ- 'that place, manner' [1], 407
a-tu 3neu sg SD I [1], 308
atta- 'maternal/paternal aunt' [142], 10
a-n(V)*k- ~ ā-n*(V)*k/-t- ~ -tt-* 'that place/time/much/many/ manner' [1], 407
*a-n*V 'there, then' [1], 407
a-nṯu 'that day, then' SD I [1], 407
appa- 'father' [156a], 10
app-am 'rice cake' [155], 10
ap-pōẓ 'that time, then', 407
amp-ali 'porridge' SD II [174], 10
ampu 'arrow' [17a], 9
amp-i 'boat' [177], 13
*a-mp*V 'there' PSD [1], 407
amm-a 'mother' [183], 10
ayy-a 'father' [196], 10
ar-ac/-aḷ 'pipal tree' [202], 12
ar-i 'a kind of tax' [216], 8
ar-V*ṇṭṭi* 'banana, plantain' SD II [205], 12
al- 'to be not' SD I, 354–5
al-a-nk- 'to shake', 277
a-l(*l*)V 'that place', 407
aw-anṯu 'he, that man' 3m sg (nom), *awan-* obl [1], 20, 211, 217, 495, 498
aw-aḷ 3f sg SD I [1], 495, 498
aww-a 'mother, grand mother' [73], 10
aḷ-amp- 'mushroom' [300], 16
aḷ-V-*kk-* 'to sacrifice' [297], 11
aẓ-i- 'to perish', *aẓ-i-ntt-* past transitive, *aẓ-i-mpp* non-past transitive, 194
aH-/ā 'that' (distal); *a-tu* 'she/it' (hum f and non-hum), *aw-anṯu* 'he' (hum m), *aw-ay* 'they'(non-men/non-hum), *aw-ar* 'men/persons' (hum), *aw-aḷ* 'she'(hum f), [1], 45, 199, 207–11, 217–18, 269, 390

aHn- (>*a(y)n-* > *e(y)n-* > *i(y)n-*, *ān-*) 'to say' [868/9], 15, 95, 143; quotative marker, 451–2
ā- 'to be, become'; *ā-k-* 'to be', *ā-kk-* 'to make'; *ān-/an-* 'to be'; *ā-p-* 'to become', *ā-pp-* 'to make' [333], 184–6, 262, 277–9, 289, 459–63
āṭ-u 'to play, dance', n. *āṭṭ-u* (< *āṭ* + *ṭ-*) [347], 10, 199
āṯ- 'to become cool, to dry up' [404], 117, 146
āṯ(ṯ)- 1pl incl nom, 310
ānt-ay 'owl' SD I [359], 13
ā(m/n)- 'cow' [334], 12, 92, 278
āy 'mother' [364], 10
ār-āy 'to investigate', *ār-āy-cci* 'research' PSD I [368 + 363], 201
ār/ar-ak- 'millet' [5265], 9
āl 'banyan tree' [382], 11
āḷ 'man/woman' [399, 400], 11

iṭ-u- (*iṭ-ṭ-*) 'to put, place' [442], 112, 293
iṯ-ay-cci 'meat' [529], 9, 10, 102
in- adj/n 'sweet' [530a,b], 394
i-ṉṯu 'today, now', 407
ir- 'to be' (copular verb) SD I, *ir-u-wu* 'a place to be' SD II [480], 8, 109, 191, 295, 496, 498–9
ir-u-ppay 'mahua tree', *Bassia longifolia* [485], 9
ir-Vl/w 'liver' SD I [546], 484
il 'house' [494], 8, 180
iẓi- 'to descend'; *iẓi-nt-* past intransitive, *iẓi-ntt-* past transitive; *iẓi-(m)p-* non-past intransitive, *iẓi-(m)pp-* non-past transitive [502], 188–9, 279
iH-/ī 'this' (proximal); *i-tu* 'this thing/woman', *iw-anṯu* 'this man', *iw-ay* 'these things/women', *iw-ar* 'these men/persons', *iw-aḷ* 'this woman' [410], 20, 45, 199, 207 (fn 2), 390, 407, 495, 498
ī 'fly' [533], 278
īr/ir-V 'two', *ir-aṇ-ṭu* 'two'(3n-m pl), *iru-war* 'two persons' [474], 46, 97, 141, 159, 197, 395
īẓam 'toddy', *īẓa-wanṯ-* 'toddy-tapper' SD I [549], 9, 11

ukir 'finger nail, toe-nail' SD I, *gōr/kōr* SD II, CD, Br.; *or-kk-* Kuṛ–Malt [561], 484
uc-V- 'to breathe', *uc-Vr* [645], 149
uṭ-ump- 'iguana' [592], 11
uṇ- 'to drink' [600], 110
uram-kkal 'grinding stone, pestle' [651], 8
ur-ay 'to rub', 118
ula-kk-V 'pestle' [572]
uḷ- 'to be, to have', *uṇṭ-u* (< *uḷ-nt-*) 'is, are' [697], 180, 187
uḷḷ-am 'mind, the inside one', 13; see *uḷ-*
uḷḷi 'onion' [705], 12
uẓ-untu 'black gram' [690], 12, 16
uẓ-u-pp- 'stag, deer' [694], 12
uẓ-uw- 'tiger' SD II [692], 12
uẓ-V- 'to plough', *uẓ-a-tti* 'farming' [688], 8, 11, 152
uHṇ-/ūṇ- (past *uṇ-ṭ-*, *uṇ-ṭṭ-*) 'to eat, drink', *ūṭṭ-* (<*uHṇ-tt-*) 'to give to eat or drink' [600], 280, 291–2
uH/ū 'yonder' [557], 45, 253–6, 390, 407
ū/uy 'meat' [728], 10
ūr 'habitation, village, town' [752], 6, 205

eṇ 'to count' [793], 13
eṇ adj 'eight', *eṇ-ṭṭu* 'eight' (3n-m pl) [783/4], 92, 111, 112, 264, 278, 395
eṯ-ay-anṯu 'chief, king' [527], 7
eṯ-V- 'red' PSD II [865], 14, 391
eṯ-V-y 'prawn' [533], 13
enk- 'to remain, be left over', *enk-al* 'left over food' (palatalization in SD I + Koṇḍa as *eñc-*) [780], 199
en-ṯ- 'sun' [869], 278
er-utu 'ox' [815], 12
er-umV- 'buffalo' [816], 12
el-ay 'leaf' PSD [497], 103
el-i 'rat' [833], 12
el, *en-ṯu* 'sunshine, sun' [829, 861], 95
el-V-mp/-nk 'bone' [839], 14, 483
elli 'tomorrow' (Tu. Te.? Br.), 407
ell-V 'all' [844], 266
eḷ-V- 'young, tender' [513], 107, 393
eḷ-V-ñc- 'black bear' [857], 12
eẓ-V adj 'seven', *ēẓ* 'seven' (3n-m pl) [910], 112, 263–4
ēk-/eHk- 'to gin cotton' [765], 8
ēṯu 'ox, bull' [917], 12
ēl 'mind, reason, knowledge' [912], 14
ēl-V- 'cardamom' [907], 9, 37
ēẓ/ eẓ-V- 'to spin' [506], 8

o- 'to be suitable'; (with incorporated tense-transitivity suffixes) *o-kk-*, *o-pp-*,

o-mp-, *o-ww-*; *okku-* 'to be together'; *okk-al* 'relatives' [924], 184, 278
*ok-*V*r*, *kō-r*, 'finger/toe nail' [561], 46
okk- 'one' CD, Tel. [990b], 261, 495, 500
oṭ-ay 'to break' PSD [946], 110, 282
oṭ-al 'body' PSD [585], 483
oṭ-unku 'to be restrained'[954], 110
*oṭ-*V*kk-* 'chameleon' [2977], 12
o̱t-a-nku 'to sleep' PSD [707], 116
on-ṯu 'one' [990c], 101, 110, 169, 260–1
*on-paṯ*V 'ten minus one' [1025] SD I, 265
oy- 'to carry' [984], 277
oḷ-an 'house' Pre-Gondi [697], 220; see *uḷ-* 'to be'
oẓ-ukk- 'to spin' [1012], 8
ōṭu v.i. 'to flee', *ōṭṭ-am* 'defeat' [1041, 2861], 8
ōtu 'to recite, read' [1052], 14
ōntti 'bloodsucker lizard' [1053], 12
*ōr-/or-*V- adj 'one' [990a], 261, 395

kac (>*kay*) 'to be bitter', n. 'bitterness' [1249], 119, 154
kañci 'gruel' [1104], 10, 16
kaṭ-/kaṭṭ- 'to tie, bind', n. *kaṭṭ-ay* 'a dam' [1147], 92, 97, 199
kaṭ-ac- 'male of cattle, heifer' [1123], 12, 16, 123–4 (fn 5), 160
kaṭ-ampu *Anthocephalus cadamba* [1116], 16
kaṭ-ay 'end, place', 407
kaṭ-al 'sea, ocean' [1118], 13
*kaṭ-*V- 'be bitter, pungent' [1135], 98
*kaṭ-*V- 'wild buffalo' [114], 12
*kaṭ-*V*-ñcc/-ntt* 'stag' [1114], 12
kaṇ 'eye' [1159a], 46, 100, 108, 196; *kaṇ-ṇīr* 'tear' [1159a + 3690a], 46, 201, 205, 483
kaṇṭ-anṯu 'husband, warrior' SD I [1173], 11, 169
katti 'knife' [1204], 9
*kan-ac*V 'dream, to dream' [1407], 123 (fn 5)
kap- ~ *kapp -/kaw-*V 'to cover' [1221, 1225], 98, 144
kapp-a 'frog' [1224], 13
kapp-am 'a kind of tax, tribute' [1218], 8
kapp-al 'ship, boat' [119], 13
*kap-*V*ḷ* 'cheek' [1357], 16
kam-kuẓi 'armpit'[1134 + 1818], 203
kay 'hand, arm' [2023], 90, 118–19, 145, 196, 484
kay-tay 'fragrant screw-pine' [2026], 16; *kay-t*V*kk-* id., 37
kay-m- (> *key-m-*) 'field' [1958], 128
*kay-*V*-l/-kk-/-mpp-* 'fish of different kinds' [1252], 13, 16
kar-umpu 'sugar-cane' SD I [1288], 12
*kar-*V*ḷ* 'bowels' [1274], 14
*kar-*V*nk* *Pongamia glabra* [1507], 16
*kar-*V*-nt-* 'to consider, intend', *kar-*V*-ntt* n. 'will, mind' SD I + Te. [1283], 14
*kar-*V*nti* 'red gram' [1213], 12
kal 'stone' [1298], 92, 118, 179, 196
kal-/kaṯ- 'to learn' [1297], 14
kala-kala onom. of 'rustle, tinkle, rattle' [1302], 486
kal-a-nku 'to be stirred', *kal-a-nkku* 'to stir' PSD [1303], 172–3, 240, 289
*kal-*V*nk-* 'covered drain, sluice' SD [1309], 13
kal-ac- 'to quarrel' [1303], 123 (fn 5)
kal-am 'boat, ship' [1305], 13
*kaw-*V*ḷi* 'a house lizard' [1338, 1399], 12, 16
kaḷ-am/-an 'an open place (threshing floor, battle ground)' [1376], 8, 9, 153
kaẓ-ut-ay 'donkey' [1364], 12
kaẓ-u-tt- 'neck/throat', SD I, *kaẓ-nt*(*t*)- Tu., CD, SD II [1366], 484
kaḷ 'toddy' [1374], 9, 1
kaḷ-/kaṇ- 'to steal' [1372], 11, 95
kaẓi (*-nt-*) v.i. 'time to pass, be spent', (*-nt-t-*) v.t. 'to spend, waste, reject' PSD [1356], 294
*kaẓ-*V*-ku/-tu* 'eagle'[1362], 13
*kaẓ-*V*t* 'paddy field' [1355], 8, 16
kā-kk-ay 'crow' [1425], 13, 91 (fn 2)
kāṇ- (<*kaHṇ-*) 'to see' [1443], 95, 196
kāṇ-ikk-ay 'gift' [1443], 6
kāṯ- 'plough-share' [1505], 9
kā(*-tt-*) 'to protect, guard' [1416], 293
kā(*-n*), *kā-ṯu* 'forest' [1418, 1438], 12, 16
kā, *kā-n-*, *kā-ṯ*V n. 'forest' [1418, 1438], 277
kā-nk- 'big clay pot' [458], 8
kāy 'fruit, pod' [1459], 12
kāy, *kā-nku* v.i.: *kā-nkku* v.t., *kā-ntu* v.i.: *kā-nttu* v.t., *kā-mpu* v.i.: *kā-mppu* v.t. 'to be hot, dry up, burn' [1458], *kā-ḷ* 'to burn, flame' [1500], *kā-r/kar-V-* 'be scorched', 9, 130, 181, 296
*kār/kar-*V 'dark, black, dark clouds' [1278], 13–14, 391
kāl 'canal' [1480], 13
kāl 'leg, foot' [1479], 179, 196, 205, 277, 484
kā-waṭi 'shoulder pole' [1417], 9
kic-ampu > *kiy-ampu* > *kī-mpu/kē-mpu* 'yam', *Arum colacasia* [2004], 6, 12, 96, 144, 197; see *kē-mpu*

kōṭ-ay 'west wind, monsoon' PSD I [2203], 13, 110
kōn-yāṯu 'temple tank, open well' [2177 + 5159], 202; see *kō-*
kōy-il 'palace, temple' (King's/God's abode) PSD [2177 + 494], 8, 202
kōl 'stick, plough-shaft' [2237], 9, 101
*kōẓ/koẓ-*V 'new, young, tender' 158–9, 393; *kōẓ-/koẓ-*V 'son, young one' [2149], 10
kōẓi 'chicken' [2248], 13

caṭa-ppī 'cowdung' (lit. bullock's excrement) [2402a + 4210], 201
*caṭ*V*caṭ*V 'cracking sound' [1659], 136
caṭṭi 'small pot' [2306], 8
*caṯ-*V adj 'six', *cāṯ-u* 'six' (3n-m pl) [2485], 263
*cat-*V- 'to read' Pre-Te. [2327], 14
*cam-*V- 'to be made, to form' [2342], 150
cay-m- adj 'five', *cay-m-tu* 'five' (3n-m pl) [2826], 263, 395
car-ac- 'snake' PSD [2359], 12, 122–3 (fn 5)
cal-/can- (*can-ṯ-* <*cal-nt-* PSD I, *can-ṯṯ-* PSD II) 'to go, pass, occur' [2781], 90, 118, 150–1, 181, 279, 295
caḷ-/caṇ- 'cool, cold' [3045], 13
*caḷ-*V- 'buttermilk' [2411], 8
caH- ~ *ceH-* (past *ca-tt-/ce-tt-*) 'to die'; PSD *caH-/cā-*, PCD *cay-/cāy-*, PND *keH-/key-* [2426], 45–6,118, 126–7, 156, 293
cār-/cēr- 'to go reach' [2484]
cāl 'ploughed furrow' [2471], 9
cāl-iy-anṯu 'nephew/son-in-law' [2410], 11
*cāl-*Vy-*anṯu* 'weaver' [2410], 11
cinki, cinki-wēr 'ginger' [429, 5535], 5, 12, 16
cin-tta 'tamarind' [2529], 12
ciy-/cī- 'to give' [2598], 123, 279
cir- 'black' [2552], 10; *cir-a-*, *cir-*V-*ḷ/-nk-* 'darkness' [2552], 13; *cir-umpu* 'black metal/iron' [2552], 10
cir 'day' CD [2553], 13
*cir-*V-*tt-* 'the low area, east' SD I [2584], 14
cil- 'to be not' [2559], 109, 354–7, 459–63, 496–7
cīk-kāy 'soapnut' [2607a + 1459], 12, 202
cīn-kk- 'darkness' [2604],13
cīn-t(*t*)-V- 'date palm' [2617], 12, 126, 168
cī-p/cay-pp- 'sweeping broom' [2599], 8
cīr-ppī 'nits' (lit. lice eggs) PSD [2625 + 4210], 201
*cukk-*V 'star' [2646], 13
cup/cow-ar 'salt' SD II, *up/ow-ar* SD I, Te. [2674a, b], 97, 98, 105, 123, 144
*cum-*V- 'to carry on head', n. 'head-pad' [2677], 9, 126
cuw- 'pipal tree' [2697], 12
*cūṭ-/cuṭ-*V- 'be hot, burn'; SD II *cuṯ-* [2654], 148
*cūr/cur-*V- 'to curl up' [2684], 126
cū-ẓ 'to see, deliberate' [2735], 13
ceṯ-ank-/-ankk- 'wing' [2591], 126
*ceṯ-*V*kk-* 'sugar-cane' SD II [2795], 12
cey-t-/coy-t- 'porcupine' [2776, 2852], 12
cer- 'to insert', 126 [2599], 126
cēr 'plough yoked to oxen' [2815], 6
cēl-āḷ 'younger sister' SD II [2783], 10
coṭ- 'to drip' [2835], 118
*coṭṭ-*V 'lame' [2838], 10
coṯ-ac- 'shark' [710], 13
col- 'to speak, relate' [2855], 15
col-(*ay*) 'fireplace' [2857], 9, 102, 123
cōṭ- 'to run', *cōṭ-am* 'boat' [2861; also see1039, 1041], 200

ñaṇṭ- 'crab' [290], 13
*ñam-*V-*l* 'peacock/peahen' [2902], 13
ñam-kōl 'plough, our stick' [297], 9 (fn 10),
ñar-ampu 'tendon, nerve, sinew, vein, pulse' [2903], 14, 484
*ñāc-*V*ṯu* 'son' SD I [2910], 13
ñāṇ/ñēṇ 'string, cord' [2908], 140
ñāṯu 'seedlings for transplantation' [2919], 9
ñāṯu 'to emit smell' [2918], 140
*ñānṯ-*V- *Eugenia jambolana* [2917], 12
ñān-ṯu/ñēn-ṯu 'day, time, today' PSD [2920], 13, 140, 407, 496, 499, 500
ñā-n/ñan- 'I' (1sg nom/obl innovated in PSD), 20, 245 (fn 21), 245–8, 269, 495, 497
ñām/ñam- 'we' (1pl incl) [cf. 3647], 14, 20, 247–8, 269

takar 'ram' [3000], 12
*taṭṭ-/taṭ-*V- 'measles' [3028], 10
taṇ adj 'cool, cold' [3045], 394
taṇṭ-al 'boatman' [3049], 3
tan-tay/tan-ṯi 'father' [3067], 10
tapa-tapa/daba-daba onom. 'walking fast' [3069], 486
tam-kay 'younger sister' [3015], 10
*tamp-*V- 'younger brother' [3485], 10

tar-/*tā-* (< *taH-r-*/*taH-*, neg and pos) 'to give to 1st or 2nd person', 198, 384–5, 496–7
tar-V- 'to churn buttermilk' [3095], 8
tal-ay 'head, hair, top' [3103], 121, 484
taḷḷ-ay/*-i* 'mother' [3136], 10
*taẓ-*V*nk-*/*-nkk* 'liver' [3120], 14, 484
tā-ṇṭu 'to dance, jump' [3158], 91 (fn 2)
tātt-a 'grand father' [3160], 10
tān/*tan-* (<*taHn-*) 'self' (3refl sg), emphatic particle SD I, 496, 498 [3196], *tām*/*tam-* 'selves' (3refl pl) [3162], 20, 198, 252–3
tāṉṯi Belleric myrobalan [3198], 12
tāli 'wedding string with a gold piece' SD I, Te. [3175], 11
tāẓ 'palmyra tree' [380], 12
tāẓ-waṭam 'a string of beads/pearls' [3178 + 5220], 202
tiṯ-V- 'to open' [3259], 159
tink-aḷ 'moon' SD I [3213], 13
tiy-am 'honey' [3268b], 96
*tir*V- 'be changed' [3251], 194; *tir-ay* 'to roll' [3244], 181; *tir-a-nku* 'be curled up': *tir-a-nkku* 'to shrivel up', *tir-i* v.i. (*-v-*, *-nt-*) 'to turn': (*-pp-*, *-ntt-*) v.t. 'to turn', *tir-u-ku*, *tir-u-mpu* v.i. 'to twist': *tir-u-kku*, *tir-u-mppu* v.t. 'to twist' [3246], 161; *tir-u-ntu* v.i. 'to be corrected' [3251]: *tir-u-nttu* v.t. 'to correct', 92, 180, 286–7, 290; *tir-uḷ* 'to turn', 118
*tir*V*-kal* 'a hand-mill' [2882 + 1298], 203
tiHn- (past *tin-ṯ-*/*tin-ṯṯ-*) 'to eat': *tī-nṯṯ-* 'to feed' [3263], 109, 281, 292
tuñc- 'to sleep' [3291], 170
*tul-ac*V 'sacred basil' [3357], 123 (fn 5)
*tuw-*V*ṯ-* 'to drizzle' [3398], 13
*tuw-*V*r* 'coral' [3284], 15
tū-nk- v.i. : *tū-nkk-* v.t. : 'to swing' [3376], 198, 289–90
tēr 'chariot' SD [3459], 9
tēr/*ter-*V- 'to become clear, to know' [3419], 14
ten, *teṯ-kku* 'south' [3449], *ten-kāy* 'coconut' (southern fruit) PSD [3449 + 1459], 12, 14, 20(fn 23), 201, 391
tepp-V- 'float' [3414], 13
teḷ-V- 'white, clear', v. 'to become clear, to know' [3433], 14
tēṯṯ- 'to recover' [3471], 112
tē- (< *tew-i-*) 'be full, satiated' [3451, 3453], 103
tē- (<*tiy-a*) 'sweet' PSD [3268a], 103
tēn-ī 'honey-bee'(lit. honey-fly) SD I [3268a + 533], 201
tēn-kk- 'teak' [3452], 12
tēḷ 'scorpion' [3470], 12, 101
tokk-/*tok-al*/*tō-l* 'skin' PSD [3559], 96, 103, 484
toṭ-V- 'to hold' [3480], 118
toṇṭ-V- 'chameleon' [3501], 12
toṯ-V 'cattle, cow' [3534], 8
*tor-*V*mp-* 'lungs' [3515], 14
toḷ-/*toṇ-* 'nine, 9/10' [3532], 14, 264, 395
toẓ-V- 'slavery' [3523], 11
toẓ-V 'cattle stall' [3526], 8
tōc-ay 'a cereal pancake' SD [3542], 10
tōṇ-ṭṭ-am (<*tōṇṭu*) 'garden' [3549], 171
tōn-ṯu 'to appear, strike to mind' [3566], 13
tō-l(<*tok-al*) PSD [3559], 8, 144; see *tokk-*
tōẓ-/*tōẓ-nt-* 'wolf' [3548], 12

nakk- 'to lick' [4353], 108
naṭ-a 'to walk' [3582], 277
nan-key 'good (wet) land' [3610], 8
na-mpu (<*nay-mp-*) 'to long for' [3602], 168
nari-(*kk*V) 'jackal' [306], 12
nal 'good, beautiful' PSD [3610], 395
naH-ay/*-att*/*-kuẓi* 'dog' [3650], 12
nāṭu 'country, place'; *nāṯu* SD II [3638], 8, 147
nā (obl of 1sg) SD II, 248, 269, 495, 499
nām-/*nam-*V- 'be emaciated' [3648], 150
nā-l, *nā-l-*nk(*k*) [3633], 46, 484
nāl/*nal-*V- adj 'four', *nāl-nk*(*k*)V 'four' (3n-m pl) [3655], 261, 395
nāḷ 'day', *nāṇ-ṭ-* (< *nāḷ-nt-*) SD II [3656], 14
nāḷ/*naḷ-*V- 'night' [3621], 13
niṯ(V)*-nay*/*-nal*/*-nāḷ* 'yesterday, completed day' [3758], 202, 407
niṯ-, *nin-ṯ-* v.i. 'to be full' [3682], 95
nil-/*niṯ-*/*niṯṯ-* 'to stand' [3675], 94
nī- (< *niw*-V-) 'be elongated' [3692], 104
nī (obl of 2sg) SD II, 250, 269, 495, 499
nī- 'to abandon' [3685], 278
nī-n/*nin-* 'thou' (2sg) [3684], *nīm*/*nim-* 'you' (2pl) [3688], 46, 249–51
nī-r 'you' (2pl) PSD, 250, 270, 310, 495, 497
nīr 'water' [3690], 46, 138
*nuẓ-*V*ḷ*/*-nk-* 'mosquito' [3715], 12
nūṯ- (obl *nūṯ-ṯ*V) 'hundred' [3729], 266
nūy 'well' [3706], 13

wēr 'root' [5535], 117–18
wēḷ (<**weH-ḷ*) 'to desire' [5528], 11, 95; see *wēṇṭ*-V

Vb^{i} + *taH*- complex verb stem SD I, SD II, 373
Vbinf + *kūṭu* 'Vb + suit' (permissive/prohibitive) SD I, SD II, 374ff.
Vbinf + *ciy*- 'Vb + give' (permissive) SD II, 380–3
Vbinf + *paṭu*- 'Vb + suffer' (passive) SD I, 374ff.
Vbinf + *wēṇṭu* 'Vb + must' (obligative) SD I, 374ff.
Vbppl + *iru*- 'Vb + to be' (perfective) SD I, 374ff.
Vbppl + *ā* 'Vb + to be' (completive) SD I, 376ff
Vbppl + *koṭu* 'Vb + give' (benefactive) SD I, 374ff.
Vbppl + *koḷ-/koṇ*- 'Vb + take' (reflexive) 374ff.
Vbppl + *pō*- 'Vb + go' (exhaustive) SD I, SD II, 374ff.
Vbppl + *wiṭu* 'Vb + leave' (completive) SD I, 374ff.
(*-w*)*-in*~ *-im*/*-ir* imperative sg/pl SD I, 357–8

B. Bound forms (grammatical markers)

-a/*-i* oblique markers, 225–6
-aṯṯ 1pl incl marker in verbs SD II, some CD and ND, 309–10
-aṯṯ obl marker SD I, SD II, *aw-aṯṯ-*, 222–3
-at n-m sg, 212–17
-ad/*-aw* 3n-m sg/pl SD II, 311
-an accusative case marker, 228–30
-an obl marker in n-h dem pronouns SD I, SD II; *at-an-*, *it-an-*, *et-an-*, *aw-an-*, *iw-an-*, *ew-an-*, Pre-Tel. obls of demonstrative and interrogative stems, 222–3
-an-Ø (<*an-ṯ-*) 3m sg SD I, 308
-an/*-in* oblique markers, 221–24, 226
-anṯ-/*-wanṯ* 3hum m suffix, *-an*/*-wan* SD I, 212–17, 308
-an-ṯṯ-/*-in-ṯṯ* complex oblique makers, 224–5
-am-t-am (deverbal noun formative), *opp-antam* 'agreement' SD I, Te. [924], 200
-ay accusative case marker, 227–8
-ay~*i*/*-ir* 2sg/pl ND, 312
-ar/*-ār* 3h pl SD I, 308
-ar/*-war* m pl/hum pl, 212–17
-al infinitive-nominal marker, 346–7
-(*w*)*-in*~ *-im*/*-ir* imperative sg/pl SD I, 357–8
-a(*w*) 3neu pl SD I, 308
-aw non-m pl/non-h pl, 212–17
-aḷ/*-āḷ* 3f sg SD I, 211–17, 308
-aH-aH/*-āH* negation marker in verbs, 46, 348–51
-ā clitic (interrogative), 388, 416–18
-ān/*-an*/*-a* infinitive markers, 346–7
-āl/*-ān* instrumental case markers, 237
-a/*-i* past-participle marker, 335
-i- ~ *-in-* past-tense marker, 291, 296–8, 300–1
-i f sg suffix in derivation, 212–17
-(*i*)*kk-ay* (noun formative), *kōru* 'to desire', *kōr-i-kk-ay* n. 'wish, desire' PSD, 200
-i-tt/*-a-tt-*/*-tt-i*/*-tt-a-* complex oblique markers, 226
-il/*-in* locative case markers, 239
-in/*-il* conditional non-finite verb marker, 338
-ī̆, *-ā̆y* 2sg suffix in finite verbs SD I, 308–9
-ī̆ r (replacing older *-īm*) 2pl suffix in finite verbs SD I, 308
-um 'also, totality, any/one (added to interrogative forms), and, even' (coordinating suffix), 413–15, 498
-um aorist future marker, 305–7, 500
-uḷ/*-uḷ-a-* locative postposition, 241; see *uḷ-*
-ē clitic (emphatic), 388, 415–16, 496, 498
-ē clitic (interrogative), 500
-ēn/*-ēm* conditional non-finite verb marker, 338
-ō clitic (dubitative-alternative), 388, 41
-oṭu/*-ōṭu* sociative case marker SD I, 237
-k-a/*-kk-a* (non-past + infinitive) optative marker SD I, SD II, 362
-k/*-nk* non-past intransitive, *-kk*/ *-nkk* non-past transitive markers, 290, 301–4
-kk- past-tense marker, 291, 299–300
-c/*-cc* past-tense marker, 193, 195, 291, 298–300
-cc tansitive–causative suffix, 285–6, 290, 300
-cc-i(*n*) perfective participle/gerund marker, a sequence of two past allomorphs *-cc-* and *-i*(*n*)- PSD, PCD, 105, 193, 291, 331–3, 496, 499
-t-al-ay (complex noun formative), *oppu-talay* 'agreement' SD I, Te. [924], 200

GENERAL INDEX

[Note: Only the unabbreviated names of languages occurring in the running text are listed below.]